ENCYCLOPEDIA OF CONTEMPORARY JAPANESE CULTURE

ENCYCLOPEDIA OF CONTEMPORARY JAPANESE CULTURE

Edited by Sandra Buckley

London and New York

First published 2002
by Routledge
11 New Fetter Lane, London EC4P 4EE

Simultaneously published in the USA and Canada
by Routledge
29 West 35th Street, New York, NY 10001

Routledge is an imprint of the Taylor & Francis Group

© 2002 Routledge

Typeset in Baskerville by Taylor & Francis Books Ltd
Printed and bound in Great Britain by TJ International Ltd,
Padstow, Cornwall

British Library Cataloguing in Publication Data
A catalogue record for this book is available from the British Library

Library of Congress Cataloging in Publication Data
A catalogue record of this book has been requested

ISBN 0–415–14344–6

FOR MY MUM AND DAD, JOHN AND ELLEN BUCKLEY

Contents

Editorial board

List of contributors

Chiaki Ajioka
Art Gallery of New South Wales, Australia

Takasue Akiko
Art Gallery of New South Wales, Australia

Anne Allison
Duke University, USA

Mark Anderson
University of Minnesota, USA

Tomoko Aoyama
University of Queensland, Australia

Noriko Aso
University of California, Santa Cruz, USA

Xavier Bensky
University of Chicago, USA

Monica Bethe
Otami University, Japan

Botond Bognar,
University of Illinois, USA

Kaye Broadbent
Griffith University, Australia

Sandra Buckley
McGill University, Canada

Catherine Burns
Griffith University, Australia

Owen Cameron
INSEAD, EEC

Lonny E. Carlile
University of Hawaii at Manoa, USA

Nina Cornyetz
New York University, USA

Romit Dasgupta
Curtin University of Technology, Australia

Mark Driscoll
University of Michigan, USA

David Edgington
University of British Columbia, Canada

Norma Field
University of Chicago, USA

Takashi Fujitani
University of California, San Diego, USA

Akiko Fukai
Kyoto Costume Institute, Japan

Tadakazu Fukutomi
International Christian University, Japan

Emilio Garcia Montiel
El Cotegio de Mexico, Mexico

Sheldon Garon
Princeton University, USA

Timothy S. George
University of Rhode Island, USA

Aaron Gerow
Yokohama National University, Japan

Michael Gibbs
University of Denver, USA

Scott Gold
Architect, Guam

Andrew Gordon
Harvard University, USA

June A. Gordon
University of California, Santa Cruz, USA

Nanette Gottlieb
University of Queensland, Australia

Jonathan M. Hall
University of California, San Diego, USA

Midori Hayashi
Independent scholar, Japan

Carol Hayes
Independent scholar, Australia

Laura Hein
Northwestern University, USA

Charles Yuji Horioka
Ōsaka University, Japan

Shun Ikeda
Australian National University, Australia

Iyotani Toshio
Hitotsubashi University, Japan

Gretchen Jones
University of Maryland, USA

Beth Katzoff
Columbia University, USA

Tanaka Kazuko
Kokugakuin University

Jeff Kingston
Temple University, Japan

Chika Kinoshita
University of Chicago, USA

Kojima Kiyoshi
Iwanami Publications, Japan

Faye Yuan Kleeman
University of Colorado, USA

Mary Knighton
University of California, Berkeley, USA

Audrey Kobayashi
Queen's University, Canada

Kogawa Tetsuo
Goethe Institute, Japan

J. Victor Koschmann
Cornell University, USA

Thomas LaMarre
McGill University, Canada

William Lee
State University of Minnesota, Akita, Japan

Seiji M. Lippit
University of California, Los Angeles, USA

Margaret Lock
McGill University, Canada

Tom Looser
McGill University, Canada

Morris Low
University of Queensland, Australia

Vera Mackie
Curtin University, Australia

Anne McKnight
McGill University, Canada

Christine Marran
Princeton University, USA

Carolyn A. Morley
Wellesley University, USA

Tessa Morris-Suzuki
Australian National University, Australia

Leith Morton
University of Newcastle, Australia

Joe Murphy
University of Florida, USA

Nakano Yoshio
City University of Hong Kong, Hong Kong

Nanba Kōji
Japan

Ian Neary
University of Essex, UK

Gregory W. Noble
Australian National University, Australia

Abé Mark Nornes
University of Michigan, USA

Maria R. Novielli
Italy

Sharalyn Orbaugh
University of British Columbia, Canada

James J. Orr
Bucknell University, USA

Mark Oshima
Independent scholar, Japan

Won-Kyu Park
Kitakyushu University, Japan

Christopher Perrius
University of Chicago, USA

Leila Pourtavaf
Concordia University, Canada

Roddey Reid
University of California at San Diego, USA

Kenneth Ruoff
Portland State University, USA

Sonia Ryang
Johns Hopkins University, USA

Naoki Sakai
Cornell University, USA

Jay Sakashita
University of Hawaii, USA

Wesley Sasaki-Uemura
University of Utah, USA

Barbara Hamill Sato
International Christian University

Mark Schilling
Tokyo International University, Japan

Mark Seldon
Cornell University, USA

Franziska Seraphim
University of North Carolina, USA

Hiraku Shimoda
Harvard University, USA

Hosokawa Shūhei
Tokyo Institute of Technology, Japan

Stephen R. Smith
Wittenberg University, USA

Joel Stocker
National Museum of Ethnology, Japan

Ichiro Suzuki
Ōsaka University, Japan

Sharon S. Takeda
Los Angeles County Museum of Art, USA

Keiko Tamura
Australian National University, Australia

George J. Tanabe
University of Hawaii, USA

Veronica Taylor
University of Washington, USA

William C. Thompson
University of Columbia, USA

Sybil A. Thornton
Arizona State University, USA

Tomii Reiko
Independent scholar, New York

Tsutomu Tomotsume
Tokyo University of Foreign Studies, Japan

Kobayashi Toshiaki

Takeyuki Tsuda
University of Chicago, USA

Uchino Tadashi
University of Tokyo, Japan

Uemura Hideaki
Japan

Andrea Vasisht
USA

Keith Vincent
New York University, USA

Alicia Volk
Art Gallery of New South Wales, Australia

Jens Wilkinson
Japan

David G. Wittner
University of Tokyo, Japan

Karen Tei Yamashita
University of California-Santa Cruz, USA

Yang Daqing
George Washington University, USA

Guy Yasko
Independent scholar, Japan

Introduction

The *Encyclopedia of Contemporary Japanese Culture* has been developed in response to the growing interest in Japan beyond a specialised readership of teachers, researchers and students in area studies. Japanese culture is now a frequent element of courses in areas as diverse as communication and media, business management, comparative popular culture, cinema, global cultural economy and gender studies. The encyclopedia is intended to be an accessible reference for both specialist readers and a more general reader seeking information on a specific topic or wanting an overview of a theme or area of contemporary Japanese culture. A reader can locate information on an individual film maker or film, or develop an overview of Japanese cinematic practice and the film industry. A lead essay on postwar social and political movements will offer a detailed history from 1945 to the late 1990s, and also guide the reader to shorter more focused entries on particular campaigns and organisations. The reader can select for themselves the depth at which they pursue a topic using the alphabetical structure, index, thematic lists and cross-referencing provided in the body of the text. This volume works committedly to extend the range of cultural practices and experience represented beyond the literature and language focus often associated with area studies, and to capture a broad perspective of contemporary Japanese life in all its diversity. The site of engagement with contemporary Japan for the entries collected here is the lived experience of everyday Japanese life. Traditional, modern and postmodern cultural practices and objects are located in the context of their contemporary consumption or circulation. Cultural value is understood as not inherent or assigned but evolving, and in a constant state of renegotiation. The focus on the contemporary does not exclude the past and historical background is developed wherever it is considered essential context for the understanding of the contemporary environment. However, overall the volume has been designed and written to allow the reader to focus on, and explore, the terrain of Japan as contemporary cultural landscape. The encyclopedia also strives to extend the notions of Japan and the Japanese beyond the popularly accepted limits of a homogeneous race defined and delimited within the geographic space of the Japanese island chain. Brazilian Japanese (in and out of Japan), *Nikkei* in North America, *japayuki* (immigrant sex workers), the Burakumin and Ainu of Japan, the Chinese and Korean populations in Japan, *gaijin*, the status of women, and the greying of Japan (the elderly) are just some of the topics developed across the volume in an attempt to reflect the complex shifts in the socio-cultural formations and politics of identity that have marked the period since 1945. The inclusion of minority communities in this volume is not intended to subsume them within a singular identity of Japaneseness but rather to challenge the historical tendancy for a myth of homogeneity and uniqueness (*nihonjinron*) and shared prosperity (Japanese economic miracle) to erase or obscure the status of these communities and the complex issues that linger unresolved between Japan and its indigenous, postcolonial and other minority communities as well as its emigrant and legal and illegal immigrant populations. The encyclopedia begins at 1945, the year of Japan's defeat and the end of the Second World War. This year also witnessed the atomic bombing of Hiroshima and Nagasaki, and the beginning of the Cold War era. The Japanese surrender led to the Allied Occupation that would continue until 1952. This volume traces Japan's trajectory from the devastation, hunger and poverty of the early postwar years to the rapid growth and consumerism of the so-called 'Japanese economic miracle', the new found prosperity and excess of the 'bubble' years, and the economic slowdown and cultural speed of the post-bubble, postmodern, information society of the 1990s. Although more than fifty years have passed since Japan's surrender and the beginning of the 'postwar' period, Japan still labours to free itself from this term. The Berlin Wall has fallen and the Soviet Union has collapsed and yet Japan continues to be described by many in the media, politics and academia as 'postwar'. Many of the entries in this encyclopedia deal with the tenacity of this designation and trace the developments over the last five decades that have worked to hinder or promote Japan's ability to step out from the shadow of a chronological designation haunted by a cold war heritage. Some authors have located their entries in historical relation to the prewar and war years in an attempt to overcome the artificial isolation or quarantining of the contemporary from the historical that continues to work against the interests and rights of certain groups in Japan e.g. Chinese, Okinawans, atomic bomb survivors.

Contemporary Japan has become a popular backdrop to many futuristic western narratives in film, science fiction, anime, television, music video etc. In a recent article the sci-fi author William Gibson described Japan as his 'prop box'. Western authors, journalists and academics too, often treat Japan as just this: a cultural 'prop box'. Major US and European dailies and syndicated network television news still regularly run sensationalised stories that highlight, and frequently distort, a narrow band of contemporary Japanese life. From Goldin's pseudo-biographical *Memoirs of a Geisha*, to Gibson's sci-fi *Idoru*, to the ficto-reportage of Greenfield's *Speed Tribes* or Bornoff's *Pink Samurai* the publishing industry has recognised that Japanese culture sells. At a minimum, this encyclopedia strives to offer an unsensationalised map of contemporary Japan that allows the reader freedom to determine their own pathways across this complex landscape. In the process of editing this volume there has been a genuine effort to avoid the

valorisation of Japan that is still representative of much written on Japanese management and industry, the sensationalising or mystifying of Japan typical of ficto-reportage and travelogues or the Japan bashing that has characterised elements of the last decade or more of journalism on Japan. There are sure to be some readers who react to certain editorial choices that have shaped this project. There is a clear focus on gender, minority identities, practices and objects of everyday life, labour and alternative social and political movements. These editorial choices reflect the understanding that the cultural sources of energy that drive change and creativity are seldom situated in the mainstream, and often challenge the normative and the status quo from the margins. Many areas of the encyclopedia strive to undo generalisations that have coloured discussions of Japanese culture since 1945. Sections of the encyclopedia dealing with areas as diverse as architecture, technology and music work to challenge the popular notion that the Japanese lack initiative and inventiveness, and specialise in copying and adapting. Dominant stereotypes are also questioned or contextualised e.g. Japanese women, tourists. Oversimplified depictions of cultural borrowing are redefined as more complex flows of influence, or as process of negotiation and renegotiation of cultural meaning in and out of Japan. This is how the US Teenage Mutant Ninja Turtles, the architect Frank Lloyd Wright, Godzilla, the abacus and mobile phones all find their way into the same volume. This is also one explanation for the focus on music in the volume. Music is an area of Japanese cultural production and creativity that is not widely written about as yet in English but there is a rapidly expanding traffic in global and local sounds into and out of Japan via the internet, DVD and MTV. As just one example our understanding of the history of US–Japan relations, Japanese urban and cafe cultures, ethnic and race relations in both Japan and the USA, and the music scene in Japan can all be inflected very differently when looked at through the filter of jazz in Japan. There will inevitably be authors, architects, artists, objects, rituals, events and places that are not covered that some will consider an oversight. The editorial task was massive and the decisions often long and hard. The input of the consulting editors was invaluable in the process of creating the entry lists. Some entries simply found no willing authors, others had to be omitted for reasons of space, and some, quite probably, were sadly overlooked. I can only hope that in the end the result is judged worth the extraordinary time and energy contributed by so many to realise a project of this scale. Asked recently if I would ever do another encyclopedia I answered 'probably not' but asked if I regretted doing this encyclopedia the answer was most definitely 'no'. The opportunity to work with so many of my colleagues has been an extraordinary and rare experience. Together I hope we have created a volume that will be both a valuable and informative resource, and a pleasure to read.

Acknowledgements

First I must thank the consulting editors, most of whom not only wrote entries themselves but also drew on their network of colleagues to develop the contributor list for their thematic area. Some went even further to provide vital support in the collection and initial editing of entries. Without the consulting editors the project could never have been realised and I thank them for their patience and endurance in what proved to be a far more marathon project than any of us imagined at the beginning. And then there are all the individual authors. Some contributed one entry and others contributed many. The number is not as important as the commitment to a project that fast became less an exercise in academics than a communal effort to see this through to the end. Some signed on at the beginning and some rushed in (more than a few were dragged or enticed!) at the final stages to help fill the gaps, to save an entry that couldn't be deleted or to add an entry that had been overlooked. Some even approached me asking to add an entry in an area they believed might have been forgotten or overlooked. I am grateful for every word that was written.

At Routledge, the project has seen a number of editors. I must thank Fiona Cairns, who has proven herself masterful at achieving the right balance of encouragement and threat to keep the project alive and moving forward. Denise Rea and Stephanie Rogers were there to deal with the nitty-gritty. At the end Tarquin Acevedo and Tony Nixon have taken charge of the details of publishing and copy-editing. To all at Routledge I can only express my deepest gratitude for endless patience and essential support. It took some courage to venture into the realm of East Asia and I hope the results will prove worthwhile and encourage more such flights of

fancy in a publishing industry where Asia is all too often put in the 'too hard' basket.

I owe thanks to the following institutions, which have hosted different stages of this project: Banff Centre, Griffith University (Faculty of Asian and International Studies), Australian National University (Faculty of Asian Studies and Institute of Art), University of California at Santa Cruz (Centre for Cultural Studies) and McGill University (Department of East Asian Studies).

And then there are the research assistants who have held this project (and me) together. The project began in Brisbane, Australia at Griffith University with the help of Kaye Broadbent and Cathy Burns. It moved next to Canberra and the Australian National University where Alison Munro balanced editing with parenting and still managed to create her own art. After a short detour to SUNY Albany the project landed in Montreal at McGill University where Leila Pourtavaf and Marc Steinberg proved relentless in their pursuit of missing details during the copy-editing stage. Each of the assistants who have worked on the project has left a very particular mark on it. I am especially pleased that Kaye, Cathy and Leila each were able to contribute entries. I can only hope that when they face a similar mountain in their future careers that someone will offer to them the same unstinting support they gave to me. I also owe thanks to Adrienne Gibb for jumping in to assist with last-minute translations.

Thanks to Nina Cornyetz for providing a model of tenacity and courage, for her love of a good time, for her affection for the canine species and above all for her extraordinary ability to laugh. Audrey Kobayashi has been there from Noosa to Waikiki to Amish country. Her intellectual integrity and the warmth of her friendship have proven a rockbed of support. Kim Sawchuk always knew when to incite outrageous behaviour and hilarity, and her confidence in me left me no option but to see this through to the last full stop. Freda Guttman offered her home and her friendship, and travelled far to be there when she was needed. Margaret Jolly remains a dear friend and a remarkable colleague. Penny Deutscher and Michael Jasper provided cheerleading and solace as required. Meaghan Morris sweated it out with me in more ways than one. I thank her for her trust and her encouragement. Gordon Bull gave me an institutional home when I needed one and most of all he gave his friendship.

Jesse and Brian gave up so much time that could have been spent together and they gave their love, which is priceless.

How to use this book

The encyclopedia contains over 750 alphabetically arranged entries. The reader can search a specific entry by alphabetical order, or by using the index at the end of the volume. It is also possible to pursue a topic or theme across the subject category lists (p. xxi), e.g. architecture, music or religion, ritual and ceremony. Cross-references are indicated in bold type in the body of each entry and related entries are indicated in the 'see also' section at the foot of each entry. Further-reading suggestions are also offered at the end of some, but not all, entries. All entries are signed and the institutional affiliation of authors at the time of publication is provided on p. ix. Entries range from short biographies to more detailed entries and overview essays for major subjects or themes. Biographical entries contain date and place of birth and death, wherever that information is available, the main profession of the individual and a concise description of their activities and works. Longer entries offer careful cross-referencing to enable the reader to pursue a topic in more detail across the volume. Names are given in the Japanese style with surname first. Exceptions to this are at the request of the contributor, as in the case of individuals who reside outside Japan and use western order for their professional name

Macrons are an ever-present challenge when rendering Japanese into English. A long vowel is indicated by the macron mark over the vowel. Other popular techniques have been converted to this format, e.g. Ohno, Ouno and Oono are all rendered as Ōno. Words used often in English such as *noh* and *butoh* are also rendered as *nō* and *butō* but readers will find the more familiar forms cross-referenced in the volume. An exception is the place name Tokyo which has been rendered without macrons due to its extensive use in this form in English. Japanese words that have become widely used in English are not translated, e.g. karaoke, sushi. All other Japanese words are either translated or explained in the text where they occur. Film entries are listed by their Japanese title and the English title is cross-referenced. Objects are also listed in Japanese and the English is cross-referenced, e.g. *ofuro* (bath). Exceptions are those objects that are used widely outside Japan and have a common English name, e.g. kites, fireworks.

To avoid confusion over currency exchange rates all yen amounts have been converted into US dollars. A timeline of major Japanese historical periods is given on p. xx to assist the reader.

Bibliographical items

These are divided into three sections:

1 Bibliography/filmography/discography – a selection of the entrant's work.
2 References – items or sources mentioned in the body of the text.
3 Further reading – suggested materials for further study.

The titles of works that occur in the text, whether book, article, film, song, etc., are translated for the most part in the body of the entry. Where both Japanese and English titles appear, Japanese is given first and the English follows in parenthesis. The Japanese names of organisations are not italicised. With the exception of political party names, most organisations are listed under their most commonly used Japanese title, e.g. Sōdōmei (Nihon Rōdō Kumiai Sōdōmei or Japan Federation of Labour). All words in Japanese organisational names are capitalised, but only the first word is capitalised in the Japanese titles of books and articles – the standard bibliographical practice in Japanese Studies. Japanese, except for proper names and titles, is italicised. The names of Japanese, Korean and Chinese authors in the bibliographical information are given in full with the surname appearing first while English and other European names appear in the form 'Smith, John'.

Timeline of Japanese history

Jōmon	c. 10,000 BC to c. 300 BC	Azuchi-Momoyama	1568 to 1600
Yayoi	c. 300 BC to c. AD 300	capital: Azuchi and Momoyama	
Kofun	c. AD 300 to 710	Tokugawa (Edo)	1600 to 1868
Nara	710 to 794	capital: Edo (Japan)	
capital: Heijo (Nara)		Meiji	1868 to 1912
Heian	794 to 1185	capital: Tokyo	
capital: Heian (Kyoto)		Taishō	1912 to 1926
Kamakura	1185 to 1333	capital: Tokyo	
capital: Kamakura		Shōwa	1926 to 1989
Muromachi	1336 to 1568	capital: Tokyo	
capital: Muromachi (Kyoto)		Heisei	1989 – present
		capital: Tokyo	

Thematic entry list

Architecture, urban space and housing

Ando Tadao
Architecture
chika
commuting
company towns
danchi
department stores
genkan
Hara Hiroshi
Hasegawa Itsuko
Isozaki Arata
Itō Toyō
Kikutake Kiyonori
kotatsu
Kurokawa Kishō
land reclamation
LDK
love hotels
mai hōmu
Maki Fumihiko
manshon
Metabolism
multifunctional polis
Nikken Sekkei Ltd
Otaka Masato
port towns
public housing
Shinohara Kazuo
shitamachi
shoji
shotengai
suburbanisation
sunshine rights
supermarkets and superstores
Takamatsu Shin
Takeyama Minoru
Tange Kenzo
Taniguchi Yoshio
tatami
temple town
toilets
tokonoma
Umeda
urban migration
waste and recycling
Wright, Frank Lloyd

Arts and performance

art, contemporary
butoh
classical dance
flower arrangements
folk performing arts
installation art
kabuki
kyogen
Living Treasures
manzai
mingei
Nihonga
noh
photography
rakugo
sculpture
sōsaku hanga
Takarazuka
Tattoos
Terayama Shuji
theatre, contemporary
theatre, tent

Fashion

Music

National identity

Religion, ritual and ceremony

Adults' Day
bonsai
Buddhism
butsudan and kamidana
Christianity in Japan
Christmas
Confucianism
death and funerals
festivals
fireworks
furusato gaeri
geomancy
gift giving
greetings
Hinamatsuri (Doll Festival) and Girls' Day
honeymoons
kites
Koinobori (Carp Kites) and Children's Day
meishi
mikoshi
mizuko jizo
new religions, Japanese
New Year
Obon
omiyage
origami
pilgrimages
religion
seasonal gift giving
seppuku/hara-kiri
Shichi-go-san (7–5–3 celebrations)
Sōko Gakkai
State and religion, separation of
State Shintō
tea ceremony
torii
Valentine's Day and White Day
weddings
wrapping
Zen

Social and political movements

against Police Duties Bill
against revision of the constitution
against teachers' rating system
Anpo struggle

anti-nuclear power
anti-US bases movements
Beheiren
circles
citizens' movements
civil development
Dōmei
environment and anti-pollution
farmers' movements
fishermans' movements
IMF-JC
Miike struggle
Narita Airport struggle
peace and anti-nuclear
Red Army
residents' movements
right-wing movements
Shinsanbetsu
social and political movements
Sōdōmei
Sōhyō
spring offensive
student movement
Tekkō Rōren
unions and the labour movement
Zengakuren
Zenkyoto

Sports and recreation

baseball
basho
coffee shops
football
Go
Golden Week
golf
horse racing
judo
karate
kendo
leisure
mah jong
national parks
ninjitsu
pachinko
skiing
sport and recreation
sumo wrestling

tennis
Tokyo Disneyland
tourism
yokozuna
youth hostels

Technology, communications and mass media

abacus
aerospace industry
anime
Astro Boy
bullet train
cameras
domestic technologies
Doraemon
environmental technologies
ero guro
exporting Japanese culture
Fuji TV
fuzzy logic
gender and technology
high definition TV
information society
Japan Broadcasting Corporation
just-in-time delivery
Kokusai Denshin Denwa
Manga
miniaturisation
mobile telephones
Morita Akio

Nihon TV
Nintendo
Nippon Telegraphic and Telephone Corporation
nostalgia boom
otaku
patents
pirate radio
Pokemon
Power Rangers
radio broadcasting
railways
robots
Sailor Moon
Sanrio
satellite broadcasting
satellite communications
Sazae-san
science and technology parks
soap operas
technology, transport and communications
Teenage Mutant Ninja Turtles
telephone sex
Tokyo Broadcasting Systems
toys
TV Asahi
TV Tokyo
Ultraman
vending machines
video and computer games
videos
Walkman

abacus

Introduced into Japan in about the sixteenth century from China, this arithmetic tool can be used for both simple and complex calculations. There is a cross bar with twenty-three or twenty-seven rows of two beads above the bar and the same number of rows of five beads below the bar. Calculations are made by moving beads up to and down from the cross bar. Each vertical row is a digit row with five units of one below the bar and two units of five above the bar. An experienced abacus user can easily outpace a calculator on addition, subtraction, multiplication and division. The larger the units calculated, the better the comparative performance of the abacus because one bead movement will represent one million as compared to seven finger movements on a calculator or computer keyboard. It has been argued that, while mathematical concepts and language usually engage the left side of the brain, people trained on an abacus also actively engage the creative right side of the brain when undertaking calculations. This is in part thought to reflect the image-based and spatialised processes of the work of the abacus. A practised abacus user will be able to perform long calculations in their head by merely visualising the movement and relational positioning of the beads in the abacus frame. Critics of the abacus in schools argued that it did not allow students to grasp conceptual operations due to its focus on accurate results and technique. Similar arguments are today being made against the extended use of calculators in classrooms, but there is no doubt that the abacus is no longer a central tool in education and is fast disappearing from daily life in Japan.

SANDRA BUCKLEY

Abe Kōbō

b. 1924, Tokyo; d. 1993, Tokyo

Writer

Abe Kōbō is recognised internationally as one of post-war Japan's most innovative authors. He was born in Tokyo but raised in Manchuria where his father was a doctor. He returned to Japan for his high-school education. During his youth he was plagued by illness. He graduated from the medical faculty of Tokyo Imperial University in 1948 but never practised medicine, instead becoming a full-time writer.

In 1951, two of his stories were awarded major literary prizes, notably *Kabe – Esu Karuma shi no hanzai* (The Wall – the Crime of S. Karma), which received the **Akutagawa Prize**. At about the same time, he commenced his career as a dramatist. In 1964, he turned his award-winning novel ***Suna no onna*** (The Woman in the Dunes) (1962) into a screenplay, which was subsequently filmed by the director **Teshigahara Hiroshi** and released under the same title. The film won the Jury Prize at the Cannes Film Festival in 1964 and has gained international renown.

He published the novel *Dai yon kanpyōki* (Inter Ice Age 4) in 1959. The same year, his play *Yūrei wa koko ni iru* (The Ghost is Here) (1958) won the

Kishida Drama Prize. His play *Tomodachi* (Friends) (1967) also won a major literary award. He founded his own theatrical troupe in 1973 and has been awarded various prizes for his scenarios and radio dramas. His other novels (many of which have been translated into English) include *Tanin no kao* (The Face of Another) (1964), *Moetsukita chizu* (The Ruined Map) (1967), *Hako otoko* (The Box Man) (1973), *Mikkai* (Secret Rendezvous) (1977), *Hakobune sakura maru* (The Arc Sakura) (1984) and *Kangarū nōto* (Kangaroo Notebook) (1991).

Abe's work is often described as surrealistic and his use of fantasy and **science fiction**-style plots represents a tendency in modern Japanese writing that has become increasingly popular over the past two decades, as we can see in the fiction of such authors as Tsutsui Yasutaka (b. 1934) and **Ōe Kenzaburō**. However, Abe's vision is essentially dark, and his narratives are often dystopias set in hospitals, with the patients being turned into distorted caricatures of humanity as a result of experiments. In this respect, his work is closer to dystopian novelists like Kafka, although critics have also read elements of political satire into his fiction, citing his famous expulsion from the Communist Party in 1962 as evidence of his political disaffection.

Select bibliography

Abe Kōbō (1996) *Fake Fish: The Theater of Abe Kobo*, trans. Nancy Shields, New York: Weatherhill.
—— (1996) *Kangaroo Notebook*, trans. Maryellen Mori, New York: Vintage Books.
—— (1993) *Three Plays by Kobo Abe*, trans. Donald Keene, New York: Columbia University Press.
—— (1992) *Beyond the Curve*, trans. Juliet Winters Carpenter, Tokyo: Kōdansha International.
—— (1979) *Secret Rendezvous*, trans. Juliet Winters Carpenter, Tokyo: Charles E. Tuttle.

LEITH MORTON

acupuncture

In acupuncture, fine needles (about one tenth the thickness of a needle used in an inoculation) are inserted at any of 365 points on the body. These acupuncture points are believed to respond to acupressure massage (*shiatsu*), needle therapy or moxabustion (see **moxa**) to redirect and balance the energy (*chi*) flows through the channels, known as meridians, that create a complex web throughout the body. An imbalance in *chi* can account for anything from a headache to infertility, back pain, asthma, liver failure and even impotency. Acupuncture is widely used for pain management in Japan today, in addition to extensive application in preventative medicine. The practice is a central element of the **traditional medicine** (*kampo*) originally imported to Japan from Korea.

Sceptics will argue that the placebo effect accounts for any perceived improvement, but Western medicine has become increasingly willing to concede the effectiveness of acupuncture and it is now included as an approved treatment in many medical benefit schemes. It is not unusual for a patient to describe sensations ranging from a slight tingling to sharp pain at points on the body, other than where a needle has been inserted. Thus, a headache may be treated by needles inserted at points other than the head, face or neck, such as the foot area or the hand. Acupuncture is usually not an isolated therapy but part of a holistic approach to balancing the flow of *chi* and detoxing the body. Diet and exercise are also incorporated in a comprehensive programme of therapy.

See also: traditional medicine

SANDRA BUCKLEY

adoption

Adoption in Japan was traditionally used to strengthen or regularise family ties. Unlike the historical Chinese preference for adopting distant relatives, adoption in Japan was usually of strangers. Today, a typical adoption involving a child would be where the child was born outside marriage and is being adopted into one or other of the parents' families. Adopting an unrelated child (the usual adoption scenario in the West) is now not uncommon. However, an ongoing problem has been that the child's adopted status will show on the family register (**koseki**). The more usual function of adoption in Japan, though, has been to solve problems of inheritance. So, numerically the greatest number of formal adoptions are of adults – often son-in-laws who are adopted so that they can carry on a family business under the original family name. Craftsmen and people involved in the traditional arts, too, may adopt an adult as the heir to that artistic tradition (and business) in the absence of a suitably talented natural heir. Another less common scenario has been adoption as a tax avoidance device, for example where a male patron adopts a mistress as a way to ensure property inheritance after his death.

See also: *koseki*

VERONICA TAYLOR

Adults' Day

Since 1948, 15 January has been set as the national day for observance of this official celebration of coming of age. On this day, 20-year-olds participate in various forms of public and family ceremonies to celebrate their official entry into adulthood. Traditionally this had occurred much earlier (usually before the age of fifteen). Changes in style and colour of **kimono** and hair accompanied the transition in pre-modern Japan, but today the occasion marks more of a shift in legal status: the right to marry without parental consent, to vote and to purchase and consume alcohol and cigarettes. City and prefectural offices offer government-sponsored ceremonies while many hotels now market Adults' Day banquets.

SANDRA BUCKLEY

advertising

Pre-war advertising was largely limited to **newspapers and magazines**, posters and, later, radio. The post-war period saw a rapid development of a vast advertising industry to match the speed and diversity of Japan's expanding consumer markets. Today, Japan's major ad agencies are powerful figures in the media world and play a central role in defining both consumer and cultural trends.

There are a number of different accounts offered for the origins of advertising in Japan. The popularisation of the actual term came with the emergence of a mass media of newspapers and magazines early in the twentieth century. Reader recognition of advertisements as an entity clearly distinguishable from the surrounding articles grew with the expansion of this mass media. The perception of department store poster advertisements as something other than art, as objects to be posted in railway stations to promote consumer goods, came later in the 1920s and 1930s with the enhancement of printing technologies. As Japan moved down an imperialist pathway towards the Pacific War, there was a significant reduction in the volume of the mass media and levels of advertising. Many of those in the advertising industry shifted their attention to the work of the national propaganda machine. With defeat, Japan first followed, and then overtook, the USA in a process of rapid post-war economic growth. Marketing and advertising know-how was imported, and with the advent of public broadcasting and television there has been no looking back from the 1960s to the present, with exceptional levels of growth in the advertising industry. By 1997, advertising had come to represent as much as 1.2 per cent of GDP. The distribution across the media was: 33.5 per cent television; 21.1 per cent newspapers; 7.3 per cent magazines; 3.8 per cent radio; and 34.3 per cent other (direct mail, outdoor poster and billboard advertising, etc.). Although cable television is not well established in Japan, the potential for advertising using the Internet, CS (**satellite communications**) and BS (broadcasting satellites) is just beginning to be tapped.

One defining characteristic of the Japanese advertising industry is that, unlike in the West, advertising agencies do not work within exclusivity-based contracts. In the absence of exclusivity, a single agency may produce advertising for a range of companies within a single commodity field. As a result, the largest of Japan's agencies have grown exponentially over the post-war period to the point where the biggest, **Dentsu**, holds 26 per cent market share, followed by Hakuhodo at 14 per cent. In all, the top five companies hold over 50 per cent of market, in what can be described as a situation of significant market domination by the majors. Needless to say, these mega-agencies have a tremendous influence on the mass media. By tightly managing the allocation of advertising space the majors are able to limit the growth and opportunities of the rest of the market. Even the largest of the global Western majors have found themselves locked out of the top ten ranking in Japan. The majors like Dentsu and Hakuhodo have each developed their own internal specialist sections for media planning, marketing, media buying, event and public relations, film and video production, space development and management, think tanks, etc. This high level of internal resources positions the majors to play a determining role in the shape of entertainment and media in Japan. The drive to expand the territory of advertising has come to play a key role in new trends and cultural developments. From the time of the **Tokyo Olympics** and **Expo 70**, event sponsorship has been a central strategy of advertising. The launch of the soccer league over the 1990s is a good example of this approach. It is a well-known fact that the establishment of the pro-soccer league (J-League) was driven from the outset by a carefully developed strategy of marketing, sponsorship and PR. In the areas of music, film, video games and Internet, content development is again intimately linked to the marketing and growth strategies of the majors with cultural content seen as a tie-up opportunity for product placement and a platform for advertising.

Although the post-war majors have clearly done exceptionally well, it must also be said that this success has not translated into international recognition. For example, other than the Japanese CM that won at the 1993 Cannes International Advertising Festival, there has been no other significant international award won by a Japanese agency. Despite 288 entries in the 1998 Cannes Festival (third in total number of entries after the UK and USA), Japan did not have a single entry in the final judging. Japanese entries are also said to be frequently booed at these events. There are a number of possible explanations for this lack of international success. In a high-pressure market, agency executives have been reluctant to risk giving sweeping freedom to their design and concept staff.

One study has suggested that a key element of the success of new designs in US CMs since the 1980s has been the concept of intertextuality. In this approach, a campaign does not rely on an autonomous and new concept but builds on previous campaigns and a familiar history of popular ads. In this way a CM is developed as an intertext: meaning is not located in the ad but created by the viewers' ability to make connections. If this has been an important new trend in international advertising, then it might explain the lack of mobility of Japanese CMs as a product of a cultural environment where there is still a strong tendency to base campaign concepts on domestic themes and images that, while very familiar and immediately recognisable to a Japanese audience, would have no point of connection for a non-Japanese viewer. An international strategy of intertextuality might even work against holding domestic market share for the majors. At the same time, this situation also works as a barrier to market entry for international agencies seeking to gain market share in Japan.

It seems unlikely that Japan's majors can continue to maintain the same level of insularity. International campaigns by such global brands as Nike and Benetton created strong reactions and gained much attention when aired in Japan. The processes of globalisation seem likely to break the wave of dominance of parochial strategies. A new generation of aggressive globally oriented agencies promises to edge Japan into a closer engagement with trends in the international advertising world. It is clear that the industry will continue to play an essential role in the definition of both existing and new media platforms into the next century. In applying their ability to shape the content and direction of new technologies Japan's major agencies will determine much of the cultural environment through media and entertainment. Japan's major advertising agencies have emerged as the primary cultural producers of our age, and this seems unlikely to change.

See also: copy writers; Dentsu

NANBA KŌJI

aerospace industry

The aerospace industry has long been cited as an example of failure of Japanese industrial policy. Decades of subsidies and a long series of consortia have failed to enable Japanese manufacturers to challenge Western leaders in the production of large commercial aircraft. In aerospace materials and components, however, Japanese firms have quietly developed significant capabilities and have emerged as major suppliers to Boeing and Airbus. Japan has also developed respected rockets and satellites. About 70 per cent of aerospace production in Japan goes to the military.

Originally, Japanese producers licensed most technology from the USA. They developed a reputation for high quality products and developed leading-edge technology in some areas, notably missiles and avionics. Limited defence budgets and a government ban on export of munitions, however, made it difficult to cut costs through economies of scale. In the mid-1980s, Japan embarked on the autonomous development of a next-generation fighter plane called the FSX. Fierce resistance from the USA eventually forced the Japanese government to drop independent development and accede to joint modification of the US F-16. US firms won a significant share of development and production contracts, as well as guaranteed access to new technologies developed in the course of the project, particularly radars and wing structures. In the end, Japanese capabilities proved less impressive than originally thought and the plane, renamed the F-2, was so expensive that the project was nearly cancelled.

In civilian aircraft, efforts at independent production such as the YS-11 turboprop of the 1960s turned into expensive failures. In contrast, high quality, reliable delivery and sophisticated engineering allowed Japanese firms to make great progress in production of parts and components for foreign assemblers, sometimes as sole suppliers. In the 1970s and 1980s, each new generation of Boeing jet liners contained a higher share of Japanese content. In the 1990s, the combination of Japanese production capabilities and a desire to assure access to the large Japanese market convinced Boeing to sub-license major parts of its new 777 transport to a consortium of Japanese aerospace firms. Airlines in Japan purchased more 777s than airlines from any other country, while Japanese aerospace manufacturers gained valuable experience in design and systems integration skills. Similarly, Japanese aerospace firms attained an increasing, though smaller, share of the responsibility in international jet engine consortia led by Western firms such as Rolls-Royce and Pratt and Whitney.

Japanese producers also licensed technology for rockets and satellites from the USA before pushing towards autonomy, but there were fewer opportunities to build up capacities as subcontractors. In satellites, a 1990 agreement with the USA opened the market for all but experimental satellites, significantly blunting Japan's progress. In rockets, Japan developed a technically impressive new launcher called the H-II and made efforts to enter the commercial launch business. In both cases, Japanese producers found it difficult to reduce costs to compete with the USA and Europe. Japanese aerospace companies have established a firm reputation for quality and sophisticated engineering. If they produce few final products, they have emerged as major suppliers of materials, parts and sub-assemblies. In the future they will need to cut costs to meet the challenges of stagnant or declining budgets for military procurement and increased competition at home and abroad.

GREGORY W. NOBLE

against Police Duties Bill

The 1958 Police Duties Bill would have significantly expanded police discretionary powers regarding search, seizure and the taking into temporary protective custody of youths and those likely to injure life, limb or property. Police would have been permitted to enter private property in order to assure the 'maintenance of public safety and order', which, the ruling **Liberal Democratic Party** announced in a separate statement, would help them prevent collective violence, as had recently occurred among feuding gangs, in labour unrest and in protests over the teachers' rating system. Memories of intrusive pre-war authoritarian police practices – such as local policemen coercing innkeepers for free meals and harassing patrons in their rooms – and anxiety that legitimate political gatherings might be deemed disruptive of the 'public order' gave rise to a broad extra-parliamentary opposition coalition of labour and student unions, academics and women's groups. The movement was unusual in the unanimity of press opposition, the extent of co-operation among labour federations and the participation of normally non-political groups such as the YMCA, the Shufuren and religious organisations. Despite an absolute parliamentary majority, the government party yielded to socialist opposition and public sentiment, allowing the bill to die in committee.

JAMES J. ORR

against revision of the Constitution

Despite its adoption under foreign Occupation, the **post-war Constitution** has been embraced by large segments of the population because of its renunciation of war (Article 9) and its guarantees of popular sovereignty and civil rights. When conservative politicians took steps towards revision in order to raise the Emperor's position, legalise the **Self-Defence Forces** and modify its other progressive elements, the left-wing and right-wing socialist parties joined together in 1954 to form Gokenren (Kenpō Yōgo Kokumin Rengō, or People's League for the Protection of the Constitution). A mass organisation with national and local affiliates, including labour unions, women's groups and religious organizations, Gokenren originally focused on preventing proponents from gaining the two-thirds control of the Diet necessary for revision, and then on conducting rallies, public lectures and commemorations on Constitution Day (3 May). Also, liberal academics formed a study group (1958–76) to counter the influence of the government-sponsored Commission on the Constitution (1956–64). As conservative administrations came to favour selective reinterpretation rather than outright revision, opposition to revision has also taken the form of lawsuits challenging the constitutionality of government practices, especially regarding the Self-Defence Forces and Article 9.

See also: post-war Constitution

JAMES J. ORR

against teachers' rating system

In the most violent and passionately contested chapter of its enduring struggle with the **Ministry of Education**, the left-wing **Teachers' Union of Japan** opposed efforts to institute performance ratings as a part of promotion and pay rise decisions beginning in the late 1950s. The government was moving to re-centralise control of education in several areas (for example textbook revisions), and the union feared efficiency ratings would restrain teachers' political freedom and so disrupt union activities. It also argued that the special nature of the teaching profession made such evaluation superficial and open to abuse. Riven by pro-communist and pro-socialist factions, at first the union adopted a hard-line strategy of day-long walkouts and physical interference with Ministry-sponsored teacher-training sessions in the newly instituted morals curriculum. **Sōhyō** and **Zengakuren** co-ordinated strike activities, most notably in violent clashes with police in Wakayama City in August 1958. With increasing member dissatisfaction and popular concern over school disruptions, moderate socialist-supported factions in the union forced a change in strategy.

Although resistance continues, since 1959 performance ratings have been rendered relatively meaningless through prefectural and local-level accommodations that assign routinely positive ratings.

See also: textbook controversies; Zengakuren

JAMES J. ORR

ageing society and elderly care

The challenge of caring for the rapidly rising numbers of elderly people has become a pressing problem in Japanese society, politics and in the economy. Although conservatives would like to rely on families to care for the aged, others call on the state and society to assume more of the burdens of elderly care. Official and public concern for the welfare of old people is of recent origin.

Despite vaunted Confucian traditions of respect for the elderly, pre-war **welfare** policies did little to relieve the aged. An impoverished old person was eligible for public assistance only if he or she lacked any relative who might provide support. The government flatly opposed the introduction of old-age pensions – the only exceptions being pensions for civil servants and Second World War-era pensions for veterans and war widows. Pre-war welfare facilities generally aimed at ameliorating the plight of children, whom, unlike the elderly, the state considered valuable national resources. Demographically, pre-war Japan was a young society. Birth rates were high, while life expectancy was only in the forties and fifties. Nor did the government move forcefully to address the problems of the elderly in the early post-war decades. Nursing homes were few. The National Pension Law (1959), though universal in coverage, fell far short of providing adequate pensions. National health insurance similarly covered all Japanese after 1958, but many older people could not afford to pay the uncovered portion of medical bills. As in pre-war days, the vast majority of the elderly lived in the same house as one of their children, with family members caring for frail parents.

As the Japanese economy grew and general poverty diminished, public attention shifted to the plight of old people. Indeed, the elderly were the focus of the monumental **welfare** reforms sponsored by the government in the early 1970s. The initiative behind the reforms came from the left-wing governor of Tokyo, Minobe Ryōkichi (see **Minobe administration**), who in 1969 introduced free medical care for the elderly. The Diet enacted a similar free medical care provision at the national level in 1972. The next year the government committed to major increases in old-age pension benefits. However, following the 'Oil Shock' of 1973–4 and the onset of slower economic growth, bureaucrats, businessmen and conservative politicians questioned whether Japan was financially capable of carrying through on its commitments to the elderly. Old people, who had recently been regarded as the deserving recipients of welfare programmes, were now described as a problem themselves.

The proponents of reducing welfare commitments coined the phrase 'the ageing society' (*kōreika shakai*) to highlight the problem in the public's mind. Japan, they noted, possessed the most rapidly ageing population among industrial societies and by 2025 would be the world's oldest. If anything, Japanese society has aged more rapidly than the conservatives predicted. While life expectancy has risen to an extraordinary eighty-three years of age for women and seventy-six for men, current birth rates have fallen to well below 1.5 children per married couple. The shrinking base of younger working people will be hard-pressed to pay for pensions and elderly care in coming decades, when each employed person will support two to three pensioners. It is anticipated that fewer children will care for elderly relatives.

Over the past twenty years, the government has offered various solutions to the ageing-society problem, though with uneven results. In 1990, a conservative cabinet proposed measures to encourage women to have more children – including childbirth bonuses and more accessible day care. These efforts did little to reverse the decline in birth rates. Officials have had more luck persuading the elderly to keep working and thus reduce some of the demands on the pension system. Since the 1970s, the government has exhorted and subsidised employers to hire, maintain and retrain older workers. Other programmes locate part-time jobs for retired people. Some 36 per cent of Japanese males aged sixty-five and older were working in 1997, compared to only 17 per cent in the USA and 4 per cent in Germany. To save additional pension funds, the Ministry of Health and Welfare succeeded in raising the age of eligibility for receiving pensions from sixty to sixty-five (which is to be phased in).

In the 1980s, conservative politicians and bureaucrats also formulated policies aimed at maintaining the family's traditional responsibility for elderly care. The three-generation family was heralded as the core of a 'Japanese-style welfare society', which would not require the massive institutionalisation of the elderly seen in European welfare states. Nursing homes expanded during these years, yet they housed a minuscule percentage of older people. More than half of those aged sixty-five and older still live with their children – compared to less than 20 per cent in Western societies. By the 1990s, however, even the bureaucrats and conservative cabinets recognised the impossibility of relying primarily on families to care for the aged. The strains on households – especially on daughters-in-law, daughters and elderly wives – has become a well-publicised social problem. Bedridden parents are living longer, while the women who give them care are increasingly re-entering the workforce.

In recent years, the government has seemingly abandoned talk of the 'Japanese-style welfare society' in favour of establishing major programmes that 'socialise' the burden of elderly care. Introduced in 1989, the 'Gold Plan' has increased the number of home-helpers, nursing-home beds and small community nursing centres. The newest, most ambitious programme is long-term care insurance (*kaigo hoken*), effected in 2000. Funded by premiums paid by all income earners aged forty and older, the system defrays most of the costs of care for physically and mentally disabled old people. For the first time, their families may choose to use these monies to pay for home-helpers, community day services or nursing homes. Whether such innovations will be sufficient to cope with Japan's ageing society remains to be seen.

See also: bedridden patients; welfare

Further reading

Campbell, J.C. (1992) *How Policies Change*, Princeton: Princeton University Press.

Long, S.O. (2000) *Caring for the Elderly in Japan and the US*, London: Routledge.

SHELDON GARON

Agnes-chan

b. 1955, Hong Kong

singer

Born in Hong Kong in 1955, she was known to her fans by her stage name Agnes-chan and is often cited as an example of the Japanese phenomenon of *idoru* **singers**. This style of sugar-sweet, innocent young girl singers dates from the launch of the girl group Sannin Musume (Three Young Girls) in the 1950s, with the first wave of radio pop music programming. Although part of the market image of the *idoru* singers of the 1990s was a more explicit seductiveness – and some of the more famous *idoru* have traded a persona of innocence for sex appeal – in the 1970s, when Agnes-chan launched her career in Japan, fans still looked to the *idoru* for purity and cuteness (the ever important quality in girl culture of **kawaii**). Agnes-chan went on to outgrow her child-like name to enter university, marry and have a family. She did not, however, choose to abandon her career at this point but continued to tour both as a television talk show personality and as a spokesperson for the peace movement. Her frequent appearances with her first son by her side sparked what became known as the Agnes debate (Agnes *ronsō*). Conservative voices came together in the media to condemn her choice to be a working mother, while the emerging feminist movement strongly supported her right to combine career and motherhood. Public opinion was sharply split and media coverage was extensive and heated. Ironically, today Agnes-chan is perhaps best remembered not for her early musical success but for the extent to which the Agnes debate brought issues of gender and work into the public domain.

SANDRA BUCKLEY

agricultural co-ops

Agricultural co-operatives (*nōgyō kyōdō kumiai*; abbreviated as *nōkyō*) provide a wide number of integrated economic and household services for farmers, including lending funds, joint purchase of production materials, guidance on agricultural technology and management, joint marketing and local savings deposit services. Their origins can be traced back to credit unions established by farmers before the Meiji Era (1868–1912), which embodied the spirit of mutual aid at a time when there were no formal co-operative organisations. In the post-war period, the Allied Occupation Forces enacted the Agricultural Co-operative Society Law in 1947, and established the present independent agricultural co-operative system (*nōkyō*) as economic organisations to replace the former government-run agricultural societies (*nōgyōkai*). Co-operatives were established at the village and township level throughout Japan, as well as federations at the prefectural level, and an apex organisation – the Central Union of Agricultural Co-operatives (JA-Zenchū) – to co-ordinate the movement nationally and to lobby governments on behalf of farmers. Membership of JA is over 9 million and includes almost all farmers in Japan as well as non-farming associate members. Despite the challenges posed by the ageing of farm labour, deregulation of agricultural markets, international competition and stagnating agricultural production, JA has provided a range of new services, including public relations, welfare for the elderly and promotion of organic agricultural products.

DAVID EDGINGTON

Ai no korida

Ōshima Nagisa's 1976 film, *Ai no korida* (In the Realm of the Senses), interprets the notorious 1936 case of Abe Sada, who killed her lover and then severed his penis. Although Ōshima developed the film stock in France and screened the film overseas due to Japanese censorship laws, he still was prosecuted unsuccessfully for obscenity over the domestic publication of the film script and stills. Western film theorists have highlighted Ōshima's interweaving of sex, politics and the camera's 'look'. The film can also be considered alongside the 1970s genre of *roman poruno*, especially Tanaka Noboru's 1975 *Jitsuroku Abe Sada* (The True Story of Abe Sada).

See also: censorship and film; pink films

JONATHAN M. HALL

AIDS

The first cases of AIDS in Japan were among haemophiliacs who became infected through tainted blood products imported mostly from the USA. These products continued to be used even after Ministry of Health and Welfare and pharmaceutical company officials were well aware of the danger of HIV infection. In the early years of the epidemic, public discourse alternated between outright discrimination and sentimental sympathy for infected haemophiliacs as 'innocent victims.' However, activist groups like the Tokyo Haemophilia Fraternal Association (Tokyo haemophilia tomo no kai) fought to shift the spotlight on to concrete issues of patients' rights and demand accountability from those who were responsible for their infection. A settlement was finally reached in March 1996 that included free treatment and compensation for all infected haemophiliacs.

The public sympathy eventually accorded the haemophiliacs, however, was not so quick in coming for those infected through sex. A series of media-driven 'AIDS panics' in the 1980s unleashed an epidemic of hysteria on a national scale. While HIV was formerly associated with foreigners, haemophiliacs and gay men, the discovery in January 1987 of an infected Japanese woman and former prostitute was seen as the first threat to the 'mainstream' of straight males. The Diet reacted swiftly with the introduction in February 1987 of a punitive 'AIDS Prevention Law' (*Eizu Yobōhō*), which proposed prison terms and fines for those who knowingly infected others. The bill sparked enormous opposition from a broad coalition of civil rights organisations, who demanded that the government focus on prevention and treatment rather than the policing of people with AIDS and HIV. Among these groups was the newly founded Japan Association for the Lesbian and Gay Movement (OCCUR), which largely came together around opposition to the proposed law.

In 1989, the law passed in a slightly less punitive version, imposing fines but not prison sentences on those whose behaviour was judged by their physicians to pose a risk to the community. The law remained in effect until 1997, when it was incorporated into a revision of the century-old 'Contagious Diseases Prevention Law', renamed the 'Infectious Disease Prevention and Treatment Law'. Together with the scrapping in 1996 of the 1907 Leprosy Prevention Law, which allowed for forced quarantine and sterilisation, the new law represented a hopeful shift of focus from control and policing to prevention and treatment. Despite these efforts, the mistrust generated by the first AIDS Prevention Law continues to deter people from being tested for HIV in Japan, leading to widespread under-reporting. As late as the autumn of 2000, the Japanese Supreme Court upheld a decision by the Dental Faculty of Kagoshima University to expel a student found to be HIV-positive.

See also: tainted-blood scandal

Further reading

Buckley, Sandra (1997) 'The foreign devil returns: Packaging sexual practice and risk in contemporary Japan', in Lenore Manderson and Margaret Jolly (eds) *Sites of Desire, Economies of Pleasure: Sexualities in Asia and the Pacific*, Chicago: University of Chicago Press, pp. 262–91.

Feldman, Eric A. and Bayer, Ronald (eds) (1999) *Blood Feuds: AIDS, Blood, and the Politics of Medical Disaster*, Oxford: Oxford University Press.

KEITH VINCENT

Ainu

The Ainu are an indigenous people whose traditional territory includes **Hokkaidō** island, the Kuril islands, southern Sakhalin and the northern-most tip of Honshū island. In 1853, the Japanese shōgunate government, in the process of negotiating the Russo-Japanese Friendship Treaty, started to unilaterally claim that the Ainu land was part of Japan proper and the Ainu people had always been Japanese nationals. After that, the Japanese government newly adopted an assimilation policy and encouraged the Ainu to accept the lifestyle of the Japanese, while urging them to abandon Ainu lifestyle and culture.

After the Meiji Restoration in 1869, the new Japanese government established Kaitakushi (Hokkaidō Colonial Development Agency) and enforced the Ainu assimilation policy through this agency. For example, in 1871, the traditional Ainu customs including earrings and tattoos for women, and *Jika Shokyaku* (burning the house of a deceased person) were prohibited, mainly because they were con-

sidered savage. In 1873 and 1876, the government started to ban the traditional Ainu ways of fishing and hunting, respectively. Furthermore, in 1877, the government completely deprived the Ainu of land rights. The Ainu people had officially been called '*Kyū-Dojin*' (former aborigines since 1878; they were studied as a 'vanishing race' by Japanese scholars in modernising Japan).

In 1945, Japan was defeated in the Second World War and forced to abandon all of its colonies, but not Hokkaidō and Okinawa. As a result, the government openly began to insist that Japan was a mono-ethnic state. In the 1950s, two reports from the government to the United Nations Secretariat and to the ILO Office stated that Japan's assimilation policy had been perfectly completed and indigenous populations no longer existed in Japan. At that time, almost all of the Japanese began to believe that the Ainu people and their culture remained only in museums and sightseeing spots.

On the other hand, in 1946, the Ainu Association of Hokkaidō (AAH) was established by some Ainu leaders to recapture lands granted under the Hokkaidō Former Aborigines Protection Act (HFAPA) of 1899, of which they were deprived during the post-war Agrarian Reform. However, the government rejected the Ainu land claims. In the 1970s, the Hokkaidō prefectural government recognised serious economic differences between Japanese and the 'descendants' of the Ainu. As a result, in 1974, the Hokkaidō Utari Welfare Programme was started in the local districts where the 'descendants' lived. However, the Japanese government at the time insisted that the 'descendants' were neither Ainu nor an ethnic group, and they could not enjoy any distinct rights.

The 1984 general assembly of the AAH passed a resolution to request the government to adopt a new law on the Ainu in repealing the HFAPA, and adopted a bill that was composed of six sections, including rights to political participation, rights to education, cultural rights and fishing rights. Two years later, the AAH started a new movement, when the then Prime Minister Nakasone Yasuhiro made notorious remarks that Japan was superior to other states because it had been a mono-ethnic state.

These remarks ignited a political movement of the Ainu people to criticise the policy of the government. A feature of the movement was attracting and mobilising international concern. In response to the Prime Minister's remarks, in 1987, the AAH sent their first delegation to the United Nations Working Group on Indigenous Populations (UNWGIP) and insisted on the existence of the Ainu as an indigenous people in Japan. In 1989, the AAH's delegation participated in the General Assembly of the ILO, which was held to adopt a revised ILO convention for indigenous people (ILO Convention No. 169). In replying to the Ainu people's request, Ms Erica-Irene Daes, chairperson of the UNWGIP, and a Greek human rights expert, visited Hokkaidō and Tokyo to investigate the present situation of the Ainu in 1991. Furthermore, the most important and brightest day in Ainu history came the following year. On 19 December 1992, Mr Nomura Giichi, the then president of the AAH, was invited to the headquarters of the United Nations in New York, gave a celebratory speech with other representatives at the opening ceremony of the International Year of the World's Indigenous Peoples. In the International Year 1993, the Ainu people invited Ms Rigoberta Menchu, Nobel Prize laureate in 1992, to their land. The Japanese government were severely concerned by the diplomatic success of the Ainu. Finally they could no longer deny the existence of the Ainu people.

At the same time, some Ainu had made painstaking efforts to revive Ainu culture and traditional customs by themselves. After some one hundred years' interruption caused by deprivation of fishing rights, in 1982, the *Ashir Chep Nomi* (a welcoming ceremony for salmon coming up the river) was held by Toyokawa Shigeo and his friends on Toyohira river in Sapporo. The first Ainu language school was opened by Kayano Shigeru, who later became the first Ainu member of the Diet, at Nibutani in 1983. The AAH has also sponsored the Ainu Culture Festival since 1989.

Under these circumstances, the Japanese government, in the reports of 1987 and 1991 to the UN Human Rights monitoring bodies, reluctantly but officially recognised that the Ainu population had maintained their own language, culture and religion, and that they should be regarded as a 'minority'. This recognition actually meant renunciation of the assimilation policy of successive Japanese governments, and it is the first transformation of the platform for ethnic groups within Japanese territory in some 140 years of modern Japanese history.

In 1994, in unstable political surroundings, the short-lived socialist Murayama administration was born, and the Ainu movement was boosted with support from that administration. Specifically, in 1996, an Advisory Committee of the Cabinet Secretary submitted a report that recommended the adoption of a new law protecting Ainu culture. Based on these recommendations, drafting was begun, and the bill proposed by the government passed the Diet in 1997 unanimously. The most important content of the Law for Promoting Ainu Culture and Tradition is that it declares that Japanese society shall be multicultural, and that the government shall support the development of Ainu culture and tradition.

However, the serious failures of the law are as follows: first, it does not recognise the Ainu as indigenous people; second, it does not stipulate any rights of the Ainu people, therefore the rights of the Ainu are not guaranteed by it; and, third, it has discriminatory by-laws relating to the repeal of the HFAPA. For example, the procedures for returning 'communal properties' of the Ainu under the HFAPA were decided unilaterally by the government. Communal properties are to be returned without any revaluation that would account for inflation and without disclosure of management records. Some Ainu groups are bringing a lawsuit against the government regarding the communal properties issue, in an attempt to make clear the history of Japanese colonisation. In 1987, two Ainu plaintiffs actually won a lawsuit over the Nibutani dam site. The Nibutani Dam Decision handed down by the Sapporo District Court recognised the Ainu as an indigenous people, and requested the government to protect their cultural rights. The Nibutani case offers some prospect that the lawsuit over Ainu communal properties could also be won in the near future.

UEMURA HIDEAKI

Ajase Complex

In 1932, Kosawa Heisaku, the founder of psycho-analysis in Japan, advanced an alternative model to Freud's concept of the Oedipus Complex. Labelled the Ajase Complex, his concept was built on the Freudian premise that children become adults by assuming their place within a social order whose rules and norms are internalised to shape the psychological desires and motivations of the self. Agreeing with Freud that such a process is universal, Kosawa disagreed that the form this universally takes is what Freud labelled the Oedipus Complex. In the case of the latter, a child is situated in a family where the father's role is central; by threatening castration, he compels the child to individuate from the mother and form an identity and love object apart from the family. In Japan, by contrast, familial dynamics are more dyadic than triangular: the family centres almost entirely on the relationship between mother and child, and there is a gradual development of this bond rather than an abrupt disrupture at the time of adolescence. In a process that barely involves the father (and his authority backed by threat), maturation is marked here by the child's ability to not break from the mother but remain bonded to her, while recognising her as a person rather than an omnipotent ideal. This is particularly apparent in the mother–son relationship.

Just as Sigmund Freud used a Greek tragedy to craft his theory of the Oedipus Complex, Kosawa adopted a tale to fashion the Ajase Complex. This is the tale of Ajase, the Japanese version of the Indian prince Ajatasatru, a contemporary of the Buddha. The story concerns Queen Idaike who, desiring a child as a means to keep her husband's affections, consults a seer and is told that a sage living in the forest will die within three years and be reincarnated as her son. Impatient, she kills the sage and immediately becomes pregnant but, fearing the curse of the sage, tries twice (unsuccessfully) to kill the foetus. Once Ajase is born, however, Queen Idaike becomes a model mother. When the boy is approaching adolescence, he discovers the secret of his birth and, disillusioned with the mother he had idealised, tries to kill her. He, too, fails, and is soon wracked with guilt that leads to odorific sores over his body. His mother

tends to him throughout his illness and, from this devotion, the son comes to forgive his mother. Queen Idaike, in turn, forgives Ajase, and the two reunite in a bond of mutual forgiveness. As analysed by Kosawa, the Ajase legend is a morality tale paradigmatic of the type of morality grounding Japanese culture: one organised through guilt and forgiveness (what he called guilt penitence). This contrasts with the guilt operating in the Oedipus Complex, motivated by fear of punishment and incarnated by Freud in his doctrine of the castration threat.

Sigmund Freud never recognised the legitimacy of Kosawa Heisaku's Ajase Complex (and thus the critique it held against the universalism and ethnocentrism of the Oedipus Complex). Denied recognition by the international community, as was Japanese psychoanalysis for close to forty years, Kosawa remained, none the less, a devoted practitioner of psychoanalysis until his death in 1968.

Further reading

Keigo Okonogi (1978) 'The Ajase Complex of the Japanese', *Japan Echo* 6(1): 104–18.

ANNE ALLISON

Akasaka

The Akasaka district of Minato Ward, **Tokyo**, is synonymous with corporate and official Japan. Streets such as Aoyama-dori present vistas of high-rise office buildings woven together with lines of heavy traffic. From any vantage point, especially the nearby Tokyo Tower in **Roppongi**, one may view a mass of office towers, some of them bearing simple signs reading 'Mori Biru 36 [or 38 or 40]' to designate more than eighty buildings raised by a developer named Mori, the third largest land owner in Japan.

Akasaka is a landscape of daytime activity. Government officials and company employees, male *sarariiman* ('salarymen') and female OL ('office ladies') pour in on crowded commuter lines each morning. The sidewalks are a sea of navy blue and grey business attire during lunchtime and the evening *rashu* (rush hour). Although Akasaka has a number of excellent, and expensive, restaurants, after dark the streets are relatively quiet, as the day population shifts back to residential districts or on to the night life in Roppongi, **Shibuya** and other entertainment areas. Akasaka has the lowest residential density in Tokyo, but its residences are extremely expensive. The most famous residents of Akasaka are the family of the Crown Prince, who occupy the Akasaka Palace, built by Katayama Otokuma in 1909, and modelled on the palace at Versailles.

AUDREY KOBAYASHI

Akutagawa Prize

The Akutagawa Ryūnosuke Prize (usually called the Akutagawa prize) is the most prestigious literary prize in Japan for new authors of serious fiction, and it still frequently launches novelists on successful careers. It was established in 1935, together with the **Naoki Prize**, by the writer Kikuchi Kan, in memory of the celebrated novelist whose name it bears. The prize is normally awarded twice a year but it is not unusual for no award to be made if, in the opinions of the judges, no story is worthy of the prize.

Since the award's inception, the *Bungei Shunjū* journal has published the prize-winning stories, which include, in the post-war era, such famous works as **Nakagami Kenji**'s *Misaki* (The Cape) in 1976, **Murakami Ryū**'s *Kagiri naku tō mei ni chikai burū* (Almost Transparent Blue) in 1977 and Yū Miri's *Kazoku shinema* (Family Cinema) in 1996. However, many distinguished writers like **Murakami Haruki** and **Yoshimoto Banana** have not been awarded the prize (despite winning several of the other numerous literary awards available). In some respects, the prize serves as much a social as a literary function, keeping literature in the public eye due to the award's high media profile.

LEITH MORTON

alcoholism

Alcoholism (*arukoru chū doku*) is a condition that is acknowledged by the Japanese, but not widely recognised. Japanese generally feel that alcoholism is rare in their country, particularly as compared to foreign countries. Opinion surveys show that the most widely held popular definition of an alcoholic is one whose hands shake because they need a drink. In practice, Japanese are far less likely than Americans to label a drinker as an alcoholic because the criteria are, in fact, more social rather than physiological. To begin with, Americans suffer from a puritanism that renders them, at best, ambivalent about the pleasures of the flesh. The Japanese, by contrast, see the pleasures of the flesh, in general, and the enjoyment of alcohol, in particular, as normal and acceptable, as long as one indulges in socially appropriate contexts. For this reason, a person whose drinking behaviour might be cause for concern among Americans may only be seen as sociable by Japanese.

On the other hand, while Americans have come to identify alcoholism as a disease and often feel some sympathy for the sufferer, Japanese are far more inclined to see those who are labelled as alcoholics as weak-willed and self-indulgent people who have a moral failing. So, where some Americans accept the label of alcoholic as an explanation for their behaviour, Japanese are more inclined to resist the label as highly stigmatising. While the surest way to gain a reputation as an alcoholic is to be an unpleasant drunk who disrupts social relations, yet persists in drinking, as long as one continues to fulfil role expectations as a spouse, parent or employee, one is unlikely to be identified as an alcoholic in Japan.

The disease model of alcoholism is also not well developed in the Japanese medical community. Physicians tend to treat alcohol-related problems symptomatically, simply warning the patient to drink less, rather than looking at a larger psycho-social syndrome. There has also been a tendency to diagnose alcoholism as an incurable psychosis, with the result that difficult drunks are sometimes institutionalised in mental hospitals for essentially custodial purposes. One trend in the medical study of Japanese alcoholism has been a focus on what is known as the Flushing Syndrome. A significant proportion of the Japanese population gets a toxic reaction from alcohol, leading to a variety of possible symptoms, such as reddening of the skin (flushing), tachycardia, headaches, nausea and dysphoria. Many Japanese physicians argue that the number of alcoholics in Japan is low because the Flushing Syndrome acts as an inhibitor against drinking.

Lay alcoholism treatment programmes exist in Japan, although they are not well known. Alcoholics Anonymous (AA) have meetings in several major cities but the membership is quite small, in part because efforts have been focused on helping skid row derelicts and in part because of cultural problems with AA principles. Far more successful in recruitment has been Danshukai, the Japan Sobriety Association. Danshukai is based on AA, but has modified its policies to be more acceptable to Japanese. While its members come from all segments of Japanese society, it has a strong middle-class following.

See also: *yobai*

Further reading

Smith, Stephen R. (1998) 'Good old boy into alcoholic: Danshukai and learning a new drinking role in Japan', in J. Singleton (ed.) *Learning in Likely Places*, Cambridge, UK: Cambridge University Press, pp. 286–303.

STEPHEN R. SMITH

alien registration

All foreigners residing in Japan for more than a year must register with their local authorities and be issued with an alien registration (*gaikokujin toroku*) card. Alien registration must be renewed every five years and the official document has to be carried at all times. A wide range of public officials are entitled to demand presentation of the card at any time – police, railway and port authorities, immigration officers.

The procedures were instigated in 1952 under the Alien Registration Law. The most controversial element of this law has been mandatory fingerprinting. Many aliens resent being put through a procedure usually associated only with criminals, and there have been a small number of cases that have gone to court in the fight to refuse fingerprinting. After years of aggressively defending

the practice, the Japanese Justice Ministry unexpectedly announced in 1998 a reform to abolish fingerprinting. The success of the bill in the Diet is not guaranteed due to continued support from the National Police Agency and conservative politicians, who favour strict screening of all non-permanent foreign residents. Permanent residents have not been required to be fingerprinted since 1993. In addition to the fingerprinting issue, many foreigners in Japan complain of the intrusiveness of the not infrequent requests from police to produce the alien registration card. This is particularly true when a foreigner moves into a new neighbourhood. The neighbourhood police-box (*kōban*) system ensures that any unfamiliar faces are quickly noticed by patrolling officers and proper documents are routinely confirmed.

See also: *gaijin*

SANDRA BUCKLEY

Allied Occupation

If any of Japan's historical experiences can be called 'unique', it is the Allied Occupation (1945–52). Following the Second World War, the USA attempted to remake Japan as a peaceful, democratic nation and to incorporate it into a new cold-war world order. **Supreme Commander for Allied Powers** (SCAP) General Douglas **MacArthur** directed the demilitarisation, democratisation and economic reform of Japan, working through the existing Japanese government but with little input from the other Allied powers and only general guidelines from Washington. The legacies of the Occupation included social and economic changes, a democratic 'peace constitution' that prohibited war and gave sovereignty and broad civil rights to the people while retaining the Emperor as a symbol, a close alliance with the USA in which Japan was subordinate, incomplete acknowledgment of the responsibility for Japan's aggression – and continuing controversies over all of these issues.

The Allies' **Potsdam Declaration** of 26 July 1945 stated that Japan's unconditional surrender would be followed by the Occupation that would supervise the establishment 'in accordance with the freely expressed will of the Japanese people of a peacefully inclined and responsible government'. The US Initial Post-Surrender Policy for Japan (29 August 1945) directed SCAP to demilitarise and democratise Japan, using but not supporting the Japanese government. MacArthur arrived on 30 August to command Allied troops throughout Japan and an Occupation bureaucracy of over 5,000 (few of whom had much knowledge of Japan) from SCAP's general headquarters (GHQ) in Tokyo. In December, Allied nations established a Far Eastern Commission and an Allied Council for Japan to supervise the Occupation, but they were of limited influence.

The Occupation authorities necessarily worked through the existing Japanese government and bureaucracy, most of which remained in place. The Home Ministry, which had controlled the police, local government and elections, was abolished, as was the military. Some 200,000 politicians, military officers and business leaders (the latter in relatively small numbers) were purged from public life. Yoshida Shigeru, a conservative former diplomat, emerged as the most important political leader of the first post-war decade, serving as Minister of Foreign Affairs from 1945 to 1946 and then as prime minister from 1946 to 1947, and again from 1948 to 1954.

Homelessness, food shortages, unemployment and inflation were severe problems in the first few years after the war, and were exacerbated by the repatriation of some 6 million soldiers and civilians from overseas. For most Japanese, simply finding enough food was an all-consuming struggle until as late as 1949. Judge Yamaguchi Yoshitada, assigned cases involving the omnipresent black markets, starved to death in October 1947 after resolving to live only on his legal food rations.

The first phase of the Occupation, from 1945 to 1949, was characterised by a focus on demilitarising and democratising Japan. Military and political leaders accused of conspiring to wage aggressive war were prosecuted for crimes against humanity and peace in the controversial Tokyo war crimes trials from 1946 to 1948. Emperor **Hirohito** was exempted from prosecution, a decision that made it impossible for the nation as a whole to fully deal with its war responsibility.

When Japanese attempts were unsatisfactory, MacArthur directed members of his staff to draft a new constitution in February 1946. After some modifications, the revolutionary document was passed by the Diet and took effect in May 1947. The **post-war Constitution** transferred sovereignty to the people, retained only a **symbol monarchy**, renounced war, broadened civil rights and provided for gender equality. Other reforms included **land reform**, which transferred land to tenant farmers, the promotion of labour unions, partial dissolution of the *zaibatsu* financial combines (see ***zaibatsu* dissolution**) and a revision of the Civil Code (see **Civil Code of 1948, the**), which reduced the authority of the family head. Education was reorganised along US lines into a single-track system.

Policy goals shifted around 1947 from democratisation to anti-communism and economic rebuilding. This change was motivated not only by cold-war fears, but also by concerns that Japan's stalled economy could make it a long-term financial burden for the USA.

Early signs of the policy shift came in response to the labour movement, which had grown more rapidly and become more radical that the Occupation expected. MacArthur banned the **General Strike** planned for 1 February 1947. Legislation prohibiting strikes by civil servants followed. In the **Red Purge** of 1950, Communist Party leaders and communist labour activists were targeted. Plans for economic deconcentration were drastically scaled back, and retrenchment policies controlled inflation and eliminated the budget deficit. After the outbreak of the **Korean War** in 1950, a 75,000-man National Police Reserve was created, despite the constitutional ban on war potential. This evolved into the **Self Defence Forces** in 1954.

MacArthur was relieved of his command by President Truman in April 1951. The San Francisco Peace Treaty, signed in September 1951, ended the Occupation in April 1952. However, Japan's independence was less than complete. Yoshida had to accept a Mutual Security Treaty keeping Japan firmly in the US orbit and allowing US bases in Japan, and to recognise the Chinese Nationalists in Taiwan rather than the People's Republic in Beijing.

Historians still debate whether the Occupation, a revolution from above and outside, put Japan back on a track from which the 'dark valley' of the

1930s and early 1940s was a temporary deviation, or whether it imposed changes that could never have been made by the Japanese themselves. After 1952, conservatives in the Diet lacked the two-thirds majority necessary to amend the Constitution, and, aside from partial re-centralisation of the police and education systems, the major Occupation reforms have stuck.

See also: Dodge Line; *zaibatsu* dissolution

Further reading

Dower, J. (1999) *Embracing Defeat: Japan in the Wake of World War II*, New York: Norton.

Schonberger, H. (1989) *Aftermath of Empire: Americans and the Remaking of Japan, 1945–1952*, Kent, OH: Kent State University Press.

Ward, R. and Sakamoto, Y. (eds) (1987) *Democratizing Japan: The Allied Occupation*, Honolulu: University of Hawaii Press.

Ward, R. and Shulman, F. (eds) (1974) *The Allied Occupation of Japan, 1945–1952: An Annotated Bibliography of Western-Language Materials*, Chicago: American Library Association.

See also the published (1975–1992) proceedings of the eight symposia on *The Occupation of Japan* sponsored by the MacArthur Memorial, later joined by Old Dominion University. Editors were first L. Redford, then T. Burkman and finally W. Nimmo.

TIMOTHY S. GEORGE

amae

The concept of *amae* is linked with the work of the Japanese psychoanalyst **Doi Takeo**. Doi developed a notion of identity in which the Japanese individual is realised not through the condition of autonomy but in the context of relationships. He identified the mother's indulgence of the child's desire for passive love as a primary dynamic of a relational individuality (which was not a contradiction to Doi). The lifelong desire for *amae*-based relationships of indulgence is then played out not only within the intimate inner circle of relations (*uchi*) but can also extend into the more distant

contexts (*soto*) of the workplace, and other relations such as doctor/patient, student/teacher.

Doi has been credited with challenging simplistic overlays of Western concepts on to either Japanese society or the Japanese psyche. He has also been criticised for his unproblematic engagement with the notion of a national psyche, and the support his work lends to theories of Japanese uniqueness (*Nihonjinron*). Doi also chooses not to analyse the dynamics of power that underpin *amae*-based relationships. Feminists have questioned the androcentric bias of his conceptualisation of the individual and the absence of gender-differentiated analysis of relationships of desire.

Further reading

Doi Takeo (1977) *The Anatomy of Dependence*, Tokyo: Kōdansha.

Rosenberger, N. (1992) *Japanese Sense of Self*, Cambridge, UK: Cambridge University Press.

SANDRA BUCKLEY

Amerika Mura

The fishing village of Mio-mura, on the south coast of Wakayama Prefecture, is erroneously known as 'Amerika Mura' in recognition of the fact that, during the early years of the twentieth century, many villagers emigrated not to America but to Canada, where they settled in the small fishing port of Steveston, in what is now Richmond, a suburb south of Vancouver.

In 1887, Kuno Gihei travelled to Canada as a *dekasegi* (see **migrant workers**). When he saw the potential for earnings in the fishing industry, he returned to his village and soon organised the emigration of many of his fellow villagers, as well as those of surrounding areas. Mio-mura became the largest of the Japanese 'emigrant villages', which sent large numbers of *dekasegi* abroad during the late Meiji and Taishō Periods. Most Mio-mura villagers worked in the fishing industry, the men on boats, the women on shore in canneries. During the Second World War, they were uprooted from their homes, dispossessed of their fishing boats and gear, and placed in internment camps. After the war, some returned to Japan, while others re-established as Japanese Canadians. There are strong links between Mio-mura and Canada today, and the village has a small museum to commemorate these links.

AUDREY KOBAYASHI

Ando Tadao

b. 1941, Ōsaka

Architect

A native of Ōsaka, Ando has based his practice there since opening Ando Tadao Architects and Associates in 1969, at the age of only twenty-eight. Ando stands out among professional Japanese architects in being largely self-taught, never working for another architect and educating himself in the decade prior to opening his own office during his travels throughout Europe, the USA, and Africa. He has made his architectural mark, not only in Japan but also in the world arena, with distinctively simple and stoic designs in exposed concrete.

Concrete, poured in carefully crafted formwork, sculpts Ando's architecture into surprisingly graceful geometric forms. In his first widely published work, *Row House in Sumiyoshi (Azuma House; located in Ōsaka, 1975–6)*, Ando reinterpreted the *nagaya*, or traditional Japanese row house. A small house only 3.3 meters wide, with approximately 62 square meters of interior area, Azuma House is also minimalist in design concept, lacking all ornament. It is divided into two parts by an interior courtyard, requiring one to go outside regardless of the weather to get from one part of the dwelling to the other. The front elevation of the house is a bared concrete wall with no windows, only a door. Although some criticise Azuma House and subsequent works for being too stark, difficult to live in or simply boring, throughout the world his work has been acclaimed for being original and direct in its use of materials and approach to form.

Over the years, Ando has attempted to forge connections between traditional concepts of architecture and modern technology and materials, and between the vernacular and modernism. Often

describing his own architectural compositions of light, natural elements, materials and form as a 'fight' to experience the lived environment more authentically, Ando also stresses an imperative for architecture to meet the spiritual needs of its inhabitants. Indeed, while several of his best-known projects are churches and a temple, his reverential attention to experiential qualities and nature's dialogue with all his architectural work is persistent.

Major works by Ando in Japan include: Rokko Housing I and II (Kobe, 1978–83); Festival shopping centre (Naha, Okinawa, 1980–4); TIME'S I/II (Kyōto, 1983–4/1986–9); Chapel on Mt. Rokko (Kobe, 1985–6); Church of Light (Ōsaka, 1987–9); Water Lotus Temple (Awajishima, 1989); and Museum of Wood (Hyōgo, 1996). Internationally, Ando's projects include: the Japanese Pavilion (Seville, Spain, 1992); Japanese Screen Gallery in the Art Institute of Chicago (1992); Peace Haven (Paris, 1995); and the Modern Art Museum (Fort Worth, Texas, 1997). In 1987, he taught a Master's course at Yale University. Ando has won numerous architectural awards, including the prestigious international Pritzker Prize in 1995, becoming the third Japanese architect to be so recognised.

See also: architecture

Further reading

Frampton, Kenneth (ed.) (1989) *Tadao Ando: The Yale Studio and Current Works*, New York: Rizzoli International Publications, Inc.
—— (1984) *Tadao Ando: Buildings Projects Writings*, New York: Rizzoli International Publications, Inc.
Futagawa Yukio (ed.) (1991) *Tadao Ando Details*, Tokyo: ADA Edita Tokyo Co., Ltd.

SCOTT GOLD AND MARY KNIGHTON

anime

Anime is the shortened Japanese transliterated word for animation. Imamura Taihei, the philosopher of media, first used the term in the 1940s in place of the Japanese word *mangaeiga* (cartoon films). Since the 1970s, the popularity of *anime* in Japan has far exceeded that of animation in any other domestic markets in the world. The market for *anime* stretches from its original base in children's fantasy and adventure into teenage romance and historical drama, male sports, science fiction, war, fantasy, avant-garde media and, finally, into pornography. Outside Japan, markets for Japanese *anime* have most often followed markets for other successful Japanese commodities such as finance capital and consumer electronics.

Similar to other US nationalistic anxieties about the proper origins of finance capital and hi-tech innovation, Japanese *anime* has been characterised as appropriated from Walt Disney and his big-budget cartoons of the 1930s and 40s. In contrast to this problematic uni-directional understanding – grounded in the supposition that modern culture and civilization originate in the 'West' – transnational critics and fans of *anime* like Ueno Toshiya configure *anime* as an effect of the crossings and double-crossings between and beyond Japan, China, Eastern and Western Europe, and the USA. *Anime* is better understood as drawing on traditions as diverse as scroll painting in China and Japan, and international influences on cinematic production of all kinds in the early part of the century.

According to Imamura, from as early as the seventeenth and eighteenth centuries Japanese painters and visionaries have constantly sought ways to 'animate'/*ugokasu* still images. Owing to its close relation to film development before and during Japan's fifteen-year war (1930–45), it was intimately linked with the domestic film studio system. In this first period *anime* was split into two camps of animators affiliated with different studios: the Seo Kosei group became the centre of propaganda *anime* for the government during the Pacific War, while the Masaoka Kenzo group rarely functioned as a propaganda organ. However, the first great *anime* artist Ōfuji Noburo (1900–61) developed outside the studios and their two *anime* groups. It was not until after the bleak ten-year period following the end of the Second World War that Ōfuji's work became recognised in and outside Japan. The mid-1950s is considered the watershed for the maturation of *anime* with Ōfuji's critically acclaimed work *Phantom Ship* (1955), the rise of new production companies like Otogi and Tōei (which

made the first feature-length colour *anime* in 1958, called *The Legend of the White Snake*) and the introduction of television *anime* contributing to a rebirth of creativity in design and production. One of the spawns for this period was the famous *manga* artist Tezuka Osamu, who used sales from his texts and television *anime Astro Boy* to build his own animation studio in 1961, Mushi Production. Here, many of the successful *anime* artists of the 1970s and 1980s began their careers. Taking advantage of the freedom offered by his own production company, Tezuka set the standard for later commercial *anime* artists by working variously in children's, adult and experimental formats.

The global popularity of *anime* in the 1980s was led by four creative artists: Miyazaki Hayao (*Princess Mononoke, Neighbour Totoro*), Ōtomo Katsuhiro (*Akira, Roujin Z*), Oshii Mamoru (*Patlabor II, Ghost in the Shell*) and Takahashi Rumiko (*Ranma ½, Yurusei Yatsura*). All four have taken advantage of commercial success in Japan to distance themselves from the closed-off, intense domestic *anime* scene where producers and consumers frequently interact, i.e. through fanzines, computer networks, *anime* magazines, specialty shops and *anime* conventions. This separation has allowed for both a greater range of artistic expression and a more sustained level of critical engagement (for example, Oshii's attacks on US imperialism and 'Americanisation', Takahashi's feminist and queer interpretations, Miyazaki's critiques of technology and Ōtomo's metafictions). It is ironic that these popular international *anime* artists have largely renounced *anime*'s sense and sensibility inside Japan. Therefore, the quality of the work of these four *anime* giants has been maintained and supported by a distance from the Lolita-like figures, super-tech machines and cybernetic entities associated with *anime* and ***otaku*** (fan) sensibilities.

Despite its increasing global and domestic popularity, by the second half of the 1980s *anime* was increasingly criticised for stagnating – limited to lots of low-quality television *anime* or formulaic, though beautiful, high-quality image work for enthusiastic fans using the new form of *OVA* (Original Video Animation). In 1996, however, Anno Hideaki and his television *anime Neon Genesis Evangelion* (1996) took advantage of a cult following in Japan, not by distancing himself from it as in the case of the four giants but by more fully immersing himself in the contradictions and pleasures of formulaic, *otaku anime*. In this way, Anno has been able to critique and open up the aesthetics and technics of *anime* through a process of implosion. Critics in Japan argue that Anno's work is responsible for reawakening the commercial *anime* scene in Japan.

Concomitant with the globalisation of the consumption of *anime* has been the globalisation of its production. Similar to the practices of outsourcing and the search for cheap labour employed by other Japanese transnational corporations, large *anime* production companies like Gainax increasingly rely on subcontracting low-tech *anime* production out to smaller Chinese, Korean and Filipino companies. These companies take the original designs, storyboards and CAD (Computer-Aided Design) images from the parent company and do the labour-intensive work that makes up 90 per cent of a television or OVA *anime* product. When the nearly finished *anime* returns to Japan, the product is fine tuned with music, voice and expensive digital enhancing. This reliance on both outsourcing to Asia and computers has brought a new importance to the role of the 'designer' in big-budget *anime*. Although central in the 1960s and 1970s, the designer's responsibility for co-ordinating the aesthetic and technological 'look' of the *anime* among many different groups has brought fame to designers like Izubuchi Yutaka of the *Gundam 2* series. These designers frequently attain levels of popularity among *anime* fans higher than creative artists, although they remain unknown outside Japan.

See also: *manga*

Further reading

Imamura Taihei (1992 [originally published in 1948]) *Mangaeiga ron*, Tokyo: Iwanami Shoten.
Levi, Antonia (1996) *Samurai from Outer Space: Understanding Animation*, Chicago and La Salle, IL: Open Court Press.
Toshiya Ueno (1998) *Beni no metarusu-tsu: Anime to iu senjō*, Tokyo: Kinokuniya Shoten.

MARK DRISCOLL

Anpo struggle

The Anpo struggle was the 1960 protest against the revised version of the USA–Japan Security Treaty (popularly know as Anpo). The ratification process provoked some of the most massive demonstrations in post-war history, turning a parliamentary dispute over diplomatic relations into a major crisis of democracy. A second Anpo struggle took place in 1970 against the renewal of the treaty, amid numerous other protests

The original Mutual Security Treaty was concluded in 1951 in conjunction with the San Francisco Peace Treaty that ended the Occupation of Japan. The 1951 treaty allowed the USA to retain its military bases in Japan and station troops there, provisions considered vital to its cold war strategy for the Far East. Japan later sought to alter other provisions that it felt impinged on Japanese sovereignty. Government officials particularly objected to the articles that allowed US troops to intervene in internal disturbances and the articles that required Japan to gain US consent before granting military privileges to any third party.

After becoming prime minister in 1957, Kishi Nobuksuke made a strong push to revise the treaty. From September 1958, the two countries carried out negotiations to that end, and, in January 1960, Kishi went to Washington to initial the revised treaty. He did not anticipate any difficulty getting it ratified and invited President Eisenhower for a state visit that summer, during which Kishi planned to present the treaty as a token of Japan's commitment to the Western bloc.

Opposition to the treaty, however, had already mounted in Japan. A coalition of 134 groups called the People's Council to Stop the Revised Security Treaty formed in March 1959, representing the Socialist and Communist Parties, labour federations, disarmament groups, organisations defending the Constitution, residents and workers concerned about the military bases, China amity associations, women's groups, student councils and minority-rights advocates. The People's Council organised a series of nineteen United Actions through June 1960, which included rallies, protest marches, petition drives and limited strikes throughout Japan involving an estimated 16 million people

Popular opposition grew because the treaty was seen as undermining post-war democracy and increasing the threat of remilitarisation. The fact that Kishi, a wartime cabinet member, had been indicted as a Class A War Criminal fuelled popular opposition. At the end of the war he declared that the treaty would be his crowning glory, so people saw Anpo as part of Kishi's political agenda to undo the democratic reforms of the Occupation and revive pre-war structures. Most prominent were his efforts to revise the Constitution, especially Article 9, which renounced military forces, and would institute a teacher rating system, centralise state control of education and pass a Police Duties Bill that greatly increased powers of arrest and detention. The treaty's military commitments prompted anxieties over Japan's remilitarisation. People retained vivid memories of the defeat and aftermath of the Second World War, so many citizens preferred a stance of unarmed neutrality. Anpo, however, committed Japan to support the USA militarily in the cold war, increasing the possibility of being drawn into a war not of its own making.

The opposition parties bottled up the treaty in committee, in order to ratify it without Upper House approval in time for Eisenhower's planned state visit, Kishi needed to extend the Diet session one month and get the Lower House to pass it by 19 May. When Socialist Party members staged a sit-in to prevent this, Kishi mobilised riot police to forcibly remove them from the chambers, extended the session and ratified the treaty in a snap vote.

The forcible ratification aroused widespread outrage and daily demonstrations, whose numbers leaped from tens to hundreds of thousands. The press was almost unanimously critical of Kishi's actions and he refused to meet with them for a week. Kishi's use of police to enforce his agenda transformed the dispute into a struggle between dictatorship and democracy, in the eyes of the protesters. Despite the massive demonstrations and the petitions of millions opposing the treaty, Kishi refused any calls to dissolve the Diet, rescind the treaty, cancel Eisenhower's state visit or resign from office.

Events peaked on 15 June when right-wing youths violently attacked citizen groups near the front gate of the Diet while riot police clashed with students at the south gate, resulting in the first fatality of the protests. Student radicals tried to force open the gate to the compound to symbolically reopen the political process that Kishi had shut down. When they succeeded in opening it, riot police attacked them with clubs and tear gas. In the mêlée, hundreds of students and police were injured and Kamba Michiko, a female student leader at Tokyo University, was killed. In the wake of the violence, Kishi cancelled Eisenhower's state visit.

For the protesters, the shock of Kamba's death was compounded by the unprecedented joint declaration of seven major daily newspapers on 17 June. The editorial implied that the protesters and opposition parties were to blame for the events and the Kishi administration claimed vindication. Two days later, the treaty 'automatically' went into effect without a vote in the Upper House and student leaders dejectedly declared the struggle had all been 'a huge zero'.

Despite the defeat, two more major demonstrations took place and Kishi resigned from office on 23 June. The ruling **Liberal Democratic Party** had to turn from its confrontational political agenda to a low-key approach emphasising programmes to promote economic prosperity. The Anpo protests also marked a shift from united-front style opposition to the rise of diverse, locally autonomous citizens' movements as agents of social and political change.

The treaty was slated for renewal in 1970, leading to a second Anpo struggle mounted by separate but related movements, including the student movement, the anti-US bases and anti-Vietnam War (see **Beheiren**) movement and the farmers' movement (see **farmers' movements**) against the Narita airport (see **Narita Airport struggle**). This meant that the 1970 Anpo struggle was not the lead political issue or the umbrella under which these various other movements were subsumed.

Despite the protests, the treaty was renewed indefinitely, as had been expected by all parties involved. However, links between the 1970 Anpo struggle and other movements meant that the defeat of the treaty struggle was not devastating and protesters moved on to other related issues.

See also: barricades; Zenkyōtō

Further reading

Packard, G. (1966) *Protest in Tokyo*, Princeton: Princeton University Press.

WESLEY SASAKI-UEMURA

anti-nuclear power

Heavily promoted by the national government, the nuclear power industry was developed with little or no consideration for local public opinion in plant site selection. As nuclear power plants came online in the 1960s and 1970s, local resentment over bureaucratic insensitivity and concern over radioactive leaks or more serious accidents led to protests and civil action by residents' groups, widely composed of housewives, others who felt their livelihoods threatened in industries such as agriculture and fishing, and concerned left-wing activists.

The well-publicised Mutsu incident (1974), in which an experimental nuclear-powered ship was refused return to port because of radioactive leakage, raised national popular awareness. The movement coalesced nationally in 1975 in reaction to a new government-sponsored system of financial inducements for municipalities accepting new plants. In 1978, a nuclear safety commission was established to divorce regulatory oversight from developmental responsibilities, but accidents at Three Mile Island, Chernobyl and nuclear power plants throughout Japan, along with evidence of investigative cover-ups, lent continued impetus to the movement. Opposition involved petitions, rallies, public fora, local plebiscites and, beginning in the 1990s, a systematic effort to gain stockholder voting rights in the major power companies (*datsu genpatsu kabunushi undō*).

See also: peace and anti-nuclear movements

JAMES J. ORR

anti-US bases movements

Movements against US military bases are typically residents' movements that oppose threats and injury to the lives and living environments of people living in the vicinity of bases occupied by the US military under the Japan–US Security Treaty. Anti-base movements began under the Allied Occupation. In 1949, fishermen in Kujū-kurihama, Chiba Prefecture, protested against US forces firing off live ammunition and the decline in the quality of life in the vicinity of a US facility, and as a result were sentenced to a year's incarceration with hard labour by a US military court. Near the end of the Occupation, in 1951, a protest movement opposed construction of anti-aircraft gun emplacements at the Yokota base in the outskirts of Tokyo.

The number and variety of protests increased markedly in the 1950s, once the security treaty became effective in 1952. Movements opposed to expropriation of local land for a US firing range in the sand dunes of Uchinada village in Ishikawa Prefecture continued from September 1952 to January 1957, when the land was finally returned to village control. Peace organisations and unions pitched in to make the movement Japan's first nationwide anti-base struggle. Farmers near Mt. Fuji began in 1955 to oppose US appropriation of former Japanese Army practice areas in Kita-Fuji and Higashi-Fuji, demanding the complete return of village commons and farm land. A combination of tactics, including sit-ins around gun platforms by members of the Shibano Village Mothers Club (Shibano-mura Ha-ha no Kai), achieved some limits on weapons use and other concessions. Also, in Okinawa, movements against land expropriation gradually expanded to become 'all island struggles'.

Some movements in the 1950s raised fundamental legal issues. In Sunagawa on the outskirts of Tokyo, residents opposed preparations to expand the runway of the US Air Force's Tachikawa Air Base. Twenty-five protestors were arrested in 1957 for allegedly breaking down fences and entering the precincts of the base, which was illegal under the administrative agreement that parallels the Japan–US Security Treaty. Seven were indicted, and, in 1959, the Tokyo District court held them blameless on grounds of the unconstitutionality of the security treaty and the administrative agreement. The decision was later overturned by the Supreme Court. Such movements began to catalyse new and sometimes lasting co-operative relationships between local residents, many of whom were farmers, and officials in local and prefectural governments, student groups, unions and left-wing political parties. The Sunagawa struggle, especially, served to build political momentum that later contributed to the **Anpo struggle** in 1960.

Massive demonstrations against US military bases also developed in the wake of the 1960 Anpo struggle. In March 1962, 100,000 protesters joined hands to surround the US air base at Itazuke, and substantially more than that gathered in October 1962 and again in January 1964 to surround the US air base at Yokota. Many demonstrations erupted in 1964 against port calls by US nuclear submarines, and, in the late 1960s, anti-base activists linked up with the anti-Vietnam War movement and the movement that would seek to terminate the Japan–US Security Treaty in 1970. By this time, movement partisans had begun to carry out detailed research and analysis of both on-base activities – much of which sought to anticipate and assess the danger of nuclearisation – and of Japanese laws and local regulations. Often, this research provided the basis for successful arguments against US activities, as in the case of opposition to US military trains in Yokohama.

In the 1970s and 1980s, anti-base struggles were often framed in environmentalist terms. In the late 1970s, lawsuits to stop excessive noise were brought against the US Air Force base at Yokota, Tokyo, and the Atsugi Naval Air Station, west of Tokyo. Successful alliances with local government in defence of livelihood and the natural environment were formed in the mid-1980s in Zushi, where throughout the 1980s citizens opposed construction of a US off-base housing facility and other installations, and on the island of Miyakejima in Tokyo Bay, where citizens voted out a local government that agreed to a Japanese government-sponsored airport that would be devoted in part to night-landing practice by US Navy flyers.

A lawsuit for noise pollution was also brought by local residents against the US base at Kadena in **Okinawa** in 1981. Indeed, at the present time, some 75 per cent of all US military bases in Japan are relegated to the tiny prefecture of Okinawa, occupying some 20 per cent of the total land area on the island. This intolerable situation has led to virtually constant anti-base protest, which has increased considerably in the 1990s A recent

example is the One-Tsubo Anti-war Landlords' Movement, in which small (one *tsubo* is 40 square feet or smaller) parcels of land within US bases have been sold by their dispossessed owners to large numbers of activists. This has greatly increased the number of voices demanding the return of land to its owners. After three US marines abducted and raped a 12-year-old Okinawan schoolgirl in 1995, Okinawa governor Ota Masahide refused to co-operate with the Japanese government in forcing the landowners to renew the US military's land leases. The Japanese government reacted by stripping prefectural officials of what little power they once had over such leases and strengthening the prerogatives of the Ministry of Justice. Other recent anti-base actions in Okinawa include the 1996–7 movement against the so-called 'offshore heliport', which is supposed to replace the Futenma Marine Corps Air Station, and women's movements against rape and other forms of military violence against women.

See also: citizens' movements; social and political movements; US–Japan relations

Further reading

Satō, S. (1981) *Chihō jichitai to gunji kichi*, Tokyo: Shin Nihon Shuppansha.

J. VICTOR KOSCHMANN

ANTI-VIETNAM *see* Beheiren

ao

Blue, it was noted in the nineteenth century, was the most ubiquitous colour in Japan. Roof tiles, shop curtains, workers' jackets, farmers' pantaloons, summer kimono (**yukata**), merchants' robes, bedding, carrying cloths (**furoshiki**) and banners were generally blue. More than a hundred years later, the popularity of indigo-dyed cloth and cobalt-blue pottery remains high, particularly in connection with folk (**mingei**) objects. Vats of blue dye are made from the fermented leaves (*sukumo*) of the Japanese indigo (*tadeai*), and produce shades from pale blue to dark navy. Experimental and traditional artists specialising in indigo use *shibori*, paste resist (*tsutsugaki* and *katazome*), ikat (*kasuri*) and inventive patterning techniques.

MONICA BETHE

architecture

During the crisis in national values that followed the defeat of Japan in the Second World War, the major trends in Japanese architecture rejected any direct use of neo-traditional elements that could be linked in any way to Japanese imperialism and its construction of a Japanese national identity. The rationalist designs of this period were largely expressed in the wave of public architecture stimulated by the immediate necessity of reconstruction of the cities that had been destroyed during the heavy bombardment of the final months of the war.

Tange Kenzō's Peace Memorial Museum in Hiroshima and his Kagawa Prefectural Office project, together with Ōe Hiroshi's 55 Year House at Hosei University, were both completed in the mid-1950s. This period saw the first lessening of the post-war financial and political crisis, and they became symbols of the spirit of peace and internationalisation that pervaded the works of Japanese architects on into the contemporary period. However, the presence of Japanese tradition was not completely eclipsed and Tange's assimilation of a modern language of design was intimately related to his interest, however muted, in shrine architecture. He was particularly drawn to the symmetry and pilotis of the atypical structure and layout of Itsukushima shrine.

Before long, in 1960, a new trend emerged with the creation of the epoch-making Metabolist Group, whose members included such well-known contemporary architects as Kisho Kurokawa, **Kikutake Kiyonori** and **Maki Fumihiko**, all disciples of Tange. Under Tange's influence the Metabolists avoided any explicit or gratuitous neo-traditional visual dimensions to their designs, but, within the original core formulation of a Metabolist architecture as a biological process, they returned to the qualities of pre-modern Japanese architectural systems: cyclical renewal, integration with nature, fragmentation, interchangeability and pre-fabrication. Rather than mere structural or formal principles, this reconsideration of tradition, sustained also by some Buddhist and nativist philosophical concepts, combined the assimilation of traditional Japanese cultural values as an element in the post-war redefinition of Japan and Japanese identity against the devastating backdrop of the war. The Metabolist ideal probably reached its clearest expression in Kisho Kurokawa's living cell. A light, prefabricated, modular capsule that plugged into a megastructure, this work incorporated many of the core Metabolist elements. It was only at the beginning of the 1970s, however, that provocative and ambitious Metabolist projects such as Kurokawa's Nakagin Capsule Building were constructed, moving theory into concrete form.

During the 1960s, the national priority fell on the New Residential Town Development Law, a project for the construction of large-scale bedroom communities at the outskirts of the cities. This led to a highly utilitarian, policy-driven period of intensive construction that paid little attention to the avant-garde projects for urban reconstruction proposed by Metabolists and other architects. From the urban perspective, the end of the post-war period was marked by the construction of the great Tokyo Metropolitan Expressway and the Shinkansen Railway that completed the transportation infrastructure of the 1964 **Tokyo Olympics**. It was Tange's National Olympic Stadium that came to symbolise the event in the popular memory, marking the first instance in Japan's post-war history of an architectural project gaining the status of monument. In the case of Tange's stadium, what was symbolised by the landmark structure was Japan's return to the world stage as a full member of the international political forum. The **Expo 70** in Ōsaka was the event that closed the decade. Intended to be a huge prototype for future city planning, the Expo site saw the materialisation of many of the core principles of **Metabolism**. What the site was remembered and applauded for, however, was its striking use of new technologies, in particular transport innovations. This performance of technological strength was understood by many to symbolise the new resources essential to Japan's post-war power.

The national project for the development and reorganisation of industrial, commercial and residential zones had the effect of reducing much urban development to the work of routine expansion. There was a marked lack of innovation of any significance for either architecture or urban planning. Some of the most interesting ideas to emerge at the beginning of the 1970s were a direct criticism of these conditions, and promoted notions of independence and individual conceptualisation as a counter to the perceived lack of distinctive character in the prevailing housing designs and urban planning trends. An important source of these individualistic and critical architectural interventions was the so-called 'third generation', a new generation strongly influenced by the student movement of 1968. This diverse movement was typified by the works of **Ando Tadao**, who began to explore the plastic possibilities of concrete and the use of light, or those of **Ito Toyo**, who was interested in links between nature and the reality of urban everyday life. Other architects from the former generation were attracted by variations in the articulations and gradation of space. Kisho Kurokawa modified his style dramatically to explore this potential in his projects during this period. **Isozaki Arata** is perhaps the major architectural presence of the 1970s. Since the mid-1960s he had been designing buildings isolated from the major centres and their urban contexts and ambiance, and his designs displayed a deep relation to a thematic of ruins (a notorious theme recurring in the continuous processes of change in the Japanese cities, and often linked, explicitly or not, to the devastation of the Second World War). Isozaki was also the critic who most severely questioned and challenged the prevailing social and architectural assumptions and conditions. Buildings such as his Ōita Medical Hall, Ōita Prefectural Library, Kita Kyūshū Municipal Museum of Beaux Arts or Kita Kyūshū Municipal Central Library reflected in superb designs his apocalyptic and sceptical attitude.

Japanese economic growth peaked during the 1980s (the **bubble economy**) and until the beginning of the 1990s was a strong support for the development of post-modern trends echoing back to the earlier proposals (1970s) of the likes of **Takeyama Minoru**, for example the 'signboard

architecture' of his Ichi Ban Kan and Ni Ban Kan buildings. The rampant rise of commercialism could accommodate and even celebrate the more extravagant designs of the proponents of post-modernist buildings. The public as well as the paying client (public and private) seemed apparently hungry for the excesses and extremes of this period of design. Ironically, post-modernism offered both an end to the problem of representation of the visual components of traditional architecture, and a return of the pre-eminence of monumental public buildings, the spaces where post-modernism was mostly frequently expressed. More than a few of these works were designed not out of nostalgia for a Japanese tradition, but under the influence of Western architectural history. **Hara Hiroshi**'s Yamato International, Kuma Kengo's M2, Tange Kenzō's Yokohama Art Museum or Isosaki Arata's Tsukuba Centre Building all exemplify this playful longing for a non-Japanese architectural past. Isozaki's Tsukuba project would become the most renowned and widely discussed example of Japanese post-modernist architecture. Other buildings such as Watanabe Makoto's Aoyama Technical College or Edward Suzuki's Pasona also became examples of the unlimited flights of the imagination that materialised on the Japanese urban landscape over this period.

The beginning of the 1990s set the pattern for the decade with a boom in international collaborations. During the 1990s, numerous major projects by, or involving, internationally renowned celebrities were completed in Japan, particularly in Tokyo: Peter Eisenman's NC Building; Norman Foster's Century Tower; Phillip Starks's Super Dry Hall; Mario Botta's Watarium; or Aldo Rossi's Ambiente International. In fact, one of the most durable, and at that time invisible, benefits of the bubble was the excellent possibility for young architects (many of whom are the present-day leaders of Japan's architectural panorama) to prove their skills in the major projects of this boom period. Some of this generation could be said to have reached their design maturity during the volatile but productive bubble years. Ando Tadao, Ito Toyo and Kuma Kengo, all mentioned above, together with Kishi Waro, Takamatsu Shin, Yamamoto Riken and Kitagawara Atsushi, all thrived under these conditions. Perhaps the last clear example of the post-modern era was Tange Kenzō's New Tokyo City Hall Complex, which became one of the most famous and controversial Tokyo landmarks. This project was an attempt to create a striking landmark symbol for Tokyo's government. It was possibly the kind of civic centre that Tokyo had been seeking to create for itself since the nineteenth century. It created a hybrid visual economy of futuristic symbolism as well as Japanese and Western traditional referents.

Even though the post-bubble period gave way to a diversity of trends, the main tendency since the middle of the 1990s has been a revalorisation of the modern. Compared to the striking designs of the former period, the present-day designs seem to be a sober meditation on modern or traditional space, materials and light. Almost all of the leading contemporary generation of architects, together with the older masters such as Maki Fumihiko and Hara Hiroshi, are actively participating in this pervasive trend. It is worth commenting that many of the present-day designs can be noted for their apparently 'involuntary' tribute or referencing to the sustained impact of the concepts and plasticity of the works of Ando Tadao, who is probably today the most internationally renowned and solicited Japanese architect. The newest generation of architects might be best represented by the works of Aoki Jun, or Sejima Kazuyo's remarkable studies in glass and transparency. Within this context, a very particular case is Ban Shigeru's cardboard tube structures and the application of this technology to the construction of provisional housing in zones devastated by natural disasters. This widely acclaimed concept was put into practice in Japan after the **Hanshin Earthquake** in 1995, and has also been trialed in other countries. Some of the more noteworthy examples of present-day architectural trends are Yamamoto Riken's Saitama Prefectural University, Kuma Kengo's Kitagami Canal Museum, Ban Shigeru's Nemunoki Art Museum, Sejima Kazuyo's HHStyle.Com and Aoki Jun's B House. Both in the processes of design and in the final design itself there has been an increasing collaboration between architectural and digital designers as animation and fuzzy-logic software open up new design and structural frontiers. Alternative building materials and new digital technologies are the two major influences shaping the more innovative designs of both everyday architecture and the high-art of international design competitions. The best of Japan's architects are now truly global names and the field of Japanese architecture is now increasingly open to the best global designs whatever the country (or countries) of origin of the architectural team.

Further reading

GA Document (magazine), Tokyo: ADA EDITA Tokyo Co. Ltd.

Hiroyuki Suzuki (1985) Contemporary Architecture of Japan/1958–1984, London: The Architectural Press.

Noriyuki Tajima (1996) Tokyo, Hong Kong: Ellipsis/Konemann.

Stewart, David B. (1987) The Making of a Modern Japanese Architecture/1868 to the Present, Tokyo and New York: Kōdansha International.

Yoshinobu Ashihara (1989) The Hidden Order, Tokyo, New York and London: Kōdansha International.

Zukowsky, John (ed.) (1998) Japan 2000, Munich and New York: The Art Institute of Chicago and Prestel-Verlag.

EMILIO GARCIA MONTIEL

arranged marriages

Omiai is the practice of arranged marriages. The go-between (nakado) is essential to this process of socio-economic negotiation between two families. From the feudal period, both the aristocracy and samurai class increasingly came to view **marriage** as an opportunity for political, economic and social alliances that promoted the interests of families, rather than a romantic match between two individuals. This practice extended into the merchant class during the Edo Period. As Japan modernised, the practice of omiai extended into the emerging urban elite and later the middle class.

In modern Japan, romantic love came to be seen as the alternative to omiai. Up until the late 1960s, arranged marriages remained the norm in rural areas while they slowly declined in the cities. By the early 1990s, a mere 12 per cent of marriages were identified as *omiai*, but this number is not completely transparent. This is because many romantic matches still begin with gentle prodding from a workplace superior or a member of one's senior–junior cohort at work or university, who sets up an initial introduction at a hosted dinner or other social event. A successful romantic match is often only formalised into an engagement when an appropriate go-between agrees to mediate between the families. While romantic marriages remain the preferred mode of finding a marital partner, surveys of young Japanese women indicate that they are inclined to think of romance as pre-marital play, while the criteria for a marriage partner are primarily based on economic security and status. As more women choose to marry later, Japanese men often cite the increasingly competitive nature of finding a life partner as a rationale for a return to a hybrid of romantic love and *omiai*.

See also: marriage

SANDRA BUCKLEY

art, contemporary

In the context of post-war Japan, the term 'contemporary art' (*gendai bijutsu*) means more than 'today's art' (the literal translation). Certainly, throughout the twentieth century, Japanese literature on art offers numerous uses of the adjective '*gendai*', in the sense of 'today's' or 'contemporary', in combination with such words as 'art' and 'painting'. However, towards the end of the 1960s, the word 'contemporary' in these phrases began to assume a distinct meaning, replacing 'avant-garde' (*zen'ei*) and denoting 'after the modern' (*kindai*).

In practice, contemporary art comprises expressions varyingly described as vanguard, progressive or new. However, the term 'contemporary art' is not a mere alternative to the more frequently used 'avant-garde art'. First and foremost, the former is a historical, institutional and theoretical construct, informed by the Japanese understanding of how the nature of vanguard practices fundamentally changed in post-war society. It should be noted that, in this context, the rephrasing of 'painting'

(see **art, contemporary**) and '**sculpture**' as *heimen* (two dimensions) and *rittai* (three dimensions) also took place around 1970.

To understand the theoretical origin of contemporary art is to acknowledge the Japanese perception that the avant-garde was finished with the Anti-Art (*Han-geijutsu*) movement. Anti-Art, which centred in and around the annual Yomiuri Independent Exhibition from 1958 to 1963, was heir to two lines in the avant-garde movement of the 1950s: politically inclined (most notably, Social Realism) and artistically inclined ('new art', advocated by Okamoto Tarō). During the period surrounding 1960 – the tumultuous year of the contested renewal of Anpo (US–Japan Security Treaty) (see **Anpo struggle**) – Anti-Art practitioners acted out the anxiety of the time in works that totally disregarded the received conventions of painting and sculpture. By the mid-1960s, however, the limitations of the Anti-Art avant-garde became evident through a series of events. First, after Yomiuri Shinbun cancelled its Independent Exhibition, primarily (but not explicitly) prompted by the excessive iconoclasm of Anti-Art in 1964, the artists were unable to create a new forum of their own with the same kind of vitality and relevance. Second, in 1967, the Anti-Art master Akasegawa Genpei was found criminally guilty for his money-based work *Model 1,000 Yen Note* (1963). The Akasegawa trial was a breaking point for the avant-garde movement, especially because it exposed the theoretical shortcomings of Anti-Art. Anti-Art's subversive gestures could be sanctioned only within the sphere of art and, above all, Anti-Art was nothing but Art. Third, lured by financial opportunities, especially, the chance to work with technology, many artists of Anti-Art and other vanguard persuasions 'avalanched into' the **Expo 70**, the state project which the left contended was an attempt to divert people's attention from the looming political crisis of the extension of the US–Japan Anpo treaty, slated for the same year.

The perception of the de-fanged avant-garde was part of a larger intellectual shift, already articulated by the art critic Miyakawa Atsushi during the years 1964 to 1966. In brief, Anti-Art, through its 'descent to the mundane', made fervent assaults on Art (*geijutsu*) as a metaphysical construct of modern times, and art (*bijutsu*) as the material means to achieve the goal that is Art. The questioning of Art/art thus helped foreground the 'collapse of the modern ideal of Art', which in turn pointed to the collapse of the 'modern' (*kindai*) as a historical paradigm, compelling a new formulation of the 'contemporary' (*gendai*). To complicate the matter, Anti-Art's failure to nullify Art in the sphere of life engendered a contradictory thesis that it was impossible for Art – a typically modern construct – to dissolve or not exist. In the late 1960s, Miyakawa's prescient observation about the end of the modern was shared by the generation of artists who came after Anti-Art, such as Sekine Nobuo and Lee Ufan, who formed the core of *Mono-ha* (literally, 'Thing School'). At this same time progressive designers and architects were debating whether modern design and architecture provided a viable premise of operation in the rapidly emerging consumerist society that is Japan. In this context, the adjective *gendai* acquired an added theoretical significance, although it should not be confused with another critical term, 'post-modern'.

In retrospect, the maturation of vanguard practices compelled the need for a new terminology. Once on the fringe of the art establishment consisting of **Nihonga** (Japanese-style painting) and **yga** (Western-style painting), the avant-garde factions were increasingly gaining entry into official culture in the 1960s. Most characteristically, instead of the establishment artists, some Anti-Art artists, such as Takamatsu Jirō and Kudō Tetsumi, were selected to represent the nation at the international biennial exhibitions in Venice, São Paulo, and Paris; thereafter, the appointment of contemporary artists (*gendai bijutsu no sakka*) to these international events became the norm, rather than an exception. By 1970, in terms of the infra-structure of art, the environment of contemporary art expanded considerably. There were museums that exhibited contemporary works regularly (most notably, the now defunct Nagaoka Contemporary Art Museum), galleries that supported contemporary artists (Tokyo Gallery and the now defunct Minami Gallery, among others), specialised schools (Bigakkō and B-Semi School), critics who wrote primarily on contemporary topics and the magazines that published them (*Bijutsu techō* was a leader of the genre). In this sense, contemporary art

became an institution unto itself. As such, it constitutes one of the three pillars of today's art world in Japan (the other two being *Nihonga* and *yōga*).

Although the theoretical birth of contemporary art dated from around 1970, it is customary to begin the discussion of contemporary art with the foundation of Gutai (Gutai Bijutsu Kyōkai; Gutai Art Association) in 1955. However, this is to adopt a broad and retroactive interpretation. The landmark event of contemporary art is decidedly Tokyo Biennale '70, curated by the art critic Nakahara Yūsuke, in that it demonstrated what the critic Haryū Ichirō called 'international contemporaneity' (*kokusaiteki dōjisei*) by presenting Euro-American examples of Minimal, Post-Minimal, and Conceptual Art, and Arte Povera, along with Japanese works of *Mono-ha* and Conceptualism. The artists working in these two directions represent the first generation that was self-conscious about contemporary art. At the same time, they were particularly aware of the institution (*seido*) of art and how it functioned externally (through the museum/gallery/exhibition systems) and internally (in governing their thinking about art). The activities of Bikyotō (Bijutsuka Kyōtō Kaiki; Artists' Joint-Struggle Council) in 1971–4 was the most radical exploration of the institutional critique, both in theory and practice.

See also: *Nihonga*; *yōga*

Further reading

Munroe, Alexandra (ed.) (1994) *Japanese Art after 1945: Scream against the Sky*, New York: Abrams.
Reiko Tomii (1999) 'Concerning the institution of art: Conceptualism in Japan', in *Global Conceptualism: Points of Origin, 1950s–1980s*, New York: Queens Museum of Art, pp. 14–27.

ソ ジ

arubaito

From the German *arbeit*, the term designates casual part-time work. Although the term is usually limited to student part-time work, it is sometimes used more loosely to describe any short-term casual work. The distinctions between *paato* (part time) and *arubaito* are not always clear but, generally speaking, *paato* positions are longer term and more regularised than the informal structure of *arubaito*. There have been movements to organise *paato* labour to improve working and wage conditions, but *arubaito* work remains largely outside formal structures and conditions of employment. *Arubaito* salaries are more likely to be paid under the table and undeclared for taxation.

SANDRA BUCKLEY

Asahi shinbun

The *Asahi*, founded in Ōsaka in 1879, is one of Japan's oldest national newspapers, along with the *Mainichi*. Under the direction of Murayama Ryōhei, president and publisher, the newspaper set its sights on reaching a mass audience. Innovative techniques like the widespread use of pictures and combining news and general-interest stories were highly successful ploys for increasing early circulation.

During the Sino-Japanese War (1894–5), the *Asahi* won acclaim for being the only newspaper to dispatch a correspondent to the front. The *Asahi* repeated this practice during the Russo-Japanese War (1904–5), but this time the *Mainichi* followed its example – and so began an ongoing competitive relationship between the two newspapers.

In 1907, when renowned writer Natsume Soseki joined the staff, fiction became an even more conspicuous feature of the newspaper. From the early 1900s, the *Asahi* assumed a liberal political stance. Its support for the 'imperial democracy' movement, and its opposition to a proposed military build-up and the Siberian Expedition earned the newspaper the wrath of the authorities. As a result, the *Asahi* became the target of a government attack and the president and chief editors, such as Hasegawa Nyōzekan, were forced to resign.

In the post-war period, the *Asahi* emerged as a critic of the Liberal Democratic Party. The *Asahi* supported the socialist-bloc countries and opposed US intervention in Vietnam. In 1987, the *Asahi*'s Ōsaka bureau office became the target of a right-wing terrorist attack that left one correspondent dead. Present circulation – morning and evening editions included – is estimated at over 8,000,000.

See also: newspapers and magazines

BARBARA HAMILL SATO

Asakusa

Asakusa lies on the eastern edge of old *shitamachi*, downtown **Tokyo**, on the banks of the Sumida River, far from the trendy districts of the western fringes. In the area surrounding Asakusa, one sees a bustling city at work, with thousands of small factories in close quarters with fishmongers, food producers and small businesses of all sorts. Many of the city's taxi drivers come from this part of the city. ***Manga*** (comics) are printed here, as well as the thousands of other paper products necessary to Japanese daily culture.

During the seventeenth century, Asakusa was the centre of the *Yoshiwara*, the licensed prostitution district. By the Meiji Period, it was a major entertainment area where *Edokko*, the people of Edo, displayed their urbane fashion. It was also the nucleus of **kabuki** theatre, and became a general theatre district prior to its destruction during the 1923 earthquake. One of the country's most famous and prosperous temples, the Sensoji, also known as Asakusa Kannon Temple, receives millions of visitors at New Year and for its summer festival and the winter festivals. The narrow surrounding streets are packed with small stores selling traditional Japanese goods. In recent years, there has been considerable interest in the revival of Asakusa, and it is beginning to show signs of gentrification.

AUDREY KOBAYASHI

ASEAN Regional Forum

The ASEAN (Association of South-East Asian Nations) Regional Forum (ARF) was established in 1994 in response to the lack of a regional security forum and the pressing need for greater communication and mutual understanding regarding security issues in the Asia–Pacific region. It was also aimed at keeping the USA engaged in the region in the post-cold-war era by providing a non-threatening environment for major power dialogue. ARF includes twenty-one member nations that are in Asia or contiguous to the Pacific Ocean. These participants are: Brunei, Cambodia, Indonesia, Laos, Malaysia, Myanmar, the Philippines, Singapore, Thailand and Vietnam (ASEAN); ASEAN dialogue partners (Australia, Canada, the European Union, Japan, New Zealand and the USA); and other invited nations (China, India, Papua New Guinea, Russia and South Korea).

ASEAN has succeeded in positioning itself at the centre of this nascent security dialogue and has played a crucial role in creating the region's first multilateral security structure. Japan and other ASEAN dialogue partners first proposed such a forum in 1990. ASEAN was initially reluctant, but warmed to the idea in response to the less stable post-cold-war security environment and the desire to keep ASEAN at the centre of the growing web of regional linkages. ARF's role has been limited to confidence-building measures, greater transparency in defence planning and arms purchases, preventative diplomacy and providing a venue for intra-regional discussion about common security concerns.

ARF functions in accord with the 'ASEAN way', meaning that emphasis is placed on non-confrontational, consensual and gradualist measures. Critics argue that the frictions and dangers in the region require a more assertive approach and point out that ARF has been left on the sidelines in dealing with critical security issues in the region. The low-key atmosphere leaves the impression that delegates meet for the sake of meeting, undermining confidence that ARF can offer practical solutions. Proponents argue that the process is essential to the resolution of problems and the diminishing of threats to mutual security, arguing that a more aggressive approach would undermine ARF as an institution and risk the withdrawal of member nations. Constructive engagement means that ARF members have a forum to air views and differences, and develop the habits of dialogue, openness and compromise. Given various disparities among ARF participants, the 'ASEAN way' may be the only viable approach, emphasising

areas of common interest and co-operation, while postponing initiatives involving divisive issues.

For Japan, ARF is an ideal forum for broadening its security profile in Asia. Multilateralising security issues in the region is important for Japan so that it can try to lessen some of the bilateral tensions between the USA and China, which involve Japan because of its own bilateral alliance with the USA. ARF allows Japan to exercise its preferred style of behind-the-scenes, out-of-the-limelight diplomacy. ARF is also convenient because the legacy of the Second World War makes it difficult for Japan to play an assertive security role in the region. By working within ARF and presenting its security profile in a multilateral context, Japan is helping its own citizens and its neighbours grow gradually comfortable with what has been a longstanding taboo.

See also: ASEAN Regional Forum; Asia–Pacific Economic Co-operation

Further reading

Almonte, Jose (1997–8) 'Ensuring security the "ASEAN Way"', *Survival* 39(4) (winter): 80–92.
Manning, Robert (1999) 'Asia's transition diplomacy: Hedging against futureshock', *Survival* 41(3) (autumn): 43–60.
Narine, Shaun (1997) 'ASEAN and ARF: The limits of the "ASEAN Way"', *Asian Survey* 37(10) (October): 961–78.

JEFF KINGSTON

Asia–Pacific Economic Co-operation

The Asia–Pacific Economic Co-operation (APEC) was established in 1989 as an informal dialogue group in response to the dynamism, growth and accelerating integration among member economies. Over the years, APEC has developed into the primary regional vehicle for promoting open trade and investment, and regional economic co-operation. APEC's twenty-one members consist of Australia, Brunei, Canada, Chile, People's Republic of China, Hong Kong (China), Indonesia,

Japan, Republic of Korea, Malaysia, Mexico, New Zealand, Papua New Guinea, Peru, the Philippines, Russia, Singapore, Chinese Taipei, Thailand, USA and Vietnam. The combined economies account for approximately 45 per cent of world trade. The most recent expansion of membership occurred in 1998 with the addition of Peru, Russia and Vietnam. The Association of South-East Asian Nations (ASEAN), Pacific Economic Co-operation Council (PECC) and South Pacific Forum (SPF) have observer status. The APEC Secretariat was established in 1993 and is located in Singapore.

In 1993, the first APEC Summit involved the leaders of member nations and has since been an annual opportunity for leaders around the region to gather and discuss primarily economic issues, in addition to crisis situations affecting the membership. In 1994, APEC produced a vision for reducing intra-regional trade and investment barriers by 2010 for developed nations, and by 2020 for developing ones. The Ōsaka Action Agenda of 1995 sought to translate this vision into reality by establishing three pillars of APEC activities: trade and investment liberalisation; business facilitation; and economic and technical co-operation. The economic crisis of 1997 spurred APEC to emphasise improving the infrastructure of trade, investment and finance, while continuing with efforts at promoting liberalisation.

APEC works closely with the business community and its many working groups involve business people from around the region. This close working relationship with private-sector interests is seen to be a source of dynamism and pragmatism. Japan has been an active and supportive member of APEC from its inception. The APEC agenda is consistent with Japan's interests and the emphasis on consensus fits well with Japanese preferences. Multilateralising economic issues is also consistent with Japan's overall objectives of avoiding the pitfalls of bilateral negotiations, which often plague its relations with the USA. The inherent confrontations involving trade and investment regimes lend themselves to less acrimonious resolution in a multilateral context.

There have been repeated efforts by Prime Minister Mahathir of Malaysia to create a separate sub-group of Asian nations, the East Asian Economic Caucus (EAEC), which would serve as a forum for Asian-only discussions and perspectives. He has pointedly invited Japan to become a founding member on numerous occasions. Japan, wary of US opposition to the EAEC and reluctant to assume the mantle of leadership, has declined. The EAEC proposal reflects concern among some APEC members that the organisation's agenda and process are dominated by the USA. The specific exclusion of the USA, Australia and New Zealand from membership of the proposed EAEC has been divisive. Japan is more comfortable with an inclusive APEC and plays an important mediating role, sometimes publicly distancing itself from US positions.

See also: ASEAN Regional Forum; Association of South-East Asian Nations

Further reading

Deng, Yong (1997) *Promoting Asia–Pacific Economic Cooperation: Perspectives from East Asia*, New York: St Martin's Press.

JEFF KINGSTON

Asian Women's Association

The Asian Women's Association (Ajia no Onnatachi no Kai) was launched on 1 March 1977. Their journal *Ajia to josei kaihō* (Asian Women's Liberation) focused on the gendered dimensions of political struggles and liberation movements, the offshore activities of Japanese companies and the international tourism and prostitution industry in the Asian region. Their journal is now called *Onnatachi no nijū isseiki* (*Women's Asia: 21*). Veteran members of the Association include **Matsui Yayori** (former editorial writer for the *Asahi shinbun* newspaper), Gotō Masako (secretary to parliamentarian Doi Takako) and feminist artist Tomiyama Taeko.

Further reading

Matsui, Y. (1999) *Women in the New Asia: from Pain to Power*, London: Zed Books.

VERA MACKIE

ASOBI *see* play

Association of South-East Asian Nations

The Association of South-East Asian Nations (ASEAN) was established in 1967 with five member nations – Indonesia, Malaysia, Singapore, Thailand and the Philippines. Brunei entered in 1984. The initial aim was to reduce intra-ASEAN tensions, promote economic development and assert influence over regional affairs. The communist victory in Vietnam in 1975 and Vietnam's occupation of Cambodia in 1978 enhanced the diplomatic role of ASEAN and accelerated co-ordination and integration of member state foreign policies. During Vietnam's occupation of Cambodia between 1978 and 1990, ASEAN matured as a regional organisation and has come to be the focus of regional diplomatic initiatives.

In the post-cold-war era, ASEAN has expanded its membership and now includes the ten nations of South-East Asia. ASEAN added Vietnam in 1995, Laos and Burma in 1997 and Cambodia in 1999. ASEAN espouses the principle of non-interference in the affairs of member states, but this policy is being tested by human rights concerns and political turmoil. Vietnam's withdrawal from Cambodia and the softening of ideological divisions in the region has been a mixed blessing; without a defining tension or cleavage ASEAN at times seems an organisation in search of a mission.

The ASEAN Free Trade Area (AFTA) has been the focus of economic diplomacy. Partially in response to the emergence of APEC (**Asia– Pacific Economic Co-operation**) in 1989, ASEAN has committed itself to lowering intra-regional trade barriers as a means to speed economic integration and develop export-oriented industries. Improved trade regimes could benefit Japan's substantial offshore production facilities scattered throughout ASEAN. However, the economic meltdown that began in July 1997 in Thailand has dampened growth, integration and enthusiasm for the AFTA initiative.

Japan has worked in, and with, ASEAN to overcome the legacies of the Second World War. Japan's Official Development Assistance (ODA) is concentrated in Asia and the government has funded major infrastructure projects in the region. The large-scale ASEAN industrialisation projects in the 1970s associated with the Fukuda Doctrine and the quiet diplomacy in brokering resolution of the Indo-China impasse set the stage for Japan's major diplomatic initiative in the post-Second World War era. Japan conceived and funded the United Nations Transitional Authority in Cambodia (UNTAC), charged with overseeing democratic elections in 1993 with the blessing of ASEAN. This was the first time Japanese troops had returned to Asia since the Second World War, an event that raised concerns both in South-East Asia and Japan. Legislation was passed in the Japanese Diet to permit the dispatch of troops overseas and to establish rigid guidelines for their deployment. Through this legislation the government sought to allay concerns that it was not abiding by Article 9 of the Constitution.

In addition, by taking a leading role in promoting political stability and democracy in Cambodia, Japan has also served notice that it is ready for a permanent seat on the UN Security Council. The problems of Cambodia continue to fester, but Japan made significant progress in burying the ghosts of its shared, traumatic history with South-East Asia. Japan's supportive economic diplomacy in the wake of the 1997 economic crisis has also enhanced its relations with ASEAN. For Japan, ASEAN has played a crucial role in broadening and deepening its regional foreign-policy posture. As a result of its strong bilateral relationship with the USA, Japan's foreign policy initiatives have largely been tentative and reactive. In Indo-china, however, Japan played a key supportive role working with ASEAN in seeking a diplomatic solution to Vietnam's occupation of Cambodia. If coping with the Cambodia situation defined ASEAN, and highlighted its limitations, the same experience was no less influential in defining the benefits and costs of Japan's low-key multi-lateralism and understated diplomacy.

Both ASEAN member states and Japan share a non-confrontational, consensus-building approach to diplomacy. As a leading dialogue partner participating in the annual ASEAN Post-Ministerial Conference, Japan has also been effective in articulating its regional interests through ASEAN.

The ASEAN emphasis on multilateralism, mutual consultation, co-operation and gradualism offer Japan a more comfortable approach to regional relations than is sometimes possible in the context of its alliance with the USA.

See also: ASEAN Regional Forum; Asia–Pacific Economic Co-operation

Further reading

Curtis, G. (ed.) (1994) *The US, Japan and Asia*, New York, Norton.

Narinne, Shaun (1998) 'Institutional theory and Southeast Asia: The case of ASEAN', *World Affairs* 161(1) (summer): 33–47.

Sandhu, K.S. *et al.* (eds) (1992) *The ASEAN Reader*, Singapore: Institute of Southeast Asian Studies.

JEFF KINGSTON

Astro Boy

Inaugurated in 1951 in a **manga** by Tezuka Osamu featuring several atomic robots, the character Tetsuwan Atomu (Astro Boy) proved so popular that in 1952 he was given his own series, which ran in the boy's comic journal *Shōnen* for more than seventeen years. In 1963, *Tetsuwan Atomu* premièred as Japan's first animated television series. The following year, the English version, *Astro Boy*, became the first animated series on US television. The *manga* and television series were eventually translated into over twenty languages, making Astro Boy, with his pointy hair, enormous eyes and rocket-powered feet, among the best known of Japanese cultural icons around the world.

Astro Boy was the precursor of an extremely popular stream of *manga* and **anime** featuring both dark and positive aspects of technological progress. Created by a mad scientist grieving for his dead son, Astro Boy had a fission reactor for a 'heart' and machine guns in his hips. None the less, he embodied innocence, bravery and morality; despite having been sold to a circus by his creator-father, he learned to love and emulate humans. He battled evil robots, saving the earth weekly in increasingly violent confrontations, before finally sacrificing himself by flying into the sun to save humanity.

See also: manga

SHARALYN ORBAUGH

atomic bomb literature

The Japanese term now most widely used to designate all atomic bomb-related literature is *gembaku bungaku*. Another term, occasionally used earlier in the post-war period, *hibakusha bungaku*, specifically referred to the literature of A-bomb survivors. However, these works are now generally subsumed under the wider category of *gembaku bungaku*. The distinction marked by these two terms – writings about the A-bomb and writings by survivors – still mirrors the nature of the debates that surround A-bomb literature.

Perhaps the earliest and the most prolific form of A-bomb literature was the testimonial, and much of this writing was also autobiographical. Across genres as diverse as diary, short story, journalistic account, historical document and poetry, those present at the time the atomic bombs fell on Hiroshima and Nagasaki, or who entered the cities soon afterwards, strive in the testimonial style to bear witness for the suffering of the victims. The 1953 collection *Surviving the Atomic Bomb: Memoirs of Atomic Bomb Victims* was compiled and edited by Yamashiro Tomoe, and brings together the transcribed and edited oral histories of twenty-three victims. *The Nagasaki Testimonies* were collected and published through a similar process of transcription and editing, and were published during the period from 1969 to 1978. The short story or novella narrated as a first-person account was a form widely used by *hibakusha*, many of whom had not considered themselves writers before, as a vehicle for the stories they felt compelled to tell. The short stories and longer works of Hayashi Kyōko, Hara Tamiki, Ōta Yōko and Kurihara Sadako offer some of the most well-known and powerful examples of these intensely personal narratives. The testimonial offered the possibility of a narrative that, while never free of artifice and technique, gestured a commitment to the 'authentic' evidencing and recording of the horror of the events of the atomic bombings. The deep motivation of these stories lies both in the desire to remember and memorialise the suffering of those who died, and the impossibility of 'making sense' or ordering the personal memories of trauma.

Poetry was also an important vehicle for these testimonials. The use of poetry in a documentary or reportative style had its precedents in the minimalist, anti-traditional realism of some early modern poetry, and in the utilitarian, rhetorical use of poetry of the social realists of the 1920s and early 1930s. Many of the *hibakusha* poets worked within the tension of the minimal form of the short, tight structure of the haiku and *waka* forms. Like the socialist and realist poets before them, the *hibakusha* poets were criticised by traditionalists for their lack of reference to, and reverence for, the depth of the tradition of these poetic forms. Long verse (*chōka*) and Western-style free verse were also used. While the *hibakusha* poets did not hesitate to use metaphor or familiar poetic images, their poems had only one referent, the atomic bomb attacks and their victims. There are numerous collections of both individual poets and collected *hibakusha* poems in Japanese, but there are only few and scattered translations available.

By the 1960s, a growing number of authors who were not themselves *hibakusha* had begun to write about the atomic bombs and the ongoing issues of nuclear threat and disarmament. In 1965, Ōe Kenzaburō published a collection of essays, first released in the journal *Sekai*, entitled *Hiroshima Notes*. The next year Ibuse Masuji published what was to become the most widely read account outside Japan of the atomic bomb experience, his novel *Black Rain*. Neither writer was himself a *hibakusha*. There was increasing attention to the issues of nuclear disarmament from the mid-1960s as Japan moved into a volatile renegotiation of the Anpo treaty with the USA (see **Anpo struggle**). The new generation of writers could not claim the authenticity of experience of the *hibakusha*, but they insisted on the right to write from their different contemporary positions as Japanese in a post-atomic world. Ōe fought long and hard to create a space for the writings of the *hibakusha*. At the same time he struggled against criticism for stepping into the space of *gembaku* literature to write as a member of a second generation striving to write about both the A-bomb experience from outside that experience, and the contemporary issues of disarmament

and nuclear threat. Ibuse also wrote a number of shorter pieces depicting the aftermath of the atomic bomb in Hiroshima, and wrote some of the more successful short stories around the Japanese experience of the Occupation period against the backdrop of the memory of the atomic bomb attacks.

In 1981, Oda Makoto's novel *Hiroshima* was released, combining a fascination with US culture and power, and a rejection of what he perceived to be Japan's easy adoption of a victim mentality. Unlike Ōe in *Hiroshima Notes*, Oda did not hesitate in either his fiction or critical essays to ask why Japan had not blamed the USA for the atrocity of the A-bombs and why it continued to accept the terms set down by the USA for Japan's place in the international community. Oda was not alone among Japanese intellectuals, both on the right and the left, who were beginning to focus on this notion of Japan's victim identity. It was over this same period that some of the harshest and most public criticism was levelled at *hibakusha* writers and their claim to literary status. From the late 1970s, key figures in the world of literature and criticism, including **Nakagami Kenji** and **Karatani Kōjin**, launched strongly worded attacks against what they saw as a tendency to attribute literary merit to *hibakusha* writing on the basis of sympathy or sentiment rather than quality of writing. Since as early as the 1950s there had been much conflict over the literary merits of much of what was being published by *hibakusha* writers and poets. Critics insisted that the *gembaku bungaku* should be recognised as something other than literature, and only those works of high enough literary standards be allowed to cross over into literature.

To this day, *hibakusha* writing has not won a place in the canon of Japanese literature. It remains a source of sadness and frustration to many *hibakusha* that it is the writings of non-*hibakusha* authors, in particular Ōe and Ibuse, that were taken up by the publishing industry, critics and public as the voices of the atomic bomb experience. Little *hibakusha* writing is translated outside Japan. The continued focus in Japanese intellectual debates on the need to overcome a post-war victim status, a concept also now widely popularised in the media, raises complex questions for the status of *hibakusha*. International calls for Japan to assume its war responsibility raise still other questions. If Japan acknowledges such wartime acts as medical experimentation on prisoners, enforced prostitution of the comfort women and massacres of civilians, what might be the impact on the international understanding of the US decision to resort to nuclear force? *Hibakusha* listen to calls for Japan to apologise and to pay compensation to countries invaded and occupied during the war, and yet they themselves continue to struggle for adequate medical coverage and care, and earn lower than average salaries. Also, of course, there is always the question of who will apologise to them? Who will take responsibility for Hiroshima and Nagasaki? As the long-term effects of irradiation take their toll, the number of *hibakusha* is dwindling rapidly. The writers among them are intensely aware of the need to capture the untold stories and to speak and write into the public spaces of contemporary Japan as loudly and as often as they can for as long as there are still *hibakusha* alive to bear testimony to the memory of Hiroshima and Nagasaki, and the lived experience of five decades of survival.

See also: atomic bombings; peace and antinuclear movements

Further reading

Treat, J.W. (1995) *Writing Degree Zero*, Chicago: University of Chicago Press.

SANDRA BUCKLEY

atomic bombings

At 8.15 a.m. on 6 August 1945, the USA detonated the first atomic bomb used against human targets about 550 meters above the city of Hiroshima, killing 140,000 of its 350,000 inhabitants and reducing the city to ashes. A massive fireball consumed nearly everything within a 1.0-km (0.6-mile) radius and caused buildings within 3.5 km (2.2 miles) to combust spontaneously. People as far away as 4.5 km (2.8 miles) from the hypocentre suffered skin burns. On 9 August, a second atomic bomb exploded over Nagasaki, killing 70,000 more people. Half of the immediate casualties attributed

to the explosions resulted from the bombs blasts, the rest from intense heat rays and high levels of radiation. Many more people, including non-Japanese, suffered long-term illnesses such as leukaemia resulting from exposure to lower dosages of atomic radiation. These victims are known in Japan as *hibakusha*.

The atomic bombings have come to be viewed in two historical contexts: first, they contributed to Japan's unconditional surrender to the Allied Powers and the end of the Second World War in the Asia Pacific, a military conflict that began with Japan's invasion of Manchuria in 1931; and, second, they marked the advent of the atomic age and a nuclear arms race between the USA and the Soviet Union during the cold war (1947–89). The bombings and their legacy of worldwide nuclear threat shaped the **peace and anti-nuclear movements** in Japan, and fostered a widespread sense of victimisation among the Japanese people.

One source of this sense was the original decision by US President Harry S. Truman to drop the bombs. He justified the action as a means to force Japan to surrender and thus avoid a US invasion of the Japanese home islands, a battle projected to cost nearly a million lives. Some evidence suggests, however, that Japan was prepared to surrender before the attacks and that Truman's decision to use the bombs was driven by the determination of US military commanders to deploy in combat a weapon that had required years and millions of dollars to develop.

Other factors contributing to this sense of victimisation included the Allies' keen interest in the scientific aspects of the explosion's effects at the expense of the medical needs of the *hibakusha*, and the comprehensive US censorship of public discussion of the bombings during the Allied Occupation of Japan (1945–52). As part of the first wave of post-war reforms initiated by the USA-led Occupation forces in October 1945, the *hibakusha* lost access to paid medical care, which was not restored until March 1957 when the Japanese government passed the so-called A-bomb Medical Law. In 1947, the USA, in co-operation with the Japan National Institute of Health, established the Atomic Bombs Casualty Commission (ABCC), which conducted scientific research into the medical effects of the bombings but did not provide medical services to the *hibakusha*. In the absence of detailed public knowledge about the A-bomb experience, the *hibakusha* became stigmatised in their own society.

Public awareness expanded with the end of the Occupation in 1952. By the mid-1950s, the atomic bomb experience had become a political issue driving popular opposition to the Japanese government's rearmament efforts and the US–Japan Security Treaty. **Citizens' movements** were triggered by the 'Lucky Dragon Incident' in March 1954, in which twenty-three Japanese fishermen were injured from radioactive fallout from a US hydrogen bomb test on Bikini atoll. The first international conference dedicated to opposition to atomic and hydrogen bombs convened in Hiroshima in August 1955. One month later, Japanese citizens founded the Japan Council against Atomic and Hydrogen Bombs (Gensuibaku Kinshi Nihon Kyogikai, or Gensuikyo). It sparked a mass movement (under the influence of the Japan Communist Party) to abrogate the security treaty and eliminate nuclear weapons worldwide.

In 1956, *hibakusha* self-help groups in Hiroshima and Nagasaki unified to form the Japan Confederation of A- and H-Bomb Sufferers Organisation (Nihon Gensuibaku Higaisha Dantai Kyogikai, or Hidankyo). Through this organisation, the atomic bomb victims themselves became part of the ideological battles that occupied Gensuikyo and its more conservative spin-offs, the National Council for Peace and against Nuclear Weapons (Kakukin kaigi), founded by the Liberal Democratic Party in 1961, and the Japan Congress against Atomic and Hydrogen Bombs (Gensuikin), established by the Japan Socialist Party in 1965. Hidankyo's long-term goal of financial compensation for the victims based on the wartime government's responsibility for starting the war finally became reality in December 1994, when the Diet enacted the Atomic Bomb Victim Support Law.

Because the horrors of Hiroshima formed the dominant images in the Japanese collective memory of the war, there was little understanding among the Japanese of Japan's wartime role as aggressor in Asia. This began to change in the 1980s and especially after the end of the cold war

in 1989, when Japan's economic and political role in Asia grew and its own population's ethnic diversity increased. For example, the definition of *hibakusha* widened to include Koreans and even Americans, many of them prisoners of war held in Hiroshima when the bomb fell, and led to new examinations of Japanese citizenship and the liability of the state. Concurrently, Japanese intellectuals linked the atomic bomb experience to Japan's responsibility for its war conduct in Asia, calling public attention to Japan's dual role as victim and victimiser in the war.

Also associated with the politics of remembering the atomic bombings is a genre of writing in Japan called A-bomb survivor literature (see **atomic bomb literature**). It is a broad category that includes journalism, memoirs, novels, poems and plays. This literature sought to bear witness to the inhumanity of the bombings and the moral vacuum they created.

See also: atomic bomb literature; peace and anti-nuclear movements

Further reading

Hersey, J. (1948) *Hiroshima*, Toronto, New York and London: Bantam Books.

Hogan, M.J. (ed.) (1996) *Hiroshima in History and Memory*, Cambridge, UK and New York: Cambridge University Press.

Minear, R. (ed. and trans.) (1990) *Hiroshima: Three Witnesses*, Princeton, NJ: Princeton University Press.

FRANZISKA SERAPHIM

Atsumi Ikuko

Feminist writer and academic

Atsumi Ikuko, former professor of English literature at Aoyama Gakuin, and a noted feminist poet and translator, published the journal *Feminist* from 1977 to 1980. The journal's subtitle, *The New Bluestocking*, referred to the pioneering feminist journal of the 1910s, edited by **Hiratsuka Raichō**. In addition to reports on the work of Japanese researchers, and translations of works from English and other languages, *Feminist* carried reports on women's issues and feminist movements from around the world, contributed to the development of **women's studies** in Japan and issued several English editions.

Further reading

Rexroth, K. and Atsumi Ikuko (eds) (1977) *The Burning Heart: Women Poets of Japan*, New York: Seabury Press.

VERA MACKIE

Aum/sarin attack

In post-war Japan's worst terrorist incident, members of the new religion (see **new religions, Japanese**) Aum shinrikyo (Teaching of Supreme Truth) released the nerve gas sarin on the Tokyo subway system on 20 March 1995, killing twelve people and injuring more than 5,000 others. Sarin is a highly toxic, odourless substance that paralyses the central nervous system and causes vomiting, convulsions and death. The nerve gas was released aboard five different trains shortly after 8.00 a.m. on a Monday morning as the trains approached Kasumigaseki, the site of many government offices.

The attack was inspired and directed by Shoko Asahara, born Chizuo Matsumoto in 1955, who founded the Aum sect in 1987. Blending various Buddhist traditions, Asahara predicted world destruction at the turn of the century and built a nearly self-sufficient, strictly hierarchical society to ensure the survival of his followers. Largely unknown until the Tokyo attack, Aum's membership never exceeded 10,000 in Japan.

In the course of police investigations after the attack, Aum was implicated in several individual murder cases and a 1994 sarin attack in Matsumoto, Nagano Prefecture, which killed seven people. Aum was dissolved in May 1995, and 427 of its members, including Asahara, were arrested.

See also: new religions, Japanese

Further reading

Kaplan, D.E. and Marshall, A. (1996) *The Cult at the End of the World*, New York: Crown Publishers, Inc.

Mullins, M.R. (1997) 'Aum Shinrikyo as an apocalyptic movement', in T. Robbins and S.J. Palmer (eds) *Millennium, Messiahs, and Mayhem: Contemporary Apocalyptic Movements*, New York: Routledge, pp. 313–24.

FRANZISKA SERAPHIM

auto industry

The automobile industry is Japan's largest and most competitive. New modes of production pioneered by Japanese firms such as Toyota revolutionised auto design and assembly. From 1981 to 1994, Japan surpassed the USA as the world's largest producer of automobiles. Output peaked in 1990 at over 13 million units, roughly one-fourth of world production. In the late 1990s, the auto industry accounted for about 10 per cent of Japan's employment and 15 per cent of exports.

Before the war, knock-down assembly plants established by Ford and General Motors of the USA dominated auto production in Japan. As the conflict in China mounted and tensions with the West increased, foreign investors were forced out while local firms concentrated on production of trucks for the military. After the war, the government banned foreign investment and strictly limited imports, but the industry's condition remained grim. In the early 1950s, massive layoffs by Toyota and Nissan provoked prolonged and bitter strikes. In the mid-1950s, increases in demand enabled private firms to resist proposals from the Ministry of International Trade and Industry (MITI) to attain economies of scale by merging the industry into two large groups. Despite this celebrated failure of industrial policy, the industry's rise was by no means unaided by the invisible hand of government: trade protection remained virtually complete until the early 1980s, while tax breaks and low-cost loans provided significant assistance in the 1950s and 1960s. Foreign firms were able to invest only in the smallest and weakest auto companies. Protection, promotion, mergers and standardisation campaigns played an even larger role in the auto parts industry.

Japanese companies brought three major strengths to auto production. First, for several decades they benefited from an inexpensive but highly productive workforce. While barriers to entry are high in the auto industry, assembly actually requires more skilled labour than capital. Japanese auto producers enjoyed access to a youthful, well-educated and flexible workforce whose wages remained well below those of Europe and the USA into the early 1980s. Intensive training and rotation programmes within Japanese firms, made possible by accommodating company unions, contributed to increasing skill levels. Second, important innovations in the organisation of factory space, material flow and work teams enabled Japanese firms to attain new levels of quality and variety, while reducing the time and investment required to design new models. 'Lean production' processes pioneered by Toyota and other Japanese firms drastically reduced the amount of inventory held on the factory floor and facilitated incremental innovation. Tying production more tightly to demand, reducing inventories and implementing statistical quality controls throughout the shop floor forced firms to eliminate defects by refining the assembly process rather than by fixing problems on an *ad hoc* basis after they occurred. Instead of treating design and production as sequential processes, Japanese auto firms delegated authority for new designs to cross-functional project teams. Extensive co-ordination and consultation led to products that were easier to build and assemble. While foreign firms learned from Japanese quality control techniques, they had a more difficult time keeping up with Japanese product cycles, which fell from five years to less than two years. Third, Japanese auto companies remained much leaner than Western firms such as General Motors, relying on affiliated but independent suppliers for all but the most critical parts. Pyramidal supply systems developed in Japan combined the advantages of co-ordination and information interchange, characteristic of vertical integration with the competitive efficiencies generated by arms-length transactions in the market. In most Japanese industries, political protection for small firms led to inefficiency, but in autos, like electronics, tiered production systems managed to combine economic and political efficiency.

Exports of cars to industrialised countries began in 1958 and accelerated rapidly from the mid-1960s. By 1980, exports totalled 6 million, accounting for just over half of total production. As Japanese cars displaced local products, demands for protection arose in Europe and the USA. In 1981, Japan agreed to implement 'voluntary' restrictions on auto exports to the USA. In order to overcome increasing barriers to exports, Japanese firms established assembly plants in North America and Europe. Japanese companies had long supplied assembly plants in Taiwan and South-East Asia, but volume remained small until the late 1980s, when a spurt of growth convinced the Japanese makers to expand investment and embark on production of 'Asian cars'. Japanese auto companies also established a dominant role in India, but they approached the Chinese market cautiously. By 1996, overseas subsidiaries of Japanese auto firms assembled over 6 million units, while exports from Japan fell below 4 million units.

At first, overseas assembly only substituted exports of parts for exports of fully assembled cars, but, as volumes increased, local production and procurement of parts increasingly supplanted imports from Japan. Pressure also emerged on the home front. In the late 1980s, diversification of consumer tastes and pressure to liberalise led to an increase in imports, particularly from West Germany. Imports captured nearly 10 per cent of the market before declining slightly in the recession of the 1990s. Japanese auto companies concentrated on compact cars until the 1980s, when the combination of increasing production costs, limits on the volume of exports and the emergence of low-end competitors from Korea encouraged them to move upmarket. Japanese makers created new luxury lines, such as Lexus (Toyota), Infiniti (Nissan) and Acura (Honda). Japanese auto producers, formerly characterised as perfectors of technology acquired from abroad, began to emerge as technological innovators, particularly in robotisation of production, emissions control and electric and hybrid cars.

After decades of extraordinary success, the Japanese auto industry faces tough challenges.

Stagnant demand, an ageing work force and continuing pressures to invest abroad have reduced the significance of the auto industry in the Japanese economy and opened strains between assemblers and large-component manufacturers, which are still competitive and capable of investing in promising foreign markets, and the smallest sub-contractors, which are unable to follow the push overseas. Still, leading Japanese firms such as Toyota and Honda remain among the most efficient and innovative auto producers in the world.

GREGORY W. NOBLE

B

baby boom

The first baby boom occurred in the early post-war period. With the return of Japanese soldiers from the battlefields and colonies created by the Asia–Pacific War, a great many Japanese couples had children. In the three years from 1947 to 1949, between 2,600,000 and 2,700,000 babies were born. Known as 'baby boomers' (*dankai no sedai*), these people came of age in the 1960s, when many of them showed interest in politics and economics through student movements and anti-war protests. This generation also began their working careers in an era of high economic growth. The Japanese middle class was expanding during a period when lifetime employment was common.

Part of this post-war generation were the mixed-race children (*konketsuji*), of Japanese mothers and foreign fathers, who were military men stationed in Occupied Japan. Many of these children experienced discrimination due to their mixed-race identities.

A second baby boom occurred from 1971 to 1973 during a period of high economic growth. Children of the first 'baby boomers' grew up to question the conventional school and career paths of their parents, and to take advantage of increased leisure opportunities in a more economically advanced and culturally cosmopolitan Japan.

See also: new generation; population

Further reading

Taichi Sakaiya (1989) 'The baby boom generation', in Tamae K. Prindle (trans. and ed.) *Made in Japan and other Japanese Business Novels*, New York: M.E. Sharpe, Inc., pp. 129–64.

BETH KATZOFF

bamboo

Along with **pine trees** and **cherry blossoms**, bamboo is one of the three dominant plant-inspired motifs in Japanese aesthetics. Several hundred varieties of bamboo grow wild in Japan. Its tall fronds are seen along rural roadsides and on mountain slopes, as well as in cultivated **gardens**, where the wind rustling its leaves creates a distinctive sound that contributes to the ambience of the formal setting. With pine branches and the plum flower, bamboo is known as one of the 'three friends of winter' because of its hardiness and resilience in cold temperatures.

The bamboo plant has many traditional uses. Its young shoots, *take no ko*, are considered a great delicacy, eaten early in the spring. Because it is strong and considered very beautiful, bamboo is widely used in building materials, furniture and an extensive range of both decorative and utilitarian items, including baskets, umbrellas, chopsticks, fish traps, farm implements, archery bows, children's toys, vases and water ladles, and the Japanese flute, *shakuhachi*. Its aesthetic qualities are particularly valued in the tea ceremony, where it is used for whisks and tea scoops. It is believed to impart a rustic quality that enhances human connections with nature.

AUDREY KOBAYASHI

Bank of Japan

Directed by the Ministry of Finance, the Bank of Japan (Nippon Ginko or Nihon Ginko) was established in 1882 to stabilise the **yen**, avoid inflation in the early years of the Meiji Period (1868–1912) and to provide funds for the growth of business and industry. As with any other central bank, it is responsible for issuing banknotes and carrying out currency and monetary controls. It also manages inflation and maintains the value of the yen (fulfilling its role as the 'guardian of the currency') by influencing financial-market operations through setting official bank interest rates, and buying or selling government bills and bonds. In addition, the Bank of Japan acts as the 'banks' bank' by offering accounts to other financial institutions. These then settle transactions between themselves by transferring funds across the accounts held by each institution at the Bank of Japan. A further role is as the 'government's bank'. Here, the Bank of Japan handles receipts and disbursements of national treasury funds, including acceptance of tax monies and payment of public works expenditures and public pensions. It also conducts accounting and bookkeeping for government agencies. Historically, the Bank conducted monetary policy with pressure exerted by the Ministry of Finance. However, a new Bank of Japan Law in 1998 requires more open disclosures through bi-annual reports of policies directly to the Diet (parliament).

DAVID EDGINGTON

banking system

The present Japanese banking system was organised after the Second World War. It has traditionally been closely regulated by the Ministry of Finance and the **Bank of Japan**, especially before the financial liberalisation of the mid-1980s. Excluding the central Bank of Japan, banks are classified into major categories:

1   Ten city banks, among the largest in the world, have branches throughout Japan and in major international centres. The largest are Dai-Ichi Kangyo Bank, Sakura Bank (formerly Mitsui Bank), Sumitomo Bank, Fuji Bank, Bank of Tokyo-Mitsubishi (BTM), Mitsubishi Bank and Sanwa Bank. Traditionally, they have sat at the very apex of Japan's well-known '*keiretsu*' enterprise groups. In October 1999, the Sumitomo and Sakura Banks merged to create the world's second largest bank, perhaps indicating that the *keiretsu* system of interlocking, mutually exclusive links between firms is breaking down.

2   Over sixty regional banks, based in the principal prefectural cities, conduct their operations primarily at the prefectural level, serving mainly small and medium-sized firms. There are also over sixty banks in the Second Association of Regional Banks.

3   Over ninety foreign banks, such as the Bank of America, have branches in Japan under licences from the Ministry of Finance. All are heavily involved in foreign-currency transactions.

Specialised banks include the following:

1   Long-term credit banks, which are the Industrial Bank of Japan, the Long-Term Credit Bank of Japan and the Nippon Credit Bank, specialise in long-term lending to promote industrial development.

2   Over thirty trust banks engage in pension and other trust fund management and administration, as well as general banking activities, providing loans to major corporations for long-term capital investments. The largest are Mitsubishi Trust and Banking, Mitsui Trust and Banking, Sumitomo Trust and Banking, and Yasuda Trust and Banking.

3   Financial institutions for small and medium business include *sogo* (mutual) banks, credit co-operatives, and labour credit associations. They take deposits and instalment savings from members and lend to members.

4   Financial institutions for agriculture, forestry and fisheries exist as co-operatives in rural

communities, where they accept deposits from members and extend loans to members and non-members. These co-operatives belong to prefectural-level associations called credit federations. At the national level is the Norinchukin Bank (Norin Chuo Kinko), the Central Co-operative Bank for Agriculture and Forestry.

5 Government financial institutions, including two government banks – the Export–Import Bank and the Japan Development Bank – are engaged in export–import finance and industrial development, respectively. There are also nine public finance corporations established for specific purposes such as housing and small-business finance.

Japan's banking system has been plagued by bad loans from property speculation during the '**bubble economy**' followed by the 'bursting of the bubble economy', leading to bankruptcies of smaller banks, mergers of large banks, and substantial reduction of employment. The government was forced to 'bail out' major commercial banks to restore confidence in the banking system. In 1998, legislation was introduced to reform the banking system, deal with large bank failures and confront the bad loans problem at the heart of Japan's economic crisis. Two major banks (the Nippon Credit Bank and the Long-Term Credit Bank of Japan) were nationalised under the provisions of the new laws.

DAVID EDGINGTON

barricades

The barricades were obstacles erected to prevent police entry on to university campuses. They were put into place by activists in the student movement, largely between 1968 and 1970. Students seized control of university buildings, graduate students stopped working and undergraduates stopped attending classes. The barricades were designed to create a space in which the ideology of everyday life could be challenged. Along with the strikes, they were conceived as an intervention in the university system as part of the larger social formation they hoped to change. The Japanese student movement was part of an international student movement that shared strategies from the mid- to late 1960s. The dominant organisation in the late 1960s Japanese student movement, **Zenkyōtō**, opposed the rationalising, bureaucratic administration of the capitalist system, and the state and the university's implication in the logic of capital. Autonomy and self-management were fundamental aspirations for Zenkyōtō. They opposed centralised bureaucratic control, and championed individual input into social decisions. They equally opposed state bureaucracy, party bureaucracy and the bureaucracy of corporate management. They promoted freedom between individuals rather than individualism. Zenkyōtō developed a critique of the university as a factory for producing social hierarchy, both between universities and within them. For example, many saw Tokyo University as a producer of elite administrators and technocrats, while Nihon University was seen as the training ground of lower management and middle-class workers. Transcripts served to rank students within each university programme.

It has been suggested that Yoshimoto Takaaki served as the intellectual leader of the Japanese student movement in a manner analogous to the role performed in the USA by Herbert Marcuse. Zenkyōtō was critical of the Leninism and Stalinism of the Japan Communist Party. For some, this raised the possibility of a return to Marx, for others the necessity of moving beyond him. Like other student movements of the time, Zenkyōtō questioned developments in the Third World. US intervention in Vietnam was seen as an extension of pre-Second World War colonial policies in developmental clothing. Indeed, Vietnam was a former French colony in which the USA determined to oppose the colonial resistance movement that had defeated the French. Zenkyōtō saw Japanese economic development and strategic alliance with the USA as a return to Japanese colonial practices of the Second World War period. Guy Yasko has argued that Mishima Yukio's confrontation with Zenkyōtō leaders during their occupation of Tokyo University nevertheless revealed that the group failed to successfully challenge the logic of modernisation.

On 18 January 1966, students at Waseda University moved towards erecting barricades and going on strike in response to a student fee hike. In

November 1966, a strike was declared at Meiji and Chuo Universities. January 1967 saw the beginning of a sixty-one day strike at Tokyo Medical School. In January 1968, students declared an indefinite strike at the Tokyo University medical school. Demonstrations related to short-term students at Nihon University began in April 1968. For many, the student movement was symbolised by the occupation of Yasuda Hall at Tokyo University on 15 June 1968. New Year 1969 saw Tokyo University, Tokyo Education University, Tokyo University of Foreign Studies, Nihon University, Chūō University, Meiji University, Yamagata University, Tomiyama University, Ōsaka University, Kobe University, Kansai Graduate School and Nagasaki University behind barricades controlled by students. Through the course of early 1969, the student groups were forcibly removed from control of the campuses, one campus at a time.

There was a cultural component to the barricades that involved group activities such as singing folk songs, attending organisational meetings and debates, and festival activities, which included music concerts. The ideological divide between those who saw the folk music movement as a challenge to the commodification of culture and those who saw a place for rock in revolution was a battle fought out on the stages erected behind the barricades. Occasionally, performers without sufficiently folk or anti-capitalist credentials were delayed in taking the stage or prevented from performing entirely. News reports of the time suggest that many students filled the dead time between confrontations with authorities with the reading of *manga*. An analysis of mid- and late 1960s *manga* that examines the degree to which *manga* sustained or undermined student activism remains to be conducted.

See also: student movement; Zenkyōtō

Further reading

Yasko, Guy (1997) *The Japanese Student Movement, 1968–70: The Zenkyōtō Uprising*, Cornell University Doctoral Dissertation.

Zenkyōtō Wo Yomu (eds) (1997) *Jokyo Shuppan Editorial Group*, Tokyo: Jokyo Shuppan.

MARK ANDERSON

baseball

Baseball is still the most popular team sport in Japan, although its pre-eminence has been challenged increasingly by soccer and basketball in recent years. Baseball has been played in Japan since 1873. It first appeared amid the social, cultural and technological spasms Japan endured on the heels of the Meiji Restoration (1868). The first Japanese team was organised around 1880, and several college teams were soon formed in Tokyo. Its introduction coincided with a surge in nationalistic sentiment aroused by the campaign to revise the unequal treaties and maintain a Japanese presence in Korea. A convergence of Social Darwinism and neo-traditionalism located the values of manliness and strength in Japan's pre-Meiji past. There was a search for a national game to symbolise the collectivist ideals and fighting spirit of the nation as it prepared for war against China. Sports journalists began to argue that baseball nourished traditional virtues of loyalty, honour and courage, and therefore symbolised the 'new bushido' spirit of the age. Japanese students, especially in the higher schools, turned to baseball in an effort to establish a new image of national Japanese manhood. Amateur baseball allowed high-school and university students to overcome a reputation for licence and indolence, establishing their credibility as a hard working and public-spirited elite.

The club representing the First Higher School of Tokyo emerged as the most formidable. On 23 May 1896, this club was the first Japanese team in history to defeat a US baseball team, punishing the expatriate Yokohama Athletic Club 29–4. This event was a watershed for late nineteenth-century Japanese national identity, in the shadow of the unequal treaties and Euro-American claims of racial superiority. Contemporary high-school baseball is dominated by the National Tournaments held each year in March and August. These tournaments, which originated in 1924 and 1915, are held at Koshien Stadium in Nishinomiya, Hyōgo Prefecture, and are commonly known as the spring and summer Koshien tournaments. The spring tournament continues to receive extensive coverage in the press and is broadcast live on national radio and television. Universities throughout Japan take part in local university leagues. As in high-school baseball, these leagues are split into spring and summer tournaments. Unlike high-school baseball, however, the focus is on the local tournaments with the national college championship earning scant attention from the media. The first professional team, the Dai Nihon Baseball Club, was organised in 1934 out of an all-star team put together to play a touring North American Major Leagues all-star team, which included Babe Ruth, Lou Gehrig, Lefty Grove and Jimmie Foxx. By 1936, seven professional teams had been formed. The current two-league system, consisting of the Central League and the Pacific League, was set up in 1950. Each league has six teams, all of which are owned and sponsored by large corporations. In 1934, the Yomiuri Shinbun organised another professional team, Dai Nippon. After a 1935 North American tour, Dai Nippon was renamed the Giants. Soon, other teams were formed. In April 1936, Japan's first professional season began at Koshien Stadium near Ōsaka. Six teams, not including the Giants, took part in three spring tournaments played near Ōsaka. From 1936 to 1939, the Tigers were the best team in Japanese professional baseball. Their chief rivals, the Giants, began to dominate after 1939.

In twenty-two seasons from 1959 to 1980, Sadaharu Oh (his father was Taiwanese) compiled a 0.301 lifetime average while setting records for home runs (868) and RBIs (1,967), and winning two consecutive triple crowns in 1973 and 1974. A nine-time Most Valuable Player, Oh also holds the single-season home run record. The most popular player in post-war Japanese baseball is Shigeo Nagashima. Nagashima played third base for the Giants from 1958 to 1974. Tenth on the all-time batting list with a career 0.305 average, the 1958 Rookie of the Year went on to hit 444 home runs with 1,522 RBIs in seventeen seasons. Nagashima earned the nickname 'Mr Giants' because of his clutch-hitting and exaggerated 'fighting spirit'. Nagashima has managed the Giants since the mid-1990s with mixed success. The Sawamura Award, Japan's version of the Cy Young Award, is named after Yomiuri pitcher Eiji Sawamura, whose brief professional career ended when he was drafted into the Imperial navy and killed in 1944. From 1936 to 1943, Sawamura pitched three no-hitters while compiling a 63–22 lifetime record with 554 strikeouts and a 1.74 ERA.

Since 1936, over 500 foreigners have played professional baseball in Japan. Japanese teams add depth to their rosters and power to their line up by signing foreign players. Each team is allowed to have four foreigners on their active roster: two pitchers and two position players. Most of the foreign players that Japanese teams sign have experience playing in either the North American major leagues or minor leagues. In recent years, players have come to Japan directly from Korea, Taiwan, China, Brazil and the Dominican Republic in increasing numbers. Friction between foreign and Japanese managers in Japanese professional baseball has been a common focus of Japanese sports journalism, in which attitudes about Japanese spirit, management style and ideology have been played off against very slowly shifting stereotypes of foreign players.

Legal challenges to the absolute monopoly of league control over players, such as free agency, came late to the Japanese leagues, but have gained some headway in recent years in radically qualified form. A Japanese major leaguer must play for ten years before becoming eligible for free agency. The remarkable proportion of Japanese Baseball Hall of Fame inductees drawn from the Ichiko High School teams testifies to the continuing hold the international aspect of the sport has on the Japanese baseball imagination. More recently, stars from the Japanese leagues such as Hideo Nomo and Kazuhiro Sasaki have had extremely successful careers as pitchers in the North American Major Leagues. Hideo Nomo was named National League rookie of the year in 1995. He threw a no-hitter and a seventeen strike-out game in 1996. Kazuhiro Sasaki was one of the elite American League relievers in 2000, piling up thirty-seven saves and an ERA of 3.14. A Japanese position player has yet to break through in the North American Majors, but in 2001 the reigning Pacific League batting champion for the last six years, Ichiro Suzuki, will attempt to change that. It will be interesting to watch his adjustment to Major League pitching as he leaves Japan in search of new challenges to overcome.

See also: Zenkyōtō

Further reading

Allen, Jim, *Jim Allen's Japanese Baseball Page*, www2.gol.com/users/jallen/jimball.html.

Roden, Donald (1980) 'Baseball and the quest for national dignity in Meiji Japan', in *American Historical Review*, 85(3) (June): 511–34.

Whiting, Robert (1990) *You Gotta Have Wa*, New York: Vintage Books.

MARK ANDERSON

basho

Basho is the term for a sumo meet or event. Each *basho* is made up of a series of fights between ranked sumo wrestlers in separate elimination matches. A *basho* lasts fifteen days and there are six per year – January in Tokyo, March in Ōsaka, May in Tokyo, July in Nagoya, September in Tokyo and November in Fukuoka. Some *basho* are also known for the season, e.g. the January *basho* is also called the winter *basho*. Each *basho* follows the same rituals without regional variation. *Basho* sponsorship tends to be national rather than regional but there is ample opportunity for corporations to capitalise on a *basho* as a fringe benefit for managers or gift for valued customers. It is no accident that the most southern *basho* is scheduled in the cooler month of November.

See also: *basho*; *yokozuna*

SANDRA BUCKLEY

BATH *see ofuro*

bedridden patients

Netakiri describes patients confined to bedcare. This practice has become controversial since the 1980s as attitudes towards elderly care have shifted, and awareness of the long-term welfare implications of the greying of the population has increased.

From the 1980s, groups representing the rights of the elderly have drawn attention to high levels of elderly confined to bedcare in the home, hospitals and elderly facilities. Concerns surfaced around the welfare of *netakiri* patients left in the care of family lacking the necessary training to avoid problems associated with prolonged bedrest: bedsores, muscular atrophy, respiratory complaints, etc. Claims that the practice of *netakiri* care was being used to limit the demands on caregivers from active and mobile elderly family members or patients led to a number of media exposés on the subject. Abused *netakiri* patients described problems ranging from infantilisation to physical violence, to excessive use of bed restraints and to overdosage of tranquillisers. Research and changing public attitudes have led to such initiatives as training programmes for family caregivers, private and public home nursing services and hi-tech digital links between home and emergency monitoring systems. Questions surrounding *netakiri* care are likely to continue to abound, with a greying population faced with government pressure to transfer responsibility for elderly care from a weakened welfare system to the private sector and families.

See also: ageing society and elderly care; welfare

SANDRA BUCKLEY

beer

Despite the popular Western image of the Japanese as **sake** drinkers, more than five times as much beer as sake is consumed. All the same, the production of alcoholic drinks out of rice has an ancient history in Japan, but barley-based alcohol was introduced by Westerners. In fact, Japan's first commercial beer brewery was established by an American, William Copeland, in 1870. Military history has influenced beer consumption in Japan. Conscription in the first half of the twentieth century exposed many a parochial farm boy to new experiences, including the taste of beer, while American beverage preferences were spread during the Occupation. Beer's popularity grew steadily from its introduction (except during the war years) but really exploded after 1960 as the post-war economic boom provided disposable income. One result is that beer lacks the working-class associations it can have in the USA; instead, it has middle-class respectability with the faintest traces of the exotic, as might wine in the USA.

Beer production is dominated by a few internationally recognised brewing corporations, such as Asahi, Kirin, Sapporo and Suntory. The mainstay of these corporations is admirable lager beer, fuller flavoured than American beers while not as heavy as many European brews; but breweries also produce numerous speciality ales and seasonal beers, packaged in a vast variety of containers, as they attempt to tap all possible markets.

Beer is first among equals for beverages of conviviality. Every visitor to Japan needs to learn the etiquette of drinking, an etiquette in which sharing is paramount. The first rule of drinking socially is that you do not fill your own glass. You modestly wait for others to pour for you, while conscientiously keeping your companions' glasses topped up. The second rule of drinking is that, when the beer bottle (or sake flask) is held before you in an offer of pouring, you should raise your cup to receive the drink. Finally, when a drink has been poured for you, you must return the favour by offering to pour for your benefactor. (Note that you can get your glass filled by offering to pour for someone else.) One consequence of this drinking etiquette is that beer is often not available by the glass; rather, it tends to be served in large bottles or cans, on the assumption that it will be shared out.

Perhaps because draft beer is sold in individual mugs, most Japanese drinking spots do not have beer on tap all year round. Draft beer is generally considered a warm-weather speciality, with taps appearing only from June to September. In summer, department stores temporarily convert their rooftops into beer gardens and, under the urban night sky, parties gather to drink mugs of beer and sample appetisers. An exception to the general rule of seasonal draft beer is the beer hall. Often run by the breweries, these establishments may affect a Germanic atmosphere, with German music and food, and great steins of beer.

Further reading

Smith, S.R. (1992) 'Drinking etiquette in a changing beverage market', in J.J. Tobin (ed.) *Re-made in Japan*, New Haven and London: Yale University Press.

STEPHEN R. SMITH

Beheiren

Soon after the USA began bombing North Vietnam and rapidly escalating its military intervention in South-East Asia, in April 1965 a group of intellectuals and artists centring around author Oda Makoto began a loosely organised protest movement known as Beheiren (Betonamu ni heiwa ō! Shimin rengō, or Citizen's Federation for Peace in Vietnam). Disillusioned by the regimented and doctrinaire character of previous left-wing protest, Beheiren's leadership hoped the movement would promote a cultural revolution in which a newly autonomous political subjectivity for the Japanese citizenry would develop. Accordingly, the movement avoided centralised leadership, encouraging individuals and groups to use the Beheiren logo for their own independently planned activities so long as they accepted the three principles of peace in Vietnam, Vietnamese self-determination and opposition to Japanese government collaboration in the war. From 1965 until Beheiren's disbandment in 1974, over 400 groups conducted monthly demonstrations and teach-ins (including a twenty-four-hour televised event on 15 August 1965), published newsletters, took out full-page advertisements in major US newspapers and provided assistance to US military deserters.

Further reading

Havens, T.H. (1987) *Fire Across the Sea*, Princeton: Princeton University Press.

JAMES J. ORR

BIKE GANGS *see bosozoku*

bishōnen

Literally 'beautiful boys', *bishōnen* refers most directly to a style of depiction of male characters in **manga** for adolescent girls. *Bishōnen* are uniformly svelte, with enormous eyes and features recognisably male, but nearly as delicate and beautiful as those of the depiction of female characters. *Bishōnen* narratives often involve a homo-erotic romance between these beautiful young men. Popularised widely during the 1970s, when glam rock made androgynous male singers into sex symbols in Japan as elsewhere, the Japanese roots of the *bishōnen* look are multiple and can arguably be traced much further back. One antecedent is a famous warrior figure from medieval history, Yoshitsune, who – at least as depicted in later *kabuki* plays – was known simultaneously for his slender, almost-feminine beauty and for military leadership. In *kabuki*, Yoshitsune is usually portrayed by an *onnagata* (male actor of female roles), underscoring his androgynous beauty. In 1848, writer Bakin used the word *bishōnen* in the title of a book about the younger, more feminine partners (*wakashu*) in the male homosexual romances that were frequently depicted in Edo art and literature. By this time the word was in common usage.

In 1914, the all-girl Takarazuka Theatre was founded; it remains popular today, mostly among women. Takarazuka inaugurated a particular look associated with the actresses who specialise in male roles: tall, slim, elegant, boyish, but still retaining female facial features. In the post-war years, Takarazuka troupes occasionally mounted plays based on popular *manga*; in turn, the visual style of the Takarazuka actresses influenced *manga* artists. Another likely influence on the 1970s *bishōnen* image were early post-war *manga* that featured characters of ambiguous or changeable gender, such as Tezuka Osamu's *Ribon no kishi* (Princess Knight), which began serialisation in 1954. Its heroine, Princess Sapphire, has both a man and woman's heart. As one or the other becomes dominant she becomes male or female. In either state, however, she is prepared to dress as a man and fight with a sword, if necessary. The *manga* that brought several of these influences together, and defined the *bishōnen* look, is *Berusaiyu no bara* (The Rose of Versailles) by Ikeda Riyoko, begun in 1972. It featured the protagonist Oscar, a young woman raised from birth as a boy, serving in the Palace Guard of Queen Marie Antoinette. The gorgeous androgyny of Oscar and the other romantic male characters in this *manga* is the epitome of the *bishōnen* look. This is, unsurprisingly, one of the *manga* made into a play by the Takarazuka Theatre. The mainstream of *bishōnen manga*, however, do not

feature cross-dressing women, but rather beautiful young men, often European, involved in homo-erotic relationships. The comic magazine for women, *June*, launched in 1978 at the height of the *bishōnen* boom, specialises in such stories. As of 1995, its circulation was 80,000–100,000, suggesting that the appeal for women readers of narratives featuring these ambiguously gendered, homosexual characters remains strong. In addition, *bishōnen*-like figures can be found in male-oriented *manga* and *anime* as well, although they usually play villains, or allies whose loyalty is ambiguous.

See also: cross-dressing and cross-gendering; *manga*

SHARALYN ORBAUGH

bonsai

Literally meaning a 'potted landscape' *bonsai* is the art of miniaturising not only a tree but, in more elaborate examples, an entire landscape of mountain, rock, water and tree. There is some disagreement over the origins of *bonsai*, although it is generally agreed that by the fifteenth century the practice was well established in Japan. The dwarfing of a tree is achieved over years of clipping new growth, trimming the root system, re-potting and training branches.

Wire, rope and bamboo supports are used to encourage branches to grow in a specific direction, resulting in the occasional humorous characterisation of *bonsai* as the torture of trees. The aesthetic of *bonsai* is grounded in the dual notion of the representation of the beauty and harmony of nature and the demonstration of the human mastery of nature. A *bonsai* tree will flower in the spring, change colours in the autumn, stand bare in the winter and green in the summer. Some *bonsai* are designed for more delicate care indoors, while others are bred to withstand outdoor exposure. A *bonsai* needs to be re-potted regularly (every two to three years) and trimmed at each new growth season. The *bonsai* artist will toil to create the effect of an aged tree using a variety of techniques to thicken and add grain and texture to the trunk. A popular style of *bonsai* leaves the upper root system exposed above the soil and will involve trimming the root system over years to create a pleasing arrangement of roots to complement the angle and density of the branches. More complex landscapes will include rocks and peaks, and even waterfalls or flowing streams in some more recent hi-tech *bonsai* design. Moss cover is another valued but fragile feature of well-aged *bonsai*. In *bonsai* produced outside of Japan, these days, you can often also find such Orientalist touches as miniature porcelain or plastic pagodas, temples, a hermit hut or even a miniaturised hermit.

Some of the most famous examples of the art of *bonsai* are hundreds of years old and are handed down from master to master. *Bonsai* is no longer an art of the elite but has become a beloved pastime for many Japanese, particularly the elderly, seeking an opportunity to nurture and grow something more demanding than houseplants in the absence of space for a home garden. National and international competitions and exhibitions provide a forum for display and the sharing of techniques traditional and new. Local *bonsai* clubs are no longer limited to Japan, and many cities and regions in Europe and North America as well as Asia now boast one or more *bonsai* clubs or associations. Websites have added a new forum for the popularisation of *bonsai* outside Japan. A *bonsai* stall is a common feature of many local arts and crafts fairs in the USA, and a number of online and mail order garden supply and florist shops now offer both pre-potted and do-it-yourself *bonsai* kits for beginners.

SANDRA BUCKLEY

bonus spending

Japanese full-time salaries are structured to include a substantial bonus. In good years, an employee may receive the equivalent of 3–4 months' additional salary in the two lump sum payments at end and mid-year. The bonus is meant to reflect management appreciation of productivity through profit sharing. However, this system has been criticised for creating significant flexibility in total salary costs. Attempts to regularise bonus formulas have met strong management resistance.

Bonus payments are scheduled close to the two gift-giving seasons. Significant portions go directly into savings or mortgage repayments and the bonus is often identified as a key factor in Japan's high level of savings. There is a marked increase in high ticket item sales at bonus time and department stores plan their purchasing and marketing to maximise sales opportunities. Price hiking at bonus season became a controversial practice in the boom years of the early 1980s. Many women's magazines carry economic advice columns in the weeks leading up to bonus season and feature articles on best consumer buys and investment strategies. Families often rely on a bonus to pay for expensive white goods and other household appliances, car downpayments, family holidays, etc. Although wives are usually the financial managers in the household, bonus spending is more often a family decision and an eagerly awaited family event.

SANDRA BUCKLEY

BOOK BROWSING *see tachiyomi*

bōsei hōgo

The phrase *bōsei hōgo* (protection of motherhood) has been used in various meanings in discussions of gender and social policy throughout the twentieth century. From 1919 to the mid-1920s, **Hiratsuka Raichō**, **Yamakawa Kikue**, Yosano Akiko and others participated in the motherhood protection debate (*bōsei hōgo ronsō*), which focused on the issue of government financial support for mothers. The Labour Standards Law of 1947 included various provisions that are known under the generic title of *bōsei hōgo*, including provision for maternity leave, nursing leave and menstruation leave, and prohibition of night work, excessive overtime and work in dangerous occupations. Provisions about night work and overtime were debated in discussions leading up the enactment of **equal employment opportunity legislation** in 1985. The debate focused on whether these so-called protective provisions could be compatible with the principle of equal opportunity. The Labour Standards Law was modified in the wake of the enactment of equal employment opportunity legislation.

Provisions directly related to maternity leave were retained, and provisions related to working hours and overtime were progressively weakened.

Further reading

Mackie, V. (1995) 'Equal opportunity and gender identity: Japanese feminist encounters with modernity and postmodernity', in Yoshio Sugimoto and Johann Arnasson (eds) *Japanese Encounters with Postmodernity*, London: Kegan Paul International.

Molony, B. (1993) 'Equality versus difference: The Japanese debate over motherhood protection, 1915–1950', in Janet Hunter (ed.) *Japanese Women Working*, London: Routledge.

VERA MACKIE

bosozoku

The subculture of the *bosozoku* (bike gangs) first gained attention from both the police and media in the 1970s. Although popularly linked to a biker gang image, the majority of *bosozoku* drive modified cars. A typical car has modified engine and exhaust, lowered suspension, wide wheels, a stereo system and mega speakers, and has a musical or other type of horn that becomes a part of the signature of the driver together with the highly stylised design of the external paintwork of the vehicle. The *bosozoku* are infamous for drag racing on city streets and cruising the night city. Stereotypes of the *bosozoku* prevail and the media enjoy sensationalising stories of these young 'speed tribes' and their alleged involvement with *yakuza*, drugs, violence and sex scandals.

Further reading

Ikuyu Sato (1991) *Kamikaze Biker: Parody and Anomie in Affluent Japan*, Chicago: University of Chicago Press.

SANDRA BUCKLEY

BOYS' DAY *see* kites; koinobori and Children's Day

BOYS' AND GIRLS' SCHOOLS *see* gender segregation in schools

Brazilian Japanese

The Brazilian Japanese are a group of *nikkei* (Japanese descendants born abroad) from Brazil who have 'return' migrated to Japan as unskilled foreign workers and have become Japan's newest ethnic minority. Currently estimated at over 230,000, they are the third largest population of foreigners after the **Koreans in Japan** and **Chinese in Japan**. The return migration of the Brazilian Japanese was initiated in the late 1980s by a severe economic crisis in Brazil, coupled with an abundance of unskilled jobs in a labour-deficient Japanese economy and an increasing wage differential between the two countries. The 1989 revision of the Immigration Control and Refugee Recognition Act enabled the Brazilian Japanese (as well as other *nikkei* from South America) to enter Japan on special renewable visas with no activity restrictions.

Most Brazilian Japanese are factory workers in the manufacturing sector and are employed mainly in small and medium-sized businesses. Although the Japanese labour shortage has become less acute because of the prolonged recession, the *nikkei* workers have assumed a critical role in the Japanese economy as a flexible and temporary migrant labour force, and their numbers continue to increase at a steady pace. Although virtually all of them come to Japan with intentions to work only for a couple of years, many have prolonged their stays and have begun to settle in Japan with their families. A vast majority of the Brazilian Japanese are of the second and third generations, who were born and raised in Brazil, do not speak Japanese very well, and have become culturally Brazilianised to various degrees. As a result, despite their Japanese descent, they are ethnically rejected and treated as **gaijin** (foreigners) in Japan because of narrow definitions of what constitutes being Japanese. As they become a permanent immigrant minority, their social integration and impact on Japanese ethno-national identity will become serious issues.

See also: migrant workers; national identity and minorities

Further reading

Keiko Yamanaka (1996) 'Return migration of Japanese-Brazilians to Japan: The *nikkeijin* as ethnic minority and political construct', *Diaspora* 5(1): 65–97.

Sellek, Y. (1997) '*Nikkeijin*: The phenomenon of return migration', in M. Weiner (ed.) *Japan's Minorities: The Illusion of Homogeneity*, London: Routledge, pp. 178–210.

Takeyuki Tsuda (forthcoming) 'The permanence of "temporary" migration: The "structural embeddedness" of Japanese-Brazilian migrant workers in Japan', *The Journal of Asian Studies*.

——(forthcoming) 'Transnational migration and the nationalization of ethnic identity among Japanese-Brazilian return migrants', *Ethos: Journal of the Society for Psychological Anthropology*.

—— (1998) 'The stigma of ethnic difference: The structure of prejudice and "discrimination" towards Japan's new immigrant minority', *The Journal of Japanese Studies* 24(2): 317–59.

TAKEYUKI TSUDA

bubble economy

Speculative 'bubbles' form when the price of assets such as land and stocks becomes inflated far beyond their fundamental value and the expected profits. In Japan, the term referred to asset inflation and speculative wealth in 1986–9. Following the rising **yen** (*endaka*) and falling export profitability in 1985–6, the government maintained a policy of very low interest rates from 1986 to 1989 to stimulate domestic demand. Money supply increased at double-digit rates for four years, allowing companies to raise capital at very low cost, driving stock market levels to unprecedented heights. Banks lent funds too freely and corporate cash surpluses were channelled into massively inflated financial and land markets. Private households and corporations took advantage of lax credit to engage in often speculative real-estate deals. Excessive speculation was finally curbed in 1989

and 1990 with increased interest rates and a ceiling on bank finance for real-estate purchases. These and other measures succeeded in halting the runaway rise in asset prices. The Nikkei average on the Tokyo Stock Exchange fell from 38,915 in 1989 to below 15,000 in 1992, while land prices declined by 200 trillion yen during 1991. This 'bursting of the bubble' choked off funds to businesses. Banks failed due to 'bad loans' and their inability to recoup either interest or capital, and the 'real' economy stagnated after 1992.

DAVID EDGINGTON

Buddhism

Buddhism was officially introduced to Japan in the mid-sixth century CE, when the king of the Korean kingdom of Paekche sent a Buddhist statue and some *sutras* to the Japanese court in an attempt to secure a political alliance. Praised for its power to fulfil wishes and for being difficult to understand, Buddhism was accepted by the powerful Soga clan, of which Prince Shōtoku (CE 573–621) was a member. The political and military ascendancy of the Soga clan allowed its leaders to overcome the critics who warned that the native deities (*kami*) would object to the importation of foreign gods.

Tied to politics from the time of its introduction, Buddhism developed as a state-supported religion during the Nara period (CE 710–84). When the first permanent capital was established in Nara, the great temple Tōdaiji was built as the cosmological and ritual centre for the new nation. A system of subordinate temples in the provinces emphasised the centralisation of spiritual and political power. Buddhist clergy were sanctioned by the state, which supported and therefore controlled monastic institutions.

Nara Buddhist temples maintained philosophical identities based on earlier doctrinal developments in India, Korea and China. With the continual flow of monks to and from the continent, Buddhism in Japan developed across a broad range of understandings typified by six schools: Kusha, Jōjitsu, Ritsu, Kegon, Hossō and Sanron. While temples gained the appearance of sectarian affiliations, Kegon for Tōdaiji, Hossō for Kōfukuji, and so forth, monks studied the teachings and rituals of several, if not all, schools. Forbidden by law to propagate their teachings freely, Buddhist clergy were confined to the study and practice of Buddhism to insure the spiritual protection of the state.

State sponsorship of Buddhism continued in the Heian period (CE 794–1185), when a new capital was established in what is now modern Kyōto. While the Nara Buddhist establishment continued to play important roles, two new schools emerged as direct imports from China. A gifted young monk named Saichō (CE 766–822) travelled to China and returned to found the Tendai school, which was based on the Lotus *Sutra*. Saichō built his monastic centre on Mt. Hiei as a centre for training monks and protecting the state. In addition to its own teachings and practices, Tendai promoted Zen meditation, the observance of the monastic precepts, a wide variety of rituals and teachings about rebirth in the Pure Land, a heavenly abode for those whose moral life produced good karma that allowed their rebirth there instead of in hell. True to its inclusive stance, Tendai Pure Land included a broad ranges of practices.

The second school was Shingon, a type of esoteric Buddhism that Kūkai (CE 773–835) studied in China. Characterised by ornate rituals designed to produce spiritual and worldly benefits, Shingon Buddhism appealed to people of all classes. While Kūkai practised Shingon in several temples in Kyōto, he established his main temple on Mt. Kōya, a remote area in the mountains far to the south of the capital. So great is the reverence accorded Kūkai that his death is believed to have brought not a final demise but a state of eternal meditation. Shingon devotees still today pray to Kūkai, believing him to be a living divine saviour.

Tendai and Shingon continued to spread throughout the country well into the Kamakura period (CE 1185–333), when a group of remarkable innovators, many of whom had studied on Mt. Hiei, founded new forms of Buddhism. Rejecting the inclusive practices of Tendai Pure Land Buddhism he learned on Mt. Hiei, Hōnen (CE 1133–212) determined that one could be reborn in the Pure Land simply by chanting the *Nembutsu*, which calls out the name of Amida, the Buddha of the Western Pure Land. As if this were not simple enough, his disciple Shinran (CE 1173–262) went one step further and declared that Amida's universal and unconditional compassion guaranteed rebirth even if one did not recite the *Nembutsu*. Hōnen's Pure Land School reduced practice to a single chant, while Shinran's True Pure Land School did away with all practices, relying on faith in the compassionate power of Amida, who promised to provide the salvation that human effort could not secure.

The tendency towards simplification continued with Dōgen (CE 1200–53), the founder of Sōtō Zen, and Nichiren (CE 1222–82), who established the school that bears his name. After studying in China, Dōgen returned to Kyōto where he was unable to find a patron and thus established his headquarters at Eiheiji in what is now Fukui Prefecture. While Dōgen required strict monasticism, he was confident that enlightenment could be experienced in the act of sitting in meditation, the only necessary practice. For Nichiren, the only requirement was belief in the Lotus *Sutra*, whose powers are invoked through recitation of the *Daimoku*, the great title of the Lotus *Sutra*.

Throughout the medieval and early modern periods, the Buddhist schools developed into sects possessing their own teachings, rituals and institutional structures. Their temples proliferated throughout the country, and their rituals and ideas influenced the development of Japanese literature, dance, music, drama, customs and politics. In the Tokugawa Period (CE 1603–1868), Buddhist sects and temples formed the largest institutional network in the nation, and were used by the government to register every citizen, making a census possible as well as providing a bulwark against Christianity. New interpretations bred new religions, some of which surpassed the earlier sects in size.

Underlying this complex landscape of Buddhist institutions are three characteristics that define Buddhism in the modern period. The first is the abandonment of monasticism such that monks have become priests living a lay life of meat eating, marriage and drinking alcoholic beverages. While nuns still observe the old clerical precepts, their numbers are few and they seldom head temples. Marriage has created a hereditary priesthood in which temples are passed from father to son. The second characteristic is the dominance of the ancient belief that Buddhism possesses spiritual power to grant people their wishes. Rituals, amulets, talismans and customs abound for the sake of gaining wealth, health, happiness and other worldly benefits. The third feature is the identity that Buddhism has with mortuary services. Funereal Buddhism is the term that defines the religion itself, and over 90 per cent of Japanese funerals are still conducted according to Buddhist rites, which, despite criticisms that they are not based on orthodox principles, ordain the deceased as monks and nuns committed to traditional practices leading to enlightenment and nirvana.

See also: *butsudan* and *kamidana*; death and funerals

Further reading

Earhart, H. Byron (1982) *Japanese Religion: Unity and Diversity*, third edition, Belmont, CA: Wadsworth Publishing.
Kitagawa, Joseph (1966) *Religion in Japanese History*, New York: Columbia University Press.

GEORGE J. TANABE

bullet train

The opening of the *shinkansen* ('new trunk line') bullet train from Tokyo to Ōsaka on the eve of the **Tokyo Olympics** in 1964 symbolised post-war Japan's move from economic recovery to high-speed growth and advanced technology. It cut the six and-a-half hour trip between the two major business centres to four hours and, eventually, to two. Pictures of the *shinkansen* with **Mt. Fuji** in the background became clichés for the new and old Japan.

The major *shinkansen* lines are broad gauge (regular lines are narrow gauge) and double-tracked, with no level crossings, and reach speeds of up to 300 km per hour. They have an exceptional safety and on-time record, but nearby residents have protested over noise and vibrations.

The original Tōkaidō Shinkansen was extended to Hakata (Fukuoka) in Kyūshū by the San'yō Shinkansen. Two lines run north from Tokyo, the Tōhoku Shinkansen (to Morioka) and Jōetsu Shinkansen (to Niigata). The Hokuriku (Nagano) Shinkansen was built for the 1998 **Nagano Olympics**, and the Yamagata and Akita 'mini-*shinkansen*' lines branch off the Tōhoku Shinkansen. Extensions of some of these lines are under construction or planned, and test runs of magnetically levitated trains for a proposed new line between Tokyo and Ōsaka have exceeded 550 km per hour. However, some of the new proposals seem to be based more on political considerations than on economic feasibility or need.

See also: railways

TIMOTHY S. GEORGE

BULLYING *see ijime*

Bungei shunjū

Popular writer Kikuchi Kan (1888–1948) founded *Bungei shunjū*, the publishing company and magazine of the same name in January 1923, months before the Great Earthquake hit Tokyo and its environs. In its early years, the magazine printed miscellaneous literary essays and fiction, but, in 1926, it was transformed into a general interest magazine. *Bungei shunjū* was a relative latecomer when compared to similar magazines such as *Taiyō*, *Chūō kōron* and *Kaizō*. However, Kikuchi's imaginative policies enjoyed immediate success: offering the magazine at a lower price than other general interest magazines, soliciting readers' contributions and introducing a round-table-discussion (*zadankai*) format as a regular monthly feature. Kikuchi, quick to note new trends, recognised the public's demand for magazines like *Eiga Jidai* (The Age of Movies) (1925) and *Modan Nippon* (Modern Japan) (1930). Both magazines attest to the company's attempt to keep abreast of changing tastes.

In 1935, *Bungei shunjū* established the Akutagawa Prize for literary fiction and the Naoki Prize for more popular novels. Both prizes remain among the most prestigious annual awards for aspiring writers. As a consequence of *Bungei shunjū*'s co-operation with the war effort, Kikuchi Kan dissolved the company in 1946. Operations resumed the following year due to the efforts of the editorial staff. In 1959, *Bungei shunjū* launched the weekly magazine *Shūkan bunshun*, similar in content to Shinchō's *Shūkan shinchō* (1956). In 1969, *Shokun* came out under the slogan: 'People, let's speak the truth. Let's use our rights to discover what is really true.' The magazine's aim was to establish a conservative forum for intellectuals. In 1976, the magazine *Bungei shunjū* received international acclaim for its investigation of the bribery scandal surrounding Prime Minister Tanaka Kakuei. As a result, Tanaka was forced to resign. To this day, the company continues to boast a liberal publishing stance and to occupy an important role in the influence of contemporary publishing on intellectual life and broader issues of public interest.

See also: newspapers and magazines

BARBARA HAMILL SATO

Burakumin

Eta, hinin and other outcaste groups, later commonly referred to as *Burakumin*, were freed from status restrictions by the *Kaihōrei* (Liberation Edict) on 28 August 1871. Discrimination and prejudice against them remained, even increased, and their socio-economic circumstances improved little, if at all, until the 1960s. The Suiheisha (Levellers' Society) was created in 1922 to oppose institutionalised discrimination, but despite its pioneering work it did little to improve living conditions and had limited impact on anti-*Burakumin* prejudice. The movement restructured itself in 1955 as the Buraku Liberation League (BLL) and with the support of the **Japan Socialist Party** and most-left-of-centre organisations it demanded that government should take the lead in opposing discrimination and providing funds to improve the daily lives of *Burakumin*. By the late 1990s, housing conditions had been transformed and levels of educational achievement greatly improved. Prejudice still remains in many regions of Japan, meaning that genuine equal opportunity can still not be guaranteed. Barriers may still be encountered in employment and when getting married.

Not everyone had fitted into the four classes of the Tokugawa status hierarchy. Leather workers and those dealing with the dead were regarded as defiled and avoided by 'normal' people, even before the Edo era. As the status regulations were periodically tightened from the late sixteenth century onwards, more were defined as outside mainstream society and while it was easy by bad luck or bad judgement to fall into outcaste status, it became hard, finally impossible, to escape. From the early eighteenth century, rural outcaste communities grew in the region bordering on the **Inland Sea** and these often had little or nothing to do with defiling occupations. They scraped a living farming, usually on marginal land. Overall the number of outcastes increased relative to the majority population and the restrictions on occupations, clothes and lifestyle became more severe until 1871.

Liberation in 1871 removed these restrictions but also ended outcaste monopolies. When modern shoe factories were built, most traditional leather workers were forced out of business. Forced out of farming by land reforms, former outcastes found work in small city factories or the mines of north Kyūshū. Formal liberation did not change attitudes. When local bureaucrats created the new family records (*koseki*), they made sure that outcastes continued to be identifiable by insisting they all take the same surname or by putting special marks on the registers. Mainstream Japanese refused to work alongside them. Their children were educated in separate schools or sat at the back of the classroom. Marriage across the caste line continued to be out of the question. Such blatant discrimination and prejudice continued into the twentieth century.

Burakumin were not passive victims in this process. Many joined the dissident rights groups of the 1870s and 1880s. In 1922, at the peak of enthusiasm for critical ideas, the Suiheisha was formed to encourage *Burakumin* to free themselves by their own efforts. It demanded that government accept responsibility for their social discrimination and urged *Burakumin* to confront those who discriminated in *kyūdan* – campaigns of censure.

Some thought the democratic revolution induced by the Allied Occupation would eliminate the material and psychological conditions of discrimination. It did not. *Burakumin* in the 1950s remained relatively disadvantaged and subject to discrimination. The BLL carried on the Suiheisha tradition: *kyūdan* campaigns continued alongside demands that government improve *Burakumin* conditions. In 1960, the government established a commission of enquiry that reported in 1965. This clarified the fact that *Burakumin* are racially indistinguishable from other Japanese and argued that it is the duty of the state to eliminate the problem of discrimination. Following a brief survey of the deprivation of most *Buraku* communities, it recommended that the government adopt a programme (the *Dōwa* policy) to transform the communities' living environment, support access to education and healthcare and educate the majority community about the error of prejudice. A Ten Year Plan was launched in 1969 to eliminate discrimination.

It took more than ten years to achieve this task and the programmes have been extended many times, most recently in 1997. By the end of the 1980s, most large urban *Buraku* had been transformed by building schemes that had put up modern apartment blocks and created clinics, schools and community centres. Priority from the 1990s was on the smaller, more remote communities.

Meanwhile, the movement campaigned against social discrimination, e.g. the accessing of *koseki* by private detectives investigating a person's background for such clients as prospective employers or parents-in-law. Local governments and finally the central government in 1976 restricted access to *koseki*. This has not stopped the detectives; only made their work more difficult.

An extensive survey of the current condition of *Burakumin* was published in 1995. Briefly put, it demonstrates improvement in income levels, educational performance and declining levels of discrimination as measured by the number of *Burakumin* marrying non-*Burakumin* (75 per cent of those under twenty-five), but shows that there remain higher than average levels of unemployment and lower access to higher education. More *Burakumin* are living outside their communities, so the question of the size of the *Buraku* population is not easily answered. Government programmes target those descendants of former outcastes who still live in areas formally defined as *Buraku* communities. By this definition, there are just over

1 million. The liberation movement works on behalf of all those who are victims of discrimination, or who would be if their status origins were known. They talk of fighting for the rights of 3 million people, but some estimates go as high as 5 million.

Over the next century, the movement wants improvements to small and remote *Buraku* communities to be completed, more stress on improving *Burakumin* living conditions beyond just the physical environment and improvements to the areas neighbouring *Buraku* communities. More broadly, it wants the government to commit to creating respect for human rights in Japan and to contribute to the UN human rights structure.

Further reading

Kitaguchi, S. (1999) *An Introduction to the Buraku Issue*, London: Japan Library.

Neary, I. (1997) 'Burakumin in contemporary Japan', in M. Weiner, *Japan's Minorities*, London: Routledge, pp. 50–78.

—— (1989) *Political Protest and Social Control in Pre-war Japan: The Origins of Buraku Liberation*, Manchester: Manchester University Press.

Upham, F. (1980) 'Ten years of affirmative action for Japanese Burakumin', *Law in Japan: An Annual* 13.

IAN NEARY

BRANDS *see burando*

burando

The Japanised English of *burando* ('brand') has come to designate the notion of recognisable brand names in the luxury market. Initially '*burando*' were exclusively foreign luxury goods such as Yves St Laurent, Gucci, Dior, etc. However, the term now also applies to major Japanese designer brand names: Hanae Mori, Comme des Garçon, Kenzo.

Luxury brand consumption remains a major feature of Japanese foreign tourism, with individuals competing to bring back the best price on the latest model of handbag, watch, scarf or jewellery. Brand names carry a significance in Japan that arguably exceeds the brand recognition in the countries of origin of many foreign luxury goods. A scarf or garment will often be worn in a style that accentuates the designer logo. *Burando aficionados* will play at naming the brand ensemble of everyone from the next commuter on the train to an *idoru* (see **idoru singers**) at a music awards night. The flooding of both domestic and international markets with cheaper imitations of new brand releases does not diminish overall sales, and is even seen as extending brand awareness and increasing consumer desire to demonstrate the purchasing power to buy 'the real thing' (*honmono*). The fact that Japanese represent 40–60 per cent of total global sales for major luxury brands has seen some design modifications to accommodate Japanese size, colour and style preferences.

SANDRA BUCKLEY

bureaucracy

While there are potentially a variety of angles from which to approach the subject of bureaucracy in Japan, the dimension that has captured by far the largest share of attention and interest among non-Japanese observers has been the role of the Japanese government bureaucracy in economic affairs. Government agencies like the **Ministry of International Trade and Industry** (MITI) and the **Ministry of Finance** (MOF) intervene extensively in the affairs of private industry on behalf of a variety of 'industrial policies'. The question that has interested observers has been whether Japan's economic success prior to the 1990s occurred because of, or in spite of, such intervention. Japan's desultory economic performance during the 1990s has caused the tide of opinion on the subject to turn to a near universal condemnation of what is now seen as the counterproductive bureaucratic coddling of inefficient industries.

The central government agencies routinely hire what are considered to be the best and the brightest graduates of Japan's top universities. In contrast to the USA, in particular, top Japanese bureaucrats tend to spend their entire careers

attached to one particular ministry. This creates a considerable *esprit de corps* that is considered by many to account for the independence and 'rationality' of such agencies in their actions. Top government bureaucrats are also known for the practice of *amakudari* ('descent from heaven') in which they take post-retirement positions in politics, local government, private corporations, think tanks and a variety of quasi-governmental entities. Such practices effectively extend the reach of the Japanese bureaucracy well beyond the confines of the government agencies proper. Also, although bureaucrats prefer to foster an air of being 'above' petty private interests, **scandals** involving bureaucrats are a periodic feature of the Japanese political scene.

The role of the bureaucracy has been equally controversial inside Japan. The arrogance of bureaucrats has long been disparaged with the phrase *kanson mimpi* ('respect the bureaucrat, despise the people'). At the same time, a job in a central-government ministry or agency has garnered tremendous power and prestige. A love–hate relationship pervades the attitudes of business toward the bureaucracy. Businesses strongly desire the protection and assistance that the bureaucracy provides but simultaneously chafe at the restrictions and red tape involved. Since the early 1980s, there has been a concerted effort to systematically reform the bureaucracy in order to adapt it more effectively to the contemporary context (the 'administrative reform' movement). Ironically, bureaucrats themselves have frequently sabotaged such efforts. More recently, legislation has been passed that will result in a major reorganisation of the central-government bureaucracy. It remains to be seen, however, to what extent this will lead to meaningful changes in bureaucratic practice.

See also: Economic Planning Agency; political economy of post-war Japan

Further reading

Carlile, Lonny and Tilton, Mark (eds) (1998) *Is Japan Really Changing Its Ways? Regulatory Reform and the Japanese Economy*, Washington, DC: Brookings Institution Press.

Johnson, Chalmers (1982) *MITI and the Japanese Miracle*, Stanford, CA: Stanford University Press.

LONNY E. CARLILE

BUSINESS/NAME CARD *see meishi*

Buta to gunkan

Imamura Shōhei's 1961 film *Buta to gunkan* (Pigs and Battleships) is considered his first great masterpiece. Noted as one of Susan Sontag's favourite films, *Buta to gunkan* is set in 1960 and deals with a *yakuza* gang living in the Japanese port city Yokosuka, a US naval base during the post-war period. While the *yakuza* live off the debris of the US fleet in Yokosuka by pimping, the protagonist of the film, a young girl named Haruko, is determined to avoid prostitution despite it being the easiest way for her to make money. Imamura's sociological details don't stray far from the anxieties of a post-Occupation period Japan and function to give the film a documentary-like feel. Filmed by Shinsaku Himeda in high-contrast black and white with energetic camera movements, the aggressive composition of the film reaches its climax in a final scene, which depicts a herd of pigs stampeding through Yokosuka streets. The film stars Hiroyuki Nagato and Tetsuro Tambo, and has received several awards including the Most Excellent Motion Picture Award from the Japanese Picture Reporters' Association.

LEILA POURTAVAF

butō

Although the first performance of *butō* is said to have taken place in 1959, this form of dance performance did not come into its own in Japan until the early 1980s. This was after a fervent period of development over the preceding decade and its popular reception at major dance and arts festivals in Europe and the USA in the late 1970s and early 1980s. *Butō* is often described as *gyaku yuīnyū* – something that has had to leave and find success elsewhere before it can come back to achieve recognition in Japan. Critics and commentators often link *butō* to the traditional performances of *nō* and *kabuki*, but in fact *butō* defines itself as anti-traditional. The movement, expressions and gestures of *butō* are characterised by provocative innovation blended with a perversion (in a productive sense) of traditional practices. The training of the *butō* performer is rigorous and renowned for its discipline of both body and mind, a quality it shares with much traditional training from martial arts to *nō* and tea ceremony. However, the years of focused work on physical and mental flexibility lead not to a predetermined range of movement and expression bounded by tradition within a set repertoire, but instead to an unlimited field of performance potential.

The figure of a white-powdered, naked body edging in torturously slow and stylised steps across a dark and empty stage, face frozen in a singular intensity of emotion is a familiar snapshot of *butō* for contemporary performance and dance audiences in and out of Japan. While most often associated with this image of bodies in minimalist slow motion, *butō*'s master performers/choreographers will not be restricted to any zone of movement or gesture by either the weight of tradition or audience expectation. A performer may suddenly lurch from painfully constrained, barely visible movement into a flailing and volatile frenzy of limbs thrown across the stage by imagined forces. A gently unfolding smile can suddenly distort into the anguished face of a silent scream that tears through the theatre. A chill can run through an audience when the eye in a frozen white-powder face of a motionless figure suddenly blinks in evil intent. The viewer can be reduced to tears by the agonising repetition of a single focused movement – a smile, a stumble, lifting a bucket of water. One of the greatest skills of the *butō* performer is the ability to isolate movement, gesture or expression in one area of the body, as large as the torso or as small as an eyebrow, and to play out meaning in a concentrated intensity in that isolated body-zone. A hand can seem to express itself independently of a body, the tension and fearfulness of the gesturing fingers and arch of the palm contradicting the calm composure of the body. *Butō* is committedly about the telling of stories but the language and structure are determinedly unfamiliar and refuse wholeness, simple resolution or predictable flows. It is often only the movement of the *butō* performers that holds the fragments of a story together in any relation to one another.

The names most often associated with *butō* outside Japan are that of the performer Ōno Kazuo and the most internationally toured group Sankaijuku. The first major wave of *butō* performance in the early 70s was more closely aligned with developments in Japanese tent theatre and installation art than with mainstream theatre or dance. Its early performances were similarly interventionist and situationalist, and performances were not limited to a theatre stage. The space of early *butō* was profoundly urban: car parks, warehouses, underground theatres, vacant lots and inner-city studios. Ōno has always been in the public limelight, renowned for his thin, bony features in white powder and women's dress, his agility defies his octogenarian years and he still performs on occasion, writes prolifically and teaches studio. It has been said that Ōno does 'not commute' between performance and non-performance but lives each as an extension of the other. His theatricality and brief if monologistic pronouncements have made him a difficult figure for Western critics and interviewers to engage with off stage. His ideas are better accessed through his multitude of essays, but few of these have been translated. Sankaijuku frequently performed with Ōno on international tours. The troupe has integrated more special effects and stage settings into its performances than are usually associated with *butō*, but this again is a sign of the flexibility of *butō* and its refusal of boundaries and limitations. The notion of 'pure' *butō* would be anathema.

Other well-known and frequently touring groups include Dairakuda-kan, Muteki-ha and Ankoku butō-ha. The term *ankoku butō* (dance of darkness) was first used by Hijikata Tatsumi, who is said to have been the founder of *butō* in the late 1950s. He popularised the name in the late 1960s and early 1970s to distinguish *butō* from other forms of dance, because the term was still widely used generically for all dance. Hijikata played an important role as the director and choreographer of some of the earliest successful *butō* pieces, many of which were performed by Ashikawa Yōko at the Theatre Asbestos-kan in Meguro, Tokyo. Hijikata

attempted to create a rural, essentially agrarian mythical ground for *butō* when he uprooted his performers from Tokyo in the early 1970s to develop the 'Tōhoku kabuki' series in Tōhoku, his birthplace. However, despite the tremendous success of this series and another return to Tōhoku in 1977, the heart of *butō* remained at the urban hub of the city, whether Tokyo, Paris – where Sankaijuku relocated itself – or New York, where Poppo Shiraeshi created his *butō* studio. It was Ashikawa Yōko who carried on the important legacy of Hijikata's work after his death in 1986. Moving increasingly into choreography herself, she worked often with the Hakutoboh troupe. Individual dancers often break away to form a new troupe or dance solo, and the openness in *butō* to this fragmentation has been attributed with much of the innovative energy of the ever transforming landscape of *butō* performance. There is also a financial motivation to keeping troupes and studios small in Japan where there is still limited government funding for the arts. *Butō* studios rely heavily on their ability to attract paying students to support performance costs.

SANDRA BUCKLEY

BUTOH *see butō*

butsudan and kamidana

A *butsudan* is a household Buddhist altar and a *kamidana* is a household Shintō shrine for ancestor worship. In some households both may be present and the two can also merge into one altar, with a mix of Buddhist and Shintō iconography and functions. A *butsudan* may contain a statue of a *bodhistattva* and/or prayer and *sutra* tablets. A small metal bell is often tapped when food or prayers are to be offered. Rice, fruit, cakes and flowers are kept as fresh offerings, and gifts brought to a family by guests are also often placed at the *butsudan* or *kamidana* before being used or eaten. A Shintō or Buddhist priest can be called to the household to offer prayers on the anniversary of the death of family members. Certain elements of family ceremonies such as betrothal, marriage and birth of a child can also be held in front of these household altars in a gesture of ancestral witnessing. Although Shintō and Buddhist beliefs regarding death and the next world differ significantly, both religions in Japan require a family to demonstrate an ongoing respect and concern for their dead, and the household altars and shrines allow regular gestures of attention. These spaces may be as simple as a wooden shelf adorned with incense and death photos, or, in some households, the *butsudan* or *kamidana* become another opportunity to display family wealth with lacquered black wood, gold, brass, silk brocade and precious iconography.

SANDRA BUCKLEY

C

calligraphy

The art of calligraphy has been identified with the life of the cultured or cultivated individual from the first introduction of Chinese writing to Japan in the 5th century. In both the Chinese and Japanese traditions calligraphy, poetry and painting have remained closely linked. Chinese characters were initially used in Japan in official documents and Buddhist texts but Japan's emerging aristocracy soon began to learn the techniques of Chinese poetry. Poetic prowess became no less important than mastery of other areas of knowledge to success in the bureacracy and cultural credentials in the court. The two Japanese phonetic systems of writing (*kana*) known as *katakana* and *hiragana* were developed in the 9th century from simplifications of Chinese characters. *Kana* became the vehicle for the rich tradition of Japanese court literature over the Heian period. A strong, usually gendered, distinction emerged with the continued use of Chinese script for public official and religious documents and the use of the *kana* syllabaries for the poetry, diaries and tales written in Japanese. Though often personal in content the poetry and diaries can't simply be classifed as private for many of these works circulated through the court, passed from hand to hand, and were discussed in the literary salons, collected and anthologised. The literary quality of any text was intricately bound up with the quality of the calligraphy. The meaning of a single symbol or character flowed from the brush stroke onto paper and blended there with colour, scent and texture. The brush lines of the word for bird could take flight with a slight upward sweep of the brush or the tangled weed of a love poem might twist into a knot of emotion and brush lines.

Over time the *kana* became marked as feminine, in part as a reflection of the central role of women as both writers and readers of the growing œuvre of courtly literature. The styles of calligraphy associated with the femininely coded kana and masculinely coded Chinese characters were distinctive and have remained remarkably consistent across centuries of calligraphy. The diaries of Heian court women pay lip service to the taboo on women learning to read or write in the Chinese style while also offering plenty of evidence that at least some women were very familiar with the Chinese classics. In both calligraphy and poetry men were free to write in both the feminine and masculine styles but cultural norms continued to limit women to the realm of the kana and Japanese styles of prose and poetry. Numerous styles and schools of calligraphy were consolidated over the centuries, some directly adopted from China and others created against the Chinese tradition or as variations on that tradition. It was the Buddhist monks who travelled between China and Japan who brought new Chinese styles back with them creating new schools and movements. Calligraphy developed into an essential element of the Zen practice of *kooan* (questions or riddles) and calligraphy lessons also became an important source of income for monks and temples. The five most widely used calligraphy styles are *tensho* (a traditional, archaic Chinese script still used in seal carving), reisho (a clerical script using squared characters), *kaisho* (heavy, thick stroked and block shaped characters), *gyoosho* (a running style that allows for some abbreviation), *soosho*, grass writing which allows for fluid linkages and abbreviations. It is the more cursive *gyosho* and *soosho* grass writing styles that are marked as Japanese and feminine while the *tensho*, *reisho* and *kaisho* forms are perceived as the domain of men's writing and closer to Chinese technique and tradition.

The tools of calligraphy are simple. The brush can be thick (*futafude*) or thin (*hosofude*). The ink is made of hardened oil or wood soot mixed with a glue made from fishbone or hide and formed into a stick. The ink stick is rubbed on the hard surface of a wetted inkstone. Water is poured into a slight indentation at the sloping end of the stone from a small often ornamental water container of metal or ceramic. The stick is blended with water until the desired consistency is achieved. A calligraphers tools are usually stored in a lacquerware box. The **washi** paper used in calligraphy can vary from the common sturdy but thin white sheets to thick textured screen paper. In the Heian period highly ornamental paper was often used to add still one more dimension to the layered meaning of calligraphic poetry or prose. Gold fibre, leaves, petals, a lightly washed landscape could create a density of interactive meaning between brush stroke, character and paper. Today there is less use of decorative or coloured paper but speciality washi stores offer a wide variety of paper for anyone wanting to experiment.

It has only been the experimentation and defiance of traditional limitations in postwar calligraphy that has seen a dramatic opening up of the gender boundaries within calligraphy. In the twentieth century calligraphy became popularised both as an essential element of public school education and through countless schools of calligraphy offering lessons in cultural centres, corporate employee clubs, temples and home tuition. The large number of middle-class women taking calligraphy as part of adult education and culture centre programs has seen the popularisation of calligraphy driven by women while the schools and their elite ranks remain dominated by men. The introduction of calligraphy into school curriculum has contributed to this process of popularisation and the extension of brush writing skills beyond the cultural elites of Japan. Today inexpensive brush sets, self-inking brush-pens, and disposable calligraphy soft tip pens encourage amateur calligraphers to experiment with brush writing styles. Calligraphy software allows online communication to reproduce the effect of brush written personal and formal styles. In the art world calligraphy is a popular area of experimentation and the traditional relationship of brush writing, poetry and landscape has become a frequent site of play for contemporary artists working with image-texts. Both Japanese and western film directors have experimented with calligraphic images allowing brush characters to flow over the surfaces of sets and actor's bodies. Japanese theatre and dance troops, especially Butō, have also drawn calligraphy to the foreground of contemporary performance space.

SANDRA BUCKLEY

cameras

The first recorded photographic image taken in Japan was a daguerreotype which belonged to Eliphalet Brown Jnr, a daguerreotypist who accompanied Commodore Matthew Perry's expedition to Japan in 1853–4. By the turn of the century, Western box cameras were introduced into Japanese society and, in 1903, the first commercially produced camera was made available by Konishi Honten (later know as Konica Corporation). Initially, most expensive camera parts such as the lens and shutter, as well as photographic techniques, were imported from the West. By the 1920s, Japanese companies began manufacturing the parts domestically and the price of cameras dropped drastically, making them available for non-professional usage. The real boom in Japan's camera industry, however, did not occur until the end of the Second World War, at which time optical manufacturers of military products began to concentrate on the development of camera technologies. By the 1950s, cameras were a common household item and camera manufacturers such as Nikon Corporation and Canon Inc. began to diversify and customise product lines. In 1962 alone, Japan produced 2.9 million cameras and replaced West Germany as the world's largest camera manufacturer. New innovations in optics and electronics continued to advance camera technologies throughout the 1970s. In 1977, the first commercial autofocus camera was made available to the mass market, while the 1980s witnessed the introduction and growing popularity of disposable cameras. An estimated 80 million disposable cameras were sold in 1986. In the 1990s, Japan's camera industry continued to grow and the country accounted for the production of 80 per cent of the world's 35-millimeter single-lens cameras.

The Japanese have long been stereotyped as camera-toting tourists. The development of the Japanese camera culture was closely linked to the growth in tourism and other consumer trends, such as the *mai kaa* (my car) and **mai hōmu** (my home) booms from the 1960s to the 1980s. Capturing the moment on camera, whether it was the first spring blossom blooming in the garden, a child's graduation, a scenic landscape on vacation or a family wedding, became an almost obligatory part of a family's or individual's performance of the new everyday life of consumerism. Success was displayed in the family photo albums and countless snapshots sent out to relatives and friends. The camera became the mechanism for recording and evidencing socio-economic mobility. While this dimension of camera culture continues to be an important part of consumer life, new technologies have seen the camera transformed from a tool of cultural archiving to a newly revitalised component of communications.

The emergence and growth of digital technologies in the mid-1990s also had a great impact on the camera industry. Japan was, and continues to be, the world's leader in the production of digital cameras, which record images on a flash-memory card instead of film. Initially made only for professional usage, in the early 1990s digital cameras were priced to be out of the reach of most consumers. However, as early as 1995 new models were developed with a reasonable retail price for the mass market. Today, the technology of digital cameras is advancing at a rapid rate and more and more Japanese are taking part in the new camera revolution. Miniaturised cameras attached to laptops and Internet-ready mobile phones are playing an important role in popularising online image-messaging, as a new feature of mobile communication technology. The capacity of individuals to now store images on disk, manipulate and enhance these images, and print their own high-quality copies is expected to have an impact on the small business owners who run the countless neighbourhood camera stores across Japan. The anticipated loss of income from film processing may result in the survival of only larger camera specialty stores and chain stores. The strong presence of imaging in contemporary Japanese culture seems to guarantee that, while cameras and the technologies of image reproduction and transmission are undergoing dramatic transformation, photography (still or video) will remain a popular element of Japanese culture even if the platform and mode of delivery undergo significant change.

LEILA POURTAVAF AND SANDRA BUCKLEY

Carol

Carol played a powerful, new, rockabilly-based kind of Japanese-language rock. They were perhaps the best Japanese rock 'n' roll band of the 1970s. Formed in June 1972, Carol was a four-person band with Yazawa Eikichi on vocals and bass, Johnny Okura on guitar and vocals, Utsumi Toshinori on guitar and, shortly thereafter, Okazaki Tomo on drums.

Their debut album, *Louisiana*, was released on Phonogram in December 1972. Yazawa's powerful, sexy, nearly rockabilly style drove fans crazy. His particular mix of English and Japanese lyrics became a trademark and effectively ended the Japanese-language rock debate. Carol raised the visibility of rock to a level that had formerly been reserved for teen pop music. Their black clothing and sunglasses made dress formerly associated with hard-case high-school biker gangs fashionable. There was a period, however, when they found it difficult to book halls for concerts due to the tough-guy image of the band and their fans.

Their first album, *Louisiana*, was followed by *Funky Monkey Baby* in August 1973. They released one more studio album and two live albums before the group split up in May 1975. Since that time, Yazawa has had an extremely successful solo career. Okura continues to work as an actor and as a musician.

MARK ANDERSON

castle towns

Castle towns, or *jōka-machi*, played a major role in establishing the pattern of Japanese urbanisation as well as urban lifestyle. Although some were built upon ancient fortifications of the Heian period, most of the castles were built during the Azuchi Momoyama period of the late sixteenth century, and became the basis for the rapid urbanization of the seventeenth and eighteenth centuries. Primarily built in the centre of flat plains, both for fortification and to provide residences for some of the largest feudal lords, or *daimyō*, they soon became centres of trade and commerce, and major transportation nodes. By the Tokugawa Period, the number of castles was limited to one for each domain. Members of the samurai class were required to live in the castle towns, thus ensuring the development of an elite urban culture. Strict rules of urban planning dictated where they could live in relation to the castle, as well as the size of residential lot, determined by rank. The *sankinkōtai* system required that *daimyō* rotate their residences between the castle towns and Edo (**Tokyo**), in order to control their movements as well as those of their families and retainers. The castle complexes attracted other activities and an urban population, housed in series of curved, narrow streets (curved so as to impede the direct flight of attacking arrows) that accommodated the growing commercial districts. More than half of the cities of more than 100,000 population today are former castle towns, Tokyo being pre-eminent.

Most of the castles are made of wood, with stone foundation walls, and rise in five to seven tiers above the surrounding area. They are painted white, with curving tiled roofs, and narrow portals to accommodate the firearms introduced by the Portuguese in 1542. Largely free of Chinese influence on their architectural style, there is perhaps no stronger symbol of the power of the samurai era.

Few of the original castles remain, most having been destroyed during the Second World War, but some of the notable original structures include the castles at Himeji in Hyōgo Prefecture, and Hikone in Shiga Prefecture. Many have been rebuilt since the war and now function as tourist sites for the reinvention of samurai heritage. Especially during the spring period of *hanami*, cherry blossom viewing, the grounds are crowded with families and young couples, strolling or picnicking. More recently, the open grounds around the famous Ōsaka Castle have become home to a significant population of homeless.

Castles have also played a major role in keeping alive the contemporary romanticised vision of the samurai in Japanese popular culture, by providing the settings for a host of samurai movies. There is perhaps no more enduring scene in the Western imagination of Japan than that of Mifuni Toshio holding court in *Shōgun*, a film set in the sixteenth century.

Further reading

Hall, John W. (1968) 'The castle town and Japan's modern urbanization', in John W. Hall and Marius B. Jansen (eds) *Studies in the Institutional History of Early Modern Japan*, Princeton, NJ: Princeton University Press, pp. 169–88.

AUDREY KOBAYASHI

censorship and film

Post-war film censorship has largely been shaped by practices developed in the pre-war and Occupation periods. Occupation authorities, while repealing the 1939 Film Law, essentially carried on that law's two-pronged approach of suppressing harmful ideas (now defined as militarism) and using cinema to shape society (now in the name of democracy). **Supreme Commander for Allied Powers** (SCAP) censors even maintained the wartime censorship procedures with both pre-production script review and inspection of the final film.

Occupation officials, hoping to leave behind a form of regulation that would inherit their aims without violating the new Constitution, which prohibits censorship, pressed the industry to found the Film Ethics Regulation Control Committee (Eirin) in 1949 as a self-regulatory organ modelled on Hollywood's Production Code. Eirin's stated goal has been to improve the status of cinema, but in reality it has mostly functioned as a means of fending off government regulation. Its main enemy has been the persistent opinion of social leaders that cinema is a pernicious medium deserving of strict censorship. Thus with the 1956 calls for government censorship to stop the *taiyōzoku* (sun tribe) films, the 1965 prosecution of Takechi Tetsuji's *Kuroi yuki* (Black Snow), and the 1972 indictments against not only Nikkatsu for the release of four 'roman poruno' films but also the Eirin inspectors who approved them, Eirin has found itself under attack from various fronts. In Japan the press has also historically been a supporter of film censorship. Faced with ongoing pressure, Eirin has been forced to revise its regulations and structure, creating, for instance, a 'for adults' classification in 1955 and an 'R' rating (under-fifteen prohibited) in 1976.

Courts have been lenient on film, acquitting the defendants in both the *Kuroi yuki* and Nikkatsu cases. However, while effectively giving official approval to Eirin's activities, they have refused to offer a clearer definition of Article 175 of the Criminal Code (covering obscenity) than the one given in a 1957 decision. This means that post-war censorship has been plagued by competing definitions of obscenity between the three sectors that regulate cinema: Eirin, the police and local authorities, and Tokyo Customs (which can confiscate films it deems 'obscene'). First the dominance of adult films in the 1970s and then the increase in international film festivals since the late 1980s (which try to show uncensored prints) have, among other factors, led to relaxation of these definitions. Customs allowed film images of pubic hair as early as 1980 and Eirin revised its code stating that 'genitals and pubic hair should not be depicted' in 1991 by adding the words 'in principal'. However, occasional citations still give foreign directors the impression that Japanese film censorship is arbitrary and bureaucratic.

Violence did not become a matter of concern until the 1990s, when the media raised worries about the link between violent images and sensational youth crimes. In reaction, Eirin revised its ratings system in 1998 to address levels of violence. Four classifications were created for greater control of movie viewing by adolescents: R-18 (adults only), R-15 (under-fifteen prohibited), PG-12 (parental guidance for under-twelve) and general audience.

See also: pink films

AARON GEROW

Char

b. 1955, Tokyo

Musician

Born Takenaka Hisato, Char (pronounced 'cha') began his recording career with the 1976 release of his self-titled debut album. His work in this period shows an affinity for the mellow R 'n' B groove of such artists as Boz Scaggs, but he also quickly established himself as a Japanese guitarist who could be seriously compared with guitar heroes from abroad.

Many continue to consider Char the finest Japanese rock guitarist to date. In short order, he was making regular appearances on television and rapidly gained a reputation for a rare combination of skill, looks and popularity. Determined to further develop his technique as a guitarist, in 1979 he went on to form a blues–rock-fusion power trio with the older rock veterans, Johnny Yoshinaga (drums) and former Golden Cups' bassist, Kabe Shogi (Johnny, Luis and Char). Their sound was somewhat suggestive of solo-period Tommy Bolin. They later changed their name to Pink Cloud (disbanded 1994). From the early 1990s Char continued to undertake new projects, including a new, Hendrix-inspired band called Psychedelix and an acoustic guitar duo known as Baho, which explored more private and personal territory. Since 1998, Char has begun performing with his bilingual son who raps in English.

MARK ANDERSON

Chara

b. 1968, Saitama

Musician

Chara is best known for her unique blend of a career as a stubbornly independent and imaginative artist with her enthusiastic embrace of feminine domesticity. Her voice has an immediately identifiable, girlish quality, which she brings to a broad range of material.

She writes all her lyrics and writes or co-writes the music for most of her songs. She signed with

Epic/Sony Records in 1990 and her earlier albums were squarely in the pop category. She released her debut album in November 1991 and continued to release an album a year until 1994. She received the Best Actress Award for her 1996 role in Iwai Shinji's *Swallowtail* and released a tie-in album, *Yen Town Band* – a work with a punkier, harder rock edge. Her fifth solo album, *Junior Sweet* (1997), saw her continue to take increasing artistic risks and her sixth solo album, the self-produced *Strange Fruits* (1999), incorporated hip-hop elements. A double live album also came out in 1999. Chara married the actor Asano Tadanobu, and they have two children. Her embrace of marriage and motherhood appears to have endeared her to younger female fans. Chara remains one of the most talented and inimitable characters on the contemporary Japanese music scene.

MARK ANDERSON

CHANOYU *see* tea ceremony

cherry blossoms

Cherry blossoms represent one of the most significant of Japanese aesthetic and popular-culture symbols. Many varieties of ornamental *sakura*, of the Rosaceae family, are cultivated in Japan, and grow wild in mountainous regions. They are a ubiquitous symbol of spring, when they cover the country in froths of many shades of pink. The wood and bark make high-quality furniture and ornamental products.

During the classical period, the practice of *hanami*, cherry blossom viewing, became popular, celebrated by picnics, dancing and poetry competitions beneath the cherry trees at approximately the time of the spring planting. *Hanami* eventually became regulated according to strict dates of the lunar calendar. The ancient capitals of Yoshino and **Kyōto** (Arashiyama) and **Tokyo** (Ueno Park) are strongly associated with cherry blossom viewing. In literature, cherry blossoms provide a dominant poetic theme, as a symbol of the spring season (see **seasons**) and a metaphor for the transitory nature of human life. The falling cherry blossom is said to depict both fleeting beauty, and the drops of blood of the samurai, whose life, like beauty, blooms ephemerally.

Today, *hanami* remains a quintessential pastime, aided by regular radio reports on the state of the blossoms. Families gather for picnics, often in large organised groups of company employees, with sumptuous picnic baskets. The sense of awe and wonder is increased whenever a slight breeze sends thousands of petals showering down upon entranced viewers. The festive atmosphere is enlivened by sake consumption, enough of which may still provide an inspiration for the composition of haiku poetry. More commonly, however, today's poetic tributes are expressed by **karaoke**, sung under the stars using portable tape machines, and lights to enhance night viewing.

Japanese cultural products abound with the image of the cherry blossom as an aesthetic trope traditionally depicted on expensive products such as kimono or lacquer boxes. It epitomises the visual arts, and is associated with purity and simplicity. The strength of this traditional imagery gives the cherry blossom tremendous power to influence the cycle of consumption. It is ubiquitous in spring, whether advertising for cars, feminine clothing or specials at the local super market. The designation *sakura* has been used for an express train, a type of 33 mm film, many bars and restaurants, and a major national bank. The image is also used to sell products and services associated with a range of liminal activities such as the beginning of the school year for children, or wedding services.

The cherry blossom has also become a symbol of international goodwill. In 1909, the City of Tokyo presented Washington, DC with more than 2,000 trees representing eleven different species of *sakura*.

Further reading

Moeran, Brian and Skov, Lise (1997) 'Mount Fuji and the cherry blossoms: A view from afar', in Pamela J. Asquith and Arne Kalland (eds) *Japanese Images of Nature: Cultural Perspectives*, Richmond, Surrey: Curzon, pp. 181–205.

AUDREY KOBAYASHI

chika

The underground (*chika*) in Japan refers not only to the extensive subway networks underlying Japan's major cities but also the linked multilevel subterranean developments that incorporate shopping malls, restaurant districts and specialised service industries. *Chika* developments depend on the density of the daytime population of the high-rise office buildings above for their business.

The first Tokyo underground track was laid as early as 1927 and is still part of the Ginza line. However, close to 95 per cent of today's subway tracks were dug since the 1950s. The railway and real-estate developers who have driven the rapid expansion of the *chika* have also promoted this underground space as a core site of consumer culture. Subways link to suburban train and bus hubs that transport downtown workers to real-estate developments, ranging from high-density apartments to free-standing family homes spread out along the commuter lines. *Chika* shopping complexes are primarily aimed at the market for daily consumables. Major downtown department stores are built down into the *chika* hubs with multiple floors of speciality foods, pre-packaged meals, fast foods and housewares, all in easy access to commuters as they move from office to subway and home. Restaurants and service industries (printers, photocopy services, dry cleaners, photo developers, travel agents, courier and parcel delivery, etc.) have also embedded themselves into the web of the *chika*, where they provide for both commuter clients and phone order delivery to the office blocks above.

Movement across downtown Tokyo is often described in terms of the most direct subway route, transfers and subway exits. Few prefer the above-ground traffic to the *chika* despite extraordinary levels of crowding at peak commuter hours. The scene of professional 'pushers' jamming people into trains in the 1980s and early 1990s was a popular image in Western media coverage of Japan, but risks of overcrowding have seen a gradual decline in the practice. Automated ticket sales and gates maintain a reasonable flow of commuter traffic despite massive peak-hour crowding. Unlike inner urban subway systems in many other countries, the *chika* are remarkably crime-free. Extensive surveil-lance networks are monitored twenty-four hours a day, but the primary concern is fire and accidents rather than crime. The **Aum/sarin attack** drew attention to the risk of terrorist activity in the *chika*. Earthquakes are another concern as urban development extends to new depths below the city. Extensive earthquake precautions are now required, but whether or not Japan's *chika* can claim to be earthquake proof has yet to be put seriously to the test. Escape strategies in the more likely case of fire remain the object of much criticism, and the sarin gas attack proved evacuation and emergency service access seriously inadequate.

As long as land prices in inner-city areas remain high, and available land scarce, the future of new downtown development looks likely to remain largely underground. There has been little innovation in *chika* architecture, which has remained functional in design. The lack of structural visibility appears to have deterred the more renowned architects, but, as *chika* expansion continues to offer substantial new projects incorporating cultural and entertainment spaces in addition to shopping and service centres, perhaps more architects will bring their design expertise underground.

SANDRA BUCKLEY

childcare

The vast majority of Japanese infants and school-age children are cared for in the home full-time by their mother. Although over 51 per cent of women of working age are actively employed, women's employment is structured to facilitate and promote the priority of child and elderly care over full-time paid labour in the workforce. Surveys consistently indicate that over 80 per cent of Japanese women believe that women should be at home caring for children and that men should work.

Childcare and the status and role of motherhood (*bosei*) are hotly debated issues within Japanese **feminism**. Some feminists embrace the notion that the Japanese attach a unique value to motherhood, and that this requires strategies for the recognition of the rights of mothers as equally important to struggles for women's employment rights. From this position Western feminists are often criticised as undervaluing the choice of full-time childcare over paid work or career. Other feminists caution against essentialism and the risks of playing into a conservative, nationalist rhetoric of uniqueness and traditional gender differentiation. Feminist historians have evidenced that the professionalisation of motherhood to the exclusion of other work is itself a product of Japan's modernisation. Women traditionally combined work in family enterprise or farm production with childcare, and wet nursing was common in aristocratic and samurai households.

Today, over 60 per cent of childcare places are in government facilities and the total number of places in private and public childcare annually exceeds demand. The core issue surrounding childcare in Japan is more complex than availability. An increasing number of Japanese companies are offering on-site childcare for all employees (male and female), supported by work breaks when employees can spend time with their child. Legal reforms to childcare and paternity leave over the 1990s have also opened up the option of men taking extended paternity leave after the birth of a child. However, neither legal nor related workplace reforms have seen a significant shift in patterns of childcare. The social and structural pressures on women to withdraw from employment on childbirth are matched only by the pressures on men to remain in the workplace and marginal to childcare.

A common compromise for women is part-time work, which offers flexibility of hours but comes with significantly lower wages and limited (if any) benefits. The recent trend towards a return to three-generational family housing reflects an attempt to combine a desire to work with the expectation that married women will take responsibility for both child and elderly care. Cohabitation with ageing parents offers home-based childcare while grandparents are still healthy. Although mothers in three-generational homes are less likely to quit the workplace permanently, the trend is still towards non-employment during the first two years of infancy and part-time employment through the school years with support from grandparents. After children leave school the mother continues part-time work as her focus shifts to elderly care. There has been significant criticism of this trend as a transfer of state welfare costs on to the domestic household and women in particular.

See also: family, gender and society; family system; gender and work

Further reading

Hunter, J. (ed) (1993) *Japanese Women Working*, London and New York: Routledge.

SANDRA BUCKLEY

CHILDREN'S DAY *see* Hinamatsuri (Doll Festival) and Girls' Day; kites; Koinobori (carp kites) and Children's Day

Chinese in Japan

Some 50,000 people of Chinese descent live permanently in Japan. About half are the descendants of immigrants from mainland China, many of whom are already fifth or sixth generation. The other half are Taiwanese, or their second or third generation descendants. Most live in several large Japanese cities, particularly Tokyo, Yokohama, Ōsaka and Kobe, and operate small businesses or restaurants. Like Koreans (see **Koreans in Japan**), Chinese born in Japan are considered to be aliens, face social and legal discrimination and are denied equal education, jobs and social welfare benefits. The Chinese are less vocal than other minorities in complaining about discrimination. Instead, they frequently rely on resources from their own community to circumvent the obstacles they face. For example, when Japanese banks refused to loan money to Chinese in the 1950s, the Chinese community established its own bank. These strategies have been highly successful, but their very success means that discrimination against Chinese is generally unrecognised.

A considerable number of Chinese traders lived in Japan as early as the 1500s. Chinese traders were also present in Nagasaki throughout Japan's 'closed period' (1639–1853), although their numbers and place of residence were strictly regulated. The number of Chinese grew rapidly after Japan was opened to Western trade in 1853. Early

Western traders living in Japan's foreign concessions brought many Chinese employees to Japan. Their numbers were soon augmented by merchants and labourers who arrived independently. By 1875, the Chinese population had reached approximately 2,500 out of a total 5,000 foreign residents. Western residents, accepting the racial characterisations of that era, believed that Chinese were unhygienic, and prone to vice and crime. Japanese officials also adopted these beliefs and introduced policies such as compulsory registration of Chinese residents. In 1899, the foreign concession system was abolished and foreigners were allowed to live anywhere in Japan. Then, laws were passed prohibiting unskilled Chinese labourers from working outside the former foreign concession areas. No other foreign nationals faced such restrictions. These laws were influenced by similar Chinese exclusion laws enacted approximately a decade earlier in the USA, Australia and Canada. This resulted in a Chinese community composed primarily of merchants and professionals living chiefly in Yokohama and Kobe. The legacy of these laws remains today in the continuing presence of Chinatowns in those two cities, and in the professional and business orientation of Japan's Chinese residents.

By 1930, approximately 31,000 mainland Chinese lived in Japan, although their numbers dropped steadily throughout the Second World War. By contrast, the number of Taiwanese increased. A few Taiwanese were engaged in business, and several thousand were students, but by far the greatest number were conscripted by the Japanese military. By 1943, this last group had reached 150,000. Many remained in Japan immediately after the end of the war, when Taiwanese briefly became notorious for their involvement in black-market activities. Other Taiwanese founded enterprises catering to the Allied military presence in Japan, such as night-clubs and cabarets. Many returned to Taiwan, so that, by 1948, the number of Taiwanese had fallen to 14,000. In 1947, Japan enacted the Alien Registration Law that classified Taiwanese, hitherto Japanese colonial subjects, as aliens. Like the 20,000 descendants of mainland Chinese, Taiwanese were now disenfranchised, obliged to register as aliens and were excluded

from employment in the public sector and from many social benefits.

Taiwanese and mainland Chinese are now treated in the same manner under Japanese law, but the two groups still comprise separate communities. This state of affairs reflects, to some extent, earlier differences in the status of the two groups. In the past, for example, mainland Chinese were only allowed to live in selected areas whereas Taiwanese could reside wherever they chose. As a result, the traditional Chinese sections of Yokohama and Kobe are still predominantly inhabited by mainland Chinese. Many Taiwanese are educated professionals such as dentists, doctors and teachers. Some operate night-clubs, coffee shops and cinemas, and some are involved in real estate and the large-scale manufacture of foods and beverages. By contrast, mainland Chinese own smaller enterprises such as shops selling foodstuffs and ethnic handicrafts in the Chinatowns of Yokohama and Kobe, or own import–export companies or Chinese restaurants. The two groups also remain separate because they have differing cultural norms, speak mutually unintelligible languages and often hold opposing political views. Political differences were accentuated after the founding in 1949 of the People's Republic of China (PRC) and the Taiwanese Republic of China (ROC), when both governments vied for the loyalties of Chinese living abroad. Today, Taiwanese and mainland Chinese maintain separate ethnic associations and run separate Chinese language schools.

Japan, which had earlier recognised the ROC as the legitimate government of China, normalised relations with the PRC in 1972. This was accompanied by a flurry of publicity concerning China. Cultural exchanges sponsored by the PRC and television series featuring China further bolstered public interest. This growth of interest prompted many Chinese entrepreneurs, who had earlier managed night-clubs or small Japanese restaurants, to begin serving Chinese food. In the 1970s, the Chinatowns of Yokohama and Kobe, which Japanese had hitherto avoided, were recreated as tourist destinations. Local residents built ceremonial archways at the entrances to Chinatown, and gave displays of lion dancing. This new version of Chinatown actually owes more to popular images of China than to the cultural heritage of local Chinese, most of whom were born in Japan. This reinvention of Chinatown is on-going. Some shops, such as grocery stores, still cater to a Chinese clientele, but an expanding number, such as restaurants and ethnic handicraft shops, are aimed at a Japanese market. Although only a tiny minority of Japan's Chinese residents actually live or work there, the average Japanese now thinks of Chinatown as typifying the lifestyle of Chinese residents in Japan.

See also: alien registration; national identity and minorities

Further reading

Vasishth, A. (1997) 'A model minority: The Chinese community in Japan', in M. Weiner (ed.) *Japan's Minorities: The Illusion of Homogeneity*, London: Routledge, pp. 108–39.

ANDREA VASISHTH

chopsticks

Used both for cooking and for eating, chopsticks are the central utensil of Japanese cuisine. They range from utilitarian wood and metal for cooking, to plastics, **bamboo** and other woods and lacquer for table use. Restaurant and take-out food is accompanied by disposable wood chopsticks and the cover wrapping offers a cheap form of advertising for the restaurant. Environmentalists continue to campaign with little success for a reduction in the use of disposable chopsticks, which are mass produced from timber harvested mainly from the rapidly diminishing forests of South-East Asia.

Cooking chopsticks are either wood or metal and can be used to carry, flip or beat foods. Their length (usually between one and two feet) allows for dexterous and safe handling of food cooking in hot broths or oil. Family members will have personal chopsticks ranging from plastic, cartoon-decorated designs for children, to elegant carved bamboo and rare woods. More expensive designs extend to hand-crafted lacquer, mother of pearl and precious metal and stone inlays. Personal chopsticks often

come in a matching carry box. It is also common to carry chopsticks to work daily together with the familiar lunchbox (see **obent**).

SANDRA BUCKLEY

Christianity in Japan

Christianity has endured a chequered history in Japan, experiencing periods of moderate success, especially during times of large-scale social change, but often encountering difficulties in acceptance due to its perceived foreign nature. Christianity was first introduced to Japan in 1549 with the arrival of Jesuit missionaries and today a variety of forms of Christianity are present in Japan, including an assortment of Roman Catholic, Orthodox, Protestant and indigenous groups and denominations. In contemporary Japan, Christianity claims approximately 1 per cent of the population.

Christianity has contributed to the development of modern Japan through its efforts in the fields of education, especially with regard to women's education, and social welfare, especially in establishing organisations designed to help those on the margins of society. The socialist movement in Japan also owes its beginnings to Christianity, as Christians were leaders of the first labour movements in Japan. The impact of Christian thought and influence has extended to other Japanese religions, including **Buddhism**, **State Shintō** and the new religions (see **new religions, Japanese**), which have incorporated Christian elements into doctrinal formulations, organisational structures and methods of propagation.

One of the more interesting areas of Christianity's development in Japan is in its attempt to produce an indigenous Japanese Christian church. The call to develop an indigenous Christian church that is self-governing, self-supporting and self-propagating stems from the fact that Japan has been the focus of concentrated missionary efforts by foreign churches. Towards this end, certain forms of Christianity have made a number of concessions to Japanese religious traditions, blending Confucian (see **Confucianism**), Shintō, Buddhist and folk elements into the religion and forming an indigenous brand of Christianity in an effort to appeal to a larger audience. For example, many Christian churches have instituted a wide range of post-funerary rites to accommodate themselves to Japanese folk religious customs, and founders of Japanese Christian groups are often accorded the type of veneration reserved for founders of other forms of Japanese religions. Moreover, some Christian groups have adopted the practice of calling on the name of God (*Nembutsu kirisutokyō*), which closely resembles the sound and rhythm of the Buddhist practice of reciting the *nembutsu*. Other attempts to indigenise Christianity include the incorporation into the practice of certain Japanese Christian churches of ascetic disciplines for spiritual training, such as water purification rituals (*misogi*) and walking across beds of hot coals.

While the struggle Christianity faces in contemporary Japan stems in part from the perceived notion that the Japanese sense of cultural identity is threatened by membership in the Christian church, there are indications that suggest Christianity is making inroads with Japanese popular culture and its youth. **Christmas**, for example, is a successful commercial festival with the young and Christian-styled weddings are becoming increasingly popular in modern Japan among Japanese couples. Whether the popularity of Christmas and Christian-styled **weddings** signifies genuine incorporation of the religion into Japanese culture or simply underscores Christianity's perceived glamorous but foreign image, however, is yet uncertain. The future of Christianity in Japan may depend instead on the development of the small but growing indigenous Japanese Christian churches.

See also: Christmas; weddings

Further reading

Mullins, Mark (1998) *Christianity Made in Japan*, Honolulu: University of Hawaii Press.

Reid, David (1991) *New Wine: The Cultural Shaping of Japanese Christianity*, Berkeley: Asin Humanities Press.

JAY SAKASHITA

Christmas

Christianity played a significant role in the processes of modernisation in Japan, with many of the new generation of intellectuals and politicians drawn to experiment with the religious beliefs they associated with the principles of democracy. However, the religious celebrations of Easter and Christmas gained little popular interest during these years beyond the most faithful followers of the new churches. It was not until the 1980s that Christmas gained popularity in Japan and this phenomenon was largely the result of a concerted marketing campaign by major department stores, keen to gain an additional gift-giving season in the Japanese consumer market. Consumer data shows that women give and receive more Christmas gifts than men. In tight consumer markets, when disposable income falls, Christmas gift-giving levels fall, suggesting that this is still seen as an optional gift season. Although Christmas falls close to one of the two annual obligatory gift seasons (*oseibo*), a Christmas gift does not replace an *oseibo* gift.

While many families decorate their homes with a Christmas tree or other ornaments, most do not produce a special seasonal meal or attend church services. The main observation of this holiday is the exchange of gifts. Christmas cards have only gained a small share of the speciality card market, partly due to the proximity to the end-of-year obligatory mailing of New Year postcards.

SANDRA BUCKLEY

chrysanthemum

The chrysanthemum (*kiku*) is widely cultivated in Japan, in a huge variety of sizes, shapes and colours. The chrysanthemum was introduced from China during the fifth century and soon thereafter widely cultivated by the nobility, who practised a chrysanthemum festival dating from the Heian period. It has two major symbolic representations, of autumn and nobility. A stylised chrysanthemum is used for the crest of the imperial household and some Japanese cultivate this flower as an expression of their admiration for the imperial family. When the chrysanthemum appears in painting it is usually highly stylised. Edible chrysanthemums are used to decorate foods, and they are a popular motif on porcelain, lacquerware and **kimono**.

Many people belong to chrysanthemum-growing clubs, and enter their plants in contests featuring spectacular blooms that have been painstakingly fertilised, trimmed and coaxed to perfection. Displays are mounted each autumn at **Tokyo**'s Meiji and Yasukuni Shrines. Also in the autumn, spectacular chrysanthemum 'dolls' are displayed in public areas. These are often life-size figures that depict storybook characters, found in a diverse range of cultural sources from *kabuki* to Disney.

AUDREY KOBAYASHI

Chūpiren

The sensational women's group Chūpiren (Alliance for Abortion and the Pill) was briefly catapulted into the international media in the 1970s through the practice of public embarrassment of men who had been guilty of infidelity. Their guerrilla tactics were enacted in a costume that included pink crash helmets, a parody of the crash helmets worn by the student left in demonstrations. Their demands for safe access to abortion and the contraceptive pill reflected their desire to see women have autonomous control over their own bodies, sexuality and reproductive capacity, demands that have been echoed by women's groups in subsequent decades.

See also: feminism; reproductive control; Women's Liberation

VERA MACKIE

cinema industry

The fact that the film industry is an oligopoly with several major companies controlling the market through a system of vertical integration (where each company has production, distribution and exhibition arms) and block booking (where theatre owners obtain a supply of films in exchange for not showing the product of any other studio) has, while helping ensure profits in a capricious business, regulated what films are made and seen. The concentration of capital existed from before the war, but the wartime government's efforts to rationalise the industry through consolidation, coupled with the post-war boom in investment in studios and theatres, finally shifted the power centre within the industry from exhibitors to producers. Film studios became modern culture factories that produced regulated commodities in large quantities, distributed to a mass audience via exhibition outlets. The position of the majors was further ensured by secret pacts in the 1950s, which eased competition, and by government restrictions on film imports.

Efforts to counter this power structure began early in the 1950s by left-wing film-makers purged from the industry, but their independent productions rarely found exhibition opportunities. The structure only began to weaken in the mid-1950s when an excess of theatres prompted fierce competition on the exhibition level and the introduction of double features. Production increased, but, with attendance declining after 1958 due to television's popularity, profits declined. The strength of the majors ebbed until several like Shin Tōhō and Daiei went bankrupt. Into this void stepped **pink films** producers, who paved the way for independent production companies formed by directors and stars. By the 1970s, the majority of movies produced were independent.

As cinema declined in popularity, the majors cut production, began expanding into other businesses like real estate and entrenched themselves around their dominant theatre networks, supported by high ticket prices. Their interest was now in showing, not producing, films, so there was little incentive to invest in new facilities and talent. The movies they showed were mostly foreign product (with Japan becoming Hollywood's major foreign market) or single, 'blockbuster' works produced with television networks and publishing houses interested in movie tie-ins. The fact that, through the *maeuri* (advanced ticket) system, these partners would buy all the tickets in advance, and in effect ensure profits, only reinforced the complacency among the majors.

The control of the majors (Tōhō, Tōei and Shōchiku) over most of the nation's theatres still enables them to prevent most independents from exhibiting at any more than a handful of locations. Their monopoly was only challenged in the 1990s by the collapse of the **bubble economy** (harming Nikkatsu and Shōchiku) and the influx of foreign theatre chains building multiplexes in the Japanese market. The appearance of the latter, however, promises little for independent producers, who still continue to target the independent film and video market with small-budget productions.

While the government has warned the industry about its monopolistic practices, its stance has basically been *laissez-faire*, doing little to direct the industry or provide aid for less commercial productions.

AARON GEROW

cinema, Japanese

The cinema is arguably the most influential form of popular culture in Japan in the twentieth century, with its visuality and new narrative forms affecting other media from literature to *manga*, and its articulations of identity and Japanese nationality impacting viewers both at home and abroad.

In spite of some Western critics' claims about the alterity of Japanese film, the majority of movies made in Japan conform to the codes of classic Hollywood cinema, subsuming filmic technique to the narrative, establishing a realistic and readable space, and presenting stories with closure and centred on identifiable characters. This style speaks of the power the US film industry culture has had over Japanese film culture, but such influences have undergone complex processes of adaptation and domestication in conjunction with Japanese culture's larger articulations of modernity, Westernisation, the nation and mass culture.

Japan's director-centred industry, for instance, has in some cases allowed far more room for filmmakers like Ōzu Yasujiro to develop alternative constructions of space and narrative. Traditional artistic and narrative forms, plus particular social and historical structures, have also shaped how films have been made and seen. Mizoguchi Kenji's *Ugetsu monogatari*, for instance, consciously cites the painted scroll in its visual style, while the *jidaigeki*

(period) film genre borrows some of its stories (e.g. *Chūshingura*), acting styles and even actors from the *kabuki* world. The basic division of Japanese film into *jidaigeki* (period films) and *gendaigeki* (modern stories set after 1868), plus other genres like *ninkyo mono* (*yakuza* film) as well as studio styles (e.g. Shochiku Ofuna style), are all specificities that must be considered in appreciating Japanese cinema, yet without essentialising their cultural foundation.

The history of post-war Japanese cinema can be narrated in the parallel developments and occasional conflicts between major studio and independent modes of production, exhibition and spectatorship. Japanese post-war cinema was largely founded on the Hollywood-based styles and the industrial reconstruction that existed from before the end of the war, but new cinematic explorations in democratising society were undertaken under the ideological imperatives of Occupation film reforms. Some of these efforts were reflected in labour movements at the studios themselves, but the breaking of the Tōhō strike in 1948 led to a purge of leftists, on the one hand, who like Yamamoto Satsuo and Imai Tadashi went on to create independent political films in the 1950s, and, on the other, the consolidation within studio cinema of a 'democratic humanistic' style with its roots in pre-war film.

The film industry was bolstered by both a late-1940s boom in theatre construction and attendance and by the win of Kurosawa Akira's *Rashōmon* at the 1951 Venice Film Festival. Japanese cinema was finally national both at home, with films now showing across the country instead of just at urban theatres, and abroad, where Japanese motion pictures gained critical acclaim and some market success. The 1950s was the golden age of Japanese film, both in terms of its cultural influence and its ability to represent the nation.

The largely all-mighty studios consolidated their markets by specialising in genre cinema and developing studio styles. Shōchiku, with Ozu and Kinoshita Keisuke, focused on lower-middle-class family dramas that often nurtured the vision of Japanese as the victims of war and history. Tōhō, with a more urban, middle-class image, promoted the humanistic cinema of Kurosawa, while also developing the monster (*kaijū*) genre and the businessman comedy. Daiei, with Mizoguchi Kenji and Kinugasa Teinosuke, focused especially on producing artistic *jidaigeki* with the foreign market in mind. It was Tōei, however, that dominated the late 1950s with a programme picture policy of star-cantered *jidaigeki* double-features offering *jidaigeki* action, spectacle and musical entertainment.

Japan was producing the most films in the world, but there were cracks in the system. Overproduction put strains on the industry as television and demographic shifts in the late 1950s began to take away cinema's audience, which hit its height in 1958. However, there were also rumblings of change among film-makers. Nikkatsu began to take advantage of an emerging youth culture with movies starring Ishihara Yujirō that, with other *taiyōzoku* films, portrayed a new lifestyle questioning post-war affluence and its humanistic culture. Masumura Yasuzō, at Daiei, specifically aimed to create a new, modern subject, free of the chains of traditional Japanese society. This fed debates among young film-makers and critics that, against the background of demonstrations against the US–Japan Security Treaty, eventually led to a series of films in 1959 and 1960 termed the 'New Wave'. Ōshima Nagisa sided with Masumura's critiques of 1950s humanism, but nevertheless faulted him for not situating his new subjects in a historical–social context. The documentarist Matsumoto Toshio placed an emphasis on the need for an alternative, avant-garde film style. These theoretical stances included a criticism of leftist independent cinema that, while political in content, had largely shared the style of major studio films.

Ōshima, Shinodai Masashiro and Yoshida Yoshishige at Shōchiku, and Imamura Shōhei at Nikkatsu, spearheaded a stylistically new form of cinema that saw in youthful alienation, sex, violence, criminality and rural life a potential critique of modern urban society in capitalist Japan. Their vision, however, was difficult to realise in the rigidly structured studios, and most, at one time or another, left their studios to form independent production companies in the 1960s. They, with figures entering fiction film from the documentary world like Hani Susumu, Teshigahara Hiroshi and Kuroki Kazuo, formed the leadership in Japanese independent art cinema in the 1960s.

This shift to independent productions, however, was partially made possible by the gradual decline of the studio system after 1960. Facing losses in profits, studios adopted sex and violence, along with widescreen and colour and to compete with television, but the inability to keep up with their own release schedule led companies to rely on independent subcontractors, especially those founded by stars like Ishihara Yūjirō, Mifune Toshirō and Katsu Shintarō. Theatres, less bound to the studios and without an adequate supply of films, turned to soft-porn pink films after 1963, which became so popular that, for periods in the 1960s and 1970s, the majority of films produced in Japan were adult movies, a situation marked by several censorship controversies.

While many film-makers went independent for political and artistic reasons, establishing forms of exhibition and distribution alternative to the dominant industry, some forms of spectatorship during the 1960s embraced a wide variety of genres both major and minor. College students, for instance, may have gone to a Tōei Katō Tai *yakuza* film one day, cheering Takakura Ken as the lone hero fighting modern authority; seen a Nikkatsu Suzuki Seijun action film the next, revelling in its exuberant style; then checked out Wakamatsu Kōji's use of the pink film to explore revolutionary politics another day; and finally paid a donation to see the documentaries of protest of Ogawa Shinsuke or Tsuchimoto Noriaki. The overall film audience after the late 1960s, however, was increasingly male, largely ending cinema's status as family entertainment, with the exception of successful series like Shōchiku's *Tora-san* comedies, whose predictable and standardised entertainment became one of the few pillars supporting major studios that were increasingly abandoning production and investing in other businesses. The Art Theatre Guild, which began sponsoring independent productions in 1967, became a crucial institution filling in this void, providing support for art-oriented independents like Terayama Shūji, Jissoji Akio, Ōshima and Shinoda.

The 1970s began with a series of shocking events: on the national level, the Asama Sanso incident and the decline of left-wing radicalism; in film, the bankruptcy of Daiei in 1971 and Nikkatsu's shift to soft porn. Nikkatsu *roman poruno* became the last vestige of the programme picture studio system, serving as the training ground for many of the great directors of the 1970s and 1980s like Kumashirō Tatsumi, Negishi Kichitarō and Nakahara Shun. Its vision of frustrated, often doomed, lovers reflected the mood of failure and pessimism. The box office for Japanese film was finally topped by that for foreign film in 1975, epitomising the decline of the once powerful domestic industry. The introduction in the late 1970s of star-studded, big-budget entertainment by producer Kadokawa Haruki, films tied in with his publishing business, helped maintain audience levels for a time. The spectacle entertainment of Kadokawa movies in the 1980s created new stars like Yakushimaru Hiroko and gave opportunities to such young film-makers as Somai Shinji and Sai Yōichi. Unfortunately, the blockbusters, becoming the trend in the industry, were often supported by corporate deals with little regard for cinematic or box office potential, and helped foster artistic lethargy and audience dissatisfaction. From the late 1970s on, animation, especially the work of Miyazaki Hayao, led the Japanese box office and became a major export product in the 1990s.

Even live-action film, once the main influence on *manga*, was now increasingly relying on *manga* adaptations to secure audiences. With the decline of the major studios, opportunities did open up for people and companies previously barred from cinema. One no longer needed long years of training as a studio assistant director in order to direct one's own film. Actors like Itami Jūzō and even some rock stars could now be found behind the megaphone. Production in 8 and 16 mm had been prominent in the experimental film world since the late 1950s, but, in the 1970s and 1980s, film-makers who had started out in 8 mm like Obayashi Nobuhiko, Ishii Sogo, Omori Kazuki and Morita Yoshimitsu were now getting the chance to direct 35 mm films. Post-1970s cinema would be marked by such waves of 8 mm film-makers entering the feature film industry. These new film-makers, spurred by a film criticism that focused on viewing cinema as cinema, often concentrated on exploring motion picture form over content, citing and referring more to past cinema than contemporary political concerns. This inward-looking cinema suffered a series of shocks from the late 1980s on: the end of Shōwa, the conclusion of the cold war, the bursting of the economic bubble; and the Aum incident. These, and the débuts in 1989 of Kitano Takeshi, Zeze Takahisa, Sakamoto Junji and others, led many critics to declare the 1990s a renaissance of Japanese film, a sense supported by revived success at foreign film festivals.

Cinema in the 1990s either tackled the emptiness and disintegration of contemporary society, as in the films of Kitano or Kurosawa Kiyoshi, or in the work of Aoyama Shinji, which tried to found micro-relations on which to rebuild a connection between self and other. This cinema, however, was rarely a unified movement, even though many films came to share a 'detached' film style favouring ambiguous long shots, long takes and over-explanatory editing. Takamine Go, Sai Yōichi and Miike Takashi challenged the myth of a homogeneous Japan through depictions of Japan's ethnic minorities; Hashiguchi Ryōsuke and Oki Hiroyuki openly explored gay sexualities; while young women like Kawase Naomi became major figures in an industry that had long shunned women directors. Such new talent gave promise to Japanese cinema entering the new century, but a restrictive industry made it difficult for any of their independent films to reach a mass audience. The work of television-related directors like Iwai Shunji and movies produced and promoted by television networks were the main films to garner such an audience. The dominance of television, the influx of new technologies like digital video and the foreign-led cineplex boom have left the state of Japanese cinema very much in flux: far from dead, but with little of the influence it once had.

Further reading

Anderson, Joseph and Richie, Donald (1982) *The Japanese Film: Art and Industry* (Expanded Edition), Princeton: Princeton University Press.

Bock, Audie (1985) *Japanese Film Directors*, Tokyo: Kōdansha.

Desser, David (1988) *Eros plus Massacre: An Introduction to the Japanese New Wave Cinema*, Bloomington: Indiana University Press.

Noletti, Arthur, Jnr and Desser, David (eds) (1992) *Reframing Japanese Cinema*, Bloomington: Indiana University Press.

Schilling, Mark (1999) *Contemporary Japanese Film*,
New York: Weatherhill.
Tadao Sato (1982) *Currents in Japanese Cinema*,
Tokyo: Kōdansha.

AARON GEROW

circles

Circles are voluntary groups that meet periodically
to discuss, write or engage in some cultural or other
activity such as singing, drama productions or
research on topics such as education. They have
emerged spontaneously in post-war Japanese workplaces, neighbourhoods and other contexts. Circle
members typically enjoy interacting informally in a
manner unconstrained by organisational, occupational or other hierarchies, and sometimes communicate regularly with other circles. In the 1950s,
circles of women, workers, high-school students
and others played an important role in formulating
and disseminating post-war values. They have also
often provided a solid foundation for **social and
political movements**, especially since the **Anpo
struggle** of 1960. A significant variant was the
circle village movement that emerged as part of a
radical organising effort among coal miners and
their families in the southern island of Kyūshū.
Circle members also often found their way into
later movements such as **Beheiren** and the
residents' movements of the 1970s. In the late
1980s, a variety of networks emerged to link circles
while attempting to preserve their autonomy.

See also: citizens' movements

Further reading

Kazuko, T. (1970) *Social Change on the Individual:
Japan before and after Defeat in World War II*,
Princeton: Princeton University Press.

J. VICTOR KOSCHMANN

citizens' movements

Citizens' movements are independent, self-gener-
ating social and political movements of citizens

taking public actions to solve problems of daily life.
The term is often used interchangeably with
residence-based environmental movements prominent in the 1970s, and includes new social
movements that developed in the 1980s and 1990s.

Many early citizens' movements grew out of
circles that sprang up in the 1950s as social
manifestations of the freedom of expression
granted politically during the Occupation. Citizens' movements adapted the circles' face-to-face,
egalitarian structures to discuss and work through
social and political problems rather than engage in
cultural activities.

Large-scale citizens' movements also formed
during the same period around the issues of peace
and democracy, such as disarmament and defending the post-war Constitution. Together with circle-
based movements, they played a prominent role in
the massive protests against the US–Japan Security
Treaty (Anpo) in 1960.

While Socialist and Communist Parties cast
Anpo as a proletarian uprising and tried to
organise a united front under their leadership, the
scale of the demonstrations was due to the influx of
ordinary citizens who saw their participation as
individual and non-partisan, serving public rather
than class or party interests.

The citizen ideal forged in the 1960 Anpo
protests carried over to movements against the
Vietnam War and the scheduled 1970 renewal of
Anpo. Several groups such as the Voiceless Voices
went on to join Beheiren (Citizens' Federation for
Peace in Vietnam), a diverse decentralised collection of independent citizen and student groups that
became a major force in the anti-war protests.

However, during the late 1960s and 1970s,
citizen movements increasingly took the form of
local residents' movements. These sprang up in
response to the contradictions of rapid economic
growth in Japan, such as industrial pollution,
environmental destruction and social displacement
due to large-scale state projects. The best-known
residents' movement formed around the victims of
Minamata disease, a medical condition caused by
mercury in the waste effluent that Chisso Corporation dumped into Minamata bay. Local opposition
to the state-sponsored petrochemical complex at
Mishima is another key example.

These movements typically distrusted political

parties and ideological agendas, and insisted on local autonomy in their struggles. They chose consensual, horizontal forms of organisation and decision-making rather than hierarchic structures and executive-style direction, and set specific, limited objectives for their movements. To overcome the problem of isolation, these movements used their newsletters and magazines for outreach to like-minded groups facing similar problems elsewhere.

The focus of citizens' movements in the 1980s and 1990s shifted to consumer issues and the search for alternative lifestyles. Social movements to combat racial and sexual discrimination, movements to promote social welfare for the disabled or the elderly and ecological movements have also become prominent. Many of these now refer to themselves as NGOs (Non-Governmental Organisations) and place increasing emphasis on networking between citizens' movements.

Further reading

Steiner, K., Krauss, E. and Flanagan, S. (eds) (1990) *Political Opposition and Local Politics in Japan*, Princeton: Princeton University Press

WESLEY SASAKI-UEMURA

civic development

Until the 1960s, local residents had little opportunity to participate in urban planning, which had long been the prerogative of administrative bureaucracies and experts. Under their direction, urban reconstruction in the wake of intensive bombing during the Second World War was carried out in a standardised fashion with little regard for local culture. However, in the context of expanding urbanisation and burgeoning **citizens' movements** and **residents' movements** in the 1960s, new civic development (*machizukuri*) coalitions began to be formed between local government agencies and residents' groups in many urban and suburban communities.

In many cases, such coalition movements also brought the new middle class of salary workers and their families, who were relative newcomers to

many suburban areas, into close working relationships with the old middle class of shopkeepers and others who were usually the mainstays of local neighbourhood associations. In addition to attempting to preserve natural surroundings and historic buildings and sites, they focused on enhancing their community's 'individuality' and attractiveness. Civic development movements and projects mushroomed throughout Japan in the 1980s in conjunction with the popular, if paradoxical, notion of 'creating hometowns' – *furusato sosei*.

J. VICTOR KOSCHMANN

Civil Code of 1948, the

The Civil Code of 1948 drastically revised the 1896 and 1898 codifications of Japan's civil law. Numerous drafts were circulated within the Japanese government before the final version was approved by the **Supreme Commander for Allied Powers**.

The Civil Code governs private (i.e. non-government) interactions and defines private rights in Japan. In its five books, it provides a legal framework for many of the issues not treated in the post-war Constitution. For example, Book 4 of the Civil Code defines the family and sets forth the legal relationships among its members, while Book 5 defines property rights and inheritance law.

The Civil Code is most praised for having abolished the pre-war family system, thereby recognising individuals as distinct legal entities, separate from the family. It also declared the property rights of men and women within the family to be equal. Despite these legal changes, however, social attachments to earlier concepts of the family system remain strong.

Further reading

Steiner, Kurt (1987) 'The Occupation and reform of the Japanese Civil Code', in R. Ward and Y. Sakamoto (eds) *Democratising Japan: The Allied Occupation*, Honolulu: University of Hawaii Press.

BETH KATZOFF

classical dance

Japanese classical dance, or *Nihon buyō*, is one of the great traditional performing arts of Japan along with *gagaku*, *nō*, *kabuki* and *bunraku*. Most of its repertory comes from the eighteenth and nineteenth centuries from the *kabuki* theatres and pleasure quarters of the Edo Period (1603–1868). However, both in terms of social structure and way of performing the classical repertory, Japanese classical dance reached its current shape after the Meiji Restoration in 1868. In other words, it became a classical art form at the same time that other forms of dance were entering Japan from the West (for example, ballet and modern dance) and was heavily influenced by these foreign genres. Today, although non-Japanese viewers often sense a deep influence of traditional theatre on such avant-garde genres as *butō*, the performers themselves mostly have very little contact and similarities come from the fact that they are both rooted in Japanese culture and that all performers, whether their genre be traditional or modern, are responding to common influences.

There are two basic forms of dance in Japanese culture, *mai* and *odori*. *Mai* emphasises spare, reserved gestures and often has many circling movements. The body is kept very low to the ground and the energy of the body is very concentrated. The dances of the classical *nō* theatre belong to *mai*. *Odori*, on the other hand, emphasises vigorous stepping movements and tends to be large and energetic. *Bon* folk dances and the dances of the *kabuki* theatre belong to this category. Before the modern period, there was no particular general term for 'dance' as we know it, just the names of different genres. In modern times, the term '*buyō*' was coined as a general term for dance by combining the character for *mai*, which can also be pronounced 'bu', and the character for *odori*, which can also be pronounced 'yō'.

The bulk of the repertory of Japanese classical dance consists of dances from the *kabuki* theatre. There are some dances that have long, complicated stories. Other dances are relatively short and lyrical with no particular story, but present some kind of *kabuki* character. This might be a character from historical legend or a colourful character from the daily life of the Edo Period in a series of entertaining dances, which may or may not have a direct relationship with that character. There are elements of both *odori* and *mai* in these dances, but usually the element of *odori* is much stronger. When these dances are performed by classical dancers instead of *kabuki* actors, the costumes, wigs and make-up are usually exactly the same as in the *kabuki* theatre. However, all female characters on the *kabuki* stage were performed by male actors called *onnagata*, and the wigs and costumes were intended to create the illusion of femininity on a male body. Thus, the *kabuki* techniques borrowed wholesale are not necessarily perfectly suited to women playing female characters. The overwhelming majority of Japanese classical dancers are women, and, although some perform male roles as well as female roles, most only perform female roles.

Another important part of the Japanese classical dance repertory is called '*jiuta mai*', or '*kamigata mai*'. These are dances from the pleasure quarters of Ōsaka and Kyōto, and are very reserved and refined. These dances are usually pure *mai* and combine abstract circling motions and fan movements with moments of very concentrated pantomime. These dances were originally meant to be performed by women and, for the most part, are performed by schools of dance that specialize in *jiuta mai*.

In the modern period, this repertory was varied in many ways. First, when a dance is performed by a classical dancer rather that an actor, it may be performed in a style called '*su odori*', in which the dancer wears only formal kimono instead of make-up and costume. This emphasises the dance as pure form, rather than theatre. Some schools reworked the classics so that they were suited to the bodies and sensibilities of women. Other times, dances from the classical *kabuki* repertory were reworked with modern, abstract settings. Often, there was a strong influence from abroad. *Sagi musume* (The Heron Maiden) was reworked under the influence of Anna Pavlova's *The Dying Swan*. Where the dancer playing a woman who is the spirit of the heron would have posed handsomely at the end of the classical version, the modern version has the character gradually sinking to the floor in lifelessness. Other artists rework the classics under the influence of such dancers as Martha Graham.

However, for all of these innovations, the main work consists of preserving and transmitting the classics of the past as they have always been performed.

Although new pieces continue to be composed, it is very difficult to create anything truly new in a genre that is so concerned with the preservation of the past. For now, Japanese classical dance largely means preserving the synthesis of old and modern, Japanese and Western, which was achieved in the twentieth century.

MARK OSHIMA

classical literature in post-war Japan

What is styled in English as classical Japanese literature is commonly known in Japan as *kogo* or *kobun*. Old Japanese or Ancient Literature was the rubric under which classical Japanese became a required component of the general curriculum in the post-war period. Another term, *koten bungaku*, broadly designates literary classics from ancient, medieval and early modern Japan.

In historical terms, *kobun* refers to literature of the ancient period, from the Nara (710–794) and Heian courts (794–1183). Linguistically, classical literature comprises texts written in the vernacular (ancient Japanese) rather than literary Chinese. Particularly important by these criteria are imperial anthologies of *waka* (thirty-one-syllable poems), women's diaries and prose tales such as *Genji monogatari* (The Tale of Genji, *c*. 1010). Although later works from medieval or early modern Japan are sometimes included on the basis of stylistic affinity, Heian literature has become not only the standard for instruction in classical literature but also its symbolic centre. This is quite different from the pre-war period.

Scholarship on classical literature is commonly organised around a history of (Chinese) influence and (Japanese) reaction. In the pre-war period, the emphasis fell to literary forms that appeared to be free of the corrupting influences of Chinese civilisation. Particularly important were poems that directly praised nature and the Emperor, such as those from the *Man'yōshū* (compiled *c*. 759). Heian poetry and tales not only seemed effeminate and decadent, but also presented a troublesome view of the Emperor. In **Tanizaki Jun'ichirō**'s first translation of *Genji monogatari* (1939, 1941), passages that dealt with the illicit relationship between Genji and the Emperor's concubine Fujitsubo were excised from the published version.

The US decision not to bomb Kyōto during the war anticipates, in many ways, the position of Heian or classical literature in post-war Japan. It underscored the idea that Heian culture had nothing to do with the feudalistic and militaristic tendencies of Japan (as seen by the Allies). The courtly tradition now promised nothing less than a new image of Japan as an insular yet refined culture, one that peacefully absorbed outside influences, one whose emperor functioned not as a ruler or commander but as a symbol of unity. This new culturalist image of Japan established an agenda for, and the relevance of, court literature in the post-war era. It also encouraged an association of courtly elegance with post-war peace and prosperity, which reached its pinnacle with the imperial burial and enthronement ceremonies in 1989. What could be more different from the wartime images of Emperor **Hirohito** on horseback in military dress than those of the current Emperor and Empress decked out in layers of patterned silks modelled on ancient court dress?

Also characteristic of classical literature in post-war Japan is the drive to make the difficult ancient texts accessible to mass-market audiences. Because course instruction tends to centre on grammar, students must turn to other materials if they wish to read classical literature. There are a number of good modern language translations. The Shōgakukan editions of Japanese classics published in the post-war period include modern translations with the original text. In the instance of *Genji monogatari*, Tanizaki made two additional, critically esteemed translations in the post-war period; **Enchi Fumiko** produced a highly readable, nuanced rendition. Recently, in 1997, the translation by Setouchi Jaku became a bestseller, and launched a Genji boom with its television specials and companion volumes. Despite the prevalence of translations, however, as the Setouchi phenomenon suggests, it is through visual culture that classical literature has often had its greatest impact.

Film versions of Heian literature have abounded, especially of *Genji monogatari*. One of the best-received efforts to bring this text closer to viewers came in 1991, with an eight-hour mini-series production that aimed to present *Genji monogatari* with authenticity and complexity, striving to replicate some of the visual devices of Heian illustrated handscrolls, and framing the story with scenes of the author, Murasaki Shikibu, at work on it. Other films are notable for drawing out the other-worldly possibilities of classical Japan. **Kon Ichikawa**'s 1987 film version of *The Tale of the Bamboo Cutter* (entitled *Kaguya*) combined costume drama with special effects, ending with the arrival of an enormous spaceship at the Heian court. In a different vein, in 1987, Sugii Gisaburō directed an animated version of *Genji monogatari* based on the early chapters, in which the brilliant colours and gaudy patterns of court life are permeated with a sense of inhuman silence and ominous distance.

Manga continue to be the most popular format for classical literature. Of *Genji monogatari* alone, there are at least five different versions now readily available in classical literature series from major publishers. The perennial favourite is Yamato Waki's thirteen-volume *Genji monogatari: asaki yume mishi* (Tale of Genji: Fleeting Dreams, 1980–93), which surpasses other versions in length and complexity. Yamato Waki deploys the style popularised by women writers of *shōjo manga* (comics for girls); images are not subordinated to a linear, logical sequence of framed events but unfurl across the page and bleed into other images, foregrounding the emotional impressions of characters. Classical literature has also found expression in the **bishōnen** *manga* (beautiful young boy) genre of *shōjo manga* as well; a series like Yamagishi Ryōko's *Hiidumo-tokoro no tenshi* (Prince Where the Sun Rises) uses the ancient court as a fantastical landscape to transform one of Japan's great cultural heroes, Prince Shōtoku, into a beautiful boy in love with beautiful boys.

A host of celebrated post-war novelists, such as Tanizaki Jun'ichirō, **Kawabata Yasunari**, **Mishima Yukio** and **Nakagami Kenji**, have written works adapted from, or inspired by, Heian prose tales; and women writers such as Enchi Fumiko and **Tsushima Yūko** have turned to such works in order to explore the possibilities for a woman's voice in Japanese literature. However, the mass-culture styles and women's issues central to *manga* versions remain in tension with the literary prestige traditionally accorded classical literature, which is only gradually and reluctantly being extended by scholars to *manga*. None the less, a new generation of young scholars has already begun to look at *manga* classics in order to raise questions about the role of visual culture, gender and readership in classical literature, and to challenge contemporary divisions between high and mass culture.

Further reading

Akiko Hirota (1997) 'The tale of Genji: From Heian classic to Heisei comic', *Journal of Popular Culture*, 31(2): 29–68.

LaMarre, Thomas (2000) *Uncovering Heian Japan: An Archaeology of Sensation and Inscription*, Durham: Duke University Press.

Takeshi Fujitani (1992) 'Electronic pageantry and Japan's symbolic emperor', *Journal of Asian Studies*, 51(4): 824–50.

THOMAS LAMARRE

Clean Government Party

The former Komeito originated as the political wing of the Sōka Gakkai (Value Creation Society), the lay organization of Nichiren Shoshu, a sect of the Buddhist religion. In 1962, the Sōka Gakkai established a League for Clean Government, which became a regular party two years later. Formal ties with the Sōka Gakkai were dissolved in 1970, although the influence of the religious group over the party remained.

The former Komeito occupied just fourteen seats in the House of Councillors (Upper House of the Diet) at its inauguration, and sent members to the House of Representatives for the first time in 1967. By the late 1970s, it became the second largest opposition party after the **Japan Socialist Party**. It has tended to stand against the traditional ideological confrontation between the **Liberal Democratic Party** (LDP) and the Social Democratic Party of Japan (SDPJ). Its supporters have tended to be young, lower-class, urban factory workers, who feel largely outside the privileged labour union or '**sarariiman**' circles of lifetime employment and large enterprises. Komeito has supported free enterprise but calls for more equitable distribution of wealth. It has advocated Japanese neutrality in foreign affairs, and a nuclear-free zone in the Asia–Pacific region.

When the LDP failed to win a majority of seats in the House of Representatives in 1993, the former Komeito became part of a coalition that established the first LDP-free administration in thirty-eight years, under Hosokawa Morihiro, and later Hata Tsutomo. This coalition ended in 1994 when it lost control over the government to a new three-way coalition formed by the LDP, SDPJ and the **New Party Sakigake**, under the leadership of Tomiichi Murayama.

In 1994, the former Komeito split into two parties – 'Komei' and 'Komei New Party'. The latter then established a new party – the New Frontier Party (NFP) – jointly with members of the Japan Renewal Party and Japan Democratic Socialist Party. The NFP failed to make substantial gains in the election of 1996 and disbanded in 1997.

Since then, Komei and the New Peace Party have worked closely together on policy and Diet manœuvres, and eventually merged into 'New Komeito' in 1998. At the end of 1999, New Komeito (together with the Reformers' Network) had fifty-two seats (10 per cent of total) in the House of Representatives, and twenty-four seats (10 per cent) in the House of Councillors, and formed the second largest opposition party, led by Takenori Kanzaki.

Komei continues as a 'middle-of-the-road' party with a philosophy that emphasises gradual reform and pacifism. On the domestic front, it pushes for policies to extend reliable systems of social security, pensions and home care, to give further encouragement for medium and small businesses, to update the employment security system and to lengthen the dole term, and to provide jobs for the estimated 3 million unemployed. Komeito also pushes for the reform of government systems by encouraging local autonomy, elimination of corruption, securing political ethics and instituting an Information Disclosure Act. In international affairs, Komeito has promoted Japan's active role in the United Nations' Peace-Keeping Operations and the curtailing of US bases in Japan.

DAVID EDGINGTON

coffee

From the seventeenth century onwards, Japanese were aware of the dark, sweet, thick beverage so prized by the Dutch and Portuguese sailors and traders. However, coffee (*kōhii*) did not become widely available for consumption in Japan until the 1910s, when it was introduced together with café culture from Europe. At this time, there was more of a fascination with the art of making coffee than the taste itself. Cafés specialised in various techniques that often proved more aesthetically pleasing than practical or a source of good tasting coffee. To this day, there are still many *kissaten* that are renowned for one or other rarefied coffee-brewing technique. The *kissaten* boom of the 1950s and 1960s saw a dramatic increase in coffee consumption, and today many Japanese will determine their favourite *kissaten* for *mōningu saabisu* (breakfast specials) on the basis of the quality of their *hausu burendo* (house blend). Coffee beans have remained relatively expensive in Japan, limiting many households to cheaper instant coffee. The arrival of Starbucks in the mid-1990s has seen a new take-out culture of coffee that is impacting on the business of many smaller *kissaten* in business districts. Japan is infamous for the ever present jar of Creap – the Japanese powdered whitener to be found by every company coffee dispenser.

SANDRA BUCKLEY

coffee shops

The first Japanese coffee shop (*kissaten*) is said to have opened in Ueno in 1888 and to have quickly developed into a favourite destination for Tokyo's emerging new literati. However, by the 1910s Ginza had emerged as the centre of *kissa* culture. Today there are over 30,000 *kissa* listed in the Tokyo phonebook. These highly eclectic shops survive usually on the loyalty of a regular local or commuter clientele. They compete with one another, not so much on pricing, because margins are limited, but by theme or specialisation: regional pottery or fine bone china, a style of music (Jazz, classical, folk, salsa), a variety of cake or confectionary, a mini-gallery, a style of brewing or a thematic décor. The architecture of *kissa* can vary from an inexpensive hole in the wall to upmarket post-modern chic. What all *kissa* have in common is coffee, and *kissa aficionados* can take you on a tour of the best coffee brewers in town. If you buy just one cup of coffee you can stay as long as you want, although few *kissa* offer a free top-up. Music *kissa* offer patrons the additional attraction of a specific style of music.

Classical-music *kissa* sometimes have no-talking areas but this is increasingly less common. *Kissa* may also offer playing tables for such games as mah jong and go, or video table tops for computerised and other electronic games. Famous bakeries will also open *kissa* outlets that offer their baked goods along with coffee, while some foreign companies have recognised this marketing opportunity and opened *kissa* specialising in their wares, e.g. Royal Doulton and Lenox. Smoke-free coffee shops are still rare in Japan, as in much of Europe.

The biggest change in the *kissa* culture has been the arrival of Starbucks, which now has over a hundred outlets in Japan and is planning to push further into the market. Take-out coffee is proving far more successful than many expected, in a culture where the tendency was either to grab a cup of instant coffee from a vending machine or to linger over a coffee and chat in a *kissa*. The major domestic competitor to Starbucks is Dotours, which has ten times more outlets but has been hit hard by the cultural currency of the now familiar and tenaciously trendy Starbucks brand. The *kissa* culture is a well established part of **gaijin** life in Japan and there are numerous websites and urban-trend magazines offering guides to the hottest and newest, as well as the oldest or most eclectic, of the *kissa* in Japan's major cities.

See also: coffee

SANDRA BUCKLEY

cohorts

One's cohorts (or in-groups) in Japan are hierarchised according to the categories of junior (*kohai*), equal (*dohai*) and senior (*senpai*). The most common sites for cohort formation are school, university, workplace and sports or other clubs. Men speak more frequently than women of their friends and colleagues in terms of these cohort categories. This hierarchy of cohort members creates a chain of responsibilities and obligations. In extreme cases, juniors can be victimised or abused as in the case of bullying in schools and hazing in the military. On the whole, these relations tend to provide important, often life-long, networks of support and mutual dependency.

See also: *giri* and *ninjo*; *uchi* and *soto*

SANDRA BUCKLEY

colours, cultural significance of

Colours in Japan carry seasonal and socio-cultural associations that are reinforced by poetic traditions. Nature is reflected and interpreted in the colours eulogised in literature and seen in clothes, food and décor. In the Heian period, combining layers of coloured garments to reflect the essence of the season became an art that continues to have repercussions in clothing design today.

For the Japanese, the correlations between colours and specific plants goes beyond associations with the flowers, and is governed by an intimate knowledge of natural dye stuffs and the dye procedures. The names of many colours are identical with their dye sources: purple (*murasaki*), indigo (*ai*) and scarlet (*beni*). Often, the value of a colour arises not only from its attractiveness, but also from the cost of its production. Purple wild-growl roots are hard to collect and also hard to dye successfully. Scarlet from safflower thistle blooms is valued at 'A pound of *beni* scarlet being worth a pound of gold.' Both purple and scarlet were ranked (reserved for the nobility) in the ancient period, and subjected to numerous sumptuary laws restricting their use by commoners during the Edo

Period. Even today, they are the most highly prized dye colours. Young girls don scarlet for celebrations, while older women choose purple.

The association of red with youth (male and female) was recorded already in the middle ages, was codified in the *nō* costumes and remains today even in Western dress. Today girls carry red satchels (boys carry black), red pencil boxes and have red lines on their sneakers. Japanese represent the sun as red and, being the most ancient of their pigments, also think of it as colour itself.

Black today carries mixed Japanese and Western associations. The formality and sobriety of black makes it suitable not only for funerals but also for weddings and, traditionally, for the crested kimono (*monzuki*) of formal wear. Seen as mysterious and magical, black is a popular fashion colour.

Blue and green are both encapsulated in the Japanese word *ao*, which can also mean inexperienced, fresh or spring-like. The most common dye source was/is Japanese indigo (see **ao**). A rank colour in the eighth century, deep blue became the colour of victory for the warrior class. In the Edo Period, the affinity of this dye for cotton led to widespread establishment of dyers specialising in indigo (*aishi*). Many regard blue as Japan's national colour.

Yellows and browns have the most varied dye sources and are the easiest to produce. Traditionally, they are associated with everyday work clothes. Subtle shades in muted combinations of earth colours echo the rustic refinement one associates with the tea ceremony utensils. Today, bright yellows, because of their visibility, are prescribed for school children's hats and umbrellas.

Other colour associations derive from religious precepts, in particular the use of colour in the mandala for esoteric Buddhism. Rich reds, yellows and blue earth pigments recall the precious stones that line the realm of the Buddhas. The lapis lazuli used to create blue pigment, for instance, is also a visualisation stone suggesting the infinite space of cosmic oceans and sky.

See also: *ao*

MONICA BETHE

comedy films

Japanese film comedy can be mapped along three axes: narrative (non-narrative gags to emotionalised narrative comedy); commercial (mass-produced entertainment towards art film); and critical (from the conservative to the satirical).

Early post-war comedy featured vaudeville veterans like Enomoto Ken'ichi offering slapstick alternatives to dire realities, or films by **Kinoshita Keisuke** and **Kon Ichikawa** satirising the 'new democratic Japan'. In the 1950s, Tōhō began mass-producing films like the *Shachō* (Company President) and *Musekinin* (Irresponsible) series, which parodied the corporate society created by the Japanese economic miracle. Against such series, which often offered comfort through repetition, directors like **Kawashima Yūzō**, **Imamura Shōhei** and Okamoto Kihachi provided blacker satirical visions of post-war Japan.

In the late 1960s, Tōhō lost its dominance as Shōchiku came to the fore with Yamada Yōji's *Otoko wa tsurai yo* (**Tora-san**) series, which preserved a *ninjō kigeki* (comedy of affinity) formula, mixing humour with tears, nostalgia with a changing Japan. Much of post-1970s comedy has been based on *manga*.

Screen comedy has been so defined by narrative that little of the variety comedy dominating television has made its way into film. Still, the 1980s and 1990s saw a new generation of satirists like **Itami Jūzō** and Yaguchi Shinobu breaking fresh ground.

AARON GEROW

comfort women

Comfort women is the English-language translation of the term *jūgun ianfu* (military comfort women), one of the euphemisms used by the military in wartime Japan for the women forced into service in military brothels in areas occupied by the Japanese military in the 1930s and 1940s. The phrase 'comfort women' is highly offensive to the women involved. A range of other terms are also employed, such as military sex slaves, mass rape victims, military prostitutes or women subjected to enforced prostitution. It is estimated that between 100,000 and 200,000 women from Korea and other Asian countries were subjected to enforced labour in military brothels, which were first set up in the 1930s in China, and subsequently in South-East Asia, the Pacific Islands and New Guinea. Many of the women were coerced or thought that they were being conscripted for other kinds of work.

Although official records of the existence of these brothels were largely destroyed after Japan's defeat in the Second World War, traces of evidence were available in military memoirs, oral histories and the war crimes tribunals that were carried out after the war. In 1970, a former military officer publicly admitted that he had been responsible for setting up military brothels in Shanghai in 1938, one year after the Nanjing Massacre. The stories of the women who had been enforced labourers in these brothels came to light in the 1970s, in interviews with Korean residents who had been brought to Japan as enforced labourers, and who had remained there after the Second World War. Japanese and Korean oral historians found that not only had hundreds of thousands of Korean men and women been subject to conscripted labour, but that many women had been forced to engage in sexual labour. The first books on this issue appeared in Japanese in the late 1970s. In the 1980s and 1990s, activists and historians in Japan, Korea and other parts of South-East Asia tried to uncover the dimensions of this history and also to bring a feminist perspective to issues of gender and human rights.

In the early 1990s, a Korean woman, Kim Hak Sun, decided to break her silence about her experiences and claim compensation from the Japanese government. At around the same time, historian Yoshimi Yoshikai found records in the archives of the Department of Defence that proved the involvement of the Japanese military, and strengthened the case of Kim and her fellow petitioners. Women from other countries also gradually spoke out. Dutch–Australian Jan Ruff O'Herne and Filipino Maria Rosa Henson published autobiographies, and members of non-governmental organisations (NGOs) collected testimonials and produced documentary films on the issue. A series of regional meetings was held, and women brought their stories into the public domain at the International Conferences on Human Rights in Bangkok and Vienna, and the United Nations International Conference on Women held in Beijing in 1995. The issue was investigated by a United Nations Special Rapporteur, and some women eventually took their claims into the Japanese courts. They were supported by a network of non-governmental organisations in the region, some of whom made links between the wartime military prostitution system, the contemporary sex industry that surrounds military installations in the South-East Asian region and incidents of recent sexual violence perpetrated by military personnel against civilian women. These contemporary issues of sexual violence were particularly acute in **Okinawa**, which hosts 75 per cent of active US military bases on only 0.6 per cent of the total land mass of Japan. In 1995, the assault of an adolescent girl in Okinawa by three members of the US military was one catalyst for a strengthening of the anti-US bases movement in Okinawa (see **anti-US bases movements**).

A tribunal convened by NGOs in Tokyo in December 2000 attracted over 5,000 participants, including sixty survivors from the Second World War, lawyers and scholars, and spectators from over thirty countries. The tribunal was jointly sponsored by organisations from North Korea, South Korea, China, Taiwan, the Philippines, Indonesia, Malaysia, the Netherlands, Japan and Burma. Mock prosecutors investigated the responsibility of high ranking Japanese military and political officials for the military prostitution system in a tribunal that had no legal force. Although women from Japan, Korea, the Philippines and other countries who had been subjected to enforced military prostitution attempted to obtain compensation from the Japanese government, it was argued that the issue of compensation had been dealt with in the San Francisco Peace Treaty at the end of the Second World War and in the treaty that normalised relations between Japan and South Korea in 1965. The Japanese government responded to the women's claims by setting up the Asian Peace Fund, a private fund that sought donations from individuals and private companies. Most of the women were reluctant to accept money from this fund and preferred to wait for official compensation. They also hoped for an apology from the government.

Further reading

Henson, M.R. (1996) *Comfort Woman: Slave of Destiny,* Manila: Philippine Centre for Investigative Journalism.

Howard, K. (ed.) (1995) *True Stories of the Korean Comfort Women,* London: Cassell.

O'Herne, J.R. (1994) *Fifty Years of Silence,* Sydney: Editions Tom Thompson.

Positions: East Asia Cultures Critique 5(1), 1997.

Watanabe, K. (1994) 'Militarism, colonialism, and the trafficking of women: "comfort women" forced into sexual labor for Japanese soldiers', *Bulletin of Concerned Asian Scholars* 26(4): 3–17.

VERA MACKIE

Comme des Garçons

Comme des Garçons is a prêt-à-porter brand name by **Rei Kawakubo**. It was established in 1973 in France. Since 1973, Comme des Garçons has launched fashion lines in evening wear as 'Comme des Garçons Noire', indoor wear as 'Robe de Chambre' and knitwear as 'Comme des Garçons "Tricot"'. There are a number of other spin-off brand names, including most notably 'Junya Watanabe Comme des Garçons', which is focused on the fashion of Watanabe who designed the Tricot (line), and has further extended itself into the perfume market. The Comme des Garçons Omotesando outlet set a new trend when it began a series of artist collaborations in the storefront display area, blurring further the line between fashion design and art. Other designer brands quickly followed with in-store artist exhibits, window displays and collaborations for launch events.

AKIKO FUKAI

commuting

The long hours spent commuting by many Japanese workers and students has led to the conceptualisation of a culture of commuting. With daily commuting time in excess of two hours, the various ways in which individual commuters pass these hours is of interest not only to academic but also market researchers.

While long days see many commuters napping on trains, there are also a number of other activities that help pass the time spent in transit between home and work or school. Print media has always been an important part of commuter culture with bookshops clustered close to stations and newspaper kiosks on platforms. Sports newspapers and comic books (***manga***) are the most popular commuter reading materials. Publishers and bookshops unashamedly promote works that target this massive commuter readership. New technologies first had an impact on commuter culture with the Walkman, which broke the monotony of the commute with music and radio. More recently, Discmans, MDs (minidisc players) and DVDs have found their way into the commute, along with palm-sized *pankons* (personal computers and organisers) that can be used for video games or as an extension of the workspace into the commute.

The density of commuter traffic through the transit system at peak hours creates a level of crowding that leads to problems specific to the commuter experience. Minor injuries from falls and pushing, along with verbal abuse, are characterised in the media as the outcome of 'peak rage'. Another common but declining problem on crowded commuter trains is the '*chikan*' – men who take advantage of anonymity to grope female commuters. A number of successful anti-*chikan* campaigns have seen a dramatic decline in reported cases. Proposals to create flexible working hours to stagger commuter numbers have received a lukewarm reception, in a country where no-one in the office wants to be seen to be departing from the status quo.

The commuter experience is heavily influenced by gender and age. A male office worker will travel to the office for a 10.00 a.m. start and will seldom expect to leave for home before 7.00 p.m. He will often find himself running for the last train home after a night of drinking with colleagues or clients. A female office worker is expected to arrive before her male colleagues and have the office ready for their arrival. If full time, she will work through until early evening but is not expected to participate in the long after-hours socialising. More and more unmarried women workers are, however, creating their own *yobai* networks of night-time entertainment. Part-time female workers will usually commute home in time to meet children after school and guide them through homework and *juku* (cram classes). Most married women in the workforce will shop for fresh or pre-prepared food for an evening meal *en route* home, or order-in meals from a local restaurant. The home commute is channelled through department store food sections, supermarkets and neighbourhood shopping streets. There is not wide acceptance of the 'big shop' in Japan, where the preference is to buy daily, and shopping and commuting are closely linked.

Children often commute long distances to attend the best schools. The comparatively high level of public safety in Japan means that it is not unusual to see even primary school students travelling alone or in groups on trains. While school children in bright yellow safety caps and carrying the traditional leather backpacks, laughing and playing as they walk through the neighbourhood to school, remains a common sight, there has also been a marked shift towards school commuting. This reflects the competitiveness within the education system that leads to even kindergarten children travelling significant distances by car or public transport in order to attend the best school they can gain entry to. Thus, from a very early age commuting has become an accepted element of the contemporary time–space configuration of movement through everyday life.

A commuter pathway is often punctuated by familiar rituals. The newspaper stand is a regular stop on the way to work, where a quick energy or vitamin drink kick-starts the day and the commuter picks up a favourite weekly or *manga*. Release dates for weekly publications are staggered so that commuters always have something new to choose from each morning. There is often a favourite coffee shop or breakfast bar somewhere between the station and the workplace, where a quick and inexpensive 'morning set' of toast and coffee is served with a smile and chat for regular customers. The day's food shopping is integral to the commute home for the working mother, but on some days she might also take time to attend a cultural centre sponsored by the department store chain linked to her commuter line, where there can be classes as diverse as cooking, French, car maintenance, carpentry, flower arranging or tea ceremony. She may pick up her child from school and drop them into after-school cram classes (*Juku*) while she does the evening shopping. A man's commute home is often staggered – both literally and figuratively. Meals with colleagues and clients are frequently followed by bars and clubs all paid for on company accounts. Male blue-collar workers too seldom commute home without stopping into a favourite bar or snack counter for a chat with friends, or a quick drink with a favourite hostess or a warm chat with the '*mamasan*'. Family meals are seldom possible except on weekends due to the very different commuter schedules of parents and children.

Driving is not the most popular mode of long-distance commuting in Japan. The combination of traffic jams and expensive parking in inner-city areas leaves many family cars garaged through the work week. High levels of truck transport create massive congestion on major arteries into and out of cities. Long hours spent in traffic have contributed to a design focus on comfort over speed. Quality upholstery, adjustable seating, single-touch computerised controls, state-of-the-art stereo, television and video monitors, and built-in satellite locating systems, offering alternative routings and traffic updates, are all standard features in recent Japanese car design. While, on the other hand, manufacturers are still required to build in a warning mechanism that triggers a beeper or other sound if the car exceeds the maximum speed limit.

There are indications that while the urban migration into Ōsaka and Tokyo continues to promote suburban sprawl (approximately half a million per annum into each centre), there is a growing trend among outer urban dwellers to relocate towards the inner wards. Ageing city apartment complexes are being replaced by design experiments in mid-density modular family complexes. Increasing vacancy rates in office blocks in the once booming Chiba City CBD indicate that the corporate sector has decided that long commutes are preferable to decentralisation. Inner-city housing subsidies are a common part of salary packages to top job candidates in an increasingly mobile, young and highly skilled workforce not inclined towards a life of commuting. In the long run, however, commuting seems likely to remain a significant feature of the cultural landscape of Japanese daily life.

Further reading

Buckley, S. (1996) 'Contagion', in C. Davidson (ed.) *Anywise*, Harvard: MIT Press, pp. 80–90.

SANDRA BUCKLEY

company towns

Japan has numerous 'corporate castle towns', cities with economies revolving around a single company's production system, many of which trace back to the Meiji Period. For instance, in the Setouchi industrial area, Onada City is presided over by Onada Cement. The nearby chemical-industry town of Ube is dominated by Ube Kosan. Omuta City, Fukuoka Prefecture, experienced a hundred-year heyday based on the Mitsui Corporation's Miike mine, the largest coal mine in Japan and the centre of an extensive industrial complex that included metal smelting and chemical processing. At the end of the nineteenth century, heavy industries – in particular steel, chemicals, ship-building and metal company towns – were often at the forefront of national industrialisation. Other company towns flourished in the second wave of industrialisation after the Second World War. Toyota City, originally named Koromo, was a commercial centre up until the 1930s, which became the core of Toyota's production system and changed its name in the late 1950s when Toyota Motor Corporation opened its second assembly plant there.

As in company towns elsewhere, the city provided infrastructure and services to keep the company's production system running smoothly. Responsibility for welfare needs of the residents has fallen to the company, which provides subsidised dormitories for young single workers or apartments for married couples. Workers shop in company outlets, attend company technical schools and receive medical services at the local company hospital. For recreation, employees take advantage of sports facilities and, perhaps, company resorts at nearby mountain or seaside locations. However, unlike many other company towns, those in Japan often developed a 'shared-fate' cultural outlook that dampened labour militancy. A post-war tradition of 'enterprise unions' in Japan also tended to make workers identify with company interests and blunt worker opposition to company operations.

Lack of balance and effective local opposition often created problems as it was easy for firms to plunge headlong into economic growth and profiteering, disregarding social responsibility and environmental harm. At the turn of the twentieth century, copper-mining towns – such as Ashio, Besshi, Kosaka and Hitachi – became notorious because of environmental pollution to farmland caused by copper refinery smoke. Later, the village of Minamata in Kyūshū prospered with the growth of Nippon Chisso's fertiliser and organic carbide plant, but Chisso's rapid expansion after the Second World War led to an increase in the volume of effluents poured into the sea, and a serious mercury poisoning case was launched in the 1950s and 1960s.

Not all company towns have been able to adapt flexibly to changing global competitive economic conditions. Those based on traditional mining, steel, shipbuilding and chemical industries have been rocked by a series of economic shocks since the mid-1970s. The effects of industrial restructuring have varied depending upon the age of local operations, degree of diversification in the local economy and success of efforts to promote new regional development. The impact on coal towns, such as Omuta in Kyūshū or Yubari in Hokkaidō, has been the most severe as companies have resorted to rapid downsizing and closures.

DAVID EDGINGTON

computers

Japan entered late into the computers world market but wasted no time in developing a concerted catch-up programme, both in manufacturing and in research. Today, Japan's computer industry is second only to that of the USA. The first digital computer was built in 1956, ten years after Sperry Rand constructed its first ENIAC system. MITI developed a research committee in 1954, the same year as the first computers were imported from the USA, with the goal of co-ordinating and encouraging both domestic R&D and manufacturing. Cross-licensing with US manufacturers was allowed from 1960, and by the mid-1960s RCA, Sperry Rand, GE, TRW, Honeywell and IBM all had agreements in place. Throughout the 1960s and 1970s, the Japanese government provided substantial R&D subsidies to promote the development of competitive domestic technologies. Unlike the USA, the Japanese computer manufacturers were not specialist companies but extensions of existing electronics or telecommunications manufacturers such as Fujitsu, Mitsubishi Electric, NEC and Toshiba. This was an important factor in the rapid start-up stage of the Japanese industry, which was able to build on the financial and R&D base of existing companies. Later, however, this became a potential disadvantage as the more secure industrial giants felt less pressure to diversify and develop new products. These companies missed out on the initial wave of the shift from mainframe to desktop and then PCs. Again, Japan had to resort to catch-up strategies. Some commentators also believe that the Ministry of Post and Telecommunications played a role in retarding new initiatives in the industry through its interventions in regulatory and licensing policy, and in its R&D priorities, especially in relation to the Internet.

By 1990, Japan had expanded both domestic and export computer sales to capture over 20 per cent of the international market. In the same year, Japan also displaced imports to win back the domestic market, claiming over 70 per cent of office computer sales and 60 per cent of mainframes. The fastest growth area was now in PCs, with the dramatic increase in home computer use. In 1994, only 14 per cent of households owned a computer but by 2000 this figure had climbed to 40 per cent (a mix of desktop and PCs), with 38 per cent of all homes owning personal computers in 1999. For reasons of space, compact PCs are rapidly displacing desktops in the Japanese market, both for home and office use, despite significantly higher prices. The higher pricing of the PC market is usually justified by the industry on the basis of manufacturing costs related to miniaturised components and the ongoing R&D costs in this rapidly diversifying area of new technology. In 1995, manufacturers shipped 5.5 million PCs. Since the mid-1990s, the accelerated popularisation of the Internet in Japan has also had a major impact on PC sales. However, the future of PCs is uncertain. The industry in Japan is watching closely the tremendous popularity of e-mail-ready digital cell phones. There is significant R&D underway into watch-sized, high-speed, Internet-ready PCs. The first prototypes were already displayed at the 2000 trade fairs in Japan and boasted 128 kilobytes of memory with the capability for flash memory card extensions. LCD units mounted on a glasses frame or lightweight headset have been designed to sit just to the side of the primary line of vision for hands-free access to e-mail and Internet. This development was originally intended for use in medical, laboratory and other scientific research environments but has been extended into a potential new platform in the fast transforming world of telecommunications.

Trends among the highly influential youth culture of Japan clearly indicate a movement towards mobile Internet access. There are some in the computer industry who believe that flexible, wearable, lightweight mobile technologies will emerge, backed up by digital tele-linked PC platforms at home. With the introduction of terrestrial digital television from 2000–1, focus is shifting to mix-media platforms combining network and satellite television, Internet, gaming and voice and video telephone. Japan is showing signs of leading the way in this new mix-media R&D and this is seen as the result of the initial decision to grow Japan's computer industry out of the existing domestic base in telecommunications and electronics manufacturing. Japan's computer manufacturers are initiating some of the more innovative global alliances across the telecommunications, computer and entertainment sectors. What is not in question today is that Japan will remain a major influence in the world of computers, whether in R&D, as a manufacturer and exporter or as an important marketplace for innovative new software and hardware imports. The highly successful

Japanese release of Windows 95 is recognised as a major factor in the mid-1990s boom in domestic computer sales. What is still on the drawing board is what the next generation of computers will look like, as both mix-media and mobility drive design innovation and consumer preference.

SANDRA BUCKLEY

computers and language

When computers first came onto the language education scene, it was initially believed that Japanese and computers were not compatible. It was assumed that it would be difficult to create software for the Japanese writing system that would be effective and efficient. It was also predicted that the operating language of computers would be English and there would be no place for languages like Japanese with different writing systems. However, the rapid development of technology and software that can accommodate the Japanese scripts has been remarkable. Today, computerisation is revolutionising written communication systems in Japan from the classroom to the office.

One can type in Japanese in the romanised alphabet (*rōmaji*) or in the *hiragana* syllabary. *Hiragana* appears on the screen and then, with one stroke of a command key, the *hiragana* is transformed into *kanji*, or the correct mix of *kanji* and *hiragana*. In some cases, a number of *kanji* options for a word are generated and the correct one must be selected. However, grammar programs enable the *kanji* software to select for contextual accuracy with low rates of error. The specialized skills needed to operate a Japanese typewriter prior to computerisation severely limited the ability to generate typed documents speedily. This led to a high level of handwritten communications in both the government and corporate sectors.

Computers are now enabling dramatic transfer of written communications into computer print and online systems. Japan is still in the early stages of the process of managing this shift and there is strong workplace resistance to the level of rapid technological transformation, a cultural change problem not unique to Japan.

While there are many immediate and obvious benefits to these advancements in computer technology, there are also a number of related concerns. It is believed now that the ability to write *kanji* among Japanese is sharply declining, whereas the ability to recognise and read *kanji* is being retained. This reflects the architecture of the *kanji* generation software, which requires only passive knowledge of *kanji* to choose the correct option on the screen. Another development in computer technology in relation to languages is the potential impact on handwriting skills. There are predictions that a new generation of Japanese growing up in a youth culture of digital communications will not develop adequate handwriting skills. Japanese schools today place a strong emphasis on handwriting and there are close ties between the practice of handwriting and the learning of *kanji*. As keyboards and touchpads become the favoured mode of writing outside the classroom, it is expected that the quality of handwriting will be more difficult to maintain in schools and after graduation.

Japanese can now be written on a special touchpad with a matching pen and be immediately transmitted and transcribed on to a display screen instead of using a keyboard. As with similar devices for English, the characters written on the touchpad are a stylised adaptation of *hiragana* that can be written in a short-hand style and still be recognised by the software. One can edit, modify or change the content in any way one wants on the screen. In government offices, private firms and educational institutions, it has become common to send internal as well as external communications by e-mail. Homepages are allowing fast and open access to necessary information. Lately, mobile phones with an i-mode facility have emerged as a popular medium for e-mail messaging, despite the small size of the display window. Internet access and e-mail exchanges are literally at one's fingertips with the added advantage of mobility and fast access. Faced with what is considered a communications and information technology boom, experts are concerned that the new technologies may enrich communication flow but dilute the richness of the written language. Others counter-argue that language is always in flux and that the new technologies will generate innovations and change that are themselves enriching.

The vast expansion of the Internet has dramatically changed language education. Students can create their own homepage in Japanese as an exercise, and can expect feedback and comments from not only classmates and teachers but also those who are outside of a traditional class. They can exchange e-mail messages in Japanese with other school students in Japan or in English and other languages with students all over the world. These exchanges of e-mail messages certainly have the capacity to enhance students' reading and writing skills. Teachers can assign, receive and return homework on the Internet and offer quick feedback. Teachers can also download written and visual images for teaching material from a wide range of sources and make use of current news available on the Internet. On the other hand, computers cannot replace teachers in language or other classroom situations. What is needed is a productive balance of proper classroom instruction and effective use of computers that offers students the best of both what the technology can achieve and access, and the knowledge and personal interaction of the teacher.

SHUN IKEDA

condoms

Condoms are the most popular form of birth control in Japan with usage rates as high as 85 per cent among young sexually active Japanese. Textured penis sheaths were a popular sex aid in the Yoshiwara brothel districts of Edo Japan but appear to have been used more for stimulation than protection or birth control. During the Meiji and Taishō Periods, some prostitutes provided their clients with condoms or used a vaginal sheath to avoid sexually transmitted diseases. During the Occupation period, the use of condoms was popularised by Allied troops, leading to many jokes and puns about bubble gum and condom-toting GIs among Japanese prostitutes and bar hostesses. The practice did, however, filter into the general sexual mores over the 1950s and 1960s. Today, condoms are widely available at convenience stores and vending machines in clubs, bars and public commuter areas around stations, and in supermarkets

and pharmacies. Resistance to legalising the contraceptive pill was a major factor in the continued high usage of condoms. Within marriage it is the wife who usually takes responsibility for purchasing condoms for birth control. Their widespread use in Japan is offered as a key factor in the relatively low incidence of AIDS, in a country that has such a well-established sex industry.

SANDRA BUCKLEY

Confucianism

Confucianism is a derivation of the name of the founder Kong Fuzi (551–479 BCE). Confucianism is not a religion as such but a political morality. Confucianism emphasises family and filial piety, the adherence to strict hierarchical structures of society, and the importance of education, as well as promoting meritocracy in administrative structures of authority. The institutionalisation of Confucian principles as state practice was instigated under both the Han (206–20 BCE) and Tang (CE 618–907) Chinese dynastic orders. The Confucian principle of a just and moral ruler was used at different times in Chinese history as the grounds for rebellion and overthrow of one ruler or dynastic order by another. Mencius (371–289 BCE) is the best known of the Chinese philosophers to further develop and refine the original teachings of Confucius.

Confucianism found its way to Japan via the Korean peninsula from the fifth century onwards. Confucian principles had a strong influence on the formation of the Japanese imperial sovereignty and its bureaucratic structures, as the Yamato clan secured its position of authority over the sixth to seventh centuries. The authority of Chinese Confucian principles and practices contributed to the authentification of this emerging ruling elite. The Japanese preference for hereditary ranking and promotions saw a rapid undermining of the notion of a meritocracy during this first wave of influence. There was not widespread interest in the Neo-Confucian shift from the political morality of institutions to the moral fabric of the individual when these teachings began to filter into Japan from the thirteenth century. It was the Tokugawa Period that saw a flourishing of Confucianism of the Ju Xi school, with its strong emphasis on classical studies and a meritocracy grounded in Confucian scholarship. Both the shōgunate and local *daimyos* embraced Confucianism as a means of enhancing their own legitimacy in a historical echo back to the Yamato strategy of the sixth to seventh centuries. The result was a return to a strong focus on classical Chinese studies and the emergence of an increasingly professionalised bureaucratic elite. The resurgence of Confucianism in this period also led to a proliferation of both elite and commoner schools, which meant that by the end of the Edo Period Japan had one of the highest literacy rates in the world. Confucianism did much to promote the inferior status of women over the Edo Period. The text *Greater Learning for Women* dictated the subordination of married women to their fathers, husbands and sons, and laid out in detail the appropriate behaviour for women. Many of the laws effecting the status of women in late Edo and even into the modern period can be traced back to this period of popularisation of Confucian-based principles of gender relations.

Although Confucianism was initially out of favour in the wake of the rapid importation of Western values and moral codes in the early Meiji Period, the emergence of *tennōsei* (emperor system) saw a return to a strong rhetoric of values of loyalty to family, father and sovereign. This Confucian resurgence was exemplified by the *Imperial Rescript on Education* issued in 1890. Although the rise of State Shintō saw the marginalisation of Buddhism, Confucian principles fortified and validated elements of the nationalist and imperialist agendas of *tennōsei*. The notion of an Asian tradition grounded in shared Confucian values provided a key platform for the Japanese concept of an Asian co-prosperity sphere. The end of the war saw Confucianism discredited and its fall from official favour. Today, Japanese conservatives are joining the political leaders of some of their regional neighbours in a return to a rhetoric of Asian values that harks back to Confucian principles, but the real depth of penetration of Confucian values within Japanese society is difficult to measure. Many of the structures of family and gender relations that are commonly identified today as Confucian in fact have their roots in the late nineteenth and early twentieth century, and the

processes of production of the modern family in policy, education and the media during those crucial decades of formation of a modern identity for the new nation state. This was a time when reinvention and remobilisation of traditional values was more common than simple continuity.

SANDRA BUCKLEY

consensus

This is the term used to describe a dominant mode of decision-making in Japan. It is a conflict-averse model in which dissenting individuals or factions are expected to move towards a majority position. A consensus outcome is achieved through consultation, compromise and concession-making, and marks an agreement to adopt a position as a group, but it does not mean that all are in agreement with that position.

Consensus depends on desire for group cohesiveness and fear of ostracisation to motivate individuals and dissenting factions to subordinate their preferred position. It has been described as coercive democracy. During the period of Japan's rapid economic growth, many US management specialists identified the technique of consensus as a major contributing factor to high production and low industrial unrest. Consensus became widely advocated outside Japan as a model for management and industrial relations. However, foreign unions remained sceptical and often pointed to fundamental structural and socio-cultural differences. Even Nakane Chie, a Japanese scholar who identified consensus as a key element in Japanese group dynamics, acknowledged that consensus processes carried a number of social costs: subjugation of minority or dissenting positions; discouragement of individual initiatives; exploitation of the fear of ostracisation; and promotion of group interests over fairness to parties outside the group.

The *ringi-sei* system is a basic element of consensus in any formal environment: workplace, committees, clubs, political parties, etc. A document is drafted after an extensive period of consultation to represent the dominant position (most often that of the strongest faction or alliance). It is then circulated and discussed among all the parties involved in the decision until each agrees to attach their seal. This process can be slow and is often the explanation for the delays that frustrate international negotiators involved in Japanese deals, who are unaccustomed to this decision-making model. That the Japanese style of consensus is a superior model to less conflict-averse alternatives should not be taken for granted. The suppression of differences in Japanese decision-making often leads to internal factional tensions that can undermine the long-term implementation of a decision, as well as impacting on the workplace environment and relations. The open office plan, also widely recognised as a Japanese management innovation, can be seen as one response to the high level of internal office factionalism promoted by the consensus process. The absence of walls and private office spaces, while apparently egalitarian, also functions to discourage open expressions of dissent. Some management and negotiation specialists reject this style of consensus for other approaches that respect and deal transparently with differences as part of the process of moving all parties towards agreement.

Further reading

Bachnik, J. and Quinn, C.J. (1994) *Situated Meaning: Inside and Outside in Japanese Self, Society and Language*, Princeton, Princeton University Press.
Nakane Chie (1970) *Japanese Society*, Berkeley: University of California Press.
Takeo Doi (1977) *The Anatomy of Dependence*, Tokyo: Kōdansha.

SANDRA BUCKLEY

CONTEMPORARY ART *see* art, contemporary

CONTEMPORARY THEATRE *see* theatre, contemporary

copy writers

The popularisation and public status of the copy writer is something that dates from the first influx of a US style of advertising and production and design systems into the Japanese advertising environment in the 1960s. There were copy writers prior to this period but, until then, those who went into copy-writing jobs were seen to be the fallen or would-be writers, designers and poets of the day. It was only from the 1960s that the profession of copy writing became attractive to new university graduates as a career in itself. It was over the 1980s, as Japan underwent an advertising boom, that ad-design, image production and catchphrases (sound bites) gained the spotlight and that top copy writers were elevated to celebrity status as gurus to the youth generation. From this period on, there was widespread recognition of both the status and professional skills of the copy writer. The shift from word copy to voice and sound, and from printed graphics to television CM mode saw the eventual disappearance of any formal distinction between print-based copy writers and broadcast-based CM planners. The national organisation of copy writers, Tokyo Copy writers Club (TCC) now includes copy writers across the full range of new media.

NANBA KŌJI

cosmetic surgery

It is difficult to access accurate statistics to assess the current state of cosmetic surgery in Japan, because it is not covered by insurance, and private clinics are reluctant to share information. Some information is available through government or university hospital facilities offering cosmetic surgery within their plastic-surgery units. One reputable unit, Shōwa University Hospital in Tokyo, reported 400 new cases in July and August of 2000 and, of these, forty-two cases were seeking assistance to correct or treat problems resulting from surgery performed in private clinics. The most popular form of cosmetic surgery in Japan today is eyelid surgery, which produces a second fold in the eyelid to create a more open eye shape. Re-profiling of the nose most often entails reduction of tissue in broad-based noses or inserts and bone reconstruction to create 'lift' in a flat nose.

Breast surgery is not as popular as in North America but a wider range of safer options are available in Japan, where approvals of new medical products are often faster. Cohesive-gel silicon implants are less likely to leak and hydrogel implants use hyaluronic acid, a natural body fluid. Japan has also made significant advances in scar tissue reduction techniques, which is a direct response to the extreme emphasis placed on unblemished skin in the Japanese aesthetic of beauty. The Japan Society of Aesthetic Surgery claims that, while their clientele was once primarily barworkers, today their major new market is women in their early twenties who are preparing for job interviews or starting to plan towards finding a marital partner. Another new cohort of women seeking cosmetic surgery in the 1990s is the generation of 'midis' (middle-aged and middle-class women), who have ample disposable income and are trying to slow down the ageing process. At the time when many of this generation of women were young, cosmetic surgery still had a bad reputation in Japan and there was a stigma attached. Now that the industry has achieved a higher reputation and the women have more money at their disposal, they are taking up the opportunity they did not pursue earlier.

The proliferation of private clinics remains a concern, and there are occasional horror stories of botched surgery sensationalised in the media. Accreditation processes for cosmetic surgeons are less stringent than in North America and there is pressure for review from within the Japan Society of Aesthetic Surgery, which considers it in its own best interest to maintain high standards and continue to enhance the reputation of the field in Japan. A significant number of Japanese women are thought to have cosmetic surgery performed in Europe and North America, where they combine vacation and healing time before returning to Japan. The Japanese clinics are keen to capture back as much of this overseas activity as possible.

SANDRA BUCKLEY

cosmetics

The first image that comes to mind when thinking of Japan and cosmetics is likely to be the dramatic, white cake make-up and deep red lips that characterise the traditional image of geisha or the female roles of the *kabuki* theatre. Make-up was limited to the world of the elite during the Heian period, when many of the ideals that continue to influence the aesthetic of feminine beauty first evolved. The white face powder (*oshiroi*) was first made from rice powder and white clay soils, but the more deadly ingredient, white lead, was imported from China around the seventh century and remained in use until the late nineteenth century. *Oshiroi* was heavily applied to the face, neck and ears to create a stark white complexion, often artfully contrasted to the natural skin colour of the neck with a carefully contoured edge at the lower neck below the hairline. Lipstick and rouge were applied from the same mix of safflower extract, a valuable commodity that was first imported in the seventh century via China and Korea from as far away as Egypt. The lips were painted onto the white cake make-up and usually rendered smaller and slightly higher than the natural lips. The practice of shaving the eyebrows and drawing in a brow-line higher up the forehead also dates from Heian and continued to be a common practice among the married women of the elite well into the nineteenth century. Blackening of the teeth (*ohaguro*) was adopted more widely and continued on in some areas into the twentieth century. Even in the early post-war years, one could still occasionally meet an older women whose teeth showed lingering black stains.

Today, this traditional make-up is limited to the stage and the world of the geisha and *maiko* (apprentice geisha) but cosmetics remain a major part of women's and, increasingly, men's daily lives. The annual value of the Japanese cosmetic market, which includes skin care products, is estimated at an astounding US$13 billion. The market is dominated by the domestic producer Shiseido, followed by Kanebo and Kose. Max Factor is the one foreign brand to have made significant headway into the Japanese cosmetic market and it has achieved this by duplicating the tied-retailer distribution system of the Japanese cosmetic giants. Shiseido, for example, has more than 25,000 small retail outlets all tied by tight contracts to Shiseido. In return for exclusivity, the cosmetic companies assure high prices by blocking secondary wholesaling and discount outlets. The risk of competition from imported cosmetics has been limited by the requirement that importers must present a full disclosure of content. In the world of cosmetics, where content is the secret everyone protects, this essentially means that only the original manufacturer is in a position to import. The government has recently relented to pressure to modify this requirement, as calls for deregulation and reduction of protection in the cosmetics market have increased since the mid-1990s. The long lines of Japanese tourists at the Chanel or Dior cosmetic counters at duty free make more sense when you know that there is often more than a 100 per cent differential between Japanese and duty-free prices. International brand names have relied on growing consumer pressure to push for deregulation. Their reliance on the Ministry of Health and Welfare for import approvals makes them reluctant to create tension with the government. The cosmetic industry has begun to respond with a loosening of the tied-retailer structure and the creation of new, less expensive lines for distribution in supermarkets and chain stores. There is still a reluctance to tolerate discounting of top-end product lines.

Skin care is a major segment of the cosmetic market in Japan and in this area advertising constitutes a lion's share of corporate expenditure, along with new product development. The launch of men's cosmetics and skin care ranges from the early 1980s has seen an explosion in sales, with skin care and hair care products for men now the fastest growing new target markets. Male make-up, especially foundation and lip creams, are becoming an accepted element of contemporary men's fashion and there appears to be much less anxiety about issues of masculinity and make-up than has been the case in North America, where this has proven a cultural stumbling block to opening up this new market area. Scandals surrounding cosmetic safety and testing in the 1960s and 1970s saw consumer groups establish their own testing facilities and this has kept pressure on cosmetic companies to comply with safety and health regulations, and to disclose more information on product content. Advertising for cosmetics has attracted a lot of attention from feminists concerned with such issues as the use of Western models to represent an ideal of beauty and the over-emphasis on physical characteristics, and the

face in particular, as the mark of beauty. There has been an increase in the use of Japanese models over the 1990s, although the face of Caucasian and Japanese mixed-race models remains a popular feature of cosmetic advertising. There is an intrinsic irony to this market that actively promotes the notion of a uniquely blemish-free Japanese complexion and a particularly refined Japanese sense of make-up, while relying heavily on non-Japanese models in its promotional materials.

SANDRA BUCKLEY

CRAM SCHOOL *see juku*

Crazy Cats

A comic band formed in 1955 by Watanabe Productions, with the jazz drummer Hana Hajime as leader. They were at first known as the 'Cuban Cats', but their popularity increased because of gags they worked into their performances in the style of Franky Sakai and the City Slickers, so they changed their name to the Crazy Cats.

Ueki Hitoshi, Tani Kei, Inuzuka Hiroshi, Yasuda Shin and Ishibashi Eitaro were the founding members, but, in the 1960s, Sakurai Senri was added and, in 1971, Ishibashi departed. They performed on Fuji TV's *Otona no manga* (Adult Manga) and Nippon TV's *Shambondama holiday* (Soap Bubble Holiday) without instruments and had some popularity as entertainers. Ueki's vocal recording of *Sudara fushi* (Hang Loose Melody) became a great hit. Ueki's performance in the *Musekinin otoko* (Irresponsible Man) film series in particular had a great impact on 1960s popular culture. At present, the various eccentric members have matured as middle-aged performers, and they remain emblematic of a group of entertainers made possible by the television era.

Further reading

Schilling, Mark (1997) '*Musekinin otoko* series', in *The Encyclopedia of Japanese Pop Culture*, Tokyo: Weatherhill, pp. 151–4.

Yano Yoshikazu (1994) 'Crazy Cats', in *Taishu bunka jiten*, Tokyo: Kobundo, p.219.

MARK ANDERSON

crime

Crime trends in post-war Japan are reflected in the Statistics on the Number of Penal-Code Offences reported to the police, which is titled *Hanzai hakushō* (The White Paper on Crime) and issued annually by Hōmu Sōgō Kenkyūjō (Research and Training Institute, Ministry of Justice).

According to these official statistics, in 1946, the year immediately following the end of the war, the total number of Penal-Code offences (excluding traffic-related professional negligence) was 1,384,222 cases. This was almost double that of 1945 and peaked at 1,599,968 in 1948. These figures reflect the period of intense social disruption that followed the end of the Second World War. After this, the figures declined steadily, with only minor fluctuations, finally reaching 1,190,549 in 1973, the lowest recorded between 1946 and 1987. Since 1987, however, there has been a gradual increase to 1,899,564 in 1997, the highest post-war figure. In terms of crime trends, the rate of non-traffic Penal-Code offences reported to the police (number of crimes reported to the police per 100,000 population) was 1,893 in 1946. This figure peaked at 2,000 in 1948, the highest in the post-war years. The rate of non-traffic Penal-Code offences steadily and clearly decreased from the late 1950s through the early 1970s, with only minor fluctuations. In 1973, the crime rate reached its lowest figure, 1,091, or just one-half that of 1948. Since 1974, however, this rate has gradually increased and reached 1,506 per 100,000 in 1997.

Post-war Japanese crime trends are noteworthy in several respects. The increasing trends starting in 1974 are mainly due to the increase in minor theft (e.g. shoplifting and bicycle thefts). Post-war crime statistics show that larceny is always the most prevalent offence, comprising more than 80 per cent of all non-traffic Penal-Code offences reported to the police. Therefore, it can be said that larceny determines the general trend in overall non-traffic Penal-Code offences. In contrast with the patterns for larceny and overall non-traffic Penal-Code offences, the number and rate for violent crimes (e.g. homicide, bodily injury, robbery, rape), comprises less than two per cent of total crime, and showed either a gradual downward trend or remained fairly stable since the 1960s. In the case of homicides, for instance, even though there was an upward trend from 1946 until 1955, peaking at 3,081 cases in 1954 (a 3.5 per cent increase), the number and rate of homicides shifted to a steadily decreasing trend thereafter. The 1990s have seen homicide rates consistently levelling off at the rate of 1.0 per cent from 1990 to 1997 to reach the lowest figure of the post-war years.

Japanese crime rates are remarkably low when compared to crime rates in many other advanced industrial countries, notably the UK, France, Germany and the USA. Thus, it is reputed that Japan with a relatively low crime rate (especially violent-crime rate) is successful in controlling crime. However, it needs to be noted that Japan's remarkably low crime rate is a relatively recent phenomenon, beginning in the late 1960s and that, until this time, the overall reported crime rates in Japan were not very different from those in major advanced industrial countries. After that time, however, while Japan's rates generally continued towards declining or stable trends, crime rates in the other advanced countries showed relatively steep increases or otherwise rising trends, so that since the late 1960s a significant difference has appeared between crime rates in Japan and the other advanced countries. Finally, despite the low-crime reputation, the current state of criminality in Japan is not as optimistic as many assume. During the past two decades, Japan has had trouble with the growth of specific types of crime, such as juvenile crimes, drug offences, organised crime (*bōryokudan* offences), crime committed by foreigners, white-collar crime, crime involving environmental pollution, etc.

It remains true that, unfortunately, little quantitative and empirical research exists on the levels and patterns of Japanese crime and the social mechanisms that discourage criminal activity in Japan. One recent piece of quantitative and criminological research (Park 1998), however, examined which factors affect the national crime trends in post-war Japan. It was found that economic affluence combined with economic equality and the high efficiency of police and court activities appear to be important determinants of crime trends in post-war Japan; age structure and social bonding variables appeared the least likely to have any explanatory power. While this empirical research did not directly bear on the problem of cross-national differences between crime rates in Japan and other advanced industrial countries, the research findings suggest that the fundamental differences between crime rates in Japan and other countries may be explained by the differential process of economic development across countries, and the degree of legal controls exercised in each society. If this is the case, it would be useful for future researchers to focus on structural explanations relating to social, economic, legal and political factors. Although the 'unique Japan' or cultural perspective dominates cross-national comparative research as an explanation of Japan's low crime rate, the empirical findings seem to imply that one does not necessarily have to call upon any unique cultural factors or cross-cultural differences to account for post-war Japanese crime trends.

See also: *kōban*; legal/judicial system; prostitution, regulation of; sexual violence/ domestic violence

References

Park, W. (1998) 'Trends in crime rates in postwar Japan: A structural perspective', Kitakyushu-Daigaku Hou-Sei Ronshu, *Journal of Law and Political Science* 24(1–2): 143–250.

Further reading

Fujimoto, T. and Park, W. (1994) 'Is Japan exceptional?: Reconsidering Japanese crime rates', *Social Justice* 21(2): 110–35.

Merriman, D. (1988) 'An economic analysis of the post World War II decline in the Japanese crime rate', *Journal of Quantitative Criminology* 7: 19–39.

Park, W. (1997) 'Explaining Japanese low crime rates: A review of the literature', *International Annals of Criminology* 35(1–2): 59–87.

Shikita, M. and Tsuchiya, S. (eds) (1992) *Crime and Criminal Policy in Japan from 1926 to 1988*, New York: Springer-Verlag.

WON-KYU PARK

cross-dressing and cross-gendering

Cross-dressing and cross-gender performance are not new to Japan. There is a long history of gender mobility in both classical and popular performance and literature. This openness to a notion of the performativity of gender identity seems in stark contrast to the apparently strict gender boundaries experienced in everyday life.

The **nō** and **kabuki** are both traditional theatre forms still performed today in which all the actors are male. Reforms in the Edo Period banned women from the stage, a move largely motivated by the desire to undermine links between the theatre and prostitution. In *nō*, an actor will always don a mask to portray a female character, while in *kabuki* make-up and hairstyle as well as costume transform the male actor into the figure of his female role. It is the stylised movements and gestures of the *nō* actor that map a mask of femininity across the entire body of his performance. The voice and movements of the *kabuki* actor portraying a woman are far from realistic, but the flow, pitch, rhythms and rich costuming of the performance are intended to designate, not duplicate, the feminine. The term for a male *kabuki* actor in a female role is *onnagata* – the female form. Among historians and playwrights of the *kabuki* it has frequently been asserted that it is the male *onnagata* who can best step into the form of the feminine. Feminist theatre and literary critics point to the essentialist assumptions of this notion of the feminine. What is important here is the distinction between the realistic capture of a representation and the performative art of rendering a form or figure. Cross-dressing and cross-gendering are premised on the understanding that gender is performative and that the masculine and feminine form can be occupied by any body, male or female.

The most well-known example of cross-gendering in contemporary performance outside the *nō* and *kabuki* is the **Takarazuka**, an all-female review troop based outside Ōsaka. This troop is exceptionally popular with a female audience of adult women and middle- and high-school age girls, and it is the young women who play the male roles (*otokoyaku* – male role) who are the most popular pin-ups, with huge fan clubs of devoted female admirers. The Takarazuka management has been at great pains since the theatre's inception in 1914 to deny the existence of homosexual relations between its actors or between the fans and actors. Despite this, there have been occasional scandals taken up by the media sensationalizing the private lives of troupe members. Similarly, the media delights in every opportunity to expose even the slightest hint of a homosexual relationship on the part of a *nō* or *kabuki* actor. However, these spaces cannot be characterised as simply homosexual, even though as spaces of gender fluidity one of the gender identities that can occupy these spaces is that of the homosexual. There has already been much written on the need to distinguish between the contemporary politics of gay identity both in Japan and elsewhere and the Japanese historical and contemporary conceptualisation and experience of 'same-sex' (*doseiai*) relationships. At least some of these distinctions also apply to any analysis of gender fluidity in these theatrical contexts.

The multiple tensions generated in scenes of love and desire played by same-sex actors are a crucial element of the performativity created in Japan's theatrical spaces, a performativity that flows on stage, and between the actors on stage and the audience, and within the audience.

The play on these cross-gendering tensions is not limited, however, to the theatre and actors. The entertainment world of Japan has always been closely linked to the **mizushōbai** – the realm of drinking, eating, popular entertainment and prostitution. Whether in the tea houses of Edo, the jazz cafés of inter-war Japan or the bars, clubs and cafés of today, there has always been a space for gender bending within the *mizushōbai*. This may take the form of on-stage performance or it may be the clients themselves who are cross-dressing and creating the fluid environment of gender bending. Some bars today are exclusively male or female, with waiters or hosts/hostesses cross-dressing to offer services to a 'straight' clientele – but any

simple line between 'straight' and non-'straight' is already bent in these performative contexts. The flows of sexual desire are unpredictable and this is part of the desirability of entering these spaces. Karaoke bars offering businessmen a wardrobe of dresses, stockings and stilettos remain popular in the entertainment districts. The cross-dressed businessman might serenade his male or female co-workers or both. A new generation of clubs specialise in an array of cross-dressing niche markets for young working women looking for after-hours entertainment, in what they describe as a male-free environment. Here, again, gender and desire are in flux.

There have been only a few examples of popular entertainers who have carried their cross-dressing identity beyond the boundaries of the *mizushōbai* into the wider entertainment domain of television, and the space allowed these performances is largely limited to the realm of comedy. In comics (**manga**), cross-dressing and gender bending or confusion are popular narrative lines. The first cross-dressing characters appeared in the *shōjo manga* of the late 1960s and 1970s, and the young female readers reacted as enthusiastic fans of the beautiful and androgynous hero(ine)s. The theme of gender confusion or gender bending has now found its way into the full range of *manga* markets, and was especially prevalent in adult pornography in the 1990s. In literature, too, there have been a number of notable cross-gendered characters, but perhaps the most well known of recent times was the figure of Eriko – the father/mother in **Yoshimoto Banana**'s *Kitchen*. Eriko's popularity with readers has been offered as one explanation for the fact that, in a popular film version of *Kitchen*, s/he is not murdered early in the story but lives on to happily fall in love with her male analyst. Both the film and novel skirt the issue of Eriko's sexuality while playing intensely on the narrative theme of gender bending.

In the mainstream of everyday life in Japan, the boundaries of identity remain firmly fixed and there is still only limited tolerance of any blurring of gender lines. In a situation where the social fabric of gendered identity is so tightly woven, perhaps we should not be surprised by a fraying at the edges into temporary and localised unravellings of orderly gendered identities.

See also: Takarazuka

Further reading

Buckley, S. (1996) 'Contagion', in C. Davidson (ed.) *Anywise*, Harvard: MIT Press, pp. 80–90.

SANDRA BUCKLEY

cultural geography

The strong bond between culture and landscape is deeply etched in the Japanese national imagination. This bond is woven through a huge range of texts and cultural practices, as primary material in the construction of social identity. We might begin with the creation myth, which claims that the Japanese islands are the progeny of the god Izanagi and the goddess Izanami, who, together with their offspring, established a divine status for all aspects of the physical landscape. This basic concept is carried forward in the beliefs of **State Shintō**, in many respects a religious geography that establishes a moral thread between people and landscape. The romance of the foundation myth is reinscribed upon the contemporary landscape in ways that are both enduring and contradictory.

The physical landscape has been modified according to the ways in which the Japanese people have imagined its possibilities. Japan is an island archipelago, made up of four major islands, and thousands of smaller ones, stretching for 3,800 km (2,360 miles) between 24° N and 42° N latitude. It is separated from the Asian mainland by a sufficient distance to have helped maintain political autonomy, with a considerable degree of cultural exchange, particularly in the adoption of major cultural practices from China. These include written script, the practice of **Buddhism** (an esoteric contrast to the earthly practices of Shintō), major art forms, city planning, agricultural practices and government systems, all of which had influenced the development of the Japanese landscape during the classical period.

Settlement has adapted the natural landscape to suit major cultural developments. The precipitous emergent coastlines of the west and north-west were eschewed in favour of the large central plains, particularly the Yamato Plain, considered the cultural and spiritual centre of the country, where the extensive Chinese systems of living were most thoroughly imposed. It was here, during the eighth century, that the ancient capitals of Nara and **Kyōto** were established as the centre of power and refinement. The system of wet-**rice** agricultural production using hydraulic principles imported from China centuries before, spread out to form the base of the country's wealth and social structure. Access to these areas established the spatial pattern of class and wealth that has, with many modifications, been carried forward to contemporary times.

However, these flat areas were relatively small and inaccessible in a country of mountains and rivers, where geo-tectonic conditions have profoundly influenced settlement patterns and land use. More than 60 per cent of the land is mountainous, the result of volcanic activity that has produced infertile and inaccessible land, but also a deep reverence for the mountains, and an overwhelming aesthetic appreciation for the volcanic form epitomised by **Mt. Fuji**. Originally, the mountains were the abode of small lumbering villages, and Buddhist temples, once separated from the secular cities in order to reduce their political influence.

By the late sixteenth century, warfare dominated as a means of controlling political affairs, and territorial power became a stronger and stronger factor in the development of the cultural landscape. The basic urban structure was established by building **castle towns** as centres of military control and administration, surrounded by rice-producing lands and connected by a carefully controlled system of transportation, the most significant feature of which was the Tokaido. The Tokaido was the nation's first 'highway', connecting the Yamato, or **Kansai**, area to Edo (now **Tokyo**), in the **Kantō** area, a military centre that occupied the country's largest coastal delta and grew to be the most powerful centre of all. Throughout the Tokugawa Period (1615–1868), the nation became strongly consolidated, based on a geographical system of controlling the whereabouts of the samurai (military and administrative class) from Edo, the world's largest city until the late nineteenth century. Edo dominated a growing urban system organised around military castles (see **castle towns**). In between, the Japanese rural countryside flourished or languished largely in relation to the centres of power. The farming classes who inhabited the rural areas made up the dominant social group, their lifestyle richly influenced by both the classical traditions of Yamato and the folk traditions that derived from a more direct relationship with the indigenous landscape. In smaller numbers, and lower down on the social scale, fishing communities were established along the coastline, to provide the major significant traditional source of protein, in a country where Buddhist proscription prevented the consumption of mammals.

Traditional cultural texts reflect this blend, steeped in the aesthetics that surround the practices of Buddhism and strongly reflected in the moral/ aesthetic system of samurai values. Augmented by flora, the image of Fuji-san combines with that of **pine trees**, **cherry blossoms**, and **bamboo**, all of which grow naturally but have been extensively cultivated, to form the major elements in the Japanese canonical landscape, inspiring poetry, visual arts and contemplative **gardens**. Water also provides a significant source of poetic and artistic imagery, in the form of waterfalls on short, rapid mountain rivers, or the sea, which provides dramatic vistas all along the Tokaido, framed by pine trees, and dotted with fishing boats.

The contemporary landscape shows traces throughout of these foundational elements, adapted as deep tradition, but just as often as contradiction, or parody. The interior plateaux and deltaic plains that provided a setting for intensive rice cultivation have been built up into urban conglomerations as dense as any in the world. The coastline that inspired artists and poets for centuries has largely been submerged under massive **land reclamation** projects that extend urban development even further. Ancient highways such as the Tokaido (stretching from Tokyo to **Ōsaka**), which were once strictly controlled access routes in a country where mountainous terrain made travel difficult, are now channels for the *shinkansen* (**bullet train**), arguably the fastest, most efficient and most well-used transportation system in the world. Mountains are tunnelled, or surmounted by impressive spiral bridges, to render

meaningless the barriers of topography. The short, fast rivers are virtually all dammed, to make Japan completely self-sufficient in hydro-electric power. The seas surrounding Japan that provided fish as a major dietary staple now struggle against the effects of pollution created by massive industrial complexes that line the new coastline. Classical images of mountains, cherry trees, pine and bamboo, which translated the natural landscape into a set of highly stylised aesthetic principles, are now conveyed in high powered advertising images pumped out of television sets or plastered in crowded train stations. The Japanese landscape thus resonates with tension between the ultramodern and the putative traditional.

Tension between urban and **rural life**, long established in Japan's political and social geography, remains one of the major motifs of modern Japan. Traditional reverence for agrarian life continues in the relative and disproportionate economic and political power afforded the rural areas, which tend also to be strongly conservative and to support the governing status quo. While land prices are exceptionally high, both in the cities and in the established agricultural regions, in the rural areas recent landscape transformations feature large, substantial houses, a gesture both towards the concentration of resources and the esteem of rural living. Urban areas, in contrast, are increasingly densely built up, with massive tower blocks, and living quarters that are considered cramped by most of the inhabitants. Scarcity of land and density of housing also mean that the daily geography of **commuting** to work, education, shopping and other activities is overwhelming. Workers commonly commute long distances, usually by train, either from suburban areas to central cities, or across metropolitan zones from one section of the city to another.

If Japanese cities are oppressive in their sheer expanse and concentration, they are also fantastic, ultimate expressions of post-modern architectural creativity. The areas surrounding Tokyo Bay, Ōsaka's **Umeda** and **Kobe**'s Port City pile innovation upon parody to form urban landscapes that, until very recently, would have defied imagination. From a scaled-down replica of the Statue of Liberty outside a building in Tokyo, to edifices in Ōsaka created in strange geometric shapes around thirty-storey-high air passages large enough to accommodate a small airplane to a gigantic temple to consumerism erected ziggurat-like above **Kyōto**'s Central Station, Japan's new skyline has a Disney-esque quality that merges the fact of form with the fiction of a Utopian imaginary. Despite a slowdown during the early 1990s, buildings continue to vie with one another to create a more spectacular impression upon the overloaded urban landscape.

However, this is not without contradiction. The ultramodern corporate world stands in stark contrast to the small scenes of conservative tradition in the form of temples, shrines and pocket-sized gardens that still dot the inner cities, and still provide the nucleus of rural villages and towns. In contrast, although it is popular to deny that Japan is a class-based society (and it is true that the range of income between the rich and poor is smaller than for most countries), there remains a very strong spatial separation of the advantaged from the disadvantaged. The *Burakumin*, traditional outcastes, live in segregated and under-serviced areas of cities. People of Korean (see **Koreans in Japan**) background or, more recently, *dekasegi*, migrant workers brought from South-East Asia or South America (most of the latter of Japanese ancestry) to work in low skilled and low paid jobs, are also pushed into distinct and denigrated neighbourhoods. The Ainu, indigenous people who occupy the northern islands, continue their quest for recognition of their cultural autonomy and land rights.

The cultural geography of the everyday is also highly gendered. Whereas men often spend long hours on commuter trains, women lead a much more circumscribed existence. Many housewives are confined to *danchi*, suburban housing developments consisting of vast tracts of crowded high-rise housing. Other women face commutes to work in addition to efforts to accommodate the complicated travel patterns of other household members, including children who commute regularly to school. At night, the pattern is even more distinctive, as men move into the world of restaurants, bars and expense accounts, while women's activities are more closely contained within the home.

The diurnal geography of movement to and from work and home is disrupted on weekends, when Japanese cultural activities take on yet another pattern – of leisure. The recreational landscape exists as a dialectical other to the more staid scene of everyday work, and people alter themselves accordingly, with different clothes, added colour (see **colours, cultural significance of**) and different modes of movement and transportation. Rush hour trains become less crowded, while the highways become more clogged with family groups using automobiles for excursions to Japan's huge number of recreational sites, which include massive shopping areas, traditional shrines, temples, **gardens** and galleries, beaches and spas, **golf** courses, temples to natural sublimity such as Mt. Fuji, or an increasing array of theme parks, the most significant being Disneyland, in Chiba Prefecture, east of Tokyo. However, if these places represent a contrast from more prosaic landscapes of work, they are still highly regulated, excessively crowded, and geared to frenzied consumerism.

Finally, Japan is part of an international cultural geography, also based primarily on consumerism. In the late nineteenth century, Japan was prodded reluctantly into the international world, but assumed its international role with a zeal that had disastrous effects in the events leading up to and during the Second World War. This also included the establishment of a system of international conglomerates, *zaibatsu* that, despite their putative dissolution after the Second World War, have significantly shaped the rapid emergence of Japan as an economic power. While the industrial landscape has come to dominate much of coastal Japan, a geography of global standardisation has permeated the domestic landscape, now fully equipped with the televisions, camcorders, computers and sound systems that make Japan both the instigator and the recipient of global technology and global consumption patterns. As a counterpart to globalisation, however, the Japanese continue to re-imagine themselves according to deeply held ideas of their unique identity, in a continuous interplay between the local and the global.

See also: architecture; gender and work

Further reading

Cybriwsky, Roman (1998) *Tokyo*, Chichester: John Wiley.

Kornhauser, David (1982) *Japan*, London and New York: Longman.

Morris-Suzuki, Tessa (1998) *Re-inventing Japan: Time, Space, Nation*, New York: M.E. Sharpe.

AUDREY KOBAYASHI

culture centres

From the early 1980s, there was an explosion of culture centres offering resources from adult education courses, to library and video loan facilities to counselling. The primary target group of these culture centres has remained housewives, the group with the most control over the day-to-day expenditure of household disposable income. While city and prefectural governments have sponsored the establishment of many community-based culture centres, there has also been strong participation from the retail sector.

The culture centres of major department stores now frequently offer a menu of adult-education courses closely linked to consumer activity – cooking classes, kimono instruction, art classes, foreign languages linked to overseas group travel, etc. Department store culture centres can include art galleries, classroom spaces, drop-in centres and advisory services, ranging from family relations to health and finance. Seibu is the chain best known for recognising the commercial opportunities of creating a full service from commuter line to consumer outlet, and cultural facilities designed to fit the varying needs and schedules of full-time housewives, as well as full- and part-time employed women. The activities of government-sponsored culture centres tend to be more closely linked to local political issues and to have a stronger interest in women's rights when compared to the more commercially driven programmes of the department stores. The leisure industry boom of the 1990s has seen a rapid diversification of commercial offerings that overlap with the activities of culture centres, and there has been a relative decline in the status of culture centres in recent years as middle-class women have sought a wider range of options in the growing commercial leisure market.

SANDRA BUCKLEY

cultured pearls

Although the Chinese are credited with innovating the production of cultured pearls, it is Japan that is renowned today for both pearl cultivation and jewellery. The brand of Mikimoto is synonymous with quality pearl production. Mokichi Mikimoto began experimenting in pearl cultivation in the early 1890s and finally patented the technique for cultivating spherical pearls in 1908. Japanese pearl divers found their ways to such far flung locations as Broome in remote north-western Australia, as others tried to compete unsuccessfully with the Japanese hold on the pearl market over the first half of the twentieth century. Over 70 per cent of the salt-water pearls on the international market are produced in Japan today and the USA consumes close to 25 per cent of that market. Not even 1 per cent of the pearls sold today are natural rather than cultivated pearls. Other than scientific testing, the fastest and surest test of natural versus cultivated pearls is the 'grit test' – when rubbed against a tooth a natural pearl will feel gritty while a cultivated pearl will be smooth. A cultivated pearl takes approximately three years to grow to full size and has a life of some 400 to 500 years. Today, almost perfect spherical pearls remain the most popular, but there is an entirely new market in imperfect pearls, often sought after by connoisseurs for their unique form and colouration.

SANDRA BUCKLEY

Cupola no aru machi

Set in Kawaguchi, a tough steelmill town, *Cupola no Aru Machi* (The Street of Cupolas) was the 1962 feature debut of director and scriptwriter Urayama Kirio and a representative film of star Yoshinaga Sayuri. Then a teenage hitmaker for the Nikkatsu studio, which made *Cupola*, Yoshinaga played Jun, the pure-hearted but spunky daughter of a hard-drinking, hard-headed craftsman who refuses to adapt to new mass-production methods. Though *Cupola* treats various social problems, including labour disputes, the educational difficulties of working-class children and the prejudice encountered by a Korean boy who befriends Yoshinaga and her younger brother, it never descends to the level of a tract, remaining instead a singularly clear-eyed study of Japanese society in the early post-war years. At eighteen, Yoshinaga became the youngest-ever recipient of the coveted Blue Ribbon prize for her portrayal of Jun.

MARK SCHILLING

D

DAISAN NO SHINJIN *see* Third Generation, the

dajare

'*Dajare*' is a coined word that comprises '*da*' ('no good' or 'of inferior quality') and '*sh(J)are*' ('pun' or 'play on words'). Because there are a large number of homonyms in Japanese, word play is relatively easy. Even if words are not homonyms, if you intend to make a pun with words of similar sounds, you can usually convey the humorous intent with relative ease. Except perhaps on formal occasions, a good number of Japanese enjoy the conversational skill of this type of word play in both speech and writing. Even in the emerging e-mail culture of today there is much word play, both intentional and accidental. In the traditional arts of the theatre, from *kabuki* to the more humorous *kyogen* and *rakugo*, there is a love of artful punning. *Share* abound in traditional poetry in the style of the '*tanka*' where one word is so often inhabited by multiple meanings, which can in turn allude to another poem altogether. This skill in poetry is an important measure of the poets' artistry and their knowledge of the tradition. At the same time, the readers' appreciative knowledge of poetry is challenged as they unfold the layered ambiguities of a poem.

In speech, the *dajare* is often a quick throw-away remark or quip delivered with wit and humour. A frequent response is '*Dajare ja nai?*' – 'Isn't that a pun?' – uttered in a half-disapproving but always humorous way. In the arts, the *share* continues to be appreciated as a refined form and in everyday life the *dajare* is social condiment to be sprinkled in amiable interaction.

SHUN IKEDA

danchi

Danchi, in general usage, refers to multi-storey apartment complexes that incorporate many features of Western dwellings, including flush toilets and standardised dining/kitchen layouts. *Danchi*-style apartment buildings first appeared *circa* 1925 in Aoyama and Daikanyama under the auspices of the Dōjunkai, a non-profit government organisation established in 1924 to provide affordable collective housing with modern conveniences to the middle classes, in the wake of the 1923 Great Tokyo Earthquake. Some 12,000 publicly subsidised apartment units were constructed before Dōjunkai was taken over by the government's Jūtaku Eidan (Public Housing Agency) in 1941. Following the Second World War, housing shortages resulted in public housing projects across the country. From 1955, the Japan Housing Corporation facilitated *danchi* development to meet housing shortages for workers, standardising the 2DK (dining/kitchen, with two rooms) and 2LDK (living room, dining/kitchen, with two rooms) layouts. Since 1981, Toshi Kiban Seibi Kōdan (Housing and Urban Development Corporation) has expanded *danchi* into often large-scale residential projects that contain numerous support, service and community facilities. High land prices have put the ideal of a detached single-family home beyond the reach of most middle-class urban dwellers, leaving them few choices outside of increasingly large-scale *danchi* complexes or expensive high-rise **manshon**, or condominiums. Many older *danchi*, lacking contemporary amenities such as lifts, are in critical need of renovation.

See also: manshon; public housing

ICHIRO SUZUKI AND MARY KNIGHTON

day labourers

Day labour is by no means unique to Japan, but there are significant differences in the profile of this section of Japan's workforce. Labour specialists often refer to Japan's floating workforce of day labourers, contract labour and part-timers as an essential element of the flexibility that allows Japanese management to contract and expand the workforce according to fluctuating demand. Part-timers are the fastest growing category of labour in Japan, quickly replacing contract labour, and women of all ages play an important role in this sector. Often denied access to long-term or career-track opportunities, women, and more recently the elderly, resort to part-time work despite significant salary differentials with full-time colleagues and the frequent lack of benefits and union representation. Part-time work also allows women to meet the social pressure to remain the dominant caregiver in a household. By contrast, the majority of day labourers are male, forty-five or over, single or never married, and either homeless or transient. Day labourers, unlike contract and part-time workers, live at the margins of Japanese society.

Only the minority are successful in securing work more than half of the time. The primary areas of work are skilled and unskilled construction and demolition. Day labourers canvas for work seven days a week at predesignated pick-up sites (*yoseba*) around Japan's urban centres. The most infamous day labourer district is San'ya in the Tokyo area. The more skilled and reliable workers will affiliate with a labour broker and can expect more regular employment and wages on completion of work (often minus a broker fee). The conditions of work for day labourers are notoriously treacherous, and accident and injury rates are high. An injury is often the difference between life as a day labourer and homelessness and unemployment. The strong links between the construction industry and organised crime (*yakuza*) means that there is an inevitable criminal presence, which can function in a distinctly benevolent mode towards the day labourers but also sees occasional outbursts of violence. Day labourers will often speak of the *yakuza* protecting their interests and standing up for them against police and contractors.

The culture of the day labourers is intensely homosocial with strong, if short-term networks of support among the men who live in the cramped boarding rooms of these districts. With many spending more time looking for work than working, the culture of day labourers is at one level a culture of non-work, combining long hours of solitariness as well as a gaming, betting and drinking. The need to get out of cramped boarding houses brings the men together in the bars, cheap *kissaten* and gambling facilities that abound around the *yoseba* districts. Illegal immigrants are not as common as Japanese who have fallen out of the mainstream but these two subcultures live side by side in the *yoseba* districts. Few day labourers tell their stories uncensored and there is tremendous distrust of outsiders, which inhibits the work of even the best-intentioned researchers and welfare workers. Police surveillance is high, which places additional pressure on illegal immigrants. Day labourers often share their everyday spaces with illegals and the women of the *mizushōbai*, many of whom are themselves illegal immigrants. The future of day labour within the Japanese economy is at best uncertain. While at the time of the Tokyo Olympics construction boom there were estimates of 15–20,000 day labourers in the San'ya district alone, the faltering construction industry of the late 1990s has seen that population fall to 6–5,000. Some estimate that as many as 40 per cent of the San'ya workers are over sixty. As work becomes scarcer, squatter tents and cardboard dwellings are replacing crowded boarding houses, and charity and welfare services are providing an essential level of services and food to this increasingly marginalised population.

SANDRA BUCKLEY

Dazai Osamu

b. 1909, Kanagi; d. 1948, Tokyo

Writer

Dazai Osamu was one of the most popular authors of fiction in post-war Japan. Born Tsushima Shūji, he was the tenth son of a wealthy land-owning family in Kanagi, a town in Aomori Prefecture on the north-eastern tip of Honshū. After completing his schooling in Aomori, Dazai entered Tokyo Imperial University in April 1930 to study French. Six months later, after agreeing to marry a geisha called Oyama Hatsuyo, Dazai attempted suicide with a bar girl, the first of a number of attempts on his own life.

By 1933, Dazai had adopted his pen name and was starting to establish a reputation as a budding author and abandoned any attempts at studying. His first collection of stories, entitled *Bannen* (The Final Years), appeared in June 1935 during a period of physical and mental decline. Only five months later, Dazai was admitted to a mental hospital where he finally cured a drug addiction and recovered much of his physical strength. Other suicide attempts followed until 1938, when Dazai separated from Hatsuyo and began writing in earnest once again. He remarried in 1939 and, by this time, had published various stories including 'Mangan' (A Promise Fulfilled, 1938), 'Fugaku hakkei' (One Hundred Views of Mt. Fuji, 1939), 'Joseitō' (Schoolgirl, 1939) and 'Hazakura to mateki' (Cherry Leaves and the Whistler, 1939). Dazai received a literary award for 'Schoolgirl' and the war years saw his fame as a writer increase.

'Kakekomi uttae' (I Accuse, 1940) was Dazai's version of Judas's betrayal of Jesus; this story was followed by 'Hashire Merosu' (Run Melos!, 1940), 'Tōkyō hakkei' (Eight Views of Tokyo, 1941) and his first full-length novel (in the form of a play) *Shin Hamuretto* (A New Hamlet, 1941). During wartime, Dazai wrote *Udaijin Sanetomo* (Sanetomo, Minister of the Right, 1943), a novel based on an account in a thirteenth-century chronicle of the life of the shōgun Minamoto Sanetomo (1192–1219). In late 1944, Dazai wrote a long memoir of a trip back to his family home in Tsugaru entitled *Tsugaru*, which Japanese critics have acclaimed and generally treat as a novel.

Dazai's two most important novels were written after the war: *Shayō* (The Setting Sun, 1947) and *Ningen shikkaku* (No Longer Human, 1948). The former work tells the story of a declining aristocratic family that cannot adapt to post-war changes. The latter work chronicles the life of a character remarkably similar to Dazai, but whose sensitivity and sincerity doom him to unhappiness.

Dazai's fiction often constructs versions of Dazai himself and frequently is based upon his own life. His style has a peculiar brilliance, shifting from first to third person and back again, interjecting the narrator into the text in an intimate and powerful way that has attracted many readers. The extreme circumstances under which he lived much of his life, his addiction, drinking, womanising, illnesses and attempted suicides all contributed to a tragic figure that particularly appealed to the imaginations of young female readers, resulting in an almost cult-like following over the 1970s and 1980s during a revival of interest in his life and works. Dazai did finally succeed in taking his own life in 1948 when he drowned himself in a double suicide with a woman, an early death under romantic circumstances that only intensified the tragic aura of his life and writings.

Further reading

Dazai Osamu (1958) *No Longer Human*, trans. Donald Keene, New York: New Directions.

Lyons, Phyllis (1985) *The Saga of Dazai Osamu: A Critical Study with Translations*, Stanford, CA: Stanford University Press.

LEITH MORTON

death and funerals

The Japanese understanding of death and burial practices has derived over centuries of interaction between the distinct but not incompatible beliefs and practices of Shintō and Buddhism. Many Japanese today, when asked to describe death and the afterlife, present a blend of Shintō spirit beliefs and Buddhist tales, and a mix of rituals from both traditions.

Within Shintō, each person is believed to host a spirit or *tama*, which departs the body on death.

During illness, the *tama* hovers outside the living body and many of the Shintō rituals and prayers associated with illness are intended to encourage the *tama* to linger and to exhort the departure of any harmful spirit or curse that might be endangering the ill person. There are various Shintō scenarios for the afterlife of the *tama*. In some versions, the spirit of the dead departs to the peak of a holy or sacred mountain. Offerings are made at a shrine at the base of the mountain, but the living do not ascend to the peak. The spirits are also thought to depart across water to the land of Tokoyo or to Yomi, the dark underworld of the dead. In Shintō, there is no active notion of heaven and hell as distinct destinations determined by action in life. All spirits travel to the same destination, but the transition is not always smooth and the living have an obligation to dedicate prayers and offerings to the dead for thirty-three years. Only after that length of attentive nourishment will the spirit take up its permanent place in the ancestral spiritual domain. Neglected spirits, spirits without descendants to care for them, spirits of those who die wishing for revenge and spirits of those who died violently or under extreme circumstances can all heap curses and disaster on the world of the living unless carefully placated. Within Shintō, it is also believed that the spirits return to this world at certain times of the year (e.g. **Obon**) when the living welcome and make offerings to them in thanks for their continued benevolence.

In Buddhism, an individual's actions accumulate in their karma and it is the weight of this karma, for better or worse, that is said to determine one's destination in the next life. Death is viewed not as an end or passage to an afterlife but as a step to the next life, with the ultimate goal of achieving a level of enlightenment needed to attain nirvana. All who die pass into a transitional or in-between state of darkness, where they stay for a period before rebirth into one of the six realms according to their karma – hell dwellers and demons/hungry ghosts/animals/*ashura*/humankind/gods (above these six sit the Buddhas in the ultimate state of nirvana). The major Buddhist sects in Japan have tended to focus on devotional techniques to bypass this dark state and move directly to the next stage of rebirth. Buddhist belief in rebirth situates the living and the dead in a very different relationship from Shintō. Buddhism does not place the same taboos and pollutions on death and this offers a real opportunity for these two belief systems to complement one another.

Japanese Buddhism is often described as 'funereal Buddhism' because so much of the work of the temples and priests is focused on funeral rituals and rites, and prayers for the dead. The historical decision that all families must register at a temple promoted the role of Buddhism as the locus of ancestral care and worship. Family graves were moved inside the temple compound and temple member households came to rely on the priests for the related devotional rituals, which became something of a blend of Shintō and Buddhist practices. Many families will maintain a link to both a temple and a shrine but rely heavily on the temple for matters relating to death and burials. This role has become a crucial source of economic stability for Buddhism in Japan, with priests holding virtually a captive market in what has evolved into a very expensive area of ritual practice.

In many households there will be both a *kamidana* (Shintō) and a *butsudana* (Buddhist) for offerings for the dead, while some households simply have a hybrid of both. When talking about the fate of their ancestors, many Japanese will fluctuate back and forth between Buddhist and Shintō elements of afterlife, vengeful and benevolent spirits, karma and rebirth. While Buddhist priests will deal with the handling of the corpse and burial, Shintō priests may be called upon to deal with the pollution of death when a person has died at home or after the body has been laid out for viewing. Also, both religions offer various services to eliminate the threat of a lingering or vengeful spirit. While Buddhism has taken up much of the institutionalised ritual of death, the relationship of families and communities to their ancestral spirits remains closely linked to Shintō practice through popularised festivals and celebrations. In death, as in so many other things, the Japanese are resourceful in making the most of the full range of options available.

See also: Buddhism; State Shintō

SANDRA BUCKLEY

DEATH BY HANGING *see Kōshikei*

Democratic Party

The Democratic Party of Japan was founded in 1996 from members of the Social Democratic Party and Shintō Sakigake. In 1997, after the dissolution of the New Frontier Party (Shinshin-tō), the Democratic Party became the largest opposition group in the Diet. In April 1998, the party picked up more members by merging with three other smaller parties. Led by the charismatic Naoto Kan, the Democrats were the biggest winners in the July 1998 Upper House elections, picking up nine seats for a total of twenty-seven. Naoto, perhaps the most popular politician in the country at the time, led the fight to oust former **Liberal Democratic Party** (LDP) Prime Minister Hashimoto. Naoto rose to popularity by challenging the power of the bureaucratic powers in the government when he was Minister of Health and Welfare in 1996 under a coalition government. He exposed ministry bureaucrats for covering up the sale of HIV-tainted blood (see **tainted-blood scandal**). This experience led Naoto and Hatoyama Mikio to organise a new party to reform the system. The Democratic Party's views tend to be progressive and centrist, seeking more open markets, greater deregulation and greater tax cuts. At the beginning of 1999, the Democratic Party controlled fifty-six (22 per cent of total) seats in the Upper House and ninety-four (19 per cent) seats in the Lower House.

DAVID EDGINGTON

Democratic Socialist Party

The now defunct Democratic Socialist Party (DSP) was once a major 'middle of the road' party in Japanese politics. It was established in 1960 when right-wing members of the **Japan Socialist Party** (JSP) broke away to form their own group. The foundation of the DSP represented the fifth of seven schisms in the socialist movement in Japan between 1947 and 1978. Ideological differences within the movement, the increasing salience of defence and foreign-policy issues in Japanese

politics, conflict within the labour movement and declining prospects for political advancement for right-wing members within the JSP hierarchy were among the major factors precipitating the split.

The primary political support base of the DSP was Dōmei (the Japanese Confederation of Labour), the former conservative private-sector labour federation, which provided roughly one-third of its political funds, and mobilised most of its votes. While Dōmei provided DSP support, the former Sōhyō (General Council of Trade Unions of Japan) provided similar support to the JSP. Apart from conservative labour, small business was the other contributor to this party. It had a concentrated regional support, especially in Aichi, Kanagawa and Ōsaka Prefectures, all urban concentrations of unionised private-sector workers and small businesses. The DSP also retained some backing from intellectuals who saw the party as a moderate, socially progressive, non-radical alternative to the communists.

Like the **Liberal Democratic Party** (LDP) and the Komeito parties, it supported the security treaty with the USA and the Self-Defence Forces. As the most conservative of the opposition parties, it often formed coalitions with the LDP. The DSP's major formal policy goals were the attainment of a welfare state in Japan through major expansion of social security benefits and an intensification of anti-unemployment counter-measures. However, while its stance was fairly similar to other opposition parties on social welfare issues, it diverged sharply on many questions of defence and economic policy, for example, strongly supporting the active development of nuclear power for commercial purposes.

The support for the DSP had declined steadily from its founding and especially in the late 1980s, after it was revealed that party chairman Tsukumoto Saburō received 5,000 shares of stock from Recruit (see **Recruit scandal**), and was later forced to resign. None the less, it entered into the anti-LDP coalition of eight parties that ruled under Prime Minister Hosokawa from 1993 to 1994. The formation of Rengō in 1989 brought together many of the unions in Sōhyō and Dōmei; however, this did not lead to unification of the DSP and the JSP. After 1994, the JSP joined the LDP in a coalition government, while the DSP decided to disband itself to join the New Frontier Party (Shinshin-tō or NFP) in 1995 (together with the Japan New Party and Komeitō), which went on to win substantial seats in the 1995 House of Councillors (Upper House of the Diet). Many former SDF Diet members then joined the Democratic Party when it formed in 1996, which after the dissolution of the New Frontier Party became the largest opposition group to the LDP in the Diet.

DAVID EDGINGTON

Dentsu

Established in Tokyo in 1901, Dentsu initially functioned as the Japanese Telecommunications Corporation and combined both telecommunications and advertising. From 1936, it shifted exclusively to advertising. It is now Japan's largest advertising agency with a staff of 5,683 staff (1998) and a complex structure of highly resourced, specialised departments.

In 1973, Dentsu was named the top advertising agency in the world by the trade magazine *Advertising Age* and, again in 1998, it was ranked fourth in gross income, and the top ranking independent agency. It holds 22.3 per cent of Japan's market share, almost twice that of its nearest competitor, Hakuhodo. This level of market dominance is possible because in Japan there are no client exclusivity limits. Thus, as a fully independent, in theory Dentsu could run campaigns at the same time for Toyota, Honda and Nissan. Fifty per cent of Dentsu's sales are in television marketing, followed by newspaper, sales promotion, magazines and radio, in that order.

In the post-war period, Dentsu and, in particular, Yoshida Hideo – often referred to as the pioneer of the advertising world – leant great weight to the push for public television broadcasting and promoted the development of national networks with a vision of this space as an influential platform for the rapid growth of both the media and advertising. Dentsu has maintained a central and powerful role in shaping broadcast and new-media technologies and their content. From the time of the Tokyo Olympics and Ōsaka Expo,

Dentsu has positioned itself as the leading event manager in the country and demonstrated a strong interest in the production of a national image for Japan both domestically and internationally.

With offices in thirty-two Japanese cities, and an international network extending over thirty-four countries and forty-six cities, and with twenty-three affiliates within the Dentsu group, this is now unquestionably a reputable and influential international agency. Dentsu has also moved aggressively into the world of cyber-advertising and is the Japanese representative of Yahoo. In addition, Dentsu offers extensive new-media research, cyber-think tank facilities and international production and PR liaison in print and broadcast media, as well as digital communications. Dentsu is committed not only to developing advertising for new digital platforms but is also actively designing innovative content options. As part of its commitment to continued growth Dentsu is planning a share float in 2001 as a source of R&D and growth capital. There are also plans for a centralisation of services and facilities in the Tokyo area in a new office building scheduled for 2002.

Dentsu will certainly have an important role in any future internationalisation of Japan's domestic advertising market. There has been strong criticism of barriers to entry from international majors and Dentsu is well placed to open up the market to global trends and competition. Dentsu has achieved a position as leader in the advertising industry, an industry that is now arguably the primary source of Japan's new cultural products.

See also: advertising

NANBA KŌJI

department stores

Japanese department stores, formally referred to as *hyakkaten* but now more commonly known as *depāto*, are prestigious large-scale retailers offering high-quality service and a wide variety of brand-name goods, from clothing and accessories to books and electronics. According to a 1997 survey, 66 per cent of the respondents said that he or she visited a department store or similar establishment at least once a week, and annual *depāto* sales in 1998 came to 9,063 billion yen. Fierce competition exists between the major department stores, often clustered together in urban centres, particularly at train and subway station complexes. Rather than slashing prices, however, this rivalry is generally pursued by cultivating a distinctive store image through advertising, obtaining exclusive rights to designer lines and holding special events ranging from toy fairs and fashion shows to concerts and art exhibits.

Early in the twentieth century, certain prominent retail establishments with centuries of history behind them, such as Mitsukoshi, Shirokiya and Takashimaya, reorganised as modern department stores. Self-consciously patterned after European and US models, these stores contributed greatly to the formation of new modes of urban mass consumption. Previously, clerks selected items to show to a customer waiting in the front area of a store, or sent goods on order directly to the customer's home. However, one key aspect of reorganisation as a department store entailed reshaping store space to allow customers to wander at will among display cases, free to comparison shop or simply browse. This new consumer–commodity interaction was pioneered at late nineteenth-century national expositions and product centres known as *kankōba*, but department stores took this to new heights, introducing further innovations, show windows, rest areas, restaurants, home delivery and the employment of young women as clerks and store guides. Shopping was transformed from a mundane task to a respectable leisure activity for the whole family. Targeting the growing white-collar sector, department stores eagerly assumed responsibility for educating consumers in the ways of a 'modern lifestyle' through tutorials, model room displays, cultural exhibits and store journals featuring essays by prominent intellectuals.

From the late 1920s, the so-called 'traditional' department stores were joined by 'terminal' department stores built by such railway companies as Hankyū and Tōkyū to capitalise on growing numbers of middle-class commuters. Terminal department stores initially concentrated on the sale of daily necessities, but soon moved into luxury items and sponsoring cultural events. Established department stores also began to take advantage of the opportunities offered by railway and subway hubs to expand and orient themselves toward a broader clientele.

During the Second World War, department stores contributed to the war effort by staging patriotic exhibits, sending goods to the warfront and complying with government regulations regarding civilian consumption, but increasingly suffered from shortages in supplies, reduced personnel and damage from Allied air raids. In the immediate aftermath of defeat, Mitsukoshi reasserted its cultural profile by offering art exhibits and a temporary home for *kabuki* productions, setting an example for its competitors. Department stores were still plagued by shortages and inflation during the early years of the **Allied Occupation**, but by the early 1950s sales began to climb. As incomes doubled and massive numbers of Japanese moved from rural areas to metropolitan centres, department stores did their best to feed a growing appetite for consumer goods during the heyday of high economic growth. They also continued to play a central role in the cultural scene, collaborating with newspapers to outperform national museums in drawing millions to the first Japanese exhibits to showcase original overseas masterpieces, such as works by French Impressionist masters. They also held, and still hold, shows featuring avant-garde as well as traditionalist Japanese artists, who regard such an opportunity as a sign of having 'made it'.

While some department stores had established regional, even overseas, branches well before the war, the 1960s and early 1970s marked a period of rapid expansion. Department stores have faced a series of ongoing challenges from superstores from the 1960s, suburban shopping centres from the 1970s, and a mid-1970s shift in consumer spending patterns, often described as the fragmentation of the mass market. In response, department stores have been investing more energy into diversification and the formation of joint partnerships.

No more striking illustration of various post-war trends exists than the terminal department store Kikuya, established by the Keihin Kyūkō railway line in 1940 at Ikebukuro Station. Renamed Seibu in 1949, the store flourished during the suburban real-estate boom and extension of the subway system of the 1950s, and in turn contributed to the transformation of its backwater surroundings to a vital commercial district. Seibu has come to rival the venerable Mitsukoshi as Japan's leading department store with the creation of a corporate image geared towards younger consumers, and by tapping into shifting market trends with such speciality stores as the boutique outlet Parco (1969) and the thematically organised shopping and arts centre SEED (1986). The Seibu Saison Group also includes supermarkets, convenience stores and hotels. Other department stores have also sought to rejuvenate their corporate images, experimenting with niche marketing, credit sales and information-based services.

The basic layout of major department stores, however, remains similar to the pre-war, class-inflected model of foods in the basement, clothing and accessories on the first and central floors, and each new level more expensive and exclusive than the one below. Upper floors usually feature house-wares, stationery, books and other miscellaneous items, while the top floor is reserved for major exhibits and special sales. It should also be noted that the department store sector is distinctive in that an estimated 70 to 80 per cent of both customers and employees are female, and this sector is unusually open to the employment of women as management and specialists as well as clerks.

Further reading

Lein, F. (1987) 'Department stores in Japan', *Institute of Comparative Culture Business* Series, no. 116, Tokyo: Sophia University Press.

MacPherson, K. (ed) (1998) *Asian Department Stores*, Honolulu: University of Hawaii Press, pp. 141–281.

NORIKO ASO

dialects

There is a standardised Japanese (*hyōjungo*) widely accepted and used throughout the nation, but it is well known, too, that each local area has its own dialect both at a lexicon level and at a phonological level. In extreme cases, two people from different dialect areas cannot understand one another well.

However, not all dialects are as isolated and intensely localised as this. Even in the pre-modern Edo Period (1600–1868), before standardised Japanese was created, and especially in the early to mid-nineteenth century, domestic trade flourished and trading merchants travelled, mainly by ship, from the large commercial centres (e.g. Ōsaka and Kobe) to many parts of Japan, including the remoter Hokuriku and western Tōhoku regions. As a result of these early trade contacts, there remain linguistic traces of the influence of Kansai (Ōsaka, Kobe and Kyōto area) dialect in some Hokuriku and Tōhoku dialects despite the geographic distances involved.

With a rapid spread of broadcasting media, mainly radio and television, *hyōjungo* (standardised Japanese) has become prevalent everywhere in Japan. Standardised textbooks and a uniform national system of language learning strictly monitored by the Ministry of Education have also contributed to the successful overlay of *hyōjungo* across the diversity of local dialects. Some people are concerned about the gradual decline of local dialects, as younger generations tend to adopt *hyōjungo* as their own 'native tongue' and neglect or reject local dialects as unfashionable or too traditional. However, the more common pattern of dialect usage is context based – *hyōjungo* in the classroom and other formal or official contexts, and dialect in informal settings. Even young Japanese who might opt not to use dialect for a period of time still interact with dialect speakers in their everyday lives and often revert to dialect usage when older if they remain in the local area.

Massive early post-war levels of rural to urban migration into the Kansai, Kinki and Kantō regions played another important role in the consolidation of *hyōjungo*. People who aspired to work in the big cities, Tokyo in particular, adopted *hyōjungo* as the normative medium of communication. Dialects were considered tainted or negatively marked as indicators of lack of sophistication or education. In the popular media, from television to comics, dialects became the object of much humour and even derision. In what some consider an extension of the never-ending cultural rivalry between Kansai and Kantō regions, the Ōsaka dialect has remained far more markedly present in commercial and official contexts and many Ōsaka people insist with pride on speaking the

immediately recognisable *Ōsaka-ben* (dialect) wherever they are doing business. Kyōto is another city
that takes great pride in its dialect and locals are
often loath to subordinate it to any pressure to shift
into standardised Japanese.

More recently, there has been a re-evaluation of
the negative marking of dialects and even school
curricula are shifting towards an acknowledgement
of the intrinsic cultural value of maintaining and
respecting local dialects, while also promoting
hyōjungo fluency. Television programmes and films
have shifted from the use of dialect for mere local
flavour, or to create easy caricatures and stereotypes, to now working to depict dialects with an
appreciation of the cultural significance and
important subtlety of nuance that can be achieved.

There is a growing acceptance of local dialects on
national radio and television, and there has been a
trend to restore local dialects in regional radio and
television broadcasting, although some areas still
remain the domain of *hyōjungo* – especially the
newsdesk. Another recent shift in attitude has
occurred among the young, who are increasingly
taking up dialect as a distinctive marker of difference
and even extending its use to exaggerated levels that
have been coined hyper-dialect. In this context,
dialect functions almost as an accessory in the highly
performative and stylised realm of Japanese youth
culture. While some local dialects have already
disappeared, many have survived, and there are
strong indications that the recent re-evaluation and
restoration of the validity of dialects will see them
maintained into the future alongside *hyōjungo*.

SHUN IKEDA

dietary patterns

Traditional Japanese dietary patterns had **rice** as
the staple food and **seafood** and vegetables as
okazu (side dishes). In underprivileged families and
during times of emergency, rice was often supplemented or substituted by other crops such as barley,
beans, millet and sweet potatoes. The centrality of
rice, however, was indisputable: *okazu* was regarded
as something that enhances appetite. While the
production of rice is closely related to **State
Shintō** rituals, the influence of **Buddhism** is

evident in vegetarianism in the Japanese diet. Meat
was not widely eaten until Meiji. Since transportation and distribution of fresh foods were limited,
each region had its specialties. Food was eaten
fresh, or with simple cooking such as boiling and
grilling. The culinary ideal was to maximise the
natural flavour of seasonal ingredients. For preservation, salt, *shōyu*, **miso** and vinegar were used,
and hence *okazu* tended to be salty.

Although the basic pattern of rice and *okazu* has
been maintained throughout the post-war period,
the balance, quantity and quality of food have
changed remarkably, as the nation became more
affluent. Between 1965 and 1985, the consumption
of rice per capita decreased by about 30 per cent,
and the consumption of potatoes halved. Almost all
the other items, including vegetables, fruit, meat,
seafood, eggs, sugar, fat, milk and dairy products,
have increased dramatically in the same period.
This clearly shows the trend away from rice and
towards a variety of *okazu*.

Dietary patterns are closely related to lifestyle.
Average time spent for food preparation in the
household decreased from three hours in 1970 to
two-and-a-half in 1990. This is partly due to the
use of electrical appliances such as freezers and
microwave ovens, but more importantly it is
supported by the huge food-processing and dis-
tributing industries, and the increased use of
restaurants and take-away foods. Supermarkets
and convenience stores are full of ready-to-eat or
easy-to-cook foods. Families can enjoy meals at
reasonable prices in 'family restaurants' and fast-
food chains. Besides speed and convenience,
variety has widened considerably. With the 'gourmet boom' of the 1980s and 1990s, 'ethnic' cuisines
from the Middle East and South-East Asia were
added to the already popular Japanese, Chinese,
French and Italian food.

The Japanese diet, with its high intake of
vegetables and low intake of animal fat, is regarded
as healthier than that of other industrialised
nations. There are, however, some problems. Food
safety is undoubtedly one of the most serious issues.
The increased efficiency in food production and
processing has created a situation where the
consumer is unknowingly exposed to various toxic
chemicals and preservatives. From the 1970s
onwards, various groups and individuals have

urged the government and industry to improve safety standards and regulations. Another important issue is the notable drop in food self-sufficiency. While the 1970 figure shows 60 per cent, in 1990 it was a mere 46 per cent, the lowest by far among industrialised countries. Many have been warning against the economic and ecological implications of this.

TOMOKO AOYAMA

discipline in schools

Discipline in Japanese schools begins on the first day of school with rituals and routines of acceptable behaviour. These routines are reinforced through classroom organisation as well as by parents and society at large. Each class is divided into small groups, called *han*, who are responsible for each other. Students take turns serving as class monitors, calling the class together, assisting the teacher and initiating activities. The teacher is thus freed from much of the classroom management. Students become accountable not only for their own behaviour but also that of their *han*. Rarely are individual students disciplined. Fear of embarrassment and shame play a significant role in curtailing deviant behaviour. Similarly, the desire to fit in with the group norm inhibits much independent delinquent behaviour.

Tannin, or home-room teachers, are responsible for the discipline of their students. These teachers pride themselves in knowing their students well enough to maintain control without overt coercion. They conduct home visits that provide parents with guidelines for student behaviour. Students also receive a small rule book, *seito techō*, to inform their behaviour and dress. A photograph shows a student in appropriate attire, including length of hair, length of uniform, etc.

JUNE A. GORDON

divorce

Divorce, like marriage, is governed by the Civil Code in Japan, but in practice is a matter of consent between the parties. More than 90 per cent of divorcing couples in Japan dissolve their marriages as they created them – by agreement. The parties' agreement is effected through registration under the Family Registration Law. Family registers are kept at local government offices, for example the local City Hall, and are a consolidated record of birth, death, marriage, divorce, adoption and name-change for each household. The usual procedure is for both of the divorcing parties to seal the notification of divorce with their personal seal and then to file this at the local government family registry. Fraudulent use of the other party's seal is not unknown, but the sealed notification has presumptive validity.

Where a married couple disagrees about the divorce, or disputes property, or where custody of children must be decided or ratified, a judicial divorce in the Family Court is required. Typically, the Family Court compels the parties to undergo court-annexed mediation with a view to reaching a negotiated outcome that can then be ratified. Some studies have pointed to a tendency of Family Court mediators in the past to urge reconciliation rather than divorce in cases where children are involved, in part because some social stigma still attaches to divorce in Japan. Another factor has been that schemes of automatic spousal maintenance and non-custodial access to children were not well developed, so that a non-working woman being divorced by a husband would in many cases face a difficult economic future. Spouses can make claims relating to the division of property, but they must do this within two years of the divorce.

Following the Second World War and the wide-ranging revision of Japan's Constitution and Civil Code, the principle of no-fault divorce was introduced. Grounds for divorce under Article 770 of the Civil Code are:

1 acts of unchastity;
2 malicious desertion;
3 a spouse's whereabouts are unknown for three years or more;
4 incurable mental illness; or
5 any other serious reason.

The last ground was arguably a provision allowing no-fault divorce, but, until the 1980s, the courts interpreted the Code narrowly and disallowed simple claims of incompatibility on social policy grounds. Since then, divorce has become more common and the legal culture has slowly adapted to this social change.

Because the Civil Code still requires that a married couple adopt the same surname, the party in a divorce who adopted the other party's name at marriage resumes their own surname at the time of divorce, and notifies this to the family registry.

One of the gender anomalies remaining in the Civil Code is that a divorcing woman is prevented from remarrying until six months after the date of the divorce. The rationale for this limitation is to allow paternity to be established in the case where the woman was pregnant at the time of the divorce.

VERONICA TAYLOR

documentary film

The Allied Occupation attempted to reconstruct Japan in its own democratic image through documentary and newsreels. To this end, radical film-makers who had quietly waited out the war were called upon to lead the post-war industry. Despite suppressions of early works – such as the atomic bomb film **Nihon no higeki** (A Japanese Tragedy) – and an elaborate system of censorship, most documentarists in the mid-1950s were aligned with the Japan Communist Party. A notable exception was Kamei Fumio, who made independent documentaries about the atomic bombings and protests against US military bases. Most documentary film-makers, however, worked in journalism and PR. Young film-makers under the wing of Hani Susumu, then head of Iwanami Publishing's PR film unit, began identifying with the politics of the New Left and went independent around 1960. For the next fifteen years, the independent documentary scene was vibrant with powerful and innovative film-making. Two figures tower above the others: Tsuchimoto Noriaki, the director of the **Minamata series**, and Ogawa Shinsuke, whose collective made a series of films on the Sanrizuka Struggle at the construction site of Narita Airport. As this generation made its finest works in the mid-1970s, brilliant first films by Hara Kazuo and Suzuki Shirōyasu signalled the appearance of a new breed of documentarist. The new

films eschewed collective production for a more artisanal mode that focused primarily on the self and its relationship to the world, a trend that became increasingly depoliticised as television became virtually the only distribution route for documentary.

ABÉ MARK NORNES

Dodge Line

The Dodge Line is also known as the Dodge Plan, but in Japanese is often called the Economic Stabilisation Programme (*keizai antei kyūgensoku*). In the immediate post-war years, Japan experienced high inflation and serious economic hardship. In December 1948, a series of anti-inflationary initiatives were recommended to the Japanese government aimed at wage and price control, and increased fiscal stability. Measures included increased raw-materials production, a foreign exchange rate set at 360 yen to the US dollar, reduced credit and the winding down of the Reconstruction Finance Bank, privatisation of international trade and export expansion, balanced budgets, increased food supplies, wage and price controls, and decreased government intervention in the marketplace. The USA pushed for these initiatives as a means of reducing Japanese dependency on US financial aid and strengthening the Japanese economy as one part of the US cold-war strategy in the region. While there was a reduction in consumer prices and a zero inflation rate for the period of the Dodge reforms, there was also a related increase in unemployment that affected the hardest hit areas of Japanese society. Joseph Dodge, for whom the plan is named, was a US banker posted to Japan as General Mac-Arthur's financial adviser from 1949 to 1952.

SANDRA BUCKLEY

Doi Takeo

b. 1920, Tokyo

Psychiatrist

The work of Doi Takeo, one of Japan's pioneers in

psychiatry, is associated with the social and psychological characteristic of the Japanese people called *amae*, or the concept of dependency, which has no direct equivalent in English. Drawing on a wide range of material from psychoanalysis, anthropological and literary theory, he defines *amae* as the desire 'to presume upon another's love', 'to bask in' or 'indulge in another's kindness'.

Amae no Kōzo (Anatomy of Dependence), published in 1971, became a best-seller. In it, he sees *amae* not only as the way the Japanese reconcile the dilemma between *giri* (obligations) and *ninjo* (feelings) (see **giri and ninjo**), but also as the fundamental formation of the mother–child relationship. Following the American Ruth Benedict, author of *The Chrysanthemum and the Sword* (1946), Doi belongs firmly in the tradition of the psychosocial school of Japanese culture, which, in the process of constructing the national culture, sometimes promotes roles that contribute to inequality and discrimination. Moreover, it is worth remembering the context in which Doi's book was written. The analysis of *amae* that Doi offers is considered by some a reflection of the post-war relationship between the USA and Japan. Doi's work remains both widely used and controversial.

MIDORI HAYASHI

Dōmei

Dōmei is short for Zen Nihon Rōdō Sōdōmei, a union federation created in the image of **Sōdō-mei**, the Japan Federation of Labour. It was founded in 1964 by rightist unions in opposition to the leftist policies of the dominant labour federation, **Sōhyō**. Dōmei disbanded in 1987, its unions (along with most of Sōhyō's) joining the new nationwide federation, **Rengō**. Dōmei's formation in 1964 coincided with the formation of the transfederation metalworking union association, **IMF-JC**, and like the latter represented the disenchantment of most large private-sector unions with the increasing dominance of Sōhyō by public-sector unions. The mid-1960s marked a watershed in Japan's post-war economic growth, the moment when heavy industry consolidated its control over the economy and heavy industrial unions took the leading position within the labour movement. Although a number of important heavy industrial unions remained outside of Dōmei (especially the steelworkers, **Tekkō Rōren**), Dōmei rapidly became home to the largest number of private-sector and heavy industrial unions (from 1967 representing more of them than Sōhyō). Dōmei allied closely with the **Democratic Socialist Party** (Minshu Shakaitō), the right wing that split from the Socialist Party in 1960.

Further reading

Ikuo Kume (1997) *Disparaged Success*, Ithaca: Cornell University Press

MICHAEL GIBBS

domestic-labour debates

The first debate on domestic labour was triggered in 1955, when Ishigaki Ayako published an article criticising women who gave up their professions for marriage. Others argued that being a housewife should be recognised as a profession, or argued for the importance of the political activities of women who mobilised as housewives. In 1960, Isono Fujiko and Mizuta Tamae engaged in a debate on how society should value domestic labour. Some contributors to the debate suggested that women's domestic labour should be considered in the calculation of their husband's salaries, or that women should receive a special allowance in recognition of their labour. The economic value of domestic labour also proved to be of interest to several Marxist theorists, who attempted to apply Marxist theories of value to this question. A similar debate had erupted in the early twentieth century, and some feminists suggested that the possibility of this same debate recurring in the second half of the century indicated the tenaciousness of the 'good wife, wise mother' (*ryōsaikembo*) philosophy in Japan. Even since the passage of EEO legislation in the 1980s, there have continued to be occasional public revivals of the debate over women's paid and unpaid work, and the related status of motherhood.

See also: Agnes-chan; feminism; Housewives' Association; motherhood; Mothers' Convention

Further reading

Ueno, C. (ed.) (1982) *Shufu ronsō o yomu*, 2 vols, Tokyo: Keisō Shobō.

VERA MACKIE

domestic technologies

The electric fan, in 1916, was the first household electric appliance to be manufactured in Japan. From 1930, electric clothes irons began to be mass produced and were the most popular electric appliance before the Second World War. Electric refrigerators and vacuum cleaners were available but very expensive. After the war, electric fans and mixers sold well, followed by washing machines. During the *denka būmu* (boom in electric appliances for the home) in the mid-1950s, household electric appliances, especially the television, washing machine and refrigerator, grew in popularity. Other housekeeping appliances entered the home too, such as vacuum cleaners and dryers. While they are often seen as labour-saving devices that enable women to undertake paid work outside of the home, their choice of appliance is often already shaped by product design and technology. An emphasis on market research in Japan does provide scope for housewives to help shape products, but the relative absence of women at the design and technical level reflects the gendered distribution of power within Japanese society.

Even the home itself can be considered a technological construct designed to isolate women from men, to domesticate them and to separate the public domain from the private. Japanese houses have long been vulnerable to fires and burglaries. Neighbourhood safety campaigns, and the safety-oriented narrative that underpins much of the advertising for domestic household products, all serve to emphasise a strong public expectation that the housewife is basically at home most of the time and responsible for the safety of both the physical structure and the family members. Housewives consequently have felt obliged not to leave their home for more than two or three hours lest they tempt fate. Surveys of part-time married women workers often show this concern as a contributing factor to the choice of part-time over full-time work. Large-scale *danchi* housing blocks may have been seen as improving these conditions of isolation, but they ironically served to only intensify this problem. Lifted out of her familiar local community the housewife found herself living in an attractively modern and new environment, but at another level this move was experienced by many as a virtual solitary confinement in a concrete box, without community. The so-called 'apartment dwellers' (*danchi zoku*) played a major role in the spread of household electric appliances, with most residents of Tokyo's big housing complexes enjoying relatively large disposable incomes, much of which was poured into appliances. Housewives were intent on improving the material quality of life in this new urban environment, even if there was little opportunity to overcome the socio-cultural impoverishment of *danchi* living.

The world's first transistorised portable radio set was produced in Japan in 1955, the first domestic television was produced by Hitachi in 1959 and Sony produced the world's first fully transistorised TV set in 1960. Colour broadcast transmissions began in 1960. Sanyo produced a rotary washing machine in 1953 and, by 1960, 40 per cent of households had a washing machine. By 1963, 90 per cent of households had televisions. By the mid-1970s, Japan produced over half the world's colour televisions and exported three quarters of them. Since the late 1970s, major technical advances linked to semiconductor technology have seen the growth of consumer electronics, with manufacturers such as Matsushita Electric (using the brand names National and Panasonic), Sanyo Corporation, Sony Corporation and Sharp Corporation being especially prominent. Products such as hi-fi systems, compact-disc players, video cassette recorders and video camera recorders have more recently entered the home as standard home entertainment technologies. Many of the products have been based on foreign technology, such as transistors and integrated circuits (IC), but the Japanese technology companies, in collaboration with such advertising and marketing giants as Dentsu, have excelled in commercialising ideas from abroad in products that emphasise high quality and relatively low pricing. Electronic goods have often been light, thin, and small. The Japanese electronics has seen an increasing trend towards offshore production with goods imported back into Japan, as well as being exported throughout the world under Japanese brand names. These brands are now household words everywhere where there is the domestic buying power to sustain an import market for high-quality electronic appliances.

MORRIS LOW

Doraemon

The cartoon character, *Doraemon* is a robot cat with a nuclear reactor in his chest, but he represents the innocent, whimsical aspects of technological innovation rather than their darker side. Doraemon debuted in 1970 as the creation of the brilliant *manga* team of Hiroshi Fujimoto and Motō Abiko, jointly known as Fujiko Fujio. When the pair split in the late 1980s, Fujimoto took over *Doraemon*. *Doraemon*'s fame soared in 1979, when, in addition to appearing as a regular *manga* serial, it was made into an animated television cartoon. Since then, *Doraemon* has also appeared annually in a feature film, timed to coincide with children's spring break.

A huge cat one day materialised before lazy and nerdy elementary-school student Nobita Nobi. Sent from the future by Nobita's frustrated descendants, *Doraemon*'s mission was to whip the disappointing boy into shape. Although *Doraemon* frequently exhorts Nobita to improve, he eventually always rescues the perennially bungling boy. *Doraemon*'s powers are many, but primary is the pouch on his stomach, from which he pulls a variety of gadgets. Although *Doraemon*'s simple humour is designed to appeal to young children, the story has achieved enormous popularity around the world, and with people of all ages.

SHARALYN ORBAUGH

double suicide

Double suicide (*shinjū*) or love suicide has been sensationalised, even romanticized, in Japanese literature and theatre. Certain *kabuki* and *bunraku* plays depicting *shinjū* were occasionally banned during the Edo Period due to the rash of love suicides they apparently encouraged. Chikamatsu Monzaemon was especially renowned for his tragic *shinjū* plays. The theme has remained popular with modern playwrights, film-makers and authors. A small number of major Japanese authors attempted double suicide over the twentieth century. Perhaps the most famous case is **Dazai Osamu**. Among the general public, the number of double suicides is difficult to ascertain. Many cases end in one death and a failed attempt that is then treated as a homicide by police. There is also a tradition of committing *shinjū* at remote sites of famous love suicides. One of the more popular locations is a dense and lonely area of woodlands at the base of Mt. Fuji. The Japanese Self Defence Forces and police collaborate once a year to mount a search for bodies in this area. Officials count double suicides in the statistical category of deaths related to problems in personal relationships. This is in part an attempt not to draw attention to the phenomenon in any way that might encourage further sensationalising than already occurs in the media around this practice. *Ikka shinjū* is the term used to describe a family love suicide in which a family dies together.

SANDRA BUCKLEY

DOUBLE SUICIDE [FILM] *see Shinjūū ten no amijima*

drop-outs

Ochikobore literally means 'those who have fallen behind'. Due to the demanding curriculum, the lack of attention paid to students with special needs and the belief that academic success is the result of hard work and not individual difference, slow learners tend to fall behind. The number increases as the years progress and entrance exams for high school approach. A child who drops out of the educational system will have a difficult, if not impossible, time re-entering. While there are night schools for students who are working during the day, these schools are not geared towards entrance to college and the status and careers available to college graduates.

Most drop-outs are relegated to physical jobs, manual labour or *furiitaa*, a relatively new term that is difficult to translate but means something like temporary wage earner. The work requires more responsibility than *arūbaitō*, or summer temp work, but there are usually no benefits and it is not seen as long term. While this would be the bane of the older generation, the young justify this new niche in terms of freedom from a system that demanded a lifetime commitment to the same employer. The flip side of this is no security and low wages.

JUNE A. GORDON

drug addiction

In 1999, the Japanese public were shocked by headline stories of large caches of drugs confiscated from Japanese fishing boats. Asian-produced amphetamines are finding a new and lucrative market in Japan's cities and rural areas. The high level of internal organisation and extensive international crime networks of Japan's *yakuza* are playing a key role in the rapid expansion of the drug market. Some anti-drug activists also point to high levels of collusion between police and *yakuza* as another factor in the recent increase in drugs reaching the streets. The years 1998–9 saw an almost constant stream of media exposés of police corruption, and this has only added to scepticism over the ability of the police to deal with the drug traffic. It has been the Coast Guard that has played the central role in recent drug seizures.

A total of 1,976 kilograms of amphetamines was seized in 1999, four times the 1998 figure and higher than the combined total for the five years before that. There is growing concern over the dramatic increase in illegal amphetamine sales and use, and this constitutes the most serious area of drug use today. It is estimated that 2 per cent of the population have used amphetamines. This group of drugs has a long history in Japan. Speed was first developed in Japan in 1888 and was already in use as an illegal stimulant in the bar and café culture of pre-war Japan. Cocaine, marijuana and magic mushrooms are also in use but not on the same scale. Police, teachers and the medical profession are also attempting to mount campaigns against the growing practice of glue-sniffing among teenagers.

While speed addiction used to be associated with the *yakuza* and prostitutes, it is rapidly became a youth addiction problem. More intense when injected than ingested, speed is creating a new health crisis with 60 per cent of users said to carry Hepatitis C. A recent (2000) survey from the Prime Minister's Office indicates that 15–19-year-olds are shifting away from an outright condemnation of all drug use. They are also describing increased access and exposure to drugs. The major obstacle to drug rehabilitation programmes is the tendency for families to deal with addiction behind closed doors rather than risk the reputation of the household. This has also limited the ability of police and the courts to pursue traffickers due to the reluctance of users to give evidence and risk public exposure for their family.

SANDRA BUCKLEY

E

earthquake preparedness

The Japanese archipelago is located at the intersection of four tectonic plates, creating a highly volatile level of volcanic activity over the centuries and an ongoing fear of earthquakes, localised lava flows and tidal waves. In 1991, Mt. Fugendake erupted after 200 years of dormancy, killing forty-three people. In 1995, the Kobe Earthquake, measuring 7.2 on the Richter scale, killed some 5,500 people. Since the 1970s, there has been increasing public tension as scientific and popular predictions of a major quake in the Kantō region have intensified media coverage of the associated risks.

Government response to the perceived risk has focused on the concept of readiness or preparedness. From the municipal to national levels, organised campaigns have trained communities in emergency response procedures, established neighbourhood evacuation sites and emergency service centres, and communication networks. In the wake of the Kobe disaster, there was considerable criticism of the delay in adequate rescue response and aid operations. Some Kansai officials claimed that the earthquake preparedness campaigns and resources had been excessively focused on the Kantō region at high cost to the victims of the Kobe quake. More closely integrated and nationally co-ordinated rapid-response strategies have been developed since 1995. Critics of the community level of implementation of earthquake preparedness point to the intrusive intervention quality of regular household preparedness checks by local authorities, and compulsory household participation in community emergency drills.

While there is widespread acceptance of the need for extensive preparation for another major quake, there is also growing pressure for less intervention at the household level and more investment in nationwide rapid-response teams and multi-tiered emergency aid programmes.

SANDRA BUCKLEY

eating disorders

In the early 1990s, eating disorders among young women began to draw serious attention. While some commentators related the problem to the increased participation of women in the workforce, others, particularly feminist critics, emphasised the social pressure on women to control their body image.

The former view was based on the statistical fact that the number of women suffering from anorexia nervosa increased in direct ratio to the number of women working outside home. Eating disorders, like refusal of motherhood, were regarded as an unhealthy symptom of women seeking superficial equality with men. This view was strongly criticised by feminists, who believe major causes of eating disorders are the 'beauty myth' (Wolf 1991) created by the media, and the frustration and stress of women in male-dominant society.

While in previous periods eating disorders were discussed purely as medical issues, they were for the first time recognised widely as social and women's issues. In the late 1980s and early 1990s, women writers such as Matsumoto Yuko, Ogawa Yoko,

Nakajima Azusa, and Oshima Yumiko dealt with the issue in their fiction, essays and *manga*.

References

Wolf, Naomi (1991) *The Beauty Myth: How Images of Beauty Are Used against Women*, London: Random House, Vintage Books.

TOMOKO AOYAMA

Economic Planning Agency

The Economic Planning Agency (Keizai Kikaku Chō) was founded in 1946, originally as the Economic Stabilisation Board, the central agency in charge of economic planning and control. Its successor, the Economic Deliberation Board, in the first half of the 1950s drew up a Five-year Plan for Economic Self-Support, the first of what were to become regular economic plans. At the same time, the Board changed its name to the Economic Planning Agency, and is today an agency reporting directly to the cabinet and attached to the Prime Minister's Office. Despite widespread use of the term Japan Inc., Japan has never been a centrally planned economy and the purpose of these plans is to provide economic projections, identify economic and social challenges facing the nation, assist in providing a consensus in the government and co-ordinate the policies of various ministries. Perhaps the most famous of its plans was the 'Plan to Double National Income' (1960), which ushered in a period of high economic growth. Recent plans have emphasised social welfare, new technologies, market liberalisation and the ageing of the population. The present plan is titled 'Ideal Socio-economy and Policies for Rebirth (1999–2009) and focuses upon policies necessary to overcome the current recession and to rejuvenate the economy, the 'new era of knowledge' and preparations for a declining population.

DAVID EDGINGTON

economic recovery

The Japanese economy in the years immediately following the Second World War hardly appeared capable of survival, much less growth and 'miracles'. Between 1945 and 1953, the economy none the less returned to, or even exceeded, pre-war highs by most statistical measures; the process, however, took a winding and uncertain path.

The awesome task of recovery began amid the ashes of defeat. The bombing of 119 cities left physical infrastructure in ruins while repatriation of 7 million soldiers and colonists, and cessation of military production left 13.1 million people unemployed. Fuel and raw materials were in severe shortage, a poor harvest reduced rice yield by one-third and inflation ran rampant as black markets fetched thirty to forty times the normal price. Initially, Occupation authorities assumed no responsibility for economic reconstruction and the Japanese government was left to control prices through the Economic Stabilisation Board (ESB), finance loans for capital investment through the Reconstruction Finance Bank (RFB) and strategically allocate precious raw materials through the priority production programme. Such Keynesian deficit financing, however, exacerbated inflation and weakened purchasing power, and did not represent real growth.

The so-called 'reverse course' in 1947 led the Occupation authorities to favour expansion and encourage foreign trade, as it sought to build up Japan as 'a bulwark against communism'. It was also during this period that the ESB drafted the Five-year Economic Rehabilitation Plan (FERP). Adopted in May 1948, the plan aimed to return production and living standards to 1930–4 levels by 1952. Inflationary practices of the RFB and government subsidies, however, caught the attention of Joseph Dodge when he arrived in February 1949 as the financial adviser to SCAP. As a free-market promoter, Dodge imposed deflationary policies that compelled the government to balance its budget, reduce RFB loans and subsidies, and fix the exchange rate at 360 yen to the dollar. Such advocacy of deflation and stabilisation was tough medicine, for it increased business failures and unemployment, and decreased the growth rate from 1949 to 1950, thus temporarily stunting recovery.

What provided a critical stimulus to the economy was the outbreak of the Korean War in June 1950. US military orders to the sum of

US$2.3 billion, or 'special procurements' poured into Japan and suddenly brought production to full capacity, swinging the balance of payments into the black. The fortuitous war boom greatly accelerated recovery, as can be seen in various production indices, which largely achieved or surpassed the goals of the 1948 FERP on schedule. Statistics confirm that, by 1955, the overall Japanese economy had recovered to pre-war levels. For example, GDP per capita in 1946 was only 62 per cent of its pre-war peak, but in 1955 it was 136 per cent. Industrial output was 31 per cent and 187 per cent, export 7 per cent and 75 per cent, consumption 57 per cent and 114 per cent, and wages 30 per cent and 118 per cent, respectively. In its White Papers for the 1955 fiscal year, the Ministry of Finance made the famous proclamation 'the postwar is now over. Growth through recovery is over', thus signalling the end of the recovery process and the beginning of high-speed growth.

See also: Dodge Line

Further reading

Allen, G.C. (1958) *Japan's Economic Recovery*, London: Oxford University Press.

Hiromi Arisawa (ed.) (1994) *Showa keizai shi*, vol. 2, Tokyo: Nihon Keizai Shuppansha.

Takafusa Nakamura (1981) *The Postwar Japanese Economy: Its Development and Structure*, Tokyo: University of Tokyo Press.

Yoshio Kobayashi (1963) *Sengo Nihon keizai shi*, Tokyo: Nihon Hyōron Shinsha.

HIRAKU SHIMODA

education

Contemporary Japanese education cannot be understood without looking at its historical context and acknowledging the way it has been shaped and influenced by other countries and cultures. Of all those to whom it owes a debt, none is greater than that to China, which has most profoundly formed Japanese 'character' both morally, in terms of values, and literally, in terms of script. Confucianism, which arrived in Japan around CE 600, serves as both the philosophical and moral backbone of Japanese education. Through the mandatory reading of classical Confucian texts, students internalise the significance of respectful hierarchical relationships in allowing for harmonious social relations. Respect for learning, and for books in general as conduits of tradition and culture, has enabled Japan to have one of the highest literacy rates in the world.

In the mid-1500s, due to increased trade with Western countries, particularly Portugal, Spain, the Netherlands and England, Japan became exposed to new skills and technology as well as languages. Jesuit missionaries, in their effort to comprehend Japanese culture, actively engaged in the printing of dictionaries and texts. While the content served religious purposes, it also began the process of adding yet another script, **katakana**, to the already complex writing system adapted from Chinese. A hundred years later, the Tokugawa government, headed by a warrior class called samurai, banned Christianity and closed Japan to the outside world for nearly 200 years. Education for the samurai class focused on knowledge of the Confucian classics and martial arts. People of lesser status received a more practical education in reading, writing and arithmetic, most of which took place in village temple schools called *terakoya*.

The leaders in the Meiji Period (1868–1912), therefore, inherited a fairly literate society that would provide the foundation for the transition from feudal society to modern nation. The government sought out Western ideas, particularly in education, to assist in bringing about this change. Japan was receptive to Germany's hierarchical view of society, along with its emphasis on learning, order and morality, which reinforced established Confucian values. Countering these inclinations came the US ideal of an egalitarian, democratic society. The 1920s found Japanese teachers embracing the progressive views of John Dewey and advocating child-centred, experiential learning. Teacher unions attempted to retain these values even as the country moved towards a more authoritarian and militaristic stance in the period leading up to the Second World War. At war's end, the Occupation leaders attempted to reshape the structure of Japanese education based on the US model. While having a physical resemblance to US education, in the sense of the 6–3–3 grade structure and other modern reforms, Japanese education remains an amalgamation of influences.

It could be argued that pre-school and the first six years of compulsory education in Japan are devoted to character development, as laid out in the Confucian classics, including the acquisition of behaviour and attitudes deemed appropriate for survival and success within contemporary Japanese society. Although official 'moral education' takes up only one hour of class time per week, its influence permeates every action and word. This is in spite of the fact that there are no compulsory moral-education texts, a significant factor when one realises the role of prescribed and approved texts for all other subjects. Teachers' discretion in this area is therefore crucial, and inadvertently plays a major role in the selection of teachers. During these early years, students are taught to take responsibility for their learning and the school environment. They participate in a range of leadership roles, which involve reinforcing routines and rituals that teachers in most other countries would normally assume. Student monitors rotate responsibility over the course of the year for calling the class together and dismissing it, taking the roll call, making announcements and organising classroom, club and out-of-school activities. As a result, there is minimal resistance to a teacher's authority. In general, young people accept their role as students and that of the teacher as authority. Transitions between activities are both quick and efficient. Self-discipline and group collaboration are not only expected but institutionalised. Parents are expected to reinforce these habits while creating a supportive educational atmosphere at home. During the first weeks of school every year, teachers visit the home of each of their pupils to understand the family situation and study environment. These visits are seen as essential in developing a strong school/home partnership. Schools often set boundaries for children's time and movements, recommending times students should get up and go to bed and when and how long they should study. Studying also takes place during summer holidays with projects often due at the end of the break. Parents are similarly instructed as to when they are to visit the school and talk with the teacher. Outside of these meetings, parents do not play an active role inside of the school.

The movement from primary school to middle school marks a distinct change in curriculum, pedagogy, attitude of teachers and student relationships with teachers. Whereas much of primary-school learning takes a hands-on demonstration approach, in which students are expected to engage in the learning experience through questioning and defending their views, middle school takes on a more formal lecture and transmission mode of learning. Curricular goals shift from student development to data acquisition as ninth-grade examinations approach. Teachers are perceived as strict and less available to students. During this period, many more students and parents turn to outside assistance in the form of private tutoring or cram classes called *juku* to supplement in-class schoolwork in order to acquire the knowledge required to pass the examinations. Two important assumptions underlie much of Japanese elementary and secondary educational practices. One is that virtually all children have the ability to learn well and to master the regular school curriculum. The second is that certain habits and characteristics, such as diligence and attention to detail, can be taught. The premise is that all children have equal potential. Differences in student achievement are thought to result largely from the level of effort, perseverance and self-discipline, not from differences in individual ability. Hence, students in primary schools are not grouped according to ability. Promotion to the next grade is not based on academic achievement, but is automatic. While the end of middle school also marks the end of free, compulsory education, approximately 90 per cent of students continue on to some form of high school (see **school system**). At this point, the competition that has existed all along, but which has remained veiled, is exposed as students enter high schools that are assiduously ranked.

See also: juku

JUNE A. GORDON

EMBRACING see *Ni tsutsumarete*

employment and unemployment

Among advanced industrial societies, Japan has maintained the lowest rates of unemployment during most of the post-war era. Indeed, the government and public have firmly supported policies that promote nearly full employment – sometimes at the expense of market efficiency. Japan's official unemployment rates varied between a mere 1 and 2 per cent during the 1960s and 1970s, and remained below 3 percent in the 1980s. Japanese statistics tend to underestimate true unemployment because they do not include: 'discouraged' workers who have stopped actively seeking work, yet are available; involuntary part-time workers who had sought full-time employment. Nevertheless, even when the figures are adjusted to account for these two categories, Japan still boasted the lowest unemployment rates among OECD nations in 1993. Amid the economic stagnation of the 1990s, the numbers of unemployed have risen steadily (to nearly 5 per cent in 2000), although rates remain far below those in most European economies.

Japan's commitment to maintaining employment evolved from a number of sources during the twentieth century. In the century's early years, employers dismissed workers with few restraints, and the state did little to assist the unemployed. An unemployment insurance bill failed in the Diet in 1922. During the slow growth years of the 1920s, central and municipal governments responded more actively to unemployment. A nationwide system of public labour exchanges was established, as were public-works projects for the unemployed. The Great Depression, which struck Japan hardest in 1930 and 1931, resulted in 1.5 to 2 million unemployed, or 15 to 20 per cent of the workforce. At their peak in 1931, public-works projects offered employment to 58,000 labourers daily. However, officials strove to limit such relief employment, fearing that workers would develop a sense of the 'right' to relief.

The shock of the Depression did much to shape new approaches to unemployment. While cool to massive public-works projects, the bureaucrats stepped up efforts to encourage companies to keep workers on the job and thus pre-empt social unrest. In the numerous Depression-era labour disputes over dismissals, the police routinely instructed employers to adopt other measures short of layoffs, such as shortening hours. In 1937, the government championed the Retirement Fund Law, which compelled medium and large firms to offer retirement or severance pay. Workers, for their part, focused their efforts on resisting layoffs and demanding higher severance pay. Even employers began accepting some obligation to assist dismissed workers, and they also offered job security and other benefits to maintain their most skilled workers.

In the aftermath of the Second World War, unemployment again became a pressing social problem. With factories bombed and the economy in shambles, millions lost their jobs. The revived labour movement, which grew to 6.7 million members by 1948, made job security its leading demand, and many employers were forced to promise that no workers would be dismissed. Although employers later excluded most women and temporary workers from job security guarantees, a substantial portion of the workforce – the 'regular employees' – secured a virtual entitlement to employment at their firm until retirement age. From the mid-1950s, unions negotiated understandings whereby regular workers would not be dismissed in case of productivity drives or technological innovation. In addition, the **Japan Socialist Party** joined with sympathetic bureaucrats to sponsor the first Unemployment Insurance Law in 1947. The **post-war Constitution** further emboldened the unions to insist on greater state involvement in relieving unemployment. Article 27 states 'All people shall have the right and obligation to work.' The Unemployment Counter-measures Law of 1949 significantly expanded the pre-war system of unemployment relief works. The bureaucrats and public, however, remained uneasy with the concept of unemployment insurance and relief works, which they believed rewarded the idle. They were particularly wary of relief projects, in which day labourers lingered for years and affiliated with the militant communist union. In the late 1950s, a group of bureaucrats and scholars formulated a new approach. Rather than depend on stop-gap relief and unemployment insurance, they proposed comprehensive intervention in the labour market so as to prevent or minimise unemployment before it happened.

The acrimonious labour dispute at the Mitsu-Miike Coal Mine in 1960 convinced the government of the need for proactive policies to maintain employment. Coal mining became the first of several declining post-war industries to face radical reductions in personnel. Recognising the explosive potential of structural unemployment, bureaucrats and the ruling **Liberal Democratic Party** introduced new measures to assist workers to shift into expanding sectors of the economy. Under the revised Unemployment Insurance Law (1963), government subsidised retraining, offered housing assistance to encourage workers to move to new jobs and expanded employment programmes for workers aged forty-five and older. In the 1970s, the Diet enacted some of the world's strongest employment maintenance legislation. The Employment Insurance Law (1974) enabled the state to systematically subsidise employers who were willing to keep workers on the job. Also passed were the Temporary Measures for Workers Displaced from Specific Depressed Areas (1978) and the Temporary Relief Law for Workers Displaced from Specific Depressed Industries (1977). The latter law required employers in depressed industries to formulate detailed plans to help displaced workers find new employment.

The economic slowdown of the 1990s has sorely tested post-war Japan's commitment to maintaining employment. Hard-pressed companies have responded by cutting back recruitment of young people, encouraging older employees to leave and occasionally dismissing regular employees. Many Western observers predict that Japanese firms may soon jettison guarantees of job security in favour of more flexible employment practices. Thus far, the Japanese government and public have vehemently expressed their opposition to the dismissal of regular employees, accusing the job-cutting corporations of forgetting their obligations to society and exacerbating unemployment. The consensus behind governmental intervention to promote employment remains strong.

See also: management systems, Japanese; Plan to Double Income; part-time work

Further reading

Gordon, A. (1987) 'The right to work in Japan: Labor and the state in the Depression', *Social Research* 54(2): 247–72.

Milly, D. (1999) *Poverty, Equality, and Growth*, Cambridge: Harvard University Asian Center.

SHELDON GARON

Enchi Fumiko

b. 1905, Tokyo; d. 1986, Tokyo

Writer

Lauded by critics, Enchi was famous for marshalling motifs of the canon, most frequently Heian period (794–1185) women-authored literature, to a stinging indictment of modern female socio-political disempowerment. She wrote plays in the 1920s and 1930s, enjoyed substantial recognition in the new theatre movement. Her *Banshun sōya* (A Turbulent Night in Late Spring, 1928) was the first play by a woman performed at the new theatre playhouse. Next, Enchi turned to prose – first with little success. Unpublished through the Second World War, Enchi was also seriously ill. However, *Himojii tsukihi* (Days of Hunger, 1954) won the Women's Literature Prize. Her most celebrated works, many available in English, followed. *Onna-zaka* (The Waiting Years, 1957; literally 'Woman-slope'), awarded the **Noma Bungei Prize**, narrates family matriarch Tomo Shirakawa's miserable life as procurer of increasingly younger concubines for her husband's insatiable sexual appetite. Her *Onnamen* (Masks, 1958) relates widow Mieko Toganō's revenge on her now deceased, previously philandering husband, which consists of complex manipulations to produce a baby with the Toganō name but no Toganō blood.

Enchi sought to reclaim a female voice and empowerment that modern Japan imagined had once informed pre-modern arts, particularly female-authored *monogatari* (tale fiction), but had been lost within subsequent male inhabitation of this supposedly feminised origin. *Onnamen* is indebted to **nō**, and in *Nama miko monogatari* (The Tale of the False Shamaness, 1965) and *Saimu* (Tinted Fog, 1975) Enchi borrowed themes and characters from

Heian *monogatari* and invented late Heian texts. Frequently, Enchi's invented classics disclose secrets of female sexuality left out of the canon. Often choosing ageing women as protagonists, Enchi's texts detail their exclusion from circuits of sexual exchange, in spite of their vibrant sexual desire. Many narratives opposed the modern reification of maternity, depicting mutually hostile mother– daughter relationships. After Enchi, portrayals of women split between rage and maternal love were common in women-authored Japanese narratives.

Repeatedly, Enchi wrote about female rage and jealousy, born of political and socio-cultural oppression, Buddhist doctrines on female sin and pollution, and latent, repressed sexuality. These women's rage finds its ultimate outlet in shamanistic spiritual possession. For Enchi, female psychology was personal, and yet inseparable from the collective, socio-political experience of being a woman in modern Japan.

From 1967 to 1972, Enchi translated into modern Japanese *The Genji monogatari* (The Tale of Genji), the most revered text of the Japanese canon. She won the Tanizaki Jun'ichirō Prize in 1969, the Distinguished Cultural Achievement Award in 1970, the Grand Literary Prize in 1972 and the Order of Cultural Merit, presented by the Emperor in 1985.

See also: women's literature

Further reading

Cornyetz, N. (1995) 'Bound by blood: Female pollution, divinity, and community in Enchi Fumiko's *Masks*, *US–Japan Women's Journal*, English Supplement 9: 29–58.

Ruch, B. (1994) Beyond absolution: Enchi Fumiko's *The Waiting Years* and *Masks*', in B.S. Miller (ed.) *Masterworks of Asian Literature in Comparative Perspective*, Armonk, NY: M.E. Sharpe, pp. 439–56.

NINA CORNYETZ

endaka

The rapid appreciation of the **yen** against the US dollar after 1985 was triggered by a meeting of the Group of Five industrial nations at the Plaza Hotel in New York. The doubling of the yen's value quickly reduced the export competitiveness of many industries and created a recession in Japan (1986–7). The steel and shipbuilding industries were among the most affected sectors. *Endaka* set the scene for higher levels of consumer spending on imported manufactured goods. Japanese firms relocated more manufacturing operations abroad, while developing more added-value and technologically intensive goods at home. Future growth in employment took place in services, especially in finance and leisure industries.

DAVID EDGINGTON

Endō Kenji

b. 1947, Hitachinaka City

Singer and songwriter

Endō Kenji debuted as a folk singer, but is perhaps more known as a rock singer and songwriter who played acoustic guitar. At a time when antiestablishment folk dominated the late 1960s scene, Endō's tough but poetic observations on everyday life made a striking impression.

His vocals ranged from a quiet whisper to an ebullient shout. Endō Kenji made his recording debut with *Hontōdayo* (Really!) in 1969. His second album, *Niyago*, was released by URC in April 1970 and featured the band Happy Endo in a supporting role. *Manzoku dekirukana* (Can I Be Satisfied?), his third album, received *New Music Magazine*'s Third Annual Japanese Rock Award. The single from that album, 'Curry Rice', proved to be his greatest hit. His work records the quiet desperation of everyday life in a cramped apartment matched with an openness towards the future and an underlying wit and sense of hope. Endō was one of the first to successfully avoid the *enka*-style phrasing of earlier attempts to write rock lyrics in Japanese. Endō Kenji continued to release quality work throughout the 1970s and 1980s. He still intermittently reappears on the Japanese music scene, reminding his listeners of his distinct intelligence, wit and sensibility.

MARK ANDERSON

Endō Shūsaku

b. 1923, Tokyo

Novelist

Endō Shūsaku is generally acclaimed as the most important Christian author Japan has produced, as well as one of the few Japanese writers to have an international readership and reputation. He was born in Tokyo in 1923 and lived from the ages of three to ten in Manchuria, but returned to Japan with his mother in 1933 after her divorce from her husband. He was baptised as a Christian the following year in accordance with her wishes. In 1943, Endō entered Keiō Gijuku University in Tokyo, boarding at the dormitory where he got to know the Roman Catholic philosopher Yoshimitsu Yoshihiko, who was to greatly influence him. In 1947, he graduated with a major in French and began to make his living as a literary journalist. In 1950, Endō was selected to go abroad for study, and in June he set sail for France to study French literature at Lyons University. He eventually returned to Japan in 1953, where a year later his mother died. His first work of fiction was published in 1954 and the following year he was awarded the **Akutagawa Prize** for his novella *Shiroi hito* (White Man). This signalled the beginning of a long and productive career as a writer of fiction and drama.

In 1958, Endō's novel *Umi to dokuyaku* (The Sea and Poison) was awarded two major literary prizes. The story concerns Japanese doctors conducting medical experiments on captured US servicemen during the war, and focuses on the emptiness in the heart of the physician narrator. Another novel, *Kazan* (Volcano, 1959), soon followed, with the protagonist an apostate priest called Durand, one of many such in Endō's fiction. Both novels deal with the issue of a pagan Japan.

The same year, Endō published *Obakasan* (Wonderful Fool), a popular novel written in an easy style, like much of his fiction. This novel tells the story of a Christ-like figure called Gaston Bonaparte, who befriends a gangster who eventually betrays him. In 1966, Endō published *Chinmoku* (Silence), a historical novel that deals with the apostasy of a Portuguese priest called Father Rogrigues in seventeenth-century Japan. It was awarded a major literary prize. *Samurai* (The

Samurai, 1980) is a meditation upon the same issues, describing the journey of three samurai to Japan in the seventeenth century.

The novel *Skyandaru* (Scandal, 1986) focuses on sexuality through the device of the doppelgänger, positing two contrasting good and evil selves in the same person. *Fukai kawa* (Deep River, 1993) attempts to create a different vision of Christianity drawn from Asian, specifically Buddhist, sources. This struggle to evolve an Asian version of Christianity perhaps lies at the heart of much of Endō's fiction.

Select bibliography

Endō Shūsaku (1990) *Wonderful Fool*, trans. Francis Mathy, Harmondsworth, Middlesex: Penguin Books.
—— (1986) *Stained Glass Elegies*, trans. Van C. Gessel, Harmondsworth, Middlesex: Penguin Books.
—— (1982) *The Samurai*, trans. Van C. Gessel, New York: Vintage Books.
—— (1968) *Silence*, trans. William Johnston, Tokyo: Charles E. Tuttle.

LEITH MORTON

enjo kōsai

This term is translated as 'compensated dating' but is used to describe the phenomenon of high-school girls being paid by older men to accompany them on dates. The money is used primarily to buy brand-name products. This arrangement can include sex but not in all cases. There has been widespread sensationalised press coverage of *enjo kōsai* in Japan from the mid-1990s. Organisations such as the Japan Youth Research Institute openly criticise the media for the over-exposure of the issue that has led to it being perceived by schoolgirls as a trend rather than a social problem. Police have begun to pay closer attention to *enjo kōsai* after a number of cases revealed sex between businessmen and under-age teenagers. However, in media interviews the police have focused more on the issue of the expensive consumer tastes of the high-school girls than on the adult men paying for their company. The issue of what constitutes paid sex and prostitution has been a grey area for police and schoolgirls alike. Questioned if they are paid for sex, many will answer 'no', but asked if they have given oral sex, they will answer 'yes'. *Enjo kōsai* is not being used to raise funds for subsistence. The girls involved tend to come from middle-class families and already have access to some pocket money, but pursue *enjo kōsai* in order to be able to afford a wider range of expensive luxury designer brands. The practice of *enjo kōsai* raises many questions about the attitude of these young students towards their own bodies and sexuality. It also draws attention to the pressure to compete in a youth culture where identity, status and belonging are so closely bound up with buying power and demonstrated consumer knowledge of trends and brands.

SANDRA BUCKLEY

enka

A type of sentimental Japanese and East Asian popular music, often identified with melancholy, homesickness, heartache and tradition. Etymologically, *enka*'s origins were in the late 1870s with songs written to propagate the Freedom and Popular Rights Movement. At the time the Youth Club was founded in 1888, a compound word was created that meant speech in song, *enka*. Musicologically, the types of songs now identified with *enka* were known as *ryūkōka* before the Second World War and thought of as modern pop. At some point between the 1950s and the 1960s, this style of pop music came to be identified with nostalgia for lost Japanese tradition (much as US 'country music' diverged from its Afro-American blues roots into a primordial white past), in self-conscious opposition to more 'foreign-sounding' pop known as *kayōkyoku*, folk, rock and post-bop jazz. It was at this point that the word *enka* came to designate a style of music with its contemporary generic connotations.

Various related types of popular music flourished at the time of the Sino-Japanese War. Around 1900, the song 'Strike bushi', which satirised the prohibition of prostitution, became popular. Direct criticism of the government gradually receded and the style came to be linked with the sentiments of farming people's lives. *Shōka* (choir song), *ryōka* (dormitory songs), *gunka* (military songs) and parodies of various Western song types proliferated. Enka came to have an upper-class, cosmopolitan image, and were also often sung by students. As its protest connotations receded, Enka came to be associated with such things as disappointment in love.

As Japan entered the Taishō Period, the 78 r.p.m. record became the primary medium of song. The first successful pop music record was 'Sendō kouta' (The Boatman's Song, 1918), with music by Nakayama Shimpei, generally regarded as an important founder of *enka*. From this time on it was common for films to be made out of hit songs (*kouta eiga*).

With progress in recording techniques, orchestral recordings of popular song also began to appear, forming the basis of Shōwa Period popular song style on records. With the Shōwa era, the songwriter Koga Masao appeared. He was raised in colonial Korea, and some have suggested that he brought elements of Korean song to Japan. (Indeed, the iconic post-war *enka* singer, **Misora Hibari**, was a resident Korean. Since the 1960s, vocalists from Korea, Hong Kong and Taiwan have been increasingly important in the world of Japanese *enka*. With such songs as 'Kage wo shitaite' (Longing for Shadows) and 'Sake wa namida ka tameiki ka' (Is Sake Tears or Sighs?), Koga's songs defined an era. Many feel that Koga's contribution to the melodic style of post-war *enka* was even more formative than that of Nakayama. In the pre-war period, Koseki Yūji, Makime Masa and Ōmura Yoshiaki were among the songwriters who followed Koga. Shigure Otowa, Nagata Mikihiko, and Shimada Yoshifumi were representative pre-war lyricists.

Post-war *enka* influenced by contemporary pop was written by songwriters such as Endo Minoru, Yoshida Tadashi, and Funamura Tōru. As lyricists, Hoshino Tetsuro and Takahashi Kikutaro leant their hands to countless, similarly pop-inflected compositions. Their work includes such songs as Miyako Harumi's 'Suki ni natta hito' (Person I've Come to Love, 1968), Mori Shinichi's 'Minatomachi Blues' (Harbour Town Blues, 1969) and

Koyanagi Rumiko's 'Seto no hanayome' (Bride from Seto, 1972).

Disappointment in love, separation and home-sickness appear in the lyrics of *enka* songs to the point that harbours, tears and rain are said to be the primary elements of *enka*. There are a variety of singing styles and forms commonly referred to as *enka*. It might be more accurate to classify them according to whether their lyrics are sentimental or sad than according to musicological style. Musi-cally, however, there has been a sense of stagnation since at least the 1980s. It is doubtful that *enka* was ever 'the music of the Japanese nation' or 'the heart of Japan' (*Nippon no kokoro*) as a popular saying would have it, but given the fragmentation of the contemporary music scene such a claim would now be patently false. At the present time, young people appear to be growing distant from *enka*. Karaoke has become essential to sustaining some degree of *enka*'s previous popularity. It nevertheless bears watching whether or not people born after the 1970s and raised on rock and pop will become interested in *enka* as they grow older or whether new varieties of *enka* with more youth appeal will emerge.

See also: Kankoku kayō

Further reading

Hosokawa Shuhei (1977) 'Enka', in *Taishū bunka jiten*, Tokyo: Kobundo, pp.83–4.

Komota Nobuo, Shimada Yoshifumi, Yazawa Tomotsu and Yokozawa Chiaki (1981) *Nihon ryūkōkashi*, Tokyo: Shakai Hisosha.

Yano, Christine (1998) 'Defining the modern nation in Japanese popular song, 1914–1932', in *Japan's Competing Modernities*, Manoa: University of Hawaii Press, pp. 247–64.

MARK ANDERSON

enlightenment intellectuals

People called enlightenment intellectuals have appeared twice within Japan's modern history. The first time was the period immediately follow-ing the Meiji Restoration and the second was the period immediately following Japan's defeat in the

Second World War. Both movements were closely associated with debates over conditions of moder-nisation. The first enlightenment intellectuals gathered in a group called the Meirokusha, which was established in 1873. The members of the Meirokusha included Mori Arinori (1847–9), Fukuzawa Yukichi (1835–1901), Katōū Hiroyuki (1836–1916), Tsuda Mamichi (1829–1903), Nishi Amane (1829–97), Nakamura Masanao (1832–91) and Nishimura Shigeki (1828–1902). At Japan's starting point as a modern state they worked at introducing European and US social institutions and enlightenment thought across the fields of politics, economics and culture. They not only had a large influence on the milieu known as '*Bunmei kaika*' (civilization and enlightenment) but also worked as its leaders. The post-war enlightenment intellectuals were a group that, from a foundation of primarily social scientific training, advocated 'the modernisation of Japanese society' as the guiding principle for Japan's post-war reconstruc-tion. Included among them are Ōkōchi Kazuo (1905–84), Ōtsuka Hisao (1907–96), Maruyama Masao (1914–96), Kawashima Takeyoshi (1909–92), Takashima Zenya (1904–90), Shimizu Ikutarō (1907–88), Uchida Yoshihiko (1913–89), Masuda Shirō (1908–97) and Taketani Mitsuo (1911–). Under post-defeat conditions they defined and criticised wartime Japanese fascism as a form of '*chōkokkashugi*' (ultranationalism) deriving from Ja-panese society's backwardness. By expounding a post-war ideal of '*shimin-Shakai*' (civil society) originating in the West, they gained great influence over the leaders of Japan's reconstruction. This intellectual current is today called 'post-war enlightenment'.

These two currents of thought are very different in terms of the period and context within which they emerged, and a direct intellectual genealogy cannot be indentified. None the less, they are usually discussed in tandem as two groups of intellectuals that played a similar role in modern Japanese history. This is because each accepted and developed in Japan the modern West's thought of reason and enlightenment; each worked to indicate the 'road that ought to be followed' for modernisa-tion during the two most important transition points in modern Japanese history: In each case this intellectual and political effort had a major effect on a broad spectrum of people. To view both groups as the models for Japan's modern thinkers seems to have become the standard, official self-interpretation in modern Japan, as shown by the fact that a portrait of Fukuzawa Yūkichi, one of the central figures of the Meiji Enlightenment, appears on the 10,000 yen note.

In order to understand the claims made by the post-war enlightenment, and the extent of its influence on post-war Japanese society, it is best to examine two essays that were published in the year following defeat, 1946. The first is Maruyama Masao's 'Chōkokkashugi no ronri to shinri' (The Logic and Psychology of Ultranationalism)'and the second is Ōtsuka Hisao's 'Kindaiteki ningen-ruikei no sōshutsu' (The Creation of Modern Human Types). Maruyama argued that wartime Japanese fascism was based upon a unique backward 'ultranationalism' that differed from German Nazism. It differed in that spiritual authority and political power were unilaterally possessed under the name of the emperor system and had yet to achieve a key condition of modernity: a formal legal apparatus that is morally value neutral. Ōtsuka further developed this argument, pointing out that at the foundation of this backward form of state sovereignty lay a pre-modern condition of ethics and human subjectivity. In Japan, he argued, these fundamental causes interfered with the development of modern forces of production. Maruyama and Ōtsuka did not understand Japan's defeat as the breakdown of an imperialistic aggression that the modern nation state had carried out, but proposed at the very beginning of post-war Japan the interpretive schema that presented defeat as an effect brought about by the 'backwardness' of the state and society. In this schema the demand for society's 'modernisation' came to be narrated as an ethical imperative born from 'reflection' upon Japan's defeat in war. In narrating this imperative, the post-war enlightenment intellectuals drove people towards economic and social reconstruction by seeking the recovery from defeat in war through the 'completion of modernisation'. They came to be seen as the spiritual leaders of 'post-war Japan'.

Within the broad context of the 'post-war', this standpoint of the post-war enlightenment intellectuals might be said to have a certain overlap with the USA's position towards post-war Japan (and the post-war world) in which it came to understand itself as the 'teachers of modernisation and democratisation' in an occupied Japan. Of course, having an affinity for Marxism, and being situated within the post-war world in which the structure of the cold war was becoming increasingly clear, these intellectuals opposed Japan's integration into the USA's anti-communist world strategy. Nevertheless, from the symbolic meaning of 'modernisation', the enlightenment intellectuals, in fact, in parallel with US self-consciousness *vis-à-vis* Japan, had indeed positioned themselves as the 'teachers of modernisation' for post-war Japan. Within the structure of this discourse, it can be said that they worked, in the same manner as the USA, at reproducing within their students a consciousness of a 'backward Japan' and came themselves to desire the continuation of the teacher–student relation.

Post-war enlightenment intellectuals can be seen as having used the discursive strategy of 'enlightenment from the lecture podium' in that the majority of them held posts as university professors. They each achieved a certain success in some academic field and, while forming their own school of thought, wrote articles and editorials for a general public against an academic backdrop. As a result, the post-war Japanese discursive situation came to display a certain number of characteristic aspects. First, through university education their enlightenment discourse was inherited by the next generation of university professors, bureaucrats, journalists and others. With their sphere of influence continually expanding, their discourse came to be shared by the leaders of every sphere of Japanese society and evolved into an institutional knowledge that transcended academism. Second, as enlightenment discourse thus achieved institutionalisation through academism in spite of its 'left-wing liberal' character, it simultaneously came into an oppositional relation with the discourse of 'right-wing conservatism', widely popularised in the mass print media. Thus, the fundamental schema of the relations of polemical opposition in post-war Japan were established. Third, the student uprisings, which occurred throughout the world at the end of the 1960s, erupted in Japan as overlapping critiques both of the 'modernisation' line of post-war Japan, and of the enlightenment intellectuals as advocates of institutionalised 'modernism'.

When, in the 1980s, the post-modernist trends came to the fore, post-war enlightenment thought, whose keynote was modernism, lost its base of support and at once retreated into the background. However, in the late 1990s, with the deaths of such central supporters as Maruyama Masao and Ōtsuka Hisao, post-war enlightenment thought underwent something of a revival, but has now been transfigured into a more clearly nationalistic form. This revival cannot be dissociated from the transformation of the world under globalisation. The era and society called 'post-war Japan' are facing challanges that shake their very foundations.

NAKANO YOSHIO

enterprise unions and gender

Historically, unions in Japan have accepted the lower wages of women workers to concentrate on protecting the wages and conditions of their 'core' male membership. Japan's enterprise unions are androcentric, and although the strategy of male union officials in the post-war period has moved beyond the pre-war strategy of exclusion, women comprise only 17 per cent of union members. Their representation does not improve at committee level, with women comprising only 3.5 per cent of the total union movement's committee membership.

As early as 1885, women textile workers organised boycotts and walkouts in an attempt to force company owners to take responsibility for improving living and working conditions. Women textile workers organised Japan's first strike on 12 June 1886, when they walked out over attempts by the owner to increase their work hours and lower wages. The success of this strike established a precedent for strike action. Disputes spread beyond the textile industry as some actions received the support of male co-workers. All of these strikes took place without the benefit of, or assistance from, an organised union movement.

Japanese unions were not legally recognised until 1947 with the enactment of the Trade Union Law, but, despite the lack of legal recognition, these labour organisations continued to form and reform in the prewar period. The Yū aikai (Friendship Association), Japan's first union, allowed women to become associate members when it formed in 1913. In 1916, it established the first women's bureau and, in 1917, women were upgraded to full-member status. **Yamakawa Kikue** outlined the function of the women's bureau in Article 3 of the *Fujinbu Teze* (Women's Bureau Thesis) as working for all members and to deal with issues common to the working class. Opposition to the creation of women's bureaux developed into a struggle over the status of women in unions and, while the debate was indirectly concerned with the larger issue of the function of trade unions, women's bureaux became the battle ground to conduct this struggle. Those opposed to the creation of women's bureaux were in the majority and so, in 1927, Fujin dōmei (The Women's League) was established outside the union movement to address 'women's issues'.

In Japan's post-war union movement, male union officials and male unionists continue to have problems with women workers, who still accept the role of women as nurturers and carers, and as 'cheap' workers with their role in paid work defined as secondary. Evidence of the number of women using the legal system to resolve discriminatory employment practices indicates that when discriminatory employment practices are acknowledged by enterprise unions they are issues beyond their bargaining and negotiating scope.

A major issue facing Japan's post-war union movement is declining union membership. Women comprise the majority of non-unionised workers and, despite union officials arguing that women are not interested in unions or workplace issues, the wealth of empirical evidence indicates the contrary. Women have become a scapegoat that prevents or even protects unions from addressing their own organisational and structural problems.

Further reading

Miller, R.L. and Amano, M.M. (1995) 'Trade unions in Japan', *New Zealand Journal of Industrial Relations* 20(1): 35–48.

KAYE BROADBENT

entrance examinations

Examinations drive the Japanese educational system. With few exceptions, all students must sit for the entrance examination for the high school of their choice. While some private institutions require examinations at earlier points in students' academic careers, high-school and college/university entrance examinations dominate the lives of Japanese youth and their families. The high school that one attends is pivotal to one's choice of university and career options. While the knowledge of the impending exam process looms over the life of all Japanese children, the intensity of the preparation kicks in during middle-school years. *Juku*, private tutorial programmes, which prior to this level of schooling served social, cultural and remedial functions, begin to focus more clearly on examination preparation. Family life is similarly affected as students spend long, intense hours studying with minimal outside distraction. Mothers carefully monitor their child's health, and are fully aware of the relationship between nutritious meals, quality sleep and the ability to concentrate in school.

The period of preparation for the exams as well as the exam itself is called examination hell. Students sit for five one-hour exams with an hour lunch break. Middle-school students are allowed to take the entrance examination for only one public high school at a time. They may, however, take a public and private exam simultaneously. Each prefecture develops their own examination based on the guidelines from the *Monbusho Kouta*, the **Ministry of Education**, which prescribes the curriculum throughout the K-12 years. Students who do not gain admission to either a public or private high school may take the exam for a special trade high school. Due to an equitable K-8 education, girls do as well as boys in the high-school entrance competition. However, a smaller proportion of girls continue on to university, reflecting cultural and historical norms as well as inequity in job opportunities after graduation.

University applicants may take exams for as many schools as they desire but usually they sit for three to six, as the cost of each exam is quite high. Two sets of exams are given for university admission. The first is a standardised general exam given to all applicants and scored the same day as the exam. These results are announced on television and in the newspapers. Depending on these scores, students then decide which university exams they are eligible to take. Each university has their own qualifying score. The exam for public institutions covers five subjects: Japanese language, mathematics, science, social studies and English. Private schools offer a choice of tracks, either language arts (English, Japanese and social studies) or science (English, mathematics and science). The second exam differs for each university and includes an essay. Private schools reserve seats for students who are academically strong and have previously attended good private schools. These students do not have to take entrance examinations. Students who fail the examination to the university of their choice often spend a year or more in intensive study before they try again.

JUNE A. GORDON

environment and anti-pollution

While there may have been elements of environmentalism in peasant uprisings dating back to the Tokugawa Period, the origin of the contemporary environmental movement can be traced back to the struggle, in the late 1880s and early 1890s, against pollution caused by the Ashio copper mine, in Tochigi Prefecture, north of Tokyo. The government eventually settled the issue by resettling the people living downstream of the mine, but it became a major social issue at the time, and was taken up in the Diet thanks to the dedication of Tanaka Shōzō, a progressive politician who was deeply involved in the movement.

At the time, Japan was undergoing a rapid process of industrialisation, and was quickly becoming one of the most heavily polluted countries of the world. During the early twentieth century, and in the period of fascism leading up to the Second World War, there were isolated struggles on environmental issues, but they never managed to coalesce into anything like a national movement. The progressive forces that existed at the time, such as the Japan Communist Party and Japan Socialist Party, were largely dominated by the labour movement, and environmental issues inevitably took a back seat to economic growth and the promotion of material affluence.

However, a major change was occurring in terms of environmental degradation. During the late 1880s, most of the problems involved mining, and thus took place in rural areas, but in the early years of the twentieth century this began to shift to urban areas, as Japan began its second phase of industrialisation, based on heavy industries. In Ōsaka, the smog was particularly serious, and in 1925 an organisation called the Ōsaka Urban Association was formed, and led a fairly active campaign against the air pollution. There was very little citizen involvement, however, in this and other movements of the time.

The defining event, nationally, was the Minamata disease affair, which first came to attention in 1956. Like the Ashio mine issue seventy years earlier, it involved industrial pollution, this time mercury being dumped into Minamata Bay by a chemical company, Chisso. In this case, however, the government was not able to solve the problem through force. Though for many years it dragged its feet, and Chisso did its best to absolve itself of any responsibility, the victims persevered, holding rallies and sit-ins at the company's headquarter building in Tokyo and at the Ministry of Health and Welfare. Eventually, the company was forced to accept responsibility, and, though the case still drags on today, the victims have at least received some compensation.

In the years following that, people around the country, prompted by the awareness raised by the Minamata issue, began forming movements to stop companies from polluting in their own areas. One case was the Itai-itai disease (in Japanese, *itai* means 'it hurts'), another illness caused by the dumping of industrial waste, this time cadmium, into a river. Another was Yokkaichi asthma, caused by air pollution in an industrial zone in Mie Prefecture, near Ōsaka. Cases of Minamata disease were also uncovered in Niigata Prefecture, leading to more lawsuits.

These struggles presented a threat to both the government and Japanese industry, and culminated in the adoption, in 1967, of the Pollution Counter-measures Basic Law, as well as the establishment, in 1971, of the Environment Agency. Thus, the organised efforts of victims of pollution throughout the archipelago, mainly in the form of lawsuits against polluting companies and the government, led to some improvement of environmental quality in Japan.

However, a second turning point came in the late 1970s and early 1980s, when Japanese environmentalists began to take an interest in affairs beyond Japan's borders. For example, the Asian Rare Earth affair, in which a Japanese company was found to be causing pollution in Malaysia, increased awareness among the Japanese movement that to some extent the clean-up of the Japanese archipelago was being achieved at the expense of people in other Asian countries. It turned out that many companies, in reaction to the stricter controls in Japan, were essentially exporting pollution overseas.

During this period, several groups, including JATAN (Japan Tropical Forest Action Network) and the Sarawak Campaign, were formed specifically to oppose the environmental destruction in other countries (notably Malaysia and Indonesia) that was being carried out for the benefit of Japanese consumers and by Japanese multinational corporations.

The Rio Earth Summit in 1992 also served to expose many Japanese citizens to environmental issues on a global level, and the number of people involved in these activities increased in subsequent years. Though many groups emerged during this period, they were hampered by a lack of willingness of private firms to make donations, exacerbated by the difficulty in registering such groups as legal organisations and by the lack of any tax deduction for donations. Observers, especially from Western Europe and the USA, have often been struck by the small size and cramped space used by Japanese environmental organisations. The situation may have improved somewhat following the passage, in 1997, of a law providing a status for non-profit organisations. However, the situation is still quite difficult.

At present, there are many organisations working on a variety of issues, but for the most part they are fragmented into groups specialising in specific issues. For example, there are conservation groups such as the World Wildlife Fund Japan, working to conserve species of animals, and numerically these groups form the largest section of the movement. Another important area of activity is waste and recycling; this sector is mostly composed of housewives who are also active in consumer co-operative activities. The links between groups in different areas working on the issue of nuclear power are for the most part weak. There are a few organisations, such as Citizens' Forum 2001 Japan, which try to incorporate the different aspects of environmental issues, but they have yet to become large organisations with solid resources.

See also: environmental technologies; Miike struggle; Minamata disease

JENS WILKINSON

environmental technologies

Japan has a long history of advanced environmental technology, the evolution of which has been stimulated by, and run parallel to, industrial development. After the Meiji Restoration, and in the inter-war years, mining pollution stimulated technological innovation. Rapid industrial development following the Second World War caused severe air/water pollution, posing an immediate public health threat. Pollution became a political issue, stimulating widespread protest. Initially underestimated by the **Liberal Democrat Party** (LDP), the election of anti-pollution (see **environment and anti-pollution**) parties to local and prefectural positions stimulated the governing party. In the early 1970s, new laws were passed. The government and Japanese industry invested heavily in environmental technologies, leading the way in fields such as desulfurisation, pollution abatement, waste disposal/recycling (see **waste and recycling**) and energy conservation, while supporting nuclear power-related technological research. The overall effect has been to radically reshape the domestic landscape, with energy consumption and efficiency figures among the developed world's best, and a widespread network of laws and regulations in place.

Japanese innovation is encouraged by self-interest. Technological innovation and industrial relocation (to South-East Asia) removed or in effect exported most traditional polluting activity. How-

ever, other environmental problems have emerged as the economy develops. Gains made from energy efficiency and pollution abatement technology have tailed off, while **leisure**/lifestyle/conservation-related problems proliferate. Vehicular related air quality remains a serious issue, as does limited public support for nuclear power. New technologies, and social change, are needed for Japan to meet challenging greenhouse gas emission/domestic energy consumption targets.

Geographical constraints (mountainous countryside and high population density) and cultural patterns (high consumption rates) mean Japan must address environmental problems that other countries will not face for several years, encouraging energy and environmental technology innovation. Industrial pollution from Asian neighbours threatens Japan's environment (as well as the very domestic resources that support Japanese regional economic activity). These nations offer emerging markets for Japanese environmental technology. The Japanese government supported international/bilateral initiatives, and research projects co-ordinated by universities and ministries further support innovation. The Research Institute of Innovative Technology for the Global Environment (RIITE), the United Nation's Environment Program (UNEP), International Environmental Technology Center (IETC) and the National Institute for Environmental Studies (NIES) are all engaged in research that will shape future technologies.

See also: environment and anti-pollution; land reclamation; Miike struggle; Minamata disease; waste and recycling

Further reading

Cameron, O. (1996) 'Japan and Southeast Asia's environment', in M. Parnwell and R. Bryant (eds) *Environmental Change in Southeast Asia*, London: Routledge, pp. 67–94.

—— (1996) 'The political ecology of environmentalism in Japan', doctoral thesis: University of Cambridge.

OECD (1977, 1993), *Environmental Policies in Japan*, Paris: OECD.

Salisbury, T. and Oya, S. (1997) *Japanese Research on*

Environmental and Energy Technology, Tokyo: British Embassy, Science and Technology Section Report.

Wallace, D. (1995) *Environmental Policy and Industrial Innovation*, London: RIIA/Earthscan.

OWEN CAMERON

equal employment opportunity legislation

The campaign for equal-opportunity legislation in Japan was spearheaded by the **International Women's Year Action Group** and a group known by the abbreviation Tsukuru Kai (Women's Group to Frame Our Own Equal Employment Opportunity Law). A coalition of forty-eight organisations contributed to the national campaign. These groups also used international publicity, through the international conferences of the United Nations International Decade for Women, in order to bring further pressure to bear on the Japanese government. Japan, since 1947, has had a constitution that outlaws discrimination on the grounds of sex, race creed or social status. In addition, the Labour Standards Law (Rōdō Kijun Hō) of 1947 upheld the principle of equal pay for equal work but did not specify other forms of sexual discrimination.

The Equal Employment Opportunity Law (EEOL) (Danjo Koyō Kikai Kintō hō) became effective on 1 April 1986. It is based on a philosophy of 'equality of opportunity' rather than 'equality of result' and is not backed up by affirmative action programmes. Discrimination in retraining, welfare, retirement and retrenchment is prohibited, and employers are required to make efforts to abolish discrimination in recruitment, hiring, transfer and promotion. There is no explicit reference to indirect discrimination. Where a dispute arises, there are three stages of reconciliation – within the organisation, through the Women's Bureau of the Department of Labour or through the Equal Opportunity Conciliation Board. It is no longer permissible to designate certain jobs as 'for males' or 'for females', but many large companies have circumvented such provisions by labelling white-collar jobs as either 'management track' or 'clerical'. In practice, males are automatically channelled into the management track, while female recruits are asked to make the choice between a clerical or management track position.

For women who are able to continue in full-time permanent positions, there are provisions for maternity leave and nursing leave in the Labour Standards Law. In discussions leading up to the implementation of the EEOL, most controversy centred on what was called **bōsei hōgo**, 'protection of motherhood'. In amendments to the Labour Standards Law, those provisions directly connected with maternity and nursing leave were retained. Restrictions on overtime for women workers were removed for women in management and professional positions, but retained in some occupations. With respect to both male and female working hours, daily overtime limits were modified and replaced with a variable system. The Labour Standards Law has undergone further modification in the years following the enactment of the EEOL.

Most new jobs in recent years have been part-time (see **part-time work**) or temporary positions, usually filled by older women after responsibilities for **childcare** have been eased. The increase in the use of women's labour has been most apparent in information and service industries. Another trend is the use of workers employed on temporary contracts through agencies, known as the *haken* system. Technological change has also created a new class of computer outworkers. The Labour Dispatch Law of 1985 and the Part-Time Workers Law of 1993 attempted to address the situation of part-time and seconded workers (see **gender and work**). The Childcare Leave Law of 1991 made it possible for men as well as women to take parenting leave, but in practice it is usually women who take parenting leave, while the generally higher paid males retain their full-time commitment to the workforce.

Further reading

Lam, A. (1993) *Equal Employment Opportunities for Japanese Women: Changing Company Practice*, in J. Hunter (ed.) *Japanese Women Working*, London: Routledge.

Steinhoff, P. and Tanaka, K. (1994) 'Women managers in Japan', in N.J. Adler and D.N.

Israeli (eds) *Competitive Frontiers: Women Managers in a Global Economy*, Cambridge: Blackwell, pp. 79–100.

Sugeno, K. (1992) *Japanese Labour Law*, Seattle: University of Washington.

VERA MACKIE

ero guro

Ero guro is the contraction of the Japanese transliteration for erotic-grotesque nonsense. *Ero-guro-nansensu* was a dominant mode of aesthetic modernism in Japan during the 1920s and 30s. It influenced mass-cultural forms as diverse as the detective and horror novel, commercial design and softcore pornography. *Ero-guro* also strongly impacted the social scientific fields of sexology, psychology and urban anthropology. However, its biggest influence was registered in the explosion of *ero guro* mass-culture magazines.

The principal *mobo* (modern boy) magazine *Shinseinen* introduced the two main *ero-guro* writers Edogawa Rampo and Yumeno Kyūsaku. Rampo's popular detective and horror novels drew on his wide-ranging knowledge of early Shōwa intellectual thought, including Freudian psychoanalysis, gender and sexuality studies, and criminology. Yumeno Kyūsaku's fiction took up the themes of sexuality, schizophrenia and Japanese colonial imperialism. Another important *ero guro* figure was Ozaki Midori, whose work provided feminist treatments of the thematics found in the male *ero guro*: hybridity, the uncanny, human–machine couplings, necrophilia and S&M.

Ero-guro influences and distinct genres continue to be popular and widespread in contemporary cultural forms, such as *manga*, *anime* and film. What is often not recognised is the continuity between pre-war and post-war fascination with *ero guro* themes in popular culture

Further reading

Silverberg, Miriam (1991) 'The modern girl as militant', in Gail Lee Bernstein (ed.) *Recreating Japanese Women, 1600–1945*. Berkeley: University of California Press, pp. 239–66.

MARK DRISCOLL

EROS PLUS MASSACRE *see Eros purasu gyakusatsu*

Eros purasu gyakusatsu

The film *Eros purasu gyakusatsu* (Eros plus Massacre, 1970) was directed by Yoshida Yoshishige This self-reflective monochrome film depicts the shooting of a film about the ideological and romantic conflict in the lives of Taishō anarchist Osugi Sakae and feminist Ito Noe, who were both murdered by a gendarme in the aftermath of the 1923 Tokyo Earthquake. The historical incident on which the film is loosely based is the violent entanglement of two feminist revolutionaries, Noe and Itsuko, who compete, struggle and even attempt to kill Osugi in a triangular politics of desire. This story gets told through a female student radical researching the Taishō era who 'interviews' Noe's daughter 'Mako' played by Okada Mariko, who also doubles as Noe. As the identity separating Noe and Mako dissolves, so does the time separating the two diegeses of past and present. In this, his most artistically successful 'intellectual' film, Yoshida uses flashback and anachronistic juxtapositioning of historical figures and modern technology to impede diegesis in one of the most radically dialectical avant-garde films ever made in Japan.

CHRISTINE MARRAN

experimental film and video

After introducing developments in the New York experimental-film scene through articles in the late 1940s, Takiguchi Shūzō formed Jikken Kōbō in 1951, which established the post-war avant-garde cinema. Their first films included Takiguchi's *Kinecalligraph* (1955) and *Silver Wheel* (1955), which was directed by Matsumoto Toshio, Yamaguchi Katsuhirō and musician Takemitsu Tōru. From here, the energy shifted to Nihon Daigaku's Film

Society, where now-classic films like *Conversation between a Nail and a Sock* (1958) and *Sain* (1962) were produced. In the late 1960s, film-makers pooled their energies in the Japan Film-makers' Co-operative, before creating the Underground Film Centre in 1971 under the leadership of Kawanaka Nobuhiro, Tomiyama Katsue and Nakajima Takashi. They started a Cinematèque in **Terayama Shūji**'s Tenjōsajiki Theatre Troupe, featuring a bi-monthly 'new works showcase'. By 1976, when Tenjōsajiki closed down, they had shown some 650 works. Renaming themselves Image Forum, they were the centre of the avant-garde into the 1990s, with a regular screening programme, classes in production and history, a distribution list and an excellent film journal. Since Image Forum concentrated primarily on film, other organisations promoted video art, beginning with Video Hiroba (1972) and followed by Video Gallery Scan and Video Cocktail, which was probably the first group formed by artists who actually had their start in video and not film or other arts. While there was overlap with radical documentaries (see **documentary film**) in the 1960s and 1970s, most experimental film and video in Japan has had a structural orientation rather than towards social criticism.

ABÉ MARK NORNES

Expo 70

Expo 70 was held in Ōsaka. Seventy-seven nations participated in this world exposition. For Ōsaka, the Expo offered an opportunity to position itself in the eyes of the world, as well as the rest of Japan, as no less of a vibrant and international city than Tokyo. Ōsaka was attempting to differentiate itself from Tokyo by promoting the Kansai region as a centre for new research and development in science and technology. Consistent with this goal, the Expo featured a strong theme of new science and space technology, and exhibits included an Apollo spacecraft and a moon rock exhibit. The park facilities themselves also foregrounded Japanese and, in particular, local Kansai transport and technology industries, with a state-of-the-art public transport system including a new monorail and

electronic cars. Sixty-four million people attended Expo 70.

SANDRA BUCKLEY

exporting Japanese culture

Although Japan has long been recognised as a major exporter of a wide range of consumer goods, there has been little attention paid to the role Japan plays as an influential exporter of culture in the contemporary global marketplace or in more local regional contexts within Asia. The dominant myth of Japan as imitator rather than innovator has added to the tendency to ignore the significant role played by Japan as cultural exporter over the late twentieth century.

An excellent example is hand-held video games. Not only has Japan captured the giant share of the hardware market with the extraordinarily successful Sony Gameboy, but Japanese game designers are also dramatically impacting the cultural space of **play** and fantasy of an entire generation of Gameboy users through their definition of the nature and parameters of that play. This is embedded not just in software code but also the narrative, dialogue, image and sound/music of the games marketed. The same can be said for the highly popular Japanese *anime* that fill much of the international primetime television scheduling for children. Then there is the Playstation or Nintendo plugged into so many middle-class homes around the globe. Many parents and children are oblivious to the Japanese origins of much commercial contemporary children's programming and gaming.

By their very nature, the cultural commodities of these global markets are not easily pinned to one site of origin or production. A new release game might be wholly designed in Tokyo or San Francisco, or perhaps the narrative and dialogue are written in the USA, the graphics created in the Philippines and the sound, voice and music recorded in Germany while the plastic casing is moulded and assembled in China. While some games are designed for global release, others continue to be first tested and launched in Japan and then translated and, if necessary, adapted to other markets. The widely popular **Pokemon** Gameboy cartridge discs are not released in their English version for up to six to twelve months after the Japanese release. This has the additional effect of creating a high level of overseas market anticipation and significant pre-orders, as with the 2000 release of the Silver and Gold Pokemon versions.

The rapidly expanding home video game market now rivals the annual 'consumer spend' for the film and home video industries, and it is the Japanese-owned Sony Playstation and Nintendo that dominate this major market in gaming and home entertainment. One of the key challenges faced by all the new digital gaming platforms is piracy and the related problem of online providers who sell access and pirated versions to subscribers. As in the music industry, web-based providers of low-cost pirated additions are proving difficult for companies to monitor and control. The extensive-ness of the market for pirated games, music and video in Asia is raising serious questions about the future of more familiar notions of ownership and copyright. It may become necessary over time for the Japanese companies that dominate these rapidly transforming 'culture markets' to reconsi-der the structure of profit and royalties, and the related processes of distribution and sales. In the music industry, Sony has already taken up a strong position in the legal fight to limit or break the MP3 music technologies at the same time that it continues to refine the MP3 technologies. This apparent contradiction reflects the complex new reality. With the shift to third-generation wireless technologies with rapid, high-quality data-sharing features, the potential to control the flow of copyrighted materials in the culture markets can only continue to decline. Both the software and hardware innovations of Japan's new technology industries will continue to have a dramatic impact on the future of the cultural formations of everyday life at the interface of communication, information access, entertainment and consumer activity.

Japan's role as a cultural exporter functions differently at a regional level than it does globally. While contemporary Japanese music is hardly known in the USA and Europe (with the possible exception of some jazz and classical composers and performers), in the night-clubs and in the local MTV and other television or radio-based music

programming Japanese singers, songwriters, pro-ducers, recording labels and television networks are a major influence. Similarly, Japanese television programming from game shows to soaps and tele-dramas are dubbed and captioned all across Asia. Some game shows are franchised to regional networks for local production. A popular Japanese detective drama may run in Hong Kong dubbed in Cantonese, with Mandarin subtitles. Japanese film also has a strong presence in the Asian region with most domestic Japanese box office successes quickly optioned for regional distribution. In contrast to this, there is a very selective distribution and captioning of only a few Japanese films per year targeted at a Western art film audience. There is no question that since Kurosawa Akira's *Rashōmon* won the Venice Film Festival in 1951 major Japanese directors have captured the attention of interna-tional film critics and gained a foothold in the art film market overseas. Much has been written on the influence of Ozu and the early Kurosawa on Western film-makers from Hitchcock to Bergman. The cinematic innovations of contemporary Japa-nese film-makers continue to affect film-making from Hollywood to Hong Kong. Japanese com-mercial films have not, however, gained a major viewing audience outside Asia.

Fashion and food are two other areas in which there has been extensive cultural export of Japanese taste and aesthetics. The widely afford-able instant ramen noodle – a hot snack favourite among children across the world – and the now almost inescapable sushi bars that dot the restau-rant districts of major cities everywhere are the two prime examples of the new global popularity of Japanese cuisine. The top restaurant list of a major city will almost always include a Japanese restau-rant or a Pacific-fusion restaurant. The immensely popular but still usually upmarket fusion cuisine is strongly influenced by the ingredients, tastes and presentation of Japanese food blended with local specialities, whether the seafood of California, the exotic fruits and vegetables of Australia, the meats of New Zealand or the spices of Thailand. The extraordinary success on cable television of the eclectic skills of Japan's Iron Chefs exemplifies this new status afforded Japanese cuisine.

In the realm of fashion Japanese designers have created their own brand names and characteristic styles over the 1980s and 1990s to win a permanent place on the international runways of fashion for such names as Kenzo, Hanae Mori, Yohji Yama-moto, Comme des Garçons, Comme ça Mode and others. It is worth noting, though, that for the most part the figure that has carried these fashions into the global spotlight has been that of the tall, thin Western model and not Japanese models. While Asia remains the primary market for these Japanese brand designers they secure that brand image in the fashion magazines and shows of Europe and the USA.

See also: anime; karaoke; manga; Pokemon; toys

SANDRA BUCKLEY

extra-curricular clubs

Extra-curricular clubs play a major role in the lives of both students and teachers in Japan. They are seen as building strong interpersonal skills, group loyalty, healthy competition, physical and emo-tional strength and a respect for order, all characteristics it is considered will enable students to survive and succeed in Japanese society.

Clubs are organised along hierarchical lines complete with *senpai*, students who are older, demanding obsequious behaviour on the part of their younger peers. Clubs are most popular in junior and high school, tapering off as the demands of exam pressure increase. Every child is encour-aged to join a club. Topics range from sports to music to ***manga*** (comics). Clubs meet after school and on weekends. Those who refuse to join a specific club are recommended to form a club for those who refuse to join a club. If a student tries to change clubs or escape practice without a good excuse, they are severely criticised or reported to their home-room teacher. All teachers are required to take on at least one main club activity and put in the long hours to coach, train and guide students towards success, particularly in competitive clubs. Saturday and Sundays are often filled with games or training.

JUNE A. GORDON

F

family, gender and society

From the late nineteenth century, travel books about Japan always included a chapter on Japanese women, which focused on dress, hairstyles and other aspects of physical appearance, and such stereotypes as that of the geisha. Most commentators on contemporary societies, however, prefer to focus on gender relations, that is, the relations between men and women in a particular society, rather than treating men or women as discrete categories. Cultural analysts attempt to explain how particular ideologies of masculinity and femininity come to prevail in the cultural forms of a society. The concept of gender relations can shed light on the dynamics of several spheres of Japanese society: the family, leisure, the workplace, the education system, the legal system, the political system and government policies. Masculinity and femininity form a major focus of popular culture: the masculinity of the *sarariiman*, the femininity of the education mother or the gender bending to be found in *manga*, the **Takarazuka** review or the novels of **Yoshimoto Banana**.

Whereas individuals under the pre-war political system were seen as subjects whose limited rights were granted by the Emperor, the Japanese people are now positioned as citizens with inalienable rights, including the right to freedom from discrimination. The **post-war Constitution** of 1947 guarantees that all of the people are equal under the law and there shall be no discrimination in political, economic or social relations because of race, creed, sex, social status or family origin. The Electoral Law was revised in December 1945,

making it possible for women to stand for office and vote in the first post-war national election in April 1946. The Labour Standards Law in 1947 stated the principle of equal pay for equal work. Until **equal employment opportunity legislation** became effective in 1986, Article 14 and Article 90 of the Constitution were often cited in litigation in cases of discrimination. In the 1970s, several women commenced litigation against companies that had discriminated against women in wages, promotion or retirement provisions. Although these cases referred to equality provisions of the Constitution, such expensive and time-consuming cases highlighted the limitations of the system, and the need for more specific and effective legislation against discrimination. This became a focus for groups such as the **International Women's Year Action Group**, who lobbied the government to ratify the Convention on the Elimination of all forms of Discrimination against Women (CEDAW). Ratification was followed by revision of the education system (in particular a revision of the domestic science curriculum, which would now be taken by both boys and girls), revision of discriminatory provisions of the **Nationality Law** and the enactment of an Equal Employment Opportunity Law (EEOL), which became effective in April 1986.

The post-war education system is formally based on egalitarian principles. Most young people go as far as senior high school. Although the numbers of males and females advancing to higher education are roughly equal, women are disproportionately represented in two-year colleges. Streaming into different kinds of institution and different disciplines still affects the likelihood of gaining employment in career-track occupations. Under the post-war Civil Code, provisions related to marriage, **divorce** and inheritance are based on equality between husband and wife, and equality between siblings. Divorce is granted almost automatically by mutual consent of both parties, and the grounds for judicial divorce are the same for husband and wife. Divorce by mutual consent is relatively unproblematic, but contested divorces require mediation. The *koseki* (household registration) system, however, still shows traces of the pre-war patriarchal family system. Each household has a family head, usually male. Under the present registration system, both spouses must have the same surname, and in almost 98 per cent of cases, the husband's surname is chosen (see *fūfu bessei*).

Married women who earn less than a moderate threshold are exempt from income tax, while their husbands may, in addition, receive a dependent-spouse rebate. Under the national insurance system, if the wife earns less than this threshold she will be included as a dependant on her husband's health insurance with no extra premiums. The inadequacy of state assistance for supporting mothers also acts to keep women within the existing nuclear family. In addition, private companies provide benefits to married male employees in the form of special allowances and welfare benefits, resulting in an even greater widening of the gap between male and female earnings. All of these practices privilege a heterosexual couple in a nuclear family with the male partner as primary breadwinner, and act as a disincentive for wives to earn an independent income.

Women who return to work after the minimum period of maternity leave may take advantage of nursing leave (thirty minutes at each end of the day), and many workers use this time for taking children to and from childcare. Both public and private **childcare** facilities are available. Most public facilities, however, only cater for children over one year old. Parents who only take the minimum period of childcare leave may have difficulties in finding adequate childcare for babies under twelve months old. In addition, most childcare facilities operate from 8:00 a.m. to 6:00 p.m., so that some parents have to find additional childcare before or after these hours. The conditions of work for elite male employees make it difficult for most males to share in domestic labour. Long working hours and commuting hours mean that men are rarely seen at home during the daytime, giving rise to an extreme sexual division of labour in most homes with children. Due to the increasing tendency to live in apartments or houses in the outer suburbs, the sexual division of labour is reinforced by a spatial division, with housing estates in dormitory suburbs largely populated by mothers and children during the daylight hours. In the 1980s and 1990s, the problems of *tanshin funin* (so-called company bachelors, separated from their families through company transfers) received media attention, and the coining of the phrase *karōshi* (death from overwork) reflected a public consciousness of the extremely stressful conditions of work for many elite male workers in Japan, where yearly working hours exceed other OECD countries.

The care of the aged (see **ageing society and elderly care**) and disabled is overwhelmingly carried out by women within the family, an issue becoming more and more pressing with the rapid ageing of Japanese society. In recognition of this situation, a new insurance system for the care of the aged was implemented in the 1990s. An ever-increasing proportion of the population is over the age of sixty-five, due to greater life expectancy and declining birth rates. After the immediate post-war baby boom of 1947, birth rates declined steadily. Falling birth rates and a trend towards nuclear households have resulted in a steady decline in household size. Abortion (see **reproductive control**) is relatively accessible, thanks to a clause of the Eugenic Protection Law of 1947 (amended as the Law for the Protection of the Maternal Body in 1996), which allows abortion on economic grounds. Condoms are widely used, but the use of the contraceptive pill has been strictly regulated, with restrictions finally being removed in the year 2000. The steadily decreasing birth rate (now less than replacement rates) is at times the focus of conservative panic, resulting in regular attempts to have the economic-reasons clause removed from the abortion law.

The relationship between domestic labour and waged labour determines the choice of many women to re-enter the labour force as part-time workers (see **part-time work**). Part-time workers and home-based workers, in addition to being subject to inferior working conditions, are marginalized from union representation, as most labour unions (see **unions and the labour movement**) focus on full-time permanent workers. From the period of high economic growth of the 1960s, women were increasingly involved in paid labour outside the home. However, because of the difficulty of combining paid work with domestic responsibilities, women tended to leave full-time employment in the years when they had peak responsibility for childcare, and return to part-time work when children reached school age. Married women who combine domestic responsibilities with waged work now outnumber full-time housewives.

Young men and women are streamed into different tracks in the educational system, so that many women have already been selected out of the possibility of progressing to an elite occupation by their choice to study at a two-year junior college, or to major in humanities rather than law, science or social sciences. Thus, there is a much larger pool of males than females who are qualified to enter the management track of large corporations or elite positions in the bureaucracy. Although it has generally been easier for women in the public sector to continue in full-time employment after marriage, thanks to legal guarantees in the public sector that pre-dated the framing of equal opportunity legislation, we can observe a similar marginalisation of women in decision-making positions in the public sector. Despite the fact that both women and men are present in most workplaces, the white-collar workplace is often constructed as a masculine space, with women being positioned as decorative non-workers or support labour, as designated by such labels as **office ladies** (OLs).

The masculinisation of middle-class workplaces is extended into the practices of after-hours entertainment in bars and hostess clubs. For women, however, these bars and clubs are workplaces (see **mizushōbai**). While prostitution (see **prostitution, regulation of**) is technically illegal, state policies take the form of regulation rather than prevention. The relationship between masculinity and work takes different forms in blue-collar workplaces, where skill and endurance form important elements of working-class masculinity, and women workers are relegated to marginal status as part-timers. The entry of immigrant workers from South and South-East Asia has highlighted the interaction of class, race, ethnicity and gender in the labour market (see **Japayuki-san**). Immigration policy officially prohibits the entry of workers to engage in unskilled labour, but several industries are now dependent on the labour of illegal immigrant workers. Female workers, often from South-East Asia, are likely to be engaged in domestic work, entertainment or prostitution. Male workers may come from the Middle East or other Asian countries, and are likely to be employed in small-scale factory production or construction work. The fact that most are illegal immigrants means that they may be exploited all the more efficiently. Such organisations as the **Asian Women's Association** have been involved in advocacy for these marginalised workers.

State institutions, policies and practices are implicated in the shaping of gender and class relations in various ways. Responsibility for welfare is often delegated to private companies and the private family. Although welfare policies are decided on at the national government level, implementation may be the responsibility of local governments. Conservative policies on welfare have emphasised a Japanese-style welfare state where women bear the brunt of welfare provision. Other policy areas also reveal gendered assumptions. For example, those provisions of the Labour Standards Law directed at women are known under the generic phrase **bōsei hōgo** (protection of motherhood), suggesting that women are primarily viewed as mothers, and that the state attitude to women is a protective one.

The gendered divisions in the home and the workplace are reinforced by stereotypical portrayals of men and women in the mainstream media and popular culture. In Japan, a distinction is made between the mass-communications media, or *masu-komi*, characterised by high capital investment and high market penetration, and the more informal networks of communication between members of specialised political groups, known as **mini-komi**. Feminist media (see **feminist publishing**) in Japan provide an alternative forum for the discussion of gender issues. Several groups have shown an interest in the problem of **pornography**, linking violent pornography with sexual harassment and sexual violence against women. The mass media has also responded to changes in gender relations with the creation of magazines, television programming and advertising targeted at ever more specialised niche markets of men and women.

Further reading

Allison, A. (1994) *Nightwork: Sexuality, Pleasure and Masculinity in a Tokyo Hostess Club*, Chicago: Chicago University Press.

Brinton, M.C. (1993) *Women and the Economic Miracle: Gender and Work in Postwar Japan*, Berkeley: University of California Press.

Buckley, S. (1994) 'Altered states: The body politics of "being-woman"', in A. Gordon (ed.) *Postwar Japan as History*, Berkeley: University Of California, pp. 347–72.

Dasupta, R. (2000) 'Performing masculinities? The salayman at work and play', *Japanese Studies* 20(2): 189–200.

Mackie, V. (1995) 'Equal opportunity and gender identity', in J. Arnasson and Y. Sugimoto (eds) *Japanese Encounters with Postmodernity*, London: Kegan Paul International.

Nuita Y., Yamaguchi, M. and Kuba, K. (1994) 'The UN convention on eliminating discrimination against women and the status of women in Japan', in B.J. Nelson and N. Chowdhury (eds) *Women and Politics Worldwide*, trans. E. Clarke, New Haven: Yale University Press, pp. 398–414.

VERA MACKIE

FAMILY REGISTER see *koseki*

FAMILY REGISTRATION see *koseki*

family system

The term *ie*, or family system, is used to describe the formal household unit of an extended patriarchal family structure that was enshrined in the legal code of pre-war Japan. The post-war Constitution guaranteed equal rights of all individuals and eliminated many discriminatory elements of the pre-war code, which had promoted the rights of some at the expense of others, especially women and female children who were consistently subordinated to the will of the household head, father, parents-in-law and husband. The household was the organising structure of many areas of law and policy, such as taxation, family registration (*koseki*), nationality and citizenship, inheritance, etc. The term *ie* stood for both the physical structure and hierarchical relations of the household members and the family members themselves. The position of head of household was usually inherited by the eldest son or, in the absence of a son, the husband of a daughter or other appropriate male heir could be officially adopted into the family register. It was the respect for the father and head of household positions that was extended to the unquestioning respect for the Emperor in State Shintō as Japan moved towards militarisation under the emperor system. It was for this reason that the Occupation targeted the *ie* system in its post-war legal and social reforms.

In pre-war Japan it was common for all family members to remain actively involved in the primary occupation of the traditional household, whether fishing, rice cultivation, *nō* acting, ceramics, restaurant or retail. Younger sons and daughters might marry out or bring marital partners into the main household, depending on the wealth of the family and available space. Branch households were obligated to remain closely linked to both the daily activities and rituals (ancestor worship etc.) of the main household. In post-war Japan it is usually only families in which there is an ongoing craft, art or business under way, or where there are significant financial and property resources, that the traditional practices and structure of *ie* can still be found. The nuclear family has become the norm, even though it is still often the case that elderly parents may reside close to an eldest son or other adult child. Children select their own education path, careers and marriage partners, although there is arguably still more direct involvement of parents, and mothers in particular, than in North America or Europe (see ***kyōiku mama***). The Liberal Democratic Party has attempted at different times since the 1980s to revive a notion of *ie* through the so-called 'Japanese-style welfare system', which calls on the family to accept an increasing level of welfare function transferred from the state.

Ongoing, if gradual, shifts in attitude towards divorce, single parenthood, gay relationships and adoption have all seen the shape of the Japanese family continue to diversify over the 1980s and 1990s. Other factors impacting the family have included the rise in 'career bachelors' (***tanshin funin***), living separately from their families on work assignments, and higher rates of widowhood related to increased deaths among male middle-aged white-and blue-collar workers. Today, the absolute authority and omnipresence of the father and household head has been replaced by concerns over the absent father, overworked, seldom at home when children are awake and reliant on the mother/wife for household management.

SANDRA BUCKLEY

farmers' movements

The grassroots farmers' movement expanded explosively in the early post-war period, but its ascendancy was short lived. An organising drive among farmer activists of various political stripes began immediately after the war, and in February 1946 the Japan Farmers' Union (Nihon Nōmin Kumiai, or Nichinō) emerged as a unified organisation. In February 1947, Nichinō estimated that its 6,000-odd member unions represented over a million people. Although dominated by right-wing socialists, Nichinō's local unions were often more radical than the centre. Farmers rose up spontaneously in this early period in order to rectify local abuses of power, to call for the abolition of a compulsory governmental system of crop deliveries and to democratise the distribution of rations.

Developing in the midst of this early dynamism of the farmers' movement was the programme of **land reform** carried out under the Allied Occupation. 'Land to the tillers' had been the consistent slogan of the Japan Farmers' Union before the war, and the prospect of finally owning some land, along with fear of the vigorous

resistance against expropriation by former landlords, stimulated tenants to organise. However, once the reform was completed such activism was fated to decline.

The first split in the farmers' movement occurred in July 1947, when the pre-war organiser and right-wing socialist Hirano Rikizō withdrew his faction to form the All-Japan Farmers' Union (Zenkoku Nōmin Kumiai), and Nichinō split again in 1949. Although the total number of union members continued to grow, reaching some 2.5 million by 1948, the 1950s was an era of declining strength for the organised movement, especially at the local level.

Even so, the 1950s saw farmers form *ad hoc*, local organisations to combat tangible threats to land rights and livelihood. There were ninety-one cases recorded between 1952 and 1960 in which at least fifty rural protestors touched off police intervention and/or physical violence. Most of these dealt with land rights issues and arose out of disputes regarding changes to local boundaries, water rights or the establishment or expansion of military bases. Movements against US military facilities resulted in a number of violent protests over the 1950s.

Following the stagnation of the post-war farmers' union movement, the political demands of farmers have been expressed through the national organization of the Union of Agricultural Co-operatives (Nōgyō Kyōdō Kumiai, or Nōkyō). Nōkyō's thousands of branch co-operatives in rural areas have annually purchased virtually all the grain produced by Japanese farmers and turned it over to the government in exchange for payment at fixed rates, which it transfers back to the local co-ops and into the hands of farmers. Then, each year during Diet deliberations, Nōkyō has transported these same farmers to Tokyo in the thousands to demonstrate for substantial raises in the price of rice. Rather than just a movement, Nōkyō has become a giant financial conglomerate, or trading company, that also acts as a political pressure group.

Japanese farmers retain their willingness to protest spontaneously and vigorously when threatened by such intrusions as military facilities, dams, development projects and airports. Their protracted resistance against Narita Airport provides just one example (see **Narita Airport struggle**).

Further reading

Sugimoto, Y. (1981) *Popular Disturbance in Postwar Japan*, Hong Kong: Asian Research Service.

J. VICTOR KOSCHMANN

fashion

Until 1868, the year that the Meiji government came into being, there was a long period in which there existed a policy of national isolation. During this time, Japan cherished and nurtured its own cultural and traditional dress, the **kimono**. However, with the Meiji Period, Japan pursued a policy of rapid Westernisation, which extended to Japanese dress. Yet, this trend applied primarily to men's and boys' fashion. While Western-style clothing for women did find its way into Japan and saw the emergence of the *moga* (modern girl) styles, there was extensive criticism of the shift from traditional dress to Western styles among women. Although Western fashion for men was equated with modernity and contemporaneity and encouraged, for women it was equated with an abandonment of traditional values of womanhood and often frowned upon. It was not until after the Second World War that new women's fashions finally began to develop in earnest and were less encumbered by, but never completely free of, moral critique.

After the war, the Westernisation of Japanese dress developed at great pace and spread widely among all Japanese people. Fashion information flowed into Japan from the USA and France in a proliferation of imported and local fashion and style magazines. As schools teaching dressmaking and design emerged one after another, there was an explosion in the production of Western garments. Dressmaking, both professional and home-based, became an important part of life, and from this trend emerged the first of Japan's professional designers. The shape of the industry was also changing as the traditional textile industry transformed itself and the apparel industry in response to the new market demands. The ease of this transformation reflected the excellence of design and manufacture of the traditional culture of the kimono industry and its ability to transfer that skill base to the new fashion technologies.

Hanae Mori appeared on the world scene as a Japanese designer in the 1960s. She achieved renown in the USA for her designs in luxurious Japanese silks. In 1976, she was accepted as a member of the Parisian *haute couture*. In 1970, **Takada Kenzō** attracted immediate attention in world fashion when he made his debut in Paris with designs that mixed Japanese pattern and colour with the sensibilities of the Parisian urban scene. By the mid-1970s, designers such as Yamamoto Kansai, **Miyake Issei**, and others had established their reputations in Paris, London and New York. In particular, it was Miyake Issei who drew attention with his 'one cloth' concept designs that were a fusion of Western and Oriental elements. In his active role as a world designer, Issey Miyake (as he came to be known) constructed a foundation for the future reputation of Japanese designers. The 1970s was the time of Japan's rapid economic growth and a dramatic rise in the standard of living and levels of disposable income within a fast growing middle class. The fashion industry in Japan attracted increasing interest and the domestic designer brand market grew along with the economy.

The 1980s saw the emergence of designers like Rei Kawakubo and Yamamoto Yōji, who in turn participated in the Paris collections. Their style, a Japanese aesthetic, which seemed to be such an expression of the contemporary moment, was so different from Western styles that it drew much righteous indignation and was sensationalised in the fashion world as the 'Japan Shock'. The designs were baggy as though made to conceal rather than flatter the human body. The style was deliberately shapeless and made to look worn and torn, and often colourless, featuring only black and white. Ultimately, these designs disrupted the dominant Western fashion aesthetic and flew in the face of *haute couture*. However, despite the fact that the designs of Issey Miyake, Rei Kawakubo and Yamamoto Yōji were the product of a cultural sphere so far removed from the sensibilities of *haute couture* and Western fashion, they still achieved an extraordinary appeal. Japanese fashion came to be characterised variously as 'world clothing', 'global fashion', 'post-apocalypse chic', etc.

The Japanese designs had no limits or restrictions in terms of gender, size or time of day – it was often both day or evening wear, one-size and androgynous. These designs had such novelty and achieved such popularity that, by the end of the 1980s, 'Japanese fashion' had its own unique currency in high fashion throughout the West and Asia, and still remains a major influence on emerging young designers everywhere.

AKIKO FUKAI

feminism

Feminist thought and feminist activism in Japan has a history dating back to the late nineteenth century. As part of a more general development of liberal thought and notions of human rights, women argued for women's rights (*joken*) from the 1880s. Socialist thinkers also debated the 'woman question' (*fujin mondai*) in the first decades of the twentieth century. The feminist literary journal, *Seitō* (Bluestocking), edited first by **Hiratsuka Raichō** and then Itō Noe, appeared from 1911 to 1916. Until 1922, Article 5 of the Public Peace Police Law prevented women from attending, holding or speaking at political meetings or belonging to political organisations. The Electoral Law also prevented women from voting or standing for public office. After the modification of Article 5 in 1922, it became possible for women to form organisations to lobby for women's suffrage. The League for the Attainment of Women's Suffrage was formed in 1924, led by **Ichikawa Fusae**. Bills for women's suffrage passed the Lower House in 1930 and 1931 but failed to pass in the House of Peers. Autonomous women's organisations were gradually co-opted under the total national mobilisation system of the Second World War.

In post-war Japan, women were initially active in such organisations as the **Mother's Convention** (Hahaoya Taikai), consumer groups, pacifist organisations and the **Housewives' Association** (Shufuren). In the 1970s, women's organisations took on a more explicitly feminist character. Some women had participated in the New Left and student left organisations that protested against the renewal of the US–Japan Security Treaty in 1960,

and which brought universities to a standstill in 1968 and 1969. Women, however, became disillusioned with the sexism of the left, and formed their own groups to explore issues of sexuality, reproductive control and identity. Women's liberation groups were known both by the Japanese phrase for the women's liberation movement (*josei kaihō undō*) and by the transliteration of women's liberation from English. The media soon started to abbreviate this to *ūman ribu* (women's lib) (see **Women's Liberation**). Such groups as the Fighting Women Group (Gurūpu Tatakau Onna) and the more sensational **Chūpiren** (Alliance for the Legalisation of Abortion and the Pill) focused on **reproductive control**. The Fighting Women Group were particularly interested in challenging conservative attempts to make it harder to obtain abortions, while Chūpiren also focused on the legalisation of the contraceptive pill. Women's liberationists set up the Shinjuku Liberation Centre, which provided an influential base for consciousness raising and political campaigns. Women's liberationists also carried out a series of weekend camps as a site for feminist discussion and consciousness raising.

International Women's Year in 1975 and the subsequent United Nations Decade for Women provided a focus for reformist activities by such groups as the **International Women's Year Action Group**. Another group, led by feminist poet Atsumi Ikuko, published a feminist journal called *Feminisuto* (Feminist) from 1977 to 1980, including two English editions. Words like *feminisuto* (feminist) and *feminizumu* (feminism) gradually became accepted terms. Feminist thought also contributed to the development of **women's studies** in Japan, in particular **women's history**. With slightly different emphases, feminist thinkers refer to women's studies (*joseigaku*), theories of women (*Joseiron*) or research on women (*josei kenkyū*). The term gender (*jendaa*) was originally associated in Japan with a rather idiosyncratic use of the term by Ivan Illich. More recently, gender has come to be used in Japan to refer to the structured relationships between men and women in a given society, and the cultural constructions of masculinity and femininity. This has led to new coinages such as gender research (*jendaa kenkyū*). Feminist women historians, in particular, have often provided a crucial link between activism and feminist research. This link was exemplified around the issue of the so-called **comfort women**, where campaigns for compensation have been supported by key historical research.

Feminist groups are currently engaged in issues that involve the gendered dimensions of relationships between Japan and other countries in the Asian region, prompted by an interest in the situation of immigrant workers in Japan, and in the situation of workers in the tourism industry and multinational factories. The **Asian Women's Association**, led by journalist **Matsui Yayori** has focused on these issues since its formation in 1977. Immigrant women, and women of the Korean and Taiwanese resident communities, are also dealing with issues where gender, class and ethnicity interact. Post-structuralism, post-modernism,- and post-colonialism have had an influence on feminist thought in Japan in recent years, with major works being translated from European languages, and theorists from within Japan actively adapting these theories to their own situation.

Further reading

AMPO: Japan–Asia Quarterly Review (eds) (1996) *Voices from the Japanese Women's Movement*, New York: M.E. Sharpe.

Buckley, S. (1997) *Broken Silence: Voices of Japanese Feminism*, Berkeley: University of California Press.

Mackie, V. (1996) 'Feminist critiques of modern Japanese politics', in Monica Threlfall (ed.) *Mapping the Women's Movement: Feminism and Social Transformation in the North*, London: Verso, pp. 260–87.

Tanaka, K. (1995) 'The new feminist movement in Japan, 1970–1990', in Kuniko Fujimura-Fanselow and Atsuko Kameda (eds) *Japanese Women: New Feminist Perspectives on the Past, Present and Future*, New York: The Feminist Press, pp. 343–52.

VERA MACKIE

feminist publishing

The networks of communication among women's groups in Japan include small-scale newsletters and more established journals, e-mail networks and bulletin boards, publishing ventures and specialist bookshops. In Japan, a distinction is made between the mainstream communications media, or *masu-komi*, characterised by high capital investment and high market penetration, and the more informal networks of communication between members of specialised political groups, known as **mini-komi**. Feminist groups have largely been characterised by the use of channels of communication outside the mainstream communications industry. The feminist media were formerly characterised as countless handwritten and roneoed newsletters, but newsletters can now be produced with professional graphics, typefaces and layout, thanks to the ready availability of cheap personal computers, desktop publishing facilities and high-quality photocopiers. The Internet has also transformed the channels of political communication, both within Japan and in the networks of non-governmental organisations (NGOs) in the Asian region. Bookshops such as Ms Crayon House in Tokyo and Shōkadō in Kyōto and Ōsaka carry books and journals on gender studies, but such publications are also becoming increasingly visible in mainstream bookshops.

Most women's movement publications are ephemeral, reflecting the creation and dissolution of *ad hoc* groups and coalitions around specific topical issues. Other publications, *Agora* or the *Asian Women's Liberation* (now called *Women's Asia: 21*) have demonstrated remarkable longevity, and have become an accepted part of the feminist cultural scene. The Asian Women's Association has also issued regular English-language editions in order to integrate the group into international channels of communication. Other publications try to bridge the perceived gap between academic research and feminist activism. While the publications of the Japan Women's Studies Association are firmly on the academic side of the divide, other journals bring together popular history and more academic feminist history (see **women's studies**; **women's history**). Shōkadō has also acted as a specialist publisher, issuing a Japanese translation and adaptation of *Our Bodies: Our Selves*, and a collection of documents on the Women's Liberation Movement in Japan. Other specialist publishers include Domesu Shuppan, which specialises in women's history and the history of education in

Japan. There are also several other publishers, who, while not specialising in women's studies materials, have lists of publications of interest to women's studies researchers, such as the facsimile editions of several early feminist periodicals.

Another function of feminist media in Japan to provide a critique of the representation of women in mainstream media. More recently, several groups have shown an interest in the problem of **pornography**, and several activists link violent pornography with sexual harassment and sexual violence against women. While the feminist media are produced by women and for women, women are poorly represented at the editorial level on most mainstream publications. Given the poor representation of women in decision-making mass-media positions, it is unsurprising that feminist issues are largely neglected or trivialised in the mass media. Mainstream publishers have also, however, recognised the development of new markets among women with the creation of magazines (see **newspapers and magazines**) targeting working women and ever-more clearly defined niche markets.

Further reading

Buckley, S. (1997) *Broken Silence: Voices of Japanese Feminism*, Berkeley: University of California Press.

VERA MACKIE

festivals

Festivals are an important and integral part of community life in Japan. Although the immediate post-war years saw a period of curtailment of many traditional rituals, by the late twentieth century national, regional and local festivals and celebrations had undergone a major revival. Over the 1980s and 1990s urban communities were encouraged through government support to re-establish, or in some cases even invent, local festivals as a focus of community activity. This revitalisation of festivals has been welcomed by many as a validation of traditional values of family and community, but there are also those who criticise

the trend as an unwanted revival of older, conservative traditions of community organisation and who caution against the risks of a nostalgia for a romanticised or even fabricated past. Feminists have pointed out that the notion of family often celebrated in contemporary formations of festivals, old and new, is the modern family constructed on a myth of the deep traditional roots of the household system (*ie*).

Both the timing and nature of regional festivals vary across Japan in accordance with the tremendous range in climate and geography from one end of the archipelago to the other. When the farming communities of Hokkaidō are already commencing the rituals that welcome the long months of winter snow, the rice-growing villages of Kyūshu are preparing the paddies and performing rituals for the next rice planting aided by the new generation of multi-yield grains as much as the benevolence of the local *kami* (gods), who are the benefactors of the rituals and offerings. Many of the local festivals of Japan are linked to the cycle of seasons and food production. Regional festivals can celebrate or call on the gods for anything from a bountiful rice crop to a successful whale hunt or an abundant pearl harvest. Other festivals are bound to religious or ritual calendar events such as the Birthday of Buddha (8 April, known in Japan as the Flower Festival), Gion festival and the Autumn Equinox or New Year. Another category of festivals or celebration are set by government decree and include Children's Day, Health and Sports Day and Respect for the Aged Day.

Festivals throughout Japanese history have combined the same complex elements that characterise almost all festivals everywhere. It is a time of excessive play and unruly and raucous behaviour, where, for the period of the festival, there is a surface performance of the disappearance of difference of rank and position. Festivals also involve an extraordinary level of planning and co-ordination, and today there is always close collaboration with local authorities, especially the police. Festivals, for all the appearance of egalitarianism, both celebrate and consolidate the wealth and power of those sponsoring the event. The lines of power and influence are drawn and redrawn in the details of community organisation and co-operation that support the festival. These hierarchies of influence may disappear in the moment of the event but are essential to its realization. While some festivals are now sponsored by local or prefectural government, there is often still a strong role to be played by the temples or shrines that are called upon to provide the essential validation of the ritual elements of the festivities. Annual festivals have become an important contribution to the economic viability of many temples and shrines, through both official and household contributions paid in remuneration for festival-related activities, and through other opportunities such as tourism-related sales of souvenirs, entrance fees, amulets, etc. Local communities, particularly in remote and agricultural regions, have also come to often rely on the annual economic injection of tourism for festivals. Some regions and towns now have active promotional strategies to bolster international and national festival tourism. Internet sites have become an important new promotional tool offering everything from historical background to travel information and accommodation bookings.

The modern festivals of Japan, those that have historical roots in communities, those that are a modern invention of tradition and those that are a celebration of the modern (health and sports day), have become the object of much attention and study. Festivals have always been deeply implicated in economic and political networks of influence, locally and nationally. Festivals are also often the site of renegotiation of lines of authority and identification – who has influence over whom. It is not suprising that, as the Japanese contemporary cultural and political landscapes have become more open to the celebration of diversity, there has been an increased national interest in minority community celebrations of distinctive histories and traditions – Brazilian-Japanese and Fillipino community Mardi Gras, Chinese New Year in Yokohama's Chinatown, etc. For the most part, however, the majority of Japan's contemporary festivals remain essentially linked to notions of community and family that are purported to have their roots in tradition but are often inventing these same notions as they perform them. The strong renewed interest of government in the financing and promotion of festivals can be seen as evidence of the potential role these events are seen to play in creating exactly what they are supposedly celebrat-

ing – a sense of community. The Cultural Protection Law of 1975 and the more recent Matsurihō (Festival Law) encode the importance of festivals for both the protection and promotion of traditional practices and artefacts, while also making explicit the government's intention to promote tradition and nostalgia for the past as essential ingredients of wholesome and viable contemporary community structures and environments.

See also: folk performing arts

SANDRA BUCKLEY

film criticism, Japanese

Writing on cinema virtually came to a standstill at the end of the war as film magazines were forcibly consolidated or stopped publication for lack of resources. The boom in cinema attendance after August 1945, however, sparked a revival in film journalism, mostly along the lines of pre-war criticism. There was a renewal of pre-war journals like *Kinema junpō* (Movie Times) and *Eiga hyōron* (Film Comment), combining industry reportage with criticism, and fan magazines like *Eiga no tomo* (Film Friend). Criticism could roughly be divided into three schools: the cultured, impressionistic criticism of film as art (Iijima Tadashi, Tsumura Hideo); reviews of entertainment films written in a popular style (Yodogawa Nagaharu, Futaba Jūzaburō); and left-wing criticism (ranging from the documentary realism of Imamura Taihei to the Socialist Realism of Iwasaki Akira and Uryū Tadao).

It was the latter's tendency to judge cinema according to a politically defined reality that became the target of criticism in the late 1950s, as young film-makers like Matsumoto Toshio argued in such journals as *Eiga hihyō* (Film Criticism) and *Kiroku eiga* (Documentary Film) for alternative realities through avant-garde technique. Some studio directors also contested the dominant cinema in writing, either, like **Masumura Ya-suzō**, on the basis of European modernism, or, as with **Ōshima Nagisa**, through a critique of post-war subjectivity.

This set the stage for the diversification of critical discourse in the 1960s, even as a drop in publications mirrored the decline in the industry. *Eiga geijutsu* (Film Art, edited by Ogawa Tōru) and *Eiga hyōron* (under the editorship of first **Satō Tadao** and then Satō Shigeomi) offered an eclectic range of writing, mostly by non-film specialists like the sociologist Tsurumi Shunsuke, the literary critic Hanada Kiyoteru and writers like Haniya Yutaka, **Mishima Yukio** and Yoshimoto Takaaki. *Kikan firumu* (Film Quarterly), with Yamada Kōichi, became the organ for avant-garde, experimental film (see **experimental film and video**), while a new *Eiga hihyō*, featuring Masuda Masao and Adachi Masao, advocated a radical cinema as part of its New Left political stance.

The dominant tone of post-1970 criticism was set by *Shinema 69* (Cinema 69 – later '70' and '71'). Young critics like **Hasumi Shigehiko**, Yamane Sadao and Hatano Tetsurō steered clear of both non-cinema-specific discourse and the political criticism of the Old and New Left to argue for the study of film as film. Hasumi influenced a whole generation of critics from Matsūra Hisaki to Umemoto Yōichi, but his general aversion to the academic analysis of film, especially the consideration of ideology, economics and other non-cinema-specific determinants, drew criticism from former students like **Yomota Inuhiko**. University film studies, which began before the war, increasingly present an alternative discourse, with strong programmes existing at Nihon, Waseda, Kyōto and Meiji Gakuin universities. Film scholars like Makino Mamoru lament, however, that not nearly enough has been done to change the view persistent in Japanese society that cinema is not an object worthy of scholarly study.

Further reading

Iwamoto Kenji (1987) 'Film criticism and the study of cinema in Japan', *Iconics* 1.

AARON GEROW

film, English-language criticism on

Although foreign-language commentary on Japanese film has a history nearly as long as Japanese cinema itself, it was not until the late 1950s and the initial development of film studies as an academic discipline that substantial criticism began to appear outside the realm of journalism. The pioneering volume of English-language Japanese film analysis, co-authored in 1959 (and updated in 1982) by Joseph L. Anderson and Donald Richie, *The Japanese Film: Art and Industry* remains today the most comprehensive survey of Japanese film, its studio system, its directors, its social and historical contexts, as well as its aesthetic and cinematic systems. Indeed, diversification and specialisation within the field of Japanese film studies have made such a wide-ranging volume no longer imaginable. Following this key contribution to the national film studies rubric, Richie completed a complementary *auteur*-based approach with his 1965 volume *The Films of Akira Kurosawa*, one of the first books in film studies wholly dedicated to the analysis of a single director's *œuvre*. In this light, the two foundational volumes in Japanese film studies also must be considered pivotal texts in the emergence of *auteur*- and national-cinema approaches.

Today, the relationship between Japanese film and the larger discipline of film studies is considerably more uneven, with Japanese film playing a regular, but peripheral, role as an easily summoned example of non-Western film culture. It is frequently cited as a cinematic languages in variance with classical Hollywood norms or as a distinct national cinematic tradition. Only recently has there emerged a significant body of English-language scholarship, often based upon research conducted in Japanese, capable of contesting both its predecessors' essentialising claims about Japanese culture and film studies' formalist tendency to examine Japanese cinema apart from its historical context. Mitsuhiro Yoshimoto's survey of the politics of US criticism on Japanese film breaks criticism after the war into three roughly subsequent periods of film analysis, each with its own dominant ideology. The first of Yoshimoto's periods, from the 1950s to the 1960s, is characterized by its interlocking humanism and essentialism. In other words, criticism on Japanese film frequently resorted to a concept of common humanity, often hinged upon the figure of the director as '*auteur*', which simultaneously relied on an uninterrogated notion of Japanese cultural difference from Euro-American societies. The burden of Japanese film criticism, in this mode, was to analyse or explain Japanese films through explanations of the purported nature of Japan and the Japanese, as well as to laud those films that were able to address universal concerns at the same time as figuring their supposed Japaneseness. Needless to say, such approaches often overlooked vast political and social differences within Japan.

The late-1970s saw the emergence of a different model: film studies' theoretical concern with Japanese cinema, where attention was often focused around key directors. Films by **Ōzu Yasujirō** and by **Ōshima Nagisa**, and other directors from the Japanese New Wave, came to occupy an important place in the formalist, psychoanalytic and post-structuralist analyses published in the British film theory journal *Screen* and the US *Wide Angle*. In the process, Japanese film became the site of heated theoretical debates involving leading figures in film studies: David Bordwell, Edward Branigan, Stephen Heath, Kristin Thompson, Maureen Turim and Paul Willemen, among others. A representative text of this period, a continued target of criticism and one of the most polemical and exciting works in Japanese film studies is Noël Burch's *To the Distant Observer: Form and Meaning in Japanese Cinema* (1979). Burch draws upon Japanese film-making practice in an effort to mark the politically radical possibilities inherent in its differences from classic Hollywood but, in his frequent location of this radicalism in the vague space of Japanese tradition, Burch ends up falling into an Orientalist trap of reifying Japanese culture. Although appearing much later than these initial debates, David Bordwell's boldly authoritative study *Ozu and the Poetics of Cinema* (1988), and Maureen Turim's psycho-analytic, feminist work in *The Films of Oshima Nagisa: Images of a Japanese Iconoclast* (1998), can be seen as richly developed descendants of this theoretical attention to the language of cinema and the contestation of established modes of representation.

In recent decades, history as an organising trope has risen to prominence within the field and with it an increased attention to the local specifics of Japanese film. David Desser's ground-breaking survey of the Japanese New Wave, *Eros purasu gyakusatsu* (Eros plus Massacre, 1988), sought to locate it 'within a particular historical, political, and cultural context', namely the Japanese 1960s. In a similar vein, Donald Kirihara has examined director **Mizoguchi Kenji** amid the context of 1930s culture, and Kyoko Hirano's *Mr Smith Goes to Tokyo* (1992) has surveyed Japanese film culture under the Allied Occupation. However, recent work also has seen a subordinate tendency towards the interfacing of thematic and theoretical projects within a historical perspective. For example, Mick Broderick's edited anthology *Hibakusha Cinema: Hiroshima, Nagasaki, and the Nuclear Image in Japanese Film* (1996) does not limit itself according to period or director, but rather engages with a broad range of filmic media from studio products and independent or experimental film to documentary and *anime* to deal with Japan's atomic experience. Isolde Standish's *Myth and Masculinity in the Japanese Cinema* (2000) crosses a limited number of genres spanning the twentieth-century that each figure the tragic male hero and a shifting crisis in masculinity. While Darrell William Davis's *Picturing Japaneseness* (1996) can be understood as a survey of 1930s and early 1940s film, the book's theoretical approach, coupled with its analyses of films in the immediate post-war and beyond, demonstrate its main concern to be the cinematic construction of a Japanese national identity. Research by Miriam Silverberg and others on non-Japanese cinema in Japanese film culture signals a much needed move towards placing Japanese film studies in a global, political perspective. Likewise, current attention among historians to Japanese colonial and wartime cinema suggests a productive questioning of the very notion of nation within Japan film studies. Finally, the renewed attention to women and gender, and newly critical attention to sexuality that have emerged in the late 1990s also portend that currently ascendant historical models will only undergo further productive questioning.

Further reading

Lehman, Peter (1987) 'The mysterious Orient, the crystal clear Orient, the non-existent Orient: dilemmas of Western scholars of Japanese film', *Journal of Film and Video* 39(1) (winter): 5–15.

Mitsuhiro Yoshimoto (2000) *Japanese Cinema in*

Search of a Discipline, Kurosawa: Film Studies and Japanese Cinema, Durham: Duke University Press.

Nolletti, Arthur, Jnr and Desser, David (eds) (1992) *Reframing Japanese Cinema: Authorship, Genre, History*, Bloomington: Indiana University Press.

JONATHAN M. HALL

film festivals

Japanese cinema initially rose to international prominence following the Second World War because of key awards received at Europe's top film festivals. **Kurosawa Akira**'s *Rashōmon* (1950) was a surprise winner of the 1951 Venice Festival's Golden Lion, its top prize. Next, **Mizoguchi Kenji**'s films were honoured at Venice over two consecutive years: *Saikaku ichidai onna* (The Life of Oharu, 1952) received the 1952 Golden Lion, followed by the 1953 Silver Lion for *Ugetsu monogatari* (Ugetsu, 1953). Kinugasa Teinosuke's *Jigokumon* (Gate of Hell, 1954) was then awarded the 1954 Grand Prize at Cannes and a US Oscar a year later. These films and others, revelations to the West, later received distribution that helped introduce Japanese culture and customs worldwide. Since then, Japanese films have frequently played important roles in international film festivals.

Imamura Shōhei, for example, became only the fourth international director to have two films garner Cannes' Golden Palm, cinema's most prestigious film festival award. In addition, a number of special film collections, including 'Before *Rashōmon*' (Japanese films before 1950), 'Women in Japanese Cinema', and director-based series, have been exhibited in prominent film festivals, particularly Locarno and Rotterdam, and significant cultural institutions worldwide since the 1970s, further introducing Japanese culture and film.

Film festivals are also important inside Japan. The Tokyo International Film Festival was originally organised in 1985 with an emphasis on young cinema. It has evolved into a major international event, complete with a competition and sidebars. New, emerging voices are now nurtured by the Pia Film Festival and the Image Forum Film Festival. The Yamagata International Documentary Film Festival, first spearheaded by documentary filmmaker (see **documentary film**) Ogawa Shinsuke in 1989, has also commanded considerable international acclaim. Finally, the non-competitive Fukuoka International Film Festival actively promotes Asian cinema.

WILLIAM C. THOMPSON

film, literature and screenplay

Post-war Japanese cinema already counted on a firm link with the literary world. Already, starting from the second decade of the last century, not only were the adaptations of literary works increased but gradually, beginning with the theories of the 'movement for pure cinema' (*Jun eiga undō*) by Kaeriyama Norimasa, the definite autonomy of the screenplay as the main feature of the film was affirmed. This, therefore, made the psychological depth that already existed in literature also possible in the cinema. In the totally Japanese tendency to codification, the adaptations lay within the already existing division between *jun bungaku* (pure literature) and *taishū bungaku* (popular literature for the masses). In particular, costume films, which were utilised as a means of spreading nationalistic theories during the war period, and which were later forbidden by the Occupation Forces following the war, belonged to the latter category.

During the 1950s, *jun bungaku* was the source from which the authors of this Golden Age drew their subjects. In spite of the fact that there were still many directors who, like Ozu, preferred to create original topics, often working in collaboration with a staff of screenplay writers to craft and create personal styles, many other directors drew on the wealth of famous modern novels. Among the most frequently adapted works are those by Kawabata Yasunari, Tanizaki Jun'ichirō and Shiina Rinzō. Many classical works have also been revived, and Meiji Period fiction has also proven a popular source of cinematic material. Perhaps the best-known such adaptation in the West is *Rashōmon* (1950) by Kurosawa, based on tales by Akutagawa Ryūnosuke. Directors like Toyoda Shirō, Gosho Heinosuke, Kinoshita Keisuke and Kon Ichikawa directed works with a strong visual impact drawing from the refined *jun bungaku* narrative repertoire. However, at the end of the 1950s, depictions of young people's unease and a moral violence, which had never been seen before, increased. This began with the work of the writer/screenwriter Ishihara Shintarō, in the literary world and subsequently in the cinema. Depictions of disaffected young protagonists continued to gain momentum, if in a politically different way throughout the 1960s. The films of Ōshima Nagisa exemplify this trend and also typify the trend away from the literary world. The screenplay, together with the movie camera, began to emerge as the dual trademarks and tools of the author/film-maker.

At the same time, *taishū bungaku* remained a strong reference point for genre movies. Most notable are the screenplays of the numerous *yakuza eiga* (gangster films), which repeat the structure of famous popular works such as *Chūshingura*, or which are adaptations of commercial bestsellers, like the works of Kadokawa Haruki. Significant collaborations between directors and writers include Teshigahara Hiroshi–Abe Kōbō, Shinodai Masashiro–Terayama Shūji and, more recently, Yanagimachi Mitsuo–Nakagami Kenji. Authors came to increasingly collaborate not only with the director but also in the creation of the screenplay.

Since the 1980s, new cultural expressions have challenged the literary world's influence on cinema, above all *manga* and advertising. Both of these forms favour rapid visual messages conveyed by images to the development of in-depth narrative. The strong presence of independent directors has, in addition, favoured the growth of screenplay writers not linked with the system, who often experiment with directing. The new generation of independent screenwriters/directors has seen a proliferation of original, often intensely personal and highly recognisable cinematic signature styles.

MARIA ROBERTA NOVIELLI

fireworks

Sometimes mistakenly described in Western media as Japanese, fireworks are a Chinese invention dating from about the tenth century. *Hanabi* (fire

flowers) quickly found their way into the festivals and celebrations of Japan but never came to play as significant a ritual role as in China. Today, fireworks are still a popular feature of most festivals and have a close association with summer festivities. Children take great pleasure in simple, hand-held sparklers as a pastime on long hot summer evenings. As in China, the loud noise of exploding fireworks is thought to chase away vengeful or bad spirits, but few Japanese who join in the revelry of community festivals today are aware of any greater significance than the immediate excitement and exhilaration of the overwhelming sound and smell of exploding fireworks overhead. The image of fireworks lighting the sky over a festival is a popular nostalgic motif among Japanese film-makers and writers.

SANDRA BUCKLEY

fishermen's movements

Movements among fishermen emerged rapidly in the context of widespread unionisation after the Second World War, and the organisation rate among fisheries workers is overwhelmingly high compared to that in other industrial sectors. About 80 per cent of crew members on seagoing fishing vessels belong to the All-Japan Seamen's Union (Zen Nihon Kaiin Kumiai), and virtually 100 per cent of crew on small and medium-sized coastal fishing vessels are members of the All-Japan League of Fishing Vessel Crew Member Unions (Zenkoku Gyosen Rōdō Kumiai Dōmei). Local movements among fishermen have arisen frequently to combat threats to livelihood from environmental pollution and other sources. Fishermen were at the forefront of the long struggle against mercury poisoning of coastal fishing waters that caused **Minamata disease**; they also achieved passage of important laws on water quality by opposing the Honshū Paper Company's Edogawa plant in 1958–9. Fishermen have participated in many other **citizens' movements** and **residents' movements**, against US bases in Chiba and elsewhere, pulp and cement plants in Ōita Prefecture, a nuclear power plant in Mie

Prefecture and docking by the nuclear-powered ship 'Mutsu' in Aomori Prefecture.

J. VICTOR KOSCHMANN

fishing

Fishing is one of the oldest Japanese occupations. Fishing villages once dominated the cultural landscape of the coastal areas, especially around the **Inland Sea** and the submergent east and southeast coasts. In recent times, fishing as a way of life occupies less than 1 per cent of the population, as machinery and electronic equipment have replaced labour while also increasing catches. While fishing has become less labour intensive for men, however, women have entered the modern fishing labour force in greater numbers, concentrating in fish processing and fish farming. Fish consumption remains a central aspect of Japanese culture.

After the Second World War, Japan quickly rose to become the first ranked country in the world in total annual catch. Their highly sophisticated modern equipment has been criticised internationally for its indiscriminate methods, especially for the threat to dolphins, which become tangled in the equipment. Yet, they continue to seek catches far into international waters, despite cutbacks in recent years due to higher fuel costs and the imposition of 200-mile limits around the coastal waters of other countries. Fishing still represents an important economic activity in the waters closer to Japan. By the 1960s, there had occurred a serious reduction of fish stocks in national waters as a result not only of over-fishing but also of industrial pollution and disturbance of the coastline through **land reclamation**. Since enactment of very tough environmental protection laws over the past two decades, marine life has gradually begun to flourish again.

The Japanese rely more and more heavily on aquaculture, especially for shellfish and crustaceans in the shallow coastal waters, and for freshwater species such as eel, carp and trout in inland ponds. In addition, the Japanese farm and consume more seaweed than any other country. Its myriad varieties are used in countless ways as a basic ingredient in most Japanese cooking.

In a country where Buddhist strictures traditionally forbade consumption of meat, fish and seafood have always represented, along with soybean products, one of the major sources of protein. Although meat consumption has increased in recent years, fish still retains its dominant position, averaging approximately 90 grams per person per day. Fish preparation and consumption are highly developed arts. 'Raw fish' in the form of **sashimi** (plain raw fish) and **sushi** (pickled rice often garnished with raw fish) represent Japanese cuisine to many non-Japanese. Trendy restaurants, with licences, specialise in cooking the **fugu**, or 'puffer' fish, a rather bland, large-boned white fish that contains poisonous glands whose contents can cause death to humans if not expertly removed. Certain fish, such as carp (*koi*) are associated with meals surrounding festive occasions, and are prepared in highly ornamental ways, emphasising the fact that eating is a cultural production of the highest order.

See also: fishermen's movements; whale meat and whaling

Further reading

Kalland, Arne (1990) 'Sea tenure and the Japanese experience Resource management in coastal fisheries', in E. Ben-Ari, B. Moeran and J. Valentine (eds) *Unwrapping Japan: Society and Culture in Anthropological Perspective*, Manchester: Manchester University Press, pp. 188–204.

AUDREY KOBAYASHI

flower arrangement

Literally meaning 'bringing life to flowers' but translated more liberally as 'animating flowers', *ikebana*, the Japanese art of flower arrangement, dates from the fifteenth century and is believed to have derived from earlier Chinese Buddhist rituals of flower offerings. *Ikebana* survived Japan's modernisation as an important cultural skill for any young woman seeking a good marriage. *Ikebana* schools, temples, cultural centres and individual tutors continue to make a lucrative industry of training the young women of Japan in the art of flower arranging.

Although there are numerous schools of flower arrangement, the dominant schools follow the core principle of three main stems, or axis, each of reducing height. The visual balance between these three primary stems is reminiscent of the spatial relations of the aesthetics of architecture. *Ikebana* is not an art form that simply presents the natural beauty of flowers but is an intensely interventionist art form. It takes the natural characteristics of a stem as its point of departure and then works to maximise the potential of the stem, whether through something as minimal as placement and angle or as radical as cutting, bending or binding. A stem may be wired and twisted to create a desired balance or imbalance. The spaces between the three primary stems can then be filled, or not, with minor or secondary stems, blooms, leaves or branches to realise the desired visual density or sparcity of the arrangement. Not unlike *bonsai*, there is no hesitation to intervene dramatically to transform the natural shape or inclination of a branch, stem or flower. The aim is to bring to life or animate rather than simply display, and this aesthetic allows the artist extensive licence for experimentation within the parameters of their particular school of *ikebana*.

The stand, vase or tray that functions as the base has always been integral to the overall *ikebana* design and there has been much freedom to experiment with base materials – wood, pottery, glass, cement, rock, plastic, etc. However, there has only recently emerged a greater flexibility to the inclusion of non-flora within the arangement itself. A 1999 digital technologies exhibition in Tokyo featured a series of *ikebana* designs that incorporated computer components and wiring. There has been some experimentation with the use of light as a feature, e.g. a light beam or fluorescent tube functioning as a stem or axis. Virtual *ikebana* has also emerged as a new area of collaboration between digital and floral art, producing mixed designs of real and virtual stems through such innovations as video, backscreen or holographic projections and animation. Online instruction and information websites are also increasingly popular with Japanese and international *ikebana* clubs seeking a wider membership.

The impact of the aesthetics of *ikebana* on Western styles of floral presentation has been profound over the last decades of the twentieth century. A new genre of minimalist floral design has gained extensive popularity outside Japan, challenging more familiar arrangements. From hotel lobby displays to wedding bouquets and private dinner party décor, volume and colour have given way to spatial design and simplicity. In Japan, the art of *ikebana* remains popular for all adult age groups and particularly among women. Women in their early twenties are encouraged to take *ikebana* classes as a part of their preparation for marriage, and '*midi*' women (middle-class and middle-aged) also often return to *ikebana* as one of their mid-life leisure activities. *Ikebana* classes often become an important social grouping for women outside family and neighbourhood. For the *midi* housewife, coffee outings, restaurant meals, *ikebana* exhibits and competitions, and occasional excursions and tours offer opportunities for friendships and a socially acceptable context for travel and activity beyond the domestic sphere of the home.

The scene of a woman carrying the carefully wrapped parcel of long *ikebana* stems on her way home from class is a familiar one in Japan. Flower shops specialise in offering pre-cut seasonal stems at special prices for home arrangements, while *ikebana* schools usually provide a pre-selected range of stems for their students. Most middle-class households will have a fresh *ikebana* arrangement prepared by the mother, daughter or grandmother of the family each week and placed in the entrance way (**genkan**) or displayed in the **tokonoma** alcove. Businesses, restaurants and hotels, too, prominently display professionally prepared *ikebana*, while some businesses even sponsor *ikebana* classes for their employees. *Ikebana* remains perhaps the most widely pursued of the traditional art forms in Japan today.

SANDRA BUCKLEY

Folk Crusaders, the

The Folk Crusaders are best known for a strangely eerie tune, 'Kaettikita yopparai' (The Reincarnated Drunk), a surrealistic neo-1920s jazz song of sorts.

It features vocals recorded at various speeds somewhat reminiscent of the Chipmunks, as well as an intermittent collage of other musical sources including the Beatles and Beethoven. The Folk Crusaders were formed in August 1965. They decided to split up in 1967 and recorded a self-produced album to commemorate their work together, which had one original song on it, the aforementioned 'Kaettekita yopparai'. It became wildly popular among younger listeners of Radio Ōsaka, eventually reaching number one. When finally released nationwide, it was a smash hit that sold 2,700,000 copies. The song was such a huge hit that the band agreed to get back together for a year, and wrote an album's worth of songs for a major label release, *Kigen ni sennen* (Second Millennium of the Imperial Era). The Folk Crusaders were notable for their eclectic originality and their pioneering use of the studio as an important tool in the creative process. A founding member of the band, Katō Kazuhiro, later went on to form Sadistic Mika Band, one of the most important Japanese bands of the 1970s.

MARK ANDERSON

folk music

Through the 1980s and early 1990s, folk music came to be thought of as the most uncool of musical genres, but there was a time in the late 1960s and early 1970s when it was nearly chic. At that time, a movement arose in opposition to the existing power structure. This movement held up opposition to the establishment as its standard – this aspect of the international student movement was articulated in Japan as well as in Germany, France, England, Korea and the USA (among many others). The folk music of the time became symbolic of this social and political struggle.

As a musical style, folk travelled from the USA to Japan during the 1960s. Japanese folk was stimulated by the modern folk of Peter, Paul and Mary, the Brothers Four, the Kingston Trio and Joan Baez. In Tokyo, groups sprang up that performed covers of Peter, Paul and Mary, the Brothers Four and the Kingston Trio. A modern folk movement known as college folk was born in

Japan as well. In 1963, a Student Festival was organised, which attracted over 6,000 attendees. It featured performances by Moriyama Yoshiko, the Modern Folk Quartet (featuring Mike Maki) and, the highlight of the event, a performance of the Broadside Four (which included Kurosawa Akira's son Hisao) with Joan Baez. It has been said that, by the time of the Tokyo Olympics (1964), performing a folk song had enough cultural cache to improve a male student's appeal to the opposite sex. As a cultural force, however, folk was not as widely popular as the contemporary surf bands and the group sounds bands that succeeded them. There were Japanese language folk hits such as Mike Maki's 'Bara ga saita' (A Rose Has Bloomed) in 1966, and Moriyama Yoshiko's 'Kono hiroi nohara ippai' (This Wide Plain is Full) in 1967, but the earliest folk acts predominantly sang in English or sang Japanese translations of originally English language folk songs. These particular hits were seen by many as simply a new variety of pop music, especially as neither Maki nor Moriyama wrote their own songs.

During the 1960s, the image of college youth changed from the traditional Ivy League look to that of long haired, unwashed teens in jeans. This style became an international symbol of student protest. Just as anti-war and anti-establishment protests were gaining ground internationally, the scheduled 1970 extension of the US–Japan Security Treaty led to an increase in the intensity of Japanese New Left student protest in the late 1960s. In such high-profile actions as the occupation of Shinjuku station on International Anti-War Day (October 1968) and the seizure of Yasuda Hall at Tokyo University in (January 1969), a large-scale struggle between the state and mobile forces for change came to national attention. Japanese-language folk songs with a political and social message were written in the context of this developing situation. In December 1966, Takaishi Tomoya made his recording debut with 'Kago no shima Blues'. Nakagawa Goro, who greatly admired Takaishi, wrote such songs as 'Entrance Exam Blues'. Okabayashi Nobuyasu burst on to the scene in 1968. This variety of politicised folk music defined itself in opposition to commodified popular music such as *kayōkyoku* and, above all, *enka*.

While they had almost no connection with the pop music industry or modern folk, intellectuals aligned with the Alliance for Peace in Vietnam provided support for acts of this sort in the form of promoting concerts and building stages. Given this support, such performers became extraordinarily popular. As the centre of this activity was in Kansai, these acts became known throughout the country as Kansai Folk acts. The Folk Crusaders and their huge hit, 'Kaettikita yopparai' (The Reincarnated Drunk), emerged from this scene in late 1967. Music of this style came to be known as underground folk. As Takaishi and Okabayashi's songs were quite politicised, they were sung at the meetings of such groups as the Alliance for Peace in Vietnam alongside such revolutionary songs as the 'Communist International'. At this point in time, major record labels were cautious about recording and releasing these sorts of songs as a business proposition. In response to this opportunity, the Takaishi office opened the Underground Record Club (URC) as a co-operatively organised, independent record label. URC Records pioneered the folk era with LP record releases of such artists as Okabayashi Nobuyasu, Takaishi Tomoya, Nakagawa Goro, Takada Wataru and Itsutsu no akai fusen (Five Red Balloons). Fashionably politicised folk was in large part associated with the cutting edge URC artists.

At a time when Okabayashi's own song 'Tomoyo' (Friends/Comrades) was being sung at political rallies, he disappeared in the fall of 1969. In 1970, he attempted to remake himself as a rock singer with the support of the band, Happy Endo, but he was already beginning to lose both political and popular appeal. Takaishi Tomoya himself left the Takaishi office in 1969. It seems that the songs of these two had begun to lose their power as a result of changes in political circumstance. The US–Japan Security Treaty was automatically extended in June 1970. By the time the third annual All-Japan Folk Jamboree opened in 1971, the politically informed songs of these two seemed to have been sucked into a historical backdraft. The third annual All-Japan Folk Jamboree featured such diverse URC recording stars as Endō Kenji and Five Red Balloons, but, between 1971 and 1973, all the major acts on URC records moved on to major record labels. In other words, under-

ground folk had almost completely disappeared by 1973. While their lyrics and music still continued to develop, and they had the support of rock musicians such as Happy Endo, the work of most folk artists tended to move towards pop at this point. Politicality became overshadowed by the effort to create an indigenous, urban Japanese pop. This is the beginning of the genre known as New Music. For folk and rock hold-outs such as Shinohara Akira, many of these early 1970s folk singers 'became *enka* singers in jeans'.

Further reading

Tatsuka Hideki (1994) 'Yogaku kabaa kara originaru songu e', in *1970 Ongakujin hyakka jiten* Tokyo: Gakusha Kenkyūsha, pp. 20–1.

Shinohara Akira (1996) 'Folk no shinjitsu', in *J-Rock 1968–1996: Best 123*, Tokyo: Kōdansha Bunko, pp.48–53.

MARK ANDERSON

folk performing arts

Japan is home to a wide variety of folk performing arts (*minzoku geinō*), many of which are still regularly performed; however, due to changing lifestyles and demographics, in recent decades a large number of local performance traditions have died out and many others are facing a similar prospect. The total number of local folk performing arts groups active in the post-war period has been estimated at between 20,000 and 30,000. Most of these arts have their origins in ritual or in entertainments to celebrate ritual events. Today, local **festivals** are still the most frequent occasion for the performance of the folk performing arts.

The most widely accepted classification system, which was devised by the pioneer scholar of folk performing arts, Honda Yasuji (b. 1906), groups the diverse variety of folk performing arts into five major categories: *kagura*, performances associated with Shintō shrines and festivals; *dengaku*, dances related to rice-planting rituals; *furyū*, summer processions and other entertainments, usually found in urban areas; *katarimono* and *shufukugei*, narrative and celebratory arts; and *toraigei* or *butaigei*, imported and other stage arts, including folk varieties of **nō**, **kyōgen**, **kabuki** and the puppet theatre. Among the most well known of the folk performing arts are Hayachine Kagura (Iwate Prefecture), Kurokawa Nō (Yamagata Prefecture) and Mibu Kyōgen (Kyōto).

Since the Meiji Period (1868–1912), social change and the diffusion of new forms of entertainment have threatened the continuation of the folk performing arts. The Second World War and the early post-war period of reconstruction also made it difficult to carry on local traditions, as did the period of high economic growth in the 1960s, which saw rapid industrialisation and large-scale migration to the cities. The sense of crisis engendered by these developments prompted the government to revise the Cultural Properties Protection Law in 1975. Under the revision, a new category of cultural properties, *juūyō mukei minzoku bunkazai* (Important Intangible Folk Cultural Properties), was created to recognise important examples of the folk performing arts. Since then, more than a 150 different folk performing arts groups or traditions have been so designated. The revision also empowered prefectures and municipalities to make their own designations.

Such government efforts to preserve and promote the folk performing arts have been only partially successful. While many nationally designated groups receive the attention of scholars, the media and tourists, as well as frequent requests to perform, many of those lacking designation are left to struggle on in relative obscurity. The problem is perhaps most severe in rural areas, many of which are now suffering from depopulation and ageing, which is making it increasingly more difficult for performing groups to recruit new members. A more recent government measure, the so-called Matsurihō or 'festival law' of 1992, met with criticism from some scholars for what was seen as an attempt to turn the folk performing arts into tourist attractions.

Further reading

Lee, W. (2000) 'Japanese folk performing arts today: The politics of promotion and preservation', in S. Scholz-Cionca and S. Leiter (eds) *Japanese Theatre and the International Stage*, Leiden: Brill.

Thornbury, B. (1997) *The Folk Performing Arts: Traditional Culture in Contemporary Japan*, Albany, NY: State University of New York Press.

WILLIAM LEE

food and drink

Although you may still be asked in some restaurants if you want a 'Western style' (*yōfu*) or 'Japanese style' (*wafu*) meal, this simple categorisation is fast breaking down. Your Western-style meal might be a plate of spaghetti with meat sauce, a pork curry or a steak, while your Japanese meal could be *tempura*, a bowl of noodles (*ramen*) or deep fried pork cutlets (*tonkatsu*) – all dishes historically imported into Japan. While traditional Japanese dishes remain a mainstay of daily food preparation and consumption, there has also been an undeniable internationalisation of the Japanese diet since the late nineteenth century, which has accelerated over the last several decades. The foreign origins of many items remain evident in their names – *pan* (bread), *sūpu* (for non-Japanese soups), *biiru* (beer) and so on. The popular and crowded cafés that line the shopping streets of the major designer-brand and youth culture districts serve menus that mix a selection of European café food and a new global Asian cuisine with Japanese snack food.

Food remains an essential element of daily life that receives a level of attention that many foreigners visiting Japan, who are more accustomed to taking the details of their daily food intake for granted, may find surprising. Whether the carefully prepared lunchboxes (**obentō**) brought to work from home, the long discussions over which local restaurant to order-in lunch from, the nightly ritual of deciding on the preferred cuisine for a group dinner or the daily ritual of housewives rushing to buy fresh produce or pre-prepared dishes for dinner, food is often at the forefront of conversation and daily interaction in the workplace and at home. The sheer density of restaurants in Japanese urban centres, from fast-food and snack outlets to high-class restaurants, is an indicator of the Japanese attention to food as part of everyday life. This has not, however, always been the case, and many of the foods today identified as traditional Japanese cuisine have only found their way from the tables of the elite into the popular diet over the twentieth century, and more particularly the period from the 1960s to the present.

The contemporary love of good food is itself one more manifestation of the effects of the intense consumer boom that began with the rapid increase in household disposable income during the so-called '**Japanese economic miracle**' and the **bubble economy** period. The high levels of expenditure on boxed sets of seasonal food during the gift-giving seasons, a major source of business for department stores and food retailers, dates from this period. The custom of gift giving was transformed in the wake of major marketing campaigns by domestic food and drink manufacturers and major department stores, and today is all too often an exercise in consumer extravagance and brand name snobbery that evidences the buying power and consumer taste of the giver. Many foods now eaten regularly, such as beef and pork, were only introduced into Japan in the late Edo and early Meiji Periods. Even the custom of eating *sushi* or *sashimi* with soy sauce is a recent development, replacing the traditional dipping vinegar. For many Japanese, fresh fish was a rarity and smoked and cured varieties were the norm, but only as an accompaniment to the main dish of rice. Soup, pickles and side dishes of cooked vegetables, fish, whale or boar were served to add taste to a bowl of rice. Even as Japan became familiar with modern Western-style cuisine and eating habits, the notion of a main course of meat with side dishes of vegetable and carbohydrates (potatoes, rice, bread) never displaced the centrality of rice to the Japanese meal.

The food shortages of the immediate post-war years and memories of meagre wartime rations still leave many older Japanese, who grew up in households with the war and transwar generations, critical of the excesses of today's food culture. The shift to larger portions, greater variety and higher food prices might be criticised as extravagant but the majority of Japanese today are oblivious and simply love to love food, spending a significant proportion of their disposable income on fast food and restaurants. A handful of biases remain from the hardship of the war years, such as the widespread reluctance to eat grains other than white rice. Even in an age of health food restaurants and organic produce many still consider brown rice and other unbleached grains to be the food of hard times, and seek out more exotic options like Canadian wild rice, Indian and Mexican breads, etc.

As the Japanese economy strengthened, consumer buying power increased and tastes became increasingly diversified. Japan's agricultural sector responded by transforming significant areas of arable land from rice cultivation to fruit, vegetable crops and dairy pasture. The government, keen to encourage farmers to diversify from the heavily subsidised rice crop, offered subsidies to experiment in new food crops. To this day Japan relies on imports for the majority of its food despite its reputation for market protection. The high level of fish consumption is met today by Japan's massive fishing fleets, which venture as far afield as the Antarctic waters. The aggressive fishing technologies of the fleet have been widely criticised but there has been little response from the Japanese consumer beyond such limited campaigns as 'dolphin-free tuna'. Even in the face of international outrage over Japan's recent renewed attempts to increase its whale catch, sales of whale meat continue to increase again as this protein source has found its way back into the everyday diet. After decades of rejection resulting from overexposure during the early post-war decades, when whale meat was used extensively in government school lunches, whale meat is now re-emerging as a trendy source of protein with a rash of whale meat cook-books and speciality restaurants.

The Western image of Japanese cuisine, as it has found its way into the restaurant districts of the world's major cities, is one of an aesthetic of simple and refined presentation verging on artistic creation, minimal servings and fresh, high-quality produce, and, of course, high prices. However, for most Japanese the daily decision over where to eat lunch or go out together for dinner with co-workers ends in a snack or fast-food restaurant or a neighbourhood speciality restaurant serving fish, noodles, curry, *tempura*, *sushi* or some other affordable fare. Much of the love of food in Japan is also a love of the social interaction of eating with friends or family, and for adults this always extends also to drinking. Beer is widely popular, including a range of domestic and imported beers from standard brands to boutique brews, followed closely by *sake* and whiskeys, and more recently also wines. The popularity of dining out among women workers has prompted a new range of alcoholic beverages with a higher sugar content targeted at women, and packaged for what market research considers a more feminine design for labels, bottles and advertising. The culture of *kissaten* (coffee shop) entertainment among older middle-class women is a popular feature of social activity among friends, and there is a wide range of *kissaten* in any city offering specialisations in coffee blends, brewing techniques, music, exotic pastries and cakes, feature décor, sales of chinaware, imported teas and coffee beans, etc. Faster, cheaper *kissaten* service commuters, and there is a wide variety of *kissaten* and café-bars featuring state-of-the-art architectural and interior design, music, new food and drink trends, etc. to capture the attention and money of the booming urban youth culture.

The top-end restaurant market in Japan is beyond the budget of most individuals. It has been driven to a pricing level beyond that of all but the finest restaurants anywhere else in the world by the power of the corporate expense account. Meals costing upwards of $500 per person are not unusual. The best restaurants, especially the more elite and traditional Japanese establishments, may also offer geisha to serve the meal for a further cost to the host. It is not at all unusual for Japanese travelling overseas to comment that they can eat a higher standard of Japanese restaurant cuisine for less in Sydney or New York than in Tokyo.

At home it is the local restaurant that delivers steaming hot bowls of noodles, plates of *sushi* or Chinese stir-fry to the door and then comes back to carry away the dirty dishes at the end of the night that is perhaps the most familiar and welcome restaurant cuisine at the end of the day. Many housewives still committedly buy fresh produce every day and prepare a home-cooked meal, but there is no shame in buying pre-prepared foods, and supermarkets and department stores specialise in ready-to-serve take-out meals that can be bought *en route* home. An exorbitantly expensive dish of finely sliced *fugu* fish or abalone wrapped in gold leaf may be a rarified cuisine for a foreign visitor to Japan, but even to a Japanese it is far from standard fare.

Food remains closely linked to ceremony and ritual in contemporary Japan. Festivals are commonly marked by special foods such as the *mochi* (rice cakes) on Boys' Day or the sweet *sake* and festive rice of New Year. Food offerings are regularly placed at family shrines and altars (see **butsudan** and **kamidana**), and seasonal foods play a major part in the everyday ritual passage of time. From poetry to pop music, television dramas and advertising billboards, there is a strong focus on seasonal variations in food. Summer is linked in every child's mind to the taste of salted watermelon and crushed ice, while autumn is the season of dried persimmons. Supermarkets and department store food sections will carry seasonal speciality dishes for every time of the year. Regional food specialisations are a favourite souvenir to bring home from travels and can play an important part in the local economy of tourist destinations. Train travel remains popular in Japan and tourists and business travellers alike will look forward to buying the station *obentō* (lunchboxes) of the regions they are passing through. As the Japanese diet has become more internationalised and sales of imported foods have shifted from speciality stores to local supermarkets, there has been a reverse exoticisation of Japanese traditional and regional foods and cooking techniques, with television cooking programmes, cookery schools, kitchen supply stores and online retailers all marketing to the renewed interest in traditional Japanese dishes and ingredients. It is this revalidation of Japanese cuisine that fuels the massive popularity of the highly stylised kitsch cuisine wars of the *Iron Chef* television programme, where top Japanese chefs are pitted against Chinese and Western-style chefs, and judged by a team of Japan's cultural and culinary elite.

It has been the move towards a healthier diet in the West that has seen the successful export of such Japanese foods as tōfu, *miso* and seaweed. Shiitake mushrooms are now available in many local European or North American greengrocers alongside bean sprouts, white radish (*daikon*) and instant *wasabi*. It is the common instant noodle that has made the greatest in-roads into international food markets, with many major Western food manufacturers now producing their own home-grown version of three-minute noodles to capture a share of the youth fast-food market. Many supermarkets now feature a *sushi* corner, and sandwich bars also often offer a take-out pack of inexpensive *sushi*. At the same time that the Japanese diet has been undergoing a substantial internationalisation, there has been a parallel if gradual flow of influence from Japan into the health and fast-food markets, and the more up-market fusion cuisine of the Asia–Pacific region.

SANDRA BUCKLEY

foreign food

Japanese cuisine is often characterised as unique, but there are many elements that originated elsewhere. The earliest influences can be traced to China and Korea, and include such core dishes of Japanese cooking as **tōfu** and bowl noodles (*ramen*). The next wave of foreign influence came with the arrival of the Portuguese and Spanish in the sixteenth century, with the introduction of some European ingredients and preparation, e.g. batter, deep frying, savoury sauces and cake dough. The nineteenth and twentieth centuries have seen the incorporation of a wide range of Western and Asian cuisines into both restaurant and home cooking.

A thousand years of evolution of local Japanese variations makes the distinction of Chinese or Japanese origin often almost meaningless. Neighbourhood restaurants specialising in distinctive national and local dishes of China and Korea proliferated in the 1920s and 1930s around urban industrial centres where significant numbers of Chinese and Korean workers were located during Japan's colonial period. Today, both cuisines remain popular foods for take-out and home delivery. Chinese cuisine has also achieved a place for itself in Japan's contemporary *haute cuisine* along with French and Italian cooking. Most elite hotels boast both a top-ranking Chinese and European-style restaurant among their guest services.

Early contacts with Spanish and Portuguese also introduced dried and salted meats, and a preference for sweet sauces over traditional vinegar and dark soy. Meat did not become a significant ingredient until the 1800s due to Buddhist prohibitions. Initially, meat only found its way on to the plates of wealthy Japanese and a small contingent of foreigners. These elite origins of meat consumption are still evidenced in the rarefied production techniques associated with **Kobe beef**. 'Mountain whale' or wild boar is the only meat with a long history in Japanese cuisine. Sugar, which is now found in many basic Japanese sauces and broths, was not widely available until the nineteenth century. The cultivation of sugar-cane played a still relatively unexplored role in Japan's colonial policies of the twentieth century.

The taste for **coffee**, **beer** and **whiskey** dates from the rapid introduction of European foods in the late nineteenth century and each played an important role in the emergence of cafés, music clubs and dance halls in early twentieth-century urban culture. Also dating from the Meiji Period is a love of curry. Instant curries are an unexpected element of Japanese home cooking and curry on rice is featured on the menu of most family and neighbourhood restaurants today. Spicy fish roe is a regular addition to a traditional rice and *miso* breakfast, and chillied pickles and meats are frequent local delicacies. While the application of chillies came via Korean and Szechwanese cooking, Japanese instant curries have more in common with British adaptations than original Indian dishes. While Japanese style spaghetti with meat sauce, ketchup omelette or ice cream sodas may have little in common with any Western-origin dish, in addition to these popular adaptations there is an exceptional tradition of Western cooking that has produced many great chefs and world-renowned restaurants, supported by a culture of corporate expense accounts that can afford the very best.

In the home, bread is just as likely to accompany a main course as rice, cereal and croissant are popular breakfasts and school lunches include sandwiches and frankfurters as often as rice balls. On the street McDonalds, Starbucks and Häagan Dazs vie with noodle counters and sushi bars for prime locations. Increased overseas travel by Japanese and a steady, if still limited, increase in migrant labour, together with the worldwide globalisation of the culture of food has seen the emergence of neighbourhood restaurants featuring anything from Thai curry to African couscous or Brazilian paella. International cuisine is now as Japanese as Japanese cuisine is now international.

SANDRA BUCKLEY

fūfu bessei

This term refers to the practice of couples adopting separate surnames. The introduction of Japan's *koseki seido* (registry system) in the Tokugawa Period (1603–1868) as a way of controlling population movement also mitigated against women retaining their single names.

Prior to 1995, the registration of a marriage between Japanese nationals involved a woman adopting her husband's surname. This practice was reinforced by employers insisting married women change their surnames after marriage. With the growing number of married women choosing to continue their careers after marriage, the issue of women retaining their single surnames has gained support. A number of court cases have gained media attention as women took action against employers insisting women adopt their husband's surname. In protest of this practice couples choosing not to register their marriage were forced to accept that the state would consider their children to be illegitimate.

In 1995, a report proposed the introduction into the Civil Code of a choice for married couples allowing them to use separate surnames but, where children are present, a selection of one family name must be made. Children of married couples with separate surnames can change their surnames under special circumstances with permission from the Family Court.

KAYE BROADBENT

fugu

Fugu (blowfish) is a delicacy in Japan and traditionally served raw in transparently thin slices.

Its taste is described as slightly numbing or tingling, the side-effect of safe levels of traces of the poison that renders *fugu* deadly if not prepared with precision. *Fugu* chefs must be licensed. Preparation involves the careful excision of the liver containing the deadly poison that regularly claims connoisseurs as victims (three to four people die per year but there are many more minor cases of *fugu* poisoning). *Fugu* restaurants are easily identified by their familiar shingle of a puffed-up blowfish.

SANDRA BUCKLEY

Fuji TV

Fuji TV (Fuji Terebijon) was founded in 1959 with support from a number of sources, including the radio broadcasters Japan Cultural Broadcasting (Nippon Bunka Hoso) and Nippon Broadcasting (Nippon Hōsō), Sankei Shinbun and several movie companies. Today, it is the key station in the FNN network of twenty-eight affiliates. Fuji is renowned for its popular quiz and game show programming and has actively pursued an image as an innovator in youth culture over the 1990s. This has marked a shift away from its earlier reputation as a conservative broadcaster, perhaps a leftover of its links to the educational and cultural agendas of its original radio broadcast sponsors. Fuji today promotes itself as a leader in new media technologies in broadcasting and entertainment. It has developed, in collaboration with Sankei shinbun and Mitsubishi electric, a new system of online news access that is a text based service delivered by a terminal connected to a home television monitor and viewer. Fuji TV has been actively pursuing opportunities to export programming. Its most well-known crossover programme today is the cartoon *Dragonball*, which, after an initial success in France, became widely popular in the USA and Canada in the late 1990s together with translations of the comics (***manga***) and action figure sales. Fuji has also been developing strong regional collaborations and seeking Asian markets for its programming.

SANDRA BUCKLEY

Fukasaku Kinji

b. 1930, Mito, Ibaragi Prefecture

Film director

Fukasaku was inspired to become a film-maker by Marcel Carne's *The Devil's Envoys* and the films of Kurosawa Akira. He studied screenwriting in the arts department of Nihon University. In 1953, following his graduation, he entered Tōei, where he served as an assistant director on nearly forty films before making his directorial debut in 1961 with *Furaibō tantei: akai tani no sangeki* (Rogue Cop: Red Valley Tragedy). In the 1960s, he worked with action stars Takakura Ken and Tsuruta Kōji in the *ninkyō eiga* (chivalry film) genre and, in 1969, co-directed the Japanese segment of *Tora, Tora, Tora* for 20th Century Fox.

In 1973, with *Jingi naki tatakai* (Battles without Honour or Humanity), Fukasaku launched a nine-part series about a gang war in Hiroshima that became an enormous hit and paved the way for more realistic portrayals of gang life. In 1982, his comedy *Kamata Koshikyoku* (Fall Guy) swept the film awards.

Best known as an action director, he returned to the genre in 1992 with *Itsuka gira gira suruhi* (The Triple Cross), but the film was not a box office success. Other films of the 1990s include *Chūshingura gaiden yotsuya kaidan* (Crest of Betrayal, 1994) and *Omocha* (The Geisha House, 1999).

Further reading

R. Tomita (ed.) (1997) *Illustrated Who's Who of Japanese Cinema: Directors*, Tokyo: Kinema Junpo.

MARK SCHILLING

Fukuoka

Fukuoka is the largest city on the island of Kyūshu. It is an important regional administrative and marketing centre, and the terminal of the *shinkansen* (**bullet train**) line from **Tokyo**. Although popular sentiment traces Japanese historical roots to the Yamato Plain, the area surrounding Fukuoka has some of the oldest archeological sites of the Jōmon and Yayoi periods. Fukuoka's major historical significance, however, is as the gateway to the rest of Asia, for it was from here that contacts with what are now China and Korea were made. Fukuoka was thus a conduit for the transmission of Chinese cultural practices.

Today, Fukuoka markets itself as the 'Asia Pacific city', thus hoping to attract business to its extensive convention facilities and hi-tech R&D parks. Like all Japanese cities, its marketing strategy includes heavy reference to the surrounding 'natural' beauty, including Hakata Bay Park, its many museums and its distinctive **meibutsu** (local crafts), which include weaving, traditional dolls and high-quality scissors.

AUDREY KOBAYASHI

furoshiki

A square cloth used to tie and carry, the *furoshiki* is no longer popular among younger Japanese but remains in wide use among older Japanese and in rural areas. *Furoshiki* can be made from any number of textiles but cotton prevails in the heavy-duty *furoshiki* still used by some traditional merchants to haul produce from warehouse to shop, or shop to customer. The scene of a young apprentice bent under the weight of a heavy *furoshiki* hung over his back was a popular image in woodblock prints of Edo Japan. Today, one is more likely to see a beautifully decorated silk *furoshiki* dangling from the hand of a kimono-clad figure carrying a gift to a wedding or some other formal or ceremonial occassion. There is an art to the knotting techniques of the *furoshiki*, which originated in the Edo Period when people carried their clothing and toiletries to the bathhouse where it doubled as a bathmat. Despite obvious environmental advantages the *furoshiki* seems to be fading slowly from popular use in a consumer culture where a brand designer shopping bag or wrapping paper carries far more social value among image-conscious Japanese.

See also: wrapping

SANDRA BUCKLEY

furusato gaeri

This is the practice of returning to the home of the main branch of the family for festivals and religious or other ceremonial events. The anniversary of the death (see **death and funerals**) of a parent or family head, the annual *Obon* and **New Year** are common reasons for this ritual return. The extensive post-war population migration from remote and rural areas into Japan's major urban centres saw a growing emphasis on the obligation of extended family members to undertake an annual *furusato gaeri*.

Furusato gaeri is increasingly perceived as a burden involving not only precious vacation time but also the cost of travel and mandatory **gift giving**. Some households contine to follow the practice devotedly as a link to their roots and a way of exposing younger generations to family history and traditions. While the practice continues, the weakening links between second- and third-generation city dwellers and their rural relatives has seen a trend towards less regular *furusato gaeri* after the death of the parents of the first generation of urban migration. Advertising campaigns by travel agencies, domestic airlines and railways still target the nostalgia of this family pilgrimage and the 1990s even saw some travel companies offering a rent-a-*furusato* experience for urban families with no rural household of their own. With the collapse or disappearance of many rural family homes, the *furusato gaeri* has become linked to the need to maintain prayers and offerings to ancestors and the washing of gravestones. Many local temples and shrines now offer prayer and cemetery services to families unable or unwilling to undertake the ancestorial obligations of *furusato gaeri*.

See also: family system

SANDRA BUCKLEY

fuzzy logic

This term found its way from the realm of artificial intelligence and computer technologies into the broader public domain as a popular advertising marker for new domestic technologies from the early 1990s. Fuzzy logic came to describe any remote-access system for domestic technology or environmentally sensitive computerised household management system.

Fuzzy-logic technology supports telephone-based coded access to computerised household controls for everything from air conditioning to bath heating, oven controls and home phone messaging. Self-adjusting systems are also available that can operate window shades, activate garden sprinklers, set outdoor lighting, adjust interior temperature and water heater settings and a range of other options aimed at maximising comfort and energy efficiency in response to changing environmental conditions.

While fuzzy-logic technology has been marketed as liberating the homeworker from the domestic space, there has been extensive feminist critique of these systems as just one more tool that keeps the homemaker plugged to her domestic responsibilities, this time via her mobile phone. Fuzzy logic is also the term applied to the now widely available and popular remote medical alert systems that link 'home alone' and *netakiri* patients (see **bedridden patients**) and elderly to twenty-four-hour hospital monitoring systems, which register fluctuations in vital indicators and can dispatch emergency services or authorise delivery of medical supplies and prescription drugs as required.

Further reading

Buckley, S. (1996) 'Guided tour of the Japanese kitchen', *Society and Space* 14: 441–61.

SANDRA BUCKLEY

G

gagaku

Gagaku is the traditional music of the Imperial Court. The term was used in both the ancient Japanese and Korean kingdoms to refer to music of the court. Traditionally, *gagaku* has been divided up into music thought to have been brought from the Tang dynasty (CE 600–1000), *togaku*, the music of ancient Korea, *komagaku*, and native Japanese music used in Shintō ritual. Recent research on the close interaction between the Paekche, Koguryō, and Silla kingdoms (ancient kingdoms of the Korean peninsula), and the Yamato Wa kingdom (an ancient kingdom of the Japanese islands tied to the imperial family) may require revision of this standard framework. As early as 1921, Tanabe Hisao suggested that Li dynasty court music may have been the origin of Japanese *gagaku*, albeit in a colonial context that altered the ramifications of the assertion. The logical consequences of this position for the imperial institution still have yet to be addressed in the contemporary consensus on Japanese *gagaku*. This is both a question of fact concerning early historical records involving ancient kingdoms on either side of the Japan Sea and a question that impinges upon Japanese ideologies of colonial empire prior to 1945. The issue is thus also contemporary in that it directly bears on the task of decolonising contemporary Japanese culture and the emperor system's place within it.

The majority of the surviving *gagaku* compositions are classified as *togaku*. These are performed as both concert pieces and as dance pieces. *Togaku* is thought to include compositions from Asian kingdoms other than Tang, but their exact origins are not clear. The compositions classified as *komagaku* are usually performed as dance pieces. They are thought to include pieces from Silla, Koguryō and Paekche. As might be expected, there are more 'native' compositions in the *komagaku* genre than in the *togaku* genre. The most central form of Shintō ritual music is the *kagura*. Folk *kagura* are said to have pre-dated their appropriation by the court. When they became part of court ritual, they were renamed *mikagura* (court *kagura*). *Rōei* and the sometimes bawdy *saibara* are also conventionally classified within *gagaku*, usually under the rubric of *togaku*. The categories of *togaku* and *komagaku* appear to date from the early Heian period. At that time, *gagaku* was performed by members of the court and schools of professional musicians. With the advent of the warrior kingdoms in the Kamakura period (CE 1185–1333), *gagaku* lost its official ritual status and was preserved only by the professional musical schools. Subsequent to the Meiji Restoration (1868), surviving members of the *gagaku* schools were incorporated as official musicians for the Imperial Court ritual of the new Meiji nation state. Members of this same official institution continue to this day to perform for all official imperial functions as well as offer the occasional public concert.

Further reading

Garfias, Robert (1975) 'The sacred mikagura of the Japanese Imperial Court', Selected Reports, Institute of Ethnomusicology, University of California at Los Angeles.

Shuhei Hosokawa (1998) 'In search of the sound of

empire: Tanabe Hisao and the foundation of Japanese ethnomusicology', *Japanese Studies* 18(1): 5–20.(May).

MARK ANDERSON

gaijin

The term *gaijin* is derived from Chinese (*gwaijin*) and can be found in dictionaries from the eleventh century as a designation of 'outsider'. The status was mainly applied to foreigners but could also describe someone from outside a family. The term did not find its way into popular usage, however, until the Meiji Period and the reopening of Japan to extensive foreign contact after 1868. *Gaikokujin* (person of a foreign country) was the term used in official documents and print media, while *gaijin* (outside person) became the more colloquial term.

Although initially applied mainly to caucasian Westerners, it is now used to designate all foreigners including other Asians and blacks. The term *kokujin* (black person) is still used extensively in Japan, although younger Japanese are more likely to use the less derogatory Japanisation of the English, *burakku*. Members of overseas Japanese immigrant communities are designated separately, as are members of Korean and Chinese immigrant communities in Japan. Foreign residents in Japan often react negatively to the label of *gaijin*, which today carries strong negative connotations of exclusion. Exclusion and exclusivity are, however, often two sides of the same coin in Japan, where the separate status attributed to *gaijin* can also bring many benefits – higher salaries, expatriate living conditions, a veneration of foreignness sometimes bordering on adulation, etc. Japanese who have worked hard to become fluent in a foreign language often complain that *gaijin* receive job priority and better salaries as teachers in the many language schools that dot Japan's cityscapes. The top paid models on Japan's catwalks are tall Caucasian blondes and there is an elite (and relatively small) corps of *gaijin tarento* (foreign talent) who have gained tremendous popularity in the Japanese media. The combined talents of these foreign media stars are their fluency in the Japanese language and their usually exaggerated performance of certain *gaijin* stereotypes. Most *gaijin* are highly critical of the *tarento* for confirming these stereotypes and capitalising on the outsider status that can frustrate *gaijin* as they move through everyday life.

Gaijin of colour or from Third-World countries experience far more exclusion than exclusivity. While there are countless stories of the hospitality and generosity of Japanese host families, neighbours or teachers, accounts of daily encounters ranging from misunderstanding to discrimination are also common. Even after almost a decade of official government rhetoric of internationalisation, *gaijin* support groups and national associations point to a lingering tolerance of racial slurs and stereotyping in the media and advertising, and a lack of substantial curriculum development in schools to address issues of racism, cross-cultural communication and comparative cultural studies. The initial AIDS education campaigns in Japan outraged many foreigners for what was perceived as a labelling of AIDS as a *gaijin* problem imported to Japan.

The total number of foreign residents in Japan remains relatively low, with 64 per cent of a population slightly in excess of 1,000,000 being North or South Koreans who are not labelled *gaijin*. The total *gaijin* population also includes all residents of less than ninety days, illegal residents and diplomats. There are many legal and other institutional as well as socio-cultural barriers to any foreseeable dramatic increase in the *gaijin* presence in Japan. Efforts to recruit foreign nationals into university and industrial research and teaching positions as part of the internationalisation process have had limited success. While even in the early 1980s *gaijin* were relatively rare on the streets of Tokyo, in 2000 the sight of foreigners moving through the CBD, lined up in a supermarket, riding a scooter down the shopping street or riding in the subway barely warrants comment for most urban Japanese. Outside the major centres, however, *gaijin* may still find themselves surrounded by excited school children wanting to touch a blonde head of hair or try out their English skills. Many caucasian *gaijin* are also frustrated by the assumption that all foreigners speak English.

While *gaijin* are no longer such an oddity, those who are living long term in Japan point out that there are still many areas in which major improvements could be made to facilitate *gaijin* life, e.g. better multilingual signage, wider access to translation services in dealing with government departments and the police and courts, affordable international school programmes, improved school services for foreign children attending mainstream schools, etc. At the same time that foreign children experience much adulation in school there can also be high levels of discrimination, which go unnoticed in an environment of low awareness of issues of racism. *Gaijin* often comment on the lack of international programming on Japanese television and the need for more bilingual broadcasting of news and current affairs through the extension of existing dual-soundtrack services. While imported foods are no longer limited to small and expensive speciality markets, high tariff duties still put most familiar foreign imports into the luxury-food category and off the weekly shopping list for many *gaijin*.

Dating a *gaijin* is popular among young Japanese, male and female. Caucasian women have been popular workers in the bars and clubs of Tokyo since the 1960s. The working conditions of these women vary dramatically from the hardship experienced by many East and South-East Asian women working in the *mizushōbai* (sex and entertainment industry). The 1990s also saw a new trend in strip clubs and bars featuring *gaijin* men for a female Japanese clientele. The rate of international marriages remains low and the Japanese partner can still face strong opposition from family. Mail order brides from South-East Asia have become a familiar part of rural communities where there is a shortage of Japanese women willing to stay or move to an agricultural life. However, the problems faced by these imported brides have been substantial and there are now a number of active support groups around the country providing counselling and help to these women, who often experience extreme isolation and discrimination.

One of the most frustrating elements of *gaijin* life is the issue of language. Every *gaijin* has a favourite silly tale on the topic. When Japanese is studied in schools it is called *kokugo* (national language) but when it is studied by non-Japanese it is called *nihongo* (Japanese language). There is a committed belief in the difficulty of the Japanese language for

foreigners and a strong sense of language as an essential and defining element of Japanese identity. Foreigners may be praised for their linguistic skill, but this praise is itself a mark of the impossibility of ever making the transition from the outside (*gaijin* and *nihongo*) to the inside (*nihonjin* (Japanese national) and *kokugo* (national language). Fluency is remarkable and remarked upon, thus emphasising and not erasing difference. For *gaijin*, language functions as an insurmountable barrier to entry often experienced as profoundly as the more obvious physical differences of ethnicity.

See also: alien registration

Further reading

Yokoyama, T. (1994) '*Gaijin*: The foreigner in Japan', in A Ueda and M. Eguchi (eds) *The Electric Geisha*, Tokyo and New York: Kōdansha, pp. 175–84.

SANDRA BUCKLEY

GAIKOKUJIN TOROKU *see* alien registration

gangster films

Gangster films, or *yakuza* films, developed in the 1960s and disappeared in the early 1970s. The real core of the genre, the 'chivalry films' (*ninkyō eiga / kyōkaku eiga*) demonstrate a particular concern with the social dynamics of militarism, as they examine the network of obligations, loyalties and betrayals that coerce the individual into violence. Films pit ordinary working men against organised crime in the defence of traditional culture and values (e.g. **Makino Masahiro**'s 1964 *Nihon kyōkaku den* (Tales of Japanese Chivalry)) or pit syndicate members in a bloody fight to the death with their bosses, implicated in imperialist schemes on the mainland (e.g. Yamashita Kosaku's 1968 *Bakuchiuchi: sōchō tobaku* (Gambling House: Presidential Gambling)). In Fukasaku Kinji's 1962 *Hokori takaki chōsen* (The Proud Challenger), a former reporter, purged during the 1950s, discovers evidence of Japanese collusion with the CIA in South-East Asia. Read against the 'cruelty of the samurai code' films, the gangster films reveal that, unlike the samurai, the common man is able to lash out against his superiors when betrayed because the commoners' values of humanity (*Jingi*) are never superseded by the samurai code of loyalty.

Further reading

Schrader, Paul (1974) '*Yakuza-eiga*: a primer', *Film Comment* 10: 9–17.

SYBIL THORNTON

gardens

Gardens have been a part of Japanese culture since antiquity. The earliest chronicles provide descriptions of gardens consisting of ponds and surrounding foliage on the grounds of the imperial residences. The principles of classical gardening were developed during the Heian (794–1192), Kamakura (1192–1393) and Muromachi (1393–1572) periods, in gardens that were integral to Buddhist, especially **Zen**, temples, as well as the homes of the samurai classes, who favoured much more simple gardening principles than those found in the Imperial Palace. Many of the oldest gardens survive in the city of **Kyōto**. Purists believe that all gardens created since the classical period are inadequate imitations of the great gardens, and that Japanese people in the present cannot appreciate the true significance of gardens in their lives. There is no question, however, that gardens occupy an unusually significant place in Japanese culture.

Japanese gardens express a cultural bond between people and nature, constructed to impart a sense of nature's ability to regulate the world and human experience, of the harmony of that world and of the purity and goodness of an appropriate relationship with nature. The garden is heavily imbued with symbolism meant to express a number of key themes that include the profundity and eternity of nature and the human connection to nature, which is both fleeting (the life of the individual) and eternal (the continuity of life), all expressed with the highest artistic sense. Although the principle of natural harmony owes much to the ancient Chinese principle of *feng shui* (geomancy), the style of Japanese gardens bears little resemblance to those in China.

There are three major forms of classical gardens: those covering a fairly large area and consisting mainly of rocks, plants and water, intended for strolling; compact dry-stone gardens (*karesansui*) intended for quiet contemplation; and tea gardens, in which the stones, gates and shrubbery are designed to lead one to the tea house in an appropriate preparatory atmosphere for the **tea ceremony**, *chadō*. Although the stone garden is well suited to individual contemplation, strolling and tea gardens are intended to be enjoyed in groups, especially groups of five, the number believed to promote the greatest social harmony. Among the most famous examples of the three garden forms, all located in Kyōto, are: the Katsura Detached Palace, a strolling garden; Ryōanji Zen Temple, a dry-stone garden; and the tea gardens of the Imperial Palace.

Japanese gardens are built to a high level of conformity, with strict rules for the quality and placement of every object in relation to every other. This is based on principles originally laid out in the tenth-century treatise *Sakuteiki* (The Way of Gardening). Gardens are begun by situating the space in relation to the surrounding landscape, or **keshiki**, so that views from the outside are 'borrowed' or incorporated into the structure of the garden. Items placed within the garden are often meant symbolically to convey some aspect of larger nature, and include pebbles to represent a stream or river, large rough stones to represent the Japanese coastline and complex patterns of rocks and vegetation, from miniature mosses to tall trees, to depict valleys and forests. Stone lanterns pay tribute to the temple and provide points of spiritual focus. Stones are set very deeply in the ground and represent the 'bones' of the garden, placed carefully in relation to ponds (or stone representations of water), with careful attention to the interplay of colour, texture and light, as well as the changing effects of the **seasons**. The effects are very subtle. Ostentatious floral displays are eschewed, and the smallest details, such as variations in the structure of mosses, often represent the most impressive garden effects.

In the *karesansui* gardens for which the Zen temples of Kyōto are famous, the art of symbolism is taken to its highest forms, with sand and stones, and occasionally and very sparingly plants, used to create an abstract and highly spiritual sense of the relationship to nature. This nature is both inspirational of the highest aesthetic qualities, in themselves an expression of goodness, and a didactic guide to correct behaviour, intrinsically tied to aesthetic principles. The intention is to create a dialectical sense of natural harmony.

Despite the importance of classical gardens, Japan has been influenced in many ways by modern gardens as well. During the Meiji Period, international gardeners were commissioned to provide settings for the new institutional buildings or to design public parks. Although parks in Japan are built on a much smaller scale than in Western countries, they provide an important setting for family outings, including cherry blossom viewing (see **cherry blossoms**). Western influences are also seen in the introduction of flower beds and rock gardens, and a stronger sense of realism in the public gardens of large cities such as **Tokyo**.

In the post-war period, parks have also been set aside as large, protected 'natural' areas, such as **Mt. Fuji**, or Miyajima, an island off the coast of Hiroshima Prefecture. Smaller parks comprise the huge strolling gardens built by Tokugawa lords, such as Lord Matsudaira of Takamatsu, whose gardens have become Ritsurin Park. Parks cater to the popular pastimes of walking and hiking, and present an image of nature as full size and sublime, in contrast to the miniaturised and stylised depictions of the classical garden. They usually contain within their boundaries Shintō shrines, which represent a much less stylised form of relationship with nature, in which the landscape itself bears spiritual qualities.

In Japan today, gardening represents one of the most important cultural activities, and almost no home is without its garden, whether in the form of elaborate, professionally maintained formal gardens that signify the homes of the wealthy, or simple collections of potted plants or *bonsai* on the balconies of *danchi* apartment units. Many people, especially the retired, belong to garden societies, and among the most popular of recreational outings are visits to the famous gardens.

Those in **Kyōto** are so crowded with visitors that it is often very difficult to invoke the air of contemplation for which they were intended.

See also: *bonsai*; national parks

Further reading

Osamu Mori (1962) *Typical Japanese Gardens*, trans. Atsuo Tsuruoka, Tokyo: Shibata.

AUDREY KOBAYASHI

gay and lesbian literature

Japanese gays and lesbians are not the first groups to look back into a literary heritage for a past on which to ground a contemporary politics and practice. Furthermore, Japan has a long history of texts amenable to such re-readings. Iwata Jun'ichi's monumental bibliography *Nanshoku bunken shoshi*, compiled in the late 1930s, contains short descriptions of 1,093 works containing some form of reference to male homo-eroticism stretching from the tenth to the twentieth century. Some of the highlights of this tradition have been anthologised in English translation in *Partings at Dawn: An Anthology of Japanese Gay Literature*. The seventeenth-century *Great Mirror of Male Love* is also available in English translation. While representations of female homo-eroticism are certainly to be found in pre-modern texts, such as the late *Heian Torikaebaya* (The Changelings) and *Wagami ni tadoru himegimi* (A Princess in Search of Herself), their incorporation into something like a 'lesbian canon' has only recently begun. The lesbian past tends rather to be found in readings of early twentieth-century writers such as Yoshiya Nobuko, Tamura Toshiko, Hiratsuka Raichō and Miyamoto Yuriko.

Post-war Japan's best-known gay writer is, of course, Mishima Yukio, although his reputation as such is more firmly established outside of Japan than in his home country. None the less, his *Confessions of a Mask* (1949) and *Forbidden Colours* (1951) remain classic descriptions of homosexual life in a relentlessly heteronormative society. However, it was only after Mishima's death (coming just a year after Stonewall) that writers began to write from a self-identified gay or lesbian perspective. The poets Takahashi Mutsuo and Ishii Tatsuhiko, whose work is included in the Miller anthology mentioned earlier, might be included in this category. Hashimoto Osamu's *Hasu to katana* (The Lotus and the Sword) is a brilliantly campy analysis of Japanese homosociality as it appears in the work of Natsume Sōseki and other canonical writers. Also, Matsūra Rieko's 1994 novel *Oyayubi P no shugyō jidai* (The Apprenticeship of Big Toe P) is a hilarious meditation on the 'lesbian phallus'.

However, perhaps the most self-consciously gay, lesbian or 'queer' writing is to be found in the community-based alternative publications known as '*mini-komi*'. Modeled on the consciousness-raising strategies used in the Japanese feminist movement since the 1970s, these publications print personal testimonies, promote amateur poetry and fiction, and offer a wide range of information including advice columns and support network information. Gay *mini-komi* publications have played an important role in disseminating accurate information regarding AIDS and offering a space for gay men and women to write in various genres about AIDS. These publications have local circulations in hard copy but are increasingly available online to a wider readership.

Further reading

(1983) *The Changelings: A Classical Japanese Court Tale*, trans. Rosette Willig, Stanford: Stanford University Press.

Hashimoto Osamu (1986) *Hasu to katana*, Tokyo: Kawade bunko.

Ihara Saikaku (1991) *The Great Mirror of Male Love*, trans. Paul Schalow, Stanford: Stanford University Press.

Iwata Jun'ichi (1973) *Nanshoku bunken shoshi*, Toba, Miwa Prefecture: Iwata Sadao.

Kakinuma Eiko and Kurihara Chiyo (eds) (1993) *Tanbi shosetsu: gei bungaku bukku gaido*, ed. Byakuya shobō.

Matsūra Rieko (1994) *Oyayubi P no shugyou jidai*, Tokyo: Kawade bunko.

Miller, Stephen D. (ed.) (1996) *Partings at Dawn: An Anthology of Japanese Gay Literature*, San Francisco: Gay Sunshine Press.

Mishima Yukio (1971) *Forbidden Colours*, trans. Alfred H. Marks, London: Penguin.

—— (1958) *Confessions of a Mask*, trans. Meredith Weatherby, New York: New Directions.

KEITH VINCENT

gay male identity

Gay male identity emerges only in explicit opposition to homophobic oppression. To the extent that Japanese homophobia works by ignoring rather than openly condemning homosexuality, Japanese gay male identity has remained largely circumscribed within the protected private spheres of bars, cruising areas, literature and the arts. Relatively few people in Japan express or admit to an outright disgust with homosexuality, the police do not raid gay bars or cruising spots and none of Japan's major religious groups find it profitable to bully homosexuals. With the exception of a brief period in early Meiji, the Japanese legal system has never criminalised consensual same-sex relations. However, an unspoken consensus makes it all but impossible for Japanese gays to come out to family or work colleagues. The result is to make gay identity in Japan largely a pre-political question of individualised sexual 'preference', or '*shumi*'. Moreover, modern Japan has become an extremely homosocial society where the divide between 'men loving men' and 'men promoting the interests of men' is policed almost exclusively through the social unspeakability (and thus unknowability) of homosexuality.

This situation has given rise to a persistent myth, current both inside and outside Japan, that the Japanese are somehow more tolerant of homosexuality than the rest of the world. However, regardless of whether one agrees or disagrees with this particular manifestation of Japanese exceptionalism, it seems clear that the comparison serves to obscure rather than reveal the realities faced by Japanese men who love men. This situation is made worse by the global spectacle both of homophobic violence and of gay male culture in the USA and elsewhere outside Japan, which tends to divert attention away from local realities. Thus, Japanese homophobia still remains largely 'in the closet' as a result of a rather queer dynamic by which heteronormative violence there can be elided through ritual comparisons to the situation abroad.

A graphic illustration of this 'problem with comparison' was to be seen on the popular television programme *Kore ga hen da yo Nihonjin* (Aren't the Japanese Strange?) in 1999. The show has a regular cast of fifty 'foreigners', from almost as many countries, who confront an equal number of Japanese guests invited to defend some aspect of Japanese culture that has been judged to be 'strange' by the foreigners. Three episodes of the show in 1999 were devoted to the question, raised by an African member of the regular cast, as to whether the Japanese were not too forgiving of homosexuality. All fifty Japanese guests for these three shows were identified as lesbian or gay (by way of little signs hung around their necks) and vigorously defended their culture's embrace of sexual diversity against a barrage of attack by 'foreigners'. The most vociferously homophobic foreigners were almost without exception people of colour from developing countries. One man from India went so far as to argue that he would kill his own son if he found out he was gay, at which point the discussion came close to degenerating into a bar-room brawl. When one indignant gay Japanese announced that the homophobic sentiment seemingly shared by all the representatives from Africa was the reason why their countries had not developed properly ('*Dakara anato no kuni ga hatten shinaindayo!*'), the Japanese viewing audience was allowed to bask luxuriously in its own moral (and hence, it was implied, economic) superiority. Meanwhile, the small number of Western foreigners present aligned themselves with the Japanese gays and lesbians in earnest calls for greater tolerance. Throughout the entire show the only indication that Japan itself remains a highly heteronormative society was to be found in the screen distortions that covered the faces and identities of about one third of the gay and lesbian Japanese in the studio. Much could be said here about the way a certain First-World conception of global gay identity serves to naturalise uneven capitalist development, but the point here has to do simply with the way a rhetoric of comparison can obscure local realities.

In recent years, sexual orientation has, for some at least, become a viable category of identity on which to base appeals for civil and human rights. In 1997, the Japan Association for the Lesbian and Gay Movement (otherwise known as OCCUR) won a protracted legal battle against the City of Tokyo, which had refused to allow homosexuals to use any of the city's youth hostels. Gay and lesbian pride parades have been held since the mid-1990s in both Tokyo and Sapporo, and in the fall of 2000 activists finally succeeded in pressuring Tokyo's Human Rights Commission to include sexual orientation in its list of protected categories. The brutal gay-bashing murder of a young man in a Tokyo cruising park on 11 February 2000 brought into horrific relief the reality of homophobic oppression in Japan. The murder happened after OCCUR had already documented dozens of incidents of gay bashing in similar spots around Tokyo. The cumulative effect of these efforts by activists is to force recognition of the fact that the visibility both of homophobic and heteronormative violence, and of an oppositional gay identity, is not a given but a product of conscious efforts of resistance and identification.

Further reading

Kawaguchi Kazuya, Kazama Takashi and Vincent, Keith (1997) *Gei Sutadiizuu* (Gay Studies), Tokyo: Seidosha.

Pflugfelder, Gregory M. (1999) *Cartographies of Desire: Male–Male Sexuality in Japanese Discourse*, Berkeley: University of California Press.

Itō Satoru and Yanase Ryōta (2001) *Coming out in Japan*, trans. F. Conlan, Melbourne: Trans Pacific Press.

KEITH VINCENT

Gendaishi Techo

The monthly journal *Gendaishi Techo* (Modern Poetry Notebook) was established in 1959 by the large poetry publishing house Shinchōsha under the direction of its long-serving editor Oda Kyū. Shinchōsha often produced individual poetry collections of the poets included in the magazine. From the first a commercial venture (and sometimes criticised as too journalistic), the magazine played an important role in helping to establish the reputation of new poets and to nurture the growth of modern free-style verse. The various editors had their own idiosyncratic styles, with, for example, Shimizu Yasuo, who took over the editorship in 1962 (Oda later returned), placing more emphasis on new thought and overseas poets. The journal has often published important manifestos on poetics and also run special issues on art, thus exercising an influence far wider than poetry circles alone.

Notable special issues include the volume on the thinker Yoshimoto Takaaki in August 1972, the Mother Goose translation number in March 1976, the issue on women poets in September 1991, the number on new directions in Japanese cinema in July 1994 and the issue on the Californian poet Gary Snyder in March 1996.

LEITH MORTON

gender and technology

Technology is implicated in every sphere of life: the use of electrical appliances in the home, the use of game boys, tamagotchi and other computer games in leisure, the use of telephone clubs (*terekura*) to arrange assignations, the use of the Internet in work, leisure and political activism, the changing uses of technology in the workplace including computerisation and robotics, the choice between public transport systems and private automobiles, the use of reproductive technology, and training in scientific and technological fields in the education system. All of these uses of technology have gendered dimensions. This starts in the education system, where most girls are gradually streamed out of scientific and technical areas, and thus under-represented in those professions. Nevertheless, technological change continually transforms the conditions of work for both men and women (see **gender and work**).

Computerisation has created new classes of technological outworkers since the 1980s, and unions (see **unions and the labour movement**) and the legal system have found it difficult to adapt to the needs of these workers. Reproductive technology affects the lives of women, whether this concerns access to safe surgical abortion (see **reproductive control**), the availability of the contraceptive pill, the development of *in vitro* fertilisation or the possibility of determining the sex of unborn children. The use of electrical appliances in the home has affected the lives of housewives, with labour-saving devices often making it easier to combine domestic labour with paid labour (see **domestic technologies**). Even a technology such as nuclear power can be seen to have a gendered dimension if we consider that the workers in the industry are overwhelmingly male, while the anti-nuclear campaigns in Japan are often primarily led by women, and more specifically housewives. The gendering of technology also has a profoundly international dimension as a direct result of the offshore activities of Japanese companies. Employment in the offshore transnational factories, where the bulk of Japan's technology products are manufactured, is heavily gendered at various levels. Line work and component assembly are areas where there is a heavy concentration of female employees, while lower management levels are dominated by local males and upper management by male expatriate Japanese executives. Agrarian transformation in South-East Asian countries encourages men and women to leave agricultural occupations, but female labour is preferred in this routine assembly work, reflecting the gendered segmentation of labour markets and stereotypes about suitable occupations for men and women. Feminist groups across the Asia–Pacific region are working in collaboration to develop a better understanding and awareness of the relationship between the conditions of Third World women working on Japanese factory assembly lines, and the comparatively affluent lives of the Japanese women who surround themselves with the finished products of this labour.

Further reading

Low, M. (1992) 'Towards a gendered approach to teaching about the history of Japanese science and technology', in V. Mackie (ed.) *Gendering Japanese Studies*, Melbourne: Japanese Studies Centre.

Morris-Suzuki, T. (1989) *Beyond Computopia: Information,*

Automation and Democracy in Japan, London, Kegan Paul International.

VERA MACKIE

gender and work

Japan's economy shifted, in a period of fifty years, from a reliance on agriculture to becoming a major service provider. These structural changes have been accompanied by significant changes in the composition of the workforce. It is the case that women are a significant proportion of the contemporary paid workforce (40.5 per cent in 1996) but this is not a recent phenomenon. Women have been, and remain, crucial to Japan's economy, with the female workforce undergoing a shift towards a greater number of married women.

In exploring historical trends in paid employment for women, what emerges is that women have always had a presence in paid work but have not been encouraged by either government or business to remain permanently in the paid workforce. Women have had very little choice about their role and position in the labour market but have been moved into and out of the labour market to suit the needs of governments and business. In Japan, continuity exists between the pre- and post-war period constructions of women in that, ideologically and materially, women have consistently borne much of the burden and responsibility for the restructuring of employment in Japan.

Despite a continuous presence in the workforce, women in paid work have generally been perceived by male employers and full-time colleagues as a temporary or auxiliary workforce assisting male co-workers and sustaining the stability of the full-time male workforce. Women workers and the work performed by women have been predicated on gender ideologies incorporating the sexual division of labour, which defines women in relation to their role in the family, potential or real, as wife and/or mother.

Central to understanding the relationship between women and paid work in Japan is an understanding of the sexual division of labour. Distinctions between jobs that are designated as 'women's' and 'men's' work remain, but the sexual division that defines the content of women's and men's work is subject to change. Shifts in the discourse on the sexual division of labour have had an impact on the ways in which women participate in the paid workforce in Japan.

It is impossible to understand employment for women in Japan without acknowledging the strength of the ideology of *ryō sai kenbo* (good wives, wise mothers). Recent manifestations of *ryō sai kenbo* embodied in *otoko wa shigoto, onna wa katei* (men at work and women at home) have had a significant impact on the construction of paid work for women in Japan. The modified expression *otoko wa shigoto, onna wa katei to shigoto* (men at work and women at home and working) reflects not only changes in women's work lives, but that there has been no concomitant change for men. Despite recent legislation to address access to employment opportunities and equity issues, the existing sexual division of labour in the labour market and family remains unchallenged.

In the Meiji Period (1868–1912), the government institutionalised the Confucian value system that prevailed among the ruling warrior class into the newly created Meiji Civil Code. With Japan's emergence as an industrialising nation, the Meiji government focused on developing Japan's industrial base. In focusing single-mindedly on this goal, the government was concerned with controlling and regulating Japanese society. *Ryō sai kenbo* clearly identified government expectations of the roles of women. What is also evident is the tension resulting from its focus on industrialisation, the need for labour to satisfy the expanding industrial sector and the need for the production and reproduction of labour.

Tension has existed between governments and employers over the appropriate 'use' of women's bodies. In constituting women as wives and mothers, government policies aimed at women workers have stressed protecting women in their maternal role (*bōsei hōgo*). Yet *bōsei hōgo* has meant employers have not been able to utilise the labour of women as flexibly as they would like. The introduction of the Equal Employment Opportunity Law (EEOL) in 1986 involved a reduction in *bōsei hōgo*, but has done little to resolve the contradiction for women in fulfilling a variety of roles.

The underlying assumptions determining the construction of the role of women, and the impact of this on the formulation of labour and welfare policies encouraging women to enter or exit the paid workforce, have been modified depending on specific historical circumstances. As paid and unpaid workers, women and the contributions of women are central to the domestic restructuring of the Japanese economy, yet the constitution of their role has remained focused on the role they fulfil as caregivers of husbands, children and aged dependents.

Employment practices combined with welfare policies privilege women either remaining full-time housewives or returning to the paid workforce as part-time workers. Age limits imposed by many Japanese companies, to circumscribe eligibility for regular work for both women and men, tend to reduce employment opportunities for women more than for men. Age-based retirement policies have been successfully challenged legally, but age-based employment criteria that contravene EEOL guidelines have not received the same attention. For women with dependent children and general skills returning to paid work after their last child begins primary school, the choice is restricted to paid work opportunities such as part-time work, piecework, temporary or dispatch work.

Since the 1970s, successive Japanese governments have reduced spending on welfare services to encourage 'families' (read women) to care for children and aged relatives at home rather than at state expense. Because of the absence of caring institutions, most women in nuclear families can re-enter the workforce only after their last child begins school, and then exit again to care for elderly family members when their carer responsibilities resume. Employers benefit from this workforce that has few employment options because it is locked into domestic responsibilities, and governments benefit by not having to provide the welfare services that it has privatised or transferred to the family. Looked at in this way, paid work for women should not be separated into regular and part time, but instead viewed as an integrated employment pattern existing within lifetime employment practices to complement social, economic and political needs and demands. In restricting women's employment opportunities to low-paid temporary or part-time jobs, employers are able to offer substantially higher wages and other financial and non-financial benefits to their 'core' male workforce.

Further reading

Brinton, M. (1993) *Women and the Economic Miracle: Gender and Work in Postwar Japan*, Berkeley: University of California Press.

Kondo, D. (1990) *Crafting Selves: Power, Gender, and Discourses of Identity in a Japanese Workplace*, Chicago: University of Chicago Press.

Lam, A. (1992) *Women and Japanese Management: Discrimination and Reform*, London: Routledge.

Roberts, G. (1994) *Staying on the Line: Blue-Collar Women in Contemporary Japan*, Honolulu: University of Hawaii.

KAYE BROADBENT

gender segregation in schools

Gender segregation increases over time within the Japanese school system. All public compulsory schooling (K-8) in Japan is co-educational. Boys and girls form mixed study and work groups called *han* and sit together in class. Many private schools are also co-educational but some are single sex. While the majority of students attend co-educational high schools, the students who choose to attend special occupational schools may find the diversity of their peer group affected by their career choice. Girls tend to occupy most of the places in commercial high schools as boys fill the slots in mechanical, agricultural and fisheries high schools.

Even though girls receive basically the same education as boys, males are privileged within families in terms of higher education. Most young women attend two-year colleges, *tankidai*, rather than four-year universities. Women with two-year college degrees have greater access to jobs than women with university degrees or those with only a high-school degree. These two-year colleges cater only to women students; some of them are more academically rigorous than the traditional four-year university. Women who fail the entrance examination to the university of their choice seldom become *rōnin* in order to retake the exam although this is a common practice among young men seeking access to elite schools.

JUNE A. GORDON

General Strike, the

The General Strike planned for 1 February 1947 was banned on 31 January by General Douglas **MacArthur**, who headed the **Allied Occupation**. This was a dramatic turning point in labour history and in Occupation policies.

The strike was planned by an alliance of public- and private-sector workers who were frustrated by inflation and encouraged by early Occupation policies promoting unionisation. By shutting down major industries and government offices, they hoped to gain wage concessions and bring down the cabinet of Yoshida Shigeru. Much of the strike leadership came from the communist-dominated Sanbetsu Kaigi (Congress of Industrial Labour Unions of Japan).

Photographs of strike co-ordinator Ii Yashirō drying his tears symbolised the disillusionment of the radical left with the Occupation. The aborted strike may be seen as the beginning of a 'reverse course' in Occupation policy, from democratic reform to the rebuilding of Japan as a cold-war ally of the USA. Labour was split in the aftermath, with radical groups such as Sanbetsu losing influence, and new laws prohibited civil servants and workers in government enterprises from striking.

Further reading

Cohen, T. (1987) *Remaking Japan: The American Occupation as New Deal*, ed. H. Passin, New York: Free Press.

Moore, J. (1983) *Japanese Workers and the Struggle for Power, 1945–1947*, Madison, WI: University of Wisconsin Press.

Redford, L. (ed.) (1980) *The Occupation of Japan: Economic Policy and Reform*, Norfolk, VA: Mac-Arthur Memorial.

TIMOTHY S. GEORGE

genkan

Genkan (entrance hall) literally means 'entry to mystery' in a reflection of its origins (roughly thirteenth century) as a transitional space between the outside world and the inner world of a Zen temple. The most common design was a simple roofed walkway with tiled floor. Other religious and official buildings, and samurai and aristocratic residences soon also adopted the architecture of the *genkan*, but it was not until the modern period that it became a common feature in most residences, regardless of class. Today, it is an important and standard feature of domestic architecture and retains its value as a transitional space. It is also a functional space where family and visitors remove shoes before stepping up into the house. The surface is most often concrete or tile although a rougher surface of riverbed stones is also popular.

The *genkan* is swept and washed down regularly and a storage area is provided for shoes. It is common for there to be some display of ornaments or flower arrangement, and there is a popular notion that you can discern a lot about a family by the state of their *genkan*. Although it would save space to reduce the entrance area, this is seldom considered as an option in designing a home. The space of the *genkan* still carries some association with status and few are willing to appear squeezed spatially or financially by skimping on the *genkan*. Even in standardised apartment complexes there is an allowance made for a reasonable *genkan* space.

SANDRA BUCKLEY

geomancy

The principles of geomancy have gained a new popularity outside Asia under the Chinese name of Feng Shui, although this is only one element of a wide range of practices that come under the broad rubric of geomancy. Geomancy is concerned with the relationship of humans and natural forces or energy, of heaven and earth and the power or force of geographic locations and natural formations.

From the earliest written Japanese records there is evidence of divinational practices grounded in geomancy. Both the classical literature and official documents from the Heian period make frequent mention of directional prohibitions limiting movement on certain days of the lunar calendar. Today, elements of geomancy continue to surface in fortune telling and traditional healing, where a client might be advised to avoid specific directions or locations on certain dates, or conversely to favour a direction in selecting a location for a holiday or a recuperation. The number of Japanese who actively consult a geomancy specialist when choosing the site or architecture of their home, date and location of a wedding etc. has dramatically declined but there remain many popular expressions in everyday Japanese that continue to keep some of the more basic concepts of geomancy in popular circulation even if only at the level of folklore or superstition.

SANDRA BUCKLEY

geta

This traditional Japanese footwear is made of two types of wood – a softer wood for the base and a sturdy hard wood for the support platforms the base sits on – and a thong of cloth or soft leather. The foot sits lightly on the base and the toes are not forced far into the fork of the thong. This requires a walking motion with a slight forward tilt over the front edge of the *geta*. They are still widely worn in the summer time with the cotton lightweight **kimono** (*yukata*). *Geta* are also closely associated with the image of the *yakuza* (gangsters), who will often wear them even with trousers. Children enjoy wearing decorative *geta* for festivals and many families still keep *geta* in the entrance way (**genkan**) to wear when working in the garden.

SANDRA BUCKLEY

gift giving

In addition to the two gift-giving seasons (mid-year and year end) there is an extensive culture of gift giving in Japan, which operates in close relation to the complex social hierarchies that order obligation and responsibility. Gift giving is seldom an exchange in Japan with the exception of the imported custom of Christmas.

As in many Asian cultures, gift giving can often take the form of cash. Children are frequently given money by older family members on such occasions as a birthday, graduation, coming of age ceremony or New Year. When attending a wedding or funeral, one is expected to present a cash gift that is determined by a combined calculation of past obligation, relative economic status and closeness to the family. Money gifts are offered in specially decorated white envelopes.

Gifts of food are also offered on a ritual basis when visiting someone's home. A family member is expected to bring home souvenir gifts (*omiyage*) for family, friends and workplace colleagues after a trip. Seasonal or local speciality foods are popular *omiyage*. Honeymoon couples are also expected to bring home presents for family members and those who offered a money gift at their wedding. A household will offer a gift to the attending doctor when a family member is hospitalised. A company will deliver seasonal gifts to loyal customers twice a year. A family may deliver a basket of fruit to a teacher or tutor on a child's successful exam results. Gift giving is not limited to the living. For thirty-three years after a death family members will continue to offer prayers, incense, flowers and seasonal fruits to the dead spirit. Just as there are department stores that offer a full gift service to help a family or business meet its seasonal and other gift-giving obligations, there are also temples and shrines that offer contracts to service obligations to the dead.

Gift giving continues to be an essential element of the fabric of contemporary Japanese society. The pattern of gift giving and receiving of any individual, household or organisation maps a field of hierarchical relations – social, economic, political, etc. The flow of gifts is said to lubricate the relations of obligation generated through networks of support. Critics of the intense level of gift giving in Japan point to the economic pressure this can create in times of hardship, when one is most likely to draw on these networks. Households and companies alike plan their budgets to accommodate the high cost of the two obligatory gift seasons. Some schools are encouraging parents to review the amount of money children spend on birthday and Christmas presents for friends after significant media attention has fallen on the extent to which issues of rivalry and competition are played out around extravagant gift giving between school age children. The culture of gift giving is, however, now so intimately linked to Japan's retail and marketing sectors that it is hard to imagine any significant decline in this culture of gift giving in the near future.

SANDRA BUCKLEY

Ginza

The Ginza district of **Tokyo** is named for the national mint (*gin* means 'silver'), which Tokugawa Iyeasu located there in 1612, and which remained for 200 years. The Ginza is known throughout the world, however, as the epitome of Japanese cultural style, and as the most expensive real estate anywhere. Many Tokyo residents, especially the older ones, believe that only in The Ginza are the shops and the service of the highest quality. It is also a major entertainment district, a centre for contemporary *kabuki* theatre and home to the **Takarazuka** theatre.

The Ginza is best known for its nightscapes, although the quaint lanterns and low wooden structures that depicted a quintessential Japan in nineteenth-century woodblock prints have given way to massive rainbows of neon and towering department stores that line the major streets such as Chūō-dōri and Harumi-dōri. Known as Japan's 'Fifth Avenue', this is one of the best spots in the world for window shopping. Since the 1960s, however, the Ginza has gradually lost its appeal for the younger generation. Its expensive shops and traditional restaurants seem staid in comparison to the radical chic found on the western slopes of the city.

AUDREY KOBAYASHI

giri and ninjo

Giri (social obligation) and *ninjo* (human feeling) are now most commonly explained in the context of **Doi Takeo**'s description of the structure of Japanese self and society. Doi places *giri* within

the category of forms and actions that locate the self in relation to society, while *ninjo* falls within the inner, intimate realm of the self.

The extent and form of social obligations (*giri*) is determined along an axis of social relations from inside (*uchi*) to outside (*soto*) (see **uchi and soto**). An individual moves across a number of significant groups within which she or he carries an insider status, and obligation may accumulate to the individual or indirectly at the level of all or part of the group. Obligation is thus often experienced as communal. Human feelings (*ninjo*) are for Doi properly located in the inner space of the self and do not circulate in the realm of the social but remain intimate and hidden. He describes two types of *ninjo*: spontaneous (parent–child, sibling) and officially condoned (master–pupil, neighbours). He speaks of *giri* as the vessel and *ninjo* as the content of relations, and links both to **amae** (indulgence of dependence). For Doi, *ninjo* welcomes or nurtures dependence while *giri* binds us in relations of dependence.

Further reading

Takeo Doi (1977) *The Anatomy of Dependence*, Tokyo: Kōdansha, p. 33

SANDRA BUCKLEY

GIRLS' DAY *see* Hinamatsuri (Doll Festival) and Girls' Day

Go

A strategy-based board game originating in China as early as 1300 BCE, Go is thought to have first come to Japan in the sixth to seventh century via Korea. The game possibly derived from a process of divination where black and white stones were cast onto a geomancy chart or mapped surface. Over time, this surface is thought to have been refined into a board marked with the nineteen horizontal and vertical lines that still form the grid of the contemporary game.

Go is played by two people and is built on the principle of capturing territory. One person plays with white stones and the other with black. The stones are said to have life and can be killed by the strategic placement of stones to surround or render dead the stone(s) of the opponent. Areas of the board can also be rendered as dead spots reducing options for the other player to gain territory. Unlike some other Asian board games, the aim is not the capture and removal of the majority of the opponent's pieces but to capture the maximum territory on the board. A completed game may have many stones, both black and white on the board. It is the configuration of the stones that will determine the final winner by total territory held. Players will stake out and claim territory, strategically blocking the opponent's opportunities while positioning for short- and long-terms gains. A less experienced player can be allocated an appropriate handicap at the beginning of the game.

Go is said to be played by some 30 million people worldwide. It is generally accepted that the game was extensively refined after its arrival in Japan. Older variations of the game are still played in parts of China and Korea, but it is the Japanese version that is recognised internationally and sponsored by the International Go Federation. The game continues to have a wide following among young Japanese, at least in part due to the popularity of student Go clubs in schools and universities. It remains more popular among males than females at all age groups. Television broadcasts of master matches as well as instructional programmes also promote the popularity of the game. Bookshops carry shelf after shelf of instructional books, as well as detailed diagrams of alternative game plans and pictorial records of famous games and master players.

There is now a rapidly expanding phenomenon of online Go and this has seen a new expansion of the game into the digital domain with a global following. Diehard traditionalists argue that the face-to-face encounter of the game is an essential element of Go and dismiss the online game sites and clubs as a passing fad. Others argue that the digital medium is well suited to the long delays that often characterise the time between moves as each player contemplates their strategic options before placing the next stone, and of course online games can be 'watched' by a diverse and widely dispersed audience. There are many jokes in Japan about Go

addiction and some would argue that there are even more Go widows than golf widows.

SANDRA BUCKLEY

Godzilla

Godzilla (Gojira) is one of the few instances in Japanese popular culture where the phenomenon is of a similar order of magnitude in Japan and abroad. As a 400-foot tall, grey-green monster icon, as an eponymous movie series and as a progenitor of its own genre of horror film, Godzilla exists in the international pop-consciousness as a permanent legacy.

Honda Inoshiro's original *Gojira* (Tōhō, 1954), filmed in black and white with a special effects team that cut its teeth on battle scene in wartime movies, is a grim, sombre story of an enormous prehistoric monster who wreaks havoc on Tokyo after being disturbed in the depths of the Pacific by hydrogen bomb testing. *Godzilla, King of the Monsters*, distributed in 1956, takes extraordinary liberties with the original: dubbing sporadically, leaving stretches of dialogue untranslated and interpolating scenes of a US 'witness who learns'. And yet it retains the austere power of the monster's foray undiminished, and, with the inspired transliteration of the title, the US version achieves its own absurdity. Its unprecedented success at the box-office in the USA launched the series as an international money-maker for Tōhō studios.

The series comprises twenty-four films to date, and may be usefully divided into early, middle and late-nationalist periods. The early Honda films (1954–61) feature a single protagonist-monster and layer a conflict between science and nature over geo-political concerns with nuclear war and environmental destruction. Tense, engaged and punctuated in their treatment of extremely massive objects by moments of great visual poetry, these early Honda films contain virtually all that is cinematically and philosophically interesting in the series. *Kingkong tai Gojira* (King Kong vs Godzilla, 1962) ushers in a middle period characterised by twin protagonists or tag-teams of protagonists, displacement of the austere dialectic of science and nature by a pro-wrestling aesthetic and concomitant introduction of an increasingly farcical stable of monsters. Honda loses his stamp on the series during this period of assembly-line production, and films which had transfixed early post-war audiences with their devastated cityscapes and figuration of nuclear catastrophe degenerate here into child's fare. This defusing at the level of production of the political unconscious that structures the early films is mirrored at the critical level in the USA, where an initial incomprehension gives way to a strategy of camp celebration in reviews by 1962. The launch of the Gamera series during this period by the rival Daiei gave shape to the *kaijū eiga* genre, though Gamera never achieved the iconic status of Tōhō's Godzilla.

Exhausted by 1975, the series endures a ten-year dry spell until *Godzilla* (1985), which handily resolves the central contradiction of the Godzilla myth, of why a monster generated from US hydrogen bomb testing returns again and again to wreak havoc in Tokyo, by superimposing the threats of Godzilla and an errant soviet missile. The 1998 Hollywood remake brackets the late-nationalist period with an interesting twist in that this figuration of nuclear horror finally comes to roost in Manhattan, the site that lent its name to the project that stirred Godzilla from his slumbers to begin with. One has to return to the original Honda films, though, to catch a glimpse of the interplay between the dark, sublime beauty of massive objects, kinaesthetic pleasure in urban apocalypse and raw outcropping of political unconscious that has seared this icon into our collective national psyches.

Select filmography

Godzilla (1985).
Gojira tai Mekagojira (1974).
Kaijū daisensō (*Monster Zero*) (1965).
Mosura (*Mothra*) (1961).
Rodan (1956).
Gojira no gyakushu (*Revenge of Godzilla*) (1955).
Gojira (1954).

JOSEPH MURPHY

GOJIRA *see* Godzilla

Golden Week

This week falls at the end of April and runs into the first week of May. A combination of national holidays in sequence, this week offers a rare opportunity for Japanese to enjoy a full week of vacation. Many workers feel pressured to distribute their holidays over the year in short stretches across long weekends. Golden Week is a time of high sales for both domestic and international travel. Most large businesses operate only on a skeleton staff for this week and foreign businesses and tourists are well advised to mark this week on their calendar as a blackout period when it is not wise to schedule visits to Japan.

SANDRA BUCKLEY

golf

Golf is perhaps the imported sport most often associated with Japan. It has always been a joke among Western businessmen that if you can't play golf you can't do business with Japan. Even if this is an exaggeration, there is no doubt that golf is a major sport in Japan with 2,200 golf courses across the country (ninety in the Tokyo region alone) and more than 10 million active players. Although golf has long had the reputation of being outrageously expensive, the late 1990s saw a major international push by leading courses to promote Japan as an affordable and attractive tourism destination for avid golfers.

The weaker yen and tighter domestic economy have led golf clubs to go online in an attempt to entice a new casual client base to Japan through golf tourism. Clubs are creating short-term memberships and opening up non-membership privileges for the first time for visiting foreign golfers. Some clubs are also looking at creating wider membership reciprocity with selected foreign clubs. It is worth noting that the Japanese courses are opting to attract an elite business clientele from overseas rather than explore the opening up of membership to a wider cross-section of Japanese.

While golf is widely played in Japan, club access remains intensely stratified across public courses and private clubs. The vast majority of hours spent playing golf take place at the practice ranges that dot the Japanese landscape and not on a course. There are many reasons that combine to keep the majority of golfers off the course and firing golf balls at a practice range into a distant green net from an elevated platform. There has been little data collected on the life of the practice range golfer even though he or she typifies the golf experience in Japan. Eighteen holes on a course is the dream of most golfers. The cost of membership to clubs is formidable for the average middle-class wage earner with upfront fees in the late 1990s often commencing at US$500,000. Corporate memberships take up much of the access at elite clubs. Ironically, while membership may be at capacity, daily usage rates (especially weekdays) are often very low due to this dominance of corporate accounts.

In addition to attempts to attract overseas golfers more and more clubs are offering 'ladies packages' on weekdays in recognition of the significant disposable income in the control of upper mid-dle-class women seeking new leisure activities. Access to public courses is also difficult with complex rules and regulations, and often even tougher social barriers for newcomers.

Most neighbourhoods have a small pro-shop selling equipment and golf wear, and there are large speciality retail areas in each major urban centre. Online golf retailing is also a new and rapidly expanding area of e-commerce in Japan. Japanese community groups and environmentalists often point to the injustice of large tracts of precious local land being devoted to a sport that few, if any, locals have access to except as employ-ees serving the elite non-local clientele. This tension exemplifies the nature of golf in Japan. It is not merely a sport but a necessary social and career passport for many who make the coveted transition from strenuous hours on the practice range to the golf course. Practice ranges are most often built on land that is less desirable for other development and so can frequently be seen beside railroad lines or at the margin between residential and industrial land. As one way of locating ranges closer to residential or office development some entrepeneurs have resorted to roof-top locations.

At least as important as a player's handicap is their ability to perform appropriately in the golf milieu in everything from their choice of club brand to the tastefulness and currency of their golf wear, knowledge of golf trivia, the quality of their golf anecdotes, their ability to tell a good scotch from a bad at the nineteenth hole. The golf section of Japanese bookstores is always one of the larger and more popular areas with rows of books not only on mastering your stroke but also on golf fashion, etc. Golf is never just a game in Japan and those determined to make a corporate career for themselves pursue the game as seriously as they do many of their workplace assignments. With few managerial positions to be had there is a strong perception that it is the fringe skills that lead to the fringe benefits and promotion, and golf is at the top of the list, perhaps second only to the complex and virtually compulsory rituals of after-hours drinking and entertaining with colleagues or clients. Golf is a crucial lubricant of the networking that can open or close doors for upwardly mobile careers.

The extraordinary mini-economy that has been spawned by the sport of golf has generated a class of broker/entrepeneur in Japan that specialises in negotiating individual and corporate memberships to clubs with waiting lists that can run for years. These brokers have also helped to promote golf course development as a lucrative field of invest-ment. The popularity of golf among Japanese has also had an impact off-shore with predicted Japanese usage underwriting a number of new elite courses in such golf tourism destinations as Singapore, Thailand and Australia. Even some of the historic and famous courses of Europe and North America have been partially reliant on attracting Japanese golfers to sustain new develop-ment and improvements. While in many parts of the world golf has gone through a gradual process of popularisation that has led to wider access to even some of the more famous greens around the world, in Japan golf has remained an elite pursuit with the majority of golfers having to content themselves with hours spent at local practice ranges. These ranges now actively compete with one another for market share with high-quality bars and restaurants, pro-shops and coaching, along with the latest in hi-tech equipment, including computer simulations that offer on-screen access to the best and toughest greens. As the top clubs vie to attract an overseas elite to

Japan's courses, budget-priced international golf tours offer many Japanese golfers their chance to progress from astro-turf to grass offshore.

See also: leisure

Further reading

Ben Ari, E. (1998) 'Golf organization and body projects', in S. Linhart S. and Frustuck (eds) *The Culture of Japan as Seen through Its Leisure*, Albany, NY: SUNY Press, pp. 139–61.

SANDRA BUCKLEY

GOOD WIVES AND WISE MOTHERS *see ryōsai kenbo*

green parties

Green parties have proliferated in Europe with policies that promote ecology, gender equality, pacificism, anti-nuclear platforms and an egalitarian and participatory ethos that sets them apart from the more traditional parties. There is really no equivalent in Japan, and currently no green party is represented in the Diet (national parliament). From the 1980s onwards, however, an ecology party known as the Network Movement (NET) launched challenges in local elections in the largest cities of Japan, such as Tokyo, Yokohama, Kawasaki, Fukuoka, Sapporo and Chiba City, and so may be considered to play a role similar to the German Green Party in the political system. NET is a social movement party whose formal members and candidates for election are all women, even though the founders were men. NET's parent organization is the Seikatsu Club (Livelihood Club) (SC), a consumer co-operative that espouses green values, especially recycling and mutual aid. In 1996, the party successfully obtained 123 seats in prefecture, city, ward and village assemblies. The party was a ruling coalition partner in the local governments of Kamakura, Kawasaki, Fujisawa, Zushi and Machida cities. Its success reflects urban voters shifting concerns towards green issues, and

the increasing ability of Japanese women to participate in politics.

DAVID EDGINGTON

greetings

Many visitors to Japan are quick to comment on the highly stylised and formal process of greetings. The Japanese use of name cards (***meishi***) is well known as an essential element of any new business transaction. The level of formality of greetings is context driven and relates directly to the relevant hierarchies of gender, age, seniority of position, in-and-out group (***uchi* and *soto***) dynamics, etc. The *meishi* plays an important role in the exchange of basic information needed to assess the appropriate form for the exchange of greetings that follows, e.g. order of speech and seating in a group situation, level of honorific speech, depth of bow.

Various explanations are offered for the ritual depth of Japanese greeting styles but each at some level focuses on two primary axes of influence: insider–outsider relations of proximity and vertical relations across a hierarchical grid of key variables. In contexts of high proximity, e.g. school friends of the same cohort, the level of formality in greetings is minimal. If a new teacher is introduced to this same group of students their attitude will shift immediately to the appropriate level of politeness. If the teacher is a male and introduced by a female school principal, he in turn will speak with deference towards her when addressing her or speaking of her to the students during the introduction. In this context, the female principal's gender is secondary to her job status but in a meeting of principals this same woman may choose to inflect for a higher level of honorifics when being introduced to a new male colleague than when introduced to a female colleague of the same rank. These decisions are strategic in both a short-term and long-term sense. In the short term it facilitates effective communication to accurately assess context and interact appropriately. In the long term the female principal may have less respect for her male colleague than her female colleague, but by adhering to codes of gender hierarchy she does not necessarily condone she may position for future support and loyalty (what some Japanese feminists have described as a realist strategy of context-based language use).

Greetings are integral to any movement across a transitional space. This can be an architectural space (a room, house, shop), or a relational space (approaching a group or individual) or an inter-active layering of both. For example, if friends meet at a funeral service, the formality of the context overrides the proximity of the relation and they may bow to one another and exchange a level of polite greetings in a way not appropriate if meeting in a café. Greetings may be short, but are expected and appropriate responses are always forthcoming – although in the case of a superior or elder this may be no more than a grunt or even silence. In any situation where a greeting is required moving into the space, then there will also be an appropriate formality for exiting that space. A female office worker will still today walk backwards out of a doorway in order to be able to bow to her manager as she departs his office space.

In some contexts a greeting will incorporate an appropriate gift offering. Department stores specia-lise in providing both gift selection and wrapping services to facilitate this integral element of social interaction in Japan. The staff of smaller local shops and restaurants will still greet each and every customer as they enter and leave. Rather than abandon this essential ritual, many larger Japanese businesses, including department stores, supermar-kets and banks, will employ young women to stand at the main entrance and elevator or escalator threshold to greet and bow to arriving clientele. An entire training industry has grown up around teaching staff the appropriate use of honorific greetings and the art of bowing. While many older Japanese lament that the younger generations are losing the art of greetings, in reality the rituals are showing a remarkable tenacity. Even the rapid popularisation of the non-face-to-face communica-tions of e-mail and mobile phones has not seen an abandoning of the etiquette of greetings but a transformation of traditional forms to fit the speed and efficiency of these new technologies.

See also: gift giving; seasonal gift giving; *uchi* and *soto*; wrapping

SANDRA BUCKLEY

Gross National Product

Gross National Product (GNP) is the total amount of added value of goods and services produced by a nation, indicating the nation's economy. During the period of rapid growth between 1957 and 1972, Japan's GNP doubled every eight years or so, and it overtook the GDP of France, Germany and the UK by the end of the 1970s. Because GNP growth has been faster than the rate of population increase, the rate of GNP per capita has also been growing at a higher rate than other major industrial countries. Following rapid appreciation of the **yen** (*endaka*) after 1985, Japan's GNP per capita in current dollars began to exceed that of the USA. Due to the high cost of housing and other necessities in Japan, however, these figures do not correspond to the relative difference in purchasing power. In other words, a dollar can buy more in the USA than its yen equivalent in Japan. The changed economic conditions of the 1990s following the 'bursting of the **bubble economy**' brought a much slower rate of GNP increase. After the turmoil of the 'Asian financial crisis' in 1997 and 1998, Japan recorded respectively a 0.4 and 2.2 per cent contraction in GDP, the first time in post-war Japan that the economy shrank for two consecutive years.

DAVID EDGINGTON

group sounds

Group sounds (GS) popularly refers to a type of band that played electric instruments and sang pop-rock songs with vocal harmony. Japanese journalism has often identified this general ap-proach with the Beatles. The Beatles made a trip to Japan in the summer of 1966 (29 June 1966–3 July 1966). Instrumental surf bands had already begun to proliferate, so bands organised around the group concept and playing electric instruments were no longer unusual. Beatlemania was no less extreme in Japan and became a media event that explored the moral decline of Japanese girls and the qualities of the Beatles which may have inspired it (long hair, amplification, rhythm). Many bands with electric instruments moved from the Ventures model (instrumental surf band) to the Beatles model with relative ease. This was the beginning of GS.

Japanese GS bands are comparable to contemporary US garage bands in that both often followed an ethic of amateurism and the prevailing style gradually evolved from pop-rock to psychedelic. The two GS pioneers, the Spiders and the Blue Comets, were both originally rockabilly and country–western bands, but the Spiders' first album was comprised entirely of original songs in the Liverpool musical style (1966). The Blue Comets, on the other hand, have been referred to as 'a band with electric instruments that sang melancholy songs'. In this sense, the bands classified as GS did not uniformly take the Beatles as a model. In the wake of these two bands, over a hundred bands made their recording debut in the year between 1967 and 1968. One complaint often heard from Japanese musicians of the era is a sense that Japanese pop and rock was following the lead of the USA and the UK, and that the world of Japanese popular music was behind the times.

The most important of the new bands, the Tigers, made their debut in February 1967, fronted by Sawada Kenji. Shoken's sound was somewhat harder and more R 'n' B oriented than that of the Tigers. Other notable GS bands included the Golden Cups, the Jacks, the Flowers, the Carnabeats, the Bunnies, the Jaguars, the Village Singers, the Mops, the Purple Shadows, the Dynamites, the Fingers and the Ox.

In late 1968, the Blue Comets' release 'Sayonara no ato de' (After Goodbye) put further distance between the Blue Comets and the more rock 'n' roll variations on the GS sound. From this point on, GS bands came to be identified with kayōkyoku, as light *enka*/pop that had surrendered any claim to rock authenticity. At this point, Anglo-American New Rock (a Japanese journalistic term for hard rock, progressive rock, US West Coast sound and the singer-songwriters of the late 1960s and early 1970s) also made its appearance. The stronger bands such as the Jacks, the Golden Cups and the Flowers evolved along with New Rock. While The Jacks became increasingly psychedelic, the Golden Cups went on to explore the jazz-blues approach of the Paul Butterfield Blues Band. The Flowers became the Flower Travelin' Band, a power-rock group that developed the heavy metal

and art rock sounds of Black Sabbath and King Crimson while advocating English-language lyrics (they felt Japanese language lyrics lacked an authentic rock feeling). As early as 1965, many of these bands already played light pop music with electric instruments rather than rock 'n' roll. It has often been suggested that writing lyrics in Japanese resulted in *enka*-flavored songs even with bands who sounded very good when covering English-language rock material. While Happy Endo is generally credited with creating Japanese language rock, the Jacks and their songwriter Hayakawa Yōichi also deserve recognition for pioneering a more rock 'n' roll approach to songwriting with Japanese lyrics. As most GS bands couldn't compete with the rising tide of New Rock, many of them had no choice but to move even more wholeheartedly into one of the more pop-oriented, kayōkyoku styles.

Further reading

Kurozawa Susumu (1994) *Nihon rock ki GS hen*, Tokyo: Shinko Music.
Shinohara Akira (1996) *J-Rock 1968–1996 Best 123*, Tokyo: Kōdansha, pp. 369–71.

MARK ANDERSON

Gunzō

The monthly literary journal *Gunzō* (Group Portrait) was established in 1946 by the celebrated publisher **Kōdansha** in a deliberate attempt to add a journal specialising in serious literature to its existing stable of publications. *Gunzō* has made an enormous contribution to literature and literary criticism: many of the major post-war works of fiction and criticism have been published in its pages. Important novelists whose works were printed there included **Ōe Kenzaburō**, **Ibuse Masuji**, **Mishima Yukio**, Shimao Toshio, **Nakagami Kenji**, Sata Ineko, **Tsushima Yūko** and Hayashi Kyōko.

Such significant works of criticism as Ito Sei's monumental twenty-four-volume history of the literary world and Honda Shūgo's famous study of the 'White-birch' literary coterie were first serialised there also. Similarly, numerous intellectual debates were played out in its pages – the debate over the obscenity trial of the Japanese translation of D.H. Lawrence's *Lady Chatterley's Lover* being among the most notable. However, it is for the quality of its fiction that *Gunzō* has been most acclaimed, with, for example, parts of Haniya Yutaka's modern classic *Shiryō* (Ghosts) published intermittently in the journal from 1975 to 1994.

LEITH MORTON

H

Hadaka no shima

Forgotten by 1950s Japanese industrialisation, a family labours on a tiny, barren island. The film documents a year of intentionally tedious repetition and arduous tasks: rowing to get water; carrying water buckets up the steep slope; and watering crops. Two events interrupt this labour: a joyous excursion to sell a fish the children have caught; and the sudden death of the older son. Lacking any dialogue, the soundtrack alternates between ambient sound and repetitive, sonorous music. Directed by **Shindō Kaneto** and shot entirely on location in 1960, with a shoestring budget and minimal crew, *Hadaka no shima* (The Island) won the Grand Prix at the Moscow Film Festival.

NINA CORNYETZ

haiku and tanka

The two main genres of traditional poetry, haiku and *tanka*, were both profoundly affected by Japan's defeat in the Second World War. Both types of poetry had been closely associated with patriotic and xenophobic verse, thus the defeat created a crisis in confidence on the part of poets who composed these verses. This crisis was exacerbated by attacks upon the artistic and aesthetic values associated with traditional modes of poetry, and the intrinsic merit of these genres.

Such important literary critics as Odagiri Hideo (b. 1916) and Usui Yoshimi (1905–87) published essays in the immediate aftermath of the war that suggested that traditional poetry was dead and should be abandoned. Their focus was on *tanka* but the critic Kuwabara Takeo (1904–88) concentrated his attack on haiku in his famous critique 'Daini geijutsu' (A Second-rate Art, 1946), where he demonstrated that it was impossible to distinguish between the works of haiku masters and stated his belief that it was impossible to tell apart masters and inferior amateurs unless one was an expert. He followed this essay two months later by another attack, this time on *tanka*, and in very similar terms.

Although many rebuttals were offered, a great many poets lost confidence in the genre of haiku. In response, new types of haiku sought to continue a pre-war modernist tradition that broke with the old rules in relation to vocabulary, and prosody to achieve a new popularity. Haiku were written on political subjects, with ideological overtones, by acclaimed haiku poets like Nakamura Kusatao (1901–83). Avant-garde haiku poets led by Kaneko Tōta (b. 1919) tried to establish haiku on the same level as modern *vers libre* (*shi*), namely, as a serious medium of artistic expression. Poets like Katō Ikuya (b.1929), Mihashi Toshio and Nakamura Enko used similar techniques to modern *shi* poets – obscurity, abstractness, conceptual themes – to compose haiku.

Several important women poets emerged in the post-war era as a force in contemporary haiku. Especially noteworthy is the poet Hosomi Ayako (1907–97). Although Hosomi began publishing haiku in the pre-war period, her haiku took a personal turn in 1951 when she gave birth to her first child at the age of forty-four. After that, she began to compose poetry about her husband and child; her award-winning 1952 collection *Fuyubara* (Winter Roses) contained many such poems. Her 1956 collection *Kiji* (Pheasant) continued this theme. Hosomi kept on writing ever more prolifically and, by the time of her 1978 collection *Mandara* (Mandala), was firmly established at the forefront of contemporary haiku.

Kadokawa Haruki (b. 1942), the heir to the Kadokawa publishing empire, emerged in the 1980s as an important haiku poet. After a successful career as a movie producer, Kadokawa became involved in various scandals and was jailed at the end of the 1990s. Nevertheless, his position as a significant haiku poet seems secure. A recent trend in haiku has been the popularity among middle-class professionals of '*renku*' or linked haiku, composed by small groups of poets – a return to the medieval origins of the genre.

Contemporary haiku is supported financially by a large network of associations and journals published by those associations. Senior haiku poets judge competitions and edit journals as professionals. By 1996, it was estimated that between 3 and 4 million amateur haiku poets existed in Japan supporting this vast network of prizes, journals and haiku schools. This connection between art and Mammon has led several critics to raise questions yet again about artistic standards.

Tanka was possibly even more shaken than haiku by post-war attacks on the genre. The deaths in the same year of the great *tanka* poets Saitō Mokichi (1882–1953) and Origuchi Shinobu (1887–1953) also played a role in creating the perception that *tanka* had seen its best days. The immediate response was a wave of avant-garde *tanka* that challenged the dominant realist school led by the Araragi group established by Saitō. This emphasis on consciously intellectual or aesthetic poetry paralleled a similar movement in haiku circles. Two particularly important poets emerged as part of the anti-realist post-war reaction: Nakajō Fumiko (1922–54) and Terayama Shūji (1935–83). Nakajō had been inspired by the call from Origuchi in 1950 for women to take up the challenge and revitalise *tanka*. Her first *tanka* collection *Chibusa sōshitsu* (The Loss of My Breasts, 1954) about her mastectomy after she had been diagnosed with breast cancer shocked the *tanka* world, not simply because of its autobiographical

content, but also because of the strongly erotic nature of much of the poetry. The pallid realism of the Araragi school was left exposed for all to see.

Terayama adapted techniques from haiku and modern *shi* into his *tanka*, something that came easily to him, as he was an accomplished poet in both these genres. This caused much controversy, as did his emphasis upon ornamentation and satire, which was contrary to the prevailing emphasis on sincerity. His first *tanka* collection *Sora ni wa hon* (In the Sky, Books, 1968) established him, together with the poet Tsukamoto Kunio (b. 1922), as the twin leaders of avant-garde *tanka*. Later, the poet Okai Takashi (b. 1928) joined this group to complete the trio of post-war *tanka* modernists. The most popular *tanka* poet in Japan is **Tawara Machi** (b. 1962). Tawara burst on to the *tanka* scene in 1987 with her first collection *Saradakinenbi* (Salad Anniversary). This volume took the country by storm, selling nearly two-and-a-half million copies nationwide. The book virtually single-handedly re-established the popularity of *tanka* among young readers and led to a massive revival in the fortunes of this genre of verse. Tawara's light-hearted monologue on love and everyday life as experienced by a young woman was only the first in a number of *tanka* collections by Tawara, who has no rivals in the public eye.

Further reading

Hiromi Taki (1994) 'The controversial debut of Terayama Shūji as a Tanka poet', *Japanese Studies: Bulletin of the Japanese Studies Association of Australia* 14(3): 51–65.

—— (1990–1) 'Grief at the loss of my breasts: On the *tanka* of Nakajō Fumiko', *The Journal of the Oriental Society of Australia* vols 22–3: 156–69.

LEITH MORTON

hair debate

The source of many cartoons and media jokes, this debate was representative of the tensions around censorship issues over the 1990s. The ban on public display of pubic hair dates back to legal code written in the Meiji Period at a time when Japan was intent on establishing its moral credentials in the eyes of the West. The lifting of the ban has been strongly opposed by anti-pornography groups including many feminists in Japan, for it is seen to be one of the few legal controls consistently implemented in an environment where the producers and distributors of pornography are for the most part allowed to self-police content.

Anti-pornography activists consider the airbrushing and various other computer-based technologies for blurring the 'offending' portion of images to be at least a limited control of explicit content. Those calling for the lifting of the hair ban argue that explicitness is in the mind of the beholder and not the image itself. The ban impacts not only pornographic film, video and photo magazines but also the exhibition of traditional erotic woodblock prints (*shunga*), commercial films, any foreign or Japanese art or photography depicting nudity, the massive market in adult comics, video and computer games. The area of the arts that has seen the least stringent application of the ban has been dance and performance, and more recently some contemporary theatre.

The full frontal nude scenes central to the cross-gender storylines of two foreign films, *The Crying Game* and *Orlando*, brought the hair debate to the fore in the mid-1990s. There was no shortage of public intellectuals and social critics willing to express their view on the controversy as it captured extensive attention in the editorial pages and feature articles of newspapers, magazines and television talk shows. At the peak of the hair debate (1993–5), media coverage ranged from comedy to sensationalism and staid intellectual exchange. Some magazines and television shows attempted to test the law at this time but the authorities were quick to advise management that they should comply with the expectation of the media industry to self-monitor content.

Although there has been a relaxing of the law in the case of certain imported artworks and art films, critics of the ban argue that the decisions finally still rest in the hands of the authorities and that this is an intrusion of the state into cultural production and consumption. The battle over the pubic-hair ban has made for some unexpected alliances as

artists, film-makers and gallery owners fight alongside the pornography industry for the right to free images of the naked body from the white fuzz of the censors' airbrush. In relation to the hair debate, feminists remain divided between those who are anti-censorship and those who are anti-pornography. In the absence of other forms of censorhip, anti-pornography groups argue that the removal of the ban would amount to a free licence on content to the pornography industry. The availability of pornography through vending machines raises issues of access for minors, but whether or not the hair ban significantly curtails the level of explicitness or violence in the comics and videos on sale at these street vending machines is a contentious point between those who defend and oppose the ban. There is no indication that the ban will be completely lifted in the near future and so we can anticipate further eruptions of the hair debate around the censorship of the exhibition or publication of specific 'offending' works in the years to come.

SANDRA BUCKLEY

hakama

The *hakama* is a loose fitting, often pleated trouser tied by a cord at the waist. Although today it is considered a part of men's formal wear it has also been worn by women at different times in history, most notably the Heian period. The *hakama* are worn over an under-**kimono** and paired with a **_haori_** jacket when worn by men. The careful co-ordination of colour, cloth and pattern are as important in the formal dress of men as in a woman's choice of kimono. Women's *hakama* are traditionally worn with an over-kimono (*kosode*) and in the early Meiji Period, as a compulsory modern education system was established, it was the *haori* and *kosode* that were designated as the school uniform for many girls' schools. *Hakama* are still worn in the *nō* theatre, and the traditional arts of archery and kendo and in some religious rituals and ceremony.

SANDRA BUCKLEY

Hakuhodo

Founded in 1895, the second largest of Japan's advertising agencies has 3,493 employees (1998) and, like **Dentsu**, it offers clients an extensive range of services. In the pre-war period, its strongest client base was with publishers of newspaper advertising. This seems to have contributed to Hakuhodo's slowness in engaging with the post-war development of public television broadcasting, something which gave Dentsu an irreversible edge in the market. Even so, Hakuhodo consistently holds in excess of 10 per cent of national market share. Hakuhodo has some twenty domestic affiliates, branches in eighteen cities and thirteen offshore affiliates in twenty-three cities. According to *Advertising Age*, Hakuhodo's gross income ranked the company tenth in the international advertising world in 1997, and it was placed ninth on the list of independent agencies worldwide that same year. One affiliate, Hakuhodo Institute of Life and Living, has gained a strong reputation as an independent think tank over recent years. The research and concept development success of the Institute has spun off into the new growth business of content development for music, film and programming. Following a similar pathway into new digital technology as Dentsu, Hakuhodo has launched its own Internet business development unit and this too features a content development section.

NANBA KŌJI

Hamaguchi Kuranosuke

b. 1917, Kōchi Prefecture

Songwriter

Kuranosuke graduated from Waseda University in engineering, then went on to work for an iron and steel company. After the war, he received a degree in business from Aoyama Gakuin. While still in school he began playing guitar with such groups as the Sakurai Ketsu Orchestra. After playing guitar in various genres such as Hawaiian and jazz, he formed a group called the Afro-Cubano Orchestra. Hamaguchi was the singer for the band. They appeared on NHK's *Kōhaku uta gassen* three years running in the mid-1950s (1954–6). In 1958, he turned to songwriting. 'Kiiroi sakuranbo' (Yellow Cherry) took off as a hit. After that, he wrote many hits such as 'Aishite, aishite, aishchyattanoyo' (I Loved, Loved, Loved You), 'Namidakun sayonara' (Goodbye Tears) for Sakamoto Kyū and 'Hoshi no furamenko' (Flamenco of the Stars). His 1966 'Bara ga saita' (A Rose Bloomed), was an early impetus toward the 1960s' boom in folk song popularity. He has continued to write songs into old age.

Further reading

Ito Tsutomu (1994) 'Hamaguchi Kuranosuke', in *Taishū bunka jiten*, Tokyo: Kobundo, p. 622.

MARK ANDERSON

Hanae Mori

b. 1926, Shimane Prefecture

Fashion designer

Hanae Mori graduated from Tokyo Women's University in 1951 and went on to establish her own shop, 'Hyōsha'. In New York in 1965, she launched her new line featuring rich and colourful Japanese patterns gorgeously splashed across dresses made of Japanese silk. This established a foothold for her in the Japanese fashion world. In 1977, she became the first Japanese to gain acceptance into the Paris *haute couture* association and she continues to launch her collections in France. She has received many awards both inside and outside of Japan. As a Japanese designer she has been active worldwide as a pioneer creating opportunities for other Japanese designers. In 1996, she was the first fashion designer in Japan to be awarded a commendation at the highest rank for contributions to Japanese culture. Her fashions are known, like Kenzo's, for the flamboyant and bold use of colour. Unlike many of her compatriot designers Hanae does not shy away from more traditionally recognisable Japanese motifs such as butterflies, blossoms, fans, etc., although she is in no way limited to Japanese sources for her stunning print designs. Her patterns and styles have won her a wide following within an older market segment than some of her fellow Japanese brand designers.

AKIKO FUKAI

Hanakozoku

The 'Hanako tribe' refers to the avid readership and cultural mileu that formed around the immensely successful young women's magazine *Hanako*. One of a number of consumer marketing magazines that emerged from the 1980s, it targeted a new generation of working women with substantial disposable income and personal savings. Articles and photo features were accompanied by specific product and distribution information. The magazine drove new lifestyle trends among its target readers and made and broke many businesses and brand names as it became increasingly influential in shaping consumer patterns in the highly niche-oriented Japanese market.

SANDRA BUCKLEY

Hanshin Earthquake

On 17 January 1995 at 5:46 a.m., a major earthquake of 7.2 on the Richter scale hit the Kobe–Ōsaka metropolitan area, also known as the Hanshin region, killing 5,502 people, injuring 41,521, leaving more than 300,000 others homeless and raising serious questions about Japan's preparedness for domestic disasters. The earthquake was the most destructive to strike Japan since the Great Kantō Earthquake in 1923. The Hanshin Earthquake lasted 20 seconds and caused fires and landslides, and fully or partly destroyed 207,283 buildings, mostly two-storey, traditional Japanese wooden structures. In addition, nine bridges collapsed, a 500-meter-stretch of the elevated Hanshin Expressway fell on its side, many modern high-rises suffered foundation damage and more than 90 per cent of Kobe's new port facilities, built on landfill, were destroyed.

Despite an acute national awareness of predictions that a devastating earthquake would strike a major Japanese metropolitan area, the central government's response to the crisis was slow and inadequate. The absence of clear leadership, together with bureaucratic turf wars, initially paralysed the nation's crisis management system. Internal communication networks failed and political leaders and rescue workers were forced to rely on television coverage for information during the emergency's first critical hours. Prime Minister Tomiichi Murayama did not order full mobilisation of the Ground Self-Defence Forces until the following morning. Aid offers by foreign countries and international organisations were initially rejected or postponed because of bureaucratic confusion and/or the inability of government officials to identify needs.

After bureaucratic hurdles were overcome, however, relief efforts were co-ordinated and many non-governmental organisations (NGOs), private businesses and individual volunteer groups joined with official agencies to help the injured and begin the rebuilding process. In contrast to the widescale riots that took place in the aftermath of the Great Kantō Earthquake, evacuation of the affected population to temporary shelters in parks, gymnasiums and undamaged public buildings proceeded efficiently. Criminal activity was almost non-existent; for example, no felonies were registered and reported burglaries amounted to only one-sixth of those filed during the same time period in 1994.

The earthquake shattered the local economy, forcing worker layoffs and threatening the city's significance as one of the world's major cargo ports. Rebuilding the Kobe port has taken preference over that of other local industries, such as synthetic-shoe manufacturing, 90 per cent of which was destroyed (accounting for 9 per cent of the national output), and the city's fifty sake breweries, which produced one-third of the nation's sake. While foreign ships were re-routed to Ōsaka and Yokohama, whose ports compete vigorously with Kobe for cargo lanes to Asian countries, Kobe harbour facilities were rebuilt with state-of-the-art technology and its functions upgraded to better serve the expanding Asian market. In general, Kobe's economy rallied at a fast pace and recovered to 80 per cent of pre-quake levels within three years.

Further reading

The Japan Times Special Report (1995) *The Great Hanshin Quake*, The Japan Times: Tokyo.

FRANZISKA SERAPHIM

haori

This is a style of jacket worn by men and women over a **kimono** or together with the men's trouser garment known as *hakama*. It falls to somewhere between the hip and knee, and ties in the front with two short cords at mid-chest level. *Haori* can vary from light, almost transparent summer-weight, materials to heavy lined silk and linen. The texture and pattern of a *haori* is carefully matched to that of the kimono or *hakama*, and seasonal variations in colour, cloth and pattern are considered an essential element of the aesthetic of this traditional style.

SANDRA BUCKLEY

Happy Endo

A strong case can be made that Happy Endo is the band that first defined the form of Japanese rock. Even after their break-up, the individual members continued to be central to the Japanese music scene. They are most commonly cited as the band that first successfully made music with Japanese lyrics which felt and sounded like rock 'n' roll.

Happy Endo effectively broke the hegemony of the *enka*-style of Japanese song lyric composition. The band's members, Matsumoto Takashi (drums), Hosono Haruomi (bass), Ōtaki Eichi (vocals and rhythm guitar) and Suzuki Shigeru (lead guitar), came together in March 1970. Hosono and Ōtaki's decision to form the band came out of a shared enthusiasm for the sound of Buffalo Springfield. Their first public appearance was on 12 April 1970 at the Rock Rebellion Festival and was followed by several concerts performed on the '**barricades**' – sections of college campuses under the complete control of student protesters. They received the Japanese Rock Award from *New Music Magazine* in April 1971 for their first album. Happy Endo

gained national prominence as the backing band for the Kansai-based political folk singer, **Oka-bayashi Nobuyasu** and were central to his transition from folk to electric rock. Happy Endo's second album was also an instant classic. Their third studio album was recorded in Los Angeles.

Hosono and Suzuki went on to play in the bands Tin Pan Alley and Caramel Mama. Tin Pan Alley was the dominant studio backing band of the 1970s. They played behind the early recordings of Matsutoya Yumi and Yoshida Minako, among many others. Hosono was later a founding member of Yellow Magic Orchestra. Ōtaki founded Niagara Records, released successful vocal harmony-based solo albums, and wrote a series of successful commercial jingles. Matsumoto became a full-time lyricist and wrote countless hits recorded by other artists through the 1970s and 1980s. In many ways, their individual careers embodied the 1970s trend of **New Music**: a form of expression where the musician and songwriter were able to wrest artistic control from the record companies, while not seriously challenging the commodity status of popular music.

The underground folk and rock of 1969 and 1970 was rapidly reintegrated into the larger social and business community. Musicians had become artists at the expense of surrendering overt commitment to social revolution or reform. For its part, from the start, Happy Endo had already translated these issues into a question of purging popular music of the melodramatic sentiments of *enka*, and using formal experimentation and artistic modernism in a manner resonant with both the Beatles and Ōshima's earlier approach to challenging the codes of Japanese film production.

MARK ANDERSON

Hara Hiroshi

b. 9 September 1936, Kawasaki, Kanagawa Prefecture

Architect

Trained at the University of Tokyo (1955–9), Hara was one of the oldest in a new generation of avant-garde New Wave architects who, active from the late 1960s and through the 1970s, were sharply critical of both the prevailing modern architecture and, particularly, contemporary urban developments in Japan. Yet, unlike many of his more radical contemporaries, such as Andō Tadao, Ito Toyo and Hasegawa Itsuko, Hara derived his design theories from his extensive studies of vernacular architecture and indigenous settlements, while conducting regular and frequent research trips in European, Asian and African countries in an attempt to bridge the avant-garde and the ethnic in urban architecture.

Thereafter, he followed a unique anthropological approach to design, similar to the one forwarded by the members of Team Ten in Europe. His early works, the so-called 'reflection houses', such as the Awazu Residence (1972) in Kawasaki, his own Hara Residence (1974) in Machida near Tokyo and the Niramu House (1978) in Chiba, display a negative attitude towards the chaotic and volatile conditions of the Japanese city while focusing upon the internal order and other critical aspects of dwelling. They were all shaped along sequences of centrally and symmetrically arranged, ritualistic spaces and appeared as hollowed-out cavities. Many of them implemented small-scale, metaphorical urban elements, including plazas, landmarks, streets and intersections, and so could be regarded as attempts to create imaginary scenes of cities in miniature.

After the 1970s, in addition to his continued residential works, Hara received commissions for larger, public buildings such as the Sueda Art Gallery (1981) in Ōita, the Tsurukawa Nursery (1981) in Machida and the Josei Primary School (1987) in Naha, Okinawa. At this time, his architectural approach began to change, becoming more receptive to the natural and built landscape. Having internalised the metropolis by creating exterior-like interiors, he now seemed to turn this model inside out, making his new buildings metaphors of 'cities within the city'. In the Tasaki Museum of Art (1986) in Karuizawa, the Iida City Museum (1988) and particularly in the Yamato International Building (1987) in Tokyo, the boundaries or transition between architecture and the surrounding environment are ambiguously defined. In his 'architecture of modality', extensively and intricately layered walls, imprinted, translucent or

transparent and reflective glass and polished aluminium surfaces, as well as fragmented elements, create an elusive atmosphere. These buildings, while evoking images of fictive vernacular villages, also allude to such natural phenomena as clouds, mist or mirage. They reveal Hara's long-standing resistance to modernist and, particularly, constructivist architecture.

In his investigations of the perceptual qualities of architecture and, through them, the relationship between reality and fiction, Hara has developed a profound interest in the latest electronic and information technologies. Inspired by them, he has been designing what he calls 'modal spaces of consciousness'. The 1990s witnessed the completion of increasingly large and significant complexes, in which the previous mode of design is complemented by the imaginative application of high technology, as in the spectacular Umeda Sky Building (1993), an inter-connected skyscraper in Ōsaka, and the Sapporo Dome (2001), an indoor–outdoor sports and entertainment facility in Sapporo. The explicitly futuristic, spaceship-like design of the Miyagi Prefectural Library (1997) in Sendai and the huge Kyōto Station Complex (1997), featuring a uniquely shaped and dynamic atrium, complete the list of Hara's most recent urban-scale projects. The exceptional quality of these works demonstrates Hara's continued significant role in contemporary Japanese architecture.

Further reading

Bognar, B. (1990) *The New Japanese Architecture*, New York: Rizzoli International.

—— (1985) *Contemporary Japanese Architecture: Its Development and Challenge*, New York: Van Nostrand Reinhold.

Fawcett, C. (1980) *The New Japanese House: Ritual and Anti-ritual Patterns of Dwelling*, New York: Harper & Row.

—— (1978) 'Hiroshi Hara: An introduction', *Archit. Assoc. Q.* 10(4): 4.

Frampton, K. (1986) 'Twilight gloom to self-enclosed modernity: Five Japanese architects', in *Tokyo: Form and Spirit*, exhibition catalogue, Minneapolis, MN: Walker A. Cent., pp. 221–41

Hara Hiroshi (1993) 'Learning from villages: 100

lessons (1987)' in Y. Futagawa (ed.).*Hiroshi Hara, GA Architects 13*, Tokyo: ADA Edita, pp. 88–91.

—— (1993) 'Yukotai theory 1968–1993', in Y. Futagawa (ed.) *Hiroshi Hara, GA Architects 13*, Tokyo: ADA Edita, pp. 32–4.

BOTOND BOGNAR

Hara Kazuo

b. 1945

Film-maker

A leading documentary film-maker whose works include *Sayonara CP* (Goodbye, CP, 1972), *Kyokushiteki erosu koiuta* (Extreme Private Eros: Love Song, 1974), *Zenshin sh ōsetsuka* (A Dedicated Life, 1994) and the especially brilliant *Yukiyukite shingun* (The Emperor's Naked Army Marches On, 1987). Through what he terms 'action documentaries', lively films made in close collaboration with his subjects, Hara calls into question what he considers to be an artificial distinction between so-called documentary films and fiction films.

The subjects of Hara's films, ranging from the poet suffering from cerebral palsy who is portrayed in 'Goodbye CP' to the radical feminist at the centre of 'Extreme Private Eros: Love Song', all are individuals who call into question the values of mainstream society. 'The Emperor's Naked Army Marches On', one of the most commercially successful documentary films produced in post-war Japan, focuses on Okuzaki Kenzō, a veteran who forces into present consciousness repressed wartime memories ranging from Emperor Hirohito's complicity in the war to the cannibalism committed by Japanese soldiers in New Guinea.

Further reading

Ruoff, Jeffrey and Ruoff, Kenneth (1998) *The Emperor's Naked Army Marches On*, Wiltshire, England: Flicks Books.

Ruoff, Kenneth and Ruoff, Jeffrey (1993) 'Japan's outlaw filmmaker: An interview with Hara Kazuo', *Iris: A Journal of Theory on Image and Sound* 16: 103–14.

KENNETH RUOFF

Hara Setsuko

b. 1920, Kanagawa

Actor

A huge film star and symbol of post-war women, Hara coaxed the defeated Japanese male towards rebuilding and democratic reform. She played strong women who suffer with dignity, such as aristocrats who lose status but remain loyal to leftist husbands (**Kurosawa Akira**'s *No Regrets For Our Youth*, 1946) or peasant parents or in-laws (Ozu's **Tokyo monogatari** (Tokyo Story)). Her image was 'pure' – moral, sincere, well-bred, radiant – but could be passionately assertive, even feminist, as in **Naruse Mikio**'s *Yama no Oto* (Sounds from the Mountain, 1954), in which she plays a wife who leaves her unfaithful husband. In *Ozu's Banshun* (Late Spring, 1949), as a faithful daughter she moves from resistance to acceptance of marriage so evocatively that one hardly notices that her husband never appears on-screen.

CHRISTOPHER PERRIUS

Harajuku

This district in the eastern area of Shibuya-ku (ward) is the site of Meiji-Jingu (Meiji Shrine), one of the major religious sites in Tokyo, as well as Yoyogi Park and Yoyogi National Stadium. Visitors to Harajuku can arrive by subway at Omote-sandō station or on the Yamanote line at Harajuku station. These two stations stand at opposite ends of a long shopping boulevard featuring many popular foreign and Japanese brand name stores, as well as some of the more famous street cafés in Tokyo. The surrounding streets and alleys are a haven of youth culture and fashion, and a stark contrast to the Issey Miyake, Yohji Yamamoto and Comme des Garçons styles on display in the boutique windows of the main boulevard.

Harajuku fashion has been described as '*oserterizer*' fashion. The streets are lined with crowded speciality boutiques devoted to anything from temporary tatoos to neo-goth accessories or recycled Elvis or rock 'n' roll fashion. Hair styles can run the full gamut from dreadlocks to skinhead or purple punk. New fads come and go in a season or maybe two – like the death-defying platform shoes of 1999–2000 or the retro '*ganguro*' blend of surfer and mod rocker style, with its layered fashion, bleached blonde or red-dyed hair and dark artificial face tan. When most people think of Japanese fashion it is the mix of playfulness and austerity of the brand designers that comes to mind, and yet for the majority of young Japanese it is what is happening on the streets around Harajuku that determines where they will spend their fashion budget. There are entire magazines devoted to glossy photo displays of the latest in Harajuku trends accompanied by an encyclopaedic detail of retail and pricing information.

Harajuku is also home to café culture, and the street cafés are a favourite place to be seen among the new class of media and digital savvy entrepreneurs in Tokyo. *Gaijin tarento* (foreign television personalities) and fashion models are also often to be found intently involved in a conversation on their mobile and checking their palm pilot while sipping a café latte. Harajuku is a place to see, and be seen, for all who want to be noticed. This area is also home to the famous Kinokuniya supermarket, which specialises in luxury imported and domestic foods, and has an extensive range of ready-to-eat take-out gourmet meals and a world-class French bakery. Every night there is a long line of taxis outside the supermarket waiting to rush the upmarket clientele home to enjoy their evening meal.

At the other end of Omote Sandō, a walk through the gardens of the Meiji Shrine is a wonderful respite from the metropolis. Although a replica of the original structure, it is a chance for many foreign visitors on a rush trip through Tokyo to experience the beauty of Japanese landscape gardening and to visit an excellent example of Shintō architecture. There are often prayer services or other ceremonies underway, especially on weekends. Behind Harajuku station stretches Yoyogi Park, where amateur dance troupes, musicians and street performers fill the main road into the park on weekends and present carefully choreographed pieces for the crowds they attract. Everyone seems to have their own home-burnt CD to sell. On the weekend, parts of Harajuku are closed to traffic and the whole area takes on the air of a consumer paradise. Harajuku on a Sunday, rain or shine, is the perfect place for anyone seeking a snapshot of the lifestyle now known globally as 'Tokyo Street'.

SANDRA BUCKLEY

Hasegawa Itsuko

b. 1941, Shizuoka Prefecture

Architect

After graduating from Kantō Gakuin University's College of Engineering, Hasegawa worked for famous architects **Kikutake Kiyonori** and Shinohara Kazuo before opening Hasegawa Itsuko Atelier in 1979. She came into prominence as one of Japan's leading architects after winning several major design competitions, beginning with the Shōnandai Culture Centre design proposal in 1986.

It may be her design for the Fruit Museum in Yamanashi City for which she is best known: several structures of crescent and dome-like shapes in varying sizes are partially buried or sprouting from the hillside slopes, their facilities wrapped in ribbed steel frames and clear glass to heighten the paradoxical sense of both exposure to the elements and containment from them. They house facilities for the museum, a workshop space, a conservatory and an indoor park called the Fruit Plaza. Hasegawa has said that each of the structures represents a different phase in the sensuous and physical life of fruit, from germination as a seed to their ripening.

Other well-publicised works by Hasegawa include the Sumida Culture Factory (Tokyo, 1994), University of Shiga Prefecture Gymnasium (1995) and Niigata Performing Arts Centre (1999).

Further reading

(1995) *JA: The Japan Architect* 19(3) (autumn).
Hasegawa Itsuko (1993) *Itsuko Hasegawa*, Academy Editions: London.

MARY KNIGHTON

Hasumi Shigehiko

b. 29 April 1936, Tokyo

Film critic, literary critic and French
literature scholar

Hasumi is arguably the most influential film critic
in Japan. In 1968, he started publishing criticism in
Cinema 69, a film journal aspiring to a new critical
discourse. Fostered by Cahiers du cinéma and post-
structuralism, his theoretical stake resided in
casting light on formal details of film, and the
thresholds of the film medium that inevitably
determine such details. He served as the editor-
in-chief for *Lumiére* (1985–8), to which he also
contributed a number of important interviews with
technicians and directors.

Select bibliography

Hasumi Shigehiko (1997) 'Sunny skies', trans.
Kathy Shigeta, in David Desser (ed.) *Ozu's Tokyo
Story*, Cambridge: Cambridge University Press,
pp. 118–29.

CHIKA KINOSHITA

Hattori Ryōichi

b. 1907, Ōsaka

Songwriter

An early jazz-influenced songwriter, in 1926
Hattori Ryōichi became a member of the NHK
Central Broadcast Symphony Orchestra. He
studied under the orchestra's conductor and
learned songwriting. Later he turned to jazz. After
working for some time as a saxophone player, he
became a staff songwriter for Columbia in 1936.
He wrote his first hit song in 1937, 'Wakare no
blues' (The Break-up Blues). Compared to Koga
Masao as a modern Japanese songwriter, where
Koga wrote many pieces steeped in Japanese
sentiment, Hattori appears to have been raised
on jazz and wrote many songs with a jazz-pop
flavour. After the Second World War, songs with
the sort of rhythm characteristic of 'Tokyo boogie-
woogie' injected a degree of vitality into the

desolate post-war scene. Later surveys place his
'Aoi sammyaku' (Blue Mountains) at the top of the
list of songs most beloved by Japanese audiences.
Hattori became the head of the Association of
Japanese Songwriters upon the death of Koga
Masao. Apart from the composition of innumer-
able popular songs, he has also continued to devote
considerable energy to compositions for orchestra.
Among popular music songwriters, he is known for
his exceptionally broad interests and abilities.

Select bibliography

Hattori Ryōichi (1982) *Boku no ongaku jinsei*, Tokyo:
Nihon Bungeisha.

Further reading

Ito Tsutomu (1995) 'Hattori Ryōichi', in *Taishū
bunka jiten*, Tokyo: Kobundo, p.615.

MARK ANDERSON

Heisei era

Heisei is the Japanese name given to the reign of the
country's current emperor Akihito. *Heisei* began
with the death of **Emperor Akihito**'s father,
Hirohito, on 7 January 1989, which brought the
Shōwa Period (1925–89) to a close. According to
the Japanese calendar, which numbers years within
each imperial reign, the year 1989 officially
became Heisei 1.

Based on two quotations from classical Chinese
literature, '*heisei*' has been interpreted to mean 'the
attainment of peace at home and abroad, in
heaven and on earth'.

Although a change of imperial reigns does not
entail political change in Japan (the emperor is a
constitutional monarch), political events occurring
during the first years of *heisei* both contributed to,
and fed on, a sense that a new historical era had
begun. First, the beginning of *heisei* coincided with
a loss of voter confidence in the **Liberal Democratic Party** (LDP), the party in power since
1948, and led to a realignment of political parties
in 1993.

Second, the end of the cold war facilitated Japan's deepening integration in East Asia and promoted debates on Japan's legitimate role in international affairs. Third, the ascendance of Emperor Akihito, a popular national symbol, untainted by the wartime militarism, spurred a more open public discourse about Japan's **war responsibility** towards its Asian neighbours.

In 1993, a series of bribery scandals involving the LDP leadership, a reformed electoral system and the slowing economy contributed to the end of the long political era marked by the LDP hegemony. A volatile coalition government came to be opposed by a loose federation of reformist factions, which created the New Frontier Party (Shinshintō) in December 1994. Consisting primarily of disaffected LDP members led by Ozawa Ichirō, it focused on deregulation, administration reform and a higher international profile for Japan.

Domestic and foreign demands for more active Japanese participation in international politics increased in the wake of the 1991 Persian Gulf War and resulted in The 'Peace-keeping Operations (PKO) Bill', passed in the Diet in 1992, which allowed Japan's **Self-Defence Forces** (SDF) to be deployed overseas in non-combatant positions for the first time since 1945. Under this law, Japanese troops were dispatched to Cambodia in December 1992 to help monitor elections, a clear departure from Japan's practice of limiting its participation in international affairs to financial contributions ('chequebook diplomacy').

An integral part of the debates accompanying changes in both domestic and international politics was the issue of reforming a consensus on how to assess Japan's colonial wartime past. In a break with earlier conventions, Emperor Akihito in April 1989 personally apologised to the visiting Chinese premier for Japan's wartime aggression against China. Since then, Japanese prime ministers have extended further formal apologies to Asian nations, but have streadfastly rejected demands to provide state compensation to non-Japanese war victims.

Further reading

Leitch, R.D, Kato, A. and Weinstein, M.E. (1995) *Japan's Role in the Post-Cold War World*, Westport, CN and London: Greenwood Press.

Fujitani, T. (1992) 'Electronic pageantry and Japan's "symbolic emperor"', *Journal of Asian Studies* 51(4): 824–50.

FRANZISKA SERAPHIM

HELP Women's Shelter

HELP Women's Shelter (Josei no Ie) was established in 1986, the centenary year of the **Women's Christian Temperance Union** (WCTU) in Japan. The shelter provides temporary accommodation and referral to lawyers, medical practitioners or social workers for women needing advice on domestic violence, marital problems or immigration issues. Most clients are immigrant women, but Japanese women also use the shelter when they cannot be dealt with by other facilities. HELP volunteers are also involved in educational activities and networking with other non-governmental organisations.

Further reading

Ōshima, Shizuko and Francis, Carolyn (1989) *Japan through the Eyes of Women Migrant Workers*, Tokyo: HELP Asian Women's Shelter.

VERA MACKIE

HIBAKUSHA *see* atomic bombings

high-definition TV

No product better illustrates the dramatic reversal in evaluations of Japan's technological prowess than high-definition television (HDTV). In the 1980s, HDTV seemed proof of Japan's emerging dominance in electronics; by the mid-1990s, it became a symbol of Japan's backwardness in open digital systems and its inability to create new technological architectures.

Japan's HDTV technology embodied three major improvements: superior image resolution (over twice as many vertical scanning lines as conventional television, elimination of ghost images and better colour separation), a wide aspect ratio similar to movies and CD-quality sound. HDTV was implemented at two levels: Hi-Vision, a broadband studio standard containing nearly five times the information of standard television signals; and MUSE (multiple sub-Nyquist sampling encoding), an analogue transmission standard that compressed television signals into 8 MHz, the space available on direct broadcast satellites. NHK, Japan's national broadcaster, pioneered HDTV research in the 1960s. As the technology neared fruition, initial foreign support and admiration turned to fear. In 1986, Europe and the USA rejected MUSE as an international standard. NHK persisted anyway. It entered technology alliances with private electronics firms to develop key enabling technologies and gained financial and regulatory support from the **Ministry of International Trade and Industry** (MITI) and the **Ministry of Post and Telecommunications** (MPT), as well as the ruling **Liberal Democratic Party** (LDP). However, for many years the high cost of MUSE decoders and the large screens required to take full advantage of HDTV retarded penetration of Hi-Vision.

In the early 1990s, unexpected breakthroughs in the USA in digital signal compression, Internet technology and communications satellites combined with the onset of the Heisei recession in Japan to convince many that Japan's HDTV, with its use of analogue compression and emphasis on quality over quantity and economy, was completely outmoded. After overcoming resistance from NHK, private broadcasters and the electronics firms, MPT eventually succeeded in killing MUSE and moving to digital television technologies based largely on international standards. Formerly excluded foreign firms such as News Corporation and Hughes Electronics used the new digital transmission techniques to establish a powerful position in Japanese broadcasting.

Many of the problems of HDTV stemmed from the fact that Japan, traditionally denigrated as a copycat, embarked on Hi-Vision before the underlying technologies were mature. None the less, US and European breakthroughs in digital television depended fundamentally upon techniques and equipment developed in Japan. Even after the switch to digital transmission, Japanese firms remained dominant suppliers of much of the hardware.

GREGORY W. NOBLE

Hihyō kūkan

The journal *Hihyō kūkan* (Critical Space) was begun in 1991 by social critic Asada Akira and social-literary critic and philosopher **Karatani Kōjin**. The first issues were published by Fukutake Shōten; in 1994, Ōta Shuppan took over and it hence became *Hihyō kūkan II*. Unlike *Gendai shisō*, the first source for contemporary intellectual thought, the editors of *Hihyō kūkan* were determined to avoid the rote format of theme-based issues (that is, the election of a topic by the editors, and solicitation of essays on these topics) to allow for greater flexibility and range. Avowedly eclectic, although humanities and social sciences dominate, *Hihyō kūkan* has been open to virtually any intellectual field or topic, including: literary criticism, Marxism, modernism, post-colonialism, queer theory, religion and cultural studies. Every issue includes a discussion by Karatani and Asada, often a roundtable with at least one invited guest, e.g. Fredric Jameson on the topic of 'After the Gulf War', in 1992. Often, there is an essay by Karatani himself. Most articles are recent intellectual interventions by contemporary leading Japanese and non-Japanese scholars, writers and intellectuals, but there are also contributions from junior scholars. At the back, a literary narrative is serialised.

NINA CORNYETZ

Hinamatsuri (Doll Festival) and Girls' Day

Although Girls' Day (3 March) and Boys' Day (5 May) have been officially combined as Children's Day since 1948, Japanese families continue to follow the custom of celebrating these events separately. Girls' Day is known as the Doll Festival. A set of doll figurines of the Emperor, Empress and their court in full Heian costume is displayed on a tiered stand in descending rank. The daughter of the house invites friends to share ceremonial foods and sweet sake.

Much of the ceremony, as well as some of the games, performed on this day are linked to the future marriage of the daughter of the household. Superstition has it that any delay in putting the dolls away after 3 March will lead to delays in finding a husband. A *Hinamatsuri* display can be a simple home-made set of **origami** dolls or might include real embroidered silk clothes for an extended entourage of porcelain or carved wooden courtiers with many miniaturised accessories, foods, flowers, gifts, etc. Deluxe models on sale in major department stores boast hand-painted miniature plates and bowls, edible miniature fruits and sweets, and even real gold hair ornaments, and gold threaded embroidery. Many girls still dress in kimono for the day's activities. The richness of the display and the food served to invited girlfriends has long been the source of considerable competition between friends and households. The doll sets are often inherited, but if there is not an heirloom set in the household then a set will be made or bought new with the birth of the first daughter, and may then be lovingly added to year after year.

SANDRA BUCKLEY

Hiratsuka Raichō

b. 1886, Tokyo; d. 1971

Feminist pioneer

Hiratsuka Haruko (pen-name Raichō) was the daughter of a prominent bureaucrat and was educated at Japan Women's College and Tsuda Umeko's English College. She was the founding editor of the feminist literary journal Seitō (Blue-stocking), a participant in the debate on the protection of motherhood (see *bōsei hōgo*), and a founding member of the New Women's Associa-tion. Her poetic phrase, 'In the beginning, woman was the sun' is widely quoted. In post-war Japan, Hiratsuka was primarily associated with the co-operative movement and the pacifist movement.

Select bibliography

Hiratsuka Raichō (1971) *Genshi josei wa taiyō de atta: Hiratsuka Raichō Jiden*, 4 vols, Tokyo: Ōtsuki Shoten.

VERA MACKIE

Hirohito, Emperor

b. 1901, Tokyo; d. 1989, Tokyo

Hirohito was emperor of Japan from 1926 to 1989. His reign of more than six decades encompassed Japan's attempt to dominate Asia by military means, the crushing defeat that followed and then Japan's recovery and development into the second largest economy in the world. He was heir to an imperial line that, according to the official ideology of Imperial Japan (1890–1945), was said to descend directly from the Sun Goddess Amaterasu. Un-surprisingly, Hirohito had a sheltered if privileged childhood. After he graduated from elementary school, a special institute was established for his education, which he attended together with a few companions who were expected to show him utmost deference at all times. He became regent in 1921 for his mentally enfeebled father, Emperor Taishō, and ascended to the throne at the age of twenty-five upon his father's death in 1926.

In 1924, Hirohito married Kuni-no-miya Na-gako (1903–2000), daughter of a collateral house of the imperial family. As was appropriate at the time, the marriage between Hirohito and Nagako was arranged by an initial formal introduction rather than being a 'love match'. Emperor Hirohito made one important break with custom regarding married life, however. After becoming emperor, he went on to abolish the courtesan system at the court. This significant cultural reform resulted from Hirohito's commitment to monogamy. No one ever has been able to provide evidence that he was anything but a faithful husband to Nagako during more than fifty years of married life. This was true even though his advisers, when Nagako had delivered four daughters but no son several years into their union, urged him to make use of the courtesans to produce an heir to the throne. He refused, and in 1933 an heir, Akihito, was born.

Hirohito was the constitutional and spiritual leader of his country throughout the Fifteen-Year War (1931–45). During the Occupation (1945–52), he worked closely with General Douglas **Mac-Arthur** and other Allied Occupation authorities, who shielded him from prosecution as a war criminal. Much attention has focused on whether or not Hirohito bore war responsibility, and, if so, to what extent. Shortly after Japan's surrender in August 1945, Emperor Hirohito dismounted his white horse, abandoned his military uniform and officially was transformed into not only a pacifist but a family man, who democratically walked among the people. Recently, more and more historical works based on documents that became available after Hirohito's death in 1989 have stressed his active if not necessarily decisive role in the tremendously complex decision-making process that characterised Imperial Japan.

See also: symbol monarchy

Further reading

Bix, Herbert P. (2000) *Hirohito and the Making of Modern Japan*, New York: HarperCollins.

Dower, John W. (1999) *Embracing Defeat: Japan in the Wake of World War II*, New York: W.W. Norton/ The New Press.

Irokawa Daikichi (1995) *The Age of Hirohito: In Search of Modern Japan*, New York: Free Press.

Large, Stephen S. (1992) *Emperor Hirohito and Showa Japan: A Political Biography*, New York: Routledge.

Ruoff, Kenneth J. (2001) *The People's Emperor: Democracy and the Japanese Monarchy, 1945–1995*, Cambridge, MA: published by the Harvard University Asia Center and distributed by Harvard University Press.

KENNETH RUOFF

historical drama

There are many sub-genres of films set in Japan's feudal past, usually 1603–1868. The *jidai geki* (period play) was initiated in the 1920s by leaders of modern theatre as the nihilist rebellion film combining social criticism and murderous sword fights. Humanism was introduced by comedies mocking authority and tragedies examining the consequences of militarism and misplaced loyalties. The tradition survived in such films as Kobayashi Masaki's 1962 *Seppuku* (Harakiri), **Kurosawa Akira**'s 1962 *Tsubaki Sanjurō* (Sanjuro) and **gangster films** of the 1960s that were remakes of earlier films. *Rekishi eiga* (historical films) appeared after 1937 in response to government demands for films expounding nationalist ideology. Hopes were frustrated by themes such as loyalty to family over loyalty to lord (Kumagai Hisatora's 1938 *Abe ichizoku* (The Abe Clan)), grim aftermath scenes vitiating any notion of heroic battle (Kinugasa Teinosuke's 1941 *Kawanakajima kassen* (Battle of Kawanakajima)), and actors and shooting style associated with politics and themes inimical to government policies (**Mizoguchi Kenji**'s *Genroku chushingura*, 1941–2). The *rekishi eiga* survived as *jidai eiga* (period films), faithful recreations of the past like Mizoguchi's 1952 *Saikaku ichidai onna* (The Life of Oharu). Except for the occasional art film and television film, both genres died out shortly after 1970.

SYBIL THORNTON

history

The subject of history in post-war Japan has been intensely controversial. It has also been extremely varied, both in form and in substance, and hardly ever a topic of detached, dispassionate inquiry. Its practitioners have been deeply engaged with matters of the present as well as the past. Above all, it has been defined, some might say haunted, by the legacy of the Second World War.

Marxian approaches dominated the professional practice of history from the early post-war years through to the 1960s, and beyond in some fields. This meant that the periods and the problems of European history, the original source of Marxian analyses, were applied directly and sometimes mechanically to Japan. Much of this writing combined a commitment to scientific analysis of the past with the desire to offer a blueprint to remake the future. The somewhat formulaic search to describe the class structure of society could be abstract and, at times, lifeless, but this practical engagement also gave historical study considerable power and sweep. Much valuable work resulted.

Japan in the immediate post-war era had only been an industrial society with a significant class of wage labourers for little more than fifty years. Thus, historians focused much attention on analysis of land systems, both pre-modern and modern. They asked who were the landlords, and who were the cultivators. They looked at ancient and medieval society for evidence of the transition from slavery to serfdom. They looked at Tokugawa-era society for evidence of hand manufacture, the beginning of a shift towards capitalism and the emergence of a wage labour force. In looking at the history of industrial capitalism, their key concern was the character of the working class. Since workers did not lead a successful revolutionary movement before the Second World War, analysis focused on the structural peculiarities or distortions of the labour force that prevented this. Economic historians identified a so-called *dekasegi* (migrant worker) pattern. They argued that workers in the industrial revolution in Japan, both men and women, were usually temporary migrants from farm villages to factories. They claimed that the passivity of the Japanese working class resulted from this temporary commitment to industrial labour.

When they examined the Meiji Restoration of the mid-nineteenth century, post-war Japanese historians directly carried forward the controversy that had raged in the 1930s between the 'Lectures' School (kōza ha) and the 'Labour–Farmer School' (rōnō ha). At issue was the class character of the movement to overthrow the Tokugawa government and, most importantly, the class character of the Meiji political order that followed. Adherents of the Lectures school (named for a collection of essays published in the 1930s as *Lectures on the History of the Development of Japanese Capitalism*) argued that the absolutist Meiji state, with the Emperor at the apex, was a semi-feudal alliance of military warriors and landlords. The position of commercial and industrial capital was weak, so Japan had experienced only an incomplete bourgeois revolution. As in the analysis of the working class, this analysis stressed the distorted characteristics of

modern Japanese historical processes when compared to patterns assumed to have characterised Europe. The Labour–Farmer school, on the contrary, saw Japan's experience as more comparable to that of the West. Adherents argued that capitalists held considerable power in the Meiji system, so that by the 1910s and 1920s an industrial bourgeoisie was ascendant in the parliamentary system. In the 1930s, this was more than an academic debate, since one's conclusions influenced one's political strategy. If a bourgeois revolution had not been completed, a political activist might support it as a necessary step in a longer process of change. The political immediacy of the controversy receded by the 1960s, as did work directly addressed to the debate.

In the early post-war era, a concern with explaining the trauma of the immediate past, and a desire to shape a different future, sparked important philosophical as well as historical inquiry in search of the agents or subjects of a contemporary transformation of society. Among Marxists both in and outside of the Japan Communist Party, a vigorous argument called 'the subjectivity debate' unfolded in the immediate post-war era. Participants sought to identify the 'subject' or agent of revolution in Japan. They were concerned to remedy a perceived 'lacuna' in traditional Marxian thought that left little room for the free thought and actions of independent subjects. Some, most prominently Umemoto Katsumi, promoted a revisionist Marxism from within the communist left (although they were sharply criticised by more orthodox party members). Others, most prominently the brilliant political philosopher Maruyama Masao and the economic historian Ōtsuka Hisao, articulated a non-communist liberal stream of modernism that was likewise concerned to find historical precedents for the creation of a society of free-thinking, humane individuals. They turned to history, both to identify promising sprouts of modernity in aspects of the Japanese past, and to find the sources of what they saw as a more powerful modern spirit in the Western past.

From the 1960s into the 1970s, alternative lines of historical inquiry emerged. Among the most important was the call for an indigenous 'people's history'. The young historian Irokawa Daikichi brought a compelling passion both to his writing and to the excavation of forgotten documentary sources. He and others argued that Marxists and liberals alike had wrongly imposed Western models or standards on Japanese experience, producing a distorted negative view of the common people in Japanese history. They drew on pioneering ethnographic work of the pre-war era by scholars such as Yanagida Kunio. Like their predecessors, they looked to folk culture and social history to uncover an indigenous spirit of an autonomous people not yet corrupted by capitalism and not yet wholly dominated by an oppressive modern state. The 'people's historians' were no less engaged in an effort to change present conditions than that of the Marxists and modernists they criticised. They condemned not only the pre-war state but also the power of the state bureaucracy and private corporations in their own time. Their work was criticised by some as romantic, but it brought to light valuable new sources and made a convincing case that the countryside and cities of Tokugawa and Meiji-era Japan, in particular, were lively sites of popular initiatives in culture and politics.

One important new development of the 1970s was the emergence of women's history and, later, gender history. Mainstream (male) historians initially reacted sceptically. However, as a 'second wave' of feminism gained strength in Japan from the 1970s, focused on lifestyles and knowledge as well as the legal and economic reforms demanded by earlier women activists, interest in women's studies and women's history spread considerably. By the late 1980s, well over a hundred universities and colleges offered courses in women's studies. A new generation of scholars, for the most part women, undertook important projects to collect and publish historical documents as well as to produce their own historical studies. In the field called simply 'women's history' (*Josei shi*) they brought to light the neglected story of the minority of women who played roles as political activists and cultural rebels seeking rights and equality. They also developed a parallel field of 'history of women's lives' (*Josei seikatsu shi*), and began to examine the experiences of ordinary women in history, as mothers and wives, as workers and as members of their broader community.

The 1980s witnessed a particular boom in study of, and interest in, the Edo or Tokugawa era.

Japan's pre-modern past, including Tokugawa times, had long been a source of professional and popular historical interest. After the Meiji Restoration, the Edo era especially had come to figure as the mirror of Japan's modernity. In some renderings it was a dark time of 'feudalism' that was, or should have been, repudiated in modern history. In other views it was the source of positive developments that made Japan's 'successful' modernisation possible. Reflecting the buoyant optimism of the present moment, the Edo evoked in the 1980s tended to be a bright and cheery time of intellectual ferment and popular innovation. The city of Edo was the administrative capital of the shōgun, but in the Edo boom its aspect as a site of carnival among commoners was stressed more often. Likewise, innovative work on medieval times in the 1980s and 1990s, notably that of **Amino Yoshihiko**, focused attention on groups on the margins of society, such as outcastes. Historians of the 1980s and 1990s in general showed increased interest in minority groups in both pre-modern and modern times. They stressed the importance of studying people on the margins, not only to remember a 'forgotten' past but to offer a new and fuller understanding of the tensions that defined the larger culture and society.

Beyond the work of professional historians, intellectuals or government officials, history in post-war Japan has exerted a broad claim on popular imagination. In book publishing and comics, in movies (including *anime*), in theatre such as *kabuki* as well as modern drama, and on the ever present television, one finds huge fascination with all periods of the Japanese past (and with world history as well). Works in these media have been endlessly popular, whether focused on Japan's ancient origins, on swashbuckling, scheming or heroic medieval-period warriors, or on modern experiences both personal and public. Two of the most watched television shows for decades (although ratings dropped in the 1990s as more viewing options became available) were the weekday morning historical soap opera and the Sunday evening historical drama on the public television network, NHK. Each cycle of the morning drama runs six months and examines the ordinary history of modern times. The heroine is always a young woman overcoming all manner of difficulty in a life that might stretch from Meiji times through to the Second World War, or from the war through to the present. The Sunday drama runs a full year, and takes up favourite moments and figures in the public and political history of Japan, especially the life and times of military rulers from Minamoto Yoritomo to Tokugawa Ieyasu. Popular interest in history has more local dimensions. For several decades, local governments from the town and village to the prefectural level have commissioned important multi-volume collections of documents and reminiscence, as well as some monographic studies. Also, unofficial groups of women and men, some part of various political movements, others simply gatherings of people interested in telling and preserving 'their own' histories, have met to exchange and record memories of their lives and those of their parents and people around them.

Over the entire post-war era, the question of Japan's responsibility for the Second World War has remained central to all views of the recent past. Scholars on the left have tended to blame military and bureaucratic elites together with venal, illiberal politicians and monopoly capitalists for pursuing ill-advised policies of expansionism and military conquest without regard to the human costs. They see popular support for the war as the result of censorship, manipulation of the education system and mass media, and outright suppression of dissent. Ienaga Saburō's work, translated into English as *The Pacific War*, is a powerfully argued example. Others, such as Maruyama Masao, have argued that ordinary people – in his case the 'lower-middle classes' – gained local power and status from the war and played an active role in promoting it to advance their own place in society. Such views hold in common the assumption that the war was both strategically unwise and morally unacceptable. In contrast, many government officials and conservative intellectuals have put forth a very different understanding of history. They defend Japan's motives as pure. They claim that the nation was leading a war to liberate Asia from the grip of Western imperialism. They point to the fact that the Japanese occupation of South-East Asia ended Dutch and British colonial rule and began the process by which the French were ousted from Indo-China. They give less attention to the inconvenient facts of Japan's own colonial

rule in Korea or Taiwan, or later in Manchuria and China. The first major statement of this position was *In Affirmation of the Great East Asia War*, written in 1963 by Hayashi Fusao, a writer of proletarian fiction in the 1920s who converted to an ultranationalist position in later years.

Arguments over 'war responsibility' have, if anything, increased in their intensity as the war has receded into the past. Although high-school textbooks in fact came to treat the war in a more balanced and detailed fashion from the 1950s through to the 1980s, in the early 1980s the government sparked major controversy at home and abroad when it modified the wording in high-school textbooks to render the start of the China War an 'advance' rather than an 'invasion'. In the early 1990s, renewed controversy erupted when a Japanese historian uncovered government documents confirming that the military had a direct role setting up the wartime system of so-called 'comfort stations', essentially brothels for the convenience of Japanese soldiers near the frontlines in China and South-East Asia. Most of the '**comfort women**' were Korean. Significant numbers were slaves rather than prostitutes, as they were taken by force, deceived as to the nature of their 'work' and received no pay. Those surviving comfort women who themselves came forward, as well as supporters in Japan and around the world, condemned the government for having denied its role until that time. They demanded apologies and compensation.

They also sparked a nationalistic backlash. Beginning in the mid-1990s, a new wave of 'revisionist' historians condemned what they called a 'masochist' historical consciousness that stressed the dark side of the Japanese past. Some went so far as to deny that the Nanking Massacre of 1937–8 had taken place. They called for a history, in particular as taught in the schools, that would instill pride in the 'Japanese people' by stressing achievements such as Japan's rapid emergence as an independent modern state. Echoing Hayashi's position in the 1960s, they characterised the Second World War as a noble endeavour to liberate Asia from the yoke of Western imperialism. They argued against teaching children about subjects such as the comfort women or military atrocities. They also provoked counter-criticism at home and abroad. As the twenty-first century began, intense debate continued over how to characterise a national history and how to situate it as part of a global or international experience.

ANDREW GORDON

Hokkaidō

Hokkaidō is the most northern of Japan's four major islands. Its colder climate is similar to that of eastern Canada. Until the nineteenth century, Hokkaidō was home almost exclusively to the indigenous **Ainu** people, who now number only about 20,000, pushed to the edges of Japanese society. Their human rights claims receive little attention.

During the Meiji Period, Hokkaidō was romantically defined as the new frontier, where young men travelled to seek fortunes in gold mining, or to develop new farming areas. Also considered a frontier of knowledge, Hokkaidō was heavily influenced by US specialists who were instrumental in establishing educational institutions, town planning and farming systems. As a result, Hokkaidō's landscape is quite different from the rest of Japan, resembling the USA in many ways.

Hokkaidō is a major tourist destination, especially for young people attracted to skiing, mountain climbing or hiking. The tourist industry continues to trade upon the image of the wild frontier, a practice that too often also casts the Ainu people in the role of exotic local attractions.

Sapporo, Hokkaidō's largest city, became famous as the site for the 1972 Winter Olympics (see **Sapporo Olympics**). It hosts one of the world's foremost annual winter ice sculpture contests, and is home of the brewery for Sapporo beer.

AUDREY KOBAYASHI

homonyms

As in other languages, there are many homonyms in Japanese, and these are called '*dō-on i-gi go*' (literally meaning 'same-sound' and 'different meaning' word). A frequently cited reason for the richness of homonyms in Japanese is the level of borrowing of Chinese sound words (kango) into Japanese during the Nara and Heian periods, when Chinese script was adapted for the writing of the Japanese language. Chinese, too, is renowned for the number of homonyms and a love of word-play. In speech, it is usually understood from the context which particular word the speaker is using among the words with the same sound. However, it sometimes happens that the speaker needs to explain which particular word he or she is trying to use when similar words exist in the same context. For example, when talking about schools, the word '*shiritsu*' refers to two different types of schools and the speaker needs to specify whether the word '*shiritsu*' he or she is using is either '*watakushi-ritsu*' (private) or '*ichi ritsu*' (municipal) schools. In writing, when *kanji* is used, the misunderstanding of meanings rarely occurs, because each *kanji* has a distinct meaning and the reader can immediately tell what the writer is trying to convey. It may be less distinct when a homonym word is written in *hiragana* only.

This is why a large number of Japanese still argue that *kanji* writing is necessary and important to avoid ambiguity and misunderstanding among homonyms. It is a common sight in Japan for someone to sketch a *kanji* character out on the palm of their hand to clarify a misunderstanding over a homonym. A classic example of a telegram (which was usually written in *katakana* before the days of fax and e-mail) often quoted is '*Kisha no kisha, kisha nite kisha su*'. This literally means, 'Your company's journalist will return to your company by train.' The abundance in homonyms in Japanese leads to a relative ease in indulging in 'share' – pun or play on words (see **dajare**). Not only nouns, but also verbs, adjectives or adverbs – in fact, any parts of speech – can be a target of a Japanese play on words and this type of verbal word-play is much enjoyed as a skill in daily conversation, as well as in more formalised styles of stage humour such as *rakugo* and *manzai*.

SHUN IKEDA

homosexuality and Japanese film

Representations of both female and male homosexualities are neither rare nor understated in post-war Japanese cinema. Genealogically, many can be traced respectively to masculinist fantasies of lesbian sexuality or to tropes of homosocial hypermasculinity. Lesbian desire and sex, when linked to male voyeurism, are suggestively figured in Masumura Yasuzō's 1964 adaptation of the **Tanizaki Jun'ichirō** novel *Manji* (Quicksand) (less successfully dramatized by Yokoyama Hiroto in 1983) and are also the basis for more regular, but often less interesting, depictions in the softly pornographic '*roman poruno*' of the 1970s. Both the reframing of masculinity in 1950s '*taiyōzoku*' youth films and the homo-erotic hypermasculinity that became a stock trope in the 1960s '*yakuza*' genre (and parodied by director **Suzuki Seijun** in *Koroshi no rakuin* [Branded to Kill, 1967]) are important predecessors to contemporary images of male homosexuality.

The first explicit cinematic representation of a gay (and male transvestite) subculture, Matsumoto Toshio's 1969 *Funeral Parade of Roses*, was also the first to suggest male homosexuality in relation to politics, although not necessarily homosexual ones. In its wake have followed numerous avant-garde and experimental works that politically figure male homosexuality, including Nakamura Genji's 1983 *Utsukushiki nazo* (Beautiful Mystery), a parody of Mishima Yukio's fascist homo-eroticism, and Sato Hisayasu's unbalanced *Kurutta butōkai* (Muscle) (1988), a meditation on sexuality under authoritarian power. Meanwhile, Yazaki Hitoshi's 1980 *Kazetachi no gogo* (Afternoon Breezes) severed the conventional link in Japanese cinema between lesbianism and male voyeurism, while foregrounding psychological aspects of lesbian love. This psychological emphasis and the theme of unrequited love have become dominant tropes in recent cinematic representations of Japanese lesbianism, problematically pursued in Sasaki Hirohisa's 1994 *Nachuraru ūman* (Natural Woman) and Satō Toshiki's 1996 *Atashi wa jūsu* (Juice for Me), but far more successfully in Shindō Kaze's 2000 film, *LOVE/JUICE*.

With the gay boom of the early 1990s, male homosexuality saw an increase in its cinematic fortunes. Easily misread as part of an emergent cinema addressing a gay male spectatorship, Najajima Takehiro's *Okoge* (1992) and Matsuoka Jōji's *Kirakira hikaru* (Twinkle) (1993) targeted

heterosexual female spectators with the problematic suggestion of male homosexuality as solution to the social constraints placed upon women by Japanese patriarchy. In this regard, key gay boom films must be considered as indebted to the narrative escapism figured by male homosexuality in *shjo manga* as to any increased social concern for sexual minorities. Two accomplished pieces based in part on popular *manga* include Nakahara Shun's sensitive lesbian coming-of-age story, *Sakura no sono* (The Cherry Orchard) (1990), and Kaneko Shūsuke's 1999 *Nen no natsuyasumi* (Summer Vacation), where four cross-dressing actresses play young schoolboys in performances reminiscent of **Takarazuka** Theatre.

Recent films directed by 'out' directors have signaled the rise of a queer Japanese cinema. London-based Nakata Tōichi's subtle but consistent positioning of gay identity in *Minoru and Me* (1992) and *Ōsaka Story* (1994) have provided a powerful precedent for gay and lesbian documentary. Also, Hashiguchi Ryōsuke's teen drama *Nagisa no shindobatto* (Like Grains of Sand) (1995) sets homosexual and heterosexual desire in dialogue, while the experimental œuvre of Ōki Hiroyuki addresses the pursuit of desire in *Anata ga suki desu, dai suki desu* (I Like You, I Like You Very Much) (1994) and his trademark homo-erotic visual lyricism in *Kokoro no naka* (Inside Mind) (1999). Such small-budget productions by gay male directors provide stark contrast to establishment director Ōshima Nagisa's provocative, yet ultimately suspicious, aestheticisation of male homosexuality in *Gohattō* (Taboo) (1999). Independent lesbian work has not seen the financial support or public acclaim of even small-budget gay works, but recent shorts by Takashi Toshiko, as well as Shu Lea Cheang's Tokyo-based work (*Fingers and Kisses*, 1995 and *I.K.U.*, 2000), suggest that Japanese queer film will only continue to grow.

Further reading

Grossman, Andrew (ed.) (2001) *Queer Asian Cinema: Shadows in the Shade*, Binghamton: Harrington Park Press.

JONATHAN M. HALL

honeymoons

The honeymoon has become an integral part of the wedding experience for young Japanese over the post-war years. The trend gained momentum in the 1960s as families and young workers began to accumulate new levels of disposable income that could support the more expensive wedding ceremonies and honeymoons being promoted by hotels and travel agencies. The high-profile media coverage of the honeymoons of a number of famous Japanese entertainers further boosted popular interest in this addition to the marriage rituals. Today, honeymooners make up a significant and influential share of Japan's tourism market and also make an important contribution to the local economies of the more popular domestic and international honeymoon destinations.

The average cost of a honeymoon in the late 1990s was $8–9,000. Honeymoons follow the dominant Japanese pattern of short trips of five to seven days. Traditionally, weddings are scheduled on auspicious dates on the Chinese calendar and this leads to honeymoon congestion at stations and airports on these dates. The vast majority of honeymoons are bought as package group tours. Even today, few young Japanese are willing to risk a catastrophe *en route*. Some agencies market a full package deal of wedding plus ceremony with online simulations for the bride and groom to practise the rituals and get to know their honeymoon destination in advance.

The high cost of domestic weddings has created a new and still expanding market in offshore wedding packages for bride and groom with selected family and friends travelling with them. In many Hawaiian hotels it is not unusual to see a honeymoon couple breakfasting together with both sets of in-laws. The distribution of honeymoon souvenirs on returning home has become integral to the wedding ritual and honeymooners dedicate much of their time away to shopping for these obligatory gifts for family and friends.

See also: arranged marriages; divorce; gift giving; tourism; weddings

SANDRA BUCKLEY

honne and tatemae

Honne (inner feeling) and *tatemae* (public performance) can be best understood through an example. A wife might be praised for not crying at her husband's funeral. Faultless execution of the formal ceremony and proper treatment of each guest (*tatemae*) would be seen as far more indicative of the depth of her inner feelings (*honne*) than a public expression of grief. The translation of these two terms as 'on-stage' and 'off-stage' similarly focuses on the sense of public and private expression or performance. Any exposure of *honne* is limited to the most intimate relations of one's inner circle (*uchi*) (see **uchi and soto**).

SANDRA BUCKLEY

horse racing

Horse racing in Japan offers one of the few areas of legal gambling. While treated as seedy and disreputable in the early post-war period, it had once been an elite cultural and sporting event and operated under the patronage of the Meiji Emperor. It regained a respectability over the last two decades of the twentieth century as the result of a concerted effort to revamp racing to appeal to the entire spectrum of Japanese society. Television live and delayed broadcast of races and related special-interest programming have played an important role in securing this broader based audience. Gambling remains a key element of the racing scene but no longer dominates the popular perception of the sport.

Japanese horse racing comes under close government control with the Ministry of Agriculture managing the largest and most profitable courses around the country. Gambling at these courses is the source of substantial annual revenue, and various government agencies have co-operated closely with both the national and regional racing associations to expand the socio-cultural base of participation in racing and to improve both the safety conditions of the races and the standard of care for horses in the stable towns that surround the tracks. As the Japanese Racing Association strove over the 1980s to attract more foreign entries to the high-stakes annual cup races, they worked hard to improve on the quality of stables, handling and veterinary conditions to overcome a reputation outside Asia that conditions in the region fell behind those in Europe, Australia, New Zealand and North America. Government agencies also co-operated in reviewing quarantine, import–export and tax laws that had discouraged extensive foreign participation on the Japanese race circuit.

The first permanent track in Japan was built in Ueno Park and the races became a popular event among the early Meiji elite. As in the USA and the UK, fashion played a large part in the involvement of the upper crust of Tokyo's socialites, while politicians, diplomats and industrialists used the race track as a favourite location for both socialising and power brokering. Historians of Japanese horse racing trace the beginning of the end of the prestigious nature of racing to the introduction of legalised betting in the late 1880s. Gambling had been traditionally linked to gaming in the brothel and theatre districts of Edo and was tainted by its association with the underworld of urban crime, which provided many of the patrons of this marginalised world of Edo. Although in the first instance betting was a novelty for the Meiji elite it soon attracted a new set of patrons from among the emerging *yakuza* (gangster) culture. Although gambling remained officially under government control there was increased illegal betting on and off track, and gradually the climate of gambling and its new clientele began to overtake the more fashion- and status-oriented concerns that had attracted the new wealth of the industrialists, the old money of the aristocrats and the power hungry of the political scene to all brush shoulders. By the turn of the century, horse racing and the track culture came to be seen as part of the underside of Japan and not something respectable citizens would want to be associated with, and it was this image of horse racing that prevailed across the twentieth century.

In the cartoons and *manga* of the mid-1980s, day and contract labourers, immigrant workers, un-employed and *yakuza* were depicted as the clientele of the race tracks. Stereotypes of seedy, untrustworthy and often violent gamblers abounded in popular narratives of track life. Recurring *manga* storylines of the day commonly involved the

exposure of a *sararii* man as an addicted gambler frittering away his family's savings secretly at the track or the appearance of a gangster at the home of an upstanding citizen who turns out to be in debt for illegal bets. The discovery that the man was a racing devotee would bring shame on the family. Exposed as a gambler, he might be fired from his job. Similar themes around horse racing and gambling were not uncommon in the increasingly popular television genre of night-time police dramas. However, the late 1980s saw a dramatic shift in the popular perception of horse racing. The emergence of a horse by the name of Oguricap and a popular jockey Take Yutake captured the imagination of the public with some considerable assistance from the media who latched onto these parallel stories. Oguricap's rise to fame, as it moved from the regional circuit to prominence in the ranked cup races of the central circuit, was matched by the growing success of the handsome young pedigree jockey who would finally ride Oguricap to a permanent place in Japanese race history and popular memory with their win in the 1990 Arima Kinen cup race.

The media frenzy that surrounded these two was at its peak from 1989–90 and saw a shift in all media coverage of horse racing from its status as a marginal and tainted sport to primetime news with focus stories and programming. Horse-racing *manga*, serialised cartoons, novels and films championed the lives of famous horses and jockeys, and presented the track as a place of adventure, heroism and romance. From this point forward, there was a new credibility for horse racing that saw the emergence of a more heterogeneous audience. While gambling has remained a significant part of track culture there is now a noticeable range of sub-cultures within the track, which includes again a more upmarket space of corporate boxes, closed paddock functions, private-stand parties and a return of track fashion and a new-found social respectability, especially among middle class women. The almost entirely male domain of the track has been transformed by a rapid influx of women attracted to the sport by the media staging of fandom for handsome star jockeys and cult-like devotion to a stable, horse or trainer. A whole range of commercial merchandising has emerged around this new life of Japanese horse racing, which caters to every level of the expanded audience from knick-knacks and souvenirs to mascot dolls and figurines of both horses and jockeys, and an entire range of affordable to expensive brand name men's and women's track fashion with appropriate horse and racing motifs.

SANDRA BUCKLEY

hot springs

The vulcanic nature of the Japanese archipelego results in an abundance of natural hot springs, or *onsen*. There are more than 1,000 *onsen* resorts throughout the country, but they are particularly notable on the island of Kyūshū and in the central alpine region of Nagano Prefecture. The sulphuric *onsen* water is highly valued for its therapeutic properties. Entire towns, such as Beppu on the north coast of Kyūshū, have been established around the hot springs, catering to a range of recreational activities from skiing in the alpine region, to establishments catering to the sex trade. A legend claims that when the Buddhist sage Kukai struck his staff on a rock, hot water spewed out, thus creating the tradition of the natural steam bath. In Shintō mythology, the gods bathed after creating the world, thus establishing rites of purification.

A visit to a hot spring is a major form of weekend recreation in Japan, undertaken either as a family outing or by company employees in an organised excursion. Facilities range widely from fairly simple public bathing establishments (*sentō*), supplied by natural hot water, to luxurious resorts. The pools may be very elaborate, built of natural stone with luxurious fittings. Those in the mountains typically have huge plate-glass windows through which one may view spectacular scenery. Many are built outside in the open air. Attendant facilities include the famous 'hot sands' of Kyūshū, where one is immersed for a period of time in the sand, through which mineral-laden steam flows naturally.

The *onsen* excursion provides not only an opportunity for a relaxing and therapeutic physical experience but also, perhaps more importantly, a social occasion. In addition to utilising the spa facilities, one may pass the weekend with group walks, special meals and, as with nearly all social occasions, evenings of **sake** drinking.

Although it is sometimes piped into buildings for heat or for cooking food, especially in up-market *onsen* resorts, use of hot spring water is highly regulated by Japanese law.

See also: *keshiki; ofuro*

AUDREY KOBAYASHI

housewife

The most common Japanese term for housewife means 'person at the back of the house' (*okusan*) and is a literal description of the location of the domestic space of the kitchen and hearth in traditional architecture. The role of housewife is highly professionalised in contemporary Japan and intimately linked to the valued role of **motherhood**. The choice of full-time homemaker is strongly defended by many Japanese feminists and the number of full-time homemakers or housewives remains high by comparison with other advanced economies.

A wide range of women are captured under the category of *okusan*: young married working women before childraising, full-time homemakers with school age children, middle-aged women whose children have married and left home, middle-aged and older women caring for grandchildren or elderly parents. There is no transition in a Japanese woman's life cycle as clearly differentiated as that from unmarried to married. Wife and housewife are synonymous. With marriage she takes on the responsibility for household management and this new role brings with it strong family and community expectations of a new mode of self-presentation from hairstyle to wardrobe and speech patterns. Magazines for women in their twenties carry regular articles about the future life they will lead as housewives and advise on how to adjust to a new life where their own pleasures will be subordinated to the interest of husband and child. The pre-marriage years are presented as a time of freedom, self-indulgence and high consumerism. By contrast, a housewife is expected to commit any disposable income to the family budget first. Even before children are born savings plans are in place for housing and educational costs. Anything that might be judged excessive spending on herself will be sure to catch the attention of family members and neighbours alike.

The expectation that a married woman would quit her paid employment for her role as housewife began to soften by the 1970s, and, by the 1980s, the expectations that a woman would resign from employment on becoming pregnant or after a birth had also shifted. The majority of working women do, however, still leave the workforce at least temporarily from the birth of the first child to the time all children are in school. A mix of domestic work and paid part-time external work or home-based contract work characterises the employment options available to most housewives with children. A housewife is usually responsible for all aspects of household management from budgeting and savings to shopping, cleaning, family vacations, tutoring for school age children, house repairs and so on. The husband and father remains heavily reliant on the housewife's role to create a problem-free environment: a calm and functional space from which he can commute. The hours spent by husbands and fathers in the family home remain strikingly low as a result of strong demands for men to commit to long hours in the workplace.

Even before marriage, the majority of women begin preparing for the role of housewife through courses in more traditional areas such as flower arranging or tea ceremony and in more practical areas such as household economics and cooking. Even today, the completion of these preparatory courses can influence the successful pursuit of an arranged marriage.

Household problems ranging from financial difficulties to a child's bad grades at school or even untidy rubbish bags can all be taken as reflections on the professionalism of the housewife. A large part of her work is presenting the household to the public in a manner befitting the family's socio-economic status (real or desired). Her skill in everything from outfitting her children to the appearance of the garden and her regular hanging out of the family bedding impacts her standing with family and neighbours, and the assessment of her degree of professionalism. A housewife is essentially managing the public performance of a happy and functional household.

A housewife involved in part-time or full-time paid work outside the home cannot adjust the standard of this performance of domestic responsibilities. The hiring of domestic help is judged harshly as a failure to fulfil one's role. Surveys often reflect the view that career women experience even greater pressure in order to prove that their paid work is not detracting from their housewife role. Some feminists have pointed to the unjustness of this situation at a time when, in reality, the role of housewife has now been extended to include earning supplemental income. In response, more conservative sociologists have described this pattern as the social contract of gendered work in Japan and point to the long hours and loss of family time as the high price paid by men. Feminists challenge the notion of contract on the grounds that this implies choice for the housewife and her working husband, while currently the range of negotiable lifestyle options falls within a very narrow band of social tolerance.

A wave of books, both academic and popular, over the late 1990s has drawn attention to the life cycle of Japanese women and, in particular, the period now widely referred to as the '*midi*' years between mid-40s to mid-50s. These years have been identified as a time in the life of a middle-class woman when she continues to fulfil her role as housewife but has a period of renewed leisure activity. With her children reaching adulthood, a partner earning a mid-career salary and focused on the workplace, her in-laws and parents usually still in good health and independent, and no grand-children yet to care for, the *midi* housewives have been identified as a new and influential consumer market for everything from group travel to health clubs, adult education courses and a wide range of leisure and sport activities. The *midi* is also seen to be a powerful buying force in the fashion and entertainment industries. Since the late 1980s, car manufacturers in Japan have developed specific models and features for this group of consumers. The importance of communication, networking and information access to this age group of housewives has also captured the design attention of the new digital and wireless technologies industries. However, while there is a new tolerance, even promotion, of the rights of *midi* housewives this is presented as a period of indulgence prior to taking up the weighty responsibilities of health care for ageing parents and occasional child care for grandchildren to allow their own daughters and daughters-in-law some time to seek external paid work. While the life-cycle pattern may have changed, the underlying assumptions of the housewife role have remained remarkably stable in Japan.

See also: gender and technology; gender and work; part-time work

SANDRA BUCKLEY

Housewives' Association

The Housewives' Association (Shufu Rengōkai, or Shufuren) was formed in 1948 at a time of post-war food shortages. The Association was led by Oku (née Wada) Mumeo (1895–1997). Oku had been a founding member of the New Women's Association and was also a suffragist, a labour activist and an active member of the co-operative movement, and would later become a Diet member.

Shufuren aimed to promote a stable lifestyle from the standpoint of consumer economics. The Association's symbol, a **rice**-serving spoon (*shamoji*), placed its members firmly in the kitchen as housewives, and also signified a nationalist identity through its association with the quintessentially Japanese food, steamed white rice. The Housewife's Hall, completed in 1956, housed a wedding reception centre, lodgings, marriage-counselling services, family-planning advice and space for adult education classes. The Association protested about price rises of consumer goods and lobbied for improved quality of consumer goods. By 1963, the Association was participating in national and regional government inquiries on consumer issues. The Association remains an influential lobby group and its massive national membership gives it the capacity to mobilise extensive support on consumer reform issues and questions of consumer safety and pricing.

Further reading

Narita, R. (1998) 'Women in the motherland: Oku Mumeo through wartime and postwar', in J.V. Koschmann (ed.) *Total War and 'Modernization'*, Ithaca: Cornell University Press, pp. 139–58.

Robins-Mowry, D. (1983) *The Hidden Sun: Women of Modern Japan*, Boulder, CO: Westview Press.

VERA MACKIE

HYAKKATEN *see* department stores

I-novel

The I-novel (*shishōsetu* or *watakushi shōsetsu*) is considered one of the central genres of modern Japanese fiction. It refers to an autobiographical form written in either the first or third person that is presumed to depict the author's own experience with varying degrees of fictional mediation. Ranging in content from the scandalous revelation of private affairs to contemplative sketches of everyday life, the I-novel has been denigrated by some critics as a deviation from the modern novel, while lauded by others as a unique product of Japanese literary tradition.

The origins of the I-novel are typically traced back to the publication of Tayama Katai's Naturalist work *Futon* (The Quilt, 1907). This work, which revolves around a middle-aged artist's attraction to his young female pupil, was received by some readers as a direct account of the author's own experience. Although Katai's novel (an exploration of the conflict between romantic ideals of love and corporeal desire) was not strictly autobiographical, it became most influential for what was taken to be its confessional form.

During the 1910s, in an intellectual atmosphere that emphasised the value of the self and of private concerns in general, confessional fiction became increasingly prominent. This included works by Naturalist writers such as Chikamatsu Shūkō and Shimazaki Tōson, as well as those associated with the Shirakaba (White Birch) school such as Mushanokōji Saneatsu and Shiga Naoya.

It was in the 1920s that the term *watakushi shōsetsu* first came into general circulation, as the diverse works of personal fiction were first conceived as forming a distinct genre. During this period, it was defined as a rejection of conventional requirements of plot and narrative structure, and as an exploration of the inner reality of the author's self. This conception of the I-novel can be seen as a reaction against the dynamic transformations taking place in literary practice during the 1920s, which included the emergence of a powerful Marxist literary movement and the new forms of literary and artistic production associated with mass culture. The I-novel was thus formulated as a rejection of popular fiction as well as an attempt to delineate a uniquely Japanese form of writing. Subsequently, the concept of the I-novel served as the foundation for the idea of 'pure' literature (*junbungaku*) in Japan.

The presumption that the I-novel is an indigenous literary genre has been largely shared by both its admirers and detractors, despite the existence of autobiographical fiction in other traditions. The writings of Shiga Naoya, for example, are frequently cited as the culmination of the Japanese I-novel. The essence of Shiga's writings, from his essayistic sketches to his novel *An'ya kōro* (A Dark Night's Passing, 1928–37), is typically said to lie in their evocation of an 'Eastern poetic spirit' through lyrical depictions of daily life and of the natural world.

Conversely, critics have also characterised the I-novel as a departure from the proper development of the modern European novel. This line of critique, which was largely shaped by an influential essay written by Kobayashi Hideo in 1935, became especially prominent in the post-war period as intellectuals turned a critical eye on Japanese cultural institutions. The I-novel was used in this period as a standard by which to evaluate modern Japanese literature in general.

Writer and critic Itō Sei, for example, analysed the I-novel as representative of modern Japanese fiction and, while positively evaluating certain aspects of the form, critiqued its rejection of a broader social perspective. Similarly, Nakamura Mitsuo cited the emergence of the I-novel as a critical turning point in modern literary history that foreclosed the development of a genuine realism in Japan, in favour of a withdrawal into an asocial interiority. Maruyama Masao went even further, analysing the I-novel as a marker of Japan's unaccomplished modernity. Maruyama argued that the rejection of fictional mediation in representation was analogous to the rejection of the political institutions of modernity in Japanese society.

Despite such persistent critiques, however, the representation of personal experience has remained an important touchstone of literary expression for each generation of writers. In the immediate post-war period, for example, writers such as **Dazai Osamu** and Shiina Rinzō depicted their experiences of extreme physical and emotional devastation in their writings. In particular, Dazai, who committed suicide in 1948, became emblematic of what critic Hirano Ken referred to as the 'destructive' type of I-novelist (as opposed to the 'harmonising' type, symbolized by Shiga). His final work *Ningen shikkaku* (No Longer Human, 1948), a fictionalised account of his own life, stands as a monument not only to an intensely personal crisis but one extending throughout post-war Japan as well.

In subsequent years, such prominent figures as Shimao Toshio, Yasuoka Shōtarō, Shōno Junzō and Yoshiyuki Junnosuke based their writings on autobiographical materials, while also inserting an ironic distance between themselves and their protagonists. Even writers who are not typically categorised as I-novelists have incorporated the depiction of personal experience as key aspects of their literature. **Ōe Kenzaburō**, for example, established himself as one of the most powerful voices of his generation with the publication of *Kojinteki na taiken* (A Personal Matter, 1964), a work based largely on Ōe's own experiences surrounding the birth of his handicapped son. Yet his novel is also a self-conscious examination of the conventions of the I-novel. As its title suggests, the underlying theme of *Kojinteki na taiken* is precisely a critical examination of the borderlines between the private and the public, between self and other.

In addition, writers such as **Ōba Minako** and **Tsushima Yūko** have at times used the I-novel form to explore issues of gender and women's subjectivity, focusing in particular on their own marginalised status in relation to Japanese society. These writers have pushed the boundaries of the I-novel in new directions, exploring the ethical and political significance of private life. In this sense, the tradition of autobiographical fiction remains a significant force and continues to shape contemporary Japanese literature in a variety of ways.

Further reading

Fowler, Edward (1988) *The Rhetoric of Confession: Shishōsetsu in Early Twentieth-Century Japanese Fiction*, Berkeley: University of California Press.

Hijiya-Kirschnereit, Irmela (1996) *Rituals of Self-Revelation: Shishōsetsu as Literary Genre and Socio-Cultural Phenomenon*, Cambridge: Council on East Asian Studies, Harvard University.

Suzuki, Tomi (1996) *Narrating the Self: Fictions of Japanese Modernity*, Stanford: Stanford University Press.

SEIJI M. LIPPIT

Ibuse Masuji

b. 1898, Hiroshima Prefecture; d. 1993, Tokyo

Writer

Ibuse Masuji is best known as the author of *Kuroi ame* (Black Rain, 1966), a novel about the A-bombing of Hiroshima, which became a bestseller both in Japan and abroad, and has been much praised for its frank yet compassionate rendering of life in the aftermath of the explosion. Ibuse was born in the village of Kamo in mountainous eastern Hiroshima Prefecture. In 1917, he graduated from a local middle school and left for Tokyo where he enrolled at Waseda University. However, he left the university in 1922 without graduating.

After a series of jobs, and publications in various journals, by 1929, Ibuse had begun to make an impact on the literary world with such stories as 'Koi' (The Carp, 1926), 'Sanshoouo' (Salamander, 1929) and 'Yane no ue no Sawan' (Swan on the Roof, 1929). The following year, he published his first collection of short stories entitled *Yofuke to ume no hana* (Plum Blossom by Night). During the 1930s, Ibuse worked on a short story published in four parts in 1931–2 called 'Kawa' (The River) and also a full-length historical novel entitled *Sazanami gunki* (Waves: A War Diary), loosely based on the twelfth-century *Heike monogatari* (Tale of the Heike), which was published in 1938. In the same year, he published another historical novel *Jon Manjiroo hyōryuuki* (John Manjirō, the Castaway: His Life and Adventures) for which he was awarded the prestigious **Naoki Prize**.

After the war, Ibuse wrote a number of well-known satirical anti-war stories including the allegorical 'Wabisuke' (1946) and 'Yō hai taichō' (Lieutenant Lookeast, 1950). In 1956, Ibuse published his second 'castaway' story, the historical novel *Hyōmin Usaburō* (Castaway Usaburō) concerning the crew of a rice ship that drifted off course in 1838. However, the major novel that Ibuse wrote during the post-war era is *Black Rain*.

This work is based on extensive research, with Ibuse personally interviewing fifty survivors of the atomic bombing. The novel tells the story of Yasuko, the niece of Shizuma Shigehiko, and her unsuccessful attempts to find a husband due to rumours that she was exposed to the A-bomb. The various flashbacks to the past are related through the devices of Yasuko and her uncle's diaries. The diaries recount the horrors of the bomb blast in a dry, unsentimental fashion, which renders their accounts all the more powerful. The story of Yasuko's own illness is interwoven into the narrative and it is the tension around her fate that drives the narrative.

Much of Ibuse's later fiction written in the decades after *Black Rain* consists of memoirs of places and times that held a special significance for the author. The wry humour and spare writing characteristic of Ibuse are still in evidence but subdued, as memory

came to claim centre stage. With Ibuse's death in 1993 Japan lost one of the more powerful literary voices of the trans-war generation.

Select bibliography

Ibuse Masuji (1988) *Pools of Water, Pillars of Fire: The Literature of Ibuse Masuji*, trans. John Whittier Treat, Seattle and London: University of Washington Press.

—— (1971) *Lieutenant Lookeast and Other Stories*, trans. John Bester, Tokyo: Kōdansha International.

—— (1969) *Black Rain*, trans. John Bester, Tokyo: Kōdansha International.

LEITH MORTON

Ichikawa Fusae

b. 1893, Aichi Prefecture; d. 1981, Tokyo

Suffragist and parliamentarian

Ichikawa worked as a teacher and journalist before positions in the Yūaikai union federation, the New Women's Association and the Tokyo Office of the International Labour Organisation. On her return from the USA, where she met leading US suffragists, she devoted herself to the suffragist cause. After briefly being purged by SCAP for co-operation with the wartime regime, Ichikawa became an independent member of the House of Councillors for much of the post-war period, her popularity being attributed to her campaigns for women's issues and against electoral corruption.

Further reading

Ichikawa Fusae (1974) *Ichikawa Fusae jiden: senzen hen*, Tokyo: Shinjuku Shobō.

VERA MACKIE

Ichikawa Raizō

b. 1931, Kyōto Prefecture; d. 1969, Tokyo

Film actor

Raizō was the epitome of the *binan* (handsome

male) period film star. Adopted into a famous **kabuki** family, he starred in 154 films at Daiei Studios, which ranged in genre from literary adaptation to modern spy movie. It was his image as a stern-faced loner, who seemed to hide a tragic, fateful past behind his beautiful visage, which won him many fans, especially female ones. Raizō died of cancer at the age of 37, but enjoys fervent popularity decades later.

Select filmography

Nemuri Kyoshiro series.
Shinobi no mono (Band of Assassins) series.

AARON GEROW

idoru singers

The *idoru* singers of Japan were the product of pop music programming on Japanese radio in the 1950s as the Japanese music industry began to develop its own homegrown version of the US pop idols. The first successful television music shows accelerated the *idoru* marketing industry through the 1960s. The *idoru* phenomenon has been described as the 'art of celebrity', not the art of singing. What marks the success of one *idoru* start-up act over another is seldom musical talent but rather a consistent and highly professionalised image and well-developed marketing strategy. The style of the *idorus* has shifted over time with the absolute purity and cuteness of the early *idoru* giving way to a more explicit seductiveness and open expression of sexuality. *Idoru* singers usually do not demonstrate a wide range of vocal style for the strategy of their managers is to create a formula for success and stick with it over the career of the singer. Modifications are made in presentation and dress to adjust for age, but another characteristic of the female *idoru* is their apparent agelessness. Though the term is used most consistently to describe female performers, the style of presentation and image marketing has also become associated with a new generation of male singers and rock bands also typified by their showcase looks, youthfulness and formulaic image.

An *idoru* is usually expected to launch one hit song per year from a new release album and it will be that hit song that is performed over and over again on the primetime television music shows. Both the choreography and musical performance are fixed and fans prefer little variation, singing and dancing along in synch with their favourite *idoru*, gesture for gesture, note for note. The type of originality that can lead to different concert versions of the same song for some pop idols elsewhere often leads to complaints and disappointment from Japanese *idoru* fans. While there have been some foreign performers who have been groomed for a successful *idoru* launch in Japan, there has yet to be a successful crossover into North American or European pop music by a Japanese *idoru*. There is, however, a massive following of Japan's *idoru* in Asia where record sales are high. The formula has been exported across the region by Japanese networks sponsoring local *idoru* competitions. It has been suggested by some that the recent popularity of image-based boy and girl bands moulded in the musical equivalent of 'boot camps' is a North American adaptation of the formulaic *idoru* phenomenon.

SANDRA BUCKLEY

ijime

Ijime, or bullying, is the systematic, long-term abuse of a schoolchild by his or her peers. All cases involve the isolation and ostracisation of the victim. While not all cases lead to physical violence, in Japan one's status as an 'outsider', *kawarimono*, can be far more brutal than physical harm. *Ijime* more often leads to suicide than to homicide. *Ijime* reflects the intolerance of a conformist society where the unofficial motto is: '*deru kugi wa utareru*', or 'the protruding nail gets hammered down'. While bullying exists in all societies, it is particularly heinous in Japan where the social group is far more cohesive and far less tolerant of individuality. Due to the emphasis on conformity and equality, students are fairly homogenous to the degree that the slightest distinctions can bring about brutal teasing and hazing. These differences might include dressing unusually, being too far ahead or behind academically, asking questions, refusing to join a club, having questionable parentage, being poor, etc. The importance of group cohesion is rigorously reinforced throughout the educational system. Schools are hierarchically organised with the assumption that the younger will follow in the ways of the older, *senpai*. Bullying is on the increase and largely responsible for a phenomenon known as the school refusal syndrome.

JUNE A. GORDON

IKEBANA *see* flower arrangement

Ikiru

Ikiru (1952) was directed by **Kurosawa Akira**. A tribute to the possibility of human will in which petty official Watanabe Kanji (Shimura Takeshi), given six months to live, and failing to find solace in hedonism or family, toils to have a playground built for a poor neighbourhood. Often compared to *Citizen Kane*, it is highly acclaimed as both a meditation on modern identity with universal appeal and a densely drawn portrait of Japanese social tensions. The post-war social system is critiqued through portrayals of empty pleasure-seeking in urban nightlife and heartless (male) bureaucrats who badmouth Watanabe at his funeral (while the neighbourhood women pay their respects). The two-part narrative structure makes brilliant use of the flashback.

CHRISTOPHER PERRIUS

illegitimacy

The social stigma of illegitimacy is slowly waning in Japan, but the *koseki* system of family registration becomes a permanent record of one's status at birth. Where a man has children outside marriage, he can formally acknowledge the child and record the child (and heir) in his *koseki*. Where a child is not acknowledged, the mother may record them in her family's *koseki*. Sometimes a single mother will petition to establish her own family register and enter the child there. It is not uncommon for the

illegitimate birth to be disguised as a legitimate birth or to be corrected through adoption.

See also: adoption; *koseki*

VERONICA TAYLOR

Imai Tadashi

b. 1912, Tokyo; d. 1991

Film director

Imai Tadashi was born into a conservative family in 1912. While studying history at Tokyo University, he joined a communist youth league and was arrested for his 'radical' activities on more than one occasion. In 1935, he became an assistant director at J.O. Studio, mainly due to his communist activities, which had placed a severe limit on his employment options. Imai began his own film-directing career during the Second World War with a series of nationalist films that countered his political convictions. However, his most noteworthy films, which portray his social commitments, were not made until the 1950s. Among them was 1950's *Dokkoi ikiteiru* (And Yet We Live), which was the first independently produced Japanese film made outside the control of large capital. In 1954, Imai released the three-part film *Nigorie* (Muddy Waters). Based on stories by Ichiyo Higuchi, *Nigorie* exposed the cruelty of the feudal system during the Meiji era. Among his other important films are *Mahiru no ankoku* (Darkness at Noon) (1956), *Yoru no tsuzumi* (Night Drum) (1958) and *Bushido zankoku monogatari* (Cruel Tales of Bushido) (1962).

Due in part to his left-wing politics, Imai was greatly influenced by Italian neo-realism, and, in particular, De Sica's works. However, as several critics have noted, unlike conventional neo-realist cinema, Imai's works were never overly sentimental. As such, his films have often been referred to as a *nakanai* realism (realism without tears). Known for the informality of his cinematic style, Imai's signature as a director is most often the themes and content of his work. Although his work has been criticised as being rough and lacking continuity, it is these very same elements that give Imai's films the pleasant sense of sincerity, honesty and spontaneity for which he has been praised. Imai was most popular among critics who rejected the New Wave directors for their pure aestheticism and obsession with style, which they considered tedious and repetitious. For those critics, Imai's overt social concerns, in an era of New Wave directors, emerged as refreshing. Imai continued to make films throughout the 1970s and early 1980s including *Ani imoto* (Brother and Sister) (1977) and *Himeyuri Lily Tower* (The Tower of Lilies) (1982). He passed away in 1991 soon after the release of his last film *Senso to seishin* (War and Youth).

Further reading

Bock, Audie (1978) *Japanese Film Directors*, Tokyo, New York and San Francisco: Kōdansha International.

Mellen, Joan (1975), *Voices from the Japanese Cinema*, New York: Liveright.

LEILA POURTAVAF

Imamura Shōhei

b. 1926, Tokyo

Film director

Over his fifty-plus year career, Imamura Shōhei has crossed the divide between fiction and documentary film in several different phases. After graduating from college, he entered Shōchiku's Ōfuna studios, and worked on Ōzu Yasujiro's *Early Summer*, *The Taste of Green Tea Over Rice* and *Tokyo Story*, before moving to the newly revived Nikkatsu Studios in 1954, where duties included scriptwriting for comedy director Kawashima Yūzō. Imamura's first feature, *Stolen Desire* (1958), was a programme picture about a group of travelling actors; it established a pattern for the unruly, carnivalesque and slightly vulgarian populist energy celebrated throughout Imamura's productions. Although he began directing at the same time, Ōshima Nagisa started at Shōchiku; despite their commonality of anti-melodramatic form, Imamura's *dochaku* nativism emerges in contrast to Oshima's unequivocally *nouvelle* modernist stance.

Imamura's nativism is often depicted by the foregrounding of characters who are somehow exiled from structures of power guaranteed by the state, living in far-flung regions, speaking slang and dialect and who are often impoverished or struggling to make a living. This sentiment is perhaps most vividly seen between *Pigs and Battleships* (1961) and *The Deep Desire of the Gods* (1968). The darkly humorous *Pigs and Battleships*, set in the base-town of Yokosuka, was made the year after the protests that followed the signing of the first USA–Japan Security Treaty. *The Deep Desire of the Gods* depicts a salaryman's transgression, and repetition, of creation myths in a primitivist Okinawa, both geographically and temporally remote from the modern mainland, and on the verge of 'modernising' tourist and economic development. Its ethnographic fantasy shifts to ethnographic method in films beginning with 1963's *Insect Woman*, the story of the 'instinctually' driven Tomé, sparked by Imamura and co-writer Hasebe Keiji's field notes taken upon encountering a brothel madam, and shot, like later documentaries, with location sets and simultaneous sound, maximising the narrative's 'reality effect'.

The 'human' as an object of knowledge also structures the 1966 film *The Pornographers*, and Imamura's most compelling film, *A Man Disappears* (1967). A true story like *Vengeance Is Mine* (1979), it begins as a documentary investigating the disappearance of a salaryman who has left his fiancée; clear demarcation of fact-versus-fiction disappears, as does the clinical nature of the film production itself, as during the process of collecting information, the fiancée falls for the investigator. Characters far from the confines of bourgeois life also populate Imamura's television documentary trilogy of 'throwaway people': in *In Search of Unreturned Soldiers* (1971), three soldiers desert and remain in Thailand and Malaysia; in the follow-up, *Muhomatsu Returns Home* (1973), a soldier returns to Japan to visit for the first time since leaving for the front; and *Karayuki-san* (1973) concerns an elderly woman who was coerced into working in military brothels in imperial South-East Asia during the war.

Following his 1997 Palme d'Or prize at Cannes for *Unagi*, Imamura continues to produce theatre in Tokyo and to supervise the Japan Academy of Visual Arts.

Further reading

Imamura Shōhei (1999) *Cinematheque Ontario Monographs*, No.1, ed. James Quandt, Bloomington: Indiana University Press.

ANNE McKNIGHT

IMF-JC

IMF-JC stands for International Metalworkers' Federation-Japan Council; in Japanese, Kokusai Kinzoku Rōren Nihon Kyōgikai (Kinzoku Rōkyō). It was founded in 1964, with the assistance of the International Metalworkers' Federation, by several Japanese unions, including the Electrical Workers and the Shipbuilders. The Yahata Steel union joined as an observer, although the steelworkers' federation, **Tekkō Rōren**, waited until 1966. Since the formation of IMF-JC coincided with the formation of a new right-wing nationwide labour federation, **Dōmei**, later the same year, left-wing unionists and supporters of the **Japan Socialist Party** and **Japan Communist Party** regarded the IMF-JC with suspicion. Indeed, from 1967, IMF-JC unions would take the lead in the annual **spring offensive** of labour, but did so in a way that minimised disruption of production and increased co-operation between big labour and big business. The leader of IMF-JC in the 1970s, Miyata Yoshiji from Tekkō Rōren (and originally from Yahata Steel), exerted a considerable moderating influence on the demands of labour during the recession of 1974. The formation of IMF-JC occurred as the metalworking industries of steel, automobiles, shipbuilding and electronics were achieving their greatest influence within the Japanese economy.

Further reading

Ikuo Kume (1997) *Disparaged Success*, Ithaca: Cornell University Press.

MICHAEL GIBBS

IMPACTION *see Inpakushon*

Imperial Household Agency

The Imperial Household Agency is an extra-ministerial bureau within the Prime Minister's Office that is charged with managing the affairs of the Emperor and the imperial family (*kōzoku*). Although much diminished in size, power, independence and prestige in comparison to its pre-war predecessor, it has none the less inherited some of the Imperial Household Ministry's functions and executes them in a manner that is considered appropriate for the **symbol monarchy**.

The most striking feature of the Imperial Household Ministry that existed from 1885 to 1945 was its power and independence from the civil government, an arrangement paralleling the Emperor's legal and symbolic status as a monarch who not only reigned but also ruled. While some of the Ministry's income came from the national treasury, most was revenue from the imperial household's enormous landholdings and investments in banking and industry. The Ministry's approximately 6,200 officials were placed in twenty-six offices. Their duties ranged from those of bureaucratic administration – for example, accounting, public relations, arranging imperial tours, overseeing the Peers' School, as well as managing imperial estates, mausoleums, museums, the Korean royalty and the aristocracy (*kazoku*) – to attending to the personal needs of the Emperor and imperial family, and serving as the Emperor's liaisons to the civil government and military.

Between 1947 and 1949, the Ministry was reorganised as an agency within the Prime Minister's office. It now employs about 1,150 officials in seven offices and its expenses are paid out of the national budget. Government bureaucrats more often than not do not desire assignment to the Agency, and usually transfer out to more desirable ministries within a few years of their arrival. Nevertheless, the Agency executes functions that are essential to sustain the symbolic dimensions of the post-war nation state. Most obviously, it continues to administer cultural resources that enhance the dignified and traditional qualities of the Emperor and the nation. Thus, it serves as custodian of the imperial and state seals, the imperial mausoleums and other cultural treasures such as the Shōsōin Treasure

House and the Kyōto Imperial Palace. Furthermore, it maintains a Board of Ceremonies and its Office of Ritualists presides over the sacred rites of the imperial household (kōshitsu saishi).

Many critics of the current imperial system, however, argue that the Agency's obstruction of public access to such sites as the imperial mausoleums and refusal to make its archives more open to scholarly scrutiny are inappropriate for a democratic society and to the imperial household's status as a publicly funded entity. Likewise, although the Office of Ritualists is legally defined as a private body serving the imperial family in order to maintain the separation between the state and religion, many have argued that this separation exists in name only. The Office is funded by the national treasury and plays a prominent role in public ceremonials of the imperial household such as funerals, enthronements and weddings. During such televised imperial ceremonies, the Agency arranges to either hide the most religious looking of such rituals or indicates that the rituals are the 'private rites' of the imperial household. However, many point out that these are merely pro forma attempts to stay within the law and that the so-called sacred rites of the imperial household were key elements of state-sponsored religion (or State Shintō) prior to 1945.

Just as importantly, the Agency tightly guards the public images of the Emperor and imperial family, giving rise to the phrase, 'the chrysanthemum curtain'. It plans all imperial outings and controls the content and flow of information about the imperial household to the media. Members of the press wishing to cover the imperial household must register with the Imperial Press Club. Agency officials monitor questions at press conferences and can blacklist troublesome reporters. While many critics of the Agency's 'chrysanthemum curtain' policy have been arguing for a more 'open imperial household', others express concern that increased media attention and less than reverent representations of the imperial household in popular culture have diminished the imperial household's mystery and majesty.

See also: Hirohito, Emperor

Further reading

Murakami Shigeyoshi (1980) *Kōshitsu jiten*, Tokyo: Tōkyōdō Shuppan.

Titus, David Anson (1974) *Palace and Politics in Prewar Japan*, New York: Columbia University Press.

TAKASHI FUJITANI

IN THE REALM OF THE SENSES see *Ai no korida*

income levels

Prior to the Second World War, Japan had the lowest levels of income and wages among industrial nations. The causes included the abundance of poor farming families in rural districts and severe government supression of organised labour in the industrialised cities. After the war, however, these conditions were greatly changed. The removal of restrictions on labour union activities, the high demand for labour due to an expanding economy and special income support mechanisms for farming households led to rising private incomes and consumption for virtually all Japanese. Other quality-of-life indicators have also improved, including health care and life expectancy. Despite high food prices and housing costs, the quality and diversity of the Japanese diet has increased, and housing and public amenities have improved greatly. Income differentials have also decreased, and while Japan is by no means a completely egalitarian society, its distribution of income is among the most equal of industrial nations. Some groups remain relatively less well-off, including female employees, workers in small firms, the aged and Korean (see **Koreans in Japan**) and **Burakumin** minorities. As elsewhere, the distribution of wealth is considerably less equal than income. Indeed, the impact of the 'bubble economy', the current economic slow down and restructuring, led to an increasing disparity of wealth and incomes during the 1990s.

DAVID EDGINGTON

individualism

The Japanese terms for individual and individualism (*kojin/kojinshugi*) have carried a negative taint since their popularisation in the Meiji Period. Studies of Japanese identity over the last century have consistently focused on the relational quality of the experience of self. Individualism has often been treated as a Western corruption or dilution of an essential characteristic of the formation of Japanese identity.

The relational model of identity locates self as one unit, but not isolated, in a continuum of relations from self to family to group to nation. This model has been criticised as deeply implicated in conservative and nationalist mechanisms of nation state identity formation during the period of Japan's modernisation leading up to the Second World War and, again, more recently, with the reconfiguration of these same mechanisms in the guise of a rhetoric of uniqueness (*Nihonjinron*). During the Meiji Period of early modernisation, individualism was synonymous with liberation from the constraints of a relational identity bound to family and other appropriate groups. It was associated with the right to form unexpected and uncondoned relations but remained bound to a desire for the reciprocity of relations, a seeking out of new territories of communal formations, rather than any conceptualisation of a self-autonomy.

The last decades of the twentieth century have seen a renewed public focus on the so-called 'selfish' or 'self-focused' generations. A resurgence in individualism is blamed for everything from increased domestic violence to school refusal, declining birth rates and increased **divorce**. The intensification of consumerism is popularly linked to this process of becoming 'selfish' and regularly conflated with a culture (cult) of the individual.

Television programming, films, comics, advertising, pulp fiction and popular magazines are all blamed for promoting a consumption-based aesthetic of individualism: a trend seen as both symptomatic of, and contributing to, an erosion of traditional values of family and social relations. Critics of this apparent nostalgia argue that while high consumerism in recent decades has seen a growing fragmentation of niche markets this hyper-differentiation of consumer trends and goods should not be confused with diversification or radical difference. The dominant consumer drive remains conformity to criteria of inclusion in a more finely articulated field of consumption: a field in which individualism functions as just one more item in the lexicon of marketing and product development.

Scholars who have played a key role in the development of theories of Japanese self and society, such as Nakane Chie and Takeo Doi, have unproblematically posited notions of a national character and Japanese behavioural traits in a language that lends itself to essentialist understandings of an intrinsic Japanese nature. And yet, the Japanese **school system** labours from kindergarten to high school to create and sustain group-oriented identification and behaviour patterns. While this strong focus in education is argued by some to be a defence against the incursion of individualism, others argue that Japan's group-based structures of relational identity formation have always been a construction (nurture) of socio-cultural and political institutions and not essential (nature) to being Japanese.

Further reading

Rosenberger, N. (1992) *Japanese Sense of Self*, Cambridge, Cambridge University Press.

SANDRA BUCKLEY

information society

Japan was one of the first countries where the term 'information society' (*Jōhō shakai* or *jōhōka shakai*) was used. The term refers to a number of things including the impact of computerisation, the importance of information processes in producing consumer products (*vis-à-vis* labour and material costs) and the growth of information industries such as software production. Although Japan is well known for the production of communications and computer hardware, and video and computer games, until the late 1990s it had lagged behind the USA (the major importer of Japanese computers) in information technology and the use of computers both in the workplace and the home.

There has, however, been a rapid popularisation of e-mail, Internet culture and online marketing that has seen the emergence of new interfaces with computer technology better suited to the Japanese context than the desktop and portable PC access that still dominate US markets.

One reason for Japan's apparent lag into the 1990s can be found in the popularity of Japanese-language word processors from the 1980s. These can be considered an interim form of technology. The popularity of efficient, portable personal word processors may well have discouraged many Japanese from using personal computers. Even once Japanese word-processing software became widely available, many consumers still opted for the increasingly inexpensive word processor. One can also point to the weakness of computer education in Japanese schools and universities, a continuing concern among Japanese educators, as a further factor in the delay of Japan's entry into a broad-based information society. The complication of having to romanise Japanese in order to use early computer keyboards is also thought to have limited enthusiasm. With new software equipped to handle bilingual text, dual-character keyboards, automatic translation and rapid Japanese character selection programs, the obstacles to computer-based communications are now negligible. Early teething problems saw many Japanese reliant on commercial computer schools and software support companies for their IT (information technology) training. The majority of mid-size and larger corporations now employ an internal IT team and this has created a new class of highly skilled technical workers who are extremely mobile by comparison with many other areas of the Japanese full-time workforce. Another important factor through the 1980s was the fact that Japanese hardware and software differed depending on the maker, and the Japanese government was reluctant to recommend one over another. The reality was that NEC accounted for up to 70 per cent of Japan's personal computer market and this dominance had a direct and, some would argue, limiting impact on consumer choice and new product development.

Interface with the Internet and digital communications and culture in Japan has been distinguished by a shift away from a reliance on keyboard-based systems. The success of the Japanese hand-held video game industry (starting with Gameboy) and the extraordinary popularity of inexpensive comics (*manga*) are just two contemporary examples of the strong preference for visual and mobile forms of entertainment and information. This factor in combination with a variety of other variables such as commuter-oriented lifestyles, a dominant urban and highly mobile youth culture, the collapse of any hard distinction between spaces of work and non-work, and an overall acceleration of everyday life have all combined to favour mobile, hand-held, hard-copy free, fast, remote access technologies. Internet cafés and neighbourhood PC bars offering low-cost remote Internet access have proliferated in Japan's major urban centres from the mid-1990s. The growing popularity of the mobile phone as the primary access to the Internet shows how a non-keyboard-based techno culture can bypass the PC. The monopolistic role of NTT in telecommunications initially constrained the development of the mobile phone market, so that this technology really only became popular among Japanese youth and in the business world after about 1994. Not surprisingly, NTT DoCoMo has rapidly emerged as the leading mobile telecommunications carrier in Japan. A greater percentage of the Japanese population has mobile phones compared to the USA, where a higher proportion have PCs in the home. Japan illustrates how multimedia culture is not necessarily centred around any single technology platform.

The advent of wireless access has contributed to dramatic growth in Internet use. It is considered that 1995 was the first year in which the Internet really took off. By October 1997, Internet users were estimated to have reached 10 million and, by 2000, this number had doubled. The Internet is already embedded in Japan's social infrastructure. It is estimated that, by 2005, 50 per cent of access in Japan will be via cellular phones. This trend is not unique to Japan but also characteristic of other Asian urban cultures, for example, Hong Kong and Singapore. The level of innovation in both the miniaturisation and multifunctional capabilities of mobile telephones has been driven in Japan by this major Asian market potential. It has only been in the late 1990s that USA-based telecoms have also come to recognise the opportunities in this area of new technology. Increasingly, urban youth and business people alike are keen to leave their PC behind in favour of a compact mobile 'handy' that can interface simply with an office or home PC or an e-mail modem at a favourite Internet café.

One concern has been the extent to which globalisation and new digital technologies in an information society might lead to the homogenisation of cultures, with the transmission of massive quantities of cultural data across vast distances. The prominence of English on the Internet has led to calls for improvements in English-language teaching in Japan, lest a lack of fluency should hamper the Japanese from taking advantage of the opportunities offered by digital culture and electronic commerce (e-commerce). Japanese-language websites servicing online shoppers have grown dramatically, but English continues to dominate the Internet. A survey in 1999 of hundreds of millions of web pages by Excite@Home showed that English was the language for 72 per cent, followed by Japanese with 7 per cent and German with 5 per cent. Issues of privacy, data piracy and online fraud and other crimes are arising in Japan just as elsewhere. Laws relating to broadcasting, publishing, copyright, patents, censorship, licensing and other relevant areas of jurisprudence are notoriously conservative in Japan and will require substantial modification to accommodate the ethical challenges and speed of change in an information society.

E-commerce offers many exciting opportunities, but presents problems as well. Although Japan has the highest credit card penetration rate in the Asia–Pacific region, they have the lowest propensity to use it. Many people prefer to pay by cash. Ninety per cent of mail order sales are cash on-delivery or paid via bank transfer. Local convenience stores (*konbini*), which operate around the clock, are set to become payment and distribution centres for online vendors with the rapid installation of touch screen access terminals. The Japanese have been reluctant to buy from unknown vendors but alliances with convenience store chains is seen as a way of overcoming the problem. Lower prices may be too appealing to resist. The Internet gives Japanese consumers the option of obtaining retail products at a discount, something that has been strongly discouraged by manufacturers in the past. Once ordered, Japan's express-delivery services (*takkuhai bin*) will ensure that products arrive in a timely manner, something that has proved to be a problem with online shopping elsewhere. An entirely different set of trade tensions are brewing over Internet access to certain foreign goods heavily taxed in the domestic market as imports. Sony has recently announced its move into the banking arena in recognition of the new online future of finance from household purchases to stock markets. In a banking environment that remains surprisingly cumbersome, the option of fast and simple online transactions is attractive to the consumer and investor alike.

Who are Japan's online shoppers? Women are increasingly using the Internet with 43 per cent of housewives estimated to be online in 2000. The new economy is offering them not only consumer products but career and educational opportunities and chances for advancement which are not available to them in the 'old', more patriarchal off-line economy. Young Japanese are increasingly choosing to work for Internet start-up companies, where advancement is based on merit, gender is less important and there is at least the promise of high financial returns. Information and other electronic technologies have the potential to bring about not only greater consumer choice but even political change. Websites have been constructed for social protest as well as campaigning and fund raising by political parties. Women's groups, still a powerful source of political lobbying and social change, have increasingly moved online to replace the print media of their established *mini-komi* networks. Hackers have been known to attack the official websites of Japanese government ministries, in acts of what have been dubbed 'cyber-terrorism', and the corporate sector is also far from immune from hacker raids and viruses.

Despite an initial lag-time in information technology, Japan is now increasingly abreast of Europe and the USA in the development, production and consumption of new communication and information technologies. The innovation in mobile phone and other compact hand-held modem access to the Internet is an exciting technological trend with special appeal to the youth market, and a fast expanding market potential beyond Asia. There is every indication that reality is rapidly catching up with fiction as Japan approaches the futuristic images of itself that have been commonplace in popular science fiction for decades. No-one travelling through Tokyo today can help but be struck by the intensity of the flow of information that is now so integral to daily life.

Further reading

Gottlieb N. (1995) 'Technology and language policy: Word processing in Japan', *Asian Studies Review* 18(3).
—— (1993) 'Written Japanese and the word processor', *Japan Forum* 5(1).
Morris-Suzuki, T. (1988) *Beyond Computopia: Information, Automation and Democracy in Japan*, London: Kegan Paul International.

MORRIS LOW AND SANDRA BUCKLEY

Inland Sea

The Inland Sea, Seto Naikai, is a shallow sea between Honshū, Shikoku and Kyūshū extending approximately 3,667 square miles. It is famous for its beauty, which has, however, been seriously affected by vast industrial development along its flat shores, and extensive pollution. Especially on the Honshū coast, the natural coastline memorialised in traditional woodblock prints and contemporary photography has been massively reshaped by **land reclamation**. The Seto Naikai consists of over 1,000 islands completely surrounded by the Inland Sea National Park (Seto Naikai Kokuritsu Kōen). It is still a major area of tourist activity, and includes many shrines and temples throughout the islands, the most famous being those of the Shikoku pilgrimage. Although the **fishing** industry has been seriously affected by pollution, the Japanese still savour the many species of seafood from the shallow waters, and recent efforts to reduce pollution levels have had considerable effect. The best and freshest **sushi** restaurants are said to be close to the Seto Naikai.

See also: fishing; *keshiki*

AUDREY KOBAYASHI

Inoue Hisashi

b. 1934, Yamagata Prefecture

Writer and playwright

Inoue Hisashi spent his childhood in Tōhoku (i.e. north-east Honshū). His father died young, and when his mother had financial difficulty in supporting the family, he and his brother were sent to an orphanage run by Roman Catholic priests. He was baptised a Christian. However, his view of Christianity is completely different from that, say, of **Endō Shūsaku**. For Inoue, the Christian God is the god of those Fathers who looked after children at the orphanage with love and devotion. This love is depicted in many of his autobiographical stories and in a series of comic novels whose protagonist is a French Roman Catholic priest. While studying at Sofia University, Inoue started working part time for a popular theatre in **Asakusa**. Surrounded by professional performers (comedians and **striptease** artists), he learned many techniques essential to entertaining an audience. From the late 1950s he wrote radio and television scripts, including educational programmes and children's drama such as the immensely popular *Hyokkori hyōtan-jima* (The Floating Island Gourd, NHK Television, 1964–9). In the early 1970s, he established his name as a playwright and novelist, winning major theatre/literary prizes including the **Naoki Prize**.

Inoue's writing, be it drama, fiction or essays, is noted for its extreme playfulness, its punning and allusions. He played an important role in the so-called parody boom of the 1970s. His insistence on entertaining the reader is clearly intended as a revolt against establishment and authority, and against the tradition of 'serious' modern Japanese literature. It is a legacy of the comic writing (*gesaku*) of the Edo 'scribblers', some of whom Inoue depicted in his fiction such as Tegusari Shinju (The Love Suicide in Manacles, 1972) and in his drama on Hiraga Gennai. While his energetic and acrobatic use of language has captivated Japanese audiences, it has created difficulty for translators: only a few of his texts have been successfully translated into English.

Inoue is known also for his extensive and intensive research in a wide range of fields including modern and classic literature, language policies, stylistics, history, education, technology, agriculture and law. In his didactic and/or polemic essays and lectures, Inoue displays not only his knowledge of, and passion for, each topic but also his skills in producing logical and comprehensive argument. He combines all of these skills with his long-term concern for Japanese agriculture in the novel *Kirikirijin* (The Kirikirians, 1981). Kirikiri, a fictitious small agricultural village in Tōhoku, is a Utopia, and its declaration of independence from Japan is a revolt of the periphery against the centre. Inoue has also published a number of lectures, essays and commentaries on the production of **rice**, insisting that the undermining of domestic rice production would lead to devastating environmental destruction.

Further reading

Aoyama, Tomoko (1994) 'The love that poisons: Japanese parody and the new literacy', *Japan Forum* 6(1): 35–46.

Cohn, Joel R. (1998) *Studies in the Comic Spirit in Modern Japanese Fiction*, Cambridge, MA, and London: The Harvard University Asia Center.

TOMOKO AOYAMA

Inoue Yōsui

b. 30 August 1948, Fukuoka Prefecture

Singer-songwriter

Inoue Yōsui was a singer-songwriter instrumental in taking serious popular music taste from folk to the range of pop-rock styles known as New Music. Inoue's first album, *Danzetsu* (Rupture), was a huge hit when released by Polydor in May 1972 and sold over 510,000 copies. His early sound was an eclectic mixture often said to be evocative of such songwriters as Paul McCartney and Roy Orbison. His music was smart, melancholy and melodic. His

second album, *Yōsui II Sentimental* (October 1973), sold 490,000 copies. The follow-up, *Inoue Yōsui Live* (July 1973), sold 790,000 copies and set a sales record. *Kōri no sekai* (World of Ice) successfully grafted a more R 'n' B edge on to his sound, selling over 1,310,000 copies – a figure that still remains a Japanese LP sales record. In 1975, he founded For Life Records with Yoshida Takurō but moved into a sales slump over the next decade until the release of *Handsome Boy* in 1990. On this record he turned towards a more **enka**-like style and sales rebounded. Inoue had two more studio releases in the 1990s and his style in this period is considered reminiscent of the music of Yamashita Tatsurō. Inoue's work of the early 1970s was distinguished enough that he is widely thought to have been a significant influence on the development of Japanese pop rock. His co-founding of For Life Records also stands as one of the earliest challenges to major record label control of the Japanese popular music market.

MARK ANDERSON

Inpakushon

Inpakushon (Impaction) is a left-wing journal published by former **Zenkyōtō** radical and indefagitable anti-emperor and anti-war activist Amano Yasukazu. Reporting and reflecting on a broad spectrum of struggles, from the environment to peace movement, it provides a forum for exchanges of ideas and experiences from both within and without Japan. *Inpakushon* first appeared in 1979 under the name of *Impakuto* (Impact), as other popular intellectual journals affialiated with the new left such as *Gendai no me*, *Ryūdō* and the first **Jōkyō** were either faltering or had already disappeared. Without breaking completely from its own roots in the New Left, *Impakushon* has made its mark by emphasising movement and activists' experience to a greater degree than typical left-wing journals. As part of their stress on experience, both *Impakushon* and its affiliated press have also extensively documented oppositional movements, especially those of the late twentieth century.

GUY YASKO

installation art

Installation art originally emerged in Europe and the USA in the late 1960s as an extension of the concept of sculpture. Since the English word 'installation' was imported to Japan in the late 1970s, however, it came to be used without a clear definition to refer to everything that could not be categorised as either painting or sculpture. Roughly speaking, 'installation' in Japan denotes a kind of art that is made up of single or multiple three-dimensional parts placed in relation to each other in a given space, and whose life is generally limited to the period of the exhibition. Prior to the introduction of the term itself, however, some artists – several artists of Gutai Bijutsu Kyōkai (Gutai Art Association) of the 1950s and of Mono-ha (School of Things) of around 1970 – had already attempted to achieve a new method of expression. Gutai Bijutsu Kyōkai was founded in Ōsaka in 1954 by Yoshihara Jirō (1905–72), who encouraged some twenty member artists to create 'what has never existed before'. Based on this principle, the member artists produced experimental works using unorthodox materials and unusual methods. In the Outdoor Gutai Art Exhibition in 1956, Motonaga Sadamasa (1922–) used polyurethane sacs, each of which was filled with various coloured waters and tied the ends between trees. Yoshihara Michio (1933–) made a hole in the ground with an electric light buried at its bottom. The idea of utilising and conforming to the nature of the site was novel at the time, as conventional sculpture was considered to be static, isolated objects.

Mono-ha refers to a group of artists in Tokyo, from the late 1960s to the early 1970s, who shared an interest in a radical presentation of the natural state of things deriving from East Asian philosophy. Using primarily natural materials such as stone, wood, earth and water, the artists aimed to eliminate entirely the trace of the artist's hand in the making of the work, and to present 'world as-is' interventions. They preferred installation for its temporary nature. In 1968, Sekine Nobuo (1942–) composed an outdoor piece entitled *Phase-Mother Earth*, in which he dug a large cylindrical hole in the ground, while, set off to one side, was an equal-sized earthen cylinder of the soil excavated. Suga Kishio (1944–) simply exhibited two wooden blocks of different lengths set diagonally in two open window frames at a museum in *Unnamed Situation I* in 1970. One of the theorists of Mono-ha, Lee U Fan (1936–) sought the total experience of the spatial and temporal relationship among the various elements composed of the work in *Relatum* in 1971, by placing several large rocks on cushions set apart in a gallery space apparently at random. The other Mono-ha artists, Koshimizu Susumu (1944–), Yoshida Katsurō (1943–) and Narita Katsuhiko (1944–92) also created installation works.

In the mid-1970s, a next wave of Japanese artists developed large-scale installation works with which they extended the philosophy presented by Mono-ha. They mainly used wood to create site-specific works that embraced the environment. Toya Shigeo (1947–) sculpted large tree trunks with a chainsaw to shape animistic totems giving a spiritual power to the site. Endō Toshikatsu (1950–) exhibited massive wooden forms, coated with oil or tar and burned until their surface was utterly carbonised. Toya and Endō refocused on the subject matter that Mono-ha had aimed to destroy, in the process of applying symbolic meanings to their works. It was Kawamata Tadashi (1953–) who brought a social dimension into installation art. At the beginning of the 1980s, he started constructing lumber scaffolding that would eventually wrap existing buildings. He placed emphasis on the process of the creation rather than the result of it, and worked to involve the local public – the lumber was salvaged within the city and the construction was assisted by public volunteers.

Once the term 'installation' took root in Japan, many Japanese artists eagerly embraced the concept, and in the early 1980s it became a fad. Japanese installation art in this period can be divided into two types. One may be categorised as constructive installations such as the works by Saitō Yoshishige (1904–). He presented large-scale installations composed of black-lacquered wooden boards assembled in loose, asymmetrical arrangements on the floor. The other type was installation created under the influence of the 'New Wave' movement, which responded to the burst of Neo-Expressionism in paintings in Europe and the USA at the end of 1970s to the early 1980s. In their installation works, the artists filled up spaces with brightly coloured figurative images, creating a sense of pop culture. Yoshizawa Mika (1959–)

was representative of this trend. Since the late 1980s, individual artists have taken a more diverse approach towards installation art. New media and technology, and political and social issues, have been dealt with in installation works. Miyajima Tatsuo (1957–) has designed objects and installations composed of hundreds or thousands of light-emitting diodes (LEDs) since 1987. The LED components, usually in dark rooms, are counting in linear rhythm from one to nine at different speeds to each other. He thus investigates the concepts of time and infinity with these works. Kasahara Emiko (1963–) has questioned sexual identity using floral motifs in her installation works. Yanagi Yukinori (1959–) has reconsidered the Japanese imperial system. He exhibited a billboard-size neon of the Japanese flag, *Hinomaru* (Rising Sun), in 1993. Tsuchiya Kimio (1955–) is another artist who refers to global social issues such as urban environment. Nakahara Kōdai (1961–), on the other hand, has concentrated on an extremely personal world. In his *Making of Nakahara* in 1992, his installation contained portraits of himself and his parents and video screens focusing on parts of the body, revealing the biological connection between himself and his parents.

The early 1990s saw the exposure of contemporary Japanese art to the worldwide art scene. The above-mentioned artists have constantly shown their works at the major international exhibitions. Recently, Naitō Rei (1961–) was the solo representative at the Japanese pavilion at the 47th Venice Biennale in 1997. She constructed a large tent of flannel, inside of which nothing but several light bulbs were placed. By severely restricting entrance to the tent and by limiting access to ten minutes, the artist aimed to question today's busy lifestyle and the absence of humanity.

TAKASUE AKIKO

International Women's Year Action Group

The International Women's Year Action Group (Kokusai Fujin Nen o kikkake to shite Kōdō o Okosu Onnatachi no Kai, or Kōdō Suru Kai), formed in January 1975, was one of the groups that argued for the implementation of **equal employment opportunity legislation** in Japan. Many of the group's members were educated working women such as teachers or public servants, and their actions reflected these women's concerns. The group was renamed the Women's Action Group (Kōdōsuru onna tachi no kai) in 1986, and has continued campaigns on working women's issues, education and the media.

Further reading

Mackie, V. (1996) 'Feminist critiques of modern Japanese politics', in M. Threlfall (ed.) *Mapping the Women's Movement: Feminism and Social Transformation in the North*, London: Verso, pp. 260–87.

VERA MACKIE

Ishiguro Kazuo

b. 1954, Nagasaki

Writer

Whether or not Ishiguro should be included in a volume on Japanese contemporary culture is not something everyone will agree upon. He grew up in the UK as the child of Japanese parents and in a Japanese-speaking household, but has repeatedly asserted that he identifies himself as an international writer more than British or Japanese. He was awarded a hotly contested British literary award, the Booker Prize, in 1989, for his novel *The Remains of the Day*. It is the insistence of so many critics on the Japanese influences in his work and the significance of his Japanese heritage that begs his inclusion in a project on contemporary Japanese culture. Ishiguro describes growing up in the South of England (Surrey) and receiving a typical middle-class schooling. He also admits to having been teased as a child for being different and being aware of not meeting other 'non-English' people for years on end. He has described how 'nobody's history seemed to be my history'. He studied creative writing with Malcolm Bradbury after graduating from Kent University. His early short stories and television scriptwriting have been overshadowed by the success of his four major novels: *A Pale View of Hills* (1982), *An Artist of the Floating World* (1986), *The Remains of the Day* (1989) and *The Unconsoled* (1995).

The central characters of both *A Pale View of Hills* and *An Artist of the Floating World* are Japanese, and each narrative is haunted by war memories. In *A Pale View of Hills*, the protagonist Etsuko has left behind a husband in Japan and is now widowed by her British second husband. Her Japanese daughter commits suicide as an adult and the relationship with her English-born daughter is ridden with tensions. A visit from this younger daughter drives a narrative in which Etsuko explores tentatively and fearfully the flow of memories between the years she spent in Nagasaki after the atomic bombing, her decision to bring her first daughter with her to the UK and her sense of responsibility for her suicide. The memory landscape that emerges is marked by the impossibility of forgetting. Similarly, in *An Artist of the Floating World*, the elderly painter Masuji Ono has relocated from Japan to England and the narrative follows the floating world of his uncertain memories as he struggles with his desire to distance himself from his role as a patriotic Japanese during the war and his sense of his own inconsequentiality. His uncertainty and self-doubt extend from his war responsibility to his art and his relation with his two daughters.

These first two novels are often spoken of as Ishiguro's 'Japanese novels', despite their English setting. With *The Remains of the Day*, Ishiguro made a clear decision to attempt to write a novel that would allow him to establish his identity and reputation as a writer of English fiction. He succeeded. His story is of a butler, Stevens, undertaking a motor tour of the English countryside with Ms Kenton, who was once in service in the same household. Stevens tours the memories of his years in service over the 1930s and 1940s from his vantage point in 1956. Facing old age and retirement, he rejects the possibility of redundancy for the world of manners in which he sees the butler as a central instrument of propriety. Ishiguro examines the dynamics of power and dependency in the British class system. The work was immediately compared to the brilliance of Dickens, Austen and James for Ishiguro's ability to capture the intimate detail of class. The book was made

into a film starring Anthony Hopkins and Emma Thompson.

Ishiguro's next novel *The Unconsoled* is difficult to imagine ever being successfully made into a film. The narrative follows a famous English concert pianist, Ryder, to a European city where he is to give a recital. Time is in suspension in this narrative. There is no linear progression either in the events related in the city leading up to the recital or in the constant eruption of memories into the time-present of the story. People and spaces fold in and out of one another without apparent connection, in an unpredictable and disquieting patchwork that refuses to resolve itself to allow Ryder or the reader to grasp 'reality'. Ishiguro is often described as fascinated with memory and repressed emotions. He describes his willingness to follow a thought or internal monologue for pages as evidence of not being afraid of slowness or letting things almost come to a stop. A comparison made often between his writing and Japanese fiction is his repeated use of a first-person narrative reminiscent of the Japanese **I-novel**. Ishiguro is however reluctant to accept these Japanese linkages and pronounces his strongest influences to have been the English and Russian realists, Ford Maddox Ford, Forster, James and Kafka.

Further reading

Schaffer, B (1998) *Understanding Kazuo Ishiguro*, South Carolina: University of South Carolina Press.

Wood, M. (1998) 'Discourse of others: Ishiguro Kazuo', in *Children of Silence: On Contemporary Fiction*, New York: Columbia University Press, pp.171–81.

SANDRA BUCKLEY

ISLAND, THE *see Hadaka no shima*

Isozaki Arata

b. 1931, Ōita City, Ōita Prefecture

Architect

Before opening his own office in 1963, Isozaki

pursued advanced studies at Tokyo University under Professor **Tange Kenzō**'s tutelage. While greatly influenced by the modernism of Le Corbusier and Oscar Niemeyer, along with Tange's reinterpretations of modernism in light of Japanese traditions, Isozaki continues to reinvent his own aesthetic in full consciousness of himself as their successor; he refuses pre-defined frameworks or ideologies while employing irony or allusion in his architecture to cite the past in the present. Critics have hailed Isozaki as a leading post-modern, and even deconstructivist, architect since the 1980s, but he has come to reject these labels.

In his controversial Tsukuba Science Centre (1983), Isozaki rebelled against the state's implicit demand for a symbolic, representative architecture by first fragmenting, then reassembling, myriad architectural 'quotations' into a patchwork of historical references at the Tsukuba site. He created what he felt was a new 'fictional place' that expressed the 'hollowness of the center' (Isozaki: 58). Specifically, he constructed skewed buildings around a central sunken plaza to cite in concave fashion the ascent of the Capitoline Hill in Rome, and reversed the tile colours of the Senate Building piazza while mimicking its well-known pattern; he alluded to classical mythology with a bronze sculpture of a laurel tree in a prominent site location; he selected ornamental forms based on works by architects and artists as diverse as Constantin Brancusi, Clauda Nicolas Ledoux and Giulio Romano; and, finally, he compared the missing subject of 'the state' in Tsukuba's design to the missing king and queen in Velázquez's painting, *Las Meninas*. For Isozaki, such quotation forces the loss of any original 'meaning' and allows the regeneration of meanings to circulate in the decentred 'texts' that are his projects. Harsh criticism of the Tsukuba Science Centre dismissed Isozaki's work as trendy post-modern jargon and charged the project with being merely decorative and derivative, even plagiaristic. Many Isozaki projects since Tsukuba de-emphasise intellectual 'play' in favour of startling site programming, massive buildings in pure geometric forms, grid-work structures and patterns, bright colours and creative collaboration with other artists, as in the Nagi Museum of Contemporary Art (Okayama, 1993).

Projects spanning Isozaki's prolific career include the Ōita Prefecture Medical Association Hall (1960), Ōita Prefecture Library (1966), Festival Plaza at Expo '70 (Ōsaka), Gunma Prefecture Modern Art Museum (1974), the Los Angeles Museum of Contemporary Art (1986), Barcelona Sports Hall (1990), Kita Kyūshū International Conference Centre (1990), Team Disney (Orlando, 1991), Centre of Japanese Art and Technology (Crakow, Poland, 1994), Domus: Interactive Museum about Humans (La Coruna, Spain, 1995) and Kyōto Concert Hall (1995). Isozaki is also credited with designing 'the White House' in Shinjuku in the late 1950s, an atelier for artists with Neo-Dadaism Organizer.

Further reading

Isozaki Arata (1989) 'Of city, nation, and style', in Masao Miyoshi and H.D. Harootunian (eds) *Postmodernism and Japan*, London and Durham: Duke University Press, pp. 47–62.

(1996) *GA (Global Architecture)*, Document Extra, 05: Arata Isozaki. Tokyo: ADA Edita, Ltd.

SCOTT GOLD AND MARY KNIGHTON

Itami Jūzō

b. 1933, Kyōto

Film director

Born in May 1933, Itami Jūzō was the son of the famous Japanese director Mansaku Itami (1900–46) and perhaps the best known of post-New Wave Japanese directors. Prior to beginning his film-making career, Itami worked as a graphic designer, a television talk-show host, an essayist and, eventually, an actor. He played the father in the film *Kazoku geemu* (Family Game). In 1984, at the age of fifty, he wrote and directed his first film *Osōshiki* (The Funeral), starring his wife Miyamoto Nobuko. A satirical look at the Japanese way of handling the social ritual of a death, *Osōshiki* had great box office success and went on to win many Japanese motion picture awards. Itami soon became famous for his un-Japanese sense of humour and his second film *Tampopo* (1986), about a young widow's search for the perfect noodle, gained him international recognition. His next few films continued his tradition of dealing with loaded issues in Japanese society with a light-hearted comic touch. After his 1992 release *Minbo no onna* (The Gentle Art of Japanese Extortion), Itami was attacked by three armed *yakuza* members, aggrieved over their depiction in the film. The attack left him with a permanent knife scar on his face. In total, Itami made ten films in his fourteen years as a director. Soon after the release of his last film *Marutai no onna*, he committed suicide in December 1997 at the age of 64 by jumping off an eight-storey building in the Azabudai area of Tokyo.

Further reading

Stone, Judy (1997) *Eye on the World: Conversations with International Filmmakers*, Los Angeles: Silman James Press.

LEILA POURTAVAF

Ito Toyo

b. 1941, Seoul, Korea

Architect

One of the most outstanding representatives of the so-called New Wave of Japanese Architecture, Ito came to prominence in the mid-1970s. He graduated from the University of Tokyo in 1965 and subsequently worked in Kikutake Kiyonori's office for four years, until 1969. In 1971, he established his own office in Tokyo and began producing, like many of his young contemporaries, private residences. Although his association with the Metabolist master left its mark on Ito's architecture of simple structures and innovative use of ordinary materials, his outlook on design did not share the primarily technology-oriented preoccupation of the Metabolism movement; Ito's work was to unfold away form the goals of Metabolism in both architecture and urbanism. This was already well demonstrated by his first completed project, the Aluminium House (1971) in Fujisawa; it represented first of all a decisively non-monumental architecture, and an informal, or

rather non-formal, language that Ito has maintained throughout the years, even though his work has developed in several divergent stages. His course in design can be characterised by a consistent progress towards increasingly lighter structures, where lightness should be understood both literally and figuratively, that is to say, as a sign of a new architectural paradigm engendered by a non-modern discourse and thought.

The early 1970s were times of significant changes in Japan, as the onset of the energy crisis and the resulting economic recession ushered in the demise of modernism in this country, while also signalling the beginning of post-modernism in architecture as well. As the economy was stagnating, most architects at the outset of their career received few commissions and were able to design only residential buildings, many of them for the members of their own family. The private residence assumed the role of forwarding the most innovative and often radical architectural ideas. Kazuo Shinohara was one whose designs became influential and Ito, like several of his contemporaries, such as Hasegawa Itsuko and Yuzuru Tominaga, started to pursue similar lines in their individual architectures. Ito's White U House in Nakano (1976) in Tokyo, with its enclosed, and strictly inward-oriented reinforced concrete architecture was an anti-urban statement, a rejection of the deteriorating urban conditions of the megalopolis.

A change in Ito's attitude was signalled by the PMT Building (1978) in Nagoya, which featured a thin and softly undulating aluminium façade in front of a standard skeletal structure, and acted as a mask or a mere architectural sign. Subsequent projects, such as the House in Chūōrinkan (1979) and House in Hanakoganei (1983), revealed not only an increasing simplicity of design, but also an innovative yet straightforward use of ordinary and increasingly lightweight materials, along with Ito's growing uninterest in preconceived forms. Acutely aware of the social conditions and urban developments of the Japanese city, which have been shaped by both the onslaught of commercialism and new information age, Ito recognised the irrepressible dynamics and mobility in contemporary urban life. In order to respond to the new, nomadic lifestyles, he has shifted the focus of his architecture once again; his own Ito Residence (1984), the 'Silver

Hut' in Tokyo, with its insubstantial materiality and tent-like cover, became a type of residence for the new urban nomads, and an architectural paradigm of temporality, where if not always or necessarily the physical entity of the structure, then the range of its acquired meanings, assumed the quality of impermanence.

Accordingly, Ito's subsequent projects were conceived in the spirit of lightness, temporality and ephemerality; among these were the 'Nomad' Restaurant (1986) in Tokyo and the House in Magomezawa (1986) in Chiba, while several installation projects for the dwelling of Tokyo's Nomad Women (1986 and 1989) also have to be mentioned. The 'bubble economy' of the 1980s and early 1990s resulted in an unprecedented building boom in Japan, a time when architects could hardly meet the growing demand for the large number of new designs whose commercial value often resided in nothing else than its striking sign quality. Ito began to receive larger and larger projects, in which he intended to both benefit from the accelerated developments, and was simultaneously critical of their trivial inferior architectural products. One of the most successful architects in Japan to be able to reconcile the contradictory nature of such intentions, Ito came to represent best the true avant-garde in architecture in these times. His success is attested to by such outstanding major works as the Guest House of Sapporo Breweries (1989) in Eniwa, Hokkaidō, the Yatsushiro Municipal Museum (1991) in Yatsushiro, the Shimosuwa Municipal Museum (1993) in Nagano Prefecture and the ITM Building (1993) in Matsuyama.

In seeking out the most appropriate modes and means of responding to the fast-changing conditions of the Japanese city and urban culture, Ito has utilised a wide variety of means: the latest electronic and computer technologies, new structural systems and a sensitive reliance on natural elements or phenomena being the most important. His Tower of Wind (1986) in Yokohama uses an extensive system of electric lights, along with a computer software program that runs it, to monitor and visually display the changes in the direction and velocity of wind, the level of surrounding urban noise and the passing of time. The Lyric Hall (1997) in Nagaoka and many others, including the above-mentioned Guest House on Hokkaidō

and the Museum in Yatsushiro, apply and shape earth or the land itself, not only as landscaping material but as an integral and significant part of architecture, creating in this way an inseparable unity between nature and artifice. The embodied design ideas and tectonic resolution of his latest large-scale project, the Mediatheque (2001) in Sendai, are an example of an architectural and engineering bravura that, in most respects, surpasses the even high expectations attached to each new project by Ito.

Further reading

Bognar, Botond (1999) *Toyo Ito: Blurring Architecture*, exhibition catalogue, Milano: Edizioni Charta.

—— (1978) 'Collage and superficiality in architecture', in K. Frampton (ed.) *A New Wave of Japanese Architecture* (Catalogue 10), New York: IAUS (Institute for Architecture and Urban Studies), pp.68–9.

Ito Toyo (1993) 'A garden of microchips: The architectural image of the microelectronic age', *JA Library* 2 (Toyo Ito): 4–15.

—— (1988) 'Architecture sought after by android', *JA, The Japan Architect* June: 9–13.

—— (1982) 'In Search of a Context, 1971–', *JA, The Japan Architect* April: 54.

Roulet, S. and Soulier, S. (1995) *Toyo Ito: Architectural Monographs No 41*, London: Editions du Moniteur.

—— (1995) *Toyo Ito: 1986–1995*, Madrid: El Croquis.

BOTOND BOGNAR

Iwanami publishing house

The Iwanami publishing house, Japan's representative academic publisher, was established in 1913, the year before the First World War, by Iwanami Shigeo, a Kanda bookstore owner. The following year, Natsume Sōseki wrote the novel *Kokoro* and entrusted its publication to Iwanami. In 1916, Iwanami was able to build the foundation of its reputation on an edition of Soseki's complete works, which was published promptly after the writer's death. Iwanami publishing established itself with a strong focus on philosophical works. In its early years, it was the only publishing house so actively engaged in the fertile ground of academic publishing. The emergence of Iwanami was promoted by the flow of background events often referred to as Taishō Democracy, and characterised by a trend towards liberalisation that had begun during the First World War. This period produced what was called Taishō 'culturalism', represented by groups such as 'the White Birch Society'. It was not insiginificant that at this same time the university system was finally advancing and fostering a level of education which produced men of real talent. The developments in academic publishing contributed in important ways to the realisation of the fruits of this new age of learning. Iwanami staff forged many close relations with those within the academies in Kyōto and Tokyo, resulting in what some considered a virtual monopoly of academic publishing.

Iwanami firmly established its reputation in the publishing world in the pre-war years, but there was much more that Iwanami achieved above and beyond its monopoly of academic publishing. It was instrumental in the establishment of numerous 'systems' that are still in operation today and which are fundamental to the Japanese publishing world. First, in 1927, taking up a German model for literary collections (Reclam Universal-Bibliothek) as its example, Iwanami established a series of small collected works (*bunko*) that quickly became known as Iwanami Bunko. The series produced a continuous stream of publications of Western and Asian classics. Other companies quickly followed suit, and to this day the *bunko* format has remained a dominant model in Japanese publishing and innumerable *bunko*-style series have been released. In 1928, Iwanami established the series entitled 'Trends in World Thought' (*Iwanami kōza sekai shichō*) and after the war this *kōza* style proliferated across publishing houses and also became an established format. The *kōza* format consisted of an edited work that organised groups of international researchers to contribute written work around specific themes or problematics, with the goal of systematically making academic fields accessible to a wider readership. A *kōza* series could consist of anywhere from ten to more than thirty volumes. In the process of developing and

promoting the *kōza* approach, Iwanami wedged itself even deeper into the academy. At the same time, it was becoming conscious of the needs of the general reader and began tirelessly publishing works directed towards the wider public. In 1938, the Iwanami Shoten launched Pelican Books. The style of these new publications was defined by a tendency to retain an academic focus while, at the same time, aiming at an intervention in the general reader's awareness and knowledge of current affairs. To this day, this mixed style has remained a precious and popular tool within the publishing world.

The republication of Sōseki's complete works in a new edition was also a significant event, not only because of the expanded readership but also for the style of editing it established, which became the model for collecting the complete works of an individual author. The Iwanami publishing house standardised the practice of collecting the complete works of not only literary writers but also other scholarly writers of a given period or epoch. A primary characteristic of their 'system' was the notion that anyone, any author, could tip the market scales in academic publishing (*kibo o kakudaisuru*). This philosophy of publishing continued to support Iwanami's market position into the post-war period.

Post-war academic publications that deserve special mention are: the 1955 publication of the *Kōjien* dictionary; the 1957 publication of *The Classical Japanese Literary Compendium*; and the 1963 publication of *The Complete Catalogue of National Texts*. *Kōjien* sold over a million copies and went on to become known as 'the people's dictionary'. *The Classical Japanese Literary Compendium* was a compilation of one hundred volumes drawing together the major classical literary works produced before the Meiji Period. It sold some 1.2 million copies. This was the first exercise since the Meiji Restoration in close textual analysis and commentary, and is said to have set the standard for Japanese classical literature. *The Complete Catalogue of National Texts* was a comprehensive catalogue that listed over half a million written works in Japan, for the thousand-year period preceding Meiji. An enterprise of this colossal scale and significance demonstrated Iwanami's tremendous power and capabilities, and ensured its position of leadership in the world of academic publishing.

In the post-war period, perhaps the most important development was the 1946 publication of the magazine *Sekai*. The defeat in the Second World War led to a realisation among the Japanese people of the necessity of radical reform and the role of social criticism. *Sekai* organised an impress-ive and diverse frontline of critically aware individuals committed to the realisation of the potential of peace and democracy. In the academy of the post-war period the influence of Marxism was very strong. The magazine not only achieved high esteem and prestige among academics but also within the broader post-war world of social criticism, an environment that *Sekai* played no small role in nurturing. An important factor in the impact and success of *Sekai* was a mature editorial policy guided by the popular intellectual credo of the day, 'from the middle road to the left'.

Before the Second World War, the academic publishing tradition had been closely linked to the authority and influence of Iwanami. However, the period of high economic growth saw not only a diminishing of the power of critique but also a significant diluting of the persuasive power of Marxism within the academy. Since the 1970s, Iwanami publishers has also entered a period of decline. Post-cold war Japan has swayed markedly to the political right, and at the same time the decline of the publishing industry has added to a state of stagnation. What this suggests is that the possibilities for academic publishing in Japan are diminishing, along with the previously substantial marketplace.

KOJIMA KIYOSHI

J

Jacks, the

Formed in 1966 by Hasegawa Yoshio and Takahashi Matsuhiro with a focus on original material, the Jacks were a band that prefigured the transition from folk to rock, which soon took place in the Japanese music scene as a whole.

The Jacks made their major-label debut in September 1968 with Vacant World, on Toshiba Records. Hasegawa's compositions are widely acknowledged to have been important in developing the rock idiom in the Japanese language. The band's concerts were among the first psychedelic rock experiences on the Japanese scene, and their eclectic combination of Jazz, R 'n' B and gloomy psychedelia was a fundamental turning point in the development of Japanese rock and pop culture. They were an important part of the underground scene in the late 1960s, acquiring an extremely devoted group of fans who remember them fondly to this day. After the release of a second album, *Jacks Super Session* in June 1969, they made a public statement declaring they were disbanding in July and gave a farewell performance at the first All-Japan Folk Jamboree in August of the same year. Even after their break-up, their influence on the Japanese music scene remained very strong, the number of artists they affected really being incalculable.

MARK ANDERSON

Japan Foundation

Established in 1972 by special legislation of the Japanese Diet, the Japan Foundation declared its goal to be the promotion of cultural exchange and mutual understanding. It has an endowment of some 16 billion yen supplemented by private and government annual donations and grants. The Foundation funds projects that promote Japanese studies and international exchange with Japan, with a strong focus on language teaching and translation, as well as academic research and the arts. There have been some very public and heated debates over the role of the Japan Foundation in setting the research and teaching agenda for Japanese Studies outside Japan. The Foundation's role in the development and implementation of internationally standardised testing for Japanese language proficiency and its close involvement in curriculum development have attracted some criticism. The new Kyōto-based research facilities for international scholars of Japanese Studies have further fuelled debate over what some perceive to be an excessively interventionist role on the part of the Foundation as the primary source of major research funds in the field of Japanese Studies. Others counter-argue that the Japan Foundation functions along very similar lines to the Goethe Institute or Alliance Francaise and is not unique in its international promotion of domestic policies of national language and culture.

SANDRA BUCKLEY

Japan Broadcasting Corporation

The Japan Broadcasting Corporation, or NHK (Nippon Hōsō Kyōkai) as it is popularly known, is a public broadcasting system. NHK falls under the rubric of a non-profit organisation. Unlike commercial stations that depend on advertising income, or public broadcasting in the USA that solicits donations from listeners, viewers and companies, NHK relies almost entirely on revenue collected from viewers.

Law states that all companies and viewers owning television sets should be subject to a contract with NHK, regardless of whether or not they intend to watch NHK's programmes. This law, which initially called for the creation of a company independent of government and industry, in fact, led to the creation of the NHK broadcasting 'empire'. NHK maintains three radio stations and five television channels, which include satellite broadcasting. Its programmes cover a wide range of topics from news, sports, talk shows, dramas, music, foreign language programmes and shows for children, NHK's history reveals its close relationship with the government. In 1925, three independent radio stations in Tokyo, Nagoya and Ōsaka began radio broadcasts. However, the following year these stations were integrated because of a government order that aimed to establish a nationwide network with a strong financial base – so began NHK. Government guidance included the regular checking of all news and programmes to be aired, and retired high-level bureaucrats were given major executive positions in the company.

In spite of the democritisation of broadcasting during Japan's Occupation period, NHK has continued to be influenced by the government. The company is obligated to report both its budget and nominations for its Board of Directors to the Diet for approval.

BARBARA HAMILL SATO

Japan Communist Party

The Japan Communist Party (JCP) was first organised in 1923 in the wake of the Russian Revolution as an illegal political group that was suppressed during the military years. It originally won a large percentage of the vote in the Diet elections of 1949, but was far less successful thereafter as it was perceived to be tied to a belligerent USSR. The Allied Occupation purged top JCP leaders following the outbreak of the Korean War in 1950. In response, and with the encouragement of the USSR, many JCP leaders adopted a policy of violent terrorist acts. These lost the party public support and, in 1952, it lost all of its thirty-five seats in the House of Representatives election. The party remained part of the international Moscow-controlled communist movement until the early 1960s, when the fortunes of the JCP revived under the leadership of Miyamoto Kenji, who stressed independence from Moscow and Beijing, and the 'parliamentary road' of non-violent, electoral politics.

Since then, the JCP has taken an independent line, but its policies have continued to emphasise the nationalisation of big business, promotion of voluntary co-operatives and comprehensive social welfare. In 1976, the party announced a new set of policies and, in 1979, gained thirty-nine seats in the House of Representatives. The party was financially independent through sales of its popular newspaper the *Akahata* (Red Flag). As a result, the JCP was least mired in 'money politics', and so earned an increased respect from voters, especially at the level of local government. Even so, it lost ten seats in early 1990 as a result of voter disgust with the party's Chinese counterpart following the Beijing 'Tianamen Square Incident' in 1989. Moreover, the JCP was excluded from the coalition of parties that eventually ousted the Liberal Democratic Party (LDP) in 1993 to form government in that year. Up until the mid-1990s, the JCP continued to be marginalised in Japanese politics due to its persistently unpopular stance on certain issues, such as its opposition to the US–Japan Security Alliance. However, it was one of the chief beneficiaries of the vote for the Upper House (House of Councillors) in 1998. The reason was not so much because the Japanese voters turned towards communist ideology, but more because the communists represented the one party that seemed organised and thoughtful about its policies at a time of widespread electoral disillusionment.

The perception was that all political opposition parties except the JCP had merged the substance of their policies with the governing LDP line. The Communist Party's platform emphasised reform, especially on questions dealing with the proposed increase in the consumption tax, freeing Okinawa of US military bases and improving the pension, welfare and medical services. The communists, in 1999, were the fourth opposition party and controlled twenty-three seats (9 per cent of total) in the House of Councillors (Upper House), and were the fifth largest opposition party with twenty-six seats (5 per cent) in the House of Representatives (Lower House). It is the only major party in Japan that has had no experience as a ruling party. Partly in consequence it continues to act independently of other opposition parties.

DAVID EDGINGTON

Japan Socialist Party

The former Japan Socialist Party (JSP, or Nippon Shakaitō) was traditionally the largest opposition party to the **Liberal Democratic Party** (LDP) in the post-war years. Established in 1906, it disbanded a year later because of suppression by the Japanese government. It reformed in 1947 and won a plurality of seats in the House of Representatives, which enabled it to form a coalition government. However, factional fighting between the party's left-wing and right-wing brought down the government in 1948, and the party was soundly defeated by conservative groups in the 1949 elections. The JSP participated in two coalition governments in the 1990s and has consistently played a major role in defining the political landscape of Japan at both the national and local levels.

After the 1949 defeat, the left- and right-wing factions finally agreed to unite in 1955, but by 1961 the moderate conservative wing of the JSP had split off to form the Democratic Socialist Party (DSP or Minshatō). The JSP made electoral gains against the governing LDP under popular chairwomen Doi Takako, following the 'Recruit Scandal' of 1989 and the introduction of a consumption tax by the government in the same year. In 1991, the

party changed its English name to Social Democratic Party of Japan (SDPJ). It formed part of a coalition government that took power from the LDP in 1993. As the coalition dissolved the next year, the socialists entered into an unprecedented coalition with their long-time rival, the LDP, to stay in power. Prime Minister Tomiichi Murayama's socialist-led government lasted from 1994 to 1996, when the LDP reclaimed majority control in the coalition. Following Muruyama's resignation as Prime Minister and Party Chair in 1996, the SDPJ changed its Japanese name to Shakai Minshutō (Social Democratic Party) and dropped the 'of Japan' from its English name to become the Social Democratic Party (SDP). Doi Takako, the outgoing speaker of the Lower House, agreed to head the SDP and cut its ties with the LDP in an effort to buoy its election chances. Although it now generally supports the US–Japan Security Treaty, the party in the past had opposed efforts to broaden Japan's military role. The SDP, which traditionally has been a party that relied heavily on unions for its support, has seen its popularity wane greatly in the past few years with the significant weakening of the union movement. The SDP now controls thirteen seats in the Upper House and fifteen in the Lower House. Other socialist parties in Japan support a stronger left-wing ideology but with the support of far fewer voters, e.g. Socialist Workers' Party, New Socialist Party. The dominance of Japanese post-war politics by the LDP has meant that there has not been a widespread understanding outside of Japan of the real extent of the influence and role played by the JSP in shaping Japanese politics from its position as a strong oppositional voice.

DAVID EDGINGTON

Japanese American literature

Recognition of a growing body of US writing as Asian US literature has occurred only in the last two decades. The production of Japanese American literature is tied to the history and economic circumstances of Asian immigration to the USA, to a history of discrimination, Asian exclusion acts and restrictive immigration laws, as well as the events of the Second World War – wartime hysteria and the internment of citizens of Japanese descent and their parents in US concentration camps during the war. Also significant is the activism by ethnic minorities in the 1960s and 1970s, resulting not only in the recovery of earlier writing but the encouragement of new writing and literary criticism.

Up until the 1970s, published examples of this literature were few. Certainly, pre-war immigrants wrote about their experiences in diaries, letters, newspapers, poetry and fiction, but this work without translation has not yet participated in the broader field of US literature. Notable among early immigrants who published work in English are Sadakichi Hartmann, Etsu Sugimoto, Bunichi Kagawa and Taro Yashima. Hartmann cultivated a persona as a bohemian, and, as early as 1908, wrote and published poetry, stories and plays based on his interests in Japanese and European literature of the avant-garde. In the 1920s and 1930s, Sugimoto wrote novels about life in Japan, and Kagawa wrote self-reflective poetry about his identity as a Japanese American. Taro Yashima was the pen-name for Jun Atsushi Iwamatsu, who during and after the war wrote about his persecution in Japan as a political prisoner. Yashima later became known for his illustrated books for children.

It took another generation educated in the USA to create a literature grounded in local history and community. However, *nisei* writers who managed to publish their work, despite the necessities of daily survival and the impact of prejudice during and surrounding the war years, were exceptions. Toshio Mori was one of the few in the 1930s to publish stories in literary journals outside the community. However, his collection of stories, *Yokohama, California*, descriptive of a fictional Japanese American community, could not be published until after the war in 1949. Hisaye Yamamoto, who began writing in the 1930s for the Japanese American press, published her essays and stories in national journals after the war. Years later, in 1988, these stories were collected in *'Seventeen Syllables' and other Stories*. In 1953, Monica Sone published her autobiography, *Nisei Daughter*, about her childhood in Seattle and internment in Minidoka. In 1959, Milton Murayama published *All I Asking for Is My Body*, set in pre-war Hawaii, but this work would only finally gain recognition in the 1970s, when it was republished in 1975. Wakako Yamauchi, who began writing in the 1950s, adapted her short story 'And the Soul Shall Dance' for the stage in 1977, but, while frequently anthologised, her collection of short stories, *Songs My Mother Taught Me*, was not published until 1994.

Nisei writing was largely kept alive through publications in local Japanese American community newspapers such as the Los Angeles *Rafu Shimpo*, the San Francisco *Hokubei Mainichi* and the Japanese American Citizens League's *Pacific Citizen*, and, during the war years, in camp publications. It was in the 1970s that *nisei* writers were 'discovered' by the next generation of Asian US writers hungry to find a past upon which to build, encouraging the republication and anthologising of this writing. One of the most notable discoveries was the work of John Okada, resulting in the republication in 1976 of his novel *No-No Boy*. This novel, first published in 1957, is considered perhaps the first literary novel of Japanese American literature. Written in unflinching prose, Okada describes the hard realities and emotional conflicts of post-war USA for Japanese Americans – for those who fought the war, for those who refused to fight, and for those who were incarcerated in internment camps.

Other *nisei* would also write about the internment and their immigrant families. Artists Mine Okubo and Estelle Ishigo drew pictorial accounts of camp life. Okubo's *Citizen 13660*, published in 1946, was republished in 1983. Ishigo, a Caucasian woman married to a *nisei* internee, illustrated and wrote *Lone Heart Mountain* in 1972. Jeanne Wakatsugi Houston with James Houston published the memoir *Farewell to Manzanar* in 1973. Canadian Joy Kogawa published her novel about the Canadian Japanese internment, *Obasan*, in 1981. Yoshiko Uchida, well known for her young adult books about *nisei* childhood, published her autobiography *Desert Exile* in 1982. Mitsuye Yamada published two books of poetry, *Camp Notes* in 1976 and *Desert Run* in 1988. Karl Yoneda wrote *Ganbatte: Sixty Years Struggle of a Kibei Worker* in 1983. In 1990, Tōru Kanazawa wrote a novel based in Alaska, *Sushi and Sourdough*. Hiroshi Kashiwagi wrote the satiric play *Laughter and False Teeth*, published in the anthology

The Big Aiiieeeee! in 1991. Poet Albert Saijo, known for his travels with writer Jack Kerouac, published his beat-styled poetry in *Outspoken Rhapsody* in 1997.

Like Milton Murayama, other *nisei* in Hawaii have written about immigrant families on the islands. Playwright Edward Sakamoto wrote a trilogy of plays later published in *Hawaii No Ka Oi: The Kamiya Family Trilogy* in 1995. Jon Shirota, also a playwright, wrote *Lucky Come Hawaii and Pineapple White*, published in 1965 and 1972.

Several *sansei* poets have been particularly influential in the uncovering of an Asian US literary past and securing a place for this genre by editing important anthologies. Lawson Inada was one of the first poets of his generation to publish his work in a book-length anthology, *Before the War: Poems as They Happened*, as early as 1971. In 1974, he also co-edited one of the first and most famous anthologies of Asian US writing, *Aiiieeeee!: An Anthology of Asian American Writers*. Similarly, Janice Mirikitani published her own work of poetry, *Awake in the River*, in 1978, but also edited the Japanese American anthology *Ayumi* in 1980. Amy Uyematsu, co-editor of the first Asian US textbook, *Roots: An Asian American Reader*, published her book of poems *30 Miles from J-Town* in 1992. Poet Garrett Hongo, along with two books of poetry published in the 1980s, *Yellow Light* and *The River of Heaven*, and a memoir, *Volcano: A Memoir of Hawai'i* in 1995, also edited two books of Asian US work, *The Open Boat: Poems from Asian America* (1993) and *Under Western Eyes: Personal Essays from Asian America* (1995). A series of Japanese American anthologies under the heading *Fusion* was also edited by James Okutsu in the 1980s.

Like *nisei* writers, *sansei* have based their themes in regional homes or sites. David Mas Masumoto has written about a California farm community in his collection of short stories, *Silent Strength* (1984), and his memoir, *Epitaph for a Peach: Four Seasons on My Family Farm* (1995). R.A. Sasaki's stories in *'The Loom' and Other Stories* (1991) are based in San Francisco, as is Julie Shigekuni's novel *A Bridge between Us* (1995). Chicago-born Cynthia Kadohata published *The Floating World* (1989) set in the Midwest, but her second novel, *In the Heart of the Valley of Love* (1992), is set in Los Angeles. Sesshu Foster's book of poetry, *City Terrace: Field Manual* (1996), is set in east Los Angeles. Los Angeles-born Rick

Noguchi explores surfing in his book of poetry, *The Ocean Inside Kenji Takezo* (1996). Mystery writer Dale Furutani has published a second book in his *Ken Tanaka* sleuth series, *Death in Little Tokyo* (1997). Although Karen Tei Yamashita writes about Los Angeles in her novel, *Tropic of Orange* (1997), her first two novels are set in Brazil and based on her study of Japanese immigration to that country. Sylvia Watanabe has written a collection of short stories set in rural Hawaii, *Talking to the Dead* (1992), and Juliet Kono collected her poems in *Hilo Rains* in 1988. Also from Hawaii, Lois-Ann Yamanaka has worked the local pidgin into her writing and is the author of poetry, short stories and two novels, *Blu's Hanging* (1997) and *Heads by Harry* (1999). Many such writers from Hawaii have been supported and launched into publication by Bamboo Ridge Press. Canadian playwright Rick Shiomi has written about his community in Vancouver in plays such as *Yellow Fever* (1982) and *Uncle Tadao*. Linda Watanabe McFerrin's novel *Namako: Sea Cucumber* (1998) is set around a US military base in northern Japan. Also set in Japan is Ruth Ozeki's novel, *My Year of Meats* (1998).

Sansei, as well as younger *nisei* and post-war *issei* writers, some of mixed heritage, have recorded family and community histories and reflected on issues of identity. Momoko Iko's play *Gold Watch*, produced in 1971 and published in *Aiiieeeee!* in 1974, is the pre-war story of a rural immigrant family. James Masao Mitsui, from Washington, published in 1974 the first of three books of poetry, *Journal of the Sun*, describing scenes from evacuation, camp and family history. Similarly, Lonny Kaneko published a book of poetry, *Coming Home from Camp*, in 1986. Playwright Philip Kan Gotanda has, since the 1970s, written plays with particular attention to the development of *nisei* characters, among them *Songs for a Nisei Fisherman* and *The Wash*. David Mura, known for his open concerns about sexuality, published his memoir, *Turning Japanese*, in 1991 and his second book of poetry, *Colours of Desire*, in 1995. Holly Uyemoto was only eighteen when she published her first novel, *Rebel Without a Clue* in 1989. Ai, of mixed heritage and native of the South-west, is the author of five books of poetry, among them, *Killing Floors* (1978) and *Sin* (1986). Playwright Velina Hasu Houston used her Japanese and African American parentage as the subject of her plays, *Asa Ga Kimashita* (1993) and *Tea*. New York-based poet Kimiko Hahn, who published her third book *The Unbearable Heart* in 1997, has taken personal stories and traditional Japanese literature as themes for her work. Japanese-born Kyoko Mori has written two novels and a memoir, *The Dream of Water* (1995), tied to her experiences as a young immigrant.

For a comprehensive bibliography and understanding of the literature through the 1980s, Stan Yogi's article, 'Japanese American literature', published in *An Interpretive Companion to Asian American Literature*, edited by King-Kok Cheung, is an excellent source.

At present, the designation 'Japanese American literature' seems tenuous as writers of mixed heritage and multiple languages, writers of recent immigration and writers of Japanese descent in Latin America make their appearance, contribute new voices and inevitably expand the definition of American literature itself.

KAREN TEI YAMASHITA

Japanese cuisine overseas

Japanese immigration in the early twentieth century saw the first Japanese restaurants in the USA and South America with the local Japanese population supporting nieghbourhood establishments. The wave of restaurants and bars that developed across Asia to service a Japanese clientele during Japan's colonial and miltary expansions shut down rapidly with the defeat in 1945. A new wave of popularity developed gradually over the 1970s and again it was mainly first- and second-generation local Japanese families together with war brides who established a new generation of restaurants specialising in dishes easily adapted to a meat-oriented diet, e.g. *sukiyaki*, *shabu shabu* and *teppanyaki*. Today, it is sushi that is most often associated with Japanese cuisine overseas. Over the 1980s and 1990s Japanese cuisine has won a place for itself in the emerging global culture of food. Such key culinary trends as nouveau cuisine, nouveau Californian and Pacific Rim cuisine are strongly influenced by Japanese aesthetics of food preparation and presentation.

The most recent trend in exported Japanese food has been the rapid popularisation of Japanese-style noodles, ranging from the instant cup-of-noodles to fast-food noodle counters and upmarket gourmet noodle restaurants.

SANDRA BUCKLEY

Japanese economic miracle

The 'Japanese miracle' is commonly used to refer to Japan's recovery from the economic setbacks of the Second World War and the subsequent rapid growth of its economy from 1955 until the 1973 Oil Crisis. In addition to generating a keen interest in Japanese economic institutions and processes, the political and sociological changes wrought by Japan's 'miraculous' economic success profoundly shaped contemporary Japanese culture.

The appellation 'economic miracle' had earlier been applied to West Germany and other European countries and their recoveries from the Second World War. What distinguished the Japanese miracle from these was the historically unprecedented rapid rate of economic growth involved and the fact that Japan was an Asian country. Japan's real **Gross National Product** grew at an average annual rate of 10.0 percent between 1955 and 1973. This was nearly double the 5.6 percent of France and Italy, the two countries that had the highest contemporaneous average growth rates among the major industrialised countries. Japan's high growth rate naturally sparked the interest of economists, particularly in light of the fact that Japan's economic policies seemed to run counter to what was deemed appropriate in conventional economic thinking. Considerable energy was therefore channelled into explaining the reasons for Japan's superlative performance. A major part of this debate was over the degree to which 'industrial policy' on the part of the Japanese state fostered or hindered growth. Another bone of contention was the role of culture in the Japanese miracle. Initially, a popular interpretation was that certain features of Japanese 'tradition' were uniquely fitted to the task of modernisation. Among such 'traditional' values was group-oriented co-operative behaviour that was seen as essential not only in enterprise management but in fostering co-operation between business and government. Likewise, traditional forms such as the Japanese *ie* (household) were seen to have provided elemental patterns for distinctive institutional arrangements like the so-called Japanese employment system.

Beyond the debates over what 'caused' the 'miracle', it is clear that this period had profound political, sociological and cultural impacts. The promotion of the Japanese miracle performed an important political function domestically. Facilitation of the GNP growth emerged as a publicly emphasised government policy following the 1960 climax of the **Anpo struggle**. The **Liberal Democratic Party** (LDP) government of Ikeda Hayato abandoned the conservatives' earlier emphasis on 'hawkish' political issues and sought instead to maintain a 'low posture'. The government's fixation on GNP growth was epitomised in the quite popular **Plan to Double Income** launched in 1960. The LDP government, furthermore, engaged in conscious efforts to use government policies to assure that the fruits of the 'miracle' were spread widely throughout the population, and in particular among the less productive agricultural and small-scale retail sectors that were key constituencies of the ruling party. Although strongly contested at the margins, GNP growth was widely embraced and became something close to a source of national identity for a large segment of the population. It was not until the miracle's waning days during the early 1970s that accelerating inflation and rampant pollution problems tarnished this faith. Even thereafter, however, popular identification with Japan's economic success remained as a prominent trait.

Japan's social structure was transformed dramatically over the course of the 'miracle'. In 1955, for instance, a majority of Japan's working population was engaged in agriculture or in some other self-employed capacity. Twenty years later, this figure had dropped to just 30 per cent while the number of employees grew to 70 per cent, making Japan a nation of *sarariiman*. A massive shift of population from the countryside to Japan's major cities also occurred during this period transforming Japan from a predominantly agrarian to an urban-based country. In a counterflow, industrial development policies pursued by the government encouraged the movement of industry to the countryside, facilitating access of rural populations to industrial and service sectors jobs. The **family system** was dramatically transformed, with the older extended family being increasingly replaced by smaller nuclear units. **Income levels** grew substantially over the course of the 'miracle' and with this a mass consumption society emerged amid an increasingly 'post-industrial' population.

Cultural change was also induced by the Japanese 'miracle'. Even prior to the Second World War, popular culture in Japan had a relatively well-developed 'mass' quality, and such tendencies were strongly abetted by the changes that accompanied the 'miracle'. Economic growth during the miracle raised overall income levels and helped to reduce the socio-economic gaps that divided the rich and poor. It was precisely during the period when the Japanese miracle was at its height that popular opinion polls began to show that over 90 per cent of the Japanese considered themselves to be **middle class**. The mechanisation of housework through a variety of household electrical appliances freed up time for **leisure** activities, especially among housewives. Increased incomes also made possible the dispersal of access to the mass media for households of all strata. Radios, television and telephones became household fixtures, as did a wide variety of other communication and entertainment technologies. The result was the development and permeation of a distinctive mass culture that both built on domestic cultural forms and incorporated a wide range of 'Western' influences.

Internationally, the Japanese miracle clearly helped to increase Japan's power and influence. The country's economic 'success' not only inspired Asian leaders like Malaysia's Mohammed Mahathir to use economic growth as a way to calm internal social tensions, but also provided Japan with the surplus capital to facilitate comparable 'miracles' elsewhere in Asia through foreign direct investments and foreign aid. On a global scale, it is clear that the Japanese 'miracle' laid the foundation for Japan's current 'economic superpower' status.

See also: bureaucracy; management systems, Japanese; urban migration; village depopulation

Further reading

The Correspondents of the Economist (1963) *Consider Japan*, London: Gerald Duckworth and Co.

Yasusuke Murakami and Patrick, Hugh (eds) (1988–92) *The Political Economy of Japan*, vols 1–3, Stanford, CA: Stanford University Press.

LONNY E. CARLILE

Japanese influence on Western fashion

Over the 1970s, Japan had a strong impact on international fashion design. After the Second World War, the Westernisation of fashion progressed rapidly, the economy prospered and in step with the growing domestic economy Japanese fashion showed significant development. Mori Hanae became known in the USA with her designer line of women's fashion in Japanese silk. After this she became the first Japanese person to gain entry into the Parisian *haute couture*. The year 1970 saw a shift worldwide from *haute couture* to prêt-à-porter. When **Takada Kenzō** had débuted in Paris, his unpretentious, everyday clothing designs were an immediate hit. These clothes had their origins in images of Japanese farmers' dress and people-oriented workers' clothes. **Miyake Issei** was also just becoming known in Paris and New York in the early 1970s. His idea for clothing was a flat design that came from the concept of using only one piece of fabric or panels as in the production of kimono. A guiding principle for Western clothing is that the garment is three dimensional, fitting over the contours of the body. While for Japanese clothing the idea is to hang the cloth flat on the body and let the left-over fabric drape down. The spaces that are opened up on the garment in this design method are something that is distinctly Japanese. From the end of the 1980s came Miyake's Pleats series, which developed another innovative method where the pleats were added to the garment after all the cutting and sewing, in opposition to the conventional method. In this way, the contemporary Japanese textile and fashion industry has utilised the latest technologies creatively while still maintaining a firm grip on the foundation of the Japanese textile tradition: an absolute respect for fabric.

In the early 1980s, Rei Kawakubo and Yamamoto Yōji created a stir when they participated in the Paris collection. From a Western conception of beauty based on symmetry, their designs, which consisted primarily of black with an asymmetry created from rips and torn, draped fabric, seemed to have no relation to the contours of the body.

They appeared shabby and, above all, incomprehensible. However, one could say that this style represented the peculiar Japanese sense of beauty based on the notions of '*Wabi*' (the inherent beauty in disparity) and '*Sabi*' (the inherent beauty in solitude) – terms that may help create a cultural context for the quiet, asymmetrical simplicity of their designs. Japanese fashion captured the world's attention with these unexpected design concepts that seemed so opposed to familiar Western design. Into the 1990s Japanese fashion continued to have a subtle but undeniable influence on some of the most basic assumptions of style, texture and colour in Western design houses. Today, some of the leading European designers openly acknowledge their debt to Japanese design and openly gesture in their own designs to the trends pioneered by their Japanese colleagues.

AKIKO FUKAI

JAPANESE PAPER *see washi*

JAPANESE TRAGEDY, A *see Nihon no higeki*

Japayuki-san

'*Japayuki-san*' is a popular, but increasingly contested, label for South-East Asian immigrant women to Japan, stereotypically denoting those involved in the 'sex and entertainment' industry (**mizushōbai**), a range of occupations including singing and dancing, hostessing and prostitution.

The word *Japayuki-san* is a pun on the name of the *Karayuki-san*, the women who travelled from Japan to South-East Asia in the late nineteenth century, often being put to work as prostitutes. The word '*Karayuki-san*' is composed of three elements: '*Kara*', an archaic word for China, but here referring broadly to any overseas destination; '*yuki*', from the verb 'to go'; and '*san*', an honorific title. The word '*Japayuki-san*' replaces China with Japan, and thus refers to immigrants who come to Japan. While '*san*' is a non-gender-specific title, the word '*Japayuki-san*' generally refers to women, and can also connote sexualised occupations. One can now see male immigrant workers referred to as '*Japayuki-kun*', using the male-specific title '*kun*'. The word *Japayuki* also has currency among networks of migrant workers in South-East Asia and the non-governmental organisations who engage in advocacy for such migrant workers.

The coining of such labels as '*Japayuki-san*' and '*Japayuki-kun*' in the 1980s in Japan, and the spread of the word '*Japayuki-san*' to the countries that send migrant workers to Japan, reflects the changing economic relationships between Japan and other Asian countries. In the late nineteenth century and early twentieth century, it was Japan that sent emigrant workers to Hawaii, the USA and Latin America, with the *Karayuki-san* travelling to South-East Asia and as far afield as Australia, the West Coast of the USA and even Madagascar. Nowadays, it is Japan that attracts workers from South and South-East Asia, and North and South America. Although the government does not recognise the importation of unskilled labour, there is a small elite class of sojourners who work legally in banking, computing, business and education. Other immigrant workers enter Japan legally on trainee, student or entertainment visas, or may illegally overstay on tourist visas. They work in construction, manufacturing or the service sector.

Some commentators refer to *gaikokujin rōdōsha* (foreign workers), a label that focuses on foreignness, while sidestepping the distinctions between legal and illegal visa status. Advocacy groups prefer to refer to *kaigai dekasegi rōdōsha* (overseas migrant workers), or *Ajiajin dekasegi rōdōsha* (Asian migrant workers). The Immigration Department categorises people according to their visa status, legal or illegal, while some commentators refer to documented and undocumented workers. Statistics are compiled according to alien registration records and apprehensions of those who overstay or engage in activities not permitted under their visa category. Because so many immigrant workers are in Japan illegally, it is difficult to obtain reliable statistics on their numbers.

In the 1970s, labour migration to Japan largely took the form of small numbers of skilled migrants from First-World countries, but new trends emerged in the 1980s with workers from South-East Asia entering Japan to take up jobs in the service sector, manufacturing and the construction industry. Rising numbers of illegal immigrant workers reflected the rapid growth of the Japanese economy in the mid- to late 1980s, the rapid appreciation of the yen from 1985 and the disparity between wage levels in Japan and other countries in the region. The high proportion of women from South-East Asia reflects the contemporary situation in Thailand and the Philippines. Industrialisation and agrarian transformation have determined young women's migration from rural areas to cities or overseas, while local economies may be dependent on the remittances of these emigrants. An initial pattern of feminised migration into the female Japanese service sector shifted to also include significant numbers of male workers in construction and manufacturing. Migration was not halted by the recession in the Japanese economy in the early 1990s, or the Asian economic crisis of the late 1990s, because Japanese wages are still far ahead of those in other countries of the region.

Despite the relatively small number of workers involved, immigrant labour has become an important structural feature of construction, manufacturing and service industries in Japan. Particular regions provide different proportions of male or female workers, with quite distinctive employment patterns for male and female immigrants. In alien registration statistics, those countries with striking gender imbalance in favour of males have been Bangladesh, Iraq and Pakistan. Females are disproportionately represented in statistics from the Philippines and Thailand. Similar patterns appear in statistics on illegal immigrants. Among legal workers by residence status, entertainers are the largest single category. Entertainers enter Japan under a legal visa category, but this status often masks employment in hostess bars or massage parlours. Illegal male workers are overwhelmingly employed in construction and factory labour – those jobs described as dirty, difficult and dangerous (*kitanai, kitsui, kiken*) – while the largest categories for illegal immigrant women are bar hostess, factory work, prostitution, dishwashing and waitressing. The largest suppliers of immigrant workers by nationality are South Korea, Thailand, China, the Philippines and Malaysia. The year 1988 marked a major a turning point, with significant increases in total numbers of illegal immigrant workers from a wider range of countries and males outnumbering females for the first time.

Further reading

Asian Women's Association (eds) (1998) *Women from across the Seas: Migrant Workers in Japan*, Tokyo: Asian Women's Association.

Komai Hiroshi (1996) *Migrant Workers in Japan*, London: Kegan Paul International.

Mackie, V. (1998) "'*Japayuki* Cinderella girl'': Containing the immigrant other', *Japanese Studies* 18(1) (May): 45–63.

Piquero Ballescas, Maria Rosario (1993) *Filipino Entertainers in Japan: An Introduction*, Quezon: Foundation for Nationalist Studies.

Ventura, R. (1992) *Underground in Japan*, London: Jonathan Cape.

VERA MACKIE

Japlish

The Japanese language has always demonstrated remarkable flexibility in periods of intense contact with other cultures. The eighth to ninth centuries saw the adaptation of Chinese characters to the writing of Japanese, and the borrowing of much Chinese vocabulary. Today, as much as 50 per cent of Japanese vocabulary is of Chinese origin. The more recent exposure to English and European languages has seen the emergence of Japlish, which refers to the forms of adaptation of English vocabulary into the Japanese sound system.

Japlish loan words are closely linked to new trends in consumer and popular culture, and so

even the term *nauii* (nowy), which was used to describe new trends over the early to mid-1990s, has now itself fallen out of popular use. English words are first rendered into a Japanese pronounciation and then frequently abbreviated:

supermarket – sūpaa maaketto – sūpaa
apartment – apaatomento – apaato
department store – depaatomento sutoaa – depaato
word processor – waado purosessaa – waapuro

Japlish is written in *katakana*, the syllabary used for imported words (excluding Chinese) The creation of Japlish is largely driven by copy writers in the major advertising agencies, who drive new products and market concepts through extensive media campaigns, often structured around a new Japlish term or product name. Less careful use of Japlish has led many foreigners in Japan to collect the more outrageous and humorous examples that can be found in advertising, on T-shirts, posters, postcards and stationery.

SANDRA BUCKLEY

jazz, classical

Jazz was introduced to Japan around 1920 as the Japanese colonial empire was expanding from Taiwan and Korea to include German possessions ceded to it by the Treaty of Versailles (in the South Pacific and on the Chinese mainland). The introduction of jazz was facilitated by years of training in European classical music. Formal training from the late nineteenth century rarely included study of traditional Japanese music. Jazz came to be associated with social dancing in the 1920s. The first centres of jazz activity were in Ōsaka and Kobe, in the dance hall and the café. The top Kobe bands were of Filipino origin. Jazz bands from this US colony were the primary channel for the transmission of live performance techniques to Japan.

There are a number of figures who have been offered as the first Japanese jazz musicians, including Kikuchi Shigeya, and the Masudas. It is said the Masudas started playing jazz after the 1923 Kantō Earthquake. Ida Ichiro is generally credited with the professionalisation of the Japanese jazz music world. Some claim that he brought jazz from Ōsaka to Tokyo in April 1928. He predominately played tunes by the Caucasian band leader Paul Whiteman. Whiteman 'orchestrated' jazz, and his approach largely defined jazz in Japan at this time (Whiteman is now perhaps best known for having commissioned 'Rhapsody in Blue'). The dominant recording companies in the 1920s were affiliates of Euro-American corporations: Polydor, Nippon Columbia and Nippon Victor. These companies began domestic production of popular music in the late 1920s and created the Japanese song genre known as *ryukoka*. The jazz song was a sub-genre of *ryukoka*. Nippon Columbia and Nippon Victor both released versions of Nimura Sadaichi's 'My Blue Heaven' and 'Song of Araby'. Subsequent jazz songs tended to follow the same format – lyrics were usually sung in both Japanese and English. Hattori Ryoichi was perhaps the first Japanese jazz song composer. Hattori is often credited with having invented the Japanese blues. The most famous jazz vocalists in inter-war Japan were Japanese-American singers who recorded and performed in Japan. Japanese-American performers became important because of their ability to sing jazz songs convincingly in both English and Japanese. Their story is an important chapter in Japanese-American history that has yet to be written.

The first sound motion picture released in Japan, the 1929 American musical short *Marching On*, featured a jazz soundtrack. Jazz became a broad topic of conversation with the release of the movie soundtrack tune, 'Tokyo March' (1929). 'Tokyo March' almost single-handedly defined the image of the modernist generation for better and worse. Its pulsating rhythm track, references to public dancing, alcohol, passion of the moment and Marxist boys with long hair provoked conservative ire. The national radio network NHK soon prohibited its airplay. Jazz became even more widely popular in the early 1930s. It nevertheless continued to occupy an ambivalent position in Japanese culture. For musicians, a trip to the Japanese colonial frontier of Shanghai served as a jazz proving ground and source of legitimacy second only to visiting the USA. In this way, Japan's purported rollback of Euro-American colonial power in East Asia in the late 1930s ironically brought Japan closer to the cultural

currents nationalist ideologues identified with the US enemy. It is interesting to note that the fascination with African American culture as primitivism so important to European modernism was largely missing from the writings of Japanese jazz critics of the 1930s. E. Taylor Atkins has suggested that perhaps primitivism held less appeal to a non-Western nation so intent on having demonstrated its modernity.

In editorials, jazz was pointed to as a root cause of Japan's increasing intimacy with the Western world, and the concomitant erosion of 'traditional' culture. For some, Japanese society and culture as such were threatened by dance hall culture. One of the reasons jazz was so controversial was its purported ties to alternative gender roles: according to some the rhythm of jazz was the impetus for the lifestyles of the era's playgirls and playboys, imagined as the promiscuous modern girl (*moga*) and the foppish modern boy (*moba*). Yet jazz was not only a form of music – it symbolised Japan's complex relation to global cultural trends. Rather than submerge themselves within the stream of modernist Americanism, many Japanese musicians attempted to compose a pan-Asian jazz compatible with the pan-Asian ideology of Japan's expanding, colonial empire. The cosmopolitanism of the 1920s, however, quickly gave rise to the policy of 'culturism'. Intellectuals and government officials of various stripes called for a return to (an imagined) traditional culture. Popular music was to play an important part in the spiritual mobilisation of the people. Military songs (*gunka*) and a new type of music known as light music (a transparently Japanised form of jazz song) were to promote the social consensus jazz was alleged to have disturbed. While there was apparently no single, enforceable jazz ban in place throughout the period, in official circles jazz was clearly seen as the music of a decadent enemy.

These debates concerning jazz strongly resonate with contemporaneous challenges to Eurocentrism in Japanese philosophy of history expressed in such influential roundtable discussions as 'The Standpoint of World History and Japan' (Chūō kōron, 1941). Older models of world history that had been grounded in a narrative of European development, were replaced by a conception of world history as a moral war between the USA and Japan to be fought out on the Chinese mainland. Within this schema, Japan not only stands in 'for' and acts 'on behalf of' East Asia but the historical agency of the entire non-Western world is confined to Japan alone. Interestingly, this schema similarly privileges the USA as the historical agent that exclusively represents 'the West'. In other words, this 1940s Japanese critique of Eurocentrism can be seen as not only having failed to challenge Japanese and US nationalisms but as having directly reinforced them. This variety of mutual historical narcissism tended to erase the rest of the world from world history.

In the post-war period, jazz regained the ambivalence of the pre-war period. While it sometimes expressed the optimism of a Japan in ruins looking toward the future (e.g. the music of **Misora Hibari**), for conservatives it still figured an anti-social stance that subverted youth and infected Japan from abroad (jazz in the Sun Tribe films). The Allied Occupation was certainly an incomparable opportunity for Japanese musicians seeking direct contact with US jazz performance tradition. Throughout the Occupation, Japanese jazz musicians were also steadily employed in the entertainment of US troops. From this point on, Japanese jazz enthusiasts often expressed an infatuation with African American culture somewhat reminiscent of the beat poets in the USA. Terayama Shūji, for example, conceived the notion of the 'yellow negro' as expressive of Japanese oppression as a 'yellow race' comparable to that of the oppression of African Americans. At present, racialised stereotypes persist with astonishing tenacity in discussions of popular music. Many of these conceptions were first articulated in US conversations about jazz. The situation is further exacerbated when the conversation is expanded to include discussion of Japan.

The culturism of post-war US Japan studies and Japanese neo-conservatism bears significant responsibility for the situation. If white Americans can't play the blues, where does this leave the Japanese? Atkins has outlined a chronology of strategies of authentication: first, replication of US jazz practice and lifestyle; second, trips to Shanghai and the USA; third, asserting an affinity with the non-white races; and, fourth, efforts to indigenise or nationalise jazz. This chronology demonstrates that even present-day alternatives remain largely trapped within the

positions mapped out in the pre-war and wartime Overcoming Modernity debate. Each alternative appears to reinforce rather than challenge Japanese and US nationalism, a shortcoming that continues to be characteristic of many present-day Japanese challenges to Eurocentrism.

As long as the ideology of jazz is tied to authenticity of expression, the antinomies of identity politics will be difficult to avoid, i.e. 'It's a black thing, you wouldn't understand', 'This is *the* Japanese understanding of X', 'You play jazz very well for a Japanese musician', etc. The connection of jazz to State Department promotion of the American Way during the cold war also suggests that increasing attention needs to be paid to the implication of African American art (in addition to the entertainment industry) in the articulation of US empire.

Jazz was an important aspect of radical Japanese student culture of the 1960s and 1970s. It was perceived as a marginal, minority music that challenged a Japanese status quo defined by the canon of Western classical music and the disposable musical products of the culture industry. By the mid-1970s, jazz had carved out a relatively stable niche for itself in Japan. Over the past fifty years, jazz has increasingly come to be treated as a form of high art in both Japan and the USA. Japan is the richest jazz market in the world. The Japanese market for jazz recordings has kept older American recordings available more consistently than the US market. A number of very gifted jazz and jazz-influenced performers of the post-war period came from Japan: Akiyoshi Toshiko, Moriyasu Shōtarō, Sato Masahiko, Shiraki Hideo, Togashi Masahiko, Watanabe Sadao, Yano Akiko and Yamashita Yōsuke. Given these facts alone, jazz clearly also has a legitimate place outside the direct experience of the African American community. Regardless of where jazz in Japan may ultimately go from here, it survives as a trace of various Japanese culture wars conducted over the better part of the twentieth century, as an essential chapter in the world history of jazz, African American music, Asian American history and US media culture.

Further reading

Atkins, Everett Taylor (1997) 'This is our music: Authenticating Japanese jazz, 1920–1980',

Ph.D. dissertation, University of Illinois, History Department.

DeVere Brown, Sidney (1980) 'Jazz in Japan: Its sources and developments, 1925–1952', Proceedings, Annual Meeting, South-west Conference on Asian Studies, New Orleans, pp. 127–39.

Koichi Uchida (1976) *Nihon no jazu-shi* Tokyo: Swing Journal-sha.

Masahisa Segawa (1975–7) 'Nippon no jazu shi', *Swing Journal*, twenty-three-part serial from July 1975 to June 1977.

Moore, Joe B. (1998) 'Studying jazz in postwar Japan: Where to begin?', in *Japanese Studies* 18(3): 265–80.

Shoichi Yui (1975–7) 'Nippon popyura ongaku shi', *Min'on*, thirty-five-part serial from January 1975 to December 1977.

Shuhei Hosokawa (1989–94) 'Seiyo ongaku no nihonka, taishūka', *Music Magazine*, sixty-one-part serial from April 1989 to April 1994.

MARK ANDERSON

jazz, free

Free jazz first took off in Japan via import records in the early 1960s. The Jazz Academy formed in 1961 with guitarist Takayanagi Masayuki at its centre, and launched musicians such as Kikuchi Masabumi, Togashi Masahiko, Toyozumi Yoshisaburō and Watanabe Sadao. This core group of challenging musicians later metamorphosed into the New Century Music Research Centre.

Those who listened to the classical jazz (see **jazz, classical**) of the 1963 Gin Pari (Ginza Paris) club sessions would have found the emergence of free jazz unexpected. Free jazz moved into the limelight after the John Coltrane Quintet visited in 1966, and became more acceptable in the jazz *kissa* cafés so vital to its dissemination. For musicians impatient with hard-bop and four-beat jazz, Coltrane's performance introduced a new musical syntax – a tense collaborative relationship based on free rhythm and free sound. Jazz *kissa* customers, mainly students, intellectuals and curious bohemians, listened intently to jazz records, rarely broadcast on the air, at a high volume unplayable anywhere else. Takayanagi's breaking of conventional jazz guitar technique followed in the wake of Coltrane; an additional impetus was made by Sato Masahiko's return from the Berklee School of Music in 1968.

In 1969, three pivotal free jazz units formed: New Directions, made up of Takayanagi Masayuki (g, 1932–91), Yoshizawa Motoharu (b, 1931–98), Toyōsumi Yoshisaburō (d, 1943–); the ESSG (Experimental Space Sound Group), made up of Togashi Masahiko (ds, 1940–), Sato Masahiko (p, 1941–), Oki Itaru (tp, 1941–); and the Yamashita Yōsuke Trio, which also included Moriyama Takeo (ds, 1945–) and Nakamura Seiichi (ts, ss, 1947–). These groups played largely in Shinjuku jazz *kissa* frequented by anti-establishment youth such as the Pit Inn New Jazz Hall and Taro. Writer Nakagami Kenji captures this atmosphere in his essay collection *Destroy It, Said Ayler*.

As seen at the 1970 Berlin Jazz Festival, even mainstream jazz artists like Hino Teramasu engaged with free jazz rhythm and tone structure. Few free jazz musicians flaunted their politics, but some collaborated with leftist movements, as seen in the sympathy held by free jazz critics like Hiraoka Seimei and Aikura Hisato for the student movements, the Yamashita Yōsuke Trio's 1969 performance of 'Dancing Kojiki' at the Waseda barricades or the improvisational soundtrack by Togashi Masahiko and Takagi Masateru to the Wakamatsu Koji/Adachi Masao film *A.K.A. Serial Killer*, based on Nagayama Norio's crime spree. Attracting the most concert-goers was the Yamashita Trio, with their energetic, over-the-top performances, dubbed 'sports jazz' by Yamashita.

The most charismatic improviser surfacing in the 1970s was Abe Kaoru (as, 1949–78). Renowned for his dramatic live performances, his music took from Anthony Braxton's *For Alto* and early Albert Ayler, and emphasised self-destructive rather than constructive improvisation. Abe was rapidly mythologised after his early death; his impact is seen in the many albums recorded and posthumously distributed by fans.

The biggest event in the early 1970s was the fourteen-day festival Power and Inspiration that took place in Shinjuku in 1973. Featuring free jazz supergroups, the festival also introduced bands such as Now Music Ensemble, led by Fujikawa Yoshiaki (as), which later became the Eastashia

Orchestra, as well as Nakamura Tetsuya, who had played in New York with Joe Bowie (tbn) and Oliver Lake (as). While not free jazz proper, groups such as the Seikatsu Kōjyō Iinkai (Committee to Improve Daily Life), formed by Umezu Kazutoki (as) and Harada Yoriyuki (p), mixed free improvisation with quirky humor.

The fact that the first recording in 1975 by conservatory-trained improvisers Umezu and Harada took place in New York with Ahmed Abdullar (tp), William Parker (b) and Rashid Shinan (ds) shows the increasing contact of Japanese free jazz with musicians abroad. Oki emigrated to Paris in the mid-1970s, while Toyozumi temporarily lived in Chicago. Beginning with Cecil Taylor's 1973 visit, and the 1974 visit by the Art Ensemble of Chicago, free jazz players began to tour regularly in Tokyo. Visits to Japan facilitated by the critic Aida 'Aquirax' Akira in the late 1970s by Steve Lacey, Derek Bailey and Milford Graves provoked collaborations with Japanese musicians.

Free jazz developed more loosely in the 1980s, focusing on improvisation and crossing over into underground music and contemporary music (*gendai ongaku*). Saxophonist Shinoda Masami of the Seikatsu Kōjyō Iinkai played with Jagakara, a powerful funk group, and led the radical brass trio Compostela. Pianist-composer Takahashi Yūji, who studied under Iannis Xenakis, played with Togashi Masahiko and Sato Masahiko.

Guitarist and turntable musician Ōtomo Yoshihide, who has studied under Takayanagi, has performed with experimental musicians such as Jon Rose, composed the music for Chen Kaige's *The Blue Kite* and written for Japanese *koto* and *shamisen* ensembles. Ties to folk-ethnic music can be seen in Umezu Kazutoki's Betsu ni nani mo klezmer band, and Sakata Akira's performances with Ainu musicians.

In the 1990s, the term 'free jazz' encompasses nearly any type of free-form improvisation, particularly acoustic improvisation. Many musicians, such as the Fedayien trio, Nonaka Goku (ds) and his Ningen Kokuhō (National Living Treasure) and Fuwa Daisuke's big band Shibushirazu, have strived to maintain ties to classical jazz syntax as well as to improvisation. Priority on working in different styles (including the classical four-beat

jazz and rock beat), and in emphasising collaboration, distinguishes them from earlier free jazz.

In the late 1990s, it is no longer simple to isolate out free jazz from other genres. The acceleration in cross-Pacific traffic in musicians was accompanied by changes in style. Currently in Japan, the factor that unifies musicians working in the realm of jazz – which is to say often playing at jazz clubs, recording on jazz labels and finding themselves in the record stores filed under 'Japanese jazz' – is most likely the fact that they are producing music in the loose association of musicians who prioritise improvisation. In this respect, Japan's free jazz continues in synch with the international improvisation music scene.

Select discography

The Gin Pari Session, *Three Blind Mice*, 1963.
Sato Masahiko Trio, *Palladium*, Toshiba Express, 1969.
Togashi Masahiko Quartet, *We Now Create*, Nippon Victor, 1969.
Yamashita Yōsuke Trio, *Mina no sekandoteema*, Nippon Victor, 1969.
Abe Kaoru, *Mort à credit*, ALM, 1975.
Seikatsu Kōjō Iinkai, *This is music is this?*, Disk Union, 1978.
Power and Inspiration 14, *Trio*, 1973.
Nonaka Goku and Ningen Kokuhō, *Jolly*, Chocolate City, 1990.
Fedayien, *First*, Chocolate City, 1990.
Takayanagi Masayuki and Abe Kaoru, *Kaitaiteki Kōkan* (Destructive Communion), DIW, 1990 1970).

Further reading

London Musicians' Collective (1996) *Resonance* 4(2).

HOSOKAWA SHŪHEI, TRANS. ANNE McKNIGHT

JETRO

JETRO – Japan External Trade Organisation (Nihon Bōeki Shinkōkai) – was established by MITI in 1958 to consolidate Japan's efforts in export promotion. The chief function of JETRO prior to the mid-1970s was to provide information to help Japanese companies, both large and small, expand exports. JETRO offices were set up in major overseas cities to collect market information and provide services to firms interested in expanding exports. As Japan's exports flourished, and its balance of trade surplus became a political problem in the 1980s, JETRO's major role changed to promote imports to Japan. JETRO also supports a wide range of specialist services and facilities for foreign firms in Japan itself, including Business Support Centres located in major Japanese cities that assist overseas business people in launching their marketing efforts in Japan. On top of providing free office space, these are staffed with advisers who provide complementary consulting services. Special support is also given to overseas housing companies in the form of subsidised Imported Housing Exhibitions ('model home parks') in suburban locations, which introduce Japanese consumers to popular models of imported housing. Similarly, JETRO provides a number of Imported Automobile Showrooms to exhibit imported automobiles and auto parts to consumers.

DAVID EDGINGTON

jinsei annai

'Life advice' is the term often given to describe the extremely popular advice columns published in the daily newspapers and weekly and monthly magazines in Japan. While the majority of advice columns appear in women's magazines, there are also a number of major news dailies offering the same service to readers. The *Yomiuri* is one of Japan's largest circulation dailies and has one of the most well-known newspaper advice columns. The majority of letters come from women under thirty and the most popular topics are related to marital and household issues. The role of the advice column in Japan needs to be placed in context for its full significance to be understood. The extensive population migration from rural areas into cities over the post-war period, combined with the emergence of the nuclear-

family model and new patterns of high-density urban housing and suburbanisation, have seen an increasing number of young married women struggling with problems in isolation from family members, long-term friendships or well-established community networks. These columns, as they have proliferated over the post-war years, offered women a venue where their questions and concerns could be aired with relative anonymity and receive a serious reception and a reputable response.

Advice columns flowed over into other areas of print media, perhaps most notably comics (**manga**). In the 1990s, it is common for *manga* to carry an advice column focused on the target readership. Teenage girls write in seeking advice on everything from contraception to **enjo kōsai** and domestic violence. *Bishonen* comics, which have a high-school, teenage-girl readership and a young-adult, gay male readership, cater to a wide range of questions concerning sexual identity and sexual practice. At a more mundane level, the wide range of consumer guide magazines offer help in locating products, pricing comparisons and questions of taste and trends. The less consumer-focused advice columns offer an opportunity to follow shifting patterns of uncertainty and change in the lives of readers, especially young women, over the last five decades. The mini-komi alternative media produced by minority groups such as Korean Japanese (see **Koreans in Japan**) or migrant brides, gay rights groups, feminist grass-roots groups, etc. has also taken up the advice column as an important vehicle for allowing community members both to seek a voice for issues they have no other venue for, and to hopefully receive some useful feedback or advice from experts or even just the shared experiences of other readers.

Further reading

McKinstry, J. and A. (1991) *Jinsei Annai: Glimpses of Japan through a Popular Advice Column*, New York: Sharpe.

SANDRA BUCKLEY

Jōkyō

Making its first appearance in 1968, during the height of the student movement, the New Left journal *Jōkyō* (Situations) brought together unorthodox currents in left-wing thought (both from Japan and abroad) and practical experiences from protests. Though *Jōkyō* was and is open to many currents of thought from radical conservatism to Trotskyism, many of the early editors and contributors had been members of the Bund (League of Revolutionary Communists). The New Left philosopher Hiromatsu Wataru provided much of the initial financial outlay and published many of his most significant pieces in the journal. *Jōkyō* writers and editors attempted to politicise intellectual life, and, at the same time, to present the best of New Left theory to activists, especially those in the student movement. The early *Jōkyō* ran reportage on foreign movements, New Left reinterpretations of Marxist theory and manifestos from the Zenkyōtō movement. Feeling that the journal had lost the connection between theory and practice it had originally forged between the student movement and intellectuals, Jōkyō ceased publication in 1975. In an attempt to reinvigorate radical critiques within Japanese political and intellectual life, Koga Noboru and others revived the journal in 1990.

GUY YASKO

jōyō kanji

From 1946, the Ministry of Education stipulated a set of 1,850 **kanji** (characters) as '*tōyō kanji*' for people to use in daily life. These characters were considered the minimum number for functional adult literacy and were required learning over the period of compulsory education. However, in 1981, the number of characters was increased to 1,945 and these were renamed '*jōyō kanji*', meaning 'frequently used'.

It is the aim of the government that *jōyō kanji* embody a standardised norm and are widely used in general social life including laws and decrees, official documents, newspapers, periodical magazines, visual media and so forth. The existence of this basic set of *jōyō kanji* does not restrict the use of other *kanji* in science and technology, art and other special academic fields. The range of *kanji* used in place names and personal names far exceeds *jōyō kanji* with many specialised readings, and this requires the extensive use of the syllabic *hiragana* to gloss the pronunciation of these less common characters on public documents and signage.

SHUN IKEDA

Joryū Bungaku Prize

The Joryū Bungaku (Women's Literature) Prize was originally established in 1946 but was re-established in its present format in 1961 by the Fujin Kōron Magazine where the results are published. The prize is normally awarded once a year to the best work of fiction by a female author or authors. Most major women novelists have been awarded the prize, for example, in 1963 the distinguished novelist Nogami Yaeko won the award for her novel Hideyoshi to Rikyū (Hideyoshi and Rikyū), in 1973 the equally famous author Kōda Aya won it for *Tō* (The Fight), first published in 1965, and in 1975 the eminent novelist **Ōba Minako** won it for *Garakuta hakubutsukan* (The Junk Museum). Other important works awarded this prize include **Tsushima Yūko**'s *Choji* (Child of Fortune) and the novelist and critic Takenishi Hiroko's *Kangensai* (Symphony), both in 1978. In 1980, the prominent novelist Sono Ayako won the prize for *Kami no Yogoreta Te* (Watcher from the Shore) and three years later the author Hayashi Kyōko won the award for her novel *Shanhai* (Shanghai).

LEITH MORTON

jūdō

Kano Jigorō founded the modern sport of jūdō in 1882 when he opened the Kōdōkan School of Jūdō based on the *jujitsu* unarmed combat techniques of the samurai. He was active in the repopularisation of martial arts in Japan after a period of disenchantment with these traditional sports in the wake of rapid Westernisation. Today, the

International Foundation of Jūdō is located in Paris and the sport is popular worldwide with some 5 million members of registered clubs. Jūdō for men was first included in the Olympics in 1964 at the Tokyo Games and women's olympic jūdō was approved from 1992. Jūdō is one of the more popular school club activities in Japan.

Jūdō literally means 'the gentle way' and this sport involves three groups of fighting techniques – throwing, grappling and attack on vital points. A match is won when one of the contestants is awarded a full point by the judge. If no point is won then the judge can determine the winner or call a draw. Agility and mental focus combine in this sport to create smooth and flowing movements. An important element of jūdō is learning to use the other party's force and strength of attack to your own advantage. The goal is to pin down or overwhelm the opponent using any of the approved techniques. Kicking and hitting are not allowed. The loose white top and trousers worn in jūdō are similar to those worn in karate but the upper garment is made of a heavier weave. Belts are coloured to represent the system of ranks (*dan*) and classes (*kyū*) originally developed by Kano.

SANDRA BUCKLEY

juku

Juku is the Japanese term for private tutorial, enrichment, remedial, preparatory and cram schools that form a parallel system of education to government schools. Since government schools are theoretically bound by the principles of equality and conformity, *juku* become the place where students are differentially assisted depending on their needs. Students are often grouped by ability rather than grade level. There are both non-academic and academic *juku*, with the academic rigor increasing over time and peaking at middle school in preparation for high-school entrance exams. *Juku* range in form from huge corporate office spaces serving thousands of students at one time to private lessons in the home of a tutor. *Juku* usually meet after school and after extracurricular activities, that is from 7:00 to 10:00 p.m. and on weekends. Since *juku* are supported with student

fees, not all students can attend; however, most families find ways to pay the costs. Parents perceive *juku* as a way to provide increased educational and social opportunities for their child. *Yobiko* is a specific form of *juku* for **rōnin**, high-school students who have not passed the exam to the university of their choice. The focus is on examination preparation, usually for one year, full time.

JUNE A. GORDON

JUMIN UNDŌ *see* residents' movements

just-in-time delivery

The concept of just-in-time (JIT) delivery can be traced to the 'lean-production' manufacturing system developed by Toyota Motor Corporation since the 1950s. Often referred to as the Toyota production system, the JIT system is the product of incremental improvements by Toyota over several decades. The distribution networks of US supermarket chains helped inspire the JIT system, which was first applied by Toyota in 1963.

The system is geared to producing what individual customers want, when they want it. JIT ensures that only the necessary items in the necessary quantities are produced at the necessary time, thus reducing the need for inventories of parts. Each workstation in a factory determines its output by consultation with the next workstation and informs suppliers of what is required. The requirements are communicated by *kanban* (cards or signs). The necessary component must arrive at the appropriate workstation at the specified time for the JIT system to work. A factory line sequence schedule specifies the order in which various products come through assembly lines, ensuring that one product is completed as the next is introduced. If defects are found at any stage, components cannot be immediately replaced so the entire factory line must stop. The process encourages zero defects and the higher the product and component quality the lower will be the cost of production. The *kanban* system is an information system that circulates the cards in Toyota factories, and among suppliers and their factories. While it reduces high inventory costs, it is, more importantly, part of the transition from mass production to a more flexible manufacturing system that seeks to reduce production defects, increase productivity and reduce the cost of production. One of the outcomes of the JIT system has been that not only Toyota but its parts suppliers have been forced to rationalise their production and management. Computerisation and online ordering systems have further streamlined JIT processes in the 1990s.

Although the JIT system has attracted worldwide attention since the 1970s, there are difficulties associated with transferring JIT abroad due to the need for close working relationships with a small number of proximate suppliers. Related labour issues, such as multi-skilling and flexible work schedules, often generate union resistance in other management–labour cultures.

Further reading

Cole, W.E. and Mogab, J.W. (1995) *The Economics of Total Quality Management: Clashing Paradigms in the Global Market*, Cambridge, MA: Blackwell Publishers.

Womack, J.P., Jones, D.T. and Roos, D. (1991) *The Machine that Changed the World: The Story of Lean Production*, New York: Harper Perennial.

MORRIS LOW

K

kabuki

Kabuki, which until the early twentieth century flourished as a form of popular theatrical entertainment, has in the post-war period taken a position alongside **nō**, *kyōgen* and the *bunraku* puppet theatre as one of Japan's classical performing arts. Originating at the beginning of the Edo Period (1600–1867) as a stage entertainment performed principally by women, by the end of the seventeenth century *kabuki* had evolved under government-imposed restrictions and the influence of *bunraku* into a complex theatrical art performed by an all-male cast. In its heyday, several troupes and theatres operated in each of the three major cities, Edo (Tokyo), Kyōto and Ōsaka. Unlike many Western forms of drama, *kabuki* has always been primarily a performance art, with an emphasis on acting skill and visual presentation rather than dramatic text or plot.

With the coming of Western influence in the Meiji Period (1868–1912), attempts were made to reform *kabuki* into a more realistic and restrained literary theatre. Although some new plays reflecting the changing times were added to the repertoire at this time, the reform effort was gradually abandoned as other, more directly Western-inspired theatrical genres began to emerge.

The post-war period has seen *kabuki*'s transition from a popular to a classical theatre. The period itself began with a sense of crisis, due both to the death of several leading actors during or shortly after the war and to the ban imposed by the Occupation authorities on the performance of many classic *kabuki* plays because of their supposed 'anti-democratic' sentiments. The ban was eventually lifted, however, and *kabuki* survived the crisis, but popularity has never returned to pre-war levels. Many of the efforts in the post-war period to promote *kabuki* have, indirectly at least, contributed to its transition into a classical theatre. The government-funded National Theatre, for example, which opened in 1966, has provided a venue for the staging of classical *kabuki* plays free of the demands of commercial production.

Important also have been the efforts of actors such as Nakamura Ganjirō (b. 1931), who, continuing the work of early post-war producer, director and critic Takechi Tetsuya (1912–88), has attempted in his performances to recreate the *kabuki* of the early Edo Period. In contrast, another actor, Ichikawa Ennosuke III (b. 1939), has attempted to draw the crowds back to the *kabuki* theatre both by reviving spectacular but long-neglected plays from the nineteenth century and by creating new *kabuki* spectacles known as 'Super *kabuki*'. Other leading actors whose performances have helped maintain an interest in *kabuki* include Matsumoto Koshirō IX (b. 1942), Nakamura Kichiemon II (b. 1944), Ichikawa Danjurō XII (b. 1946), and the *onnagata* (player of female roles) Bandō Tamasaburō (b. 1950). Today, many of the top actors also sometimes take on roles in other forms of theatre, as well as occasionally appearing in films or television series. There is regular television broadcasting of *kabuki* plays, which is intended to promote new audience interest in live theatre performances and is often accompanied by commentary and interviews with actors and musicians.

Performances of *kabuki* are held regularly at the Kabuki-za and the National Theatre in Tokyo, the Minami-za in Kyōto and the Shōchiku-za in Ōsaka, as well as less frequently in other theatres around Japan.

Further reading

Brandon, J. and Leiter, S. (eds) (forthcoming) *Kabuki Plays on Stage*, 4 vols, Honolulu: University of Hawaii Press.

Kominz, L. (1997) *The Stars Who Created Kabuki: Their Lives, Loves and Legacy*, Tokyo: Kōdansha International.

Leiter, S. (ed.) (2001) *The Kabuki Reader: Essays in Japanese Theatre History and Performance*, Armonk, NY: M.E. Sharpe.

Okamoto Shiro (2001) *The Man Who Saved Kabuki: Faubion Bowers and Theatre Censorship in Occupied Japan*, trans. S. Leiter, Honolulu: University of Hawaii Press.

WILLIAM LEE

Kadokawa

Kadokawa shoten was founded in Tokyo in 1945 by Kadokawa Gen'yoshi., a Japanese literature scholar. Following the leads of Iwanami (1927) and Shinchōsha (1928), Kadokawa launched a successful paperback series, Kadokawa Bunko in 1949, which offered works in modern Japanese literature at affordable prices. A paperback publishing boom ensued.

Kadokawa's second venture was the publication in 1952 of the sixty-volume *Shōwa bungaku zenshū*, a series that included representative and entertaining literary works from the Shōwa Period.

Kadokawa Haruki succeeded his father in the business and continued to make strides in marketing paperback books. Kadokawa's aim was to promote a new genre of multi-media publishing. He initiated a tie-up between book publishing and the film industry, calling his venture 'media-mix'. Kadokawa stressed that books sold movies and movies sold books.

In the 1980s, Kadokawa Haruki took on another challenge when he put out *Tokyo Walker*, a weekly magazine guide to movies, plays, exhibitions and other events. This venture led to the marketing of a weekly television guide called *The Television*. Kadokawa is famous for its annual prize awarded for the best work in literature and history.

BARBARA HAMILL SATO

KAIJŪ EIGA *see* monster films

kanji

Japanese is written using three scripts: *kanji* (Chinese characters) and the two phonetic scripts, *hiragana* and **katakana**. *Kanji* were imported from China in the sixth century or earlier because Japan had not yet developed a writing system of its own. The differences between the Chinese and Japanese languages were such, however, that characters alone were not sufficient to write down Japanese. The *kana* scripts were therefore developed from characters around the tenth century and came in time to be used as a supplement to characters, representing things like Japanese verb and adjective inflections and grammatical particles.

Different dictionaries give different estimates of the exact number of characters available; the largest (*Daikanwa Jiten*) lists 49,964. Nobody is expected to write or even read all these, of course. Even before the post-war script reforms limited the number of characters for general use, surveys indicated that the actual number in use was around 6,500. The *Jōyō kanji* list, established by the National Language Council (Kokugo shingikai) in 1981 to replace the slightly smaller *tōyō kanji* list of 1946, recommends 1,945 characters for general use. In actual practice, most newspapers and other general texts use around 3,000 characters when those used for personal and place names are added in. Characters usually have more than one pronunciation, depending on the context. These pronunciations are known as *on* (Chinese) and *kun* (Japanese) readings. When a character is used to write a Japanese word, it is pronounced with its *kun* reading. When it is used to write a Sino-Japanese word, it is pronounced with its *on* reading Some characters have more than one of each type. The post-war reforms sought to limit the number of readings each character could have, as well as simplifying the shapes of some of the more complex *kanji*.

These reforms revolved around issues of education and literacy. People had been arguing since 1866 that limiting the number of characters in general use would free children to spend more time at school on other studies. Later on, democracy came to be seen as an important factor as well; the complexity of the script prevented many people from developing a grasp of political problems reported in the press and limited the use of printed materials in campaigning. Office automation and printing also came into the arguments for reform, because of the difficulties presented by the large number of *kanji*.

The invention of character-capable word-processing technology in the late 1970s effectively solved the problem of how to produce printed documents efficiently with *kanji*. Some people (e.g. Hannas 1997) nevertheless argue that the relative difficulty of inter-computer communication when characters are used will eventually lead Japan to adopt the alphabet. Characters seem unlikely to disappear in the foreseeable future, however, and Japanese script is now widely utilised on the Internet.

References

Hannas, W.C. (1997) *Asia's Orthographic Dilemma*, Honolulu: University of Hawaii Press.

Further reading

Gottlieb, N (1995) *Kanji Politics: Language Policy and Japanese Script*, London: Kegan Paul International.

Seeley,C. (1991) *A History of Writing in Japan*, Leiden: Brill.

NANETTE GOTTLIEB

Kankoku kayō

What most people refer to as Korean song (*Kankoku kayō*) in Japan are the *enka*-style songs that appeared in the late 1920s. While Korea was a Japanese colony in the 1920s, various record companies such as Nippon Columbia, Nippon Victor and Teichiku sought sales on the Korean peninsula, set up branches in Keijo (present-day Seoul) and began producing records for the Korean market.

In the creative department of each company were numerous songwriters who had studied songwriting in Japan as foreign students and then returned to Korea. These songwriters produced many hits over the 1930s, for example 'Takyoku gurashi' (Living in a Foreign Country). Sano Ryōichi concludes, 'that these songs laid the foundation for Japanese enka style melodies, beginning with Nakayama Shimpei, is undeniable'. This is a very strong claim in that Nakayama was at Nippon Victor from its inception in 1927 and had a national reputation as a songwriter. He is often characterised as 'the father' of Japanese popular song. The suggested link to Korean influence would be controversial in the often conservative Japanese audience of *enka*. This type of song has continued to the present, but the golden age of 'Korean song' in this sense was from the mid-1950s to the 1960s. The famous title songs of many film melodramas were written by Korean songwriters such as Baku Shi Chun, Fan Mun Pyon, Son So Gu and Baku Chun Soku. In the 1970s and 1980s, pop music displaced the *enka* mode in Korea where it had also remained popular. The *enka* style continues to recede in both Korea and Japan as singers and songs are becoming more visually oriented. Serious investigation into the 'ethnicity' of the *enka* style itself, i.e. whether it may be thought of as Korean, Japanese, both, etc., as well as its relation to the colonial period has only just begun in recent years.

References

Sano Ryōichi (1994) 'Kankoku kayō', in *Taishū bunka jiten*, Tokyo: Kobundo, p. 176.

MARK ANDERSON

Kansai

The Kansai occupies south central Honshū, encompassing **Nagoya** to the East, the ancient capitals of Nara and **Kyōto**, and the international cities of **Ōsaka** and **Kōbe** on the west. The region derives its name, meaning 'western barrier', from the Kamakura period, when the *bakufu* rulers set up a military outpost to control the western warlords. The Kansai is often depicted as everything that its rival area, the **Kantō**, is not: traditional, commercially sophisticated and, especially in Kyōto, resplendent with the gardens, temples, shrines and architecture that define traditional Japanese landscape aesthetics. The Kansai is also heavily developed industrially, and home to Matsushita, the largest Japanese electronics firm. Much of the area is still highly productive agriculturally, including extensive tea cultivation in Nara Prefecture, and has some of the country's richest rice cultivation in Shiga Prefecture. The oldest settlements, including the earliest wet-rice agriculture, occurred in the Yamato area that includes Kyōto and Nara, and extends eastward to Hikone. Kansai people are known for their distinctive **dialects**, and for strong involvement in the arts, both traditional and modern. The Kansai region is also associated with the *yakuza*, Japan's version of organised-crime syndicates.

AUDREY KOBAYASHI

Kantō

The Kantō is Japan's largest alluvial plain, about 100 km in diameter, consisting of some 13,000 km^2. It comprises four prefectures, it lies barely above sea level and was in the past subject to flooding by the five major rivers – the Ara, Naka, Sagami, Tama and Tone – that criss-cross its surface. There is little evidence of the rivers today, however, as they have been channelled into concrete conduits that underlie one of the world's most developed urban agglomerations of more than 30 million people. Kantō's major cities include **Tokyo** and **Yokohama**, both of which have been considerably extended by landfill to make the former Tokyo Bay part of the Kantō Plain. There is little agricultural land left in the area, although farming still occurs intensively in the northern section, and around Narita Airport to the east, where conversion of farmland represented

a major cause for **farmers' movements**. The plain is surrounded by mountains, which form a natural basin subject to climatic inversions that exacerbate problems of air pollution in the urban area. The most famous mountain is Fuji-san (**Mt. Fuji**), which rises to the south of the area, can still be seen on clear days from Tokyo but is now often hidden behind a veil of air pollution.

AUDREY KOBAYASHI

karaoke

Karaoke refers to the amplification of a previously recorded instrumental track together with live vocals input through a microphone. '*Kara*' is the reading of a character meaning empty and '*oke*' is an abbreviation for the English term 'orchestra'. Thus the term 'karaoke' means 'empty orchestra'.

There were various precursors to karaoke: first, professional singers who made touring and television appearances at which they sang along to a prerecorded instrumental track; second, jukeboxes of popular records minus the vocal track with a microphone attached to the jukebox; and, third, machines with prerecorded musical tracks on piano designed for the purpose of singing along. Beginning in the early 1970s, karaoke devices with echo and prerecorded tracks including a guide melody were developed, largely for use in drinking establishments. These were produced for home use in the late 1970s. The mid-1980s saw the invention of the karaoke box – small individual or group sound boxes. These originally used cassette tapes, but in the 1980s there was a shift to CDs, laser discs and big screens. Karaoke was at first a means for middle-aged men to sing *enka* ('traditional pop') in bars. With the emergence of the karaoke box, younger and older men and women became able to sing a variety of musical genres without having to go to a bar. It is probably safe to say that the karaoke box market is now generally dominated by customers between the ages of 14 and 35, although family outings are not uncommon.

Contemporary genres available for performance include *enka*, pop, dance pop, rock, heavy metal, classic and contemporary Euro-American pop and rock, and Chinese and Korean pop. Karaoke provides an opportunity for Japanese who like singing to express their enthusiasm together. Karaoke people affords the opportunity to sing solos or duets before a usually supportive and enthusiastic audience. Beyond satisfying social demands for group activities by supporting performance in a common space, individual song selection and performance style also assure a measure of individual self-expression. There are a number of social problems associated with karaoke such as neighbourhood noise pollution. The karaoke box has also become an oasis of private space available to young people who typically live at home, especially important for young couples. Among conservatives, the karaoke box is seen to contribute to the decline of morals among contemporary Japanese young people.

Karaoke occupies a very important place as a site for social interaction generally and figures centrally in the financial calculations of the Japanese popular music industry as a whole. In recent years, manufacturers have made a concerted effort to export both equipment and recorded media to Korea, China and South-East Asia. Recent research has turned to investigating the possibility that karaoke perhaps has its origins in the pre-1945 Japanese colonies. It can be argued that karaoke helped lead the recent charge of Japanese pop culture exportation most recently spearheaded by animated film and television. Future research will clearly have to explore karaoke in an international context.

Further reading

Ogawa Hiroshi (1994) 'Karaoke', in *Taishu Bunka Jiten*, Tokyo: Kobundo, p. 162.

MARK ANDERSON

karate

Literally meaning 'empty hand', this is a form of unarmed combat. The range of modern techniques known by this name first came together as a unified set of movements in Okinawa in the seventeenth century. Although karate is often described as a Japanese sport it developed in Okinawa before those islands were Japanese territory and many Okinawans still proudly declare the local roots of this now internationally popular sport. Karate derived from the Chinese kick-boxing techniques of kung fu (*quan fa*) in the seventeenth century, a time when Okinawa had tributary relations with China and there was extensive trade between the two. It is part of the folklore of karate that, after the Japanese Shimizu clan laid claim to Okinawa, locals were not allowed to carry weapons for fear of rebellion and karate became a popular form of unarmed defence. Modern karate gained wide recognition in Japan after a series of demonstrations by the Okinawan master Gichin Funakoshi in 1905. The Federation of Karate Organizations was established in 1964 and monitors and accredits the diversity of styles practised around the world today. There are said to be some 23 million people worldwide training in karate in the late 1990s. The sport is perhaps most reknowned for the spectacle of tile and board smashing practised at the higher ranks. Karate involves a wide range of strikes, kicks and thrusts but the aim is to stop short of direct impact on the body. Competitive sparring matches are judged for potential 'killing' points, while there are also individual competitions where style and form (*kata*) are judged. Belts are awarded by colour as in most other martial arts in Asia.

SANDRA BUCKLEY

karōshi

karōshi (literally, 'death from overwork') refers to the condition where victims collapse and die, often due to a sudden cerebral haemorrhage or cardiac arrest, as a result of work-related fatigue: a combination of excessively long working hours and intense responsibilities, compounded by irregular and unhealthy lifestyle habits. Victims are typically believed to be middle-aged managerial males. However, *karōshi* victims also include a significant number of female employees, and span various ages and occupations.

Although *karōshi* is not a new phenomenon, it only started receiving attention from the late 1980s, due to the efforts of concerned legal and medical groups.

Underlying the problem have been such features of Japanese corporate culture as long working hours, after-work socialising and an inability to take extended holidays. Moreover, current structural readjustments in the workplace are further aggravating these pressures on employees.

Despite widespread publicity and numerous litigation cases, the response from the government in acknowledging *karōshi* and offering compensation has been slow. According to the Ministry of Labour, only seventy-eight cases were officially recognised in 1996. Support groups, however, estimate the annual number of victims to be close to a thousand.

See also: management systems, Japanese

Further reading

Ministry of Labour (1999) *Heisei 10 Nendo Rōdō Hakusho*, Tokyo: Nihon Rōdō Kenkyū Kikō.
National Defence Counsel for Victims of karōshi (1990) *karōshi: When the Corporate Warrior Dies*, Tokyo: Mado Sha.

ROMIT DASGUPTA

katakana

'*Katakana*' is one of the three writing systems in modern Japanese. '*Kata*' means incomplete or immature and '*kana*' means a basic written script. Like '*hiragana*', it derives from '*Man'yo-gana*' and is comprised of symbols for forty-eight 48 syllables in all.

It is believed that *katakana* was invented at the beginning of the Heian period by Buddhist monks who wanted to jot down readings and annotations in the limited space of the margins of *kanji* texts, or between lines in the Buddhist texts when they listened to lectures. It was necessary to invent a syllabary with a small size and the fewest possible number of strokes for rapid writing. There were some variations in shape and the number of strokes when *hiragana* and *katakana* were developing, but by end of the Heian period the shape and number of strokes were more or less unified. Each *katakana* derives from a part of a certain *kanji* as opposed to *hiragana*, which derives from a grass style (running

style) writing of a certain *kanji*. The current standard *katakana* was stipulated in 1900 (Meiji 33) by the Ministry of Education.

Katakana is used for the following usages nowadays:

1 foreign place names and personal names;
2 words in foreign languages (except Chinese) and '*gairaigo*' (loan words or words from foreign languages adopted in Japanese);
3 **onomatopoeia** and exclamatory remarks;
4 slang and '***dajare***';
5 names of fauna and flora
6 some academic and technical terms such as computer-related language;
7 proper nouns such as company names and brand names; and
8 emphasis in advertisements.

Among these, (1) and (2) are the most frequent usages. *Katakana* feature extensively in commercial advertising, where there is a frequent use of foreign loan words as well as the invention of new 'trend' words that come into vogue for the life of a product or fashion and often fall out of use again. Some of these *katakana* words gain sufficient currency to become a permanent part of daily speech.

SHUN IKEDA

Katō Shidzue

b. 1897, Tokyo

Birth control campaigner

Katō (formerly Ishimoto, née Hirota) Shidzue observed the lives of the poor in mining villages with her first husband, a mining engineer. She met family-planning advocate Margaret Sanger in the USA, and attempted to promote birth control in Japan, being arrested for these activities in the 1930s. She has been a leader of the family-planning movement throughout the post-war period, and has served in both the House of Councillors and the House of Representatives.

Further reading

Ishimoto Shidzue (1935) *Facing Two Ways: The Story*

of My Life, New York: Farrar & Rinehart (reprint: Stanford: Stanford University Press, 1986).

VERA MACKIE

Katō Tai

b. 1916, Kobe; d. 1985, Kyōto

Film director

The Nephew of the famous director Yamanaka Sadao, and a director himself, mainly of historical films, Katō began working in the cinema as assistant director for Tōhō and Daiei. In 1951, he became director for a small company, Takara, with the film *Kennan jonan* (Trouble with Swords and Women). Katō gradually shed some of the most rigid genre conventions, including heavy make-up, to bring about a realistic configuration of the moral vulnerability of characters, particularly women. This is exemplified in the famous three episodes he made for the 'Hibotan bakuto' (The Red Peony Gambler) series, which belonged to the starkly male domain of the *yakuza*. Critics have recently reappraised his work, underlining Katō's original filming technique, of low-angle long takes.

MARIA ROBERTA NOVIELLI

Katsu Shintarō

1931, Tokyo; 1997, Tokyo

Film actor

A cultural icon whose character was as freewheeling off-screen as on. Initially saddled with handsome male leads at Daiei, Katsu became famous by discarding vanity to play eccentric and unsightly characters both earthy and boisterous, principled and rebelliously violent in such series as Akumyo (Tough Guy), Heitai yakuza (Hoodlum Soldier) and the long-running Zatoichi, in which he played the blind masseur/master swordsman. His image as a rugged individualist was fostered by both his independent production company, where

he sometimes wrote, directed and starred in his films, and his arrests for drug possession.

AARON GEROW

Kawabata Yasunari

b. 1899, Ōsaka; d. 1972, Kamakura

Writer

A writer of sensual-erotic, deeply aesthetic narratives, in 1968 Kawabata became the first Japanese to win the Nobel Prize for Literature. Surprise greeted the award, as Kawabata was then regarded as so quintessentially Japanese as to be beyond appreciation by non-Japanese. Apparently, his aesthetics also resonated with a much larger readership and this became even truer after the award.

Early in life, Kawabata suffered devastating losses: his parents as an infant, his grandmother and sister shortly thereafter and then his grandfather. Such tragedy undoubtedly contributed to the undercurrent of loss that permeates his work. He began publishing stories, poetry and very short 'palm of the hand stories' while attending university. His *Izu no odoriko* (The Izu Dancer, 1926) won substantial acclaim. Other celebrated works available in English include: *Yukiguni* (Snow Country, 1948), *Senbazuru* (Thousand Cranes, 1949) and *Yama no oto* (The Sound of the Mountain, 1949).

Kawabata was affiliated briefly with the Neo-Sensualist literary coterie that rejected the then-dominant naturalist literature. Kawabata argued that attention to sensory perception could stimulate a new mode of Japanese literary expression. The associative prose to which Kawabata aspired was, he believed, inspired by modern **Zen**, *mono no aware* (heightened, emotive awareness of the transience of things), and the Japanese classics' mediated interweaving of humanity and nature. Kawabata's tales frame human event in the cycles of seasonal changes. Protagonists observe and record their mental reactions to an ever-changing environment. When protagonists become active, their occasional deeds yield only questionable power over the greater forces of time, space and nature. Trees shed their leaves in autumn, human beauty fades over time, people age and die – regardless of human effort.

Kawabata highlights momentary flashes of perceived beauty against bleak backgrounds. As objects of furtive, unrequited erotic-sensory arousal, appreciated from a physical and psychic distance, women emerge as features of the natural landscape. Beauty is rendered more poignant when it is momentary, when the flow of time is halted to behold wondrous moments that cannot last: the first buds of spring, childhood *naïveté* and female virginity. At the moment of its blossoming, purity already is tinged with decay. Desire stripped of the possibility of sexual union is the pinnacle of erotic and emotional arousal for Kawabata's protagonists. Sexual consummation would render the pure impure: beauty can only be preserved by distance. These themes, suggested in his early works, were boldly fetishised in his later *Nemureru bijo* (House of the Sleeping Beauties, 1961). Throughout his corpus, the prose is lyrical, the sequences episodic and the mood established through perceptual contrasts – directing the reader firmly along the surface of the text, away from psychological interiority.

Kawabata mentored **Mishima Yukio** and **Ibuse Masuji**, who matured into acclaimed authors. His death appears to have been suicide, although no note was found. Mishima's 1970 suicide is thought by some to have affected him deeply and possibly influenced his own suicide.

Further reading

Kawabata, Y. (1968) *Japan The Beautiful and Myself,* trans. E. Seidensticker, Tokyo: Kōdansha International.

Miyoshi, M. (1974) *Accomplices of Silence: The Modern Japanese Novel,* Berkeley: University of California Press.

NINA CORNYETZ

kawaii

Kawaii (cute) can describe everything from clothing to toys to children and animals. However, in Japan, cuteness has a unique place in a consumer culture fascinated with trends and fads. Cuteness is a recognised marketing tool for a target audience of youth and adult female consumers. From Little Kitty to **Pokemon**, Sailor Moon and Pengu the market is flooded with brand names linked to 'cute' characters that adorn everything from keyrings to stickers, T-shirts, trading cards, bath towels, chopsticks, lunchboxes, bedspreads, handkerchiefs, stationery, cookie cutters and the list goes on. The quality of *kawaii* is most often linked to the figure of the ***shojō*** (young girl) and the character of the *kawaii shojō* can occur almost anywhere in Japanese popular culture – comics, television comedy, drama, pop idols (***idoru* singers**), pornography or animation. While cuteness can be a simple description of physical characteristics ('she's so cute'), it also often describes the accessories and gestures of the *shojō* or is used as a common element of the vocabulary of the *shojō* who performs her own cuteness through her acclamation of cuteness all around her – '*aaa kawaiiii*' ('it's so cute') is the rallying cry of the *shojō*.

SANDRA BUCKLEY

Kawashima Yūzō

b. 1918, Aomori Prefecture; d. 1963, Tokyo

Film director

Kawashima entered Shōchiku in 1938 and earned his first directorial assignment in 1944. Nonsense comedy became his forte in the post-war period, but his talents did not fully blossom until he moved to Nikkatsu with his assistant **Imamura Shōhei** in 1955. His depiction of 'active escape' from confining reality in *Bakumatsu taiyōden* (Sun Legend of the End of the Tokugawa Era) and *Kashima ari* (Room For Let) established him as a master of comedy, while his virtually experimental style in films like *Shitoyakana kemono* (Elegant Beast) have ensured his status as a leading post-war director.

AARON GEROW

kayōkyoku

The term *kayōkyoku* refers to popular music created in Japan that falls outside the categories of folk or rock. It often carries the pejorative connotation that the musical decisions are made by promotion companies and talent agents rather than by musicians or by the performers themselves. It also implies that the performing artists were likely chosen for their appearance rather than their musical ability. In other words, it is a category defined in opposition to folk, rock and new music – styles of music that are associated with artistic control and vision. Historically, it seems that the term *kayōkyoku* was coined when NHK radio began broadcasting. Prior to that time, the same type of music was referred to by such terms as *ryūkō kouta*. For sales purposes, the record companies sometimes referred to the music as *ryūkōka*, sometimes as *kayōkyoku*. While *kayōkyoku* originally referred to popular music in general, its meaning has narrowed. Japanese popular music was greatly influenced by US popular music in the post-war period. Song styles strongly identified with Euro-America came to be referred to as pop while styles that appealed to, or evoked, a particularly Japanese sensibility came to be known as **enka**. *Kayōkyoku* is situated between pop and *enka* – while it is somewhat Japanese, it does not strike one as native, yet sounds familiar in an urban context.

Kayōkyoku history largely takes place between the 1920s and the present, but may be divided up into four main periods. The first era is from the mid-1920s until militarisation in 1938. The second era is the period of mobilisation during the war. The third period is from the loss of the war until the high-growth period. The last is from the time of the oil shock in 1973 to the present.

In 1928, various Japanese record company divisions were formed with foreign capital: Nippon Columbia, Nippon Polydor and Nippon Victor. In addition to importing and selling recordings produced abroad, they also began recording Japanese material. The first epoch-making recording to be produced by a record company and which became a hit was Nippon Victor's 'Kimi Koishi?' (I love You), released in January 1929. While popular songs were originally folk songs, from the Shōwa Period record companies aimed to produce a fashion for particular song styles. To this end, the record companies organised stables or teams of songwriters, lyricists and singers. They gave birth to a new style of popular music that combined lyrics evocative of traditional Japanese sentiment with songs composed in Western song form. Of course, this was an essentially different music from the *ryūkōka* of the Taishō Period or the *zokukyoku* that emerged from the Edo Period.

With electricity, recordings were made electronically and radio broadcasts and talking films were developed. While these three mass media influenced one another, they also expanded *kayōkyoku* and brought about a great revolution in popular music. The first new song intentionally written and recorded for a film was the title song 'Tokyo March' (May 1929). With talkies, the number of hit title songs released exploded. Victor was most successful at first, and then Columbia responded with the song-writing combination of Koga Masao and Fujiyama Ichirō. Polydor never was the leading record company, but they greatly changed the course of *kayōkyoku* with Tokai Rintarō's performance of 'Akasaka no ko mamoriuta' (Song for the Child of Akasaka). On a number of songs they added *samisen* to the orchestra to evoke a Japanese atmosphere and captured the attention of the popular music world.

From the late 1930s, the popular music world began to respond to growing patriotic, militarist sentiment. Before the end of 1937, the Cabinet Information Department commissioned a march with the intent of unifying national thought. They made a public call for lyrics and music for a 'Patriot's March'. From this point on, record companies quickly changed their approach to emphasise military and patriotic songs. They released one song after another promoting militarism and imperialism. The Asahi, Mainichi and Yomiuri newspaper companies also shifted their policies in accord with this trend and awarded prizes for reader contributions who wrote suitably patriotic compositions. These were then repeatedly broadcast on radio.

Because the Japanese situation changed so quickly with the loss of the war on 15 August, from mandated militarism to a rejection of it, record companies were somewhat at a loss as to how to respond. It was in this context that the light quality of Misora Hibari's 'Ringo no uta' (The Apple Song, October 1945) became a great hit. In such light-hearted musical fare, Japan found a starting point for the psychological energy necessary to rebuild. Thanks to military procurement, with the Korean War the Japanese economy began to revive. In 1949, 12-year-old Misora Hibari had a string of hits that startled her adult competition. There were also songs by Yoshida Tadashi with an urban flavour such as 'Let's Meet in Yurakuchō' and 'I Love You More than Anyone'. With the development of television broadcasts from February 1953, and the proliferation of entertainment and women's magazines, singers became extraordinarily popular – much more so than the songs they sang. From 1965, music trends clearly reflected the coming of age of television. The visual elements of *kayōkyoku* and fashion began to supersede listening with the increasing popularity of television music programmes.

The first folk boom occurred in 1966. Such songs as 'Where Have All the Flowers Gone' and 'The Rose Has Bloomed' became hits. Folk songs imbued with Japanese themes and politics became popular among young people. As Arai Yumi's first album, *Hikōki Gumo* (Airplane Clouds), set out in one new direction, '**New Music**' emerged as another current. Music industry people began to refer to the growing and diversifying rock and techno-pop field as 'New Music', in opposition to the previous forms that came to be referred to as *kayōkyoku* in a new sense of the word. Even within *kayōkyoku* there remained the narrower category of songs of irrepressible longing known as '*enka*'. New Music musicians usually refused to appear on pop music television shows in an effort to break the perceived tie between pop music and idol singers, but their songs became 'image songs' for television advertising campaigns with corporate tie-ins. Since 1976, when Ogura Yoshi's 'Wavering Gaze' was used as the campaign song for a cosmetics commercial, there has been a consistent connection between television advertising and New Music. Companies pay highly for the use of such songs. This sort of marketing has become the driving force of the *kayōkyoku* world.

Since 1975, *kayōkyoku* has split off from idol singers, pop music, New Music and rock. One reason for this is that the musical needs of the popular song have become more diverse. It also reflects a frivolous, stunted era in which the hit cycle has become both more intense and extremely short. However poorly promotion may be done, it is becoming difficult not to have a million seller.

Further reading

Ito Tsuyoshi/Tsutomu (1994) 'Kayōkyoku', in *Taishū bunka jiten*, Tokyo: Kobundo, p. 159.

Nagata Akeji (1996) 'Kayōkyoku no rekishi', Tokyo: Kobundo, pp. 160–1.

MARK ANDERSON

Keidanren

The Federation of Economic Organizations (Keidanren, abbreviation for Kezai Dantai Rengokai) is one of Japan's four main business organisations of the *zaikai* (economic community), which serve different purposes but maintain close contact and co-operative relations with one another on matters of common and mutual interest. The other three are Nikkeiren (Japan Federation of Employers' Associations), Keizai Dōyōkai (Japan Association of Corporate Executives) and Nissho (Japan Chamber of Commerce and Industry).

Keidanren was established in 1949 by merging several pre-war economic and industrial groups. Its members now include around 120 industry-wide groups, representing manufacturing, trade, distribution, finance and energy, as well as over 1,000 major corporations (including many foreign firms). Keidanren is a private and non-profit economic organisation that attempts to influence the government (especially MITI, the **Ministry of International Trade and Industry**) to adopt policies that reflect a consensus of ideas within the business community. Keidanren also facilitates political contributions from the business community to the **Liberal Democratic Party** (LDP). Keidanren's policy committees address issues such as taxation, the fiscal system and transportation. Their policy statements are endorsed as Keidanren official policies and given to government and political parties. In recent years, Keidanren has developed *ad hoc* committees to discuss economic co-operation with overseas countries, as well as engaging in public relations at home to foster support for the Japanese business community.

DAVID EDGINGTON

keigo

'*Keigo*' means 'revered words' in Japanese. It basically refers to the linguistic system that reflects the relational social contract of a mutual performance of respect. Thus, it is often referred to as an 'honorific system'. This 'honorific system' exists in any language in different forms, but the Japanese *keigo* has unique features in that it has special grammatical forms to express one's reverence to other people.

In *keigo*, there are three functional styles for the demonstration of respect. The first style is exaltative (*sonkei*) where you exalt the person you respect by raising the person's status above your own level, thereby showing your respect. Normally you do this by inflecting the main verb, which refers to the respected person's action using a formula pattern (e.g. '*yomu*' to '*o-yomi ni naru*'), but some verbs have a totally different form to designate exaltation (e.g. '*meshiagaru*' for '*taberu*' and '*irassharu*' for '*iku/kuru/iru*'). These verbs are not numerous, but need to be learnt by heart. The second style is humble (*kenjō*), where you lower your own status in relation to the person you respect to show reverence. Normally, you do this by changing the main verb that refers to your own action into a formula pattern (e.g. '*o-mochi suru*' for '*motsu*'). However, there is a restriction on the use of this style in that your own action must have something to do with the person you respect. You cannot use this humble form unless your own action has some bearing on that person. The third style is polite (*teinei*), where you demonstrate your politeness for the occasion or situation and not for persons involved by using certain forms of sentences or expressions. You do this by using the polite sentence final form (the so-called *desu-masu-* style) as opposed to the non-polite sentence final forms (the so-called *da-de aru*-style).

Sometimes a prefix is used with nouns to display politeness such as *o Tegami* (letter), *o-cha* (tea), *go-*shōkai* (introduction) and *go-jitaku* (home). Normally, you need to show your respect to those who are senior to you in age or social-status. When both elements conflict, it is usually the case that social status takes primacy. Another important dimension to the 'honorific system' is the relations of respect between in-group and out-group (***uchi* and *soto***). The closer you feel to people you associate with, the less you need to demonstrate respect. This '*uchi*' (in-group) consciousness works not only at an individual level but also at a group level. Therefore, people do not normally use *keigo* among family members. However, you need to use *keigo* towards your in-laws. Your working environment is also '*uchi*' and when you deal with people outside of that group ('*soto*') the outsider is addressed with a respect that honours but also reinforces the relational distance. Within a workplace *uchi* group '*sonkei*' (exaltation) forms are used towards those who are senior in age or status. However, as soon as you deal with someone who is out-group, you refer to your in-group seniors using a *kenjō* (humble) form to lower the status in respect towards the out-group. In such contexts, respect is also functioning as an indicator of formality and lack of intimacy.

Needless to say, *keigo* is not simply expressed by linguistic form, but also through the intricate display of facial expressions and gestures including bows and refined manners. An arrogant attitude is not compatible with respectfulness and *keigo* usage. At the same time, an excess of *keigo* results in an obsequious effect and may sound presumptuous. *Keigo* needs to be used appropriately and in good measure or it can have an unintended negative effect. *Keigo* is an essential social lubricant in the complex net of vertical and horizontal relations that suffuse Japanese daily life.

SHUN IKEDA

kendō

'The way of the sword' is a traditional form of fencing that uses a two-handed sword crafted from bamboo. The art of sword fighting was an essential element of samurai skills, but over the Edo Period emphasis shifted from armed combat to the discipline and cultivation of technique. Teaching the art of sword fighting became one way for samurai to make a living in an era of more extensive peace. Some 200 schools had emerged by the end of the eighteenth century, each with its own variations in form. Kendō is practised in protective gear consisting of quilted cloth panels, a hard chest plate, padded gloves and a thick, loose trouser skirt. Cuts, thrusts and blows can only be delivered to certain areas of the body – left or right torso, top of head, left or right wrist, left or right flank and the throat. Each strike has to be called as it is delivered. Kendō is a part of the compulsory physical education programme in many high schools and also a popular after-school club activity. The All-Japan Kendō Federation was formed in 1952 and the International Kendō Federation in 1970. The international following of kendō does not compare to the tremendous popularity of judo or karate, which may in part be due to the significant costs associated with the sparring gear. The sound of pounding feet and the sharp loud call of a kendō strike are familiar sounds when walking around Japanese neighbourhoods after school, while kendō practice is underway in school gyms and play-grounds.

SANDRA BUCKLEY

keshiki

Keshiki means 'scenery', a concept with particular cultural constructions in Japan, referring not simply to the surrounding landscape, but to landscapes that conform to natural ideals, viewed through a highly conformist lens that merges physical elements – water, rocks, trees, topography – with concepts of natural harmony and aesthetic inspiration, expressed in a variety of forms that include painting, gardens (as landscape art) and poetry, particularly haiku (see **haiku and *tanka***), which is specifically directed towards landscape. The ideals of landscape composition were codified by the great *ukiyoe* (woodblock) painters of the Tokugawa Period, most notably Hiroshige, whose scenes along the Tōkaidō still represent the epitome of landscape tastes.

The entire Japanese landscape has been modified by human intervention of one kind or another,

and much of the original scenery altered beyond recognition by industrial development, urban sprawl and **land reclamation** along the coastlines. Even so, maintaining a few particular scenes in pristine condition has remained a high priority. Such scenes transcend the modern landscape to depict the perfect place, much like set designs for a play. Such scenes include the perfect cone of **Mt. Fuji**, the isolated island and pines of Matsushima, the sacred precincts of Ise Shrine and picturesque Miya-jima.

Customs regulate proper scenic viewing. Each site is believed to change seasonally (see **seasons**), so visits occur accordingly, including the viewing of **cherry blossoms** in the spring and maple leaf viewing in the autumn. Both these can be enjoyed from dining rooms or *ofuro* (bath houses) built to capture and display notable landscape features.

AUDREY KOBAYASHI

Kikutake Kiyonori

b. 1928, Fukuoka Prefecture

Architect

Along with **Kurokawa Kishō** and Kawazoe Noboru, Kikutake helped found the **Metabolism** Group in 1960 in time for the World Design Conference hosted in Tokyo. Kikutake is credited with having come up with the term 'metabolism' to describe the Group's fundamental philosophy of futuristic urban change and regeneration. His 'Ocean City' and 'Tower-Shape Community' proposals, included in the Metabolist manifesto, promoted megastructures with modular, removable, and changeable parts for collective housing projects built over the sea and vertically into the air, respectively. He partially realised the former design in his Aquapolis project, a city block-sized marine 'city' built for the 1975 Expo in Okinawa; with this, Kikutake attempted to show how a floating structure, or artificial island habitat, could co-exist harmoniously with nature, recycling its waste and attentive to environmental concerns. Into the 1990s, Kikutake advocated 'eco-polis' planning and a return to the basic principles that grounded the insights of the Metabolism Group, insisting that technology and nature do not have to be at destructive odds. His striking design for the Edo-Tokyo Museum (1990) re-asserts history and tradition as integral to, and continuous with, the future of Japan's capital city.

MARY KNIGHTON AND SCOTT GOLD

kimono

Kimono can be used in its more general sense of 'clothing' but is also used specifically to describe the wrap-around ankle-length traditional garment worn by both men and women. The kimono is worn with the left side folded across the right and tied with a sash (*obi*). Kimono appear to have been in use since the Heian period and possibly earlier. A modern kimono will be lined or unlined depending on the season and this will also determine appropriate textiles, with silk and linen favoured in the summer and lined silk and light wool in the winter. The colour and pattern of a kimono will be selected to reflect the nature of the event or seasonal variations. White or red silk kimono are worn by brides while black is worn for funerals (see **death and funerals**) and by wedding guests (see **weddings**). Lightweight unlined and decoratively patterned *yukata* are a familiar feature of the summer landscape.

Men made the move from kimono to Western-style dress (*yōfuku*) much more speedily than women during the rapid Westernisation of the Meiji Period. While Western dress was considered modern and stylish for men, the imported Western styles for women were often derided as unfeminine and a threat to Japanese traditional values. It was really in the post-war period that women were finally free to more actively pursue imported fashions and their local variations. Today, kimono are usually reserved for special ceremonial occasions including weddings, funerals, graduation ceremonies, **Adults' Day**, *Shichi-go-san*. Even today, it is often the case that when a more formal event requires a woman to wear a kimono, a man is likely to don the somewhat dated Western-style morning suit still reserved for such occasions in Japan.

A kimono is usually worn over an under-kimono with a white edging that is displayed as a lining slightly exposed at the neck edge of the kimono. A man's *obi* can be stiff and narrow or a wide and soft long sash folded over into a narrow wrap and tied low on the waist. Women's *obi* are wider and stiff, and often beautifully embroidered or embossed to create a seasonal or ceremonial theme in co-ordination with the textile, colour and pattern of the kimono. As the kimono has become more rarefied, both the art of knotting an *obi* and dressing a kimono are now often learnt in kimono schools rather than passed down from mother to daughter. The care of kimono has also been commercialised with cleaning and folding services. A kimono should be taken apart and cleaned panel by panel and then carefully re-stitched and folded and wrapped with special paper. Fewer families are able to afford the expense of a good-quality kimono and the related care, and this has led to a growth in rental outlets, despite the widespread aversion to wearing used clothing.

The art of the kimono has undergone extensive re-invention in the 1980s and 1990s. Japanese brand designers like Yamamoto, Kawakubo and Miyake have often played with the design of the kimono in their global fashion lines, but just as importantly some of Japan's renowned designers have also experimented in kimono design. A number of top designers now have a summer line of *yukata*, *obi* and **geta**. In another interesting development, a number of overseas Japanese designers have made their reputations with eclectic sculpted designs that use kimono and *obi* fabric in unexpected textural juxtapositions with satin, tuille, wool, cotton and linen. While the fundamental art of the kimono remains remarkably consistent, even this traditional garment is not beyond the playful interventions of contemporary fashion trends.

SANDRA BUCKLEY

Kinoshita Keisuke

b. 1912, Hamamatsu; d. 1998, Tokyo

Film director

Born in 1912, Kinoshita Keisuke is one of Japan's most popular directors, best known for his satirical social commentaries. His love for movies began at a young age and, when his parents refused to let him follow his cinematic interests, he ran away from home and began working in the processing laboratory of Shochiku. He later became an assistant cameraman, studied scenario writing and by 1936 became an assistant director to Shimazu Yasujirō. He directed his first film, *Hanasaku minato* (The Blossoming Port) in 1943. In 1946, he won the Kinema Jumpo Award for best film for his fifth picture *Osone-ke no asa* (Morning for the Osone Family). He received the same award for *Nijushi no hitomi* (Twenty-four Eyes) in 1954, and again in 1958 for one of his most famous works, *Narayamabushi-ko* (The Ballad of Narayama). This latter film is an adaptation of Fukazawa Shichirō's 1956 novel, which tells the story of a 69-year-old woman's journey to the summit of Mount Narayama, where she is to die. The film fuses modern cinematic techniques with traditional Japanese *kabuki* techniques, as well as making extensive use of Kinoshita's trademark long, panoramic shots. Among his other popular films are 1951's *Karumen kokyō ni kaeru* (Carmen Comes Home), the first Japanese colour film, and 1952's *Karumen junjosū* (Carmen's Pure Love). Both films feature the same comic figure named Carmen, a young female stripper from Tokyo who lives for her dance art. Kinoshita was interested in exploring the lives of 'common people', and female protagonists in his films, such as Carmen, often stand in for the essence of the common people. Many of Kinoshita's films involve the politicisation of feminine figures, a gesture that is also prevalent in the works of Mizoguchi and Imamura. Kinoshita is infamous for his very personalised style, which was the result of his tight control over all aspects of the production process. The same actors re-appeared in many of his films and his crew was usually composed of a close circle of friends and family. His brother, for example, wrote music for many of his films, while his sister wrote his scripts and his brother-in-law was his cameraman. For this reason, his cast and crew were often referred to as the 'Kinoshita family'. In total, he, along with his cinematic family, are responsible for over forty films, most of which had a great deal of box office success and achieved critical acclaim. Soon after the release of his last film *Chi Chi* (Father),

Kinoshita died in December 1998 at the age of 86 as a result of a cerebral infection.

Further reading

Anderson, Joseph and Richie, Donald (1982) *The Japanese Film: Art and Industry*, New Jersey: Princeton University Press.

Bock, Audie (1978) *Japanese Film Directors*, Tokyo, New York and San Francisco: Kōdansha International.

LEILA POURTAVAF

Kitano Takeshi

1947, Tokyo

Comedian and film director

While first gaining fame through the acerbic humor of his *manzai* (comedy team) act, the 'Two Beats', Kitano, also known as 'Beat Takeshi', became in his own right one of the dominant personalities of the 1980s and 1990s in the diverse worlds of television, publishing and film. With such works as *3–4 × 10-gatsu* (Boiling Point) and *Sonatine*, his deadpan violence and narratively elliptical style established him as the leading film director of the 1990s, a status confirmed internationally when *Hanabi* won the grand prize at the 1997 Venice Film Festival.

AARON GEROW

Kitaro

b. 1953, Toyohashi

Musician

Born Takahashi Masanori, Kitaro began his music career while still a student as a member of the rock band Far East Family Band. When this group disbanded in 1976 he abandoned rock for new age music releasing his first album *Astral Voyage* in 1978. His musical score for the television documentary *Silk Road* (1980) rocketed him to international acclaim. He has produced a large repertoire of New Age record releases, which now have a dedicated following among New Age devotees and he is regularly listed among the top world performers of this genre of music. His concert tours are sell-out successes across the world, despite being regularly panned by critics as visually overpowering events laced with special effects rather than artistic prowess. He is renowned for his annual retreats or cleansings when he travels to remote locations with a select group of musicians, where he is said to drum ritually until his hands are blistered and bleeding. His televised New Year performances from the mountain location of his Japanese home and studio base in Nagano Prefecture became a much anticipated event among New Age music fans. Kitaro now also has a mountain studio/home in Boulder, Colorado. It was no suprise when he was featured as a key artist and composer in Japan's Millennium celebration event. His spectacular and dramatic performance in this internationally broadcast event saw a sudden spike in his world sales. Today, the music videos, DVDs and CDs of such Kitaro classics as *Silk Road* (1980), *Kojiki* (1990) and *Mandala* (1996) continue to outsell many newer and more experimental artists of the genre.

SANDRA BUCKLEY

kites

The earliest references to kites in Japan are traced to the tenth century, but they are thought to have originated in China some 2,000 years ago. There is also some evidence of kites in ancient Greece. In Japan, the kite was first both an ornament and toy of the aristocracy and a tool of warfare used to carry messages and send signals across a battlefield. By the Edo Period, kites had become a popular amusement among all classes. Kite wars and races have remained a featured event of many local festivals. The most famous kite event is the launching of *Ō-Dako* (giant kites) at Children's Day celebrations (5 May). These monster kites can weigh us much as a ton and seem to defy gravity when they take to the air. Painted carp-shaped kites (*koinobori*) are flown outside the home of any family with a son on this day (traditionally designated as

Boy's Day). The carp symbolises the wish for the good health and well-being of the son. Originally hand-crafted in paper or silk, synthetic *koinobori* are now a popular year-round house decoration outside Japan. Today, the most complex models are three-dimensional aerodynamically designed structures that can achieve astounding heights and speeds. Trick kites have developed into a popular competitive pastime among young and old alike in Japan and elsewhere.

See also: *Hinamatsuri* (Doll Festival) and Girls' Day

SANDRA BUCKLEY

kōban

The *kōban* (police box) is a familiar sight to anyone who has lived in a Japanese urban neighbourhood. Most often located close to the major transport hub for trains, underground or buses, these non-residential facilities provide a full-time police presence.

The officers are expected to become familiar with the faces and movements of their jurisdiction and patrol by foot and on bicycle in twenty-four-hour shifts. Any unfamiliar situation or individual is investigated. An officer from the designated *kōban* will visit the home of any new resident as a formality. Foreigners can be asked to present their alien registration papers or passport.

The extent to which the *kōban* embeds a police presence within neighbourhoods has frequently been attributed as a major factor in low urban crime rates. Even so, in neighbourhoods that have a higher percentage of minority populations (e.g. **Burakumin**, Korean-Japanese), transient Japanese workers, immigrant workers (legal and illegal), bar and entertainment workers (see **mizushōbai**) and prostitutes (see **prostitution, regulation of**), the *kōban* can be experienced as a source of surveillance and even harassment. Human rights advocates also identify the role of the *kōban* in implementing public-safety campaigns (e.g. earthquake and fire prevention) as a potential invasion of privacy, for few households really feel free to refuse the offer of a home safety visit from their local *kōban*.

SANDRA BUCKLEY

Kobayashi Akira

b. 1938, Tokyo

Actor and singer

After attending Meguro High School in Tokyo, Kobayashi attended Meiji University and subsequently went to work for the Nikkatsu Film Company. He was promoted as a youth star in the 1956 *Ueru tamashii* (The Starving Soul). In 1963, he made his singing debut with the title song to his film *Onna wo wasureru* (To Forget a Woman). The B-side of the record, 'Dainamaito ga hyakugoju ton' (150 Tons of Dynamite), became a hit. In 1964, the unfortunately titled 'Gitaa wo motta watari dori' (The Migrating Bird with a Guitar) became a hit, and the American Western-flavoured Watari dori series began. Akira became popular as an action star. As a fellow Nikkatsu star, he was frequently compared and contrasted with Ishihara Yūjirō. Like Yūjirō, he had a degree of success as a singer. Akira had several big hits, including 'Junko' and 'Kita e' (To the North). His personal life was very eventful and the object of much media coverage. Both his marriage in November 1962 to **Misora Hibari** and their divorce in June 1964 captured much popular attention.

Further reading

Ito Tsutomu (1995) 'Kobayashi Akira', in *Taishu bunka jiten*, Tokyo: Kobundo, pp. 271–2.

MARK ANDERSON

Kobayashi Masaki

b. 4 February 1916, Otaru, Hokkaidō;
  d. 4 October 1996, Tokyo

Film director

His experiences as a prisoner of war during the Second World War set the tone for several of Kobayashi Masaki's films. *Kabe atsuki heya* (The Thick-Walled Room, 1953) depicts punishment of lower-level war criminals whose superiors remained free. *Ningen no jōken* (The Human Condition, 1959–61) centres on a young pacifist attempting to confront Japanese militarism. *Tokyo saiban* (The Tokyo Trials, 1983) is a documentary (see **documentary film**) assembled from the 1948 war crime trials. His samurai films *Seppuku* (Harakiri, 1963), awarded a Special Jury Prize at Cannes, and *Jōi-uchi* (Samurai Rebellion, 1967) feature warriors confronting hollow codes of ethics. Although free of social messages, the sumptuous *Kaidan* (Kwaidan, 1964) also received a Special Jury Prize at Cannes for its stylised adaptation of four Lafcadio Hearn ghost stories.

WILLIAM C. THOMPSON

Kobe

Kobe is the capital of Hyōgo Prefecture, located 30 km west of **Ōsaka** on the Seto Naikai (see **Inland Sea**). It is Japan's second largest port after **Yokohama**. As an international gateway, Kobe has long been viewed as a city with strong Western cultural influences. During the late nineteenth century, international traders set up operations there to create a sizeable cosmopolitan population. Attendant institutions included schools, restaurants and cultural facilities. Kobe is also known for its fashion industry and for '**Kobe beef**', meat from cows carefully fed and tended to produce very tender cuts.

Kobe's Port Island represents one of the world's largest artificial islands, and a **land reclamation** project of mythic proportions. Connected to the mainland by monorail, it is a major complex of state-of-the-art container facilities, hotels, conference and entertainment facilities and housing for 20,000 people. It was created by removing material from the Rokko Mountains north of Kobe and depositing it by conveyor belt into the former harbour.

In 1975, the **Hanshin Earthquake**, centred on Kobe, resulted in massive damage to the islands and the entire city. 5,500 people were killed and 415,000 injured. Also, 100,000 houses were destroyed and 185,000 badly damaged. It has taken several years to repair the damage, especially to the traditional wooden houses that do not stand up well to earthquakes.

See also: Hanshin Earthquake

AUDREY KOBAYASHI

Kobe beef

This beef has become almost legendary. It is well marbled with fat and extremely tender. Pricing of Kobe beef can soar to $400 a pound around festive seasons when it is in high demand. Kobe beef is always processed in Kobe but, today, in an attempt to meet ever-increasing demand, a limited number of Australian and US beef ranches are raising the cattle according to traditional husbandary techniques. The breed of herd used for Kobe beef is called *wagyū* and it has been an essentially closed herd since the seventeenth century. Kobe beef ranched overseas must be *wagyū* stock.

The cows are fed beer to encourage appetite during the summer heat and are rubbed down with sake to improve coat and skin, which Japanese farmers believe also adds to the quality of the meat. The Japanese herd seldom has grazing pasture and so massage is used to combat the lack of exercise. The level of fat marbelling exceeds prime beef categories in the USA. Needless to say, there is an art to cooking Kobe beef. It should never be more than seared and is best cooked over an open flame or on preheated cast-iron. If more than lightly cooked the fats melt and due to the high fat content the meat quickly becomes saturated. The key is to heat the meat through without breaking down the marbelling.

SANDRA BUCKLEY

Kōdansha

In 1909, Noma Seiji, a former middle-school teacher and member of the clerical staff at Tokyo Imperial University, made his foray into the world of publishing with the founding of Kōdansha. The following year, the company's first magazine, *Yūben*

(Dynamic Speeches), a collection of speeches in digest form, came out.

Two years later, Noma published *Kōdan kurabu* (Storytelling Club), an easy to read magazine devoted to a traditional kind of storytelling and aimed at a general reading audience. The advertisements for the magazine included the words 'fun', 'interesting' and 'beneficial reading'. In 1914, when *Shōnen Club* (Boys' Club) came out, the same words were used to attract young readers. These two publishing successes led to the publication of *Moshiro kurabu* (Interest Club) in 1916. Anxious to attract women readers, *Fujin kurabu* (Woman's Club) was launched in 1920. This was followed in 1923 by *Shōjo kurabu* (Young Girls' Club), which was supposed to complement the magazine launched for boys.

Noma's magazines drew on the ideal that there are various pathways to success in life. Noma's philosophy reached its high point with the publication of *Kingu* (King) in 1925, the first magazine to sell 1,000,000 copies in its first printing, a mass magazine from its inception. Publishing magnate Noma's string of magazine successes resulted in Kōdansha being called a 'magazine kingdom'.

After the Second World War, Kōdansha's first project was the publication of *Gunzō* (1946), a literary magazine that provided an opportunity for writers to publish new works. This project led Kōdansha to expand its operations. In addition to publishing books and magazines for a mass reading audience, Kōdansha made a commitment to promote mainstream Japanese literature.

In 1963, Kōdansha began publication of English-language books with the establishment of Kōdansha International. Kōdansha presently publishes books and mass magazines on topics as varied as beauty, cooking, fashion, health, business and science. It also has a significant stake in the comic industry.

BARBARA HAMILL SATO

kodo

The term *kodo* has come to be used outside Japan to describe the art of the Japanese drum (*taiko*). It is in fact the name of the drumming group that has become synonymous with *taiko* since its formation in the 1980s.

Originally a breakaway group from the Onde-koza (Demon Drummers) troupe, Kodo established itself on Sado island where the forty performers of the troupe train along with hopeful apprentices under a very strict regimen. There are different drumming techniques and drums vary in size. The most impressive of the drums are mounted on wooden blocks or played lying on their sides on the floor. The act of beating the drum is intensely physical and the Kodo troupe members are renowned for their muscular bodies, agility and endurance. A loincloth and sweat band are usually all that is worn during a *kodo* troupe's performance but in other local and amateur performances it is common to wear a **haori** marked with the symbol of the *kodo* club, a local sponsor or the temple or village. Many local *kodo* drumming groups have sprung up around the world and particularly among immigrant Japanese communities. *Taiko* drumming also remains a popular element of Japanese festivals and some religious celebrations.

SANDRA BUCKLEY

Koinobori (carp kites) and Children's Day

On 5 May (Children's Day), any house where there is a male child will traditionally fly a carp kite for each son in the household. The carp is a traditional Chinese symbol of good health and well-being. The custom was initially limited to warrior households but spread across the town culture of merchants over the Edo Period. By early Meiji, it was a recognised element of household celebrations of Boys' Day. In 1948, the government redesignated 5 May as Children's Day, combining Boys' and Girls' Day in a single national holiday. However, tradition has prevailed and families still celebrate these two events separately on 3 March and 5 May.

Originally made from paper, these kites are today largely mass-produced in synthetics, although more expensive silk and paper models are still handcrafted. The differing quality and size of the kites is often the source of considerable neighbourhood rivalry between families striving to achieve the grandest display. The kites are flown from the doorway or eaves of the house. The colour and movement of *koinobori* flying from so many homes makes for a pleasant transformation of residential streets and apartment buildings. These brightly coloured kites have also become a popular year-round house decoration in other countries.

See also: kites; *Hinamatsuri* (Doll Festival) and Girls' Day

SANDRA BUCKLEY

Kokusai Denshin Denwa

Kokusai Denshin Denwa (KDD) (International Telegraphic and Telephone Corporation) was incorporated in 1953 and was, until the 1990s, the uncontested largest provider of international communication services including telex, facsimile and phone. KDD has been an influential presence in satellite and optical communications research domestically and internationally. However, since the privatisation of **Nippon Telegraphic and Telephone Corporation** (NTT), KDD has faced increased competition and now contends with other major international service providers such as DDI and IDO, and of course NTT. In 1998, KDD formed an alliance with Teleway, the third largest domestic service as part of a strategy to remain competitive with NTT and to develop a seamless international and domestic network. The combined cable, fibre optic and satellite services of this alliance far exceed current demand but it is intended that with the introduction of 3-G (third-generation) technologies this capacity will offer a market advantage as multimedia delivery puts increasing pressure on existing competitor networks. KDD also has a market and research and development edge in such areas as video conferencing, rapid data transfer and internationally integrated digital services as a result of its traditional specialisation in international communication services for industry and government. KDD is actively seeking international alliances to further strengthen its competitiveness in the face of

NTT's massive financial success with DoCoMo's mobile platform technologies since the late 1990s.

SANDRA BUCKLEY

Kon Ichikawa

b. 1915, Mie

Film director

Born in November of 1915, Kon Ichikawa began working in the animation department of J.O. Studio upon graduating from high school. He later worked as an assistant to Kurosawa Akira at Tōhō Studios on films including *Shichinin no samurai* (Seven Samurai) (1954) and *Kumonosūjō* (Throne of Blood) (1957). His early influences, however, were US genres such as the Western, and US directors Charlie Chaplin and William Wellman. He made his first film *Musume Dojo-ji* (The Girl at Dojo Temple) in 1946. In the 1950s, Ichikawa began a series of collaborations with his wife Wada Natto, a screenwriter. Among them were *Ashi ni sawatta onna* (The Woman Who Touched the Legs) (1952) and *Pu san* (Mr Poo) (1953), both of which inserted a Western style of comedy into Japanese drama. This period was followed by a decade of anti-war films, which included his first major internationally acclaimed film *Biruma no tatekoto* (The Harp of Burma) (1956). The film tells the story of a Japanese soldier who transforms into a monk after bearing witness to the tragic state of Burma after the Second World War. In 1960, he received a Golden Globe Award for Best Foreign Film and a special prize at the Cannes Film Festival for his 1959 picture *Kagi* (Odd Obsession), which tells the perverse tale of a Japanese family inflicted with impotence, betrayal and incest. A film that makes it difficult for the audience to empathize with any of the characters, *Kagi* captures Ichikawa's dark humour with a claustrophobic intensity. It is also the film that led many critics to accuse Ichikawa of embracing an empty aestheticism and nihilism that equated all things to form alone, an observation that Ichikawa never denied. Other major works of his include a series of adaptations of major modernist literary works by canonised writers such as Natsume Sōsekei, *Kokoro* (The Heart) (1955), and

Mishima Yukio, *Enjo* (Conflagration) (1958). He later experimented with the documentary style in 1965's *Tokyo orimpikku* (Tokyo Olympiad), which focuses on the stress of being an athlete. One of Japan's most accomplished directors, he is also regarded as a brilliant cinematic stylist, and has had a great deal of international success. Ichikawa has continued to direct a number of films, including a host of historical ones such as *Koto* (Koto the Ancient City) (1980), and a remake of *Biruma no tatekoto* (The Harp of Burma) (1985). The latest additions to his prolific filmography are *Shinjushichinin no shikaku* (Forty-seven Rōnin) (1994), *Yatsuhaka-mura* (The Eight-tomb Village) (1996) and *Dora heita* (Dirt Soldiers) (1999).

Further reading

Bock, Audie (1978) *Japanese Film Directors*, Tokyo, New York and San Francisco: Kōdansha International.

Mellen, Joan (1975) *Voices from the Japanese Cinema*, New York: Liveright.

LEILA POURTAVAF

Korea–Japan relations

When Japan's thirty-six-year colonial rule came to an end in 1945, the Korean Peninsula became divided and has remained so until this day. Negotiations to normalise relations with the Republic of Korea (South Korea) began soon after Japan regained independence in 1952, but made little progress during the 1950s due to mutual antagonism over issues concerning reparations and territorial adjustments. Fervently nationalistic, South Korean President Syngman Rhee refused to compromise. The claim by a Japanese government negotiator in 1954 that Korea's demand for compensation for Japan's harsh colonial rule should be offset by its positive legacies effectively derailed negotiations and ignited waves of mass protest in Korea. Actions such as South Korea's seizure of Japanese fishing boats within what Rhee defined as a 199 nautical-mile coastal territory further soured the atmosphere. Negotiations resumed and made progress soon after Park Chung-hee came to power after a military *coup* in 1961. The two governments signed a secret memorandum that year, establishing the basis for property settlements and economic co-operation, and went on to normalise diplomatic relations in 1965 by signing the Treaty on Basic Relations between Japan and the Republic of Korea. The treaty declared all treaties or agreements between Japan and Korea before, or on, 22 August 1910 null and void. Japan recognised the government of the Republic of Korea as the only lawful government in Korea in accordance with United Nations resolutions.

Supplementary agreements dealt with other areas of dispute such as property rights, fishing rights and the legal status of Korean residents in Japan. Japan agreed to provide a grant of $300 million, and added another $500 million in long-term government and private credits. In exchange for Japan's economic aid, the Republic of Korea renounced the right to seek reparations. Tokyo and Seoul have enjoyed close ties since normalisation, despite such incidents as the 1971 abduction of prominent dissident Kim Dae-jung from a Tokyo hotel by Korean government agents. President Park, a graduate of the military academy in Japan-dominated Manchukuo, emulated many of Japan's economic policies, while Japanese investment and loans played an important role in enabling Park's authoritarian developmental state to move the South towards export-led rapid economic growth. In 1967, regular ministerial conferences were inaugurated, and a Japan–Korea Co-operative Committee was set up two years later by leading businessmen from both countries. By the 1990s, the Republic of Korea was Japan's third largest trading partner, while Japan was Korea's second largest. During Korea's financial crisis of 1997, Japan pledged $10 billion assistance, the largest recorded bilateral contribution ever.

Japan's relations with the People's Democratic Republic of Korea (North Korea) have remained largely frozen throughout the post-war period. In the 1950s, Japan repatriated many Koreans – some with their Japanese spouses – to the North at their request. Bilateral trade began in the 1960s, but is dwarfed by the trade between Japan and South Korea. Visits to North Korea by Korean residents in Japan were inaugurated in the 1970s, as were the exchange of cultural and sports delegations. In response to calls from the North Korean leadership to normalise relations since the 1970s, Japan finally adopted a 'cross-recognition' policy, provisional on China and the Soviet Union also recognising South Korea. Colonial legacy has cast a long shadow over post-war relations between Japan and the two Koreas. Korean residents in Japan, most of whom were brought in as labourers under harsh conditions during the Second World War and constitute the largest ethnic minority in the country, continue to face considerable discrimination even in the wake of some recent significant legal reforms regarding citizenship rights. Since the 1980s, both Koreas protested against the Japanese government's alleged screening of textbooks to downplay its aggression in Asia and also demanded an official apology in the wake of the revelation of the sexual slavery of Korean women by Japan's military forces during the Second World War. Japan's government-sponsored Asian Women's Fund, which sought to compensate those victims through private channels, received much criticism in Korea for its lack of recognition of Japanese government responsibility.

Relations between Japan and South Korea saw further improvement in recent years, especially after the latter's transition to democracy. In his visit to Japan in 1998, Republic of Korea President Kim Dae-jung vowed to move beyond the past and look forward to future co-operation, while the Japanese government renewed its apology for past transgressions. The Republic of Korea took the necessary steps to remove restrictions on Japanese popular culture that had been in force since the end of the war. Korean and Japanese scholars expanded the collaborative efforts in historical research – first began in the mid-1960s – and made substantial progress in the 1990s. The two countries are scheduled to co-host the 2002 World Cup Football Games. Even their military forces began limited joint exercises, an unprecedented move to promote co-operation. Only the long-standing territorial dispute over the jurisdiction over Takeshima (Dokto in Korean) – a small island occupied by South Korea but claimed by Japan – remains to be resolved, along with issues relating to fishing rights in regional waters.

Japan's relations with the People's Democratic Republic of Korea remain estranged, however.

Inter-governmental negotiations for diplomatic normalisation began in the early 1990s, after the recognition of Seoul by China and the Soviet Union, but failed to produce any breakthrough. After the disintegration of the Soviet Union, North Korea came to be viewed as the major threat to the security of Japan. Renewed allegations of North Korea's abduction of Japanese citizens, intrusions into Japanese waters by North Korean 'spy boats' and reported nuclear facilities in North Korea have all contributed to the further deterioration of relations with North Korea. While Japan offered famine relief to the North and pledged participation in the KEDO project in North Korea in exchange for its abandonment of nuclear facilities, Pyongyang's launching of a test rocket over Japan in 1998 produced an outcry in Japan and brought the relations to an all-time low. More than fifty years after its colonial rule ended in Korea, Japan has yet to fully normalise relations with its closest but divided neighbour.

See also: comfort women

Further reading

Lee, C. (1985) *Japan and Korea: The Political Dimension*, Stanford: Hoover Institution Press.

Hughs, C. (1999) *Japan's Economic Power and Security: Japan and North Korea*, London: Routledge.

Hyun, I. and Okonogi, M. (eds) (1995) *Korea and Japan: Searching for Harmony and Cooperation in a Changing Era*, Seoul: Sejong Institute.

YANG DAQING

been examples of few depictions of Japanese since then, and again they have been primarily negative. Kwon-Taek's *Jokbo* (Family Tree Book, 1978) centres on an aristocratic patriarch who, forced to adopt a Japanese name to protect his family during the colonial period, commits suicide to apologise to his ancestors. Im's *Jangkuyui adeul* (The General's Son, 1990–92) features a Korean gangster fighting Japanese *yakuza* to protect Korean shop owners. In the conspiracy-filled *Munzoonghwa* (The Rose of Sharon Has Landed, 1995) South and North Korea discover their real enemies are the USA and Japan. *Kimyui jeonjaeng* (Min's War, 1992) depicts a second-generation Korean-Japanese man facing discrimination while living in Japan.

Since the mid-1990s, Korean films have depicted a shift in attitudes towards Japan. Younger Koreans are more strongly influenced by Japanese pop culture, and Japanese films have been legally released in Korea since 1998. Attempts to depict Japanese more objectively include *Kkangpae sueob* (Hoodlum Lessons, 1996), in which two Korean gangsters who end up in Japan learn *yakuza* ways, and Park Chul-Soo's *Kazoku cinema* (Family Cinema, 1998) featuring a dysfunctional Korean-Japanese family as the subject of a documentary film. *Kazoku cinema* is based on the work of the same name by the Korean-Japanese author **Yū Miri**. Both films, which were mainly shot in Japan, indicate South Korea re-examining its image of Japan.

WILLIAM C. THOMPSON

Korean images of Japan in film

In 1942, Japan closed all film companies in Korea, replacing them with a single Japanese propaganda machine. Resurrected following the Second World War, Korea's film industry initially featured themes of nationalism and liberation from Japanese rule, along with stories about martyrs and patriots. Choe In-gru's *Jayu manse* (Victory of Freedom, 1946), was the most important of the new post-war films. It depicts freedom fighters and their underground operations.

Although South Korea's film industry re-emerged following the Korean conflict, there have

Korean-Japanese literature

Korean-Japanese literature refers to the work written in Japanese by Koreans resident in Japan. The writings of these resident foreigners represents a literary phenomenon that has become increasingly visible since the 1960s. Their work presents a complex mosaic of national, cultural and individual identities, embodying a tension in Japanese society that has been largely ignored by critical discourse. Their status as resident foreigners allows them to be simultaneously inside and outside Japanese society, providing a distinctive and alternative view.

Most Koreans resident in Japan are descendants of those who came, or were brought, to Japan when Japan colonised the Korean peninsula between 1910 and 1945. Japan has actively promoted a homogeneous national identity and resident Koreans are still denied a number of basic civil rights, such as voting and access to public office. Korean-Japanese can become naturalised Japanese citizens, although many see this as a betrayal of their national heritage and political freedom; or they can become *zainichi chōsenjin*, which translates as 'Koreans residing in Japan', a status that denies them the freedoms of Japanese citizenship. While the first generation wanted to return home and was focused on the early re-unification of Korea, the later generations, who were born in Japan and speak only Japanese, often are more inclined to live within Japanese society and work for ethnic freedom.

Central to the work of Korean-Japanese writers is the relationship between personal identity and the notional homelands of Korea and Japan. Their work explores the resulting tension, attempting to reconcile Korean history and tradition with the real conditions of life in Japan. Their Korean cultural inheritance exists primarily as fragments in their everyday life, and their longing for a homeland is sustained as much by imagination as by any geographical or physical link. Korean-Japanese writing actively incorporates the cultural, historical and linguistic inheritance of Korea, exploring the discrepancy between socially imposed roles and an individual's sense of self, and examining how identity is challenged when separated from native tradition and a physical 'homeland'.

The awarding of the **Akutagawa Prize**, a prestigious award for new writers, to three Korean-Japanese has brought their work and its primary concerns to the attention of Japanese literary circles. These three writers are part of a new phenomenon in Korean-Japanese writing in that they write for a Japanese readership as well as their own ethnic group. **Yi Hwe-Sung** was the first to receive the prize in 1972 for *Kunuta o utsu onna* (Women at the Washing Stones), a tale of a young boy's early loss of his mother. **Yi Yang-Ji** was the second, winning in 1989 for her novel *Yuhi*, a story of a young Korean-Japanese woman, who travels to Korea in pursuit of the spirit of her motherland

only to find herself unable to cope with the resulting fracturing of her identity. **Yū Miri** became the third awardee with *Kazoku Shinema* (Family Cinema) in 1997, a story of a young woman who is confronted by the daily reality of a family coming apart while filming a family reunion.

See also: Koreans in Japan; Yi Hwe-Sung; Yi Yang-Ji; Yū Miri

Further reading

Field, N. (1993) 'Beyond envy, boredom, and suffering: Toward an emancipatory politics for resident Koreans and other Japanese', *Positions* 1(3): 640–70.

Mitsios, H. (ed.) (1991) *New Japanese Voices: The Best Contemporary Fiction from Japan*, New York: The Atlantic Monthly Press.

Paik, N. (1993) 'The Idea of a Korean National literature then and now', *Positions* 1(3): 553–80.

Ryang, S. (ed.) (1999) *Koreans in Japan: Critical Voices from the Margin*, London: Routledge.

CAROL HAYES

Korean schools

Prior to the First World War, Korean children in Japan were educated separately from Japanese children. Even after integration in 1922, they were still denied the opportunity to study their own language and history, and often adopted Japanese last names. About 90 per cent of Korean long-term residents possess Japanese names in addition to their Korean birth names. Currently, the majority of Korean children of school age attend Japanese schools. Of the Korean schools attended by 20 per cent of Korean children, most are affiliated with North Korea. Korean schools provide students with a cultural, historical and linguistic foundation not found in Japanese schools. The focus is on the Korean peninsula. Often, the history of Japan is taught as part of world history while students learn the Korean language and use it in daily conversation and refer to each other by their Korean names. Japanese language is taught as a second language. Uniforms tend to be based on traditional national dress, though some follow Japanese patterns, especially in primary school. North Korean high schools, similar to Japanese high schools, place a great emphasis on club participation. Since students who attend Korean schools are all Korean, they are not conscious of their ethnic identity in the same way as Korean students who attend Japanese schools. Thus, they do not experience their ethnicity negatively, as a minority that can still experience discrimination in mainstream schools. Those who criticise the Korean schools argue that they do not foster integration and that the Korean culture and language taught do not reflect the reality of contemporary North Korea. Should North and South Korea finally be re-unified, the fate of these schools may depend on whether or not the divisions between North- and South-affiliated Korean communities in Japan can also be overcome.

JUNE A. GORDON

Korean War

This refers to the military confrontation between the Democratic Peoples' Republic of Korea (DPRK), backed by the Peoples' Republic of China (PRC) and the USSR, on the one hand, and the Republic of Korea (ROK) and the UN, as represented by the USA, on the other. Armed hostilities began on June 25 1950 when DPRK pushed across the 38th parallel into ROK in an attempt to re-unite the two Koreas, and concluded with an armistice on July 27 1953.

At the end of the Second World War in 1945, Korea was divided along the 38th parallel, the north of which was occupied by the Soviets and the south by the Americans. This temporary division was made more meaningful when Kim Il-Song established the DPRK in the north and Syngman Rhee established the ROK in the south. When DPRK forces drove into ROK in 1950, the USA managed to secure UN approval for intervention against DPRK and provided the bulk of the fighting force. By the summer, DPRK pushed the ROK and US forces back to Pusan on the southeast coast. The USA counter-attacked in September by landing at Inch'ôn and advanced into North Korea as DPRK forces retreated across the border.

The conflict assumed a new tone, however, when the US forces continued their push toward Yalu River and threatened the PRC border. The PRC responded with a massive counter-attack that eventually led to a stalemate along the 38th parallel. The armistice of 1953 confirmed the 38th parallel as a demilitarised zone demarcating the two Koreas.

As **MacArthur** mobilised US troops to Korea, he counted on Japan as an important staging area. Japan fulfilled the US expectation of being the 'workshop' of non-communist Asia. 'Special procurements', or orders for US military necessities, were a magnificent windfall for the struggling Japanese economy. Virtually all industries reaped the benefits of huge demand for goods ranging from metal products and textiles to medicine and food items. In particular, the automobile industry received a much-needed boost in the form of a $13 million order for 7,079 trucks. Services such as repair works and personnel support were no less lucrative. All told, Japan filled orders totaling $2.3 billion from June 1950 through to 1953, making for a so-called special-procurements boom that produced an annual GNP growth of over 10 per cent and a trade surplus of $430 million in 1950. Even after hostilities ceased, $1.75 billion in additional orders came in between 1954 and 1956, largely for reconstructing war-torn South Korea.

While Prime Minister Yoshida called the conflict a 'gift of the gods', the war boom was not without its attendant problems, including inflation, goods shortage, hoarding, speculation and capital scarcity. Furthermore, the emotional ambivalence that some Japanese profiteers might have felt is perhaps best captured by the president of Toyota who is quoted as having described, 'a mingling of joy for my company and a sense of guilt over another country's war'. In the political realm, the war confirmed Japan's strategic value in cold war geopolitics and revived conservative trends such as SCAP's consideration of Japanese rearmament.

Further reading

Cumings, Bruce and Halliday, Jon (1988) *Korea: The Unknown War*, London: Penguin.

Dower, John W. (1999) *Embracing Defeat*, New York: Norton.

Iriye Akira (1974) *The Cold War in Asia*, Englewood Cliffs: Prentiss Hall.

Johnson, Chalmers (1982) *MITI and the Japanese Miracle*, Stanford: Stanford University Press.

Stueck, William (1995) *The Korean War: An International History*, Princeton: Princeton University Press.

HIRAKU SHIMODA

Koreans in Japan

Approximately 70,000 Koreans live in Japan as foreign residents. This figure does not include Koreans who are naturalised as Japanese citizens, the precise number of whom is not known. The majority of Koreans in Japan are permanent residents who were either colonial immigrants or are their descendants. In the late 1980s, the number of new immigrants from South Korea rose. The alien statistics compiled by the Japanese government include both permanent residents and newcomers under the category of 'Koreans', thereby obscuring the diverse constitution of Koreans in Japan.

During the Japanese colonial rule over Korea from 1910 to 1945, Koreans migrated to Japan in search of jobs and better living conditions. With the outbreak of the Pacific War, hundreds and thousands of Koreans were brought to Japan as a wartime workforce. In 1945, there were more than 2 million Koreans living in Japan. In the first several years following the end of the war, the majority of Koreans were repatriated. The outbreak of the Korean War in 1950 made it difficult for those Koreans still in Japan to return to Korea, thereby generating the population who would become the core of Japan's Korean resident communities. Prior to the Korean War, in 1948, separate states of North Korea and South Korea had emerged in the peninsula, dividing the nation.

These two antagonistic states reflected the politics of the cold-war confrontation. North Korea, supported by the USSR and led by the former anti-Japanese guerrilla fighters including Kim Il Sung, joined the communist camp; South Korea, directly governed by the US military, was regarded as the only legitimate state of the 'free world'. It was only in 1965 that Japan entered formal diplomatic relations with South Korea, while no diplomatic relation has been established between Japan and North Korea even today. The 1965 normalisation enabled Koreans in Japan to obtain South Korean nationality. The possession of South Korean nationality was a necessary pre-condition for acquiring permanent residence in Japan. Consistent with cold-war relations, only those who associated with South Korea were given better civil status in Japan, while those who did not opt for the South Korean government were left with hardly any civil-rights. It was only in the early 1980s that Koreans without South Korean nationality gained access to permanent residency in Japan. The political division in the peninsula was thus reproduced in the expatriate community of Koreans in Japan, resulting in the emergence of political organisations each supporting the different regimes of North and South. Chongryun, the North Korea-supporting organisation (est.1955), operates Korean ethnic schools from elementary to the graduate school level, runs its own credit union and has multiple media companies, among other activities. Mindan, the South Korea-supporting organisation (est.1945), also owns credit union and print media facilities, but on a lesser scale than Chongryun. During the cold-war years, the North–South confrontation swayed the life of Koreans in Japan, especially those of the first generation who regarded the partition of Korea as a temporary measure and upheld the belief that they would eventually return to Korea.

The situation of Koreans in today's post-cold-war Japan appears much different. The prolonged sojourn of Koreans in Japan saw the replacement of first-generation values with those of the Japan-born generations who are culturally more Japanised and look towards a future settlement in Japan, rather than a return to Korea. In the 1990s, the life in general for Koreans in Japan has improved. Due to the long boom period of the Japanese economy, the economic base for Koreans in Japan has been stabilised. There have also been improvements in the legal system concerning alien registration and foreign residents' rights. Today, the permanent residence status of Koreans in Japan guarantees a wider range of residential rights.

See also: Korea–Japan relations; Korean-Japanese literature; Korean schools

Further reading

Field, N. (1993) 'Beyond envy, boredom, and suffering: Toward an emancipatory politics for resident Koreans and other Japanese', *Positions* 1(3): 640–70.

Ryang, S. (ed.) (1999) *Koreans in Japan: Critical Voices from the Margin*, London: Routledge.

SONIA RYANG

koseki

Japan records its citizens' personal details such as date and place of birth, death, marriage, divorce and adoption in a single document, the *koseki* (family register). An individual's place of residence is recorded in a different documents (*jumin tōroku*). Although the *koseki* looks like a simple administrative document, it has a powerful social significance. Historically, it established the identity of the (male) head of the household (*koshu*) and the birth order of children, which determined rights and obligations in relation to inheritance. It also determined Japanese nationality. During Japan's colonial period, *koseki* registration became substantive proof of Japanese nationality. Today, when a prospective school or employer or marriage partner looks at a *koseki* extract, they can tell a family's regional origins; whether divorce has occurred; whether a person was born legitimate, illegitimate or adopted; the structure of the family and, in some cases, the racial origins of family members. This information allows systematic discrimination against, for example, people of *Burakumin* (outcaste) origin, people of Korean or Chinese descent and anyone with a non-standard family structure. For this reason, public access to copies of the *koseki* are now restricted.

See also: *Burakumin*; family system

VERONICA TAYLOR

Kōshikei

The 1968 fiction film *Kōshikei* (Death by Hanging) participates in director **Ōshima Nagisa**'s extended concern with the Japanese oppression of Koreans. *Kōshikei*'s deceptive documentary beginning, a problematisation of the death penalty, is only prelude to a complex meditation on fantasy and the social manufacturing of a marginalised other. When R., a resident Korean, 'refuses' to die at his hanging, losing only his memory instead, the executioner's staff re-educate him in his identity, all in order to hang him again. The film's experimental technique and biting social critique together make it a superior example of the *nouvelle vague*.

See also: Koreans in Japan; minority representation in film

JONATHAN M. HALL

kotatsu

The *kotatsu* is a low-legged table covered by a quilt and with a heating mechanism under the table. People sit on *zabuton* (cushions) at floor level with their legs tucked under the quilt where the warmth is captured. A removable table-top secures the quilt and acts as a working and eating surface. The origin of the *kotatsu* can be traced to the central cooking hearth. By the fourteenth century, a seating platform had been introduced at the edges of the hearth and, over time, the cooking and sitting functions separated and a cover was placed over the sitting area where a charcoal burner offered a concentrated, if localised, source of heat in the otherwise unheated and drafty Japanese housing. In homes where there is a *kotatsu* it still functions as a centre of family life in the colder months. Usually located in the family eating room next to or opening on to the kitchen, the *kotatsu* is used for meals, homework or games, and is often set up in view of the television. Western-style tables are becoming more common in larger apartments and homes, where dining and living areas are also more likely to be structurally separated. The basic principle of providing heat close to the floor has carried over into the widespread use of heated rugs and floors in Western-style living areas.

SANDRA BUCKLEY

Kurahashi Yumiko

b. 1935, Shikoku

Writer

In a career spanning four decades, Kurahashi Yumiko has established herself as one of the most important authors of the post-War era, known for her daring experiments in style, her ironic appropriations of Western and Japanese tales and her unique understanding of feminism.

Kurahashi is perhaps still best known for her first major work, the controversial political satire 'Parutai' (Party). Combining echoes of French existentialist writings with stinging lampoons of the young left-leaning intellectuals that populated the university campuses in the 1960s, the short story gained both rave reviews and criticism from the critics and established Kurahashi as one of the most important writers of the 1960s. Together with Ōe Kenzaburō and Abe Kōbō, she defined a new kind of literature that was heavily influenced by Western theory and methodology yet uniquely Japanese in its outlook and social context.

Kurahashi first tried her hand at writing after failing to get into medical school. Later, she attended Meiji University and majored in French literature. Like many young intellectuals of her generation, Kurahashi was influenced by Sartre, Camus and Kafka; her early works show a distinctively existentialist tendency. Early short stories such as 'Kai no naka' (Inside the Shell), 'Hebi' (Snake) and 'Kon'yaku' (Engagement) have a surreal, allegorical quality that is often compared to Kafka. Kurahashi eschews 'I-novelistic' realism (see **I-novel**), considering it unseemly for writers to expose their personal life to their readers. For her, writing is a performative act intended to create a fictitious 'anti-world' (*han-sekai*).

In 1966, Kurahashi spent a year as a Fulbright scholar in the creative-writing programme at the University of Iowa. This experience paved the way for one of Kurahashi's most productive periods,

during which she completed several major novels. The self-reflective novella *Baajinia* (Virginia, 1968) drew on her experience in the USA in a meditation upon the ultimate impossibility of bridging the cultural gap between East and West. The most notable achievement of this period was *Sumiyakisuto Q no bōken* (The Adventure of Sumiyakist Q, 1969), a grand political satire that explored the ideology and revealed the absurdity of a revolutionary movement. In 1971, Kurahashi wrote her signature novel, *Yume no ukihashi* (Bridge of Dreams, 1971). Inspired by the *Tale of Genji*, this lyrical tale of incest and *jouisance* is interwoven with the chaos created by the campus unrest of the early 1960s. Kurahashi was also drawn to Greek tragedies and *nō* plays, and this interest is reflected in a series of experimental short stories collected under the title *Han higeki* (Anti-tragedies, 1972).

Kurahashi's subsequent career has consisted, for the most part, of a series of variations on and refinements of her writings from this early period. The protagonist Keiko in *Bridge of Dreams* appears in later works such as *Shiro no naka no shiro* (A Castle within a Castle), *Shunposhion* (Symposium) and *Kōkan* (Fraternity). Through these works, Kurahashi has brought into being a fascinating female character, an intelligent, sophisticated, privileged woman who has matured through the years. Kurahashi has not lost her satirical edge, either. The political satire that she was famous for earlier in her career surfaces again in *Amanonkoku ōkanki* (The Record of the Journey to the Amanon Empire), which pokes fun at the concept of a feminist Utopia. Her talent for rewriting and reinterpreting pre-existing texts, already demonstrated in *Anti-tragedies*, reappears in her *Otona no tame no zankoku dōwa* (Cruel Fairy Tales for Adults), a humorous collection of parodies of fairy tales from around the world.

Positioned at the juncture of the pre-war and post-war generations of women writers, Kurahashi stands out for her rich imagination and her unyielding anti-establishment stance.

Select bibliography

Kurahashi Yumiko (1998) *The Woman with the Flying Head*, trans. A. Sakaki, New York: M.E. Sharpe.
—— (1989) 'The monastery' ('Kyosatsu'), in Van

C. Gessel and Tomone Matsumoto (eds) *The Showa Anthology*, trans. C. Haynes, Tokyo: Kōdansha International.

—— 'Partei' ('Parutai'), in Y. Tanaka and E. Hanson (eds) (1984) *This Kind of Woman, Ten Stories by Women Writers 1960–76*, trans. Y. Tanaka and E. Hanson, New York: G.P. Putnam's Sons.

—— 'To die at the estuary' ('Kakō ni shisu'), in H. Hibbett (ed.) (1977) *Contemporary Japanese Literature: An Anthology of Fiction, Film, and Other Writing Since 1945*.trans. D. Keene, New York: Alfred A. Knopf.

FAYE YUAN KLEEMAN

Kurokawa Kishō

b. 1934, Nagoya

Architect

Kurokawa graduated from the Department of Architecture, Kyōto University, and the Graduate School of Architecture, Tokyo University. By 1960, at the age of only twenty-six, he had made his mark on the architecture world as a founding member of the **Metabolism** Group. His Nakagin Capsule Tower (Tokyo, 1972) exemplifies Metabolism's emphasis on the prefabricated, modular unit.

Persistently theoretical in his approach to architecture, Kurokawa continues to elaborate his basic tenets of architecture via biological metaphors such as 'metamorphosis' and 'symbiosis', embracing French philosopher Gilles Deleuze's notions of 'nomadism' and 'rhizome' as well. A prolific writer, Kurokawa's seminal works include *Urban Design, Homo Movens, Thesis on Architecture I and II, The Era of Nomad, Philosophy of Symbiosis* and *Hanasuki*. His 1987 'New Tokyo Plan, 2025', which seeks to recentre the capital on to reclaimed land in Tokyo Bay to accommodate future population growth by non-Japanese as well as native residents, while alleviating overcrowding in 'Old Tokyo', is reminiscent of **Tange Kenzō**'s 1960 'Plan for Tokyo Bay'. His major works include: the National Ethnological Museum (Ōsaka, 1977); the National Bunraku Theatre (Ōsaka, 1983); Nagoya City Art Museum (1987); Hiroshima City Museum of Contemporary Art (1988); Museum of Modern Art (Wakayama, 1994); Japanese Studies Institute (Bangkok, 1985); Japanese-German Centre (Berlin, 1988); Chinese-Japanese Youth Centre (Beijing, 1990); Melbourne Central (1991); Pacific Tower (Paris, 1992); New Wing, Vincent Van Gogh Museum (Amsterdam, 1998); and Kuala Lumpur International Airport (1998).

Select bibliography

Kurokawa Kishō (1997) *Each One a Hero: The Philosophy of Symbiosis*, Tokyo: Kōdansha International, Ltd.

—— (1994) *The Philosophy of Symbiosis*, London: Academy Group, Ltd.

SCOTT GOLD AND MARY KNIGHTON

Kurosawa Akira

b. 1910, Tokyo; d. 1998, Tokyo

Film director

Japan's most celebrated film director, both domestically and abroad, and also, as one critic writes, its 'most undervalued', Kurosawa Akira authored a diverse *œuvre* of thirty films that includes pioneering uses of film technology as well as innovations in the two major categories of Japanese film, the historical film (*jidaigeki*) and contemporary social drama (gendaigeki). Kurosawa's remarkable competence within established genres coupled with his concurrent contestation of their tropes, his regular preference for narratives that revolve around unyielding characters in the face of overwhelming social conditions, his stubborn perfectionism in the film-making process and the regular use of actors Mifune Toshirō and Shimura Takashi, as well as the wide acclaim his films garnered in their figuring of Japan's experience of modernity, were each factors that contributed to making Kurosawa an internationally recognised film *auteur* in the 1950s and beyond.

After giving up hopes for a career as a painter, Kurosawa began work with PCL Studios (later to become Tōhō) in 1936, where he was trained under Yamamoto Kajirō. Kurosawa's first film as director was the popular, lyrically beautiful jūdō action film *Sugata Sanshirō* (Sanshiro Sugata, 1943). Other early films include the modernist-influenced propaganda piece *Ichiban utsukushiku* (The Most Beautiful, 1944) on the wartime factory effort, and the twelfth-century *jidaigeki Tora no o o fumu otokotachi* (The Men Who Tread on the Tiger's Tail, 1945), not screened commercially until after the end of the Allied Occupation. Kurosawa's independent, virtuous and strong-willed characters made his films useful at one level for furthering post-1945 US doctrines of 'individualism' and 'equality', yet recent critical work by Yoshimoto Mitsuhiro has suggested how Kurosawa's Occupation-era films, such as *Waga seishun ni kuinashi* (No Regrets for Our Youth, 1946) and *Nora inu* (Stray Dog, 1949), might contest dominant post-war ideologies. The 1950 *Rashōmon* (Rashomon), the first Japanese film to win major awards at the Venice Film Festival and the American Academy Awards, not only launched Kurosawa's international career but was also widely responsible for drawing worldwide attention to Japanese cinema.

Other films from the 1950s, including *Ikiru* (To Live, 1952), *Shichinin no samurai* (Seven Samurai, 1954) and *Ikimono no kiroku* (Record of a Living Being, 1955), epitomise Kurosawa's attention to individuals as they exist within social institutions of power, and the social critique evident in the early 1960s films *Warui yatsu hodo yoku nemuru* (The Bad Sleep Well, 1960) and *Tengoku to jigoku* (High and Low, 1963) suggest an increasing pessimism of social vision. Attacked by **Ōshima Nagisa** and other directors of the Japanese New Wave in the 1960s for a cinematic and narrative conservatism, and experiencing increasingly troubled relations with Japanese studios that could no longer afford the large production budgets he demanded, Kurosawa found himself unable to secure film financing domestically and turned in the mid-1960s to foreign capital. A brief affair with Hollywood ended in disaster when Twentieth-Century Fox removed him from the director's seat of *Tora, Tora, Tora*, leading the director into a nearly fatal depression. Kurosawa's production dwindled, but in his remaining decades he completed seven more films, including the MosFilm-funded *Dersu Uzala* (1975), the Shakespearian epic *Ran* (1985) and the self-referential *Madadayo* (1993).

Further reading

Goodwin, James (1994) *Akira Kurosawa and Inter-textual Cinema*, Baltimore: The Johns Hopkins University Press.

Mitsuhiro Yoshimoto (2000) *Kurosawa: Film Studies and Japanese Cinema*, Durham: Duke University Press.

Price, Stephen (1999) *The Warrior's Camera: The Cinema of Akira Kurosawa*, Princeton: Princeton University Press.

Richie, Donald (1996) *The Films of Akira Kurosawa*, Berkeley: The University of California Press.

JONATHAN M. HALL

Kyodo and Jiji News Agencies

The two major pre-war Japanese news agencies were amalgamated in 1936 to form the Domei News Agency for the period of Japan's war effort. After defeat, Domei was replaced by the wire services Kyodo Tsūshin and Jiji Tsūshin but there was considerable continuity between these agencies and their pre-war predecessors. Kyodo remained closely linked to the large and influential advertising agency Dentsu. Kyodo and Jiji agreed to share the market with Kyodo functioning as a co-operative, and sourcing general news for the news industry while Jiji was to operate as a for-profit organisation sourcing economic news for publishers and business.

Both agencies were quick to establish overseas services after the end of the Occupation. Jiji focused on developing facsimile-based communications and English-language services. JIJIWIN, an English economic news service, was established in 1982. Kyodo focused on Japanese language communications and developed important technology for Japanese character type and transmission. In 1965, Kyodo World Service was established as the English international news service of the Kyodo system. The agreed division of new services (news sector versus business world) has broken down as each agency continues to encroach into the others' traditional markets. There has been growing criticism of the biased selection of materials for translation into English for international transmission, with a tendency to under-represent domestic stories portraying a negative image of Japan. There has been some gradual redressing of this imbalance as more foreign reporters with Japanese language skills are recruited by international agencies and networks. Kyodo today employs more than 2,000 and is fully funded by its members and subscriptions. Jiji employs 1,400, who are also the majority shareholders in the agency. Both agencies now offer extensive online services in addition to standard print media releases.

Further reading

Cooper-Chen Anne (1997) *Mass Communication in Japan*, Ames, Iowa: Iowa University Press.

SANDRA BUCKLEY

kyōgen

Kyōgen, Japan's oldest comic-acting tradition and the companion to the serious *nō* drama, dates back some 600 years. Trained from childhood, *kyōgen* actors traditionally perform in three distinct roles: as the interlude player (*aikyōgen*) within a *nō* play (most often, a man of the area or a god of a subsidiary shrine); in the danced role of Sambaso for the New Year's ritual *Okina Sambaso* performance; and, most frequently, as the performers in the 250-some short comic skits (*honkyōgen*) performed on the *nō* stage between two *nō* plays during a day's performance. While the former two roles are not meant to be overtly comic, the broad gestures, unique intonation and whimsical design on the costumes lend a common earthiness to all of the *kyōgen* roles. Unlike the *nō*, which is based on dance movement and music, *kyōgen* acting relies on mime and verbal play. The movement is highly stylised but the setting, the mimetic depictions, the character-types, the costume and the props are all recognisable as part of everyday life in the sixteenth century. In this sense, *kyōgen* offers a realistic counterpoint to the symbolic nature of the *nō*.

Kyōgen plays are generally twenty to thirty minutes in length and require only two to three main actors. For most plays, the plots turn on such simple comic devices as mistaken identity (*Hanago*, *Buaku*, etc.), reversal of roles (*Bushclover Daimyō*,

Poison, etc.) and tricksters outsmarting country bumpkins. There are a number of plays, however, with a darker, more poignant tone such as *The Blind Man Goes Moon Viewing* (which tells the story of a blind man who is first befriended and then tripped up by a passerby). Such plays are possible because the humour in *kyōgen* tends toward an ironic identification of the viewer with the main character (the butt of the humour) rather than the satiric or slapstick humour of medieval European farce.

The staging of *kyōgen* plays is simple, requiring few props and relying on repetitive patterns for blocking movement on the stage. For example, the main character tends to open the play by announcing who he is and why he is there (the name announcement scene). He may then make a circle of the stage (a travel scene) and then call upon a neighbour or servant (calling out the neighbor scene). The simplicity of the staging allows the gesture and costume of the characters to stand out in contrast. Mimetic movement (often exaggerated) is precisely choreographed; for example, the toasting of chestnuts with only a fan as a prop and the popping of the hot chestnuts back and forth in the hands, etc. The costumes, as well, have a simple, bold appeal. In particular, the vest (*kataginu*) worn over the robes by many of the characters (especially the master and servant) is considered characteristic of *kyōgen*. The vest is made of a stiff hempen material and displays across the back any one of a number of whimsical drawings, such as a giant turnip, a dragonfly, rabbits, crabs and so forth. Unlike the patterns on a *nō* robe, the *kyōgen* design is simple with only a few objects represented against a plain, solid background. Masks are rare in *kyōgen* since among the various mimetic movements are the laugh, the cry, anger, feat and surprise, all accomplished through manipulation of the face. In some instances a mask is identified with a specific character type, such as the *Ofuku* mask of the young girl (big round cheeks and a tiny mouth), the old-man mask and animal masks, to name a few. Just as often, however, masks appear as props on stage and are donned and taken off to further the mechanism of the plot, in particular in plays turning on the device of mistaken identity.

Today, two of the original three *kyōgen* schools remain, the Okura and the Izumi. The Sagi school appears to have died out at the end of the Tokugawa Period, when the *nō* and *kyōgen* theatre no longer could expect government patronage. In the 1970s and 1980s, *kyōgen* experienced a remarkable boom in popularity and this resulted in *kyōgen* actors travelling abroad. Although *kyōgen* is still normally seen on the *nō* stage, actors today also perform in other settings such as performance halls, or on various outdoor stages independently of the *nō*. Because *kyōgen* is a theatre of mime, it is easily accessible and has found a wide audience both at home and abroad.

CAROLYN A. MORLEY

kyōiku mama

The neutral meaning of *kyōiku mama* reflects a self-sacrificing woman who dedicates her life to providing an optimal learning environment for her child, which includes a quiet space to study with desk, light and a range of acceptable educational accoutrements, the quality of which is often dictated by either the school or peer pressure. Over 95 per cent of all elementary-school children have their own desks in designated study areas. While Japanese parents, in general, feel that it is their responsibility to give their children the best education possible, the onus falls upon the mother. If a child falls behind her/his peers, it is the mother who takes the blame and shame. As a result, the mother tries to instill in the child an awareness that academic success is important to more than just the child. The mother–child bond provides strong emotional support for the child in a highly competitive environment.

Kyōiku mamas monitor their children's lives to esure maximum access to educational opportunities. They find appropriate tutors and *juku*, ensure that their children associate with the right peers and, in general, direct children's free time towards study. The average Japanese child is also not expected to help around the house with chores or allowed to take an outside job for income. If money is needed to pay for the extra costs, whether it be *juku*, private school, college or more educational amenities, mothers will often take **part-time work**.

Studying is encouraged and supported in the Japanese home. *Kyōiku mamas* work with their children on a daily basis, helping with homework or drilling them on lessons. Inexpensive study guides are available at local bookshops. These are designed to supplement the government-approved texts and are indexed to pages and chapters in the official texts. During school vacations, parents are provided with guidelines on student behaviour, including suggested times to get up and go to bed, as well as the amount of time that should be spent studying. Mothers are often pressured into accepting this role through community and societal expectations. Those who resist in the name of providing a more balanced or liberal situation risk their child's ostracisation from peers, the ire of their teacher and potential consignment to a low-status high school and/or job. In a country where community acceptance is still a part of everyday existence, the possible embarrassment is profound. With few exceptions, once a child fails, the entire family suffers a loss of self esteem.

While many in the Western world attribute a great deal of Japanese educational success to *kyōiku mamas* and see parental involvement in the academic lives of children as an asset, some Japanese do not always see *kyōiku mamas* in such a positive light. Pressure on students can result in a child lashing out at the parents and, in particular, the mother. This is as true for very intelligent children as for those who find the academic rigour overwhelming. If the pressure is too great, even students who have strong potential may simply refuse to do well in school in order to shame and undermine their mothers. Some observers claim that the *kyōiku mama* phenomenon is the main cause of students dropping out, *ochikobore* (see **drop-outs**) and a contributing factor in 'school refusal' cases.

JUNE A. GORDON

Kyōto

Kyōto is the capital of Kyōto Prefecture, but more widely known as the imperial capital of Japan from the Heian Period (794) to 1868, after which the capital was officially moved to Edo, which was in turn renamed **Tokyo**. It is the cultural and religious centre of Japan and a major site of tourism activity for more than 30 million visitors annually. Its cultural artefacts were protected during the Second World War, when the Allies made a special agreement to refrain from bombing Kyōto. Situated on a plain surrounded by mountains, at some distance from the seacoast, Kyōto is known for its relatively cold winters and its hot, humid summers.

Kyōto is also a major industrial centre, most noted for the production of handicrafts, particularly silk and ceramics, as well as lacquer ware, dolls, religious paraphernalia, and masks, fans and other props used in the traditional performance arts of **nō**, **kabuki** and *bunraku* (puppet theatre). Kyōto's most important economic activity remains cultural production.

Unlike most Japanese cities, Kyōto was originally laid out according to Chinese cosmological principles, on a north–south oriented grid. Its wide avenues, many of which are still lined with willow and cherry trees, are ironically well adapted to contemporary traffic. Kyōto's elegant old wooden homes are slowly giving way to modern buildings, although Kyōto remains relatively low-rise compared to other major cities. Kyōto is well known for its progressive urban government, whose concern for planning is evident in the high level of street maintenance, and in the wide range of civic buildings and recreational projects. Throughout, Kyōto is a landscape of intense cultural expression. Its universities, art galleries, museums, palaces and, above all, temples run the full gamut from the oldest traditional to the newest pop culture, but with a deeply cultivated air of grace, elegance and decorum found nowhere else in Japan. The streets ring with the Kyōto dialect, a distinctive form of **Kansai** speech, considered by Kyōto residents to be the most distinguished form of Japanese, and by those from Tokyo to be stilted and old-fashioned. It is not uncommon to see women on the streets dressed in traditional **kimono**, while men tend to be dressed more conservatively than in other cities. The many priests, students and academics provide a distinctive contrast to modern chic. The residents of Kyōto celebrate their cultural heritage in an almost constant series of festivals, the most famous being the Gion Festival during which, every July, neighbourhood groups parade through the streets carrying ornate floats, most of which have been maintained for centuries by generations of neighbourhood association members. In the autumn, the *Jidai Matsuri* (Festival of the Ages) brings thousands of people to parade through the streets wearing period costumes that reflect Kyōto's history.

One of the most striking aspects of Kyōto's urban landscape is its neigbourhood variety. In the eastern hills, tree-lined 'Philosopher's Walk' winds along beside opulent but subdued private residences and a string of temples, large and small. In the west, the Nishinjin district houses Japan's major producers of fine silk; its streets are filled with the sounds of shuttles clicking, from houses especially designed to accommodate the weaving process. In Shita-Machi, the centre of the city, one moves from the elegant wooden homes along and close to Karasuma-dori, the main north–south axis, east through a maze of small streets teeming with commerce, where one can find everything from a huge variety of traditional foods to priceless antique art works, towards Gion, Japan's most famous entertainment district. Here is the home of the original *kabuki* theatre, and here developed the high arts of female entertainment by the *geiko* (known elsewhere as 'geisha') and *maiko* (apprentice *geiko*). The area is still one of Japan's most flourishing pleasure districts, where infinitely complex gradations of gender, sexuality and sophistication are negotiated in the most elegant (and expensive) surroundings.

As a spiritual centre, Kyōto has approximately 1,500 Buddhist temples and 300 Shintō shrines, many of them located in the surrounding hills, separated somewhat from the secular urban world, where they were once disallowed, to prevent their interference in civic affairs. One of Kyōto's major temples, however, Nishi-Honganji, the headquarters of Jōdō-Shinshū, Japan's largest Buddhist sect, is situated in central Kyōto, very close to today's central train station, a symbol of the dominant role that this institution has played in Japanese affairs. Also close to Kyōto Station is Tōji, with its five-tiered pagoda (representing the five unifying principles of the universe) whose postcard image has conveyed Japan to thousands throughout the world. Tōji is the site of one of the most popular of the monthly temple fairs, where people flock to find food and a range of goods from slightly used to antique. The more significant destinations for Japanese visitors, however, are the many famous temples with their collections of art and contemplative gardens. These include Kiyomizu-dera, older than Kyōto itself; Nanzen-ji, which epitomises the austere style of the Zen sect; Ginkaku-ji, the 'Silver Pavillion', surrounded by an exquisite Zen garden; Daitoku-ji, where one may sample Zen temple food; Kinkaku-ji, recently built and resplendent in gold leaf, in contrast to the subtle Zen style; or Ryoan-ji, the site of the most famous Zen garden, built of dry stones. Ironically, it is difficult to enjoy the contemplative ambience of the garden as it was intended, because of the huge crowds that flow through in regulated tours.

See also: Buddhism; gardens

AUDREY KOBAYASHI

L

land reclamation

The Japanese coastline, particularly along the eastern and south-eastern submergent coasts, has undergone massive extension to accommodate the rapid post-war expansion of industry. From **Tokyo** Bay, which began to be filled from as early as the eighteenth century, to the southern tip of Honshū, there is an almost continuous ribbon of landfill, comprising 160,000 hectares protected by 10,000 km of dykes. The Tokyo Bay Highway Loop connects Tokyo, **Yokohama**, Kawasaki, Kisarazu and Chiba in a series of artificial islands and tunnels. **Kansai** International Airport, opened in 1994 as the country's second most important transportation hub, was constructed entirely on the former **Ōsaka** Bay. Perhaps the most famous example is Port Island, built with fill transported from the nearby Rokko Mountains, to extend the city of **Kobe** with major container port facilities, hotels and conference centres. It was severely damaged, but withstood a major earthquake in 1994. Japanese engineers are sought worldwide for their unique expertise in artificial-land management systems. Although the massive landfill is usually rationalised by the expressed need for flat land to develop industrial and transportation systems, the loss of Japan's picturesque coastline is also lamented. Especially along the **Inland Sea**, some of the most famous vistas have been preserved as a form of landscape museum.

AUDREY KOBAYASHI

land reform

Land redistribution was perhaps the most successful of all the reforms carried out during the **Allied Occupation** of Japan following the Second World War. At the end of the war, nearly half of the population lived in the countryside, and nearly half of all farm land was worked by tenants. The Occupation considered this a dangerous stumbling block to political and economic democratisation. It sought to create a new class of yeoman farmers by purchasing landlords' 'excess' holdings and reselling the land to the former tenants, and by 1950 only 10 per cent of farm land was tenanted.

Pre-war tenant unions and reformist bureaucrats had lobbied without success for land reform, but wartime controls weakened landlords' influence. Under pressure from SCAP (**Supreme Commander for Allied Powers** General Douglas **MacArthur** and his headquarters), the Diet passed a bill for limited land reform in December 1945. SCAP and the other Allies rejected a Soviet proposal that land be expropriated without compensation, but forced the Japanese government to pass a second, more comprehensive land reform bill in October 1946.

By 1950, national, prefectural and local land commissions completed the complicated task of deciding what land the government would buy, to whom it would be sold and what the price should be. The government purchased all land held by absentee landlords, and all land held by resident landlords beyond a certain amount (which averaged three hectares outside Hokkaidō, where 12 hectares was the limit). Tenants were given thirty-year mortgages at 3.2 per cent interest. Prices were calculated using 1945 figures, and hyperinflation of the early post-war period meant that this massive land transfer did in fact amount to virtual expropriation. After the reforms, owners were allowed to rent out small portions of their land, but rents had to be in cash rather than kind and could not be more than 25 per cent of the value of the crop.

The reforms resulted in dramatic changes in the political economy of the villages, though social relations changed more slowly. Land reform did not create larger farms, but the incentives provided by ownership led to increased agricultural productivity, partly through small-scale mechanisation and the use of chemical fertilisers and pesticides. Farm families' standard of living improved further during the post-war period as rural residents found it possible to devote less time to farming and more to jobs in nearby towns and factories.

Capable bureaucrats and willing volunteers at the local level carried out this massive, foreign-ordered land transfer remarkably smoothly. The land reforms succeeded because they provided immediate, tangible economic and social benefits to millions of people. Farmers' lives were improved significantly, and rural voters came to provide important support for the conservative governments that led post-war Japan.

Further reading

Developing Economies 4(2) (1966) (special issue on land reform).

Dore, R. (1959) *Land Reform in Japan*, Oxford: Oxford University Press.

Fukutake, T. (1967) *Japanese Rural Society*, trans. R. Dore, Ithaca: Cornell University Press.

Redford, L. (ed.) (1980) 'The Occupation of Japan: economic policy and reform', Norfolk, Virginia: MacArthur Memorial (proceedings of a 1978 symposium).

TIMOTHY S. GEORGE

language

Approximately 125 million people in the Japanese archipelago speak the Japanese language (usually called *kokugo* inside Japan and *nihongo* outside it). Sizeable communities in South America, Hawaii and California also speak it as the result of earlier waves of migration to those areas. Japanese is the main language spoken in Japan. Since Japan was never colonised by another country, its language has never faced the kind of struggle for dominance against the language of a colonising power seen in other parts of Asia. Regional **dialects**, the minority languages in use among various ethnic groups and the powerful influence of English mean that the linguistic landscape is still far from one-dimensional.

The standard form of Japanese, or *hyōjungo*, which is spoken and understood throughout the country, is based on the speech of the Tokyo dialect, in particular the dialect of the inner Yamanote area of the city. This variant was designated the standard by the National Language Research Council in 1916. The standard language is used in writing and in formal-speaking situations. When people are interacting casually, however, they usually speak a variant called *kyōtsūgo* (common Japanese). This is close to Standard Japanese in all its main features but less formal; it includes contractions, for example, and people living in regional areas might include expressions from their local dialect. Regional dialects, which were accentuated by the political segmentation of Japan during its feudal period, do remain, and some of them are quite markedly different from those of other areas. However, the over-arching use of the standard language throughout Japan overcomes any communication difficulties this might cause.

In addition to the national language itself, there are a number of minority languages spoken in Japan. These include **Ainu**, Korean (see **Koreans in Japan**), Chinese and English, with Okinawan also being spoken in the southern islands of the archipelago. The Ainu community, located predominantly in the northern island of Hokkaidō, is small in size (around 24,000 are officially registered). Private language schools in Hokkaidō teach the Ainu language; since the passing of the Ainu New Law in May 1997, they have been helped by government support. The Foundation for Research and Promotion of Ainu Culture was set up by the Hokkaidō Development Agency and the Ministry of Education in September 1997 to implement the provisions of the law, which include the promotion of the Ainu language. The Foundation trains Ainu language instructors, broadcasts Ainu-language radio courses, holds an Ainu language speech contest and conducts Ainu language classes in fourteen areas in Hokkaidō and the Kantō area around Tokyo. The diminishing number of native speakers of Ainu as the population ages is an important consideration underlying both the training of teachers and the dissemination of the language itself.

The ethnic Korean minority in Japan (see **Koreans in Japan**) numbers around 650,000. Most of these are permanent residents who come from families who chose to remain in Japan after Japanese colonial rule in Korea came to an end in 1945 or were isolated in Japan by the Korean War and subsequent partition of North and South Korea. Their communities, in particular Chongryun, the North-Korea-supporting General Association of Korean Residents in Japan, work hard to maintain the Korean language, running their own schools up to and including tertiary level where education is conducted in that language. However, language proficiency among the second, third and now fourth generations has been decreasing. Chinese, both Cantonese and Mandarin, is spoken in communities found in the Tokyo area, the Kansai region and Nagasaki; the small number of Chinese schools in Japan have a bilingual policy of instruction. In Okinawa, the Ryūkyūan dialects are widely spoken in addition to Japanese; the standard variety among them is the Shuri dialect of Okinawa.

Although English is not spoken widely in Japan, the study of the language is compulsory (though not by law) in middle and high schools, so that most Japanese leave school having studied English for six years. Many then go on to further study at university. The teaching of foreign languages in Japan has been fostered in recent years through the Japan Exchange and Teaching (JET) programme, which was established in 1987 with the aim of promoting internationalisation at the local level. A feature of this programme is the team teaching approach of using Assistant Language Teachers (ALT) in classrooms in tandem with Japanese teachers of English, French and German.

Teaching the Japanese language to non-Japanese is now a growth industry both inside and outside Japan. The spectacular performance of the Japanese economy in the 1970s and 1980s led to a push to spread the teaching of Japanese to overseas learners through the activities of the Japan Foundation, established in 1972. While the Foundation's activities are not limited to language promotion, it has been active in fostering such programmes, both by bringing teachers to Japan for development work and by establishing active language institutes in other countries. Within Japan itself, the study of Japanese as a foreign language at both universities and private language schools has boomed, particularly in the wake of a government decision to increase the number of foreign students studying in Japan.

The language itself has changed in various ways in the post-war period. One very noticeable feature of the lexicon, for example, has been the increasing popularity of both loanwords from English and other languages, and neologisms created from corruptions of loanwords. Preferring the sophisticated image they believe using a foreign word gives, many people will use a loanword even when a perfectly functional Japanese alternative exists: for example, *biggu-na* instead of *ōkii* for 'big'. This trend shows no sign of diminishing, as a perusal of any popular magazine or advertising catalogue shows. Scores of Japanese magazines have foreign words, predominantly English, as their titles, e.g. *Outdoor, Motor, Flash, Class* and so on. The spread of computers in particular has brought with it a plethora of new terms from English, such as *mausu* (mouse), *fuairu* (file), *kurikku* (click) and so on. To take an extreme example, *ko-garu-go* (high-school girl-talk) is liberally sprinkled with English terms, many from US pop culture, which may have been adapted to fit Japanese grammar. *Hageru* in this dialect, for example, is a verb meaning to buy a Häagen-Dazs ice cream, formed by adding the *-ru* verb ending on to the first part of the trade name.

An issue that has gained prominence in some areas since the 1970s has been the protests against

language considered by its targets to be discriminatory either in terms of outright denigration or of
inappropriate linguistic stereotyping. Terms that
have attracted comment have been, as in other
countries, those relating to minority groups. in
Japan's case, these have included **Burakumin** (a
group of Japanese traditionally considered outcastes
because of the nature of their occupations), Ainu,
women, people with disabilities, certain occupations
and ethnic groups such as the large Korean
community. Since the mid-1970s, mass-media
organisations have had lists of prohibited words –
such as *eta* (the characters used to write this word
mean 'great pollution') for *Burakumin*, *kichigai* (madness) for extreme enthusiasm of any sort and so on –
and lists of words that are used to replace them. This
has led to political correctness debates of the kind
also found in other countries; the lists have been
criticised by opponents, in particular by some
members of the Japan Writers' Association, as being
unacceptable attempts to restrict freedom of expression. Others, however, see them as evidence of
an increasing sensitivity to the needs of minority
groups in the language of public debate. As
elsewhere, the debate continues from time to time.

Japanese is written with a combination of **kanji**
(Chinese characters as used in Japan) and two
phonetic scripts, *hiragana* and **katakana**. In
written Japanese, the predominant feature of the
post-war period has been the implementation of
script reforms that have limited the number of *kanji*
in common use, modernised *kana* spelling, rationalised the number of ways any one character can be
pronounced and simplified some of the more
complex character shapes. These and other reforms, introduced immediately after the war, were
the results of a push to democratise the script and
make the written language of public life more
accessible to all by simplifying language education.
They later became the focus of bitter argument
during the 1960s, when opponents of the reforms
argued that they imposed unacceptable limits on
freedom of expression and had led to a decline in
the literacy standards of children educated in post-
war. In 1981, the character list was amended
slightly to raise the total recommended for general
use from 1,850 to the current 1,945. The National
Language Council of Japan (Kokugo Shingikai)

completed a twenty-five-year cycle of revision of
the post-war reforms in 1991.

One of the major issues relating to script since the
early 1980s has been the impact of word-processing
technology in Japan. The difficulties that a large
character set placed in the way of machine input and
output meant that Japan never had a successful
typewriter age. Once machines were developed that
could handle characters electronically without
needing a large keyboard, however, these obstacles
were to a large extent overcome. Businesses and
private users alike took to the technology rapidly, so
that, during the 1980s, stand-alone word processors
(i.e. a single machine incorporating keyboard, LCD
screen and printer) sold in increasingly large
numbers. Later, after the use of personal computers
began to spread, word-processing software packages
also began to sell well. Many people have questioned
whether the habit of using a word processor, with the
attraction of being able to retrieve large numbers of
characters from its memory banks relatively easily,
will mean that people will eventually lose their
ability to write characters by hand. If the widespread
use of computers and word processors continues, as
it seems certain to do, we may see changes in
national script policy, with more characters being
taught in schools for recognition and fewer for
reproduction. The National Language Council is
examining this issue. Meanwhile, because this
technology exists, Japan has been able to construct
a substantial Japanese-language presence on the
Internet. After a slow start, Japanese rapidly climbed
to a position as equal second most common
language after English on the Internet (neck and
neck with Spanish) after only a couple of years. The
Ministry of Post and Telecommunications calculated that the number of characters found on
Japanese web pages one year actually exceeded the
number found in print sources produced that year.

See also: Ainu; *Burakumin*; Chinese in Japan;
computers and language; dialects; Japan
Foundation; *kanji*; Koreans in Japan; Korean schools

Further reading

Backhouse, A.E. (1993) *The Japanese Language: An
Introduction*, Melbourne: Oxford University Press.
Gottlieb, N. (1995) *Kanji Politics: Language Policy and*

Japanese Script, London: Kegan Paul International.

Maher, J. and Yashiro, K. (eds) (1995) *Multilingual Japan*, Avon, England: Multilingual Matters Ltd.

Miller, R.A. (1980) *The Japanese Language*, Tokyo: Charles E. Tuttle.

Neustupyn, J.V. (1987) *Communicating with the Japanese*, Tokyo: The Japan Times.

Ryang, S. (1997) *North Koreans in Japan: Language, Ideology and Identity*, Boulder: Westview Press.

NANETTE GOTTLIEB

LDK

Many foreigners arriving in Japan and struggling to find their first apartment to rent come up against the mystery of LDK. All apartments are categorised according to their **tatami** mat size, even if they do not include any *tatami*. A six-*jo* room is a six-mat room and is referred to as I(one)K. IDK is a six-mat room with a kitchen. ILDK is six-mat room plus kitchen and living room. 2LDK would indicate two six-mat rooms with kitchen and living room, a quite generous space for a single person by Japanese housing standards. Rooms are frequently multifunctional and the living room of a ILDK or 2LDK might also serve as a bedroom with futon bedding stored in a cupboard during the day.

SANDRA BUCKLEY

legal/judicial system

Japan is often characterised as having a civil law (i.e. European-style) legal system. In fact, Japan's legal system, like those of other countries, is now a hybrid model. From the eighth century, Japan imported legal concepts and models of government from China, and, until the seventeenth century, state law in Japan was basically administrative rules for government officials, and locally administered criminal codes adapted for Japanese use. Unification of the country under the Tokugawa shōguns (1600–1868) led to the creation of national legal rules and adjudication by government officials – mainly in cases concerning criminal offences; land and water disputes; taxation; inheritance and the control of the samurai (warrior bureaucrat class). Merchant guilds and associations developed private commercial law governing areas such as contracts, product quality and loans. Family law and local governance were developed through custom. Official legal rules and dispute resolution were mainly used to maintain social order and control in a class society where the Tokugawa rulers had only precarious control over the provinces. Tokugawa law officially discouraged litigation, but, by the Meiji Period (1868–1912), economic change had forced the development of a highly sophisticated system for adjudicating commercial and civil disputes.

After the fall of the Tokugawa, Meiji reformers were forced to reform completely the legal and judicial systems. The catalysts for change were the unequal trade treaties forced on Japan by the USA, the UK and European powers. The Meiji government resolved to actively study and adopt the key legal institutions that would mark Japan as a civilised power in the eyes of the West. So, a Parliament was created under the Constitution of 1889 and Japan adopted European-style codified law that covered civil, commercial, criminal and procedural law. Customary law continued to be recognised in a limited way through the Codes and in the attempts of the new, independent judiciary to reconcile traditional values and norms with newly imported legal concepts. As a colonial power, Japan imposed its European-style laws and legal institutions on its colonies Korea and Formosa (present-day Taiwan). After independence, both countries reverted to national legal systems, but remain closely linked to trends in Japanese jurisprudence and law reform.

A second convulsive change in Japan's legal system occurred with Japan's loss in the Second World War. The **Allied Occupation** authorities under SCAP (the **Supreme Commander for Allied Powers**) interpreted the **Potsdam Declaration** as a mandate to democratise Japan. The Constitution was rewritten by the Occupation authorities in consultation with Japanese advisers to make the Cabinet accountable to the Parliament; to introduce a Bill of Rights, including gender equality; to limit the Emperor's role to symbolic head of state and – more controversially – to renounce Japan's right of war (Article 9).

In line with the new Constitution, the Civil Code (see **Civil Code of 1948, the**) was reformed to guarantee equality of the sexes and to abolish discrimination in legal treatment based on differences in status under the feudal household (*ie*) system. The Occupation reformers introduced Anglo-American legal principles in areas such as administrative and commercial law. One example is the Anti-monopoly Law of 1947, designed at the time to break down the economic power of industrial conglomerates (*zaibatsu*), the forerunners of the *keiretsu* (interrelated companies) that became central to Japan's business and economic growth between the 1960s and 1990s.

Today, Japan has a legal system that is much closer to those of other industrialised countries than it is to other legal systems in Asia. It is a unitary system (i.e. a single jurisdiction). Japan's courts are, in ascending order, Summary Courts, District Courts, High Courts and a single Supreme Court of fifteen justices. Its highly educated judiciary has a reputation for impartiality. Lawyers, prosecutors and judges are selected from those who have successfully passed a national bar examination and who then complete an eighteen-month training period at the Supreme Court Judicial Training Institute. Prosecutors and judges become career bureaucrats, while lawyers enter private practice. Most bar exam candidates study law as undergraduates at university but this is not essential; most bar preparation is actually undertaken at private specialist coaching colleges (*yobikō*).

Japan's relatively low number of lawyers and judges has often been interpreted as a deliberate policy by government to discourage litigation. Certainly it has far fewer judges than its nearest point of comparison in the civil law world, Germany. Japan's bar examination is also artificially difficult, for many years permitting a pass rate of only 1.5 per cent or 1,500 people per year, now lifted to about 2,000 per year. Foreign lawyers may practice in Japan, but have been prevented from expanding their operations by restrictive rules that govern foreign lawyers, Japanese lawyers (*bengoshi*, or barristers) and other legal professionals (such as tax attorneys, patent attorneys and scriveners who are equivalent to solicitors).

Japan's legal and judicial systems, however, are now the subject of wide-scale pressure for reform.

Since 1999, a government-appointed Commission on Reform on the Legal System (*shihōkaikaku iinkai*) has been examining, among other thing, how to: improve citizens' access to lawyers; increase legal aid; bolster alternative dispute resolution outside court settings; improve access to the courts; review a public defender system for accused criminals; consider the introduction of a jury system; increase the number of legal professionals; strengthen legal ethics; reform legal education in universities.

Many commentators see a strong continuity between Japan's contemporary legal structures and those of the Tokugawa and Meiji Periods (patriarchal families; gender inequality; social hierarchy; strong government; deference to the bureaucracy). Some have characterised the Japanese legal system as a public regime that was designed primarily for the convenience of the state and for key economic institutions such as *keiretsu* corporations, rather than to allow citizens to assert their individual rights or to challenge the state or claim redress from others. Landmark departures from this trend include the Minamata disease litigation and related cases where the courts upheld claims by groups of tort victims against both government and corporations. Counter-examples include the prevalence of financial and government scandals in which prosecution is a very recent 1990s phenomenon, and in the area of human rights, where there is a contrast between Japan's strong record on ratifying international human rights conventions, and a reluctance to implement them domestically. As Japan enters the twenty-first century, however, after more than a decade of economic recession and structural reform, policy makers are increasingly seeking answers to social problems in law. Custom, the importance of relationships and informal means of resolving problems live on, but are being overlaid with increasingly complex legal regulation.

See also: Allied Occupation; Civil Code of 1948, the; Minamata disease; Potsdam Declaration; scandals

Further reading

Baum, Harald and Nottage, Luke (1998) *Japanese Business Law in Western Languages: An Annotated*

Selective Bibliography, New York: Fred Rothman and Co.

Haley, John O. (1998) *The Spirit of Japanese Law,* Athens: University of Georgia Press.

Iwasawa Yuji (1998) *International Law, Human Rights, and Japanese Law: the Impact of International Law on Japanese Law,* Oxford and New York: Clarendon Press.

Oda Hiroshi (1999) *Japanese Law,* Oxford: Oxford University Press.

Ramsayer, J. Mark and Nakazato Minoru (1998) *Japanese Law: An Economic Approach.* Chicago: University of Chicago Press.

Taylor, Veronica (1997) 'Beyond legal orientalism', in V. Taylor (ed.) *Asian Laws through Australian Eyes,* Sydney: LBC.

—— (1997) 'Consumer contract governance in a deregulating Japan', *Victoria University of Wellington Law Review* 27(1): 99–120.

VERONICA TAYLOR

leisure

Leisure (*riijaa*) has become a new catchphrase in contemporary Japan, from government white papers on health to advertising campaigns for sports clubs and feminist research on the family. Rendered in Japlish and written in *katakana*, the popular script of ad copy, it is marked as both an imported concept and a market commodity but it also designates a new area of policy and economic and cultural development. Since the early 1990s, *riijaa* has emerged as the growth industry of the new Japanese lifestyle orientation but it is far from a mere consumer trend.

Outside Japan, 'leisure' is not a concept commonly linked to the popular image of the Japanese: working hard for long hours and devoted to the corporate good. This image, while still prevalent, is the product of the period of the so-called '**Japanese economic miracle**', which was indeed a time of much personal sacrifice by individuals, families and communities in the interests of the rapid expansion of the Japanese economy. The '**Plan to Double Income**' policy over this period saw a dramatic increase in household disposable income, but the intense consumerism of the ***mai hōmu*** and *mai kaa* booms in this same era saw household spending re-channelled back into the further expansion of the domestic manufacturing base. Vacations and week-ends were sacrificed not only for the good of the company but to boost the seasonal bonus payments needed to support high levels of household consumer activity and the rapidly rising cost of living.

The economic slowdown of the post-bubble period has seen both government and corporate sectors striving to promote a new culture of leisure, encouraging employees to take regular annual vacations and rotate between six- and five-day workweek rosters. There has also been an increase in official national and regional holidays. On the one hand, all this can be understood as a new commitment to the quality of life and physical well-being of Japanese workers. On the other hand, some critics of the new policies point to economic motivation, citing the fact that many companies do not offer full salary for vacation time even on mandated holidays. The shorter working week and increased annual vacation also facilitate a reduction in work hours without resort to layoffs. At another level, the leisure boom has played a key role in promoting the related service and IT sectors as the new drivers of domestic economic performance over the 1980s and 1990s in the face of declining household consumption of high-end consumer goods. This growth in individual and household leisure expenditure has also been a partial counterbalance to the reduction in corporate spending in the service sector, due to restructuring of tax laws effecting deductions for client entertainment and corporate-sponsored vacations and other fringe benefits.

Since the mid-1980s, national, prefectural and municipal governments have invested in leisure infrastructure from park facilities, to gymnasiums to community entertainment and **culture centres**, incorporating a broad base of services including cinemas, Internet cafés, indoor stadiums, pools, theatres, art and craft workshops, exhibition spaces, video and computer gaming centres, health spas and golf practice ranges. The private sector has also moved extensively into the leisure market, expanding beyond the localised government facilites into an extraordinary array of user-pay consumer options from low-budget to luxury leisure products. Critics of the leisure culture argue that it has become just one more area for the intensification of consumer differentiation. The high cost of participation in Japan's new leisure culture has led to considerable debate over the real impact of *riijaa* on the Japanese work ethic and family. The impact of the emerging leisure culture on such markers of Japanese contemporary society as 'the absent father' are still unclear. Although there is much lamenting by older Japanese in the popular media that the leisure generation has abandoned the work ethic for a more selfish and family-oriented way of life, there is still no marked shift in workplace participation levels, vacation draw-down statistics or productivity levels that would support the notion that there has been significant change. It remains unclear whether the new leisure culture will produce the touted values of individual and family leisure time or merely promote new areas of segregated consumer activity target markets.

SANDRA BUCKLEY

Liberal Democratic Party

The Liberal Democratic Party (Jiyū Minshūtō, or LDP) has been Japan's dominant political party for more than forty years. The LDP was founded in 1955 by the incorporation of two conservative parties, the Liberal and Democratic Parties of Japan, in response to the uniting of socialist political factions as the **Japan Socialist Party** in the same year. This act created the so-called '1955 system' where confrontation between the LDP and Japan Socialist Party was seen as a domestic mirror of the 'cold war'. Between 1955 and 1993, the LDP held the majority of seats in the Japanese Diet (parliament) with the Japan Socialist Party (now the Social Democratic Party, SDP) in opposition. During that time, all of Japan's prime ministers and most cabinet ministers were LDP.

The LDP has enjoyed widespread conservative support among farmers, business, professionals, government workers and non-unionised workers. A dominant mix of pork-barrel politics and status quo policies has protected agricultural and business interests. The LDP traditionally identified itself with administrative reform, but also supported general goals such as rapid export-based economic growth, close co-operation with the USA in foreign and defence policies and, since the 1980s, administrative reform, but supported a wide and growing range of government services, including medical insurance, old-age pensions, a minimum wage and improved working conditions, and various other social welfare programmes. The party has, in addition, defended rice and other staple crops from competitive imports. On particular issues, however, the party has almost always been divided into factions, producing highly eclectic and often contradictory positions propounded as official party lines. While this diversity has given the party the benefit of breadth and versatility, it has also caused disunity, and inertia in decision making.

Funds expended in the never-ending vote-gathering activities of rival LDP factions were supplied mainly by conservative businesses associated with particular faction leaders. Reacting against the excesses of 'money politics', the public handed the LDP its first significant defeat in the 1989 House of Councillors (Upper House) election, when it lost its traditional majority. Following the 'bursting of the **bubble economy**' in 1990, Japan's economic problems became more intractable, and voters became further disillusioned. In 1993, the LDP split again and failed to achieve a majority in the Lower House of Representatives election of that year, when the 'Shinsei Party' and the 'New Party Initiatives' (NPI) were established and a multi-party anti-LDP returned to power in 1994 in an unprecedented coalition with its old nemesis, the left-of-centre **Japan Socialist Party** (JSP). In 1996, the LDP reclaimed the prime ministership as Hashimoto Ryutarō replaced his JSP coalition partner Murayama Tomiichi. The coalition was broken in June 1998. Unable to stimulate the economy, Hashimoto resigned in July 1998 after the LDP were defeated again in the House of Councillors because voters opposed his financial policies.

In November 1998, the LDP organised a new coalition cabinet with the Liberal Party, and in January 1999 these parties organised a coalition cabinet under Prime Minister Obuchi Keizo, LDP President. A coalition agreement was also concluded with New Komeito and the Reformers' Network in October 1999, when the LDP had a majority in the Lower House but a minority in the Upper House.

DAVID EDGINGTON

Liberal Party

The Liberal Party was formed in 1998 with forty-two Diet members from the former New Frontier Party. Its outspoken Chairman Ozawa Ichirō rose to prominence in 1993 as leader of a breakaway faction from the **Liberal Democratic Party** (LDP), which later formed the Shinseito Party (Japan Renewal Party), a core member of the coalition government under Prime Minister Hashimoto. While Hashimoto was Prime Minister, it was commonly agreed that Ozawa was the more powerful figure. Following the fall of the Hashimoto government in 1994, Ozawa was a key figure in the **New Frontier Party** (Shinshintō) opposition. When Shinshintō dissolved in 1997, the Liberal Party adopted its basic philosophies and policies. The Liberal Party policy platform generally follows Ozawa's popular reform manifesto, *A Blueprint for the Renewal of Japan* (1993), which urges substantial political and administrative reform and the need for Japan to become a 'normal nation' with less government regulation and more participation in international affairs. Following failure of the LDP to gain a majority in the upper chamber (House of Councillors) in 1998, the Liberal Party joined the LDP in a coalition under Prime Minister Obuchi Keizo, and now controls twelve seats in the Upper House and thirty-nine in the Lower House.

DAVID EDGINGTON

libraries

Japan's first libraries date back to before the Nara period. These were the clan repositories of records which included clan and local histories, and religious and ritual documents. From the centralisation of power around an imperial court there was a thorough recording and storing of historical, legal and religious materials. *Bunkō* (archival repositories) were kept throughout history by elite households and were sometimes made available for teaching and scholarly work. *Buke bunkō*, or warrior archives, were the storehouse of everything from tales of battle to legal documents, maps and even battle plans. The substantial and irreplacable collections of some samurai and aristrocratic households eventually won local or national government sponsorship in the modern period, as a reflection of their value as a national resource and heritage. Prior to Meiji, the dominant vehicle for the collection and archiving of literary texts and other historical archives was the private household or family *bunkō*.

Public collections and broad-based access to archives were practices observed in Europe and North America by some of the early Japanese intellectuals to travel abroad after the Meiji Restoration in 1868. The Japanese government was quick to act and the first public library was established in 1872. Public response, however, did not match government enthusiasm. During the Edo Period, access to affordable mass-produced woodblock publications had been a contributing factor to high levels of pre-modern literacy. Lending libraries that charged a fee to borrow materials were also popular and carried over into the modern period, actually growing in number and popularity until the war and then resurfacing again in post-war Japan. Today, these local commercial lending libraries still frequently outnumber public libraries in less populated regions. Many writers of popular fiction write specifically for the lending-library market, responding quickly to new trends among readers. Storytellers, combining illustrated cards and scrolls with the art of a good tale, were also a familiar part of the cultural landscape of Japan from the Edo Period through to the post-war period, and it was only the arrival of television that finally brought an end to this street profession in the 1950s. All in all public borrowing libraries did not win a place quickly in the reading culture of modern Japan. The preference among the wealthy and intellectuals for building their own personal, often highly specialised libraries has supported a significant trade in second-hand and antiquarian book sales. The value of these family collections has meant that, when the collector dies, those who inherit often sell rather than donate the collection to a library, in a culture not known for a strong history of philanthropic giving. The wide base of general readers in Japan remain very comfortable with buying or renting affordable editions from a neighbourhood bookstore or lending library. Much of the popular fiction and illustrated materials available in these local outlets would not have found its way onto the shelves of government-funded public libraries. Bookshops and lending libraries also serve a dual function as a meeting place in a neighbourhood, especially for students, a role the more austere and hushed setting of the library can not compete with.

The National Diet Library of Japan was not established until 1948 and the majority of Japan's regional and city libraries date from the 1960s onwards after a major insertion of government funding into public cultural institutions. The national government also funds national university libraries, and collections in some museum and research institutes, prisons and the teaching and professional archives of national hospitals and courts. Private universities have received some limited national government support for their collections in an attempt to redress the 1970s imbalance of a 1:3 ratio in comparison to national university collections. The late start-up for many major libraries has led to some difficulty in compensating for lack of longitudinal depth to collections. Moves towards specialist collections and the avoidance of regional duplication are being promoted together with inter-library loan systems. The number of large collections in private family or institutional holdings also creates some issues of broader access and archival preservation. Private collections are not always catalogued for easy use and some private collections contain extremely valuable historical materials, but these are not always fully documented or adequately housed. There are still occasional accidental discoveries of rare scrolls and texts in family storehouses.

One of the greatest challenges facing the Japanese library system since the Meiji Period has been the need for multiple cataloguing systems to accommodate materials in Western languages, and both Chinese and Japanese. The Nippon Decimal Classification system was instigated as a variation on the Dewey system in 1929 and remains in wide use for Japanese and Chinese materials. Scientific and international research institutes prefer the Universal Dewey system. A number of key teaching and research libraries such as Tokyo University (with over 6 million volumes) have developed their own internal cataloguing systems, which further complicates the situation. The major issues facing the computerisation of libraries in Japan are the different focus on title and author of the Japanese systems (title) and Western systems (author). There is also the problem that Japanese bibliographers and cataloguers have focused on classification options by title or author, and have not developed adequate subject categories to allow for a simple integration of Japanese collections with the detailed subject classifications of Western systems.

Most libraries have continued to house their often substantial Western-language volumes separately from their Sino-Japanese collections, rather than try to deal with the difficulties of integration. Another major factor impeding computerisation is continued disparities in romanisation techniques for both Japanese and Chinese, and the ever present problem of standardising macron signatures. There has been extensive experimentation with the Nippon Cataloguing Rules developed in 1943 and reworked in 1965. This system is generally thought to be more flexible and adaptable to each of the current problems of integration and standardisation. The push for computerised information technologies is being driven by the National Diet Library with strong encouragement from the scientific research community, which is keen to see a rapid move to a more standardised national and international network of libraries and other data banks.

SANDRA BUCKLEY

literacy

The literacy rate of the Japanese is usually put at 99 per cent. This is extremely high when one considers the complexity of the language and how literacy is defined. Traditionally, the ability to both read and write almost 2,000 **kanji**, or Chinese-derived characters, is considered as baseline for literacy. This level of comprehension is usually attained by the end of middle school, which marks the end of nine years of compulsory education, and is the requirement for reading a national newspaper. Three separate writing systems co-exist to make up the Japanese language. Two of these, *hiragana* and **katakana**, consist of forty-eight phonetic symbols each. The third system, *kanji*, is composed of Chinese characters, each of which can be read or pronounced in several ways, depending on the context. These characters usually are visually complex units requiring from one to twenty brush strokes each. In regular text, Chinese characters are combined with the phonetic symbols according to carefully prescribed rules to form words and sentences. There are also two different ways of writing and reading text. The first is to read from left to right, horizontally, as in Western books. The second is to read vertically from top to bottom, starting with the column on the far right. In Japanese-language classes, textbooks are printed vertically and children write their compositions in similar form. In arithmetic and science, textbooks are printed horizontally, and notebooks for these subjects must be kept in similar fashion. As a result, Japanese children spend one-fourth of their time in primary school mastering their own language. During the first year they learn to read and write the two forty-eight character phonetic systems and a few Chinese characters. Each year thereafter, approximately 200 Chinese characters are added, along with their various readings and rules of spelling for common words. Calligraphy is a daily practice as there is a 'right' way to shape characters and preferred techniques for the use of traditional brushes and ink. Brush calligraphy is an increasingly rarefied skill.

Even though pre-primary education in Japan is not a part of compulsory education, most Japanese parents send their children to either half-day or full-day pre-school. These schools tend to be philosophically opposed to early academic learning, seeing the need for group interaction and the acquisition of socially acceptable habits, attitudes and behaviour as far more important for success in later schooling. Still, most children begin the first grade of compulsory education already having learned how to read and write the basic phonetic system from their parents. The pace of the system that assumes that all children have the ability to

maintain a certain level of learning can disadvantage those who fall behind. There is some research that suggests that, although students enter school well prepared in reading, by fifth grade a significant number of them have not been able to keep up (see **drop-outs**).

JUNE A. GORDON

literary criticism

In Japan, the notion of literary criticism encompasses a larger range of meaning than in the West, frequently including what would be considered intellectual and cultural criticism elsewhere. Consequently, literary criticism in post-war Japan presents a diverse and complex picture: a mixture of professional critics (often employed, if only in a visiting capacity, in colleges) who write book-length studies of major writers and intellectual trends, as well as short pieces in newspapers and magazines; and university-based scholars of literature who, driven by the 'publish or perish' syndrome, write numerous specialist scholarly articles in professional journals but also book-length studies. In addition, working authors frequently write practical criticism on literature, as well as producing literary journalism for a broad audience.

Contemporary academic criticism of Japanese literature is not radically different from the kind of literary criticism taught in Western universities. The major schools in the West – traditional textual/historical analysis, psychoanalysis, structuralism, Marxism, semiotics, feminist critiques, etc. – have their counterparts in Japan, although Japanese scholars are often more eclectic, blending Western elements with traditional Japanese hermeneutics. Nevertheless, a list of major literary critics in post-war Japan would extend for many pages, and would need to be broken down into periods and genres, as most critics, whether academic or not, specialise in particular periods, and often genres.

There are distinctive Japanese traditions of both academic and professional literary criticism that date back at least to the nineteenth century, if not well before. One of the major post-war professional critics of Japanese literature and thought, the poet

Yoshimoto Takaaki, can be seen as the heir of the major pre-war thinker Yanagita Kunio. Both men were profoundly influenced by Western thinkers, in the case of Yoshimoto, originally by structuralist writers like Claude Lévi-Strauss, but both strove to develop their own unique critical systems. In *Gengo ni totte bi towa nanika?* (What is Beauty in Language?, 1965), Yoshimoto offered rhetorical critiques of classical poetry and modern fiction, and in *Masu imeeji ron* (On Mass Images, 1984) of contemporary fiction, as part of an ongoing effort to establish broad critical and cultural schemata specifically suited to Japanese conditions.

Japanese traditions of academic criticism are generally conservative and, especially in the case of pre-modern literature, concentrate on textual exegesis, annotation and commentary. Literary history and biography are often the focus of studies of modern literature, with Tokyo University scholar Komori Yoichi typical of an older trend of scholarship in emphasising the larger cultural context in his 1995 book, *Sōseki o yominaosu* (Re-reading Sōseki), on the great pre-war writer Natsume Sōseki. However, at the same time, his use of narratological theory in books like *Kozo to shite no katari* (Narrative as Structure, 1988) provides another critical perspective from which to read literature.

Further reading

Suzuki Sadami (1998) *Nihon no 'bungaku' gainen*, Tokyo: Sakuhinsha.

Yoshimoto Takaaki (1972) *Kyōdo gensōron in Yoshimoto Takaaki zen chosakush*, vol. 11, Tokyo: Keisō Shobō.

LEITH MORTON

literary journals

This entry will focus on a selected group of current academic literary journals, rather than mass-circulation literary magazines. There are two important, exceedingly well-known and well-read journals named *Kokubungaku* (National Literature). The older journal has the full title of *Kokubungaku: kaishaku to kanshō* (Interpretations and Appreciation) and commenced publication as a monthly in 1936.

This journal is published by the Shibundō company and is often referred to colloquially as the *Shibundō Kokubungaku* to distinguish it from its namesake, known as the *Gakutōsha Kokubungaku*, named in turn after its publisher. The *Shibundō* journal has been edited by a distinguished group of scholars of Japanese literature beginning with Fujimura Saku (1875–1953), its first editor, and including such influential figures as Hisamitsu Sen'ichi (1894–1976), who dominated debates over classical Japanese literary studies in the pre-war period. Originally, the journal was a coterie publication but from 1954 it was commercially produced. In the pre-war period, it concentrated on classical literature, especially on philological commentaries on famous works. From 1950, it adopted a policy of producing special issues on a single topic or author, and henceforth focused on modern literature, normally adopting the pattern of a series of commissioned or invited articles.

The *Gakutōsha Kokubungaku* has the full title of *Kokubungaku: kaishaku to kyōzai no kenkyū* (Studies of Interpretations and Materials) and commenced publication in 1956. The journal soon became a monthly, originally under the editorship of Hosaka Kōji, and was the journal of a scholarly association, though in reality it was sold as a commercial journal. Issues are produced on themes ranging from individual authors or works to special editions containing, for example, specialised dictionaries. Modern topics and authors predominate (although it does have special issues devoted to early modern, medieval or classical literature), and articles are commissioned. It is not unusual for there to be a number of special issues over a period of several years on the same author or text. For example, the famous novelist Natsume Sōeki (1867–1916) has been the subject of numerous special issues. Thus, it is possible to trace changing fashions in criticism by examining successive special Sōseki issues.

Another important journal is *Kokugo to kokubungaku* (Language and National Literature), which commenced publication in 1924, originally under the editorship of Fujimura Saku, who was then a professor of Japanese literature at Tokyo University. For many years after, it was edited by a Tokyo University team of scholars, though it is published by Shibundō. It is a refereed journal that is open to submissions of articles on Japanese literature and language. The journal is edited by a scholarly association, appearing roughly every month and carries many regular features like book reviews, news of the profession, etc. It also has a column that reviews the contents of other scholarly journals. Approximately every hundred copies an index appears. The journal has a strong but rather conservative reputation, with more articles on classical literature than the two *Kokubungaku* journals, and with fewer numbers on a single theme.

The journal *Nihon bungaku* (Japanese Literature) commenced publication in 1949, originally as a quarterly, but from 1952 it has been a monthly. It is also currently edited by a scholarly association and thus resembles *Kokugo to kokubungaku* in that it carries news of the profession and has a strong focus on high-school and junior-college scholarly audiences, as well as the traditional university market. It also has a strong practical emphasis aimed at teachers of Japanese language and literature, with special issues on pedagogy, book reviews, research reports and special numbers on its annual conferences. Thus, it resembles similar journals published in the West by associations like the American Modern Language Association (MLA). It is not as relentlessly theme- or topic-driven as the more commercial *Kokubungaku* journals, with a great deal of diversity in a typical issue, occasionally carrying articles on obscure writers or texts (both classical and modern), rather than an exclusive focus on canonical topics or authors.

The Iwanami company, famous as a publisher of affordable paperback editions of serious literature since 1927, has published the commercial journal *Bungaku* (Literature) since 1933. The magazine has gone through various editorial permutations, but since 1957 has been a quarterly journal edited by an in-house editorial board. It publishes invited or commissioned articles and often produces issues on special topics like translation or gender. The main focus is on Japanese literature but the journal sometimes has issues on non-Japanese writers or texts. *Bungaku* is known for its occasional invitations to foreign scholars to contribute articles and also for its publications of original archival research and bibliographies.

Two well-known scholarly journals of modern Japanese literature are *Nihon kindai bungaku* (Modern Japanese Literature) and *Shōwa bungaku kenkyū* (Studies in Shōwa Literature). The former commenced publication in 1964, while the latter began in 1980. Both journals are published bi-annually by scholarly societies whose editorial boards referee submissions of articles on modern Japanese literature from members of the respective associations. Hence, both resemble journals published by such overseas scholarly associations as the Oriental Society of Australia. Special issues are not as numerous as the more commercial journals and both journals carry book reviews, author or text bibliographies, research reports, etc.

Smaller academic societies publish similar specialist journals on literature, like the annual journal *Geijutsushijōshugi bungei* (Art Literature), established in 1979, which focuses on modern literature, along the same lines as the two journals just mentioned. Numerous specialist scholarly associations that publish annual journals on only one author or, rarely, on one text have arisen in recent years, as have specialised scholarly journals on traditional genres of poetry or drama (and some date back many decades). Naturally, mass-circulation monthly literary magazines like *Bungakkai* (The Literary World, established 1947) or *Shinchō 45* (established in 1982) occasionally carry scholarly articles on Japanese literature written in an accessible style, as well as original stories and articles.

LEITH MORTON

literature

In many ways, post-1945 Japanese literature differed dramatically from that of the pre-war. With the loss of the Second World War and the Allied Occupation, huge literary issues were hotly debated – many well into the 1980s, some beyond. Of these, the most important were: literary representations of national and individual subjectivity (*shūtaisei*); literary function (entertainment value versus the dominant pre-war, transcendentalist view of literature as a vehicle for personal truth, and thus 'authenticity' valued over fictionalized possibility); and a gendered structure that regulated content and style by the author's sex.

The problematic of national and individual subjectivity was linked to that of modernity. In journals and newspapers writers pondered: Was Japanese literature sufficiently modern? Which pre-modern elements bore responsibility for writers' general lack of opposition to the war? Pre-war literature and ideology were re-evaluated as negative (feudalistic) factors conducive to Japanese fascism and imperialism. How then, writers asked, were they to break with the past, and exorcise any trace of 'semi-feudal' attitudes? How were they to discover or invent a speaking subject of their texts that embodied the new ideals of democracy and modernity?

Under the Occupation, wartime censorship ended and literature revived. New, ambitious literary journals formed: *Shin Nihon bungaku* had a communist literary agenda; *Kindai bungaku* advocated aesthetics, democracy and socialism. One writer, the radical **Sakaguchi Ango**, aware that history is continually rewritten, argued in essays like his 1946 'Daraku ron' (On decadence) that Japan's contemporary needs were better met by airplanes and trains, than by temples and shrines. Vehemently rejecting the Emperor's symbolic divinity, Ango held that modern Japaneseness was not to be found in reproductions of classic culture or myth. Conversely, as early as his 1949 *Kamen no kokuhaku* (Confessions of a Mask), **Mishima Yukio** had begun his endeavor to revive, although ironically as myth, the Emperor as divine symbol in an increasingly aesthetic-fascist, narcissistic attempt to reorder history in keeping with his personal, erotic mythology. Later works like *Taiyō to tetsu* (Sun and Steel, 1968) further polished Mishima's obsessive, personal vision. Many established writers, such as **Kawabata Yasunari** and **Tanizaki Jun'ichirō** avoided the political by personalising post-war sociocultural and economic rupture, discontinuity and loss. Nostalgically turned towards an imaginary (personal and cultural) past, these inward-directed narratives (such as Tanizaki's *Sasameyuki* (The Makioka Sisters 1948), or Kawabata's *Yama no oto* (Sound of the Mountain, 1952)) were the obvious successors to the complete subjugation of wartime art to fascist political agendas. Even Marxists shifted the focus from class to individual. Socialists Hayashi Fumiko and Takahashi Kazumi sought literary authenticity, writing self-referential narratives that drew heavily on their own life experiences.

Nihilist **Dazai Osamu**, like Ango a member of the decadent '*burai-ha*' coterie, enjoyed extensive recognition and even after his suicide his popularity continued to grow. He is best remembered for *Shayō* (The Setting Sun, 1947).

Following the optimism of the 1947 Constitution, the unsettling events of the 1950s – the **Korean War**, the Bikini incident – were greeted with a strengthening of the **peace and anti-nuclear movements** and anti-Anpo (the US–Japan Security Pact) (see **Anpo struggle**) demonstrations. Political distrust and social disquiet spawned literature of disruption and disorder. Literary coteries and their mentor–disciple system essentially died. In their wake, established journals such as **Shinchō**, literary awards and social critics remained to evaluate and provide commentary for literary movements and writers. Unmentored, young, male writers such as Yasuoka Shōtarō and Shimao Toshio (see **Third Generation, the**) emerged with a shared disdain for pretty style, black humour, exposés of personal (and cultural) shame, degradation and humiliation (often related to the recent world war depictions of domestic disorder and miserable poverty) and hallucinating, untrustworthy protagonists. As these writers matured, their writing did too and their plots became less extreme. In the absence of the refuge of classical culture they explored narrative spaces of psychic and/or material disintegrations. Anyone or anything, including culture, ideology or institutions, that had survived the war had done so only in flawed, dysfunctional and disfigured forms.

A resurgence of women writers began in the 1950s and continues to the present. Many women-authored texts were called *monogatari* rather than *shōsetsu* proper. While *Monogatari* culled themes and characters from folklore and the classics, *shōsetsu* were considered modern, constructed works more like the Western novel. In her *monogatari*-like *Onnamen* (Masks, 1958) and *Onnazaka* (The Waiting Years, 1957), **Enchi Fumiko** made innovative, subversive use of the canon to chronicle women's psychological, yet communal, emotional and sociopolitical discontent. She often wrote fiction evocative of magical realism and depicting female spirit-possession. Many of her themes, like problematising the reification of maternity as female mission, carried over from women's pre-war literature, and were explored by subsequent women authors including **Ōba Minako**, or updated and contemporised in **Tsushima Yūko**'s *Yama o hashiru onna* (Woman Running in the Mountains, 1980). Tomioka Taeko dwelled on 'liberated' female sexuality divorced from familial values; Kōno Taeko shocked readers with brutal sado-masochist imaginaries. Different critical expectations attended writing by women and men. By and large, because women writers were grouped into the category of *joryū bungaku* (**women's literature**), they were lauded for personal narratives about love, jealousy, maternity, sex – 'natural' and 'bodily' matters. Too much abstraction, so critics held, did not suit women.

By the early 1960s, the Miike mine strikes (see **Miike struggle**) had taken their psychic toll, the anti-Anpo movement had failed and Japan was contemplating relative economic stability. The late 1960s hosted student movements (see **student movement**) and the **Tokyo Olympics**, and saw creative energy shift from literature to film. Folklorist Yanagita Kunio and Buddhist philosophers Nishida Kitarō and Watsuji Tetsurō regained importance and popularity, countering the late-1940s rejection of anything Japanese. Nationalism revived and 'innocent', classical-cultural attributes were used to rearticulate notions of a modern, so-called unique Japanese sensibility, albeit now divested of fascism. Maverick **Abe Kōbō** turned from surrealism to humanist allegory, setting up isolated fictional worlds in both film and narrative to explore existential problems. Even as Kawabata became the first Japanese to win the Nobel Prize for Literature in 1968, the second Japanese to do so, humanist **Ōe Kenzaburō**, was heading up a literary movement antithetical to Kawabata's Zen-inspired, mournful and nostalgic, aesthetical-poetic prose. In a raw, new, compellingly prose Ōe struggled, like the third generation but employing brilliant irony, with issues of political, social and, yet always also, individual guilt and culpability. For Ōe, not only was the war survived in flawed forms, but history itself lost all rationality, or coherent pattern and direction. The protagonists of his *Mizu kara waga namida o nuguitamō hi* (The Day He Himself Shall Wipe My Tears Away, 1971), or *Warera no*

kyōki o ikinobiru michi o oshieyō (Teach Us to Outgrow Our Madness, 1969), cannot move beyond moments of psychic rupture symbolised by a brain-damaged child, an insane father or the Emperor's radio announcement of surrender. Like most Japanese writers, Ōe drew heavily from personal experience. Conversely, **Ibuse Masuji**'s 1966 *Kuroi ame* (Black Rain) was criticised for using a first-person, diary format to invent an account of the lingering effects of radiation poisoning from the nuclear blasts. The use of the first person to narrate personal response to actual event, which, after all, the author had not experienced, was considered deceitful.

Mishima Yukio staged his final performance, what some have described as a farce, in the form of his doomed attempt at a *coup d'état* with his personal army. This event provided a stage for his public, ritual suicide in 1970. It was, many felt, the end of an era. Literature fragmented. After Ōe, writers increasingly spoke from, or depicted, the social margins. Speaking 'legitimately' as a survivor, Hayashi Kyōko published her autobiographical *Matsuri no ba* (Festival sites, 1975) about the Nagasaki atomic bombing and built a career as a writer exclusively documenting her status as *hibakusha*, or atomic bomb victim.

Other writers inherited the trajectory begun by Sakaguchi in the immediate post-war, and challenged dominant Japanese axioms on national identity, the Emperor and Japanese culture. **Murakami Ryū** wrote explicit accounts detailing alienated youth violence, sex and drug addiction, even as middle-class Japanese enjoyed an ethnic 'boom' and consumed multiculturalism and the exotic within the Japanese heartland. **Nakagami Kenji**'s trilogy of *Misaki* (The Cape, 1975), *Kareki Nada* (Withered Tree Beach, 1977) and *Chi no hate, shijō no toki* (The End of the Earth; The Supreme Time, 1983) exploded one after the other on to the literary market with brutal attacks on the canon, dominant renderings of history and the myths of Japanese homogeneity. **Kurahashi Yumiko** and Kanai Mieko transformed French post-structuralist theory into wild fictional fantasies oblivious to axioms of novelistic realism, humanism, psychological interiority and causality. **Inoue Hisashi**'s *Kirikirijin* (People of Kirikiri, 1981) brought regional dialect to this hilarious, satirical tale of a rural village that declares independence from Japan.

By the mid-1980s, a crop of determinately irreverent young writers – lumped together under the rubric of 'post-modern' – were blurring the distinction between popular fiction and literature, outraging their seniors, and delighting young readers. Called frivolous, apolitical, and amoral, their fictional topographies are given form by the social massification, global capitalism and indiscriminate commodity consumption that shaped the 1980s. The once-radical Ōe, like many senior writers, laments the loss of what he understands to be any serious, responsible or sustained sociopolitical agenda in their texts. Peppering their prose with *katakana*, mixing **science fiction**, cyberpunk, pornography, detective stories and even classic *monogatari* into unrecognisable, disjunctive pastiches, the young writers of the 1980s and 1990s rejected the problematic of national identity in favour of anything 'trans-': trans-national, transhistorical, trans-geo-political, trans-gender, transsexual. Some of these writers incorporate the canon in a manner reminiscent of rap 'sampling'. Snippets of classics are lifted out of their originary context and capriciously circulated in completely unrelated contexts, often deconstructing or parodying the apparent intent, or significance, of the source text. Other writers reject the classics altogether. Paradigmatic post-modernist Tanaka Yasuo's infamous *Nantonaku, kurisutaru* (Somehow, Crystal, 1980) had some 400 notes on purchasing brand-name items mentioned in the text. Bestselling author **Murakami Haruki** invented quirky, trans-temporal dreamscapes in dispassionate narrative style. Shimada Masahiko cleaved to his ethic of parodic deconstruction and Lyotardian language games, writing satires often made serious by his critique of the enduring imperial system, global capitalism and rampant consumerism. *Manga* (comic) inspired **Yoshimoto Banana**'s single-dimensional depictions of consumable popular culture, while the popular **Yamada Eimi** scribed female sexuality complicated by colonialist power-politics and racial stereotypes. With the economic 'bubble' burst, literary explorations of alternative sexualities blossomed. Matsuura Rieko publicly proclaimed herself a lesbian. More explicitly and publicly than before, Takahashi

Mutsuo's books and poems celebrated male homosexuality, while in *Iesu iesu iesu* (Yes yes yes, 1990) Hiruma Hisao's 17-year-old male prostitute-protagonist suffered the delights of degradation. **Yi Yang-Ji** and **Yū Miri**, both Korean-Japanese women, brought some measure of political consciousness to their deeply personal narratives of the 1970s and 1990s, respectively, if only by virtue of their ethnic origins and in the critical commentary that frequently foregrounded those origins.

All told, the young writers of the present day are reshaping Japanese literature once again. Speaking for their own generation, their fictional worlds are inundated with mixed ethnicities, the high-tech, paranoia and alienation, moments of extraordinary, anonymous and/or spontaneous violence, information overload, economic globalisation and depression, radical shifts in time and space surface vying with and content, and upheavals in 'normative' sex and gender performances.

Further reading

Mitsios, H. (ed.) (1991) *New Japanese Voices: The Best Contemporary Fiction from Japan*, New York: Atlantic Monthly Press.

Miyoshi, M. (1991) *Off Center: Power and Culture Relations Between Japan and the United States*, Cambridge, MA: Harvard University Press.

Schalow, P.G. and Walker, J.A. (eds) (1996) *The Woman's Hand: Gender and Theory in Japanese Women's Writing*, Stanford: Stanford University Press.

Snyder, S. (ed.) (1999) *Ōe and Beyond: Fiction in Contemporary Japan*, Honolulu: University of Hawaii Press.

NINA CORNYETZ

Living Treasures

This is the popular term for the group of traditional artists and artisans designated as Bearers of Important Intangible National Assets (*Jūyō mukei bunkazai hojisha*). These men and women include among others potters, *kabuki* actors, weavers, musicians and dyers. They each are designated a Living Treasure for the invaluable and irreplacable knowledge (intangible assets) they possess in their area of specialisation. The aim of identifying these individuals is not only recognition of their individual contribution to their craft or art but, at least as importantly, the acknowledgement of the need to preserve and create opportunities for the continuation of their area of creative work and the tradition it represents. There are eighty-five recognised areas of skill in which this designation can be given. Each year, any new 'Treasures' are announced in the spring by the Agency for Cultural Affairs within the Ministry of Education.

SANDRA BUCKLEY

Lockheed scandal

The Lockheed scandal, news of which broke in 1976, resulted in the conviction of former Prime Minister Tanaka Kakuei for bribery. The scandal symbolises the 'money politics' that grew along with the post-war economy. The Lockheed corporation paid Tanaka ¥500 million (US$1.6 million) through the Marubeni trading company to insure that All Nippon Airways bought its passenger jets. It also paid US$6 million to right-wing fixer and suspected former-war criminal Kodama Yoshio, and US$1 million to Osano Kenji, a powerful businessman who had made his fortune in the post-war black market.

Tanaka had been forced out of the premiership in 1974 by money scandals. The Lockheed affair made it clear that corruption was widespread. Yet, the Liberal Democratic Party remained in power, and, despite his trial and 1983 conviction, Tanaka remained a Diet member and increased his power as 'kingmaker'. He was by far the most powerful politician in Japan until he suffered a stroke in 1985.

Further reading

Farley, M. (1996) 'Japan's press and the politics of scandal', in S. Pharr and E. Krauss (eds) *Media and Politics in Japan*, Honolulu: University of Hawaii Press, pp. 133–63.
Hunziker, S. and Kamimura, I. (1994) *Kakuei Tanaka: A Political Biography of Modern Japan*, Los Gatos, CA: Daruma International.

Johnson, C. (1986) 'Tanaka Kakuei, structural corruption, and the advent of machine politics in Japan', *Journal of Japanese Studies* 12(1): 1–28.
Mitchell, R. (1996) *Political Bribery in Japan*, Honolulu: University of Hawaii Press.
Schlesinger, J. (1997, 1999) *Shadow Shoguns: The Rise and Fall of Japan's Postwar Political Machine*, Stanford: Stanford University Press.

TIMOTHY S. GEORGE

love hotels

Love hotels are the popular short-stay hotels (hourly to overnight rates) that have captured international attention due to their extraordinary architecture and theme-based room designs. Building design can vary from fantasy castles to space-ships or even a volcano. Theme rooms are equally eclectic: S&M, Versailles, safari, warzone, shuttle, samurai. Although often sensationalised in commentaries on the underside of Japan, love hotels are closely linked to essential elements of Japan's modernisation – urban crowding, commuting and motorisation. Though now primarily associated with short-stay liaisons and roadside prostitution rings, the phenomenon of short-stay hotels initially developed as accommodation for a new breed of car commuters, travelling salesmen and truckers in the wake of the expansion of commercial road transport and the *ōnaaduraibaa* (owner-driver) boom of the 1960s. These roadside hotels vied with one another through extravagant façades to capture the eye of weary travellers. In the early 1970s, they had become linked to prostitution and were known as love hotels. They began to appear in towns and cities around major road and rail commuter hubs as well as on the edges of entertainment districts. They offered inexpensive, private space not only for prostitutes and their clients, but also for couples in cities where apartments are cramped and often uninviting, and a suburban home and bedroom is a long commute away. By the mid-1970s, their illicit reputation was firmly established and today love hotels remain a popular location for the seedier storylines of film and television dramas.

SANDRA BUCKLEY

M

MacArthur, Douglas

b. 1880, Little Rock, Arkansas, USA;
d. 1964 Washington, DC, USA.

US army general, Supreme Commander
of Allied Power in Japan, 1945–51.

Having commanded the US forces in counter-attacks against Japan during the Pacific War, General MacArthur accepted Japan's surrender aboard the USS Missouri in September 1945. Placed in charge of the **Allied Occupation** of Japan, MacArthur wielded extraordinary authority in Japan and *vis-à-vis* Washington. Convinced of the efficacy of using Emperor **Hirohito** for the purpose of Occupation, MacArthur successfully foiled attempts to remove the Emperor or to put him on trial. Motivated in part by political ambition for the Republican presidential nomination as well as by Christian zeal, he pushed for many sweeping reforms in Japan that would have been considered revolutionary in the USA. Awe-inspiring and disarming in style, MacArthur rarely intermingled with the Japanese, yet his larger-than-life presence was felt everywhere. He was sometimes compared to a modern-day *shōgun*. MacArthur was relieved of his duty in 1951 by President Truman due to their differences over the conduct of the war in Korea.

See also: Allied Occupation; Hirohito, Emperor; Supreme Commander for Allied Powers

Further reading

Schaller, M. (1989) *Douglas MacArthur: The Far Eastern General*, New York: Oxford University Press.

YANG DAQING

mah jong

The fast moves and loud sounds of mah jong tiles being mixed and slammed varies dramatically with the slower and more solemn pace of Go. Mah jong too originated in China and its earliest precursors date from the second century BCE. However, the form of the game that is so popular today was not developed until the 1870s and the basic rules were settled by the early 1900s.

Mah jong is played with tiles marked with symbols of differing value and power. The tiles themselves are today often made from plastic, but more valuable sets are crafted from bamboo, bone and ivory or rare wood. A winner holds four sets of three tiles and an 'eye' made up of two tiles. A three- or four-tile set can be either a run of the same suit or sets of matching tiles. The possible mix of these sets and their combination with other special tiles (e.g. winter, dragon, wind) provide for a multitude of variations in the game. Four players begin the game with thirteen tiles each and pick up and discard tiles until there is a winner. Players discard and pick up strategically to try and block or bluff other players, and the best players are renowned for their ability to surmise and memorise the location of tiles in and out of play around the table. A winner calls out the words 'mah jong'.

Mah jong is played extensively in Europe and North America, where it was introduced in the 1920s by expatriots returning from Asia and quickly became a high-society parlour game most popular among woman. In North America and Europe today, it is played widely by middle-class women and has a similar status to bridge. Mah jong is also a popular pastime in Asian immigrant communities but in this context it is played mostly by men and is closely linked to gambling. In Japan it is also a gambling game and crosses class lines. While the popular image of the game is of a seedy back room with tatooed *yakuza* hunched over a table shuffling and slamming tiles, in reality mah jong has a much wider following and might be played in locations as diverse as a cheap bar, a high-stakes gaming parlour or a student dormitory. In Japan, women players are in a minority and mah jong has not become the society game it has in the West. The noise, drinking, betting and fast speed of mah jong all contribute to the tension and excitement at the heart of the continued popularity of this game. Unlike Go, there has been less success for mah jong as an online game because of the limitations and close monitoring of online gambling sites.

SANDRA BUCKLEY

mai hōmu

The 'my home' trend describes a phenomenon dating from the 1960s. The period of rapid economic growth and income-doubling policy saw an increasing number of Japanese able to contemplate the purchase of their own home. Real-estate developers responded with a well-stratified range of housing from free-standing single-family homes to less expensive medium- and high-density apartment blocks.

The *mai hōmu* boom continued even after the housing market began to slow over the 1970s, as this first wave of home-owners turned their attention to trading up to the next level of housing or indulged in cycles of consumer good upgrades. The *mai hōmu* generation has been criticised by some as typifying a new **individualism** marked by a shift away from extended family interests to a consumer-driven nuclear-family structure. One outcome of the *mai hōmu* boom was a corresponding increase in car sales – a trend that similarly came to be called *mai kaa*. The high cost of land drove developers out of the inner urban areas and, despite close links between rail and real-estate developments, car ownership became another high priority. Many of the concrete apartment blocks developed and sold as co-operatives during the *mai hōmu* boom are now facing serious structural and financial problems that can be traced back to the initial speed of construction and contracting.

See also: civic development; urban migration

SANDRA BUCKLEY

Mainichi shinbun

The *Mainichi* boasts the oldest history of Japan's national newspapers. Its roots go back to Tokyo's first daily newspaper, the *Tokyo Nichi Nichi* (1872), and the *Ōsaka Nippo* (1876), the darling of the business community. The *Mainichi* got its start as news organ of the Rikken seitō (Constitutional Government Party) (1882), but in 1888 it became the *Ōsaka Mainichi*.

Under the editorship (1897) of future prime minister, Hara Takashi (Kei) (1897) and later president, Motoyama Hikoichi (1903), it was the first newspaper to put out local editions, include periodic supplements, and establish overseas branch offices.

In 1911, the *Ōsaka Mainichi* bought out the *Tokyo Nichi Nichi* and became the only newspaper besides the *Asahi shinbun* to have bases in Ōsaka and Tokyo before the Second World War. A tie-up with the United Press International wire service was concluded in 1923.

The end of the Second World War ushered in a period of growth for the newspaper. However, by the 1970s, the oil crisis, economic recession, a domestic scandal over the reunion of Okinawa and lax management policies resulted in the newspaper's bankruptcy. New leadership has attempted to alter the *Mainichi*'s course, but its circulation figures remain below those of the *Asahi* and *Yomiuri*.

Famous for its 'scoops', the *Mainichi* has been a frequent recipient of the much-coveted annual prize for investigative reporting. The *Mainichi* was the first to criticize Japan's importation of tainted blood, which resulted in the spread of the AIDS virus and many deaths.

Present circulation – morning and evening editions included – is approximately 4,000,000.

BARBARA HAMILL SATO

Maki Fumihiko

b. 1928, Tokyo

Architect

Maki graduated from the Architecture Department at Tokyo University in 1952, and later from Harvard University and Cranbrook Academy of Arts. Maki's career began as an original member of the **Metabolism** Group in 1960. Elaborating on his essay 'Group Form', co-authored with Ōtaka Masato and included in the Metabolism manifesto, Maki wrote *Investigations in Collective Form* (University of Washington, 1964) as an inquiry into architecture's relation to its larger urban context. In Daikanyama Hillside Terrace Apartments (Tokyo, 1967–92), Maki's design 'metamorphosed' through six different phases over twenty-five years, enfolding into its layers his changing ideas about the project's internal and external spaces and their dialogue with the ever evolving topos of the city itself. An urban planner and self-avowed modernist architect, Maki received the international Pritzker Architecture Prize in 1993. Major projects include the Okinawa Aquarium (1975); the Spiral Building (Tokyo, 1985); the Nippon Convention Centre at Makuhari Messe (Chiba, 1989); the Tokyo Metropolitan Gymnasium (1990); the Fujisawa Shonan Campus of Keio University (1985–92); Yerba Buena Gardens Visual Arts Center (San Francisco, 1993); and Izar Büro Office Park (Munich, 1995).

Further reading

(1994) 'Fumihiko Maki', *JA: The Japan Architect* 16(4) (winter).

SCOTT GOLD AND MARY KNIGHTON

Makino Masahiro

b. 1908, Kyōto; d. 1993, Tokyo

film director

Makino's reputation is based on his combination of high social realism and fast, hard-hitting mass action scenes. In 1927, he was placed first (*Street of Masterless Samurai*), fourth, and seventh in the Best Ten list; in 1929, first and third. His stunning 1953–4 series *Jirocho – Record of Three Provinces*, and the 1964–5 *yakuza* film series *An Account of the Chivalrous Commoners*, featured the same style and techniques that had first made him famous.

Further reading

(1976) *Nihon eiga kantoku zenshu*, special issue of *Kinema jumpo* 12(24).

SYBIL THORNTON

management systems, Japanese

A number of distinctive characteristics have marked the Japanese approach to worker–management relations in the post-war period, especially in the larger companies. The Japanese employment system is based on three essential institutions: career-long employment (*shushin koyō*), a seniority system (*nenkō jōretsu*) and enterprise unionism. Because newly recruited male labourers traditionally came to urban factories from rural villages, they tended to respond to a paternalistic pattern of labour management relations and sought the security of a permanent community. The system continues today in a modifed form with recruitment of new graduates from universities and colleges on the basis of interviews and competitive exams. New employees commit themselves to their employers, who in turn guarantee job security and periodic promotions, unless normally acceptable behaviour is violated, until retirement. The stability of these systems has been shaken with the recent economic slowdown.

The salary gap between workers and managers is not as wide as in many US and European firms. Traditionally, starting pay is low and rises with seniority, which counts for more than merit in the early years. Firms also offer security of employment, incentives and a pervading sense of teamwork to promote harmony and consensus. An adversarial relationship is avoided wherever possible. Managers, although rigorous in their demands of workers, are also careful to keep in touch with them. Management uniforms are often the same as those of workers. They occupy multi-person offices, open and near the factory floor, not in remote luxury in a top floor suite. Managers regularly visit the factory floor, talking to employees at their work stations, and showing readiness to adopt suggestions for improvements from workers' group discussions ('quality control circles') both on grievances and on possible new technical methods.

Major advantages to the management style include social cohesion, a relatively equal distribution of rewards and worker identification with company goals. From management's viewpoint, an obvious disadvantage is that it makes flexible hiring and firing of the permanent workforce virtually impossible. Career-long employment is guaranteed, however, only to regular blue- and white-collar workers. Temporary workers have been used in the post-war years as a 'safety-valve': contracted in boom times and discharged during economic downturns.

In the past fifteen years or so, there has been opposition to the overwhelming demands and organisational straightjacket of business and corporate life in Japan. A young generation of workers is not as content with this system. In view of the very high cost of living, young married men are scarcely able to wait for a salary they consider viable. Similarly, many workers in all categories, but particularly those in management, have become restive under the heavy time demands made by firms. Working long hours, even on weekends, leaves little time for families. A heavy burden, physical and emotional, has been known to cause a '**koroshi**', or death by overwork.

Moreover, the extended recession of the 1990s has put extreme pressures on business to maintain profitability and has led to an erosion of the system. Skilled managers and blue-collar workers alike can today find themselves dismissed or facing reduced pensions and benefits.

See also: Japanese economic miracle

DAVID EDGINGTON

manga

The Japanese word for comics is *manga*. The comic format in Japan has achieved a level of popularity that outstrips the performance of this genre of popular culture in North America or Europe. In Japan, the market extends from children's fantasy to teenage sports and adventure, in addition to a rapidly growing adult readership of special interest titles and pornography. The most popular titles sell 2–3 million copies per issue. The comics are cheap 'read and trash' publications bound on recycled paper. A single *manga* contains multiple serialised storylines and is usually 3–400 pages long. Regular *manga* exhibitions and festivals attract crowds of devotees of the more popular artists and comic characters. The fact that comic graphic art is now recognised as a distinct area of study in university design departments reflects the popularity and legitimacy *manga* have achieved in Japan.

The term *manga* is said to have been first coined by the Edo woodblock artist Hokusai Katsushika (1760–1849) to describe the comic woodblock images that were so popular in that period. Even the better known and more successful woodblock artists such as Hokusai were not above producing pornographic *manga* for a lucrative market in images of the brothel and theatre districts. A more important precedent of the modern *manga* was the illustrated storybook librettos for the theatre of that same period. The overlay of written text and images in these woodblock books guided the less literate reader. Throughout the early years of Japanese modern fiction, the practice of serialised illustrated short stories and novels continued this tradition of image-texts. The highly visual nature of Japanese ideographs and pictographs has also been cited as an explanation of the collapse of image and writing into a blur of movement and words on the pages of the *manga*. There is no doubt that, to the unfamiliar eye, the processes for reading or decoding a *manga* are not immediately apparent.

The first appearance of European and US satirical comics in the late nineteenth century led to a brief period of political comic art in Japan, but for the most part *manga* have not emerged as a strong vehicle for political satire. The US style of newspaper comic strips was common in the 1910s and 1920s, fitting well with the existing practice of illustrated serialised stories. The Second World War saw the frequent use of *manga*-style propaganda. With an influx of American comics during the Occupation, *manga* publishers began to opt for a bound book format rather than the comic strip of the pre-war years. The Occupation authorities tolerated the *manga*, which they mistakenly considered to be a simple by-product of US influence.

Throughout the 1950s and early 1960s, comics for children and teenagers dominated the market. It was not until the late 1960s that *manga* began to emerge as a major form of post-war Japanese popular culture attracting diverse target readerships across age groups. Increased surplus income over the 1960s led to increased domestic consumption. Even as early as 1960, 90 per cent of households owned a television set. It was the rapid advent of cheap home entertainment through television that saw the demise of more traditional forms of children's entertainment. By contrast, *manga* moved into a period of rapid popularisation.

The first new wave of post-war comics were aimed at a target audience of teenage males. The most successful of these was *Shōnen Magazine*, which was launched by **Kōdansha** in 1959, and reached weekly sales of 1 million by the mid-1960s. Other major publishing houses were quick to enter this apparently insatiable market. The more popular weeklies and monthlies for boys regularly sell in excess of 3 million copies. Just as rapid commercialisation of the Edo woodblock prints was the direct outcome of technological developments in the printing industry, the dramatic growth in *manga* production in the 1960s can also be linked to innovations in the technology of commercial presses resulting in high volume, low-cost print runs.

The comic artist often referred to as the father of the post-war *manga* boom was Tezuka Osamu. He produced many famous titles that continue to appear in regular reprints. His most internationally known work remains *Tetsuawan Atomu*, which was popularised outside Japan as *Astro Boy*. Tezuka was particularly enamoured of Disney animation graphics and also introduced a range of cinematic techniques into *manga*, e.g. close-ups, frame cuts, suture, pan shots and frame bleeds. These techniques are now the everyday graphic tools of the *manga* artist. There has been a considerable reverse flow of influence from the Japanese comics industry into recent European and North American markets as artists and readers gain access to ongoing *manga* innovation through international speciality comics outlets and online websites.

Throughout the 1960s, there was a proliferation of *shōnen manga* (comics for boys). Adventure stories featuring **robots** and future worlds were common in the late 1950s and early 1960s. The 1964 **Tokyo Olympics** also saw a rapid growth in the genre of sports *manga*. Another rapidly expanding area was the sword fight *manga*, featuring samurai, ninja and other traditional martial-arts figures. This genre also flourished in film and television with more popular *manga* titles converted to animation for television.

After the extraordinary success of comics for boys, the industry was quick to recognise the next potential target market. *Shōjo Friend* and *Margaret* were the first two *manga* for girls to capture a major readership. Throughout the 1950s and early 1960s, the majority of the artists of the new *shōjo manga* (comics for girls) were male. The dominant storyline was 'the quest', where the female protagonist was carried along a trajectory of adventure or romance towards either the happy ending of a reunion or the tragic ending of a separation. The risk of loss or threat of danger were standard devices for creating tension to entice the reader back for the next month's instalment.

By the late 1960s, women began to enter the ranks of the comic artists. As teenage girls who had grown up as devotees of the *manga* began to seek a place for themselves within the industry, the narrative structures of the *shōjo manga* became far more complex and moved beyond the normative boundaries promoted by earlier male comic artists.

The first major shift came with *Seventeen*'s serialisation of Mizuno Hideko's *Fire* from 1969 to 1971. The hero Aaron, a US rock star, was good looking but unruly and rebellious. *Fire* was the first postwar *manga* to depict sexually explicit scenes. Another obvious shift was the focus on a male protagonist. In the earlier *shōjo manga* the female protagonist had remained at the centre of the narrative.

The shift to male protagonists took a further turn with Ikeda Ryoko's *Rose of Versailles* (*Margaret*, 1972–4). In this work, heterosexual love was replaced by male homosexual love complete with *beedo sheenu* (bed scenes) depicting young homosexual couples. Although *Rose of Versailles* was the most influential of the new *bishōnen manga* (beautiful young boy) genre, it is quite problematic to describe the relationship between its heroes as homosexual. The protagonist of *Rose of Versailles* is a girl who has been raised as a boy by her/his family. Storylines of young, attractive homosexual, bisexual and transgendered lovers pursuing one another across exotic and fantastic landscapes of mountains, forests, chalets and palaces are a far cry from the comics read by US teenage girls in the 1960s.

It was the *bishōnen* comics that first broke the public taboo on the representation of sex in the *manga* in the late 1960s and the 1970s. This trend saw the emergence of the magazine *June*, which specialises in *bishōnen* stories to this day. The primary target readership of *June* remains teenage girls but today the extensive crossover readership includes a significant gay male following. For a period in the 1970s, the *shōjo manga* were a major testing ground for the censorship laws. In addition to the homo-erotic *bishōnen* stories, the popular and influential comic artists branched out into stories of lesbian love and increasingly explicit representations of heterosexual sex scenes. What made it possible for the *shōjo manga* to go as far as they did was the so-called *beedo sheenu*. As long as the characters did not roll over or come out from under the bedsheets completely, there was no technical breach of the law, which only prohibits the display of pubic hair and penis. The bed sheets crept further and further off the body and occasionally an artist would risk a standing embrace or full-body profile, but the representation of sexual scenes in the *bishōnen manga* continued to rely upon innuendo and anticipation rather than explicitness.

It was the new range of adult comics that appeared from around the mid-1970s that finally ended the suspense that had built up around the hide-and-seek graphics. The cinematic techniques or pornographic film and photography quickly became the stock and trade of the graphic artists of these 'adult' comics. There are two main streams of pornographic *manga*, the *ero manga* (adult comics for men) and *reedeezu komikku* ('ladies' comics'). There are a wide variety of rapidly changing subgenres such as Milky comics featuring masturbation and Rori comics specialising in Lolita storylines. A survey of comic shops and industry catalogues showed in the vicinity of 180 pornographic titles for either men or women in the summer of 1989. This only includes weeklies, bi-monthlies and monthlies, and not the extensive range of special issues, reprints and collected works.

Many of the companies now publishing pornographic comics are small and highly specialised, and extremely sensitive to any enquiry regarding sales or profits. Increasing tensions in the relationship between the police, the publishing industry and the anti-pornography movement have sensitised publishers to all forms of scrutiny. Some larger, more reputable publishers also carry pornographic titles and are equally reluctant to offer any breakdown of sales figures. Feminists and other interest groups have formed occasional coalitions to fight the increase in teenage-oriented pornographic titles, unmonitored vending machine sales of *ero manga* and breaches of the publishers' code of self-censorship. However, for the most part, the *manga* industry has ignored official and unofficial pressure. *Ero manga* are not an isolated or insignificant phenomenon in Japan but rather a fast growing and widely accepted area of Japanese contemporary popular culture, with an increasing readership among both male and female adults.

The pornographic *manga* may be the fastest growing segment of the comics market but they still only constitute one fraction of the massive weekly sales of *manga* in Japan. Titles often have a short shelf life while the range of weekly, bi-weekly and monthly comics on the market seems to proliferate endlessly. A baseball player, sushi chef, housewife, sumo wrestler, submarine captain, young career woman or even bottle-toting toddler can be the unexpected star of a new hit *manga*. High adventure, violence and the supernatural abound in young boys' and girls' comics, but surprisingly many storylines are focused on the mundane, mirroring the hopes and disappointments of daily life. The comic is the quintessential 'throw away' read; priced at the same amount as a cup of coffee, they are left on the seat of the train or coffee shop to be picked up by someone else.

The comic has become so familiar a part of contemporary Japanese culture that it is now a common medium for official publications seeking a wider, popular readership. One of the best-selling histories of the Shōwa Emperor's life was published in *manga* form after his death. Nakasone Yasuhiro published a *manga* history of his political career when seeking to re-establish his electoral popularity. Conservative Diet members resorted to the *manga* format when attempting to justify their support for increased defence spending, and the Ministry of Health and Welfare has taken up the style of the *manga* to illustrate its **AIDS** education brochures. This new proliferation of 'official' *manga* publications reflects the extent to which the *manga* graphics and narrative style have been recognised as a familiar and accessible vehicle of communication. There is perhaps no other culture in which the comic has so successfully permeated popular contemporary cultural practices as has the *manga* in Japan.

See also: *anime*; pornography; robots

Further reading

Buckley, S. (1991) '"Penguin in bondage": a graphic tale of Japanese comic books', in C. Penley and A. Ross (eds) *Technoculture*, Minneapolis: University of Minnesota Press.

Schodt, F. (1983) *Manga Manga*, Tokyo: Kōdansha.

Tsurumi Shunsuke (1987) 'Comics in post-war Japan', in *A Cultural History of Post-war Japan*, New York: KPI Limited.

SANDRA BUCKLEY

Manji

This film, *Manji* (Passion, 1964; Daiei, 91 minutes), was a strong vehicle for the actresses Wakako Ayako and Kishida Kyoko. A faithful film version of the work bearing the same title by Tanizaki Jun'ichirō, it begins with the affair of a woman hopelessly attracted to her young female friend. Intertwined with the former's relationship with her husband and the latter's with her young lover, the structure develops like a spider's web towards death. In this film, which according to its director Masumura Yasuzō represents an important step towards his renewed interest in Europe, the characters are strongly dominated by their egos and an unceasing sense of dissatisfaction. This effect is further highlighted by the unsettling visual impact of the constant movement in eroticised scenes.

MARIA ROBERTA NOVIELLI

manshon

Manshon are apartment buildings with rental or condominium units, having modern facilities that render them relatively luxurious and distinguish them from more utilitarian public housing, or **danchi**; the very loan word 'mansion' advertises to consumers the 'my home' (*mai homu*) ideal of owning one's own dwelling. Detached two-storey tract homes sold by developers (*tateuri jutaku*) in outlying suburbs compete with *manshon* to fulfil this dream. Public corporations and developers virtually synonymous with *manshon* projects include such 'brand names' as Lion's Mansion and Park Homes. *Manshon* tend to emphasise Western style, or else to mix Western- and Japanese-style interior designs; units are predictable throughout the industry, and do not differ substantially from the different size options for DK and LDK layouts in *danchi*. It has become increasingly difficult to tell the difference between *danchi* and *manshon* since their exteriors are no longer persistently concrete in the case of the former or tiled for the latter; indeed, during the bubble economy the Housing and Urban Development Corporation (HUDC) built *manshon*-like *danchi* that were expensive even by commercial-market standards, resulting in unsold units during the subsequent recession. The term 'ghost *manshon*' was coined for these vacant and grossly discounted properties.

ICHIRO SUZUKI AND MARY KNIGHTON

manzai

A New Year's blessing rite in medieval times, *manzai* had become an attraction at entertainment centres such as the Ikutama Shrine in Ōsaka by the early eighteenth century. From the end of the nineteenth century to the late 1920s, *manzai* developed into a popular entertainment in the thriving variety halls of Kansai. At first interspersed in other performances of song and dance popular at the time, it eventually became the most diverse variety act. By the late 1920s, features of other performance genres based on comic repartee were incorporated into *manzai*, which already included an array of music, dance, physical action (impersonations, skits) and comic dialogue. Concomitant with industrialisation, urbanisation and economic recession, large, inexpensive performance venues for *manzai* opened in this era in Ōsaka. It grew more popular than its rival, *rakugo*, and continues to be the genre in which Japan's comic entertainers are most commonly trained.

The *manzai* dominant today is characterised by the antagonistic yet friendly, fast-paced dialogue performed by two or more people in wit (*tsukkomi*) and fool (*boke*) roles. This *shabekuri manzai* appeared in 1930 with the debut of Yokoyama Entatsu and Hanabishi Achako, a team created and managed by the production company Yoshimoto Kogyo, based in Ōsaka. Yoshimoto executives promoted this new *manzai* by skillful use of the mass media, especially radio and film. Also, the performers shifted from kimono to Western suits, from song and dance to dialogue alone, and from references to historic plays and music to anecdotes about modern life. *Manzai* entertainers have become staples of Japanese popular culture and are strongly associated with the dialect, culture and people of Ōsaka, largely through the powerful influence of the mass media and Yoshimoto's successful dominance of the Japanese comedy market. Dozens of companies now train or market (or market the training of) *manzai* comedians. Since the mid-1980s, the majority of lower-tier *manzai* entertainers, as well as some of the top *manzai* entertainers, have been graduates of Yoshimoto's 'New Star Creation' (NSC) schools in Tokyo and Ōsaka, a media-oriented system that no longer relies on master–apprentice relations and which can quickly lead to diverse careers in a multi-media entertainment.

Further reading

Maeda Isamu (1975) *Kamigata Manzai Happyakunen-shi*, Ōsaka: Sugimoto Shoten.
Tsurumi Shunsuke (1979) *Tayū Saizō Den: Manzai o Tsuranuku Mono*, Tokyo: Heibonsha.

JOEL STOCKER

market research

There had been exposure to the theories and methods of Western market research in pre-war Japan, but it was a US study tour by top Japanese management in 1955 that saw the substantial adoption of the concept. It was felt by the members of the study tour that Japanese business development would be limited without the expertise and technologies of marketing. A Marketing Focus Group was formed and from the 1950s a number of initiatives were undertaken. Professors of marketing were brought from the USA to address Japanese management. From the 1950s to the present, there has been an ongoing pursuit of enhanced marketing research technologies and the introduction of computers has seen a continuous pursuit of new and enhanced data-anaylsis techniques. There are now a significant number of specialist-market survey companies.

With the dramatic growth of market survey companies, the current state of Japan's markets can now be segmented and analysed through such diverse engines as consumer surveys, trend surveys, product surveys, market-potential surveys, etc. The expertise of sociologists, psychologists, statisticians and the like is essential to the ongoing accuracy and enhancement of the data analysis that guides the market. However, the recent introduction of

Point of Sales (POS) systems in banks and ATMs has exponentially increased the level, speed and detail of data collection, which in turn has created a demand for accelerated analysis.

The decision to launch a new product in the intensely differentiated and complex Japanese market is made only after extensive data analysis has indicated market entry and market share potential. To ascertain product viability, a simple demographic study will no longer suffice. It may be necessary to analyse lifestyle trends, consumer patterns, market competitiveness, product placement potential and much else. Even after a product launch, the need for data continues in order to measure and improve product knowledge, advertising impact, product recognition, market reception, customer profile, etc. Information on reasons why consumers do or do not purchase the product, product performance feedback, repeat purchase data and other analysis all combine to shape new marketing campaign strategies and product R&D.

NANBA KŌJI

marriage

Attitudes to marriage in Japan have shifted, with the most significant change occurring for women. The average age at first marriage has increased for both sexes standing at 27.5 years for women and 30 years for men (1996). In two decades, the age at marriage for women has increased by three years, one year greater than that for men. Greater numbers of women are pursuing tertiary education with professional skills, and are either consciously choosing to remain single or feeling less compelled to marry for social or economic reasons.

In the 1980s, the impact of women choosing a single life led to a focus on *yome busoku* (shortage of wives), a problem particularly affecting sons in farming families. This concern prompted a number of rural local governments to organise bachelor tours to countries in the region including the Philippines and Sri Lanka to seek wives. There was a boom in *kokusai kekkon*, or a marriage where one partner (usually the wife) was from overseas. From the mid-1990s, the concern has focused on the implications of later marriages for the projected dramatic decline in population, as evidenced by the declining number of children per family (1.5) and the related issue of family-based welfare provision.

See also: ageing society and elderly care; family system; marriage migration; welfare

Further reading

Hendry, Joy (1986) *Marriage in Changing Japan*, Vermont: Tuttle.

KAYE BROADBENT

marriage migration

From 1975, the typical 'international marriage' (*kokusai kekkon*) changed from the pattern of non-Japanese husband/Japanese wife to Japanese husband/non-Japanese wife. Although one popular label for the women in these marriages is *Ajia Hanayome* (Asian brides), they actually come from such diverse regions as the Philippines, China, Korea, Thailand, Sri Lanka, Brazil, Peru and more recently Russia. The pattern is that women from poorer countries come to Japan to provide domestic labour, sexual labour, reproductive labour and childcare for husbands in Japanese households. For a time, local governments were involved in promoting such marriages, but now tend to delegate this to private brokers. While women who migrate to rural areas have become the focus of media attention, those women who marry husbands in urban areas have received less attention.

In addition to those who enter the country specifically as wives or fiancées, some immigrant women who initially enter as labour migrants marry local men, while others become entangled in sham marriages that guarantee their residence status. As these women and their children become part of local communities, notions of community and nationality are being challenged at the grassroots. Volunteer workers in shelters deal with various issues related to women in these international marriages. Most of this welfare activity is carried out by private volunteer organisations dependent on subscriptions and donations. Some have been funded by private foundations, and a few progressive local governments have provided assistance to non-governmental organisations. Some women seek shelter from domestic violence by husbands or partners. Others seek to regularise the nationality status of their children. In order for the child of a Japanese father and non-Japanese mother to receive Japanese nationality, it is necessary for the father to give official acknowledgment (*ninchi*) of the child (see **Nationality Law**). If a woman's visa category is spouse of a Japanese national, divorce will mean that she loses her residence status, and she will need to apply to the Department of Immigration for special permission for continued residence in Japan. While some women may be happy to return to their country of origin in such circumstances, the situation is more difficult for women with children.

These marriages have been the subject of television programmes, documentary films and books. While these programmes and publications have made the issue more visible in mainstream culture, members of immigrant communities and advocacy groups have been critical of the stereotypical portrayal of immigrant women in popular culture in Japan.

See also: Asian Women's Association; HELP Women's Shelter; Japayuki-san; marriage

Further reading

Suzuki Nobue (2000) 'Between two shores: Transnational projects and Filipina wives in/from Japan', *Women's Studies International Forum* 23(4):431–44.

VERA MACKIE

Marusa no onna

An international comedy hit, directed by **Itami Jūzō**, *Marusa no onna* (A Taxing Woman, 1987) depicts a woman tax investigator combating business corruption at the height of the 1980s **bubble economy**. Miyamoto Nobuko, Itami's wife and star of all his films, combines sweetness with discipline and competence in her characters, which have become more assertive through Itami's *Tampopo, Marusa no Onna* and its sequel, and on to

Minbo no onna, in which she played a lawyer who battles *yakuza* extortionists. *Minbo* provoked a knife attack on Itami. He committed suicide in 1998, allegedly depressed in part by *yakuza* harassment. Itami's playfully narrated parodies have introduced to the world Japanese characters and attitudes well outside the mould of stereotypical conformity.

CHRISTOPHER PERRIUS

Marxism

The history of Marxism in post-war Japan starts again in 1945 with the liberation of many wartime political criminals by the Allied Occupation administration. The legalised Japan Communist Party had already won thirty-five mandates in the parliamentary elections in 1949. With the relaxation of the ban on publication, numerous Marxist literatures flowed into the book market. Most political discussions held were, therefore, more or less about questions as they were put forward by Marxist-oriented intellectuals: What was the nature of the war in Asia and the Pacific? How could national militarism have come into being? What are the peculiarities of Japanese capitalism and how can it be criticised? What was and is the emperor system that survived the war? Is Japan already modernised or not? Was the Meiji Restoration a bourgeois revolution or a radical change in feudalism?

Some of these questions, of course, were directly caused by the defeat. The main part of the discussions, however, was based on the pre-war *shihonshugi ronsō*, 'debates about Japanese capitalism', carried out by the communist scholars of the Kōza school (Noro Eitarō, Yamada Moritarō, Hirano Yoshitarō) and the Rōnō school (Yamakawa Hitoshi, Kushida Tamizō, Sakisaka Itsuo, Ouchi Hyōe) in the 1920s and 1930s. The Kōza school, which held the leadership of the newly founded Japan Communist Party, maintained that Japan had not been modernised enough and so remained a half-feudalistic system. The Rōnō school, by contrast, found the capitalist factors more important than the feudal ones in the analysis of Japanese society. This difference can be seen in their respective revolutionary strategies; whereas the former strived for bourgeois revolution by democratising the half-feudalistic system, the latter directly aimed for socialist revolution.

Only after the war did a new discussion become possible and it especially stimulated the new generation: the 'debate about subjectivity' was first sparked in 1946 by such literary critics as Hirano Ken (1907–78), Honda Shūgo (1908–), Ara Masato (1913–79) and Odagiri Hideo (1916–). It revolved around the question of whether Marxism provides scope for 'subjectivity' at all. The debate was subsequently held among philosophers such as Umemoto Katsumi (1912–74), Kozai Yoshishige (1901–90), Matsumura Kazuto (1905–77) and Kuroda Hirokazu (1927–). Should Marxism hold to the ideas of historical necessity and scientific objectivity and, if so, wherein lies the scope of the freedom of the individual? Although from the theoretical standpoint these debates did not produce any significant results, they were important at least in preparing discussions between Marxists and existentialists in the 1960s, which were mainly prompted by Sartre. Another important subject representing the debates of this era is the atomic bomb, which was, of course, not the monopoly of the left but rather a common topic for all camps. The protest movements against atomic and hydrogen bombs, however, were started by the left and, indeed, still come from the initiative of leftist camps.

From the late 1940s until the beginning of the 1950s, the political situation of the Japan Communist Party and other leftist groups was quite severe. Quite a few demonstrations and strikes were suppressed during the 'Red Purge' under the command of the GHQ (General Headquarters). The Japan Communist Party, meanwhile aiming for a peaceful revolution under the Allied Occupation, still had to experience the critique of the Moscow Cominform (1950). The Social Democrats split from the Japan Communist Party as a result of this situation, and another splinter group from the JCP leadership lost the support of the general public because it attempted to organise a violent revolt in many cities. Khrushchev's subsequent critique of Stalin and the unrest in Hungary in 1956 left the entire leftist camp in utter chaos. From then on, three main oppositional forces were formed in the Japanese left: commu-

nists, social democrats and the so-called anti-Stalinist (and at the same time anti-JCP) new left. The peak of their activities could be found in the protest movement against the US–Japan security treaty in 1960 (the so-called **Anpo struggle**), which they led together with sympathetic liberals. In the end, however, it failed because of police intervention and discordance among the participating groups.

However, the intellectual discussions at that time were not without result. All through the 1950s, investigations about the nature of Japanese fascism initiated by the liberals Kuno Osamu (1910–99), Maruyama Masao (1914–96), Tsurumi Shunsuke (1922–) etc. were fruitful, and it was energetically debated among Marxists whether Japan, in regard to its capitalism, could be seen as an independent country or rather as one subordinated to the USA. Parallel to this development, the scientific branches of Marxism gained much success. The economist Uno Kōzō (1897–1977), for example, claimed that science and ideology should be strictly separated. He put down the Marxian conception of capitalism to the principles of value, population and profit-balancing, and again acknowledged Lenin's theory of imperialism in his theory on the stages of the development of capitalism. Uno's theory, until the beginning of the 1970s, had great influence, especially on the sectors of economic planning in the government and on large financial and industrial institutions where Marxist-oriented scientists played an important role.

The modernistic political scientist Maruyama Masao could never have developed his well-known critique of Japanese ultranationalism had he not closely examined the pre-war works of Marxist scholarship. Also, the historian and Weber specialist Otsuka Hisao (1907–96) attempted to construct a new model of the civil society by synthesising the theories of Weber and Marx. The liberal economists Uchida Yoshihiko (1913–89), Mizuta Hiroshi (1919–) and Hirata Kiyoaki (1922–95) also established their own picture of the civil society and qualified the conception of Marxism on the basis of their detailed reading of Marx and Adam Smith.

In the field of literature, the critic Yoshimoto Takaaki (1924–) must be mentioned. Already shortly after the war, he focused on the conversion of the leftist intellectuals to conservatism as a central theme, and sharply criticised the Japan Communist Party policy from the viewpoint of the 'common people'. In the 1960s, he became a charismatic figure among students, especially among the new left who were critical of both Stalinist and social democratic stances. The theory they sought after was offered by the philosopher Hiromatsu Wataru (1933–94). Hiromatsu, who published a new edition of 'the German Ideology' by Marx and Engels on the basis of critical analysis, looked for a Marxism that was neither subordinated to scientism nor to existentialist humanism. His interpretation of Marx, which strictly distinguishes between early and late Marx on the basis of his own theory of reification, made it easy for the next generation to integrate French structuralism into the Marxist camp.

During the student movements at the end of the 1960s, existentialism and phenomenology were quite popular. Marxists had to conduct rigorous readings of Sartre's 'Critique of dialectic reason', for example. At that time, the critical theory of the Frankfurt School – Marcuse, Fromm and, in particular, Habermas – and structuralism – Althusser, Foucault and Lévi-Strauss – were introduced to Japan. Both of these new trends in the end contributed to the modification and even questioning of the old picture of Marxism. Instead of the stiff political and economic theories, a critique of culture became popular among students and even protests were organised more diversely than before – a phenomenon that was also apparent in Europe and the USA.

The student movements, however, ended with acts of violent terrorism among the activists, which precipitated the total collapse of the radical leftist movement. From then on, the new left has scarcely been of any political importance. As in Europe, the former student activists mostly turned to environmental-protection movements, feminism, anti-discrimination movements and so forth. The subject of Marxism has neither been popular in the academic field nor in journalism since the 1980s. After the fall of the Berlin Wall, the second largest party, Japan Socialist Party, was almost dissolved and the communists have in the mean time changed their course to the right. Political apathy, therefore, prevails. Nevertheless, this does not simply mean that Marx's critical body of thought has entirely

vanished in Japan. It survives inconspicuously in various intellectual activities and protest movements. The popular literary critic **Karatani Kōjin** (1941–), the economist Imamura Hitoshi (1942–) and the feminist **Ueno Chizuko** (1948–), among others, meanwhile demand that one read and confront oneself theoretically with Marx again.

What does this historical development of Marxism in post-war Japan reveal? First, it reveals that Japan and, in particular, Japanese Marxism in no case took a special course. Many problems, the critique of Stalinism, the unrest in the Eastern bloc, the examination of existentialism, the student movements, the shock of (post-) structuralism, feminism and ecology, etc. with which Japanese Marxism was perforce confronted had to be dealt with contemporarily all over the world. Corresponding to the so-called 'globalisation of capitalism', these problems have become more and more international and borderless. Japan, of course, has its own specific problems: the critique of the emperor system, a self-critical responsibility for the former colonialism in the People's Republic of China and North and South Korea; the critique of the globalisation of Japanese capital; upholder of the peace movement as the only country with atomic bomb victims; a critique of discrimination against minorities; and so forth. These tasks, however, are not solvable by Japan alone. A restriction of the problems to a national level is rather questionable. The further the world system becomes internally connected, the more global must become its solutions. Regardless of whether one calls these critical activities Marxist or not, Marx's thought will itself be handed down as long as capitalism is incapable of solving its own problems.

See also: Anpo struggle; Japan Communist Party; Japan Socialist Party; Red Purge; student movement

KOBAYASHI TOSHIAKI

Masumura Yasuzō

b. 1924, Honshū; d. 1986

Film director

Born in Kofu on the island of Honshū, Masumura's

love for cinema developed at a very young age with the films of Kurosawa Akira. He briefly studied law at Tokyo University, but graduated with a degree in philosophy. While still in college, he began working as an assistant director at Tokyo's Daiei Studio. In 1950, he won a scholarship to study film-making at the Cento Sperimentale Cinematografico in Rome, where he was instructed by great figures in Italian neo-realist cinema such as Federico Fellini and Michelangelo Antonioni. Upon returning to Japan in 1954, he once again worked at Daiei Studio, this time as an assistant to prominent Japanese directors Kenji Mizoguchi and Kon Ichikawa. His first major release, 1957's *Kuchizuke* (Kisses), tells the story of a poor, alienated young man and his turbulent relationship with his girlfriend. The film, with its focus on youth rebellion, is considered an important precursor to Japan's New Wave cinema. The influence of Italian neo-realism is felt both in *Kuchizuke* and throughout Masumura's filmography in his preference for location shooting, and his focus on lower-class people. Thematically, however, his films often counter neo-realism through the depiction of a fictional world where human desire and eccentric individuality flourish against the constraints of social systems. From the late 1950s to the early 1970s, Masumura produced an impressive body of work. Among them were *Kyojin to gangu* (Giants and Toys) (1958), *Kuro no shishosha* (The Black Test Car) (1962), *Shisei* (Tatoo) (1966) and *Akai tenshi* (Red Angel). Made in 1966, and set during the Sino-Japan war, *Akai tenshi* is a twisted tale of an army nurse who performs sexual favours on an amputee war victim in exchange for blood in order to save the life of her rapist. The film is representative of the sort of excessive yet erotic behavior that Masumura's characters often engage in. It is his female protagonists in particular who possess a kind of irrepressible and overt sexuality. This eroticism is representative of a more general exploration of political freedom, and, in the 1960's and 1970s, became a popular trope among the emerging New Wave directors.

LEILA POURTAVAF

Matsuda Seiko

b. 1962, Fukuoka

Singer

Matsuda Seiko is an idol singer (see ***idoru singers***) who has paradoxically also been described as 'independent' in that she has come to manage her own career to some degree. Seiko made her recording debut in 1980. Her first three singles were smash hits used in television ad campaigns. As a vocalist, Seiko has been described as having a 'crystalline' voice and has recorded songs written by such New Music legends as Otaki Eichi, Matsumoto Takashi and Hosono Haruomi. In the idol singer context, she stands out for her musical ability. As for her image, Seiko initially played up a mix of the sexualised girl-next-door with a teasing pre-adolescent look of the *shojo*. Often compared now to Madonna, Seiko has changed her image to that of the independent woman. She is seen as an alternative to a life bound to the conventions of loveless marriage. From the late 1980s, she began to undergo significant **cosmetic surgery** including breast enhancement and eyelid 'Europeanisation'. Despite the mountain of negative press stemming from her countless extra-marital affairs prior to her divorce in 1997, Seiko forged an innovative style of guiding the Japanese media's insistent objectification of her image to her own benefit.

MARK ANDERSON

Matsuda Yusaku

b. 1950, Shimonoseki, Yamaguchi
 Prefecture; d. 1989, Tokyo

Actor

Matsuda made a total of twenty-five films, beginning with *Abayo Dachiko* (So Long Dachiko) in 1974 and concluding with *Black Rain* in 1989 – the year he died of cancer at the age of forty. Beginning with his role as the long-haired Detective Jiipan in the 1973 television series *Taiyo ni hoero*, Matsuda frequently played rebels who casually flouted authority while living by their own moral codes. After winning success on both the big and small screen with such roles, he branched into more serious drama with *Kagerō-za* (Heat-Haze Theatre), a 1981 Suzuki Seijun film in which he portrayed a contemporary playwright led into a destructive world of illusion by his love for a mysterious woman. Abroad, Matsuda is best known for playing the sardonic tutor in Morita Yoshimitsu's *Kazoku Game* (The Family Game, 1983) and the feral outlaw in Ridley Scott's aforementioned *Black Rain*.

Further reading

Editorial Work (eds) (1994) *Yomigaere! Tantei Monogatari*, Tokyo: Nippon Television Network Corporation.

Yamaguchi Takeshi (1994) *Matsuda Yusaku Hono Shizuka ni*, Tokyo: Shakai Shososha.

MARK SCHILLING

Matsui Yayori

b. 1934, Kyōto

Feminist journalist

Matsui Yayori was educated at the Tokyo University of Foreign Studies. From her appointment to the **Asahi shinbun** newspaper in 1961, Matsui took an interest in issues of gender and development in the Asian region and the networks of activists in the region. In 1977, Matsui helped found the **Asian Women's Association** and its journal *Asian Women's Liberation*, which appeared in both Japanese and English. On retiring from the *Asahi* newspaper, she set up the Asian Women's Resource Centre.

Select bibliography

Matsui Yayori (1999) *Women in the New Asia: From Pain to Power*, London: Zed Books.

—— (1989) *Women's Asia*, London: Zed Books.

VERA MACKIE

Matsutoya Yumi

b. 1954, Tokyo, Hachiōji

Singer, songwriter

Born Arai Yumi, Matsutoya Yumi (nickname Yuming) reached music world renown in 1969 after Katsumi Kahashi recorded 'Ai wa totsuzen' (Love, All of a Sudden), a song she had written at the age of fifteen. Arai's first album, *Hikōki gumo* (Airplane Clouds), was released in 1973 and forged a new musical idiom between folk, rock, pop and *enka*.

Yuming incorporated influences from progressive rock and European pop to produce a sophisticated, upper-middle-class female Japanese voice and sound in a contemporary musical and journalistic world dominated by discussions of folk music and social critique. This musical idiom is generally thought to have been first realised on her third For Life Records album *Cobalt Hour*, featuring the single 'Ano hi ni kaeritai' (I'd Like to Return to that Day). Yuming is credited with coining the phrase 'New Music', which caught on as a catchphrase for the various musical styles of early-1970s musicians recording for independent labels with roots in the folk-music boom. While their styles were quite various, they shared an *auteur* approach to popular music which demanded that artistic control be placed in the hands of the songwriter and performer.

Arai changed her name to Matsutoya Yumi after marrying her keyboardist and arranger, Matsutoya Masataka (1976), who has produced every album she has recorded since her debut on For Life Records. Yuming has maintained an image of balancing work and home life, which ties in to her upper-middle class image and resounding popularity from the 1970s to the early 1990s. Each succeeding Yuming album set new sales records through the early 1990s. She is still among the leaders in career album sales. For many, Yuming was a representative voice of the 1970s and 1980s, for better and for worse. She self-consciously distanced her musical output from politically oriented folk towards a more artistically focused medium of expression, often coded by male critics as a move from the public to the private sphere. Her later work reiterates pronouncedly Orientalist motifs and landscapes, which she shares to some degree with 'progressive' rock in Europe and the USA, but which are also inflected by her insistently feminine, not to say feminist, voice.

Matsutoya Yumi is surely one of the most familiar Japanese pop culture icons who is both female and to some degree in charge of her own career and artistic direction (while deferring to her husband as head of the household and the recording studio). She is clearly a female artist who made a name for herself on the basis of her ability as a songwriter rather than her physical appearance or her voice (which notoriously strays wildly out of tune in live performance). She may be considered both an influence on, and a reflection of, Japanese popular culture generally from the mid-1970s to the late 1980s. Her work and her image raise important questions about gender, class and ethnicity in Japanese popular music of the period.

MARK ANDERSON

mazaakon

The concept of mother complex, rendered into Japanese as *mazaakon*, dates from the late 1980s and early 1990s and was first popularised in the works of feminist scholar **Ueno Chizuko**. Ueno rejected the Oedipal model as inappropriate for the analysis of the Japanese mother–son relationship. The pronounced absence of the typical working Japanese father from the home and the weak romantic and/or sexual relationship between husband and wife did not support an Oedipal model. The male child did not experience jealousy in relation to this weakened paternal presence and could demand the full attention of the mother. This intense relationship was not subject to any traumatic disruption, and by the teen years the mother herself could become so dependent on the relationship as the site of her own identity formation that she would resist the son forming attachment to another female. This then functioned as an explanation for the over-investment of mothers in their son's educational and career performance, a fixation that fed into a growing contemporary urban mythology of mother–son incest that was popularised in the

media at the same period. *Mazaakon* was also offered as an explanation for the level of interference of a mother in her son's married life and related problems between husband and wife.

See also: Ajase Complex

SANDRA BUCKLEY

meat

Meat was not a part of the Japanese diet until the last 200 years due to a traditional Buddhist prohibition. The one exception was wild boar, which was eaten by local villagers in areas where it could be hunted and also treated as a delicacy by the samurai elite, popularly known as 'mountain whale'. The explorers, sailors, traders and missionaries who arrived from Spain and Portugal over the sixteenth century brought with them dried and salted meats, but it was not until the next wave of contact with the West in the nineteenth century that a broad-based taste for meat would develop. Increased meat intake has been a major factor in a 50 per cent decline in rice consumption between 1950 and the mid-1990s.

While there is no doubt that meat consumption is increasing, it is also important to recognise differences in regional dietary patterns. In the western region of Japan, including **Ōsaka**, **Kyōto** and **Kobe**, pork is the main meat consumed, while in the north-eastern and northern regions beef is far more popular than pork. Beef consumption doubled over the period from 1950 to 1990 but with strong concentrations in the **Tokyo** area and Tōhoku and **Hokkaidō** to the north.

Initially, meat was rarely treated as a main course in the Western style but served as one more of the array of side dishes that accompanied rice or was mixed in with vegetables in a broth-based meal where noodles remained the staple. Today, despite relatively high prices, it is not uncommon for meat to appear as the staple for a family meal. Significant increases in national average height and growth rates among children are attributed to school milk and high-protein lunch programmes, and increased meat consumption at home. Ground and chunked beef, diced chicken and pork cutlets are the most popular cuts in Japan today. Preparation methods still rely heavily on soy-based sauces – *shoyu* and **miso** – and grilling (*yakimono*), deep frying (*agemono*) and simmering (*nimono*) are the most frequent cooking techniques for meat. In a country where the treatment of indigestion is the stuff of both folklore and primetime advertising, meat is usually marinated or tenderised before cooking.

The recent boom in pre-prepared foods available in food halls of major department stores and supermarkets, together with home delivery services, have contributed to higher meat consumption without any substantial increase in time or effort. A dramatic increase in the array of international cuisines available, not only in the major urban centres but even in smaller regional towns, has been another factor in increasing the variety of meat dishes now familiar to Japanese consumers. It is **Kobe beef**, however, that remains the most expensive and elite of the meats on the Japanese market. The health food boom of North America and Europe has been slow in reaching Japan but it is not expected that the upward trend in meat consumption will end, even with the first signs of a shift towards reduced fat intake.

SANDRA BUCKLEY

meibutsu

Meibutsu means 'famous product', and refers to distinctive, usually handcrafted, items produced in particular places throughout Japan. Typical examples of *meibutsu* include wooden dolls (*kokeshi*) produced in Akita Prefecture, inlaid wooden boxes from around the city of Hakone near Mt. Fuji or decorative lanterns from Gifu Prefecture. Porcelain and ceramic products are highly regional in style, the most famous including Arita ware from Northern Kyūshu and Satsuma ware from Southern Kyūshu. *Meibutsu* also include food products, such as *soba* (buckwheat noodles) from Nagano Prefecture, *ocha* (green tea) from Shizuoka Prefecture and a huge variety of *senbei* (rice or wheat crackers) and *manju* (sweet rice and bean cakes) produced differently in each locality. *Meibutsu* may be associated with particular neighbourhoods: silk products from the Nishijin district of **Kyōto**, or

yomogi danbo (mugwort-flavoured *manju*) from Yomogi in **Tokyo**.

While *meibutsu* are fascinating in themselves and for the remarkable range of their cultural geography, they are also significant as ***omiyage***, obligatory gifts to family, friends and colleagues after even a short trip out of town. The gift must be evocative of place, and appropriate for the season (see **seasons**) and event. While *meibutsu* are traditional, marketing strategies are modern; every region of Japan now has a website advertising its *meibutsu* and offering online sales.

See also: gift giving; *omiyage*; wrapping

AUDREY KOBAYASHI

meishi

The *meishi* (business/name card) is a key social tool in interaction with Japanese business contacts. Each new association opens with a formalised exchange of business cards. The language of this exchange in Japanese is largely predetermined by an etiquette of hierarchy and is directly tied to relative status in a complex grid of variables including status of the company of employment, ranking of individual position, age and gender. Two individuals meeting for the first time do not launch into conversation before assessing the information on the face of the card for comparative status. Without this information, the appropriate levels of honorifics and gestures of respect cannot be determined. The name of the individual is almost secondary to this status-related information.

The practice of exchanging cards came to Japan during the period of diplomacy leading up to the opening of Japan from the mid-1800s but the practice fast took root and gained a social significance far greater than in the European cultures in which it originated. The formal and highly stylised process of announcing a visitor within Japan's aristocratic and samurai cultures also focused on rank and family, clan or other affilliated status. The exchange of business cards quickly emerged as a vehicle for compensating for the more abbreviated information exchanged in the Western style of greeting of the day.

SANDRA BUCKLEY

menopause

The Japanese term *kōnenki* is usually translated as menopause, but to most people *kōnenki* conveys the idea of a gradual ageing process starting around age forty to forty-five and continuing until sixty. The end of menstruation is just one sign among many, including changes in eyesight, hearing loss and stiffening of joints, which suggests to women that they are growing older. Many Japanese consider that ageing men also experience *kōnenki*, a term that was created at the end of the nineteenth century under the influence of German medicine to convey the idea of a mid-life transition. To this day, ageing in Japan is thought of by many primarily as a social process in which the position of an individual in a family takes precedence over biological changes of ageing.

Research has shown that a relatively small number of Japanese women experience symptoms thought to be universally associated with the end of menstruation. Reporting of hot flushes and night sweats is very low. Preliminary findings indicate that this is also the case in other Asian countries, and dietary practices and possibly genetics are implicated. It is of note that there is no word in Japanese that refers to a hot flush.

MARGARET LOCK

Metabolism

Promulgated by the Metabolism Group of 1960, Metabolism theories attempted to bridge the gap between nature and technology by espousing large-scale projects or city planning proposals that could organically change, regenerate and adapt to growing population needs and the high-tech modern demands of the future's urban environment. The name Metabolism itself underscores the Group's explicit intent to transform, or 'metabolise' (*shinchintaisha suru*), society itself through the revitalisation and reorganisation of architectural space in cities.

The Metabolism Group was organised to represent new ideas by younger Japanese architects at the 1960 World Design Conference hosted in Tokyo; Tokyo University professor and architect **Tange Kenzō** headed the Conference Programme Committee. Group members included: former *Shinkenchiku* (New Architecture) journal editor and critic Kawazoe Noboru; architects **Kikutake Kiyonori**, Ōtaka Masato, **Maki Fumihiko** and **Kurokawa Kishō**; industrial designer Ekuan Kenji; and graphic designer Awazu Kiyoshi. They presented proposals, sketches or essays in their 'manifesto', *Metabolism 1960: The Proposals for a New Urbanism* (Tokyo: Bijutsu Shuppansha), published in both English and Japanese for the conference. The dramatic futuristic contents of the conference exhibit and manifesto included 'Ocean City' (Kikutake); the essay 'Toward group form' (Maki and Ōtaka); 'Space City' (Kurokawa); and the essay 'Matter and man' (Kawazoe). The bilingual manifesto and conference announced the Group's claim to international status, while also stressing its distinctively Japanese origins, drawing attention to their resolute breaking away from excessive Western influence.

The most striking characteristics of Metabolist design and theory can be enumerated: an emphasis on technology and machines co-extensive with the organic and biological; interchangeable parts and renewable modular structural units; moveable or capsule-like living spaces; walls that serve not just structural purposes but also contain housing units or life-support equipment; references to atomic-age living; a lexicon of dividing cells, nerves, 'Golgi body' structures, disease, anthropomorphic and plant forms; attention to 'systems' over 'forms'; and monolithic urban projects or megastructures that adapt and 'naturally' shrink, grow or die with the population's growth and lifestyle changes. Important Metabolist projects, many never built, include: Kurokawa's DNA-like helix structures and the Nakagin Capsule Tower (Tokyo, 1972); Tange's 1960, Kikutake's 1961 and Kurokawa's 1987 Plans for Tokyo Bay; Kikutake's spinal-cord-like 'moveable house', 'Sky House' Movenet structures and Aquapolis (Okinawa, 1975).

Metabolism did not end in 1960; rather, it has been regularly revived, especially at science and technology fairs such as the Ōsaka Expo (1970), the Okinawa Expo (1975) and the Tsukuba Expo (1985). Besides the independent success of Kurokawa, Kikutake and Maki, members of the original Group have worked together over the years in collaborative and corporate ventures: the company Communication Design Institute K.K. (Kawazoe, Ekuan and Kikutake) and the National Museum of Ethnography in Ōsaka (1977; Kurokawa, Kawazoe and Awazu). In 1981, the Metabolism Group reunited to found their company Keikaku Rengō K.K. (Planning Federation), which planned the '85 Tsukuba Expo and the 1989 Yokohama Showcase at Minato Mirai 21, and designed the Kawasaki City Museum (1988).

Further reading

(1991) 'Special report: Metabolism, 1960–1990s', *Approach* (winter), Ōsaka: Takenaka Corporation.

SCOTT GOLD AND MARY KNIGHTON

middle class

As measured by surveys, the overwhelming majority of Japanese think of themselves as 'middle class'. While some scholars characterise Japanese society as a 'new middle mass', critics counter that significant inequality along class lines persists. Whether 'middle class' describes all Japanese, the segment of people whose occupations or lifestyles defines them as middle class has grown steadily during the twentieth century.

The pre-war decades saw the emergence of two distinct middle classes. The 'old middle class' was comprised of shopkeepers, owners of small workshops and 'middling farmers'. From the 1910s to 1930s, the old middle classes increasingly recognised their collective interests *vis-à-vis* big business and large landlords. Their trade associations secured business-tax reform and an anti-department store law. As early as the 1890s, a smaller, but self-conscious, 'new middle class' arose among those in the new professions of law, journalism, education, engineering and medicine. Their status rested on higher education and 'Western' knowledge. By the 1920s, the new middle class included large numbers of salaried employees in government and the expanding corporations. In middle-class homes, women assumed the privileged status of **housewife** (*shufu*), who managed the household, read the new housewives' magazines and partook of inter-war consumer culture.

In the post-war era, the new middle class gradually supplanted the old middle class. According to the 1985 census, some 35 per cent of the employed populace could be considered new middle class; another 35 per cent were working class, followed by the old middle class (25 per cent) and capitalists (5 per cent). Inevitably, the old middle classes have declined in the face of urbanisation, white-collar employment and large-scale production and commerce. None the less, Japan's old middle classes have done much to slow their decline. Well-organised farmers and shopkeepers lobbied the political parties to secure substantial protections (e.g. subsidised rice prices and restrictions on large-scale stores).

Meanwhile, the new middle classes surged amid post-war economic growth. The narrowly based 'salaryman' culture of the 1920s became the norm for many post-war families during the 1950s and 1960s. Supporting this 'enterprise society' was an expanding meritocratic educational system, marked by competitive entrance examinations. Nearly all Japanese complete high school and a significant proportion go on to higher education. Large companies recruit university-educated men, who work most of their lives at the same firm. Educated young women routinely work as **'office ladies'** before marrying salarymen. A great many women became full-time housewives, who bolster the enterprise society by educating their children, saving at high rates and managing their homes and communities so their husbands can work long hours in the full-time paid workforce.

The post-war growth of the new middle class further contributed to a homogenisation of a middle-class culture that spread beyond those in middle-class jobs, particularly to well-paid blue-collar workers and their families. Companies instructed workers' wives in middle-class home-making, and many workers' families similarly strive to place their children in the most highly regarded universities.

See also: housewife; motherhood

Further reading

Ishida, H. (1993) *Social Mobility in Contemporary Japan*, Stanford: Stanford University Press.

Vogel, E. (1963) *Japan's New Middle Class*, Berkeley: University of California Press.

SHELDON GARON

Mifune Toshiro

b. 1 April 1920, Tsingtao, Shantung province, China; d. 24 December 1997, Tokyo

Actor

Mifune Toshiro is the Japanese film actor best known in the West, epitomising the Japanese *tateyaku* (the noble, virile protagonist in Japanese theatre and cinema), Mifune generally developed his roles through his attention to gestures, at times small and naturalistic, at other times charged and animal-like. He is particularly remembered for appearances in sixteen **Kurosawa Akira** films, including: *Rashōmon*'s (1950) untamed bandit-rapist; the comically brash would-be samurai in *Shichinin no samurai* (Seven Samurai, 1954); the handsome thief of *Donzoko* (The Lower Depths, 1957); and the gruff but dedicated doctor nicknamed *Akahige* (Red Beard, 1965). Also known for his legendary samurai roles in Inagaki Hiroshi's films and as Toranaga, the title role in the television series *Shōgun*, Mifune also founded his own production company in 1963.

WILLIAM C. THOMPSON

migrant workers

Between the latter half of the 1980s and the early 1990s, over a million foreign workers entered Japan and the foreign (long-term resident) population reached more than 1 per cent of the population as a whole. This trend was noted by immigration specialists, particularly since Japan has moved, within a short period, from achieving high economic growth without the introduction of foreign workers to accepting immigrants. However, these immigrants, whether workers who are Brazilians of Japanese descent or those from Asia, as well as those born in Japan (*zainichi*), all have a long connection to the history of Japanese immigration since the formation of the modern Japanese state. The history of migration began with that of the emergence of the modern state and expanded with the development of capitalism. The first migrants were Japanese who emigrated to the sugarcane fields of Hawaii in 1868, 'emigration year one', and later to places like Australia for pearl diving (1883). Immigrants such as European and North American diplomats and merchants entered Japan, as did their Chinese and Korean domestic servants. However, the number of people leaving and entering Japan increased significantly as industrialisation intensified from the latter half of the nineteenth century.

Until the beginning of high economic growth in the 1950s, Japan was basically a nation of emigrants. Emigration from Japan grew first as part of Asian indentured migration within the world economy, then increased further with the spread of Japanese imperialism as Japanese migrated to colonies or countries inside the territory of Imperial Japan. In the first case, Asian workers were sent in the form of indentured labour to the farms and construction sites of North and South America, and South-East Asia. They replaced the labour force of the outlawed system of slavery. Japan, too, sent emigrants officially and in groups to Hawaii, North and South America, and other countries. Many emigration companies and shipping firms were established, and the official figures alone show over 700,000 Japanese emigrated before the Second World War. Mass emigration also occurred sporadically after the Second World War, and, by the start of economic growth in the early 1960s, over 500,000 people had left Japan. In the second case, as Japan developed as a modern state and its imperialism grew, emigrants were sent first to settle in areas such as Ezo (present-day **Hokkaidō**) to strengthen Japan's frontier. Then military personnel, administrators, merchants and prostitutes, as well as labourers, were sent to countries under Japan's colonial rule such as Taiwan, Korea, Manchuria and other countries in South-East Asia and the South Sea Islands. Emigration to the colonies was intended to increase Japan's influence, maintain local control and to protect industrial interests and sources of food, and other essential resources.

Although the modern state tends to exclude outsiders, it is still necessary for it to incorporate foreigners in various ways. During industrialisation, in particular, one of the basic problems for Japanese capitalism was how to acquire and maintain a stable, good-quality, low-paid work-force, while at the same time the country continued to send emigrants overseas. The creation of low-paid workers and the adjustment of their appalling working conditions in the early stages of capitalism continued to be the most pressing issue for industrialisation. The supply of labour basically depended on the huge flow of population from the country to cities with some augmentation by workers from abroad.

The entry of foreigners into Japan may be divided into three periods, from the point of view of labour supply conditions. The first, the national formative period, was from the mid-nineteenth century to the beginning of the twentieth. The second stage was from the 1920s to the Second World War: the age of heavy chemical industrialisation and imperialism. The third stage was the post-1960s period, when fresh labour supply from the country dramatically decreased and the labour market became rigid. The first period, which saw the initial steps in the formation of the modern Japanese state, was also the period in which the division between foreigners and Japanese nationals was formed, and the period in which the modern city was shaped in opposition to agriculture-based communities. People who had lost their means of support moved to large cities such as **Tokyo** and **Ōsaka**, where they became part of the urban lower classes. In **Okinawa**, particularly, in spite of being included in the nationalisation process, Okinawans were marginalised and discriminated against as labour. The amount of foreign labour flowing into Japan greatly increased in the second period, in which the modern labour market was formed. With heavy chemical industrialisation the gap grew between large companies, which needed to maintain a stable workforce, and small/medium-sized companies, which depended on a flexible supply of casual labour. Large numbers of workers from colonies like Korea flowed into these smaller companies and into areas such as mining, where working conditions were very harsh. In the shift to a wartime economy in the late 1930s, these workers were included in national mobilisation and over 2,000,000 foreign workers were mobilised, including forced labour.

There was little foreign labour introduced in the high-growth period following the Second World War, but the price of this was the disintegration of rural society, which proceeded at such speed that the rural population dropped from over 50 per cent of the entire Japanese population in the years immediately after the war to under 10 per cent in the 1970s. The rural population was no longer able to supply fresh labour and, in addition, the labour market lost its flexibility due to a rise in the school-leaving age and social security policies. This change or hardening of the labour market manifested itself in the absolute shortage of labour that occurred during the 'bubble' economy of the 1980s. This caused an unavoidable and necessary influx of workers from overseas. The government turned a blind eye to large numbers of illegal immigrants who entered by such 'side doors' as language study, as well as by 'back doors' such as staying beyond visa expiry dates. The entry of foreign workers peaked in 1993 and after that declined rapidly as the economy entered a depression. Even so, since the second half of the 1980s, changes in the Japanese economy have encouraged an overall trend towards legal immigration and long-term stays.

See also: Brazilian Japanese; Japayuki-san; migrant workers; national identity and minorities; Nikkei in North America

IYOTANI TOSHIO

Miike struggle

The Miike struggle was a 282-day strike in 1960 by coal miners in Kyūshū, the most protracted in post-war history. It is frequently portrayed as the last gasp of militant labour unionism. Miike was the site of one of Mitsui Mining's largest mines and was a bell-wether for smaller mines throughout Kyūshū and **Hokkaidō**. The company began rationalising the mines in 1959 to break the strength of the union and facilitate the transition from coal to oil as Japan's primary energy source. After colluding with other firms to prevent competition during the strike, Mitsui laid off 1,500 miners in December. The union rejected the notices and Mitsui began a lockout on 25 January 1960. The miners responded with an all-out strike. Mitsui formed a second company union and mobilised police and hired goons to break the picket lines. The struggle peaked in July when 20,000 miners and supporters confronted 13,000 police at the mine entrance. The two sides finally submitted to government arbitration and the Japan Coal Miners' Union accepted a settlement upholding the firings over the objections of the Miike local. Despite its defeat, the strike forced government and big business to begin creating social-welfare programmes providing for workers' continued livelihoods.

WESLEY SASAKI-UEMURA

mikoshi

This particular scene is a popular one among tourists, film-makers and television crews alike as they seek out local flavour and ritual in contemporary Japan: a band of men from the local shrine community, dressed only in coiled loincloths, balance a heavy wooden portable shrine high on their shoulders. Chanting together, often to the rhythm of the *kōdō* drum beat, they seem to achieve the impossible and heave the shrine still higher in the air as all watch hoping that no one will stumble and that the shrine will again descend safely onto their shoulders. The team weaves its way precariously, hot and sweaty, through the neighbourhood streets. Once a year, at the main shrine festival, the local deities are paraded through the streets surrounding the shrine, safely ensconced in the weighty carved wooden recesses of a *mikoshi*. It is believed that the deity returns to the community once a year to bring goodwill and protection. The emergence of the deity into the community while

celebrated is also accompanied by all the necessary offerings and prayers to encourage the deity to depart again satisfied and not linger beyond the end of the festivities.

The right to be among the *mikoshi* bearers is a privilege and the source of many a community feud between male rivals, young and old alike. These days it is sponsorship of the shrine that is as likely as anything to determine who is in and out, and who has the best positions. The revitalisation of traditional festivals and the invention of new ones has seen a higher profile for the *mikoshi* of old. The nostalgic revival of festivals since the 1980s has seen new sponsors and shrine donors financing the refurbishment and aggrandisement of many local *mikoshi*.

See also: festivals; State Shintō

SANDRA BUCKLEY

Minamata disease

Minamata disease, first discovered in 1956, is a disease of the central nervous system caused by eating fish and shellfish contaminated with organic mercury discharged by the Chisso Corporation chemical factory in the city of Minamata in Kumamoto Prefecture in Kyūshū. It was one of the 'Big Four' pollution cases in which victims sued the polluting companies in the late 1960s. Minamata disease was Japan's worst case of industrial pollution, and came to symbolise both the dark side of high growth and the flowering of the citizens' group movement.

It took several years to confirm the cause of the 'strange disease' that attacked nerve cells, afflicting its victims with numbness and tremors in the extremities, loss of hearing and taste, constriction of the visual field, mental disorders and sometimes death. There were congenital victims as well. As suspicion began to focus on the factory, social pressures worked to protect the company that supplied half the city's tax income and a quarter of its jobs. The Ministry of Health and Welfare disbanded its research group and buried its 1959 preliminary report suggesting mercury as the cause, while Chisso (named Shin Nihon Chisso Hiryū until 1965) promoted counter-theories. Researchers confirmed in 1961 that the organic mercury was created inside the factory in the production process for acetaldehyde, but only after Chisso stopped using mercury in 1968 did the government officially conclude that Chisso's mercury caused the disease.

Victims' demands for compensation have resulted in three so-called 'final and complete' solutions to the Minamata disease issue. In 1959, Chisso agreed to make 'sympathy payments' to patients, in return for a ban on further demands, even if the company's waste was proven to be the cause. Prior to this, Chisso's own secret experiments had proven that its mercury was the cause. Chisso also installed waste treatment equipment, but did not announce that it did not remove mercury.

In the late 1960s, as activist citizens' groups appeared nationwide and another outbreak of Minamata disease occurred near a factory in Niigata Prefecture, Minamata came to national attention. In 1973, after victims won their lawsuit, Chisso accepted legal responsibility and began paying reasonable compensation to those certified by the government as Minamata disease victims. By 1999, 2,262 victims had been certified. Court cases continued after 1973 over certification and government responsibility, while government loans kept Chisso alive and able to continue making compensation payments. A government-brokered agreement implemented in 1996 had compensated 11,152 uncertified victims by 1999, but only in return for promises never to apply for certification or sue the government. Nevertheless, this was likely to be the last 'solution' to the Minamata disease issue, since the average age of patients was in the late seventies.

The most heavily polluted areas of Minamata Bay were dredged in the 1980s, largely at Chisso's expense. In 1997, Kumamoto's governor declared the fish in the bay safe, and the net that had surrounded the bay since 1977 was removed.

Further reading

Huddle, N. and Reich, M. (1987 [1975]) *Island of Dreams: Environmental Crisis in Japan*, New York: Autumn Press and Cambridge, MA: Schenkman Books.

Ishimure, M. (1990) *Paradise in the Sea of Sorrow: Our Minamata Disease*, trans. L. Monnet, Kyōto: Yamaguchi Publishing House.

Mishima, A. (1992) *Bitter Sea: The Human Cost of Minamata Disease*, trans. R. Gage and S. Murata, Tokyo: Kosei Publishing Company.

Smith, W. and Smith, A. (1975) *Minamata*, New York: Holt, Rinehart & Winston.

Upham, F. (1987) *Law and Social Change in Postwar Japan*, Cambridge, MA: Harvard University Press.

TIMOTHY S. GEORGE

Minamata Series, the

Director Tsuchimoto Noriaki started his career making educational and industrial films for the high-growth economy at Iwanami Productions. When he quit to make films independently, he ended up at Minamata where the dimensions of the mercury poisoning by Chisso Corporation were only beginning to be understood. In a series of powerful films Tsuchimoto carefully documented how mercury entered the food chain and affected the human body; this in the face of corporate and governmental denials. As a whole, his series of thirteen films charts the depth of the tragedy while sensitively following the victims as they make sense of their lives.

ABÉ MARK NORNES

mingei

Mingei refers both to articles produced by traditional craftspeople for everyday use and to the movement to protect and promote such crafts, which began in the 1920s and still continues today. The term itself was coined in 1926 by Yanagi Soetsu (Muneyoshi) (1889–1961) as an abbreviation of *minshū no kogei* (crafts of the common people). Both 'folk art' and 'folk craft' have been used as English equivalents, but Yanagi himself preferred the latter in order to distinguish *mingei* from works of 'high art'. Typical *mingei* include: pottery, lacquer ware, textiles, baskets, furniture and other household items, and Japanese paper (*washi*). Yanagi's 'discovery' of *mingei* and the subsequent *mingei* movement can be said to reflect both a consciousness of modernisation and the way in which the modern Japanese have turned to traditions for a source of identity.

Early in his career, Yanagi had been a student of Western art and literature, and a frequent contributor to the avante-garde magazine *Shirakaba* (White Birch). In 1914, he published a major study of the poet William Blake. Soon thereafter, however, he began to turn his attention to East-Asian art, at first to Korean ceramics of the Yi Dynasty (1392–1910), but later also to Japanese pottery and other hand-crafted objects, especially of the Edo Period (1600–1867). Yanagi's interest in crafts was stimulated by his association at this time with the British etcher and potter Bernard Leach (1887–1979) and Japanese potters Tomimoto Kenkichi (1886–1963), Hamada Shoji (1894–1978) and Kawai Kanjiro (1890–1966). He was also not unaware of the work of William Morris (1834–96) and of the English Arts and Crafts movement of the 1880s and 1890s. Just as Morris's call for a return to the crafts was a response to the mechanisation of work brought about by the Industrial Revolution, so can the *mingei* movement be seen as a reaction to Japan's own period of industrialisation that began in the late nineteenth century and which, by the 1920s, was threatening to drive the remaining traditional crafts out of business.

As understood by Yanagi, *mingei* can be defined as items which:

1 are designed to be used;
2 are made by anonymous craftsmen and women rather than known artists;
3 are made by hand;
4 exhibit local characteristics; and
5 are produced in sufficient numbers so as to be readily available and inexpensive.

For Yanagi, what was remarkable about such items is that, although they are not made with any conscious aesthetic intention, they none the less possess a certain beauty. This beauty, he argued, derives from the nature of craftwork itself. Drawing on the Buddhist notion of *tariki* (reliance on a greater power), he saw the beauty of *mingei* as a result of the way in which the craftsman, rather than asserting himself as an artistic creator, submerges his identity into his craft, its tradition and the people. In this way, according to Yanagi, the craftsperson can be said to surrender his or her self to nature, and it is thus nature that is ultimately the source of the beauty of *mingei*.

In 1931, Yanagi and his friends founded the Japan Folk Craft Association and began publishing the magazine *Kogei* (Crafts). Support for the movement grew, and in 1936 the association opened the Japan Folk Craft Museum (Nihon Mingei-kan) in Tokyo, which ever since has been the centre of the *mingei* movement. These activities represented two of the *mingei* movement's aims, namely collecting examples of *mingei* and promoting an appreciation for their special qualities. A third aim was to revive the crafts themselves. Here efforts were less successful, and it was not until the post-war period that the decline was arrested and production of *mingei* increased.

One of the factors leading to the popularity of *mingei* in the post-war was government recognition. In 1954, a revision of the 1950 Cultural Properties Law made possible the designation of certain skills or traditions as 'intangible cultural properties' and the notion of '**Living Treasures**'. This resulted in *mingei* and the movement receiving a new level of media attention. What contributed more than anything to the growth of interest in *mingei* was the economic boom of the 1960s. As incomes rose and Japan became flooded with consumer goods, a veritable *mingei* boom developed that continued into the early 1970s. Traditional craftsmen, especially potters, found themselves scrambling to keep up with demand. The number of craftsmen increased and production facilities were expanded. Not surprisingly, among the works most in demand were those that the Cultural Properties Law and the *mingei* movement had identified as exemplifying the *mingei* ideal. The increased demand, however, only made it more difficult for that ideal to be maintained. Prices rose, some craftsmen turned to more modern methods (including mechanisation), others stopped using local materials and all became more conscious of aesthetic demands and thus self-conscious of themselves as artists. Competitive exhibitions organised by the various crafts associations such as the annual *Dentō Kogeiten* (Traditional Crafts Exhibition) also contributed to the transformation of the craftsperson into the artist–craftsman.

Today, there are many museums throughout Japan devoted to the preservation and display of historical *mingei*. There is also a healthy antique business. As for the contemporary production of *mingei*, although the boom has long since subsided, many problems remain. Craft traditions that do not receive recognition continue to die out. Most of those that do receive recognition, however – whether through promotion by local governments for the purpose of **tourism**, designation as intangible cultural properties or publicity from the Japan Folk Crafts Museum, the official voice of the mingei movement – are certain to survive for the foreseeable future. Few if any, however, can qualify as true *mingei*, at least according to the strict definition of the term. In this sense, the *mingei* movement could be said to have been doomed from the beginning. For while it was born of, and continues to reflect, an attempt to find value and, one could argue, a sense of national identity in traditions, Japanese society continues to move ever farther away from its past, making it all the more difficult for such traditions to be maintained.

Further reading

Japan Folk Crafts Museum (ed.) (1991) *Mingei: Masterpieces of Japanese Folkcraft*, Tokyo: Kōdansha.

Moeran, B. (1997) *Folk Art Potters of Japan*, Honolulu: University of Hawaii Press.

Yanagi, S. (1972) *The Unknown Craftsman: A Japanese Insight into Beauty*, adapted by B. Leach, Tokyo: Kōdansha.

WILLIAM LEE

mini-komi

In Japan, a distinction is made between the mainstream communications media, or *masu-komi* (mass communication), characterised by high capital investment and high market penetration, and the more informal networks of communication between members of specialised political groups, known as *mini-komi* (mini-communication). *Mini-komi* were originally handwritten and roneoed newsletters, but may now be produced with professional graphics, typefaces and layout, thanks to the ready availability of cheap personal computers, desktop publishing facilities and high-quality photocopiers. The Internet has also transformed the channels of political communication, both within Japan and in the networks of non-governmental organisations (NGOs) in the Asian region.

VERA MACKIE

miniaturisation

While Japan has produced one of the world's most famous giants in the form of the monster Godzilla, this country has also gained an extraordinary reputation for miniaturisation – the process of scaling down standard-size models without reducing functionality. This is most evident in the electronics industry – domestic white goods in particular – and personal communications technology (e.g. mobile phones).

An obvious factor has been space. Although television advertising focuses on 'full size' or 'American models', the majority of Japan's domestic white-good sales are models only marketed in Asia. Production of full-size models is focused on exports to countries like Australia, Canada and the USA, where domestic space and market taste reflect a preference for bigness over compactness. The notion of miniaturisation in fact only applies if the standard is accepted as the US/full size. A full sized cooker with four hotplates and oven remains a rarity in Japanese homes where most household food preparation is still limited to a two- or three-burner benchtop cooker. An array of mini-convection ovens, toaster ovens, rice cookers and compact microwaves are stacked in highly innovative space-saving layouts of shelving and draws. Streamlined washer-dryer combinations stow away in a narrow corner cupboard or under a bench. An average family can stack its top-end DVD, CD, tape and video cassette and HDTV, AM/FM receiver and satellite connection into a wall unit the size of the average US family television screen. The compactness of mobile phones, palm computers and organisers makes the models available in most of Europe and the USA look clumsy and gargantuan by comparison. Miniaturisation and compactness have ceased to be merely functional and are now a well-defined consumer aesthetic of everyday life and a potential source of market edge for designers and manufacturers.

SANDRA BUCKLEY

Ministry of Education

The Ministry of Education, Science, and Culture, commonly shortened to Ministry of Education, or **Monbusho Kouta**, sets minimum standards for curricula, examinations, the number and qualifications of teachers, the size of buildings and grounds. It also approves guidelines for textbooks, provides financial assistance to the prefectures and municipalities, and authorises and supervises the establishment of colleges and universities. Japan has a three-tiered structure for governing and administering education with national, prefectural and municipal components, all under the general supervision of national authority, the Ministry of Education. The Minister of Education is appointed by the Prime Minister. The normal term for an Education Minister is about two years as cabinet positions are frequently rotated under Japan's parliamentary system. The Ministry of Education is involved with the Cabinet and the Diet (the national legislature) in developing the budget and drafting legislation for education in Japan. Monbusho draws on the advice and recommendations of standing advisory councils composed of specialists outside the Ministry. The Central Council for Education is the most powerful of the groups and is concerned with fundamental policy issues. In addition to its education responsibilities, Monbusho is responsible for administering government services for science and culture, including national museums, art galleries and some national research institutes. Each of the forty-seven prefectures has a five-member board of education whose responsibilities include appointing the prefectural superintendent of education and the daily operations of public schools within that prefecture. The prefectural governor is responsible for the administration of post-secondary institutions and private schools.

The Course of Study in Japan, which is decided by the Ministry of Education, is the basic guiding principle for all educational curricula. While the Course of Study does not specify how teachers are to teach, the curriculum content and the sequence of instruction is set for each subject and grade level at the national level. Teachers are encouraged to come up with strategies that will enhance student understanding of the material. Textbooks are written and published by commercial publishers, although the content is based closely upon Monbusho guidelines (see **textbook controversies**). Schools select from an approved list. These books are then purchased by the government and given to children in both public and private schools free of charge. The books, which tend to be concise and lightweight, become the personal property of the students. Students are expected to clear their desks every afternoon and take their books home with them for study.

JUNE A. GORDON

Ministry of Finance

The Ministry of Finance (Ōkurashō, or MOF) is the government agency responsible for financial matters, including budgeting, stocks and bonds, regulation of the banking system and international monetary affairs. The Ministry was founded in 1869. In the post-war period, the MOF, together with the **Ministry of International Trade and Industry**, played a significant role in Japan's economic success, and it has usually been considered the most powerful and prestigious agency in the Japanese government. Its power stems largely from its control over the budget since other ministries and agencies must come to it for funds. Accordingly, the Budget Bureau has the highest status within the Ministry. The Ministry's Tax Bureau is responsible for tax policy, revenue forecasting and supervision of tax administration. The Financial Bureau is in charge of foreign exchange and Japan's balance of payments. The Banking Bureau and the Securities Bureau oversee banking and services business, respectively. Other bureaux deal with customs and tariffs, local government finance and so on. As in all Japanese ministries, MOF officials rely heavily on administrative guidance to implement their policies. Over the last decade, however, the Ministry has lost many of its former powers. Financial scandals in the 1990s concerning payoffs involving ministry officials further weakened the Ministry's standing.

DAVID EDGINGTON

Ministry of Foreign Affairs

The Ministry of Foreign Affairs (MOFA, or Gaimushō) was established in 1869 by the Meiji government (1868–1912) to develop formal relations with Western countries after more than two centuries of national seclusion. The influence wielded by the ministry has varied considerably. In its early years, it stood at the summit of the bureaucratic hierarchy, reflecting in part the prominence accorded foreign relations by a nation newly opened to the outside world. Only the Foreign Ministry had the linguistic expertise and administrative resources to gather intelligence on foreign countries, analyse overseas legal and political systems, and negotiate military, political and trade treaties. It has remained at the heart of Japan's international relations even as other government departments and agencies have developed comparable levels of overseas expertise and specialisation.

During the late Meiji Period, however, the ministry's monopoly on foreign-policy decisions was challenged by the Japanese military, especially following the Sino-Japanese War of 1894–5, and the Russo-Japanese War of 1904–5, and finally the First World War. By the time of the Manchurian Incident of 1931, the military had clearly usurped much of the ministry's control over foreign-policy decision making. In 1933, a committee, comprising the prime minister and ministers of foreign affairs, finance, the army and the navy, was formed to co-ordinate foreign policy. After the outbreak of war with the USA in 1941, a military-dominated wartime council further eroded the ministry's diplomatic functions. However, with the abolition of the military in the post-war period, the ministry

regained most of its former powers. Japanese foreign relations and economic issues are closely related; consequently, MOFA works closely with the Ministry of International Trade and Industry (MITI) to co-ordinate trade policy and address 'trade friction', for example with the USA. MOFA also co-operates with the Ministry of Finance over issues such as foreign aid, international finance and tariffs, and with the Ministry of Agriculture, Forestries and Fisheries regarding agricultural imports from overseas, and fishing rights.

The Ministry comprises ten bureaux, two departments, the Minister's Secretariat and over 4,600 employees. The Foreign Policy Bureau addresses planning of basic and middle- or long-term foreign policy and the co-ordination of policies formulated by other bureaux, placing special emphasis on national security, arms control and disarmament, non-proliferation, nuclear energy, science co-operation and other scientific affairs. The Multilateral Co-operation Department addresses Japan's co-operation with the United Nations, human rights issues, refugee-related matters and global issues such as the environment, population issues and narcotics, The Asian Affairs Bureau is responsible for policies concerning Asian countries, including the protection of Japanese nationals and their property in these countries, intelligence over Korea, Taiwan, Sakhalin, China and South-East Asia. Other regional affairs bureaux include North America, the Middle East, Africa, Latin America and the Caribbean, Europe and Oceania. The Economic Affairs Bureau takes charge of the protection and promotion of Japan's interests relating to treaties of commerce and navigation. The Economic Co-operation Bureau works on Overseas Development Assistance, the Japan International Co-operation Agency (JICA, an overseas technical-aid agency) and overseas investment issues. The Treaties Bureau takes charge of the conclusion of treaties and other international agreements, matters of international law and legal matters concerning foreign relations. Finally, the Intelligence and Analysis Bureau conducts general analyses of the international situation and collects necessary information.

DAVID EDGINGTON

Ministry of International Trade and Industry

The Ministry of International Trade and Industry (MITI, or Tsūshō Sangyō – Tsūshanshō for short) was established in 1949, from a reorganisation of the former Ministry of Commerce and Industry and the Board of Trade. MITI played a central role in the development of Japan's post-war industrialisation and expansion. From its beginning it regarded the promotion of exports as a primary objective; however, industrial expansion, the rationalisation of enterprises and technological improvement were also considered to be prerequisites for trade expansion.

Until the 1960s, MITI adopted restrictive import barriers through high tariffs in order to protect infant industries such as computers and electronics. It also restricted direct investment in Japan from overseas until the early 1980s. At the same time, through various industrial policies, it targeted growth industries (initially coal, electric power, steel and shipbuilding, but later consumer and industrial electronics and high-tech industries) that would enjoy growth in world markets. With power to license industries, allocate foreign exchange and approve loans and investments for large companies through the Japan Development Bank, MITI exercised a strategic influence. It also had many indirect and close ties to both big business and Japan's elite political circles. MITI's informal 'administrative guidance' of Japanese companies adjusted marketing strategies, and guided business investments. It also operated the effective Japan External Trade Organisation, which promoted Japanese trade around the world. This close relationship between government and business gave rise to the term 'Japan Incorporated' during the economic growth period of the 1960s.

Since the late 1970s, the success of Japanese exports has led to persistent trade surpluses with major trading partners, such as the USA and the countries of Western Europe. Mounting 'trade friction' and foreign pressure to reduce the surpluses led MITI to promote foreign imports. In the 1990s, it started to emphasise the quality of life and consumers' interests, in contrast with the past one-sided emphasis on producers' interests.

The growing liberalisation of the Japanese economy and internationalisation of Japanese corporations led to a decline in MITI's influence over the economy and companies.

MITI activities today continue to cover a wide range of industrial fields, including the development of basic industries (steel, new chemical materials, bio-industries), machinery and information industries (electronic equipment, robots, industrial machinery, automobiles, aircraft, information processing, etc.) and consumer goods industries (textiles, ceramics, household goods, housing materials and service industries). In addition, affairs related to foreign trade and investment, advanced technologies, environmental protection and industrial location, energy and patents are also among MITI responsibilities.

In policy making, MITI has had to address how Japan's industrial might can locate itself within a global economy. It participates in a wide range of international fora, including bilateral and multilateral economic negotiations, and international organisations. In the 1990s, MITI has also had to meet the challenge of Japan's struggling economy. This has included the need to create new industries to respond to the 'hollowing out' of domestic industry that has stemmed from the movement of many manufacturing operations overseas. MITI continues to promote technological developments, entrepreneurship and economic structural reform.

DAVID EDGINGTON

Ministry of Post and Telecommunications

This Ministry of Post and Telecommunications (MPT) has control of Japan's postal system and through the national network of post offices it also operates Japan's postal savings system, life insurance sales and pension programmes. All are extremely lucrative businesses. The postal savings system has been both praised and criticised for promoting high levels of domestic household savings, which in turn have been seen to limit consumer spending, compared to the USA where saving levels are lower. Through its regulatory powers the MPT also has significant indirect control over radio and television broadcasters, and Japan's major telcos, Nippon Telegraph and Telephone (NTT) and International Telegraph and Telephone (KDD – Kokusai denshin denwa).

There has been some concern expressed over the Ministry's close relationship with major domestic broadcasters, especially NHK and its telcos, and the impact of this on open-market competition for foreign companies. The Ministry is also widely considered to be conservative and cautious in its policy development and awarding of licences for new technologies. This has been seen as a factor in such areas as Japan's slow move to Internet communications, the final failure of Japan's early HDTV strategy and its slow shift from analogue to digital communications and broadcasting. In the initial post-war period, the Occupation established the Radio Wave Management Commission to control the Japanese broadcast systems according to the US model, and assigned it similar powers to the Federal Communications Commision (FCC). However, in 1952, the Japanese government located all broadcast-related policy and regulation under the jurisdiction of the MPT. The Japanese MPT opted to replace competitive selection with a 'collaborative' approach in which the MPT mediates alliances between potential competitors rather than selecting one. This has functioned to both restrict foreign-market participation and to favour existing players in the media marketplace over newcomers. It is this alliance-based model that is seen to have restricted open-market competition across broadcast and communications industries and to have created virtual monopolies.

The 1990s have seen significant change, however, as satellite television has found the media giants Murdoch and Turner edging into Japanese broadcast space. The telco explosion of mobile technologies has also led to a rapid proliferation of new services from increasingly global alliances. Even the traditionally stable area of postal services has been shaken up with the successful arrival of Fed Ex and UPS, and variations on Mailbox services across the country. In an attempt to define a new role for itself, the post offices have recently been approved as outlets for foreign-cash and credit card ATM services in a radical expansion of foreign banking beyond the brick and mortar of the major banking institutions. The MPT does seem to be showing signs that it has recognised the need to reinvent itself to keep pace with the rapid transformation of the communications space it is meant to both monitor and develop.

Further reading

Cooper-Chen, A. (1997) *Mass Communication in Japan*, Ames: Iowa State University Press.

SANDRA BUCKLEY

Minobe administration

Minobe Ryōkichi (1904–84) served as the governor of Tokyo Prefecture from 1967 to 1979. Because of his family background (son of a liberal pre-war constitutional scholar, Minobe Tatsukichi), his policies and the centrality of Tokyo, Minobe was the best known of the many progressive governors and mayors of major urban areas. By the early 1970s, these included Kyōto (governed by Ninagawa Torazō from 1950 to 1978), Ōsaka, Kobe, Yokohama, Kita Kyūshū, Kanagawa and Saitama. Most of these governors and mayors, including Minobe, were officially unaffiliated but backed by a coalition of leftist parties, citizens' groups and small-business leaders. These local successes for the left in the midst of thirty-eight years (1955–93) of unbroken control of the national government by the conservative **Liberal Democratic Party** (LDP) were the result of scandals, pollution, dissatisfaction with the LDP and the rise of citizen politics, as well as the general tendency for voting patterns to be more progressive in larger, more urban districts.

Minobe, an economics professor, ran on the slogan 'blue skies over Tokyo'. Though one of his first pronouncements was a call for a ceasefire in Vietnam, he was best known for increasing citizen input into decision making, and for his pollution and welfare policies. Under Minobe, the Tokyo Metropolitan Government established a Citizens' Office to handle suggestions and complaints, and to co-ordinate relations with citizens' groups. Tokyo also began the burning of sludge from primary sewage treatment before dumping it in the sea, though residents of areas where it was dumped, and activists in the Bureau of Waterworks, continued to press for better treatment of waste. Minobe declared a 'war on garbage', which included the promotion of recycling as well as the construction of incinerators to reduce the huge volume of garbage used as landfill in Tokyo Bay. In this 'garbage war', however, he was caught between citizens opposing incinerators in their neighborhoods and others hoping the incinerators would reduce the volume of garbage transported through or dumped in their areas.

In 1969, Tokyo Prefecture under Minobe began providing free medical care for citizens over seventy, as well as subsidies towards medical expenses for children. The former became national policy in 1973, exemplifying a trend in which many more liberal pollution and welfare policies were initiated at the local and prefectural levels before being made national policy by the LDP. Therefore, the replacement in the late 1970s of many progressive mayors and governors, including Minobe, with conservatives may mean not that the progressives had failed but that they had forced the conservatives to adopt their policies.

Further reading

Calder, K. (1988) *Crisis and Compensation: Public Policy and Political Stability in Japan, 1949–1986*, Princeton: Princeton University Press.

McKean. M. (1981) *Environmental Protest and Citizen Politics in Japan*, Berkeley: University of California Press.

Reed, S. (1986) 'The changing fortunes of Japan's progressive governors', *Asian Survey* 26(4): 452–65.

Steiner, K., Krauss, E. and Flanagan, S. (eds) (1980) *Political Opposition and Local Politics in Japan*, Princeton: Princeton University Press.

TIMOTHY S. GEORGE

minority representation in film

The situations of Japan's various minorities, including its *Burakumin* (outcaste) and Korean communities, seldom appeared in pre-war or wartime films, for reasons both commercial and political. In the post-war period, with the sudden shift to the glorification of democratic values, including the value of human equality, the barriers to films with minority characters began to crumble, if not totally disappear. Among the first was Abe Yutaka's 1948 *Hakai* (Broken Commandment), a film based on a Shimazaki Tōson novel of the same title that depicted *Burakumin* life in pre-war Japan. Other post-war films with *Burakumin* themes include the 1960 Kamei Fumio documentary *Ningen mina kyōdai* (Men Are All Brothers) and the Imai Tadashi two-part drama *Hashi no nai kawa* (River without a Bridge), with part one appearing in 1969 and part two in 1970. *Burakumin* activists protested the Imai films, claiming that they reinforced the prejudices which they ostensibly opposed. In 1992, the Buraku Liberation League sponsored the production of a remake of *Hashi no nai kawa* by Higashi Yoichi.

Honest cinematic depictions of Koreans were likewise rare in the pre-war and wartime years. Also, in the first post-war decade, the subject of Koreans in Japan was off-limits for Japanese filmmakers, who feared, with some justification, that the least appearance of prejudice would provoke a reaction from Japan's recently liberated Korean subjects. The first to break this taboo was Uchida Tomu with *Dotanba* (They are Buried Alive), a 1957 film that depicted Korean miners rescuing their Japanese comrades from a mining accident.

Other ground-breaking movies with Korean characters and themes were Imamura Shōhei's 1959 *Nianchan* (My Second Brother), the first film to make a Korean character its hero, Imai Tadashi's 1961 *Are ga minato no hi da* (Pan-Chopali) and Urayama Kirio's *Cupola no Aru Machi* (The Street of Cupolas). The post-war film-maker most actively critical of Japan's treatment of Koreans was Ōshima Nagisa, best known for such films as the 1967 *Nihon shunka-kō* (Treatise on the Japanese Bawdy Song), the 1968 *Koshikei* (Death by Hanging) and the 1983 *Senjō no Merry Christmas* (Merry Christmas Mr Lawrence).

During this same decade, Korean film-makers began using their Korean names and openly expressing their Korean identities. Among them were director Sai Yoichi, actor Cho Bang-Ho, director Kim Soo-Kil and cinematographer Kim Duk-Chul. In 1993, Sai swept Japanese film awards for *Tsuki wa dotchi ni deteiru* (All Under the Moon), a film about the romantic and professional adventures of a cynical Korean cabby, played by Kishitani Gorō.

In the 1980s, with the rise of Japan's bubble economy, Asian workers began flooding into Japan and, by the end of the decade, the representation of minorities in Japanese film began to expand accordingly. The first director to portray this new influx was Obayashi Nobuhiko in *Pekinteki suika* (Peking Watermelon), a 1989 film based on a true story about a Chiba vegetable seller's devotion to Chinese students living in a nearby dorm. The film was quickly followed by others of similar tendency, including Ōtomo Katsuhiro's 1991 *World Apartment Horror*, Tashiro Hirotaka's 1991 *Afureru atsui namida* (Swimming with Tears) and Yanagimachi Mitsuo's 1993 *Ai ni suite Tokyo* (About Love, Tokyo).

At the same time, minority voices from other segments of Japanese society began to be heard, including gays, Okinawans, AIDS victims and the disabled. Among the more notable were: Okinawan film-maker Takamine Go, whose 1989 *Untama Giru* was a magical realistic exploration of Okinawan myth and legend; gay director Nakajima Takehiro, whose 1992 *Okoge* helped launch a brief gay boom; and Tengan Daisuke, the director and scriptwriter son of Imamura Shōhei, whose 1993 *Muteki no handicap* (Invincible Handicapped) was an unsparing look at the world of disabled professional wrestlers.

In the middle of the decade, more commercial and established directors began to produce films on Asian-in-Japan themes, such as Koyama Seijirō with 1995 *Mitatabi no kaikyō* (Three Trips across the Strait), and Horikawa Hiromichi with *Asian Blue Ukishimamaru Sagon* (Asian Blue), both of which examined the plight of Koreans drafted into Japan's war effort.

In 1996, a young director named Iwai Shunji presented a new image of Asians in Japan in *Swallowtail Butterfly* (Swallowtail), a fantasy about a near-future Tokyo whose Asians will stop at nothing to make a yen, but none the less have more vitality than the grey Japanese masses around them. The film's box office success inspired Japanese film companies to make a spate of Asian-themed co-productions with Asian partners. Like *Swallowtail*, these films rejected both idealism and condescension. Instead, they tended to be packages of Japanese and Hong Kong talent, in which attitude and style counted for more than message. The most commercially successful was Lee Chi Ngai's 1998 *Fuyajō* (Sleepless Town), starring Kaneshiro Takeshi as a half-Japanese, half-Taiwanese hustler in Shinjuku's Kabukichō entertainment district. In the film, Kaneshiro's character becomes mixed up in a Chinese gang war, while pursuing a passionate affair with the former lover of a man he is trying to kill. Far from being a passive victim, Kaneshiro's hustler is a morally ambiguous character in an underground world where Japan serves as a mere backdrop. In this film and others like it, the Asian outsider is not only tolerated, but actively celebrated as a new type of hero in a society that no longer easily produces the native variety. In the space of five post-war decades, Asians and other minorities have gone from taboo to trendy in Japanese films.

Further reading

Sato Tadao (1994) *Nihon eiga shi*, Tokyo: Iwanami Shoten

Schilling, Mark (1999) *Contemporary Japanese Cinema*, New York: Weatherhill

MARK SCHILLING

minyō

In its narrow sense, *minyō* refers to the subdivision of folk song that is sung by adults. The term *minyō* was already in use in the Edo Period (1600–1868), but other terms such as *fuzokuga* were more widely used until it began to be used to translate the German term, *Volkslied*, and the English, folk song, in the mid-Meiji Period at the behest of Mori Ōgai and Ueda Bin. The vast majority of songs that continue to be sung seem to have had their origins after the medieval (*chūsei*) period. Popular songs that arose between the Bakumatsu and mid-Meiji Period became known throughout the entire country. From mid-Meiji, regional folk songs were introduced to the centre with increasing rapidity. In the process, they were refined and technically improved.

From the late Taishō through early Shōwa Periods, a New Folk Music Movement occurred. Many folk songs were written taking different areas of the country as their subject matter. With the rapid changes in society and lifestyle that followed the end of the Second World War, the frameworks that supported village structure began to crumble, and the situation of *minyō* also radically shifted. Songs related to democracy and work songs related to productive labour rapidly came on the scene. In recent years, each regional locale has formed a *minyō* preservation society. Semi-professional folk singers have emerged, as have singers who have become nationally famous on radio and television. *Minyō* began to lose the qualities that had characterised it up to this point, the form became rigid and formalised, and the mode of distribution moved to the mass media, becoming homogeneous and standardised. After the rapid economic growth period, the accelerated diversity of popular taste and values brought about by the mass media saw *enka* take over the position of an index for the revival of tradition, and this largely was in turn sustained by the dissemination of karaoke. Today, *minyo* has become a genre confined to an elderly mass audience.

Further reading

Kuma Tahei (1994) 'Minyō', in *Taishū bunka jiten*, Tokyo: Kobundo, p.777.

MARK ANDERSON

Mishima Yukio

b. 1925, Tokyo; d. 1970, Tokyo

Novelist

Mishima Yukio remains the Japanese writer with the greatest name recognition outside of Japan. This reputation is due as much to his extraordinary ability to invent himself as a media persona and latter-day samurai as to the interest of his literary output, which included everything from 'pure' literature, to potboilers to sophisticated critical writing.

With his first major novel *Confessions of a Mask* (1949), Mishima set out the themes that would pre-

occupy him for the rest of his life. The novel's first-person protagonist, who suffers from such a surfeit of self-consciousness that he claims to remember his own birth, is tortured by a painful awareness of the gulf that separates his inner self from his outer persona. 'What people regarded as a pose on my part,' he claims, 'was actually an expression of my need to assert my true nature, and…it was precisely what people regarded as my true self which was a masquerade' (p. 27). In typical adolescent fashion he imagines that he is alone in his affliction, and his loneliness is only exacerbated by the fact that he is attracted to other boys and feels compelled to pretend otherwise. Envious (and desirous) of the uncomplicated (heterosexual) desire of other boys, which he imagines 'arises from [their] being [themselves]', he describes his own desire as 'the fierce, impossible desire of not wanting to be myself' (p. 119). Thus blurring the lines between desire and identification, the 'I' of *Confessions of a Mask*, for all his alienation and loneliness, seems to have been able to speak for an entire generation disillusioned by the crisis of cultural and individual identity in the wake of Japan's defeat.

It is worth noting that outside of Japan Mishima is not only the best-known Japanese writer, but known best as a 'gay' novelist with a campy sensibility. In his own country, however, his sexuality is politely ignored under the shadow of his fascist leanings and he is reviled by feminists as a shameless misogynist. This discrepancy is partly to be explained by the particular trajectory of his career. The productive tension between surface and depth that made *Confessions* such a moving testament to the alienated nature of desire gradually gave way in Mishima's work to an unabashedly cynical commitment to surface performativity. Rather than self-conscious and self-hating homosexuals, more and more of his protagonists became grimly homosocial 'men of action'. In 1966, he offered unbidden his support and love to the emperor system by forming a private army of attractive young men in designer uniforms called the 'Shield Society'. It was in 1970, in the company of several of these young men, that Mishima disembowelled himself after having forced a group of unimpressed members of the Self-Defence Forces to listen to his plea that they return to their samurai values. How seriously we take Mishima's appeal to return to those values will determine whether his life and work will be remembered as the last exemplar of a romantic notion of Japaneseness, or a queer critique of modern identity itself.

Select bibliogaphy

Mishima Yukio (1959) *The Temple of the Golden Pavilion*, trans. Ivan Morris, New York: Knopf.
—— (1958) *Confessions of a Mask*, trans. Meredith Weatherby, New York: New Directions.
—— (1956) *Sound of the Waves*, trans. Meredith Weatherby, New York: Knopf.

Further reading

Nathan, John (1974) *Mishima: A Biography*, Boston: Little, Brown.

KEITH VINCENT

miso

Fermented soy bean paste is a Japanese dietary staple. It is most frequently consumed in the soup named *miso-shiru*, commonly consumed at breakfast or after a main course. In addition to soups, *miso* is also used in a wide number of dishes including sauces and broths, as baste in grilled foods and it is often added to pickling pots.

The two main types of *miso* paste are white (light), which is mixed with rice, and red (dark), which is mixed with barley. Quality of *miso* varies according to yeast base, texture and period of maturation. *Miso* can be set aside to season for just a few weeks or up to several years. There are many famous regional *miso* pastes available in speciality stores or bought home as **meibutsu** gifts from travel.

Miso has recently gained popularity outside Japan with a new generation of global chefs, always ready to experiment with the wide range of *miso* flavours, and also among the health conscious seeking alternative sources of protein. Despite being a major producer of soy beans and a supplier

to the Japanese market, the USA uses the bulk of its soy crops for export or domestic animal fodder.

SANDRA BUCKLEY

Misora Hibari
b. 1937, Yokohama; d. 1989

Singer, actress

Born Kato Aeki, Misora's recording career as a vocalist spanned forty years (1949–89). She is still best remembered for her childhood recordings, which brought hope and cheer to many struggling to rebuild out of the immediate post-war ruins. While her music was prominently featured in radio dramas and film soundtracks, she also acted and sang in a considerable number of films.

Misora made her recording debut in 1949 on Columbia Records with 'Kappa boogie-woogie'. Her next release, 'Kanashikii kuchibue', was featured on a radio drama and became a national hit. Her third single, 'Watashi wa machi no ko', from the film, *Tokyo Kid*, had similar success. Her status as a representative Japanese singer dates from this period. Hibari recorded over 1,401 songs and her career may be neatly divided between the 78 r.p.m. record era and the era of the $33\frac{1}{3}/45$ r.p.m. hi-fi record. Her best-selling song was 'Yawarakai', which reached 1,800,000 in sales. She had many hits and received the best song award from the record industry in 1960 and 1965.

Misora's younger brother, Kato Tetsuya, was prosecuted for gang-related activity in 1973. Misora was unceremoniously excluded from NHK's *Kohaku uta gassen* for the first time in eighteen years that same year, although typically NHK did not publicly acknowledge any connection between the two events. Misora bore a deep-seated grudge and refused to appear on NHK for years afterwards. Misora is generally regarded as the representative *enka* singer of her generation. Her vocal technique, however, owes at least as much to the US Broadway and jazz performance tradition as to any other. She rarely used her throat or vibrato in the standard *enka* manner. She was renowned for her remarkable ear, and, while she is said not to have understood a word of English, her recordings of US jazz tunes with English lyrics may still be the most natural and idiomatic English language recordings by an entertainer born and raised in Japan.

Significantly, published Japanese and English accounts of Misora's career have so far failed to mention that both she and her family were Korean-Japanese holding Korean passports (see **Koreans in Japan**). It is deeply ironic that the most representative vocalist of the 'most Japanese' musical genre turns out to have been Korean-Japanese. In more recent years, a very high proportion of *enka* singers in Japan have been of avowedly Korean extraction. Along with the colonial Korean upbringing of an important *enka* songwriter, this situation suggests the importance of pursuing ties between the development of *enka* and the Japanese colonial occupation of Korea. From the 1960s, *enka* was largely positioned as a marker of family, melodrama and tradition in Japanese popular culture in opposition to folk, rock, soul and pop. Many Japanese hold on to fond memories of the lasting image of the later Misora with her Las Vegas-style costumes and feathers. Her music and personal struggles, however, record traces of a much more complex post-war Japanese social history. Misora Hibari died of pneumonia, 24 June 1989.

MARK ANDERSON

Miyake Issei

b. 1938, Hiroba

Fashion designer

Miyake Issei (or Issey Miyake) is perhaps the most immediately recognisable and internationally known of Japan's fashion designers. He went to France after graduating from Tama Fine Arts University. In Paris, when he was training at the *haute couture* fashion house of Givenchy, he encountered the events of May 1968, and this was to have a great influence upon his design concepts. From France he went to New York and then, in 1970, upon returning to Japan, he established his company Miyake Designs. He released collections in New York in 1971 and then in Paris in 1973. In 1977, Miyake designed a line inspired by a return

to the origins of Japanese clothing, in particular the **kimono**. This play on traditional design remains a feature of much of his contemporary work with additional recent influences from ethnic styles and colours. In the late 1990s, Miyake Issei's new designs began to experiment with bolder colours in a break with the sombre tones he has become known for.

His notion of 'One Cloth' designs marked a significant new design concept both from a stylistic perspective and as a production technique. In 1992, he launched another striking innovation with his 'Pleats Please' series. His original shapes were created with careful attention to the relation between form and body, and form and material. He developed a new pleating technique in which the pleats were created after the garment was already cut and sewn. This was the exact opposite of the way that it was normally done. Tightly pleated textiles have become a virtual trademark of Miyake Issei style, with many cheaper imitations also now on the market. To this day, the appeal of his designs surpasses national borders. He has collaborated with artists and film-makers in projects around the world and has become one of the best-known Japanese designers. His contribution to fashion has been acknowledged with a number of important awards both internationally and in Japan.

AKIKO FUKAI

Miyako Harumi

b. 1948, Kyōto

Singer

Born Kitamura Harumi, she made her recording debut in 1964 with 'Komaru kotoyo' (You Upset Me). This song did not fare well, but in the same year her song 'Anko tsubaki wa koi no hana' (The Anko Camellia is the Flower of Love) won the New Artist Award from the Japanese recording industry.

With her distinctive, moaning style of singing, 'Namida no renraku fune' (The Ferryboat of Tears), 'Bakattcho debune' (Idiot! Outgoing Ship) and 'Suki ni natta hito' (The Person I Came to Love) also became hits. She emerged as an unavoidable presence among female *enka* singers. Her 1976 hit 'Kita no shuku kara' (From a Northern Waystation) was somewhat of a departure for her and yet it won both record of the year and the Japanese popular-music award. In 1984, she retired from the popular music world with the release of the song 'Futsū no obasan ni naritai' (I Want to Become an Everyday Woman). She has subsequently done some work as a music producer and has also worked as a news commentator. She gave a special performance on the first part of NHK's music programme *Kohaku uta gassen* in 1989, then finally made a comeback as a singer in 1990.

Select bibliography

Ishikawa Koichi (1994) 'Miyako Harumi', in *Taishū bunka jiten*, Tokyo: Kobundo, pp. 769–70.

MARK ANDERSON

Miyamoto Yuriko

b. 1899, Tokyo; d. 1951

Writer

Miyamoto Yuriko is remembered as one of only a small number of Japanese writers who consistently stood by a radical socialist politics throughout her career, despite periods of imprisonment and torture, and ongoing harassment and surveillance. She began writing early and published her first novel at age seventeen in the literary journal *Chūō kōron*, *Mazushiki hitobito no mure* (1916). Her second husband, Miyamoto Kenji, published a biography to accompany the release of her complete works in 1951, after her death. He went to great lengths to emphasise that her writings should not be categorised as 'women's writing' (*joryū bungaku*) because this would not reflect the far wider significance of her work. While his opinion may represent a biaised view of *joryū bungaku*, he is not alone in his opinion that Miyamoto was one of the great writers of the trans-war generation.

Miyamoto traveled often to the rural community of her grandfather's birthplace as a young girl, and there she developed a strong commitment to a politics of the oppressed classes through her exposure to the poverty of the rural areas of Japan. She travelled to the USA to study at Columbia University in her twenties, where she met and married her first husband. He too was Japanese but the marriage was a failure from early on and they divorced after only five years. Miyamoto's relationship with Yuasa Yoshiko, a female scholar of Russian literature was both romantic and professional, and they lived together for seven years after her divorce. During this period, Miyamoto completed her semi-autobiographical account of a failed marriage, *Nobuko* (1925). In this work, she analyses the institute of marriage and its limiting effect on women's creativity and life choices. She traveled to Russia with Yuasa in 1927 and chose to remain there for three years. On her return to Japan in 1930 she joined the Communist Party and became a key figure in the All-Japan Proletarian Writers' Association. It was in the early 1930s that she met Miyamoto Kenji, a left-wing literary critic and key figure in the Communist Party. In 1932, she ended her relationship with Yuasa to marry him. Only months later he was arrested for his communist activities and soon after that she was also taken into custody. They spent the war years apart with Miyamoto in and out of prison, while her husband was jailed in Hokkaidō from 1933 to 1945. Unlike so many other writers and intellectuals, she never abandoned her political convictions in the face of Japanese fascism. Her writing through the war years continued to deal with issues of poverty, the status of impoverished women, imprisonment and police brutality. Little of her work got past the wartime censors. In the post-war years before her death in 1951, she wrote prolifically and with the same political intensity and conviction to leftist politics. She rejoined the Communist Party, founded the Women's Democratic Club and edited the publication *Working Women*. Her most well-known fiction remains the trilogy that begins with *Nobuko*, continues with *Futatsu no niwa* (The Two Gardens, 1947), relating her years with Yuasa, and ends with the story of the Russian years in *Dōhyō* (Signpost, 1950). *Fūchisō* (Weathervane, 1946) is an astoundingly powerful and beautiful tale of the reconstruction of post-war life in Japan, the rebirth of the possibility of a radical politics and the reunion of a couple separated by imprisonment over the war years.

This, like all of her works, was criticised by some as 'too difficult' for a woman's text. Her writing, like her life, refused to settle into stereotypes of womanly behaviour. Her years with Miyamoto Kenji are explored in detail in their published letters, *Jūninen no tegami* (Twelve Years of Letters,1952). That her work is still not widely available in English reflects the double bind of gender and politics. There continues to be a tendency for the literary-left tradition to be disregarded and women writers remain seriously under-represented in English translation.

See also: Marxism; women's literature

Select bibliography

Miyamoto Yuriko (1991) 'The family of Koiwai', trans. Mizuta Lippit, *Japanese Women Writers*, New York: M.E. Sharpe.

SANDRA BUCKLEY

Mizoguchi Kenji

b. 1898, Tokyo; d. 1956

Film director

A prolific film-maker, Mizoguchi was famous for his Social Realist, sympathetic portrayals of suffering women, often geishas and prostitutes, and as a formalist master of *mise-en-scène*. Born into a poor family that kept getting poorer, his sister Suzu was given up for adoption, and later sold into prostitution as a geisha. Although a wealthy client eventually married her (and in fact she ended up supporting her biological family), these events apparently inspired Mizoguchi's obsessive filmic representations of women in similar miserable circumstances. Before becoming a film-maker, Mizoguchi studied painting and literature, and his films often adapted Japanese classics. Making his directorial debut in 1923, early in Japan's film history, with *Ai ni yomigaeru hi* (The Resurrection of Love), a film held to have shockingly realistic depictions of poverty and deeply critical of class inequities, Mizoguchi went on to make over eighty films. He was most celebrated for the films he directed in the 1950s, such as his *Saikaku ichidai onna*

(Life of Oharu) – the story of a high-class courtesan's descent in status to the equivalent of a street walker – which won him the International Director's Prize at the 1952 Venice Film Festival. The French New Wave critics and film-makers in particular, including Jean-Luc Godard, revered Mizoguchi. There are no existing prints or negatives of the vast majority of Mizoguchi's films from the 1920s into the 1930s. In the surviving 1936 *Gion no shimai* (Sisters of the Gion), the story of two impoverished geisha, the young, manipulative Omocha (literally: Toy) who embodies modern values, and the self-sacrificing, old-fashioned Umekichi, there are already many thematic and formal signatures of Mizoguchi-as-*auteur*. Like in *Life of Oharu*, and the 1955 *Yokihi* (The Princess Yang Kwei-Fei), the geisha of *Gion no shimai* are in worse straits at the conclusion than in the beginning. That is, although Mizoguchi's films are overtly sympathetic to women, they frequently trace, in curiously loving detail, the downward spiral of women from bad to tragic circumstances.

Mizoguchi's formal signatures include: extraordinary mastery of depth-of-field sometimes emphasised by low-key lighting; predominance of long shots; long takes (parsimonious editing); a fluid, gracefully moving camera; frequent decentring or blocking of actors and actors gazes from spectatorial view; a frequent absence of overt dominants; reticent use of reverse field; slightly high camera angle; innovative time transition devices and avoidance of opticals. In his *Mizoguchi and the Evolution of Film Language*, David Bordwell used an analysis of Mizoguchi's *mise-en-scène* to counter André Bazin's Hegelian theory of the historical development of film.

See also: women in film

Further reading

Bock, A. (1978) *Japanese Film Directors*, Tokyo: Kōdansha International.

Bordwell, D. (1983) 'Mizoguchi and the evolution of film language', in S. Heath and P. Mellencamp (eds) *Cinema and Language*, Frederick, MD: University Publications of America.

McDonald, K.I. (1983) *Cinema East: A Critical Study*

of *Major Japanese Films*, London and Toronto: Associated University Presses.

NINA CORNYETZ

mizuko jizō

Mizuko jizō is the name given to small statues of the Bodhisattva Jizo that are purchased as part of the practice of *mizuko kuyō* – the memorialising of a foetus. Jizo is the protector of children in the other world. The rituals observed by many women after an abortion are not traditional practice but date instead from the 1970s, when Japan saw the rapid popularisation of the notion that women who undertook an abortion were at risk of attack from an avenging or angry foetus spirit.

Historically, there has not been a strong stigma attached to abortion, even after its criminalisation in the Meiji Period. Despite Buddhist prohibitions, attitudes have historically remained largely pragmatic. In post-war Japan, the abortion rate in relation to live births has been estimated to be as high as 60 per cent. The post-war legalisation of abortion in cases of economic hardship has not changed the fact that many doctors still do not officially document the procedure for fear of prosecution. The 1970s saw a boom in spiritualists, diviners and fortune telling, with a related explosion in a fear of spirits and a belief in possessions and spirit attacks. The 1970s also saw a widespread anti-abortion campaign by the influential new religion Seichō no Ie (House of Growth). The media, in particular talk radio and tabloid press, quickly latched onto the possibilities of sensationalising the idea of the vengeful foetus. The Seichō no Ie campaign shared much in common with the rhetoric of the Moral Majority in the USA and there was an extensive exchange of propaganda between the two movements. In the meanwhile, spiritualists capitalised on the potential income to be made from offering memorialising services to placate these angry foetus spirits and some Buddhist temples, recognising the same opportunity, began offering *mizuko kuyō* services. Special areas were created in temple compounds for the display of *mizuko jizō*, where a woman could continue to come and make offerings and prayers.

Many women acting on their fear or distress sought a one-time solution that could free them from a lifetime of risk and offertory obligations. Spiritualists and Buddhist priests were quick to oblige for the right fee. The purchase, naming and memorialising of a *mizuko jizō* statue became a widely practised element of these rituals. The practice continues to be widespread but is no longer the focus of the same level of media attention.

Further reading

Hardacre, Helen (1997) *Marketing the Menacing Foetus in Japan*, Berkeley: University of California Press.
LaFleur, William (1992) *Liquid Life: Abortion and Buddhism in Japan*, Princeton: Princeton University Press.

SANDRA BUCKLEY

mizushōbai

While 'water trade' is the literal translation of *mizushōbai*, in Japanese the term has none of the romantic connotations often attached to the English when it appears in popular fiction or the media. The term describes the entire space of relations and work of the sex and entertainment industry. The Japanese term refers to any trade where drinks are served, and in this way is not unlike the English description of a favourite bar or pub as a 'watering hole'. The world of *mizushōbai* is populated by the women sex workers, hostesses, waitresses, prostitutes, masseuses and the men who are their clients, as well as their bosses and the *yakuza*, who have a central role in the management, financing and internal policing of the sometimes violent culture of this major sector of Japan's shadow economy.

See also: alcoholism; *nopan kissa*; peep shows; pink salons; pornography; sex tourism; soapland; striptease; *yobai*

Further reading

Allison, Anne (1994) *Nightwork: Sexuality, Pleasure and Corporate Masculinity in a Tokyo Hostess Club*, Chicago: University of Chicago Press.

Buckley, Sandra (1996) 'Contagion', in *Anywise*, New York: Anyone Corporation.

SANDRA BUCKLEY

mobile telephones

Mobile telephones are not just a technological change in Japan but a major cultural influence. In 2000, there were 10 million e-mail-ready mobiles in operation in Japan, and mobile service subscriptions outnumbered landline subscriptions for the first time (56.7 versus 55.6 million). With the explosion of cellular phone e-mail transmission, Japan is set to move from one of the slowest countries to take up Internet communications to the top rank for Internet usage. The slow take-up of Internet was a reflection of several factors, including low household usage of computers, largely considered a result of limited and multi-functional domestic spaces (e.g. a dining area becomes a television area before becoming a sleeping space). The Ministry of Post and Tele-communications (MPT) was also sceptical about the Internet and slow to approve licenses, and **Nippon Telegraphic and Telephone Corporation** (NTT) was notoriously expensive and slow in responding to requests for new lines, as well as being faced with limited growth capacity.

Internet communications, like computer usage, were focused on larger corporations until the late 1990s when the MPT approved the linking of Internet services to cellular platforms. This shift in access has seen a dramatic 'democratisation' of Internet access and a matching transformation of user profile. The corporate male white-collar worker is fast being overtaken by the urban female teenage and young adult markets. Tokyo streets, subways and cafés are now the site of mail chat as people scramble to read and type messages while negotiating their way through crowded streets and trains. The fifteen-key touchpad and miniaturisation of phones have led to new levels of innovation in abbreviation to facilitate quick and easy messaging. An example would be the popular online abbreviation for the new-year greeting from '*akemashite omedetō gozaimasu*' into '*ake ome*'. The market leader in mobile telephones, NTT's

DoCoMo, has added over 200 picto-symbols to its messaging to further enhance speed on the new 'i-mode' smart-phone models. A phone symbol plus *kure* (a short and fairly curt form of *kudasai* – please) is used to abbreviate 'phone me'. Interestingly, and much to the concern of some language specialists, these symbols are being used instead of characters (**kanji**). Abbreviated syntax and symbols are also beginning to find their way into speech or handwriting. Some women are now using in daily speech, among friends, the same informal and masculine forms now utilised in e-mail-speak, which were previously not accessible to them. Many e-mail users now touch type, allowing them to continue a conversation or other activity while returning e-mail messages.

The boom in mobiles is also itself reversely linked to e-mail access. Many Japanese were deterred from mobile phone use due to issues of privacy when speaking in public and also out of politeness to others. E-mail messaging allows fast, mobile text-based communication without these complications. E-mail messaging time is cheaper than phone calls, both due to lower rates and a tendency for shorter communications. Many young people now carry two phones – one for personal and one for work-related calls. An entire industry has grown up around accessorising mobile phones. As they become smaller, they also become increasingly integrated into fashion for both men and women. In addition to the constant stream of new shapes, sizes and colours of phones on the market, there is an ongoing proliferation of decorative attachments. Clothing and leather-good brand names compete to design the most innovative techniques for combining fashion and wearable mobile technology. Other innovations include vending machines that offer a ¥200 service in alternative phone ringing tunes. One such service, Capcom, offers some 20,000 song options and is compatible with the three major selling brands of mobiles. DoCoMo has also developed and launched a new range of miniaturised folding keyboards as extensions to mobile phones. They collapse into the size of a make-up compact for easy storage in handbag or briefcase, and allow more convenient messaging and broader Internet access.

Both NTT and its major competitor **Kokusai Denshin Denwa** (KDD) are set to ride the current wave of cellular platform LCD digital communications into positions of global leadership. What was perceived as a 'PC lag' in Japan has ironically proven the impetus for Japanese innovation in third generation (3-G) technologies. Given the limited hours Japanese spend at home in this commuter-oriented society and the intense mobility and speed of Japan's urban culture, the cell phone is likely to remain the dominant platform for communications for the foreseeable future and 3-G technologies will see the rest of the world moving increasingly in this same direction. The cultural significance of this phenomenon is expected to be extensive and the first signs of this impact are already generating some legislative response from government, with attempts to limit usage in public spaces such as trains and a call for a ban on hand-held cell phone use while driving. The cell phone has already captured the imagination of film and television script writers, with the world of e-space and cell phones sparking many storylines around the new ethical dilemmas and social tensions of the changing dynamics of inter-personal communications and relationships promoted by mobile technologies.

SANDRA BUCKLEY

mochi

This glutinous **rice** cake is usually mass-produced but *mochi* making still plays an important role in winter **festivals** and **New Year** ceremonies. When prepared traditionally, hot steamed rice is beaten in a large wooden mortar until it forms a thick, sticky paste that is rounded into individual *mochi*. Mochi can be served grilled or added to winter broths and the popular winter treat of sweetened red bean soup (*oshiruko*). The term *mochi* is also used for the soft, sticky rice cakes served with **tea**. These are stuffed with sweet pastes and often wrapped in aromatic leaves or decorated with frosted seasonal motifs.

SANDRA BUCKLEY

Monbusho Kouta

Monbusho kouta is the standard reference for children's songs in modern Japan. Until the late

Edo Period, as a feudal society there were songs that groups of children sang together at play. With the entrance into modernity, songs written by adults for children were born as one aspect of children's culture. Among these children's songs, those written in the Meiji era were known as *kouta*, and those from the mid-Taishō as *dōyō*. Those known as *kouta* were not written by popular poets or democratic activists; rather, they were written by the Education Ministry (Monbushō) as part of the practical bureaucratic management of state education policy. As the Education Ministry's director of music approval, Izawa Shuji mobilised instructors at the Tokyo Teachers' School, members of the Imperial Household's Gagaku Association and instructors of the Tokyo Music School to compose music and lyrics. Textbooks from 1881–4 and 1887 were filled with adaptations of Euro-American songs that had Japanese lyrics attached to them ('Chocho'/Butterfly, 'Hotaru no hikari'/Light of the Firefly). After the six-volume music textbook of 1911, which was composed in accordance with the new Monbushō textbook regulations of 1903, there was an increase in songs that had both music and lyrics written by Japanese composers ('Hato' (Pigeon), 'Momiji' (Maple), 'Kisha' (Train)). Several of these powerfully expressed the fundamental emotions of childhood. However, as the *Monbushō kouta* left out fa to shi in the musical scale they had a quiet and peaceful sound. After Taishō, the *dōyō*, which included the fa and shi steps of the scale in their melodies, were also admitted into the curriculum.

Further reading

Kami Shōichiro (1994) 'Monbushō kouta', in *Taishū bunka jiten*, Tokyo: Kobundo, p. 793.

MARK ANDERSON

monster films

The successful genre of monster films (*kaijū eiga*), initiated by Tōhō in 1954 with 'Gojira' (**Godzilla**), directed by Honda Ishirō, was then taken up by other companies including Daiei. The anger and destruction of the monsters are outstandingly spectacular thanks to a combination of the innovative use of basic special effects and attempts at scientific realism. Each generation of monster owes much to its predecessors. Not to be forgotten are Matango, Mothra, Radon and Biollante. After a period of decline at the end of the 1960s, monster films regained popularity in the 1970s, with both adult and youth audiences. In these more recent films, the monster is represented as either an external threat to, or as the protector of, Japanese identity.

See also: Godzilla

MARIA ROBERTA NOVIELLI

MONO-HA *see* installation art

Mori Shinichi

b. 1947, Yamagata

Singer

Mori Shinichi has been one of the more important *enka* singers since the mid-1960s and has proven his capacity to change with the times, carrying this genre of music with him through new stages of engagement with contemporary music trends. Born in Yamagata but raised in Kagoshima Prefecture, Mori made the first step towards his career when he won a musical competition on Fuji television and became an understudy of Charley Ishiguro. He made his recording debut in 1966 with the song 'Onna no tameiki' (A Woman's Sigh). Despite the fact that his uniquely husky voice became the object of satire and derision early on, his series of hit songs – 'Hana to chō' (The Flower and the Butterfly), 'Inochi karetemo' (Even if I Die), 'Toshiue no hito' (An Older Person), 'Minatomachi blues' (Harbourtown Blues) and 'Ofukurosan' (Mother) – quickly established the popularity of Mori's idiosyncratic style of *enka*. This was in part due to the success of a new strategy of using cable radio as the centerpiece of promotion for *enka*. In 1974, he won the Japan Record Award for the song 'Erimosaki' (co-written by Okamoto Osami (lyrics) and Yoshida Takuro (music)), which represented a cross-over between *enka* and the folk

and pop-rock of New Music. Today, Mori is recognised for having the vocal talent and flexibility to perform both older-style *enka* and New Music-inflected styles. In terms of his image, Mori stands as an undisputed and immensely popular icon of contemporary *enka*.

Further reading

Ishikawa Koichi (1994) 'Mori Shinichi', in *Taishū bunka jiten*, Tokyo: Kobundo, p. 791.

Koizumi Fumio (1984) *Kayōkyoku no kōzō*, Tokyo: Tōjusha.

Komota Nobuo, Shimada Yoshinobu, Yazawa Kan and Yokozawa Chiaki (1995) *Nihon ryūkokashi, shita*, Tokyo: Kaisha Shisōsha.

MARK ANDERSON

Morita Akio

b. 26 January 1921, Nagoya City;
d. 3 October 1999, Tokyo

Businessman

An engineer by training, Morita Akio is best known as an entrepreneur, businessman and the co-founder of Sony Corporation. Morita was the eldest son of a famous sake-brewing family in Nagoya. From a young age, he was groomed for, and expected to, assume leadership of the 300-year-old family business. After graduating from Ōsaka Imperial University with a degree in physics in 1944, however, he joined the Japanese Imperial Navy's Wartime Research Committee, advancing to the rank of lieutenant. It was as a naval officer that Morita met Ibuka Masaru with whom, in 1946, he co-founded Tokyo Tsūshin Kōgyō Kabushiki Kaisha (Tokyo Telecommunications Engineering Corporation), a small radio repair business, set up in the ruins of a bombed-out Tokyo department store. The company was renamed Sony in 1958, by combining the Latin root for sound, *sonus*, with the American slang, 'sonny-boy', symbolic of the company's youthful and innovative staff.

Known to be energetic, autocratic, impulsive and stubborn, Morita managed company finance and business strategy, turning Sony into an international household name. In 1950, he and Ibuka built Japan's first magnetic tape recorder from salvaged parts. Their first great international success was marketing the world's smallest transistor radio in 1955. Five years later, the pair marketed the world's first all-transistor television. In 1965, Sony and Morita marketed the first video-tape recorder for home use. Illustrative of Morita's style of management, he overrode company opposition and halted a new advertising campaign on a hunch, after deciding to rename what was to become his most famous product, the Walkman, in 1979.

Morita became president of Sony's US subsidiary in 1970. In the same year, Sony became the first Japanese company listed on the New York stock exchange. He became chairman of Sony in 1976, and remained in that position until 1994. The author of several books, including his autobiography *Made in Japan* (1986), Morita outraged US corporations and the US Congress for his scathing criticism of US corporate practice and culture in *The Japan that Can Say no* (1989), which he co-authored with Ishihara Shintaro.

Select bibliography

Morita Akio (1986) *Made In Japan: Akio Morita and Sony*, with Edwin M. Reingold and Mitsuko Shimomura, New York: Dutton.

Morita Akio and Ishihara Shintaro (1991) *The Japan that Can Say no: Why Japan Will Be the First Among Equals*, trans. Frank Baldwin, foreword by Ezra F. Vogel, New York: Simon & Schuster.

—— (1989) *No to ieru Nihon: shin nichi-bei kankei no kado*, Tokyo: Kobunsha.

Further reading

Nathan, John (1999) *Sony: The Private Life*, Boston: Houghton Mifflin.

DAVID G. WITTNER

motherhood

The concept of motherhood has been hotly debated in Japan since the earliest stage of modernisation in the Meiji Period. The figure of the mother has remained strongly implicated in the rhetoric of identity of the Japanese modern nation state. While pre-modern treatises on womanhood had not been uncommon, these were written for the elite and were less concerned with the role of mother than those of wife and daughter, or daughter-in-law. It was not at all uncommon for women of the aristocracy and samurai class to employ the services of wet nurses and for children to move between the households of relatives at the convenience of the parents. The notion of motherhood as the primary role of married women with children, and the isolation of child-rearing from other forms of labour was a product of a modernising Japan and its move towards more Anglo-European ideals of family. A notion of moral behaviour measured against a perception of Judeo-Christian standards drove a series of early Meiji reforms ranging from bans on mixed public bathing to a gradual institutionalisation of motherhood as the moral centre of the modern family – as distinct from the head of household, which was clearly designated as the role of the father. Here, Western ideals and Confucian principles blurred with real practice into a framework for a new patriarchal extended family. As the mechanisms of State Shintō and imperialism went into gear over the first three decades of the twentieth century, women, and motherhood in particular, became the focus of policy and government intervention.

The first of the so-called 'housewife debates' erupted in this era with leading female political and intellectual figures at odds over the right of women to work in the paid workforce and the impact of working mothers on the family. As the public debate continued, the government passed increasingly interventionist eugenic policies and motherhood protection measures (*bōsei hōgo*) as essential elements of its mobilisation of the society in the interest of the Emperor and nation. After the war, many of these laws were erased or modified under SCAP, but some others have remained the focus of feminist reform campaigns, most notably the abortion law and 'protective' elements of the employment laws that discriminated against women. Even after decades of women working in the fields and factories over the war years, the 'housewife debate' still resurfaced in the midst of the economic prosperity of the 1970s and 1980s.

Experts on both sides of the debate analysed women's active involvement in paid work during the period of economic recovery to assess the impact on the family.

Although the UN Decade of the Woman saw the Japanese government set in motion EEO legislation, the eventual passage of this 'toothless' policy in the mid-1990s has not resolved the tensions surrounding the status of motherhood versus the proliferation of other possibilities: working mother, childless couples, career woman, single mother, single father, etc. Over the 1990s, attention has also been drawn to the fate of absent fathers overworked and isolated from their families by the demands of the workplace. Death by overwork (**karōshi**) is now a recognised phenomenon. Some social commentators are asking if there is room for a renegotiation of the hard and fixed gender divide of paid work in the workforce and unpaid domestic work, which could allow both sexes greater flexibility and benefit the family as a whole. The debate continues in such diverse forums as popular television dramas, *manga* comics, abortion law reform campaigns, school curriculum development and media advertising. Should a woman's primary role be motherhood or does a woman have the right to pursue paid work? What is missing are the policies and infrastructure (day care, elderly care, equal pay and pensions, taxation credits etc.) to enable working mothers to freely pursue both or either choice with all the necessary support for themselves and their families.

See also: *bōsei hōgo*; Hiratsuka Raichō; *ryōsai kenbo*

Further reading

Buckley, Sandra (1993) 'Altered states: The body politics of being woman', in A. Gordon (ed.) *Postwar Japan as History*, Berkeley: University of California Press, pp. 347–72.

SANDRA BUCKLEY

Mothers' Convention

The first Mothers' Convention (Hahaoya Taikai), held in June 1955 in Tokyo, focused on opposition to nuclear war. This meeting was linked with the World Mothers' Convention meeting in Lausanne in July 1955. By 1960, the National Meeting of the Convention was backed up by regional meetings and study groups, and delegates were a combination of individuals and representatives from around sixty affiliated groups. As 1960 was the year of controversy over the renewal of the US–Japan Security Treaty, this was to prove the most politicised of the annual meetings, which have continued through the post-war period.

Further reading

Tanaka, S. (1988) 'Nihon ni okeru hahaoya undō no rekishi to yakuwari', in Sōgō Josei Shi Kenkyūkai (eds) (1988) *Nihon Josei Shi Ronshū 10: Josei to Undō*, Tokyo: Yoshikawa Kōbunkan, pp. 170–88.

VERA MACKIE

moxa

Moxa or *moxabustion* is a traditional medicinal practice used in conjunction with acupuncture and utilising the same points on the skin. The treatment involves burning a small cone or stick of crushed herbs selected for their healing powers in different combinations on, or over, the skin. Although the skin was traditionally allowed to blister, today heat is applied more sparingly and only sometimes leaves a redness or black mark. Each stick or cone burns for just a few minutes before it is removed. *Moxa* is often used for rapid relief of intense pain or discomfort, and is attributed with an anaesthetic effect. Although there is some evidence that the treatment stimulates the autonomic nervous system, both patients and doctors outside Japan have remained less willing to experiment with *moxa* than with other elements of traditional Asian medicine such as acupuncture.

See also: acupuncture; traditional medicine

SANDRA BUCKLEY

Mt. Fuji

Mt. Fuji – Fuji-san – at 3,776 m, 12,385 ft, is the highest mountain in Japan, on the border of Shizuoka and Yamanashi Prefectures, about 100 km south-west of **Tokyo**. Although it is an active volcano, it last erupted in 1707. Its almost perfect volcanic cone is perhaps the most beloved landscape icon in Japan, representing ideals of beauty, symmetry, majesty and sublimity. It has become symbolic of the nation itself. The use of the honorific 'san' is both a mark of respect and an anthropomorphisation that expresses the strong feelings that Japanese people have for Fuji-san, and the mythological relationship between the Japanese islands and people.

The popular anthem, 'Fuji ga yo', a Meiji-era romantic ballad, is sung on social occasions when the mood turns slightly maudlin, as well as by Japanese people all over the world when they are feeling homesick. Mt. Fuji is the single most oft-painted scene in the Japanese landscape, and was an especially popular backdrop for the pre-modern *ukiyoe*, woodblock prints of the Meiji Period, when it was most often depicted as a backdrop for scenes of the city of Tokyo.

While dense industrial development now crowds the base of Fuji-san, the mountain itself has by legislation remained undeveloped, and is a popular climb. Thousands ascend Fuji-san annually for recreation and religious pilgrimage. The mountain is considered sacred by Fujikō, a sect combining elements of **Buddhism** and **State Shintō**. A pilgrimage, *ohachi meguri*, consists of walking around the eight small peaks that surround the rim of the crater. The climb takes five hours from the fifth station, which can be reached by road. Today, climbers are more likely to sport sophisticated imported climbing gear than the traditional garb of pilgrims. Climbing season is July and August.

Fuji-mi, or Fuji view, is almost as important as physically climbing the mountain. *Fuji-mi* increases the status of places all around. Although the peak is often obscured by air pollution, thousands flock to the best viewing sites, especially when Fuji-san shows itself on a weekend, whether from the distance of the Tokyo Tower in **Roppongi**, or from selected viewing sites along its slopes and around the base. The experience of *Fuji-mi* is

enhanced when combined with *hana-mi*, cherry blossom viewing (see **cherry blossoms**), on its lower slopes in spring. Like cherry blossoms, Fuji-san has become a major consumer icon, the name of a bank, film and other products, and a strong evocation of tradition and beauty. It is a telling manifestation of the Japanese nation's reinvention of itself, and of the enduring and harmonious bond between people and nature.

AUDREY KOBAYASHI

multifunctional polis

In 1987, the Japanese government proposed the development of a so-called multifunctional polis (MFP) in Australia: high-tech research and a development project based around a sustainable-environment community. The next year, a feasibility study was commenced and by 1990 there were strong rumours in the Australian media that the project could be approved. As the economic and political costs of the proposed MFP became clearer, enthusiasm at both ends of the Pacific waned.

In 1991, the first meetings of an MFP International Advisory Committee took place in an attempt to combat growing criticism of the project. Public concern centred on rumours that the MFP was to be staffed by Australians but inhabited exclusively by Japanese, and that the site would be developed as an exclusive hi-tech Japanese enclave. More than fifty leading Japanese companies expressed interest in the MFP and its research development potential and, in 1995, the Australian government went as far as to allocate $8 million dollars in funds to the project for the 1995–6 fiscal year. At this time, an initial population of 100,000 was being reported in the media. Despite a significant push for national approval of a site outside Adelaide in South Australia, plans were finally abandoned.

The futuristic sci-fi quality of the MFP worked to both attract attention and controversy as rumours multiplied and local tensions deepened. The failure of the MFP can be attributed to many factors, not least of all were the absence of a comprehensive media strategy and a lack of recognition of the public-relations sensitivities in a country where there had already been a number of strong campaigns over the 1980s and early 1990s opposing Japanese investment and real-estate developments. The weakening of the Australian currency and overall economy only added to local claims that Japan was simply looking for a legitimate basis for a new mode of colonisation, thinly disguised in a rhetoric of globalisation and hi-tech research.

SANDRA BUCKLEY

Murakami Haruki

b. 1949, Kyōto

Writer

Murakami Haruki is one of the most popular authors of serious fiction in contemporary Japan. He was born in Kyōto, but soon after the family moved to Kobe where Murakami was brought up. Murakami left home at the age of nineteen to attend Waseda University in Tokyo, where he majored in film and theatre studies. He was married in 1971 while still a student and opened a jazz coffee shop. Graduating from Waseda in 1975 with a thesis on the journey motif in the US cinema, Murakami began his career as a novelist by winning the Gunzō New Author's Prize in 1979 with his story 'Kaze no uta o kike!' (Hear the Wind Sing).

Soon, Murakami was translating F. Scott Fitzgerald and writing articles on US film and literature. An ironic, 'cool', first-person male protagonist is often employed in his fiction. While these protagonists often sound almost trans-Atlantic in their admiration of US popular culture, for Murakami, what is being described is always also Japanese popular culture.

In 1981, Murakami decided to become a full-time writer. Between 1981 and 1999 he has published eight full-length novels, which have won many literary prizes and which have all been translated into English, several volumes of short stories, various volumes of essays and works of non-fiction, including *Andaguraundo* (Underground) in 1997 – a study of the human impact of the gas attacks on the Tokyo subways. He has also produced numerous translations of contemporary US fiction by such authors as John Irving, Raymond Carver and Truman Capote.

His famous tetralogy of novels, 'Hear the Wind Sing', published between 1981 and 1988, are *1973 no pinbōru* (Pinball, 1973), *Hitsuji o meguru bōken* (A Wild Sheep Chase) and *Dansu dansu dansu* (Dance dance dance). They feature the young narrator simply referred to as '*boku*' ('I') in a series of complex relationships with friends, partners and lovers, focusing, initially, on the impact of the suicide of a former lover. In the last two novels, love becomes entangled with politics, and also a kind of hyper-real fantasy. The final novel deals with right-wing conspiracies and murder, but seen through the plot device of the narrator pursuing a mystery, a not uncommon device in Murakami's fiction, usually linked to a mysterious woman with whom he is involved.

The theme of history and its impact on subjectivity emerge strongly in this tetralogy. Haruki juxtaposes late twentieth-century Japan, with its easy accommodation of Western popular culture, with the legacy of the Second World War, and the atrocities associated with it. The subjectivity Haruki creates and constantly interrogates is that of the urbanised, disconnected self of the younger generation of modern Japan. This theme re-emerges in *Nejimaki-dori kuronikuru* (The Wind-up Bird Chronicle), published in 1997, a further examination of Japan's past as it impinges on the present.

Select bibliography

Murakami Haruki (1997) *The Wind-up Bird Chronicle*, trans. Jay Rubin, London: The Harvill Press.
—— (1991) *Hard-Boiled Wonderland and the End of the World*, trans. Alfred Birnbaum, New York: Kōdansha International.

LEITH MORTON

Murakami Ryū

b. 1952, Nagasaki

Writer

Murakami Ryū lived close to the US base at

Sasebo and has written and spoken openly of his experiences growing up in the shadow of the US military presence. His fiction has often explored both this continued military presence in Japan and the extent of the collapse of any meaningful distinction between the categories of US and Japanese popular culture for the post-war generations in Japan, who grew up on Bob Dylan, Elvis, the Beatles, jazz and the Rolling Stones, along with the equally eclectic mix of Japanese folk, **Yellow Magic Orchestra**, an array of *idoru singers* and Japanese Noise bands (see **Noise Music**). Murakami refuses any simplistic rejection or damnation of US popular culture at the same time as he actively critiques the impact of the Anpo treaties and the US military presence. His rendering of Japanese post-war youth culture is grounded in the complexity of the day-to-day negotiations of difference and identification, rather than in any self-referential national literary or cultural tradition. His favourite characters include the camp followers who moved from one US base to another in the 1960s and 1970s, immersing themselves in the hedonistic lifestyle of the marginal hybrid culture of music, bars, alcohol and drugs, coffee shops and base prostitution. His unapologetic depictions of the underside of Japanese life continue to win him both praise and rejection from literary critics.

His first major success came with the novel *Kagirinaku tōmei ni chikai burrū* (Almost Transparent Blue, 1976). He won the prestigious **Akutagawa Prize** for this work, which explores the excesses of the lives of a group of young Japanese living close to the Yokosuka US Airforce base. His explicit depiction of sex, drugs and abusive and racist language was dismissed by some as gratuitous and sensationalist, but this critique is almost too easy and does not engage with the confrontational style that spans Murakami's works up to his most recent serialised novel *Exodus* (1998–9). In *Exodus*, Murakami creates an alternative world of disenchanted Japanese youth in an Internet alliance and then follows them as they flee the rapid economic decline of Japan in 2001 to create an independent state in the remote north of Hokkaidō. Perhaps the most controversial line in the novel is the statement from the leader of the youth defectors that Japan is a country with everything but hope. His earlier

novel *Koinrokkaa beibiizu* (Coin Locker Babies, 1980) offered another controversially stark, yet strikingly candid, critique of the ethical bankruptcy of a society where consumer culture is constantly reaching new levels of excess while two infants are left abandoned to die in station coin lockers. In *Tokyo Decadence* (1992), Murakami created a film version of his own manuscript in which he depicts the volatile and disturbing relationships between an S&M prostitute and her customers against the backdrop of the underside of Tokyo's nightlife.

Murakami has become a focal point of those who still want to draw a distinction between a notion of pure literature and popular literature. His writings are rejected as post-modern pastiche and he is accused of lacking intellectual and literary sophistication or style. However, these criticisms ring hollow after too many repetitions in the face of his continued ability to capture a broad-based readership in Japan and internationally, and his committed, if confrontational, engagement with contemporary cultural nodes of ethical crisis. Murakami's strategy has always been to perform the crisis 'in the face' of Japanese society, as one critic describes it, rather than pretend an intellectual distance. Murakami's fictional works are his best expression of the view that the objectivity and distancing mechanisms and self-referentiality of Japanese 'pure literature' are what are shallow and pastiche. What is certain is that his work will remain controversial.

SANDRA BUCKLEY

museums

The Meiji government took reports of Western cultural institutions to heart in its determination to establish a modern model of education and learning. It had established the first public library in 1872 and in the same year the Ministry of Education Museum (*Monbushō hakubutsukan*) was launched with its first public exhibition. It was the perceived link between cultural institutions and education that saw the Ministry of Education take much of the initiative in early museum development. The Museum of Education (*kyōiku hakubutsukan*) opened in 1877 and its exhibits were used as an opportunity to showcase new disciplines and fields of study. There was a strong focus on the sciences and the latest and best new technology and scientific knowledge were placed on display and archived. The museums were intended to not only educate the public but also offer research, teaching and learning facilities for fledgling university departments.

The 1890s saw the opening of both the Imperial Museum of Kyōto and the Imperial Museum of Nara. These institutions would develop collections that incorporated cultural and historical archives and exhibits. Ethnography and archaeology were both rapidly emerging disciplines that would soon come to play a crucial role in the weaving of a narrative of national identity essential to the realisation of Japan's imperialist agenda. It is no accident that these cultural institutions, established in the area of Japan's old capitals (Nara and Kyōto) were labelled 'Imperial' and not 'National', for the processes of formation of Japan's modern nation state identity were already being channelled through the body of the imperial institution. The curatorial practices of Japan's pre-war museums actively contributed, at both the grassroots level though exhibitions and at the level of research and archive development, to Japan's emergent colonial aspirations.

The early post-war period saw the renaming of a number of museums that had played a major role in pre-war myth-making. The Imperial Museum of Kyōto (renamed in 1924 as the Imperial Gift Museum of Kyōto) was renamed again as the National Museum of Kyōto in 1952. The Museum of Education was re-established as the National Science Museum in 1949 and the Ministry of Education Museum became the Tokyo National Museum in 1952. Just as the museums had been seen to have a key functional and symbolic role in the creation of Japan's modern identity, so the Occupation and early post-war governments also saw these institutions as important vehicles in the production of the identity of a rehabilitated and newly democratic Japan. The archives of Japan's cultural institutions included invaluable ethnographic and archaeological collections as well as historical archives. The curatorial work of the museums was now to redefine the national and international value and significance of their

archives and reposition themselves in the cultural landscape of post-war Japan. Materials that had once been the authenticating props of Japanese imperialism would now be reorganised into the historical narrative background for the Japanese economic miracle.

Government funds for cultural projects beyond the revitalisation of the education system were limited during the 1950s. However, a number of bills guaranteed a significant flow of funds into libraries, museums and other cultural facilities from the 1960s to the 1980s. Both the National Museum of Modern Art (1952) and the National Museum of Western Art (NMWA) (1959) were able to begin expanding their collections and to commission new buildings. The NMWA collection was initially based on the personal collection of Matuskata Kōjirō, a wartime industrialist. The bulk of the collection was in France at the end of the war and awarded to the French under the San Francisco Peace Accords, but France donated the collection to the Japanese nation. Many of the works in Japan's current collections were purchased by Japanese industrialists during the period of heady growth of the inter-war years. This has created some controversy, but not on the same scale as the Nazi theft of European masters. There is little information publicly available on the level of art, historical or archaeological materials that were moved to Japan from the colonised countries of Asia. The contemporary traffic in pirated archaeological materials and religious iconography, especially out of China, Thailand and Burma, is a source of more controversy today, with Japanese private collectors often accused of encouraging this illicit market.

The 1980s was known for its museum boom. With rapid economic growth, both private and public museums flourished. Architects from across the world were commissioned in a frenzy of construction. While there has been criticism of the architectural value of some of the projects completed during this period, the museum boom saw many regional centres create their first local cultural facilities, a direct goal of the government funding campaigns. The LDP were pursuing policies of decentralisation and regional development over the 1980s and this extended to cultural institutions and programmes. This was also the period when Japan was riding the wave of **nihinjinron** (theories of the Japanese). In an attempt to explain Japan's extraordinary economic success there was again a resort by Japanese and Western scholars and politicians to notions of essential Japanese qualities. This time, however, ethnicity was ostensibly subordinated to technology and culture. By the end of the 1980s, there were some 2,600 museums operating in Japan and many of these were dedicated to craft and everyday life or technological innovation. The Electric Energy Museum was opened in 1984, the Subway Museum in 1986 and the Cultural Museum of Kyōto in 1988.

Specialised collection museums include everything from kites to salt, whiskey, clocks, toys, cameras and a myriad of regional arts, crafts and local historical archives. Not infrequently the curatorial practices of local museum collections create contemporary narratives of identity that echo or even extend pre-war narratives of Japanese ethnicity, but the area of curatorial critical practice and research in Japan remains relatively new, even in the late 1990s. Many of the directors and curators of the smaller regional museums have continued to draw on old models of museum management, acquisition and exhibition. The tendency to strive to 'out-authenticate' the next village, town or region was at least in part driven by funding structures that pitted projects against one another, at a time when the government agenda was clearly one of creating narratives of Japaneseness that could establish continuity between traditional society and the contemporary Japanese miracle.

The 1990s saw a slowdown in the number of new museum constructions. While the 1980s saw Japan gain a reputation for buying the best pick of the international art market and driving up auction prices, the 1990s were marked by Japan's museums developing a more actively collaborative international role. This is most evident in Japan's growing role in the expanding domain of international touring exhibitions, which draw together works thematically from across international and national museum collections. Japanese museums have also begun regularly exhibiting new Japanese artworks in the major international and regional biennales and festivals. Private museums often function more on a gallery model than that of the museum, despite using the title. It is not unusual for a private gallery to have a 'stable' of artists, both established and fledgling, who rely heavily on the sponsorship of the institution. This is partly a consequence of the continuing dearth of public funds for artists. Another very distinctive element of Japanese museum life is the role of department stores. From the trendy Parco to the conservative Mitsukoshi, department stores actively promote themselves as cultural institutions and host art and other museum-style exhibitions of international quality in dedicated art spaces within their major shops. Guided tours and lectures are offered, just as they would be in a museum, and exhibition themes may extend into related speciality sales of food, fashion, furniture, etc. Here, the department stores and museum gift shops are both pursuing a strategy of profitably linking the culture of consumption and cultural consumption.

SANDRA BUCKLEY

N

Nagano Olympics

The 18th Winter Olympics were held in Nagano in 1998. After the various difficulties that had marred the 1996 Summer Olympics in Atlanta, the IOC seemed greatly relieved at the efficiency and problem-free execution of these games and was open in its praise of the Japanese organising committee. Japanese television audiences for the games increased by 50 per cent over previous winter Olympics and the dedication of Japanese audiences both at home and at the Olympic sites was rewarded with five gold medals for their team, the most gold won in winter Olympics by Japan. Although US television audience levels were disappointing and there was much criticism of CBS's untimely and fragmented coverage of events, audiences in other countries where there is a high interest in winter sports, such as Austria, Germany and Canada, were significantly higher than past years. The Olympics were, as always, marked by financial controversy, this time focused mainly on the high level of government funds invested in the creation of a new bullet train line that could carry passengers from Tokyo to Nagano City in just ninety minutes.

Korean-Japanese worked to create an awareness around the Olympics of their own distinctive and tragic history in Nagano. Unknown numbers of Korean labourers died in the final years of the war due to cave-ins and explosions when they were forced to work on the creation of a bunker, located deep underground in the alps, intended for the Emperor and the top levels of the military and government. The bunker was never completed and many Japanese were quoted as saying they knew nothing of this history until it came out in the domestic media coverage of these Olympics.

The Nagano Olympics were the first online Olympics to attract a significant web-audience. Some 620 million hits were recorded at the official site. The impact of the Internet on future Olympic broadcast coverage is being developed around research on user trends at Nagano and Sydney 2000. The IOC is hoping that the Salt Lake City location for 2002 will see a renewed interest in the winter games in the USA, the major source of advertising sponsorship.

SANDRA BUCKLEY

Nagoya

Nagoya, capital of Aichi Prefecture and Japan's fourth largest city, is located almost exactly in the centre of Honshū, along the Tōkaidō (Eastern Sea Road), the ancient road linking the areas of **Kantō** and **Kansai**, and now the route of the bullet train. Originally one of the **castle towns**, Nagoya's primary function historically has been as a regional market centre, and only recently has it become known as a port (see **port towns**). It is a major industrial centre for automobiles and construction materials, and has a well-developed high-technology sector, supported by internationally known research institutes. As a centre of technical innovation, Nagoya is famous as the place where **pachinko**, a pinball-type game was invented.

Most of the vast numbers of Japanese pachinko machines are still manufactured here.

Nagoya is the city where people stop on the way to somewhere else, whether literally just passing through on the *shinkansen* (**bullet train**), or changing trains for one of the interior cities or small coastal towns, or as a stage in the life course. Nagoya's many colleges and universities attract thousands of students to live in the city temporarily, while the surrounding industrial areas are a major destination for *dekasegi* workers seeing temporary employment.

AUDREY KOBAYASHI

Nakadai Tatsuya

b. 13 December 1932, Tokyo

Actor

Nakadai Tatsuya is one of the few Japanese actors with distinguished careers in both cinema and theatre. His diverse characterisations in both are generally generated inwardly. Nakadai first studied at the Haiyūza actors' training school. When working in film, he could perform straight romantic and comic roles effectively, but his jaded, roguish characters are more remarkable. His most memorable roles include those of the idealistic soldier in **Kobayashi Masaki**'s *Ningen no jōken* (The Human Condition, 1959–61), the dual role of concerned warlord and shadow warrior in **Kurosawa Akira**'s *Kagemusha* (1980) and the confused, ageing warlord in *Ran* (1985), Kurosawa's adaptation of *King Lear*. His stage work comprises both *shingeki* ('modern theatre'), featuring a highly acclaimed *Hamlet*, and roles in other Shakespeare, Gorky, Ibsen and Chekhov adaptations, and avant-garde, including work with **Abe Kōbō**'s theatre group.

WILLIAM C. THOMPSON

Nakagami Kenji

b. 1946, Shingū; d. 1992, Shingū

Writer

Canonised in the late 1990s, Nakagami Kenji first exploded onto the literary market with texts permeated with class rage and on ironic relation to dominant Japanese ethics. He is particularly remembered for his renderings of history and the canon in the face of the 1960s rush of consumerism, and his critical response to the massification of information and the jaded literary world. Graduated from high school, aged eighteen, Nakagami moved to Tokyo from rural Shingū. There he encountered jazz and the student riots, and read voraciously. Deeply influenced by William Faulkner, particularly *Absolum Absolum*, Nakagami's writing is also indebted to **Ōe Kenzaburō**, **Tanizaki Jun'ichirō**, Izumi Kyōka and Origuchi Shinobu. Nakagami died prematurely, at age forty-six, of kidney cancer.

Critics separate Nakagami's narratives into two categories: realistic texts set in the present and in the odoriferous *roji* (alleys; in Nakagami's texts associated with the **Burakumin** or outcaste ghettos) of an underclass unrepresented in the canon; and narratives set in pre-modern times (*monogatari*, or tale fiction), often inspired by oral folklore. In many texts Nakagami attempted to link the two textual topographies of realism and folklore.

Nakagami's most celebrated texts include: the trilogy of *Misaki* (The Cape, 1975), *Kareki nada* (Withered Tree Beach, 1977), and *Chi no hate shijō no toki* (The End of the Earth, the Supreme Time, 1983), which chronicles protagonist Akiyuki's attempt to come to terms with his irregular paternity and his older brother's suicide. Akiyuki's identity struggle drives him to intentional incest with his half-sister in *Misaki*, the killing of his half-brother, a provoked crime of passion, in *Kareki nada* and to arson in *Chi no hate shijō no toki*. A breath-taking orchestration flows throughout his writings, be it the maze of family relations in *Kareki nada*, or the genealogy of *Sennen no yūraku* (A Thousand Years of Pleasure, 1982), the tale of six young male outcastes, or the descriptive seaside and mountain panoramas that alternate with depictions of human brutality. Persistently, Nakagami put into question the categories of the sacred and the profane – binaries integral to Japanese discrimination discourse, while imbuing his texts with sombre violence, pulsing eroticism and shocking crudeness. The prose is a masterful mixture of convention and innovation. Like repeating chord formations, certain motifs recur: a brother dead of suicide, a derided father, the cries of protagonists into a deathly silence of 'Who am I?', 'Help me' and 'What does it all mean?', and certain tropings, such as that of the *roji* or the false holy man, or masculinity itself, as sites for multiple deconstructions of dominant Japanese literary and cultural axioms.

By 1999, only *Misaki* and *Fushi* (The Immortal, 1980) were translated into English, but most of Nakagami's texts were available in French.

Further reading

Cornyetz, N. (1999) *Dangerous Women, Deadly Words: Phallic Fantasy and Modernity in Three Japanese Writers*, Stanford: Stanford University Press, pp. 130–52.

Zimmerman, E. (1999) 'In the trap of words: Nakagami Kenji and the making of degenerate fictions, in S. Snyder and P. Gabriel (eds) *Ōe and Beyond: Fiction in Contemporary Japan*, Honolulu: University of Hawaii Press, pp. 130–52.

NINA CORNYETZ

Nakajima Miyuki

b. 1952, Hokkaidō

Singer and songwriter

Nakajima Miyuki was very important in establishing the genre of New Music in early 1970s Japan. Nakajima entered the Yamaha Popular Music Contest in May 1975. By September of the same year, she had already made her professional recording debut with her own composition, 'Azami jo no rarabai' (Lullaby of Lady Thistle). Her second composition, 'Jidai' (The Age), was released in November of the same year and won the grand prize at the Japanese World Music Awards. Her third song, 'Wakare uta' (The Break-up Song), sold over 700,000 copies.

The style of song she writes is an amalgam of pop and folk styles, though some of her critics have accused her of simply founding a new genre of *enka*. Her lyrics discuss trials facing women, especially the emotional difficulties arising out of romantic relationships. The gloom of her lyrics has been the subject of some debate, but the words are also generally written from a perspective with at least one eye toward the future. After 1976, she began to write songs for others such as Ken Naoko, Sakurada Junko and Eto Shizuka. 'Jidai' became a hit once again when it was used as the featured song for the Shochiku film, *Downtown Heroes*, in 1988. In recent years, Miyuki has worked as a DJ in the course of which her bold, earthy radio persona has added complexity to her rather more proper stage image.

Further reading

Kitagawa Junko (1994) 'Nakajima Miyuki', in *Taishu bunka jiten*, Tokyo: Kobundo, p. 574.

Nagano Osamu (1994) 'Nakajima Miyuki', in Fujibayashi Hitoshi (ed.) *1970 Ongakujin hyakka*, Tokyo: Gakūshū Kenkyusha, pp. 150–1.

MARK ANDERSON

Nakane Chie

1926, Tokyo

Social anthropologist

Nakane Chie's social anthropological works on Japanese society are considered to be among the most well-founded. Based on comparative studies of social structures, not between Europe/USA and Japan as commonly happens, but between other Asian societies, such as Tibet, India and Korea, and Japan, Nakane advocates the uniqueness of social relationships in her own country. She calls these relationships *tate-shakai*.

In Nakane's view, beyond the illogical surface appearance, there is a deep structural or latent logic of social mechanisms supporting *tate-shakai*, conditioned by two constitutive psychologies of the society's members. The first is the obsessive self-consciousness within the social hierarchy, deriving from the strong emotional attachment of Japanese people to their environment of belonging. The second is an extreme competitiveness based on a 'primitive' sense of human equality, radically different from traditional European democracy. These psychological structures are determined by the homogeneity of Japanese society and almost never found elsewhere, including Asia. In this way, Nakane's thesis can said to be dependent upon the stereotype of Japanese social homogeneity.

Selected bibliography

Nakane Chie (1970) *Japanese Society*, Berkeley: University of California Press.
—— (1967) *Kinship and Economic Organization in Rural Japan*, London: Athalone.

MIDORI HAYASHI

Nakayama Shimpei

b. 1887, Nagano Prefecture; d. 1952

Songwriter

Nakayama Shimpei was one of the most important songwriters in Japanese popular music history. In 1906, he became a student of the critic and dramatist Shimamura Hōgetsu. In 1908, he entered Tokyo Music School. He made his professional debut in 1914. Often referred to as the father of Japanese popular music, he wrote more than 6,000 songs over the course of his career.

Shimpei's début was the music for 'Kachusha no uta' (Kachusha's Song, 1914), a song written for the role played by Matsui Sumako in Shimamura Hogetsu's dramatic adaptation of Tolstoy's *Resurrection*. Sumako went on to record the song for Oriental Records, selling over 3,000 copies. It saw explosive popular success. Both Sumako and Shimpei became nationally recognised figures as a result of this song. When Hōgetsu gave Shimpei the lyrics he had asked Shimpei to write a song that combined Japanese folk melody with Western melody. Shimpei used nonsense words to write the melody, a technique that became a trademark of his songwriting style. This song established Shimpei's reputation and he continued to write for the stage until the late 1920s with great success.

Shimpei played an important part as a songwriter for the New Folk Music movement. He self-consciously created the Japanese *yonanuki* minor pentatonic scale (without four and seven) as a synthesis of Western diatonicism with the melodic structure of nineteenth-century Japanese songs. 'Sendomacr; kouta' (The Boatmen's Song, 1921) was the first popular song to use this scale. This song became one of the models for later popular Japanese song style. It established a mode that was thought to reflect traditional Japanese sound, yet was filtered through Western music theory. 'Sendomacr; kouta' may have had the longest lived popularity of any Japanese song.

With the advent of the recording industry in Japan, songs came to be written expressly for recording purposes. It was at this point that the locus of the Japanese music industry shifted from live performance and sheet music sales to radio broadcast and record sales. Shimpei became the main songwriter for Nippon Victor upon its foundation in 1927 and wrote many *ryūkōka*. His songs were the first popular songs ever recorded in Japan. He was also the best-selling children's song composer.

Further reading

Fujie, Linda (1989) 'Popular music', in Richard G. Powers and Hidetoshi Kato (eds) *Handbook of Japanese Popular Culture*, New York: Greenwood Press, pp. 197–220.
Ito Tsuyoshi/Tsutomu (1994) 'Nakayama Shimpei', in *Taishū bunka jiten*, Tokyo: Kobunkan, p. 576.
Kitahara Michio (1966) 'Kayōkyoku: An example of syncretism involving scale and mode', *Ethnomusicology* 10(3): 271–84.
Komota Nobuo, Shimada Yoshifumi, Yazawa Tamotsu and Yokozawa Chiaki (1981) *Nihon ryūkōkashi (Senzen-hen)*, Tokyo: Shakaishisosha.
Nakamura Toyo (1991) 'Early pop song writers and their backgrounds', *Popular Music* 10(3): 263–82.
Yano, Christine R. (1998) 'Defining the nation in Japanese popular song, 1914–1932', in *Japan's Competing Modernities*, Honolulu: University of Hawaii Press, pp.247–64.

MARK ANDERSON

Naoki Prize

The Akutagawa Ryūnosuke Prize (usually called the Akutagawa Prize) is the most prestigious literary prize in Japan for new authors of serious fiction, and still frequently launches novelists on successful careers. It was established in 1935, together with the **Naoki Prize**, by the writer Kikuchi Kan, in memory of the celebrated novelist whose name it bears. The prize is normally awarded twice a year but it is not unusual for no award to be made if, in the opinions of the judges, no story is worthy of the prize.

Since the award's inception, the *Bungei shunjū* journal has published the prize-winning stories, which include, in the post-war era, such famous works as **Nakagami Kenji**'s *Misaki* (The Cape) in 1976, **Murakami Ryū**'s *Kagirinaku tōmei ni chikai burrū* (Almost Transparent Blue) in 1977 and Yū Miri's *Kazoku shinema* (Family Cinema) in 1997. However, many distinguished writers like Murakami Haruki (b. 1949) and **Yoshimoto Banana** have not been awarded the prize, despite winning several of the other numerous literary awards available. In some respects, the prize serves as much a social as a literary function, keeping literature in the public eye due to the award's high media profile. ·

LEITH MORTON

Narita Airport struggle

The Narita Airport struggle (more commonly known as the Sanrizuka struggle, or Sanrizuka *tōsō*) was the longest and the most violent of the post-war citizens' movements. The roots of the movement stretch back to other popular struggles against modernisation and the state, such as the long struggle against the Ashio Copper Mine in the early twentieth century. The Narita struggle went much further than other citizens' movements in that it began as a struggle over land and came to question the very idea of 'citizenship' and the legitimacy of the state. The Narita struggle also radicalised the citizens' movement by bringing in New Left students, who became key players in the defence of the farmers' land.

The airport struggles began in 1962, as the government began planning a new international airport for the Tokyo region, and continued until well after the 1978 debut of the airport, some nine

years behind schedule. The government chose Sanrizuka, near Narita in Chiba Prefecture, as the site of the new airport in 1966. The Vietnam War had increased military air traffic at Haneda Airport as well as US bases in the Tokyo area, and, with Tokyo airspace saturated, a remote airport became necessary. Sanrizuka had the attraction of lying near the Emperor's horse stables and a former imperial villa. It was, in fact, the government's second choice for the new international airport; it had abandoned an earlier site in Chiba in the face of determined resident opposition.

The Narita Airport Struggle took a New Left turn very early on. Though the anti-airport struggle remained under the direction of local farmers, New Left activists far outnumbered locals in the anti-airport coalition. The **Japan Communist Party**'s youth group, Democratic Youth (commonly abbreviated to Minsei), had participated in early protests against the New Tokyo International Airport Corporation's surveying and planning in the autumn of 1967. These early protests were violent, with many injuries on the anti-airport side. When the Minsei criticised the anti-airport group's strategy and violence, outraged farmers and residents banned them and the JCP from further participation in their struggle. Farmers asked the New Left groups from Sanpa Zengakuren ('Three Faction' **Zengakuren**) and the Hansen Seinen I'inkai to replace the Minsei. Of the various New Left factions, the most dominant sect in the airport struggle was the Trotskyist 'Core Faction' (Chūkaku-ha). Though rifts inevitably developed, the New Left groups remained faithful to the struggle. The New Left groups opposed the new airport and its location for several reasons. First, the New Left stressed the connection between the airport and the Vietnam War, and American/Japanese imperialism. Moreover, along with Chiba farmers, they questioned the legitimacy of the state's claim to represent the general welfare. As in the Ashio and Minamata struggles (see **Minamata disease**), the New Left and the anti-airport coalition questioned the legitimacy of sacrificing Japanese people in the name of the general welfare.

The fighting for the airport was more than fierce. The first violent clash between airport opponents and the state occurred in October

1967. The Sanrizuka-Shibayama United Airport Opposition (Sanrizuka-Shibayama Rengō Kūkō Hantai Dōmei) tried to prevent the Airport Corporation from surveying. As the state and the Airport Corporation were carrying out their second round of forced evictions in 1971, more than 16,000 farmers and activists gathered to resist. Three police died in the series of battles that spanned several weeks. So determined were anti-airport farmers that they chained themselves to trees to obstruct surveying crews, and attacked construction workers and their police bodyguards after first anointing themselves with faeces and urine. Others buried themselves in the ground to block construction. The anti-airport protesters resisted by building steel towers to block the landing approaches to the airport in 1971. These remained standing until 1977, when riot police tore them down. In the fight to protect the towers, veteran New Left activist Higashiyama Kaoru died from a direct hit from a police tear gas cannister.

The anti-airport coalition sabotaged the construction of the jet fuel pipeline to the new airport. Through their New Left contacts, anti-airport forces also enlisted the aid of Chiba-area railway workers, who blocked and threatened to block shipments of jet fuel to the airport. Just as the new airport was scheduled to open in 1978 (nine years behind schedule), members of the Trotskyist Fourth International broke into the airport's control tower through the airport's sewage system, occupying it and destroying equipment. The damage to the tower set back the opening of the airport by two more months.

After the destruction of the control tower, battles between the opposition and police often centred around the 'solidarity huts' (danketsu koya). Police attacked the solidarity huts under the provisions of the Narita Area Emergency Facilities Act, which gave them (unconstitutional) powers to exclude anti-airport activists from the area and prevent their meetings.

When the airport finally opened in May 1978, it was with only one of three planned runways. The airport opposition's persistent campaign of low-level sabotage tactics forced the Airport Corporation and the state to sink vast amounts of money and resources into merely protecting the airport. Moreover, security concerns precluded connecting

the airport directly to railways until 1990, making the airport one of the world's most inconvenient and unpleasant for travellers. The Anti-Airport struggle breathed new life into the New Left after the collapse of the **Zenkyōtō** movement and the **Red Army**'s terrorist escapades by bringing it into contact with farmers and working people. The anti-airport struggle also brought Sanrizuka farmers into a network of oppositional groups ranging from the New Left, Chiba workers and members of New Left labour unions, and their counterparts in similar struggles throughout Japan. The movement thus brought new breadth and depth to both citizens'/residents' movements and the New Left.

Further reading

Apter, D. (1984) 'A 60's movement in the 80's', in S. Aronowitz, F. Jameson, S. Sayres and A. Stephanson (eds) *The Sixties without Apology*, Minneapolis: University of Minnesota Press, pp. 70–90.

Apter, D. (1984) *Against the State*, Cambridge, MA: Harvard University Press.

GUY YASKO

Naruse Mikio

b. 20 August 1905, Tokyo; d. 2 July 1969, Tokyo

Director

Naruse Mikio was an inconsistent director of *shōmin-geki* (melodramas centred on common people), who made a number of highly regarded films during two separate time periods. Born to a poor family in central Tokyo, his adolescence was marked by insecurity and unhappiness. This, coupled with the loneliness he felt following his father's early death, became key to his best work.

Naruse, who directed his first films in 1930, received considerable acclaim for the comical *Tsuma yo bara no yō ni* (Wife! Be Like a Rose!, 1935), which was among the first Japanese films exhibited in the USA. Shortly afterwards, his career began a long decline, and did not rebound until 1951, when he discovered popular novelist

Hayashi Fumiko's works. In total he adapted six Hayashi books to much acclaim: *Meshi* (Repast, 1951); *Inazuma* (Lightning, 1952); *Tsuma* (Wife, 1953); *Bangiku* (Late Chrysanthemums, 1954); *Ukigumo* (Floating Clouds, 1955); and the autobiographical *Horoki* (Lonely Lane, 1962). Naruse's bleak melodramas from the 1950s and 1960s, including non-Hayashi adaptations such as *Iwashigume* (Herringbone Clouds, 1958) and *Onna ga kaidan o ageru toki* (When a Woman Ascends the Stairs, 1960), strongly identified with Hayashi's female protagonists. They quintessentially depicted lonely women either outside the traditional family system or placed in harsh and seemingly inescapable situations. Most of these heroines were intelligent and strong, but accepted exploitation by men and society in general. In the end, they proved to be self-respecting and determined survivors forced to cope with life's betrayals and bleakness.

WILLIAM C. THOMPSON

national identity and minorities

National identity is a complex and much debated phenomenon. It refers to the sense of belonging that links individuals to the modern nation state. In all modern nations, governments have sought to foster this sense of belonging through education, rituals, ideas and symbols. Japan is no exception. A sense of belonging is also created at the level of popular culture, by the sharing of familiar traditions or new fashions. Different visions of national identity therefore exist side by side, and these visions change over time.

In modern Japan, notions of national identity have mobilised a wide variety of different images and symbols. Some images date back to the second half of the eighteenth century, when a group of scholars sought to define a distinctively 'Japanese' world-view, in contrast to the Chinese philosophies, which had long exerted a dominant influence on intellectual life. These scholars of *kokugaku* (national learning) – including Motōri Norinaga (1730–1801) and Hirata Atsutane (d. 1843) – drew inspiration from the ancient myths and folk beliefs of Japan, which they depicted as a truly indigenous

'Way of the Gods' – Shintō – in contrast to the imported notions of Buddhism and Confucianism. They also drew a distinction between a spontaneous 'Japanese' empathy with nature and 'Chinese' modes of thought, which they presented as being rigid, formal and scholastic.

From the middle of the nineteenth century onwards, issues of national identity became a major concern for policy makers. The new, centralised Meiji state needed to assert its authority over a country where local domains had previously provided a primary focus of political loyalties. The government also wanted to create a strongly united country capable of resisting the pressures of the Western imperial powers. Japan in the early Meiji Period was a country of considerable regional diversity, where customs and dialects varied between one area and another. One task for the new government was to define which form of the Japanese language was the 'standard' to be taught in schools and used for official purposes. After considerable debate, the form of Japanese spoken by the educated classes in Tokyo was selected for this purpose. The creation of the modern Japanese state also involved the incorporation of Hokkaidō and Okinawa, which had previously only been tenuously linked to Japan. Notions of national identity, including the imposed use of 'standard' Japanese, were used by the state in its attempt to assimilate the people of these regions, and (from 1895 onwards) of Japan's colonial empire.

Ideas derived from *kokugaku* were among those mobilised by leading Meiji politicians and intellectuals to foster a new sense of Japanese national identity. A cornerstone of official constructions of nationhood in the Meiji Period was the image of the Emperor. Previously a shadowy and invisible ceremonial figure, the Emperor now became the focus of a set of 'invented traditions' derived partly from Shintō practices and partly from Western notions of royalty. At the same time, however, Meiji leaders also drew on Confucian tradition to emphasise the importance of loyalty to superiors and the centrality of the family in national life. The role of the Emperor was closely linked to an ideology that stressed the importance of the *ie* (patriarchal family). In fact, this hierarchical family structure had historically been prevalent mainly among the ruling warrior class. From the mid-nineteenth century onwards, however, it was increasingly held up as the model for all Japanese citizens. The nation was frequently depicted as a 'family state' (*kazoku kokka*), in which the Emperor occupied the position of father and head of household.

The construction of national identity also focused on educating the population about the significance of symbols such as the red-and-white rising sun (*hinomaru*) flag, originally used on shōgunal ships in the Tokugawa Period, and officially designated as 'the national flag' for use on merchant vessels in 1870. The production of a national anthem proved more difficult. In 1882, after various efforts at collaboration between Japanese and foreign musicians, the ancient poem *Kimigayo*, set to a new tune by a Japanese court composer with harmonies by a German music instructor, was recognised by the government's music academy as the official national song. Such symbols of identity as flag and anthem, however, could be used differently by different sections of society. While the government employed them to promote a sense of national unity and loyalty to the state, the same symbols were used in the 1880s by popular rights activists, as part of their campaign against a government that they criticised for placing personal interests over the interests of the Japanese people as a whole. Meanwhile, official efforts to instil a sense of national belonging into the population made use of imported, as well as indigenous, ideas. Ethics education in state schools, for example, gave a prominent place to Shintō creation myths, but also, from the early twentieth century onwards, taught young Japanese citizens to model themselves both on the heroes of Japanese history and on figures such as Benjamin Franklin, Florence Nightingale and Edward Jenner.

Ideas of nationhood are shaped, not just by official symbols such as flags and anthems but also by a repertoire of images created by public intellectuals and the mass media. In Japan, from the late nineteenth century onwards, one important set of images depicted a unique relationship between Japanese people and their natural environment. This imagery was powerfully influenced by the writings of the philosopher and historian Watsuji Tetsurō (1889–1960), who argued that the Japanese have tended neither to dominate nor to submit, but rather to harmonise and work with nature. Other contemporaries of Watsuji's also looked for the sources of national identity in the cultural and philosophical dimensions of Japanese life. Philosopher Nishida Kitarō (1870–1945), for example, emphasised distinctive forms of selfhood and consciousness related to Japan's Buddhist traditions, while the folklorist Yanagita Kunio (1875–1962) sought to balance the obsessive drive towards modernisation by recording the indigenous traditions of rural Japanese society.

A further important theme in debates about national identity was the question of the racial origins of the Japanese. The introduction of Western theories of archaeology, anthropology and racial science in the late nineteenth century provoked intense debates within Japan around this topic. Some writers, like the Meiji political thinker Katō Hiroyuki (1836–1915) emphasised the racial homogeneity and 'purity' of the Japanese people. For them, the Japanese people were a literal 'family' linked by bonds of blood to the imperial family. However, others, like anthropologist Torii Ryūzō (1870–1953) and historian Kita Sadakichi (1871–1939), stressed the fact that the Japanese *minzoku* (ethnic group) had emerged from the intermingling of waves of immigrants from various parts of North-East and South-East Asia, and the Southern Pacific in the centuries before the formation of the Japanese state in the seventh to eighth centuries of the common era (a view that is widely accepted by scholars today). These debates were played out against the background of Japan's colonial expansion into Asia from the Meiji Period to the end of the Pacific War. As a result of that expansion, Koreans and Taiwanese came to be officially designated as 'Japanese subjects', without being accorded political rights equal to those of other Japanese. During the pre-war period, debates about the racial 'homogeneity' or 'hybridity' of the Japanese population often became entangled in policy debates between those who favoured maintaining a clear separation between Japanese colonisers and colonised populations, and those who favoured an assimilationist approach to the colonies.

In the 1930s and 1940s, as Japan engaged in war, first on the Asian continent and then throughout the Pacific, questions of identity and national pride became ever more deeply politicised. The Kokumin Seishin Sōdōin Undō (National Spiritual Mobilisation Movement) of 1937–40 aimed to imbue all citizens with a sense of pride in Japanese culture, as well as disseminating the values of hard work, hygiene and thrift, through activities such as radio broadcasts and public lecture tours by prominent public figures. Even at this time, however, the sources of national identity remained an issue of debate. Some saw Japan's claim to hegemony in East Asia as based on the nation's rapid and successful industrialisation; others emphasised the unique status of the Japanese imperial tradition; others again argued that Japan was culturally superior because it had refined traditions imported from other parts of Asia to a uniquely high level.

The profound shock of Japan's defeat in the Pacific War, and the loss of the colonial empire, resulted in a radical change in images of nationhood. With the political changes of the Occupation period, the Emperor and State Shintō were displaced from their central position in official definitions of national belonging. From this period onwards, far more emphasis was placed upon cultural features that were seen as distinctive to Japan. A key role in the formation of this new cultural image of Japanese national identity was played by the evolving genre of thought known as **Nihonjinron** ('theories of the Japanese'). These post-war definitions of Japanese culture and identity derived not only from the work of Japanese authors themselves, but also from the writings of foreign scholars. One particularly significant influence was the work of US anthropologist Ruth Benedict, whose famous study *The Chrysanthemum and the Sword* (1946) emphasised the group consciousness of the Japanese, and the power of *giri* (obligation) (see **giri and ninjo**) and *haji* (shame) as sources of social discipline. During the 1960s and 1970s, images of Japanese cultural uniqueness were further developed by Japanese scholars such as **Nakane Chie**, who contrasted the vertical structure of Japanese social institutions to the horizontal structure of their Western counterparts, and **Doi Takeo**, who saw emotional indulgence/dependency (**amae**) as the key source of Japanese group consciousness. These writings tended to emphasise the cultural homogeneity of Japanese

society, a feature widely believed to be associated with the absence of significant ethnic or linguistic minorities in Japan. The belief in ethnic homogeneity as a defining characteristic of the nation was most famously (and controversially) articulated by then Prime Minister Nakasone Yasuhiro in 1986. Contrasting Japan to the multiracial USA, Nakasone argued that the absence of ethnic minorities in Japan for the past 2,000 years made it easier for Japan to become an 'intelligent society'.

During the post-war decades, however, images of Japanese cultural uniqueness were always complex and contested. Many social critics saw the distinctive characteristics of Japanese culture as obstacles to progress as much as sources of national pride. Meanwhile, the experience of military defeat and post-war democratisation had created new images of national belonging. For many people in post-war Japan, the 1947 Constitution, with its official renunciation of war, became a significant focus of national identity. Notions of Japanese homogeneity have also been strongly contested. Prime Minister Nakasone's 1986 comment on this subject evoked protests from many quarters, particularly from representatives of **Ainu** and resident Korean groups (see **Koreans in Japan**). From the early 1980s onwards, the growing presence of foreign migrants in Japan helped to create an increasing awareness of cultural diversity, and encouraged some to argue that Japan should redefine itself as a multicultural society.

Debates about cultural diversity in Japan (as elsewhere) have raised important issues of the definition of 'majority' and 'minorities'. In the Japanese case, for example, the **Burakumin**, descendants of social groups who were subject to discrimination in the pre-Meiji Period have continued to be seen as a distinct 'minority'. However, descendants of members of the ruling warrior cast, though equally a 'minority' in numerical terms, rapidly ceased to be seen as a distinct group within society. Ainu and Okinawans are commonly defined as 'minorities', but people from other outerlying islands, some of whom also have quite distinctive histories and cultural traditions, are not. 'Majority' and 'minorities', in other words, are not naturally existing categories, but are defined and redefined in response to changing historical and political circumstances. For many people, an awareness of national identity is not something that plays a major part in everyday life. It becomes important only in times of social instability or change, or when they experience discrimination or encounters with the 'foreign'. How strongly people feel a sense of national identity, and how they choose to interpret and represent that identity, depends upon social position, gender, generation and life experience, and whether they are defined by others, and define themselves, as belonging to the 'majority' or 'minority'.

Further reading

Morris-Suzuki, T. (1998) *Re-Inventing Japan: Time, Space, Nation*, New York: M.E. Sharpe.

Vlastos, S. (ed.) (1998) *Mirror of Modernity: Invented Traditions of Modern Japan*, Berkeley: University of California Press.

Yoshino, K. (1992) *Cultural Nationalism in Contemporary Japan*, London: Routledge.

TESSA MORRIS-SUZUKI

national parks

Japan has twenty-eight national parks (*kokuritsu kōen*) and a further fifty-five limited or semi-official national parks (*kokutei kōen*). All national parks fall within the jurisdiction of the Office of the Prime Minister under the Environmental Protection Agency (EPA). Hiking, camping and winter sports are extremely popular in Japan and, while these activities guarantee the continued preservation of Japan's national parklands, this recreational use is seen by environmentalists as a threat to preservation. Use of the parklands is facilitated by an excellent national network of public and private **youth hostels** and inns.

The largest of Japan's national parks is the protected area of the **Inland Sea**. This park incorporates a hundred islands over an area stretching 400 km from east to west. Economic activity is not prohibited in the parklands and this has led to some international and national criticism of land management policies under the EPA. For example, oyster- and pearl-harvesting activities

continue in some coastal park areas. Here we see direct tension between local traditional lifestyle, economic need and environmental protection. Similarly, issues of logging and damming have occurred in the central and northern highland parklands, while hunting and **fishing** access remain controversial in **Hokkaidō**'s parklands, where traditional **Ainu** lifestyles, **tourism** and commercial interests frequently are in conflict in the determination of park management policies. Some parklands include significant national monuments such as temples or shrines. The Nikko parklands, site of the Tōshōgu black-and-red lacquered shrine buildings just outside Tokyo, are an example of the attempt to combine both the management of historical and environmental protection.

Despite the impact of intensive deforestation and pollution, the inaccessibility of much of Japan's rugged highlands has seen the preservation of spectacular tracts of unspoiled forest beyond the reach of agricultural or commercial development. The extraordinary popularity of **skiing** in Japan has seen major incursions into parklands under limited protection. The large-scale development of ski slopes and related tourist facilities has an inevitable impact on surrounding wilderness areas.

SANDRA BUCKLEY

Nationality Law

Japan's defeat in the Second World War left many people with claims to Japanese nationality, due to their forced removal to Japan (mainly from Korea and Taiwan), voluntary migration, interracial marriage or extra-marital birth. The Occupation authorities decided to divest Korean and Chinese residents of their Japanese nationality, in the (mistaken) belief that they would choose to, and be able to, return home (see **Potsdam Declaration**). The Alien Registration Law in 1947 was introduced to record and control these now foreign residents of Japan, and has been controversial ever since. Japan's post-war Nationality Law of 1955 recognised only Japanese nationals and foreigners; the intermediate category of permanent resident was recognised only in the 1980s, in acknowledgement of the fact that Korean and Chinese settlement in Japan would be permanent.

Since the Meiji-era Nationality Law of 1899, Japan had sought to fuse ethnicity, language and nationality. Until recently, Japanese bureaucrats insisted that people applying to naturalise as Japanese be able to prove their assimilation by changing their names to Japanese-sounding ones and showing that they had blended into their workplace and neighbourhood. Many second- and third-generation Koreans and Chinese chose not to naturalise under these conditions.

Initially, the 1955 Nationality Law continued the principle of patrilineal nationality, i.e. a child's nationality would follow its father's. In 1985, the Law was revised in line with Japan's ratification of the Convention on the Elimination of Discrimination against Women. The Law now allows a child to acquire Japanese nationality from either its mother or its father. Illegitimate children can acquire Japanese nationality once they are recognised by a parent who is a Japanese national. Parents of children who are eligible for Japanese nationality when born outside Japan must 'reserve' this by notifying diplomatic officials and registering the birth. Dual nationality is avoided by requiring those holding Japanese and foreign nationalities to retain or relinquish Japanese nationality before the age of twenty-two. Conditions for naturalisation are now the same, regardless of gender. A Japanese national whose spouse or parent is non-Japanese is now able to use a foreign name, expressed in *katakana* (phonetic script for foreign-origin words) as his or her name and enter this in the family register (*koseki*).

These changes had unintended consequences for Koreans in Japan. Every child of a Korean-Japanese marriage will now acquire Japanese nationality and will have to confirm their nationality as adults. Over time, almost all Koreans resident in Japan are likely to become Japanese – an enormous challenge to their political and ethnic identities. The 1985 reforms did, however, benefit stateless children, particularly those of Japanese mother and US servicemen fathers who were otherwise ineligible for basic social welfare payments and social services. The most recent reform in Nationality Law has come from the courts, in response to the problem of stateless children born to foreign mothers (often sex industry workers) in Japan and unknown Japanese fathers. In these cases, the Supreme Court has held that the child is entitled to receive Japanese nationality – a major departure from the cultural idea that Japanese nationality and ethnicity should be fused.

See also: Allied Occupation; Korean War; *koseki*

Further reading

Fukuoka Yasunori (1993) *Zainichi Kankoku/Chōsenjin* (Japan's Resident Koreans), Tokyo: Chūkō Shinsho.

Ōnuma Yasuaki (1993) *Tan itsu minzoku shakai no shinwa o koete* (Beyond the Myth of a Monoethnic Society), Tokyo: Tōshindō.

VERONICA TAYLOR

natto

Natto is a fermented soy bean dish that originated in north-east Japan. It is made in speciality shops across the country and even among Japanese remains something of an acquired taste. During the fermentation, the beans are stored at over 100 degrees Fahrenheit. The consistency is sticky, and *natto* fans boast of being able to tell regional differences from texture, taste and colour – usually a rich, dark brown. *Natto* is most often eaten as a side dish with rice. Many a foreigner has been offered this pungent dish to test their assertion that they love all Japanese food.

SANDRA BUCKLEY

NETAKIRI *see* bedridden patients

New Frontier Party

The New Frontier Party (NFP) (Shinshintō) was Japan's second largest party to the **Liberal Democratic Party** (LDP) in 1994–8. It came into being as an 'anti-LDP' coalition in December 1994 after the fall of the Hosokawa coalition government in June of that year, to hasten Japan's transition to a two-party political system and to form an opposition party to the coalition of the LDP, SDP and Sakigake in a government under then Prime Minister Hosokawa.

The nine parties that formed the NFP lacked policy cohesion, however, and were far apart on a wide number of sensitive policy issues (e.g. Japan's defence forces). They included: Shinseitō (Japan Renewal Party), like **New Party Sakigake**, formed by a group of conservative politicians who left the LDP in the summer of 1993 on an agenda of political and administrative reform; the Japan New Party, originally the political arm of the **Sōka Gakkai**; the Democratic Socialist Party, and a moderate party of ex-socialist parliamentarians; Komeitō (Clean Government Party). The NFP moved into opposition in 1994 following the formation of a new coalition between the LDP, **Japan Socialist Party** and Sakigake under Prime Minister Murayama.The NFP, under President Toshiki Kaifū, finally split up at the end of 1998 into six parties, the largest being former NFP president Ozawa Ichirō's **Liberal Party**.

DAVID EDGINGTON

new generation

Members of the generation born during the 1960s and early 1970s, the *shinjinrui* became young adults during the heyday of Japan's **bubble economy** in the 1980s. Beginning in the mid-1980s, they were disparagingly called the new generation by people born in the first **baby boom**. The *shinjinrui*, in turn, negatively refer to their parents and bosses as the old generation or *kyūjinrui*. Neither group appreciates its appellation, but both express difficulty in understanding the ways of the other generation.

Not easily definable, the *shinjinrui* have been compared to affluent post-war adults in other countries like the 'DINKS' (Dual Income No Kids) in the USA and the 'new youth' in France. Because many *shinjinrui* work in, or are otherwise active in, the arts, they are often thought of as being more creative than their forebears. *Shinjinrui* are also characterised as cultivating an image of individual-

ism, and as questioning the social expectations and standards created during the previous generations.

Another generation has recently appeared (*choshinjinrui* or *shinshinjinrui*), the children of the second baby boom generation. This generation is strongly influenced by the internationalism of the new forms of entertainment and information media.

BETH KATZOFF

New Music

New Music is a type of artist-directed Japanese pop that emerged in the early 1970s and incorporated rock modes, although there are many competing definitions. New Music can be credited with transferring the lion's share of artistic control from the record companies to the musical artists themselves in the case of exceptionally talented and self-directed artists. The representative faces of New Music are Arai Yumi (later, **Matsutoya Yumi**), Yoshida Minako and **Yano Akiko**.

All three are prodigiously talented and strikingly original songwriters and they each perform, almost exclusively, their own materials. Yano Akiko is further recognised as a fine, jazz-inflected pianist (she played on the **Yellow Magic Orchestra** (YMO) world tour). Yoshida Minako deserves far wider recognition as the great R 'n' B vocalist she is. Over the course of her career, Yoshida Minako moved from a Carole King-derived singer–songwriter approach to a much harder, more soulful sound with a melancholy undertow. Matsutoya Yumi developed an eclectic, bouncy, yet doggedly determined feminine melodic voice, with ballads often set in a lush, self-consciously exotic and vaguely East Asian tonality. Yumi set new Japanese pop-music sales records with each successive release in the late 1970s and 1980s and emerged as one of the most prolific and successful songwriters in the pop-music history of the world.

Caramel Mama/Tin Pan Alley was the backing band for all three of these performers at the beginning of their careers. They also played a decisive role in the development of New Music. In fact, if you trace the activity of this band it constitutes a veritable history of New Music *per se*.

Caramel Mama was formed in early 1973 as a backing band for recording sessions. Its members were Hosono Haruomi on bass, Suzuki Shigetaka on guitar, Matsutoya Masataka on keyboards and Hayashi Tatsuo on drums. Hosono and Suzuki had previously been members of **Happy Endo**, while Hosono went on to co-found YMO. From 1974, the band changed its name to Tin Pan Alley. In addition to the founding members, at various times they recorded with Yoshida Minako, Yano Akiko, Sato Hiroshi and **Sakamoto Ryūichi**. They undertook a very broad variety of musical activity and effected a significant transformation of the Japanese pop world. They disbanded in 1977, bringing to an end an immensely influential musical presence in the Japanese music scene. Caramel Mama/Tin Pan Alley was involved with Ōtaki Eichi and Sugar Babe (featuring **Yamashita Tatsurō**), Arai Yumi, Matsumoto Takashi, the Moonriders and the **Sadistic Mika Band**. From this perspective, they were involved in almost all of the fundamental transformations of Japanese pop in the 1970s and early 1980s, and their influence cannot be over-estimated. Other artists conventionally associated with New Music include **Inoue Yōsui**, Nakajima Miyuki, Yamashita Tatsurō and **Yoshida Takuro**.

Further reading

Shinohara Akira (1994) 'New music to Caramel Mama/Tin Pan Alley', in *J-Rock 1968–1996: Best 123*, Tokyo: Kōdansha Bunko, pp. 134–5.

MARK ANDERSON

New Party Sakigake

The New Party Sakigake (meaning 'harbinger') was formed in 1993 by ten breakaway **Liberal Democratic Party** (LDP) Lower House members led by Masayoshi Takemura after a no-confidence vote against the Miyazawa Cabinet. Sakigake's major policy platform has been to reform political and bureaucratic systems in favour of a more 'people-oriented' political system (e.g. providing NGOs with legal status). It won thirteen extra seats in the 1993 Lower House election and

joined in the ensuing coalition government with the Japan New Party (JNP). Chairman Takemura became Chief Cabinet Secretary under Prime Minister Morihiro Hosekawa. In 1994, Sakigake withdrew from the coalition to a position of 'co-operation' with the government, without cabinet representation, but later rejoined a coalition with the LDP and Social Democratic Party (SDP), with Takemura as finance minister. Sakigake gained three seats in the July 1995 Upper House (House of Councillors) election, but suffered a major blow in 1996 when popular Minister of Health and Welfare, Naoto Kan, left the party to start the Democratic Party. After the 1996 Lower House election, Sakigake controlled only three seats in the Upper House and two in the Lower House, and has focused mainly on environmental and 'quality of life' issues.

DAVID EDGINGTON

new religions, Japanese

The term Japanese new religions refers to a large, amorphous collection of religious groups and movements that have emerged since the start of the nineteenth century in Japan. Japanese new religions are eclectic and syncretistic, often incorporating Buddhist, Christian, Shintō and folk religious elements along with features from spiritualism, the occult and science fiction. There is no agreement as to the number of Japanese new religions that exist, with some scholars counting thousands of such groups while others limit the number to several hundreds. Neither is there agreement on the terminology or typological casting utilised. The labels new religion, new new religion, new age and new spirituality movements are used with little consistency to refer to a host of contemporary religious interests and developments. Moreover, there is little agreement as to the causes and factors that gave rise to the new religions.

Since the number and variant types of religious groups that have arisen since the nineteenth century cross a significant span of both time and trends, it is not surprising that Japanese new religions display a diverse array of characteristics that present a challenge to any attempt at generalisation. There are, none the less, certain themes and traits that scholars have identified. Japanese new religions offer a world-view that enables followers to make sense out of nonsense. They propose a new paradigm in which the uncertainty of the world can be influenced and interpreted, if not controlled, by the accumulation of spiritual merit and the acquisition of supernatural power. This is especially appealing to those who are increasingly dissatisfied with the apparent spiritual desolation of modern society or who view the risks and demands of modernity as overly stressful and empty of meaning. There are also apocalyptic leanings in the world-view of an increasing number of new religions, stemming from the growing recognition of the problems of modern industrial society and the limits of science and technology. The world-view proffered by new religions addresses these concerns by fostering the belief that members can help the world avoid a cataclysmic end through their devoted practice or that the followers themselves will survive such an apocalypse.

Japanese new religions often centre on the powerful personality and charisma of founders and leaders. Their teachings and interpretations of tradition and spiritual practice are viewed as vital for salvation, and followers will turn to them for guidance and remedies for the problems of life. The religious insights and powers founders possess are believed to have been procured through their own devoted and arduous spiritual practice. Not surprisingly, many founders of new religions are highly venerated, believed by their adherents to be the manifestation or expression of a new or traditional *kami* or god.

The vitality and dynamism of many larger Japanese new religions are linked to their close-knit organisational structure, where members find camaraderie and counselling. Smaller cell-groups within the religions serve as vehicles for the dissemination of teachings and are frequently the means for immense growth for the religions. In new religions that utilise this type of setting, it is often the case that senior members are responsible in part for the spiritual development of junior members and junior members in turn are invited to emulate the examples set by the leaders of the religion. The trend among many new religions that have arisen or gained prominence over the past two decades, however, is towards a more individualised practice. Organisational structures are less fixed and are designed to appeal to individuals seeking a more privatised spiritual experience, instead of the close networking of social relations featured in many of the older new religions. These more recent new religions promulgate through audio tape-recordings of teachings, videotape and publications, instead of home meetings, which allows the individual the freedom to pick and choose his or her own course of spiritual practice.

Proselytism is a prominent feature among many of the new religions and its emphasis in the groups' practice provides the impetus and means for growth. The ability of followers to successfully bring in new converts is linked to their spiritual development and successful proselytism is viewed as clear evidence of the legitimacy and significance of the particular new religion for contemporary society. Moreover, many Japanese new religions seek to spread their teachings to people and countries beyond Japan, establishing branches abroad and attaining an international presence that lends support to their perceived universal relevance. While there is ambivalence among the new religions concerning the use and direction of science and modern technology in contemporary society, Japanese new religions also deftly employ technological advances to help spread their message. Traditional print and media broadcast are commonly utilised to disseminate teachings or advertise their religious practices.

A sense of control over material and spiritual matters through the development and cultivation of spiritual faculties is one of the distinctive features among Japanese new religions and one of the main reasons why they are attractive to a large number of people. An emphasis on personal transformation, incorporates a wide range of individual and communal practices designed to refine one's character. Popularly referred to as *kokoro naoshi* (polishing the soul), such religious practices include on an individual level meditation and other psychological techniques for reaching higher levels of consciousness, chanting or fasting, and at the group level communal cleaning of parks, public toilets and other voluntary activities.

Experimentation with the spiritual dimension of life, which offers respite from the mundane world of work and study, is also a hallmark of Japanese new religions. Japanese new religions offer followers the opportunity to develop their own spiritual faculties or supernatural powers that provide the ability to perceive mysterious phenomena. The prominence of mystery and experimentation can also be viewed as an expression of the reaction against scientific materialism and increasing rationalism prevalent in modern society. Many view the established religions of Japan as exhausted and stagnant when faced with the challenges of modern life and turn instead to the new religions as an antidote to the perceived impotence of the older religious traditions. Critical of the failures of modernity, on the one hand, but aware of the limitations of a pre-modern world-view, on the other, individuals seek religious alternatives to address problems of spiritual, social and emotional malaise. Viewed in this light, Japanese new religions are a product of, and impetus for, religious change and dynamism in contemporary Japanese society.

Further reading

Davis, Winston (1980) *Dojo: Magic and Exorcism in Modern Japan*, Stanford, CA: Stanford University Press.

Hardacre, Helen (1986) *Kurozumikyō and the New Religions of Japan*, Princeton, NJ: Princeton University Press.

Inoue Nobutaka (ed.) (1991) *New Religions: Contemporary Papers in Japanese Religion*, Tokyo: Institute for Japanese Culture and Classics, Kokugakuin University.

JAY SAKASHITA

New Year

Since 1872, when Japan adopted the Western solar calendar, New Year celebrations and rituals have begun in the hours leading up to 12.00 a.m. of 1 January. Today, families are just as likely to take this rare cluster of holidays as a chance for an overseas vacation as they are to follow the tradition of travelling back to the main-branch household. Even so, this is a time of year when public and private rituals abound. Community celebrations are focused around neighbourhood or village temples and shrines. The midnight ringing of the temple bell at Japan's most famous New Year sites is broadcast annually on national television. Much of the ritual associated with New Year remains closely linked to agrarian traditions. While urban celebrations are generally limited to the first three or seven days of the new year, in rural areas there is a distinction made between these early celebrations of the Greater New Year and the more agrarian festivities and rituals of the Lesser New Year that fall around the fifteenth day.

Pine and bamboo displays welcome the god of the New Year at the entrance to homes. Special foods are painstakingly prepared and served in tiered lacquer boxes. Today these traditional dishes can be ordered and delivered to the home. Celebratory rice with soy beans, sweet soy bean soup and rice cakes are important dishes in this season and thick sweet sake is drunk to welcome in the New Year. The wide regional variations in rituals make for popular television viewing along with specially produced New Year historical dramas. A visit to the local temple or shrine to offer New Year prayers, purchase a new year talisman, sip sake and join in the often raucous celebrations remains a favourite way for many Japanese to see in the New Year.

SANDRA BUCKLEY

newspapers and magazines

In the 1870s, newspapers as a business took off in Japan. Early newspapers were divided into two types: first, opinion papers, or newspapers that served as sounding boards for political debate, known as *ō shinbun* ('big' newspapers) and, second, easy-to-read newspapers that centred on entertainment and were considered recreational reading, known as *ko shinbun* ('small' newspapers). Within a period of fifty years, the distinguishing characteristic of Japanese newspapers was the emergence of nationwide dailies like the *Asahi* and *Mainichi*, both of which boasted circulation figures of over 1,000,000 by the late 1920s. However, with Japanese newspapers and publishing companies reluctant to release their true circulation figures – a practice that continued until after the Second World War – it is difficult to establish exact circulation figures. National newspapers publish morning and evening newspapers and are primarily distributed on a subscription basis as a set. Nevertheless, nationwide newspapers are not the only newspapers to provide information. Local newspapers that cater to provincial concerns also have large followings. By the late 1920s, local newspapers such as the *Kahoku hinpō*, *Sanyō shinpō* and *Nagoya shinbun* existed throughout the country, and they, too, enjoyed a surge in circulation at this time. After the Second World War, the Constitution guaranteed newspapers freedom of the press. However, the practice known as self-censorship often curtails the reporting of issues related to such topics as the imperial family and religious groups.

By the 1920s, mass magazines had emerged as another media force to be contended with, a result, among other things, of industrial capitalism and the expansion of education. Women's magazines like *Fujokai* (Woman's World), *Shufu no tomo* (The Housewife's Companion) and *Fujin kurabu* (Woman's Club), which no longer catered to elite, upper-class women but a wide-based popular readership, were the first to achieve the status of mass-circulation magazines. Acquiring mass readership meant meeting the demands and wishes of a new, more diversified audience of readers. Noma Seiji, Kōdansha's founder, editor and publisher, was the mastermind behind the publication launch of *Kingu* (King) in 1925. *Kingu* became the first mass magazine to achieve a circulation of 1 million within one year of its founding, and it enjoyed the acclaim both of men and women in urban and rural areas.

From their inception, most newspapers and magazines, irrespective of their audiences, used fiction to attract readers. Illustrated serialised novels like Natsume Sōseki's *Wagahai wa neko de aru* (I Am a Cat), *Hototogisu, mon* (The Gate) and *Meian* (Light and Darkness) were an important element in the emerging form of print media. This practice continues today. The emergence of newspaper and magazine magnates in the 1920s established the colour and tone for Japan's contemporary media. In the early 1920s, when plans for radio broadcasting began to materialise,

leading newspaper companies rushed to apply for permission to operate radio stations, fearing that radio would become a serious competitor to nationwide newspapers. However, at this time, the government refused their requests. Instead, a public corporation for radio broadcasting was established, which proclaimed broadcasting stations to be non-profit, 'private' organisations. In fact, with the establishment of Nippon hōsō kyōkai (NHK: **Japan Broadcasting Corporation**) in 1926, broadcasting fell under the watchful eye of the government. Since over half of Japan's families owned radios by the 1940s, it was fitting that the Shōwa Emperor's announcement of Japan's surrender in the Second World War and his own denial of divinity were both brought to the public by radio.

Following the Second World War, the newspapers' ambitions to enter broadcasting were finally realised with the first permission granted to establish commercial broadcasting stations. From that time, almost all newspapers had a capital investment in broadcasting. Indeed, the advent of television was but a step away. Today, five nationwide television networks have close capital and personal relationships with newspaper companies such as **Asahi shinbun**, **Yomiuri shinbun**, **Mainichi shinbun**, **Sankei shinbun** and **Nihon keizai shinbun**. After much haggling, NTV (**Nihon TV**), a private company established mainly with capital from Yomiuri shinbun, was the first to receive government approval for a television license in July 1952. Although NHK was the second to win government approval, actually it became the first to telecast on 1 February 1953. In addition to NHK, which exists primarily on fees collected from viewers, over one hundred privately owned television networks that depend on advertising revenue for their livelihood also operate actively. While the four main commercial stations (Nihon TV, **Fuji TV**, TBS or **Tokyo Broadcasting Systems** and Asahi Television) have their headquarters in Tokyo, all operate local television stations, though the parent companies assume most of the responsibility for programming.

In the case of magazines, with the exception of Iwanami shoten (**Iwanami publishing house**), which made its name by promoting paperback series, today's major publishers such as Chūō kōron, **Kōdansha**, **Bungei shunjū** and **Shoga-kukan** owe their successes to the publication of a diverse range of magazine genre. These publishers are also major players in the field of book publishing. Severe competition between publishers, the push to bolster advertising revenue and a lack of original planning is as worrisome in book publishing as it is in magazine publishing. Another profitable segment of the publishing industry is the area of popular print-based entertainment. Comics now constitute the largest segment in publishing and sports newspapers are the biggest sellers at newsstands. By the late 1960s, children no longer held a monopoly over comics readership. Shoga-kukan began publishing *Biggu komikku* (Big Comic), a weekly comic for adult readers, in 1968. Within ten years, it had amassed a circulation of over 10,000,000. It is perfectly natural to read comics in the company cafeteria and while commuting to and from work in Japan, where the *manga*/comic has a very different status from the comic book in North America.

Sports newspapers, in contrast to comics, are gender differentiated and targeted at a male reading audience. Like other tabloid newspapers, the headlines are in large print and in colour, and photographs are plentiful. Sports newspapers such as *Deirii supōtsu* (Daily Sports), *Hōchi shinbun* (Hōchi Newspaper), *Sankei supōtsu* (Sankei Sports) and *Tokyo supōtsu* (Tokyo Sports) not only contain the results of **baseball** and **soccer** games, boxing, wrestling, **tennis** matches, **golf** tournaments and fishing information, but also carry news on a more personal level that concerns the daily lives and gossip surrounding the athletes. Entertainment for men, like gambling (boat racing and horse racing), and information about drinking and sex are standard fare in sports newspapers. Comics, on the other hand, are published for both men and women. While comics generally are not read by people over fifty years of age, sports newspapers are enjoyed by men of all ages and classes.

The digitalisation trend in information industries has been influential in several ways. Because of the initial financial burden of digitalisation, broadcasting companies have been forced to look for varied and powerful investors. Digitalisation has seen the proliferation of over 200 channels. However, at this stage in development, it is unclear whether broad-casting stations will increase and become more diverse, or will decrease through a market-based rationalisation. Although NHK already has as many as eight television channels and radio stations, it would like to expand further, despite extensive criticism directed against the scale of this plan.

From the user's standpoint, digital communication, particularly **mobile telephones**, now glut the market. Over 50 per cent of young people, including high-school students, spend a significant amount of time each day on the phone and anywhere from $100 to as much as $200 a month for service charges. This is claimed to be an important reason why young people have cut down on their purchases of books and magazines. The print media's ability to adapt to the new digital platforms of information transfer and consumption will be essential to the publishing industry's survival into the future. No-one is seriously questioning the future of the book as yet in Japan, but what a book or newspaper might look like by 2010 and how books might be read are certain to be different from the familiar forms of today.

BARBARA HAMILL SATO

Ni tsutsumarete

By the end of the 1980s, Suzuki Shirōyasu and Kawanaka Nobuhiro had already established personal documentary as an experimental film genre (see **experimental film and video**). However, Kawase Naomi's *Ni tsutsumarete* (Embracing, 1992), a tender record of the director's search for a father who left her at age three, came to represent a new generation of young women filmmakers (see **women in the film industry**), including Miura Junko, Utagawa Keiko and Takefuji Kayo, who pointed their cameras at themselves and their families in order to explore their origins and identity. In Kawase's case, this use of the camera to establish personal relations was continued in her Cannes award-winning feature *Moe no Suzaku* (Suzaku, 1997).

AARON GEROW

NIGHTCRAWLING *see yobai*

NIHON BUYO *see* classical dance

Nihon keizai shinbun

Nihon keizai is the only national newspaper that primarily reports economic news. It was founded originally in 1876 as a weekly journal under the name *Chūgai bukka shinpo*. Although it became a daily newspaper in 1885, it was not until 1889, when it took the name *Chūgai shōgyō shinpo*, that general news articles were incorporated.

The newspaper went through a second name change in 1946, at which time it joined the ranks of other Japanese national newspapers under its present name *Nihon keizai shinbun*. The newspaper has domestic offices, which stretch from Hokkaidō to Kyūshū, and a large overseas network, as well. Its rise in circulation mirrors Japan's period of economic growth, particularly during the 1960s.

True to its name, *Nihon keizai* carries detailed accounts pertaining to domestic and international economic and trade issues, financial trends, stock information, changes in corporate personnel and other business-related matters. The newspaper takes pride in introducing up-to-date industrial developments and the latest commercial products. *Nihon keizai* has become indispensable reading for people interested in and connected with any aspect of the business sector.

In comparison with the **Asahi shinbun**, **Mainichi shinbun** and **Yomiuri shinbun**, the newspaper's layout and headings are extremely plain.

In the 1970s, *Nihon keizai* made an initial move towards becoming a media giant by publishing various books and magazines related to finance and management, and presently it plays an important role in publishing computer journals.

Present circulation – morning and evening included – is approximately 2,000,000.

BARBARA HAMILL SATO

Nihon no higeki

For one of the first films of the post-war period, the Allied Occupation enlisted the talents of producer Iwasaki Akira and director Kamei Fumio, the only two film-makers to be imprisoned for war resis-

tance. Drawing on old propaganda films, Kamei used brilliant editing to offer an alternative history of the war. He demonstrated how information was filtered through structures of power, revealing the lies of the wartime media. The film was finally suppressed because its angry critique of the wartime leadership and the Emperor was not consistent with the SCAP decision not to pursue the Emperor as a war criminal, This decision set the tone for the Occupation's film policy and left Iwasaki and Kamei victims of their liberators.

ABÉ MARK NORNES

Nihon TV

Nihon TV (NTV) was launched in 1953 by the president of **Yomiuri shinbun**, Soriki Matsutaro, who applied for a television licence when he recognised the need for wider audiences to be established to satisfy the advertisers who would ultimately support commercial broadcasting. He set up big-screen television receivers in central public locations to encourage new viewers. Newspapers at the time reported traffic jams caused by the crowds that gathered to watch the broadcast of major events. NTV is the key station in the now extensive Yomiuri NNN (Nippon Television Network Corporation) network of thirty affiliates. The Yomiuri connection predictably has led to extensive sports coverage of baseball and, in particular, the Yomiuri Giants. The station also became renowned for its late night programme *11 p.m.*, which specialised in provocative content. News coverage is also a popular element of the station's programming, with the public perception that the shorter NTV news is a more accessible and popular news style than that of NHK.

SANDRA BUCKLEY

Nihonga

Nihonga (Japanese-style painting) is an aspect of Japan's modernisation project that began in the Meiji Period (1868–1912). Its goal was to at once preserve tradition in Japanese art and forge a modern cultural identity. While the tension between tradition and innovation inevitably marked the evolution of *Nihonga*, artists struggled to pay balanced attention to their own East Asian heritage and the expressive possibilities in Western painting.

In practice, *Nihonga* encompasses paintings executed primarily in traditional materials (e.g. ink and glue-based mineral pigments), supports (e.g. paper and silk) and formats (e.g. hanging scroll, handscroll, screen), although the medium has evolved considerably over the past century (e.g. the use of panels and synthetic pigments). The term, which literally means 'Japanese painting', was first coined during the 1880s as a means to distinguish the pictorial practice grounded in the native tradition of *shoga* (calligraphy and painting) from **yōga** (Western-type painting) that employed Western media, formats and modes of representation. As modern institutions of art, such as salons/exhibitions, schools, museums and art associations, were introduced, the distinction between *Nihonga* and *yōga* increasingly gained a divisive political significance.

Aside from aesthetic and formal matters, numerous other issues surround *Nihonga*. Above all, its history is closely tied to that of art institutions and art patronage in Japan. The intricate rivalry and comradeship between the Tokyo and Kyōto circles demands a nuanced reading of the evolution of *Nihonga* as a whole. Considered to embody Japan's cultural essence, it was a major ingredient in the government's cultural policies, including representation in the world's fairs and other international expositions, and its contribution to the formation of the nation's booming crafts industry was vital. In this light, its wartime role, though less visible than that of *yōga*, was significant and thus remains to be re-examined.

In post-1945 Japan, despite a number of efforts to revitalise it, *Nihonga* has been more often than not faulted for mindless craftsmanship and vulgarity of taste. As with the case of *yōga*, the crisis of *Nihonga* is generally attributed to art establishment politics involving the high-stakes art market, powerful and wealthy patrons and the traditional master–disciple relationship, the last of which is tightly intertwined with the rigid structure of the official salon and art associations in Japan. However, the fact remains that *Nihonga* is the most familiar and popular form of art today, still enjoying large audiences at exhibitions and in the print media.

Further reading

Conant, Ellen P., Owyoung, Steven D. and Rimer, J. Thomas (1995) *Nihonga: Transcending the Past – Japanese-Style Painting, 1868–1968*, St Louis: St Louis Art Museum.

Morioka Michiyo and Berry, Paul (2000) *Modern Masters of Kyōto: The Transformation of Japanese Painting Traditions – Nihonga from the Griffith and Patricia Way Collection*, Seattle: Seattle Art Museum.

TOMII REIKO

Nihonjinron

The *Nihonjinron*, or discourse of Japanese uniqueness, refers to the sort of publications, visual presentation and oral lecturing that are produced or performed in journalism, academia, schools and so forth, and has an obsessive focus on the unique and exceptional features of the ethnic Japanese. It purports to explain to the Japanese as well as to the non-Japanese audience in terms of cultural traits how unique and distinctive the Japanese are as an ethnicity. The authors of the *Nihonjinron* are mostly Japanese, but it has also been written and lectured about by non-Japanese authors. This type of discourse can be traced back to pre-war or wartime works such as Watsuji Tetsurō's *Fūdo* (Climate and Culture) and Ruth Benedict's *The Chrysanthemum and the Sword*, but it enjoyed an unprecedented popularity in the 1960s and 1970s. Since the 1960s, a variety of *Nihonjinron* have been produced: some insisted on Japanese uniqueness in reference to Japanese particularism (Robert Bellah), to Japanese language (Suzuki Takao), to some collective psychoanalytic trait (Doi Takao and Kawai Hayao) or to the Japanese sense of 'milieu' (Augustin Berque).

The conceptual scheme of the *Nihonjinron* is fairly simple. It draws upon a number of academic disciplines – cultural anthropology, national history, sociology, linguistics, philosophical anthropology, national literature, climatology, psychoanalysis and ethnography – in addition to the literary genres of autobiography and travelogue. Generally speaking, however, *Nihonjinron* does not require that the argument be organised consistently or open to cross-examination. It is often a mixture of auto-biographical travelogue with random references to academic writings in the humanities and social sciences. There are a number of unexamined assumptions without which the discourse of Japanese uniqueness cannot be sustained. First of all, the Japanese as a group must be an unproblematic given, so that Japaneseness is taken to be a natural, ethnic–national identity. The political or historical constitution of such an identity is rarely examined. Second, it is assumed that the ethnic Japanese share a national culture, which is represented according to the trope of an organic unity. To be Japanese means to internalise such a national culture. Third, the unity of Japanese national culture is supposed to coincide with the unity of the Japanese language. Therefore, the structure of the Japanese language is assumed to reflect the structure of Japanese culture, and vice versa. Fourth, the Japanese are the ones who speak the Japanese language as their native tongue, so that the Japanese are expected to be pre-programmed innately by their own native language.

Under these assumptions, the behaviour patterns of the Japanese are explained sometimes in terms of the nature of Japanese culture or sometimes by appealing to the structural features of Japanese language. Since culture, language and ethnic community are all understood as organically unified entities, the generous and unrestricted use of synecdoche is granted in the discourse of Japanese uniqueness. One instance can be referred to as exemplary of the Japanese as a whole; the observation of a particular case is generalised so as to determine the image of the Japanese people. Precisely because of laxity and the lack of critical precision in the discourse of Japanese uniqueness, its assumptions remain unexamined no matter what explanation about Japanese uniqueness may be forged. Also, the Japanese are unique almost always in contrast to the West; Japanese culture is predominantly identified in comparison or in co-figuration (that is, two terms figured in mutual reference to one another) with the putative traits of the West.

Consequently, *Nihonjinron* offers ideal opportunities in which the stereotypical images conceived of Japan by Westerners are repeatedly reproduced and preserved. In the discourse of Japanese uniqueness by Japanese authors these stereotypes are relatively positive and sometimes overtly narcissistic, while non-Japanese authors tend to offer negative stereotypes. Yet, the basic operation is always the same in that the West and Japan are figured in reference to one another in the manner of transference.

Nihonjinron insists upon the fixity of ethnic and racial identity, and should be viewed as a so-called 'differential racism' that appeals not to physiology but culture for the justification of its discriminatory practices.

NAOKI SAKAI

Nikkatsu Action

Nikkatsu Action, less a genre than mode or style that reigned at the Nikkatsu studio from the late 1950s to the early 1970s, was centred around young male stars like Ishihara Yūjirō, Kobayashi Akira, Akai Keiichirō, Shishido Jō, Takahashi Hideki and Watari Tetsuya. It encompassed many genres like the detective, gangster (see **gangster films**), spy and even cowboy film; it also experienced historical stages like 'mood action' and 'new action'. What defines the line as a whole is a hero who is constantly pursuing an identity distinct from society. The fact that post-Anpo (see **Anpo struggle**) society could not promise true fulfilment of this individual subjectivity seemed to explain why these heroes frequently operated in a *mukokuseki* (nationless) landscape divorced from the real Japan. The work of veteran Nikkatsu directors in Hong Kong strongly affected that cinema's action genre and the discovery of **Suzuki Seijun** abroad in the 1990s has spread the mode's influence to the West. Representative films include *Kurutta kajitsu* (Crazed Fruit), *Akai hankachi* (Red Handkerchief), the *Wataridori* (Rider with a Guitar) series, *Koruto wa ore no pasupōto* (A Colt Is My Passport) and *Kurenai no nagareboshi* (Red Shooting Star).

AARON GEROW

Nikkei in North America

Nikkei means 'of Japanese lineage', and refers to Japanese emigrants and their descendants, primarily in North and South America. Travel to other countries was forbidden by the Tokugawa government, but support for international *dekasegi* (temporary emigration for labour purposes) became a policy of the Meiji government, for whom rural unemployment was a problem. The first known permanent emigrant was Nagano Manzo, who went to Canada in 1977. A small group known as the *gannen mono* (first-year people) travelled to the USA in 1885. However, the major exodus of emigrants occurred to Hawaii, with a small number in 1868, and larger numbers through the 1880s, when thousands of *dekasegi* left Japan under labour contracts, the largest of which were with the plantation owners of Hawaii. They came primarily from the south-western parts of Japan, Kyūshū, Hiroshima, Okayama and, in the case of Canada especially, Wakayama and Shiga. Although the objective of such labour was to earn enough money to return to Japan and become better established in agriculture – and the majority did so – a significant number remained abroad, as the pioneers of today's *Nikkei* communities. Throughout the early decades, many moved to mainland USA and to Canada, where they worked in agriculture, fishing, sawmills and other primary industries. Today, the *Nikkei* make up the single largest ethnic group in Hawaii, and they have significant communities in Los Angeles, San Francisco, Seattle, Vancouver and Toronto.

The early *Nikkei* faced intense discrimination. They were denied the civil rights of other residents, such as the right to vote or to own property or hold public office. In the major cities, they lived apart in distinctive communities broadly referred to as 'Little Tokyos' (although, ironically, *Nikkei* from Tokyo were rare). The early communities were comprised almost entirely of men working on contract in the primary industries. Women came to join their husbands in large numbers only after official steps were taken to limit the free movement back and forth between North America and Japan, through 'Gentlemen's Agreements' written in 1906 in the USA, and in 1908 in Canada. Thence, many young women arrived as 'picture brides', in marriages arranged by the two families through

an exchange of photographs. While the men worked in primary industries, the largest number of immigrant women worked as domestic servants.

The economic bases of the early *Nikkei* communities varied. In Canada, *Nikkei* were by the First World War the largest single ethnic group in the sawmill industry, and their community on Powell Street in Vancouver was located close to that city's major mills. Other Canadian communities were established along the Pacific Coast, in fishing, mining and logging villages, and in the interior valleys in farming communities. In the USA, there were logging and fishing communities in the Pacific North-West, and farming communities throughout Washington, Oregon and California. The largest community in Los Angeles was heavily involved in service industries, most notably landscape gardening, where they still maintain a significant presence. The largely urban *Nikkei* communities were for the most part self-sufficient, with their own schools, churches, newspapers and services.

In both countries, *Nikkei* communities quietly but persistently pushed for the civil and economic rights enjoyed by other citizens, but made little progress. Immigration to the USA was completely cut off in 1924 and to Canada in 1928. During the 1940s, in response to public agitation against them, the two governments moved to uproot the 120,000 US and 21,000 Canadian *Nikkei* from their homes, and dispossess them of their property and rights. Actions against the *Nikkei* in Hawaii were limited, but the mainland US *Nikkei* were removed from the coastal areas and sent to internment camps. In 1943, when, as a result of a court case challenging the constitutionality of actions against them, the majority were released, most returned to their pre-war homes. Conditions for the Canadian *Nikkei* were much more harsh. The Canadian government held more sweeping powers than the US; *Nikkei* there were similarly placed in interior camps, in forced labour camps or sent to work as farm labour on the prairie provinces, but, although most were freed by the latter years of the war, they were not allowed to return to coastal British Columbia (whence more than 90 per cent had originated). Instead, they were forced to relocate either to eastern Canada or to Japan. Almost none of their property was returned, and the measures against Japanese Canadians were not lifted until 1949.

Rebuilding the shattered communities after the war was a long and difficult process. In the process, *Nikkei* communities became much more geographically dispersed, and largely urbanised, more so in Canada, where the government undertook official dispersal programmes and made it nearly impossible for many years for *Nikkei* to re-enter agriculture. Community institutions such as churches and co-operative associations had been dismantled during the 1940s, and, in their absence, the *Nikkei* became much more fully integrated into mainstream institutions. They also turned to education as a means of improving their social and economic conditions, so that, in both countries today, the younger generations are among the most highly educated of ethnic groups. They are also highly intermarried with other ethnic groups. Some social scientists have advanced a 'model minority' theory to account for this apparent success, but such interpretations are resisted by *Nikkei* communities. Over the past decade or so, there has been a renewed interest in *Nikkei* history, culture and community, motivated in part by the redress settlements that were signed in both countries in 1988. Since the settlements there has been a proliferation of *Nikkei* scholarship and artistic activity, and considerable investment in community infrastructure in the form of community centres, museums and artistic projects.

See also: Amerika Mura

Further reading

Adachi, Ken (1976) *The Enemy that Never Was: A History of Japanese Canadians*, Toronto: McClelland and Stewart.
International Nikkei Research Project, http://www.inrp.org.
Lyman, Stanford M. (ed.) (1977) *The Asian in North America.*, Santa Barbara, CA: ABC-Clio Books.

AUDREY KOBAYASHI

Nikken Sekkei Ltd

Nikken Sekkei Ltd, with approximately 2,500 employees, has long been the largest architectural firm in Japan. Originally an architectural design department of Sumitomo Corporation when first established in 1900, Nikken Sekkei went independent and took its current name in 1950 with a staff of only ninety-two people. Since 1950, it has completed well over 14,000 projects in Japan and in forty countries around the world, covering virtually every category of building type and project: office and other commercial buildings; industrial facilities; transportation projects; commodity distribution facilities; urban and site planning; and civil engineering works.

Nikken Sekkei provides engineering as well as architectural services. Unlike other big-name architectural firms, Nikken Sekkei does not promote individual designers' talents but has preferred to concentrate instead on its corporate (*kaisha*) image and highlight its teamwork capabilities. Nikken has been at the forefront of engineering and technological advances in architecture, creating numerous landmark buildings. For example, the San'ai Dream Centre of 1963 in Ginza, a cylindrical glass tower, was one of the first buildings to incorporate curved glass windows. According to Nikken Sekkei, it was also 'the first of a new building type to emerge in Japan in the 1960s – the multipurpose building whose main function is to communicate commercial information' (Frampton and Kudo: 111) by means of the building itself. The Palaceside Building (1966) excited public attention for maximising its height so near the private compounds of the Imperial Palace, not to mention for extending six floors underground. Two narrow rectangular buildings staggered to fit on the irregular site footprint and linked by a central corridor, the Palaceside Building's design is marked by unusually long spans for its square office bays and by service cores housed separately in two flanking cylindrical towers. The Pola Cosmetics Home Office (1971) was one of the first projects in Japan to employ an integrated rather than separate double-core system, and its spans are more than double the length of those in the Palaceside Building.

The Shinjuku Sumitomo Building (1974), C. Itoh & Company's Headquarters (1980), the Shinjuku NS Building (1982) and the NEC Headquarters (1990) are examples of Nikken Sekkei's skyscrapers that develop various atrium concepts and reveal Nikken Sekkei's impressive in-depth studies of this architectural form from both functional and aesthetic viewpoints. Other widely known and significant Nikken Sekkei projects within Japan include: Tokyo Tower (1958); Narita Airport (Chiba, 1973); Nakano Sun Plaza (Tokyo, 1973); Portopia Hotel (Kobe, 1981); Toyota Head-quarters (Tokyo, 1982); Taisho Marine & Fire Insurance Co. Head Office (Tokyo, 1984); Chiba Port Tower (Chiba, 1986); Tokyo Dome (Tokyo, 1988); PACIFICO Yokohama (1994); Ōsaka World Trade Centre (1995); and Nagano Dome (1996) for the winter Olympic Games. Overseas Nikken Sekkei projects include the Headquarters for the Islamic Bank (Jeddah, Saudi Arabia, 1993); Korea World Trade Centre (Seoul, 1988); Cairo Opera House (1988); and the China World Trade Centre (Beijing, 1990).

References

Frampton, Kenneth, and Kudo Kunio (eds) (1990) *Nikken Sekkei: Building Modern Japan 1900 –1990*, Princeton Architectural Press: New York.

SCOTT GOLD

ninjitsu

Ninjitsu is the form of martial art that has captured much attention outside Japan, where it is often sensationalised for its association with supernatural skills. Meaning 'stealthing in', *ninjitsu* is the martial art form that developed within the samurai class around highly secretive techniques of espionage and assasination. The ninja were used to raid enemy castles and camps, and were frequently assigned to spying or killing missions. The art of *ninjitsu* is said to date back some 800 years but not a great deal is certain about its history or origins. According to folklore surrounding this somewhat mysterious martial art, ninja are said to have been trained from childhood in a wide range of knowl-edge and skills including not only fighting techni-ques but also meditation, alchemy, meteorology, explosives, astronomy and medicine. Utilising a wide array of technologies, ninja gained a reputa-tion for disguise, concealment, disappearing, rapid movement and extraordinary agility and balance.

Many of the popular Edo tales of ninja describe acts of flying, slipping through impossibly narrow spaces, walking upside down on ceilings, long periods without air and so on. At least some of these supernatural abilities may have simple explanations in the wide range of scientific knowl-edge that was integral to their training. There has been a revival of *ninjitsu* outside Japan since the 1970s, at least partly spurred on by the popularity of images of ninja in both Japanese and Western comics, film and television. There is little standar-disation across clubs or schools and the legitimacy of some claims of links to traditional masters are challenged by leaders of other martial arts. Concern has been expressed that, while there are legitimate clubs, there are also cases where a fascination with the ninja myth has become linked to street fighting techniques and the use of purportedly traditional ninja weapons – metal knuckle covers, short swords, fighting sticks and flying blades.

SANDRA BUCKLEY

Nintendo

In the early 1980s, a hundred-year-old Kyōto-based company pioneered a new 'platform' type of arcade-based video game, *Donkey Kong*, followed by *Mario Brothers*; the instantly popular games remain classics of the medium. In 1983, Nintendo released its home-based 'Famicom' system, quickly revitalis-ing the flagging home gaming industry. In 1985, this 8-bit system was released in North America as NES (Nintendo Entertainment System), together with its updated game, *Super Mario Brothers*. Soon Nintendo had captured 80 per cent of the world-wide home gaming market. A few years later, the company released the Gameboy, a hand-held game player featuring the wildly-popular *Tetris*.

In 1989, although Nintendo had designed a more powerful machine, the company inexplicably held back its release. This allowed rival company Sega to swoop in with its 16-bit machine and innovative games to take over most of Nintendo's market.

In 1996, Nintendo released an even more powerful, 64-bit system. Also, in May 1999,

Nintendo finalised a deal with IBM and Matsushita to produce the next generation of video game players in a DVD format. Nintendo remains the best-known icon of the video game revolution, especially with the smashing popularity of *Pokemon* on Gameboy in the late 1990s.

SHARALYN ORBAUGH

Nippon Telegraphic and Telephone Corporation

Nippon Telegraphic and Telephone Corporation, or Nippon Denshin Denwa, is known in Japan by the acronym of its English translation, NTT. Before privatisation, NTT was a public corporation. Both before and after privatisation, it was positioned as the largest provider of telephone networks, with 71 per cent of the market in 1998. All other carriers have to rely on NTT local networks for access to domestic households.

NTT established fully automated telephone services from 1958 and facsimile services were added in 1973. NTT was capitalised at ¥780 billion in 1985 when it was launched as a joint stock company under a holding company. There had been pressure for a complete break-up of NTT, but finally it was divided into east- and west-coast businesses under a holding company and allowed to develop an international network. While NTT's limited capacity for network expansion and slow service were frequently cited reasons for the slow uptake of Internet access in Japan, the company has undergone a renaissance since the inception of its mobile service provider DoCoMo. NTT is now the innovator and market leader in new 3-G technologies utilising the mobile phone as a platform for digital communications. It has powerful alliances with Microsoft, with plans for 3-G technology launches early in the first decade of the millennium. NTT has been traditionally focused on the domestic telephone market and this remains true of DoCoMo with the vast majority of mobile subscriptions limited to domestic use. Access to international networks remains costly and largely the domain of corporate and institutional subscriptions.

See also: Kokusai Denshin Denwa; mobile telephones

SANDRA BUCKLEY

Nixon shock

On 15 July 1971, US President Richard Nixon surprised the world by announcing his upcoming visit to the People's Republic of China, effectively ending decades of US hostility toward Beijing. Tokyo, which had recognised Taiwan instead of mainland China in 1951 under US pressure and had faithfully followed the US policy, was not consulted and was notified only minutes in advance. Nixon's decision to bypass Tokyo, which was partly influenced by his frustration with Japan's position in the failed textile talks underway at the time, caused widespread and lasting indignation in Japan and brought about the resignation of the Sato Cabinet. A few months later, a new Japanese Prime Minister would make his own visit to Beijing and established diplomatic relations with China.

Exactly a month later, on VJ Day, President Nixon delivered another shock with his New Economic Programme, which included the unilateral abandonment of the gold standard. This new policy brought about a major increase in the international value of yen. Together, these shocks signalled a new era in post-war US–Japanese relations, in which Japan could no longer expect preferential treatment from the USA.

See also: US–Japan relations

Further reading

Kusano, A. (1987) *Two Nixon Shocks and Japan–US Relations*, Research Monograph No. 50, Princeton: Princeton University Woodrow Wilson School Center of International Studies.

YANG DAQING

nō

Originally a product of the fourteenth century, the *nō* theatre has come to be viewed as a more historical repository of 'traditional' Japanese identity. Western texts on Japanese economic practices use *nō* masks for cover photos, while Japanese newspapers describe the workings of the national Diet as *nō*-like. Post-war avant-garde theatres, movie directors and even *anime* creators have all used elements of the *nō* as a means of referring to fundamental Japaneseness. Although only a very small percentage of the population actually attends the performances, the *nō* has continued to play an important role in post-war imaginings of what it is to be Japanese.

Centred around just one principal character (the *shite*), *nō* performances consist of: a set of musicians (drums and flute), sitting stage right; a chorus, sitting stage left; and the actor himself. The *shite*'s lines are shared alternately by the chorus and by the actor, and in a sense the 'character' is produced out of the ensemble of the musicians, the chorus and the actor's dance. The structure of the plays themselves, the stage properties and the acting style all are formed in such a way as to deny reference to the immediate world of the present. Props are almost non-existent; the most ubiquitous object is a fan, which can be used to symbolically represent almost anything.

The plays are written in archaic poetic language, and all of the actors' movements are slow and fully choreographed (there are approximately 200 fixed movements, or *kata*) – there is thus no intrusion of the everyday. The stories, too, almost uniformly carry one from the present to the past. Typically starting out in the 'present', in the latter part of the play the present is revealed to be in truth some well-known world in Japan's literary past, with which the *shite* longs to be (and sometimes is) reunited. In all of these ways, the *nō* is focused on a more stable, originary (if mystical) past, rather than on a present-oriented world of change. The plays draw on imagery from a variety of sects of Buddhism, Shintō and other Japanese ritual practices.

Although the *nō* began under the patronage of fourteenth- and fifteenth-century shōguns, much of the theatre as it exists today was formalised only in the early modern Tokugawa Period (1600–1868). Many of the definitive characteristics, including the stage, the slow speed, some of the acting styles, etc., were codified under law by the Tokugawa shōguns,

who were themselves interested in presenting an image of timeless continuity rather than worldly change. The Tokugawa shōguns made the *nō* their official ceremony of state, and used the *nō* to help create a state-wide system of ritual performances, which helped to unite provincial lords under the control of the shōgun. It was only in the Meiji Period (1868–1912), however, that the *nō* came to be associated with a national Japanese identity. During an early ambassadorial trip to Western countries, Iwakura Tomomi (1825–83) was taken to the opera. Though Iwakura had previously found the *nō* uninteresting, in this new context, he came suddenly to think that the *nō* was an absorbing and appropiate counterpart to the West's opera. Iwakura was then instrumental in governmental decisions to use *nō* as an appropriately native Japanese drama for the entertainment of foreign diplomatic visitors. This decision was bolstered by the reaction of foreign visitors, notably US President Grant, and Minnie Hauk of the Prussian Court, who praised the beauty of the *nō* as 'Japan's most ancient drama'.

In the immediate post-war era, unlike **kabuki**, the Occupation forces allowed the *nō* to continue largely as it was. *Kabuki*, for them, was thought of as a Tokugawa-era product, and therefore potentially 'feudal' in character – in opposition to the allied forces' aims of promoting capitalist democracy. The *nō*, on the other hand, was taken to be a more innocent form from a more distant time – the tie of the *nō* to the Tokugawa shōguns was ignored – and thus was not subject to censorship in the way that *kabuki* was. This image of the *nō* as free of political and economic interest, and as in essence a pre-modern form, has been institutionalised by post-war scholarship. Scholars have tended to focus primarily on *nō*'s fourteenth- and fifteenth-century history, and especially on the writings of Zeami Motokiyo (1363–1443), considered along with his father Kanami Kiyotsugu to be founders of the *nō*.

Patronage of the *nō* in the post-war period has come primarily from private sources, but by the mid-1970s the national government was also contributing substantial support. In 1982, a national *nō* theatre building was constructed in Tokyo. The national educational television station broadcasts *nō* plays on New Year and other public holidays, so that the *nō* continues to serve as a marker of something like a national ritual calendar. Perhaps the most significant post-war development has been the new popularity of *takigi* (bonfire) *nō*. *Takigi nō* is held outdoors, ideally under torchlight though electric lights are now often used. Originally it had religious connections, as with the Kasuga shrine in Nara. However, as its popularity increased dramatically in the post-war period, largely following the growth of Japan's economy, by the 1980s towns, shrines and temples throughout Japan had created their own *takigi nō* celebrations. *Takigi nō* performances are typically more casual than indoor *nō*, and they have brought in a broad new audience; generally, these performances are viewed as entertainment spectacles rather than moments with great depth of meaning.

The five traditional *nō* schools (Kanze, Hōshō, Komparu, Kongō and Kita) have remained conservative in approach, keeping to a canon of approximately 250 plays and discouraging innovation. In 1959, a *shite* actor from the Kanze school (Kanze Hideo) was asked to leave the traditional *nō* world for becoming too involved with acting in non-traditional plays, movies and other projects, though twenty years later he was allowed to return. Traditional schools have, however, made some attempts to expand beyond the many 'returns to Zeami', and in the 1990s a revivalism movement sought to expand the possibilities of *nō* by resuscitating plays that had gone unperformed for 200 or more years. A very few newly written plays have been performed by these schools, such as Yokomichi Mario's *The Hawk Princess* (based on William Butler Yeats's use of the *nō* in *At the Hawk's Well*). Avant-garde theatre directors such as Suzuki Tadashii have long used the *nō* in more experimental blendings of theatrical styles, and bilingual projects initiated with Western actors have had long-standing success.

While the *nō* traditionally is performed exclusively by men, women none the less are integral. The amateur actor associations that provide a large percentage of funding for the *nō* are populated by far more women than men – men more commonly simply practice the chanting. The first foreigner to become an official member of the Nō Association (*Nōgaku Kyōkai*), as a *shite* actor, was a woman (Rebecca Teele). By some measures, the *nō* at the end of the twentieth century found itself in one of its most successful eras. Leading actors from the five *nō* schools collectively have well over a million students, the number of performances is higher than at any previous time and actors themselves say quality is higher than it once was.

Further reading

Brandon, James (ed.) (1997) *Noh and Kyōgen in the Contemporary World; Noh-Kyōgen*, 3 vols, Honolulu: University of Hawaii Press.

Keene, Donald (ed.) (1970) *Twenty Plays of the Noh Theatre*, New York: Columbia University Press.

Komparu Kunio (1983) *The Noh Theater Principles and Perspectives*, New York: Weatherhill/Tankosha.

Komparu Nobutaka (1987) *Takigi Noh*, Tokyo: Gurafikkusha.

Nakamura Yasuo (1971) *Noh, the Classical Theater*, New York: Walker/Weatherhill.

TOM LOOSER

NOH *see nō*

Noise Music

'Noise' is a contested term, as hybrid and inchoate as the acoustic cultures it refers to. These gathered critical mass in the mid-1980s through bands like the Boredoms and Hijō Kaidan.

About the only thing that artists active for nearly twenty years like Haino Keiji share with sound experimenters like Ikeda Ryōji and Makigami Kōichi, pop-influenced bands Melt-Banana and the Boredoms or sampling artists such as Ōtomo Yoshihide is a complicated, often antagonistic relation to post-war 'information culture'. Disidentification with information and narrative might be manifested in live performance or recording through high volume and density, distortion, interference and polyphony, manipulation of sound objects and technology, alternative networks of production and distribution, and a sense of pleasure in dissonance for both performer and listener.

Like techno-pop and Japanese *musique concrète*, recorded noise took from the 'official culture' of electronic music inaugurated upon the NHK electronic music studios' founding in 1955. Noise also fell under the sway of the post-aleatory avant-garde, as well as prog rock, psychedelia, punk's do-it-yourself anti-aesthetic and free-jazz improvisation (see **jazz, free**). Noise artists such as Akita Masami (Merzbow) see noise as a conceptual category that serves as the abjected unconscious of music.

Select discography

Tokyo Flashback, vols 1–4 (PSF).

ANNE McKNIGHT

Noma Bungei Prize

The Noma Bungei Prize can be awarded in three categories: literature, scholarship and the fine arts. It was established in 1941 by a bequest of Noma Seiji (who died in 1938), the founder of the **Kōdansha** publishing empire. The prize is normally awarded once a year and the categories in which prizes are awarded are often varied, so that, for example, in 1957 the women novelists **Enchi Fumiko** and Uno Chiyo won the award for their novels *Onnazaka* (The Waiting Years) and *Ohan*, respectively, but in 1958 the cultural critic Kobayashi Hideo won it for his study *Kindai kaiga* (Modern Painting).

The list of authors awarded this prize reads like a roll-call of the intellectual elite of post-war Japan. It includes both Japanese Nobel Prize-winners for literature, **Kawabata Yasunari** and **Ōe Kenzaburō** in 1954 and 1973, respectively, for their novels *Yama no oto* (Sound of the Mountain) and *Kōzui wa waga tamashii ni oyobi* (The Floodwaters Have Come unto My Soul), and the distinguished critics Yoshida Ken'ichi and Etō Jun, both in 1970, for their studies *Yoroppa no seikimatsu* (*Fin-de-siècle* Europe) and *Sōseki to sono jidai* (Sōseki and his Times).

LEITH MORTON

noodles

The two main types of noodles eaten in Japan are *soba* (buckwheat-based) and *udon* (wheat-based).

Noodles are most often eaten in a steaming-hot broth but are also served cold in the summer with a light dipping sauce on the side.

The buckwheat *soba* noodle is thin and round, and can be brown or bleached white. A green variety of *soba* is produced with the addition of green **tea** to the dough mix. *Udon* are usually a flat noodle and are wider and bulkier than *soba*. Noodle shops offer speciality and regional varieties that include, among other flavourings, *shiso* (Japanese coriander) flakes, chilli, garlic, sesame seed and cracked pepper corns. Many Japanese soup- and broth-based meals end not with a bowl of rice but the addition of noodles to the steeped broth. Noodle chefs fiercely guard the secret of their basic broth. The director Itami Jūzō even produced a movie about one chef's struggle to create the perfect noodle broth. Noodles are a popular quick lunch and snack food, and noodle restaurants and bars abound. Instant cup-noodles have proven a successful fast-food export for Japan, while, at the other extreme, beautifully presented box sets of high-quality noodles are a frequent choice of seasonal gift.

SANDRA BUCKLEY

nopan kissa

A contraction of '*no panty kissaten*' the term describes a popular but limited phenomenon that emerged from the early 1980s. Faced with a downturn in business with the economic slowdown and the proliferation of cheap clubs and **pink salons**, some *kissaten* sought to pull back clients by offering something more than the traditional fare of light food and drinks. '*Nopan*' waitresses offered tantalising glimpses as they bent over tables and counters, or, in some extreme cases, walked across reflective glass surfaces. The trend was generally short lived.

SANDRA BUCKLEY

Northern Territories, return of

In 1945, in accord with the Yalta agreement, Soviet troops occupied and began developing the Kurile islands, which extend north from Hokkaidō. Japan had gained jurisdiction over the Kuriles in an agreement of 1875, and built military facilities there during the war. Disagreement over the islands' ownership forced Japan and the Soviet Union to sign a declaration rather than a peace treaty in 1956. Japanese movements for return of the so-called Northern Territories (*hoppō ryōdo*) have been co-ordinated by the Northern Policy Head-quarters (Hoppō Taisaku Honbu), which was created in 1972 by ex-Prime Minister Satō Eisaku and remains under the Prime Minister's office; they have also been funded largely by the Japanese government. Most movement activists are former residents of the islands, although some conservative politicians and businessmen, fishermen and others also participate. A broader movement has been impeded by disagreements and confusion relating to the issue, strong economic incentives to co-operate with Russia, the absence of Japanese residents on the islands and the ageing of former residents.

Further reading

Stephan, J. (1974) *The Kuril Islands: Russo-Japanese Frontier in the Pacific*, Oxford Clarendon Press.

J. VICTOR KOSCHMANN

nostalgia boom

Nosutarujii is a term now completely integrated into everyday Japanese. It found its way into the mainstream of popular culture over the 1970s at the hand of the copy writers and market research-ers of such major advertising companies as Dentsu. The focus of the original wave of nostalgia advertising campaigns were the cultural artefacts and everyday objects of the Meiji and Taishō Periods. The cultural details of Japan's early modernity became the commodity fetishes of a Japan moving rapidly into its own particular articulations of early post-modernity. The so-called new or third generation of Japanese (*shinjinrui*) led

the consumer trends in everything from fashion to travel, food, literature and television dramas. It even became popular to select children's names from speciality publications listing popular girls and boys names from the Meiji and Taishō Periods, names long abandoned as old fashioned. It was the first generation of young women workers of the post-war period whose disposable income became the primary target of many of the nostalgia consumer campaigns. The 1970s Discover Japan tourism campaign launched by Japan National Railways typified the marketing strategies of the initial nostalgia boom. Whether the promotion of rail travel to historical and famous sites in Japan, the popularisation of rustic village-style furniture and artefacts, or the marketing of traditional recipes for fast foods, the nostalgia boom crafted an imagined relationship to a historical past. This allowed a post-war generation of young consumers the first opportunity to identify positively with a notion of Japaneseness, and encouraged them to look back comfortably through a lens that carefully crafted a past edited for popular consumption and artificially cleansed of the lingering issues of wartime memory and responsibility that still haunted both the past and present of older generations. In this way, the initial nostalgia boom in Japan is perhaps best understood not as a simple longing for a distant past but as being deeply implicated in mechanisms of forgetting that have been essential to imagining Japan's post-war present. Nostalgia remains a popular mechanism for triggering consumer interest and buying with even the 1960s and 1970s now having found there way into more recent nostalgia campaigns in the media and advertising.

Further reading

Ivy, M. (1995) *Discourses of the Vanishing: Modernity Phantasm Japan*, Chicago and London: University of Chicago Press.

SANDRA BUCKLEY

O

Ōba Minako

b. 1930, Tokyo

Writer

Ōba Minako is one of the most well-known women writers of contemporary Japan. She was born the eldest daughter of a naval doctor. Her family moved frequently during her childhood due to her father's profession. Ōba experienced the effects of the war years first-hand when her school was appropriated as a factory site. By the end of the Second World War, she and her family were living just outside Hiroshima. The memory of witnessing the mushroom cloud over Hiroshima and the experience of being conscripted to care for bomb victims in the aftermath of the atomic explosion have together had a significant but implicit role in shaping her concerns as a writer over the years. Ōba has seldom spoken openly of her work as an aid worker among the *hibakusha*, though she admits that the memories of the period haunt her still.

Ōba claims that her desire to become a writer dates back to her first reading of Victor Hugo at age eleven. T.S. Eliot and Dostoevsky are important influences she has often named in discussing the emergence of her distinctive narrative style. Ōba agreed to marry several years after graduation, at the age of twenty-four, on the condition that her husband would not obstruct her desire to pursue her writing. They moved together to Alaska in 1959 as a result of her husband's work and remained there until 1970. She states that much of her attention was taken up with her role of housewife over this period. Despite this, she took

advantage of this time away from the constraints of the normative expectations a Japanese housewife would have faced in Japan in order to travel extensively alone in Europe. It was the publication of her short story 'Sanbiki no kani' (Three Crabs) in 1968 that brought her instant acclaim as a writer in Japan. The work was awarded both the **Gunzō** Literary Prize and the **Akutagawa Prize**.

Ōba's writing is frequently described in terms of the intensity of her depiction of the desires of both the men and women who inhabit the pages of her texts, and the intricacy of the psychological workings of the complex and unpredictable characters she crafts. Ōba has never championed herself as a feminist but her work has been well received by feminist critics in Japan for the strength and depth of her women characters. Ōba's women have a credibility often lacking in post-war representations of Japanese women written by well-known male writers. They are also a far cry from the subtle style of questioning of traditional roles that characterised the work of some other post-war women writers of a slightly older generation, such as Ariyoshi Sawako and Sata Ineko.

Ōba wrote two other short stories that were also published in 1968, 'Kōzu no nai e' (Formless Painting) and 'Niji to ukihashi' (The Rainbow and the Floating Bridge). Ōba was not only skilled in the portayal of complex personalities but also became known for her capacity to capture the wild, harsh and unpredictable beauty of natural landscapes: a coast shrouded in fog in 'Kiri no tabi' (Journey Through Mist), the threatening wilderness of 'Higusa' (Fireweed) and the desolate and remote island burial ground of 'Aoi kitsune' (Pale Fox).

The themes of uncertainty and fragility of both national and individual identity continued to be developed in detail in her long novel, *Urashimasō* (Urashima Grass). It was in *Sanbiki no kani* that Ōba first demonstrated her extraordinary skill at crafting highly charged dialogue, a trait that her readers have come to anticipate in her writing. The electric exchanges between the female protagonist Yuri and her husband weave a picture of a marriage that falls outside the stereotypes of Japanese married life. Language is never innocent as it passes between Ōba's characters.

In *Sanbiki no kani*, as in so many of the works that would follow, Ōba questions the absoluteness or stability of the identity of her characters, throwing them into circumstances that test their own sureness of how well they know themselves. Her montage-like movement back and forth through time and space also acts to disrupt any familiar sense of the unfolding of a character for the reader. This movement keeps the history of the characters and the events of the story in flux just as it prevents identity from settling comfortably or predictably on anybody moving through the pages of Ōba's texts.

Ōba has gone on to win various prestigious awards as she continues to weave her tales of unfamiliar but ordinary people traversing unfamiliar (though often Japanese) locations. She won the 14th Women's Literature Prize in 1976 for 'Garakuta hakubutsukan' (The Garbage Museum) and the 1982 Tanizaki Prize for her novel *Katachi mo naku* (Shapeless). There is no doubt that Ōba is one of Japan's best post-war writers and hopefully as more of her work is translated she will find herself a well-deserved place in the forum of contemporary world literature.

See also: literature; women's literature

Select bibliography

Ōba Minako (1985) 'The Pale Fox', trans. S. Kohl, in Van C. Gessel and Tomone Matsumoto (eds) *The Showa Anthology Vol. 2*, Tokyo: Kōdansha International.

—— (1984) 'The Three Crabs', trans. Y. Tanaka and E. Hanson, in Y. Tanaka and E. Hanson (eds) *This Kind of Woman, Ten Stories by Japanese Women Writers 1960–76*, New York: G.P. Putnam's Sons.

—— (1982) 'The Smile of a Mountain Witch', trans. N. Mizuta Lippit, in N. Mizuta Lippit and K. Iriye Selden (eds) *Stories by Contemporary Japanese Women Writers*, New York: M.E. Sharpe.

—— (1981) 'Fireweed', trans. Marian Chambers, *Japan Quarterly* 28(3).

—— (1980) 'Sea Change', trans. J. Bester, *Japanese Literature Today* 5 (March).

SANDRA BUCKLEY

obentō

Obentō (boxed lunches) are Japanese meals, packaged in boxes, which are portable. *Bentō* (o is honorific and both *bentō* and *obentō* are commonly used) refers to the container, a box that is laquer or wood for special occasions and plastic, metal or disposable cardboard for everyday use. The boxes are small – rarely larger than 7×5 inches (though they are bigger for special occasions or rituals, as at **New Year**) – and have partitions (often removable) to separate different foods. The aim is to prepare an entire meal that can fit, compactly yet elegantly, into the confines of the *bentō*. The culinary principle thus duplicates that of Japanese food more generally; there should be multiple courses, all small and presented in a plethora of morsels, dishes, tastes, textures and colours. The *mélange* of dishes that covers a Japanese table at mealtime thus is reproduced in the *obentō* where multiple courses are packed into a box to be transported and eaten elsewhere.

The tradition of *obentō* goes back for centuries, but, like the tea ceremony, it was originally a custom reserved for ritual occasions and adopted more by ritualists and elites. Recently, however, *bentō* have become much more a fixture of everyday life; sold at train stations (*ekiben*), small shops, department stores, sports stadiums and kiosks, they are the Japanese version of carry-out fast-food. Office workers eat them for lunch, tourists while travelling, families on outings and flower-viewers while gazing up at cherry blossoms. The commodified form of *obentō*, as common as it is, however, is based on the homemade version with its associations of loving mothers making fresh, delicious and eye-pleasing food for their families. The management of home and hearth by mothers, in contrast to fathers, is still strong in Japan and food is both a representation and icon of domestic attachments. The same attentiveness mothers often devote to meal preparation at home, particularly dinner time, is carried through in the *obentō* they send with their children to school (and sometimes work for an older child still living at home).

While children eat school-prepared lunches during grade school and middle school, they bring *obentō* during their nursery-school and high-school years (though schools differ somewhat). Mothers making *obentō* spend as much as thirty minutes each morning. They prepare multiple-coursed meals (averaging five separate courses, according to one friend), carefully arranged and prepared to please as much as feed their child. The principles that guide this *obentō* making are nutrition, beauty and freshness; the aim is to design the contents using contrasting colours and textures, give a balanced meal and add fresh foods that are appealing to the eater. Husbands may also receive *obentō* from wives though workers often go out for lunch these days. A typical *obentō* would be a three-sectioned box with rice (which appears in most *obentō*) in the largest section, *tempura* and sesame-seeded spinach in the other two, pickles in a tin cup, slices of apple in another tin and a plastic container with *tempura* sauce. A pickled plum dots the rice. Wrapped in a *furoshiki*, *bentōs* are accompanied by chopsticks, (spoons, if needed), napkins, cups and, sometimes, additional containers. Ideally, the appearance is neat, orderly, pretty and appealing: the perfect meal.

Further reading

Allison, Anne (1996) 'Japanese mothers and obentōs: The lunch box as ideological state apparatus', in *Permitted and Prohibited Desires: Mothers, Comics, and Censorship in Japan*, Boulder, CO: Westview HarperCollins, pp. 81–122.

Richie, Donald (1985) *A Taste of Japan*, Tokyo: Kōdansha.

ANNE ALLISON

obi

The *obi* is the sash worn with kimono. The *obi* we are familiar with today came into wide use from the Edo Period. A woman's *obi* can be 3–4 m in length and 30 cm wide. The silk material of the *obi* is stiff and there is an art to tying the special ornamental knots that secure it. Today, all women wear the *obi* tied to the back but it was traditionally worn to the front by married women. Men's *obi* can also be stiff but are narrower and knotted more simply. Another style for men is a long and much wider soft silk *obi* that is folded over into a narrow band worn below the waist. A woman's *obi* is worn high on the waist, girdling the mid-section and flattening the breastline.

SANDRA BUCKLEY

Obon

Obon (the Festival of the Dead) is officially set between 13 and 16 July, according to the Western solar calendar, but it is widely celebrated on the same dates in August much closer to harvest celebrations in rural areas. This period of ritual and festival is a mix of both Buddhist and earlier indigenous practices and beliefs. Families pay for a priest or nun to visit family graves or household *butsudan* and offer prayers for the souls of long-dead ancestors, while other prayers are offered for the souls of more recently deceased family whose spirits still linger between this world and the next. In addition to these clearly Buddhist ritual prayers and offerings, there are many other rituals that mark *Obon* which run counter to Buddhist prohibitions, including the giving of gifts of raw fish and the offering of wild meats and fish to the souls of ancestors at the *Tama Matsuri* (festival of souls). On the night of the 13th, lights are placed outside the home to guide the ancestors back while in the countryside families will walk to and from the graveyard with paper lanterns. Various offerings accompany the many festivities and rituals of the next days and these are all finally placed in a small vessel and floated down a stream or out to sea. In some locations these rafts are set alight, creating a beautiful spectacle. In some areas, a small bonfire in the temple grounds symbolises this same sending off of the spirits. **Fireworks** are an integral part of *Obon* celebrations and this festival season is especially known for its *Obon* dances (*bonodori*). The late-summer evening scene of families clad in cotton **yukata** and walking through the popular food and game kiosks that surround the local temple at *Obon* is a favourite image often drawn upon by Japanese writers and film-makers.

SANDRA BUCKLEY

Occupation literature

The **Allied Occupation** of Japan lasted nearly seven years, from 2 September 1945 until 28 April 1952. The Occupation government, known as SCAP (**Supreme Commander for Allied Powers**), was headed by General Douglas **Mac-Arthur**. From September 1945 until September 1947, the Civil Censorship Detachment (CCD) of SCAP was responsible for the 'pre-censorship' of all printed matter in Japan: newspapers, magazines, books, dramatic scripts, etc. Pre-censorship meant that all these materials had to be submitted to SCAP prior to publication. In October 1947, most books and magazines were transferred to 'post-censorship'. Although CCD's responsibilities continued formally until October 1949, very few items were subjected to examination after December 1948.

Pre-war censorship within Japan had been capricious and punishments sometimes severe, with leftist sentiments and pornography the most frequent targets. In contrast, SCAP was seen as surprisingly lenient toward sexual explicitness and freedom of political expression, although anything that appeared 'ultranationalist' was expressly prohibited. Some writers took advantage of the new freedom to explore the sexual body in ways that had been impossible in pre-war Japan.

There were, however, relatively severe limits placed on depictions of the atomic bombings. Some *hibakusha* writers' accounts of their experiences were written soon after the bombings, but could not be published until 1949. Graphic depiction of food shortages, fraternisation between Allied personnel and Japanese citizens or Allied soldiers' involvement with the black market was also forbidden.

The *Dai-san no shinjin* (third generation of new writers) who emerged prominently during this period were for the most part young men with military experience. They included Yasuoka Shōtarō, Kojima Nobuo, Shimao Toshio and **Endō Shūsaku**. In general, the Occupation period writing of these young men is dark, sometimes humorous, sometimes surrealistic, but always expressing a sense of disempowerment and humiliation – the psychological effects of life under Occupation. A typical story is Kojima's 'Kisha no naka' (On the Train. 1948). The story's protagonist, Sano, is a teacher, whose material wellbeing and social status have been decimated by the war. On a long train ride from the countryside, where he has obtained black-market rice, Sano experiences multiple incidents of humiliation and discomfort, while his impatient wife berates him for being feckless. In the end he is robbed of his hard-won rice. In contrast, the fiction produced by Occupation women writers tends to focus on the day-to-day realities of life – the difficulty of surviving and caring for children alone in the ruined cities, in the midst of food shortages worse than those of wartime. Women's fiction also explores the new types of families being created after the chaos of war. A typical example is Hayashi Fumiko's 'Dauntaun' (Downtown, 1948), which features a young widowed mother, Riyo, who, after the war, meets a repatriated soldier abandoned by his wife while he was imprisoned in the Soviet Union. The two begin a new life together in the ruins of downtown Tokyo, but, when the man is suddenly killed in an accident, the woman once again has to struggle on alone. Despite her feelings of despair, Riyo finds hope in the kindness of other struggling survivors.

SHARALYN ORBAUGH

OCHIKOBORE *see* drop-outs

Ōe Kenzaburō

b. 1935, Shikoku

Writer

At the award ceremony for the 1994 Nobel Prize for Literature, Ōe Kenzaburō gave an acceptance speech titled 'Japan, the Ambiguous and Myself'. It was, of course, a parody of the acceptance speech presented by Kawabata Yasunari when accepting the same award some three decades earlier, 'Japan, the Beautiful and Myself'. In this speech, Ōe, though full of admiration for Japanese literature as envisioned by Kawabata, nevertheless made a courageous break from that tradition. Instead, he laid claim to the heritage of the generation of Japanese post-war writers and expressed an affinity with writers and poets from all parts of the world, such as Yeats and Kim Chi-ha.

Ōe Kenzaburō was recognised as a talented, up-and-coming writer even before he graduated from the French department of Tokyo University. Under the tutorage of the renowned scholar of French literature Watanabe Kazuo and heavily influenced by Sartre, Ōe wrote short stories such as 'Kimyō na shigoto' (A Strange Odd Job) and 'Shisha no ogori' (Lavish are the Dead), works that to this day are still considered among his best. Ōe was awarded the Akutagawa Prize in 1958 for 'Shiiku' (Prized Stock), a pastoral yet intense tale of a young boy's coming of age during the chaotic days at the end of the Second World War. 'Shiiku', together with *Memushiri kouchi* (Nip the Bud, Hit the Child), led the critic Etō Jun to locate Ōe at the vanguard of a 'New Literature'.

The Anpo Movement (see **Anpo struggle**) of the early 1960s, protesting the Mutual Security Treaty with the USA, was a turning point for Ōe's writing. His provocative and highly politicised essays and novels became a must-read for college students involved in the campus uprisings of the day. He was the youngest member of a group of Japanese writers who visited China in 1960 and was often sought out as a spokesperson for his generation. Ōe's politics brought an end to his amicable relations with Etō Jun and a long-term antagonism developed between Ōe and more right-leaning writers such as Etō, Ishihara Shintarō and Mishima Yukio.

After a number of novels, some highly controversial, Ōe's life was changed and his writing career redirected by the birth of his eldest son, Hikari, in 1963. Hikari suffers from a brain defect and is severely retarded. In the summer of the same year, Ōe took a research trip to Hiroshima to investigate the victims of the atomic bomb. The convergence of these two events produced works that detail his life with his son, such as *Sora no kaibutsu Agui* (Agui the Monster in the Sky) and *Kojinteki na taiken* (A Personal Matter), as well as an essay collection meditating on human dignity and resilience in the face of catastrophe, *Hiroshima nōto* (Hiroshima Notes). Gone were the frustrated, cynical and nihilistic young men who populated his early works. Instead, a thoughtful, pensive and mature persona emerged from his writings, prepared to take on the burdens of an imperfect world yet struggling to find a hope of salvation. Ōe's subsequent sojourns in Okinawa and North America provided him with an awareness of the impact of global geo-politics on landscapes and localities, and, interestingly, also made him re-examine his own personal journey. Influenced by Mikhail Bahktin's ideas of carnivalistic energy and grotesque realism, and by the theory of margin and centrality advocated by anthropologists Victor Turner and Yamaguchi Masao, Ōe completed his massive masterpiece *Man'en gannen no futtobōru* (The Silent Cry). In this work, which was awarded the Tanizaki Prize, he traced the origin of his imaginative energy back to the tiny Shikoku village where he was born and raised. Ōe would further explore the same themes in an even more fantastical and mythical format in *Dōjidai geemu* (The Contemporaneous Game) and *M to T no mori no fushigi* (M and T and the Magical Forest).

Ever a prolific writer, Ōe toyed with the idea of retiring from writing after his Nobel award. Fortunately, this ominous prophecy did not materialise and Ōe continues to write. His humanistic outlook on life and global vision assure that his literature will remain a beacon of social conscience to his generation.

Select bibliography

Ōe Kenzaburō (1996) *A Healing Family (Kaifuku suru*

kazoku), trans. Stephen Snyder, New York: Kōdansha International.

—— (1996) *An Echo of Heaven (Jinsei no shinseki)*, trans. Margaret Mitsutani, New York: Kōdansha International.

—— (1994) *The Pinch Runner Memorandum (Pinchi ranna chosho)*, trans. Michiko N. Wilson and Michael K. Wilson, Armonk, NY: M.E. Sharpe.

—— (1989) 'The Clever Rain Tree' ('Atama no ii reintsurii'), trans. B. de Bary and C. Haynes, in Van C. Gessel and Tomone Matsumoto (eds) *The Showa Anthology, Vol. 2*, Tokyo: Kōdansha International.

—— (1985) *The Crazy Iris and Other Stories of the Atomic Aftermath*, ed. with an introduction by Ōe Kenzaburō New York: Grove Press.

—— (1995) *Hiroshima Notes (Hiroshima nōto)*, trans. David L. Swain and Toshi Yonezawa, New York: Marion Boyars.

—— (1977) *Teach Us to Outgrow Our Madness: Four Short Novels*, trans. John Nathan, New York: Grove Press.

—— (1974) *The silent cry (Man'en gannen no futtobōru)*, trans. John Bester, New York: Kōdansha International.

—— (1969) *A Personal Matter (Kojinteki na taiken)*, trans. John Nathan, New York: Grove Press.

FAYE YUAN KLEEMAN

office ladies

Office ladies or OL, as the name suggests, refers to women hired to provide support for male colleagues by performing roles traditionally associated with women. Formerly known as *shokuba no hana* (literally, office flowers), they are seen as decorative but insubstantial and transient. OLs are hired to perform light secretarial duties including photocopying and to serve tea to clients and male co-workers. Japanese employers expect women to fulfil the roles of 'company wife' or 'cute daughter', roles that confirm women's subordinate position and define them primarily in family terms (see **gender and work**).

On recruitment, women workers seeking full-time work face a 'choice' between pursuing a career-track, *sōgō shoku* (a career-track employment path similar to their male co-workers), or a clerical track, *ippanshoku*. Jobs for OL in the clerical track are badly paid with poor conditions and few opportunities for training and promotion compared with colleagues in the career-track. The trade-off for OLs is that they are rarely expected to work beyond 5 p.m., with little expectation of attendance at after-work socialising.

The lack of both challenging employment opportunities and adequate childcare policies, combined with social expectations and management pressure ensure that the majority of OLs quit after marriage or the birth of the first child.

KAYE BROADBENT

ofuro

Although the term *ofuro* literally means 'bath', its cultural significance goes far beyond the concept of bodily cleansing. Bathing is one of the most significant rituals in the Japanese day, and one of the most important practices through which interpersonal relations are acted out.

In traditional rural settings, the *ofuro* was housed separately from the main residence, and consisted of a wooden, copper or iron tub. In the metal tubs, which could be heated directly with a wood fire, a wooden plank floated on top of the water, to be submerged by the weight of the occupant's body as protection against direct contact with the hot-tub sides. In urban areas, only wealthy houses boasted private *ofuro*; most people attended neighbourhood public bathhouses, *sento*, featuring large common bathing areas, usually segregated by gender. Nowadays, most private homes have interior *ofuro*. The style varies from a small, simple tub of moulded fibreglass that is part of a mass-produced bathroom complex, to large elaborate pools in wealthier households. Many people, including students who live in small, modest quarters, still use the *sento* on a regular basis. Even those with a bath at home still occasionally attend the *sento* for it is a place as important for social gathering as for bathing.

The *ofuro* has two primary design features. It is intended for use in a seated, rather than a reclining, position; and it is intended for soaking only. Washing is done on a small stool outside the tub.

Typically, one washes cursorily before entering the tub for a long soak, then spends a lengthy time outside scrubbing the body thoroughly, using a variety of specially designed brushes and washing cloths. One then rinses thoroughly and re-enters the tub for another soak.

The etiquette of the *ofuro* expresses the gender and age structure of the household. It is the duty of the wife/mother to clean and fill the *ofuro* each evening. It is the prerogative of the head of the household to enter the *ofuro* first, followed in order by elders, sons and daughters in order of diminishing age and, finally, the wife/mother. Small children commonly bathe with their mothers. Guests are invited to enter first, with exhortations to please bathe *go-yukkuri* (take as much time as you like). Conversely, those leaving the *ofuro* always offer a ritual apology to the next person in line for having gone before.

The etiquette of communal bathing also follows clear guidelines. While nakedness is not considered shameful, it is rude to stare. Conversation flows freely in the *sento*, but with eyes averted. It is customary to cover genitals, especially while standing, with a small white towel that is also used for washing and, when wrung out, for drying.

In contemporary Japan, the more expedient daily shower has become more and more popular, but it is still important for most people to be able to relax in the *ofuro* at least once or twice weekly.

See also: hot springs

Further reading

Clark, Scott (1992) 'The Japanese bath: Extra-ordinarily ordinary', in Joseph J. Tobin (ed.) *Re-Made in Japan: Everyday Life and Consumer Taste in a Changing Society*, London and New Haven: Yale University Press, pp. 89–105.

AUDREY KOBAYASHI

Ogawa Shinsuke

b. 1935, Mizunami; d. 1992, Tokyo

Film director

Expelled for political reasons from Kokugakuin University, in 1960 Ogawa joined Iwanami Productions where he met directors such as Tsuchimoto Noriaki and Kuroki Kazuo. He became independent in 1963 and established himself a director in 1966 with a documentary on the student world, *Seinen no umi* (The Sea of Youth). His militant type of cinema was best expressed in a documentary series dedicated to anti-**Narita Airport struggle**, a true picture of human nature captured in the everyday life of the local people. A similar sensibility is realised in the portrait of the rural life in Magino, Yamagata prefecture, in *1000 nen kizami no hidoke – Magino mura monogatari* (Magino Village – A Tale, 1986). Ogawa was a pioneer of the influential Yamagata Documentary Film Festival.

MARIA ROBERTA NOVIELLI

oil shocks

After the outbreak of the Fourth Arab–Israeli War in October 1973, Arab members of OPEC announced a price hike of crude oil and an incremental reduction of oil exports to countries that were friendly with Israel. The announcement produced an immediate impact on Japan – the largest oil-importing country with less than two months of oil reserve – and set off a nationwide panic. Housewives began hoarding daily necessities ranging from laundry detergent, sugar and salt to toilet paper. The government faced stark choices. Some LDP politicians proposed price control laws reminiscent of the wartime controlled economy, but this approach was eventually rejected. The Tanaka Cabinet instead adopted Urgent Measures on Petroleum Policy, raising the oil price 1.4-fold to suppress overall demand and cope with price inflation. Altogether, Japan reduced oil imports by 20 per cent and reset its oil reserve to thirty days.

As three quarters of Japan's total energy consumption depended on imported oil, the crisis effectively ended the decade of double-digit economic growth and produced negative real growth rate for the first time in the post-war period. In 1974, retail prices rose 31.4 per cent, while consumer prices rose by 24.3 per cent. The crisis also produced long-term consequences. In response to labour union demands for pay increases, companies began to hire more part-time workers and low-cost female workers during and after the recession. Japanese factories enforced strict energy-saving measures, thus hastening the ongoing shifts in the industrial structure from high-energy-consumption heavy industries such as steel and petrochemical to more value-added industries. Subsequently, Japan's oil imports never again reached the peak level of 1973. Overall, recovery was quick and Japan's economy registered a respectable 8.7 in 1975.

Japan was hit with another Oil Crisis later in the decade. After the Iranian Revolution of 1979, Arab oil-producing countries again reduced production and nearly doubled oil price over the next two years. Drawing from lessons of the first crisis, the Japanese government resorted to monetary policy by raising interest rates to curb capital investment. As a result, despite the rising cost of imported oil, the government was able to successfully control price inflation in Japan.

As 85 per cent of Japan's imported oil came from the Middle East and North Africa, the Oil Crisis brought about some adjustments in Japan's Middle Eastern policy. In November 1973, Japan followed European countries and called on Israel to return the territory occupied in the 1967 war and to respect the rights of Palestinians under the UN charter. Vice-Cabinet Minister Miki Takeo was dispatched on a special mission to the Middle East to explain Japan's new policy. At its meeting in December, OPEC agreed to treat Japan as a friendly country and restored the oil supply quota to pre-crisis levels. On the other hand, Japan's support for Palestinian independence, as well as its friendly relations with Iran after 1979, would in turn complicate its relations with the USA.

Further reading

Miyoshi, S. (1974) 'Oil shock', *Japan Quarterly* 21(2): 143–51.
Sato, R. and Suzawa, G. (1983) 'Japan's adjustment to the oil shocks and labor productivity growth', in *Japan Relations: Towards a New Equilibrium*, Cambridge, MA: Harvard University.

YANG DAQING

Okabayashi Nobuyasu

b. 1946, Shiga Prefecture

Singer and songwriter

Okabayashi is the single most identifiable icon of the politicised wing of 1960s Japanese folk music, the Ōsaka underground folk scene. His message songs gave great energy to the political movement, student resistance and anti-war movement from 1968 to 1971. Like Dylan in the USA, he participated in a general shift from folk to rock.

Okabayashi's first performance at an underground music festival was in March 1968. His first record went on sale in September 1968, 'Yamatani Blues'/'Tomoyo' (Companions). 'Kusokuraebushi' (The Eat Shit! Ballad) was supposed to be his first release, but its sale was banned due to the lyrics: 'The Emperor also depends on *kami* (paper/gods) in the toilet.' His first album, *Danzai seyo* (Condemn me), was released in August 1969 and his second, *Miru mae ni tobe* (Leap Before You Look), in June 1970. On the second album he was backed by the rock group **Happy Endo**. In 1971, Okabayashi suddenly quit music and moved to the country. He seldom appeared on stage after this, but in 1975 **Misora Hibari** recorded his song 'Tsuki no yoru kisha' (Train on a Moonlit Night). In 1985, he again began performing live. As he entered the 1990s, he began to explore traditional Japanese folk song (*minyō*).

Further reading

Kato Chikara (1994), in *1970 Musician's Dictionary*, Tokyo: Gakushū Kenkyūsha, p. 26.

MARK ANDERSON

Okinawa

Until 1879, the Ryūkyū archipelago (which now forms the Japanese Prefecture of Okinawa) was an independent kingdom, though the Ryūkyū Kingdom had long paid tribute both to China and to the southern Japanese domain of Satsuma. Archaeological finds show that the archipelago was inhabited at least 17,000 years ago. Around 6,000 years ago, the northern islands of the archipelago were home to people who created shell-mounds and used pottery similar to that found in Honshū, while the southern islands seem to have been more closely linked to South-East Asia. Between the twelfth and fifteenth centuries of the common era, communities in the Ryūkyūs centred around large fortified stone 'castles' known as *gusuku*. (Some 300 *gusuku* sites still remain in Okinawa today.) Gradually, political control was consolidated into three kingdoms, and in 1429 the kingdoms were united under the control of the Shō Dynasty, who ruled the Ryūkyūs until their incorporation into the Japanese state. During the early part of the Shō period the kingdom became a thriving centre of trade with connections stretching from South-East Asia and China to Japan and Korea in the north. In 1609, however, the Ryūkyūs were invaded by the southern Japanese domain of Satsuma, which forced the Kingdom to pay tribute to Japan. Despite heavy tax burdens imposed by Satsuma, however, the Ryūkyū rulers continued to maintain close links to China. During the seventeenth and eighteenth centuries, local crafts such as textile weaving were also developed to a high level. The brightly coloured *bingata* textiles regarded as characteristic of Okinawa culture began to be widely used during this period.

After the incorporation of Okinawa into the modern Japanese state in 1879, Okinawans were subject to assimilationist policies. Particularly after Japan's defeat of China in 1895, assimilationist policies were introduced to replace Okinawa's distinctive religious traditions with emperor-centred Shintō and to enforce the use of 'standard Japanese' language. The Okinawan language is commonly treated as a dialect of Japanese, though Okinawan and modern 'standard' Japanese are mutually incomprehensible. During the first part of the twentieth century, the speaking of Okinawan in schools was prohibited, and children who disobeyed this rule were forced to wear 'dialect tags' as a mark of disgrace. At the end of the Pacific War, Okinawa became the only part of Japan to experience a land invasion. Some 150,000 inhabitants were killed during the 'iron typhoon' of the Battle of Okinawa in 1945. After Japan's surrender almost all of the surviving population of Okinawa were interned by the Allied forces, and many returned home from the internment camps to discover that their land had been taken for use as military bases. Besides, although the post-war peace settlement resulted in the restoration of sovereignty to Japan under the 1951 Treaty of San Francisco, Okinawa continued to be occupied by the USA until 1972. Heavy handed Occupation policies and human rights violations by the US military created strong popular support for a movement demanding the reversion of Okinawa to Japan. The movement reached a peak during the 1960s, and contributed to the decision to end the Allied Occupation, officially announced in 1969. Since the return of Okinawa to Japanese rule in 1972, however, the continued presence of US bases has remained a crucial issue of debate; by the mid-1990s, Okinawa Prefecture, with 0.6 per cent of Japan's land area and 1 per cent of its population, contained 75 per cent of the land allocated for US bases in Japan. Economic inequalities between Okinawa and Japan have also been a continuing subject of contention. Okinawa consistently comes last in the ranking of prefectures by GNP per capita. Development policies directed towards Okinawa have focused on large-scale tourist and infrastructural projects, which have caused severe environmental disruption in many parts of the archipelago. Some local citizen's movements therefore call for an alternative model of development based on smaller-scale and more environmentally sensitive approaches. During the 1990s, the bases issue became the focus for strong demands by many Okinawans for greater local autonomy. A widespread anti-base movement emerged in 1995, after the rape of a local schoolchild by a group of US servicemen. This has led to plans to scale down and reorganise the bases. Many see the reorganisation plans, however, as merely transferring the bases problem from one part of the islands to another. In response to the distinctive social and political concerns of the region, some Okinawans call for a devolution of power that would allow the archipelago to play a more active role as a bridge between Japan and other parts of Asia, and some have even put forward demands for independence. On the other hand, others emphasise the need for Okinawa to become a more active and assertive participant in Japanese national life. Recent years have seen not only political controversies but also a cultural revival movement centred particularly on traditional forms of music and crafts such as pottery and textile weaving.

TESSA MORRIS-SUZUKI

Okoge

Directed by Nakajima Takehiro, the 1992 film *Okoge* is representative of Japanese 'gay boom' cinema from the early 1990s in its suggestion that male homosexuality offers heterosexual women an alternative space of relationships to patriarchy. Critically successful amid an increased visibility of male homosexuality in the Japanese media, *Okoge* received art-house distribution in Europe and the Americas, where it was frequently hailed as breaking 'taboos'. The film's departure, albeit a limited one, from homophobic stereotypes, its depiction of gay male sex and its strong dose of humour also contributed to *Okoge*'s international reputation, despite the disturbingly simplistic logic of its story.

See also: homosexuality and Japanese film

JONATHAN M. HALL

omiyage

The custom of buying souvenirs for family and friends and for oneself while travelling has a long history in Japan. Traditionally, the souvenir was a local speciality that could range from tea, to rice cakes to weaving or wood carving.

Contemporary travellers still actively seek out **meibutsu** (famous local goods) to bring home. The streets leading up to tourist attractions are lined with local speciality shops and if you miss the chance to buy a souvenir in town there are always souvenir outlets at stations and airports. This custom has done much to support Japanese cottage industries, which have relied heavily on the trade in souvenirs in the modern period. The buying power of Japanese tourists has also significantly shaped an international market in souvenirs heavily weighted towards Japanese taste. A major goal of Japanese travellers overseas is to hunt down appropriate gifts for family and friends at home. The honeymoon couple is under particular pressure in this regard, for the souvenir is an important gesture of thanks to all those who contributed cash gifts towards the wedding and honeymoon. The targeting of luxury brand goods as both personal souvenirs and gifts by Japanese international tourists has also had a major impact on that high-end market.

SANDRA BUCKLEY

onigiri

These firm rice cakes are formed through repeated pressing and rotation of the cooked rice granules in the palm of the hand until a tight, solid shape is formed, most often a triangle. At the centre of an *onigiri* is a small, bite-sized, tasty treat: salmon, pickled vegetable, sour plum, tuna. The rice cake is then wrapped in toasted seaweed. *Onigiri* are extremely popular both in lunchboxes and picnics. Recently, more gourmet *onigiri* have found their way on to phone-order delivery menus in upmarket business districts. Railroad concessions and fast-food outlets sell single, wrapped *onigiri* for both breakfast and lunch. Green tea and *onigiri* remains a favourite snack for all ages.

SANDRA BUCKLEY

onomatopoeia

Onomatopoeia in Japanese is abundant. It is a sound symbolism to describe actual sounds (*giongo*) such as the sound of wind (*pyūpyū* or *byūbyū*), actual voices (*giseigo*) such as a dog's barking (*wanwan* or *kyankyan*) or someone's laughter (*hahaha* or *hohoho*), movements and situations (*gitaigo*) such as '*suisui oyogu*' (swim smoothly) and emotive feelings (*gijōgo*) such as '*ujiuji suru*' (to be bashful or hesitant). Whereas in English sound words are most often found in cartoons and comics in varied forms of noun, verb, adjective and adverb, onomatopoeia is frequently used in both spoken and written Japanese and is an important element of the language. It is usually classified as an adverb. '*Giongo*' and '*giseigo*' are often followed by a particle '*to*' or are used by themselves. '*Gitaigo*' and '*gijōgo*' are often followed by either particle '*to*' or '*ni*' and are used by themselves. Some onomatopoeic words are closely linked with specific verbs, thereby forming an idiomatic expression. On the other hand, new onomatopoeic words, '*giongo*' and '*giseigo*' in particular, can be easily understood from the context and you can create your own with ease. They are extremely popular in advertising. A few examples have derived from Western languages such as '*chikutaku*' from 'tick-tock' and '*jiguzagu*' from 'zigzag'.

SHUN IKEDA

organ transplants

The majority of organs available for transplant are taken from patients who have been declared brain dead. In Japan, after thirty years of contentious debate, the organ transplant law was passed in October 1997, making the condition of brain death legally recognisable as the end of human life, but only under very specific circumstances. Prior to this law, though the criteria for brain death was recognised by the Japan Medical Association in 1985 and skilled physicians and necessary technologies were available, it had not been possible to carry out organ transplants except by using living donors. As a result, some Japanese patients in their desperation have gone overseas to receive transplants.

The first heart transplant performed in Japan was carried out in Sapporo in 1968, but the surgeon was arrested for murder shortly thereafter, although the charge was dropped for lack of evidence three years later. This case is widely recognised today as one of malpractice and deception, and it set the tone for the public debate that followed. Over the years, twenty other doctors have been charged with murder in connection with organ procurement from brain dead bodies, but none have been convicted.

It is often assumed that opposition to recognition of brain death is due to religious beliefs or cultural tradition. Careful analysis suggests that a lack of trust in the medical profession is probably more important, particularly because informed consent has not been routinely practised in Japan. Many people believe that brain death might be prematurely declared in order to procure organs. The media has fuelled this mistrust. Television programmes have discussed such issues as the possibility of misdiagnosis, and sensationalised stories of healthy infants born from brain dead mothers.

Groups opposed to the recognition of brain death exist throughout Japan. They include doctors, lawyers and well-known intellectuals, and certain of these individuals appear regularly in the media. Surveys from several countries, including the USA and Sweden, have shown that people are often uncomfortable, as are the Japanese, with the idea of cutting into a very recently deceased relative. However, in North America, once brain death is declared, by far the majority of medical professionals and most families of brain dead patients believe that both body and person are dead. In contrast, in Japan, for perhaps the majority, a brain dead patient is still a living person, because life remains in the body. The person is not located, for most, in the brain. The Organ Transplant Law is designed to accommodate this position by permitting only individuals who have signed organ donor cards, and whose families are in agreement, to be declared legally dead should they be diagnosed as brain dead. Those people who have no declared intention of donating organs but who are diagnosed as brain dead are not legally dead until the heart stops beating. It was one and a half years after the law was passed before the first legal organ transplants making use of brain dead donors were carried out.

MARGARET LOCK

origami

The art of paper folding is closely linked to both religious ritual and gift-giving traditions in Japan. Before the Meiji Period, it was largely limited to the aristocratic class and was only widely popularised as the higher-quality paper used in origami became more affordable. Through a series of folds a flat sheet of paper is transformed into three-dimensional shapes ranging from a simple frog to the complex folds of a kimonoed woman of the court. The practice is thought to have come to Japan from China during the Heian period.

Traditionally, gifts were delivered with an ornamental or decorative origami attached. Symbolic folded paper was also linked to a number of Shintō events and rituals, ranging from the simple tying of knotted paper to branches when offering prayers to the more intricately folded white paper adorning ropes around a shrine or *torii*. Special shrine paper was also folded into shapes to represent sacred deities before important prayer events or festivals. The most familiar form of origami outside Japan remains the crane. It is one of the simpler foldings and the practice of creating a thousand cranes (*sembazuru*) strung and hung on thread as a gift for a friend at times of illness or hardship has spread among children outside Japan.

SANDRA BUCKLEY

Ōsaka

Ōsaka is the centre of the **Kansai** district, and Japan's second largest city after **Tokyo**. Ōsaka's recently expanded Kansai International Airport is also the second largest international gateway to Japan.

Ōsaka's background and reputation revolve around commerce. In a country where merchants were the lowest rank of the pre-modern class system, for this commercial focus it has always been looked down upon by the rest of Japan. It is a city of bustle, business and brusque entrepreneurial exchange. Ōsaka originated as the port for the Kansai area, in particular for **Kyōto**, which is only a half-hour away by fast train. It is known as the 'city of a thousand bridges' for the many bridges that cross its canals, but these are primarily for moving goods rather than for sightseeing.

The people of Ōsaka are untroubled by their rough image. They continue to speak a distinctive, low-pitched regional dialect, and to take pride in their cultural achievements, which include the development of *bunraku* (puppet theatre), and having been the birthplace of both the famous

haiku poet Bashō Matsuo and Japan's best-known playwright, Chikamatsu Monzaemon.

As a major transportation, manufacturing and commercial centre, Ōsaka was heavily damaged during the Second World War, much of the city reduced entirely to ashes. In the years after the war, new and substandard housing went up quickly, so that, by the 1960s, Ōsaka had the largest areas of slum housing in Japan. Over the past three decades, there has been considerable urban redevelopment, with much of the population, as well as much of the industry, being moved to suburban 'New Towns', large centrally planned developments, with a variety of housing and commercial services provided in town centres. In the past decade, the redevelopment focus has returned to the downtown, where in the **Umeda** district one may see examples of Japan's most innovative post-modern architecture, soaring over vast underground shopping complexes.

Ōsaka is also the home to three of the largest marginalised Japanese populations. The majority of the Japanese-Korean population (see **Koreans in Japan**) is in Ōsaka, many having been relocated there after being pressed into labour by the military authorities during the Second World War. In addition, Ōsaka has extensive neighbourhoods occupied by **Burakumin**, the people traditionally designated as outcastes in Japanese society. Both these groups have become much more strongly activist in recent years, advocating improvements in human rights and economic conditions, including improved housing conditions. They now have strong allegiances with dispossessed groups in other parts of the world. Finally, Ōsaka is the centre for the *yakuza*, Japan's controversial underworld organisations, whose distinctive style of dress is seen on many Ōsaka streets and in many bars and clubs.

AUDREY KOBAYASHI

Ōshima Nagisa

b. 1932, Kyoto

Film director

Regarded as the most influential film-maker of the Japanese New Wave generation, Ōshima Nagisa is also among the most controversial figures of Japanese cinema. He attended Kyōto University where he studied law and political history. Upon graduating, Ōshima began his film career in 1955 when he joined the film company Shōchiku, first as a screenwriter and later as a director. His earlier works had a gangster film sensibility with an abundance of sexually explicit and violent imagery, and always politically radical content. He gained recognition in 1960 with his second full-length feature *Seishun zankoku monogatari* (Cruel Story of Youth). In the same year, Ōshima left Shochiku when one of his films, *Nihon no yoru to kiri* (Night and Fog in Japan) was withdrawn from public screening by the studio for political reasons. His controversial break with the big studio led him to form his own independent production house. Like many of the post-war Japanese artists and intellectuals, Ōshima's films provide a commentary on the cultural and political tensions of post-war Japan. Ōshima himself, however, rejected his country's great cinematic figures and the history of Japanese cinema as a whole. He despised Kurosawa, Ōzu and other post-war humanists for their reliance on big budgets and their failure to engage with socio-political issues, and instead was more interested in the emerging feminist and French-inspired leftist movements, as well as European New Wave directors such as Godard and the Yugoslav director Dusan Makevjev. Accordingly, Ōshima's later works were characterised by their difficulty, which was designed to illicit a reaction from the audience, and was executed through techniques such as extreme long shots, voice-over narration and aggressive composition. Many of Ōshima's films in the late 1960s and early 1970s aimed their attack at the Japanese family structure. These included 1969's *Kōshikei* (Death by Hanging), and 1972's *Gishiki* (Ceremony), which showed the emptiness of Japanese values in the face of a politically repressive and authoritarian corporate society full of violent crimes, pollution and overcrowding. He is, however, best known for his 1976 film *Ai no korrida* (In the Realm of the Senses), which sparked a huge debate around censorship in Japan and abroad due to its graphic sexual content. In 1978, Ōshima received the best director's award at Cannes for the sequel of the film titled *Ai no borei* (Empire of Passion). His prolific filmography also includes two British co-produced films that were released in the 1980s, *Merry Christmas Mr Lawrence* (1983) and *Max, Mon Amour* (1986). After suffering from a stroke in 1996, Ōshima took a brief break from cinema. He recently returned in the spring of 2000 with *Gohatto* (Taboo), which was a Golden Palm Award nominee at the Cannes festival.

Further reading

Bock, Audie (1978) *Japanese Film Directors*, Tokyo, New York and San Francisco: Kōdansha International.

Desser, David (1988) *Eros plus Massacre*, Bloomington and Indianapolis: Indiana University Press.

Oshima Nagisa (1992) *Cinema, Censorship, and the State: The Writings of Nagisa Oshima 1956–1978*, trans. D. Lawson, Massachuset: MIT Press.

Turim, Maureen C. (1998) *Films of Oshima Nagisa: Images of a Japanese Iconoclast*, California: University of California Press.

LEILA POURTAVAF

Otaka Masato

b. 8 September 1923, Fukushima Prefecture

Architect

Otaka received his degree in architecture from the University of Tokyo in 1947. In 1949, he joined Maekawa Kunio's office, where he worked for several years. In 1961, he opened his own office in Tokyo. Otaka, together with Asada Takashi, Awazu Kiyoshi, Kawazoe Noboru, **Kikutake Kiyonori**, **Kurokawa Kishō** and **Maki Fumihiko**, was a founder of the Metabolist Group (see **Metabolism**) in 1960. Forwarding new directions in urban design, he and Maki collaborated in competition projects, including one for Shinjuku Redevelopment (1960) in Tokyo, and jointly published a study on 'group' forms in architecture and urban design. Somewhat akin to structuralist design methodologies, the study proposes a more flexible relationship between a formal/functional ensemble and its constituent parts than in traditional (modernist) compositions.

Otaka investigated these ideas in a series of urban projects such as a mixed-use development (1962) in Sakaide featuring an urban platform raised above the ground; and several buildings for Japanese agricultural co-operatives. His Tochigi Prefectural Conference Hall (1969), a prefabricated reinforced concrete structure that extensively utilises post-and-beam construction, demonstrates the principle of using a larger-scale 'primary' structural frame, and smaller 'secondary' ones in a system that arguably allows for easier changes in function and form. The largest, most successful – and best-known – project by Otaka to date is the Motomachi and Chōjūen High-rise Apartments (1973) in Hiroshima. As part of an extensive urban development along the river, the numerous multi-storey residential blocks have been laid out in a zigzag pattern so as to accommodate the lower-level community and commercial facilities among them in a park-like setting. The high-rise blocks benefit again from the combined system of construction: a 'primary' steel frame and 'secondary' reinforced concrete frame, well articulated also in the façades. In later designs, Otaka emphasises the role of some steeply pitched 'traditional' roof forms, which, as seen in the Gumma Prefectural Museum of History (1979) in Takasaki; and the Cultural Centre (1984) in Fukushima, was also one of the pre-occupations of several Metabolist architects.

Further reading

Bognar, B. (1995) *The Japan Guide*, New York: Princeton Architectural Press.

—— (1985) *Contemporary Japanese Architecture – Its Development and Challenge*, New York: Van Nostrand Reinhold, pp. 143–8.

Kurita, I. (ed.) (1970) *O tani sachio, Otaka Masato, gendai Nihon kenchikuka zenshu* (complete collection of modern Japanese architect), Tokyo, p. xviii.

BOTOND BOGNAR

otaku

The word '*otaku*' means 'you' in polite Japanese, so it is a puzzle how this commonplace word has come to designate millions of Japanese pop-culture fans around the world, particularly fans of **manga** and **anime**. In Japan, the word has connotations similar to 'nerd' or, worse, is even sometimes used to suggest an obsession bordering on psychopathy. Outside Japan, however, the term *otaku* is used for the most part positively among *manga* and *anime* fans to designate the true *aficionado*.

The origin of the term has been traced to Nakamura Akio, who used it in the title of a 1983 magazine column devoted to his impressions of the amateur *manga* movement, 'Otaku no kenkyū' (Studies of *Otaku*). The media, ever alert for new signs of youth rebellion, picked up the term and made it a household word. The *otaku* were presented as just the latest trend in the ongoing degeneration of Japanese youth after the Second World War – degeneration into infantile, irresponsible, individualistic non-conformers. University students who spent time reading and drawing *manga*, watching *anime* and memorising countless details about their favourite fantasy worlds instead of preparing for productive lives seemed to epitomise the faults of the '*shinjinrui*' (literally: the new humans) of the affluent 1970s and 1980s. However, while the *otaku* may share the *shinjinrui* fixation on the detailed perfection of consuming, they limit their consumer preoccupation to a single, often marginal, area of cultural practice rather than an entire '**burando**' lifestyle. *Otaku* are committedly anti-lifestyle. In the late 1980s, the word *otaku* came to be associated with Miyazaki Tsutomu, serial killer of pre-school-aged girls, because Miyazaki's apartment was found to be filled with *manga* and *anime* videos – many of them pornographic. Formerly, the term had often been used to suggest mildly aberrant social behaviour, but hereafter the media associated the word *otaku* with genuine psychopathy. In the early to mid-1990s, cultural critics produced an endless stream of analyses of the *otaku* as a new and negative phenomenon in Japanese society.

The term came to be used almost always pejoratively, to refer to a person who is obsessive about any of a wide range of hobbies. These include computers, non-animation television programmes and even something as obscure as shipping statistics – anything that requires detailed (but superficial) knowledge, and that can take up a lot of time without necessarily requiring regular human interaction. Although the term 'loner' is sometimes used to describe *otaku*, they are not necessarily isolated in their pursuits. Many of the new *otaku* subcultures are grounded in multimedia and Internet technologies that create intense levels of online communication and information sharing. While the Internet *otaku* may be isolated, she or he is often not alone but operating within a complex local to global network.

The term has also become widely popularised outside Japan in *anime*, *manga* and Internet circles where it has gained a global cultural currency that is far more positive than its Japanese origins. *Otaku* are not averse to gathering together to share and accumulate more information about their field of interest. Local, national and international *anime*, *manga*, RPG (role-playing games), video game and hacker conventions and trade shows draw massive numbers of *otaku aficionados*. Certain cultural texts gain cult status when they are taken up by an international *otaku* subculture, e.g. *Space Ship Yamato Gundam*, *Macross* or *Maison Ikkoku*. *Otaku* create entire online fantasy worlds around storylines and characters extrapolated from the original.

There is increasing evidence in Japan that *otaku* tend to be among the top-performing students and while they resist involvement in group activity they also reject participation in gangs and bullying. A high level of techno-fluency among children and home access to computers and multimedia equipment support the continued growth of hi-tech *otaku* subcultures in Japan. Some researchers of the phenomenon trace the roots of the *otaku* trend to the highly fragmented structure of areas of specialised knowledge in education, and the strong emphasis on fact-based learning and testing rather than critical thinking. The fragmented accumulation of detail is certainly a characteristic of *otaku* culture and has led to the popularisation of such labels as information fetishism and info-mania. The desire to resist the continued emphasis on group-oriented identity is another commonly cited influence among *otaku* and, again, new technologies play an important role in opening up channels of non-conformist networks of identity and cultural practice.

Further reading

Kinsella, S. (1998) 'Japanese subculture in the 1990s: Otaku and the amateur manga movement', *The Journal of Japanese Studies* 24(2): 289–316.

SHARALYN ORBAUGH AND SANDRA BUCKLEY

Ōzu Yasujirō

b. 1903, Tokyo; d. 1963, Tokyo

Film director

A prolific studio director and exacting film stylist, Ōzu Yasujirō achieved his current international prominence only after his death. Although his work won early acclaim among Japanese critics, his late overseas recognition can be attributed in large part to a carefully understated attention to the daily life of Japan's bourgeoisie and working class that confounded exoticist, Western expectations of Japanese film. Subsequently burdened both at home and abroad with the reductive label of being 'quintessentially Japanese', much criticism today continues to locate Ōzu in relation to a putative Japanese national identity at the risk of ignoring the formal experimentation and unique stylistic rigor that the director developed across an *œuvre* of fifty-three films in tandem with regular cinematographers, first Shigehara Hideo and later Atsuta Yūharu.

Ōzu was hired in 1923 by Shōchiku Studios, where he worked as an assistant cameraman and assistant director until directing his first film, a sword-fighting drama, in 1927. Although he would remain with Shōchiku across his career, Ōzu quickly abandoned historical settings in favour of the contemporary in films such as the comedic *Umarete wa mita keredo* (I Was Born, but, 1932), the gangster story *Hijōsen no onna* (Dragnet Girl, 1933) and the melodramatic *Ukigusa monogatari* (A Story of Floating Weeds, 1934). The latter genre of 'home drama' became Ōzu's speciality and his studio's most familiar commodity. Ōzu conceived the story for many of his films, receiving credit under the pseudonym James Maki, and worked frequently with noted Shōchiku screenwriter Noda Kōgo. After the war, Ōzu made some of his most well-known films, including *Bakushu* (Early Summer, 1951), *Tokyo monogatari* (Tokyo Story, 1953), the film widely considered his masterpiece, and *Samma no aji* (An Autumn Afternoon, 1962), his final film.

Ōzu's career also included military service in China from 1937 to 1939 and a stint making propaganda films in Japanese-occupied Singapore. Active across a broad swathe of Japanese film history extending from the so called 'silent-film' era through to two pre- and post-war 'golden eras' of Japanese film culture, this masterful director was a frequent recipient of Japan's top film awards, receiving the Kinema Jumpo first prize in three consecutive years in the mid-1930s, and winning even more numerous post-war honours. A director slow to adopt technological innovations such as sound and colour, and one who gradually narrowed down the range of narrative and cinematic elements found in his films, Ōzu has been portrayed widely in Western film criticism as a 'formulaic' master, as 'a uniquely Japanese director'. Such characterisations not only risk Orientalising stereotypes but end up ignoring Ōzu's experimentation and innovation in film form. Ōzu's use of a 360-degree space, which meant trumping conventions of classical Hollywood film-making, the distinctively low-height ratio of his camera and the narrative ellipsis of key story developments are some techniques that warrant careful viewing.

Further reading

Bordwell, David (1988) *Ozu and the Poetics of Cinema*, Princeton: Princeton University Press.

Desser, David (ed.) (1997) *Ozu's 'Tokyo Story'*, Cambridge, UK: Cambridge University Press.

JONATHAN M. HALL

P

pachinko

Pachinko is a vertical pinball game that is often claimed to be the single most popular leisure activity in the country. Once an inexpensive game where winnings were traded in for small prizes, biscuits, chocolates or cigarettes, Pachinko is now far more professionalised both in terms of gaming technology and the skill base of players. The clammer of ball bearings, clatter of mechanisms, dinging of bells and ubiquitous loud music entice passers-by in off the streets to line up for their plastic basket of ball-bearings and wait their turn for a favourite machine.

Pachinko is said to have developed in the immediate post-war years in Nagoya, where factories associated with wartime heavy industries found the manufacture of pachinko gaming machines a convenient alternative application of stocks of sheet metal, aluminium and ball bearings. The game flourished and so did the gaming industry. Pachinko was at first openly linked to gambling but the general crackdown on gambling in the 1950s saw a shift to token prizes. Only regular customers would still know where they could go to trade their chocolate bars and sweets for the real prize money. Initially, pachinko was played mostly by blue-collar workers and the parlours were concentrated around the stations and entertainment districts of working-class areas. However, by the 1960s, the games were becoming more sophisticated in design and pachinko parlours were springing up around stations everywhere and even on neighbourhood shopping streets. The Tulip model of the 1960s and Fever model of the 1980s attracted a broader base of pachinko loyalists, while computerisation over the 1990s has led to another generation of game that is faster, sleeker and potentially more attractive to the video game generation.

Dedicated pachinko players think nothing of spending $2–300 in a sitting. It is difficult, though, to estimate the full extent of the gaming economy generated around pachinko, but estimates placed annual spending in excess of US$200,000,000 by the early 1990s. This figure is certainly an underestimate due to the extent of the shadow economy surrounding pachinko. Critics link gaming culture to poverty levels and also question the solitary and addictive nature of pachinko. There are regular calls for research into pachinko addiction and the real extent of covert gambling linked to the parlours. The *yakuza* remain closely, if not openly, involved in pachinko operations, both through their control of large sections of the gaming industry and their involvement in gambling rings. In recent years, parlours have worked hard to enhance their image. Some parlours promote themselves as hi-tech, while others boast the best vintage models. Discount hours for the elderly and special family prize days are aimed at the home-makers and elderly left behind in the suburbs during the day. Many parlours have actively targeted a young female white-collar market. New façades, 'feminine' interior décor, smiling and attentive male hosts, more attractive prizes and dedicated 'ladies' corners' are some of the strategies for catching a larger share of the disposable income of this significant sector of Japan's consumer economy.

SANDRA BUCKLEY

part-time work

The construction of part-time work in Japan has changed during the post-war period, but this segment of the workforce has remained feminised. As a form of paid work, part-time work is increasing in significance, and is intrinsic to Japan's wider 'lifetime' employment. In the late 1990s, women comprised 73 per cent of the part-time workforce. The retail, wholesale and hospitality industries boast the largest number of part-time jobs with approximately 45 per cent of all jobs constructed as part time. Of the part-time employees in the private sector, almost half are employed in small companies (ten to ninety-nine employees).

Part-time work was introduced in factories during the war period, and viewed as auxiliary to the duties performed by the 'core' full-time workforce. The high industrial growth of the 1960s and the restructuring of the Japanese economy away from manufacturing to service industries in the late 1970s saw an explosion in the number of part-time jobs. Employers actively recruited married women to cope with the shortfalls in labour as the traditional source of labour, high-school leavers, continued their education.

Since the mid-1980s, the construction of part-time work has shifted. An important change has been the increase in the number of hours constituting 'part time'. Working hours in a growing number of part-time jobs are comparable to those worked by full-time women workers, but without the equivalent wages, benefits and conditions paid to full-time workers. In the 1990s, part-time work has evolved from simple repetitive tasks to, in some occupations, specialised work involving the handling of specific tasks or the supervision of small departments. Empirical studies suggest that with the growth in part-time work, a gender hierarchy is developing within the part-time workforce that replicates the structure existing in 'lifetime employment' practices. Male workers employed part time are receiving higher wages, better conditions and more promotion and training opportunities in a wider range of occupations than women employed part time.

The introduction of the Part-time Workers' Law, in June 1993, provided for the first time a framework for the regulation of part-time work. Two criticisms of the law focus on its lack of powers to enforce compliance and its exclusion of more than 50 per cent of part-time workers who work more than thirty-five hours per week. Complicating the picture further is the inconsistency of definitions of 'part time' between sections of the Japanese bureaucracy and that included in the Part-time Workers' Law.

Definitions based on the number of hours worked are the general criteria for defining a part-time worker but these are problematic as they exclude part-time workers working beyond thirty-five hours per week. A worker's employment conditions, wages and other financial benefits are determined by the number of hours worked, job content, qualifications or skill level. The construction of the category of part-time work is based on assumptions about the type of paid work appropriate for women and the assumption that a sexual division of labour, which prioritises women's domestic work and nurturing role, is natural and exists objectively.

See also: enterprise unions and gender; gender and work

Further reading

Kondo, D. (1990) *Crafting Selves: Power, Gender and Discourses of Identity in a Japanese Workplace*, Chicago: The University of Chicago Press.

Roberts, G. (1994) *Staying on the Line*, Honolulu: University of Hawaii Press.

KAYE BROADBENT

PASSION *see Manji*

patents

Originally based on a Spanish model, Japan's first Patent Law was enacted in 1871, only to be suspended the following year. A second Patent Law was enacted in 1885, and was superseded numerous times. The present law, the Patent Law of 1959, is a descendant of the second law. Considered an industrial property law, the Patent Law is based on the belief that a patent system plays a vital role in a nation's economic development by providing protection and financial incentive to inventors whose endeavours will significantly contribute to the country's industrial development.

The Patent Law is distinguished from the Utility Model Law, which is concerned with the protection and promotion of devices that are not as advanced as inventions. The Patent Law grants applicants exclusive rights to produce, use and sell the invention for fifteen years, but no more than twenty years, from the filing date. Patent rights do not prohibit the use of patented inventions by individual consumers for non-business purposes, for testing or research, by vessels (or equipment thereon) passing through Japan or to items existing in Japan prior to the patent filing date. Patentees can assign, sell or grant licences to the patent. In the case of unauthorised use of a patented invention, the patentee may seek redress for the infringement. Penalties for patent right violation include financial compensation, reimbursement for losses and criminal liability in the case of intentional patent violation. Patentees must pay an increasing annual fee and if the fee is unpaid patent rights are terminated.

The Patent Office is an extra-ministerial bureau of the Ministry of International Trade and Industry dealing with issues related to industrial property law and trademark registration – including patent and utility-model application examination, trademark registration, accreditation of patent attorneys and determination the technical validity of patent infringement claims. Although criminal and civil infringement cases are tried in Common Court, only the Patent Office can determine cases regarding the validity of a patent, or engage in proceedings to invalidate an existing patent. Patents can only be filed by the inventor or a successor in title; only representation by a patent attorney or attorney-at-law is permitted. Throughout the 1970s and 1980s, many Japanese politicians, journalists and academics have cited the number of patent applications as evidence of Japan's high level of innovation in science and technology. For a number of reasons, low patent application fees, a first-to-file system (based on application-filing date, not date of invention) and on-request patent examinations, Japan has a comparatively high rate of patent applications. There is, however, a great difference between the number of patent applications and number of accepted patents. National pride is the impetus behind this 'medal count' mentality, which recognises the sheer volume of often frivolous patent applications rather than the lesser number of high-quality patents that are granted to Japanese inventors.

Further reading

Doi, T. and Shattuck, W.L. (1977) *Patent and Know-How Licensing in Japan and the United States*, Seattle: University of Washington Press.

Foster, R. and Ono, M. (1970) *The Patent and Trademark Laws of Japan*, second edn, Asahi: Tokyo.

Kinmonth, E.H. (1987) 'Japanese patents: Olympic gold or public relations brass', *Pacific Affairs* 60(2): 173–99.

DAVID G. WITTNER

peace and anti-nuclear movements

Japan's post-war peace movement has its roots in an enduring popular pacifist sentiment that is the legacy of Japan's utter defeat and extreme civilian suffering at the end of the Second World War. Encompassing numerous **citizens' movements** and often involving broad participation from those otherwise not politically active, the peace movement has included activism against Japanese remilitarisation and attendant issues such as the constitutionality of the **Self-Defence Forces**, the US security treaty and its renewal (see **Anpo struggle**) and military base expansion (see **anti-**

US bases movements). It has also included other protest activities, most notably against the Vietnam conflict (see **Beheiren**) and nuclear weapons testing. Although the peace movement has typically been dominated by liberal and left-wing intellectuals and activists, especially in the early post-war years, by marshalling broad pacifist and anti-nuclear sentiment it has compelled conservative governments to restrain military build-up and adopt anti-nuclear policies. From the 1970s, much of its energy shifted to environmentalism and civil rights movements. After the Persian Gulf War of 1991, the government overcame the movement's formerly rigid opposition to the overseas dispatch of the Self-Defence Forces, even under United Nations auspices. Although the constitutionality of military forces and the probity of such overseas mobilisation are now generally accepted, pacifist sentiment remains strong in supporting the peace movement's efforts.

During the Allied Occupation, Soviet-sponsored global initiatives such as the World Peace Council led to the establishment of organisations like the Japan Peace Committee (Nihon Heiwa Iinkai), which promoted the Stockholm Appeal against nuclear weapons. In reaction to the shift in US policy toward the remilitarisation of Japan, liberal and left-wing intellectuals affiliated with the progressive journal *Sekai* organised what might be called the first major indigenous peace organisation in the late 1940s. The Peace Study Group (Heiwa Mondai Danwakai) gained the support of the Socialist Party and its affiliated labour federation Sōhyō when it declared its four peace principles for ending the Occupation: a comprehensive peace treaty with all former belligerents, no foreign military bases, diplomatic neutrality and no rearmament.

In the midst of the Korean War, Prime Minister Yoshida Shigeru committed to partial rearmament and a post-Occupation security treaty with the USA in exchange for a separate peace treaty with the USA and its allies. Although the Occupation had officially ended and Korean War procurements provided a much needed stimulus to Japan's economy, the continued US military presence and anxiety about being drawn into a nuclear conflict by the alliance kept pacifist sentiment strong and lent support to an anti-US bases movement. While resentment over social disruption and appropriated farmland caused by base expansion meant local protest was broad based, the larger peace movement was often considered a left-wing movement because of the assertive leadership taken by left-wing activists, politicians and student radicals, and because of the inevitable anti-USA tone that accompanied protest against policies of the pro-USA government.

The anti-nuclear movement was dominated by liberal and left-wing activists until a non-partisan ban-the-bomb movement arose in response to the Lucky Dragon incident of March 1954. This Japanese tuna trawler was caught in radioactive fallout from an unexpectedly strong hydrogen bomb test blast at the Bikini Atoll, and returned to port with a radioactive catch and a crew suffering from radiation poisoning. Municipal and prefectural resolutions condemning the testing occurred spontaneously across the country as the media reported on the crew's condition, raising anxiety regarding Japan's continued vulnerability to nuclear fallout, termed 'ash of death'. A ban-the-bomb petition campaign conducted by a housewives' group in the Suginami Ward district of Tokyo inspired a national petition movement. Characterised by an inclusive strategy that avoided earlier ideologically divisive tendencies, this ban-the-bomb movement garnered over 30 million signatures (over a third of the population) by promoting awareness of a uniquely Japanese mission to acknowledge atomic bomb victimhood in the cause of world peace. In August 1955, the newly formed anti-nuclear bomb organization, the Japan Council against Atomic and Hydrogen Bombs (Gensuibaku Kinshi Nihon Kyōgikai, or Gensuikyō), began sponsoring annual ban-the-bomb conventions with international representation. Regional affiliate Gensuikyō organisations attracted non-partisan political support, the Diet enacted legislation providing limited medical assistance for Hiroshima and Nagasaki A-bomb victims, and the anti-communist Kishi Nobusuke administration felt compelled to adopt an ostensible anti-nuclear weapons policy in the late 1950s.

In 1959, Gensuikyō was split over disagreement on joining the Anpo struggle, and then again in the early 1960s over the communist faction's refusal to condemn Soviet and Chinese nuclear testing.

Conservative parties and the Dōmei labour federation formed the National Council for Peace and against Nuclear Weapons (Kakuheiki Kinshi Heiwa Kensetsu Kokumin Kaigi, or Kakkin Kaigi), while the Socialist Party and Sōhyō formed the Japan Conference against Atomic and Hydrogen Bombs (Gensuibaku Kinshi Nihon Kokumin Kaigi, or Gensuikin). The three organisations held separate conferences, except for a period in the late 1970s and early 1980s when they temporarily joined forces to submit a ban-the-bomb petition, with over 20 million signatures, to the United Nations special session on arms control. In the late 1990s, Kakkin Kaigi and Gensuikin held joint conventions again, their support for the Comprehensive Test Ban Treaty making participation difficult for Gensuikyō.

The anti-nuclear movement has consistently campaigned for expanding government assistance for *hibakusha*, protested against nuclear bomb testing and performed a watchdog role in assuring government compliance with its three non-nuclear policies (no possession, production or entry of nuclear weapons). In promoting the idea of a special Japanese pacifist mission during the cold war, the movement helped restrain Japanese military expansion. Progressive elements of the movement have also worked to establish *hibakusha* aid as state compensation rather than simply a form of public welfare, a distinction important to the question of **war responsibility**.

See also: against revision of the Constitution; student movement

JAMES J. ORR

peep shows

The peep show has a long history in Japan. Travelling performance troupes in pre-modern Japan often included a peep show featuring either nudity or some form of human or animal physical deformity. For a brief period in early Meiji, aboriginal peoples and rare animals were also imported into Japanese peep shows. Although some provincial troupes continued the peep show even after 1945, this style of entertainment was largely overtaken by the striptease shows popu-

larised during the Occupation. The contemporary variation of the peep show box features a glass window, two-way microphone and curtain. The women on display are often illegal immigrant sex workers. This is one of the lowest paid jobs in the sex industry.

SANDRA BUCKLEY

people's history

The project of the *minshūshi*, 'people's history', which has been trying to construct a representation of 'non-elite' people, is an influential intellectual movement that began in the 1960s. In the 1950s, a combination of the flourishing of local histories and a strong Marxist belief that history is guided by popular struggle for emancipation, led historians to turn their attention to the lives of common people who did not have access to power and knowledge. The *minshūshi* movement was launched by Irokawa Daikichi (1925–), one of the most well-known historians. While participating in the movement against the Security Treaty of 1960, Irokawa began to research the Freedom and Popular Rights movement of the 1870s and 1880s in the villages of the Kantō region. Irokawa was seeking out local origins of an indigenous, grassroots democracy, which he believed should have become dominant instead of the ideals of democracy and modernisation. He saw these two options as representing distinctive 'top down' versus 'bottom up' trajectories in Japan's transition from the Edo Period. Through this project, Irokawa and his colleagues carried out careful and painstaking research, which included the remarkable discovery of draft constitutions drawn up by local liberals in the 1880s. They also uncovered other important records and accounts of the Chichibu Rebellion, a large political protest launched by the *gōnō* (wealthy peasants), and of Liberal Party demands for tax relief from the Meiji government in 1884.

Beginning with their validation of peasant rebellions as one of the main issues of history, *minshūshi* researchers established a strong place in university departments of history. The *minshūshi* movement later came to be concerned with issues of subjectivity and autonomy in the 'lower classes' or marginalised groups. Here, a focus on the history of women and the oppressed gained attention for the first time in the academy. It is also important to note that *minshūshi* has come into existence and continued to collaborate closely with Japanese ethnography and folklore studies. The historians of the *minshūshi* to some extent share the perspective of the ethnologist Yanagita Kunio, who evaluated the meanings of the vital energies, everyday lives and consciousness of the common people and was very concerned about their hardships under modernisation and industrialisation. Although the scholars of the *minshūshi* have, like Yanagita, been accused of romanticising the notion of *minshū* (the people or masses), they were still able to preserve their critical standpoint in relation to the contemporary political situation of Japan and its modernization processes. This standpoint also extended to the determining role of the Japan–USA relationship after the Asia–Pacific War. In addition to Irokawa, most acknowledge Kano Masanao, Inoue Koji, Haga Noboru, Yasumaru Yoshio, Hirota Masaki and Fukaya Katsumi as representative historians of this group. Among these, Yasumaru Yoshio (1934–), well-known for his argument of 'conventional morality' (*tsūzoku dōtoku*), has extensively theorised the methodology of *minshūshi* as intellectual history based on a well-developed critique of not only modernisation theorists such as Maruyama Masao and Robert N. Bellah but also the dogmatic Marxism that had played a central role in the formation of the academic discipline of history in post-war Japan. Yasumaru defined the *minshū* as a 'self-constituting, self-disciplining subject' on the one hand, but on the other hand he historicised the vulnerablity of *minshū* to subjugation under modernisation. Moreover, through the study of such new religions as Kurozumikyō, Konkokyo, Tenrikyō or Omotokyō, which arose over the period from the late Edo through to Meiji, Yasumaru and his colleagues examined the genealogy of the popular thought of 'world renewing' (*yonaoshi*), or the Utopian movement of 'non-elites', as a counter-movement against modernisation and industrialisation. This work was careful not to simply reduce these movements to a call for a restoration of feudalism or an anti modernism.

The trajectory of *minshūshi*, which began as a positivistic, and sometimes romantic, movement

later adopted the theory of Max Weber and the theoretical works of phenomenological sociology and cultural anthropology. The impact and intellectual significance of *minshūshi* in the Japanese context is comparable to the studies of E.P. Thompson or Eric J. Hobsbawm, the study of *mentalité* by the Annales school or subaltern studies. Although the larger movement of *minshūshi* has lost some of its initial influence among intellectuals in the wake of the end of the Cold-War and the related collapse of the authority of Marxist models, the view point of minshūshi remains alive in the continuing work of peasant studies and social history in Japan.

Further reading

Gluck, Carol (1978) 'The people in history: Recent trends in Japanese historiography', *Journal of Asian Studies* 38(1) (November): 25–50.

Irokawa Daikichi (1973) *Shinpen Meiji seishinshi* (revised version), Tokyo: Chuo Koronsha.

—— (1970) *Meiji no Bunka*, Tokyo: Iwanami shoten. (English translation: Marius B. Jansen (ed. and trans.) (1985) *The Culture of the Meiji Period*, Princeton: Princeton University Press.)

—— (1964) *Meiji seishinshi* (The Spiritual History of the Meiji Period), Tokyo: Koga Shobo.

Takashi Fujitani (1998) 'Minshushi as critique of Orientalist knowledges', *Positions* 6(2) (fall): 303–22.

Yasumaru Yoshio (1977) *Deguchi nao*, Tokyo: Asahi Shinbunsha.

—— (1970) *Nihon no kindaika to minshu shiso* (Japanese Modernisation and Popular Thought), Tokyo: Aoki Shoten.

TSUTOMU TOMOTSUNE

photography

Photography has had a long and varied history in Japan since its introduction in the mid-1880s. From the early twentieth century until the present, Japanese photographers have debated the nature and function of their medium, variously emphasising its social role or expressive capabilities. The Japanese word for 'photography', *shashin*, means to 'copy truth' or 'represent reality'. Given the photograph's unique capacity to function both as a truthful document and as a constructed fiction, the twin poles of objectivity and subjectivity and their relation to 'reality' have formed the parameters for this discursive field. Perhaps more than any other artistic medium, photography has played an instrumental role in exploring, representing and constructing images of what it has meant to be Japanese in the face of modernisation, Westernisation and industrialisation.

The romantic pictorialism of early twentieth-century art photography (*geijutsu shashin*) was made obsolete with the industrialisation and urbanisation that came in the wake of the 1923 earthquake. Under the banner of New Photography (*shinkō shashin*) and *Neue Sachlichkeit*, photographers such as Horino Masao, Watanabe Yoshio, Yasui Nakaji and Kojima Yasuzō exploited the mechanical eye of the camera to capture the 'undiscovered beauty' of the modern industrial city and the new types who inhabited it. Publications on domestic and foreign photography became more numerous, and Japanese photographers experimented with a variety of techniques, including photomontage, photocollage, solarisation and photograms. From the mid-1930s until the end of the war, photographic practices polarised in response to a changing social and political climate. Photojournalism (*hōdō shashin*, practised by Kimura Ihei, Natori Yonosuke and Domon Ken) flourished under state sponsorship, its 'straight' style co-opted to accommodate nationalist ideology in propaganda magazines such as *Nippon*, *Front* and *Shashin Shūho*. Avant-garde photography (*zenei shashin*, practised by Ei-Kyū, Matsubara Jūzō and Kawasaki Kametarō), by contrast, was executed in a subjective, often surrealist mode, and critically portrayed the destruction of the individual body at the hands of nationalism and censorship. Ultimately, *zenei shashin* was suppressed by the militarist state.

Photographers working in the years immediately following Japan's defeat in 1945 were confronted with the charred ruins of a civilisation and a devastated populace struggling to rebuild and redefine itself. They used their medium as a tool to preserve memories of the catastrophic effects of the war, and as a means to question, reaffirm or problematise Japanese identity. The principle format for such endeavours has been the photo book, a series of photographs on a common theme, juxtaposed and linked into a narrative sequence.

In the 1950s, Hamaya Hiroshi adopted a documentary, almost ethnographic, approach to portray the traditional Japanese way of life, exploring the relationship between people and the land in order for 'the Japanese to understand the Japanese' (Yukiguni, 1956, and Ura Nihon, 1957). Domon Ken, who formed the Shudan Photo group in 1950 in support of 'pure' and 'unstaged' realism, photographed atomic bomb victims with a similar sense of objective detachment, using photography as evidence of the unspeakable (Hiroshima, 1958).

This documentary or realist approach held sway until the late 1950s, when the influence of *Subjektiv Fotografie* was felt among a new generation of photographers. While they shared the realists' social concern, for the Junin-no-me and Vivo groups photography was primarily a means of expression, a vehicle to convey the photographer's response to his or her subject. This new approach was stimulated through collaboration with artists in other genres, especially architecture, literature, dance, film and theatre. Ishimoto Yasuhiro returned from study at the New Bauhaus in Chicago to photograph the Katsura Palace, questioning the nature of Japanese culture and pursuing a Japanese sensibility in the tactile qualities of the photograph (Katsura, 1960). Hosoe Eiko expressed the traumatic memories of his wartime youth by metaphorically narrating a Japanese folk tale with *butō* dancer Hijikata Tatsumi (Kamaitachi, 1969); he also collaborated with the writer Mishima Yukio in an erotic series of elaborately staged portraits (Barakei, 1963 and 1971). Tōmatsu Shōmei, committed to 'building a dam against the flow of time' and exploring the political issues of the post-war period, photographed the effects of the atomic bomb on Nagasaki ('Nagasaki: 11:02', 1966 and *The Hiroshima–Nagasaki Document*, jointly authored with Domon, 1961). Tōmatsu's photographs of US military bases evoke the clash of cultures between conquered and conqueror (Okinawa, 1969), and his treatment of the Shinjuku riots of 1968 and its youth culture is an essay on political and physical violence, eroticism and death (*Oh, Shinjuku!*, 1969).

The 1970s largely saw a retreat from social mission into the interior landscape of personal subjectivity. Moriyama Daidō photographed the fragmented experience of urban life from the position of a voyeuristic hunter-photographer in search of authenticity, itself composed of fleeting, accidental experiences in the everyday (*A Hunter*, 1972). Rejecting the frame and structure, Moriyama's images are grainy, blurred and nearly unmediated representations, strung disjunctively together in existential essays. Araki Nobuyoshi's autobiographical series, a visual 'I-novel' (*shishō-setsu*) is composed of intimate images of himself and his wife from their wedding, honeymoon and everyday life (*Sentimental Journey*, 1971). Araki's work attempts to escape from 'lying photographs'.

Since the 1980s, there has been little concern among photographers to define or work from a position of 'Japaneseness', and a variety of approaches towards expanding the possibility of the medium are vigorously being explored. The 1980s and 1990s also saw the acceptance of photography into the realm of fine art, as photographers exhibited their works alongside painting and sculpture in art museums, and artists appropriated mass-media photographic images in their own multi-media works. Morimura Yasu-masa, whose photographs critically deconstruct the cultural authority of art historical codes and the stability of identity, exemplifies this trend. Fukuda Miran and Hirakawa Noritoshi use photography in conjunction with painting, sculpture or video to expose and critique conventional systems of art and society. Michiko Kon's photographs of fetishistic objects meticulously crafted from fish are a critical yet playful comment on consumption and desire. Sugimoto Hiroshi's time-exposed series of land-scapes are a means of depicting 'condensations' and 'metaphors' of the abstract concept of time. Satō Tokihiro's photography records his own relation with, and movement throughout, a space, the trace of which remains as trails and points of light in a time-exposed photo. Hatakeyama Naoya's images of Japanese limeworks and the concrete city of Tokyo are 'like negative and positive images of a single photograph', an attempt to link the geography of the present city with the sediment of time and history.

Further reading

Dower, John W. (1995) *The Founding and Development of Modern Photography in Japan*, Tokyo: Tokyo Metropolitan Museum of Photography.

—— (1980) *A Century of Japanese Photography*, New York: Pantheon Books.

Hiraki Osamu and Ishiwata Maya (eds) (1996) *Japanese Photography Guide*, Tucson, AZ: Nazraeli Press.

Holborn, Mark (1994) *Liquid Crystal Futures: Contemporary Japanese Photography*, Edinburgh: The Fruitmarket Gallery.

—— (1986) *Black Sun: The Eyes of Four: Roots and Innovation in Japanese Photography*, New York: Aperture.

ALICIA VOLK

pickles

In a diet where rice has traditionally been the staple, pickles (*tsukemono*) are at the heart of the meal and not a mere side dish. Pickles are carefully selected to complement the rest of a meal and might be chosen for any combination of taste, colour, texture and seasonality. Most pickles are vegetable based but some regional specialities include meat or fish. Pickles are usually eaten at the end of the meal and are often accompanied by a bowl of *miso*. Pickles can be commercially bought and most neighbourhood markets, food halls and supermarkets will have at least one stall lined with the wooden barrels and pottery crocks used to season the pickles, sitting open to display an array of richly coloured and aromatic delicacies. Pickles are a popular gift for travellers to carry home. Each region, town or village will boast its own special recipe for pickles, which can be bought gift wrapped in local speciality shops or at railway station kiosks. If you forget to buy a gift of pickles before leaving for home they are often on sale on board tourist trains. When guests come to eat, many households will still proudly pull out a crock of pickles made with the family's own traditional recipe.

SANDRA BUCKLEY

PIGS AND BATTLESHIPS see *Buta to gunkan*

pilgrimages

The pilgrimage is no longer one of the main motives for travel in Japan as it was in the Edo Period when hundreds of thousands of pilgrims visited the more popular destinations each year. There are records of mass pilgrimages to the Shintō shrine at Ise that numbered as many as 3 million. Ise remains a popular destination for contemporary pilgrims. When the imperial government collapsed in the Muromachi period the shrine lost much of its financial support and resorted to raising funds through regional patronage and annual pilgrimages sponsored by dedicated Ise associations across the country. Today's Ise pilgrims travel as individuals or in the familiar Japanese group tours but their presence remains essential to the survival of the local economy. There is much in the structure of the historical pilgrimage that can be linked to contemporary tourism.

The sun goddess Amaterasu Ōmikami is enshrined at Ise shrine, lending this site tremendous significance in the cosmic and spiritual order of agrarian life in pre-modern Japan. All wanted to travel at least once in their lifetime to Ise but few villagers could afford the trip or the time. Ise associations collected money to sponsor representatives from the village to make the trip on behalf of all members, and this trip quickly became an adult rite of passage for young men. The adventures of the pilgrimage to Ise became the stuff of many popular tales and songs. Along the way, different groups would travel together, often creating rare opportunities for villages and regions to hear news of one another. The shrine offered not only a spiritual experience but also a lively pleasure quarter in the precinct between the inner and outer shrines. The custom of village pilgrim groups continued well into the twentieth century, even after the disbandment of Ise associations, and this structure of travel is often linked to today's group tours, which are also frequently made up of people from the same village, neighbourhood, apartment complex or company. The pilgrims to Ise were required to bring back gifts of local speciality foods and crafts for their sponsors at home, and this custom of **omiyage** (souvenirs) remains an important element of contemporary travel, especially for **honeymoons**, which are also often paid for in part by gifts of money from wedding guests and family (see **weddings**).

Although the period of State Shintō saw a decline in pilgrimages to Buddhist temples during the early twentieth century, the post-war decades have seen a return to the temple sites that had been popular among Edo pilgrims. A famous Shikoku pilgrimage to eighty-eight temples scattered across some 1,000 km retraces the steps of Kōbō Daishi and still attracts pilgrims of all ages, who can ride the island trains and buses between sites if they are not ready for the long commitment of travelling on foot. The *Bandō sanjūsandō* (Thirty-three sites of Bandō) is another pilgrimage route to thirty-three Kannon temples in the Kantō region (once also known as Bandō). There is a similar thirty-three-site Kannon pilgrimage route in Kansai and both remain popular destinations. The nostalgia boom promoted by such national travel campaigns as Exotic Japan and Discover Japan in the 1970s and 1980s did much to bolster travel to pilgrimage sites, although the motivation of these waves of domestic tourists was more consumerist than spiritual. None the less, the boost was important to these regional local economies.

Although historically, women were discouraged from travel and even prohibited from some temple and shrine sites for reasons of pollution, today, women make up the majority of pilgrims. Promotional campaigns encourage women in their mid-life years to enjoy the departure of their children from the home as a time to pursue their spiritual lives. However, the groups of women drinking and laughing in the local restaurants or singing loudly over beer and boxed lunches on the train attest to the fact that these modern women pilgrims also get a great deal of pleasure from their trips away from home in the company of friends new and old.

See also: Buddhism; nostalgia boom; *omiyage*; State Shintō; tourism

Further reading

Kato Akinori (1994) 'Package tours, pilgrimages and pleasure trips', in A Ueda and M. Eguchi (eds) *The Electric Geisha*, Tokyo and New York: Kōdansha, p. 59.

SANDRA BUCKLEY

pine trees

Along with **cherry blossoms** and **bamboo**, pine trees represent one of the three major plant-inspired decorative motifs in Japanese culture. Pine trees are admired for their strength and ability to withstand the weather, and associated with superior and enduring character. The pine is a symbol of winter, and considered most beautiful when it is lightly dusted with snow. Combined with bamboo, it is used at New Year to create *kadomatsu*, a kind of decoration placed on the gate of every home. It provides an important subject for art works, especially *sumi-e*, black and white drawings made from ink produced from the ashes of burnt pine. Paintings of pine trees provide the dominant backdrop for *nō* theatre sets, modelled upon the stark outline of pines from Matsushima (Pine Tree Island), one of the three famous sites of Japan.

Although the aesthetic inspiration comes from nature, pine trees in domestic gardens – where they represent one of the fundamental landscape components – are carefully pruned and trained to take on shapes that are believed to improve upon their natural beauty. This idealised conception of nature is carried forwards allegorically in a range of texts from poetry to advertising.

AUDREY KOBAYASHI

pink films

Pink films are low-budget, commercial, soft-core pornographic films produced in the mid-1960s as part of the independent film production movement that emerged following the major studio slump of that period. Stories are structured around sex scenes; the average budget of ¥30–35,000,000 has remained consistent for thirty years. Production occurs on location, usually in under a week; films show in specialised adult, or occasionally art-retro, cinemas.

By the late 1960s, the new pink industry was produced, distributed and screened by mini-studios.

While new markets and modes of independent production were forming, works such as Wakamatsu Koji's sexually and politically transgressive films, drew from student and leftist movements (see **student movement**). In both mainstream and avant-garde productions, sexual fantasies generally appealed to a male spectatorship. Occasional there were female directors, including Yoshiyuki Yumi and Hamano Sachi. Young directors such as Suo Masayuki, Kurosawa Kiyoshi and Oki Hiroyuki have broken into film-making via pink films.

From 1972–88, Nikkatsu produced over 500 bigger-budget *roman poruno* (romantic pornography) films, some by major *auteurs* like Kumashiro Tatsumi and Tanaka Noboru. Idiosyncratic, sometimes de-eroticised 'pink *nouvelle vague*' films by directors like Zeze Takahisa and Sato Toshiki emerged in the 1990s.

See also: women in film; women in the film industry

Further reading

Weisser, T. (1998) *Japanese Cinema Encyclopedia: The Sex Films*, Miami: Vital Books.

ANNE McKNIGHT

Pink Helmets

The 'Pink Helmets' was the nickname for the group Chūzetsu Kinshihō Hantai shi Piru Kaikin o Yōkyū suru Josei Kaihō Rengō (usually shortened to Chū-P-Ren or **Chūpiren**). The group formed around Enoki Misako and others on 14 June 1972 to battle proposed pro-natalist revisions to the 1947 Eugenics Protection Law. The proposals would have eliminated the right to abortion except in cases of birth defects by eliminating the Economic Reasons Clause, under which some 80 per cent of abortions in Japan were performed. The **Chūpiren** also fought conservative attempts to make birth control pills available only under doctors' prescription. (Until then, birth control pills were only available from pharmacists for relief of menstrual pain.)

Many of the group's members had participated in the student movement during the **Zenkyōtō** period, and the 'Pink Helmets' used many of the

New Left's confrontational tactics to press for women's reproductive and sexual rights. Like radical students, the Chūpiren used the mass media to bring its agenda to public attention. The group went to the workplace to confront men who had impregnated and then abandoned women. They brought forth testimony from older women on such issues as abortion, birth control and sex. Later feminists criticised Chūpiren for its uncritical attitudes towards birth control pills and sexual liberation, but there is no doubt that Chūpiren contributed in important ways to women's sexual and reproductive freedom.

GUY YASKO

Pink Lady

Pink Lady was a packaged, late 1970s female pop duo who combined robotic, synchronised choreography and sensual dress with innocent lyrics and television commercial tie-ins for unrivalled commercial success (Nemoto Mitsuyo, Masuda Keiko).

Idol singers for the disco era, their careers charted new commercial territory and served as a model for such later performers as **Matsuda Seiko**. Pink Lady released their debut single, 'Police Inspector Pepper', in summer 1976. While this song reached number four on the charts, their next nine releases were each number one hits. From their fourth to their eighth releases, each record sold over 1,000,000 copies. Over a hundred varieties of licensed Pink Lady merchandise were ultimately offered for sale. At the height of their popularity, Pink Lady briefly played Las Vegas. In 1979, they hosted a summer replacement show on NBC and released their first and last English-language single, just breaking the Top 40 at number thirty-seven. By 1981, Pink Lady's popular success had precipitously declined and they retired. Pink Lady remains both a symbol of Japanese popular music as sexualised commodity and an icon of the late 1970s Japanese pop culture they partially defined.

Further reading

Kitagawa Junko, (1994) 'Pink Lady', in *Taishū bunka jiten*, Tokyo: Kobundo pp. 656–8.

Schilling, Mark (1997) *The Encyclopedia of Japanese Pop Culture*, New York: Weatherhill, pp. 187–90.

MARK ANDERSON

pink salons

Pink salons are a cheaply priced combination of the *kissaten* style of food and drink, and the sexual services of club hostesses. Pink salons are most often found clustered around stations and suburban fast-food districts. Clients pay a time-based cover charge for a hostess. Drinks and food are extra. In addition to keeping her client's glass filled and offering entertaining and flirtatious dialogue, the hostess will provide masturbatory sexual services to the client. Some pink salons offer booths but in many there is no more privacy than the cover of a table and dim lighting.

SANDRA BUCKLEY

pirate radio

Unlike in North America or Western Europe, after the 1970s Japanese radio did not advance toward 'liberalisation' (*'jiyūka'*). It continued to be dominated by the monopoly of NHK and a few other public broadcasting stations. In the latter half of the 1970s, as urban culture and consumerism (*shōhi seikatsu*) became more diversified, the demand among young people for more varied broadcasting, especially FM stations, grew stronger every day. However, the strong psychological impact on the Japanese collective consciousness of the suppressive control of the airwaves before and during the war meant that there were hardly any pirate radio stations which had the output that could cover large areas. Even after the war the control of the airwaves was extremely strict, and the occasional attempts at pirate radio broadcasts were shut down soon after going on the air. In the 1980s, Mini FM held a real fascination for people and, in spite of continuing strict control of the airwaves, a half-legal 'pirate radio' movement began to spread.

Long before this, children were already playing at radio transmission using 'weak airwaves', condoned under broadcast law without a license.

Tetsuo Kogawa, who was inspired by the free radio movement in Italy and France, saw a radical and activist potential in this micro-level child's play and began to experiment with the technology. Thus, the Mini FM boom was actually an accidental coming together of this trend towards the use of 'weak airwaves' and a more general change in people's attitudes. 'The Season of War', as it was called, was over and people were starved for something more radical in broadcast content. The demand was growing stronger for the eternally unchanging mass media to begin to offer something different. For this reason, an interest in the free radio Mini FM grew even within the mass media. This new medium of entertainment, which at first had spread solely by word of mouth, began to flourish as a result of coverage in the mass media. Taking advantage of this boom in Mini FM, the major electronics suppliers decided to maximise on the marketing opportunity and launched new model lines at reasonably affordable prices. Sales figures climbed and it is estimated that several thousand Mini FM stations sprung up across the country. However, the majority of this influx of Mini FM stations merely reproduced the form and content of the already existing FM stations. Thus, there were few people who recognised or worked to develop the full extent of the potential of Mini FM. Because of this, many of these stations folded very quickly, disappointed by limited transmission space and relatively low audience numbers. Then, in September 1985, the Mini FM boom essentially came to an end due to a single incident widely reported in the newspapers and weekly magazines, in which a Tokyo station in Minato ward known as KY FM was found to be in violation of broadcast law.

The Mini FM movement in Japan had started ten years before the micro-radio movement in North America, and yet Japanese radio audiences only experienced for a very short time the media version of the freedom of the 'legally illegal': a brief moment in which the 'illegal' became a tolerated space of broadcast experimentation. Despite the fact that in many regions of the world in the 1990s micro-radio activity became quite lively, in Japan Mini FM radio, much less pirate radio, has resurfaced only sporadically. Why is it that in Japan there are so few attempts to break 'the law' for the sake of liberty and freedom? What kind of

activity could again shake up a media-saturated Japanese society? Those still actively focused on the potential of radio-style broadcasting in the digital age look to the possibility of a new wave of media piracy, prompted by technological innovations that again offer the prospect of developing broadcast opportunities one step ahead of regulation.

TETSUO KOGAWA,
TRANSLATED BY ADRIENNE GIBB

Plan to Double Income

The Plan to Double Income (*Shōtoku Baizō Keikaku*) was an economic plan developed under the leadership of Prime Minister Hayato Ikeda in 1960, designed to bring about the doubling of real national income from 1961 to 1970 by an annual growth rate of at least 7.2 per cent. While the groundwork of economic growth had been laid in the early 1950s, Ikeda pursued a policy of lowering interest rates and taxes to stimulate economic activities in the private sector, and adopted an aggresssive policy of capital investment in infrastructure – building highways, high-speed railways, subways, airports, port facilities and dams. The goal of a doubled national income was reached some time in 1967.

DAVID EDGINGTON

play

Play (*asobi*) in Japanese culture is not understood in the same way as **leisure** (*rijaa*). While leisure is being marketed as a non-work related and usually family-centred activity, *asobi* has a very different status and history. The most popular space of *asobi* in Japan today is the realm of the ***mizushōbai*** – the world of bars, clubs, restaurants and prostitution (see **prostitution, regulation of**). In this space of play, Japanese men step outside the limits of appropriate and proper behaviour that bound everyday life in the family and the workplace. Here they can shout at their boss, deride a fellow worker, be pampered like a small child by a fawning hostess, act out sexual fantasies in the privacy of a sex club or just drink too much and become excessively loud. On company trips, colleagues spend several days indulging in *asobi* at corporate expense at resorts designed to entertain and encourage excessive behaviour.

Even the immensely popular game of pachinko can also be understood in terms of excess; hours spent funnelling metal balls into a slot machine in isolation from everyone around you and disconnected from the usual circuits of work and family. This should not be misunderstood as meaning that *asobi* is not related to work, for it is very often an extension of work but functions differently with different dynamics and there is a silent social contract that there is no overflow of consequences from the space of *asobi* back into the workplace or family. Therefore, a man can shout at his boss but not have to apologise or suffer reprimand the next day, or flirt with a hostess, even sleep with a single, female co-worker or a prostitute, and not consider that it affects his wife or family. Indeed, many Japanese wives also speak of their husbands' *asobi* activities as something they are not concerned with so long as the husband is discreet and does not allow any impact on the family. In fact, there are any number of inevitable effects on the family and workplace as a result of *asobi*, but these are largely ignored or hidden, e.g. gambling debt, alcoholism, STDs, sleep deprivation, absentee fathers. etc.

The relationship of women to *asobi* is not unproblematic. Women play a crucial role in facilitating *asobi* for men, either as active participants (hostesses, entertainers, etc.) or as wives who simply tolerate the husband's absence and related expenses. Opportunities for women themselves to indulge in *asobi* are, however, limited. While *asobi* is considered an integral part of men's lives, women experience a need to justify and explain any activity that might be seen as self-indulgent rather than an extension of their role as wife and mother. Young unmarried women have a great deal of freedom to play and do so actively: eating out, going to bars, travelling, playing sports and dating. However, with marriage there is tremendous social pressure for a woman to adopt the appropriate behaviour of a wife. Although a husband may be out drinking, it is expected that the wife will come home from work, shop and have a meal prepared and waiting for him on his return, no matter how late he is. Many young wives still admit that they

feel it is wrong for them to go to bed before their husband returns home, even if they have to go to work themselves the next day or get up to prepare children for school. Women do take advantage of free time to play sports, attend adult education courses, learn traditional or other crafts and arts, etc., but these activities are often presented as a part of the performance of her role as a professional housewife and mother. Participating in local clubs and neighbourhood recreational activities and self-improvement through courses are all seen as part of her self-presentation as a model middle-class wife and mother. It is when a woman reaches her '*midi*' (middle-age and middle-class) stage in her life-cycle that she is again briefly allowed a period of more unhindered *asobi* in between her years of caregiving to children and the next stage of elderly care for ageing parents and in-laws.

Asobi is intimately bound up with such complex issues as gender-differentiated work (paid and unpaid), sexuality and sexual practice in the family and in the sex industry, **alcoholism** and **karōshi** (death from overwork). Japanese social commentators and researchers argue that there is a long history of *asobi* in Japanese popular culture dating back to the pleasure quarters at pilgrimage destinations (see **pilgrimages**), the brothel districts of the major urban centres and the riverbed entertainment districts on the margins of towns and cities. Feminist scholars reject this long history of *asobi* as a reason for not challenging the gendered nature of play in its contemporary forms and the gender divides and inequities it promotes between men and women and between women – married and unmarried, working and non-working, sex worker and wife.

SANDRA BUCKLEY

poetry

Post-war modern free-style verse (*shi*) continued many of the trends established prior to the Second World War. However, the impact of the war also helped modern poetry to gain a stronger foothold among the reading public, as traditional genres of poetry suffered a backlash from a close association with patriotic wartime values. As many, if not most, of the major pre-war poets had written such verse, and were subsequently obliged to keep a low profile in the immediate aftermath of the war, this created an opening for new, young poets not tainted by any association with the past.

The most influential poet in this group was Tanikawa Shuntarō, who has since become the best-known and most widely read poet in contemporary Japan. Tanikawa burst onto the scene in 1952 with his collection *Nijū oku kōnen no kodoku* (Two Billion Light Years of Loneliness). Tanikawa's verse was fresh and new, his focus on the quotidian issues of daily life came in sharp contrast to other older, post-war poets, like Ayukawa Nobuo and Tamura Ryūichi, who still focused on the war and unresolved issues arising from it. Tanikawa's poetry rarely grappled directly with politics, in stark contrast to the post-war school. It was this disengagement from ideology and a turn to a new sensibility that proved immensely popular among readers.

A quite different but, in some respects, similar response to the war can be found in the poetry of Yoshioka Minoru, whose two major collections of the time, *Seibutsu* (Still Life, 1955) and *Sōryo* (Monks, 1958), continue an older, pre-war tradition (which was actively discouraged by the wartime authorities) of the avant-garde. Yoshioka was the heir to poets of the jazz era of the 1920s, like Nishiwaki Junzaburō, although Nishiwaki and others like him continued to write poetry. Yoshioka's verse exploited semantic ambiguity and indeterminacy – often utilising collage, a favourite avant-garde technique – to create a sense of conceptual displacement that was both playful and serious. His poetry is, at times, difficult and obscure but a focus on the complexity of meaning can easily be seen as another kind of response to the debased language of ideology born of the totalitarian politics of war.

Yoshioka was equally as influential as Tanikawa, and a host of poetry about language, and the philosophical conundrum of meaning, began to be written. A group of women poets who looked to Yoshioka and the tradition he represented emerged more or less at the same time. Tomioka Taeko broke new ground in collections like *Okaeshi* (Return Gift, 1957) and *Onna tomodachi* (Woman Friends, 1964), which explored notions of sexuality and 'the speaking subject' in ways that call into question the conceptual categories that define male–female relations. Female colleagues of Tomioka like Shiraishi Kazuko, Yoshihara Sachiko and Shinkawa Kazue found other modes of poetic expression more congenial than the adoption of Yoshioka's conceptual verse. Shiraishi began as a performance poet – poetry written for oral recitation underwent a revival in the 1950s and 1960s – but soon moved on in such collections as *Seinaru inja no kisetsu* (Seasons of the Sacred Lecher, 1970) and *Sunazoku* (Sand Clan, 1982) from 'beat poetry' to complex meditations on religion and identity.

Poetry with a strong interest in language and the conceptual games inherent in the act of playing with words continued to find followers in the decade of the 1960s and beyond. Poets like Takahashi Mutsuo and Yoshimasu Gōzō, and such younger poets as Hiraide Takashi and Asabuki Ryōji, shared a common interest in extravagant fantasy or, better, a fantasia of words. Takahashi's verse in collections like *Bara no ki, nise no koibito tachi* (Rose Tree, Fake Lovers, 1964) and *Ōkoku no kōzō* (The Structure of the Kingdom, 1982) has lines of surprising beauty juxtaposed beside ugliness, and deals frankly with homosexual passion. Yoshimasu is possibly the best-known performance poet in Japan and in books like *Sōsho de kakareta kawa* (River Written in Grass *Ecriture*, 1977) he constructed complex myths in language as violent as it was lyrical. Hiraide and Asabuki's verse is less lyrical, perhaps, but more rigorous in pursuing the endless permutations of language.

Poets associated with the politically charged works of the 1960s, which arose partly as a reaction to debates over national identity inspired by anti-USA riots, such as Yoshimoto Takaaki and Amazawa Taijirō, came to be somewhat critical of their successors in the 1970s and 1980s. Yoshimoto wrote a famous polemic against language-centred poetry in 1978, arguing that much contemporary poetry was simply rhetoric, and that the solipsism of these poets rendered their verse meaningless.

Tanikawa Shuntarō's 1968 collection *Tabi* (Journeys) anticipated the shift to language and the debate over meaning, as he came increasingly to focus on the efficacy or otherwise of language itself. In his prize-winning collection *Seken shirazu* (The Naïf, 1993), Tanikawa's investigations of the process of writing take on a strong autobiographical colouration as his themes become increasingly personal; the long poem written on the death of his father is as much an interrogation of the futility of words to express true meaning as an expression of grief.

A similar journey into the inability of language to represent despair was undertaken in Soh Sakon's celebrated 1968 collection *Moeru haha* (Mother Burning). Soh's long book-length poem attempts to grapple with the death of the poet's mother during an incendiary raid in the Second World War and the subsequent burden of guilt. This harrowing and tortuous self-scarification asks, as many poets did in the aftermath of the war, whether art is possible in the face of the abyss. The war has never entirely disappeared as a theme in contemporary Japanese poetry. Moreover, the atomic bombs dropped on Hiroshima and Nagasaki continue as powerful and enduring themes in the poetry of those who either survived the bombing or live as witnesses to these horrific events.

Further reading

Morton, Leith (ed.) (1993) *An Anthology of Contemporary Japanese Poetry*, New York: Garland Publishing Inc.

Yoshimoto Takaaki (1972) *Kyōdo Gensōron in Yoshimoto Takaaki Zen Chosakush*, vol. 11, Tokyo: Keisō Shobō.

LEITH MORTON

Pokemon

Pokemon is a media-mix (electronic game, cartoon, comic, movie, cards, merchandise) children's entertainment that became a sensational hit in Japan and globally in the late 1990s. Along with his staff at Game Freak, Tajiri Satoshi spent six years creating the original Gameboy game, which Nintendo bought and released in February 1996. The game blended his two childhood pastimes, insect collecting and video games, into a new digital recreation that combined a concern for nature and preservation with the potential of new communication technology. Initial predictions were modest (because of Gameboy's waning popularity in 1996), but *Pokemon* did well, leading its marketers to develop it across other media. In summer 1996, *Pokemon* came out as a serialised comic in *Korokoro komikku*; cards by Media Factory followed in the fall; the television *anime* produced by Terebi Tokyo débuted in April 1997; toy merchandise by Tomy appeared the same spring; and the first movie hit the screens in the summer 1997. Besides these major media, there has been a concatenation of tie-in merchandise – pencils and stationery goods by Enikkusu, curry and condiments by Nagatanien, and chocolate and sweets by Meiji Seioka – as well as a host of highly visible launch campaigns for *Pokemon*. These included ANA aircraft painted with *Pokemon* motifs in the summer of 1998 and a train promotion by JR the same summer. *Pokemon* exports began in 1997 to East Asia (Hong Kong, Taiwan), hit the USA in 1998 and have subsequently spread around the world (from Australia, South Korea, Indonesia and Mexico to Germany, Israel, Canada, France and Colombia). In 2001, it is fading, though still popular in most of these marketplaces.

The basic concept of *Pokemon* is of an imaginary universe inhabited by wild monsters that children capture and then retain in balls they keep in their pockets. There are 151 pokemon (now expanded to 260 with the latest gold and silver Gameboy game editions) and the goal is to catch them all (*getto suru*, which becomes 'gotta catch 'em all' in English). Pokemon, which start out wild (*yasei*) until caught, are amalgamations of features both fantastic and animal-like. There is a typology of different creatures (water, grass, legendary, strange) and each pokemon has unique powers, characteristics and features that grow as they develop through fights. Some pokemon can evolve. New pokemon are captured through two main methods, matches (*taisen*) and exchanges (*kōkan*), which largely depend on strategy. In the television *anime*, the story revolves around three main humans: Satoshi (Ash in the English version), the 10-year-old boy trying to be the world's best pokemon trainer; Kasumi (Misty), the 10-year-old girl accompanying him on his trek; and Takeshi (Brock), the 15-year-old more interested in studying pokemon than capturing them. Three movies have been released in Japan (two in the US), five different Gameboy versions have been released and there are endless tie-in products and spin-off merchandise. There were also live shows in Japan and a kick-off campaign in the USA that turned Topeka, Kansas, into Topikachu for a day. The most popular pokemon is Pikachu, the yellow, red cheeked, electric-super-powered, mouse-type pokemon that is Satoshi's main pokemon and rides constantly on his shoulders in the *anime*.

Across the different media, *Pokemon* is a form of play that is said to involve exploration, discovery, collection, capture, mastery, communication exchange and animal care. Throughout the progression of the game/story, pokemon shift in status across a diverse range of possibilities: possessions, tools, companions, friends, pets, objects, monsters and weapons.

ANNE ALLISON

POLICE BOX *see kōban*

political economy of post-war Japan

Japan's distinctive political economy was a post-war development, created out of compromises between business and government, and management and labour, and influenced by global developments, notably the foreign policy of the USA. It is characterised by an unusually tight integration of major social institutions, a major role for the state in the economy and a relatively equal distribution of income, although those conditions changed enough in the 1990s to raise doubts about the system's future.

Surrender marked the failure of a national economic strategy that had relied on imperial expansion, oligopoly and tight control at home. Domestically, the Japanese elite could no longer enforce very low wages on the urban population or very high rents and taxes on the rural population. The new post-war government could not attain legitimacy without granting most Japanese greater economic security, higher wages and a better standard of living.

Allied Occupation reforms changed the legal and political framework for economic activity. Most important were **land reform** and new laws legalising organisation, collective bargaining and strikes by labour unions. The biggest firms were also broken up under a *zaibatsu* **dissolution** policy. Other forms of wealth disappeared either in wartime air-raids or in post-war hyper-inflation, making incomes (see **income levels**) in Japan far more evenly distributed than ever before.

Post-war Japanese social organisations were integrated far more tightly into a single system than in many other nations. After major struggles that neither won outright, workers and managers agreed on guidelines that created an extremely stable labour market (see **management systems, Japanese**). Employers hired only recent school graduates for their core workforce and promised them lifetime employment. Schools 'sorted' young people and determined their lifelong career opportunities. Women were relegated to part-time and temporary work, creating a national 'standard' **middle-class** family of full-time male breadwinner and female home-maker who juggled **part-time work** on the side.

Other laws strengthened the hand of government bureaucrats (see **bureaucracy**), especially at the **Ministry of Finance**, the **Economic Planning Agency** and the **Ministry of International Trade and Industry**, created in 1949. Tax incentives, control over foreign currency and regulation of export licences, banking (see **banking system**), credit and interest on savings (see **saving**) were some of the ways the ministries practised 'administrative guidance' over private firms. These measures were, in general, accepted by business leaders. Japanese business leaders rejected the heavy handed state interference they had experienced during the war, but they also feared a return to the chaotically competitive conditions of the 1920s. Managerial autonomy in a stable environment, rather than a free market, was their goal.

In late 1946, the Japanese government adopted an economic policy that emphasised economic growth and development in the direction of a sophisticated high-wage economy. An early success was the **priority-production** policy, which concentrated on coal and steel. It committed the economy to heavy industrial production.

In 1949, spurred on by US efforts to reintegrate Japan into the global economy, Japanese planners added a commitment to a high-value-added economy with sophisticated export goods. The 'rationalisation plan' involved upgrading the quality of goods produced through infusions of imported technology in order to sell abroad. This strategy required the co-operation of industrial workers and a literate, trained workforce. One of the two major labour union federations, **Shinsanbetsu** (see **Sōdōmei**), institutionalised co-ordinated nationwide bargaining over wages and working conditions as part of this system with the invention of the **spring offensive** in 1955.

The post-war Japanese political economy was profoundly shaped by the patronage of the USA. The rationalisation policy required extensive US inputs of capital and technology. The US government also supplied the crucial first post-war export market by giving Japanese firms most of the contracts to supply materials for the **Korean War**. The Japanese government agreed to support the USA in its strategic decisions in return for access on favoured terms to the USA-designed trade system.

The 1950s and 1960s can be characterised as a period of high-speed growth. A significant policy change was the 1959 transformation of the rationalisation policy into 'industrial structure policy'. The collapse of the coal and textile industries showed that rationalisation was not equally possible in all sectors. Each had become a declining industry; that is, neither could be made internationally competitive through injections of technology. The 'industrial structure' policy targeted 'infant' and declining industries, which later included oil refining, petrochemicals, steelmaking and shipbuilding. Workers refused to shoulder the whole burden of declining industries' reduced fortunes, and the 1960 **Miike struggle** ultimately concerned government policy towards 'sunset' industries. Recognising that declining industries were inevitable led to the development of a 'soft-landing policy' of unemployment compensation for workers and payments to local governments.

The final key to the high-speed growth of the 1950s and 1960s was increased domestic consumption. The **Plan to Double Income** of 1960 championed redistribution of economic benefits within the context of economic growth. The plan reaffirmed government responsibility for social welfare, vocational training and education, although at lower levels than in Europe. The plan's greatest innovation was to redefine economic goals to include Japanese consumers as well as producers. The government promised to double average household incomes within a decade, and, gratifyingly, the standard of living did jump dramatically. The new wealth created the mass market that made high-speed growth possible.

While government policy was important, it only indirectly affected most economic decisions. Private firms seeking profits and market share were the main engine driving economic growth. Major Japanese firms and horizontally organised *keiretsu* groups competed fiercely with each other to buy new technology, increase their productivity and quality of goods, and capture higher market shares. They also incorporated smaller firms as subcontractors into vertically integrated groups. However, business leaders worked closely with bureaucrats and politicians. During the long reign of the **Liberal Democratic Party**, large firms and major business associations were the main financiers of the party, paying for electioneering and cash gifts from politicians to their constituents. In return, the businessmen enjoyed easy access to political and bureaucratic leaders. Many of them – notably in agriculture, construction and retail sales – enjoyed cartel-like legal and political protection from new competitors.

After 1960, the economy grew an unprecedented 12 per cent annually. Consumer goods proliferated. Wages rose an average of 10 per cent annually (in real terms). Although labour's share of **Gross National Product** (GNP) began shrinking from the early 1960s, the absolute standard of living for farmers and workers increased markedly. By the 1970s, the huge income gap between urban and rural households and the grinding rural poverty (see **poverty and the poor**) of the pre-war era had disappeared. New problems developed, however: rural areas were depopulated while congestion; planned obsolescence; environmental degradation and inadequate transportation systems became an enduring feature of urban life. Meanwhile, the ties between the Japanese and the international economies became increasingly complex. The 1946 strategy worked politically through to 1973 to elevate economics as a central political theme of Japanese society. It also mediated political tension by taking elements proposed by various different groups and weaving them together into a single post-war settlement in Japan.

However, a number of trends culminated in the early 1970s to bring an end to the period of high-speed growth. Japan closed the technology gap that had powered growth for twenty years. Manufacturers could no longer buy more efficient technology and install it into their plants for quick productivity increases. Also, agriculture had shrunk so much that it could no longer provide a pool of low-productivity workers available for more high-productivity jobs. The Japanese were most unprepared for changes in the global political economy, especially US demands that Japan curb its ballooning trade surplus with the USA. Then, in 1972, the USA devalued the dollar against the yen, recognised the People's Republic of China (see **Sino-Japanese relations**) and temporarily banned soy bean exports – all major 'shocks' to the Japanese political economy. The OPEC embargo followed in 1973, demonstrating the inhospitality of the world beyond the US patronage umbrella. The Japanese suddenly confronted the inescapable relationship between economic diversification and increasingly complex ties to the global economy.

None the less, by 1980, the Japanese economy seemed strong again. Many firms had cut costs substantially by becoming far more energy efficient and technologically sophisticated. They also began marketing their goods far more aggressively overseas, exacerbating trade friction, especially with the USA. Yet policies changed little. Japan's interdependence with the global economy accelerated in the mid-1980s with a new and massive yen revaluation (see *yendaka*) in 1985 and emerging labour shortages. At first, there were few structural changes in the domestic political economy. Employment levels held steady except in declining industries. So did wages, although they declined as a percentage of GNP. Japanese employers still felt a strong obligation to retain all the employees to whom they had promised lifetime employment. They even began hiring young women for core jobs. Government resources were concentrated in securing a soft landing for workers and local communities hardest hit by global competition. Yet, in retrospect, it is clear that several trends of the 1980s undermined the Japanese post-war political-economic system.

One result of the yen revaluation was a surge of Japanese investment overseas rather than at home. Some firms wanted low-wage, pollution-tolerant sites in Asia. Others wanted to build manufacturing plants in North America and Europe to fend off potential protectionism legislation. Second, Japanese firms took advantage of easy credit in the 1980s to buy up Japanese real estate, stocks and securities, causing the prices of real estate and land to soar. Third, the banks and the government both allowed firms to borrow without meaningful fiscal safeguards. One result was that organised crime, which had enjoyed covert patronage from both major corporations and political leaders throughout the post-war era, also expanded its influence in the economy in the 1980s. Finally, the post-war trend towards wealth equality reversed. While workers' household incomes increased about thirteen-fold between 1960 and 1990, urban land prices increased about twenty-eight-fold. General standards of living were still rising but, by 1989, the gap between rich and poor was far larger than thirty years earlier.

The sudden collapse of the stock market in 1990 and subsequent economic depression revealed the weaknesses of what became known in retrospect as the **bubble economy** of the 1980s. Japanese companies could not pay back the loans they had confidently taken out in the 1980s. Banks, holding billions of yen in bad loans, could not lend new funds. Real economic growth slowed to nothing. New college graduates, especially women, searched desperately for jobs. High-school students saw little point in cramming for college entrance exams if good jobs were no longer assured at the other end. Meanwhile, firms fired employees, even some of the permanently employed ones. The Liberal Democratic Party, which had controlled the Diet since its founding in 1955, lost power in 1993 after voters became disgusted with a series of revelations about corruption and frustrated with economic recession. Government and businesses quarrelled over new solutions. The social tensions created by inequality, instability and insecurity, all of which had seemed to be waning earlier in the post-war era, reappeared as Japan reached the end of the twentieth century.

Further reading

Brinton, M. (1993) *Women and the Economic Miracle*, Berkeley: University of California Press.

Gordon, A. (1998) *The Wages of Affluence*, Cambridge: Harvard University Press.

Hein, L. (1990) *Fueling Growth*, Cambridge: Harvard University Press.

Johnson, C. (1982) *MITI and the Japanese Miracle*, Stanford: Stanford University Press.

Katz, R. (1998) *Japan: The System that Soured*, Armonk, NY: M.E. Sharpe.

Murakami, Y. and Patrick, H. (eds) (1987–92) *The Political Economy of Japan*, 3 vols, Stanford: Stanford University Press.

LAURA HEIN

population

The population of Japan is approximately 125 million, the world's seventh largest. With an area of 377,643 km (145,808 square miles), Japan is one of the most densely inhabited countries. Moreover, the population is heavily concentrated in the narrow, urbanised coastal strips, where 78 per cent of the population lives in 28 per cent of the area, in the most dense concentrations found anywhere. Japan has one of the world's lowest rates of natural increase, 0.24 per cent in 1997, a result of one of the lowest birth rates (9.5 per thousand). It is projected that the population will continue to grow slightly until 2005, but drop consistently thereafter, to about 100 million by 2050. The low natural increase is offset by a low death rate (7.3 per thousand), with the result that Japan also has one of the world's most rapidly ageing societies. Whereas those over age sixty-five currently make up about 15 per cent of the population, that figure is projected to grow to about 33 per cent by 2050.

Life expectancy is high, 77.19 years for men and 83.82 years for women.

Associated with these dramatic demographic figures are some interesting cultural trends. Japan has a very high abortion rate (28.3 per hundred live births, or over 300,000 annually), which makes the experience of abortion common among Japanese women. Throughout the country, shrines dedicated to unborn children receive thousands of small *jizō* (see **mizuko jiz**), with offerings from mothers who have undergone abortions. In contrast, in a highly developed culture of motherhood, mothers lavish tremendous devotion upon children, especially in **education**. More children are growing up without siblings in smaller households. Young people spend more time in school as education levels climb, marry later and enter the labour force later. The mean age at first marriage is 26.6 for women, and 28.5 for men, an increase of more than two years for men and nearly four years for women, since 1946. This trend means more single-person households, but also more people living with their parents into early adulthood.

The changing composition of the workforce has wide implications for contemporary lifestyles. Over the past thirty years, the labour force participation of men has declined somewhat, due mainly to a legal reduction of the age of retirement to sixty. Women's participation, however, has increased substantially, both for women in their twenties, a very high percentage of whom leave the workforce after marriage, and for women in their forties, who return to the workforce after their children enter higher education. The resulting pattern represents the well-known 'M-curve' of labour force participation. The centre of the curve is flattening out in recent years, as more women defy established norms to remain in the workforce through their reproductive years.

Japan has an active culture of ageing, reflected in cultural industries such as group tours, and recreational activities such as elderly aerobics classes and gateball, a game similar to croquet that swept the country during the 1980s. The elderly now occupy a significant consumer niche market for every conceivable product, carefully adapted for ageing consumers.

See also: education

AUDREY KOBAYASHI

pornography

Sensationalist commentaries of contemporary Japanese culture savour the details of a long history of pornographic tales and images in both Japan and China, and tantalise the Western reader with perversities, old and new. However, the extensive pornography industry in Japan today owes at least as much to the equally long tradition of pornography in the West for both its content and the structure of the market.

There are many examples to be drawn from Japanese cultural texts of pre-modern tastes in everything from incest to bestiality and paedophilia. However, what renders these examples unique is the unfamiliarity of the contexts and modes of representation, and not the practices themselves, for we can find equally disquieting and graphic examples elsewhere across cultures and time. This argument is not intended as a justification of Japanese pornography but rather as a caution against the Western appetite for myths of Oriental sexual perversity. In pre-modern Japan, pornographic storytelling and images were common fare in the repertoires of itinerant performers and storytellers. Precedents for sexually explicit depictions do date back to the earliest collections of Japanese myth and folklore. Even the classic *Tale of Genji* has sexual references, which Arthur Waley either excluded or rendered into Latin when working on his translation in the 1920s. That there was an openness and familiarity in pre-modern Japan to many themes that would be labelled pornographic by contemporary censors has been cited as both precedent and justification for tolerance of the extensive pornography industry in Japan today. Critics of this cultural-continuity argument point out that there are also examples of pre-modern cultural texts that depict rape, incest and sexual violence in an unfavourable light.

Pornography in contemporary Japan, as in many other countries, is closely linked to the sex industry and bar culture. Stores specialising in pornographic materials ranging from commercial videos to sex aids are located in the same marginal urban spaces as bars, clubs and brothels, essentially quarantined from inner urban residential, sub-urban areas and school zones. However, given current levels of urban density and mixed-use real estate a full demarcation of pornographic zones is not possible. There is also the added complication in Japan of vending-machine consumption. Street vending machines selling pornographic photo magazines and comics are commonplace. Although there has been extensive campaigning against this unmonitored access to print pornography, surveys of school-aged children indicate that access to pornographic materials can most often be traced to the home and not vending machines. DM (direct mail) marketing accounts for over 20 per cent of Japanese mail and courier deliveries, and this is rapidly becoming the primary marketing strategy of Japan's pornography industry. Pornographic comics and magazines carry extensive DM advertising, and this marketing has now expanded to include a rapidly growing adult female audience. The extraordinary popularity and volume of pornographic *manga* (comics) targeted at highly diversified adult and teenage markets is one aspect of Japanese pornographic production that is arguably unique. The cultivation of the adult female and teenage male readers of pornographic *manga* has led to a further expansion in what is already the largest sector of the print media after newspapers.

The term video in Japan was for years synonymous with pornographic rentals and this created a marketing dilemma for home video distributors, and was at least in part responsible for the initial success of Japan's WOWOW satellite movie station over neighbourhood video rental outlets. There are close ties between the shadow economy of the *yakuza* and the financing and management of pornographic clubs and video production houses. While a surprising number of Japan's leading cinematographers today began their careers directing pink (porn) movies, today's video technologies have shifted the style of Japanese pornographic video to low-tech, low-budget hand-held videocam footage with rough edits, ad lib dialogue and minimal sets.

Strip clubs, on-stage sex shows, hostess bars, peep shows, etc. are usually clustered together around consumer hubs and stations. While the daytime clientele is largely rank and file *yakuza*, blue-collar workers and unemployed, the night trade is supported by the expense accounts of the Japanese white-collar **sarariiman**. Pornography and prostitution (see **prostitution, regulation of**) are the two main sources of income for the **mizushōbai** and the entertainment accounts of the corporate sector feed this shadow economy. The Japanese taxation office expends extraordinary effort trying to track the mostly undocumented profits of this significant sector of the national economy. There is limited police intervention in the monitoring of pornographic performances and video and other pornographic sales, partly due to Japan's stated preference for a policy of industry-based self-censorship. Some claim that a flood of police corruption cases over the 1990s is, however, evidence that there is substantial co-operation, if not collusion, between some local police, producers of pornography and *mizushōbai* management.

The issue of censorship is one area that distinguishes Japanese pornography from that of other countries. The now infamous 'hair law' prohibited the public display of pubic hair and this essentially amounted to a ban on the representation of genitalia in everything from classic woodblock prints, to pornographic video to Hollywood film. Airbrushing and digital modification are the two preferred censorship techniques, but artists, international film distributors, museum curators and publishers, not to mention pornographers, have all become increasingly innovative in the application of the ban, leading to a gradual erosion in the letter of the law. Recent appeals have seen the courts prepared to exempt works of artistic significance and this has opened the door to increasing flexibility in both industry self-censorship and legal enforcement.

Historically, there has been little focus on the conditions of Japanese women working in the pornography industry. It was the plight of foreign sex workers and minors that finally captured the attention of activists and the media over the 1990s. This can be seen as a reflection of the pariah status of Japanese women who make their living in the shadow world of the *mizushōbai*, and pornography in particular. They have been seen not as victims but as social outcastes. Post-war feminists and

conservatives alike have campaigned against the sex industry in the name of the Japanese family. Feminists have mounted critiques of the sexual exploitation of women's bodies in everything from advertising to hard-core video, but there has been little work done on the real conditions of everyday life of the Japanese women who still form the majority of the workers in the pornography and sex industries. More recently, there has been a growing recognition in feminist research and anti-pornography groups of the intimate interrelatedness of this extensive shadow economy and the stability of the mainstream economy and its mainstay, the Japanese family.

See also: hair debate

Further reading

Buckley, S. (1991) '"Penguin in bondage": a graphic tale of Japanese comic books', in C. Penley and A. Ross (eds) *Technoculture*, Minneapolis: University of Minnesota Press.

SANDRA BUCKLEY

port towns

There are approximately 4,000 port towns on the harbours of Japan's coastline, most of them along the submergent southern and eastern coasts. The oldest ports are on the island of Kyūshū, established during the classical period, when Japan had extensive relations with the Asian mainland. The sex industry was established early in these ports, as a result of young women being brought from East and South-East Asia, a practice that continues today. During the Tokugawa Period, when Japan maintained a strict policy of isolation, ports did not develop, and coastal settlements consisted mostly of small fishing villages. The exception was Nagasaki, where, starting in the seventeenth century, the Portuguese were allowed to maintain a small trading settlement on a strictly controlled artificial island built in the harbour. During the Meiji Period, as international trade expanded, ports became important urban centres. The major ports, such as **Kobe** and **Yokohama**, had sizeable international populations, and were regarded as Japan's most cosmopolitan cities. Today, Japan's ports boast huge container facilities, largely the product of **land reclamation**.

AUDREY KOBAYASHI

post-war Constitution

The Japanese people changed from imperial subjects to democratic citizens when the Constitution of Japan took effect on 3 May 1947. It was drafted in six days by a small group of Americans, modified by the Japanese government and passed by the Diet, and promulgated by Emperor **Hirohito**. It replaced the 1889 Constitution of the Empire of Japan (the 'Meiji Constitution'), to which it was technically an amendment. The new 'Peace Constitution' transferred sovereignty from the Emperor to the people, guaranteed a broad range of rights and renounced war.

The Allies' **Potsdam Declaration** of July 1945 promised the establishment 'in accordance with the freely expressed will of the Japanese people of a peacefully inclined and responsible government'. In October 1945, **Supreme Commander the Allied Powers** (SCAP) General Douglas **MacArthur** made it clear to Japanese leaders that the Constitution would have to be revised. One revision project led by former Premier Prince Konoe Fumimarō ended with his suicide in December 1945 on the eve of his arrest as a war criminal. A government committee headed by legal scholar Matsumoto Jōji proposed making the Cabinet responsible to a more powerful Diet (legislature), reducing the Emperor's powers but not taking away his sovereignty, and expanding but still qualifying civil rights. A number of other proposals were put forward by civic groups, political parties and individuals.

MacArthur feared that a popular backlash against a conservative government draft would result in a Constitution that eliminated the throne, which he considered essential to stability. Directives that might be forthcoming from the Far Eastern Commission, set up by the Allies to supervise the Occupation, could have the same result. So, he ordered members of his Government Section to write a draft on their own, and, although the

Constitution they created is one of the world's most progressive, MacArthur's primary goal was a conservative one: to protect the Emperor.

The SCAP draft was presented to the government on 13 February 1946, accompanied by warnings that only minor changes would be accepted and that there was no other way to guarantee the preservation of the Emperor. The document was shockingly revolutionary. Sovereignty was transferred to the people from the Emperor, who was made only 'the symbol of the State and of the unity of the people'. Civil rights could no longer be restricted by law, and went beyond even those in the US Constitution to include equality of the sexes, collective bargaining for labour, academic freedom, the right to work and to receive an education and 'the right to maintain the minimum standards of wholesome and cultured living'. The prime minister was to be selected by and from the Diet. The cabinet was to be responsible to the Diet, and could be brought down by a vote of no confidence. Most remarkably, Article 9 renounced war and prohibited the maintenance of military forces.

Negotiations between SCAP and Japanese officials resulted in only one major change, which made the Diet bicameral rather than unicameral. The government then presented the draft as its own, and the Emperor, who was required by the Meiji Constitution to initiate constitutional amendments, announced his approval. During Diet deliberations, the wording of Article 9 was changed to make it possible to argue that the Constitution did not prohibit military armament for purposes of self-defence, so that it reads:

Aspiring sincerely to an international peace based on justice and order, the Japanese people forever renounce war as a sovereign right of the nation and the threat or use of force as a means of settling international disputes.

In order to accomplish the aim of the preceding paragraph, land, sea, and air forces, as well as other war potential, will never be maintained. The right of belligerency of the state will not be recognised.

The Emperor promulgated the new Constitution of Japan on 3 November 1946, the birthday of his grandfather Emperor Meiji, and it took effect six months later.

A revised election law gave women the right to vote in 1946, and other new laws were passed to implement the provisions of the new Constitution. These included important revisions to the Civil Code (see **Civil Code of 1948, the**) to reflect the new equality of the sexes and reduce the authority of the head of the household.

Though the Supreme Court has the authority to judge laws and government actions unconstitutional, it has rarely done so. In particular, it has avoided any definitive judgement on the constitutionality of the **Self-Defence Forces**, established in 1954 despite Article 9.

When Japan regained its independence with the end of the Occupation in 1952, conservatives wished to amend the Constitution to expand the role of the Emperor and explicitly allow rearmament. However, despite the conservative parties' dominance of post-war politics, they never gained the two-thirds Diet majority required to initiate constitutional amendments. Even if they had, it is not likely such changes would have gained the necessary majority in the national referendum that would follow Diet passage of a proposed amendment. Opinion polls have consistently shown a majority of Japanese supporting the 'peace Constitution'. Though it was authored and imposed by Americans, it clearly drew on a strong pre-war legacy of demands for democracy and meshed with a war-weary people's desire for peace. At the end of the century, however, post-cold war uncertainties in East Asia seemed to carry the potential for weakening this popular pacifism.

Further reading

Dower, J. (1999) *Embracing Defeat: Japan in the Wake of World War II*, New York: Norton.

Gordon, B. Sirota (1998) *The Only Woman in the Room: A Memoir*, Tokyo: Kōdansha International.

Henderson, D. (ed.) (1968) *The Constitution of Japan: The First Twenty Years, 1947–1967*, Seattle: University of Washington Press.

Inoue, K. (1991) *MacArthur's Japanese Constitution: A Linguistic and Cultural Study of its Making*, Chicago: University of Chicago Press.

Koseki, S. (1997) *The Birth of Japan's Postwar Constitution*, ed. and trans. R. Moore, Boulder, CO: Westview Press.

TIMOTHY S. GEORGE

postal savings

Japan's *ūbin chokin seido* (postal savings system) was established in 1875 and is by far the largest financial institution in the world; in fact, its deposits are five times greater than those of the Bank of Tokyo-Mitsubishi, the largest private bank in the world. The postal savings system is convenient (deposits, withdrawals and transfers can be made at any post office in Japan) as well as innovative (it offers types of accounts not offered by private banks) and has been credited with helping to raise Japan's personal saving rate. Most of the deposits collected by the postal savings system are funnelled via the Shikin Un'yū-bu (Trust Funds Bureau) of the Ministry of Finance to government financial institutions, public corporations, local governments, etc., and it has also been credited with helping to finance Japan's economic growth and development. Some argue that the system should be privatised but this proposal has been shelved, for now. The postal savings system is slated to be converted into a public corporation in 2003, and from 2001 it will be required to manage all of its funds rather than work through the Trust Funds Bureau. It has managed some funds independently since 1987.

See also: saving

CHARLES YUJI HORIOKA

Potsdam Declaration

On 26 July 1945, the USA, Britain and China issued the Potsdam Declaration as the ultimatum to Japan, calling on its government to proclaim 'unconditional surrender of all Japanese armed forces' or to face 'prompt and utter destruction'. Its stipulation included demilitarisation and demobilisation, punishment of war criminals, removal of obstacles to democratisation, material reparation and loss of territory in accordance with the 1943

Cairo Declaration and Occupation of Japan till all objectives have been accomplished.

The Japanese government, still hoping to broker a conditional surrender through the Soviet Union, was deeply divided. In particular, it was concerned with the status of the imperial institution, not clarified in the declaration. Strong pressure from the military led Prime Minister Suzuki Kantarō to announce that the Cabinet 'would offer no comment [*mokusatsu*]', essentially ignoring the Allied demands. Japan's failure to promptly accept the Potsdam Declaration, coupled with the Allies' insistence on unconditional surrender, brought about grave, albeit unforeseen, consequences. Two weeks later, after two atomic blasts on Japan and the Soviet entry into the war, the Japanese government indicated willingness to accept all Allied demands, 'with the understanding that the authority of the Emperor shall not change', thus bringing the war to an end.

YANG DAQING

poverty and the poor

Post-war Japan experienced a dramatic decline in the numbers of its citizens living in poverty. By 1970, the Economic Planning Agency proclaimed the nation to be on the verge of the 'dissolution of poverty'. Although pockets of destitution and homelessness persist, Japan today registers some of the lowest rates of poverty and income inequality among the world's advanced economies.

Poverty constituted an endemic social problem throughout the pre-war era. The pattern of pre-war industrialisation emphasised low-cost production for export while slighting the development of a home market made up of well-paid workers. In the countryside, large numbers subsisted as tenant farmers, and those who migrated to the cities often swelled the ranks of the urban poor. Pre-war public assistance measures relieved only a small fraction of the destitute. The standard of living rose for most Japanese between the late nineteenth century and 1930s, yet improvements in ordinary people's lives lagged far behind the aggregate economic growth.

Millions more became impoverished in the wake of Japan's defeat in the Second World War. These were people who lost their homes, wealth or livelihood due to US bombing, and who faced massive unemployment, hyperinflation, loss of Japan's overseas dominions and the war deaths and wounding of family members. As late as 1953, officials estimated that 45 per cent of the population lived either below the defined subsistence level or just barely above it. Under the Daily Life Security Law (1946; revised 1950), the government granted public assistance to many more people than in pre-war times. None the less, a mere 3–4 per cent of the population received such assistance in the early 1950s. Income inequality continued to grow during the 1950s.

Beginning in the early 1960s, the numbers of Japanese living in abject poverty rapidly declined, and the gap between rich and poor diminished. The reduction in destitution was in part related to the state's expanded **welfare policies** – notably national health insurance, national pensions and higher levels of public assistance. However, the decline in poverty may be primarily attributed to post-war Japan's rapid economic growth.

Other explanations pinpoint various government policies that were not anti-poverty programmes *per se*, yet successfully improved the living standards of targeted sectors of society. Various measures have aimed at protecting and maintaining the many small proprietors and farmers, whose families might have suffered economic deprivation under freer markets. Moreover, to ameliorate rural poverty, the state has actively encouraged economic development projects and social services in depressed regions. Another set of programmes aids minority groups, whose members disproportionately suffered deprivation. In the case of the largest minority, the **Burakumin**, the government has significantly raised living standards with programmes of assistance and services. Overall, income gaps have lessened due to the equalising benefits of Japan's system of nearly universal education through high school.

This is not to say that Japan has eradicated poverty. The vast majority of the nation's poor neither appears on public assistance rolls nor lives on the streets or in identifiable slums. Less than one-third of households whose income qualified them for public assistance actually received such aid over the past three decades. Many Japanese do not apply for relief because they fear the public stigma, or because their relatives support them. At the same time, government policies have helped render poverty invisible by frequently discouraging the truly needy from seeking assistance. The authorities administer stringent, humiliating means tests, and they ferret out distant relatives who are expected to support the needy in lieu of public monies.

Who are the poor? The two largest categories of public-assistance recipients are the elderly and those lower-income families caring for a disabled individual. As Japan becomes a rapidly ageing society (see **ageing society and elderly care**), the number of elderly people without sufficient means has grown. It is noteworthy that Japan's single-mother households do not constitute a large category of the poor. The nation, boasts officials, has thus far avoided the 'feminisation of poverty', as seen in the USA. In 1997, single mothers headed a mere 8 per cent of households receiving public assistance. Although Japan's **divorce** rate has risen steadily in recent years, it remains low compared with most Western nations. Moreover, few Japanese children are born out of wedlock (a mere 1 percent in 1992). Japan's relatively stable families are more than an innate cultural trait. Government and company policies actively discourage single mothers who seek economic independence. Officials often refuse to grant assistance to single mothers, or demand that the women first seek support from their parents. **Day labourers** and the homeless make up the poorest ranks of the Japanese. Most are adult males who are estranged from their families. Day labourers generally live in cheap lodging houses near *yoseba*, gathering places where contractors hire them for construction jobs. Some are **migrant workers** from other Asian countries. The *yoseba* are primarily found in the big cities – notably Ōsaka's Kamagasaki area and Tokyo's San'ya. Estimated in the early 1990s at one to two-hundred-thousand men nationwide, day labourers eke out a minimal living between periods of unemployment. Most are in their fifties or older, and commonly in poor health.

The homeless constitute the smallest, though most visible, category of the poor. In the late 1990s, the government estimated their numbers nationwide at 16,000. Most lived in Ōsaka and Tokyo. To be sure, the numbers of homeless in New York City alone far exceed the national totals in Japan. Also, the present population of Japan's homeless and day labourers is much smaller than that of the impoverished early post-war years. None the less, many Japanese fear a steady rise in homelessness and casual labour if the economic stagnation of the 1990s continues.

Further reading

Fowler, E. (1996) *San'ya Blues*, Ithaca: Cornell University Press.

Garon, S. (1997) *Molding Japanese Minds*, Princeton: Princeton University Press.

Milly, D. (1999) *Poverty, Equality, and Growth*, Cambridge: Harvard University Asian Center.

SHELDON GARON

Power Rangers

The Mighty Morphin' Power Rangers (MMPR), with their signature cry 'It's morphin' time!' débuted on US television in 1993. Two movies and seven television series later, the Power Rangers are still going strong. The television series completed so far are: *Mighty Morphin' Power Rangers* (145 episodes); *Mighty Morphin' Alien Rangers* (ten); *Power Rangers Zeo* (fifty); *Power Rangers Turbo* (forty-five); and *Power Rangers in Space* (forty). As of spring 2000, *Power Rangers Lost Galaxy* was still airing. The year 2000 also saw the début of a new series, *Power Rangers Lightspeed Rescue*.

The television programmes are jointly produced: Tōei Studios in Japan providing action scenes from previously released Japanese series (with the actors in colour-coded fighting suits and helmets), and a US studio providing scenes shot with American teenaged actors (dressed like normal high-school students). Aimed at young children, the Power Rangers' popularity has in turn produced a huge market for the affiliated toy action-figures, made by the Japanese company Bandai.

While this kind of live-action battle programme for young children was new to US audiences in 1993, it has a longer history in Japan. Called '*sentai*' (group fighter) shows, the five-person colour-coded fighting unit has been familiar since *Go Renjaa* (Five Rangers), broadcast in 1975. Like the various Power Rangers incarnations, each new *sentai* series in Japan may begin with a new threat from different enemies, but all return to the time-honoured narrative formula once the storyline is established. The action scenes for *MMPR* were taken from an early 1990s series called *Jū Renjaa* (Ten Rangers). New *sentai* shows remain popular; *MMPR* was even reverse-imported to Japan.

MMPR and its sequels demonstrated some key differences from the Japanese series whose scenes they borrow. While most *sentai* series include one female ranger (usually the 'pink' one), the US series' team featured two girls and three boys; an African-American, an Asian-American, a Hispanic and two white characters.

In *MMPR* the Power Rangers were recruited by an ancient interdimensional being named Zordon to fight the evil Rita Repulsa. Five normal high-school kids in California, these teenagers brought various talents to the group and were given individual powers as they learned to morph into Power Rangers. Each Ranger rode a fighting vehicle, known as a Dino Zord, which combined the strength of the ancient dinosaurs with technological power from the Morphing Grid. These Zords could in turn link together to form a more powerful fighting unit, called a MegaZord. In every series, the mounts/vehicles of the Rangers have had various possibilities of combination into larger fighting units. This concept is no doubt related to the popularity of other 'transforming robots' in Japanese popular culture. As new Power Rangers series have come out, each has updated the original five-Ranger concept to fit the latest fads among their young audience. The latest release, *Power Rangers Lightspeed Rescue* is accompanied by toys that can 'read' the television programme and record parts of it, without any direct connection to the television set, as well as featuring **Pokemon**-style monsters.

See also: robots; toys

SHARALYN ORBAUGH

pregnancy and pre-natal care

As life-cycle and employment patterns for women have undergone significant shifts since 1945, there have been corresponding changes in the timing and experience of pregnancy and pre-natal care. Women today are having children later, exercising greater self-determination in the choice to carry to term or not and accepting fewer cultural constraints on control over their own pregnant body – at the same time as they experience increased medical and state intervention.

Prior to the Meiji Period, pregnancy had been highly ritualised, mainly through the involvement of local midwives who administered traditional treatments while also ensuring adherence to a multitude of taboos and purification ceremonies related to the notion of pollution. By the 1920s, a modern generation of midwives prided themselves in their technical and scientific training, and carefully distinguished the medical foundations of their practices from the ritualistic focus of pre-modern midwives. This may not, however, entirely do justice to the value of the traditional medical knowledge underpinning midwifery in pre-Meiji Japan. There was a move to monitor and control the conditions of pregnancy and the wellbeing of the foetus with an increasing rhetoric of eugenics over the 1920s and 1930s. In the post-war years, gynaecology and obstetrics displaced the midwife from the birthing room to community clinics, where she was limited to an educational role and monitoring pre- and post-natal healthcare.

While reform to the abortion law has allowed woman greater choice, limited access to effective birth control has left women excessively dependent on surgical termination of pregnancies when determining not to carry a pregnancy to term. While there is little stigma attached to abortion in Japan today, pregnancy outside **marriage** remains such a social stigma that few women are willing to face the associated risks of social and economic disadvantage. Pregnancy within marriage is carefully timed and the strongest factor is economics. Women have been extending their years of full-time participation in the workforce after marriage and before the birth of the first child. Pregnancies early in marriage create a personal crisis that many women choose to resolve without consultation with their spouse. While women are beginning their child-bearing years later (average age twenty-six), there also remains a strong cultural bias, supported by the exhortations of the medical profession, against pregnancy past the mid-thirties. This amounts to a dramatic shortening of the active reproductive period – average 2.2–2.5 years – (Buckley: 353).

If ritual and concepts of pollution acted to constrain pregnant women in pre-modern Japan, today it is the excessive medicalisation of pregnancy and pre-natal care that feminists and some women doctors criticise. Advocate groups for the handicapped argue that the required levels of foetal monitoring through community motherhood clinics border on eugenic screening and that women are pressured into abortion with the first sign of 'abnormality'. Though it is no longer legal to require women to resign employment on becoming pregnant, cultural attitudes are slower to change and the majority of women still quit the workforce early in pregnancy.

The wardrobe of a pregnant woman has remained remarkably unchanged over the post-war period, with a strong emphasis on plain, loose fitting wrap-around smocks and apron dresses that emphasise the newly domesticated and asexual status of the mother-to-be. The sight of a woman in the last weeks of pregnancy riding the subway or entering a theatre or restaurant can still attract judgemental looks in an odd mix of old and new taboos. While the specific experience of being pregnant may have changed, there is no question that the first full-term pregnancy still marks the most important transition in a Japanese woman's life-cycle.

References

Buckley, S. (1993) 'Altered states', in A. Gordon (ed.) *Postwar Japan As History*, Berkeley: University of California Press, pp. 347–72.

Further reading

Hardacre, H. (1997) *Marketing the Menacing Foetus in Japan*, Berkeley: University of California Press, pp. 19–100

SANDRA BUCKLEY

PRIME MINISTER'S OFFICE *see* Sōrifu

priority production

Priority production was a government economic programme to stimulate critically low industrial output in the years immediately after the Second World War. The policy was instituted in December 1946 by the first Yoshida Cabinet and was in effect until 1948. Scarcity of raw materials and capital strained industrial output, which in 1946 was less than one-third of what it had been before the war.

The government sought to resuscitate production by devoting scarce capital and resources to two prioritised industries: coal and steel. Petroleum received as American aid was concentrated on steel production. Steel was then used to improve infrastructure in the coal industry, whose increased output was then allocated to fuel the steel industry. The programme aimed to induce a cycle of increased production in which the steel and coal industries would be mutually revitalised and serve as the basis of overall industrial expansion. Under the programme, the government funnelled capital through the Reconstruction Finance Bank (RFB) and provided subsidies that allowed steel and coal producers to sell below cost. Although the programme neglected other industries and encouraged inflationary practices by the RFB, it helped increase steel and coal output dramatically and provided a foundation for later expansion.

Further reading

Dower, John W. (1999) *Embracing Defeat*, New York: Norton.

Johnson, Chalmers (1982) *MITI and the Japanese Miracle*, Stanford: Stanford University Press.

Suzuki, Takeo (1960) *Gendai Nihon Zaiseishi*, vol. 1, Tokyo: Tokyo Daigaku Shuppankai.

HIRAKU SHIMODA

private and public schools

Public schools fall into two categories: national schools, established and funded by the national government, and local public schools, established by either the prefectural or municipal government and funded by all three levels of government. Private institutions receive their income from student tuition and subsidies from national and local governments, as well as business and industry. Most elementary and junior high students attend public schools in Japan, which traditionally have had higher status, lower costs and established linkages among schools of the same rank, which can lead to certain career prospects. However, with the limit of compulsory education set at the end of middle school, private institutions begin to play a much larger role in education in order to satisfy the range of student demand. Because public school enrolment in high school is limited, competition for the best is great, leaving students who do not perform well opting for expensive private education. More than 25 per cent of high schools are private. Most vocational schools, junior colleges and special training schools are private. The status differential between public and private schools becomes more fluid at the post-secondary level where some of the best universities are private. Similarly, private schools for younger children are gaining in recognition and respect as students and parents challenge the rigidity of the public-school system and more students with diverse needs enter the system.

JUNE A. GORDON

prostitution, regulation of

In 1956, the Prostitution Prevention Law (the PPL) made prostitution illegal for the first time in Japanese history. The Occupation authorities declared that prostitution was 'inconsistent with democracy', but lobbying from Japanese social reformers and the dangers of venereal disease were also important factors.

The PPL purports to prohibit prostitution, but penalises only streetwalking, procuring, advertising and providing premises for prostitution. This reflects the view that streetwalkers in the 1950s were victims in need of protection and social reintegration. Consequently, although the law prescribes fines and imprisonment for offences, in practice women charged were directed to protec-

tive institutions for compulsory rehabilitation. No penalties are prescribed for clients. Few women today are charged or rehabilitated under the PPL. The profile of female sex workers has changed dramatically. Today's victims tend to be illegal foreign sex workers, who are typically forcibly controlled, work virtually unlimited hours, are paid less than their Japanese counterparts and receive no compensation provided for illness or injury. When detected, they are deported under immigration law. Among Japanese women, the typical sex industry worker now sees herself as either a full-time professional or a part-time freelancer. Commercial sex in contemporary Japan is a high-profile, high-tech business. The 'corporatisation' of commercial sex in Japan also reflects the widespread involvement of organised crime syndicates, the *yakuza*.

Traditional sex industry work in Japan includes: streetwalking; entertainment work (bar hostess prostitution in cabarets, night-clubs, bars, snack bars, Japanese-style inns and restaurants); bath-houses (so called 'soaplands'); new-style entertainment (see **nopan kissa**); and escort agencies. A 1948 Law to Control Businesses Affecting Public Morals established a licensing system that allows police and local government to monitor and regulate the venues in which entertainment industry businesses operate (**mizushōbai**), including **love hotels** (hotel rooms, often featuring fantasy décor, rented by the hour). Key challenges for regulators today are: the diversity of community attitudes to prostitution; fear of the spread of AIDS; the influx of (illegal) foreign sex workers; and the growing participation of ordinary women – housewives, students and office workers – in the sex industry. New forms of prostitution are much harder to detect: telephone sex services, telephone dating clubs and client lists developed through word of mouth. A hotly debated issue at present is voluntary prostitution by girls in middle-school or high-school – so-called **enjo kōsai** (subsidised dating). This has prompted reconsideration of the links between tolerance for the expansion of sex industry businesses and the relaxation of social values. Local governments in some cases have responded with ordinances making it an offence for clients to solicit under-age sex.

See also: love hotels; *mizushōbai*; prostitution, regulation of; sex tourism; telephone sex

Further reading

Buruma, I. (1984) *A Japanese Mirror: Heroes and Villains of Japanese Culture*, Penguin: London.

Mackie, V. (1988) 'Division of labour: Multinational sex in Asia', in G. McCormack and Y. Sugimoto (eds) *The Japanese Trajectory: Modernization and Beyond*, Cambridge: Cambridge University Press, pp. 218–32.

VERONICA TAYLOR

public housing

Modern public housing in Tokyo was first introduced in the 1920s by the Dōjunkai, to respond to housing needs after the Great Tokyo Earthquake. The Jūtaku Eidan (Public Housing Agency), created to rebuild and develop affordable housing after the massive destruction of the Second World War, continued its work in 1941. The Public Housing Agency was replaced by two government agencies: the Japan Housing Corporation (JHC) in 1955, which standardised the n-DK layout plan, flush toilet and Western-style kitchen for collective housing, and focused on building collective housing for workers; and the New Town Development Public Corporation in 1975, which began development of large 'bed town' communities in the suburbs of metropolitan areas. In 1981, the Jūtaku Toshi Seibi Kōdan (Housing and Urban Development Corporation, or HUDC) subsumed both of these agencies. HUDC works together with local and regional housing supply agencies formed under the 1951 Public Housing Law (*Kōei Jūtaku Hō*) to meet five-year incremental national-policy goals for collective and individual housing construction, urban renewal projects and public-facilities development. While *danchi* (plain, multi-storey concrete apartment complexes) met initial needs for emergency public housing, in recent years HUDC claims to concentrate on quality rather than quantity in its public housing and development programmes. Indeed, public housing is not stigmatised by stereotypes of inexpensive, low-quality housing, but increasingly appeals to middle- to-upper-class homebuyers; however, critics question the gentrification that is putting public housing out of the reach of the lower classes as a result of HUDC policies. Besides HUDC, local-supply corporations (*kōsha jūtaku*) and publicly operated housing (*kōei jūtaku*) agencies build housing with government or local subsidies, then locally manage and lease them to low-income, handicapped and elderly tenants.

Further reading

HUDC Public Relations Division (eds) (1993) *HUDC: Housing and Urban Development Corporation*, Tokyo: Kamiya Printing Co., Ltd.

ICHIRO SUZUKI AND MARY KNIGHTON

R

radio broadcasting

The Japanese, according to a 1995 survey, spend twenty-four minutes a day listening to the radio, compared to three hours and twenty-eight minutes watching television. Only one in five Japanese turn on the radio daily. Despite these numbers, new stations are opening across the country. In the 1980s, residents in small towns could tune into five stations including three stations from the public broadcaster NHK, and two from commercial stations. There were only two commercial stations because government policy only allowed two – one AM and one FM – for each of the forty-seven prefectures (the Japanese equivalent of a state).

Although residents in Tokyo enjoyed three more commercial AM stations along with the US Armed Forces Network, their choice of FM stations was also limited to two. However, radio broadcasting began to diversify in the 1990s with new FM stations that reflected the needs and tastes of various communities. By 1999, Tokyo residents could choose from more than fifteen stations, including eight FM stations.

Radio broadcasting in Japan began in 1925, when a private Tokyo Broadcasting Station launched its daily programming, five years after the first US station, owned by a receiver manufacturer, pioneered regularly scheduled transmissions, and three years after the BBC established its daily service. In 1926, the Japanese government consolidated Tokyo Broadcasting and two other private stations into NHK, redirecting Japan's broadcasting towards a more British model – a regulated, and yet not state-operated, public

service. NHK continued to be the sole voice on the Japanese airwaves until 1951, when the first commercial stations opened in **Ōsaka** and **Nagoya**.

Both the role of radio and its relationship with the public have greatly shifted over the years. On 15 August 1945, when Emperor **Hirohito** issued the command to **surrender** on the radio, families and neighbours gathered around radio sets, and paid full attention to his voice. Radio enjoyed predominance until Crown Prince Akihito, the current Emperor, married in 1959, and the royal wedding (see **Royal Wedding, 1959**) procession was broadcast live on television, attracting millions of first-time television viewers. The next media event, the 1964 **Tokyo Olympics**, marked the widespread arrival of a television set in the Japanese living room. Average listening hours dropped from over ninety minutes in 1960 to approximately thirty minutes in 1965. More competition came from the introduction of FM band. In March 1969, NHK started regular FM broadcasts, followed by a commercial station nine months later.

Radio found its new identity by becoming an accompaniment to other activities. A radio set became increasingly portable, affordable and thus personal, moving into bedrooms and cars. In the 1970s and 1980s, commercial AM stations captured a large following by targeting young people working alone after midnight. Students cramming for university **entrance examinations** studied while listening to freewheeling late-night shows (*shinya-hōsō*). Some hosts lent a sympathetic ear to those under pressure, and gave support and advice.

Others played music that was too progressive for either primetime radio or television, and ultimately set music trends. **Kitano Takeshi**, a comedian better known as a movie director in the West, told politically incorrect jokes in this arena throughout the 1980s. Late-night radio faced a challenge in the mid-1980s when late-night television began to offer the same intimacy and casualness. Video games, CDs and the Internet also lured the young listeners away. The older generation, however, tended to stick to the radio. In 1990, NHK Radio 1 ventured into late-night broadcasting by targeting a mature audience. The programming featured slowly paced talk by popular hosts from daytime programmes and appealed to a respectable niche of listeners in a rapidly ageing society (see **ageing society and elderly care**).

Mixed programming dominates radio broadcasting in Japan. Few commercial stations specialise in only one particular type of music or genre. Commercial AM stations offer remarkably similar segmented programming. On a given evening, all four commercial AM stations in Tokyo might carry the baseball games of the Tokyo Giants. NHK Radio 2, however, maintains a separate identity as an educational medium. More than 50 per cent of its programmes are foreign-language instruction, which deliver more than nine hours of language lessons a day.

Radio voices multiplied as budding local stations were added to foreign-language stations. The **Ministry of Post and Telecommunications** began to issue licences for Community FM stations that 'narrow-cast' to a city or a district, while traditional commercial FM stations broadcast to a prefecture. The first of these stations opened in Hakodate, Hokkaidō, in 1992, and 111 stations joined the airwaves by October 1998. The Community FM stations encourage the participation of local residents. The first foreign-language FM station, Cocolo FM in Ōsaka, became operational in February 1995, followed by InterFM in Tokyo, and Love FM in Fukuoka. A fourth station in Nagoya was scheduled for 2000. While these stations are better known for their hip US-style DJs and hot music, they provide public-service announcements for expatriate communities in French, Indonesian, Korean, Mandarin, Portuguese, Spanish, Tagalog and Thai. In the post-

Kobe Earthquake Japan, tailored information for small communities is considered vital to prevent and manage a disaster.

For listeners abroad, NHK Radio Japan has been broadcasting an international short-wave service since 1935. In addition to programmes in Japanese and English, NHK offers daily programming in twenty other languages, reaching some 18 million global listeners by its own estimate. The programmes include news as well as Japanese language lessons. Radio Japan's website – http://www.nhk.or.jp/rjnet – lists the available frequencies.

See also: pirate radio

Further reading

Japan Ministry of Post and Telecommunications (1994–8) 'White paper: Communications in Japan 1994–8'. English summary available at http://www.mpt.go.jp/policyreports/english/papers/index-e.html.

Kasza, Gregory J. (1988) *The State and the Mass Media in Japan, 1918–1945*, Berkeley: University of California Press.

Kogawa, T. (1988) 'New trends in Japanese popular cutlure', in G. McCormack and Y. Sugimoto (eds). *The Japanese Trajectory: Modernization and Beyond*, Cambridge: Cambridge University Press, pp. 54–66.

Nakano, Y. (1999) 'Japanese radio voices: Parachuter's paradox', in A. Knight and Y. Nakano (eds) *Reporting Hong Kong: Foreign Media and the Handover*, Surrey: Curzon Press and New York: St Martin's Press, pp. 131–52.

National Association of Commercial Broadcasters in Japan. Website at http://www.nab.or.jp/htm/english/englishtop0.htm.

NAKANO YOSHIKO

railways

The construction of railways in Japan commenced almost half a century after that of the USA and Britain. Railway construction was costly and technically difficult, and the government was only able to complete seventy-six miles of line before 1881. Tokyo and Yokohama were linked by rail in

1872; Kobe and Ōsaka were connected in 1874, and the line was extended to Kyōto in 1877. The hope was to construct a trunk line that would run through the main island and thereby expand government control of the country; establish market control throughout Japan and increase the mobility of the armed forces. The railways were seen as the means by which to enlighten the Japanese people about Western ways, and also as a vehicle by which to expand foreign trade.

Despite government encouragement of private enterprise, railways remained a government monopoly until 1891. The Sino-Japanese War (1894) and the Russo-Japanese War (1904–5) helped to promote further railway development. The late Meiji Period saw a railway boom, during which many private railways were constructed. In 1906, the Japanese government bought up the private railways and established the Japan National Railways Corporation (JNR). The South Manchurian Railway Company (SMR) was established by Japan in 1906, half of the original capital of the company being provided by the Japanese government. This company dominated the Manchurian economy, with control over railways, coal mines and industrial plants. The railways provided Japan with the means by which to exploit Manchuria's natural resources, and territory beyond its borders. The next few decades saw a period of intense railroad rivalry between China, Russia and Japan, in which economic and territorial rights were at stake. The period culminated in the Japanese seizure of Manchuria in 1931.

After the Pacific War, JNR hired discharged soldiers and other personnel who had worked on Japan's colonial railroads. During the Allied Occupation, JNR was transformed from a state-owned enterprise to a public corporation. JNR was left to finance the construction of new lines and the expansion of its facilities by borrowing or using its earnings. Japan pursued plans to create a new high-speed railway line that would enhance the Tōkaidō Line that runs from Tokyo to Ōsaka. Japanese airlines, roads and automobiles were relatively undeveloped and there was a visible need for railroads. The subsequent development of road transport, however, meant an eventual reduction in railway traffic. Despite this, unprofitable lines were not abolished and higher rates

were not imposed on these lines, despite the need for increased revenue. The official view that trains and railway development fostered local industry made it difficult for JNR to abolish unprofitable lines, and led to pressure to continue to expand the rail network.

During the decade-and-a-half after the Second World War, an annual loss of ¥4,000 million reportedly accrued each year from the new local lines built after Japan's surrender. In 1964, the first year of the *shinkansen* (**bullet train**) and the year of the **Tokyo Olympics**, JNR recorded its first deficit at ¥30 billion. The deficit continued to grow each year reaching ¥184 trillion in 1973. The Japanese Diet had power of authorisation over the JNR budget, and, as a result, many politicians pushed for uneconomical construction projects that were attractive to their electorates. In order to maintain the support of voters, politicians were very reluctant to approve fare increases. This made it impossible to generate sufficient revenue to cover the growing deficit. JNR accumulated a long-term debt that reached around US$109 billion in the 1985 financial year. Despite high levels of patronage, of the total 245 trunk and local lines operated by JNR, only the Tōkaidō–Sanyō line and seven other main lines between Tokyo and Ōsaka generated a profit in the 1984 financial year. JNR came to an end on 1 April 1987, with more debt than Brazil, Mexico and the Philippines combined.

JNR was replaced by six private passenger railway companies and a national freight operator. This privatisation would prevent the Diet from interfering in railway matters and produce smaller groups that would perhaps make for better management–labour relations, and engender co-operation and a more commercial spirit. The break-up and regionalisation of the railways was seen as a way they could become more focused and more competitive with road and air transport. It was also considered a good time to dispose of surplus land holdings. The total debt that had accumulated over twenty-two years was US$167 billion. The privatisation of Japan Railways in the 1980s and loss of its massive government subsidy has made it a more competitive organisation, but cost cutting has had some negative consequences. Critics suggest that a lowering of design and inspection standards may have had a part in the collapse of concrete from tunnel walls a decade later, due to incorrect materials used and reduced maintenance. The ageing of the Japanese population and decline of the birth rate suggests that there will not be significant growth in the railway industry in the future.

Japan Railway companies are turning to property development in the form of shopping centres and hotels, as well as ancillary services such as food and beverages, buses and car rental to complement their core business. West Japan Railway Company's most ambitious project to date of this sort has been the controversial refurbishment of Kyōto Station, which was completed in 1997 at a cost of ¥150 billion (US$1.07 billion). Several Buddhist organisations opposed the project that sought to create a new gateway for the city. The project is but one example of how the company is seeking to make the most of its existing stations, with an emphasis on commercial facilities such as a hotel, a department store, shopping mall and underground restaurant and shopping arcade. Kyōto Station thus has become not only a transportation hub but a destination in itself. The Kyōto station development reminds us that Japanese railways were, historically, an agent of modernisation and, today, remain an essential element of the capitalist landscape. In this and other contemporary station and rail development projects we see demonstrated the extent to which commuting and consuming have become inextricably entwined around contemporary multifunctional stations complexes.

MORRIS LOW

rakugo

Rakugo is a comic performance genre in which a professional raconteur, alone on stage, relates a humorous story to an audience. Seated on their knees and wearing traditional Japanese clothing, *rakugo* storytellers (*rakugoka* or *hanashika*) make dramatic use of their hands, facial expressions and head movements to bring a multitude of characters to life. They also occasionally use a fan (*sensū*) and a hand towel (*tenugui*) to portray a variety of objects. The ceremonial opening of a *rakugo* performance is announced by an orchestra (*hayashi*)

of drums, *samisen*, flute and gong, placed behind the stage. Literally written 'falling words', *rakugo* is also characterised by the final punchline, or *ochi*, that almost always ends the story with a witty surprise.

Rakugo traces its history to the civil-war days in the sixteenth century, when warlords wary of would-be assassins hired comic storytellers called *otogishū* to keep them awake. By the beginning of the Edo Period (1603–1868), collections of *otogishū* stories were published and storytelling spread to the common people. The first professional storytellers appeared in the 1670s as *tsujibanashi*, or 'street corner story' raconteurs. Represented by Shikano Buzaemon in Edo, Yonezawa Hikohachi in Ōsaka and Tsuyu no Gorobō in Kyōto, the *tsujibanashi* storytellers established the foundations of *rakugo*. While these street performances gradually disappeared, skilled amateur raconteurs began to tell stories at private banquets and *soba* noodle shops. The stories became much longer, adding a narrative dimension, providing more detailed descriptions and emphasising the punchline. Eventually, this led to the establishment of professional raconteurs and the first *yose* vaudeville theatres in Edo. At the end of the nineteenth century, there were almost 400 theatres and *rakugo* had become a very popular form of entertainment. One of the most renowned artistes of the day was Sanyūtei Enchō (1839–1900), who was responsible for many innovations in the genre.

Today, there are basically two categories of *rakugo*: classical, or *koten rakugo*, whose repertory was essentially fixed in the Meiji (1868–1912) and Taishō (1912–26) Periods, and *shinsaku rakugo*, featuring modern themes. Although *shinsaku rakugo* began in the Meiji Period, stories of that era are now considered classical. A *rakugo* story is composed of the *makura*, or introduction, the *hanashi*, or the story itself, and the *ochi*. The raconteur uses the *makura* to size up the audience, engage them with short anecdotes, or *kobanashi*, and provide background explanation. This is especially important for *koten rakugo*, which involves colloquial language and themes from the Edo Period that may be difficult for contemporary audiences to follow. With the advent of mass-mediated entertainment through radio and television in the twentieth century, *rakugo* saw its popularity decline, along with the number of *yose* halls. However, several *rakugo* performers, mostly from the Kansai area, have become popular television personalities. Furthermore, new trends such as innovations in *shinsaku rakugo*, the rise of female *rakugo* performers, tentative forays into English-language *rakugo* and collaborations between *rakugo* and other comic genres suggest that this centuries-old art has not exhausted its creative potential.

XAVIER BENSKY

Recruit scandal

The Recruit scandal symbolised the shocking growth of 'money politics' during the 1980s bubble economy. It was revealed in 1988 that prominent politicians had received low-priced shares in a real-estate subsidiary of the Recruit publishing and information conglomerate. When the stock was listed for public sale in 1986, its value shares skyrocketed. Many important politicians, including opposition leaders, were tainted by receiving stocks or cash from Recruit. Finance Minister Miyazawa Kiichi and then Prime Minister Takeshita Noboru resigned. Former Prime Minister Nakasone Yasu-hiro resigned from the Liberal Democratic Party (LDP).

The LDP did poorly in the 1989 House of Councillors Election. However, it used its success in the 1990 House of Representatives election to argue that its period of penance was over. Miyazawa became Prime Minister in 1991, and Takeshita continued to head the most powerful faction in the LDP. Nevertheless, it was the voter backlash and the defections of key politicians from the LDP in the wake of the Recruit scandal, the **Sagawa Kyūbin scandal** and others, as well as the consumption tax implemented in 1989, that combined to bring the LDP's thirty-eight-year reign to an end in 1993.

Further reading

Farley, M. (1996) 'Japan's press and the politics of scandal', in S. Pharr and E. Krauss (eds) *Media and Politics in Japan*, Honolulu: University of Hawaii Press, pp. 133–63.

Mitchell, R. (1996) *Political Bribery in Japan*, Honolulu: University of Hawaii Press.

Schlesinger, J. (1997, 1999) *Shadow Shoguns: The Rise and Fall of Japan's Postwar Political Machine*, Stanford: Stanford University Press.

Yayama Tarō (1990) 'The Recruit scandal: Learning from the causes of corruption', *Journal of Japanese Studies* 16(1): 93–114.

TIMOTHY S. GEORGE

Red Army

The Red Army Faction was a violent New Left organisation that formed in 1969. Growing out of the frustrations with the **Zenkyōtō** movement, the Red Army and like-minded groups turned towards more Old Left organisation and rhetoric. Still, the Red Army differed from the **Japan Communist Party** (JCP) in its call for immediate armed struggle. Battles with police and the departure of leaders after the 1971 'Yodo-go' hijacking left the group unable to carry out its plans for armed revolution. The JCP (Revolutionary Left Wing), Kanagawa Standing Committee joined forces with the Red Army in 1971, and the new group was known as the Allied Red Army (Rengō Sekigun).

The group became known for its spectacular and violent actions, including bombings and hijacking, as well as its internecine murders. In the Allied Red Army Incident of February 1972, the Red Army fought a spectacular battle with police in the mountains near Karuizawa. After the Allied Red Army Incident, Red Army murders of their own members became public. The police and the media effectively presented these murders as a means of discrediting the entire New Left. The Allied Red Army Incident thus marked the beginning of the end of New Left activism in Japan.

GUY YASKO

Red Purge

Between the end of 1949 and December 1950, Supreme Commander for Allied Powers (SCAP) General Douglas **MacArthur**, business leaders and the Cabinet of Prime Minister Yoshida Shigeru engaged in a concerted effort to curb communist influence in Japan's public life. In June 1950, the central committee of the **Japan Communist Party** (JCP) and the editorial board of the party organ *Akahata* were dissolved. During the following months, JCP members, sympathisers and suspected sympathisers employed in government, the media, film industry, schools, universities and the coal and steel labour unions were forced to surrender their jobs. A total of 10,972 private-sector and 10,793 public-sector employees were dismissed, effectively diminishing communist influence in the labour movement. This effort came to be known as the 'Red Purge'.

The outbreak of war in Korea on 25 June provided the immediate context for this action, intensifying long-standing anti-Communist sentiment among the conservative power elite. MacArthur's denouncement of the JCP on 3 May gave the purge official legitimacy. To many, the Red Purge, along with the release of militarists whom SCAP had banned from holding public office in 1946, epitomised the 'reverse course' in Occupation policy – an apparent radical switch from democratisation to cold-war ideology.

See also: Japan Communist Party; MacArthur, Douglas

Further reading

Sakamoto Y. (1987) 'The international context of the Occupation of Japan', in R. Ward and Y. Sakamoto (eds) *Democratizing Japan: the Allied Occupation*, University of Hawaii Press: Honolulu, pp. 42–75.

FRANZISKA SERAPHIM

reforestation

One of the most ubiquitous aspects of the Japanese landscape is the vast stretches of *shokurin*, cultivated forest. Except in parks and other protected areas, there is almost no natural forest in Japan. Nearly every bit of land that is too steep, inaccessible or otherwise unsuitable for agriculture is covered with trees planted in orderly rows. These rows create a distinctive and orderly patchwork pattern of various hues of green. The forests that are regularly harvested and replanted are cedar, cypress and pine for building materials, and fir for wood pulp. Some silvaculture results in highly specialised production, for example, posts used to support *tokonoma*, residential display alcoves. These trees are carefully wrapped, shaped and wired to achieve decorative effects.

See also: *tokonoma*

AUDREY KOBAYASHI

Rei Kawakubo

b. 1942, Tokyo

Fashion designer

Rei Kawakubo graduated from Keio (Gijuku) University. In 1973, she moved from being a designer to establishing the fashion house of Comme des Garçons based in Paris. In 1981, she caused a sensation when she announced her first collection, 'Black Shock'. Her clothes, with their bagginess and wrinkles, do not fit the body and completely disregard gender differences. They are known for their flat surfaces and simple lines, and are ultimately based on a distinctly Japanese inspiration. The collection defined new aesthetic boundaries in fashion. Since then, she has continued to cause sensations all over the world in her pursuit of the avant-garde, never-before-seen creation. This is a contemporary art of sculpted fashion in mysterious and unexpected forms, where fingers do not emerge predictably from the end of a sleeve where hemlines are seldom straight and where designs refuse to be worn simply: the dismantled/deconstructed garment.

AKIKO FUKAI

religion

Shūukyō, the word employed since the Meiji Period to mean religion, covers a range of meanings, but specifically connotes formal systems of doctrine and practice, especially those defined by sectarian institutions. Since many of the most common religious activities, such as visits to family graves, funerals and trips to temples and shrines, do not require association with these formal systems, the majority of Japanese report in repeated surveys that they do not have any religion, even though they regularly participate in religious activities. The word religion is thus understood in a restrictive sense and does not cover such activities. Many people identify themselves with both Shintō and Buddhism. The phrase 'born Shintō, die Buddhist' epitomises this acceptance of multiple religious identities.

Scholars of religion have questioned the usefulness of the very word 'religion' in the Japanese context, but no one has proposed an adequate alternative. Japanese and Western scholars have no choice but to use the words *shūukyō* and religion to refer to an entire spectrum ranging from formal systems to customary activities. In this broad sense, religion includes major traditions (**State Shintō**, **Buddhism**, Christianity, etc.), sectarian organizations (Tendai Buddhism, Ise Shintō, Shūgendō, Sōka Gakkai, etc.) and popular practices (pilgrimage, funerals, etc.). There is a long tradition of juxtaposing Buddhist and Shintō deities in temples and shrines, and many homes traditionally had both Shintō and Buddhist altars. Christians, who comprise less than 1 per cent of the population, tend to be more exclusive. While Christianity never attracted large numbers, it has exerted considerable influence through converts who were writers and intellectuals. **Confucianism** has also been influential far beyond its visible manifestation in institutions, and forms the underlying moral values of filial piety, loyalty and hard work.

Sectarian affiliation is most often defined by family custom rather than personal belief. Though they participate in funerals and other religious activities, many people do not even know which religious institution they belong to. While they may be certain that they are Buddhists, they often do not know their sectarian identity. This widespread phenomenon has led observers to minimise the importance of sectarian religions since, for most people, the differences between sectarian teachings and practices are insignificant to their participation in religious activities. Those who are aware of their sectarian affiliation cannot always explain the difference between their sect and another.

Although there is widespread uncertainty about sectarian identities among adherents, religious groups are highly organised, well-endowed and active. Every religious organisation must be legally registered as a religious corporation, and, as such, must have bona fide officers, a structure of authority, by-laws and defined teachings and practices. Sectarian organisations are national and even international in scope, and command substantial personnel and resources. Their temples and shrines are very visible in small towns and large cities, and serve as centres of many activities. While members may not be cognisant of the significance of their sectarian affiliation, they participate none the less in a wide number of organised activities ranging from ritual ceremonies to sightseeing excursions.

Institutional religion is a major part of the religious landscape in Japan, and is decidedly sectarian. The most popular religious activities are funerals and a range of customs related to the seeking of practical benefits. Despite the rise of non-religious funeral rites, over 90 per cent of funerals are performed according to Buddhist prescriptions. The ritual assures safe passage to a blessed post-mortem existence in a heavenly pure land, and guarantees the retention of personal and even bodily identity. Most Buddhist funerals are ordination rites in which the deceased are ritually transformed into monks or nuns who commit themselves to purification and repentance, both of which are required for dealing with the body and its imperfections that accompany them even in death. Since bodies need to be fed, food and drink are offered, as is incense, which is defined as that which feeds the soul. The care and feeding of the souls continue in annual memorial services and graveside visits. Memorial services should be carried out for forty-nine years after a person's death; thereafter, the soul becomes part of the corporate ancestors. Summer is the season for the *Obon* rites of memorial services and visits to the graves, and is one of the busiest times for travel. Graveside visits remain the single most popular religious activity in Japan.

Seeking practical benefits such as health, wealth, love and success underlies the common religion of Japan. Buddhist temples and Shintō shrines offer a wide array of talismans and charms for good luck, protection against misfortune, healing, traffic safety, success in school and many other important things in life. Although some scholars, priests and intellectuals condemn supplications for practical or worldly benefits as superstition and bad religion, the belief that deities have the power to grant one's every wish is based in the highest levels of Buddhist scripture and Shintō teachings. Temples and shrines develop specialised services, and certain sites have become famous for the particular benefits they offer. Narita-san, for example, is famed for its amulets for traffic safety.

There is a growing current of non-institutional religions that may be classed as New Age types. Bookshops are filled with books on divination, fortune telling, mind reading, prognostication, healing and channelling. These interests are new in terms of techniques, the level of popularity and the personalities claiming extraordinary powers, but the basic themes are actually very traditional: spiritual powers can better one's life in very practical terms, and spiritualists can mediate between the ordinary and the spiritual realms. This is indeed a theme common to all religions in Japan.

See also: Buddhism; Christianity in Japan; Confucianism; death and funerals; pilgrimages; State Shintō

GEORGE J. TANABE

Rengō

Short for Zen Nihon Minkan Rōdō Kumiai Rengōkai and for Nihon Rōdō Kumiai Sōrengōkai. The former means National Federation of Private-Sector Unions and the latter National Federation of Labour. The idea for Rengō originated among private-sector unions belonging to the **IMF-JC** in the 1970s. They formed the initial nucleus of the Rengō that was founded in 1987 to replace an informal association of private-sector unions, Zenmin Rōkyō. Rengō quickly grew to include a large percentage of all unions, hence the second name, which took effect from 1989, by which time most pre-existing federations, including **Sōhyō**, **Dōmei** and **Shinsanbetsu**, had disbanded. Rengō, like its predecessors Sōhyō, Dōmei and Shinsanbetsu – not to mention earlier union

federations like **Sōdōmei** and Sanbetsu – is a federation of federations. Its constituent unions, like those of its predecessors, are themselves federations. Thus, **Tekkō Rōren**, a member of Rengō and formerly of Sōhyō, is the federation of steelworker unions. The actual unions themselves, as opposed to the federations, are overwhelmingly enterprise unions, organised within one firm. Rengō has been the most successful of post-war union federations at incorporating and retaining a large union membership.

Further reading

Ikuo Kume (1997) *Disparaged Success*, Ithaca: Cornell University Press

MICHAEL GIBBS

reproductive control

Since the late nineteenth century, governments have taken an intense interest in the control of reproduction, through their attempts to regulate access to abortion, access to contraceptive methods and practices such as infanticide. Individuals and groups, on the other hand, have resisted government attempts to control individual decisions on reproduction. After a post-war baby boom peaking in 1947, the birth rate has steadily declined, and is now below population replacement rates. Decreasing birth rates have been the subject of regular conservative panics. Abortion was designated as a crime in the Criminal Code of 1882, and this was carried over into the penal code of 1907. During the wartime period, reproductive control was linked with eugenic imperatives under the National Eugenics Law (*Kokumin Yūsei Hō*) of 1940. The wartime regime was interested in the production of large numbers of healthy subjects under the slogan of *umeyo fuyaseyo* ('bear children and multiply').

In November 1945, the Birth Control Alliance (Sanji Seigen Dōmei) was formed and in November 1946 Recommendations for a New Basic Population Policy (Shin Jinkō Seisaku Kihon Hōshin ni Kansuru Kengian) were introduced by a private organisation, the Committee for Population Policy Research of the Institute for Population

Issues (Jinkō Mondai Kenkyūkai, Jinkō Seisaku Iinkai). A revised abortion law, the *Yūsei Hogo Hō* (Eugenic Protection Law) was passed in 1947, to become effective in June 1948. For most of the post-war period, there has been reasonable access to abortion, thanks to a clause of the Eugenic Protection Law that allows abortion on economic grounds. In April 1949, the Ministry of Health authorised the use of contraceptive drugs such as spermicides and devices such as condoms and diaphragms. The use of intra-uterine devices had been banned since 1931. The Family Planning Movement, which had begun in the pre-war period before suffering repression in the 1930s, was revived in the aftermath of the Second World War. Despite these developments, Japan has seen regular attempts by conservatives to smash the regulations that allowed relatively liberal access to abortion. The quasi-religious group Seichō no Ie began in the late 1950s and launched the Cherish Life Movement (*Inochi o Taisetsu ni Suru Undō*) in 1962 with various Roman Catholic organisations and campaigns for revision of the Eugenic Protection Law.

Although abortion is relatively easily available in Japan, feminists have resisted the eugenic philosophy of the various versions of the laws that regulate abortion, and have resisted the philosophy which affirms that decisions about reproductive control are a matter of government policy rather than a matter for individual self-determination. Reproductive control was a major focus of feminist activity in the 1970s (see **feminism**). Women's liberationists (see **Women's Liberation**) were galvanised by attempts to remove the economic-reasons clause from the Eugenic Protection Law in 1972, 1973 and 1974. Although they were successful in forestalling the removal of the economic-reasons clause, they actually wanted a more radical reform of the law. What has remained from these campaigns is an interest in providing women with access to knowledge about their own bodies and reproductive functions, so that they could make informed choices about sexuality, contraception and reproduction. In the 1970s, some women associated with the women's liberation movement started to talk about producing a Japanese translation of the US women's liberation classic, *Our Bodies, Our Selves*. It was not until the

1980s, however, that a group associated with the Shōkadō Women's Bookshop in Kyōto was able to tackle this work in earnest. The translation, or rather adaptation, which included a wealth of information about health facilities in Japan, finally appeared in 1988.

The Eugenic Protection Law was revised again in 1996, this time removing the eugenic provisions of the Law, which had been highly offensive to advocates for the rights of the handicapped. Many, however, are ambivalent about the new title, the Law for the Protection of the Maternal Body (*Botai Hogo Hō*), which seems once again to relegate women to a reproductive role. It was not until the year 1999 that the final restrictions on the contraceptive pill were removed. This happened just after Viagra was made available to treat impotence. In contrast with the decades it has taken to reach such a decision on the contraceptive pill, Viagra became available relatively quickly. Current interest focuses on the use of *in vitro* fertilisation techniques, and the ethics of possibly using screening technologies to predict the sex of unborn children.

See also: *Chūpiren*; gender and technology; Katō Shidzue; *mizuko jizō*

Further reading

Buckley, S. (1997) *Broken Silence: Voices of Japanese Feminism*, Berkeley: University of California Press.
—— (1988) 'Body politics: Abortion law reform', in G. McCormack and Y. Sugimoto (eds) *Modernisation and Beyond: The Japanese Trajectory*, Cambridge: Cambridge University Press, pp. 205–17.
Coleman, S. (1993) *Family Planning in Japanese Society*, Princeton: Princeton University Press.

VERA MACKIE

residents' movements

Residents' movements (*jumin undō*) are led and staffed primarily by local residents, and take up issues that are specifically regional. They protest environmental degradation as a result of air or water pollution or the negative impact of such public facilities as military bases, dams and highway interchanges, or promote better parks, day-care centres, libraries or public transportation. They are usually led by members of the local middle class, including self-employed business-people and professionals, and their activists are often women. The ideologies of such movements are typically focused on the quality of local community life, and therefore they are often susceptible to charges of 'egoism' – or NIMBYism ('Not-in-my-backyardism'). However, while in the 1970s they typically sought to defend local areas from external threats, some have gradually turned to more affirmative goals related to the building of local community.

Perhaps the best-known historical case of what by the 1970s would be called a residents' movement began in the 1890s when farmers and fishermen in Tochigi Prefecture protested against poisoning of the Sone River by the Ashio Copper Mine That incident was not finally concluded until 1972, when some compensation was paid. The post-Second World War construction of dams for hydro-electrical power stimulated opposition movements that more or less fit the above definition. Other important movements against environmental pollution in the 1950s included protests by fishermen of Urayasu, Chiba Prefecture, in 1958 against the pollution of fishing grounds in Tokyo Bay by the Edogawa plant of Honshū Paper Company. They won not only compensation but passage of important legislation regulating water quality.

The 1960 movement against the Japan–US Security Treaty, or **Anpo struggle**, was an important watershed in the development of genuinely grassroots, local movements independent of national parties, unions and other organisations. Residents' protests against the huge industrial complexes built in many of Japan's port cities, such as the oil refinery complex in Mishima Numazu, were characteristic of the 1960s, and in the course of such struggles local movements learned to carry out substantial research on technical matters related to pollution, initiate effective educational campaigns and appeal effectively to the general public.

Residents' movements were finally defined as such and widely commented on only in the 1970s, by which time residents in local areas all over Japan were being driven to activism by the impact of the

regional development that accompanied accelerated economic growth in the 1960s. The 'big four' pollution cases – mercury poisoning in both Minamata and Niigata, cadmium poisoning (Itai-itai disease) in Toyama and asthma in Yokkaichi – occurred in the late-1960s, and by 1972 there were apparently some 3,000 environmentally oriented residents' movements. They have been interpreted, variously, as signaling the emergence of an autonomous, rights-conscious citizenry willing to assert its interests in a pluralistic society, but also as evidence that affluence and an individualistic culture might have fostered a self-centered, short-sighted outlook on life that leads people to always insist that unpopular facilities like waste-treatment plants be located in other people's neighbourhoods rather than their own (the NIMBY syndrome). An oft-cited, although not necessarily apt, example is the 'garbage war' that took place in the early 1970s between Kōtō and Suginami wards in Tokyo, especially resistance in the latter against a waste incinerator. Some analysts have also contended that residents' movements are animated in part by pre-modern patterns of community solidarity and democracy, and compare them to the peasant rebellions of the Tokugawa era (1600–1868). In the 1980s and 1990s, a large proportion of active residents' movements have been directed against the nuclear power industry and its many installations across Japan.

Residents' movements have situated themselves in relation to local government in various ways. The classical pattern in the 1970s was for movement activists to conclude that central issues could not be resolved through established channels of procedure and influence, and to work independently of, and even seek to reform, those channels. However, especially in the 1980s and 1990s, many of the remaining movements have become less oppositional, organising not only to oppose damaging intrusions but to encourage positive forms of **civic development**. Those that represent interests and concerns that are broadly shared and uncontroversial throughout a local region have begun to work closely with the local governmental authorities, and in some cases have formed NGOs. In some communities, residents' groups have entered into partnerships with local administrators who consult with them openly in exchange for their participation in consensus building.

Residents' movements have not only often been successful at the local level, but cumulatively have been credited with bringing about major changes in public policy. An example is the major national policy shift with regard to environmental pollution that occurred in the early 1970s, including formation of the Environmental Agency and passage into law of strict new regulations designed to protect the environment.

See also: anti-US bases movements; civic development; environment and anti-pollution

Further reading

Broadbent, J. (1998) *Environmental Politics in Japan*, Cambridge: Cambridge University Press.

Irokawa, D. (1978) 'The survival struggle of the Japanese community', in J.V. Koschmann (ed.) *Authority and the Individual in Japan*, Tokyo: University of Tokyo Press, pp. 250–82.

McKean, M. (1981) *Environmental Protest and Citizen Politics in Japan*, Berkeley: University of California Press.

J. VICTOR KOSCHMANN

RETURN OF NORTHERN TERRITORIES *see* Northern Territories, return of

rice

Rice has been the major crop in Japan since ancient times, believed to have been introduced from China about 2,000 years ago. Originally a marshland plant, it is cultivated in wet fields using a system of hydraulic management, planted in nursery beds in April or May, transplanted to the wet fields in June and harvested in September and October. Growing rice requires careful control of the water levels throughout the growing period, and intensive cultivation, weeding and fertilisation. Although rice consumption has decreased, it remains at over 100 pounds per person annually. Rice plays an important role in Japanese religion and cultural practices. Its cultivation is marked by sequential religious rituals that in the past regulated the annual round of activities in rural areas. Both the traditional family structure and the system of social relations are built around the requirements of intensive rice cultivation. Rice was traditionally used as currency, and one's wealth and social status were measured according to one's rice stipend, or *koku*. Rice is the major offering to the gods (*inadama*). Ceremonial rice offerings are made at temples, and especially at Shintō shrines. People place a bowl of rice in the household shrine to honour local deities. When someone dies, a bowl of rice with a single chopstick stuck in it is placed near the head of the body. Japanese never, therefore, leave their chopsticks in their rice bowls. The straw from the rice plant stalk is used for a variety of traditional goods, including ropes, sandals, hats, *tatami* mats.

Fewer than 5 per cent of the population are now engaged in rice cultivation, which is now largely the domain of the elderly. Desire to maintain at least a symbolic amount of rice production has had a major effect on residential patterns, as many families live in semi-rural areas from which men commute long distances to work in cities. Economically, rice was for many years protected against competition from foreign imports, and the price kept artificially high, although in recent years the ban on importing rice has been lifted.

Rice is mostly eaten plain in a special bowl, with a great deal of ceremony. The expression to 'eat rice' (*gohan o taberu*) is generally understood to indicate eating in general. Young children are taught never to leave even a single grain of rice in their bowls. Rice is normally not served as long as alcohol is being consumed, and a hostess may signal that enough drinking has taken place and it is time to get on with the evening meal by asking if her guests are 'ready for rice?'

Rice is also consumed in many other forms, the most common being *sake*, rice wine, the major alcoholic beverage in Japan, also considered sacred to the gods. Glutinous rice (*mochi*) is pounded into cakes and stuffed with sweet bean paste (*manjū*) or eaten in soup (*ozōni*) as part of the annual New Year's festivities. Rice is also used for making noodles, and *senbei* (crackers).

Further reading

D.H. Grist (1965) *Rice*, fourth edition, London: Longman.

Ohnuki-Tierney, Emiko (1993) *Rice as Self: Japanese*

Identitites through Time, Princeton: Princeton University Press.

Robertson, Jennifer (1984) 'Sexy rice: Plant gender, farm manuals and grass-roots nativism', *Monumenta Nipponica* 39(3): 233–60.

AUDREY KOBAYASHI

right-wing movements

Right-wing movements in Japan have their ideological origins in pre-war ultranationalist groups that promoted fervent loyalty to the imperial state, gloried in Japanese continental expansion and fiercely opposed socialism and communism. Although the Allied Occupation force disbanded these groups and undermined their pre-war influence through its programmes of demilitarisation and democratisation, several were able to re-establish themselves in the early 1950s. Two prominent pre-war right-wing leaders who survived defeat and Occupation with fortunes intact were Kodama Yoshio and Sasagawa Ryōichi. Kodama, detained but not prosecuted as a class-A war criminal, used his considerable wealth to play a backroom role as fixer in conservative politics (see **Lockheed scandal**) and support patriotic organizations such as the Youth Thought Study Association (Seinen Shisō Kenkyūkai). Sasagawa, also detained as a class-A war criminal and reputed to have been a political fixer, applied profits from his speedboat-racing promotions towards philanthropic support of martial arts, religious and cultural organisations.

The right-wing movement consists of several hundred small groups, sometimes finding financial support from well-connected members of the conservative elite. Although these groups all favour constitutional revision, remilitarisation, state support for **Yasukuni Shrine**, respect for the Emperor and the promotion of patriotic sentiment among Japan's youth, and generally share antipathy toward the Communist and Socialist Parties, they have had difficulty unifying into a cohesive movement mainly because of a tendency toward intense personal in-group loyalty. During the cold war, they generally shared a pro-US, anti-Soviet bias, occasionally coming together in organisations such as the All-Japan Patriot Group Conference (Zen Nihon Aikokusha Dantai Kaigi) to oppose left-wing coalitions as in the 1960 **Anpo struggle**. In anticipation of clashes with progressive forces on the occasion of US Security Treaty renewal in 1970, groups began martial training in the 1960s, a practice that continues in most groups. There has also been considerable overlap with gangster organisations, which sometimes register as right-wing political organisations in order to avoid legal suppression.

During the campus unrest of the late 1960s, a more violence-prone segment in the right wing developed among patriotic students who sought true Japanese independence through revocation of the security treaty. These groups rejected the mainstream right-wing acceptance of what they termed the 'Y-P order', composed of the bipolar post-war international order that emerged from the Yalta accords and the anti-emperor, anti-*Volk*, anti-state domestic political order that resulted from Japan's acceptance of the Potsdam Declaration.

Members of right-wing groups have engaged in acts of terrorism, notably the assassination of Socialist Party leader Asanuma Inejirū, the attack on the residence of the president of a major journal for publishing fiction disrespectful of the imperial family (Shimanaka incident) and the harassment and shooting of Nagasaki Mayor Motoshima Hitoshi, who had stated that the Shōwa Emperor bore some measure of war responsibility. Although such acts of intimidation have reinforced taboos regarding the imperial institution, they have not had the far-reaching impact that pre-war right-wing terrorism achieved.

JAMES J. ORR

rising-sun flag

On 9 August 1999 the Japanese National Diet passed a bill legally recognizing the rising-sun flag (*nisshōki* or *hinomaru*) as Japan's national flag. Despite much heated debate about the measure and public opinion polls indicating that barely a majority of the populace desired legalisation, the ruling **Liberal Democratic Party** and its coalition parties succeeded in passing the legislation. Political turmoil around *hinomaru* is nothing new; ever since the mid-nineteenth century the rising-sun flag has been not only a symbol of national unity, but a material site around which conflicts over the meaning of Japan and its past have occurred.

The rising-sun flag, a crimson disc on white background, is a modern invention. While many living in the territory we now call Japan had previously understood the rising-sun emblem to be an auspicious symbol, national consciousness among commoners was weak or non-existent until the late nineteenth century and nothing approximating a national flag existed until 1854. At that time, the Tokugawa state (1600–1867) declared that Japanese ships should fly a white flag bearing the rising-sun emblem so they could be distinguished from foreign vessels. In 1870, the new Meiji government (1868–1912) formally adopted this policy while also ordering the flag's use in the Army and Navy. While *hinomaru* increasingly appeared in public places as Japan's *de facto* national flag, it never attained legal status as such. In fact, in 1931, the Diet defeated a bill that would have given the flag such legal support. Nevertheless, as the state accelerated its efforts to mobilise the entire population of Japan and its colonies for the war effort in the late 1930s and early 1940s, the flag became extensively and regularly employed in ceremonial activities in schools. Moreover, geographical use of the flag spread along with Japanese colonialism and expansionism, and for many became associated with precisely these phenomena. After Japan's defeat in 1945, the Occupation temporarily prohibited raising the rising-sun flag, but this directive was rescinded in 1949.

Precisely because the flag has been a symbol of the Japanese nation state and empire, it has also sparked symbolic acts of resistance. The most famous of such pre-war incidents involved the Korean runner Son Ki-jong. After Son won the marathon competition in the 1936 Berlin Olympics, the Korean newspaper *Tong-a ilbo* carried a photograph of him, but with the rising-sun emblem on his uniform blotted out. This has long been understood as a defiant demonstration against Japanese colonial rule. A comparable post-war incident took place in 1987 when an Okinawan supermarket owner and activist named Chibana

Shōichi took down and then burned the rising-sun flag at the National Athletic Meet. Chibana is known to have done this in protest against the past and ongoing discrimination and marginalisation of Okinawa by the Japanese state and mainstream population.

See also: Okinawa

Further reading

Field, Norma (1991) *In the Realm of the Dying Emperor*, New York: Pantheon Books.

Tanaka, Nobumasa (2000) *Hinomaru kimigayo no sengoshi*, Tokyo: Iwanami Shoten.

TAKASHI FUJITANI

robots

The appearance of robots in the Japanese imagination pre-dated their actual invention by several centuries. An early twelfth-century collection of stories, titled *Konjaku Monogatari Shu*, told of a device that could pour water into paddy-fields during dry seasons. This device not only helped the peasants irrigate their fields; it also provided them with a source of entertainment as neighbours competed to make their 'robot' tip water into the fields faster. Later, in the seventeenth and eighteenth centuries, Japan witnessed the emergence of robot-like puppets, called *karakuri-ningyo*, for which the Takeda-za theatre was built in Ōsaka in 1662. Robots continued to be featured in literature, children's comics and, more recently, Japanese Anime throughout the nineteenth and twentieth centuries. The theme of robots as both a source of labour efficiency and entertainment remains a central motif in the development of the robotics industry in modern Japan. Although Japan's robotics industry only dates back to the late 1960s, today Japan is the world's largest developer of robotics technology, and the producer of approximately half of the world's robots.

In 1967, the US company AMF exported the first advanced robot technology to Japan. Soon after, and based on the technology of another US company, Unimation, the Japanese company Kawasaki Heavy Industries Ltd began producing robots in 1968. Within ten years, an estimated 10,000 robot systems were being produced domestically per year, and, by 1980, this figure had doubled. While in the 1970s and 1980s the highest concentration of robot usage was in electronic machinery and automobile manufacturing, by the 1990s the economic and social role of robots had expanded and their usage began to diversify. Robot technology grew beyond the industrial field to applications in nuclear power generation, medicine, offshore development, space technologies and other areas in which robots could perform difficult and often unsafe tasks quickly, efficiently and accurately.

In the 1990s, more than forty Japanese companies were producing commercial robots, while in the USA there were only a dozen firms. By the late 1990s, a new trend emerged in the industry and those with expertise in robotics turned their attention towards the entertainment robot industry. Large companies such as Sony and Honda lead the way in developing toy animal and humanoid robots. In 1999, Sony released Aibo (Japanese word for 'partner' or 'companion'), the first commercially available robot pet. With a camera for its eyes, microphone ears and artificial intelligence software, Aibo barks, sings and wags its tail when patted on the head. The robodog was an instant hit in Japan's consumer market and encouraged Sony, along with its competitors, to continue their investment in the entertainment robot industry. The prototype for Sony's first humanoid robot, SDR-3x, was released in November 2000 and it is predicted that the robot will be available to consumers by 2005.

Today's robots, and future generations still in research laboratories, much like their fictitious predecessors, can perform increasingly complex tasks by combining artificial intelligence, sensors, speech recognition and other leading-edge technologies with human and animal appearances. One of the most recent and controversial areas of experimentation is taking place at the interface of robotics and cybernetics, with the use of 'cultivated' human muscle tissue in robotic joints as a means of facilitating greater flexibility of movement and responsiveness. The robots that once existed in the Japanese imagination through literature and comics are becoming more and more of a reality, as the gap between real and imaginary disappears with the development of new technologies.

LEILA POURTAVAF

rōnin

Rōnin, literally 'masterless samurai', are high-school graduates who have failed to obtain the exam score that they need to get into the university of their choice. Each year, about 200,000 *rōnin* study to retake the entrance examinations at special ***juku*** (cram schools) called *yobikos*. The image of *rōnin* is one of isolation and depression but this is not always the case, especially in the first year. Many *rōnin* are very capable, but either did not take high-school academics seriously or focused on extra-curricular clubs. Female *rōnin* are more stigmatised than males and few women attend *yobiko*.

JUNE A. GORDON

Roppongi

Roppongi is the most international and cosmopolitan of **Tokyo**'s distinctive districts, in the southern part of Yamonote, the 'High City' on the western side of Tokyo. Roppongi is a night landscape, which comes alive with huge crowds attending the many restaurants, bars and trendy clubs. It is a neighbourhood of glitter and excess, where one may expect to see Japan's rock stars and other high-living public personalities, as well as the exotic models, actors and television commentators from around the world, but especially the USA. In the residential streets away from the entertainment scene are many international embassies, as well as the expensive compounds of wealthy foreigners living in Japan, and the homes of Japanese who can afford to pay for a status address. In a country where mix-race relationships are still relatively rare, this is one of the few neighbourhoods where the sight of mixed couples will not turn heads. During the day, Roppongi is transformed into a much more staid atmosphere of business, similar to nearby **Akasaka**, including traffic clogged streets and busy commercial enterprises.

AUDREY KOBAYASHI

rorikon

A Japanisation of Lolita complex, the term *rorikon* describes a genre of pornography that features stories and images of pre-pubescent and pubescent girls. *Rorikon* storylines first gained a significant audience in pornographic **manga** in the 1980s, then quickly spread to pornographic video, film and photographic magazines. Some claim the genre developed as a means of bypassing laws prohibiting the depiction of pubic hair and genitals by resorting to images of sexually undeveloped girls. Whatever its origin, the *rorikon* fantasy scenario, in its many permutations, has gained one of the largest segments of the Japanese pornography market. While advertising in the earliest *rorikon manga* indicated an adult male target audience, the genre now includes monthly and bi-weekly titles that target male readers from early teen to adult. *Rorikon* pornography has been the focus of aggressive censorship campaigns by alliances of such diverse interest groups as conservatives, new religions, feminists, parent–teacher groups and incest victim support groups. The loosening of the 'hair law' over the 1990s has not seen any decrease in popularity or publication levels. Publishers and video producers and distributors are generally expected to self-censor materials before public release. This approach has, however, merely led to a tendency to develop increasingly creative techniques to push the censorship laws to their limits.

See also: hair debate; pornography

SANDRA BUCKLEY

Royal Wedding, 1959

Crown Prince Akihito's 'love match' marriage (in contrast to an arranged marriage) to the 'commoner' Shōda Michiko was widely interpreted as symbolizing postwar values such as equality and liberty held dear by the growing middle class. Interviewed by a popular weekly about the significance of the engagement, Koizumi Shinzō, director of the crown prince's education, reminded readers of Fukuzawa Yukichi's famous saying: 'Heaven never created a man above or below another man'.

The announcement of the engagement led to a 'Michiko-boom' capitalised and spurred on by magazine weeklies. The story of how Akihito and Michiko's love blossomed on the tennis courts of Karuizawa, where they first met, was recounted over and over. By 1959, a process begun in 1945 to remake the imperial house to suit a 'new Japan' had successfully produced a young imperial couple that was interpreted as embodying the essential spirit of democratic Japan. In the 1960s, the young imperial couple advanced the 'family-isation' of the imperial household by establishing a home that came across as middle class.

Further reading

Ruoff, Kenneth J. (2001) *The Symbolic Monarchy in Japan's Postwar Democracy, 1945–1995: Royalism in an Age of Popular Sovereignty*, Cambridge, MA: Published by the Harvard University Asia Center and distributed by Harvard University Press.

KENNETH RUOFF

Royal Wedding, 1993

Crown Prince Naruhito's marriage to Owada Masako ritualised the practice of princes choosing their brides from among the people. The first woman with a career ever to become crown princess, Owada was anything but average. She was educated at three of the world's most elite universities, Harvard, Oxford and Tokyo, and had earned a position in the Foreign Ministry through the demanding entrance examination. Among other things, she symbolised Japan's meritocracy.

In 1958, many young women had dreamed of being Michiko, but a prolonged discussion among women about whether or not Owada had made the right decision to give up her career as an elite civil servant in the Foreign Ministry greeted her engagement to the crown prince. To young Japanese women accustomed by the 1990s to using their considerable disposable income to support a lifestyle that included regular trips abroad, the notion of becoming a princess under the stifling supervision of the Imperial Household Agency did not necessarily hold much attraction. At their first joint press conference, held after the engagement was announced, Owada recounted a promise made by the crown prince: 'I will protect you for my entire life.' It was a frank admission of the fact that Naruhito had needed to persuade Owada to become his bride.

See also: Royal Wedding, 1959

Further reading

Ruoff, Kenneth J. (2001) *The Symbolic Monarchy in Japan's Postwar Democracy, 1945–1995: Royalism in an Age of Popular Sovereignty*, Cambridge, MA: published by the Harvard University Asia Center and distributed by Harvard University Press.

KENNETH RUOFF

rural life

The value of rural living is deeply embedded in Japanese cultural norms. A century ago, during the Meiji Period, Japan's population was 85 per cent agrarian. During the period of state-instigated industrialisation and modernisation of the late nineteenth and early twentieth centuries, the Japanese government depended heavily upon the agrarian population for its tax base, and to supply excess labour both for the new factories and for the armed forces. This stability was strengthened by instilling a strong sense of rural ideology, based upon two essential values: loyalty to the rural household, the *ie* (and, beyond that, loyalty to the Emperor); and the independence of the household through private property ownership. The household was built upon nominally Confucian concepts of loyalty and filial piety, which included a strongly patriarchal relationship between men and women. Cultural practices such as primogeniture and arranged marriages were adapted from samurai customs of the earlier Tokugawa Period, to help strengthen and value rural tradition. Also derived from the Tokugawa Period was a sense of mutual obligation that regulated relationships among households in the rural village, or *mura*. Thus valued, farmers were considered second to the nobility on the social scale, above merchants and artisans, fishermen and the *Burakumin*.

Today, the majority of Japanese live in urban areas, but many retain a romantic concept of their ties to their rural birthplaces, referred to as *furosato*. The rural population retains strongly conservative values rooted at least in part in Meiji Period values. Although the balance has begun to shift slightly, rural voters also maintain relative political power because the electoral districts are arranged to privilege their votes, a situation that in part explains the power of the Liberal Democratic Party. Many landowners have become wealthy by selling small portions of land for residential or industrial development. It is not uncommon to see large, expensive houses. In some parts of the country, such as conservative Shiga Prefecture, attempts are made to maintain the traditional exterior of rural houses as a form of status symbol. Rural families cling to agrarian ways by maintaining at least small plots devoted to **rice** cultivation.

However, agriculture no longer drives the rural economy. Although some parts of the country have thrived by cultivating speciality crops such as citrus or other fruits, or tea, in most parts of the country the major income derives from other sources. It is not uncommon for male household heads to commute to nearby cities, while their wives work full or part time in local jobs. Agricultural activity is left to the older generation of grandparents, who fear that their work will not be carried on by future generations.

Tourism plays an increasingly important role in rural life. Partly in response to the nostalgia of *furosato*, urbanites flock to rural areas to celebrate ancient farming festivals, or simply to relax in a country inn, or *minshuku*. Such activities, combined with the high level of commuting, mean that there is a very high degree of economic and cultural interdependence between rural and urban areas.

See also: family system; *furosato gaeri*; rice; urban migration

AUDREY KOBAYASHI

Russo-Japanese relations

Mutual antagonism and suspicion characterised much of the relations between post-war Japan and Russia. On 9 August 1945, the Soviet Union joined the war against Japan, three months after it abrogated the 1941 Neutrality Pact with Japan. Japan still expected Russia to act as a mediator. As Soviet forces swept across Manchuria, Southern Sakhalin and the Kurile islands, over half a million Japanese servicemen and civilians were taken to Siberia and condemned to hard labour. Up to 60,000 of them perished there.

The onset of the cold war, during which Japan was closely allied with the USA against communist powers in North-East Asia, only reinforced ill feelings among many Japanese towards their northern neighbour. Bilateral relations remained largely hostile and occasionally tense. The Soviet Union was not a signatory to the San Francisco Peace Treaty in 1952. It was not until October 1956 that the two governments signed a Joint Declaration and restored diplomatic relations. The Soviet Union repatriated those Japanese who had been convicted of war crimes, gave support for Japan to join the United Nations and granted permission for Japanese to fish in coastal Soviet waters. Dispute over the status of four small islands off Hokkaidō – known as the 'Northern Territories' in Japan – proved to be the thorniest of all problems in their relations. Occupied by the Soviet Union at the end of the war, these islands have considerable strategic importance. In 1956, the Soviet Union agreed to return two of the four islands – an offer refused by Tokyo (in part due to US pressure) and later withdrawn by Moscow after Japan renewed its Defence Treaty with the USA in 1960.

Although some Japanese companies have participated in development projects in the resource-rich Siberia and Russian Far East since the early 1970s, only limited progress has been made to realise the full potential of economic co-operation between the two countries. Bilateral trade still occupies a small share in either country's total foreign trade. Signs of improvement in bilateral relations emerged in the mid-1980s after the beginning of *glasnost* in the Soviet Union. The end of the cold war as well as the disintegration of the Soviet Union introduced new opportunities but also uncertainties. Russian President Yeltsin, during his 1993 visit to Japan, offered apologies for the death of Japanese detained after the Second World War. Japan, for its part, agreed to provide economic aid to Moscow and to improve bilateral relations. Local governments in the Japan Sea area began to promote regional exchanges in economic and cultural spheres. At the 1998 summit meeting between President Yeltsin and Prime Minister Hashimoto in Krasnoyarsk, the two governments promised to resolve the territorial dispute and sign a peace treaty by 2000. While Japan's relations with Russia have improved in general, as indicated by the frequent meeting of government leaders, the territorial dispute continues to obstruct treaty talks as of this writing.

See also: Northern Territories, return of

Further reading

Glaubitz, J. (1995) *Between Tokyo and Moscow: The History of an Uneasy Relationship, 1972–1990s*, Honolulu: University of Hawaii Press.

Hasegawa, T. (1987) 'Japanese perceptions of the Soviet Union, 1960 1980', in T. Hasegawa (ed.) *The Soviet Union Faces Asia: Perceptions and Politics*, Sapporo.

YANG DAQING

ryōsai kenbo

In the late nineteenth century, several writers promoted the idea that women should be 'good wives and wise mothers' (*ryōsai kenbo*), that their primary role was in the family in a companionate marriage and that they should receive a proper education for this role. The government built on *ryōsai kenbo* ideology in campaigns aimed at mobilising women through the educational system and semi-official patriotic organisations in the early twentieth century. The phrase is still used to denote a conservative ideology whereby women are expected to give priority to family and children rather than paid work.

VERA MACKIE

Ryū Chishū

b. 1906, Kumamoto, Kyūshu

Actor

Though he has worked under many directors, Ryu is usually associated with the work of Ozu, especially among international audiences. An early member of the Ozu 'family' and star of many of his films, Ryu's understated, tightly controlled acting anchors Ozu's signature 'quiet style'. His first big part was in *Daigaku yoi toko* (College is a Nice Place, 1935) and he appeared in such Ozu classics as *Early Spring*, **Tokyo monogatari** (Tokyo Story), *Late Spring* and *Late Autumn*.

CHRISTOPHER PERRIUS

S

Sadistic Mika Band

Sadistic Mika Band was one of the most highly regarded bands in Japanese rock music history. The band's name comes out of a word-play derived from John Lennon's Plastic Ono Band. The Sadistic Mika Band made its formal debut in June 1972. The band members were Kato Kazuhiko on vocals and guitar (formerly of the Folk Crusaders), Kato Mika on vocals, Takanaka Masayoshi on guitar, Ōhara Hiroshi on bass and Takahashi Yukihiro on drums (later of Yellow Magic Orchestra). The song 'Cycling Boogie' was released on Japan's first private label, Donuts Records (founded by Kato). After the release of their debut album, *Sadistic Mika Band* (May 1973), the keyboardist Imai joined the band and they actively began touring.

Their masterpiece, *Kurobune* (Black Ships), was produced by Chris Thomas, widely known for his work with Roxy Music, John Cale, Pink Floyd and the Pretenders. It was recorded between February and May 1974 and released in November. It combined funky R 'n' B grooves overlaid with something of a progressive rock sound. All of this was accomplished with the album still sounding like the confident work of Japanese musicians. Thematically, the song titles and lyrics explore icons of the *Bakumatsu* period (1853–68) and lost Japanese tradition, Japan's encounter with the West and the concept of time. The album received a great critical response as soon as it was released. It was the first Japanese rock album released in the UK and the USA by British and US record companies.

In June 1975, Ōhara Hiroshi left the band and bassist Goto Hideyoshi took his place. In September of the same year, they took part in Roxy Music's British tour to rave reviews. The original Sadistic Mika Band's last studio album, *Hot Menu!*, was released in Japan in November 1975. During the tour, the Katos decided to divorce. Kato Mika chose to remain in the UK after the tour, while Kato Kazuhiko returned to Japan with the rest of the band. At this point the band also broke up. After the break up, a live album, *Live in London*, was released in July 1976. The rest of the band minus the Katos released three instrumental albums as the Sadistics. Kato, Takanaka, Imai and Takahashi all went on to considerable success with important solo careers. Along with Hosono Haruomi and Sakamoto Ryūichi, Takahashi Yukihiro became a founding member of Yellow Magic Orchestra in 1978.

In 1989, Sadistic Mika Band reformed with Kirishima Karen on vocals and in April released the album *Appare*. They also played a live concert at NHK Hall. Sadistic Mika Band might not be described as one of the most talented, original and intelligent Japanese bands but they will, over time, come to be seen as an important band in the context of rock music history the world over.

MARK ANDERSON

sado-masochism

The term 'sado-masochism' (*sadomazohisumu*) entered the Japanese lexicon in the early 1950s. However, the words 'sadism' (*sadizumu*) and 'masochism' (*mazohizumu*) were familiar in Japanese intellectual circles from as early as the 1880s.

Interest in the dynamics of dominance and submission, and a curiosity about erotic bondage is evident in art and literature dating back at least to the Edo Period.

In post-war literature, authors such as **Tanizaki Jun'ichirō**, **Mishima Yukio**, Kōno Taeko, and **Yamada Eimi** are noted for their literary explorations of sado-masochism. The first popular magazine to bill itself explicitly was *SM magajin*, first published in 1968. While much of the content involved bondage, the initials for the magazine actually stood for 'suspense and mystery'. Since then, the 's/m magazine' genre has grown and includes numerous titles dedicated to sado-masochism. Author Dan Oniroku pioneered the 's/m novel' (SM shōsetsu), beginning in the 1950s. Sado-masochism frequently appears in *manga*, including the genre of 'ladies' comics', aimed specifically at adult women. In cinema, **Ōshima Nagisa**'s internationally known film *Ai no korida* (In the Realm of the Senses) is a daring exploration of sado-masochistic pleasure, while some *roman poruno* (romance porn) and *pinkku eiga* (pink films) take a more lowbrow approach. Since the 1980s, 'S&M clubs', and **love hotels** with S&M theme rooms, have gained notoriety. Sado-masochism, while perhaps not a feature of daily life, occupies an essential place in the erotic imagination of many Japanese.

GRETCHEN JONES

Sagawa Kyūbin scandal

In August 1992, Kanemaru Shin, a powerful leader in the ruling Liberal Democratic Party (LDP) known as 'the Don', admitted receiving ¥500 million ($3.5 million) in illegal contributions from the parcel delivery company Sagawa Kyūbin in 1990. The company had also arranged contacts for Kanemaru with *yakuza* organised crime groups, and given money to scores of other Diet members.

Kanemaru resigned from the Diet and was arrested in March 1993 for tax evasion. Investigators searching his homes and offices found 100 kg of gold, billions of yen in bonds and cash, and documents indicating that much of this wealth had come from construction companies seeking government contracts. Yet Kanemaru evaded prosecutors' questions and paid a fine of only ¥200,000 ($1,600). LDP leaders, while insisting the corruption was not systemic, promised 'political reform' but never delivered.

The resulting public anger compounded that caused by other scandals such as Recruit (see **Recruit scandal**) and by the consumption tax implemented in 1989. However, it was Diet members' defections from the LDP over how to respond to this public backlash and to trade and diplomatic issues that ultimately led to the LDP's defeat in 1993 after thirty-eight years in power.

Further reading

Farley, M. (1996) 'Japan's press and the politics of scandal', in S. Pharr and E. Krauss (eds) *Media and Politics in Japan*, Honolulu: University of Hawaii Press, pp. 133–63.

Mitchell, R. (1996) *Political Bribery in Japan*, Honolulu: University of Hawaii Press.

Schlesinger, J. (1997, 1999) *Shadow Shoguns: The Rise and Fall of Japan's Postwar Political Machine*, Stanford: Stanford University Press.

Woodall, B. (1996) *Japan under Construction: Corruption, Politics, and Public Works*, Berkeley: University of California Press.

TIMOTHY S. GEORGE

Sailor Moon

Unlike most successful cartoons, which begin as *manga* and are later transferred to other media, *Bishōjo senshi seiraa mūn* ('Pretty Soldier Sailor Moon') by Naoko Takeuchi débuted simultaneously as a *manga* serial (in Nakayoshi), a television animated series and a line of affiliated merchandise in 1992. *Sailor Moon* proved so popular that only three years later, in 1995, it had been translated into at least twenty-three languages.

Japanese high-school girl Tsukino Usagi (literally, 'moon rabbit'; Serena in the English version) discovers that she is a reincarnated moon princess from a civilisation destroyed 1,000 years before. Using magic artefacts from her former kingdom, she invokes 'moon prism power', thereby transforming into superhero Sailor Moon. Accompanied by similarly reincarnated companions, the Sailor Scouts, she battles evil. By day, Serena is a ditsy, cowardly teenager in a typical school uniform sailor suit, but, when evil threatens, Sailor Moon is a brave and powerful warrior, dressed in a short-skirted, sexier version of the same outfit. Sailor Moon combines elements associated with boys' comics (*shōnen manga*), such as action and battle, and those associated with girls' comics (*shōjo manga*), such as romantic storylines, cute accessories and gender-bending, perhaps explaining the story's broad appeal.

See also: *shōjo;*

SHARALYN ORBAUGH

Sakaguchi Ango

b. 1906, Niigata

Writer

Born Sakaguchi Heigo in Niigata in 1906, this was perhaps the first writer to emerge from the ranks of pure literature (*junbungaku*) to find wide popular acclaim in his own lifetime without significant damage to his literary credentials. Although he wrote a number of popular short stories and essays prior to the Second World War, it is his period of production between 1946 and 1949 that has won him a place in modern Japanese literature. In some ways, his works are weighed down by the burden of his persona as it has emerged and been embellished upon over time. Not unlike his contemporary, **Dazai Osamu**, his occasional periods of withdrawal and bouts of alcoholism and drug addiction only added to the tragic figure of the author.

The works that captured the attention and unguarded praise of not only Japan's intellectuals but a broad-based readership in Occupation Japan between 1946 and 1949 were *Hakuchi* (The Idiot, 1946), *Darakuron* (On Decadence, 1946) and *Sakura no mori no mankai no shita* (Beneath the Blossoming Cheery Trees, 1947). Of these, it was *Darakuron* that won Sakaguchi his place in the Japanese post-war

cultural landscape. Defeat and the Occupation period represented an end to Japanese imperialism but the years of SCAP control also brought their own strict censorship and firm criteria for the terms of articulation of a post-war Japan. It has been said that the Emperor's surrender address marked the end of the war but that it was Sakaguchi's essay *Darakuron* that marked the possibility of beginning to confront the past, the first step towards exploring the potential of the present and future of Japan. *Darakuron* was an unhesitating attack on imperial Japan. Sakaguchi clearly stated the culpability of the emperor system (*tennosei*) and the warrior code (*bushido*), and did not shy away in any of his work from the complex and painful immediate issue in 1946 of the complicity of the Japanese people in the war effort. He was not, however, interested in lingering on the question of responsibility or tracing historical explanations. Sakaguchi invited his readers into a freefall from the 'truths' of the past into the uncertainty and fragility of the present. Unlike the strong Marxist intellectual tradition that would take root in the early post-war period, Sakaguchi rejected the 'will of history' or the return to history as remedy for the future. He pursued a strikingly post-modern trajectory into the unpredictable realm of decay and disarray, promoting the chaotic over the orderly and inviting an immersion in the potential of an unregulated and disorderly (decadent) subjectivity not bounded by subject relations. It is no surprise, then, to find that some of the leading voices of Japanese intellectual life in the late 1990s returned to rediscover and reinvent Sakaguchi. He has been presented as a powerful echo from Japan's early post-war period into the contemporary moment of Japan's ever imminent emergence from the post-war into an as-yet uncategorised and unperiodised present in the new millennium.

His contemporary champions consider the project of *Darakuron* incomplete and their return to his works is not driven by nostalgia or recuperative strategies but rather out of a commitment to the contemporary potential of the politics of Sakaguchi's project.

SANDRA BUCKLEY

Sakamoto Kyu

b. 1941, Kanagawa Prefecture; d. 1985

Singer

Sakamoto Kyu was a rockabilly singer who holds the distinction of being the only Japanese recording artist ever to have a number one song in the USA. Released in May 1963, the song was 'Sukiyaki', and it remained at the top of the Billboard charts for three weeks. The original title was 'Ue wo muite aruko' (I'll Walk with My Head up). In 1964, 'Sukiyaki' went gold by selling 1 million copies. Sakamoto played country and western in the 1950s and moved into rockabilly in 1959. He had his first hit single in 1960, 'Itsy Bitsy Teeny Weeny Yellow Polka-dot Bikini'. 'I'll Walk with My Head up' was released in Japan in 1961, in Europe in 1962 and in the USA in 1963. It was an international hit. After a few more hits in Japan in the mid-1960s, Sakamoto became a widely known television MC. He died in a plane crash in August 1985.

Further reading

Schilling, Mark (1997) *The Encyclopedia of Japanese Pop Culture*, New York: Weatherhill, pp. 215–17.

MARK ANDERSON

Sakamoto Ryūichi

b. 1952, Tokyo

Musician and actor

Sakamoto Ryūichi is one of the handful of Japanese artists who has achieved extensive international recognition in the world of rock and pop music. He cites his own major early influences as the Beatles, John Coltrane and John Cage. His own unique style is a mix of syntho-fusion pop and jazz. He released his first solo album in 1978, *Thousand Knives*. Soon after this initial success, he formed the Yellow Magic Orchestra, which released its title album also in 1978 to immediate national and international acclaim. *B-2 Unit* (1980) and *Lefthand Dream* (1981) consolidated the band's position as a powerful influence in world electronic fusion music

but Sakamoto's determination to work in a wide range of music, including classical and soundtrack composition, as well as building an acting career saw YMO (as it came to be popularly known) disband in 1983.

Sakamoto's collaborations with Bernardo Bertolucci on the soundtracks for *The Last Emperor* (1988), *The Sheltering Sky* (1990) and *Little Buddha* (1994) further extended his international reputation as a composer of orchestral pieces and screen music. Sakamoto is frequently called upon to compose music for major international events such as the Barcelona Olympics (1992). Sakamoto is also known for combining his love of acting with his role of conducting to create an impressive stage presence at orchestral performances of his work. A 1993 reunion of YMO led to two highly successful concerts and a record release, but Sakamoto remains committed to his solo career and pursuit of international collaborations. His appearance in the Oshima film *Merry Christmas Mr Lawrence* together with David Bowie, and their provocative kissing scene, created a gay cult following for both his film work and music. Dedicated Sakamoto websites offer updated information on his career and pin-up images of this actor-musician. His music has taken a pronounced turn towards more classical influences as he works increasingly on orchestral soundtracks and commissioned works for international public events.

SANDRA BUCKLEY

sake

Sake is an alcoholic beverage brewed from rice and may well deserve to be the national beverage of Japan, although green **tea** and **beer** both qualify as serious challengers for the title.

Strictly speaking, the word sake is the generic Japanese term for any alcoholic beverage while the terms *osake* (honoured liquor) or *nihonshū* (Japanese liquor) are used to specify what in English is glossed as rice wine. Sake resembles a white wine – sometimes described as resembling a dry vermouth – in taste, aroma and appearance (non-carbonated, clear and almost colourless) but, in terms of production, it is more akin to ale. Sake, as with beer, is fermented from grain, not fruit, so complex processing is necessary to produce the sugars upon which yeast thrive. Special rice is milled down to its starch rich core, then steamed and inoculated with a mould (*kōjikin*) that breaks down starch into sugar. Water and yeast are added, and the processes of sugar production and fermentation proceed simultaneously. The top fermenting yeast can produce an alcohol content as high as 22 per cent, but commercial sake is adjusted to a standard 15–16 per cent alcohol. Like lager beer, sake is brewed at cold temperatures and considered best after a short ageing. Some sakes are sweet (*amakuchi*), while others are dry (*karakuchi*). Sake drinkers, like connoisseurs of wine, also recognise and prize regional sake (*jizake*), where such factors as the water, the rice, the weather and the brewmaster's touch can produce delightful variations on a common theme.

It is well known that sake is enjoyed hot (*atsukan*). Heated sake is served in a flask (*tokkuri*) and is drunk from a tiny thimble cup (*sakazuki*). What is less well known is that many Japanese also like to drink their sake at room temperature (*hiyazake*) or chilled (*reishu*), in which case a tumbler is used. A variation in sake is *taruzake* (barrel sake), which is stored in cedar casks. The delightful aroma of the wood is imparted to the beverage. *Taruzake* is frequently drunk from a cedar box (*masu*), the traditional measure for rice and salt and sake; a pinch of salt may be placed on the rim of the box or on the back of the hand and then tasted, tequila style, while drinking. Another interesting way of flavouring sake is to grill the dried fin (*hirezake*) of a *fugu* fish, then steep the fin in hot sake, thus giving a pleasing, smoky taste to the drink.

Just as wine and beer figure in Western cooking, sake is not only drunk but also used in Japanese cuisine. Sake has deep symbolic meanings for the Japanese. It is strongly associated with national identity as a distinctly Japanese beverage; it also plays a central part in the sacraments of **State Shintō** and, as such, is as significant as wine in Christianity.

Further reading

Kond, H. (1984) *Saké: A Drinker's Guide*, Tokyo, New York and San Francisco: Kōdansha International Ltd.

STEPHEN R. SMITH

SALARYMAN *see sarariiman*

Sankei shinbun

The *Sankei* has a reputation for being the conservative voice among Japan's national newspapers – particularly in regard to its pro-government stance on political issues. As a result, the *Sankei* occupies a special position in the newspaper community. It was founded in Ōsaka in 1933 under the name *Nihon kōgyō shinbun*. However, in 1941, in conjunction with wartime policies to ration newsprint and control press freedom, the newspaper merged with thirty-three other business-oriented newspapers located in western Japan. The following year, it assumed the name *Sangyō keizai shinbun*. In 1955, another merger occurred, this time with *Jiji shinpo* (1882), enlightenment intellectual Fukuzawa Yukichi's newspaper devoted to news and business. It took the name *Sankei jiji*. The *Sankei shinbun* came into being in 1957 and moved from an economic focus to a general-readership publication. Nationwide distribution followed, but financial difficulties besieged the newspaper. In 1958, Mizuno Shigeo, former head of a large paper company, became president and a comeback was attempted. Mizuno made it clear from the outset that the *Sankei* supported the Liberal Democratic Party. From the 1960s, the *Sankei* became a major stockholder of Nippon hōsō broadcasting company, Bunka hōsō broadcasting company and Fuji Television, creating a tie-up between newspaper, radio and television (Fuji-Sankei group). Under the tutelage of the former president of Fuji Television, there was an increase in politically charged columns supporting such controversial issues as the constitutionality of the National Defence Forces, and conservative reforms.

Today, *Sankei*'s morning and evening editions have a combined circulation of approximately 2,000,000.

BARBARA HAMILL SATO

Sanrio

Begun in 1960 as Yamanashi Silk Centre, Sanrio grew rapidly into a multinational corporation specialising in 'fancy goods' with branches all over the world after opening its first Tokyo shop in 1971. After the high economic growth period of the 1960s, the markets for large consumer goods – televisions, washers – were nearly saturated. Sanrio targeted a previously untapped market: girls. Experimenting originally with pretty stationery featuring nonsensical English phrases, Sanrio soon developed animal characters to decorate accessories for girls' pencil cases, barrettes, notebooks. In 1974, the first and best-known of the cute animal characters appeared as 'Hello Kitty'. Although most of its products are useful (e.g. lunchboxes), what Sanrio sells is an aesthetic – one of cute, wide-eyed, childlike innocence.

In Japan, girls seem to buy cute (**kawaii**) 'fancy goods' as part of a '**shōjo** lifestyle', which some Japanese cultural critics have condemned as empty consumerism, but others have seen as a creative form of identity construction. For young girls, whose lives are characterised by regimentation – school uniforms, regulated hair length, identical book bags – these cute, colourful accessories may serve to personalise everyday objects.

See also: *kawaii*

SHARALYN ORBAUGH

Sapporo Olympics

The Eleventh Winter Olympics was held in Sapporo in February 1972. This Olympics, like the 1964 Tokyo Olympics and 1970 Ōsaka Expo, marked Japan's re-emergence on to the international stage, and the world's growing acceptance of a new identity for Japan separate from its wartime activities. This winter Olympics, like the 1964 summer games, was attended by athletes from many of the countries that had been occupied by Japan. The event was renowned for the debate over participation by professional athletes. The Chairman of the IOC stood firm by his conviction that the Olympics should be a strictly amateur event, and he challenged the participation of numerous international athletes who were known to have accepted various forms of corporate sponsorship. Finally, one leading athlete was excluded in a symbolic gesture to the IOC regulations. These games brought Japan the first winter Olympic gold. The successful event was the ski-jump and, in fact, Japan also captured the silver and bronze in this event to the delight of the national audience at the games and on television. The country virtually came to a standstill for the period of the event. By 1972, Japan was clearly on the pathway to becoming a major international economic force and Japanese citizens were increasingly aware of their improved standard of living after a decade of rapid growth. The Sapporo Olympics saw an outpouring of national pride around the success of the ski-jump team. This has been interpreted by some commentators as a substitute for other expressions of national identity in a country still very unsure of how to articulate national pride and sentiment in the lingering shadow of war memories.

SANDRA BUCKLEY

sarariiman

Strictly speaking, *sarariiman* (salaryman) refers to salaried, white-collar, permanent, male employees of private-sector organisations. However, the everyday usage of the term extends across a broader spectrum, including blue-collar employees, public servants and (sometimes) female employees.

The birth of the *sarariiman* was closely linked to Japan's process of industrialisation from the Meiji Period onwards (the term itself was first coined in the years after the First World War). However, it was only over the post-Second World War decades, due to a rapid expansion of white-collar employment, that the *sarariiman* became the ubiquitous everyman of Japanese industry. A whole body of popular culture (movies, music, **manga**) exists surrounding the *sarariiman* and his lifestyle.

The emergence of the *sarariiman* was premised upon a particularly powerful and pervasive ideology of gender, which equated masculinity with work, and femininity with the household. In return for paternalistic concern on the part of the company, the *sarariiman* would be expected to devote himself to the organisation, leaving matters of the household to his spouse. However, in the context of recent social and economic changes, the *sarariiman* as the embodiment of masculinity is being challenged on several fronts.

Further reading

Beck, John C. and Beck, Martha N. (1994) *The Change of a Lifetime: Employment Patterns among Japan's Managerial Elite*, Honolulu: University of Hawaii Press.
Kumazawa Makoto (1996) *Portraits of the Japanese Workplace: Labor Movements, Workers, and Managers*, trans. Andrew Gordon and Mikiso Hane, Boulder, CO: Westview Press.
Otani Akihiro (1993) *Sarariiman no Wasuremono*, Tokyo: Magajinhausu.

ROMIT DASGUPTA

sashimi

Raw fish served fresh and thinly sliced is hardly an adequate description for the artful dish known as *sashimi*. The quality of *sashimi* is judged on a number of levels including the skilfulness of the slicing technique, the aesthetics of the presentation and, above all, the freshness and grade of the fish served.

Sashimi is eaten dipped in individual dishes mixed to taste. The soy and sake-based dip can include any combination of garnishes but the most popular are grated fresh ginger, grated green *wasabi* (Japanese horse radish) and diced or grated white radish. The delicately carved vegetables that decorate the plate can also be eaten. The slicing techniques appear simple at first glance but require a combination of experience, dexterity and top-quality knives maintained with a perfect blade edge. Freshness and quality of the fish is essential and in the early hours of each morning you will find the local *sashimi* and **sushi** chefs vying for the best of the day's catch at the fish market auctions (see **Tsukiji fish markets**). *Sashimi* is always

eaten early in the meal when the palette is clean and its subtle flavours can be best appreciated.

SANDRA BUCKLEY

satellite broadcasting

Since 1992, there has been commercially based household access to both broadcast and communication satellite channels in Japan. The three broadcast and six communication satellite channels available in that year are still operating. NHK was in an excellent position to pioneer satellite broadcasting and, even today, commercial competitors point to the advantages NHK has in this high-risk area of broadcasting given its strong influence on regulatory policies through its relationship to the Ministry of Post and Telecommunications (MPT) and its secure revenue from licensing and access to government funding and subsidies for research and development. Commercial broadcasters must rely on household subscriptions and advertising, and have had to work hard to develop marketing strategies to win both advertisers and audiences away from the traditional network stations.

In the early years of direct satellite broadcasting, the MPT intervened in an apparent move to protect NHK's position in that market and forced an alliance of commercial direct broadcasters resulting in the single station WOWOW, which specialised in movie and sports broadcasting. In a classic example of the NHK market advantage, WOWOW can be accessed from NHK dishes but is encrypted and requires the upfront purchase of a decoder. In 1997, NHK's satellite service boasted about 8 million subscribers while only 2 million households paid to access WOWOW services. NHK BS-1 offers twenty-four-hour international news services in collaboration with foreign news services, e.g. BBC (Britain), CNN (USA), KBS (South Korea), ZDF (Germany), with bilingual broadcast as a standard feature. NHK BS-2 offers broad-based entertainment and is increasingly abandoning the more traditional programming of NHK.

Communication satellites had a reputation for poorer quality compounded by inferior satellite orbits but technological improvements saw a rapid narrowing of the gap with broadcast satellites, and by the late 1990s enhanced digital compression technology enabled communication satellites to broadcast a hundred or more channels to mass audiences. Thirty-four companies were finally licensed by MPT in 1996 to broadcast satellite programming via cable distribution as PerfecTV. The global media giants, Rupert Murdoch and Ted Turner, were both attracted to this major untapped market and, despite early MPT resistance and NHK protests, have now established themselves in Japan through alliances with local networks and technology providers. Murdoch's Star TV launched J Sky B in an alliance and share buy strategy involving Sony and Fuji TV, which saw a merger with PerfecTV (now SKY PerfecTV). As the market has become increasingly competitive, NHK and WOWOW were forced to move to digital transmission for the next generation of broadcast satellites, abandoning the MPT's long-standing preference for analogue systems. The link between broadcasting and multimedia, largely digital, entertainment also made this move to digital transmission inevitable.

Satellite broadcasting is linked to a key area of cultural debate in Japan. Any visitor to Japan will be struck by the limited amount of imported programming, and many syndicated shows are 'stale'. Defenders of the high level of domestic content argue that there would be more international programming if Japanese were interested but that Japanese prefer 'local' content. This cultural argument is countered by supporters of a more internationalised range of programming, who point to the regulatory and market-place barriers to entry created by Japanese broadcasters and the MPT wanting to protect their high investment in domestic production. The rapid gain in market share by satellite broadcasters with a broader base of international programming has not seen a dramatic increase in imported programmes on the Japanese television networks, with the exception of sports events. This has led to a cultural dichotomy in broadcast content, with the larger satellite broadcasters offering more international content while the Japanese networks continue to specialise more in domestic content. This divide is also reflected in viewer profiles with youth and under-thirties audiences constituting a crucial market for satellite stations. The shift to digital

platforms for both television and digital entertainment access is expected to intensify this age-based differentiation in audience distribution.

Japan is not the only country in the Asia–Pacific region involved in this type of cultural debate around domestic and imported content issues. Korea only lifted a comprehensive ban on the importation of Japanese commercial programming in the mid-1990s. There are ongoing negotiations between the Japanese and Taiwanese governments over Japanese television and music sales into that domestic market, and the dumping of Japanese comics and animation in the Hong Kong market is a regular issue in trade magazines and conferences. The Japanese government fought the leakage or spillover of Hong Kong-based communication satellite broadcasts into Japan in the early 1990s with little success. Korean protests of cultural imperialism as a result of Japanese spillover into Korean broadcast space similarly have had little impact. With more than twenty unauthorised satellite signal footprints over Japan in 1998 alone, there has been a gradual recognition of the inevitability of spillover, and networks and governments are now opting more for collaborative strategies and regional agreements. Networks are calling for greater autonomy in these content decisions but MPT remains committedly involved in this area of regulation. For the most part, Japanese networks seem willing to play the culture debate differently depending on context. They remain more focused on developing the potential of their own export market into Asia than promoting domestic competition from other markets, especially US imports.

See also: satellite communications

SANDRA BUCKLEY

satellite communications

After nuclear power, few areas of technology policy have received as much attention and funding from the Japanese government as space development. In the 1960s and 1970s, Japanese electronics firms licensed satellite technology from the USA. In the 1980s, they strove towards autonomous production, but resistance from domestic users such as

NTT and NHK to high prices and opposition from the USA led to a market-opening agreement in 1990 that stalled domestic production of all but experimental satellites. The focus of attention then swung from manufacturing to services.

Among the major applications of satellites are mobile telecommunications, data transmission and broadcasting. Traditionally, mobile telecommunications such as cellular phones have depended upon land base stations. Satellite systems, such as the less than successful Iridium project organised by Motorola of the USA and supported by Daini Denden of Japan, make it possible to communicate to and from even the most remote and isolated spots. Users pay for the convenience and flexibility of broader access with higher connection fees. Satellite communications also make possible provision of global positioning information for marine and car navigation systems, in which Japanese firms have established a leading position. Data transmission emerged in the late 1990s with the rapid diffusion of personal computers and the Internet. Satellites are capable of beaming down large amounts of data quickly and at low cost; when necessary, users can use fixed telephone or cable lines to send small amounts of data uplink. The most lucrative application of satellite communications is television and radio broadcasting. Satellite broadcasting can provide coverage similar to cable but at lower costs. Japan's national broadcaster NHK pioneered satellite broadcasting first as a way to reach remote communities and then to provide higher-quality images, including high-definition television (HDTV). When a number of private broadcasters attempted to move into direct satellite broadcasting, the Ministry of Post and Telecommunications (MPT) forced them to form a single company called WOWOW to avoid 'excessive competition'. By 1997, NHK's satellite service boasted about 8 million subscribers while another 2 million households watched WOWOW's movies.

Technological improvements in transponders, antennas and digital data compression gradually enabled communications satellites that had originally specialised in providing corporate communications from inferior orbits to erase the gap with broadcasting satellites. Communications satellites used digital compression to broadcast a hundred or more channels to mass audiences. General trading companies led the way with PerfecTV, which was soon followed by DirecTV Japan, a joint venture of the US satellite manufacturer Hughes and Culture Convenience Club, a local video rental chain. Australian media magnate Rupert Murdoch's News Corporation then created an alliance with software distributor Softbank and electronics giant Sony called J Sky B.

Frustrated in their effort to acquire a major share in Asahi TV, they switched to Fuji TV. Eventually, J Sky B merged with and effectively absorbed PerfecTV, while NHK and WOWOW were forced to move to digital transmission for the next generation of broadcasting satellites. Satellite communications is no longer an arena for autonomous development in Japan, but technological innovations have led to a rapid growth in demand for new services.

GREGORY W. NOBLE

Satō Tadao

b. 1930, Niigata Prefecture

Film critic and scholar

Satō began writing about films while working as a telephone repair man and rose to the editorship of *Eiga hyōronka* (Film Criticism) and *Shisō no kagaku* (Science of Thought) magazines, despite his lack of formal education. In 1956, with the publication of his first book, *Nihon no eiga* (Japanese Film), he advanced to the front ranks of Japanese film criticism. In this and subsequent volumes of criticism, Satō rejected an overly ideological or aesthetic approach in favour of an analysis, which while deeply informed, focused on a film's emotional content, in a style comprehensible to non-specialist readers. Satō's essays and reviews have been widely translated abroad, and in 1982 his *Currents In Japanese Cinema* became the first full-length work of film criticism by a Japanese author to appear in English. In 1995, he published his four-volume *Nihon eiga shi* (Japanese Film History), a monumental project that he described as the culmination of his life's work.

Select bibliography

Sato Tadao (1982) *Currents In Japanese Cinema*, Tokyo: Kōdansha International Ltd.

MARK SCHILLING

saving

Japan had one of the highest saving rates in the world during much of the post-war period. Its household saving rate peaked at 23 per cent in the mid-1970s, meaning that the Japanese were saving close to one-quarter of their take-home pay. This high saving rate helped Japan to achieve double-digit rates of economic growth from the 1950s to the early 1970s by providing the funds needed to finance investment in plant, equipment and social infrastructure, which in turn was needed to expand the productive capacity of the economy.

Numerous factors have been suggested as possible explanations of Japan's high saving rate, but I consider only the most frequently mentioned ones here. First, culture: many believe that Japan's high saving rate is due to cultural factors (national character, Confucian values), but the evidence suggests that culture is not the primary explanation. For one thing, Japan's saving rate was low and often negative during the pre-war and early post-war periods. For another, Japan's saving rate showed an upward trend during much of the post-war period (1950s to mid-1970s), even though this same period is often associated with a weakening of core cultural influences.

Second, the high rate of economic growth: during the high-growth period of the 1950s to early 1970s, household incomes rose so rapidly that the Japanese could not adjust their spending habits and lifestyles fast enough to keep pace with their rising incomes. The result was an increase in savings.

Third, the low level of household assets: much of Japan's housing stock was destroyed during the Second World War, and the real value of household financial assets was greatly reduced by post-war hyperinflation. Thus, household assets were at very low levels just after the war. One factor motivating Japanese savings may have been the desire to restore assets to previous levels.

Fourth, the unavailability of consumer credit: until the 1970s, consumer credit was difficult to obtain in Japan, and this made it necessary for Japanese households to save in advance for big-ticket items such as housing, automobiles, furniture and electrical appliances.

Fifth, the bonus system: a considerable portion of Japanese employee compensation is paid in the form of semi-annual bonuses, and many scholars believe that this method of compensation encourages savings.

Sixth, government promotion of saving: the government offered a variety of tax breaks and the Central Council for Savings Promotion, a quasi-governmental agency affiliated with the Bank of Japan, engaged in activities designed to encourage people to save more.

Seventh, the young age structure of the population: until the 1970s, the age structure of Japan's population was the youngest among the developed countries. People typically work and save when they are young and retire and draw down their accumulated savings in old age. Thus, a country's overall saving rate will typically be higher, the more young people there are relative to the number of old people.

Most of the factors responsible for Japan's high saving rate no longer apply and so it is hardly surprising that there has been a precipitous decline since the mid-1970s. Moreover, this downward trend is likely to continue or even accelerate. For one thing, Japan's population is expected to become the most aged in the world by the year 2010, according to most projections. This factor alone will cause Japan's saving rate to plummet to possibly even negative levels.

See also: banking system; postal savings

Further reading

Horioka, Charles Yuji (1990) 'Why is Japan's household saving rate so high? A literature survey', *Journal of the Japanese and International Economies* 4(1): 49—92.

CHARLES YUJI HORIOKA

Sazae-san

Sazae-san is the most beloved animated character in Japan, known to all generations. First depicted in 1946 in a newspaper comic strip by Machiko Hasegawa, Isono Sazae began as a spirited, optimistic young woman, struggling to survive in the difficult circumstances of the Occupation. However, Sazae-san is better known in her married incarnation: as a twenty-three-year-old housewife with husband Masuo and toddler Tara, living in a three-generation family with her parents and younger siblings. In this form Sazae-san appeared in a *manga* that ran until 1975, and an animated television series that began in 1969, and as of 1997 was still broadcast.

The popularity of Sazae-san rests on its gentle humour and relentless reinforcement of what are perceived as mainstream Japanese values, albeit from an earlier era: the happy three-generation family, with time to enjoy each other's company; the contented full-time housewife; children who are not overstressed at school; fathers who come home early from the office; and particularly the attention to seasonal rituals and cultural practices. Sazae-san watching fireworks at a summer festival, dressed in cotton kimono and carrying a pretty folding fan, while eating traditional festival foods – scenes such as this are the backbone of Sazae-san's nostalgic appeal.

SHARALYN ORBAUGH

scandals

Scandals (always involving money but rarely sex) have been an important feature of politics in modern Japan. The essential ingredients have been present since the late nineteenth century: elections, politicians in need of money, businesses seeking government contracts, a vigorous press and an interested and informed populace. 'Money politics' reached new heights by the 1970s as a result of high economic growth. Yet opposition parties and voters were never able or willing to oust the **Liberal Democratic Party** (LDP), which governed from 1955 to 1993. The end of LDP hegemony and the uncertain political alignments that prevailed through the 1990s resulted less from voter backlash than from the defection of LDP members to form new parties.

Modern Japan's first major scandal involved the sale in the early 1880s of industries that had been founded by the government. Many were sold at low prices to friends of government officials. In the Siemens affair of 1914, a German company was found to have paid kickbacks to Japanese naval officials in return for contracts. Criticism in the Diet and violent demonstrations in the streets brought down the Cabinet.

The first major post-war scandal was the Shōwa Denkō scandal of 1948, which brought down the government after Prime Minister Ashida Hitoshi (a socialist), members of his Cabinet and other high-ranking officials were accused of taking bribes in return for arranging a low interest loan for Japan's largest fertiliser producer. In 1954, a number of politicians, including future prime ministers Ikeda Hayato and Satō Eisaku, were indicted for taking bribes from shipbuilding companies. This scandal, particularly Prime Minister Yoshida Shigeru's shielding of Satō, contributed to the fall of the Cabinet.

The **Lockheed scandal** of 1976 had the greatest effect on post-war politics. Tanaka Kakuei, who had been forced out of the premiership in 1974 by money scandals, was paid ¥500 million ($1.6 million) to persuade All-Nippon Airways to purchase Lockheed jets. Yet the affair led not to a clean-up of the political system but to Tanaka's protecting himself by becoming a behind-the-scenes 'kingmaker', by far the most powerful politician in Japan.

The 1988 **Recruit scandal**, involving cash and pre-issue stock certificates given to politicians by a real-estate company, and the 1992 **Sagawa Kyūbin scandal**, in which a package delivery company with organised-crime connections gave huge sums to leading politicians, combined to contribute to a splintering of the LDP that resulted in its 1993 election defeat. However, in other ways politics after these scandals, as after earlier ones, quickly returned to business as usual. Meaningful reforms seemed unlikely as long as business needed government favours and politicians needed more money than they could raise legally.

Further reading

Farley, M. (1996) 'Japan's press and the politics of scandal', in S. Pharr and E. Krauss (eds) *Media and Politics in Japan*, Honolulu: University of Hawaii Press, pp. 133–63.

Masumi, J. (1995) *Contemporary Politics in Japan*, trans. L. Carlile, Berkeley: University of California Press.

Mitchell, R. (1996) *Political Bribery in Japan*, Honolulu: University of Hawaii Press.

Schlesinger, J. (1997, 1999) *Shadow Shoguns: The Rise and Fall of Japan's Postwar Political Machine*, Stanford: Stanford University Press.

Woodall, B. (1996) *Japan under Construction: Corruption, Politics, and Public Works*, Berkeley: University of California Press.

TIMOTHY S. GEORGE

school excursions

School excursions are integral to Japanese education. These trips are fondly remembered by students years after their formal education is completed. Students in the same class/year travel together. Depending on the size of the school, there can be as many as 500 young people to watch over. All teachers are expected to participate, but not parents. There are two forms of school excursions: *ensoku*, or one-day trips, and *shūgaku ryokō*, a four- or five-day outing, usually in May. Teachers and students spend a great deal of time in planning for the major trip. Favourite destinations have included Kyōto, Tokyo and Hiroshima, but, more recently, Tokyo Disneyland and ski trips have been added to the list. Wealthy private schools have been known to take students to Hawaii, Taiwan, Korea or Hokkaidō.

While the obvious goal is to broaden student knowledge about their environment, the excursions serve as a significant opportunity to train students in appropriate public behaviour and etiquette. Through the planning and execution of these events, students learn to work together and take responsibility for the decisions of their peers. Maintenance of school reputation is a serious matter for teachers. Students are expected to conduct themselves with dignity.

JUNE A. GORDON

school system

Elementary and secondary schools are organised along the lines of the US 6–3–3 model with pre-schools, *yōchien*, and day-care centres, *hoikuen*, preceding formal schooling. Compulsory education, *gimukyōiku*, based on strong egalitarian norms starts at age six and stops after lower secondary school, ninth grade. This period includes six years of elementary school, *shogakkō*, and three years or middle school, *chūgakkō*. Even though high school or upper secondary school, *kōtōgakkō*, is not compulsory, over 90 per cent of students attend. The type of high school one attends is decisive in one's future education, employment and social position. While primary and lower secondary schooling is free, all high schools require some form of tuition, regardless of whether public or private. Admission to high school requires an application process and is based on competitive exams, given in March, along with recommendations of one's adviser/home-room teacher. Those who cannot attend a public or private high school for academic or economic reasons may attend vocational schools. If this is not possible, then there is night school and/or employment.

Post-secondary education includes: four-year colleges and universities, *daigaku*, some with graduate programmes; two-year colleges, *tankidai*, for women; technical colleges, *kōtō senmon gakkō*, which combine upper secondary and two-year college work; and special training schools for vocational training at both the upper secondary and two-year college level. There are both public and private schools at each level of education. Public is further divided into national and local/prefectural. While a parallel system of private schools has always existed in Japan, their number and quality are increasing. Some of these schools are called *elevetaa* schools, meaning that entrance to a prestigious pre-school or kindergarten will guarantee your space, with the right connections and funding, to elementary and junior high schools known for successful entry to the best high schools, and then on to university. Students are usually admitted to this elite system based on recommendations and interviews.

The educational philosophy in Japan assumes that all children are of equal ability and should not be singled out for special attention. Differences in student academic success are seen as the result of individual effort, perseverance and self-discipline. Students, therefore, are not grouped by ability but rather are given the same curriculum at the same speed as dictated by the **Ministry of Education** (Monbusho). Those who cannot keep up, *ochikobore*, are expected to receive outside help either from home or *juku*, but they are not held back. They move forward with their age group. In elementary school, students usually stay with the same teacher in the same room for two years. In lower and upper secondary school, the students stay in the same room together and teachers rotate to teach their subjects. The *tannin*, or home-room teacher, serves a pivotal position in the Japanese educational system, providing guidance and continuity throughout a student's academic life. They are responsible for extracurricular activities, field trips and discipline problems. In elementary school, the *tannin* is the regular teacher who teaches all subjects to the same group of students. In the upper grades, students meet with their *tannin* at the beginning and end of the day as well as for one period of an academic subject taught by the *tannin*. The home-room teacher offers crucial advice on the type of further education appropriate for each student. Based on the student's academic performance and disposition, the home-room teacher will suggest that a student take the exam for a particular high school or university. Schools pride themselves in being able to make successful matches for their students as demonstrated through high acceptance rates. Schools are ranked according to their test scores and the number of placements their students receive in the top high schools and/or universities.

Japanese school buildings are plain, but functional. Generally, they are three-storey, rectangular, concrete structures, which lack central heating and air conditioning. The lack of decoration and furnishings is believed to help the child focus on learning and building character. However, schools have excellent educational facilities such as labs, art studios and computers. Each grade occupies a separate section or floor of the building. Across the grade levels, the day flows in a similar pattern. Classroom activities begin at 8:30 a.m. with a fifteen-minute morning class meeting, which is led by the home-room teacher and student monitors. The number and duration of classes increases over the years with elementary students having four classes of about forty-five minutes with recesses. The upper grades have six class periods during the week and four on Saturday. Each class period runs for fifty minutes. In elementary schools, lunch is provided for a nominal fee and is usually eaten in classrooms with the teachers. Students both serve the meal and clean up afterwards. In some middle and high schools, students bring their own meals carefully prepared by mothers to maximise nutritional content. The school day ends at 3:00 p.m. with a ten-minute class meeting and the cleaning of the room, school building and school grounds. In the afternoon, usually from 3:30–5 p.m. or 6 p.m., most students participate in organised clubs. *Juku* lessons, for those who attend, usually occur between 7–10 p.m. On three Saturdays a month, school ends at noon, after four class periods. Class size tends to run between thirty-five and forty-five students. Each class is divided into *han*, small groups of four to six students who work as a unit for study, chores and organised activities. The *han* is essential to the Japanese way of educating young people to be responsible for each other.

The Japanese elementary and secondary school year begins in early April and is divided into trimesters that run from April to July, September to December and January to March. A six-week holiday occurs from mid-July to the end of August, with shorter vacation periods between other trimesters. During this time, students are expected to work on assignments and behave according to school rules. Out of the reported 240 days of schooling, thirty days are designated for activities such as field trips, sports day, cultural festivals and ceremonies.

Adjusting for the half-days on Saturdays, the Japanese school year contains the full-time equivalent of about 195 days of classroom instruction.

JUNE A. GORDON

school uniforms

Most public primary schools do not have uniforms, but all require something to identify the child as attending that particular school, such as a school cap or badge. Some schools require students to purchase identical athletic apparel, which is often worn during regular classes as well. Middle school begins the routine of mandatory uniforms for students who attend public school. Other aspects of personal appearance are also regulated, including hairstyle and accessories. These changes symbolize the seriousness of secondary education and the expected attitudes and demeanor. The quality of uniforms and acceptable forms of accessories such as socks and jewellery mark the relative status and economic level of schools.

JUNE A. GORDON

science and technology parks

As of March 1994, there were seventy science and technology parks actually operating and forty-one in planning. The Japanese divide these into three categories: innovation centres (26 per cent), science parks (32 per cent) and R&D parks (42 per cent). Innovation centres possess incubators to facilitate the establishment of industries, and other facilities to encourage research and information exchange. Science parks tend to be larger in scale, and are able to accommodate industries that have outgrown the incubator stage. R&D parks don't have incubators, but nevertheless attract corporate laboratories and university and government research institutes as their tenants.

Incubators are a common feature of both innovation centres and science parks, growing in popularity since 1988. There were forty-five in existence in 1993, with a further twenty being planned. The jury is still out on whether or not incubators are effective in nurturing new industries. There does appear to be a trend away from them. Whereas 64 per cent of the seventy science and technology parks have incubators, only 49 per cent of the forty-one parks under planning have this feature. Science and technology parks tend to emphasise regional development. They often lack universities and government research institutes, which ideally should be at their core. The public research institutes that do exist have mainly been established by public corporations, rather than by universities. In the past, it has been institutionally difficult for national universities to conduct joint research with private firms. Tenants of these parks tend to be large or medium-sized enterprises. Their size and company culture may work against the fostering of new firms, but most make an effort to facilitate research exchange between university, industry and government.

The majority of parks are public-sector projects managed by government, local authorities or public corporations intent on attracting private firms to their location. There are over one hundred science cities/technopolises/research cores/industrial brain areas/strategic development areas in Japan, in addition to science and technology parks. Research cores are either located in designated technopolises (twenty-six as of 1993) or in big cities. They usually consist of facilities for experimental research, research training, information and communications, and venture business incubators. Private firms become tenants in research cores. There are two science cities: Tsukuba Science City (located in Ibaraki Prefecture) and the more recently established Kansai Science City. In contrast to Tsukuba, where a university and government institutions dominate, the emphasis in Kansai Science City is on the private sector. The latter project dovetailed well with plans for the now completed Kansai International Airport, which services Ōsaka and beyond.

Further reading

Hayashi, K. (1991) 'High-technology strategies and regional restructuring', *International Journal of Political Economy* 21(3): 70–89.

Yoshizawa, J., Oyama, Y., Yamamoto, T. and Gonda, K. (1995) 'Comparative studies on science and technology parks for regional innnovation throughout the world', NISTEP Report no. 38, Tokyo: National Institute of Science and Technology Policy.

MORRIS LOW

science fiction

Until the early 1960s, science fiction in Japan was known by the Japanese equivalent *kagaku shōsetsu*, but is now simply referred to as SF (pronounced *esuefu*). While translation of Western works has been and remains an important part of the field in Japan, since the 1960s an increasing number of Japanese writers have been active in the production of a diverse range of original science fiction writing. The establishment of specialised science fiction magazines, a writers association, fan organisations and awards have all contributed to the development of the genre. Today, hundreds of titles, both translations and original Japanese works, are published each year. At the same time, the popularity of other forms of mass culture such as **manga** and **anime**, both of which have freely drawn on science fiction techniques and themes, has resulted in a blurring of the lines between traditional science fiction and these new genres.

Although there is a tradition in Japanese literature of fantastic adventure stories dating back to the Edo Period (1600–1867), the genre of science fiction can more properly be seen as the result of Western influence beginning with the opening of the country during the Meiji Period (1868–1912). Translations at this time of the works of Jules Verne and H.G. Wells helped prepare the way for Japanese writers' first efforts at science fiction, such as Yano Ryūkei's *Ukishiro monogatari* (Tale of a Floating Fortress, 1990) and Oshikawa Shunrō's *Kaitei gunkan* (The Undersea Warship, 1900). After waning for a couple of decades, science fiction writing began to make a comeback in the pages of the magazines *Shinseinen* (New Youth), founded in 1920, and *Kagaku gahō* (Science Pictorial), which followed in 1927. Many of the stories that appeared in these magazines, however, were little more than variants of detective fiction in which some new technology or gadget played a role in the crime or its detection.

Among early post-war writers, mention should be made of Kayama Shigeru (1904–75), author of *Kaijū gojira* (The Monster Godzilla), which provided the story for the 1954 film that started the popular genre of **monster films**. In 1957, an important year in the development of Japanese science fiction, the Tokyo-based fan club Kagaku Sōsaku Kurabu

(Science Fiction Club) was founded and began issuing its influential fan magazines, *Uchūjin* (Cosmic Dust). In the same year, publishing company Hayakawa began issuing its series of science fiction translations. This was followed by the company's launching of Japan's first commercially successful science fiction magazine, *SF magajin*, in 1959. Other magazines began to appear in the 1970s, including *Kisō tengai*, *SF hōseki* and *SF Adventure*. As other publishers entered the field, more and more works by Japanese authors began to appear alongside the translations. The writers themselves founded their own organisation, the Japanese SF Writers Club, in 1963. In 1980, Japan hosted the International Science Fiction Symposium. The same year saw the establishment of the multi-category Seiun Award, winners of which are chosen by the fans. In 1980, the Japan SF Writers Club introduced its own book award, the Japan SF Grand Prix.

Among the most influential of the first generation of post-war science fiction writers are: **Abe Kōbō** (1924–92), who is not always considered a science fiction writer but whose *Daiyon Kampyō-ki* (Inter Ice Age 4, 1959) clearly falls into the science fiction category; Hoshi Shinichi (1926–97), master of the science fiction short story; Komatsu Sakyō (b. 1931), a prolific writer of science fiction novels, whose *Nippon chimbotsu* (Japan Sinks, 1973) topped the bestseller list and was made into a movie (released in a severely mangled version in English as *Tidal Wave*); Tsutsui Yasutaka (b. 1934), another prolific author, whose works cover a wide range and who sometimes crosses over into mainstream or experimental fiction but as a science fiction writer is best known for his satirical and slapstick humour; and Yano Tetsu (b. 1923), who was influential in the early period as a translator but later turned to writing novels of his own. Other important authors who entered the field in the 1960s are Hanmura Ryō (b. 1933), Matsuse Ryū (b. 1928) and Mayumura Taku (b. 1934).

As science fiction began to boom in popularity during the 1970s, a new generation of writers began to emerge, including Tanaka Kōji (b. 1941), Hori Akira (b. 1944), Yokota Junya (b. 1945), Kajio Shinji (b. 1947), Kambe Musashi (b. 1948), Yamada Masaki (b. 1950) and Yumemakura Baku (b. 1951). The late 1970s and early 1980s saw yet another wave of new writers appear, most notably Kambayashi Chōhei (b. 1953), who dominated the Seiun awards in the mid-1980s and whose *Kototsubo* (Wordport) won the Japan SF Grand Prix in 1995; and the women writers Ōhara Mariko (b. 1959) and Arai Motoko (b 1960). Arai especially is known for having introduced the issue of gender roles into her science fiction stories and novels. She was awarded the Japan SF Grand Prix in 1999 for her *Chigurisu to Yufuratesu* (Tigris and Euphrates).

While science fiction can still be said to be enjoying a boom, the line separating the genre from other forms of fiction and popular culture is becoming increasingly blurred. *Manga* and media categories were added to the Seiun Award in 1978 and 1980, respectively. Among the winners of these awards have been animators Miyazaki Hayao (b. 1941) and Ōtomo Katsuhiro (b. 1954). Ōtomo was also awarded the Japan SF Grand Prix in 1983 for his *manga Domu* (A Child's Dreams). In 1996, the same award went to the monster film *Gamera 2*. Meanwhile, mainstream authors such as **Murakami Haruki** (b. 1949) and **Murakami Ryū** (b. 1952) frequently cross over into the science fiction genre, while many recognised science fiction writers have turned to writing occult or horror fantasy for the mass market. It is thus questionable whether science fiction will continue to be recognised as a distinct literary genre. This continued flow of influences between *anime, manga*, film and sci-fi literature in Japan exemplifies the high level of interactivity across media in the contemporary cultural landscape.

Select bibliography

Abe Kōbō (1970) *Inter Ice Age 4*, trans. E. D. Saunders, New York: Knopf.

Hoshi Shinichi (1978) *The Spiteful Planet and Other Stories*, trans. T. Genkawa and Bernard Susser, Tokyo: Japan Times.

Komatsu Sakyo (1976) *Japan Sinks*, trans. M. Gallagher, New York: Harper.

Further reading

Apostolou, J.L. and Greenberg, M.H. (eds) (1989) *The Best Japanese Science Fiction Stories*, New York: Dembner.

Lewis, D. (1987) 'Japanese SF', in N. Barron (ed.) *Anatomy of Wonder: A Critical Guide to Science Fiction*, New York: Bowker, pp. 474–503.

Matthew, R. (1989) *Japanese Science Fiction: A View of a Changing Society*, London: Routledge.

WILLIAM LEE

sculpture

It may be no exaggeration to say that, in the history of modern art, painting is the privileged and dominant medium, with sculpture more or less relegated to the sidelines. In Japan, too, the same disregard for sculpture can be observed. For example, in 1907, at the first government-sponsored salon, Bunten, painters were duly grouped into two sections – **Nihonga** (Japanese-style painting) and **yōga** (Western-style painting) – whereas sculptors were simply given one section, 'sculpture', into which two movements, as divergent as the two painting categories, were placed together. These movements were the revived traditional wood sculpture and the newly introduced Western carving and modelling. This basic classification system was continued in many incarnations of the official salon as well as art association exhibitions.

Over the next five decades, Japanese sculpture made its steady progress from Rodin-esque realism, to Constructivism to abstraction. Misfortune struck again in the late 1950s and into the 1960s, when Anti-Art (*Han-geijutsu*) practitioners – mostly trained as painters – produced two- and three-dimensional works, and even room-sized environments (anticipating installation art) and happenings/events (precursor of performance art), in defiance of every established convention of painting and sculpture, at the annual Yomiuri Independent Exhibition. Throughout the 1960s, Anti-Art further mutated into technology-based Environment Art (*Kankyō geijutsu*), which included early video and computer experiments. By the time *Mono-ha* (literally, 'Thing School') appeared on the horizon in 1968, it was essentially irrelevant to capture these new developments within the rubric of sculpture – so much so that, in 1969, the organisers of the bi-annual Contemporary Art Exhibition of Japan/Gendai

Nihon Bijutsu-ten decided to replace the sculpture section with that of *rittai* (three dimensions) within its 'open-entry competition' section. This change was more than linguistic, signalling a profound paradigm shift. It is not a coincidence that around this time Japan saw the rise of 'contemporary art' (*gendai bijutsu*) (see **art, contemporary**), the practice that encompasses various two-, three- and four-dimensional forms of expression, including video art, performance art and **installation art**, along with sculpture.

Further reading

Koplos, Janet (1991) *Contemporary Japanese Sculpture*, New York: Abbeville.

Munroe, Alexandra (ed.) (1994) *Japanese Art after 1945: Scream against the Sky*, New York: Abrams.

REIKO TOMII

seafood

Seafood remains the primary source of protein in Japan today, despite recent increases in meat intake. There is archaeological evidence of fish in the diets of the Jōmon and Yayoi periods, although there is some evidence that suggests fish intake fell after the establishment of rice cultivation as an alternative food source. To the present day, the combination of rice and fish, often supplemented by soy-based foods and/or seaweed, has provided a nutritionally well-balanced basic diet. Fish is seldom bought frozen in Japan but shopped for fresh as needed.

In addition to both ocean and freshwater fish, a wide variety of shellfish and crustaceans are found in popular Japanese dishes. The emphasis on seasonality of foods means that prices for seasonal seafoods can be very high for the limited period that they are available fresh in the shops and markets. It is not unusual to see a housewife or restaurant chef carrying a prized find home, live in a bucket or plastic bag. The local fish markets are always a lively centre of early-morning activity with chefs and fishmongers vying with one another for the best of the day's catch at auction. Deep-water fish such as blue fin tuna will be bought frozen as

this is the only viable means of ensuring quality due to the long distances the Japanese deep-water fishing fleets travel. The majority of Japan's consumers are unaware of the level of controversy that surrounds the high-yield technologies utilised by Japan's fishing fleets. Consumption of the once popular whale meat has fallen dramatically in the wake of environmental protests surrounding the annual Japanese whale catch.

The extensive vocabulary in the Japanese language for varieties of fish, fishing techniques and equipment, preparation and cooking, as well as fish dishes, reflects the central place of fish and other seafoods to the Japanese diet. Fish is a staple of everyday family fare and a walk through any neighbourhood in the early evening will find the air filled with assorted aromas of cooking fish. Seafood restaurants offer a wide range of specialised preparation techniques from the now more mundane **sushi** to the exotic and slightly more risky *fugu* (blowfish). It is *sashimi*, thinly sliced raw fish, that is the pinnacle of seafood cuisine in Japan. In the absence of any cooking, the emphasis is entirely on freshness, taste, skill of slicing and finally presentation. The top ranking *sashimi* chefs have celebrity status. With more women working and not having the time needed to buy and prepare fresh fish, there has been a rapid increase in seafood restaurants offering home delivery. For important family occasions and ceremonial meals, fish remains a requisite item on the menu. In the warmer summer months, it is still a popular family excursion to travel to the coast to gather shellfish and crabs or fish for shallow-water fish with hand nets along the shoreline. A simply prepared grilled seasonal fish or fresh shellfish steaming in a bowl of *miso* will still seldom fail to bring sighs of appreciation at the table.

SANDRA BUCKLEY

seasonal and festive cooking

Food is at the heart of much of Japanese ceremony and is intimately linked to the changing seasons. Gifts of food are a common element of ceremonial events as well as at the **gift-giving** seasons of mid-summer and New Year. When visiting someone's home, and even the office of a business acquaintance, it is often appropriate, if not required, to bring a suitable gift of food or beverage, which might include anything from a seasonal basket of fruit to a boxed set of summer desserts, or a gift-packaged bottle of whiskey (see **seasons**). Some professionals such as doctors are overwhelmed with food from clients during the gift-giving seasons. Anyone who travels away from home will attempt to bring back, for close friends and family, gifts of local seasonal food specialities (***meibutsu***) from their destination. The market in local seasonal food gifts is an important income source for many tourist destinations.

Not only in restaurants but also at home there is an attention to the details of seasonal shifts in food. This is at one level related to a preference for fresh foods but it also has a deeply rooted aesthetic component. The link between certain foods and seasons is embedded in the culture to the extent that there would be few Japanese who would not be able to quickly name the seasonal foods of any given time of the year. Traditional and contemporary poetry and literature, the *nō*, *kabuki*, film, comics, television and advertising all abound with references to seasonal foods and cooking: gingko nuts or persimmon in autumn; shredded ice, chilled *tōfu* or salted watermelon in summer; steaming hot, sweet red bean soup, grilled ***mochi*** and tangerines in winter; sake and ***onigiri*** under the cherry blossoms in spring.

Seasonal fruits and flowers are also placed as offerings at graves and on the family altars (see ***butsudan* and *kamidana***) at home. There are now commercial services that will care for these seasonal obligations for families too busy to keep up their ancestoral responsibilities. Some ceremonial days such as the Doll Festival (third day of the third month) (see **Hinamatsuri (Doll Festival) and Girls' Day**), Boys' Day (fifth day of the fifth month) and **New Year** entail the preparation of very specific foods. **Rice** holds a central place in these ceremonial events. ***Mochi*** rice cakes are wrapped in cherry leaves for Dolls Festival and oak leaves for Boys' Day. Celebratory red rice (*sekihan*) is prepared for birthdays, **weddings** and New Year, mixing red soy beans with glutinous rice sprinkled with black sesame. At New Year, *mochi* are served in a hot broth for breakfast after a family toast of hot spiced **sake** (*otoso*). Sake plays an important role in many ceremonies including betrothals, weddings, funerals (see **death and funerals**), naming ceremonies and coming of age. **Tea** is another beverage that has a long cultural history. Initially limited to medicinal applications and the world of the aristocracy, certain teas have retained an elite and ceremonial character, while others have become part of the fabric of daily life. Teas are also closely linked to specific regions and seasonal tastes and events.

SANDRA BUCKLEY

seasonal gift giving

There are two main gift seasons – *ochūgen* (mid-year/summer) and *oseibo* (year end). Gifts are not exchanged but offered out of obligation. A common axis of gift giving is junior to senior in the workplace, but company to customer gift giving is also a major source of business for department stores and speciality shops offering comprehensive gift services.

Younger generations will send gifts to senior family members, a patient's family will send a gift to the attending doctor, university professors and teachers may receive gifts from students or their families, politicians receive gifts from their constituents and in turn offer gifts to their patrons. The level of domestic consumption peaks at these two seasons, which also correspond to the payment of the two seasonal salary bonuses. Pre-packaged speciality foods and liquor are popular selections.

A gift should be of an appropriate value that reflects the relative status of the parties and the level of obligation or seniority. A gift wrapped in the paper of one of the major department stores carries more weight than a hand-wrapped gift. The gift is a performance of not only obligation but also the economic status and cultural currency of the giver.

SANDRA BUCKLEY

seasons

A sense of season pervades Japanese society and regulates cultural practice. It is widely believed that the seasons manifest the order and harmony that determine the world and inform human relations. Seasonally appropriate actions in daily life are required to maintain harmony. Letter writing and greetings refer to seasons using formal conventions. Homes and public places display decorations using seasonal symbols, such as **pine trees** and plum for winter, **cherry blossoms** for spring, willow for summer and maple leaves for autumn. Plastic versions of these flora festoon supermarkets in regular rotation. Seasonally appropriate gifts are given to one's superiors at mid-year and year-end to express appreciation. Seasonal conventions have roots in classical aesthetic forms, such as painting and haiku poetry, where a metaphorical seasonal reference is *de rigeur*: the bush warbler heralds spring, references to cuckoos or crickets signal summer. The passing seasons convey the ephemeral nature of life.

Seasonal conformity has more to do with social obligation than weather. Traditional clothing is strictly regulated according to sleeve length and fabric, in consideration of others who would feel uncomfortable should someone dress inappropriately. Seasonal foods, *gyōji ryōri*, are served to please one's family or guests at designated seasonal events. School children switch from summer to winter uniforms on designated days. Air conditioning and heating systems are switched on and off on set dates, regardless of temperature. Seasonality thus functions as a significant marker of Japanese social convention.

See also: colours, cultural significance of

AUDREY KOBAYASHI

seaweed

The three main types of seaweed consumed in Japan are *asakusa nori* (sheets of black *nori* served to wrap or garnish **rice**), *ao-nori* (a powdered green seaweed garnish) and *kombu* (dried kelp used in stocks). Seaweed is an important and inexpensive source of protein in the Japanese diet (see **dietary patterns**).

Japanese poetry and theatre abounds with images of young girls gathering seaweed along the shore, but since the 1500s there has been a well-established industry of seaweed cultivation and harvesting to match the demand. Today, seaweed can be bought off the shelf in supermarkets (see **supermarkets and superstores**) or connoisseurs can order regional varieties from speciality seaweed stores or gourmet food halls in the major **department stores**. Sets of high-quality seaweed and fine **tea** are a popular seasonal gift.

Kombu is the basic ingredient of the stock (*dashi*) that is essential to many Japanese dishes. The powdered *ao-nori* is used to garnish many rice and noodle dishes. Sheets of black seaweed are a crucial ingredient of sushi and the quality of *nori* will often be the trademark of a famous sushi restaurant. Sheets of *nori* can be served toasted or seasoned with a light brushing of **soy sauce**.

SANDRA BUCKLEY

Self-Defence Forces

The imperial Japanese military was abolished after the Second World War. A National Police Reserve was established in 1950, and reorganised in 1954 as the Self-Defence Forces (SDF), comprising the Ground, Air and Maritime Self-Defence Forces. Unlike the imperial military, which was responsible directly to the Emperor, the SDF is under the control of the prime minister, through the director-general of the Defence Agency, who is a Cabinet member.

The name 'Self-Defence Forces' is used because Article 9 of the **post-war Constitution** renounces war and the maintenance of military forces to settle international disputes. The SDF has always been highly controversial, but in several rulings the Supreme Court has never explicitly declared the SDF either constitutional or unconstitutional.

As the economy grew, the share of the **Gross National Product** (GNP) devoted to defence decreased by the late 1960s to under 1 per cent, a limit that was made an official target in 1976. Even at less than 1 per cent of GNP, however, Japan's defence expenditures were the third largest in the world by the late 1980s.

There were 238,000 SDF personnel at the end of 1997. All are volunteers, and women have served in the SDF since 1974. Nearly all equipment and weapons are produced in Japan, with some, such as fighter planes and missiles, produced under licensing agreements with US manufacturers. As of March 1998, the SDF had 1,100 tanks, 152 major ships (including fifty-seven escort ships and sixteen submarines) and 1,165 aircraft (including 363 fighters). Under the Three Non-nuclear Principles announced by Prime Minister Satō Eisaku in 1968, and approved by the Diet in 1972, Japan promised never to produce or possess nuclear weapons or allow them to be brought into its territory.

The USA is committed to defend Japan under the mutual security treaties in effect since 1952. The Japanese government bears part of the costs of US bases, and the SDF holds regular joint training exercises with US forces. Public opinion polls indicate broad acceptance of the SDF, the 1 per cent spending limit and the military alliance with the USA. Of the major parties, only the Japan Communist Party continues to oppose the existence of the SDF.

In the wake of criticism of Japan's 'chequebook diplomacy' in the Gulf War, SDF minesweepers were sent to help clear the area of mines in the first dispatch of Japanese military forces overseas since the Second World War. In 1992, the Diet passed legislation to allow SDF troops to participate in United Nations peacekeeping operations, and several hundred SDF personnel, mostly engineers, joined a UN operation in Cambodia. Post-cold-war uncertainties, and North Korean missile and nuclear weapons programmes, led to SDF joint exercises with South Korean troops and renewed proposals for a constitutional amendment explicitly legalising the SDF. These incremental changes gratify those who wish Japan to become a 'normal state', but rekindle fears of Japanese militarism in Asia.

Further reading

Calder, K. (1988) *Crisis and Compensation: Public Policy and Political Stability in Japan, 1949–1986*, Princeton: Princeton University Press.

Green, M. (1995) *Arming Japan: Defense Production, Alliance Politics, and the Postwar Search for Autonomy,* New York: Columbia University Press.

Harries, M. and Harries, S. (1987) *Sheathing the Sword: The Demilitarisation of Japan*, New York: MacMillan.

Hook, D. (1996) *Militarization and Demilitarization in Contemporary Japan*, London: Routledge.

Katzenstein, P. (1996) *Cultural Norms and National Security: Police and Military in Postwar Japan*, Ithaca, New York: Cornell University Press.

TIMOTHY S. GEORGE

seppuku/harakiri

A ceremonial form of suicide by disembowelment, *seppuku* was the preferred form of suicide of feudal retainers wishing to show their absolute loyalty to their lord. Only samurai above a certain level of rank were allowed to commit *seppuku* in situations such as remorse for an act of disloyalty or cowardice, faced with the dishonour of defeat or capture or to follow a lord in death.

A short sword is inserted in the left side and drawn across the stomach to the right. The stomach, and not the heart, is thought to be the centre of truth, loyalty, honour and other transrelational values, and thus the symbolism of the act. This is an extremely painful and potentially slow death and it became common practice for a comrade to decapitate from behind at almost the instant the knife stroke was completed. In some famous suicides there is reference to the suicider asking for this final blow to be delayed, extending the suffering in a last gesture of loyalty and strength. *Seppuku* is in fact very rare today but the highly publicised *seppuku* suicide of the author Mishima Yukio in 1970 briefly captured the attention and imagination of the world. The ceremony lives on, however, in the graphic images created by the film-makers and novelists who continue to sensationalise *seppuku* both in and out of Japan.

SANDRA BUCKLEY

sex aids

Sex aids are neither a modern phenomenon nor an import. The prostitution districts and travelling performer/prostitution troupes of pre-modern Japan were host to sex aid salesmen and speciality stores. The diversity of aids is clearly depicted in many of the more explicit of the early *shunga* (erotic woodblock prints). In addition to such gadgets as textured vaginal sheaths and footheld dildos there was also an extensive market in herbal aphrodisiacs and cures for impotence. The twentieth century saw the addition of new materials and technologies but many of the basic sex aid designs remained remarkably constant. The contemporary market is primarily mail order based but this has been moving increasingly online over the 1990s. Inter-active pornographic video games and computer software are a rapidly expanding sector of the market. The continued popularity of traditional herbal aphrodisiacs has been a growing target of environmental and animal rights campaigners seeking bans on the sale of products that rely on poaching of endangered species. Surveys indicate that the market for sex aids is generally not in the domestic home and marital bed but is driven rather by the extensive sex industry in Japan. Prostitutes, brothels and clubs are the major client base of the sex aid market.

SANDRA BUCKLEY

sex education

Sex education in Japan takes place at school, in home economics and physical-education classes, more than at home. With the exception of the traditional family celebration of the beginning of a girl's menstrual cycle, sex is seldom discussed in the home. Middle-school physical-education classes provide coursework in both male and female anatomy as well as the various forms of sexually transmitted disease. Students learn about HIV, the history of AIDS and its international impact. As with all Japanese coursework, students memorise detailed information, which they are then tested for in examinations.

Home economic classes are required for both boys and girls (as is industrial arts). Home economics teachers teach about types of birth control and contraception, including abortion, but there is no discussion of sexual intercourse. The student rule book, *seito techo*, admonishes students that dating and sex are prohibited.

JUNE A. GORDON

sex tourism

From the early 1970s, the practice of sex tours became increasingly common. Many corporations organised paid company vacations to the brothel districts of Seoul, Bangkok, Hong Kong, Manila and other major Asian cities. Policies of non-intervention in 'host' countries amounted to an official condoning of Japanese sex tourism. High spending Japanese businessmen gave a quick boost to foreign exchange credit. These tours became increasingly controversial over the 1970s but have still far from disappeared.

In the early 1970s, Korea's President Park Chung Hee actively promoted Japanese tourism as a stimulus for economic growth and increased foreign exchange credit. No distinction was made between sex tourism and other travel. There was an immediate expansion of the brothel districts in Seoul and the southern cities of the peninsula to meet the increased demand. The doubling of Japanese tourists (the majority male) was matched by a doubling of foreign exchange credit by 1975. However, Christian women's groups in Korea first initiated public protests against Japanese exploita-tion of Korean sex workers and then student groups followed. Japanese women's organisations were shocked into action on an issue they had not recognised until confronted by the efforts of the Korean protesters. The subsequent international alliances quickly expanded beyond Korea and Japan to the entire region. Strategies of public protest, targeted letter writing, petition campaigns and media coverage saw a gradual but significant shift in public attitude both at home and overseas towards sex tourism.

Some shifts in taxation laws affecting corporate entertainment deductions and a stigmatisation of sex tourism have seen significant reductions in the traffic of sex tourism out of Japan, but it is by no means a spent phenomenon. Although corporations are now less likely to approve group travel to these destinations, travel agents and tour group operators have shifted their focus to other potential clientele such as men in rural villages and working class blue-collar workers whose yen-traveller checks will still buy them a short-lived sense of status and wealth in some parts of Asia. Some Japanese feminists, anti-prostitution campaigners and advocates of sex workers' rights argue that the increase in Asian sex workers arriving illegally and legally in Japan since the 1980s – the *Japayuki-san* phenomenon – can be explained as a response to the decrease in Japanese sex tourism into the region. The middle-men of the sex industry have shifted their energies to brokering the importing of sex workers into Japan.

The initial campaign against sex tourism was heavily influenced by the moral outrage of the Korean Christian activists, and closely linked to an anti-prostitution platform. Over time, however, the Japanese campaign extended to a consideration of economic issues that linked Japanese investment and offshore economic development activities to the local low wages and poor working conditions that in turn promoted alternative shadow employment, like prostitution, in less developed economies. While a strong current of anti-prostitution sentiment still underlies Japanese efforts to reduce public tolerance of sex tourism, there is now also a wider recognition of the complexity of economic and political issues impacting the sexual traffic of bodies and currencies across the region.

Further reading

Matsui Yayori (1999) *Women in the New Asia: From Pain to Power*, London: Zed Books.

SANDRA BUCKLEY

sexual violence/domestic violence

While there has been a significant shift in official responses to sexual violence against women in Japan since the mid-1990s, silence continues to surround this issue. Forms of sexual violence include rape, incest, child sexual abuse, sexual harassment, prostitution, trafficking in women, pornography and domestic violence. The majority of women experiencing these forms of violence do not seek police assistance for a variety of reasons ranging from fear of retaliation to the strong social tendency to blame victims for their abuse, and the attitude that sexual and family relations are private concerns and thus not appropriate sites for policing or other outside forms of intervention. There has been no agreement on how to name certain behaviours experienced as abusive or particular legislation specifically defining the illegality of these behaviours. For example, the word 'sexual harassment' (*sekuhara*) was introduced into the Japanese language in 1988, and it was first specifically articulated as unlawful behaviour by the courts in 1994. In addition, there is no law specifically pertaining to incest, domestic violence or rape in marriage.

While sexual violence is still a neglected area of social policy and research, there is evidence of a shift in official attitudes due to the lobbying of Japanese activists and the added weight of the 1993 United Nations Declaration on the Elimination of Violence Against Women and the international attention on this issue at the Fourth World Conference on Women in 1995. In response to this pressure, Japan's 1997 Plan For Gender Equality outlines specific measures to tackle problems of sexual violence and, as a result, improved policing practices have been implemented including the establishment of private rooms where complaints of sexual assaults can be made, attempts to increase the number of female police officers available to victims, special education programmes for police officers and public awareness campaigns.

Since 1989, there have been a number of hotlines and surveys focused on sexual harassment and domestic violence, which have revealed high rates of non-reporting. This type of research is increasingly carried out by official bodies. Two major problems identified are the insufficient numbers of shelters for women fleeing violence and the inadequacy of current counselling perspectives that emphasise the importance of family over the needs of the abused women and children. The existing 300 public mother–child centres combined with the twenty to thirty privately run shelters can only accommodate about 7,000 women and their children.

See also: divorce; HELP Women's Shelter

Further reading

Hada Aiko (1995) 'Domestic Violence', in K. Fujimura-Faneslow and A. Kameda (eds) *Japanese Women: New Feminist Perspectives on the Past, Present and Future*, New York: The Feminist Press, pp. 265–8.

Shigematsu Setsu (1996) '"The law of the same" and other (non)-perversions: Women's body as a "use-me/rape-me" signifier', *US–Japan Women's Journal*, English supplement, 12: 154–77.

CATHERINE BURNS

Shibuya

Shibuya is **Tokyo**'s second busiest transportation node after **Shinjuku**, both a major rail transfer point, and the destination for thousands of central city-bound commuters daily. At the heart of Yamanote, the 'High City', the Shibuya district comprises a series of small and distinctive neighbourhoods, including a massive commercial section, a section devoted to electronics and an area of **love hotels**. However, most of all, Shibuya epitomises fashionable consumer Tokyo, designated by urban planners as a node of information and fashion. Especially the sub-district of Harajuku, it is the Mecca of up-to-the-minute chic for teenagers and young adults. Shibuya streets are spectacular fashion runways, exhibiting everything from radical to sophisticated, lined with (expensive) designer shops, and trendy bars and clubs at which to show off those fashions. Across from the station, one passes through Senta Dōri (Centre Street), a liminal passage to the world of trendy youth. The shopping extends to massive new commercial towers, anchored by the major department store chains and their many subsidiaries, all connected by underground passageways that link to the rail lines. On a Sunday afternoon, the principle shopping day in Tokyo, these centres throb and pulse with masses of eager shoppers.

See also: Harajuku

AUDREY KOBAYASHI

Shibuya-kei

Often attached to indie artists like Cornelius, Pizzicato Five and Original Love, the term *Shibuya-kei* crystallised around 1993. It refers more to an atmosphere than a strictly indie sound; a musical infrastructure laid in the 1970s underwritten by an urban street culture of design, public space and commerce.

Department stores like Parco (opened 1973) catered to young trendsetters. At the same time, a shift from recorded media in jazz *kissa* to new Shibuya live houses on modernised streets contributed to a new *flâneur* culture. A staggering concentration of record shops opened within five minutes of Shibuya station. In 1991, Shibuya's HMV opened a J-pop corner, where displays and '***mini-komi***' leaflets highlighted indie production. This new triangle of music and information distribution, artists and listeners established *Shibuya-kei* outside of the conventional ***kayōkyoku*** realm. Since the mid-1980s *neo ako* (neo-acoustic) scene, record shop information culture provided musical raw material for collector-artists. Independent labels opened, magazines like *Beikoku ongaku*, and *Bar-f-out!* included omnibus flexi-discs of new bands. DJs double-billed with bands, introducing new music to new audiences. With the millennium, *Shibuya-kei* pursues perfect three-minute pop songs in bands like Sunny Day Service and soloists like Kahimi Karie.

See also: Shibuya

Select discography

Cornelius (1998) *Fantasma*, Trattoria.

Further reading

Beikoku ongaku magazine.

ANNE McKNIGHT

Shimura Takashi

b. 1905, Hyogo Prefecture; d. 1982, Tokyo

Actor

Shimura began his acting career as a stage actor before he joined Tōhō in 1945. Soon after the war, Shimura appeared in Kurosawa's first films including *Sugata Sanshiro* (1943), *Waga seishun ni kui nashi* (No Regrets for Our Youth) (1946), *Yoidore tenshi* (Drunken Angel) (1948) and *Norainu* (Stray Dog) (1949). He soon became a permanent fixture in Kurosawa films, appearing in almost every one of them. Shimura, however, rarely played the lead role. Instead, his unaffected performances were better suited for supporting roles such as the woodcutter in *Rashōmon* and the leader of the samurai in *Shichinin no samurai* (Seven Samurai).

LEILA POURTAVAF

Shichi-go-san

There was not a tradition in Japan of celebrating birthdays but, instead, at particular stages of transition in life there would be ritual celebrations and festivity (*Shichi-go-san* or 7–5–3 celebrations). For children, 15 November marks such a celebration. Girls and boys of three, boys of five and girls of seven are taken by their families to Shintō shrines, where prayers and offerings are made by the family and the children are blessed by a priest and presented with a special sweet symbolising good health and longevity. At the age of three, girls are marked to be old enough to grow their hair; at age five, boys are presented with their first *hakama* (formal silk trouser skirt); and, at seven, a girl is presented with her first *obi* (stiff kimono sash). On this day each year, shrines are filled with the colour and noise of children and their families in kimono. Kiosks sell speciality gifts, toys and festive foods for the children and there is usually a meal of traditional celebratory dishes to follow the shrine visit.

See also: festivals

SANDRA BUCKLEY

Shinchō

The monthly literary journal *Shinchō* (The Tide) was established in 1904 by the leading publisher Shinchōsha. This journal has produced many of the major works of Japanese literature and criticism of this century. In the pre-war period, creative and critical works of such luminaries as the novelists Tokuda Shūsei, Arishima Takeo, Tamura Toshiko, **Tanizaki Jun'ichirō**, Yokomitsu Riichi and Hirabayashi Taiko, the critics Kobayashi Hideo and Watsuji Tetsurō and the poets Ueda Bin and Kubota Mantarō were all published in its pages, often at the instigation of the journal's long-standing editor Nakamura Murao.

After the Second World War, many famous works of foreign literature were first introduced to a large Japanese readership in *Shinchō*, such as Kafka's *Metamorphosis* in 1952. Naturally, the journal still continues to publish key works of Japanese literature. **Mishima Yukio**'s acclaimed novel *Kinkakuji* (The Temple of the Golden Pavilion) was serialised in the journal in 1956, as was also **Ibuse Masuji**'s masterpiece about Hiroshima *Kuroi ame* (Black Rain) between 1965 and 1966.The journal also publishes important literary documents such as the exchange of letters between **Kawabata Yasunari** and **Mishima Yukio** included in the October 1997 issue.

See also: Shinchōsha

LEITH MORTON

Shinchōsha

Shinchōsha is one of Japan's most respected publishers of Japanese literature and foreign literary works, though its publishing network includes many genres. Founded by Satō Giryō in Tokyo in 1896, Satō called his company Shin-seisha. Its first magazine, *Shinsei* (New Voice), relied primarily on unsolicited literary contributions from young writers. In spite of the magazine's popularity, financial difficulties forced Satō out of business. Satō made a comeback in 1904 with the founding of *Shinchōsha* and the magazine *Shinchō* (New Tide). In 1915, Satō launched *Shinchō bunko*, a paperback series that specialised in translations of foreign literary works. In 1927, *Sekai bungaku zenshū*, a series devoted to world literature, came out. This series, published as '*enpon*', or one-yen books, (a practice begun by Kaizōsha) paved the way for the 1920s '*enpon*' boom. The low price of the books and the fact that the series was sold on a subscription-only basis made this a profitable venture. After the Second World War, Shinchōsha expanded its readership by entering new genres of publishing, ranging from fine arts, to entertainment and even scandal. *Geijutsu shinchō*, a magazine devoted to art appeared in 1950. *Shūkan shinchō*, a recreational magazine, came on the market in 1956, the first weekly put out by a publishing company rather than a newspaper company. In 1981, Shinchōsha launched a controversial pictorial, *Focus*. This was the first weekly magazine to rely on pictures as proof for 'scooping' crimes and scandals. The 'seeing is believing' format caused a small boom, but frequent problems have arisen over the violation of privacy.

Nobel Prize winners Ōe Kenzaburō and Kawabata Yasunari, and other famous novelists including Mishima Yukio, Abe Kōbō and Murakami Karuki, have used Shinchōsha as their publisher.

BARBARA HAMILL SATO

Shindō Kaneto

b. 1912, Hiroshima

Film director

Since Shindo entered the film business in 1934, he has maintained a superlative reputation as a screenwriter, producing scripts for such well-known directors as **Mizoguchi Kenji** and **Kinoshita Keisuke**. From 1936 to 1947, he was assistant director to Mizoguchi at Shōchiku. His first film as director, *Aisai monogatari* (Story of a Beloved Wife, 1951), already hints at a tendency towards Social Realism, which gets expanded upon in his later work through anti-war themes and sympathetic depictions of the underclass living at the margins of society. In 1950, he left Shōchiku to make independent films. With his award-winning *Hadaka no shima* (The Island, 1960), made under severe financial constraints, he became internationally

known. Shindō's films occasionally border on sentimentalism but his anti-war and anti-atomic bomb films – illustrating the devastating effects on individuals and communities (*Genbaku no ko* (Children of the Atomic Bomb, 1952)); *Dai go Fukuryumaru* (The Fukuryu Vessel No. 5, 1959)) and his stark portrayals of women as outspoken, erotic and tenacious survivors of stifling social or primitive conditions (*Onibaba* (1964); *Shukuzu* (A Microcosm, 1943)) – constitute an important contribution to post-war Japanese film.

CHRISTINE MARRAN

SHINJINRUI *see* new generation

SHINJŪ *see* double suicide

Shinjū ten no amijima

Double Suicide, directed by **Shinodai Masashiro**, is a 1969 Art Theatre Guild filmic analysis rather than an adaptation of Chikamatsu Monzaemon's 1721 puppet-play. *Double Suicide* scorns realism to follow the playscript of star-crossed lovers doomed to suicide – paper-seller Jihei, courtesan Koharu and Jihei's wife Osan – replacing puppets with human actors, alternating minimalist stage sets with location shots. The tensions produced through this citation of puppet drama in modern film comment on the binding of modern Japanese aesthetics to Japanese pre-modern convention. The film offers a critique the economy of women as commodified objects of exchange.

Further reading

Bock, A. (1978) *Japanese Film Directors*, Tokyo: Kōdansha International.

NINA CORNYETZ

Shinjuku

Shinjuku is perhaps the noisiest, certainly the most crowded, of **Tokyo**'s twenty-three wards. Originally a post town on the highway running north into

Saitama Prefecture, during the twentieth century, it became a major entry to the city for the rural northern population, and was therefore looked down upon as hick and gauche by the cosmopolitan urbanites. It still carries such connotations as the major staging area for millions of suburban commuters, daily subjected to the most crowded subways anywhere. Shinjuku Station is famous for its white-gloved 'pushers', employed to ensure the maximum number of people are safely stowed in subway cars.

Up on the surface awaits all that is spectacular about Tokyo: a high-rise office plaza; department stores, theatres, restaurants and trendy meeting places filled with fashionably dressed young people, who have not yet reached levels of staid responsibility. This is a favourite area for expense account entertaining, for hanging out before or after events at the nearby National Sports Stadium, or just for hanging out. One may expect to hear political speeches broadcast from truck beds, to be harangued by religious proselytisers or to witness street happenings from Elvis look-alike contests to rap dancing. On weekends, young people shed sombre office attire for outrageous costumes that include multi-coloured wigs, and the fashions of the moment. Shinjuku is about spectacle.

AUDREY KOBAYASHI

SHINKANSEN *see* bullet train

Shinoda Masahiro

b. 1931, Gifu Prefecture

Film director

Shinoda Masahiro was born into an affluent family in Gifu Prefecture. He studied theatre history at Wasada University in Tokyo, and, in 1953, began working as an assistant director at Shōchiku's Ofuna Studio. In 1957, he worked as an assistant to Ozu on the set of *Tokyo boshoku* (Twilight in Tokyo) (1958). Unlike his New Wave contemporaries, Shinoda's sense of pictorial composition is reminiscent of the older generation of Japanese directors. He did not share Ōshima's hatred for the masters of Japanese cinema and was greatly influenced by the camera movements and editing styles of Mizoguchi and Ozu. However, while his films were formally precise, they were thematically consistent with the New Wave genre, and told stories of youth rebellion filled with drugs, violence, sex and masochism. He began his directing career in 1960, with *Koi no katamichi kippu* (One-Way Ticket for Love), a rock 'n' roll saga that tells the story of a young musician and his obsessive promoter. He had more success with his second film *Kawaita mizuumi* (Dry Lake) (1960), for which he recruited Terayama Shūji to write the script. Terayama, a poet who had no experience as a screenwriter, went on to become a frequent collaborator with Shinoda. Set during the anti-USA–Japan Security Treaty demonstrations, *Kawaita mizuumi* tells the story of a group of young activists, one of whom, discouraged by the Anpo demonstrations, decides to turn to terrorism. The film has been credited with predicting the factional terrorism of the student movement that eventuated in the 1970s. Shinoda has been producing feature films at a steady rate since the 1960. Among his most significant films of the 1960s and 1970s are *Kawaiba hana* (Pale Flower) (1963), *Ansatsu* (Assassination) (1964), *Shokei no shima* (Punishment Island) (1966), *Shinjū ten no amijima* (Double Suicide) (1969), *Hanare goze Orin* (Banished Orin) (1977) and *Yashagaike* (Demon Pond) (1979).

Shinoda has had a particular commitment to both avant-garde and contemporary Japanese music throughout his career as a director and, in the 1980s, he produced two major mainstream films that starred the popular Japanese rock singer Hiromi Go. The 1984 film *Setouchi shōnen yakyū dan* (MacArthur's Children) tells the story of the traumatic experience of a rural Japanese island in the aftermath of the Second World War defeat, which led to the seven-year Occupation period, while 1986's *Yari no gonza* (Gonza the Spearman) is a classical, but violent, adaptation of an eighteenth-century play in the tradition of *bunraku* puppet theatre. The latter won Berlin's Silver Bear award and tells the story of a samurai restricted by his strict code of honour. Shinoda continued his successful directorial career in the 1990s with 1991's *Shōnen jidai* (Childhood Days), which won several prizes at the Japanese Academy Awards.

His latest films include 1997's *Setouchi munraito serenade* (Moonlight Serenade) and 1999's *Fukuro no shiro* (Owl's Castle).

Further reading

Bock, Audie (1978) *Japanese Film Directors*, Tokyo, New York and San Francisco: Kōdansha International.

Desser, David (1988) *Eros plus Massacre*, Bloomington and Indianapolis: Indiana University Press.

LEILA POURTAVAF

Shinohara Kazuo

b. 1925, Shizuoka Prefecture

Architect

An enigmatic figure and one of the most influential designers in contemporary Japanese architecture, Shinohara Kazuo enjoys renown both at home and abroad. This stems primarily from the fact that, during his long career since the early 1950s he, as both an architect and academician/theoretician, has consistently broadened the architectural discourse in Japan, exploring new horizons with his extraordinary works, thereby also challenging the prevailing architectural ideologies and trends or fashions of the times. In so doing, he has shifted the focus of his designs several times throughout the years. Thus, although his work has always remained highly conceptual in nature, it is possible to identify four phases in his architecture. Particularly from the early 1970s on, he had a profound impact on the work of a new generation of Japanese architects including, among others, Sakamoto Kazunari, Hasegawa Itsuko and Ito Tōyō, who, within the so-called New Wave, were often referred to as the Shinohara school.

First trained as a mathematician before obtaining his architecture degree from Tokyo Institute of Technology in 1953, Shinohara in the early stages of his career became fascinated by, and explored the abstract qualities of, traditional Japanese architecture. His small wooden houses of the 1950s and 1960s, like the House in Kugayama (1954) and the Umbrella House (1961), both in

Tokyo, reinterpreted the 'simplicity' of historic residences. While featuring some elements of the typical Japanese house, these designs experimented with the symbolic value of the purest themes, such as symmetry/asymmetry and division/connection; by way of simplification they created subtle variations in perceptual qualities. Along such intentions, Shinohara's architecture became increasingly art-oriented; he declared that 'a house is a work of art'. In the 1960s, the age of industrialised and predominantly technology oriented Metabolist architecture in Japan, this position was clearly revolutionary and outside the mainstream of Japanese design.

Shinohara's second phase in the 1970s evolved as he abandoned the traditional architectural language he had investigated so far; abstract geometric forms of unfinished concrete volumes began to dominate his works, while his architecture also became more inward oriented. Residences such as the Incomplete House (1970) and the Repeating Crevice House (1971) in Tokyo, and the Cubic Forest House (1971) in Kawasaki displayed a manifest uninterest in the volatile urban environment. On the other hand, inside they all featured spatial compositions of a uniquely poetic minimalism; Shinohara aimed at the evocation of 'naked spaces'. The quality of primitive simplicity that characterised his architecture from the very beginning was even more pronounced in these projects. In his Tanikawa Residence (1974), a summer house in the woods, he shaped the floor as hard pounded earth that followed the slope of the site.

Influenced by Claude Lévi-Strauss's structural anthropology and Roland Barthes's linguistic theories, Shinohara, from the mid-1970s on, was to complement his prevailing primitivism with his new concepts of 'zero-degree machine' and 'progressive anarchy'. Two major works, the House in Uehara (1976) and the House on a Curved Road (1978), both in Tokyo, best exemplify this phase. They were designed with massive over-sized concrete columns and sturdy, diagonal braces of beams, which invade the extraordinary interiors and allude to the quality of the jungle. Slowly the issue of order/disorder (anarchy) with an invisible threshold or a curious 'gap' in between them emerged as another theme in Shinohara's architecture. While the solid and relatively simple volumes of his buildings still rejected the chaotic cityscape, now they were also to deny an overall formal unity; spatial and structural elements started to appear as parts in a machine, regarded as 'a physical system in which objects are simply joined together in a *sachlich* manner'. In other words, the objectivity of such 'functional' design excluded the need and even the possibility of the 'synthesis of form', signalling the beginning of Shinohara's quest for theoretical structures in an architecture of fragmentation.

Along with his growing fascination with such hi-tech products as the Tomcat fighter plane and the lunar landing module, the primitive machine in Shinohara's architecture acquired a more sophisticated quality. Simultaneously, the fragmentary articulation of his designs, beyond the anarchy of the jungle, found another analogy in the anarchy of the Japanese city. Accordingly, residences, such as the House under High-Voltage Lines (1982) and the Higashi–Tamagawa Complex (1983), could respond more actively to the layered, collage-like urban fabric of Tokyo. In fact, Shinohara transformed anarchy into a creative concept; what he calls 'progressive anarchy' is an operative model that recognises and responds to the chaotic nature of the Japanese city while not necessarily endorsing it.

Starting in the 1980s, Shinohara's theoretical investigations and conceptual designs have been put to the test in larger public buildings as well, not only in small, private residences. The most significant of his larger works, the Tokyo Institute of Technology Centennial Hall (1987), is a unique composition that aspires to a formal integration without synthesis. It admittedly draws from the chaotic energy, ways and means of perception, as well as the alogic of its urban nexus, but, by way of its appeal to a 'dead' machine aesthetic (unlike the unified compositions of high modernism), it also opposes the uncontrolled excesses of the existing city, especially by refusing to harmonise with the all too trivialising modes of signification and representation of the prevailing consumerist urbanism. The Centennial Hall prefigures a new, visionary city, an information-fuelled technopolis of the future.

The Centennial Hall, followed by such other works as his own Shinohara Residence (1984) in

Yokohama, the K-2 office building (1990) in Ōsaka and the Kumamoto North Police Headquarters (1991), poignantly epitomises Shinohara's career as a relentless course oriented away from the past, and attests to his conviction that 'tradition can be the starting point for creativity, but it must not be the point to which it returns'.

Select bibliography

Shinohara Kazuo (1986) 'A program from the "fourth space", *JA, The Japan Architect* (September): 28.
—— (1986) 'The context of pleasure', *JA, The Japan Architect* (September): 22.

Further reading

Bognar, B. (1990) *New Japanese Architecture*, New York.
—— (1985) *Contemporary Japanese Architecture: Its Development and Challenge*, New York, pp. 307–22.
Suzuki, H., Banham, R. and Kobayashi, K. (1985) *Contemporary Japanese Architecture of Japan 1958–1984*, New York, pp. 82–6.
Frampton, K. (ed.) (1982) *Kazuo Shinohara* (exhibition catalogue), New York.

BOTOND BOGNAR

Shinsanbetsu

Shinsanbetsu, short for Zenkoku Sangyōbetsu Rōdō Kumiai Rengōkai, was founded in 1949. Shinsanbetsu ('New Sanbetsu') aimed to be the successor to the dominant left-wing labour federation of the post-war years, Sanbetsu. Shinsanbetsu, with **Sōhyō**, founded the following year (1950), represented one of two major attempts to reorganise the nationwide labour movement in the wake of the decline of both Sanbetsu and its moderate counterpart, **Sōdōmei**. Just as the principal leadership of Sōhyō would come from the Sōdōmei, the dominant figure in Shinsanbetsu was Hosoya Matsuta, one of the leaders of Sanbetsu. Hosoya had been the only former blue-collar worker on the Sanbetsu executive council, although, like most Sanbetsu leaders in the immediate post-war period, he too was a Communist Party member. Hosoya broke with both the party and Sanbetsu policy to form an anti-communist democratic league (Sanbetsu Mindō) in 1948. Hosoya established links with the leader of the left wing of the moderate Sōdōmei, Takano Minoru, but the two ultimately failed to agree on policy and Hosoya founded Shinsanbetsu separately from Sōhyō, which became the dominant labour federation of the 1950s and 1960s. Shinsanbetsu remained a small federation, representing mainly workers in smaller-scale enterprises.

MICHAEL GIBBS

SHISHOSTOTSU *see* inovel

Shisō no kagaku

Shisō no kagaku (Science of Thought) was a widely read progressive monthly, which first appeared in 1946. In 1953–4, the journal appeared under the name of *Kaya* (Bud), but, after switching publishers, it reappeared under its original name until 1996, when it ceased publication. The early editors were members of the Science of Thought Study Group and included **Maruyama Masao**, Tsurumi Kazuko, Tsurumi Shunsuke and the atomic scientist Taketani Mitsuo. These progressive intellectuals made *Shisō no kagaku* part of an effort to explore the meanings and practice of democracy through an open dialogue with an educated, democratic public. With its long-standing commitment to the post-war progressivist values of peace and democracy, *Shisō no kagaku* allied itself with anti-Security Treaty protestors in the 1960 **Anpo struggle**. During the Anpo years, the journal had particularly close associations with the *Koe naki no kai* (Voiceless Society), which Maruyama and Tsurumi had organised. *Shisō no kagaku* enjoyed popularity in liberal and progressive circles, especially with **Beheiren** and the **citizens' movements** of the late 1960s and 1970s.

GUY YASKO

shitamachi

The *shitamachi* is literally translated as 'downtown', but it was historically an even more specific reference to 'lowlands' and was coined the 'low city' in contrast to the 'high city.' These two terms demarcated not only the geographical and topographical spaces of pre-modern and early modern Edo but also the cultural space of high and low, elite and popular culture. The low city was the domain of the merchants and artisans who serviced the needs of the high city world of aristocratic residences, temples, shrines and official buildings. It was a world of street entertainers, storytellers, peddlers, itinerants and raucous festivals, in stark contrast to the austere aesthetic of the samurai elite and the prevailing climate of neo-Confucian propriety, protocols and scholarly aspirations.

The shōgunate granted the high-lying ground of the new Edo capital to its own elite, and delegated the workers and merchants to the flatlands of the marsh areas reclaimed at the mouth of the Sumida river. The historical heart of *shitamachi* was Nihonbashi but the real territory described by this term today stretches far beyond the original eastern bank of the Sumida River. The *shitamachi* districts suffered two major blows, the 1923 earthquake and the intensive US bombing of the final months of the war. It is still possible today to undertake a tour of the older *shitamachi* neighbourhoods combining walking, subway and even ferries, a reminder of the vibrant role of the river and canal network of the old capital in the growth of Japan's pre-modern capital of Edo. Railroads and subways today often trace the routes of old canals, and many contemporary subway station names still echo the history of famous bridges, docks and river crossings of the commercial world of the low city.

A stroll through the residential and shopping streets and temple surrounds of Kanda, Asakusa, Ueno or Tsukudajima will still offer a rare view of the historical remnants and reconstruction of the old low-city urbanscape with its narrow alleys, low-level housing, **shōtengai** (shopping streets) and traditional architecture. The low city was the home of the '*edokko*', the quintessential 'child of Edo', who held up the credentials of Edo dialect and an intimate knowledge of the popular culture of the low city, in sharp contrast to the caricature of the aesthetically refined aristocrat or austere military ethic of the samurai. The *edokko* survives as a rapidly diminishing minority in the face of massive urban migration into Tokyo over the last half of the twentieth century. Popular television dramas, comedy and documentary now rarefy an often idealised notion of the *edokko*, with the same intensity and nostalgia afforded an endangered species.

Further reading

Karan, P. and Stapleton, K. (1997) *The Japanese City*, Lexington, KY: University of Kentucky, pp. 56–78.

SANDRA BUCKLEY

Shogakukan

Shogakukan, one of Japan's major publishing companies, started out in 1922, mainly as a publisher of magazines for young people. Shoga-kukan's originality can be attributed to its founder Ōga Takeo, whose career began as a clerk in a Tokyo bookshop. In 1928, Shogakukan put out a twenty-eight-volume series of humorous books for young people, but today magazines remain the backbone of the company. The first publisher to design magazines for young people at each grade level, Shogakukan's magazines were intended as supplements to be used in conjunction with school texts. By incorporating titles like *First Year Elementary School Student* – a practice considered ingenious at the time – Shogakukan's magazines caught the eye and won the recognition of school teachers. In the post-Second World War period, Shogakukan continued to focus on young people, but, in the 1960s, it also assumed the challenge of attracting adult readers. On the one hand, 1960 saw the publication of a fifty-six-volume world literature series for young people. The magazines *Boys' raifu* (Boy's Life) and *Josei sebun* (Seven), a popular magazine for teenage girls, both appeared in 1963. On the other hand, 1969 marked the inauguration of *Shūkan posuto* (Weekly Post), the biggest selling entertainment weekly for so-called white-collar workers, which included among its topics sex and scandal. In 1978, the weekly's circulation figures topped 600,000. Shogakukan has continued with this mix of adult- and student-oriented publication strategy to the present.

BARBARA HAMILL SATO

shōji

These wood and rice paper sliding doors are an essential element of Japanese traditional architecture and continue to remain a common feature in both contemporary and traditional house design. The rice paper panels of the doors allow better circulation of air in the hot summer months as well as access to filtered natural light for the inner recesses of the home. *Shōji* can be left open to create larger internal spaces or closed for privacy. The panels of natural wood and paper combine to create a visual contrast to the strong horizontal lines of black trim on *tatami* matting in traditional architecture. Mass-produced *shōji* have reduced the number of specialised artisans and put the handcrafted higher-quality *shōji* beyond the budget of the average household.

SANDRA BUCKLEY

shōjo

'*Shōjo*' literally means 'young woman' or 'girl', but the concept is far more complex than this implies. An advertising blurb for a Japanese book about the *shōjo* describes its topic like this: 'Neither adult woman nor girl-child, neither man nor woman....' The words frequently used in cultural studies texts on the *shōjo* include: 'labyrinth', 'floating', 'dreaming' and 'Narcissus'. As these terms begin to indicate, the contemporary *shōjo* is a cultural construct, symbolising a state of being that is socially unanchored, free of responsibility and self-absorbed – the opposite of the ideal Japanese adult.

It was not until the 1920s that 'girlhood' became a recognisable life stage; previously, young girls stayed at home until marriage, or were sent out to work. However, the rise of a 'middle class' and extended compulsory education for females created a space for girlhood, and schools emerged as the shared location of that experience. Writers such as Yoshiya Nobuko began to create fiction specifically for the *shōjo*; magazines and early comics were created to cater to *shōjo* taste. In buying these products, girls had a new opportunity to join consumer culture and exercise consumer choices. Early *shōjo* stories were uniformly sweet, sentimental and aesthetically pleasing. The image of '*shōjo* taste' purveyed through these media lasted well beyond the Second World War. This new stage, 'girlhood', isolated a period in life when a female was neither naïve child nor sexually active woman.

As opposed to the parallel designation for 'boys' – *shōnen* – '*shōjo*' marked off a time of minimal social responsibility. Young men were expected to prepare actively from childhood for their eventual important roles in adult society; girls only had to prepare dreamily for marriage and motherhood. The *shōjo* became an object of intense interest in the late 1980s and early 1990s, when cultural critics were decrying the excesses of consumer culture in Japan's boom economy. To the earlier images of the *shōjo* as 'dreamy' and 'sentimental' were added 'infantile', 'selfish', 'passive' and 'superficial'. When contrasted with the increasingly hectic work life of adults (particularly men), *shōjo* life was criticised as irresponsibly unproductive. In this period, the '*shōjo* state of being' was figured as potentially describing people of either sex – any young person who seemed to inhabit a world of relentless consumerism and free play, unconnected to adult society or meaningful activity, could be labeled a *shōjo*.

For young women writers and artists of the 1980s and 1990s, the label '*shōjo*' and its implication of selfish passivity has provoked a strong reaction. In the *shōjo manga* and fiction produced by women we find ruthless explorations of the tyranny of existing gender and family structures, even if those explorations are packaged in visual terms that look as 'cute' and 'sweet' as ever. The fiction of Kanai Mieko and Kurahashi Yumiko, or the gender-bending comic art of Hagio Moto and Wakuni Akisato, provide good examples of the *shōjo* concept as a tool for the critique of contemporary society.

Further reading

Honda, M., Iizawa, K., Kurabayashi, Y., Fujisaki, K., Kohama, I., Horikiri, T., Taniguchi, T., Kanezuka, S., Seo, F., Watanabe, T., Hashimoto, S., Tanemura, S. and Yagawa, S. (1988) *Shōjoron*, Tokyo: Aoyumisha.

SHARALYN ORBAUGH

SHOPPING STREET *see shōōtengai*

shōtengai

The *shōtengai* (shopping street) is a familiar feature of the Japanese urbanscape. The shopping street traditionally was characterised by low-level (one- or two-storey) free-standing or row structures featuring a shop front opening directly on to the street or pavement with storage, manufacturing or processing and housing facilities in the space behind and above the shop front. In pre-modern Japan, the long narrow *shōtengai* ran out like spokes from the central hub space of a river port or intersection of roads, a major bridge or official checkpoint. The main access route and surrounding alleys leading up to a temple or shrine gate also often developed into a *shōtengai*, offering local food specialities and souvenirs alongside inns for pilgrims and other travellers.

The *shōtengai* has remained a design feature of contemporary urban planning. New housing estates still feature a shopping street running out from the local commuter railroad and bus hub. Although today there may be a supermarket and Seven-Eleven, the continued preference for daily shopping and the intimacy of neighbourhood community have seen the survival of speciality food and service stores, for example butcher, fishmarket, dry cleaner, greengrocer, tailor, hair stylist, etc. Local restaurants along the *shōtengai* deliver cooked meals within the neighbourhood, an important element of daily life for busy housewives often also working part or full time. The *shōtengai* has generally proven more resilient to the encroachment of big business than the Main Street of the USA or the High Street in Britain. The covered shopping streets of many Japanese neighbourhoods, especially popular in the Kansai area, first developed as a modern variation on the function of the traditional *shōtengai* and the cultural space of the European arcade.

SANDRA BUCKLEY

Shūeisha

Shūeisha, a subsidiary of Shogakan, was established in 1926 to fill a demand for entertaining and recreational, rather than educational, magazines for young people.

In 1968, *Shonen jumpu* (Boys Jump), which would become the most popular comic among elementary and junior-high school students, was first released. By the late 1980s, its circulation figures had reached an overwhelming number of over 5,000,000 per week, and it is still in circulation.

Although comics account for Shūeisha's major sales, in the 1970s, the company began publishing magazines for adult readers. The short-lived women's magazine *More* (1977), and the fashion, food and travel magazine *Non-non* (1971), which targets young women, are representative examples.

Shūeisha also prints Japanese editions of foreign magazines such as *Cosmopolitan* and *Playboy*.

BARBARA HAMILL SATO

silk

Silk (*kinu*) is the luxury fabric of Japan. In the 1980s, Japan consumed 50 per cent of the world production, 33 per cent of which was home grown. Although integral to the vanishing kimono industry, silk fabric is also popular for fashion material, while silk batting is valued for its warmth and silk cording is still used extensively in industry.

This resilient, elastic, lustrous fibre is produced by silkworms when making their cocoons. The two basic ways of producing silk threads are reeling and spinning. The strongest threads are procured by reeling; that is, unravelling the unbroken cocoon filaments. To do this, the cocoons are floated in hot water to loosen the gum (*sericin*) coating sufficiently for the ends to come free. Using a bamboo whisk, a number of ends are pulled upward and wound on

to a frame and then given a twist (thrown). Several of the resultant threads may be plied together to form a heavier thread.

The reeled silk still has a protective gum coat that makes the thread strong and resilient, but dull. To remove this coat from the raw silk (*kiito*), it is boiled in an ash, alkaline or soap solution. De-gumming exposes the lustrous core, but also weakens the fibre. Generally, in Japan, silk thread is only partially de-gummed.

Raw silk forms the base for such fabrics as silk crêpe (*chirimen*) and fine plain weave (*habutae*). It is often used for warp alone, or for the warp and weft of the ground weave of a patterned cloth (e.g. *nō* costumes, *obi* sashes and woven wall hangings), where the patterned float stands out, being thicker, softer and more lustrous de-gummed thread. Raw silk thread has a body that recommends it for warp intertwine weaves, like gauze (*ra,ro,sha*).

De-gummed silk (*neriito*) dyes well and was used for the thin *nerinuki* cloth popular in the sixteenth century that formed the base for the stitch-resist patterns of *tsujigahana*. Since the Edo Period, it has been used for simple stripes and checks, for ikat (*kasuri*), and for satin weaves (*shusuori*), such as damask (*donsu*) and figured satin (*rinzu*).

The parts of the cocoon that are unsuited to reeling (beginning and end) are often hand spun to form noil (*tsumugi*), or second-class cocoon pulled and stretched to form batting (*mawata*) for lining clothes or stuffing comforters. A rural textile style adopted by some modern artists is pongee (*tsumugi*), which has reeled, partially de-gummed warps and hand-spun wefts.

A present from China in the third century including both silkworms and silk fabric marks the beginning of sericulture in Japan. Immigrant Chinese and Korean craftsmen taught the art to the Japanese, who soon set up government-sponsored workshops creating twills (*aya*) and multi-coloured fabrics (*nishiki*). By the eighth century, silk thread and cloth were important tax and tribute items produced in many areas of the country. The years of civil strife between the thirteenth and sixteenth centuries saw a marked decline in local silk farming. Chinese thread and fabric imports formed a steady trade. When, during the Ōnin wars (1467–77), many of the tradesmen of Kyōto fled the city to such post towns as Sakai, new input resulted due to their closer contact with Chinese techniques. As the silk weavers re-established themselves in Kyōto during the sixteenth century, they introduced new looms and started to weave their own satins and damasks. Under the directive of the Tokugawa government in the seventeenth century, the Japanese re-established their silk production. Inventive methods of pruning mulberry trees, experiments in cross-breeding and more efficient processing tools led to increasing proficiency of production. When Japan set out to modernise in the late nineteenth century, it already had an embryo industry waiting to be developed. By cross-breeding for uniformity (as opposed to lustre or resilience), the Japanese were able to supply much of the silk for Western stockings, exporting in 1934 as much as 45,243 metric tons.

MONICA BETHE

Sino-Japanese relations

Japan's surrender in August 1945 brought an end to the eight-year war with China, during which the Japanese forces ravaged large areas of China's eastern provinces. Manchuria, which was under Japanese control since 1931, and Taiwan, ceded to Japan after China's defeat in the First Sino-Japanese War (1894–95), were returned to China in accordance with the Cairo Declaration. Millions of Japanese were repatriated from these areas without major incidents, although tens of thousands of Japanese technical and military personnel remained to serve in China until 1948. Numerous Japanese children were abandoned in Manchuria after the war and did not become reunited with their families in Japan until the 1980s.

Though victorious in name, China soon descended into Civil War and played a negligible role in the Allied Occupation of Japan. After the Communist victory in China in 1949 and China's subsequent entry into the Korean War the following year, the USA pressured Japan to sever ties with the mainland and to establish diplomatic relations with the Republic of China (ROC) on Taiwan. In 1952, Japan signed a Peace Treaty with the ROC; the ROC in return renounced the right to reparations from Japan for damages during the war in China. In 1957, Kishi Nobusuke became the first Japanese Prime Minister to visit Taiwan, where he voiced support for ROC's endeavour to reclaim mainland China.

Between 1949 and 1972, Japan followed the US policy on political relations with the People's Republic of China (PRC) and sought to build informal relations with Beijing based on the principle of 'separation of politics from economics'. The 1950s saw the signing of the first non-official trade agreement, China's repatriation of many remaining Japanese, including those held as war criminals, as well as a variety of cultural exchanges. However, China terminated trade relations in 1958 in retaliation for Kishi's pro-Taiwan policy and an incident in Nagasaki where the PRC flag was pulled down at a trade fair by a Japanese youth. Stable trade relations were not restored until 1962 when the two governments signed the so-called 'Trade Memorandum'. Increasing radicalisation of Chinese domestic politics before and during the Cultural Revolution made further improvement impossible. Even the once intimate relationship between communist parties in China and Japan came to an open split in the 1960s due to mounting ideological polemics.

The turning point in Japan's relations with the PRC came in 1972 when Prime Minister Tanaka Kakuei visited Beijing in the wake of the **Nixon shock**. In return for Japan's diplomatic recognition, the Chinese government also renounced war reparations in anticipation of Japanese economic assistance. (Japan reduced its relations with Taiwan to semi-official status, although the two countries remained close economic partners and Japan's cultural influence in Taiwan remains strong to this day.) Bilateral relations rapidly improved in the 1970s, culminating in the 1978 Treaty of Peace and Friendship. The PRC government, which had consistently opposed Japan's defence alliance with the USA and warned against the 'revival of Japanese militarism', now welcomed Japan's defence capability as well as its alliance with the USA as bulwarks against Soviet expansion. Such momentum continued even into the early 1980s, as the Chinese government invited 3,000 Japanese youth to visit China while Japan became and remains a popular destination for Chinese students

– some 33,000 Chinese studied in Japan between 1976 and 1996, with many staying on to work. A number of bilateral government commissions were set up to develop the relationship into the twenty-first century.

As China embarked on economic modernisation from the late 1970s under Deng Xiaoping, Japan became even more important as a source of capital and technical know-how. Japan has been China's lowest ranking trading partner, while China is Japan's second. Bilateral trade reached US$57 billion in 1998. Japan is the largest provider of Official Development Aid (ODA) to China; since 1980, China has received ¥1,785 billion, making it the second largest recipient of Japan's ODA. After the 1989 Tiananmen massacre, Japan relaxed its sanctions against China ahead of other Western governments. At the invitation of the Chinese government, Emperor Akihito made an unprecedented and highly controversial visit to China in 1991.

A number of issues have also disrupted the otherwise close relations since the 1980s. Divergent views of Japan's past invasion of China have proven to be a significant problem, as the Chinese government protested over alleged Japanese government revisions to history textbooks' accounts of the war in China (see **textbook controversies**) and Japanese cabinet members made open visits to the **Yasukuni Shrine**, where Japan's war dead are memorialised. Demands by private Chinese citizens, often supported by Japanese activists, seeking reparation for wartime abuses has added a new dimension to the relationship since the early 1990s. Many Japanese, however, view these actions as mere Chinese tactics to embarrass Japan and extract further political and economic advantages. Moreover, from the late 1980s, Japan became increasingly concerned with the rise of Chinese power, and protested against China's testing of nuclear weapons by suspending part of its loans in 1995. The Chinese government, on the other hand, has expressed grave concerns over the redefinition of US–Japan Defence Guidelines and the potential expansion of Japan's defence role in the region. The unresolved territorial dispute over Senkaku Islands (Diaoyu in Chinese) – a chain of islets between Taiwan and **Okinawa** around which oil deposits were discovered in the 1970s –

is yet another irritant. Chinese in Hong Kong and Taiwan mounted several demonstrations over the disputed islands.

Although mutual perceptions sank in the late 1990s, both the Chinese and Japanese governments have striven to keep this important relationship on track. Bound by strong economic ties despite brewing strategic rivalry and suspicion, both Japan and China are seeking to define a new relationship for the new millennium.

Further reading

Howe, C. (ed.) (1996) *China and Japan: History, Trends, and Prospects,* Oxford: Clarendon Press.

Lee, C. (1984) *Japan and China: New Economic Diplomacy,* Stanford: Hoover Institution Press.

—— (1976) *Japan Faces China,* Baltimore: Johns Hopkins University Press.

Whiting, A. and Xin, J. (1990) *Sino-Japanese Relations: Pragmatism and Passion,* World Policy Journal.

DAQING YANG

skiing

Skiing was introduced into Japan by an Austrian, Major Theodore Von Lerch, in 1911. It developed into a widely popular sport in the 1950s and is now the most popular of Japan's winter sports, followed by snowboarding and skating. Over 16 million Japanese spend an average of US$900 annually to indulge their love of this sport. There are some 300 ski resorts across the country offering facilities from budget youth hostels to luxury resorts. The best snow is found in Hokkaidō where powder conditions are common on high slopes boasting long runs. The majority of Japan's ski-slopes, however, are on the main island of Honshū along the southern, central and northern alps. Here, runs tend to be shorter and with vertical drops of less than 400 m. Crowding is a problem on the Honshū slopes but this is the double bind of fast and easy rail access from major urban centres.

Japan was the first Asian country to host the Winter Olympics (1972), an honour repeated in 1998 with the Nagano Games. The climate in

Japan is well suited to a long ski season with slopes usually open from December through to spring skiing in April. Many ski destinations also feature hot springs as an added attraction. Snowfalls are heaviest on the western face of the alps where heavy winter precipitation is brought by the infamously cold Siberian air mass. Snowfalls on the eastern face of the alps are sparser and snow cover is often thin and icy in the early and late seasons. Package tours to the outstanding snow conditions of Hokkaidō's ski-slopes are a popular winter vacation. More affluent Japanese skiers are an important source of income for Europe's luxury resorts, while it was not unusual during the *yendaka* years for high schools to take advantage of the strong exchange rate to take student groups on winter tours of the US and European slopes. Devoted Japanese skiers now often take advantage of the southern-hemisphere winter to gain year-round skiing between Japan and the outstanding ski conditions in New Zealand.

Skiing has created a massive market in high-end ski gear in Japan. There are speciality shopping districts scattered across Tokyo, but Jimbōchō is renowned among avid skiers for both its bargains and range of equipment. Foreigners hoping to ski in Japan need to be forewarned that larger sized boots and ski wear are rare and expensive, but skis, blades and snowboards are available in a wide range of popular and high-quality Japanese brands. In a country where there is not a strong culture of second-hand sales or sports rental equipment, foreigners need to be careful not to assume they can hire appropriate gear at the slopes. Major tourist agencies, the airlines and railroads all offer package ski deals and brochures can be picked up easily at travel agents or information accessed online. During peak ski season it is not unusual to find skiers lined up in their sleeping bags overnight in Tokyo Station ready to fight for a seat on the first morning trains to the slopes.

SANDRA BUCKLEY

slang

Are there slang words and/or expressions in Japanese? The answer is yes and no. Yes, because slang exists as the least polite level of speech in the **Keigo** (honorific) system. No, because there very few words and expressions equivalent to the English concept of slang.

Let us look at the 'yes' case first. Depending upon whom they talk to, the Japanese use a different level of speech. Slang is used when both the speaker and the listener are in the same 'inner group' – **uchi** (see **keigo**). They are allowed by social norm to use any level of speech, including the least polite level, without offending each other. For example, '*meshi o kuu*' is used instead of '*gohan o taberu*' and '*yabai*' is adopted in place of '*abunai*' (risky or dangerous). In this context, slang is a form of more intimate or honorific-free speech.

Let's turn to the 'no' case. If the word 'slang' by definition includes so-called 'four-letter words', there is hardly any 'slang' in Japanese. People seldom resort to derogatory terms when they abuse others. They employ a different level of speech to express their anger, mockery, scorn, frustration, indignation and other emotive feelings. There are, however, just a few derogatory terms, almost equivalent to 'four-letter words' in English. '*Chikushō*', '*kuso*' and '*kusottare*' are such words, but they are seldom heard in daily life.

In Japanese, there are words called '*ryūkōgo*' (fashionable or popular language). These words or expressions are born constantly and are used by many people, sometimes only within a certain generation, and for a short while before disappearing. Few *ryūkōgo* remain in mainstream speech long enough to gain entry in authorised dictionaries. Most *ryūkōgo* are recorded only in chronicles. The contemporary and situational nature of these words or expressions lends them a linguistic currency not unlike slang but they tend to be considered trendy and lack the more negative associations of slang.

SHUN IKEDA

smoking

At the close of the twentieth century, cigarette smoking remains a common social practice in Japan, but it is taking new forms and is no longer as tightly interwoven in people's daily lives. Since the

1980s, restrictions have gradually been placed on smoking in public spaces such as public transport and workplaces in response to lawsuits by anti-smoking groups, and it would appear that a quiet revolution is underway in homes where wives and children are forcing husbands and fathers to smoke outside.

Brought by Portuguese traders, tobacco first reached Japan in the sixteenth century. Its cultivation, sale and use was banned in 1612 by the Tokugawa shōgunate until 1624, when the government decided to tax tobacco. At that time, smoking by men and women alike, in the form of long *kiseru* pipes, had become a sought-after luxury consumption. During the Meiji Period, in response to the threat of domination of the Japanese market by UK and US manufacturers, the government established the state tobacco monopoly (Japan Industrial Tobacco; later Japan Tobacco or JT) and sharply raised tariffs on imported cigarettes in 1904.

As in much of East Asia, cigarette smoking has been largely a male habit since the 1920s. In 1960, almost all men who could smoke did (80 per cent), whereas only 10 per cent of women smoked. Token and symbol of twentieth-century modernity, the tobacco cigarette was adopted in Japan during the 1920s at the same time as it was in China, France, the UK and the USA. Most likely because of the Asia–Pacific War (1931–45), individual consumption, as in Europe, did not reach the heavy levels achieved by UK and US smokers in the 1940s until some twenty-five years later. Public health advocates argue that the apparent low public awareness of the health hazards of cigarette smoking in Japan and comparably weak government policies can be largely explained by the following factors: the twenty-five-year lag in heavy smoking (shared with Western Europe), and, as a consequence, the delayed increase in lung cancer rates; the lack of publicity concerning cause of death in Japan; the majority ownership of Japan Tobacco by the powerful **Ministry of Finance** (which is also responsible for the weak tobacco health warnings); and the 1984 Tobacco Business Law that declared a healthy domestic tobacco industry to be in the national interest.

In 1985, the abolition of import tariffs introduced foreign competition and with it modern advertising campaigns targeting women and minors (under twenty years old). As of 1998, UK and US manufacturers succeeded in capturing over 28 per cent of the domestic market. (This loss of market share, together with the decline in male smoking rates, has led Japan Tobacco to begin exporting its products, especially to East Asia.) By the late 1990s, 55 per cent of men and 15 per cent of women smoked in Japan (for a combined rate of 38 per cent) compared to 28 per cent for the UK and 25 per cent for the USA; moreover, a new globalised market of smoking had emerged with 50 per cent of young smokers preferring foreign brands and young women smoking in increasing numbers (predicted by some to reach 30 per cent), for whom cigarettes are still thought to afford an image of liberation, glamour and slimness. In 1999, partly in response to pressure from anti-smoking groups, the Ministry of Health and Welfare announced the very ambitious goal of reducing the smoking rate by 50 per cent by 2010.

Further reading

Goodman, John (1993) *Tobacco in History,* Routledge: London.

RODDEY REID

soap operas

The closest approximation to US soap operas on Japanese television are the '*hirumero*' (afternoon melodramas) broadcast in limited runs every weekday for thirty minutes starting at 1.00 p.m. or 1.30 p.m. This time was opened up to dramas directed at housewives in the early 1960s, first by **Fuji TV**, with programming slots like the *Hiru no obi dorama* (Afternoon Belt Drama, 1964–present), *Okusama gekijo* (Housewife Theatre, 1964–84) and *Kao ai no gekijo* (Kao Love Theatre, 1969–present). Early stories were called *yoromeki dorama* (love affair dramas) for their focus on marital infidelities, but programming later opened up to romances, literary adaptations, historical dramas, comedies and mother-in-law versus daughter-in-law battles (a staple of Japanese 'home dramas'). Soaps were at their peak in the 1970s as rival soap companies sponsored competing shows in a fierce *shabondama* (soap bubble) ratings war.

Japanese afternoon dramas tend to present a more conservative image than their US counterparts, one matching the stereotype of the **middle-class** '*okusama*' (**housewife**). Thus, while much that threatens the family is given expression, from uncaring children to social corruption, such contradictions are usually resolved through the figure of the strong heroine who, even if not a housewife, struggles to preserve the home and its values.

AARON GEROW

soapland

This is the term that replaced the name of *toruko* (derived from Turkish bath) when Japan's bath-house owners succumbed to pressure from both the Japanese authorities and the Turkish embassy in 1985 to rename these establishments that offered a combined bath and massage service. There had already been two strong waves of anti-prostitution activity in the post-war period. The first led to the passage of anti-prostitution legislation in 1956 and the second was part of the public clean-up leading to the Tokyo **Olympics**. The 1985 legal review of prostitution laws saw the bath-house owners declaring their commitment to new regulations requiring that bath attendants be clothed at all times and that no services other than bathing and massage be offered. That infringements far exceed compliance goes without saying and today it remains possible to purchase a well-lathered soap bath followed by one of a diverse menu of exotically named massages for prices that can range from about US$100 up to well over US$1,000. While most premises explicitly prohibit intercourse with clients, many attendants do earn extra funds through intercourse for an additional charge paid to her directly. Other bath-houses simply have another hidden price list and back rooms for this additional service. Little has changed other than the name of these premises. Soapland districts are still easily recognisable for their often outrageous architecture and façades, although some discreetly presented bath-houses have found

their way into more respectable neighbourhoods. While there are many foreign sex workers employed in the soaplands today, there are still some establishments that ban foreign customers under various complex house rules. This ban reflects the continuing tenacity of the myth that AIDS is a disease imported and spread by foreigners rather than a real domestic health problem requiring extensive care, prevention and education programmes.

See also: AIDS; prostitution, regulation of

SANDRA BUCKLEY

soccer

Known in Japan as *sakka* (soccer), this sport has been a classic example of Japanese-style market development. The establishment of the Japanese Professional Football League was as much a commercial decision as it was a sports landmark. The launch of the initial ten-team J-League coincided with growing pressure for Japanese to shift priority from a culture of work to a culture of *riijaa* (**leisure**). Within a period of just four years, soccer promotion had transformed the public response to the game from mild curiosity into a national fever.

From the outset, soccer actively distinguished itself from other sports as an environment where players and spectators alike could express their individual feelings openly, loudly and even physically. Brazil not only provided most of the early imported players for the J-League but also the model for soccer spectatorship. Almost a decade after the first J-League games, the rhythms of Brazilian music and dance still underpin the chants shouted from the stands. The exuberant and even theatrical behaviour of both fans and players is as much a part of the game of *sakka* as the on-field performance of the players and teams. An entire alternative youth culture of music, fashion and even hairstyles has grown up around soccer in Japan and many fans and players pride themselves in the maverick image of the sport promoted by the J-League, its sponsors and the assorted manufacturers and commercial outlets of soccer fashion, sports gear and related paraphernalia.

While baseball was also an imported sport it had evolved differently around company-based teams. Soccer, on the other hand, was introduced and sponsored initially at the regional level by local government and then further supported by business on the sponsorship model. Baseball has a deep and strong base in the school system through inter-school sporting competitions from the local to national levels but soccer cut into the popularity of baseball by presenting itself as a new youth culture and characterising baseball as a duller sport. It was promoted as a trendy alternative to baseball offering a new and exciting sports experience for players and spectators alike. This image-based promotion of the sport in tandem with a comprehensive product development and merchandising strategy had much to do with the sport's rapid rise to primetime television programming and the spread of soccer fever from high-school leagues to Japan's 2002 World Cup bid.

Another significant factor in the success of *sakka* was its image as a truly international sport. It had the advantage of not being so closely linked to the USA over the 1990s, when Japan–USA relations were frequently strained politically, economically and on the baseball pitch. Moreover, the 1990s was not only the decade of *riijaa* culture but also of Japan's fervent government campaign for internationalisation of everything from foreign policy to education and dietary patterns. Soccer identified itself as an international sport and the J-League, together with sponsors and broadcast networks, actively promoted international tournaments and the importing and exporting of star players (although there are still caps on foreign recruitment). The J-League successfully combined a strategy of exploiting regional and home-town loyalties with a promotional rhetoric of internationalism to create the maverick consumer culture of Japanese *sakka*.

Further reading

Watts, J. 'Soccer shinhatsubai: What are the Japanese consumers making of the J-League'.

SANDRA BUCKLEY

social and political movements

Progressive Japanese intellectuals often argue that, in Japan, as in other modern industrial countries, people are reluctant to participate in and take responsibility for public affairs. They leave it to the politicians and bureaucrats, and frequently the results are autocratic government, corruption and exploitation. Yet, protest and civil strife are integral to modern Japanese history, and since the Second World War people have become especially prone to take their grievances into the polling booth, the media and the streets. Social and political movements have fluctuated in size and intensity, and changed qualitatively from one era to the next, but have played an important and occasionally determining role in post-war politics, society and culture.

Many social and political movements of the early decades of the post-war period are indebted to wartime mobilisation for their leadership, organisational patterns and even ideology. Labour unions grew rapidly by availing themselves of an earlier, enterprise-based organisational pattern, and many post-war leaders of labour unions, farmers' unions, youth groups, women's organisations and social democratic political parties also played roles in national mobilisation for total war. Moreover, it was through mobilisation that most of the rank and file of post-war political movements had been propelled for the first time into the public realm as a participant. During the war, they became accustomed to ideological conformity, organisational hierarchy and rationality, as well as control from a national centre. Belief in the formal equality of all national subjects was also intensified by the wartime experience. Social and political movements and incidents of all kinds mushroomed in the 1950s in Japan.

Incidents involving fifty or more participants and causing either human injury or property damage numbered 385 between 1952 and 1960, whereas in France between 1950 and 1960 the same sort of disturbances numbered only 163. Moreover, if police intervention is added as a sufficient criterion for inclusion, the number of incidents in Japan in the same period jumps to 945. Labour union members spearheaded popular unrest, while participation by farmers and fishermen was relatively infrequent (Sugimoto: 67, 75).

Nationally centralised union federations, political parties, peace movements and organisations of all kinds were relatively successful in bringing local groups under their wing. In the **unions and the labour movement**, national centres such as Sanbetsu, **Sōdōmei** and **Sōhyō** claimed the right to speak for organised labour just as national unions like the Teachers' Union spoke for teachers, the National Farmers' Union represented farmers, the **Housewives' Association** (Shufuren) represented housewives and, in the mean time, the communist and socialist parties competed to co-opt and control not only workers but writers, artists, women, pacifists and a whole range of other groups. Undergirding this hierarchical style of mobilising support were both formal and popular forms of Marxism as well as modernisation theory, which relied on unilinear conceptions of historical development and privileged certain social groups and parties as the unique vehicles of progress. Movements broadly consistent with this organisational pattern included not only the labour movement but the **peace and anti-nuclear movements**, the early-post-war farmers' movement (see **farmers' movements**) and movements in the late-1950s against the Police Duties Bill, **against revision of the Constitution** and **against teachers' rating system**.

Yet, hidden throughout society in the 1950s were countless small groups that remained outside the purview of national political organisation. Among these were circles of various sorts – typically focused on some form of cultural activity like singing, collecting, writing and sharing poetry – that catalysed new values oriented to voluntarism, autonomy, self-reliance, sociability and genuine egalitarianism. Such practical values resonated with the official democratic ideology but were also capable of encouraging resistance against the empty formalisms of 'post-war democracy' as an established institutional system. That is not to say that major national parties did not try to organise and subsume circles. The communists tried to turn some into party cells, or incorporate them into a united front, while the Socialist Party and Sōhyō organised others under the aegis of the National Congress of Culture (Kokumin Bunka Kaigi).

However, most circles found such affiliations to be inconsistent with their *raison d'être*.

Rather than succumbing to the hierarchical movement politics of the 1950s, circles instead helped produce a new political style that was quite extraneous to it. The major occasion for the emergence of this new style was the 1960 **Anpo struggle** over ratification of the Japan–US Security Treaty. In the course of this struggle, groups that were organised on the model of the circles, such as the Voiceless Voices citizens' group, joined with established national organisations such as the socialists, the Communist Party, Sōhyō and others, and their umbrella organization, the People's Council to Stop the Revised Security Treaty. However, the circle-type citizens' groups also resisted attempts by those organisations to subordinate them, and developed a non-hierarchical, decentralised, ideologically-pluralistic, voluntaristic mode of protest that constituted a legacy for what came to be called **citizens' movements** in the 1960s and 1970s. By most definitions, citizens' movements are decentralised, issue-specific, middle-class movements that are often touched off by national or global rather than local issues. **Beheiren**, which was virtually a direct successor to the Voiceless Voices and the major catalyst of Japanese protest against the Vietnam War, is the best example.

The Anpo struggle also provided the occasion for development of a Japanese New Left in the form of an anti-Communist Party radical student movement. Organisations such as the Bund were formed by students who had left or been expelled from the party in the 1950s, but who were still devoted to the goal of socialist revolution. These students had rebelled against the party not only on account of its narrow orthodoxy but because in its authoritarian organisational style it appeared to replicate the very emperor system that it claimed to oppose. In the course of the Anpo struggle, the Communist Party proceeded to give highest priority to maintaining its own control, even to the point of interfering with radical actions that it knew it could not direct, while the New Left students led the assault on the National Diet and pre-empted the vanguard role claimed by the Communist Party.

After the Anpo movement brought down the government of Kishi Nobusuke, a new Cabinet was formed by Ikeda Hayato. Ikeda retreated from Kishi's rightist authoritarianism and instead focused attention on rapid economic growth, which was well underway in Japan by the late-1950s; indeed, the occurrence of middle-class, citizen movement-type protest in the Anpo struggle had been to some degree made possible by that growth. Ikeda's successful '**Plan to Double Income**' programme licensed pell-mell industrialisation (later called the 'economic miracle'), whose side-effects included uncontrolled urbanisation, standardisation of employment patterns, lifestyles and gender roles, soaring consumption levels, decreased labour militancy, disruption of small-scale communal and neighbourhood life and environmental pollution on an unprecedented scale. **Residents' movements** were one result.

Residents' movements are a variety of citizens' movements that are focused on local rather than national issues and, on the whole, less 'public-spirited'. Of course, this is only a matter of degree. Residents' movements typically defend local communities from environmental pollution and other unwelcome intrusions that accompany development. They are therefore sometimes conservative in the sense that they seek to preserve the local status quo. Moreover, in contrast to many citizens' movements, they tend to reinforce negative rather than positive images of modernisation. Some commentators have compared them to the similarly-conservative peasant uprisings of the early modern period (1600–1867) of Japanese history. Yet, very often, residents' movements have been virtually indistinguishable from other citizens' movements, as in the case of resistance against US military facilities in the seaside town of Zushi, which has combined self-centred, local defensiveness with principled opposition to military alliances and the stationing of US troops on Japanese soil.

Post-war protests and other disturbances, including labour disputes, reached an initial peak in the early 1950s, and then another between 1957 and 1960, with the widespread outbreak of disputes related to education, the Anpo struggle and major strikes such as the **Miike struggle**. The third peak, from 1970 to 1973, was accounted for largely by environmentally focused residents' movements. The number of actively contentious movements has apparently declined since the early 1970s, although military bases and nuclear power plants are still powerful magnets for opposition. Yet, the decline in protest does not necessarily mean that Japanese citizens have retreated again into a purely private realm. In the 1980s and 1990s, political and social movements have continued to diversify in pursuit of a wide variety of specific goals and purposes, broadly consistent with directions among the so-called New Social Movements in other advanced industrial countries. Continuing unabated since the late-1960s is the movement against the Narita Airport (see **Narita Airport struggle**), near Tokyo. Farmers who resisted land confiscation were supported by radical students and others who attempted physically to block construction, leading to violent clashes and continuing protest, which delayed the airport's opening for some seven years and limited it to one runway in place of the three that were originally planned.

Some citizens' and residents' movements are attempting to broaden and perpetuate the impact of their concerns about the environment, social justice, minority rights and other causes by organising non-profit interest groups, but tax-exempt status is very difficult to acquire in Japan and tax laws do not encourage philanthropy. This has severely limited the development of relatively permanent, nationwide environmentalist and other organisations along the lines of Greenpeace or the Sierra Club in the USA. Others have channelled their earlier political activism into alternative lifestyle movements, such as natural foods, organic farming and communes. Citizens' movement activists and circles began to develop networks in the 1970s and 1980s, and many such networks continue to exist, reinforced by the circulation of small publications and newsletters (**mini-komi**). Some citizens' groups try to gather together with other movements periodically in order to facilitate communication and strengthen connections while retaining local autonomy

References

Sugimoto, Y. (1981) *Popular Disturbance in Postwar Japan*, Hong Kong: Asian Research Service.

Further reading

Gordon, Andrew (1993) *Postwar Japan as History*, Berkeley and Los Angeles: University of California Press.

Livingston, J., Moore, J. and Oldfather, F. (eds.) (1973) *Postwar Japan: 1945 to Present*, New York: Pantheon Books.

Sasaki-Uemura, Wesley (2001) *Organizing the Spontaneous: Citizen Protest in Postwar Japan*, Honolulu: University of Hawaii Press.

Steiner, K., Krauss, E. and Flanagan, S. (eds.) (1980) *Political Opposition and Local Politics in Japan*, Princeton: Princeton University Press.

J. VICTOR KOSCHMANN

Sōdōmei

Sōdōmei was short for Nihon Rōdō Kumiai Sōdōmei, the Japan Federation of Labour. Modelled on the American Federation of Labour, it was first established in 1912 as the Yūaikai, temporarily disbanded during the war years and re-established in 1945. Sōdōmei, like the post-war **Japan Socialist Party**, whose principal support base it was, contained a number of ideological factions, ranging from the leftist unionism of Takano Minoru to the right-wing led by Matsuoka Komakichi. Sōdōmei was stronger in private industry than its rival federation, the pro-communist Sanbetsu and its primary base of support came from veteran blue-collar workers, many of them foremen. Unlike Sanbetsu, Sōdōmei never aspired to create industrial unions; its very existence was premised on separate 'enterprise unions' for each company, factory or mine. Sōdōmei reached a peak of influence with the short-lived Socialist Party-led coalition government of 1947–8, but its influence declined thereafter. Most Sōdōmei unions joined **Sōhyō** in 1950 and the organisation itself disbanded the same year, but it was resurrected in 1951 and became a forum for opposition to the leftist policies of Sōhyō until absorbed into the new right-wing national federation, **Dōmei**, in 1964.

Further reading

Kume Ikuo (1997) *Disparaged Success*, Ithaca: Cornell University Press.

MICHAEL GIBBS

Sōhyō

Sōhyō is short for Nihon Rōdō Kumiai Sōhyōgikai. Founded in 1950, it was the leading labour federation in Japan for several decades. Its history breaks down into several periods: 1950–5, when Takano Minoru was its leader; 1955–70, when Iwai Akira held Takano's old position of general secretary; and the 1970s and 1980s, when Sōhyō became relegated to representing public-sector employees (who lacked the right to strike). Sōhyō disbanded in 1989, after its unions joined the new national federation, **Rengō**.

Sōhyō represented the resurrection of the **unions and the labour movement** after the demise of the **Japan Socialist Party** coalition of 1947–8 and the decline of the pro-communist labour federation, Sanbetsu, in 1948–9. Although both Allied Occupation officials and the conservative Japanese government had hopes that Sōhyō, which was based to a considerable degree on the anti-communist 'democratic leagues' formed in many unions during 1948 and 1949, would tame the radical thrust of the Japanese labour movement, they were soon disappointed. Under the leadership of Takano Minoru, Sōhyō aligned with the left wing of the Socialist Party to oppose the US–Japan peace and security treaties. Sōhyō took the lead in opposition to US military bases, nuclear testing and continued close ties between the USA and Japan, including the kind of investment and technology ties favoured by Japanese big business.

Takano fell from power following the failure of several overly ambitious strikes carried out by unions during the severe post-Korean War recession of 1954. His replacement, Iwai Akira, led Sōhyō towards a focus on more realistic economic struggles launched by unions against their employers. From 1955, Sōhyō mounted an annual **spring offensive**, aimed at forcing wage increase across the economy. From 1958, the flamboyant Ōta

Kaoru joined Iwai as head of the federation. Sōhyō under Ōta and Iwai did win significant wage gains for its members, but the narrow focus of its struggles reduced the greater national significance of the labour movement over time. These were the years when major employers began to shift towards non-unionised outside-contract workers. They were also the years of major defeats for labour, both in the great steel strikes of the late 1950s and in the Mitsui Miike coal miners strike of 1960. By 1970, Sōhyō had lost most of its influence over unions in private industry to **Dōmei** and the **IMF-JC**.

Increasingly outmanœuvred by right-wing labour organisations like the IMF-JC and ignored by private-sector employers, Sōhyō mounted its last major effort in 1975 – the 'strike for the right to strike' by employers of the Japan National Railways (JNR). JNR and other public-sector employees had lost the right to strike in 1948, but despite a week-long (illegal) shutdown of the railway system, the government refused to compromise and the weakness of Sōhyō was exposed. Sōhyō's influence declined rapidly in the 1980s. Its dissolution in 1989 was anti-climactic.

Further reading

Kume Ikuo (1997) *Disparaged Success*, Ithaca: Cornell University Press.
Price, John (1997) *Japan Works*, Ithaca: Cornell University Press.

MICHAEL GIBBS

Sōka Gakkai

Sōka Gakkai is the largest of the Japanese new religions and the most successful in terms of its proselytisation efforts abroad, having established branch offices and places of worship in over a hundred countries.

Founded by Makiguchi Tsunesaburō (1871–1944) in the 1930s as a devout lay-Buddhist organisation under the auspices of the Nichiren Shōshū sect, Sōka Gakkai grew rapidly in the following decades under the leadership of Toda Jōsei (1900–58) and Ikeda Daisaku (1928–), who advocated a more aggressive proselytising campaign that resulted in Sōka Gakkai emerging as one of the most prominent religious groups in the post-war era.

The chief idea behind the teachings of Sōka Gakkai lies in the notion that misfortune originates in the sin of clinging to false teachings. According to Sōka Gakkai, belief, genuine happiness and material success can only be procured through the veneration of the Lotus Sutra as interpreted by Nichiren (1222–82), the founder of the Nichiren Buddhist sect. Specifically, this is accomplished through the chanting of the *daimoku* (title of the Lotus Sutra) with faith in the *gohonzon* (mandala devised by Nichiren).

The influence of Sōka Gakkai has extended to several areas of society, including education and politics, where it has founded a major university (Sōka University) and spawned its own political party (Kōmeitō). The religion also owns one of the largest daily newspapers in Japan (*Seikyō Shinbun*) and is active in promoting cultural and social activities in various countries.

In 1991, the tension that characterised the relationship between Sōka Gakkai and Nichiren Shōshū erupted in a well-publicised and bitter split between the two religious organisations, forcing both groups to undergo processes of redefinition and restructuring. While it is difficult to obtain accurate membership figures for the religion, in the 1990s Sōka Gakkai claimed to have more than 8 million members in Japan and over a million members outside Japan.

Further reading

Metraux, Daniel (1994) *The Soka Gakkai Revolution*, Maryland: University Press of America.
Wilson, Bryan and Dobbelaere, Karel (1994) *A Time to Chant: The Soka Gakkai Buddhists in Britain*, Oxford: Clarendon Press.

JAY SAKASHITA

Sōrifu

Sōrifu (Prime Minister's Office) was created by law in 1949. It is distinct from the various ministries as it falls under the direct administration of the prime minister, although its director-general has ministerial rank. Together with the Cabinet, its major function is to co-ordinate the policies and programmes of the twelve ministries and fourteen agencies of government. Other responsibilities include providing public information on government activities, carrying out national statistics, opinion polls and decorative honours. In recent years, it has taken on a wider range of policies, such as co-operation with the United Nations (UN) peacekeeping efforts. Under 1992 legislation, the secretariat of the International Peace Co-operation Headquarters is located in the Prime Minister's Office, effectively allowing Japan to participate in UN Peacekeeping Operations by dispatching personnel to Angola, Cambodia, Mozambique, El Salvador and the Golan Heights. In 1994, the Office for Gender Equality and the Council for Gender Equality were established in the Prime Minister's Office. The Office for Gender Equality provides overall support for the Minister for Women's Affairs as well as advancement of women in Japan. Other functions include co-ordinating the reconstruction and relief programme following the Kobe (Hanshin-Awaji) Earthquake in 1995, and the promotion of administrative reform and decentralisation of government functions.

DAVID EDGINGTON

sōsaku hanga

Sōsaku hanga (creative print) is an art in which Japan has strong international presence and has continued to cross national boundaries to inspire Western as well as other Asian artists.

Sōsaku hanga, or the 'creative print', emerged in the early twentieth century and the term refers to a modern concept that the print made by an artist as self-expression is a work of art in its own right, not the reproduction of a given image. At that time, although the *ukiyo-e* print was in decline, its highly developed woodblock printing techniques were utilised in reproductions, usually works by famous artists. They were also used in *shin hanga* or the 'new print', which began in the 1910s and aimed at reviving the *ukiyo-e* repertoire of images of beautiful women, famous places and *kabuki* actors in the modern context for collectors and foreign markets. *Shin hanga* were designed by the artist and then blockcut and printed by specialists under the supervision of a publisher such as Watanabe Shōzaburō or an artist-publisher such as Hashiguchi Goyō. *Sōsaku hanga* artists, on the other hand, were inspired by modern Western art and aimed at expressing themselves through the medium of print. In order to distinguish their work from *shin hanga* and other reproductive prints, the *sōsaku hanga* artists defined this form as 'prints designed, blockcut (or etched, engraved, etc.) and printed by the artist'. This rule cannot be applied too rigidly, but it represents the general direction of *sōsaku hanga*. The print that is generally agreed among print historians as the first *sōsaku hanga* is *Fisherman* by Yamamoto Kanae (1882–1946), which was made and published in the magazine *Myōjō* in 1904. Although there was no market for *sōsaku hanga* and the word *hanga* was often jokingly punned with the English 'hunger', many artists took up the medium and developed diverse styles.

By the end of the Pacific War, *sōsaku hanga* had gained general recognition as art, particularly through its inclusion in the annual government-sponsored art exhibition. In 1938, Munakata Shikō became the first artist to win First Prize at the government-sponsored Bunten. However, perhaps the most prominent of the *sōsaku hanga* artists was Onchi Kōshirō (1891–1955), who in 1915 created Japan's first abstract image, *Bright Hours*; he became a leader of Japanese printmaking with his artistic originality and organisational skills. Among various printmaking techniques, woodcut, which reached its technical height with the *ukiyo-e* print in the Edo Period, continued its dominance over other newly imported techniques. Many artists remained attracted to the texture of wood and the specifically Japanese materials, tools and paper (*ganpi* and *baren*).

Although the Pacific War and the post-war hardship took a toll on many significant artists, survivors such as Onchi, Munakata, Maeda Tōshirō, Sekino Jun'ichirō, Kawakami Sumio and Nagase Yoshirō continued their prominence in woodcut prints into the 1970s. In copperplate prints, Komai Tetsurō became known for his poetic expression. Hasegawa Kiyoshi, who has lived and worked in France since 1920, was recognised in

France for reviving the then largely forgotten mezzotint technique. Hasegawa acted as one of the few channels between Japanese and Western printmaking.

After the war, the Japanese *sōsaku hanga* (now simply called *hanga*) began to win international recognition. Foreigners, particularly those from North America, discovered the Japanese *sōsaku hanga* and began collecting works by prominent artists such as Onchi. These individuals include Oliver Statler and Jack Hillier, who became instrumental in introducing Japanese prints overseas. Another significant international exposure was through overseas exhibitions, beginning with the 1951 São Paulo Biennial, at which Komai Tetsurō and Saitō Kiyoshi won awards. This was followed by Munakata Shikō's winning the Grand Prize in the print section at the 28th Venice Biennial in 1956. From that time onwards, Japanese print artists have continued to achieve an international success that other media such as painting have not. In 1966, Ikeda Masuo became the second Grand Prize winner at the Venice Biennial with works that conveyed the artist's response to contemporary international art movements and presented with an individual wit.

Such international exposure necessarily affected the printmaking practice in Japan. The practice of signing, dating and inserting edition numbers by the artist, which was the exception rather than the rule before the war, was quickly adopted, as it was an international rule that artists had to comply with when submitting their works to international exhibitions. After the first Japanese international print biennale in 1957, artists began to practice more in isolation rather than in 'schools', experimenting in different and more sophisticated techniques. Use of photographs, silkscreen and other new media greatly extended the possibilities of expression. Another aspect of the post-war revitalisation of printmaking was the development of print workshops, which preceded the establishment of printmaking classes at art schools and universities as part of the curriculum. The Japan Artists Association (JAA) opened the first public print workshop in 1963. This provided many young artists with opportunities to use expensive presses and other facilities, as well as receive instruction from established artists. Komai Tetsuro

was particularly devoted to teaching and was responsible for the establishment of printmaking classes at art schools. The JAA workshop was closed in 1976, having achieved the original purpose of education and diffusion of printmaking.

Noda Tetsuya is one of the internationally successful artists who combined photography and silkscreen. Installation artists, including Sekine Nobuo, and designer/illustrators, including Yokō Tadanori and Awazu Kiyoshi, brought new approaches to prints. While abstract artists such as Hagiwara Hideo, Funasaka Yoshisuke and Sugai Kumi have established themselves, since the revival in the 1970s of the 'decadent' *ukiyo-e* artists of the late Edo to Meiji Period, some print artists have taken up and reinterpreted *ukiyo-e* themes and icons. This latter group includes Yokō, Ay-o and Teraoka Masami (who has lived in the USA since 1961). Woodcut artists also developed sophisticated techniques as seen in works by Fukita Fumiaki, Yoshida Hodaka and Nakayama Tadashi, while others like Kitayama Fumio, Mori Yoshitoshi (stencil) and Sekino Jun'ichirō continued the rustic or folk style.

CHIAKI AJIOKA

Southern All-Stars

The Southern All-Stars are most strongly identified with the playful charisma of their lead singer and songwriter, Kuwata Keisuke. The Southern All-Stars' first single, 'Katte ni Sinbad', was released in June 1978 and rose to number three on the charts. It already exhibited Kuwata's distinctive rhythmic flair and nearly modernist, parodic relation to 1960s and 1970s Japanese mass culture.

The band staked its claim to lasting critical and popular recognition with their second single release, 'Itoshi no eri', an intense and soaring R 'n' B ballad since recorded by Ray Charles. Kuwata's appropriation of white blues singing style fundamentally changed approaches to vocal phrasing in Japanese popular music. His early lyrics interwove English and Japanese phonetics and semantics, creating a Gestalt effect that put his songwriting in a unique category of its own. Through the 1980s and early 1990s, the Southern

All-Stars retained the rare status of defining a period in pop music history, even as their work became increasingly adventurous and exploratory. While the songwriting of the band has rarely measured up to Kuwata's incredible gifts as a vocalist and lyricist, the band's work remains an important turning point in post-war Japanese popular music.

MARK ANDERSON

soy sauce

Known in Japanese as *shōyu*, this dark-coloured, salty sauce is a basic ingredient to much Japanese cooking. It is the product of fermented soy beans, roasted cracked wheat, salt, water and a fermenting agent.

Light soy is so named to distinguish it from the thicker, saltier and blacker dark soy that is closer in style to traditional Chinese-style soy. Today, health concerns have led to a number of new varieties of low-sodium and gluten-free soys on the market. Soy was produced by households up until the sixteenth century when the first commercial producers emerged. Kikkoman is the largest of these today and has achieved international brand recognition.

SANDRA BUCKLEY

sport and recreation

For the majority of people in pre-modern Japan, there was no simple distinction between work and non-work. This was most true for those in farming and fishing communities. Evenings might be spent away from the fields or boats but family members would still be involved in repairs to nets and lines, tools, mending clothes, pickling or drying foods, sorting grains, etc. These activities would be mixed with conversation, gossip, planning, laughter, argument, drinking and song. It was **festivals** and rituals that were designated as a space of **play** (*asobi*) and rest from work.

Although a festival might relate to harvest or planting season, the duration of the festival was one of tolerance of excess and the suspension of daily routines. **Pilgrimages** also offered an important but rare extended break from the regular routines of work with plenty of opportunity *en route* and in the grounds of the famous pilgrimage sites for *asobi*. By the Edo Period, the merchant class of the towns and cities had achieved a well-developed sense of play that included **kabuki** and *bunraku*, **sumo wrestling**, popular literature and street theatre, and, of course, for the men there was the domain of the 'gay quarters' where they could enjoy drinking and an array of entertainment from dance and song to prostitution in the tea houses and brothels of the district. Street performers, storytellers, travelling theatre troupes, cheap inns and drinking establishments offered plenty of opportunity for *asobi* for the poorer population of the cities. Among the elite, however, leisure was hardly distinguishable from other forms of personal improvement and achievement. Poetry parties and some ritual and festival events (e.g. blossom viewing) allowed for an abandonment of proper etiquette and decorum, but for the most part the aristocracy and samurai classes were bound to a relentless and demanding performance of their status that extended to their leisure and entertainment. Tea ceremony, calligraphy, flower arrangement, poetry, musical instruments and the martial arts were all activities linked to the development and enhancement of the individuals' mind and spirit rather than simply enjoyable pastimes.

It was the Meiji Period that saw the introduction from the West of distinct notions of sport, leisure and vacation time. Japan's modern elite began to indulge in resort and spa trips for pleasure as well as overseas travel, and a culture of eating out at Western-style and Japanese restaurants, and relaxing in clubs and cafés emerged as popular pastimes in the urban centres. The first cafés and clubs were expensive and upmarket, but the culture of the *kissaten* and music club or bar quickly found its way into middle- and working-class neighbourhoods. Sports such as **golf**, baseball, **skiing**, swimming and **tennis** were brought to Japan by the foreign businessmen, diplomats, government officials and educators who began arriving with the opening of Japan after 1868. The popularisation of these sports was closely linked to education, and it was the **Ministry of Education** that came to play a key role in creating an ethic of fitness and achievement that still dominates the general attitude to sports. Physical education was introduced into primary schools under the Educational Code of 1872 and in 1878 the Ministry created an Institute of Physical Education that was to play a central role in the incorporation of sport into teacher training and curriculum policy across all levels of education. From this time forward, sport in Japan became intimately linked not to leisure and entertainment but to the development of individuals, healthy and wholesome in mind and body. This would fast become a national project linked to the goals of the emerging modern identity. Although Japan and Germany both pursued a fascist distortion of this modern identity into a belief in ethnic superiority, in Japan this link, while firmly developed in relation to the rest of Asia, was far more fragile and problematic in the context of Japan's relation to the West and 'whiteness' (see **West, the**).

The term *taiiku* (nurturing the body) was used rather than sport, and still is in the school curriculum to designate the compulsory hours of exercise and sports activities. The majority of children's sport activities are located within the school system, whether through *taiiku* classes, school teams or extracurricular sports clubs. Many popular **manga**, **anime** and television dramas about teen life will feature a subplot around the long and arduous hours of often harsh training with strict discipline that characterises a lot of school sport teams. The national system of inter-school competitions actively promotes what is considered a healthy competitive attitude between schools and regions, but is also sometimes criticised in the media for the excessive pressure to win that it places on participating schools and students. Sports clubs outside schools and universities are relatively rare. Companies also offer sporting activities for employees through clubs and annual employee vacations. In **baseball**, it was these company-based clubs that eventually evolved into the regional and national leagues. In the 1960s and 1970s period of rapid economic growth, many larger companies developed their own sports facilities and resorts for the benefit of employees. Independent sports clubs were the domain of the very rich until the 1970s and 1980s, when the first wave of commercial private health clubs and sport

resorts were successfully launched to cater to the health and fitness needs of an affluent baby boomer generation beginning to seek opportunities for leisure time outside the work environment. These facilities, however, tend not to sponsor competitive teams but offer fitness and recreational facilities to individuals.

Spectator sports have been aggressively promoted by the media in Japan since the introduction of television in 1953. It was the 1964 **Olympics** that stimulated the colour television boom in Japan. Coverage of major national and international sporting events now attracts some of the highest advertising fees in commercial broadcasting. Sports newspapers make up 12–15 per cent of the daily print media in Japan and carry a mix of daily news, sports results, articles, interviews and gossip, and a now almost compulsory section of pornographic photos. While baseball has had a long history of popularity in Japan from the Meiji Period, rugby and soccer were both launched as new sport leagues under carefully developed marketing strategies linking sporting associations, broadcast networks, commercial sponsors, advertising agencies and retail outlets. Gambling has remained an ever-present element in some popular spectator sports, most notably **horse racing** and speedboat racing. Gambling is also an integral component in the non-sport recreational activities of **mah jong** and **pachinko**. **Sumo wrestling** has gained a new lease on life in post-war Japan via its television audience. Although traditionally a ritual and popular element of festival activities, sumo is now transformed into an organised and nationally regulated spectator sport that has achieved a new financial stability through commercial sponsorship attracted by the wide television audience.

Japan's **leisure** market is dominated by eating and drinking, **tourism** and gambling. There has been rapid growth led by a boom in youth sports such as skiing, snowboarding and windsurfing, but golf continues to dominate the leisure market, despite the limited access to club membership or course greens for the majority of Japanese. Travel and sport are closely linked in the youth, young adult and family segments of the leisure market. With high club fees and crowding more and more prevalent, Japanese are taking sporting vacations to overseas resorts. Tourism is something Japan has become famous, even infamous, for, and yet despite the long lines of Japanese at immigration counters in popular resort destinations and the familiar sight of group tours, even with 16 million Japanese travelling overseas each year, industry analysts estimate that by the early 1990s only 10 per cent of Japanese had participated in international travel. The tourism industry has had to develop new models for short package tour vacations to accommodate the Japanese reluctance to draw down their vacation entitlement. Even the government push to promote leisure culture since the mid-1980s has not seen a significant shift in this area. The majority of international and domestic travel is still crowded into a couple of narrow bands of annual vacation at **New Year**, **Golden Week** and **Obon**, putting tremendous pressure on services and infrastructure at these times. Japan's leisure market is clearly divided by income. White-collar males are more likely to pursue golf on practice ranges and play mah jong, while blue-collar workers are more likely to play pachinko, watch horse and speedboat racing and participate in gambling. Baseball and sumo are two universally popular sports and the national radio and television broadcasts of major matches capture huge audiences.

Martial arts in Japan continue to be widely practised, but it is difficult to simply treat them as a sport. The different schools of each of the martial arts emphasise the spiritual or inner development of the individual in addition to physical strength and adeptness. It has been argued that it is the focus on discipline and personal development, which became an essential element of the martial arts and the various *dō* (**tea ceremony**, **flower arrangement**, calligraphy, etc.) during their engagement with **Zen** philosophy over the Edo Period, that carried over into the modern notion of *taiiku*. Sport in Japan was transformed into a pursuit of an ethic of self-improvement, and less a matter of leisure than a purposeful application to a task often also closely linked to one's status. In the case of modern sports, this association saw sport become an extension of the individual's relationship to their school or workplace – one more productive activity and an opportunity to demonstrate loyalty and commitment. Sport spectatorship

in post-war Japan emerged as a rare opportunity to be non-productive and inactive in a lifestyle dominated by a work ethic. Commuter time today is also non-productive time spent disengaged from work and family, but for many commuters it is simply a chance to rest, even sleep, in the hectic schedule of the long work day (see **commuting**).

Children participate in compulsory *taiiku* activities at school and also often after-school sports clubs, but there continues to be a growing concern expressed by educators, parents and health specialists that children spend too many hours in non-physical activities. In addition to hours spent in school at their desks, many children also attend after-hours tutoring, leaving little time for outdoor play or games. Magazines aimed at the mothers of school-aged children frequently run feature articles on the dangers of a sedentary youth culture of video and computer games, Gameboys, television and online web activities. Opportunities for children to pursue undirected activities tied to no specific educational or self-improvement goals are few on the six school days of the week. The retreat into the solitary space of audio-visual entertainment during free time can be understood as a strong counter-response from children to the intensity of the level of purposeful activity and close supervision of the rest of their time. This explanation still leaves open the question of the long-term impact on children's health of an apparent shift from physical play with other children to solitary interactive video and computer games.

Government campaigns promoting leisure and family activities, along with increases in the number of official national holidays, have seen gradual changes in the attitude to taking time out from work to relax. The leisure boom has seen an explosion of new activities on to the Japanese leisure and sports market, especially in youth extreme sports. The tourism sector has also responded with a wide range of new sports-oriented family and individual vacation packages, such as ski holidays, snorkelling and diving packages with accreditation training included, hiking treks, cowboy ranch family vacations, etc. There has been a boom in golf vacations to top international courses for the wealthier clients, as well as bargain trips to greens in Florida, Hawaii and Australia. Another new market is recreational group travel for an older clientele. With the greying of Japan's population, there has been a concerted effort in the leisure industry to capitalise on the health and recreational needs of this target market. New elderly-friendly resorts and tour packages offer a range of indoor and outdoor activities mixing fitness and health assessment, and advise on relaxation, diet and exercise. Municipal and pre-fectural governments are also developing extensive new facilities for elderly recreation and sports, and offering incentives to local entrepreneurs to also move into providing private user-pay facilities for elderly care, recreation and entertainment.

Like most aspects of contemporary Japanese life, leisure, sports and recreational activity have developed into an intensely differentiated consu-mer market in which individuals participate with a level of professionalised consumerism that almost seems to outweigh the interest in the activity itself. Whether involved in horse racing, soccer, golf or extreme sports tourism, it is the equipment, fashion and accessories, standard of travel and accommo-dation and even the type of camera and luggage that function as the focus of a very public performance of consumer taste and buying power. The real risk is that, as the leisure market continues to develop, sport will increasingly become one more carefully orchestrated consumer activity and finally anything but relaxing.

Further reading

May, William (1989) 'Sport', in R. Powers and H. Kato, (eds) *Handbook of Japanese Popular Culture*, Westport, NY: Greenwood Press, pp. 167–95.

SANDRA BUCKLEY

spring offensive

The spring offensive, or *shuntō* (literally, spring struggle), began in 1955 as the new tactic of the post-Takano leadership of **Sōhyō**, the nationwide labour federation. It was not until the 1960s that most union wage struggles became co-ordinated in the spring offensives that we have come to expect every year. However, by the 1960s virtually every major union in Japan had dropped its militant stance toward management and had separated its (sometimes radical) political rhetoric from its willingness to co-operate with management on issues of wages and production. The unspoken basis of this arrangement was the virtual guarantee of 'lifetime employment' for the regular unionised workforce of major companies. Unions, from the 1960s on, would push for higher wages, though only for their own members (a shrinking minority of the workforce), but do so with a sense of security about their jobs. The number and frequency of strikes gradually declined over time as the spring offensive became institutionalised. Indeed, the union federation that increasingly took the lead in the spring offensive from the 1960s, **Tekkō Rōren** (the Steelworkers), conducted its last strike (a twenty-four-hour affair) in 1965.

Further reading

Kume Ikuo (1997) *Disparaged Success*, Ithaca: Cornell University Press.

MICHAEL GIBBS

standardised Japanese

Standardised Japanese is called '*hyōjun-go*'. '*Hyōjun*' means standard or norm. It is not '*kyōtsū-go*' (common language) designated by a state organ. In a strict sense there is no designated national language in Japan. Standardised Japanese was artificially created at the beginning of the Meiji Period in the late 1860s. Those who formed the new government came from different parts of Japan and they had a difficult time making themselves understood in their own dialects because of the phonological and lexical differences. At that time, the capital was shifted from Kyō (now Kyōto) to Edo (now Tokyo). It was decided to adopt a local dialect of one part of Tokyo as a base of a new language, because it was a neutral language to anyone from outside of Tokyo. This decision was also a symbolic rejection of the highly inflected language of the Kyōto nobles.

Nowadays, there is a standard speech accent, based on this Tokyo dialect, which NHK (Nippon Hōsō Kyōkai, or **Japan Broadcasting Cor-**

poration) announcers use. This functions like the once-familiar voice of the BBC announcers in the UK or the ABC in Australia. While there has been an attempt to open up these national broadcasters to a wider range of accents in recent years, NHK has remained tenaciously committed to *hyōjungo*. With the rapid development of broadcast media, radio and television in particular, *hyōjungo* has spread widely and is accepted by almost everyone throughout Japan as a common medium of communication. Some people are worried about the decline in local dialects because of the deluge of *hyōjungo* in the popular media. However, there are signs that there is an emerging process of revalidation of dialects in recent years as one element of a resurgence of interest and pride in local heritage and culture.

Certainly, at the level of lexicon, *hyōjungo* can be understood by anyone, anywhere in Japan. However, pronunciation and pitch or accent vary even now in accordance with local dialects when people are trying to use *hyōjungo*. It is generally encouraged that foreign learners of Japanese focus their studies on *hyōjungo*, but they will be constantly reminded once in Japan that local dialects are still flourishing and will need to cope with the variations this can produce.

In writing, it is again strange that there is no orthography in Japanese in a strict sense. However, the Ministry of Education has commissioned the Kokugo Shingikai (National Language Council) to establish some rules and regulations for written Japanese. Since the end of the Second World War, there have been many changes in written Japanese, including: the number of **kanji** that students are required to learn by the end of their compulsory schooling; rules of '*okurigana*' (the *hiragana* that follows *kanji* in verbs and adjectives); approved writing techniques for *hiragana* and **katakana**; and accepted simplified forms for some *kanji*. The recent rapid development of word-processing and other software programs for computers has in some ways solidified the standardised writing system of Japanese. Computerised character selection software requires the user to recognise the proper alternative among the many options displayed on a computer screen. These programs guide the user to the correct forms for the writing of *kanji*, *kanji* compounds and *okurigana*.

Finally, one's correct usage of the spoken or written forms of *hyōjungo* remains dependent upon an individual's overall language abilities. Fluency and proficiency in *hyōjungo* is a goal of compulsory education. The process of communication across the diverse range of local dialects still spoken in Japan has been simplified by the introduction of this normative structure of language, but critics continue to caution against a potential decline in the rich and diverse repertoire of local dialects. Unlike France, the Japanese government is not attempting to control or monitor the influx of foreign words into everyday usage and there appears to be an acceptance of the need for *hyōjungo* to remain fluid rather than a rigidly monitored regulatory structure.

SHUN IKEDA

state and religion, separation of

Japan's post-war Constitution guarantees both freedom of religion and the separation of state and religion. Article 20 of the 1947 Constitution was clearly intended to encode the **Allied Occupation**'s commitment to the dismantling of **State Shintō**. Japanese religions have characteristically demonstrated a high level of flexibility towards the mixing of religious beliefs and practices. Shintō and Buddhist rituals began converging from their earliest contact in the Nara and Heian periods. Elements of Confucian (see **Confucianism**) ritual and moral principles also filtered into both **State Shintō** and **Buddhism**. It is Christianity (see **Christianity in Japan**) that has kept itself more quarantined since it first arrival in Japan. The issue of separation of state and religion is, however, a significant break with historical precedent. Japan's ruling elite had always mixed ritual (Shintō, Buddhist and Confucian) with government functions. In the Tokugawa Period, the Buddhist temples were established as the place of register for families and became closely involved through this role in issues of governance related to family and community. State Shintō would shift these functions from temples to shrines during the Meiji and Taishō Periods as a state ideology of the family was promulgated around the figure of a divine Emperor.

Throughout the post-war period, there was, however, ongoing uncertainty around Article 20 and frequent eruptions of tension and protest over apparent breaches of the law. The mere fact that the Emperor was not removed from power, and moreover continued to perform a number of both religious and state functions, did nothing to discourage Japan's right from continuing to push for such reforms as the restoration of state sponsorhip for **Yasukuni Shrine**. The 1985 visit to Yasukuni Shrine by the then-Prime Minister Nakasone led to an immediate wave of protest from those who saw this as a symbolic rejection of Article 20. Yasukuni Shrine is the site where Japan's war dead are enshrined and memorialised. There have been other visits from senior politicians in the ensuing years and each has been met with similar media attention. Public debate over the flag and anthem are also tied to this same issue by virtue of the close linkage between State Shintō, imperialism and these symbols of Japanese identity with such deep historical ties to Japan's wartime identity.

SANDRA BUCKLEY

State Shintō

State Shintō is a term used to designate the official religion of Imperial Japan during the years between 1868 and 1945. The creation of State Shintō as a comprehensive, organisational structure that emphasised devotion to the Emperor, and its elevation to a national institution patronised by the state, can be traced to the period at end of the nineteenth century under the newly formed Meiji government (1868–1912).

Before this time, Shintō as a religion centred on native or tutelary deities called *kami* and its rituals and practices were carried out mostly on a localised level by priests of independent clerical lines or by important males in the local communities. During the period of State Shintō, however, a nationally ranked hierarchy of shrines was formulated with Ise Shrine at the top, along with a national priesthood with unified ranks. Attempts were made

to register every Japanese citizen with a shrine and each family was to enshrine a Shintō talisman in its home. Each household, thus, in theory became a branch shrine under a unified system. The creation of Japan's first national ceremonial calendar, national anthem and common flag also occurred during this period. In fact, much of what is represented today as ancient and traditional Shintō beliefs and practices were developed in conjunction with State Shintō. In short, State Shintō was created to help build a foundation of clear national and cultural identity for Japan during a time when Japanese values were perceived to be in competition against newly introduced Western ones.

Tied to the origins of State Shintō was a school of thought known as National Learning (*Kokugaku*), which influenced the formation of State Shintō during the end of the Tokugawa Period (1600–1868). Developed in the eighteenth century, National Learning attempted to return the country to an idealised past, a pure Japan before it became contaminated through contact with foreign culture and religion. Towards this end, efforts were made to separate the native Shintō from **Buddhism** (which was perceived as being foreign) and to create a standardised form of worship of Shintō deities. In such an environment of increasing nationalism, followers of other religions were at times subjected to persecution. Buddhist temples, images and other priceless treasures, for example, were wantonly destroyed and Buddhist priests were made to renounce their ordination and become Shintō priests instead. A number of new religions, too, were attacked or suffered under state intimidation. In particular the new religion Ōmoto suffered persecution as its leaders were jailed in 1921 and its headquarters destroyed in 1935.

Japan's educational system also came under the influence of State Shintō. Ideas concerning the sacredness of Japan and the notion that the Emperor was divine were ordered to be taught in school. Priests were recruited to teach in public schools and led students on periodic trips to shrines for formal worship. Shrines and priests were expected to serve the nation in fostering patriotism by encouraging such practices as formal veneration of the imperial portrait and making the Imperial Rescript on Education (1890) the ethical pillar of the nation. Making participation in shrine rites obligatory in light of the Constitution of 1889, which guaranteed religious freedom, was possible due to the state's view that State Shintō was not a religion. State Shintō was legally categorised as a government institution and its priests were government officials. From the government's point of view, State Shintō fostered moral instruction and not religious teaching. The Meiji regime then created an official religious branch of Shintō that included thirteen separate Shintō sects (Kyōha Shintō). Under this structure, the values and ideas associated with State Shintō could be nurtured and promulgated freely without any breech of the Constitution.

The cult of the war dead was also begun during the period of State Shintō. In 1869, the **Yasukuni Shrine** in Tokyo was established as a shrine for the spirits of those who had died fighting to restore the Emperor as head of state (Meiji Restoration). Yasukuni Shrine was thus dedicated to the enshrining of Japan's war dead and became one of the focal points for State Shintō. The Emperor performed rituals at Yasukuni Shrine that deified those enshrined. The war dead were then worshipped as *kami*. During the Second World War, more than 1 million war dead were enshrined as *kami* in Yasukuni Shrine. With the defeat of Japan in the Second World War and the issuance of the Shintō Directive by the Occupation authorities in December 1945, state sponsorship of Shintō officially came to an end. School trips to shrines were forbidden, altars enshrining the imperial portrait and the Imperial Rescript on Education were removed and Shintō doctrines that promoted a nationalistic ideology were removed from school textbooks. The Emperor formally renounced his divinity in a broadcast in 1946 and Shintō was completely disassociated from the state. Shintō thus began a separate existence as an explicit religious entity.

Several issues and controversies associated with State Shintō have continued into the present, however. There remains in Japan a lobby consisting of right-wing and conservative nationalists that is committed to restoring the links between government and religion. The Association of Shintō Shrines, for example, is one such group that wields political influence and lobbies for conservative positions on social issues. In much of the controversy, Yasukuni Shrine has been the symbolic centre of public debate and foreign consternation. On several occasions, the state has introduced bills to once again give Yasukuni Shrine government support. Although thus far unsuccessful in passing such bills, other manœuvres by conservative politicians have attempted to re-establish the relationship between Shintō and the state. On 15 August 1985, then-Japanese Prime Minister Nakasone Yasuhiro and his Cabinet paid formal tribute at Yasukuni Shrine, an act that created an uproar both in Japan and abroad. Disputes over state endorsement of Shintō ground-breaking purification ceremonies have also raised strong emotions on both sides of the issues and have had to be settled in Japan's supreme courts. In May 2000, comments made during a speech by Japanese Prime Minister Mori Yoshiro sparked public and international outrage when he referred to Japan as 'a land of the Gods with the Emperor as its core'. The ensuing controversy caused by the Prime Minister's remarks is evidence that issues surrounding Shintō and the state continue to play a part in the shaping of Japan's political, social and religious landscape.

See also: state and religion, separation of

Further reading

Hardacre, Helen (1989) *Shintō and the State*, New Jersey: Princeton University Press.

Reader, Ian (1998) *The Simple Guide to Shinto*, England: Global Books Limited.

JAY SAKASHITA

STREET OF CUPOLAS, THE see *Cupola no aru machi*

striptease

The first strip bars opened in the Shinjuku area of Tokyo in the late 1940s, but it would be the Asakusa area that emerged as the striptease centre of Tokyo. Nudity was not an uncommon element of much pre-modern popular theatre and peep shows were common in travelling performance troupes. There is even a reference to one of the Gods baring her genitals in a dance described in Japan's creation myth. However, the structure of an entire performance around the act of a woman stripping was new to Japan. Strip shows were expected to operate within the laws prohibiting the public display of pubic hair and male genitals. However, creative use of props and dance movement saw club owners stretching the law to the limit of its interpretation over the 1970s, and by the 1980s strip shows frequently featured client and stripper in on-stage sex. Despite occasional police crackdowns, strip clubs are generally self-policing and allowed significant leeway by the authorities. The extensive abuse of illegal immigrant workers in strip clubs over the 1990s has led to campaigns by feminists and human rights activists for stricter regulation of this area of the sex industry in Japan.

See also: hair debate; Japayuki-san; *mizushōbai*

SANDRA BUCKLEY

Structural Impediments Initiative

Structural Impediments Initiative (SII) refers to a series of discussions between US and Japanese trade negotiators in 1989–90 to address Japanese economic policies and business practices that the USA claimed impeded US exports and investments. The SII was, in part, a Bush Administration response to the stubborn US trade deficit and other problems that caused friction in the trading relationship with Japan.

SII responded to congressional pressure to deal more aggressively with Japanese unfair trade practices and to adopt a 'managed' trade policy towards Japan. It was designed to address Japan's savings rate, product distribution system and other policies long considered fundamental to US–Japanese bilateral negotiations, such as import quotas, high tariffs and government regulations. The final report called for Japan to: first, spend ¥430 trillion on public works over ten years; second, encourage personal consumption by narrowing the gap between domestic and foreign prices, and streamlining the distribution system;

third, stabilise land prices to promote housing construction; and fourth, reform transactions within 'keiretsu' (corporate groups). SII talks also produced a list of actions the Japanese side thought necessary to improve US competitiveness and so reduce trade friction. These included the US reduction of its budget deficit and an increase in the domestic savings rate. Japan also called on the USA to improve the competitiveness of its industries and to strengthen its education system and worker training programmes.

DAVID EDGINGTON

student movement

Until the late 1970s, Japanese students played a major role in post-war politics. The student movement provided a training ground and springboard for radical politics, giving rise to Japan's New Left. Between the **Anpo struggle** of 1958–60 and the **Narita Airport struggle** of the 1970s, Japanese students directly threatened the educational system and challenged state authority and legitimacy. The 1960 Anpo protests rejected the state's claim to represent the will of the people. Also, in 1968–9, the **Zenkyōtō** movement created both short- and long-term shutdowns at most universities and many high schools, and forced cancellation of university entrance exams. New Left violence in the 1970s and state repression had made activism less appealing to students by the 1980s and 1990s, and student activism declined.

The roots of the post-war student movement lie in two organisations, the Shinjinkai (New Persons' Society) at Tokyo Imperial University, and the wartime Student Patriotic Associations (SPA; Gakusei Hōkokukai). The Shinjinkai provided much of the early **Japan Communist Party**'s membership, and in fact the organisations were nearly synonymous. Part of a programme of total mobilisation, the SPA attempted to channel student organising into the war effort.

The early post-war student movement took up elements of both the Shinjinkai and the SPA. Post-war students took up the Shinjinkai's radical politics, and injected them into the universal framework of the SPA. Under Occupation reforms, students automatically became members of student autonomous councils (*jichikai*). Newly organised into *jichikai* and the **Zengakuren** (the JCP-affiliated national union of *jichikai*), students confronted universities and government officials over economic issues such as tuition fee hikes and housing. Like the pre-war student movement, the Occupation student movement allied itself with the JCP, but Zengakuren often resisted Party policies. In keeping with Party strategy, the JCP advocated a decentralised, federated student movement. Students argued that their unified, national movement was more effective, and nationally co-ordinated student actions against the '**Red Purge**', which ended in complete victory for the students, seemed to support this position.

After the JCP's decision to go underground at the Fifth Party Congress in June 1950, many students left school to foment revolution in the countryside. Student activists were the bulk of the foot soldiers for the Party's Maoist phase between 1950 and 1955. Many of these militant students resented the Party's lack of commitment to its own cause, and left the JCP after it renounced its revolutionary strategy in 1955. For the first time, students saw activity outside the party as legitimate and revolutionary. Disenchanted students and other activists joined fledgling Trotskyist organisations or simply gave up politics. Under JCP leadership, the student movement turned from revolutionary agitation in mountain districts to folk dancing and campus issues like tuition, dormitories and prices in student cafeterias, as well as democratisation of the university.

The next round of student protests crystallised around opposition to the scheduled renewal of the US–Japan Security Treaty in 1960 (see **Anpo struggle**). In 1959, Zengakuren broke away from the Communist Party when students affiliated with the New Left League of Communists gained a majority. Students were at the forefront of the anti-Anpo protests, which climaxed after the night of 15 June 1960, when Tokyo University student Kanba Michiko died after police attacked students. As the old left waited for workers to take centre stage, students took the lead against the treaty renewal. The Anpo protests thus redefined the political role of the students.

Following defeat in the anti-Anpo protests, the student movement once again turned to campus and educational policy issues. Students protested the proposed University Administration Act (Daigaku kanri hōan, or more often, Daikanho). Attempting to prevent a recurrence of the Anpo protests, the government proposed strengthening the powers of national university presidents and the Minister of Education. Ironically, though the Daikanho sought to curb student protest, vociferous student protests prevented its becoming law. Forced to abandon the bill, the government encouraged national universities, and the Ministry of Education put most of its tenets into practice informally. During the mid-1960s, students protested tuition price hikes and co-ordination of educational and industrial policies. At the same time, students also sought issues that could ignite radicalism as the Anpo Treaty had done. Students led protests against the 1965 Japan–Korea Treaty, which they argued would license a new version of Japanese imperialism. Soon afterwards, students began protesting the US presence in Japan and Japanese co-operation in the Vietnam War. The New Left 'Sanpa' Zengakuren (Three Faction Zengakuren) called students to protest harbour visits from US Navy ships carrying nuclear weapons and Prime Minister Sato's visit to Vietnam, as well as the construction of a US military hospital at Ōji.

After 1968, the Zenkyōtō movements at Tokyo and Nihon Universities gained a strong hold of the focus of the student movement. Denying the need for majorities and vanguards, Zenkyōtō organisation departed from previous student movement norms. Typically, Zenkyōtō action took the form of barricade strikes and occupations of campus buildings. Though Zenkyōtō organisations were not by nature violent, neither did they renounce violence. Zenkyōtō's voluntarism, direct democracy and radicalism appealed to students impatient with the New Left's factionalism and the JCP's parliamentarism. Zenkyōtō-style organisations shut down over a hundred Japanese universities, spread to high schools and gained some following among workers and artists, and even elements of the military. As protests spilled into the streets, the state met Zenkyōtō's challenge to hierarchies with a level of repression the movement could not match.

Disillusionment followed the Zenkyōtō movement. Though not directly connected to the Zenkyōtō movement, the violence of New Left groups such as the **Red Army** discredited radical, non-parliamentary action and the left in general. Though radical organising continued through the 1970s, with New Left students playing a major role in the **Narita Airport struggle**, by 1980, Tanaka Yasuo was depicting students as brand-obsessed consumers. By the 1990s, the individualising tendencies of consumer society and the breaking of the chain of organising and activism had left all but a handful of students politically defeatist.

GUY YASKO

suburbanisation

The post-war years have seen a wave of migration out of rural areas and smaller urban centres into the three major metropolises. More than 40 per cent of Japan's population resides today within 50 km of **Ōsaka**, **Nagoya** or **Tokyo**. In the twenty years from 1950 to 1970, the percentage of Japanese dwelling in urban areas showed a staggering increase from 38 per cent to 72 per cent. This pattern of rural to **urban migration** mirrored the shift in the economy from primary to secondary and tertiary industries, with the majority of new economic activity and employment growth in the rapidly developing industrial belt along the narrow band of the Pacific coastal plain.

Although the population growth of Ōsaka and Nagoya has levelled to, or fallen below, national figures over the 1990s, Tokyo continues to grow at higher than the national rate. As the Japanese economy has again shifted gears, this time towards a finance, services and information/communications base, Tokyo has emerged as not only a national centre but a global city acting as an essential axis of the flows of currency, information and labour at the heart of the new global economic order. The robustness of Tokyo as a business centre has seen a continued growth in demand for office space and an ongoing reduction in residential occupancy rates. In 1970, 1.6 million Japanese commuted to work in the Tokyo ward, while by 1990 this had already increased to 3.1 million.

Today, some inner wards of the CBD see a 70 per cent fall between daytime and night-time populations. The inflated land prices of the 'bubble economy' of the late 1980s only intensified the trend for migration out of the inner urban areas to the suburbs. Another significant factor in the development of the 'bed towns' was the fact that Japan's suburbanisation was not characterised by the usual pattern of increased economic activity in the suburban areas. This left many workers with little choice but to face long commutes into the metropolitan centre in order to secure employment. The commuter zone used to delimit the metropolitan area of Tokyo is 70 km.

Development in the suburban areas has focused on residential needs. Shopping centres, local branches of household-related financial services, local government, community services, health and educational facilities, construction and maintenance-related trades and family-oriented support services occupy much of the non-residential space around suburban commuter hubs. Manufacturing has been pushed to the less expensive land at the limits of urban development, creating concentrations of blue-collar worker populations at the margins of the suburban map. There is a marked gender difference in patterns of work and commuting from the suburbs. The vast majority of women living in the suburbs are either non-working or working within their municipal area and it is men, for the most part, who undertake the longer commute to the inner metropolitan areas.

The long hours and distance separating residence from workplace for so many male white-collar workers has led to a number of distinctive areas of concern. The fatigue and stress of long, crowded commuter routes places strain on the health of the commuter, workplace productivity and the quality of family life at home. There has been little research done on the nature of the commuter culture that has developed around the extended period spent daily moving between work and home The impact of the absentee father on families and strain on marital relations have become the focus of considerable research over the 1990s. Despite the **leisure** campaigns of the last decade, there is still little evidence of any significant shift in the level of participation of fathers in domestic duties and child-rearing activities. It is predicted that continued rural to urban migration, and a new wave of baby boomer babies, will see a steady increase in suburban population growth in the first decade of this millennium. This creates some urgency for the need to assess the current state of Japanese suburban life and consider options for enhancing the quality of life of families and communities as the gap between the metropolis and the suburbs continues to widen.

See also: commuting; population; urban migration

Further reading

Okamoto, K (1997) 'Suburbanization of Tokyo and the daily lives of suburban people', in P.P. Karan and K. Stapleton *The Japanese City*, Lexington: University Press of Kentucky pp. 79–105.

SANDRA BUCKLEY

suicide

Suicide rates in Japan are often mistakenly thought to be among the highest in the world, but this is more a reflection of sensationalised images of ritual suicide in popular cultural representations of Japan than the reality of Japan's suicide statistics. Japan sits around the mid-level of international tables of suicide rates but is still often described as having the highest incidence in Asia. The National Police Agency reported 33,048 suicides in 1999. Perhaps the two most striking figures that emerge from closer analysis are that 46.8 per cent of those who committed suicide were unemployed and 71.1 per cent were male, and of these men 41.3 per cent were in the age cohort of forty to sixty. Unemployment alone is not considered a motive for suicide but treated as a contributing factor. That the economic downturn and increased business closures have had an impact on middle-aged male suicide rates does seem to be gaining acknowledgment and finally some attention and action from health and welfare authorities.

In official reports, illness and mental health remain the primary influence in suicide, rating in the high 30 per cent range through the late 1990s. Counselling and psychiatric care still carry a social stigma in Japan for both the individual and their family, and this is thought to be a major influence on the reluctance of individuals to seek essential mental health care. Suicides among elderly living with family are higher than those among physically and financially independent elderly. There is evidence that some elderly choose death rather than enduring long-term chronic or terminal illness, and placing a high burden on family caregivers. The number of elderly suicides among women is significantly higher than for men. Even the longer life expectancy of women cannot fully account for the extent of this gender difference. Feminist sociologists have argued that the life-cycle of women has developed with such a strong focus on caregiving that women become demoralised when they find themselves relying on others for care in old age and often widowed. This has led to calls for the society to find ways of revaluing the last stage of a woman's life-cycle and to create a wider range of support and community options.

That almost 30 per cent of the 2,767 deaths among those in their thirties in 1998 were related to alcoholism is a stark commentary on the institutionalised drinking culture of the Japanese business world. Another characteristic of Japanese suicides is the relatively high number of under-twenty-five suicides, although there has been a marked decline in this age group as drugs frequently used in youth suicides such as tranquillisers and pain killers have become prescription drugs and harder to attain. For all other age groups, death by hanging has become the most frequent mode of suicide (over 50 per cent in 1998), although among young to middle-aged women leaping from buildings and in front of trains is not uncommon. While love suicides remain a highly popular theme in television dramas, especially police programmes, the percentage of suicides related to personal relationships remains relatively low and double suicides (see **double suicide**) of the type often represented in traditional Japanese theatre and contemporary historical film and television drama are rare.

A category of suicide that is always predictably sensationalised by the media is 'family suicide'. In most instances in Japan this is a homicide suicide and the main perpetrator is the mother and not the father, as is more often the case in Western family suicides. The mother commits suicide after taking the lives of her children and usually leaves some form of apology for her action. There is a remarkably high level of sympathy shown in Japan for these 'mother–children' suicides, which seems to reflect a widespread understanding of the levels of pressure and distress that contemporary Japanese wives and mothers can experience without condoning the mother's final action. Seventeen per cent of homicides in Japan are child murders committed by a parent (most often the mother). Child advocacy groups and women's support organisations regularly call for improved support systems, formal and informal, for women in distress. Japan has been criticised for being too slow to create government-funded suicide prevention and intervention programmes and facilities. The major source of support for potential suicides are the networks of telephone hotlines across the country. Trained volunteers staff these facilities sponsored by a number of different religious and non-religious bodies. The longest existing of these hotlines, Life-line (*inochi no denwa*), reports up to 330,000 calls annually.

Further reading

Fuse Toyomasa (1994) 'Trends and patterns of suicide in Japan: Some observations in suicidology', in J. Kovalio (ed.) *Japan in Focus*, Captus: Captus University Publications, pp. 241–63.

SANDRA BUCKLEY

sukiyaki

This beef-based dish did not come into existence until the mid-nineteenth century, after the initiation of a second period of extensive contact with Westerners and the consumption of meat. The dish is a variation on the many popular recipes that combine simmered noodles with different combinations of seafood and vegetables in broth and, like these, it is usually cooked in a cast-iron pot or flat dish over a low but concentrated flame. This style of cooking beef is thought to have originated in the

Ōsaka and Kobe areas, where there was a significant traffic in foreign sailors and traders.

SANDRA BUCKLEY

sumo wrestling

This 2,000-year-old traditional form of Japanese wrestling has long captured the imagination of foreigners, but only in the late 1990s has there been any regular coverage of sumo tournaments on television networks outside Japan. Sumo is renowned for the sheer physical size of the wrestlers. Sustaining body weights often in excess of 300 lbs and eating a specially prepared traditional diet, wrestlers combine size with strength, manoeuvrability and strategy to defeat their opponents in the ring. For their bouts the wrestlers wear a distinctive thick band (*mawashi*) wound around the belly and secured about the groin while exposing the buttocks. In official fights, a decorative 'apron' (*sagari*) is added to the front of the band. The aim of a sumo match is for one wrestler to force the other out of the ring or to cause any part of their opponent, other than a foot, to touch the ground within the circle.

Wrestlers are recruited from the nationwide circuit of amateur sumo clubs and taken into a sumo stable (*heya*), where they train long and arduous days for years before working their way up to compete in a ranked tournament (*basho*). The traditional high-protein diet prepared and eaten everyday in the sumo stable promotes the extraordinary weight and size of the wrestlers. There are six annual *basho*, each lasting fifteen days. The sumo *basho* are held in different cities with the best seats selling long in advance. These days, sumo is both a popular corporate fringe benefit for executives and their guests and a sought-after opportunity among corporate sponsors wanting to see their logo paraded at the beginning of a major bout between high-profile wrestlers. For the most part, though, sumo remains a spectator sport with a largely non-elite audience. Today, sumo wrestlers have regained the celebrity status they enjoyed in the first heyday of competitive public sumo wrestling in the Edo Period. Its association with older traditions saw a wane in popularity during the period of rapid modernisation from Meiji (1868–1914), while links between the rituals and symbolism of the imperial household and sumo dampened any possibility of revival during the early post-war period. A visit to one of the sumo stables by the Emperor was arranged as part of a strategy to create a new popularist image for the post-war Emperor. Despite an initial controversy, this visit generated broad-based media attention for both the Emperor and sumo, and reopened the way for a new popularisation of the sport. This wave of sumo popularity has been closely linked to the spread of television sports coverage and the related phenomenon of corporate sponsorship and the media creation of sports idols. Today, the top wrestlers are again seen side by side with famous actors, singers and other popular public figures – no longer the subject of woodblock prints but the sought-after feature celebrity story for weekly magazines, sports newspapers and talk shows.

Sumo is a highly ritualised performance at the same time that it is a sport of carefully mastered skills. Foreigners unfamiliar with the details of the ritual that surround each match of a tournament can find the experience slow. The time involved in the ritual purification of the ring before a match and the introduction of both the sponsors and then the wrestlers all takes far more time than the often very brief encounters in the ring. The two wrestlers engage in an intense period of silent staring broken by occasional slight movement, but only when one of the wrestlers finally lunges forward out of the semi-squatting start position does the match move from a battle of nerves to a battle of strength and skill. Seventy moves are listed as approved techniques to gain a win. The match is officiated by a figure whose role is a blend of referee and ritual master. He is dressed in traditional costume of brocaded silk and carries a ceremonial board by which he marks his decisions. The language of the sumo ring is a highly stylised pre-modern Japanese close to some ceremonial and religious chanting in intonation and style.

Sumo has faced some significant challenges in recent years. From the 1960s, the first young Hawaiian sumo wrestlers were recruited into Japanese stables to much outcry from stalwarts who saw this as an affront to a Japanese traditional sport. Although the Japan Sumo Association (Nihon Sumo Kyōkai) defended the initial decision not to promote foreigners to the top rank of **yokozuna**, the rhetoric around this debate was often highly nationalistic, even xenophobic. However, attitudes slowly shifted and a number of foreign wrestlers have gained a popular following over the 1990s and risen to high ranks, including *yokozuna*. In the year 2000, the female mayor of Ōsaka challenged the taboo on women setting foot in the sumo ring when she was refused the traditional opening role as mayor of the host city for a **basho**. She finally relinquished her stand but not before significant media attention fell on the controversy. There has also been increased interest in the health of the wrestlers whose body frames carry extraordinary levels of weight for many years. Weight control, blood pressure, heart attack, joint and bone deterioration are just some of the health problems faced both during and after a wrestling career. A number of financial and gambling scandals struck sumo in the late 1990s, together with exposés in the media of the often harsh conditions under which young wrestlers are apprenticed within the hierarchy of a stable. Despite these setbacks, there has been little impact on the tremendous popularity of this national sport, which is still capable of bringing the country to a virtual standstill for the brief minutes of a hotly contested title match for *yokozuna*.

SANDRA BUCKLEY

Suna no onna

The film *Suna no onna* (Woman in the Dunes) tells the story of an entomologist, Niki Junpei, who takes a brief research trip to the seashore. He is imprisoned in a woman's home in a surreal village of houses in deep sand pits. Forced to labour by shovelling sand for profit by the village collective, Niki tries to escape. Eventually immersed in a project that unexpectedly offers a much needed technique for collecting water, and intimately involved with the woman, Niki discovers meaningfulness. Given the opportunity to escape, he chooses to remain there instead. A visually stunning film, directed by **Teshigahara Hiroshi**, and based on **Abe Kōbō**'s book by the same title, it won the 1963 Cannes Film Festival jury prize.

Further reading

McDonald, K.I. (1983) *Cinema East: A Critical Study of Major Japanese Films*, London and Toronto: Associated University Presses.

NINA CORNYETZ

sunshine rights

Sunshine rights (*nisshōken*) stem from cultural values that place great importance on a property's right to sunlight. They are supported by a Supreme Court decision in 1972, resulting in a highly restrictive sun-shadow law (*hikage kisei*), passed in 1976 as Article 56–2 of the Building Standards Law (*kenchiku kijun ho*).

Spurred on by **citizens' movements** protesting high-rise housing projects that overshadowed and infringed upon the privacy of low-rise urban dwellers, this law (enforced since 1977) stipulates that one's building cannot cast shadows or otherwise interfere with neighbouring property rights to sunlight for more than a prescribed number of hours in a day. For example, between 8 a.m. and 4 p.m. shadows measured at a plane of 4 m from the ground on adjacent property cannot be cast for more than 2.5 hours a day within 10 m of the property line, or 4 hours within 5 m. Building heights are indirectly restricted, causing buildings designed for maximum height to be set back in order to avoid shadow-casting and resulting in the pyramid-like tops or staggered roof designs characteristic of the inner-urban skyline. Difficulties meeting sun-shadow building regulations often arise in cases of multiple adjacent properties. Zoning codes determine the permitted amount of shadow, with no restriction for commercial zoning, and the strictest laws reserved for residential zoning.

ICHIRO SUZUKI AND SCOTT GOLD

supermarkets and superstores

The appearance of supermarkets in the early 1950s changed Japan's retail scene irrevocably and created competition for the previously two dominant sectors, department stores and small family businesses.

Unlike department stores, supermarkets as an emerging industry were not subject to industry regulation, an element contributing to their rapid expansion. Due in part to the agitation of department stores and small family-run stores, the Large-scale Retail Store Law was passed in 1973. Major revisions to the size of establishment covered under, and permitted by, the Large-scale Retail Store Law in 1991 created a development explosion with the construction of large shopping centres and superstores, and supermarket chains opening new stores in suburban and urbanising rural areas.

The retail industry has relied heavily on women to provide full-time and part-time staffing needs. The expansion of the supermarket sector in the 1970s was able to absorb the growing numbers of married women retrenched from the recession-affected manufacturing industries.

In the 1980s, large supermarket chains expanded their range of services beyond the usual groceries, clothing and household goods to include travel, leisure, finance, insurance and real estate.

See also: gender and work; part-time work; *shōtengai*

KAYE BROADBENT

Supreme Commander for Allied Powers

Supreme Commander for Allied Powers (SCAP) refers to the chief executive of the Allied Occupation of Japan, as well as his General Headquarters (GHQ), which was also responsible for the US forces in the Far East. SCAP took its orders only from the Far Eastern Commission in Washington, but consulted with other Allied powers in Japan. In reality, SCAP-GHQ was almost entirely staffed by

US military and civilian bureaucrats, numbering 3,200 at its peak in early 1948. Few of them had substantial knowledge of Japan, or spoke the language. Many had experience working in the US federal government during the New Deal; others only held local positions in the USA. Most SCAP members shared a high degree of motivation and optimism.

Unlike the military government in occupied Germany, SCAP organisations approximately paralleled the existing Japanese bureaucracy. In addition to military staffs, SCAP-GHQ was divided into seventeen sections, each responsible for direct contact with a Japanese agency. All major policy decisions had to be approved by SCAP, with General Douglas **MacArthur** holding the final say. SCAP initiated or accelerated a wide range of sweeping reforms that affected nearly every aspect of Japanese society. Its Government Section essentially drafted Japan's post-war Constitution, on the basis of a few guidelines set by MacArthur himself. In addition to its unprecedented renunciation of war in Article 9, the Constitution stipulated equal rights for women, in part thanks to the vigorous efforts by female SCAP staff members.

SCAP oversaw demilitarisation and the purge of about 200,000 Japanese military, government and business leaders. In economic matters, SCAP initiated anti-trust measures and the *zaibatsu dissolution*. It encouraged labour unions and the introduction of labour standards, and promoted **land reform**, building on the previous work of some Japanese bureaucrats. SCAP also sought to democratise education in both content and structure. Though it mostly worked through Japanese bureaucracy, SCAP exercised direct control over censorship of the Japanese media, allowing no public criticism of its own policies or the USA.

During 1947–8, shifting geo-political situations in East Asia and the continued weak economy in Japan convinced policy-makers in Washington and SCAP to alter some of these reform programmes, embarking on what some have termed a 'reverse course'. The radical labour movement was suppressed, and there was a purge of the leftists (see **Red Purge**), who had at first welcomed and collaborated with SCAP. At the same time, the earlier purges of those with links to militarism were lifted. Economic deconcentration measures were halted in favour of a rapid recovery, thus allowing many business interests to regroup. Other SCAP reforms were reversed after the end of the Occupation. On the whole, however, many of the earlier reforms remained in effect. General Douglas MacArthur was SCAP until November 1951, when he was relieved of his duty and replaced by General Matthew Ridgeway. Four months later, SCAP-GHQ was abolished when the Occupation of Japan came to an end.

See also: US–Japan relations

Further reading

Dower, J.W. (1999) *Embracing Defeat: Japan in the Aftermath of War*, New York: Norton.
Schaller, M. (1985) *American Occupation of Japan*, New York: Oxford University Press.

DAQING YANG

surrender

The Shōwa Emperor's radio broadcast at noon on 15 August 1945, announcing the end of the Second World War, is the most powerfully symbolic moment in Japan's twentieth-century history. The eight years of fighting prior to **Hirohito**'s announcement that the war had 'developed not necessarily to Japan's advantage' and that Japan would now have to 'endure the unendurable' had seen nearly 3 million Japanese killed (and perhaps 15 million other Asians), rendered 9 million Japanese homeless and destroyed a quarter of Japan's wealth. Two weeks after the announcement, Japan's first foreign conquerors arrived to begin the **Allied Occupation**; within two years a new **post-war Constitution** institutionalised democracy, created a **symbol monarchy** and renounced war; and, by 1968, the '**Japanese economic miracle**' had produced the world's third largest Gross National Product.

The Instrument of Surrender was signed on board the USS Missouri in Tokyo Bay on 2 September 1945. Hirohito was spared the indignity of attending, but announced that his government had surrendered at his command and that his subjects should respect the agreement ending all hostilities and placing the government under the control of General Douglas **MacArthur, Supreme Commander for Allied Powers** (SCAP).

The Emperor's role in ending the war fought in his name has been the focus of much controversy. SCAP and the Tokyo war crimes trials described Hirohito, as he did himself, as a distant constitutional monarch unable or unwilling to influence policy decisions until the very end. More recently, documents have shown that he was well informed and closely involved in major decisions on many occasions. In February 1945, former Premier Prince Konoe Fumimarō urged the Emperor to end the war before a revolution destroyed the imperial system. Hirohito instead gambled that one decisive victory might enable Japan to end the war on more advantageous terms. However, the disastrous Battle of Okinawa began in April, hopes for Soviet mediation came to nothing and Hirohito's 'sacred decision' to end the war was not made until after the **atomic bombings** of Hiroshima and Nagasaki on 6 and 9 August and the Soviet Union's entry into the war on 8 August.

The other controversy about the surrender concerns whether the atomic bombs were necessary to end the war. Some advisers to US President Truman suggested that Japan would surrender if it were assured that the Emperor could be retained, and the US Strategic Bombing Survey estimated after the war that Japan would likely have surrendered by November even without the atomic bombs or an invasion. However, the Allies' **Potsdam Declaration** of 26 July threatened Japan with 'utter destruction' unless it surrendered unconditionally. The Japanese government at first chose to ignore the declaration, but on 9 August Hirohito agreed to its acceptance on the condition that the Allies clarify the status of the throne. They replied that after the surrender the Emperor and government would be subject to SCAP, but reiterated the Potsdam Declaration's statement that ultimately Japan's form of government, including presumably the role of the Emperor, would be determined by 'the freely expressed will of the Japanese people'. When top leaders disagreed on 14 August over whether to accept these vague assurances, the Emperor chose surrender.

Further reading

Butow, R. (1954) *Japan's Decision to Surrender*, Stanford: Stanford University Press.

Hogan, M. (ed.) (1996) *Hiroshima in History and Memory*, Cambridge: Cambridge University Press.

Sigal, L. (1988) *Fighting to a Finish: The Politics of War Termination in the United States and Japan, 1945*, Ithaca, New York: Cornell University Press.

US Strategic Bombing Survey (1946) *Japan's Struggle to End the War*, Washington, DC: US Government Printing Office.

TIMOTHY S. GEORGE

sushi

Sushi is perhaps Japan's most notable cultural export. There are various types of sushi, although most foreigners are only familiar with *nigiri-zushi* (a hand-pressed mound of **rice** covered with a strip of freshly sliced raw fish or shellfish), *makizushi* (a hand-rolled sushi with a centre filling of fish and/or vegetables rolled in rice and wrapped with an outside layer of toasted seaweed) and *temakizushi* (a vertical cone-shaped wrapping of toasted seaweed surrounding a core of fish and/or vegetables and rice). The art of not only cutting the fish but selecting the best fish at the markets, producing a perfect blend of rice wine, soy and bonito for the house sauce, and the care and sharpening of the sushi knives are just a few of the many talents of a top sushi chef. Most of the sushi chefs outside Japan have not undergone the same level of close apprenticeship as their colleagues at home. This has not stopped sushi from emerging as one of the most popular foreign foods of young affluent consumers across the world.

What many non-Japanese do not realise is the importance of the texture and flavour of the rice base in achieving a high quality of sushi. One popular method for achieving the right consistency of rice is to add the rice kernels to hot, not cold, water and then to cool the cooked rice very quickly using a hand fan, or these days even an electric one, while gently turning the vinegar and other ingredients into the rice as it cools.

If there is one secret that all foreigners should know before attempting to bite into their first morsel of sushi, it is simply to always turn the sushi rice side up and dip only the fish into the soy sauce or else the rice portion will disintegrate into a hundred pieces, much to the amusement of all around you. Most Japanese will eat sushi with chopsticks in restaurants but at home it is not at all unusual to use just fingers. As a rule, sushi should be eaten within two hours of preparation to avoid any problems of toxicity. It is safest to have raw-fish sushi prepared by a professional chef who is trained to notice blemishes and differences in texture, which might indicate that the fish is not fresh or has some form of worm or other parasite. Eating any flesh uncooked carries a degree of risk; however, a good sushi restaurant will build its reputation on the quality and freshness of its fish. The green *wasabi* mustard is also used as a partial protection against tainted fish.

SANDRA BUCKLEY

Suzuki Seijun

b. 1923, Tokyo

Film director and actor

One of the post-war's most influential cult film directors, Suzuki entered Shōchiku in 1948 but did not direct his first film until after he moved to Nikkatsu in 1954. His early work was mostly routine B-movie melodrama and youth films. As **Nikkatsu Action** began developing as a mode, Suzuki started moulding a flashy and boisterous camera and colour style in such action films as *Yajū no seishun* (Youth of the Beast), *Kenka ereji* (Elegy to Violence) and *Tōkyō nagaremono* (Tokyo Drifter), which, coupled with the art direction of Kimura Takeo, threatened to overwhelm the narrative through a unique pursuit of the nature of the cinematic image. His outrageous lack of realism gained him a cult following among intellectuals, but also the disfavour of Nikkatsu, which fired him in 1968 for his 'incomprehensible' *Koroshi no rakuin* (Branded to Kill). A collective protest politicised the event, but Suzuki did not direct again until 1978, a break during which he began acting. In his subsequent work such as *Tsuigoineruwaizen* (Zigeuneruweisen), he has shed the genre framework to pursue an art-film style, the **ero guro**

(eroticism, grotesquerie and nonsense) of the Taishō era he loves.

AARON GEROW

sword movies

The term 'sword movies' has been used to connote both *chambara* (swordfight films), a sub-genre whose name is derived from the onomatopoeia representing the background music for the silent films to which era they date back, and the much broader genre of samurai films. Such films were severely restricted by Allied Occupation forces immediately following the Second World War and were thus rarely made at that time. Thriving upon their revival in the early 1950s, they frequently depicted legendary samurai heroes and noble or daring acts and rituals, clan conflicts, protection of the innocent and the ethical path of the samurai code of *bushidō* ('the way of the warrior').

During the 1960s, these films became bleaker and more violent, often featuring nihilistic *rōnin* (masterless samurai; literally 'wave men') and other anti-heroes doomed by decaying traditions and endemic clan corruption. Although historically the period associated with the samurai class ranges from the late twelfth century until 1868, most sword films are set near or during the Tokugawa Period (1600–1868), an era of peace in Japan but the time of samurai inactivity and decline. The ultimate defeat of samurai codes and spirit during the Second World War is thus partly reflected in the themes and storylines of many of these samurai films.

The popularity of the sword film genre declined immensely during the 1970s due to changing Japanese interests, a rise in the *yakuza* (gangster) film genre, over-formulaic approaches to sword movies and a declining Japanese film box office. Since then, the few new samurai films have been primarily large-budget epics.

WILLIAM C. THOMPSON

symbol monarchy

The term 'symbol monarchy' requires explanation. Article 1 of the **post-war Constitution** transformed the Emperor from an inviolable sovereign to 'the symbol of the State and of the unity of the people, deriving his position from the will of the people with whom reside sovereign power'. The Japanese came to refer to the constitutionally redefined monarchy as the 'symbol emperor' (*shōchō tennō*) or as the 'symbol emperor system' (*shōchō tennōsei*). The term 'symbolic monarchy' is better understood outside Japan, however. These terms capture Japanese expectations for their monarchy: that its role be only symbolic and ceremonial. Although these terms imply a contrast with the pre-war monarchy that lay at the centre of the political process, they are problematic, for they suggest that the pre-war monarchy was political but not symbolic, and that the post-war monarchy is symbolic but not political. Yet the boundaries between the symbolic and the political cannot be drawn so easily.

The symbolic monarchy has been distinguished by impassioned public debates about its symbolic nature, issues which fit an expanded definition of what is political. Many of the Emperor's symbolic acts, such as Emperor Akihito's apologies during the 1990s to neighbouring countries for Japan's actions during the war, have carried political significance, although measuring their resonance is a far more imprecise enterprise than computing the increase in governmental revenues resulting from a change in the sales tax. Precisely because of its symbolic role, the monarchy has retained a certain centrality in post-war Japan. At the two extremes, left-wing groups have protested violently against the monarchy on occasion, while right-wing groups have resorted to violent action to protect the dignity of the throne. In fact, Japanese of all political inclinations have contested the meaning of the monarchy, and thus of Japanese national identity, throughout the post-war era.

There are many ways to periodise the history of the symbolic monarchy. One could divide this history into three periods: first, reform: 1945–7; second, shaping of the symbolic monarchy even while its legitimacy remained in question: 1947 to the late 1950s, early 1960s; and, third, ongoing contestation over the symbolic monarchy: late 1950s, early 1960s to the present. Both 1945, the year of Japan's disastrous defeat, and 1947, the year that the post-war Constitution went into effect,

were major disjunctures. It is difficult, however, to be more precise regarding the year that the symbolic monarchy provided for by the Occupation-era Constitution was legitimised. Other important turning points, such as the Occupation's conclusion in 1952, Crown Prince Akihito's wedding in 1959, and Emperor Hirohito's death in 1989, further complicate this periodisation.

The present monarchy, politically and culturally, has been shaped profoundly by the Occupation-era Constitution and fifty years of social evolution. Conservative Japanese regard the monarchy as the symbol of timeless Japanese culture, as the embodiment of 'traditional' customs and beliefs. The monarchy's cultural importance ranges from its central role in the national system of bestowing honour to the national holidays celebrated in its honour. One post-war interpretation has proposed that the present symbolic monarchy represents a return to the lengthy Japanese tradition of emperors serving ceremonial, cultural roles and remaining above the political process. The interpretation that the post-war symbolic monarchy represents a return to pre-modern tradition, while not fanciful in broad terms, brushes over the fact that the present monarchy has very little in common with its pre-modern ancestor. Even though the post-war evolute of the monarchy differs considerably from its pre-war antecedent, it has far more in common with its pre-war ancestor than with its pre-modern one. Not only as a politico-legal institution, but also as a cultural institution, the present monarchy is largely a construct of the modern era. An appropriate label for the post-war evolute of the imperial house would be 'symbolic constitutional monarchy under popular sovereignty', a description that hardly applies to the institution's pre-modern ancestor.

In theoretical terms, the existence of a hereditary royal family seems antithetical to democracy, the founding principle of post-war Japan. Indeed, for some Japanese, the throne has represented all that was said to be undemocratic about Japan. However, for other Japanese, the throne has served as a powerful symbol of democracy. This was the case in 1959 when the present emperor, Akihito (1933–), as crown prince wed someone from outside the former aristocracy. At a time when constitutional revision was under official consideration, the popularity of Crown Prince Akihito's 'love match' marriage (as opposed to an arranged marriage) to a 'commoner' served to remind politicians of the people's attachment to the principle of equality (Article 14 of the post-war Constitution) as well as to the principle that 'Marriage shall be based only on the mutual consent of both sexes' (Article 24). Through constitutional debates, social movements, popular discourse and manœuvring by the palace itself, the monarchy has become embedded thoroughly in Japan's post-war culture of democracy.

Until 1989, Emperor Hirohito, who had been groomed to be sovereign, remained on the throne. In contrast, the present emperor, Akihito, was groomed to be a 'symbolic emperor' under the post-war Constitution. Since ascending to the throne, Akihito has reformed palace practices that he considered to be outdated. For example, the position of 'imperial stool analyser' was abolished. Thus, Emperor Akihito's stool has not been subjected to analysis each time he has had a bowel movement, as was the case with his father. Emperor Akihito also has worked with Empress Michiko to project an informal style and to reach out to the people in ways that contrasted with Emperor Hirohito and Empress Nagako. For example, when Emperor Akihito is ready to read his statement at ceremonies such as the opening of the National Athletic Meet, he simply retrieves it from his pocket. In his father's time, a courtier formally handed over the statement at the appropriate moment.

Further reading

Dower, John W. (1999) *Embracing Defeat: Japan in the Wake of World War II*, New York: W.W. Norton/ The New Press.

Ruoff, Kenneth J. (2001) *The Symbolic Monarchy in Japan's Postwar Democracy, 1945–1995: Royalism in an Age of Popular Sovereignty*, Cambridge, MA: published by the Harvard University Asia Center and distributed by Harvard University Press.

Seizelet, Eric (1990) *Monarchie et democratie dans le Japon d'après-guerre*, Paris: Maisonneuve & Larose.

KENNETH RUOFF

T

tachiyomi

Standing and reading is the direct translation of *tachiyomi* (book browsing), which describes one of the simplest and least expensive commuter pastimes. At any time of day, but especially during peak commuter periods, there will be rows of people browsing the shelves of a bookstore or huddled around new-release magazine and comics displays. Any foreigner visiting Japan cannot help but be struck by the number of bookshops, new and second-hand, and magazine stands. No one, however, is expected to buy without browsing and many who browse buy nothing. There is no pressure on a browser who lingers over a book or magazine and there is an unstated etiquette to the culture of browsing that includes handling the materials with care, replacing books on the shelf exactly and avoiding splitting a book spine. Few books or magazines other than pornographic materials are clearwrapped in Japan. Even very expensive volumes are available on the shelf. Commuters often have alternative *tachiyomi* routes that take them home via a number of different book and magazine shops on different days, allowing them to see the full range of new publications. In a print-oriented culture with a publishing industry as large as Japan's, the sheer number of new titles can keep the most avid browser busy from week to week.

SANDRA BUCKLEY

Taifū kurabu

Sōmai Shinji produced *Taifū kurabu* (Typhoon Club) in 1985, after having turned several idol films into complex investigations of youth. This cinematic narrative depicts a handful of middle schoolers stuck at school during a typhoon and explores their adolescent sexual awakening within a restrictive social environment. However, it is Sōmai's one scene, one shot photography that masterfully combines a rhythmic festival of the body with an existential awareness of death. This long-take style not only established Sōmai as one of the leading directors of the 1980s, but it also became the dominant formal choice of independent cinema for the next decade.

AARON GEROW

tainted-blood scandal

The Japanese Health Ministry waited until December 1985 to require the heat treatment of blood products in order to prevent the transmission of HIV. As a result of this delay, 40 per cent of Japanese haemophiliacs were infected with HIV. To make matters worse, the pharmaceutical company Green Cross (Midori Jūji) continued to sell its reserves of unheated blood products even after the government's ban.

Despite the AIDS-related death in August 1983 of a haemophiliac patient, the Ministry continued to insist that Japan remained untouched by AIDS. Health Ministry documents referred to domestic cases as 'pseudo-AIDS' (*giji shōrei*) until a gay Japanese man living in New York but home for a brief visit was officially declared Japan's first case of 'genuine AIDS' (*shinsei* AIDS) on 23 March 1985. The Japanese government was determined to identify AIDS as a 'foreign' problem. The fact that some of the tainted blood used to treat Japanese haemophiliacs was imported from the USA only complicated this situation further. In March 1996, a group of Japanese haemophiliacs accepted a one-time payment of 45 million yen each from the state and five pharmaceutical firms. Subsequently, several drug company executives and government bureaucrats were convicted on charges of criminal negligence. The fact that many haemophiliacs were not told of their own infections by their doctors and unknowingly infected others highlighted the dangers of medical paternalism in Japan and helped spur a movement for patients' rights.

See also: AIDS

KEITH VINCENT

Takada Kenzō

b. 1939, Hyogo Prefecture

Fashion designer

Takada Kenzō is a clothing designer whose name has become a brand mark known across the world of *haute couture*. He dropped out of Kobe Shiritsu University and graduated from the Bunkafukush-oku (cultural dress) Institute at Godai University. He went to Paris in 1965 to pursue an international career in fashion design. In 1970, he opened his boutique, 'Jungle Jap'. In the same year, one of his designs was featured on the cover of *Elle* magazine and won him instant international attention.

Inspired by Japanese everyday clothing, his casual and unpretentious style perfectly captures the mood of the 1970s. As the standard bearer for prêt-à-porter fashion in the 1970s, his annual designer lines became the height of fashion along with the likes of Yves St Laurent. He has remained true to his love of bright colours and strong

contrasts of texture and pattern, and his designs are renowned for a colourful mix 'n' match of diverse ethnic elements with the style of *haute couture*.

AKIKO FUKAI

Takahashi Gen'ichirō

b. 1951, Onomichi, Hiroshima Prefecture

Writer

Takahashi Gen'ichirō is one of most outstanding writers and critics of his generation. Because of his father's work-related relocations, he lived in a variety of places. He attended junior high school in Tokyo but senior high school in Kobe. He enrolled in the economics faculty at Yokohama National University in 1969 but, due to his participation in radical student politics, and thus his non-atten-dance, his enrolment lapsed in 1977. According to the author's published account, he worked as a labourer until 1981. In that year, his novel *Sayonara gyangutachi* (Goodbye to the Gang) won the Gunzō New Writers' Award and launched him on a literary career.

In 1984, he published *Ōbaa za reinbō* (Over the Rainbow), which was quickly followed three months later by a photo-book *Oyogu otoko* (The Swimming Man). The following year, he published *Jon Renon tai kaseijin* (John Lennon versus the Martians). In the same year, his first collection of essays was published, the first of many such volumes to follow in the years to come. One of his suggestions formed the basis of a jointly written screenplay, which was made into the film *Birii za kiddo no atarashii yoake* (The Dawn of Billy the Kid, 1986), directed by Yamakawa Naoto.

His novel *Yūga de kanshōteki Nihon yakkyū* (Languid and Sentimental Japanese Baseball, 1987) won a prestigious literary award. His literary columns in the journal *Kaien* were published in 1989 along with cartoon illustrations under the title *Bungaku ga konna ni wakatte ii kashira* (Is it Okay to Understand Literature so Well?), and consolidated his reputa-tion as a quintessentially post-modern writer. Other novels include *Pengin mura ni hi ga ochite* (Sundown in Penguin Town, 1989), *Wakusei P-13 no himitsu* (The Secret Of Planet P-13, 1989) and *Gōsutobasutaazu bōken shōsetsu* (Ghostbusters: An Adventure Novel, 1997).

His essay collections are numerous and equally well known, many of them focusing on literary and cultural criticism. He published in serial form in 1997 a parodic history of Japanese literature. This work was in some sense a culmination of his literary criticism. He has also written on horse racing and worked as a sports commentator for television.

Takahashi has pioneered a genre-crossing pop fiction written for *aficionados*. He attacks the conventions of 'serious fiction' using comics characters, cartoons, parody and deliberate kitsch to shake up the novel. His work has achieved much acclaim.

Select bibliography

Takahashi Gen'ichirō (1997) *Gōsutobasutaazu bōken shōsetsu*, Tokyo: Kōdansha.
—— (1991) 'Christopher Columbus discovers America' in Alfred Birnbaum, (ed.) *Monkey Brain Sushi: New Tastes in Japanese Fiction*, Tokyo: Kōdansha International.
—— (1992) *Bungaku ga konna ni wakatte ii kashira*, Tokyo: Fukutake Bunko.

LEITH MORTON

Takahashi Takako

b. 1932, Kyōto

Writer

Takahashi Takako is one of many outstanding women writers who has come to public notice since the 1970s. She attended Kyōto University majoring in French literature; her graduation thesis (1954) was on Charles Baudelaire and her Master's thesis on François Mauriac (1958). She has published translations of French writers, including Mauriac. Six months after her graduation in 1954, she married the famous novelist Takahashi Kazumi (1931–71), who apparently inspired her to write fiction. Her short stories were published in various collections issued in the 1970s and established her reputation as a significant novelist. Many of her works written during this period received literary prizes, including *Sora no hate made* (To the End of the Sky, 1973), *Yūwakusha* (The Temptress, 1976) and 'Ronrii uuman' (Lonely Woman, 1977).

Takahashi established a reputation as a writer of fantasy, but with a strong erotic focus in such short-story collections as *Hone no shiro* (Castle of Bones, 1972). Her interest in Roman Catholicism became manifest after her conversion to the Roman Catholic faith in 1975. Her use of 'Gothic' motifs and dark, surrealist techniques parallels similar modes of fiction employed by her contemporaries. Other important works include 'Sōjikei' (Congruent Figures, 1972) 'Ningyō no ai' (Doll Love, 1976), *Yomigaeri no ie* (The House of Rebirth, 1980), *Yosōi seyo, waga tamashii yo* (Gird up Thyself, O My Soul, 1982) and *Ikari no ko* (Child of Rage, 1985).

After the publication of *Ikari no ko*, Takahashi became a Roman Catholic nun and entered a convent in Paris to pursue the religious life. With this decision, Takahashi abandoned writing. She lived as a nun in Paris until 1988 and then returned to Japan to enter a Roman Catholic convent of a different order. In an interview in 1994, Takahashi revealed that she had left the formal religious life in 1990 but continued her religious devotion outside the convent. In the same interview, Takahashi spoke of the possibility of resuming her career as a writer.

Takahashi's fiction is complex and powerful. Her stories vary from sado-masochistic fantasies to apparently autobiographical accounts of spiritual crises. However, this very complexity and her focus on gender issues has assured her of an important place among contemporary writers.

Select bibliography

Lippit, Noriko M. and Selden, Kyoko I. (eds.) (1982) 'Congruent figures', in *Stories by Contemporary Japanese Writers*, New York: M.E. Sharp Inc.
Yukiko Tanaka and Hanson, Elizabeth (eds) (1982) 'Doll love', in *This Kind of Woman*, Stanford: Stanford University Press.

Further reading

Maryellen Mori (1996) 'The quest for jouissance in Takahashi Takako's Texts', in Paul Schalow and

Janet Walker (eds) (1996) *The Woman's Hand*, Stanford: Stanford University Press, pp. 205–35.
—— (1993) 'The subversive role of fantasy in the fiction of Takahashi Takako', *Journal of the Association of Teachers of Japanese* 28(1): 29–56.

LEITH MORTON

Takakura Ken

1924, Fukuoka Prefecture

Film actor

Star of many Tōei gangster film (see **gangster films**) series such as *Shōwa zankyōden* (Story of the Last Gangsters of the Shōwa Era), Takakura's image as a traditional and stoic lone-wolf gangster, enduring the machinations of modernised mobsters until compelled to commit a final cathartic moment of revenge, made him the hero of both mass- and counter-culture audiences in the 1960s. The shift away from these films left him with roles on the side of the law, but leading parts in US movies like *Black Rain* and *Mr Baseball* ensured his status as a symbol of Japanese masculinity.

AARON GEROW

Takamatsu Shin

b. 1948, Shimane Prefecture

Architect

Graduated from Kyōto University (Ph.D.) in engineering research, Takamatsu Shin opened his own office, Takamatsu Shin Architect and Associates, in 1980. In the 1980s, the Kyōto-based Takamatsu first drew attention on the architecture scene with Hinaya Home Office, or Origin I (Kyōto, 1981), and followed it with a series of other machine-like architectural projects. Origin I is a heavy, dark building of red stone with bolted steel accents and concrete, without windows; its front entrance is vertically extended as a repeating cut-out door shape revealing a lit-up interior core, and finally culminating in an oval opening reminiscent of a robot's head or a Cyclops's eye. Takamatsu expresses his dark vision in stark geometric shapes

and brutal materials such as steel plates, girders and rivets; industrial cables; unfinished reinforced concrete; jointed and exposed steel pipes and ducts; black granite. The ambivalent qualities of anthropomorphic machines arouse admiration as technological feats yet also anxiety as unforgiving, anti-humanist displays. Takamatsu's Kirin Plaza (Ōsaka, 1987) appears in director Ridley Scott's gangster film *Black Rain*, dramatising the dystopic qualities of his architecture. Takamatsu's best-known works include: Origin II/III (Kyōto, 1982/1986); Ark (Fushimi, 1981); Pharaoh (Kyōto, 1983); Syntax (Kyōto, 1990); Solaris (Hyogo, 1990); and Earthtecture Sub 1 (Tokyo, 1991). Many of his larger and later works, such as Kunibiki Messe (Shimane, 1993), emphasise pure geometric forms, natural elements and interior space over industrial decadence and exterior design.

Further reading

(1993) 'Special Issue: Shin Takamatsu', *JA Library: The Japan Architect* (spring) 1.
(1994) 'The wave of neo-modern', in *JA: The Japan Architect* (summer) 14(2).

SCOTT GOLD AND MARY KNIGHTON

Takamine Hideko

b. 1924, Hokkaidō Prefecture

Film actress

One of the leading actresses in film melodrama, Takamine entered the industry in 1929 and, with a teenage image as a cheerful and indefatigable girl, by the post-war became one of the few child stars to successfully make the transition to adult roles. While she showed her acting range in such post-war satires as *Karumen kokyō ni kaeru* (Carmen Comes Home), her performances as strong but tragic women in films directed by **Kinoshita Keisuke** and **Naruse Mikio** (Ukigumo (Floating Clouds)) helped articulate melodramatically the national memory of suffering during and after the war.

AARON GEROW

Takamure Itsue

b. 1894, Kumamoto Prefecture; d. 1964, Tokyo

Feminist historian

Takamure Itsue worked as a teacher in Kyūshū before moving to Tokyo and publishing collections of poetry and essays. She edited the anarchist women's journal *Fujin sensen* and contributed to other publications. She devoted her life to **women's history**, with the support of husband Hashimoto Kenzō, and completed major works on the history of marriage systems, female emperors in pre-modern Japan and the history of women in Japan.

Further reading

Tsurumi, E.P. (1985) 'Feminism and anarchism in Japan: Takamure Itsue, 1894–1964, *Bulletin of Concerned Asian Scholars* 17(2): 2–19.

VERA MACKIE

Takarazuka

The Takurazuka Kagekidan (Takarazuka Opera Company) is an all-female musical theatre troupe based in the town of Takarazuka outside Ōsaka. The troupe was founded in 1913 by Kobayashi Ichizō, a well-known figure in both politics and entertainment. First established as the Takarazuka Girls' Choir, it was renamed quickly in 1913 to capitalise on the tremendous popularity of opera at that time. A permanent stage theatre seating 4,000 was constructed in 1923–4. By this time, the troupe was also regularly touring and performing to large audiences in other cities. The extent of the popularity of the troupe nationwide was evidenced in the decision to construct a Takarazuka theatre in Tokyo in 1934. Today, the Takarazuka remains the most well-known example of cross-gendering in contemporary performance outside the traditional *nō* and *kabuki* theatres, and the most popular live entertainment outside the arena of pop-music concerts.

Girls are recruited into the Takarazuka Music School between the ages of fifteen and eighteen, where they enter an intensive two-year period of training. Takaraziennes are selected for either an *otokoyaku* (male role) or *musumeyaku* (female role) career early in their training and develop their singing, dancing and acting towards this role specialisation. Famous *otokoyaku* may on occasion be called upon to play the role of a strong female, as in the case of Scarlett in the Takarazuka adaptation of *Gone with the Wind*, and *musumeyaku* do occasionally play a male role in comedies, but for the most part a performer remains in her assigned gender role throughout her career. The troupe is exceptionally popular with a female audience of adult women and middle- and high-school age girls. It is the *otokoyaku* who are the most popular pin-ups, with huge fan clubs of devoted female admirers. The Takarazuka management has been at great pains since the theatre's inception in 1914 to deny the existence of homosexual relations between its actors or between the fans and actors. Despite this, there have been occasional scandals taken up by the media that have sensationalised the private lives of troupe members. It is difficult to access information and opinions of Takaraziennes around the issue of sexuality due to their adherence to the 'violet code' (*sumire*) within the troupe, which not only calls for a voluntary code of silence on sexual matters, and all other sensitive or controversial content concerning the troupe and its members, but also leads to careful and strict censorship of the content of performances. While audience tension and anticipation in a scene may be built around the lead-up to an embrace or kiss between an *otokoyaku* and *musumeyaku*, any explicit reference to sex is forbidden.

More recent close studies of the history of the review troupe have begun to explore the historical and ideological relationship between the Takarazuka and Japanese modernisation debates and the militarist and nationalist agendas of the 1930s and 1940s. The troupe did tour in China three times during the period from 1939–45 and, although this element of the history of the troupe is not widely known among contemporary fans, there seems little question that there was a clear collaboration between the troupe and the colonising policies of that period. Kobayashi was himself a war Cabinet minister and he had from the inception of the troupe seen its purpose to be one of educating and enlightening young women through entertainment.

Kobayashi was heavily influenced as he developed his personal philosophy of the Takarazuka by his artistic director Tsubouchi Shikō, son of the famous Meiji intellectual and theatre specialist Tsubouchi Shōyō. Tsubouchi's own writings, and therefore Kobayashi's, need to be understood in the context of the Taishō and early Shōwa intellectual debate surrounding the place of culture. Who should produce culture for whom? Is art the domain of the elite or should there be an art and cultural movement inclusive of the middle and working classes? Or should there be a separate popularist art and culture of the masses, and if so should it be 'of' or 'for' the masses? Kobayashi favoured art produced and controlled for the masses as an educational experience. The involvement of Takarazuka in the military government's colonising strategies in China is consistent with this position.

Today, the Takarazuka has some 400 performers divided into five rotating troupes (Flower, Moon, Snow, Star and Cosmos) that perform to sold-out houses. The troupe's extravagant and luxurious sets and costuming, and flamboyant, highly stylised performances attract millions of fans per year to the full-house shows of the season's repertoire. Fan clubs are almost exclusively female and offer an astounding array of Takarazuka-related paraphernalia for sale, as well as an endless stream of information and stories about the lives and activities of the most popular actors. Online fan clubs have opened up an entirely new level of intensity of fan activity and fanaticism. There has been a strong reaction from Japanese critics to some Western feminist research that is seen in Japan to focus too much on the issue of homosexuality and the erotic tensions of the Takarazuka. It could be said that this amounts to an acceptance or even an intellectual investment by these critics in the Takarazuka's self-perpetuating myth of sexual innocence. The theatre has achieved such massive popularity that it has almost become sacrosanct and beyond criticism, and yet there seems to be much still to be gained from a critical engagement with the Takarazuka on terms other than its own self-defined image.

Further reading

Domenig, R. (1998), 'Takarazuka and Kobayashi Ichizoo's idea of kokumingeki', in *The Culture of Japan As Seen Through its Leisure*, Albany: State University of New York Press, pp. 267–84.

Robertson, J. (1998) *Takarazuka: Sexual Politics and Popular Culture in Modern Japan*, Berkeley, California: University of California Press.

SANDRA BUCKLEY

Takeyama Minoru

b. 15 March, 1934, Sapporo, Hokkaidō

Architect

Takeyama graduated from Waseda University, Tokyo, in 1958 and continued his studies as a Fulbright scholar (1959–60) at Harvard University, Cambridge, MA. He then worked for Josep Lluis Sert in Cambridge, MA (1960–1), for Harrison and Abramovitz in New York (1961–1); and for Jorn Utzon, Arne Jacobsen and Henning Larsen in Copenhagen, Denmark (1962–4). On his return to Japan, he established his own office, Takeyama Minoru and the United Actions, in Tokyo in 1965, opening a second office in Sapporo in 1975. One of the New Wave of avant-garde Japanese architects and one of the early representatives of postmodernism in Japan, Takeyama was interested in semiotics and the language of architecture. In 1971, with Takefumi Aida, Takamitsu Azuma, Mayumi Miyawaki and Makoto Suzuki, he formed the counter-Metabolist group ARCHITEXT.

His first significant buildings were Ichiban-kan (Number One Building, 1969) and Niban-kan (Number Two Building, 1970), multi-rental stores in Tokyo. Ichiban-kan is a tall, black-metal and glass structure, with horizontal stripes, while Niban-kan originally featured a combination of Op art and catalogue elements on its multi-faceted exterior (later repainted). Takeyama used the term 'heterology' to describe the relationship between entities, establishing links based on metaphor and symbol. His designs continued to be inclusive and complex, rather than exclusive and simple. Such buildings as Hotel Beverly Tom (1973), Tomakomai, Hokkaidō; Takeyama's studio Atelier Indigo

(1976) and the Nakamura Hospital (1978), both in Sapporo; the Sweet Factory (1985), Nara; and the Renaissance Building (1986), Kyōto, were created as 'kaleidoscopes of signs', which display ambiguous and contradictory qualities. Hotel Beverly Tom, for example, is encased in black metal and parodies the buildings of the heavily industrialised region in which it is situated. The spectacular large-scale Tokyo Port Terminal (1991) is again a testimony to his skill and artistry in 'reconciling polar opposites' in the paradoxical urban conditions of the Japanese city. One of his latest and largest projects, a Crematorium, Cemetery and Memorial Complex (2001), in North Yokohama, is remarkable for its integration with the natural landscape in which it is set. He has recently completed a commission to design the Central Railway Station Complex in Seoul, Korea (2002). Takeyama has also taught architecture, both in Japan and abroad, and is the author of many books on the subject.

Select bibliography

Takeyama Minoru (1983) *Language in Architecture*, Tokyo.
—— (1973) *Autobiography of an Architect*, Tokyo.

Further reading

Bognar, B. (ed.) (1995) *Minoru Takeyama*, London.
—— (1995) *The Japan Guide*, New York.
—— (1990) *The New Japanese Architecture*, New York.
Frampton, K. (ed.) (1978) *A New Wave of Japanese Architecture*, New York: Institute of Architecture and Urban Studies.
Ross, M.F. (1978) *Beyond Metabolism: The New Japanese Architecture*, New York.

BOTOND BOGNAR

Tanaka Kinuyo

b. 29 November 1909, Shimonoseki;
 d. 21 March 1977, Tokyo

Actor

Tanaka made her debut in 1924. Her early post-war screen persona embodied the spirited 'good wife, wise mother' type. The 1952 film *Saikaku ichidai onna* (The Life of Oharu), part of her extensive collaboration with **Mizoguchi Kenji**, was ground-breaking for her career. Her single-minded devotion to her occupation created a number of unforgettable performances as old women or in character roles. She was also one of the first women to direct a feature film in Japan, and went on to make six films.

See also: women in the film industry

CHIKA KINOSHITA

Tanaka Mitsu

b. 1943

Tanaka Mitsu was one of the most influential activists in the **Women's liberation** movement in the early 1970s. Disillusioned by the masculinism of the New Left movement where women were treated as assistants and sex objects, Tanaka helped establish the Fighting Women Group and the Lib Shinjuku Centre, where they published a newsletter and held discussions on the nature and experiences of women's oppression. Through the newsletter, leaflets and her book *Inochi no onnatachi e* (To Sisters), Tanaka led the discourse in the women's lib movement. Her leaflet 'Liberation from the toilet' was a monumental manifesto revealing the sexual nature of women's oppression. She is now engaged in the practice of acupuncture, which she links to the importance of women learning to cherish both their bodies and minds.

TANAKA KAZUKO

Tange Kenzō

b. 1913, Imabari, Ehime Prefecture

Architect

Tange is one of Japan's most famous modern architects, emerging in the post-Second World War period to build such national landmarks as the Hiroshima Peace Memorial Hall and Museum (1955) and the Yoyogi National Stadium for the

1964 Tokyo Olympics. Raised amid the tumultuous political events of the 1930s and educated at Tokyo University during the Second World War, Tange later taught there, training such architects as **Isozaki Arata** and **Kurokawa Kishō**. The lasting influences of Le Corbusier, Walter Gropius and Bauhaus were tempered by Tange's desire to seamlessly weld Japanese tradition and regional character to modern technology and design. He was instrumental in realising the 1960 World Design Conference in Tokyo as head of the Conference Programme Committee, situating Japanese architecture firmly within an international frame while highlighting the originality of contributions by younger architects. Tange's works, including Tokyo Plan 1960 – a megastructure composed of traffic circulation networks, giant collective housing tents and public buildings, extending from one side of Tokyo Bay to the other on vertebrae to make room for the capital's expansion – inspired **Metabolism**.

Working part time for the city planning commission during the Second World War, teaching at the nation's most prestigious university and designing mostly large, public projects for government agencies after the war, Tange's early work remains largely undistorted by the excesses of monumentality and state symbolism that critics claim is evident in more recent projects, particularly the controversial Tokyo Metropolitan Government Offices (or Tōchō, 1991). Indeed, Tange projects consistently exhibit profound restraint in ornamentation; deploy the simple structural and aesthetic appeal of concrete and beamwork; and are most striking for their massive yet defiantly light structures, as in the case of the Hiroshima Peace Memorial, a reinforced concrete block on thin pilotis. The Yoyogi Stadium dramatises Tange's use of the shell structure, a steeply pitched concrete roof shaped by use of steel suspension. The Kagawa Prefecture Offices (Shikoku, 1958), a ten-storey administrative office complex, are constructed almost totally of reinforced concrete but celebrate an elaborate system of interlocking, isolated and counter-balanced beams to invoke traditional carpentry in Japanese-style wooden architecture.

The Tōchō is conspicuously situated among the high-rise buildings of Shinjuku's west side, its Tower I the tallest structure in Tokyo at 243 m. The urban Gothic quality of the twisted towers have caused the Tōchō to be called Tange's Notre-Dame, while the façade's densely patterned grids of granite, dark glass, stainless-steel bars and aluminum panels were intended to suggest simultaneously an integrated circuit board and the beam-and-post structure of traditional architecture. Critics descry the Tōchō as oppressively symbolic and inappropriate for a democratic government building, while supporters laud it as a striking addition to the skyline.

Other major projects by Tange include: the Shizuoka Convention Hall (1953); the Tokyo Metropolitan Government Offices (1957); the Kagawa Prefectural Government Offices (Shikoku, 1958); Kurashiki City Hall (1960); the Yamanashi Press and Broadcasting Centre (1966); Expo 70 theme pavilion (Ōsaka); Hanae Mori Building (Tokyo, 1978); and Embassy for Turkey (Tokyo, 1979).

SCOTT GOLD AND MARY KNIGHTON

Taniguchi Yoshio

b. 1937, Tokyo, Japan

Architect

One of Japan's most accomplished architects, Taniguchi has made his name in the early 1980s with several remarkable projects, such as the Shiseido Art Museum (1978) in Kakegawa and the Kanazawa Municipal Library (1978) in Kanazawa. His international recognition, however, came with the completion of the Ken Domon Museum of Photography (1983) in Sakata, which remains one of his most noted designs. This project introduced a line of museums, whose designs have grown in sophistication, significance and often size as well. His latest one, the new wing of the Museum of Modern Art (MoMA) in New York, now under construction, is a testimony to his success in this regard; in 1997, he won the much discussed international invitational design competition for this work.

Taniguchi earned his first degree in mechanical engineering from the Keio University in Tokyo in 1960, before obtaining an M.Arch. degree from

Harvard University in the USA in 1964. After working in partnership with Shinsuke Takamiya for several years, he established his present office, Taniguchi and Associates in Tokyo, in 1979. Taniguchi is one of those Japanese architects who, in growing numbers after the War, were trained abroad at a time when modernism was still flourishing in the West. Thus Taniguchi, like Yoshinobu Ashihara and Fumihiko Maki – also graduates of Harvard University – has remained faithful to the best legacies of modern architecture, even in the age of post-modernism. Rather than indulging in mere stylistic adventures, as most post-modern architects did and do, he has always favoured a certain rationality of design, which he has conveyed with an increasingly sophisticated and rich simplicity. His artistry reveals affinity with Mies van der Rohe's design paradigm of 'less is more'. In this regard, though, Taniguchi's works find their precedents and inspiration not only in the achievements of modernism, but also in the traditions of Japanese architecture. Taniguchi's architecture can be characterised by the innovative use of materials, tectonic systems with a structural clarity, flexible and enlightened articulation of spatial sequences, a sensitivity to natural phenomena, particularly light, and, very importantly, a high-quality craftsmanship along with the elegant resolution of details. One of the cornerstones of traditional design, the artful mediation between inside–outside of architecture is reinterpreted in his designs by way of a quietly responsive spatial articulation, the implementation of various courtyards, as well as the frequent application of extensive roof canopies.

The Ken Domon Museum, at the shores of a picturesque pond, embraces the landscape also by way of a tranquil courtyard that carefully opens towards the water. Taniguchi's much admired design for the Tokyo Sea Life Park Aquarium (1989), boosting his international reputation, has been shaped with an attractive glass dome hovering above the entrance and a large circular pool of water beneath which the actual aquarium is situated. Several years later, he was commissioned to design a small structure, the View Point Visitors' Centre (1995) adjacent to the Aquarium. The building stretches out horizontally and is composed of a 'glass box' (7 m wide, 75 m long and 11 m high) placed on top of a reinforced concrete base. This highly transparent volume, whose 'column-free' cage-like structural system is provided by the solid steel sashes of the glass walls themselves, was designed so as to also form a gateway at the end of the 'Promenade to the Sea', which begins at the train station and forms the central axis of the park.

Taniguchi's interest in spatial transitions can be likened to Maki's intentions also in terms of addressing urban issues and the relationship between public and private realms. One of Taniguchi's most remarkable works in this regard is the Marugame Genichiro–Inokuma Museum of Contemporary Art (1991) in Marugame, where the outside urban plaza of the front side is successfully continued within the building; first under the huge canopy of the proscenium-like front façade, and then, as a long open stairway cutting through the body of the building and leading to a third floor public terrace with an outdoor café. The Toyota Municipal Museum of Art (1995) in Toyota is perhaps Taniguchi's largest project to date; combining his design skills with those of the landscape designer, American Peter Walker, he succeeded in creating a most memorable assemblage of spatial sequences through several courtyards among groups of buildings, then continuing them inside with an intricate series of galleries, softly lit through large frost-glass wall surfaces. A similar intention is seen in his Keio Shonan-Fujisawa Municipal Junior and Senior High School (1992) in Fujisawa; the articulation of various volumes and in-between outdoor public places are reminiscent of a small urban enclave. Other outstanding designs by Taniguchi include the IBM Japan Makuhari Technical Centre (1991) in Makuhari and the Tokyo National Museum Gallery of Hōryū-ji Treasures (1999), both in Tokyo.

Further reading

Bognar, B. (1995) *The Japan Guide*, New York.
(1996–1) 'Special issue on Yoshio Taniguchi', *The Japan Architect* (spring) 21.
(1999) *The Architecture of Yoshio Taniguchi*, New York.

BOTOND BOGNAR

Tanizaki Jun'ichirō

b. 24 July 1886, Tokyo; d. 30 July 1965,
Yugawara

Writer

Tanizaki Jun'ichirō's fifty-five year career spans the
reigns of the Meiji, Taishō and Shōwa emperors
and his collected works fill twenty-eight volumes.
He is best known for his novels and short stories
that often feature experimental narrative techniques, but he also wrote plays, cinema screenplays,
essays and several translations.

Born in Tokyo, Tanizaki's earliest writing
reflects his affinity and nostalgia for Edo culture,
and the influence of late nineteenth-century Euro-
American literary movements. His early works,
exemplified by his short story 'Shisei' (The Tattoo,
1910) show a marked interest in **sado-masochism**, in particular in foot fetishism and the
figure of the *femme fatale*. Tanizaki's increasing
infatuation with Western culture appears full force
in his first novel of acclaim, *Chijin no ai* (Naomi,
1925), which portrays an independent and sexually
liberated young woman. Tanizaki was keenly
interested in cinema, and wrote screenplays for
several films during the 1920s.

Following the Great Tokyo Earthquake in 1923,
Tanizaki took refuge in the **Kansai** region of
Japan. This move brought about a change in
literary interests as he became absorbed with
traditional Japanese arts and culture. *Manji*
(Quicksand, 1928–30), the story of two modern
women involved in a lesbian relationship, is a
transitional novel but shows Tanizaki's fascination
with the regional Kansai dialect (see **dialects**). His
novel *Tade kuu mushi* (Some Prefer Nettles, 1929)
reflects Tanizaki's somewhat tortured exploration
of the juxtaposition between West and East, old
and new. His finely crafted novella, *Shunkinshō* (A
Portrait of Shunkin, 1933), and internationally
renowned essay on aesthetics, 'In'ei raisan' (In
Praise of Shadows, 1933–4), both written as Japan
was beginning its colonialist expansion, are indicative of Tanizaki's deepening affinity for a more
traditional Japanese ethos.

During the Pacific War, Tanizaki produced little
fiction of his own, but instead worked on his first
modern Japanese language translation of the

eleventh-century classic *Genji monogatari* (The Tale
of Genji). He translated it twice again later in life.
During the war years he began his longest novel,
Sasameyuki (The Makioka Sisters, 1943–8), which
depicts the 1930s Hanshin upper middle class in
decline. Both projects suffered wartime censorship;
Sasameyuki was published in its entirety only in
1948.

Tanizaki's interests in sexuality, **sado-masochism** and experimental narrative merged again
in his 1956 novel *Kagi* (The Key), which created a
sensation for its bold descriptions of a couple's
erotic life, written in the form of alternating diary
entries by husband and wife. The lyrical 'Yume no
ukihashi' (The Bridge of Dreams, 1959) incorporates Tanizaki's passion for Genji and his abiding
affection for mother figures. *Ften rojin nikki* (Diary of
a Mad Old Man, 1961–2) returns full circle in its
somewhat comical depiction of an old man's erotic
attraction to his daughter-in-law's feet.

Tanizaki holds the distinction of being the first
Japanese author inducted into the American
Academy and Institute of Arts and Humanities in
1964. The Tanizaki Prize, established upon his
death, is conferred yearly on a Japanese writer for
exemplary literary production and marks the
importance of Tanizaki's legacy to the world of
Japanese letters.

See also: classical literature in post-war Japan;
film, literature and screenplays

Further reading

Boscaro, A. and Chambers, A. (eds) (1998)
    A Tanizaki Feast, Ann Arbor: Center for Japanese
    Studies, University of Michigan Press.
Chambers, A. (1994) *The Secret Window: Ideal Worlds
    in Tanizaki's Fiction*. Cambridge, MA: Council on
    East Asian Studies, Harvard University.
Ito, K. (1991) *Visions of Desire: Tanizaki's Fictional
    Worlds*, Stanford: Stanford University Press.
Gessel, Van (1993) 'An infatuation with modernity',
    in *Three Modern Novelists: Soseki, Tanizaki and
    Kawabata*, Tokyo: Kōdansha International, pp.
    68–132.

GRETCHEN JONES

tanshin funin

Tanshin funin is a term used to refer to employees who, due to work commitments, are forced to live away from their families for extended periods of time. Although the term may be applied to both male and female employees, in the context of the Japanese employment system, the overwhelming majority of *tanshin funin-sha* (*tanshin funin* individuals) are males living away from their families for periods ranging from a few months to a couple of years, hence giving rise to the term business bachelors.

According to Australian academic Yoshio Sugimoto, approximately one in five transfers of married employees in organisations with a thousand or more employees fall into the *tanshin funin* category; Sugimoto, citing Ministry of Labour figures, puts the number of *tanshin funin-sha* as close to half a million (Sugimoto: 95). The most common reasons why married employees are forced to live away from their families are a reluctance to disrupt children's education and problems associated with finding housing. Despite the disruptions to the family caused by these transfers, the nature of corporate culture in Japan makes it difficult for employees to refuse a transfer order.

References

Yoshio Sugimoto (1997) *An Introduction to Japanese Society*, Cambridge, UK: Cambridge University Press.

Further reading

NHK International and Japan Foundation (1995) *The Way of Life In Japan Series: Business Bachelors.*

ROMIT DASGUPTA

Tatakau Onnatachi

The Tatakau Onna (Fighting Women) group was formed in 1971. **Tanaka Mitsu**'s manifesto for the group provided a passionate indictment of the sexual double standards of the time, whereby women's bodies were used as the objects of male sexual gratification. They were involved in the campaign to combat conservative moves to amend the abortion law; the first Women's Liberation weekend camps held in 1971, 1972 and 1973; and the creation of the Shinjuku Women's Liberation Centre.

See also: feminism; reproductive control; Women's Liberation

Futher reading

Tanaka, K. (1995) 'The new feminist movement in Japan, 1970–1990', in K. Fujimura-Fanselow and A. Kameda (eds) *Japanese Women: New Feminist Perspectives on the Past, Present and Future*, New York: The Feminist Press, pp. 343–52.

VERA MACKIE

tatami

The rice matting used as flooring in Japan began as foldable (*tatamu*) and portable mats used for sitting and sleeping. There are slight regional variations in the size of *tatami* but they are approximately 3 feet by 6 feet (910 × 1,820 mm) and bordered by a black trim on the longer sides. Techniques for stitching vary according to quality and region and there are a number of different styles allowed for the trim. Room sizes in a home are described according to how many mats (*jo*) would fit the room, e.g. 4.5-jo or 6-jo. This measure is also used for non-*tatami* and Western-style rooms. Many contemporary Japanese homes will have only one *tatami* space and this is often the formal reception or guest room. *Tatami* is still preferred by many in bedrooms, even though a bed may replace traditional floor futon. Although the more durable wood, tiles and linoleum are increasingly common flooring materials, the practice of removing shoes at the entrance to a home continues. Today, many homes combine an unpredictable mix of *tatami*, wood, carpet and Japanese and Western-style furniture. In a traditional *tatami* room, the horizontal black lines of the *tatami* edge form a strong visual contrast to the simple vertical lines of wood and plaster walls and columns. Factory production of *tatami* keeps them affordable but

there are still professional *tatami* craftsmen producing a wide range of *tatami* styles and grades.

SANDRA BUCKLEY

tateshakai

The sociologist **Nakane Chie** located the concept
of vertical relations at the heart of her understanding of Japanese society. She contrasted a
dominant vertical structure of Japanese village
hierarchy to the horizontal structure of caste in
India. For Nakane, the hierarchies generated
within vertical social structures function as the
primary organising principle of human relations in
Japan.

The criteria determining the order of a
hierarchy can vary, but include age, seniority
(length of employment and/or rank), education
and gender. What criteria, or mix of criteria,
dominate is dependent upon the organising
principle that sustains the viability of the vertical
grouping. For example, a middle-aged woman,
graduated from two-year college and working as an
office clerk, would fall far down the workplace
ranking compared to her male university-educated
colleagues, including those younger than herself. In
a different context, however, such as the tea
ceremony class she teaches, this woman will be
treated with deference by her male and female
students regardless of age. Nakane places great
emphasis on the ordering power of the **cohorts** of
sempai (seniors), *kohai* (juniors) and *doryo* (equals or
contemporaries). This relational chain sets in
motion a lifetime of obligations and responsibilities
that can sometimes cut across another chain in
complex and conflictual ways requiring careful
social negotiations. The relationship of vertical
relations to the dynamics of **uchi and soto**
relations is also fluid and seldom uncomplicated.
Nakane has been criticised for trying to create too
simple a model that cannot capture the complexity
of the ongoing daily negotiations, which characterise the movement of an individual across their
multiple networks of community and belonging,
and refuse reduction to Nakane's vertical and
horizontal axes.

Further reading

Nakane Chie (1970) *Japanese Society*, Tokyo: Tuttle

SANDRA BUCKLEY

tattoos

The tattooist in Japan is a master craftsman, even
an artist. His clientele is, however, largely limited
today to the *yakuza* and foreigners. *Irezumi* literally
means the insertion of ink, and Japanese techniques involve the use of either combs of needles or
single needles (*hari*) to place *sumi* ink under the skin.
Shades of black, red and brown are the palette of
Japan's masters.

Figurines displaying tattoos were found in
archaeological sites dating from third to fourth
centuries BCE. There are also clear references to
tattooing in early Chinese records of contact with
Wa (Japan). Although there is evidence that these
early tattoos were linked to both ritual and
adornment, by the eighth century tattoos had
become a mark of punishment, a brand for
criminal behaviour and no longer a practice of
the elites. In the early Edo Period, there was
another shift in the value of tattoos. While they
retained their association with the criminal and
punishment, there was a widespread popularisation
of tattooing as adornment in the world of
prostitution and entertainers. The more rarefied
use of the tattoo among nuns and priests to signify
a bond with the Buddha also found a popular
expression among lovers with the proliferation of
love tattoos. It was also during the Edo Period that
the criminal underworld developed the tattoo as a
mark of identification and difference, a practice
they took to new extremes with increasingly
complicated and extensive patterns involving much
more perseverance and pain. The macabre
Museum of Tattoos in Tokyo still houses examples
of the best of the *yakuza* custom of full- and half-
body tattoos; skins sold 'in advance' by impoverished gangsters – a now illegal practice. It has been
claimed that the tattoo became the signature of
gangsters as they sort to disguise their criminal
branding under decorative markings. The extent of
the practice and its strong links to fashion and
trends in the brothel and entertainment districts

attracted the attention of the authorities and a series of restrictive edicts dramatically impacted the previously booming business of the master tattooers. By the 1840s, any public display of tattoos was banned. The practice was not fully legalised again until after the Second World War.

During this period, the tattoo became the insignia of the underworld of the *yakuza*. Despite the appropriation of the tattoo by high fashion over the 1990s, this has been one element of global fashion that has not gained ground in Japan. The strong association between the tattoo and the underworld has kept all but the hardiest of trend setters from experimenting with even stick-on tattoos. Although Japanese designers have incorporated elements of Ainu and Okinawan textiles into 'ethnic' fashion lines, they have avoided the traditional tattooing of both cultures. It is not clear what historical links there are between Ainu and Okinawan tattoos and the tattooing practices of early Japanese elites. In the heated intellectual debates over the origins of 'the Japanese race', tattoos function not as a fashion accessory but as an accessory in the formation of contentious arguments of historical evidence.

Further reading

Richie, D. and Buruma. I. (1990) *The Japanese Tattoo*, New York and Tokyo: Weatherhill.

SANDRA BUCKLEY

Tawara Machi

b. 1962, Ōsaka

Poet

Tawara Machi is one of the most popular *tanka* poets in contemporary Japan. Tawara has made *tanka* accessible to a new generation of readers. She defamiliarised everyday language by subjecting it to the traditional 5, 7, 5, 7, 7 constraint, and she revived interest in women's love poetry.

Tanka (literally, short poems) is a kind of *waka*, consisting of thirty-one syllables divided into groups of 5, 7, 5, 7 and 7. Tawara became interested in this genre, while studying at Waseda University, thanks to lectures by the poet/scholar Sasaki Yukitsuna. In 1987, only a few years after starting to compose *tanka*, she published her first collection, entitled *Sarada kinenbi* (Salad Anniversary). The collection not only won a major *tanka* prize and critical acclamation, but also proved a huge commercial success, which was unprecedented in this genre. Tawara's poems deal with ordinary, everyday scenes as observed by a young woman. Food, love, loneliness and travel are major themes of the collection but there are also sections depicting her family in her home town and her life as a high-school teacher. The title of the collection is taken from one of its poems:

> 'This tastes great' you said and so
> the sixth of July –
> our salad anniversary
>
> (trans. Juliet Winters Carpenter)

While maintaining the traditional 5, 7, 5, 7, 7 form and some of the more accessible *tanka* diction, Tawara avoids archaism and pedantry, and uses colloquial language. Products of popular culture such as rock and pop music also appear frequently in her poems. It is also notable that she often places a semantic gap (marked with ¶ below) deliberately in the middle of a syllabic group (marked with /): 'Yomesan ni/ nareyo'¶ da nante/¶ kanchhai/ nihon de¶ itte/ shimatte¶ ii no. In English translation:

> 'Marry me',
> after two canned cocktails –
> are you sure you want to say that?
>
> (trans. Carpenter)

Since her sensational debut, Tawara has been active not only as a *tanka* poet but also in other roles such as television commentator, essayist and writer of children's books. Her third collection of *tanka*, *Chokoreeto kakumei* (The Chocolate Revolution, 1997), deals with an affair between a young woman and a married man. She has also 'translated' Yosano Akiko's *tanka* collection *Midaregami* (Entangled Hair, 1901), publishing her version as *Chokoreeto-go yaku midaregami* (Entangled Hair in Chocolate Language, 2 vols, 1998). In the afterword, she hopes that the reader will find her 'chocolate language' 'sweet and a little bit bitter, not to be overeaten, and yet so tempting'.

Select bibliography

Tawara Machi (1988) *Salad Anniversary*, trans. Jack Stamm, Tokyo: Kawade Shobō.

—— (1988, 1990) *Salad Anniversary*, trans. Juliet Winters Carpenter, Tokyo: Kōdansha International.

Further reading

Strong, Sarah M (1991) 'Passion and patience: Aspects of feminine poetic heritage in Yosano Akiko's *Midaregami* and Tawara Machi's *Sarada kinenbi*', *Journal of the Association of Teachers of Japanese* 25(2): 177–94.

TOMOKO AOYAMA

taxation system

The Japanese tax system involves national taxes (*chihōzei*) and local prefectural and municipal taxes. Taxes can also be divided into direct and indirect taxes. The former are levied directly on the income and profits of individuals and corporations, while the latter are levied indirectly as consumption tax, excise tax or charged as fees. The post-war tax system was introduced by US economist and banker Carl Shoup in 1949, during the Occupation. It has been characterised by heavy dependence on direct taxes and a steeply progressive income tax system. Japanese tax rates have been comparatively low, in part due to limited spending for the Self-Defence Forces. There is an increasing demand, however, for social security programmes, especially as the Japanese population ages. Attempts at tax reform have been made over the years and a consumption tax was introduced in 1989. In 1997, this tax rate was raised to 5 per cent, including a 1 per cent tax to provide revenue for local-government finances. The ratio of taxes to national income has now surpassed that of the USA to come close to the level of West European countries. The government planned tax cuts in 1999 amounting to ¥9.3 trillion, the largest ever.

DAVID EDGINGTON

TAXING WOMAN, A *see Marusa no onna*

tea

Although tea did not arrive in Europe from China until the seventeenth century, it had reached Japan by as early as the eighth century. Today, there are many varieties of tea consumed in Japan, ranging from the powdered tea (*macha*) of the **tea ceremony** to the popular everyday coarse leaf green tea (*bancha*) and the more expensive refined leaf tea (*sencha*) served to guests in the home or at more expensive restaurants.

Regional varieties are a popular seasonal gift or travel souvenir (**omiyage**). Tea is seldom drunk without some tasty accompaniment. A traditional and still highly popular breakfast or snack consists of tea poured over a bowl of rice served with savoury or sweet spices, seaweed and roasted grain (*ocha zuke*). Types of tea once considered rustic, such as *genmaicha* (*bancha* processed with roasted varieties of rice), *sakura-yu* (a cherry leaf infusion), *mugi-cha* (roasted-barley tea) or *hōjicha* (roasted coarse-leaf tea), have gained a new following among younger generations of tea drinkers, who seek out hard-to-get, speciality brands as part of a carefully inflected aesthetics of consumption that extends from clothing and hi-tech equipment to food and drink. The highest-quality tea is called *gyokuro* (literally, jewelled dew) and is painstakingly produced from the finest new buds of the most established tea bushes. Some of the rarest teas are produced from named groves just as a fine wine can be, and, just like the best wines, these teas fall far outside the price range of most Japanese.

The difference between green and black tea lies not in the type of plant used but in the processing of the leaves. If the leaves of the tea bush are steamed before they can begin to dry out they retain a green colouring that remains even after the leaves are roasted or dried. Japanese green tea is not served strongly steeped, as is often the preference of black-tea drinkers elsewhere. Tea is usually only left for two to three minutes in the pot before serving and even less for finer teas. As a consequence, black tea is also often served lightly steeped in Japan or what many black-tea lovers would describe as weak. Although black tea has experienced a considerable market comeback against coffee since the tea bag, there has not been a similar widespread adoption of this technique for green tea in Japan. Even most offices, where the young **office ladies** prepare cups of tea for everyone from their managers and corporate guests to their male colleagues, the ease of the tea bag has generally not displaced the simple rituals of tea making.

The tea powder that is beaten into a foaming smooth consistency in the traditional pottery bowls of the tea ceremony is made from finest young tea leaves. Although historically associated with the aristocratic class, the samurai and priests, it has experienced something of a popular revival in the 1990s: everything from *macha* ice cream and sorbet to *macha* **noodles**, **mochi** and *macha* natural dyes for textiles used by a new generation of inter-nationally renowned Japanese **fashion** designers.

See also: tea ceremony

SANDRA BUCKLEY

tea ceremony

The origins of tea in Japan are traced back to the early ninth century, but the familiar austere form of the Japanese tea ceremony (*chanoyu*) practised in Japan today dates from the sixteenth century. Guests gather to partake of tea in a highly stylised and formal ceremony in which the host prepares the tea in front of the watchful and appreciative, if sometimes critical, eyes of his guests. The success of the ceremony rests not simply with the taste of the thick, frothy, warm green tea but with the skilfulness and aesthetic quality of the ceremony. The gracious and artful participation of the guests is an equally important element of *chanoyu*.

The tea ceremony is not a part of everyday life but a very refined art that is also known as *chadō* – the way of tea – and closely linked to the meditative practices of Zen. Even so, it is now possible for anyone who has an interest to join one of the contemporary *chanoyu* schools and begin lessons. This refined set of skills was once limited to the aristocracy, samurai class and priests. In its earliest form, the tea ceremony was unapologetically associated with a Chinese aesthetic of collecting

and lavish ceremony, and there was much focus on the display of rare and precious utensils. The occasion of the ceremony was also taken as an opportunity to display other art works and personal possessions of value, e.g. calligraphy, paintings, ceramics, silks, robes, etc. It was in the sixteenth century that the Zen monks and the court elite lost their hold on the ritual of the tea ceremony as a handful of tea merchants strove to create a new aesthetic that actively defined itself in stark contrast to the lavishness and excess of the court.

The tea ceremony was relocated from the large ceremonial spaces of temples and castles to a four-and-a-half mat room of wood and plain walls with *tatami* floor, where decoration was shunned. At most, there was a single calligraphy scroll hanging in an alcove with a simple *ikebana* arrangement. Over time, an even smaller tea room evolved at a mere one-and-a-half mats and the entrance was reduced to a crawl space that required everyone to kneel in a symbolic gesture of the equality of all who entered. In a space this small, there was literally no room for hierarchies. Economy of movement became essential to the ceremony and an intimacy of proximity came to characterise the interaction of host and guests. The separate structure of the rustic tea house located in a remote natural setting or in the quiet corner of a landscaped garden added another layer of distance from the business and detail of the everyday world. To this day, the calm and simplicity of the tea room afford an aura of austerity and non-worldliness for those who enter this space of contemplation and quietude.

The tea ceremony is, however, far from free of artfulness. The simplicity and austerity of the tea room or hut are carefully cultivated and crafted. The tea master strives to achieve an aesthetic of minimalism that appears free of artifice or design, but is nevertheless the product of an art of artlessness. The aesthetic term most often linked to *chanoyu* is *wabi*. *Wabi* celebrates the austere over the lavish, the rustic over the rich, the imperfect over the perfect, shadow over light. The eye of a tea master will rest in appreciation on the flaw or crack in a tea bowl. In the making of the tea, the master's fingers might linger over a knot in the bamboo of the whisk before gently placing it in the tea to stir. Perfection is subordinated to the unexpected, the irregular, the accidental character of an object. By contrast, though the ritual of the ceremony itself is followed religiously, individual flare is not valued in the tea room. Each person is there as one part of the whole of the ceremony. The tea master does not lead but rather facilitates. Subtlety and the lack of grand gestures mark the unobtrusive presence of the tea master whose role it is to animate the simple beauty of the utensils arrayed on the *tatami* and to weave the guests into the fabric of a seamless ritual.

The tea ceremony, like *ikebana*, has become one of the skills young women seek to develop in their preparation for a good marriage match. It is this more commercial side of the tea schools that often supports the ongoing pursuit of the aesthetic ideals of *chanoyu*. Wealthy patrons are also an important source of finance for today's tea ceremony schools. Unlike *ikebana*, there is little opportunity for this tradition to engage with new technologies beyond information-based websites. The very principles and aesthetic of *chanoyu* exclude the possibility of collaboration with the new. Ironically, it was the desire to innovate and depart from tradition that saw the emergence of what we now know as *chanoyu* and yet, today, the practice of the tea ceremony is set in stone in defence of tradition in a world where cultural practices are undergoing rapid and dramatic transformations.

SANDRA BUCKLEY

Teachers' Union of Japan

Teachers' unions have historically served as a counterweight to the powerful role of the **Ministry of Education**, Monbusho. They have been in the forefront of resistance to a rigid, hierarchically defined, uniform education system, which cannot, and does not, respond to the individual learning needs of children.

While teachers' unions in Japan have tended to stand for progressive ideas, including equality of access for all children and the acknowledgement of teaching the whole child, they have been greatly affected by the political and economic context within Japan. The first teachers' union, Keimeikai, emerged after the First World War as a means to protect the rights of teachers and maintain an adequate living standard. In the 1920s, as Japan moved into its more nationalistic and militaristic period, many teacher unions were disbanded or driven underground due to their ideological critique of the government's attempt to use education as a conduit for the preparation of citizens loyal to the imperial hegemonic mission. Regardless, censorship, sanctions on textbooks, imposition of uniform examinations and mandatory military drills, many teachers still strove to provide opportunities for their students to interrogate the social and political context of the time.

After the Second World War, various groups emerged to form the Teachers' Union of Japan (Nikkyōsō). Teachers who had been faithful to their government's nationalistic agenda now were asked to leave the profession by the Allied Occupation or demonstrate that their convictions had changed in support of a more democratic mission. The union, reinvigorated by the apparent removal of nationalistic overtones, began to negotiate with the post-war government in a less antagonistic approach. Soon, however, fearing the socialist orientation of the union, and the potential for it serving as a groundswell of popular resistance, the Occupation began to restrict the scope of union activities, including changing the status of teachers to that of national government employees. This allowed for greater centralisation and control of the curriculum and performance assessment.

Resistance to teacher unions has come not only from the government but also from society at large, where there was a strong public perception of teachers not as workers with rights to organise, strike, or expect certain wages and benefits but as committed, selfless individuals who have responded to a calling, a mission. Built on the Confucian system of respect for teachers and learning, those in the profession were supposed to be above the economic and political vicissitudes of daily life. Ironically, by fighting for an adequate standard of living and a more autonomous professional status, unions have, in the view of many people, lowered the status of the teachers to that of ordinary workers. One of the results of this shift in perception has been the gradual decline in union participation, particularly among incoming teachers. Simultaneously, the union has changed its strategy from one of outside provocateur to inside critic, as it attempts to bring about change in collaboration with, rather than in spite of, the Ministry of Education. As the diversity of student needs increases due to the economic and demographic challenges facing Japan, the role of teacher unions and their members will need to be both responsive and flexible.

See also: Ministry of Education

JUNE A. GORDON

technology, transport and communications

Technology has not only accelerated the pace of daily life, and expanded the sources and diversity of information and pleasure, but has also dramatically transformed the relationship of Japanese to their landscape, to their homes and to the experience of every level of their daily lives. Technological innovation and access is integral to contemporary Japanese culture. It is not an accident that Japan has come to stand in for visions of futuristic hi-tech societies for so many non-Japanese science fiction writers. The lived reality of the period from 1946 to the present has seen Japan emerge as a major centre for the development, production and consumption of new technologies across a diversity of areas ranging from the music industry to fast trains, and from mobile phones to human reproduction.

By the 1950s, a consumer-dominated culture had emerged in Japan. During the '*denka būmu*' (boom in electric appliances for the home) in 1955, the phrase **mai hōmu** ('my home') came into popular use in cultural texts as diverse as advertising and novels. It conjured up the image of a home with pristine white washing machines, refrigerators and electric rice cookers. In time, other housekeeping appliances entered the home, such as vacuum cleaners and dryers; information and entertainment technologies such as radios, television sets, tape recorders, stereo sets, personal computers and word-processors became commonplace; as did health and beauty items such as hair dryers and electric shavers; and consumable goods such as light bulbs, batteries and tapes. Many of these items were perceived as labour saving. Some have argued that these domestic technologies reflected the increasing liberation of women from the household and a related growth in leisure time. While these new technologies impacted gender roles and social hierarchies, feminists have challenged the extent to which they liberated women from domestic work. The growth of the home electronics industry that accompanied rapid economic growth reflected the increasing affluence of the population and the growth of both the domestic and international markets for Japanese goods. The entertainment and information industries reflected, at the same time as they contributed to, the rationalisation and Westernisation of Japanese life. Images and popular narratives from advertising to television programming promoted the rise of US-led democracy and an ideal of the nuclear family. Televisions were a crucial vehicle in this process, helping to introduce images of US-style family life and the material features of US culture to a broad viewing audience. Technology, and communication and media technologies in particular, played an integral role in the representation and diffusion of dominant values, facilitating rapid processes of cultural reproduction and social change.

The rise of consumerism was seen as a milestone in Japanese economic development, for the Japanese had largely freed themselves from the struggle against scarcity of the immediate post-war years and gone beyond the basic needs of subsistence. The White Paper on Japan's Economy 1961 produced by the Japanese government bore the subtitle 'Consumption is a virtue: The era of throwaway culture begins'. While the Japanese were encouraged to believe that through careful shopping they could acquire good taste, improve themselves and be happier and more attractive, consumer goods did not so much improve the material conditions of families as provide them with symbols of status. In the 1950s, for example, many people bought blenders despite the lack of fruit and fresh vegetables to blend. The development of a mass-consumer market and the status associated with purchasing power and consumer knowledge (trends, image, brand values, etc.) were integral to the social and economic change which Japan underwent in the post-war period.

Many of the new consumer products were based on technology initially introduced from overseas and then modified and enhanced in Japan, such as transistors and integrated circuits (IC), new models of television sets, refrigerators, audio goods and videotape recorders. There was an initial emphasis on high-quality, low-priced goods, but by the 1980s and 1990s Japanese electronic retail prices had become comparable to those in similar overseas markets. Japanese electronic goods are typically light, thin and small, with miniaturisation often considered a hallmark of Japanese ingenuity and creativeness. While the Japanese have been accused of lack of 'originality', this claim is often exaggerated and does not allow for the real level of significant technological innovation in Japan. What is more, even when technological design has originated elsewhere, there is no disputing the amount of creativeness required to successfully commercialise a concept or product for global distribution.

Whereas the Tokyo Olympics of 1964 celebrated feats of physical endurance, the launch of the Tōkaido bullet train between Tokyo and Ōsaka, just prior to the Olympic opening, transformed the relationship between the human body and the Japanese landscape. In the post-war period, technology has increasingly mediated the contact that the Japanese have had with their natural environment. Scenic destinations are not only more accessible but can also be captured and added to an individual or family portfolio of travel. Cameras and video-cams filter and frame the passing scenery as memorabilia or travel trophy. Television and cinema have been important in providing a window to a myriad of cultures, promoting consumerism and tourism, by transporting viewers to parts of the world they may have once only dreamed of but can now access with the flick of a switch or push of a button.

The year 1966 was dubbed the first year of the mai kaa ('my car') era, the year when the number of automobiles in Japan exceeded 10 million. The car was viewed as a way of bringing the family together, the 'my' suggesting individuality in a mass-production-oriented world. Despite the traffic congestion and the limited space in which to park cars, by the late 1980s there would be one automobile for every two people. The phrase 'mai

kaa' was but one of many beginning with mai ('my') that came into usage after 1955: maikara ('my colour television set'), maikura ('my air cooler/air conditioner') and, more recently, maikon ('my computer'). These words reflect the increasing intensity of the relationship of individual and group identity to consumerism, and new personal-use technologies in particular. This new bonding between humans and machines can be seen as an extension of experience and sensorial perception through technologies, as life seems to imitate science fiction. The degree to which identity and everyday experience are mediated through technology does effectively become cyborg-like, at least to the extent that it has become difficult to disconnect a person from the multiple technological mediations that constitute a significant proportion of daily life in Japan.

The term 'information society' was used in Japanese publications as early as 1969, in three distinct ways. First, it was understood as a society in which the progress of computerisation will give people access to reliable information, free them from clerical work and thus bring about the blossoming of 'human creativity'. Second, it is a society characterised by the increase in 'the importance of information processes relative to material processes'. That is, the price of goods tends to be a result of 'information costs' associated with the requirements of fashion, style and quality. The importance of labour and material costs declines. Finally, the third approach combines part of each of the previous two and predicts that the rise of the information society will be characterised by computerisation of commerce, finance and manufacturing, and the growth of information industries like software production.

It was foreseen that, in the information society, both the method and content of production would be changed. While some of these expectations were decidedly Utopian in nature, there is no disputing the impact of technological change on communities, imagined or otherwise, the number of social relationships the Japanese enter into on a daily basis and their experiences of self. Consumption patterns and spending power are also directly impacted by credit and risk, and other ratings determined by world financial markets. One key criteria in these determinations is the comparative ability of national economies to generate wealth via technological innovation.

The advent of Cyberspace and virtual reality has taken the relationship between humans and technology to a new level, immersing the body in artificially created environments. Computers have gone beyond being mere tools to being a way of achieving new bodily experiences. Technologies of observation have grown in sophistication, ranging from stomach-cameras that explore the inner recesses of the body to ultrasound and extending the capacity of the body, other medical innovations that have helped human vision to penetrate the body. Despite advances in other areas of medical technology, progress in the area of **organ transplants** has been limited by a widespread aversion among Japanese to transplant surgery, an aversion grounded in both religious and cultural reasons, and, some would also argue, due to lack of unbiased information. The high rate of abortion in Japan suggests that reproductive technologies aimed at controlling fertility are underused. Low-dose oral contraceptives only became available by prescription as late as September 1999. By contrast, Japan has invested significantly in a wide range of genetic-screening technologies, an area of research that is receiving close scrutiny from both women's groups and advocates of rights for the disabled.

Advances in transportation and communication, such as the subway, the **bullet train**, automobiles, airplanes, **cameras**, telephones and **computers**, have helped the Japanese, and people elsewhere, to see the world in new ways, often courtesy of technologies that have been manufactured in Japan. Commuting by bullet train and telecommuting by computers are but two examples of how advances in transportation and communication have extended the social space of the Japanese. To what extent the Japanese can retain popular notions of a unique identity in a technology-mediated and globalising world, and to what degree goods designed by Japanese but made in other parts of Asia or designed by Japanese for other markets can still be described as Japanese, all remain matters for debate. With the 'hollowing out' of Japan in the 1990s and the shift of Japanese manufacturing to other parts of Asia, more and more 'Japanese' technology is being produced

overseas. In 1996, it was estimated that over a third of Japanese car stereos and VCRs, more than two-thirds of colour televisions, and a large 80 per cent of hi-fi audio equipment made by Japanese companies will have actually been produced elsewhere. We have a situation where China and South-East Asia effectively provide the world with Japanese electrical appliances. Not only is Asia where much of Japanese manufacturing occurs, the rise of the 'new rich' of Asia is seeing the emergence of a major new consumer market, despite the problems posed by the Asian financial crisis of the late 1990s.

It was from around 1988 that the idea of an 'intelligent home', which made use of the latest home electronic goods, was promoted. The home technologies can be broadly divided into:

1 housekeeping systems (home security systems, automated lighting and heating, television camera surveillance);
2 management systems (home shopping, electronic communications, telecommuting);
3 culture systems (distance education, audio-visual systems);
4 communication systems (upgrading of telephone lines, home fax, computer-based communication).

Large-scale attempts at artificial intelligence R&D such as the Fifth-Generation Computer Project (1982–95) have met with very limited success, and there has been a far higher level of interest and investment in robotics than AI in both industrial and academic research and development. However, the highly popular **fuzzy-logic** household systems of the 1990s extended the notion of the 'intelligent home' to become the first successful consumer-oriented commercialisation of basic elements of AI research. Many of the activities and everyday experiences of the Japanese are mediated by technologies, which serve as extensions of the senses. While television sets and telephones have become commonplace, computer networks are now another familiar and accessible layer of the everyday engagement with technology. Science cities, technopolises and 'wired' public housing represent recent government attempts to regulate social relations for R&D outcomes, but the long-term effectiveness of these planned interventions is still unclear.

The Internet is seen by many as fostering a 'new economy' in Japan, which will make the most of a knowledge-based, high-tech nation. Personal-computer sales increased 74 per cent in 1995, and 37 per cent in 1996, reflecting a rapid increase in interest in the Internet. By January 1997, the number of Japanese Internet-connected host computers had reached 700,000, ranking Japan second only to the USA. By 2005, it is estimated that there will be 58 million Japanese Internet users, equivalent to 45 per cent of the population. Mobile phones have been transformed into Worldwide web browsing platforms, and Japan is said to be ahead of the USA in the area of mobile communications, with mobile phones now outnumbering conventional fixed telephone lines in Japan. The top mobile-phone company NTT Mobile Communications Network is seeking to make the most of its success and expand its wireless Internet service overseas. Its DoCoMo i-mode service offers continual Internet access from cell phones. Japan's dream of extending its vision of the future to outer space has come unstuck, with failed rocket launches said to be jeopardising Japan's fledgling commercial satellite industry. Meanwhile, back on earth, Japanese manufacturers have increasingly adopted an environmentally friendly stance. In 1997, Toyota unveiled 'Prius', the world's first car powered by gasoline and electricity. Honda followed suit in 1999 with 'Insight', a gasoline-powered vehicle that has low fuel consumption. The Japanese government has also reconsidered its energy policy in the face of mounting public opposition to nuclear plants. Plans to build sixteen to twenty new plants by 2010 are likely to be cut back.

As we enter the twenty-first century, technological innovation is seen as the key to continuing Japanese economic prosperity. The challenge will be to ensure that it improves the quality of life in a country with an ageing population and declining birth-rate. It is feared by some that too much reliance is being placed on the promise of technology alone. Without a liberalisation of immigration and an increase in foreign workers, Japan will lack the workforce necessary to sustain economic success. Feminists also point to the need for more effective and implementable reforms to ensure equal employment opportunities and job access for women. While technology may help to alleviate some of the problems Japan will face in the next decade, a more multicultural Japan that welcomes immigrants and a genuine shift towards gender equity would be two other important elements in guaranteeing a better future.

Further reading

Aoyama, Y. (1991) *Kaden* (Home Appliances), Tokyo: Nihon Keizai Hyōronsha.

Morris-Suzuki, T. (1988) *Beyond Computopia: Information, Automation and Democracy in Japan*, London: Kegan Paul International.

Plath, D.W. (1990) 'My-carisma: Motorizing the Showa shelf', *Daedalus* 119(3): 229–44.

Tada, M. (1978) 'The glory and misery of "my home"', in J.V. Koschmann (ed.) *Authority and the Individual in Japan: Citizen Protest in Historical Perspective*, Tokyo: University of Tokyo Press, pp. 207–17.

MORRIS LOW

Teenage Mutant Ninja Turtles

Despite their designation as ninja, the Teenage Mutant Ninja Turtles (TMNT) are purely US in origin. Even so, the series owes much to the influence of Japanese *anime* on both US youth audiences and trends in television production and programming. The creation of Kevin Eastman and Peter Laird, the Turtles debuted in a black and white self-published comic in 1984. The unusual name caught the attention of PBS radio and UPI, which broadcast reports about the Turtles throughout the USA. This unexpected publicity caused the first issue of 3,000 copies to sell out instantly. The second issue, of 15,000 copies, sold out as well; as did the third of 35,000. The Turtles appeared in a syndicated comic strip until 1997. In the mean time, TMNT had mutated into an animated television series, three animated feature films, a role-playing game and action figures.

The superhero turtles are named for the famous Italian artists: Michelangelo, Leonardo, Raphael and Donatello. Despite the Turtles' *ninjutsu* skills and their '*Sensei*', Splinter the rat, the creators thought that Japanese names would be too alienating for a US audience. The series aimed to appeal both to children and older comics fans by using the adolescent insouciance of the teenaged turtles to provide a fresh, humorous quality to the darker superhero comics that it simultaneously imitated and parodied.

See also: *anime*; exporting Japanese culture; *manga*

SHARALYN ORBAUGH

Tekkō Rōren

Short for Nihon Tekkō Sangyō Rōdō Kumiai Rengōkai, Tekkō Rōren is the federation of steelworkers unions. Tekkō Rōren was established in 1951 and affiliated with **Sōhyō** from 1952 until 1989, but was also a leading force within the **IMF-JC** from 1966. Although Tekkō Rōren is best known for its right-wing stance, orchestrated by Miyata Yoshiji and his followers, it was originally established by Shimizu Shinzō, a protégé of the leftist leader of Sōhyō, Takano Minoru. Tekkō Rōren unions waged several long and bitter struggles against the management of the steel industry in 1957 and 1959; their failure marked the demise of militancy in the industry. Disagreement among the major steelworker unions was an important cause of the defeats. One major union, Kawasaki Steel, did not belong to Tekkō Rōren at the time; another, Yahata Steel (by far the biggest union) was lukewarm about the struggles. Miyata Yoshiji, who took Yahata out of the 1959 strike, led the elimination of militant unionists from the leadership of Tekkō Rōren after 1960.

Further reading

Gibbs, Michael (forthcoming) *Struggle and Purpose in Postwar Japanese Unionism*, Berkeley: University of California, Institute of East Asian Studies.

Gordon, Andrew (1998) *The Wages of Affluence*, Cambridge, MA: Harvard University Press.

MICHAEL GIBBS

telecommunications

Telegraphic service and railway development were among the top technological priorities of the Meiji government's modernisation programme. The first telegraphic device was brought to Japan by Commodore Perry in 1854 and offered as a gift to the Tokugawa shogunate. This and other such technological gifts and demonstrations were intended to encourage Japan to open its doors to the outside world in order to gain access to the new inventions of the industrialising west. As early as 1872 the Nagasaki Shanghai submarine cable had been laid and by 1878 Japan had begun domestic production of telegraphic services and telephones, and a nationwide telegraphic network had been established. By 1890 public telephone services were in operation in Tokyo and Yokohama and the telephone was rapidly becoming a recognised tool of business. The image of a young Japanese woman clad in traditional kimono while speaking into a telephone became one of a number of popular symbols in Meiji and Taisho art, advertising, government publications and public campaigns promoting the notion of Japan as a modern nation state that could blend technology and tradition.

The government controlled all telecommunication services in the prewar period. There was rapid growth in telephone ownership with just 60,000 units in use in 1907, 200,000 in 1913 and 800,000 units operating in 1934. Unlike the situation in North America, the spread of telephones into the family home was slow. Throughout the pre-war period the telephone remained closely identified with industry, commerce and professional services and government. Many family businesses kept a phone but its use was largely prescribed as business oriented rather than personal. From 1938 all telecommunications were further centralised under the International Telecommunications Co in order to both achieve greater efficiency and to reinforce government control as Japan began to focus on strategies of military expansion.

The Occupation period saw a number of Ministerial changes as SCAP worked with the Japanese bureaucrats to establish an efficient operational and policy base for telecommunications. The most significant decision was the separation of postal services and telecommunications.

Nippon Denshin Denwa was established in 1952 and is known in Japan by the acronym of its English translation Nippon Telegraph and Telephone, NTT. Until its privatisation in 1988 NTT was a public corporation. Both before and after privatisation it held its position as the largest provider of domestic telephone networks with 71per cent of the market in 1998. All other carriers have had to rely on NTT local networks for access to domestic households. Kokusai Denshin Denwa (International Telegraphic and Telephone Corporation, KDD), was incorporated in 1953 and, until the 1990s, it was the uncontested largest provider of international communication services including telex, facsimile and phone. Essentially the early post-war period saw a carving up of telecommunications into two monopolies: NTT for domestic and KDD for international.

Telex services were available from 1954 and NTT established fully automated telephone services from 1958. Facsimile services were added in 1973. While NTT's limited capacity for network expansion and slow service were frequently cited reasons for the slow uptake of Internet access in Japan, the company has undergone a rennaisance since the inception of its mobile service provider DoCoMo. NTT is now the innovator and market leader in new 3-G technologies utilising the mobile phone as a platform for digital communications. The vast majority of mobile subscriptions in Japan are restricted to domestic use and international access remains costly. The privatisation of NTT also saw limited market liberalisation but NTTs control of major infrastructure has remained an ongoing barrier to entry for many potential competitors. Since liberalisation KDD has face increased competition and now contends with other major international service providers. KDD has been an influential presence in satellite and optical communications research domestically and internationally and in 1998 it formed an alliance with Teleway, the third largest domestic service as part of a strategy to remain competitive with NTT and to develop a seamless international and domestic network. The combined cable, fiber optic and satellite services of this alliance exceed current demand but it is intended that with the introduction of 3-G technol-

ogies this capacity will offer a market advantage as multimedia delivery puts increasing pressure on existing competitor networks.

The future of telecommunications in Japan is closely linked to mobile technology and the 'keitai' (mobile phone). In 2000 there were 10 million e-mail-ready mobile phones in service and, in this same year, mobile service subscriptions outnumbered landline subscriptions for the first time (56.7 versus 55.6 million). With the explosion of cellular phone based e-mail transmission Japan is set to move from its past reputation as one of the slowest countries to take up either home-PCs or internet communications to assume the top rank for internet usage. Both NTT and its major competitor KDD are set to ride the current wave of cellular platform LCD digital communications into positions of global leadership. What was perceived as a 'PC lag' in Japan has ironically proven the impetus for Japanese innovation in third generation (3-G) technologies. Given the limited hours Japanese spend at home in this commuter oriented society and the intense mobility and speed of Japan's urban culture the mobile phone is likely to remain the dominant platform for communications for the foreseeable future, and 3-G technologies will see the rest of the world moving increasing in this same direction. NTT's DoCoMo is already poised to extend its phenomonal dometic success with e-mail and Internet ready i-mode mobile phones into the international market. DoCoMo's purchase of 16 per cent of AT&T Wireless has left no doubt about NTT's global ambitions.

See also: computers; mobile phones; KDD, Ministry of Post and Telecommunications; NTT

SANDRA BUCKLEY

telephone sex

These phone-based services offer clients sex talk via a restricted toll number. Telephone sex became common from the late 1980s. Many phone boxes around stations and in entertainment districts are covered with photo stickers advertising phone sex individual and party-lines. These services offer a menu of options that can include sexual preferences and fantasy-based dialogues. The industry utilises part-time workers operating out of their homes or centralised phone banks. This work is a popular, if often hidden, source of income among female university students and housewives. Since the mid-1990s, a number of services have also offered male phone sex providers to a female client base.

SANDRA BUCKLEY

television

In the 1950s and 1960s the popular media often made reference to the three treasures of post-war Japanese consumer culture – washing machine, refrigerator and television. The rapid development of the Japanese economy over the the 50s and 60s, the so-called economic miracle, relied heavily on domestic consumption of these three electrical appliances. Household socio-economic status also became linked to the acquisition of these consumer durables. When first released on the market in 1953 televisions were beyond the budget of most households. The initial NHK broadcast on the 1st of February 1953 was received by less than 900 sets nationwide. Televisions were often displayed by the manufacturer and networks in public spaces as a marketing strategy and drew large crowds at shop display windows. As in the US and elsewhere television viewing was often a communal affair in the early years, with neighbours gathering in the home of a TV owner for the broadcast of major sporting or cultural events or the final episode of a popular series. However, mass production saw significant falls in pricing and this combined with public interest in the the television broadcast of the 1959 Royal Wedding of Prince Akihito and his commoner bride, Shoda Michiko, saw a dramatic increase in television sales. By 1960 30 per cent of households owned black and white televisions. Colour television also got off to a slow start due to high prices but this time it was the Tokyo Olympics in 1964 that saw many households scramble to raise the funds to make the shift from black and white to colour. By 1966 more than 68 per cent of Japanese cited television as their main source of information and news. The popularity of television

would have a significant impact on both radio and cinema.

In the late 1990s the diffusion rate for household television ownership had exceeded 99 per cent. Households have the television running for as much as 7 to 8 hours daily although average viewing time is lower at 3 to 4 hours. The gap between viewing time and hours of reception reflects the fact that many Japanese households leave the television running (*tsukeppanashi*) throughout the peak family hours around breakfast and dinnertime as a background to the daily activities but focused viewing of specific programming is shorter. Television programming in the 1950s and 1960s included a high proportion of imported material from the United States. This was the result of a still developing local production industry and the comparatively low cost of imports. Exposure to images of the ideal US television family of the 1950s and 60s is thought to have helped fuel demand for domestic consumer goods, especially electrical appliances and automobiles. Few Japanese families could hope to own a house on the scale of those seen on popular US programmes or a full-sized American style car, but the mai hōmu (my home) and mai kaa (my car) booms of the 60s saw Japanese families opting to spend a portion of annual bonuses on the major domestic appliances that came to represent the standard of a middle class lifestyle.

Television advertising also came to focus on idealised images of the white, middle-class American family as the model of modern consumer life. Japanese advertising agencies presented the television viewer and consumer with fantasy landscapes of US suburban life. The standardisation of domestic achitectural space in the free standing houses of suburban residential parks and mid- to high-density danchi and manshon complexes saw the incorporation, often on a miniaturised scale, of the apparent consumer values of these projections of middle-America. Larger appliances were designed into the layout of prefabricated structures. This included a television alcove or display cabinet along with space in the kitchen for the refrigerator and an external balcony or verandah for a washing machine.

By the late 1980s the majority of households owned two or more televisions. In many middle-class family homes a compact set is often located in the kitchen/dining area and a larger unit incorporating video and stereo equipment is showcased in a more formal living area or family room where guests may also be entertained. In smaller domestic spaces where there is no separate family or living room the dining area will often be an extension of the kitchen space and the television will be placed so that it can be watched by the mother from the kitchen while preparing meals, as well as from the eating area. Whatever the design or size of the house, the television is now a central element in the layout of domestic family space. It is increasingly common for children to have their own televisions in their rooms. This trend began with the introduction of interactive video games that utilized the television as a gaming platform and has only increased with the immense growth in popularity of both Playstation and Nintendo. Home computers have not been as competitive as gaming platforms in Japan within the youth market. Dramatic increases in online gaming activity since the late 90s are linked to the explosion in mobile phone technology. DoCoMo's i-mode has opened up a new frontier in handheld, mobile game technology that is shifting gaming from television to phones in a way that is freeing up this element of youth culture from the television screen even if it is only transfering the focus to a mobile and more compact screen.

The national public broadcaster, NHK, is almost fully supported (98 per cent) by reception licencing fees. Commercial networks have long argued that this system gives NHK an unfair advantage in the market. Unencumbered by an equal need to seek advertising sponsorship NHK does have the luxury of producing programming free of pressures from sponsors and the related pursuit of high ratings. The networks non-commercial status has allowed NHK to maintain an Educational channel. The main NHK station is best known for its news coverage and traditional focus on cultural programming and historical drama. NHK news is, like the BBC in Britain, regarded as the flagship of news broadcasting. Its news anchors are known for their serious style and well-spoken standard Japanese. Other stations have begun to experiment with different formats for the news desk, high profile anchors and new presenta-

tion styles in an attempt to win audience share from NHK. Nyusu Suteeshon Asahi (News Station, Asahi, NTV) is the main competition to NHK for current affairs and news coverage. NTVs more animated and interventionist commentary is preferred by some to the staid NHK news culture.

The other popular and influential format for current affairs coverage is the so-called 'wideshow' (*waidosho*). These programmes run mostly in the morning and mid-afternoon slots when housewives are identified as the prime audience or late at night when a youth and student audience also joins the target profile with an appropriate shift in advertising sponsorship. The wideshows run for one hour or longer (this is supposedly the source of the name - running across more than one 60 minute program slot) and the format is either interview-style or a panel hosted by one or more well known media figures. Content of these usually live broadcasts varies from current topical news stories to scandals and sensational or extraordinary people and events. Late night wideshows frequently venture into adults only content dealing with sex scandals, pornography and sex crimes in addition to serious forays into contemporary political and cultural issues. A typical latenight guest line-up might include a leading contemporary novelist, a manga artist, a stripper, a politician, a feminist and teacher all invited to discuss censorship and popular culture. Audience phone in and onscreen e-mails are now common elements of the wideshow format. It is the mix of the everyday and the ecclectic that seems a major audience drawcard for the wideshows. Japanese quizz and team-based shows have gained international renown, or infamy, for often requiring extraordinary levels of human endurance. A player may be asked to enter a pit of poisonous spiders, step into a bee-filled room or allow themselves to be buried underground in a box. More lightweight quiz style entertainment often features high-tech sets with assorted special affects including pilot-like seats that elevate the player, carefully strapped in for safety, higher and higher up a wall-sized game board or score tower. The excess of these early evening prime time shows mounts from season to season as the networks go to greater extremes to compete for ratings.

NHK's Sunday night historical drama, running

across the entire year, has become a feature of Japanese television viewing. These expensive and visually spectacular costume dramas generally focus on the life of the aristocratic court or the samurai class and warlords. The storylines mix the personal drama of love stories and family betrayals and scandal with the espionage and diplomacy of palace and castle politics. Sword fights and battle scenes alternate with sombre interiors and rich period costumes as well as occasional sweeping shots of Japan's most well-known natural vistas, temples and historical landmarks. Commercial networks have followed suit with regular weekly offerings of costume dramas. A blend of sword fighting and romance is the recipe for success although some producers have also introduced comedy to create a new lighter historical genre.

Contemporary and historical family or home dramas were a popular element of morning and afternoon programming throughout the 60s 70s and 80s but the focus on everyday life has now also carried over into evening programming. Dramas built around a family home, neighbourhood, school or business have become commonplace in the 8.00 to 10.00 p.m. timeslots. By 9.00 p.m. domestic detective and police dramas join mystery programs for a more adult target audience. Japanese primetime evening dramas have become a significant cultural export in the Asian region with subtitled and dubbed versions capturing strong audiences in Hong Kong, Taiwan and Singapore. Satellite broadcasting and regional syndication have extended the audience for Japanese television programming from its more traditonal and familiar domestic market to at least a regional, if not global, audience.

Foreign countries and foreigners are an important element of a diverse range of Japanese programming. Travelogues have emerged as a staple in network programming and cover every possible taste in travel from extreme sport tours to Nepal, to literary tours of London or environmental treks into the Sumatran jungle. On a less serious note many programmes sensationalise unfamiliar or mysterious elements of foreign cultures rendering them into the bizarre content of quiz or talk shows. Foreigners living in Japan (*gaijin*) have also increasingly become fodder for current affairs programmes and quiz shows. One

popular foramt pits foreigners against Japanese in an open debate on topical issues that usually degenerate into a shouting match grounded on little more than racial and cultural stereotyping. This format inevitably positions the Japanese hosts or panelists as rational and credible while the *gaijin* are presented as emotional, erratic and aggressive. The genre has been described by one foreign critic as 'United Nations meets Gladiator'. Television has emerged as a gradually expanding forum for the representation of Japan's minority communities and as a space for public debate on such issues as multiculturalism. The broadcast of the first Chinese and Korean language programming and news is a recent and welcome development for these communities. A number of successful primetime dramas have developed storylines around the experience of Chinese or Koreans in Japan and these programs have received a mixed critical response in the communities. Multicultural television programming remains a new and still tentative area of production and funding for Japanese television.

Early television production was concentrated in the network studios but the 1980s and 1990s saw the expansion of independent studios which now provide up to 50 per cent of programming for some stations. Most production is centred in Tokyo and Osaka with only minimal regional programming carried on local stations. Networks channel central programming across their national web of stations. Although news and weather contain regular regional content, local presenters are streamed into the mainstream programme and are usually allocated only brief timeslots. Some morning and evening news shows specialise in a nationwide sweep of selected regional station announcers who feed images and soundbites of information on local weather, news or events to create at least an impression of inclusiveness and regional diversity in content. Travelogues and special interest shows (e.g. art & crafts, cooking, history) frequently take the audience to remote or rarified sites across Japan and offer the urban viewer exposure to parts of Japan they might never see otherwise. It has been argued that national broadcast networks, in collaboration with their regional stations, have done a lot to bring this regional diversity to the attention of the densely urbanised Japanese population and to encourage domestic tourism and the popularity of local specialised produces in city markets and department stores. It is also argued that access to national networks promotes the rapid dissemination of information and helps bridge gaps between rural communities and the urban centres where there is a greater concentration of the resources of cultural production. Critics however also point to the role of the dominance of national broadcast networks in both radio and television in the weakening of regional cultural practices, the standardisation of spoken Japanese at the expense of local dialects and a weakening of local networks and funding for community based entertainment, cultural activity and sports.

The advent of high definition and digital television and the new mobile technology of hand held DVDs will certainly have an impact on the future of television production and reception in Japan. Japan seems positioned to continue to lead in the development of new hardware for both the domestic and export market in televisions, video and DVDs. Television audiences outside Japan are often unaware of the extent of the penetration of Japanese programming into their local markets. This is true of a significant percentage of popular children's programming from Sailor Moon to Gundam Wing and Power Rangers but is also true for adult audiences as certain Japanese production techniques and program formats find their way into other markets. The genre of 'Real TV' is often traced to Japanese human endurance programs while popular music shows in Asia and Europe are showing some influence from the production techniques of Japanese 'idol' TV performances. How Japan will respond to and manage its growing role as an increasingly influential exporter of global media culture, and whether this will impact domestic content, remains to be seen.

See also: HDTV, NHK, Nihon TV, satellite broadcasting, TBS, TV Asahi, TV Tokyo, videos, video games and computing

SANDRA BUCKLEY

temple towns

Monzen-machi means 'town in front of the gate', referring to commercial areas built up at the entrance to Buddhist temples, where one could purchase religious objects or food, or pilgrims could obtain lodging. The earliest temple towns developed in the hills, especially in the vicinity of **Kyōto**, because temples were forbidden in the city in an attempt to reduce their political influence. A string of such settlements is now incorporated into the eastern hills of modern-day Kyōto, while others remain isolated in the surrounding mountains. The most amusing story of the establishment of a temple town is that of Nagano, established after a priest was led to the spot by a cow believed to be divinely inspired. During the Edo Period, *monzen-machi* developed as part of **castle towns** or post towns. Today, the areas surrounding temples attract pilgrims (see **pilgrimages**) and tourists, and consist of very colourful streets selling an incredible array of **omiyage** (travel souvenirs), **meibutsu** (typical local products, especially food) and religious objects such as prayer beads or images associated with the temple.

AUDREY KOBAYASHI

tempura

When the Spanish and Portuguese first arrived in Japan in the 1500s, they brought a taste for battered fried foods. *Tempura* is characterised by a light and lumpy batter made with iced water, egg yolk and flour. Very fresh seafood and vegetables are dipped into the batter and quickly fried in a hot oil kept at a constant temperature – a drop of batter dropped into the oil should sizzle, sink and then rise again if the oil is hot enough. Meat is traditionally not used in *tempura*. The quality of the dipping sauce often distinguishes a great *tempura* chef.

SANDRA BUCKLEY

tennis

Tennis is said to have been introduced to Japan by Dr George A. Lealand, a US surgeon, in 1878. It was played with a soft ball until 1913, when standard balls were introduced. Tennis gained widespread popularity in post-war Japan as one of the sport clubs available in high schools. Many high schools have tennis court facilities or share daytime access to public courts. Tennis gained a major boost in the 1990s when a number of young women players broke into the higher ranks of the international professional tennis circuit. In 1996, Date Kimiko became the first Japanese woman to play the Wimbledon finals when she reached the semi-finals. Her defeat of Steffi Graf in Tokyo the same year gained major media coverage and stimulated a tennis boom over the summer months. The next year Hiraki Rika won the French Open and in 1999 Sugiyama Ai was ranked the number one doubles player by the World Tennis Association. The male tennis player Matsuoka Shūzō has not had the same international success but his media image as the handsome 'prince of tennis' has won him a massive following of female teenage fans.

Tennis facilities in the major urban centres are limited, and in most wards of Tokyo and Ōsaka access to precious hours on public courts is determined by lottery. Some schools allow public access to their courts but many do not. Hotel courts can be booked by the hour at extremely high rates. Private clubs are also expensive and closed to all but members and their guests, with long waiting lists for new memberships. Many tennis enthusiasts travel to sports resorts outside the cities, where they can book a tennis vacation package. The sight of racket-toting Japanese tourists heading to Hawaii, Australia and other locations for tennis vacations is increasingly common.

SANDRA BUCKLEY

TENT THEATRE *see* theatre, tent

Terayama Shūji

b. 1935, Aomori; d. 1983, Tokyo

Theatre troupe leader, playwright, essayist and film-maker

Terayama Shūji is best known as a playwright, essayist, film-maker and leader of the theatre troupe Tenjō Sajiki, an influential avant-garde

'ungra' theatre group. Performing in the Shinjuku scene of the 1960s and 1970s, the group was an aesthetic laboratory combining elements of surrealism and dream-work, folk culture, machines and Brecht-like theatrics of defamiliarisation, with a critique of family and national structures.

Terayama made his literary debut by winning a haiku contest in his teens. Feature film work began with screenwriting for Matsumoto Toshio's film *Mothers* (1968), Hani Susumu's *First Love* (1968) and five films in collaboration with Shōchiku New Wave director Shinoda Masaharu. Tenjō Sajiki's performances, including *Knock* (1975), used direct theatre and improvisation to theatricalise city space. Experimental films such as *Emperor Tomato Ketchup* (1970), *Throw away Your Books, Let's Go into the Streets* (1971) and *Young Person's Guide to the Cinema* (1974) theatricalised movie theatre space by directly engaging spectators, manipulating the projected image or breaking the cinematic 'fourth wall'.

Beginning with Terayama's controversial essay 'Guidance in running away from home', many works involved meditation on memory, and the disenchanting effects of memory on a relation to one's past in marginal terrains of Japan.

Further reading

Mellen, Joan (1975) 'Interview with Terayama Shūji', in *Voices from the Japanese Cinema*, New York: Liveright, pp. 282–8.

ANNE McKNIGHT

Teshigahara Hiroshi

b. 1927, Tokyo

Film director

Son of the *ikebana* master, Sōfū, Teshigahara graduated in oil painting from Tokyo University. His first documentaries date from 1953, and demonstrate strong surrealist tendencies inspired above all by Buñuel's teaching. In the 1960s, he teamed up with the writer Abe Kōbō, both members of the avant-garde group 'Seiki' (Century), and made four films characterised by a strong visual impact and tight symbolic structure based on the theme of identity in modern society. The surreal parable on human conditions shown in *Suna no onna* (Woman in the Dunes) won Teshigahara international recognition with a Cannes Jury special award in 1964. In 1972, Teshigara directed *Samaa sorujaa* (Summer Soldiers), based on a novel by John Nathan, which was ideologically weaker than his previous works. A long period of inactivity brought him closer to the world of *ikebana* and ceramics, with only occasional returns to the camera.

MARIA ROBERTA NOVIELLI

Tetsuo: Iron Man

Directed by Tsukamoto Shinya, *Tetsuo: Iron Man* (1991; black and white, 67 minutes) is a surreal tale of environmental devastation and the post-modern mutations of bodies and identities. It was a cult hit that resonated with disaffected post-bubble Japanese youth and sympathetic foreign audiences. The film's hyper-frenetic style, special effects and industrial-music soundtrack realise in live-action the motifs and images of sci-fi horror *manga* and *anime*: gory, often sexual violence wrought by bizarre monsters. In a landscape of post-industrial blight, a demon-ghost boy (Tsukamoto) takes revenge on the salaryman (Taguchi Tomoro) and his wife who ran him over in their car. Metal debris infects and painfully mutates characters into junk-heap cyborgs with super-powers.

CHRISTOPHER PERRIUS

TETSUWAN ATOMU *see* Astro Boy

textbook controversies

Throughout the post-war era, history and civics textbooks have been a major site of controversy over the meaning of the Japanese nation, its relationship to the world, especially its Asian neighbours, the remembered past and the imagined future. The most hotly contested issue has been textbook depictions of Japanese colonialism and behaviour prior to and during the Second World War, with the Ministry of Education regularly intervening to require authors to eliminate all criticism. Specific points of controversy have included whether, and precisely how, to mention Japanese actions during the 1919 uprising against Japanese rule in Korea, the Nanjing massacre in 1937 and bio-warfare unit 731. Japanese authors have also fought with government officials over descriptions of imperial rule in pre-modern times and of peaceful protest against modern government policies such as its strong support of nuclear power. Those battles show that different visions of the relationship of the Japanese state to its own citizens are at stake, as well as of Japan's external relations.

Japanese textbooks are commissioned and published by commercial publishers. However, since the Meiji era, the Ministry of Education has practised a system of textbook review and certification. The Ministry reviews all textbooks and presents authors with specific instructions for revisions or cuts that it requires for certification. Critics have long denounced this system as censorship.

One of the first acts of the Allied Occupation in 1945 was to order schools to blacken out offensive passages in their texts, such as paeans to the Emperor or glorification of Japan's military expansion. Since the days of those '*suminuri* (painted out) texts', state control of texts has moved back into the Japanese government and to the pre-publication stage of textbook preparation.

Over the last half-century, historian and text-book author Ienaga Saburō has been at the centre of Japan's textbook controversies: as a co-author of the first Japanese history text to emerge under the Occupation, and, from 1965 to 1997, as the plaintiff in three lawsuits challenging the legality of Ministry of Education censorship. He took the unusual (in Japan) step of suing in court to sustain and publicise his vision of education as a tool to train a democratically engaged citizenry. The government has insisted instead that school children should receive a bland 'official story' of the nation's past.

The issues of textbook content and censorship gained new prominence in 1982 when, for the first time, government orders to soften criticism of Japanese wartime actions led to major international tensions. The People's Republic of China, the Republic of Korea and other former victims of colonialism and war rejected the understated or minimalised descriptions of those events in Japanese texts because they saw this as strong evidence of Japan's failure to transcend its wartime expansionist ideology. In 1982, the most famous example was the government's insistence that Ienaga change his description of Japanese aggression (*shinryaku*) against China to Japanese advance (*shinshutsu*) into China.

In 1995, the same issues flared up again when a group of Japanese nationalists, led by a Professor of Education at the University of Tokyo, Fujioka Nobukatsu, claimed that Japanese texts were filled with self-hatred and demanded they be revised in ways that highlighted pride in Japan's achievements. This time, textbook mention of Asian women (known as 'military comfort women') who were enslaved to provide sex for soldiers and sailors was the precise flashpoint.

Open public discussion in Japan of Japanese aggression in Asia was rare until the early 1990s, when suddenly many Japanese began to debate questions of relative wartime suffering, war responsibility, atrocities in Asia and the need for apology and/or restitution to Japan's victims. The Japanese government issued a series of limited apologies for its wartime conduct and allowed textbooks to include brief references to the Nanjing massacre and the military comfort women. One reason for the change was the 1989 death of the Shōwa Emperor. Another was the end of the cold war. A third was the weakening of the Liberal Democratic Party within Japan. Changes in international norms of racial and gender discrimination had also led to public criticism of Japan by former military comfort women and other slave labourers, breaking a fifty-year silence. The German government's greater willingness to respond to European and Israeli criticism of German textbook accounts of the Second World War and the Holocaust focused further international attention on Japanese recalcitrance.

The major social and political shift represented by this new debate provided the impetus for Fujioka Nobukatsu's claim that Japanese children were being taught 'masochistic' history. Several of his books topped the bestseller lists in the mid-1990s, arguing for a national history that glorified

the heroes of the Meiji era and dismissing the testimony of the military comfort women and the victims of the Nanjing massacre as unproven and pernicious rumour.

All parties to these controversies see the battles over authoritative narratives of the Japanese nation as crucial to the future of Japanese national identity, thus ensuring that there will be no simple or quick resolution.

References

Hein, Laura and Selden, Mark (eds) (2000) *Censoring History: Citizenship and Memory in Japan, Germany, and the United States*, Armonk: M.E. Sharpe.

Ienaga Saburo (1993–4) 'The glorification of war in Japanese education', *International Security* (winter) 18(3): 113–27.

—— (1970) 'The historical significance of the Japanese textbook lawsuit', *Bulletin of Concerned Asian Scholars* 2(4): 3–15.

Yue-him Tam (1994) 'To bury the unhappy past: The problem of textbook revision in Japan', *East Asian Library Journal* 7(1): 7–42.

LAURA HEIN AND MARK SELDEN

textiles

From hand-loomed cloth of natural fibres to machine-made synthetic fibre woven by computer-driven looms, textiles produced in Japan range from the traditional to the avant-garde. Traditional textiles in the form of beautiful kimono, colourful festival banners, unique curtains for shop entrances (*noren*) and simple carrying cloths (***furoshiki***) are utilised every day throughout the country. At the same time, technically innovative contemporary textiles designed and produced for art, craft, fashion, interior design and industry have received world-wide acclaim.

During the Meiji Period (1868–1912), the new post-feudal government introduced a policy of modernisation in which Western culture and technology were promoted in all aspects of Japanese life. One of the first handicrafts to be adapted to Western technology in Japan was textile production. In 1872, representatives from the Nishijin weaving district of Kyōto, a city where silk weaving had flourished for centuries, were sent to Lyon, France, to research foreign weaving equipment and techniques. Upon their return, advanced weaving techniques and the mechanised Jacquard loom were introduced to Japanese weavers. These innovations helped revitalise Kyōto as a textile centre and established new industrialised textile production areas. By the beginning of the Second World War, textiles had become the largest industry in Japan.

As a result of widespread modernisation, traditional techniques used to produce hand-made textiles and objects began to languish. In the early twentieth century, a group of concerned connoisseurs, led by the art critic and philosopher Yanagi Muneyoshi (pseud.: Yanagi Sōetsu; 1889–1961), delineated the special grace and beauty of hand-made Japanese crafts. Yanagi led a folk craft movement (**mingei**), modelled after the arts and crafts movements in the UK and the USA, which brought about a new appreciation for traditional handicrafts. Textiles, often considered one of the most significant traditional crafts of Japan, exemplified the philosophy of the *mingei* movement and demonstrated the way craftspeople, working anonymously to adorn everyday, utilitarian objects, produced objects of great artistic strength and appeal. Japanese folk textiles were produced from a variety of indigenous natural materials, including such grass-bast fibres as ramie and such vine-bast fibres as wisteria. Cotton, softer and warmer than bast fibres, was introduced to Japan in the fifteenth century from India via Korea and China. It was successfully cultivated in the sixteenth century, became more readily available in the eighteenth century and replaced bast fibres as the material commonly used to produce textiles made for daily life. Clothing for farmers and fishermen were primarily made from bast or cotton cloth dyed with natural colourants. Indigo dyeing (*aizome*) was favoured because it strengthened fabric, was slow to fade and its odor was thought to repel insects and snakes. Dyeing techniques included ikat (*kasuri*), paste-resist dyeing (*tsutsugaki*), stencil dyeing (*katazome*) and tie-dyeing (*shibori*).

In 1954, the Japanese government officially recognised the importance of the traditional crafts and passed legislation to protect certain techniques as Important Intangible Cultural Properties (*mukei bunkazai*). The types of textiles that have been designated include those that have historically been significant techniques dating as far back as the seventh and eighth centuries, or are made in regions where particular climatic and environmental conditions have helped inspire and dictate methods of production. Since 1955, individual artisans and groups of craftsmen have also been recognised as Holders of Important Intangible Cultural Properties (*ningen kokuho*). This honour commonly known in the West as Living National Treasure was established to acknowledge those with traditional artistic skills so significant and rare that they warranted protection and encouragement to help ensure their continuation. The post-war recovery in the 1960s and 1970s saw an increase in the number of Japanese studying, travelling and working abroad. Informed by the fibre art movements in Europe and the USA, and encouraged by the support for contemporary crafts in their own country, Japanese artisans began creating bold and exciting two- and three-dimensional textile art that gained domestic and international recognition. Dyeing and weaving materials and techniques were being incorporated into contemporary art objects and commissioned to adorn the increasing number of modern, Western-style architectural spaces being constructed in Japan.

Japanese fashion designers also began to make in-roads on the international scene in the 1960s and 1970s (see **Hanae Mori**, **Miyake Issei** and **Takada Kenzō**). Their successful strides in synthesising Eastern and Western aesthetic elements resulted in innovative textile designs and clothing concepts that revolutionised fashion in the 1970s and the 1980s. Designers such as Miyake Issei were invited by the textile industry to experiment and create fashions using their new synthetic fabrics. These collaborative efforts often combined craft traditions with ultra-modern materials and equipment to surprising results.

Government and corporate support for textile research centres and laboratories have enabled Japanese textile companies and designers to be at the forefront in developing revolutionary new fibres, fabrics and finishing processes. Synthetic fibres have been designed to look and feel like natural fibres such as silk and leather. Metallic filaments coloured and softened through heat and chemical processes have been used alone or combined with natural fibres to create sumptuous fabrics suitable for clothing. Also, chemically engineered fibres that contain antibacterial agents, insect repellents or perfumes have been woven into fabrics that are designed to gradually release onto the wearer's body. Japan's commitment to develop such innovative 'smart' textiles that promise to improve one's health and lifestyle is simply the next phase of its rich textile tradition.

Further reading

Adachi, B. (1973) *The Living Treasures of Japan*, Tokyo, New York and San Francisco: Kōdansha International Ltd.

Braddock, S.E. and O'Mahony, M. (1998) *Techno Textiles: Revolutionary Fabrics for Fashion and Design*, New York: Thames & Hudson.

Fontein, J. (ed.) (1983) *Living National Treasures of Japan*, Boston: Museum of Fine Arts.

McCarty, C. and McQuaid, M. (1999) *Structure and Surface: Contemporary Japanese Textiles*, New York: The Museum of Modern Art.

Takeda, S.S. (1999) 'Textile innovation: Form and antiform, Makiko Minagawa', *American Craft* 59(3): 60–3.

Tsuji, K. (ed.) (1994) *Fiber Art Japan*, Tokyo: Shinshindo Publishing Co. Ltd.

SHARON SADAKO TAKEDA

theatre, contemporary

Contemporary theatre practices in the post-war period can be divided into three phases: up to the 1960s; from the 1960s to the 1980s; and the 1990s and after. In the first phase, *shingeki* (literally, 'new theatre') was the dominant mode of contemporary-theatre practice. *Shingeki*, as a new genre of theatre, emerged towards the end of the nineteenth century and established its visibility in the 1920s. It can be defined as an attempt to adapt Western-style modern theatre to a modernising Japanese cultural environment. Relying on a realist mode of representation and acting style, *shingeki* practi-

tioners tried to break away from Japanese traditional forms so that their new art could accommodate the rapidly changing conditions of Japanese society and life. Because of its leftist ideological tendency, most *shingeki* performances were banned during the Second World War and many *shingeki* practitioners were imprisoned. Thus, the end of the war marked a new beginning for the construction of the modern theatre tradition that had been suspended for the duration of the war.

Three theatre troupes – Bungaku-za (Literary Theatre), Haiyū-za (Actors' Theatre) and Mingei (The People's Art Theatre) – led the scene, and each of these companies nurtured young playwrights in addition to producing many modern Western plays. The works of Chekhov in translation were particularly popular. Various members of the *shingeki* movement, **Mishima Yukio** (1925–70) and **Abe Kōbō** (1924–93) among them, would later become literary giants in post-war Japan. As a director, Senda Koreya (1904–94) of Haiyū-za was most influential in trying to establish a standard acting style for *shingeki* by negotiating a blend of Brechtian acting techniques with a more traditional realistic mode presented against the backdrop of the contemporary Japanese cultural milieu. The post-war *shingeki* also produced many popular actors such as Sugimura Haruko (1906–97) of Bungaku-za and Uno Jūkichi (1914–88) of Mingei.

The Japanese 'economic miracle' and politicisation of the culture in the 1960s brought about a growing level of dissatisfaction and dissent among the younger generation of theatre practitioners and audience alike, and *shingeki* came to be considered outdated and dogmatic. Under the influence of the avant-garde dancer and the originator of *butō* Hijikata Tatsumi (1928–86), the renowned *butō* performer Ōhono Kazuo (1906–) and such Western theorists as Artaud and Brecht, the 1960s saw the flourishing of various kinds of experimental theatre troupes and artists. Kara Jūrō's (1940–) Jōkyō Gekijō (Situation Theatre), Satō Makoto's (1943–) Kuro Tento (The Black Tent) and Suzuki Tadashi's (1939–) Waseda Sho-gekijō (the Waseda Little Theatre) were the major forces in this underground theatre movement. **Terayama Shūji** (1935–83), coming from a slightly different perspective, also participated in these fervent years with his Tenjō Sajiki (literally, the Upper Gallery).

The name 'angura' became widely used for this movement and it derived from the fact that most of the performances took place in small spaces in the basements of buildings in Tokyo (underground). Exponents of angura positioned antagonistically towards shingeki, placing it as a Japanese modern theatre that they had to overcome. In a political gesture of returning to 'the essence', they each emphasised the physical power and stage presence of actors and their bodies, not the texts and language of the plays. Radically deconstructing accepted notions of narrative and character, they explored the immediate potential of the body of the actor. There was a certain shared affinity and understanding towards (and against) traditional forms of theatre in Japan. They abandoned proscenium staging and 'official' and familiar theatre spaces. Their attempts are usually understood in terms of a famous dictum by Hanada Seiki, a critic and writer, that 'We should overcome the modern via critical acceptance of the pre-modern.' Although it is now possible to read the body of the actor in these performances as an 'essentialised Japanese body', their exploration of the possibilities of physicality on stage remained influential for decades to follow.

Angura revolutionaries vary in their aesthetic convictions and ideological standards, but most of the exponents of Angura, except Terayama, were college graduates, i.e. a part of the cultural elite. Because of this, their scope of 'revolution' was somewhat limited. A more appropriate term for some might be 'aesthetic radical' rather than 'political radical'. In a way, their achievements can and should be compared to those of the high modernists in the Western tradition of art. While these avant-garde giants were active throughout the 1970s, radical structural changes in the socio-political sphere were being brought about through the successful implementation of the **Plan to Double Income** by 1970. There was a sense of a new stability in the society as a whole. Marxist revolution became little more than a fantasy, and the average Japanese grew politically conservative. Emerging theatre artists in the 1970s, like Tsuka Kōhei (1948-) and Yamazaki Tetsu (1946–), had to become more introverted and/or sarcastic. They were never able to overtake the work of the aesthetic radicals. Working within the framework

set by the precedents of the avant-gardists while contributing to a popularisation of angura aesthetics, Tsuka, for instance, wrote plays and directed his work to a broader audience.

The 1980s saw an unprecedented expansion of the market for theatre in the major urban centres, especially Tokyo, in accordance with the emergence of a cultural industry in the context of the late capitalist formations of the late 1970s. Audience sizes grew rapidly, and, for the first time in Japan's modern history, theatre became an attractive market prospect for entrepreneurs and producers. Purely commercial theatre activities had been in existence for a long time, but, in the 1980s, even so-called 'little theatre' practices were incorporated into the market. Many theatre buildings, both public and private, were built during this decade and most of these were no longer 'underground' but in the centre of shopping districts in downtown Tokyo. Aesthetically speaking, the emerging young theatre artists of the 1980s were working in the theatrical space opened up by angura theatre practitioners, but they did not have to define themselves as a 'cultural other' like their predecessors. What can be called an 'angura paradigm' in theatre had already become an orthodoxy, and audience members, mostly young people, were already accustomed to watching these non-linear and non-realistic narratives on stage. Journalists started to refer to the contradictory notion of a 'little-theatre boom'. Noda Hideki (1955–) of Yume no Yūmin-sha (The Dream Wonderers) and Kokami Shōji (1958–) of Daisan Butai (the Third Stage), among many others, won an extreme popularity that would have been unthinkable two decades earlier. Exponents of the 'little-theatre boom' were able to locate themselves within many other sub-cultural genres like manga and anime, not in spite of but because of their arbitrary writing style and amateurish productions. They were no longer cultural elites, but cultural icons admired because of their acceptability and popularity with youth culture.

The 1980s also saw the emergence of many female practitioners. Previously, contemporary theatre practices were totally male dominated except in the realm of actresses. Female playwrights/directors, like Kishida Rio (1950–), Kisaragi Koharu (1956–2000) and Watanabe Eriko

(1955–), became major voices during the little-theatre boom. Though not consciously feminists (at least then), these female artists are historically important because they were able to inscribe the views of female artists on to the theatre arts, for the first time in history. The theatre scene in the 1990s can be characterised by the opening of the New National Theatre for contemporary performing arts in 1997. Preceding this historical event, national public funds became available for the first time in Japan's cultural history. The Japan Arts Fund was established in 1990, followed by Arts Plan 21 in 1996 (both funds are provided by The Agency of Cultural Affairs).

Up until the 1980s, there was almost no public funding for theatre activities, forcing theatre artists to work in a market economy. With the emergence of the possibility of public funding, what was then required of them was to prove their public worth for the nation. This economic undercurrent brought a drastic change in many aspects of contemporary theatre practices during the decade of the 1990s. Along with the deteriorating economy, the festive feeling of the 1980s 'little theatre boom' slowly faded and was replaced by a sense of seriousness and commitment to a larger segment of society over the 1990s. The theoretically innovative Hirata Oriza (1962–), a playwright and director, surprised the critics with his 'quiet theatre' works, in which all of the dramatic elements are intentionally stripped away, while Sakate Yōji (1962–), a playwright and director, explores the 'invisible' suffering of the oppressed in a seemingly stable and egalitarian society.

By the mid-1990s, it had become difficult to distinguish between the mainstream *shingeki* works and little-theatre practices. The *angura* paradigm has come and gone, and more provocative works, both artistically and politically, are now found in more interdisciplinary and multimedia venues. Dumb Type (established in 1984), a collaborative of visual artists, performance artists and musicians, mounted the monumental multimedia work called S/N in 1995, which dealt with issues of sexuality and the AIDS crisis, while the works of Kaitai-sha (literally, Theatre of Deconstruction – established in 1985) seek to explore the potential of the physical body in the digital age of new technologies.

See also: theatre, tent; Terayma Shūji

TADASHI UCHINO

theatre, tent

Tent theatres were a key element in the very diverse *angura* (underground) theatre movement that developed in the 1960s and 1970s. The two most influential tent theatre companies were what came to be known as the Red Tent, founded by Kara Jūrō in 1967, and the Black Tent Theatre, organised by Satō Makoto out of three smaller groups in 1968. The principal contexts in the emergence of tent theatre, and the underground theatres in general, were the bitter, large-scale student protests surrounding the national government's renewal of the Japan–US Joint Security Treaty (Anpo) in 1960, and the emphasis on a high-growth consumerist economy that emerged thereafter as the basis for social identity in Japan. Thus, these theatres were part of a critique of the politics of nationalism, and also, more broadly, of the social conditions of consumer capitalism.

Throughout the early underground theatre movement, a tension can be seen between a desire on the one hand to develop a pre-modern, more essentially 'Japanese' mode of statement that would oppose Western forms, and on the other hand a wish to transcend the politics of Japan versus the USA, or East versus West. Especially visible in *butō*, the tent theatres also shared these tensions. But whereas *butō* generally refused specific reference to politics, the tent theatres attempted a more directly political form of critique.

Kara Jūrō (b. 1940), a seminal figure in the underground movement, is often cited as having founded the tent theatres, in 1967. Kara made strategic reference in his work to traditional Japanese theatre, especially **kabuki**. He called himself a *kawara kojiki* (riverbed beggar – a term used for the outcaste groups that had started *kabuki*), and in 1968 set up his tent in Kyōto's Shijōkawaramachi, ostensibly the very spot where the first *kabuki* performance was held.

Rather than a nostalgic return to a purer Japanese aesthetics, however, Kara's citations of *kabuki* were meant to assist in creating a different sense of history, and thereby an altered experience of the present. The impermanent space of the tent was designed, in part, to contribute to this experience. Kara was also influenced by the Situationists, and, though popularly known as the Red Tent, the true name of his company was the Situation Theatre (Jōkyō Gekijō). Thus, like the Situationists, Kara was concerned with a critique of the structures of the quotidian life that is produced by modern capitalism. By staging plays sometimes even on street corners, at the height of rush hour, Kara (and others) attempted to interrupt the repetitious time of everyday work. Also, by setting up tents in temporary spaces throughout urban environments, including the grounds of shrines and temples, Kara tried to create events within which people might somehow rethink the space of the city. In most cases, like the Situationists, Kara was in these ways interested in contesting modern life from within, rather than arguing for a romantic remove to a non-urban or more traditional world. The plays themselves drew on a wide variety of sources, including Western theatre, and his scenography often referred to contemporary city life, but the intent was to evoke an almost mythic world – surrealist rather than realist – underlying the apparently rational order of modern life. Props typically were old, used, everyday objects, and stages often incorporated trick devices, but the props and devices were generally simple, non-technical and even at times archaic. The Black Tent Theatre of Satō Makoto (b. 1943) was in many ways similar to the Red Tent, although it was thought of as more consciously political and more plainly leftist.

In the early 1980s, tent theatre achieved widespread popularity. Yet, by the mid 1980s, criticisms began to appear that these theatres were being incorporated into the general economy of leisure. Rather than in any sense interrupting or critiquing the everyday order of things, the theatres were decried as mere 'ludic escapism'. By 1990, neither Kara Jūrō nor Satō Makoto were using tents, but both continued to be influential well after this time.

Further reading

Goodman, David G. (1988) *Japanese Drama and*

Culture in the 1960's: The Return of the Gods, Armonk: M.E. Sharpe.

Kara Jūrō (1982) *Karagumi: Jōkyō gekijō zen-kiroku*, Tokyo: Parco.

Rolf, Robert T. and Gillespie, John K. (1992) (eds) *Alternative Japanese Drama: Ten Plays*, Honolulu: University of Hawaii Press.

Senda Akihiko, *The Voyage of Contemporary Japanese Theatre*, Honolulu: University of Hawaii Press.

Takahashi Yoji (ed.) (1991) *Gendai engeki '60's–'90's*, Tokyo: Heibonsha.

TOM LOOSER

Third Generation, the

Literary coteries, usually said to have begun with Ozaki Kōgyō's Friends of the Inkstone (Kenyūsha) in 1886, are such an important feature of modern Japanese literature that some periods are virtually defined by their constituent groups. The Third Generation (*Daisan no shinjin*) may well be the last literary coterie to have a significant impact on the Japanese literary scene.

First identified around 1955, the Third Generation included a group of new writers such as Yoshiyuki Junnosuke, Yasuoka Shōtarō, Shōno Junzō and Kojima Nobuo. Refusing to be wed to the abstract, experimental and politicised style associated with the post-war generation (*sengoha*), they opted for a return to the more universal themes of mundane, everyday life. Consequently, the Third Generation is characterised by a rekindled interest, in and the conscious appropriation of, the techniques of the I-novel (**shishō-setsu**).

There are various theories as to the origin of the group's name. It was first used in a critical essay by Yamamoto Kenkichi (*Bungakkai*, January 1953), who contrasted it with Usui Yoshimi's earlier use of the term 'the second wave of new writers' (*daini no shinjin*). Usui designated by this term the generation of writers that arose after the First Post-war School (*daiichi sengoha*), writers such as Noma Hiroshi, Haniya Yutaka and Shiina Rinzō, and writers categorised as the Second Post-war School (*daini sengoha*), Ōka Shōhei, **Mishima Yukio** and **Abe Kōbō**. From 1953 to 1955,

Yasuoka's *Warui yatsura* (Bad Company), Yoshiyuki's *Shūu* (Sudden Rain), Kojima's *Amerikan sukūru* (The American School), Shōno's *Pūru saido shōkei* (A Scene by the Pool) and Endo Shūsaku's *Shiroi hito* (The White Person) were awarded the prestigious **Akutagawa Prize**. Journalists began to refer to this group of up-and-coming writers rather randomly as the Third Generation, despite the fact that is was difficult to define what this group represented and who should be included in the group. In a definitive article, the contemporary critic Hattori Tatsu described three shared features of the Third Generation writers, characterising them as: 'those who spent their formative years during the war', who 'rebelled against the lofty conceptualisation of the Post-War School by rowing against the current in reviving I-novel tradition', and who 'metaphorically reflected on the economic recovery stimulated by the Korean war' (*Bungakkai*, September 1955) Further, the group generally exhibited little interest in politics, which contrasted sharply with the Post-war School's fascination with this topic. Despite the criticisms of the Third Generation as 'apolitical' and 'trapped in the quotidian', their refusal to be swayed by foreign intellectual fashions and their determination to write out of their own personal experiences are noteworthy. Prominent themes include the loss of the traditional family and the protagonist's alienation in a rapidly Americanising, materialistic society. Kojima's *Hōyō kazoku* (Embracing Family) and Yasuoka's *Kaihen no kōkei* (A View by the Sea) are the two masterpieces that best represent the dilemma faced by these writers. Ironically, since the early 1980s, members of this group have increasingly come to be identified with the establishment, sitting as judges on the panels of all major literary awards and helping to determine the canon of contemporary literature.

References

Hattori Tatsu (1955) 'Retōsei shōfugusha soshite shimin: Daisan no shinjin kara daiyon no shinjin e', *Bungakkai* 9.

Yamamoto Kenkichi (1953) 'Daisan no shinjin', *Bungakkai* 1.

Further reading

Gessel, Van C. (1989) *The Sting of Life: Four Contemporary Japanese Novelists*, New York: Columbia University Press.

FAYE YUAN KLEEMAN

TO LIVE *see Ikiru*

tōfu

Tōfu is an important ingredient of the modern Japanese diet and has recently also gained great popularity among Western consumers of health food. It is produced from warm soy milk curd moulded and then set in cold water. It has an extremely high protein content, while also being cholesterol-free and low in carbohydrates. It was first brought to Japan in the eighth century from China.

What is generally described as firm tōfu in the West is a Chinese style of pressed or drained tōfu. Japanese-style tōfu is finer and softer in texture and is whiter in colour. In Japan, most neighbourhoods will still have a local tōfu shop where tōfu is bought fresh and consumed the same day. A tōfu maker will often sell a range of textures of tōfu, which vary according to firmness. More recently, there has been some willingness to experiment with the addition of flavoured or garnished tōfus. However, there is much less variation from traditional production techniques and recipes in Japan than in the West, where tōfu and tōfu-based products are now commonly found in the refrigerator section of major supermarkets as well as in speciality health food shops.

It was the Buddhist monks who produced and consumed most of the tōfu in Japan in the first couple of centuries after its arrival from China. However, as an increasing number of temple visitors developed a taste for tōfu, local shops started up in both **Kyōto** and Kamakura, but it remained still largely unknown outside these urban centres. Tōfu became an important element of the cuisine associated with the **tea ceremony** and in this way gained favour with the samurai class.

Once farmers in colder regions began to grow extensive soy bean crops to meet demand in the cities, tōfu also started to appear in country-style cooking. Now so essential a part of the Japanese diet, tōfu has found its way into many proverbs and is often mentioned in traditional poetry and folk song. Tōfu is also linked to many popular and religious rituals. **Kimono** makers will still annually collect up the bent sewing needles from the year and stand them in a cake of soft tōfu at the family altar (see **butsudan** and **kamidana**), as a gesture of respect to the spent creative energy of these tools of their trade.

Tōfu is most often eaten in the summertime, chilled and topped with ginger, soy and shaved bonito (*hiya yakko*). In the winter it is steamed in a variety of stock-based dishes (*yudofu*), and it is always a popular addition to **miso** soup. Vinegared tōfu skins stuffed with sushi rice are also a popular snack or lunch. Grilled tōfu is not a hot dish but the name of another style of preparation where the tōfu cake is lightly grilled after pressing and then packed in cold water like other fresh tōfu. Deep frying is one more processing technique that produces the finish of a darker patina. The hot tōfu dish known as *agedofu* consists of tōfu fried in a sticky light batter, but here the frying is part of the final cooking stage rather than the production process.

SANDRA BUCKLEY

toilets

The traditional Japanese toilet is a long and narrow ceramic bowl indented into the floor, which is used in a squatting position. Despite the fact that the majority of new homes in Japan today have Western-style toilets, most public facilities offer both Western- and Japanese-style cubicles.

Public toilets for men usually have both cubicles and urinals. Some older public facilities still found in parks and temple grounds can confuse a foreign tourist who enters the male or female doorway to find that both doors lead into the same area, with women using the closed cubicles. Japan has led the way in new bathroom technologies and many homes and hotels now boast 'programmable'

toilets, with options ranging from seat warmers, to temperature-controlled bidet and dryer functions, automatic flush and seat sterilisation. The control panels leave many first-time users baffled and sometimes drenched and surprised. A small electronic music or sound box is often found on the wall, especially in public female toilets, and is activated to discreetly cover the sound of bodily functions.

The Western toilet once introduced into Japanese homes quickly became one more opportunity for home decorating. Many Japanese first complained about the coldness and lack of hygiene of a common toilet seat. The earliest popular solution was the application of socks to the two sides of a split toilet seat. This innovation both offered some softness and warmth and could be changed regularly. Homeware designers soon captured the opportunity and launched lines of matching toilet accessories including seat warmers, toilet roll dispensers, mats, cistern covers and slippers. Foreigners are often surprised at the level of decoration of the domestic Japanese bathroom and toilet. Despite design magazine images of postmodern metallic bathrooms or traditional wooden décor, the average family toilet is a visual potpourri of frills, ribbons and lace. In the home, and in many office buildings, toilet slippers are provided so that shoes or house slippers are not worn in and out of the toilet area. This is a hygiene-based tradition that has spurred another toilet fashion – designer slippers.

The toilet area in most homes remains separate from the bathroom because a combined toilet and bathroom space goes against the grain of Japanese hygiene. In many hotels there has been a move, however, to the cost-saving option of single-mould bathroom structures, a process pioneered in Japan.

From the comic fiction and street performers of the Edo Period to contemporary comedy and television sitcoms, scatological humour has always had a place in Japanese popular culture. The toilet joke has long been a standard in comic repertoires. This fascination seems to contradict the refinement of toilet décor and decorum but each is in its own way an expression of what some only half-jokingly describe as Japan's 'toilet culture'. Even a modern writer of the stature of **Tanizaki Jun'ichirō** wrote a short essay on traditional Japanese aesthetics that focused on the toilet. In this essay, 'In'ei raisan' (In Praise of Shadows 1933–4), where he recalls with great nostalgia the virtues of Japanese toilets before shiny ceramics and bright electric lights.

SANDRA BUCKLEY

tokonoma

This recessed alcove was traditionally described as the spiritual centre of the Japanese household. While generally agreed to have its origins in Zen Buddhist reflection, there are various versions of its incorporation into household architecture. Today, it is no longer limited to elite architecture but has become an essential element of contemporary homes. Even Western-style houses will still usually include a guest or greeting room and, whether it is in the Japanese style or not, this room includes a *tokonoma*. Even many small apartments may boast an abbreviated *tokonoma*. It is architecturally designed as a focal point of not only the room where it is located but also the entire house. A scroll painting hangs on the inner wall of the recess and a simple *ikebana* display sits at the foot of the alcove or on a slightly raised platform. Occasionally, there may also be an ornament or item of pottery or lacquerware on display.

The *tokonoma* reaches high towards the ceiling, creating a disruption of the lower visual lines of Japanese interiors. It is proportioned exactly in relation to the *tatami* mats if the room is in the traditional Japanese style or, on the rare occasion in contemporary architecture when it is located in a non-*tatami* room, its proportions are determined by the dimensions of the room. The floor may be of rice matting or wood, but if raised it is frequently surfaced in black lacquer. Usually, the construction materials are identical to those of the rest of the room but rare or gnarled wood may be used as a contrast if there is a beam in the design. Experimenting with this essential element of traditional design, some contemporary architects have used such unexpected materials as a matt metal or tile for the walls of the recess but the simplicity of the *tokonoma* seems to remain sacred. The artwork, flowers and objects displayed are rotated and matched to the seasons, festivals or other celebrations. The *tokonoma* offers the home-maker an opportunity to demonstrate her aesthetic sensibility in the co-ordination, seasonality, etc. of what is displayed there. The *tokonoma* has been adopted as a popular spatial thematic in contemporary Japanese installation art and remains an essential element of architectural design.

SANDRA BUCKLEY

Tokyo

Located on the **Kantō** plain, Japan's largest alluvial delta, the self-governing metropolis of Tokyo-to occupies 2,162 km^2, with approximately 12 million people in twenty-three wards and fifty-one surrounding municipalities and villages. The entire metropolitan area has more than 30 million people, one quarter of the national **population**. It is the second largest urban agglomeration in the world after Mexico City, and is expected to become the largest in the next fifteen years.

Tokyo gained prominence in 1603, when the ancient village of Edo became the political headquarters of Tokugawa Ieyasu. The next three-and-a-half centuries are known as the Edo Period. In the seventeenth century, Edo was the largest city in the world. In 1868, it was renamed Tokyo (Eastern Capital), and became the official national capital under the Meiji government. Established as the pre-eminent power in the *bakuhan* system of **castle towns** that make up Japan's urban fabric, Tokyo has remained Japan's primary urban centre, and has become a major international centre of capital. The Tokyo Stock Exchange is the third largest trading entity in the world. Tokyo ranks first in number of headquarters for the world's top 500 transnational firms, and has thirty of the top 100. It is a world leader in innovative technology, software design and consumer style.

Tokyo has twice faced major physical disasters, the Great Kantō Earthquake of 1923, and the US bombing of 1945, after which the city was quickly rebuilt along US planning lines. Its post-war **architecture** is modern and functional, contrasting with the sedate tradition of cities such as **Kyōto**. Its central business districts also exhibit some of the most fanciful and extravagant of recent international, post-modern architecture, in soaring skyscrapers that boast exotic superstructures, cultural pastiche and exorbitant construction costs. The most daring of these structures, such as Tokyo's City Hall, are crowned with massive geometric designs set into alcove-like structures built on top of the buildings to resemble giant external *tokonoma*. The most recent trend is huge multi-purpose complexes encompassing diverse cultural, educational, consumer and business functions. As use has become more and more concentrated in high-rise buildings, the floor space of central Tokyo has doubled over the past two decades, while land prices soared to the highest in the world before levelling off during the recent economic downturn.

Tokyo faces huge planning problems. Rapid growth has created massive sprawl and difficulty organising land use. It is one of the most densely populated urban areas in the world, where the majority of families live in expensive apartments of under 50 m^2. Crowding and high land prices have resulted in a strong separation of residential and business land use, with the majority of the population flung into huge suburban developments surrounding the city. The most highly developed public transportation system in the world is overloaded with commuters constantly on the move, including nearly 3 million workers travelling into the central business district daily. Japanese workers typically spend two or more hours per day in the journey to and from work. Those commuting by automobile may expect to spend even longer in snarled traffic. Tokyo's location in a natural basin subject to climatic inversions, combined with intensive industrial land use and massive automobile traffic, creates serious problems of pollution. Water supply and garbage disposal represent huge challenges. The possibility of earthquakes is ever present. Although Tokyo's crime rate is remarkably low, it has risen in recent years, partly in response to economic pressures and partially as a result of increasing political activism that uses urban sabotage as a form of protest.

However, Tokyo is vibrant and culturally exciting. It is best understood as a collection of neighbourhoods, each with strong distinctive character, divided basically into two areas: Yamanote, the elevated western district, traditionally the home of the military and political elite, known as the 'high city'; and Shitamachi, traditionally the downtown, plebeian district of commerce and artisanship known as the 'low city'. Yamanote, including **Akasaka**, **Shinjuku**, **Shibuya** and **Roppongi**, is a mecca of trendy consumerism, corporate power and international style. Yamanote is a landscape strongly regulated by time. During the week, it is perhaps the world's most intense corporate dayscape. At night, it becomes a series of huge entertainment districts, regulated by expense accounts and a sense of international chic. On weekends, it displays the biggest and best of Japanese consumerism, on a grand scale, with a multitude of shoppers intent on seeing and being seen.

Shitamachi, in contrast, includes the commercial bustle of **Asakusa** and the traditional sophistication of the **Ginza**. Land use is much more chaotic, with smaller lots, and much mixed residential and commercial use, dotted with small-scale manufacturing rather than corporate headquarters, and businesses that cater to the everyday needs of the city from food to newspapers. Beyond Shitamachi lies the futuristic landscape of the ever-developing port area, where all of Tokyo's international pretensions are written boldly upon a landscape of global symbolism.

Tokyo residents form strong opinions not only of the character of places but of the character of people who live in different parts of the city. Yamanote people are said to be distant and cold, if rich and trendy, while Shitamachi people are deemed honest, forthright and reliable. This strongly impressionistic view of Tokyo, however, belies the fact that the majority of its citizens live in the vast suburbs that ring the central city, and travel into the city for work, entertainment and consumption. For these millions, especially for the women whose domestic and work activities are confined largely to the suburbs, life is a more mundane affair than the glittering international image would indicate, a struggle for adequate housing and for reasonable commuting access to schools, work and shopping.

Further reading

Cybriwsky, R. (1998) *Tokyo*, Chichester: Wiley.

Hirai, T. (1998) 'The heart of Tokyo: Today's reality and tomorrow's vision', in G. Golany, K. Hanaki and O. Koide (eds) *Japanese Urban Environment*, New York: Pergamon, 81–105.

AUDREY KOBAYASHI

Tokyo Broadcasting Systems

Tokyo Broadcasting Systems (TBS) is the key station of the JNN broadcasting network of thirty affiliates. It operates with a sister radio affiliate of the same name. The TBS television was launched in 1955. It became known for its television drama programming and, in particular, the genre of 'television novel series'. This genre built on the highly popular serialisation of fiction on radio and in the newspapers. Other stations followed but TBS maintained the lead in this programming niche. The other major areas of programming are news and education. In the mid-1990s, TBS news was at the centre of a scandal relating to the Aum Shinrikyō, which involved the withholding of interview footage from police in 1989. TBS undertook and televised aspects of an internal investigation and the president resigned. Close to 20 per cent of TBS airtime is still news coverage or 'wide shows', which combine news, interviews and feature stories.

SANDRA BUCKLEY

Tokyo Disneyland

Tokyo Disneyland was opened in 1983 in Chiba Prefecture. It was developed by the Oriental Land Company and designed to replicate the original Disneyland in Anaheim, California. The park proved tremendously successful, despite early criticism of its US cultural bias.

The Japanese love of Disney quickly outstripped the sales performance of the original Disneyland. The launch of Japan's Disney experience was carefully orchestrated by the advertising giant **Dentsu** as a major cultural and consumer event. Despite claims to being the same as its US namesake, there are substantial differences that reflect the adaptation of the original to its new Japanese environment. Most commentators remark on the stronger focus on souvenir shopping. While there has been a recent increase in commercial allotments in the Anaheim complex (a possible reverse flow of influence), when the Chiba site first opened, shopfront space appeared to have been increased to maximise on the retail opportunity offered by the Japanese love of souvenir (**omiyage**) shopping and brand names (see **burando**).

Other differences include the final agreement by the Disney parent company to allow all performance dialogue and lyrics to be translated into Japanese. Food was controversial from the outset with strong consumer discontent at the lack of Japanese foods and the ban on all external food and drink. The popular Japanese family excursion with boxed lunch (**obentō**) was prevented by the requirement that all food be purchased from Disney concessions. After a long public outcry, some Japanese items were added to menus but the homemade *obentō* remained contraband. The general Japanese dislike of eating while walking has limited the sale of take-out fast-food and required larger seating areas at restaurants.

For the US family visiting the original Disneyland or Disneyworld, the experience is familiar yet exotic, but the Japanese family touring Tokyo Disneyland experience it as foreign, non-Japanese and most importantly as American. The developers went to great lengths to reinforce this 'foreign' quality and early advertising emphasised the chance to be in the USA without leaving Japan. There has been some shift towards a more international atmosphere over the 1990s as Japan–US relations have become more volatile; however, the underlying flavour of the Tokyo Disneyland experience remains profoundly American.

School excursions traditionally travelled to sites of great historical importance or natural beauty, but after the opening of Tokyo Disneyland it quickly became the most popular destination for school groups from across the country. This tremendous popularity forced a dramatic change in strategy among Japan's amusement park owners. A shift away from ride-based parks to theme parks marked the 1980s, and the 1990s saw hi-tech automation transform many parks into cybergame playgrounds. There has been a marked drop in teenage attendance levels and management is now grappling with how to attract a teen audience less interested in fantasy and adventure, and for whom much of tomorrowland's technology is *passé*. Issues such as the high price of Disney brand merchandise, ongoing quality problems and market saturation need to be dealt with if Tokyo Disneyland is to remain a significant cultural presence in Japan.

Further reading

Brannen, M.Y. (1992) 'Bwana Mickey: Constructing cultural consumption at Tokyo Disney', in J. Tobin (ed.) *Re-Made in Japan: Everyday Life and Consumer Taste in a Changing Society*, New Haven: Yale University Press, pp. 216–34.

SANDRA BUCKLEY

Tokyo monogatari

Considered Ōzu Yasujirō's masterpiece both in Japan and abroad, *Tokyo monogatari* (Tokyo Story, 1953) portrays the conflicts within an extended family encountering post-war change and disillusionment. An elderly couple visit their selfish, materialistic children in Tokyo and receive kindness only from the widow of their son who died in the war. Key thematic dialogue includes 'Be kind to your parents while they're alive' and 'Life is disappointing, isn't it?' The father (**Ryū Chishū**) and daughter-in-law (**Hara Setsuko**) display bravely cheerful resignation. Ozu's subtle humor infuses scenes of the parents' disorientation in the big city and during a visit to a boisterous spa. The relations between characters are expressed through meticulous compositions, such as visual rhymes in the old couple's movements.

CHRISTOPHER PERRIUS

Tokyo Olympics

The 12th Olympic Games were scheduled for Tokyo in 1940 but cancelled due to the war with China. The 18th Summer Olympic Games, held in Tokyo (10–24 October 1964) at a cost of over ¥1 trillion ($2.8 billion), enabled Japan to demonstrate its full recovery from the war and its commitment to peaceful membership in the community of nations.

Japan went to great lengths to present the best possible face to the world and to make the games smooth and successful. They were held in the fall to avoid the heat and humidity of summer, and many schools, offices and factories closed or operated on limited schedules to reduce air pollution and traffic problems.

The Olympics, held in the middle of Japan's period of rapid economic growth, were the occasion for great physical transformations. New transportation infrastructure included the *shinkansen* (**bullet train**) linking Tokyo and Ōsaka, the Tokyo Monorail between Haneda Airport and central Tokyo, and the Tokyo Metropolitan Expressway network. Major roads in the capital were widened, making parts of the city nearly unrecognisable for those who had known the city earlier. **Tange Kenzō** designed Yoyogi National Stadium, two buildings with striking curved, suspended roofs that were the venues for swimming, diving, volleyball, gymnastics and other indoor events. Kasumigaoka National Stadium, the site of the opening and closing ceremonies, soccer and track and field events, was originally built for the third Asian Games in 1958. Other buildings built in preparation for the Olympics included the Hotel New Ōtani, then Japan's largest hotel.

Of the many remarkable athletic performances in the Tokyo Olympics, none riveted the Japanese more (or prompted more to buy colour televisions) than the efforts of the Japanese women's volleyball team. Their single-minded dedication, their intensity in training and competition, and their gold medal symbolised the post-war struggle and success of the entire nation.

Select filmography

Kon Ichikawa (1965) *Tokyo orinpikku* (Tokyo Olympiad).
Waters, C. (1966) *Walk Don't Run*.

Further reading

Posey, C. (1996) *The XVIII Olympiad: Tokyo 1964,*

Grenoble 1968, Los Angeles: World Sport Research & Publications.

Seidensticker, E. (1990) *Tokyo Rising: The City Since the Great Earthquake*, New York: Knopf.

TIMOTHY S. GEORGE

TOKYO STORY see *Tokyo monogatari*

Tomioka Taeko

b. 1935, Ōsaka

Poet, writer and critic

Tomioka Taeko made her literary debut as a poet in 1957, while studying at Ōsaka Women's College. In 1960, she left Ōsaka for Tokyo, and in 1965–6 she spent almost a year in the USA. By 1970, with five poetry collections and an anthology under her belt, and with two prestigious awards and critical acclamations, she decided to bid farewell to poetry. Her declaration to abandon poetry had no political undertone. She likened it to parting with a lover of fifteen years: 'Thanks for everything, but now goodbye.' The new genre she chose was fiction. As a fiction writer, Tomioka believed she could reclaim the immediacy and concreteness, which, in her view, had been 'trampled under foot' by poetry. She made her début as a fiction writer with *Oka ni mukatte hito wa narabu* (Facing the Hills They Stand, 1971). She was nominated for the **Akutagawa Prize** a number of times, and was awarded a string of literary prizes, including the Tamura Toshiko Award for *Shokubutsusai* (The Festival of Plants, 1973), the Women Writers' Award for *Meido no kazoku* (Family in Hell, 1974) and the Kawabata Yasunari Award for one of the stories in *Tōsei bonjin den* (Stories of Contemporary Ordinary People, 1976).

The protagonists of Tomioka's fiction are 'ordinary' people (*bonjin*); even when they are criminals or eccentrics, she treats them as ordinary people. She depicts their sexuality and relationships within and without the family, at times, with dry humour and shrewd sarcasm, but usually in a simple, unattached tone. Some stories do seem to be based on her own experience or the experience

of people around her, including her father and the artist Ikeda Masuo, with whom she lived for several years. However, one would hesitate to regard these stories as **I-novel**s (*shishōsetsu*), for they are neither confessional nor confined to the writer's everyday life. It seems more appropriate to regard them, like Sherwood Anderson's *Winesburg Ohio*, which she admires, as a collective portrait of ordinary people.

After establishing her name as a novelist, Tomioka has consistently produced not only fiction but also plays, essays and criticism. Several volumes of her essays written since the late 1960s express her views on literature, language, film, theatre, feminism and many other topics. *Danryū bungakuron* (A Study of Male Literature, 1992), co-authored by **Ueno Chizuko** and Ogura Chikako, is an influential and pioneering work of contemporary feminist literary criticism. *Naka Kansuke no koi* (Naka Kansuke's Love, 1993) is a compelling biography of the poet/writer Naka Kansuke, with a focus on his love for his friend's wife and daughter. Tomioka has also published translations from Gertrude Stein and Susan Sontag, written film scripts and recorded songs composed by **Sakamoto Ryūichi** to her words.

TOMOKO AOYAMA

Tora-san

Running for forty-eight episodes over twenty-seven years until the death of lead actor Atsumi Kihachi in 1996, *Otoko wa Tsurai yo* (the Tora-san series; literally, 'It's Hard Being a Man') is credited in the *Guinness Book of Records* as being the world's longest-running film series. Tora-san, a stock Japanese folk hero, was a kind-hearted but bumbling tramp full of contradictions. An itinerant peddler who wandered throughout Japan, routinely falling in love, he was also fortunate enough to have a loving family in an old fashioned Tokyo ward. Tora-san served as a symbol of purity and freedom that no longer exist in Japan; his popularity was rooted in the conflicts of maintaining the traditional and following the influx of change within contemporary society. In tribute to this popularity, arts critic David Lewis once noted that to the Japanese people Atsumi's face was 'better known than the Emperor himself'.

WILLIAM C. THOMPSON

torii

Torii are gates located at the entry to Shintō sacred sites and shrines. Two vertical pillars support a top horizontal beam and a second horizontal beam sits slightly lower and is jointed into (and in some styles extends beyond) the vertical supports. Traditionally made of wood, *torii* can also be made of stone, copper and, in the modern age, even concrete. A *torii* marks a place where a *kami* (god) is thought to reside, such as a rock, tree or spring. A misty scene of a long row of *torii* running up a hillside or along a stream bed is a popular image of traditional Japan among photographers and film makers.

SANDRA BUCKLEY

tourism

Once a popular destination for Western tourists, Japan is now renowned for what tourism industry analysts describe as a travel imbalance. The Japanese have gained a reputation as being among the world's most affluent tourists and many destinations have tailored facilities specifically to their needs and taste. Some 16 million Japanese travel abroad annually but a mere 4 million tourists come to Japan. Japan ranks only 32nd in the world as a tourist destination and this has led to the launch of a number of initiatives by the Ministry of Transport to transform Japan's international tourism image. There has also been a transformation in the profile of inbound tourists to Japan, with a significant shift towards a higher percentage of Asian tourists. The poor exchange rate for many European currencies and the US dollar have created a sense of Japan as too expensive a vacation destination for many Westerners.

Japanese outbound tourism was relatively low up until the 1980s, although internal tourism boomed as the result of a number of highly successful domestic travel campaigns in the 1960s and 1970s.

While the strengthening of the economy saw the emergence of an affluent elite and a rapidly expanding middle class, there remained a strong work ethic and consequent social pressure not to take long holidays. Moreover, despite high domestic spending on consumer goods in the 1970s, international travel continued to be considered an extravagance. Strict government controls on foreign exchange also deterred many potential travellers. By the mid-1980s, looser currency controls and a gradual shift towards a **leisure** culture began to see a marked increase in outbound tourism, with an annual growth rate of up to 18 per cent by the 1990s. The *yendaka* phenomenon was also a major contributing factor to this boom in international tourism. In 1987, the Ministry of Transport instigated the 10 Million (yen) Programme, a promotional strategy, aimed at further encouraging growth in outbound tourism. After over a decade of managed tourism promotions and limited government support, however, only approximately 10 per cent of Japanese participated in international tourism by the late 1990s. While the failure of the industry to grow beyond this level of market penetration is offered as one reason for recent instability in this sector, market leaders argue that the mere fact that there is still so much untapped potential bodes well. The challenge is to identify new strategies and travel products that can entice more Japanese to venture abroad.

Although there is a widely held stereotype of hoards of Japanese tourists travelling in groups huddled behind a flag-carrying guide and being rushed on and off buses at one famous site or shopping complex after another, the actual profile of Japanese tourism is quite different and has diversified considerably over the 1980s and 1990s. As already noted, 90 per cent of Japanese do not yet travel abroad, and so we are not looking at a nation of globe-trotting tourists as sometimes depicted in the foreign media. The perception in popular resort destinations of crowds of Japanese tourists is more the result of a continuing preference for group tours, combined with the tendency for Japanese to travel within very narrow windows of time around the few clusters of national holidays that create a stretch of five to seven consecutive days. The guided group tour was a successful marketing strategy developed in the

1960s and 1970s to create less anxiety for travellers at a time when few Japanese knew foreign languages and even fewer had any international experience. Business travellers and groups made up the major portion of outbound travellers in this period. This was also a time when Japanese travel agencies developed the now-controversial sex tour packages to Asia, which were marketed to companies to offer employees as a form of corporate reward and organised recreational leave. While sex tourism is still a recognised market segment in Japan, pressure from feminists and governments across the region has seen a marked decrease in corporate organised sex tours. As the economy began to slow over the 1980s, the level of business travel declined and levelled out into the 1990s at a ratio of about 15 per cent business and 85 per cent tourism.

The new traveller in the 1980s was the young working woman with substantial disposable income and far less career pressure than her male colleagues in what remained a heavily gender-differentiated workplace. By the 1990s, the category of '*midi*' – middle-aged and middle-class – women had also joined the swelling ranks of female tourists. Both young working women and *midis* are now a major focus of new product development and advertising strategies targeted at capturing the imagination and spending power of these two expanding consumer groups. The image of the young Japanese woman traveller became a controversial one in Japan during the late 1980s and early 1990s as the media sensationalised stories of the Yellow Taxi – an expression supposedly popular at the time in New York where local men were said to have coined the term to describe a new wave of young Japanese girls with lots of money to spend, 'cruising' the city for foreign men. A number of novels, short stories and many magazine articles explored the motivation of these young women and their apparent preference for romance abroad before marriage at home. The Yellow Taxi seems to have been more media hype than reality. It closely reflected a growing anxiety at home over the increasing number of women delaying marriage, and related reports of growing dissatisfaction with Japanese men as potential partners in the large number of surveys on attitudes to gender and sex published in the popular 'trend

magazines' of the 1990s. As the older generation of *midis* joined the lines of tourists departing for overseas at Narita, this seedier stereotype of female tourists dropped out of the media. The tourism industry itself did much to promote a new 1990s image of the discerning, educated and sophisticated woman traveller as it sought to develop this lucrative new gender profile in the market and counter the negative impact of the media interest in Yellow Taxi stories.

Two other recent notable shifts in outbound tourism are the new market niches of family and adventure travel. With increased focus on the need for men to spend more time with their families, there has been a trend towards families travelling overseas together during peak holiday seasons. Travel brokers are rushing to develop new package offerings that cater to the very different needs of parents travelling with children. Families are also looking for more economic holiday options and this is pushing the development of a new range of budget destinations. Adventure tours or X-tours (a term used in Japan as a hybrid of extreme sports and exotic locations), either for small groups or individuals, are also becoming increasingly sought after by a new generation of young Japanese more interested in remote locations off the beaten track than standard group travel to established destinations. This trend has seen a sharp rise in tourism to Asia and Oceania among younger Japanese over the 1990s, and this in turn has generated a new popular non-fiction genre of adventure travelogues.

Destinations have remained remarkably stable over the last three decades, with Hawaii always ranking high. Japanese tourism today represents almost 10 per cent of the state of Hawaii's annual gross product. Similarly, in Australia, the tourist development of both the Gold Coast and Barrier Reef has relied heavily on a continued flow of Japanese tourists, in particular honeymooners. The impact of high volumes of Japanese tourism is often the focus of local tension at the destination. Escalating land prices and environmental issues have surrounded a number of proposals for expansive Japanese resort projects in northern Australia and in the Hawaiian islands. South Korea, USA and Hong Kong are the other most frequent destinations along with Hawaii. Many Japanese tourists explain that they prefer Asian destinations because they experience less cultural tension. Outside Asia, Hawaii offers the most problem-free destination with a significant local Japanese-American population.

While the tourism sector is keen to continue to access a larger share of market potential for outbound tourism, there is also mounting pressure on the Japanese government to take a range of steps to promote higher levels of inbound tourism to Japan. Despite some effort to improve and broaden foreign currency exchange facilities in Japan, to streamline immigration and visa procedures, to encourage multilingual signage in major urban centres and to develop international promotional campaigns, the ratio of business to tourism among inbound travellers remains close to 50:50. There is widespread agreement that the potential of both Japanese inbound and outbound tourism is only minimally developed at this time, but there is tremendous frustration within the tourism industry with an apparent lack of focus by government on the rich opportunities this sector offers. Rail remains the popular and efficient mode of transport for domestic travel, but this seems to be a deterrent to many foreign tourists. While stations and roadways close to major cities are now generally posted with romanised and Japanese signage, many foreigners when surveyed still find it difficult to navigate the rail and road systems. Domestic air travel in Japan can be very expensive, and connections to international flights are not assured and can require a change of airport. The substantial amount of time required to travel between Narita Airport and downtown Tokyo and Kansai International and downtown Ōsaka are also deterrents to the type of short-term stopover that is an important element of inbound tourism in Hong Kong and Singapore, which have successfully marketed themselves as attractive international hubs.

The 90 per cent of Japanese who do not travel overseas do fuel a healthy domestic tourist industry. Specific holiday periods such as *Obon* and Golden Week find Japan's regional airports and railroads stretched beyond capacity. Reserved seats on the famous **bullet train** (*shinkansen*) at peak periods are booked out weeks in advance and the lines for open seating are long. There are excellent and frequent express train services between major urban centres and tourist destinations. Popular honeymoon and summer vacation destinations include the southern islands beyond Kyushu and Okinawa, as well as mountain destinations in the southern, central and northern alps and Hokkaidō.

Sport and tourism are closely linked for younger Japanese and families. Ski season usually stretches from December through to April, and express trains drop skiers from Tokyo at the slopes within an hour. Beaches along the eastern seaboard are crowded in summer and on weekends, but this does not deter enthusiasts of the new boom in water sports including windsurfing, sailing and waterskiing. Hiking, mountaineering and camping have long attracted significant numbers of enthusiasts, who take advantage of the network of **national parks** and hiking trails across the island chain. Motoring is a popular weekend pastime, especially among young couples with many joining touring clubs that promote weekend motoring excursions and amateur touring rallies. Even the long hours that can be spent sitting in traffic jams getting in and out of the urban centres do not daunt these devoted roadsters. The lack of sports facilities in the cities has created a market for sports resorts offering a broad range of sports in combination with health club and hot springs facilities. As more households struggle with the high cost of family travel, a new trend towards three-generational packages has developed where grandparents' pay for or subsidise travel and get to go along. This has become humorously known as *obaatsure* (taking granny along) as a pun on the infamous pre-modern practice of *obaatsute* – leaving older village members (most often women) out on a hilltop to die in times of food shortage.

A very different type of travel is that of the pilgrim (see **pilgrimages**). Many of those who travel to famous temples or shrines are what might be termed casual or tourist pilgrims rather than religious devotees, but certain festivals and religious rituals will find tens of thousands of visitors lining up over a number of days to make an offering and a prayer for long life, road safety, good exam results, a happy marriage or whatever is thought to be the special area of spiritual influence of a given shrine or temple. Some temples and shrines have become famous for their gardens or seasonal displays of autumn colour, spring blossoms, etc.

Others may be renowned for a special ceremony or ritual, and still others for a festival offering a glimpse of local tradition. A much smaller, and ever declining, number of truly pious pilgrims wind their way across the countryside collecting charity as they go on their way by foot from one spiritual site to the next. They are immediately recognisable in their distinctive simple white garb. A very different genre of domestic tourism is the annual company holiday trips for employees.

While some larger corporations own their own resort facilities, most rely on travel agencies to create an annual employee excursion to a popular mountain or oceanside resort. Hot springs are particularly popular and many of the older and more traditional resort destinations depend on this corporate trade. Schools also undertake annual excursions to sites of historical, natural or educational interest, and this is another important source of regular income to local tourism. There are countless historical and heritage sites around Japan, not least of all the old capital of Kyōto, and these remain popular vacation destinations for all age groups.

Tourism, like so much else in the contemporary Japanese cultural landscape, is an integral element of the intensely consumer-oriented mechanisms of identity formation. Self-image as well as group identification and networking strategies interplay with individual consumer desire in a highly differentiated market place. An individual's choice of destination for their annual vacation, choice of travelling companions (or not), mode of transport, hotel, baggage, clothes, sunglasses and sunscreen are all carefully considered aspects of a public staging of self that is performed as much to be observed by those who stay at home (family, friends, co-workers) as for the enjoyment of the individual or group travelling. Tourism has come to play a crucial role in inter-personal networking and career-tracking in Japan. The professional and flawless performance of the role of tourist is one more opportunity to invest in the cultural capital that so strongly impacts social and workplace mobility.

The onerous task of souvenir buying for those at home, which takes up so much free time while travelling, is a part of the negotiation of this cultural currency. The flows of obligation and respect are, in this case, mediated through an aesthetic of tourism.

See also: leisure; national parks; pilgrimages; school excursions; skiing

SANDRA BUCKLEY

toys

Toys played a significant role in the re-establishment of the Japanese economy in the early post-war period. Although such traditional hand-made toys as carved wooden tops, kimonoed dolls or papier mâché animal figures remain popular gifts and souvenirs for Japanese and foreign tourists alike, Japanese children spend their play hours today enjoying the same action figures, transformers, Gameboys, video games, computer chip-driven dolls and furry creatures, collector cards, sticker books and so on as children in many other countries with comparable disposable household incomes. What is still not widely recognised in a global age of production and distribution is just how many of the designs and innovations of today's toy market originate with the major Japanese toy manufacturers and then are exported or pirated across the world.

Over the 1950s and 1960s, Japan gained an international reputation as a major exporter of children's toys, although its real level of toy production and consumption was still less than 20 per cent that of the USA, even by the early 1960s. Over this period 'made in Japan' became synonymous with inexpensive toys, models and games, but it also came to be associated with poor quality. In fact, Japan's rapidly expanding electronics industry would have to wrestle to overcome the market stigma left by the 'made in Japan' toy label. Quality control and product improvement strategies initiated in US manufacturing were transferred as best practice into toy manufacturing over the 1960s and 1970s, but by this time there was already a marked trend towards offshore production. Toy manufacturers have always sought out the cheapest low-skilled labour pool and, as Japanese wages began to rise and the workforce became increasing educated, Japanese consumers increasingly found themselves buying familiar local toy designs and brands now labelled Made in Hong Kong, Korea and Taiwan, and more recently China.

It was the **Allied Occupation** that first identified and promoted toys as a non-military, low-skilled manufacturing industry with high export potential. Up to 80 per cent of some toy lines were exported in the 1940s and 1950s. Domestic consumption would not become significant to the industry before the dramatic increases in disposable household income over the 1960s. The most popular of Japan's early post-war toy lines were wind-up tin **robots**. Over the 1960s, the cheap and easily broken springs were replaced by battery-operated mechanisms. A shift from sub-contract and cottage industry to consolidated production lines and systems of quality control saw a leap in product standards. Claims of toxic poisoning from lead-based paints and problems with paint adhesion on tin, leading to excessive chipping, saw manufacturers experimenting with new materials. Plastic and rubber mould designs rapidly displaced tin toys over the late 1960s and into the 1970s. Although robots have continued to capture the imagination of Japanese children, they are no longer a major export item. The comics robot hero *Mazinger Z*, created by Nagai Go in the 1970s, saw a new line of control-operated battery models that imitated the robot and pilot storylines, with children controlling their toy robots through increasingly sophisticated remote control or signalling devices.

Just as the most popular robot lines were based on characters in both Japanese and US movies and television, the emerging trend in monster movies, cartoons and animation saw the birth of the first of a still expanding menagerie of rubber and flexible plastic-mould monster figurines. **Godzilla**, in its many miniature incarnations, has remained the leader of the pack in this section of Japan's toy market.

Further improvements to mould technologies and more durable and flexible plastics supported a new line in action figures. Like *Astro Boy* (Testuwan Atom), these heroic figurines originated in cartoons and animation. Ironically, until the *Pokemon* phenomenon of the 1990s, few US children glued to their television screen watching the heroic deeds of their favourite action figure were aware of the Japanese origins of their heroes. From *Astro Boy* to

the crew of the Argo on *Star Blazers*, the fighting pilots of *Robotech*, the Mobile Suits of *Gundam Wing* or the *Mighty Morphin' **Power Rangers***, children can purchase hand-held figurines along with weapons and vehicles that create hours of role play games. It is now common for there to be two lines of figures available, an elite and more expensive line manufactured in Japan and typically better finished and packaged, and a cheaper line made elsewhere. As with *Gundam Wing* and *Pokemon* figures, the Japanese models are are often treated as collectables outside Japan, sell for much higher prices – a far cry from the stigma of 'made in Japan' in the 1950s.

It was Japanese toy designers who launched the extremely successful line of transformer or morphing toys over the 1970s and 1980s. The introduction of moving body parts into the design of robot and action figures saw designers and cartoon and animation artists begin to explore the possibilities of morphing for action figures. Transformer toys remain popular and can have a hero or his enemies morphing from a humanoid or animal-like robot form into an assault machine that might be anything from a tank, to a race car, fighter jet or attack monster. The transformations require careful motor skills for the child to manipulate the moveable parts from one form into the other, and the designs and production technology reflect a new level of quality improvement in toy manufacturing. Bandai, Tomy and Takara have led the domestic market in morphing toys, but it was Takara that captured the international export market with its highly successful *Transformers* line.

The fascination with robot toys has carried over into the age of robotics and computerisation, and the 1990s has seen ongoing experimentation with the use of computer chips in hand-held and remote-operated toys, as well as the 2000 release of affordable robotic pets such as TOMY's robot cat with its ability to walk, flip, roll over and purr. The astoundingly popular but very controversial Tamagotchi virtual pet from Bandai in the mid-1990s first drew attention to the new range of ethical issues raised for the toy industry and parents as robotics and computerisation began to transform the nature of the relationship between children and toys. Children grieving the death of the virtual pet they had forgotten to 'feed' for a day or two, or mesmerised by the evolution of a *Pokemon* character to its newest state, create questions beyond more traditional bonds of a child to a favourite toy.

While it was the California-based company Atari that first tried to tap the potential of video gaming, it was Nintendo that finally succeeded in creating a gaming technology that now rivals the film industry for both the youth and adult entertainment markets. Nintendo began its international market push in the mid-1980s and, by 1991, there were as many Nintendo platforms in private homes as PCs. While there remains a popular market in coin-operated upright and tabletop video games in amusement parks and game parlours, the video game industry is now predominantly focused on home entertainment systems viewed on either a computer or television monitor with a separate hardware platform and control peripherals. Games now extend from children's favourites like *Donkey Kong* (Nintendo), to *Crash Bandicoot* (Playstation), to *Sonic the Hedgehog* (Sega) and to hardcore pornography and M-rated violent fighting games for adult audiences. The launch of the hand-held Gameboy in 1989 reasserted Nintendo's supremacy in the vidoe game market despite challenges from new generations of Sega and Sony Playstation in the home entertainment market. Each of these three Japanese companies now maintain extensive operations in the USA, which remains the primary and most lucrative export market for video games.

The continued rapid expansion of computerised video games has raised still more questions about the transformation of the ethical field of gaming and toys, as well as impacting the very notion of play. The new relations of play conceptualised around interactive and role play video games are attracting attention from parents, educators, psychologists, doctors, government, industry censors and many others in Japan and elsewhere. The debates emerging in this area are complex and far from resolved. The significance (or not) of the fact that so much of the hardware and software design of this generation of hi-tech toys and gaming originates in Japan is a topic that has as yet received only minimum attention from specialists in cross-cultural research. What is clear, however, is that with the computerisation of the world of toys

Japan has secured its reputation for leadership in innovation, design and quality.

See also: robots; video and computer games

Further reading

Schodt, F. (1990) *Inside the Robotic Kingdom*, Tokyo: Kōdansha.
Sheff, D. (1994) *Game Over: How Nintendo Conquered the World*, New York: Vintage Books.
Yang, J., Gan, D. and Hong, T. (1997) *Eastern Standard Time: A Guide to Asian Influence on American Culture*, New York: Mariner Books.

SANDRA BUCKLEY

traditional medicine

At least three bodies of medical knowledge and practices have contributed to widely shared ideas about health and illness in contemporary Japan. The oldest of these is associated with the ubiquitous belief in animism present throughout Japanese history and still discernable today. Shintō, the name given to these animistic cults, had no comprehensive national organisation until the early 1900s, but its beliefs about purity and pollution have nevertheless exerted a profound influence on medically related practices throughout Japanese history. For example, menstruation and childbirth were associated with pollution until well into this century and these events have, therefore, been hedged with taboos. The continuing widespread custom of having children rinse out their mouths upon their return home from school is no doubt associated with fears about the incorporation into the body of dirt from the outside world.

The first corpus of medical knowledge and practices to be systemised in textual form in Japan was brought form China in the sixth century, primarily by priests who used their medical knowledge to facilitate the spread of Buddhist doctrine. Several doctors arrived around the same time, including one from southern China, who brought with him about a hundred books on theoretical medicine. An array of medicinal plant material and the techniques of **acupuncture**, moxabustion (see **moxa**) and massage, all part of the Chinese medical tradition that began to be formalised in that country from approximately 1700 BCE, were introduced to Japan at this time. East Asian medicine was the sole systematised, professional medical knowledge in Japan until the sixteenth century, when Portuguese missionaries and scholars introduced European knowledge about medicine and surgery. However, East Asian medicine continued its dominance until the second half of the nineteenth century, when 'Western' medicine was made into the official state-supported medical system.

Like the majority of other societies today, Japan has a pluralistic medical complex in which the services of the technologically sophisticated, dominant bio-medical system are covered by various comprehensive health insurance systems. After half a century of decline, the East Asian system underwent a lively revival from the 1950s and is used by many patients throughout the country. The majority attend private clinics, although the cost of some of the herbal medicine is covered by health insurance. Numerous acupuncturists, practitioners of moxibustion and masseurs own or are employed in clinics liberally distributed throughout Japan. Practitioners are generally formally trained and licensed, but both massage and moxabustion can be practised informally, often by Buddhist priests or at a hot-springs resorts. The popular form of massage known as *shiatsu* (finger pressure) commenced only in the last century, and more than 200 different schools exist today, employing a range of techniques. Patent medicines continue to be sold throughout Japan, as has been the case for 300 years; chiropractic and bone-setting specialists are numerous. Shintō shrines and most Buddhist temples sell talismans and amulets, and often provide a range of popular practices relating to health care, and a good number of shamans continue to practice in rural areas, usually in association with Shintō shrines. There is significant traffic on the part of patients of all ages across these different domains of traditional medicine in search for the most efficacious therapy or combination of treatments.

The philosophic foundations of East Asian medicine are grounded primarily in Taoism. The body is understood as a microcosm of the macrocosmic natural order and the doctrine of

yin and yang is fundamental to the entire system. A healthy body is in harmony with the macrocosm, and, although deviation from this state of balance is normal and inevitable, there is a tendency for the body to return to harmony without intervention, A serious loss of balance can be diagnosed by means of various techniques including a complex assessment of the condition of the pulse and through abdominal palpation. Diagnosis reveals the condition of the internal organs of the body. The organs are not conceptualised anatomically but primarily in terms of their physiological function and connection in the body to other systems. Treatment is directed at symptom removal, rather than the elimination of named diseases, and consists of a gradual restoration of dynamic equilibrium between body and environment, through the application of herbal medication, dietary changes, acupuncture and so on. Health and ill health do not exist in dualistic opposition, but rather are conceptualised as on a continuum.

East Asian medicine is secular. Disease causation is never associated with the ideas of retribution by the spirit world or with evil. Under the influence of Confucianism, individuals are responsible for their own health, although women are also made responsible for the health of their entire family. Preventative medicine, including appropriate diet and emotional control, is considered crucial. This is the ideal, which many people, of course, do not uphold. Individuals are essentially subordinated to the social order in Japan, and, should they become sick, it is their own bodies that must adjust, and the work environment or the taxing school system, to give just two examples, remain unchallenged.

In East Asian medicine, links between a stressful environment and illnesses are acknowledged, but therapy is directed at adjustment of individual bodies. Similarly, a mind–body dichotomy is not recognised and although an association is made between heightened emotional states and ill health, the body is inevitably the focus of therapy. The approach may be thought of as one of sociosomatics rather than psychosomatics. Neither psychiatric nor psychological therapies are part of East Asian medicine, although indigenous psychotherapies are present in Japan, the best known of which, Morita therapy, is influenced by Buddhism.

It is widely believed that herbal medicines, including those used in the East Asian system, are 'natural' and therefore do not produce side-effects. This is not the case, and practitioners of herbal medicine in Japan worry that, with the enormous popularity of herbal medicine and its increasing use by non-specialist doctors, that herbal medications will be misapplied. The quality of herbal medicines also varies widely, depending upon where they grow and how and when they are harvested, and the processing and handling conditions. With increasing commercialisation, high-quality medicines have become more expensive and less readily available.

See also: acupuncture; *moxa*

MARGARET LOCK

Tsukiji fish markets

Located on reclaimed lands in Chūō-ku beyond the Ginza and Kanuki-chō, these famous fish markets are the lifeblood of Tokyo's sushi restaurants and bars. From before dawn each morning the wholesale markets are a blaze of lights as the best of the catch from local and international waters is auctioned to the highest bidder.

In addition to the markets for which it is famous, Tsukiji is host to warehouses, wholesalers, loading bays, distribution and transport facilities. The neighbourhoods are quiet by day and alive and bustling at night. By 5.30 a.m., the retail market opens to the public. In addition to fish, you can buy every imaginable shellfish and crustacean along with endless varieties of fish roe, seaweed and seasoned pickles. Even if you buy nothing, the sounds and smells of the endless aisles and the diverse hawking styles of the stall owners make for an entertaining morning. Much of the market is closed by noon. Some of the best and freshest sushi is to be found at the market bar counters where Tokyo's famous sushi chefs take a break from searching for the special of the day to line up to eat with the stall owners, fishermen and icepackers.

SANDRA BUCKLEY

Tsushima Yūko

1947, Tokyo

Writer

After a degree in English literature, Tsushima Yūko enrolled in the graduate school of Meiji University. Her post-graduate study coincided with a tumultuous period of student protest on university campuses throughout Tokyo, and Tsushima was eventually expelled from the programme due to her long absence. Her interest in writing had begun as an undergraduate at Shirayuri Women's College, where her piece 'Modernity and dream' won a college-wide competition. She also joined the literary coterie, *Bungei shuto* (Literary Capital), and published several works under the pen-names of Angei Yūko and Ashi Yūko. In 1979, the prestigious literary journal *Mita bungaku* (Mita Literary Journal) gave her her first break and the writer Tsushima was born.

Considered by most critics to be the most accomplished female writer of her generation, Tsushima Yūko achieved this reputation despite numerous trials and tribulations. Born the second daughter of the legendary novelist Dazai Osamu, her father abandoned her in a sensational double suicide with his mistress when Tsushima was only one year old. When she was thirteen, her elder brother, who was born with Down's syndrome and was extremely close to Tsushima, died of pneumonia. In 1985, after her divorce, her 8-year-old son died by drowning in an accident. These personal tragedies might not be of importance to our understanding of her literature were it not for their frequent appearance in her stories and novels. In fact, all of Tsushima's works, in one way or the other, weave together variations of her personal experience.

In stories such as 'Yurikago' (Cradle) and 'Ikimono no atsumaru ie' (The House where Living Things Gather), the shadow of her retarded brother looms large. A prototypical brother–sister relationship is portrayed with intimacy. The usually female protagonist not only identifies with her retarded brother, but through him attains an insight into human nature. Childhood, in particular girlhood, forms the primordial psychological landscape in Tsushima's writing. 'Hi no kawa no hotori de' (By the Bank of the Fire River) explores childhood violence and the way it shapes the adult lives of two sisters, Maki and Yuri.

Families with absentee fathers and stubbornly strong, protective mothers are found in stories such as 'Mugura no haha' (Mother of Creepers), for which she was awarded the Tamura Toshiko award, and 'Waga chichitachi' (My Fathers). The intense mother–child (daughter) theme is further examined in 'Chōji' (Prized Child) and *Yama o hashiru onna* (Woman Running in the Mountains), where, instead of the point of view of a young girl, a mother's point of view is used to tell the stories.

From her earliest stories to her most recent work in 1999 ('Watashi'), Tsushima continues the journey into her own deepest inner world. Through an enquiry into the various modes of the most basic human relationships, Tsushima attempts to locate and define the multitude of positions women occupuy in the modern society. Her works, sombre, honest and unsparing, capture the dilemma and the complexity facing everyday women.

Select bibliography

Tsushima Yūko (1997) *The Shooting Gallery and Other Stories*, trans. Geraldine Harcourt, New York: New Directions.

—— (1991) *Woman Running in the Mountains* (*Yama o hashiru onna*), trans. Geraldine Harcourt, New York: Pantheon Books.

—— (1989) 'The silent traders' (*Danmariichi*), trans. G. Harcourt, in Van C. Gessel and Tomone Matsumoto (eds) *The Showa Anthology*, Tokyo: Kōdansha International.

—— (1984) 'A bed of grass', trans. Y. Tanaka and E. Hanson, in Y. Tanaka and E. Hanson (eds) *This Kind of Woman, Ten Stories by Women Writers 1960–76*, New York: G.P. Putnam's Sons.

—— (1983) 'Child of fortune' (*Choji*), trans. Geraldine Harcourt, New York: Kōdansha International.

FAYE YUAN KLEEMAN

TV Asahi

Established through links with the publisher Obunsha, TV Asahi was formerly called Japan Educational Television. It is the key station of the ANN (Asahi National Broadcasting) Network of twenty-six affiliates. It has a reputation as a news station and it revolutionised the news format with the programme *News Station* in 1985. The news anchor Kume Hiroshi, a former comedian, broke with the sombre manner and tight scripting of the NHK, which had set the standard and etiquette of newscasting since its inception. At the same time that its innovative approach to news coverage attracted audiences away from NHK at times of major news events, its rogue reputation also created scandal, as with the controversial coverage of the 'Yellow Taxi' story in 1992–3. Again, in 1993, Kume and TV Asahi were accused of biased anti-Liberal Democratic Party coverage leading up to elections.

SANDRA BUCKLEY

TV Tokyo

Terebi Tokyo Channel 12 was established in 1964 by the Foundation for Science and Technology. Like other major television broadcasters, it is affiliated with a newspaper, *Nihon Keizai*, and this leads to a strong financial focus especially to news and *zadankai* (group discussion) programming. TV Tokyo also has a strong showing of imported popular US programming. Although commercial station networks and cross-media ownership are prohibited, the affiliation with well-established newspapers can facilitate the development of regional stations. TV Tokyo expanded to include the affiliates TV Ōsaka and TV Aichi in the early 1980s, and then created the MegaTON linked affiliates covering the Nagoya–Ōsaka corridor, making it the fifth largest television broadcaster.

SANDRA BUCKLEY

TYPHOON CLUB *see Taifū kurabu*

U

uchi and soto

These two terms designate in-group (*uchi*) and out-group (*soto*) relations. When Japanese society is characterised as group oriented, what is often being described is the network of in-group and out-group relationships that determine the dynamics of everyday life across complex axes of proximity and exclusion. The most significant and long-term in-group relation is to family, but others operate with varying degrees of influence at different stages in an individual's life cycle. A university cohort, particularly from an elite university, can become a crucial *uchi* network that creates not only lifelong obligations and responsibilities but also offers extensive opportunities from career prospects, to promotions to arranged marriage. The workplace will also become a central *uchi* network, although this is more true for men than for women, who have a pattern of shorter non-career-track employment in which workplace relationships are more limited to job duration.

Individuals who share an *uchi* relationship will interact with one another within a dynamic of intimacy that determines not only mutual obligation and responsibility but also details of language and all other indicators of in-group proximity. Conversely, when interacting with someone who is out-group that exclusionary status is inflected in the distancing effect of honorific speech. *Uchi* and *soto* relations can vary between the same two individuals according to context, e.g a workplace *uchi* relationship will supersede a university cohort *uchi* relationship when two graduates of the same university class meet as representatives of their separate companies in later years. By the same token, the in-group relationship between them might facilitate a better deal for their two companies. There can also be mini-clusters of in- and out-group relations within a larger *uchi* grouping, such as a corporation or government ministry. An understanding of these internal networks of *uchi* and *soto* is essential to successfully working with any organisation.

SANDRA BUCKLEY

Ueno Chizuko

b. 1948, Toyama Prefecture

Sociologist

Ueno Chizuko is a feminist sociologist who has written extensively on the subjects of gender and power. She has endorsed post-structuralism's rejection of essentialist theoretical categories. In her most recent works, Ueno discusses the political conditions and ideologies that have led women to play an active role in the colonialism and violence of the Japanese nation state. She aims to deconstruct the category of 'woman' and its relationship to nationalism by exploring recent paradigm shifts in feminist thought, which no longer concerns itself with the denial of such simple dichotomies as 'man' and 'woman'.

VERA MACKIE

Ultraman

Like Superman, Ultraman (and dozens of eventual Ultra-siblings) came from a doomed far-away galaxy-nebula, M-78, in this case-to battle monsters on earth and in space. The creation of Eiji Tsuburaya (the special-effects man behind **God-zilla**), the Ultraman concept débuted in a 1965 television show called *Ultra Q.* Thereafter, Ultraman and his siblings were featured in at least ten television series (some animated, some live-action), more than seven movies, stage shows and *manga*. There is even an Ultraman theme park in Japan. The Ultraman phenomenon in its various incarnations has gained popularity around the world.

Early Ultraman narratives played on themes of ecological disaster, featuring mutated creatures whose monstrous behaviour stemmed from ingesting harmful substances. In 1960s Japan, such storylines were quite topical and far from atypical at a time when popular culture was emerging as a site to explore the legacy of the atomic bomb attacks. This period was also characterised by anxiety over the ramifications of space exploration. Both the positive and negative potentialities of human technology and extraterrestrial life were explored through the Ultraman stories. Much of Ultraman's continuing appeal may come from the incongruous combination of serious themes with campy, clunky visual effects. As of the late 1990s, the Ultra-warriors' idiosyncratic martial arts and 'specium beam' continued to be the featured elements in new television series and films.

SHARALYN ORBAUGH

Umeda

Umeda, to the north of Ōsaka Station complex, is the commercial hub of the Kansai region, a magnet for residents of Ōsaka and thousands who come in from surrounding areas daily. From the station, one faces a fantastical collection of architectural wonders in the innovative office towers that ring a congested and noisy commercial area jammed with shops, restaurants and enter-tainment services, many of them underground. Umeda's vast underground network, the largest in Japan, connects the train and subway stations. Dotted throughout this consumer wonderland are monuments of stained glass, 'natural' waterfalls and, in the main station area, a huge artificial tree that acts as one of the major rendezvous places in the city.

See also: *chika*

AUDREY KOBAYASHI

UNDERGROUND *see chika*

unions and the labour movement

The post-war history of Japanese unions and the labour movement can be divided into four periods. The first, dominated by the struggle between the radical unionism of Sanbetsu and the conservative unionism of **Sōdōmei**, lasted from 1945 to 1950. The second, characterised by the militant unionism of **Sōhyō**, ran from the **Red Purge** and the founding of Sōhyō in 1950 through to the Miike coal miners strike of 1960. The third period stretched through the 1960s and early 1970s, and culminated in the railway workers' 'strike for the right to strike' in 1975; in this period, public-sector unionism remained militant while that of the private sector became conciliatory towards man-agement. The fourth period, from the mid-1970s to the present, has seen the cessation of any real movement on the part of labour. So stagnant has the labour movement become that it is difficult to foresee its existing organisations again engaging in meaningful social protest. Labour may exist as a lobby, but it has come to a full stop as a movement. A return to the post-1945 context is necessary to explain how this came to be.

The sheer vitality of the early post-war Japanese labour movement would have been as inconcei-vable to observers of the social scene in the 1930s and the war years as it is dramatic and surprising from today's perspective. Although we can see the roots of post-war labour in the years before 1945 – in the growth of a working-class culture around major cities, the positive effect that the wartime labour front's rhetoric had on the social status of workers, and the economic crisis of 1945 that forced workers to organise or see their families starve – the shape of the post-war labour movement was completely new. White- and blue-collar employees allied against senior management and the capitalist class. Fully half the nation's workers joined unions. A broad spectrum of politicians and opinion makers solicited the favour of labour. Labour became the unquestioned leader of the post-war popular movement.

During the **Allied Occupation** (1945–52), Japan's first-ever Labour Union Law was passed (1945), together with Labour Relations Adjustment (1946) and Labour Standards (1947) laws. These laws, drafted by the Japanese government under the prodding and supervision of officers from the **Supreme Commander for Allied Powers** (SCAP), were meant to foster a US-style labour movement of independent but politically moderate unions. SCAP soon grew disillusioned with its foster child, however. While moderate unionists affiliated with the Sōdōmei did take the lead in establishing many unions (in some cases re-establishing pre-war unions disbanded during wartime), they soon found themselves challenged by more radical voices, affiliated with the Sōdōmei's rival, Sanbetsu.

Sanbetsu was closely tied to the **Japan Communist Party** and the far left wing of the **Japan Socialist Party**. As the standard English-language rendering of its full name (Congress of Industrial Unions) indicates, it was modelled in part on the US CIO (Congress of Industrial Organizations), just as the Sōdōmei had been modelled on the American Federation of Labour. Sanbetsu aimed ostensibly to transcend the corporate framework of Japan's 'enterprise unions', organised separately by plant, office or mine, but soon abandoned this quest for industrial unionism to work within the enterprise union framework, where it recruited the more radical elements among the workforce.

These radical elements protested what they saw as the overly conciliatory attitude of Sōdōmei unionists – many of whom were senior workers and workplace supervisors – towards management. Radicals tended to be younger, often veterans of military service, sometimes women conscripted to work in wartime factories. Their ranks also attracted white-collar employees, including some junior managers anxious about their careers and dissatisfied with the direction of corporate management. They saw no reason to be conciliatory towards bosses so closely tied to the discredited wartime regime, especially when many employers seemed inclined to lay off workers and leave plants idle in the face of SCAP's early, draconian policies.

Without formal endorsement from Sanbetsu, radical unionists began to take measures into their own hands during the first post-war year, seizing control of workplaces (what became known as 'production control') and running them on their own. Other workers went along, since the alternative was idleness or unemployment. SCAP initially refused to condemn this tactic, thus inhibiting an effective response by the Japanese government and corporate management. Sanbetsu, allied with the Communist Party, tried to channel this radical energy into a generalised political struggle, with labour in the forefront, against the conservative government and its supporters in society. Such a radical democratic revolution was, however, too much for SCAP. General Douglas **MacArthur** banned a **General Strike** planned for 1 February 1947 that would have marked the culmination of the Sanbetsu struggle.

Thereafter, Sanbetsu was on the defensive, eyed with suspicion by SCAP and abandoned by more and more unions. This did not mean, however, that the national labour movement as a whole declined in influence or lost its initiative. The elections of spring 1947 brought the Socialist Party to power, albeit in coalition with the conservative Democratic Party. Labour had unprecedented access to government and unheard of prestige in public opinion during much of 1947 and 1948. This occurred in part because of the decline of Sanbetsu and the retreat of Communist Party (CP) influence. Neither disappeared, but the claim of Sanbetsu and the CP to speak first for labour could only be taken seriously by fellow travelers and anti-communist opportunists.

Labour commanded such a huge audience on the national stage in 1947 and 1948 for several reasons. The successful post-war **land reform** muted the angry voices from the countryside that had been so conspicuous a feature of the popular movement in the pre-war era. Although women had won equal political rights with men, sexist social attitudes (not least those within the labour movement) inhibited the women's movement. In addition, the fact that the Socialist Party was in power meant that politicians vied with one another to appeal to the labour vote. Perhaps most importantly, labour itself spoke with a more articulate voice than ever before in its history. Its prestige was greatly enhanced by the presence within it of many university-educated white-collar unionists.

So long as the white-collar workers, the young radicals and the senior blue-collar workers stuck together, their union was unbeatable. The task of management was to disentangle this alliance, to win back the loyalty of the white-collar staff, to placate the senior workers and to isolate the young radicals. Some managers hit upon this strategy as early as 1946, but it was the formation of the nationwide employers' organisation, Nikkeiren, in 1948, that facilitated its widespread and successful adoption. This came just as the ruling coalition of Socialists and Democrats ran out of steam and US policy makers lost all sympathy for Japanese progressive politics; it was at this time that MacArthur stripped public-sector workers of the right to strike. SCAP now stood with Nikkeiren.

Cold war politics hit the labour movement hard, but did not destroy it or steal its militancy. The reverse course in US policy came at a time when unions were bitterly divided between reflexively pro-communist and proactively anti-communist factions. Sanbetsu and its supporters were losing influence within unions but were not without recourse. Nor were the anti-communist groups united in a positive sense. This became clear in the wake of the Red Purge, when the pro-communist factions in unions were eliminated through SCAP- and government-sanctioned mass dismissals. The new national federation that brought together all the anti-communist unionists, Sōhyō, quickly divided along ideological fault lines.

Some of the quarrelling factions that dominated the labour movement of the 1950s could trace their lineage back to the pre-war era. The right wing of the old Sōdōmei, led by Nishio Suehiro, was one. Takano Minoru, general secretary of Sōhyō in the early 1950s, was a leftist from his pre-war days.

Regional figures led their own factions, like that of Asahara Kenzo in northern Kyushu; Asahara had led the great 1920 strike at the Yahata Steelworks. The pro-communist group, though purged in 1950, also made a slow comeback during the following decade. It, too, had a pre-war lineage, but there were also important groups with no pre-war background, made up of younger blue-collar and white-collar unionists. Ōta Kaoru, the (white-collar) leader of Sōhyō in the late 1950s and 1960s, led one of these. Another powerful unionist of white-collar background was Masuda Tetsuo of Nissan and the Autoworkers Federation. In the steel industry, Miyata Yoshiji, a young (blue-collar) communist in the early post-war years, founded his own anti-communist group in the 1950s. Miyata would lead his followers to control of, first, **Tekkō Rōren** and, then, the **IMF-JC**, becoming the most powerful labour leader in Japan in the late 1970s and early 1980s.

The greatest labour struggles of the 1950s were struggles of resistance. As corporate managers set out to modernise industry and rationalise production, and as the conservative government attempted to impose its political agenda on society, the labour movement – led by Sōhyō – resisted. Lay-offs at Nissan in 1953 led to a prolonged strike and the destruction of the militant union led by Masuda. Plans by the government to revise the school curriculum and impose greater central government control over the schools led to a series of actions by the teachers' union and its allies in 1956. Lay-offs at the Mitsui Miike coal mine in 1960 led to an even longer strike and the weakening of the militant union. So many lengthy strikes occurred in the 1950s that major employers, in order to win labour peace, informally promised an end to lay-offs. They could do this, in part, because of the extraordinary growth occurring in the Japanese economy by 1960 and sustained for the next decade. This was the period when the Japanese countryside virtually emptied of young people, who flocked to jobs in the cities. The strength that these numbers brought to the labour movement brought it to a second pinnacle of influence; this was the period of greatest solidarity between organised labour and other popular movements, ranging from women's to anti-nuclear movements.

Although Sōhyō remained strong among public-sector employees and strengthened its ties to other popular movements (especially the anti-pollution movement) in the 1970s, its increasing weakness among the core male workforce in private industry signified the long-term decline of the labour movement. The growth in influence of **Dōmei** and the IMF-JC split the movement once again; the sheer success and resultant wealth of Japan's major corporations also reduced the appeal of labour militancy. Nor did organised labour really try to recruit new groups like part-time woman workers and non-unionised outside-contract workers.

Unions and the post-war labour movement have left a complex legacy. The social status of unionised workers is higher than ever before in Japanese history, but it is only a privileged minority of workers (mostly male) who enjoy this status and the social and economic security that goes with it. The labour movement has, with some exceptions, paid only lip service to the needs of working women. Nor has it been able to break out of the enterprise union framework that restricts membership and its privileges. The post-war generation of private-sector unionists, after a decade or so of internal struggle, cast their lot with their employers. As the Japanese economy grew stronger in the 1970s and 1980s, the voices of these unionists came to drown out those of their erstwhile public-sector comrades. For better or worse, the fate of the labour movement has been bound to that of the great corporations that have come to represent the face of Japan to the world.

Further reading

Gibbs, Michael (forthcoming) *Struggle and Purpose in Postwar Japanese Unionism*, Berkeley: University of California, Institute of East Asian Studies.

Gordon, Andrew (1998) *The Wages of Affluence*, Cambridge, MA: Harvard University Press.

Kume Ikuo (1997) *Disparaged Success*, Ithaca: Cornell University Press.

Moore, Joe (1983) *Japanese Workers and the Struggle for Power*, Madison: University of Wisconsin Press.

Price, John (1997) *Japan Works*, Ithaca: Cornell University Press.

MICHAEL GIBBS

urban migration

Urban migration has a long history in Japan. During the Tokugawa Period, the practice of requiring the samurai class to live in castle towns, and the *sankinkōtai* (alternate residence) system, which required members of the *daimyo* (feudal lord) class to divide their families between regional headquarters and **Tokyo**, resulted in large-scale movement to the cities of both the upper classes and their many retainers. It was also common during the Tokugawa Period for excess family members of rural families to migrate to urban areas, where work was arranged for them as apprentices or domestic servants, based on a system of patronage that connected the cities with particular rural areas. This system was expanded during the Meiji Period, when rapid population growth combined with rapid industrialisation resulted in massive migration of the rural population as *dekasegi*, or temporary migrant workers, in the new urban industries. Although the majority of such workers, if they did not hold agricultural land, eventually ended up as permanent urban residents, the vagaries of employment and the pull of **rural life** led to extensive shifting back and forth, and strengthened ties between rural and urban areas.

Since the Second World War, urban migration has reached unprecedented levels. It is offset somewhat because, with the advent of automobile travel and mass transit, many areas that were formerly rural are now part of urban systems, accessible by daily commute. In the less accessible areas, however, rural depopulation is directly linked to urban growth. Despite the fact that Japan's **population** is expected to level off and begin to decline somewhat over the next two decades, the proportion of people in urban centres is expected to continue to increase at the expense of rural areas.

Urban migrants live in a variety of residential contexts that vary regionally. In the post-war period, many moved to **company towns**, although the smaller company towns have declined in recent years. In the largest cities, most end up in *danchi*, massive apartment blocks, built to such densities that they make the former rural accommodation seem spacious. Another major destination is the 'New Towns', vast mixed-use subdivisions that ring virtually all of Japan's cities.

There is considerable debate over whether the urbanisation of the Japanese population has resulted in distinctive cultural experiences and practices. The strength of the electronics industry as a magnet for urban population growth has made Japan's population into a model of the new information society. Sophisticated electronic equipment is very significant in the Japanese lifestyle, and affects the organization of domestic space, as well as forms of communication among people. The fact that Japanese cities are extremely crowded means Japanese urbanites live in densities among the highest in the world. Some believe urban density has cultivated a strong sense of co-operation, communal spirit and consideration for others, while others feel that proximity encourages greater intolerance for those who are different, and heightened sensitivity to material acquisition, with an attendant lessening of spiritual values. Another hotly debated topic is the effect of urban migration on the traditional family structure in Japan, which depends upon the household, or *ie*, as a stable social unit. While there is no doubt that *ie* has been significantly transformed in an urban setting there is extensive debate on the positive and negative implications of urban migration for household formations and family relations.

See also: family system

AUDREY KOBAYASHI

US–Japan relations

Bitter adversaries during the Pacific War, the victorious USA and the defeated Japan co-operated remarkably well during the US-dominated Occupation. Set out on a mission to 'demilitarise and democratise' Japan, the Americans introduced massive reforms that affected all areas of Japanese life from constitutional politics to popular culture. Even though some of the reforms were scaled back and even reversed in later years, the Allied Occupation reoriented Japan and served as the basis of post-war US–Japan relations.

Internationally, as the cold war had created new lines of confrontation in Asia, the USA became the dominant power in the Pacific. When the Allied Occupation ended in 1952, Japan became a member of the US-led cold-war alliance in East Asia, and, under US pressure, forfeited diplomatic relations with the communist regime in China and began a programme of limited rearmament. By and large, the US-dominated capitalist international framework served both countries well during the cold-war era; the USA gained a reliable and economically strong ally in East Asia in its crusade against communism (a position later described by Japan's Prime Minister Nakasone as an 'unsinkable aircraft carrier'). Japan, given generous access to the vast US market and to resources in South-East Asia and elsewhere, concentrated on economic recovery and development without the burden of a large military defence or another disastrous war. While Japan was constitutionally forbidden to participate in war, its economy benefitted enormously as a major supplier to the US-led military operations in the Korean War, and later during the US involvement in Indo-china.

The military alliance based on the Japan–US Security Treaties – the cornerstone of post-war bilateral relations – was prone to controversy in Japan from the beginning. The renewal of the revised treaty of 1960, though more reciprocal and equal than its 1952 predecessor, still encountered strong opposition in Japan. During ratification hearings, Prime Minister Kishi Nobusuke rammed the treaty through the Diet in the absence of opposition parties, which had abstained from the vote in protest. Popular opposition in Japan to the alliance reached its zenith in June 1960, when the Diet building was surrounded by hundreds of thousands of demonstrators, and as many as 6 million people protested throughout the country. The tense situation forced President Eisenhower to cancel his trip to Japan.

Although the appointment of prominent academic Edwin O. Reischauer as Ambassador to Japan in 1961 helped restore some stability to the bilateral relations, the US military presence in Japan continued to be a volatile issue. The USA returned to Japan the Ogasawara Islands in 1968 and **Okinawa** in 1972, areas that had been under US possession after Japan's defeat in the Second World War. US forces in Japan were reduced from 260,000 at the end of Occupation to 40,000. Still, the USA has retained numerous military bases in Japan, especially on the island of Okinawa. Possession of nuclear weapons by US forces was particularly sensitive to the Japanese, who had been the first victims of nuclear attack when the USA bombed Hiroshima and Nagasaki at the end of the war. Again, in the 1950s, Japanese fisherman suffered from radiation fallout from US hydrogen bomb tests in the Pacific, further intensifying opposition to US nuclear weapons activity in the region or on Japanese soil. Although the USA agreed to Japan's so-called 'Three Non-nuclear Principles' (no production, possession or introduction of nuclear weapons), private admission by former US officials revealed lack of full US compliance. Military-related accidents and noise pollution caused by US facilities, in particular low-flying jets around airforce bases, were additional reasons behind continued protest from affected Japanese citizens.

Bilateral relations underwent major shifts since the early 1970s due to changing geo-political and economic factors, symbolised by the two Nixon shocks. Economic relations became an area of increasing tensions, as Japan's stunning economic growth began to be seen as a serious challenge to the USA, and Japanese exports and foreign direct investment raised alarm. Trade friction further worsened throughout the 1980s, as the US economy went into recession. When the USA confronted ballooning bilateral trade deficits with Japan and rising domestic unemployment, protectionist sentiment grew as Americans accused Japan of closed-market access. On the other hand, many Japanese came to blame the USA for failing to control its budget deficit, and even accused Americans of a poor work ethic, which further inflamed ill feeling. Relations were also strained by rising nationalism in Japan, as symbolised by the 1989 bestseller, *The Japan that Can Say No*.

The end of the cold war introduced new uncertainties in the bilateral relations. Following a 1992 incident in Okinawa, in which three US servicemen raped a Japanese schoolgirl, Japanese popular opposition to the US military presence reached new heights and sparked massive demonstrations. The Gulf War, which Japan supported with generous financial contributions but not soldiers, led to criticisms in the USA and calls in both countries for Japan to play a greater role in the alliance. The rise of China as well as the crisis in the Taiwan Strait in 1995 added urgency for a reassessment of their alliance relations. As a result, new 'Guidelines for Japan–US Defence Co-operation', which allowed Japan's Self-Defence Force to provide limited assistance to US military operations in the west Pacific, were issued in 1997 and passed in the Diet two years later. Opinion polls in Japan have indicated a greater acceptance of the military relations with the USA among the general public and major political parties, except the Communist Party.

Famously described by the former US Ambassador Mike Mansfield as 'the most important bilateral relationship', post-war US–Japan relations have also been a constant search for reciprocity and equality. Such a search continues in all areas, including culture and society, as both sides vow to build global partnership on the basis of shared values.

See also: Anpo struggle; Beheiren; Okinawa; peace and anti-nuclear movements

Further reading

Buckley, R. (1992) *US–Japan Alliance Diplomacy, 1945–1990*, Cambridge, UK: Cambridge University Press.

Funabashi Yoichi (1999) *Alliance Adrift*, New York: Council on Foreign Relations Press.

Iriye, A. and Cohen, W.I. (1989) *The United States and Japan in the Postwar World*, Lexington: University of Kentucky Press.

Schaller, M. (1997) *Altered States: The United States and Japan since the Occupation*, New York: Oxford University Press.

DAQING YANG

V

Valentine's Day and White Day

Valentine's Day came to Japan as the result of commercial marketing initiatives in the 1960s. This day quickly became an occasion on which women give gifts of chocolate to men. Within less than a decade, women in the workplace and in university classes had begun to give small chocolate gifts to all their male colleagues and friends to avoid any apparent favouritism. Men for their part showed little interest in buying Valentine's gifts for women and soon the marketers captured the opportunity to create White Day on 14 March, a day now designated for men to buy white chocolate for women friends and colleagues. The romantic side of these gifts has long been displaced by the sense of gift-giving obligation. The exchange of Valentine's and White Day gifts is far less frequent between married couples, although a man or woman might still buy the expected chocolates for work colleagues years after they stop bringing home a gift for their spouse.

SANDRA BUCKLEY

vending machines

Anyone who spends time in Japan cannot help but notice the popularity of vending machines. In a culture where commuting is a large part of everyday life, quick access to cheap snacks, drinks, tobacco and magazines along the route to and from work is a desirable convenience.

Long work hours mean that many commuters are returning home after local kiosks and fast-food stands have closed. The surrounding streets and internal alleys and platforms of commuter hubs are the popular location for a whole new genre of coin-in-the-slot hot and cold fast-food lines that can vary from cheap instant **noodles** to gourmet *onigiri*. Alcoholic beverages are sold alongside coffee and soft drinks. The taste for the convenience of vending machines has now extended to suburban drive-up vending banks specialising in cumbersome items like bulk rice, cooking oil, soy sauce, laundry soap, etc. Fresh and perishable food items such as sushi, fruit and sandwiches are a recent new commodity in this area of fast-food retail but raise more difficult issues of refrigeration.

The lack of monitoring of such purchases as alcohol, tobacco and pornography at vending machines has created some pressure for stricter controls on the location, stocking and accessibility of these facilities. Regulations in some cities and wards are now attempting to enforce certain standards and controls, and even zoning for vending machine-based commerce.

SANDRA BUCKLEY

video and computer games

The idea of enjoying games on computers was born at Brookhaven Institute in 1957 and spread throughout the world in tandem with the computer itself. During the 1960s, a number of students 'hacked' into games on IBM, DEC or FACOM systems installed at Japanese universities. However, more liberal access was rare at a time when computer mainframes were still expensive and under strict security controls. Those who enjoyed the benefits and pleasures were just the small fraction of students whose studies or research gave them access to institutional computer facilities.

The invention of a coin-operated game machine by Nolan Bushnell was quickly taken up by the Japanese amusement industry. The likes of Sega, **Nintendo**, Namco and Taito recognised the potential of the technology. By the mid-1970s, these game machines could be seen not only in amusement arcades but also in coffee shops and bars. *Space Invader* (1978) was a Japanese-designed arcade game that became a super hit, and led to an explosion in invader-game-only cafés. While the influence on under-age youth from these adult-oriented arcades and coffee shops quickly became the subject of debate over the extent of the potential social problems, computer games continued to take root as a mainstay of the popular culture of the day. For instance, the well-known musical group **Yellow Magic Orchestra** (YMO) incorporated game sounds into their debut album as part of their appeal to a youth culture. The *Galaxian* (1980) and *Donkey Kong* (1981) games followed in quick succession, enriching and expanding the appeal and uniqueness of the new video game culture.

Micro computers (CPU) made their appearance in the market in the early 1970s. These low priced CPUs created the *maikon* (abbreviated form of the English 'micro computer') boom, which spread most rapidly in the first instance among amateur radio operators who already had an established interest in portable and home-based electronic technologies. The Japanese company NEC released a training kit called TK-80 in 1976 to encourage people to buy their *maikon* product, and this fed into the first stage of development of the market. Devotees enjoyed creating and playing computer games with these NEC products or imported Apple computers. Early on, attention became focused in the media by feminist groups on the pornographic content of many of the home-grown games finding their way onto the open market through mail order and telephone sales.

Video games had to wait until the 1980s to find their way into the home as *terebi geemu* (TV games).

Seeing the success of Atari's first products for the home market in electronic games, Japanese and US toy manufacturers released a barrage of home video game platforms. In the first half of the 1980s, US manufacturers such as Epoch, Commodore and Mattel, and Japanese manufacturers such as Tomy, Bandai, Nintendo, Sega and Casio, virtually flooded the market with a succession of home and personal video game machines and platform-specific games. The *'famikon'* (Japanese abbreviation for 'family computer', known as NES in the USA), was released in 1982 from Nintendo. This platform was equipped with an optional keyboard and basic programming, and quickly took a significant share of the home video game market. This success was owed to the high-quality game software released exclusively from Nintendo for this platform. In 1984, Nintendo approved licensing of third-party game software and strengthened its virtual market monopoly and distribution network. Nintendo started out manufacturing decks of playing cards and the traditional Japanese gambling cards (*hanafuda*). They had a long history in gaming and possessed an exceptional knowledge of the Japanese games and toy market. The world-wide success of *famikon* can be in large part attributed to this depth of experience in combination with their effective strategy of blending the new technology with the popularity of video and computer games, and with the *otaku* style of fanaticism associated with such mass popular-culture markets as *anime*, *manga* and SFX.

After Nintendo, others like Sega and NEC released a stream of similar game platforms, but in vain. It was not until 1995 that Sony would finally threaten Nintendo's market position with the release of Playstation. Created by Sony's game software team, Playstation originally released *famikon*-compatible software. However, it was the new Playstation hardware that won over the loyalty of the dedicated game lovers. Playstation collaborated with third parties to develop distinctive designs for both its software and dedicated platforms, and launched a highly successful new style of promotional campaign that quickly established Playstation as the new standard in television game culture. The much more sophisticated hardware tolerated far more complex game software, adding exponentially to developmental costs. Soon, the new games, such as *Dragon Quest* and *Final Fantasy*, required as much front-end investment as a blockbuster film. This generation of role-playing games took much longer to develop to a standard for commercial release and were often rolled out in different improved or upgraded versions over a period of several years. This slowed down the growth of the game-playing population. Playstation 2 was released by Sony in 1999 to much fanfare. Years in the development stage, this platform can do as much as a quality graphic movie workstation; however, there are few third-party gaming companies in a position to create compatible game software that meets Playstation standards of endorsement. Given the high cost of this unit, a range of alternative extensions of the Playstation are being proposed that could convert it into a convenient home server or Internet terminal in addition to its gaming function.

Nintendo released the hand-held Gameboy and Gameboy Colour over the second half of the 1990s. The game **Pokemon** (Pocket Monster) played a major role in the extraordinary market success of the Gameboy technology. The media mix of television *anime* and the retail merchandising of miniatures, cards and collectibles, combined with the game, comics and CDs, was the secret recipe for both Gameboy and *Pokemon*. The inventor of *Pokemon*, Tajiri Satoshi, spent his childhood enthralled by invader games and went on to launch television game magazines and independent game software. He could be called a child of the age of video game culture. His own success story with *Pokemon* is already a myth of both the gaming and merchandising worlds. Sega, one of the few other long-term players, withdrew from the home video game market after their less successful 2001 launch of the Dreamcast platform. Sega will, however, continue to build on its strength in the arcade game market.

See also: *Pokemon*; toys

Further reading

Hirosi Masuyama and the TV Game Museum Project (eds) (1994) *Denshi yuugi jidai – Terebi geemu no genzai* (The Electronic Game Era: The State of TV Games), Tokyo: Village Center.

Tajiri Satoshi (1996) *Shin-geemu dezain* (New game design), Tokyo: Enix.

TADAKAZU FUKUTOMI

videos

The video tape recorder (VTR) was invented in the USA in 1956 and has been adopted worldwide as an indispensable tool of both broadcasting and film-making. Though initially intended for professional use, Sony, in 1965, first proposed and released a low priced individual or family use VTR. This was a reel-to-reel monochrome recorder using half-inch video tape and the release price was 200,000 yen. This reel-to-reel recorder was, however, rather hard to handle and still relatively expensive for an amateur. They were mainly purchased by schools, firms and hotels, where they ran tapes before multiple audiences. For example, in 1969, 20 per cent of Japanese high schools were equipped with a VTR system.

In the early 1970s, manufacturers agreed to a standard video cassette and this replaced the less efficient reel-to-reel system. A standardised video disc was also manufactured at this time, and video software made its way onto the open commercial market. Even as early as 1971 there existed over a hundred video software production companies in Japan, concentrated around the film, broadcast, music, newspaper and publishing industries. It was predicted that within ten years the video production industry would be worth 500 billion yen annually. In fact, after ten years it was worth about 7.5 billion yen.

The software industry envisaged the resale of existing in-house resources as video packages. This strategy did not promote easy, broad-based access to VTR technology for individual or home use. Some experimental artists like Nam June Paik worked with the medium in the 1970s, but there was limited popular use of the technology outside the media and art worlds. In the early 1980s, improved and simplified home use video cassette recorders were again successively released at lower prices. Industry standardisation of video cassette systems assisted this release and price minimisation. Sony's Betamax and Victor's VHS were the products of this next wave of VTR technology. Disc-based recording systems were relaunched in the early 1980s and the laserdisc appeared in 1981, with limited success outside of Asian entertainment markets. Personal use overtook business use of video software, reversing their ratio in total software sales over this period. In 1982, 10 per cent of Japanese households owned a VTR. This increase in household sales was in part due to new long-play VTR systems. People could enjoy such new options as video-taping extended periods of television programming at home, in addition to renting commercially available films from the increasing number of neighbourhood video rental outlets. This early boom in video rentals was met with legal problems when pornographic content in rental videos led to calls for censorship rating standards. Both the industry and the public were keen for a social consensus to be reached on the handling of pornographic content and other standards, in order that the expansion of the video market could continue. Issues of copyright and pirate videos also were commonplace in this early period. One challenge for the video rental market was to free the term 'video' from its links to pornography and clean up the image of the industry in order to reposition it as popular home entertainment.

In the late 1980s, compact video cameras, such as 8-mm VCRs appeared. As VCRs became popular among individual and family users, the VTR platform increased its importance as a standard household appliance. With the long illness and eventual death of the Japanese Emperor in January 1989, television and radio networks all voluntarily cut their entertainment programmes as part of a national gesture of mourning. During the weeks prior to the Emperor's death, programming was dominated by coverage of his ailing condition. Finally tired of this saturation coverage, people rushed to video rental stores in search of alternative entertainment. There was a shortage of rental videos during this period, but the overall long-term effect was positive with people finally opting for video entertainment as an alternative to standard broadcast programming. While this same period saw an expansion in satellite broadcast and cable television, this did not slow the increase in popularity of both rental video and video recording.

Film companies have begun to experiment with production of movies aimed specifically at video release (V-cinema) and original video animation (OVR). TSUTAYA, a major video rental franchise, has chosen to invest in DirecTV in an example of the move towards mediamix strategies in the entertainment industry, as companies with different media specialisations recognise the need to diversify their platforms and move towards flexible and collaborative strategies of organisation. One of the biggest hindrances to recent developments has remained the Ministry of Post and Telecommunications, which is renowned for its slow regulatory response to new technologies and market trends. The late 1990s saw the popularisation of digital video equipment, high-end PC and broadband communication systems. Digital movies are saved on the computer hard disk or zip drive, and no longer require a cassette tape format, and can be attached to e-mails, located on websites or broadcast on Internet television. The potential of digital imaging seems set to transform the future of home image-based entertainment and to launch a new era in cinematic culture.

See also: pornography

Further reading

Nakamura Akira (1996) *Kensho nihon bideo sofuto shi* (Study of the History of Japanese Video Software), Tokyo: Eizo Shinbun.

TADAKAZU FUKUTOMI

village depopulation

Japan's low rate of **population** growth has dramatic effects in rural areas, which have undergone extensive depopulation since the Second World War. Over the past three decades alone, the proportion of people employed in the agricultural and other rural occupations has decreased from over 30 per cent to under 6 per cent. Increasing numbers of young people migrate to urban areas, leaving behind a large elderly population, with attendant problems of housing and social-services provision. Because the rate of **urban migration** is higher for young women than for men (traditionally, elder sons are expected to continue the household and care for parents), the gender balance has become more heavily male. In some areas, especially in the north, young men for whom marriages cannot be arranged have turned to other countries, particularly in South-East Asia, literally 'importing' brides, who are expected to fulfil the traditional daughter-in-law role. In other areas, particularly the most remote and mountainous, entire villages have been abandoned, leaving empty buildings as eerie museums of the past. In only a few cases, the fortunes of these remote villages have been reversed, through innovative economic schemes such as tourism, or the creation of attractive retirement communities.

AUDREY KOBAYASHI

Wakao Ayako

b. 1933; Tokyo

Film actress

Wakao entered the film industry in 1951 and throughout the decade led all idol actresses in popularity with an image that combined ladylike decorum with the accessibility of the girl next door. While most of her early work at Daiei consisted of routine entertainment, her performances for **Mizoguchi Kenji** and **Kawashima Yūzō** (*Gan no tera* (Temple of the Wild Geese)) broadened her acting range, and those for Masumura Yasuzō (*Tsuma wa kokuhakusuru* (A Wife's Confession)) established her reputation for portraying fully sexual adult woman whose honest love for men could often be destructive.

AARON GEROW

Walkman

Morita Akio developed the concept of the Walkman in the late 1970s. It was launched on the Japanese market in 1979. Morita wanted to develop an individual sound system that allowed the listener to determine their own sound preference wherever they might be but also saved others around them from the noise. The Walkman is a portable, compact, battery-operated cassette player with options for radio and recording. Sound is channelled through a jack to earphones. The earliest models came with twin jacks to allow two listeners but this proved impractical in most busy urban settings. In the late 1990s, teenagers and adults walking around in groups each listening to their own music while still holding a lively conversation has become a common sight.

Despite initial reluctance among his own colleagues, sales in Japan were strong from the first launch but the US and UK markets lagged behind. Sony then decided to use the Japanese market brand name internationally and abandoned the US Soundabout and UK Stowaway brands. By 1981, sales had rocketed and, in 1999, the Sony Walkman had sold over 200 million units in more than 600 models. Miniaturisation has been a major trend, with units becoming smaller and lighter with each redesign. Earphones have transformed over time from the clumsy plastic headphone to compact earplugs. Sports models were developed to meet the massive market among joggers and people in training or fitness programmes. The US sports and youth markets mean that US sales alone make up over half the annual total. New lines of Walkman include an I-MAC look-alike in transparent plastic pastels, and bold metallic fashion colours intended to be both functional and a fashion accessory. Sony is positioning to maintain market share in the face of the new challenge from mobile-phone access to online music sites and MP3.

The Walkman not only created a new mode of portable personalized audio entertainment but also boosted the popularity of cassettes and weakened vinyl-record sales in the youth market to the point where the launch of commercially affordable CDs saw the demise of vinyl. The move to Discmans was predictable, as was Sony's own rapid expansion into the international music field, culminating in the purchase of CBS's Columbia and Epic labels. While the disc player has become more popular in cars, the Walkman remains the preferred sound source for those traveling on foot, despite improved anti-shock technology in Discmans. It was the Walkman that opened the way for the technological innovations in personal mobile technologies. Hand-held computers and palmpilot-style devices simply extend the same expectation into the digital domain. Now MP3 and Napster, and other online music sources, have pioneered the way for new collaborations between telcos and the music industry to offer an alternative to the Walkman, as the mobile phone becomes the preferred platform of third-generation technology providers. Mini-discs and inexpensive hand-held DVDs have taken up a share of the Asian markets but have been kept out of North America. Phones that provide e-mail and online access, cheap phone communication and personal audio-visual entertainment, and which can even be encoded to function as credit and cash cards, may finally break the dominance of the Walkman, but not in the short term. There are some who argue that the mobile phone will be redesigned to become more like a Walkman-style wearable fashion accessory as part of the process of creating a screen that can better accommodate text and image. Whatever its future, the Walkman transformed our sense of the place and time for music listening and created an age of consumers hungry for new initiatives in mobile technologies.

See also: miniaturisation; mobile telephones

SANDRA BUCKLEY

war brides

War brides, *sensō hanayome* in Japanese, are the women who married servicemen and civilian workers, associated both with the Allied Occupation of Japan and the Korean war. Migrating to their husbands' countries mainly in the 1950s, they were the first large group of Japanese women who married interracially. Many of them encountered hostility from the Japanese public towards their liaison with Occupation forces personnel and faced strong opposition from their families towards their marriages.

Due to their racial origin and nationality, immigration regulations needed to be cleared before admission to their husband's country was granted. Most of the women who married US servicemen had to wait until the McCarran–Walter Act was passed in 1952 before their migration. In total, approximately 36,000 Japanese women arrived in the USA as war brides. The Australian government banned the entry of Japanese war brides until 1952 due to the White Australia policy and their Japanese descent. After the ban was lifted, about 650 arrived in Australia. Other destinations included Canada and New Zealand.

After arriving in their new country, the war brides initially had difficulties in learning the language and customs, experiencing an acute sense of isolation. However, they put great effort into learning to adapt to, and assimilate into, the wider communities, while they raised their families. Almost fifty years after their departure from Japan, they today express pride at being good citizens of their adoptive countries. At the same time, they are also proud to have contributed towards the improvement of the mutual understanding between Japan and their countries of residence at a grassroots level.

The movement to form an international network among the war brides started in the late 1980s, when those in the USA gathered for the first time to commemorate the fortieth anniversary of their arrival. The Nikkei Internationally Married Women's Association was formed, and a similar gathering was held in Australia in 1993. The association has hosted international conventions in Hawaii (1994), Aizu-Wakamatsu (1997) and in Los Angeles (1999), and publishes regular newsletters. Through their activities, they try to correct stigmatised images in Japan of *sensō hanayome* as being camp followers who only married Occupation soldiers for material gain. The women also realised their joint experiences of migration by sharing their stories, and want their roles as postwar Japanese migrant women to be recognised both in Japan and their adopted countries.

Select filmography

Hoaas, Solrun. (1989) 'Green tea and cherry ripe', Gōshū Films.

Further reading

Spickard, P.R. (1989) *Mixed Blood*, Madison, WI: University of Wisconsin Press.
Tamura Keiko (1997) 'Border crossings: Changing identities of Japanese war brides', *Asia–Pacific Review* 8: 43–7.

KEIKO TAMURA

war responsibility

War responsibility has been one of the most important problematics for Japanese intellectuals since the late 1940s. It has been raised repeatedly, and a number of important public debates have been formed around this topic. A great number of books and articles on it have been published in the past five and a half decades.

In post-war Japan, the term 'war responsibility' (*sensō sekinin*) refers to the fact that the Japanese are to be held responsible for the collective crimes – atrocities and destruction of human lives and properties – committed by the Japanese state (including its military forces) and its citizens during the Asia–Pacific War. By extension, it also includes the oppression and brutality exercised by the Japanese colonial administrations and colonisers in former Japanese colonies prior to the defeat of the Japanese Empire in August 1945. It is a broad concept and has been subject to many different, and sometimes contradictory, interpretations, depending upon who is specifically held responsible to whom.

According to the terms of the **Potsdam Declaration**, a large number of the Japanese soldiers, a few politicians and ideologues were executed as war criminals for their alleged war crimes by the Allied Powers in the few years after the defeat. However, apart from those executions, in the first few decades of the post-war period, Japanese war responsibility was mostly regarded either as a matter of reparation between the Japanese government and the governments of the other countries whose territories (including their colonies) were invaded or occupied by the Japanese military, or as the moral problem of the Japanese state leadership that led Japanese people into a disastrous war and final defeat. Since the matters of war reparation were perceived to be mainly concerned with inter-state diplomacy and economic aid, they were rarely discussed with a view to the problem of historical responsibility for the Japanese nation as a collectivity and as individuals.

Rather, the problem was construed in terms of the responsibility of the leadership to the Japanese nation, the state being the perpetrators while the nation the victims. Central to the problem of Japanese war responsibility, as most typically illustrated by Maruyama Masao's analysis of Japanese ultranationalism published in the late 1940s, was the way the Japanese were incapable of resisting aggressive and pathological ultranationalists or of achieving a more rational and modernized organicity so as to unify more efficiently and win the war. The trait of Japanese society that was characterised as 'the system of irresponsibility' manifested itself as the lack of such an organicity, Maruyama argued. Similarly, a literary debate raised in the 1950s by Marxist poet and literary critic, Yoshimoto Takaaki, about the wartime collaboration of the communist intellectuals, was constituted around the problematic of intellectuals' responsibility to the Japanese 'people'. Thus, the issue of war responsibility for Maruyama and many Marxist writers can be summarised as the intellectuals' responsibility to the masses or 'Japanese people' for the Japanese leaders' failure in the war. It is important to note that, except for a small number of intellectuals such as Takeuchi Yoshimi who continued to be concerned with the problems of colonialism and racism in modernity, the issue of war responsibility was conceptualised without explicit reference to peoples in Asia whose lives were drastically affected by the Japanese invasion and occupation during the Asia–Pacific War. In other words, the issue of war responsibility was addressed to the Japanese by the Japanese, but the majority of Japanese intellectuals failed to be aware that they should be held responsible to non-Japanese, morally obliged to respond particularly to those in Asian countries.

It is not difficult to explain why war responsibility was debated within such a context of international insularity. Japanese intellectuals in post-war Japan could not discuss the problem of Japanese war responsibility seriously in the company of people from Asia and Oceania (virtually all those other than Americans) because they had to endorse the political settlement in which the ultimate locus of Japan's moral and judicial responsibility about the Asia–Pacific War was totally erased. Emperor **Hirohito** (Shōwa Emperor), who had been the supreme commander in all branches of the central government, colonial authorities and military forces according to the Meiji Constitution, after Japan's defeat was relieved of his judicial and political responsibility for all of the actions of the Japanese state during the war. All the policies including the declaration of war against the Allied Powers were legislated and promulgated in his name. Through deliberate and systematically orchestrated censorship, however, the Allied Occupation administration and Japanese government worked together to obscure the questions of who should be ultimately responsible to whom for war crimes and atrocities. By pardoning Hirohito, they also obscured the responsibility of those who followed his orders and commands and thereby created 'the system of irresponsibility' not before but after the war. As Edwin Reischauer's 1942 note to the US Department of War amply shows, this tactic (which the British Government also endorsed immediately after Japan's defeat) was adopted by the US government in order to use Hirohito as an extraordinarily effective puppet head of the state for the Allied Occupation of Japan.

From the 1970s, Japanese intellectuals began to engage in the problem concerning their responsibility to non-Japanese victims. Gradually, an increasing number of people understood that the issue of war responsibility was inevitably also an international issue of 'post-war responsibility', an issue of how to respond to those who still suffer from the legacies of wartime atrocities and colonial violence. The post-colonial dimension of this problem became glaringly obvious when the former '**comfort women**', Korean, Taiwanese, Filipino, Chinese, Indonesian and other victims of Japanese military sexual slavery, came forward to demand apologies from the Japanese government in the late 1980s and 1990s. At first the Japanese government denied that the Japanese military established the system of 'Comfort Stations' in China in the 1930s as a policy. However, a number of historians discovered old governmental documents as corroborating historical evidence, so the Japanese government had to concede its responsibility for the 'Comfort Stations'.

Today, war responsibility is a touchstone for a number of intellectual problems in Japan. In a manner very similar to the New Racist movements in Britain and France in the 1980s, a group of revisionist intellectuals (Jiyūshugi shikan: Liberal View of History Group) are trying to disavow Japanese war and colonial responsibility for the sake of national solidarity. Also, some conservatives argue that, in order to responsibly deal with Japan's past, the Japanese must first nurture a sense of national pride.

In any event, it is increasingly unlikely that the problem of war responsibility can be adequately examined within the confines of the sovereignty of the national state.

See also: Allied Occupation, rising-sun flag, comfort women, Chinese in Japan, Korean Japanese, national identity and minorities, surrender, textbook controversies, Yasukuni Shrine

NAOKI SAKAI

washi

The term *washi* did not come into use in Japan until after the introduction of machine-made paper products. *Washi* is used specifically to describe hand-made Japanese-style paper.

Paper is said to have first arrived in Japan from China in the early seventh century. The centralisation of government and the expansion of Buddhism both created a high demand for paper products for the keeping of records and other official documents. By the Heian period, the court required so much paper that a government-owned mill was established. It was the highly refined aesthetics of calligraphy and the flourishing literay salons of this period that also saw the development of an art of decorative papers combining textures and materials in beautifully crafted paper that was always more than simply a surface to write on. Word, ink and paper were each integral to the value of the finished work of the poet or author. Paper was also an essential element of the court architecture. It was during this period that many of the diverse varieties of paper and many paper-making techniques were refined. While the samurai culture, which dominated the period from the late twelfth-century to early seventeenth-century Japan, preferred simple and more practical paper to the luxurious varieties of the Heian court, the Edo Period with its explosion of popular literature and publishing, together with the merchant-class nostalgia for the refinement and excesses of the Heian aristocracy, led to a new flourishing of paper-making.

In the late 1920s, there were over 28,000 registered family businesses making *washi*, but by the early 1970s this had fallen to less than 900. Although there had been a limited flow of paper from Japan and China to Europe from the early seventeenth century, it was with the opening of Japanese trade relations in the Meiji Period that the world discovered the richness of *washi*. The fine, silky yet sturdy *tengujo* paper, first developed in the Gifu region, gained tremendous popularity outside Japan and was one of Japan's major export commodities throughout the 1930s. However, mechanisation of paper-making techniques and cheaper products from South-East Asia saw Japan's market hold diminish quickly. Today it is the higher quality and more expensive varieties of *washi* that sell well internationally. In the domestic market *washi* is still used extensively in arts and crafts in its finer forms, while less expensive varieties still have extensive applications in daily life ranging from school calligraphy classes, to wrapping paper, or the sturdy *shōjigami* (screen paper) that is found in many Japanese homes, both modern and traditional.

It is the *nagashizuki* style of paper making that is unique to Japan and distinguishes *washi* from other varieties of hand-made paper elsewhere. The name of the technique describes the process of discharging (*nagashi*) or casting off of excess pulp that is essential to the special characteristic weave of *washi*. The act of tossing the fibre mix across a screen and then casting off the excess is achieved through skillful hand movements that are the mark of the master paper maker. Layer on layer of finely intertwined fibres accumulate with each repetition

to create the desired texture and thickness of the paper. The slow drainage process is also characteristic of Japanese paper making and is essential to avoid clumping and tangling of the layered fibres. While *washi* artisans are increasingly rare today, extensive efforts are underway to conserve the full range of paper-making technologies and *washi* styles. Textile and paper making institutes and museums work with artisans to promote both preservation of the heritage of *washi* and experimentation through collaboration with contemporary artists, interior and furniture designers and publishers.

See also: origami

Further reading

Turner, S. (1998) *The Book of Fine Paper*, New York: Thames & Hudson.

SANDRA BUCKLEY

waste and recycling

During the early post-war years, environmental issues were placed far behind the priorities of economic recovery. By the 1970s, Japanese pollution was no longer just a national problem and had begun to attract international attention. Issues of air pollution were attacked first, with new national standards and regulatory measures. At the community level, air pollution questions were focused not only on major industrial polluters but also on the more community-based issue of waste disposal. The practice of incinerating rubbish at local facilities drew criticism and increasingly community action groups moved to block the construction of new incinerator plants. Recycling has emerged over the 1980s and 1990s as the response to the need to develop new technologies for waste management with low environmental impact.

Although there have been extensive recycling campaigns at the local and prefectural levels since the 1980s, the first substantive national legislative reform in this area did not come until the 1990s. The year 1991 saw the passage of the Law for the Promotion of the Utilisation of Recyclable Resources, followed in 1995 by the Law for the

Promotion of Sorted Collection and Recycling of Containers and Packaging and then, in 1997, the reform to the Waste Disposal and Public Cleansing Law. Ambitious targets have now been set for recycling rates for both households and industry, e.g. 56 per cent of paper in 2000, 85 per cent of steel cans and 80 per cent of aluminium cans by 2002. The national recycling rates had come within 2 per cent of these targets by 1999. However, rates for PET (plastic bottles) remain low and are a priority area in recent campaigns as well as the focus of new recycling technology initiatives. Although over 21,000 tons of PET bottles were recycled in 1997, this constituted less than 10 per cent of the total PET bottles in distribution.

New technologies to extrude recommercialised PET pallets for use in industrial fibre offer some promise for increased plastic-bottle recycling. One difficulty for recycling facilities is the seasonal shift in consumption levels of PET bottle products such as soft drinks and mineral waters, with off-season and peak-season rates varying by as much as 30 per cent. The continued annual increases in PET bottle sales mean that this is one rubbish problem that is not going away.

Local incineration plants are slowly being replaced by such alternative technologies as fermentation, which produces cheap, reusable compost, and pulverising and compressing, which produces solid fuel bricks or pallets. Some composting facilities have been able to sign advance contracts for up to five years of recycled waste with agricultural co-operatives. Recycled solid fuel is being extensively tested by utility companies as an alternative fuel in power generation. There has also been a marked trend towards community-based treatment facilities, where local government and the community collaborate to develop and manage recycling and rubbish disposal facilities. Sometimes contracts are allotted to commercial providers but usually with strict terms and conditions set and monitored by nominated local representatives. Increasingly, recycling is emerging as a profit-generating operation and there is a growing industry vying for community and commercial contracts.

Although landfill was a highly popular form of rubbish recycling throughout the 1980s and into the 1990s, there has been increased community concern over the health hazards of landfill in residential developments and some official concern over the structural stability of landfill development for residential, commercial or industrial sites. Persistent subsidence in some existing landfill developments, especially where there has been coastal extension, has led to caution in approvals for new projects. The need to more carefully monitor the disposal of potentially hazardous wastes in landfills is under ongoing review, with strong community pressure for guarantees of long-term safety.

Surveys of Japanese over the 1990s have indicated a number of contradictions in attitudes towards waste disposal and recycling. While most Japanese show a high awareness of the need to recycle at the household level and to manage rubbish disposal at the local level, and there is a strong connection made between high levels of consumption and increased waste, there is little agreement that there should be any curtailment in consumption of disposable products and packaging. The popular focus is on improved technologies for recycling rather than waste reduction strategies for the consumer household. The highly professionalised role of the Japanese housewife extends to a very public performance of a responsible attitude to rubbish and recycling. While households may not be inclined to reduce their level of waste, there is a significant investment of time in the careful separation and preparation of waste and recycling. In many areas, rubbish must be separated into dry and wet non-recyclable trash, aluminium and steel cans, PET, paper and cardboard. Each of these categories is placed in separate standardised containers and often labelled by household name before disposal at a central pick-up point in the neighbourhood. Putting rubbish out except on bin days after the designated hour is frowned upon by neighbours, and some zealous communities even resort to transparent rubbish bags or bins to encourage a clean and orderly disposal of rubbish. Rather then create a desire to produce less rubbish or to protest against this highly regulated routine of rubbish disposal, recycling has become an integral element of household ritual and neighbourhood dynamics. On a more global scale of awareness, campaigns to encourage Japanese to boycott disposable wooden chopsticks and lunchboxes were briefly popular and captured media attention, but then fizzled away. Environmentalists trying to link local issues of waste disposal to global issues of deforestation describe a sense of frustration at the public resistance to translating these connections into action in everyday consumer practice.

In a country where there is a cultural aversion to the use of second-hand goods, where the new is always sought after by affluent, informed and aspiring consumers and where the aesthetics of packaging and wrapping often outweigh environmental concerns, it is unlikely that rubbish and recycling will cease to be urgent environmental issues in the foreseeable future. In the meantime, Japan is rapidly emerging as a major innovator in recycling and waste management technologies.

SANDRA BUCKLEY

Watanabe Hamako

b. 1910, Yokohama

Singer

Born Kato Hamako, Watanabe Hamako graduated from the Musashino Music School in 1933, and made her début the same year on Nippon Victor Records with the song 'Hitori shizuka' (Alone and Quiet). In 1936, 'Wasurechai iyayo' (Don't Go Forgetting Me) became an enormous hit. The record sold 100,000 copies and Watanabe became a star. Unfortunately, sale of the record was prohibited after three months as the Home Ministry considered its coquettish lyrics too *risqué* to pass ideological muster. Her music continued to remain controversial throughout her career.

'Wasurechai iyayo' was described as 'a song of carnal desire which displays the coquetry of a prostitute [*shofu*] as if before one's eyes'. It seems that after this official incident, at least for some time, there were those who considered Hamako not to be a proper singer. The decision to ban the song was handed down at about the time of the February 26th Incident (a failed *coup* attempt by a clique of young army officers) and just before war in China broke out. Remarkably, as 'Wasurechai iyayo' was so popular, Hamako's record company insisted that she continue to record material with a

similar tone. All of it was banned. This comedy of cultural production sheds some light on corporate attitudes towards state censorship in the late 1930s.

Hamako moved to the Nippon Columbia Record label and rode the continental melody boom, emerging with another mega-hit, 'Shina no yoru' (Chinese Nights). This song was also considered improper and was nearly banned. From this point on, she had a string of hits including: 'Aikoku no hana' (Flower of Patriotism), 'Soshū yakyoku' (Soviet-Manchuria Night Song) and 'Ōrin chin tsai rai' (When Will You Return?). Hamako went on a goodwill tour of Imperial troops in mainland China, Taiwan and domestic Japanese military hospitals in order to overcome her damaged reputation. At the time of Japan's surrender she was captured in North China, and she continued to be interned there for another ten months.

She made a post-war comeback in 1947 with 'Ame no orandazaka' (Dutch Hill in the Rain). Her success continued with the hit, 'Sanfuranshisuko no Chaina Taun' (San Francisco's Chinatown). Her next release was a song that expressed hope for the release of Japanese war criminals and it called forth a strong social reaction. Before the end of that same year, she set out for an actual Filipino prison where Japanese were interned and sang the song in front of the Japanese war criminals. As a result of this effort, the sentences of the men in question were commuted and they were allowed to return to Japan without incident. In 1972, she received a medal of honour and a prize for special service from the Japanese recording industry.

Further reading

Komota Nobuo, Shimada Yoshifuni, Yazawa Tamotsu and Yokozawa Chiaki (1994) *Nihon ryūkokashi*, Tokyo: Shakaishisosha, pp. 15, 33.
Suzuki Kazutoshi (1994) 'Watanabe Haruko', in *Taishu bunka jiten*, Tokyo: Kobundo, p. 870.

MARK ANDERSON

weddings

The Shintō ritual of the Japanese wedding ceremony is usually only attended by the couple together with the immediate family of the bride and groom, and the go-between and his or her partner. A Shintō priest presides over the ritual sharing of sake, the recitation of an oath of betrothal by the groom and offerings to the *kami*. It is usual for the couple to wear kimono for this part of the ceremony. After this ritual, friends, family and workplace colleagues gather for a formal reception. Buddhist, Christian and civil ceremonies are still in the minority, but many temples are trying to develop a new source of income by promoting Buddhist nuptials.

The post-ritual reception is focused around a meal accompanied by speeches, toasts and singing. Today, it is most common for the reception to be held in a hotel or wedding centre where everything from kimono hire to menus and flowers can be handled by specialised staff. Many hotels also offer a Shintō sanctuary so that the entire wedding can be located in-house. A couple is expected to change clothing several times during the reception and the quality of the kimono and Western attire worn is a measure of the grandeur of the event. It has become popular for the bride to include a white wedding dress in her range of outfits. The white dress along with the giving of an engagment ring, the exchange of wedding rings and the honeymoon have all been imported into the Japanese ceremony and are now accepted practice. Some wedding facilities also offer a chapel where the couple can add a brief Christian service to their wedding celebrations.

Few today can afford the cost of the kimono worn for the wedding and these are commonly rented for the occasion. Traditionally, kimono were hand-sown in silk and handed down as family heirlooms or, if damaged, they could be sewn into the colourful cloth cover of traditional futon bedding. A mother or grandmother may offer the elaborate decorations to be worn in the bridal hairstyle or these too can be rented. In the early stages of the ceremony, the bride wears a cloth cover over her hair and decorations, and this piece is known as the *tsuno kakushi* (concealer of horns) and symbolises the woman's obedience towards the man. There is much remaining in the symbolism of the Japanese wedding that designates the subordinate position of a wife to her husband in traditional gender roles.

The entire wedding celebration has taken on such an immense scale and developed into a major symbol of socio-economic standing that for many families the event has become a financial burden. Many guests will offer money as a gift, which is in turn used to cover the cost of the ceremony, honeymoon and obligatory gifts for guests. On average, these cash gifts only amount to some 50 per cent of the expenses incurred. The cost of a Japanese wedding has escalated over the last two decades to the point where foreign locations have become an increasingly attractive option. The average cost of a wedding in Tokyo in the mid-1990s was US$30,000 with a further US$8–9,000 for the honeymoon. Several international tourist destinations now feature Japanese wedding packages, including everything from international travel to a chapel wedding, reception, hotel accommodation and honeymoon itinerary for the happy couple and a small entourage of family and friends. The comparatively low cost of a Barrier Reef, Banff or Waikiki wedding has attracted over 35,000 couples annually to travel abroad to take their vows. Weddings in Japan today are a marketing bonanza for the tourism and hotel sector, but there are signs that couples are beginning to resist the pressure for upscale weddings, just as their parents are also beginning to wonder at the long-term planning needed to save in advance for the exorbitant cost of a daughter's future marriage. Home weddings and an array of budget wedding venues are appearing on the market to meet a new demand for alternatives to the current high-cost wedding industry.

See also: arranged marriages; divorce; gift giving; marriage

SANDRA BUCKLEY

welfare

During the first half of the post-war era, Japan ranked low among industrial nations in terms of its welfare programmes. In recent decades, however, Japan has taken on the trappings of a Western-style welfare state. As measured by expenditures on social security as a percentage of GDP, the Japanese welfare state approaches those of the USA and UK, though it is far less generous and comprehensive than the French, German or Swedish variants. Whether Japan should become a high-level welfare state is a contentious issue today, as the nation confronts the needs of a rapidly ageing society (see **ageing society and elderly care**).

Historically, the Japanese government has been reluctant to spend heavily on constructing a social safety net. In the pre-war decades, the regime eagerly financed military and industrial development, while opposing measures to establish old-age pensions, unemployment insurance and a minimum wage. Aside from providing relief to the countryside at times of crop failures, the central state's welfare programmes remained confined to two modest poor laws. The first of these – the Relief Regulations (1884) – aided less than 0.05 per cent of the population. The second, the Relief and Protection Law (effected 1932), expanded the scope of public assistance, yet excluded all potentially employable poor people and even a majority of those who qualified for aid. Big-city governments adopted more activist measures towards ameliorating poverty during the 1920s. Urban authorities sponsored labour exchanges, day nurseries and cheap lodging houses.

In general, pre-war Japanese officials were averse to instituting costly welfare mechanisms, which they believed were bankrupting governments in Europe and creating popular dependency on the state. To ward off a European future, the authorities encouraged families and communities to bear the burden of caring for the poor and elderly. Beginning in 1918, prefectural governors appointed community leaders in each neighborhood to serve as 'district commissioners' (*hōmen iin*), who concentrated on morally reforming the poor – rather than providing material assistance. Ironically, welfare programmes advanced considerably after Japan embarked on war with China in 1937. Seeking to develop the nation's 'human resources', the regime expanded day care and granted allowances to fatherless families. Veterans and war widows became entitled to pensions. Most enduring was the National Health Insurance Law (1938), Japan's first universal welfare measure that covered the entire populace.

The aftermath of the Second World War induced few changes in the country's historically low-cost welfare system. The most immediate challenge was relieving widespread poverty (see **poverty and the poor**) in the wake of defeat. The Daily Life Security Law (1946; revised 1950) granted public assistance to greater numbers, yet aided a mere fraction of the needy. Renamed 'welfare commissioners' (*minsei iin*), the pre-war district commissioners continued to administer public assistance in ways that denied adequate benefits to the poor. In retrospect, the most important early post-war change was the Occupation's introduction of the legal 'right' to welfare benefits and the state's corresponding obligation to promote social welfare. Article 25 of the **post-war Constitution** (1946) stipulated that 'all people have the right to maintain the minimum standard of wholesome and cultured living'.

Gradually, the government – prodded by scholars, the **Japan Socialist Party** and bureaucrats – endorsed welfare measures that provided universal benefits to all Japanese. A new National Health Insurance Law (1958) and the National Pension Law (1959) took effect, although benefit levels remained low over the next decade. Increasingly, attention shifted from the diminishing problem of poverty to the plight of old people. In 1969, the left-wing governor of Tokyo, Minobe Ryōkichi (see **Minobe administration**), introduced free medical care for the elderly. At the national level, the ruling **Liberal Democratic Party** – eager to arrest the steady drop in its popularity – sponsored an across-the-board expansion of universal welfare programmes. The Diet approved free medical care for the aged in 1972, and in 1973 the government committed itself to sharp increases in pension benefits.

As luck would have it, the Japanese economy experienced the 'Oil Shock' of 1973, within months of the government's embrace of a fully fledged welfare state. Many bureaucrats, businessmen and conservative politicians thereupon questioned how such costly commitments could be financed in an era of slow growth. They voiced particular concern about funding pensions and health care as Japan became an ageing society (see **ageing society and elderly care**). By the late 1970s, conservatives strove to persuade the public of the wisdom of cutting back on welfare commitments. The nation need not establish a Western-type 'welfare state', they argued; it already was blessed with a 'Japanese-style welfare society', in which three-generation families, communities and firms cared for their own. Indeed, during the 1980s and 1990s, the government chipped away at earlier commitments to welfare expansion. In 1985, officials cut future pension benefits, while raising current contributions. Nine years later, the Diet agreed to raise the age of eligibility to receive a pension from sixty to sixty-five (to be phased in after 2001). To contain the costs of institutional care, officials have also increased the numbers of home-helpers and recruited millions of local volunteers to assist old people at home.

Despite these efforts, Japan's welfare state is necessarily expanding. The numbers of physically and mentally disabled old people grow, and more and more families (especially wives) are finding the burdens of caregiving overwhelming, and even oppressive. Officials themselves now recognise the limits of relying on Japan's vaunted 'family system'. In 2000, the government responded by introducing long-term care insurance. This innovative pro-gramme 'socialises' the burden of elderly care, funding home or individual care from premiums paid by all income earners aged forty and older. Japan shows no signs of becoming a high-tax, cradle-to-grave welfare state like Sweden, but the Japanese public appears increasingly willing to bear the costs of welfare for, at least, elderly citizens and their families.

See also: ageing society and elderly care; poverty and the poor

Further reading

Campbell, J.C. (1992) *How Policies Change*, Prince-ton: Princeton University Press.

Garon, S. (1997) *Molding Japanese Minds*, Princeton: Princeton University Press.

SHELDON GARON

West, the

The West is a peculiar sort of social imaginary. It is supposed to indicate a certain group of people called 'Westerners' in terms of their residential area, traditions, race and pedigrees. It may appear to be a proper name and its propriety is expressed by the capitalisation of its first letter. Whereas 'west' suggests a direction, 'the West' retains the devotion of an area in the direction of the setting sun. Accordingly, it is generally believed that the West is, first and foremost, a geographic index. Although it derives from the directional adverb, the natural tendency is to assume that it should point to a geographic area on the surface of the earth. However, since the earth is a globe, there is no fixed location that can be designated by 'west' and any point in the world can potentially be so called. The West as the delimitation of 'west' must then be diacritically distinguished from that which is not the West, that is, the Rest of the world. Only in so far as it is distinguished from the Rest, can it refer to something other than a mere west. In this respect, the West is dependent upon how the Rest is determined and the binary opposition of the West and the Rest prescribes the meaning of the word 'the West'. Thus, the West can be imagined to be a fixed and identifiable referent only when the Rest is thought of as a fixity.

As a geographic index, however, it sustains no coherence. The majority of those who live in countries in Western Europe believe themselves to be Westerners, but at the same time some white people in South Africa, for instance, might also insist that they are 'Westerners'. Conversely, non-Caucasians in North America are rarely recognised as 'Westerners' even if the majority of residents in North America claim, perhaps since the end of the Second World War, that they are in the West. So it may appear that the West is primarily a racial index. However, once again, this assessment contradicts the historical fact that Eastern Europe has been generally excluded from the West, not only during the period of the cold war but throughout the twentieth century. Furthermore, we now know that whiteness itself is historically so contingent that it is hardly an index of a stable identity.

Just like the racial notion of whiteness, the West does not cohere as a concept, and is excessively over-determined. This does not mean that the West has ceased to be a reality whose objectivity is globally accepted. This is why the West must be understood as a social imaginary on a global scale and as functioning only as one term of the binary opposition of the West and the Rest.

The Japanese use of this word 'the West' is no exception. It is excessively over-determined, and it is closely associated with the racial fantasies of whiteness. Yet, generally speaking, the racial notion of whiteness is organised loosely enough to allow those groups who would be excluded from being white in other regions in the world, such as peoples from the Middle East, to be recognised as such. This can be said about the West as well. Of course, the West itself is essentially a phantasmal type whose differentiation from other types is determined in the scenarios of imagined satisfaction in a given configuration of desires. In Japan, this differentiation is drawn predictably between Japan and the West, so that the West often serves as a standard against which something specifically Japanese is measured and fixed.

The Japanese word '*seiyō*' originally meant 'the western seas' in relation to China, the Central Kingdom, then believed to be the centre of the universe. In the mid-nineteenth century, the same word was adopted as a translation for 'the West', and since then the word has scarcely been used with the old Sino-centric signification.

Typically in **Nihonjinron** (discourse of Japanese uniqueness), Japanese cultural is predominantly identified in comparison or in co-figuration (that is, two terms are figured in mutual reference to one another) with the putative traits of the West. Although the last 130 years have seen many academic and journalistic attempts to compare Japan with other societies in Asia, what gives the majority of the Japanese the characteristic image of Japanese culture is still its distinction from the so-called West. In terms of industrial development, the secularisation of religions, the pervasiveness of scientific thinking, the sense of hygiene, the dominance of economic rationality in everyday life and the loss of traditional communities, many aspects of Japanese society appear to be just as Western as, or even more Western than, any in Western Europe and North America. Yet, the Japanese appear hesitant to include themselves in the West. For, given the culturalist constitution of Japanese identity today, the loss of the distinction

between the West and Japan would result in the loss of Japanese identity in general.

Although largely speaking the Japanese believe that there is some substantive entity called the West, the West serves an ideological function in organising desires in Japanese social formation, and implies a set of features that are perceived to be lacking in the Japanese way of life. Until the 1970s, the Japanese imagined the West to be a guidepost indicating their future and the goal towards which Japanese society must progress. Accordingly, the transformation of Japanese society was thought of as a progress in modernisation, and there was a general consensus that modernisation was invariably Westernisation.

For the last two decades, however, the power of the West as a co-figuring social imaginary seems to be fading in Japan. For one thing, an increasing number of young Japanese are aware of 'non-Western' aspects of societies in Europe and North America as well as 'Western' aspects of life in Japan. The figure of the West is neither as threatening nor alluring as before. It seems that the West is losing its grip on Japanese desires.

NAOKI SAKAI

whale meat and whaling

There is a long history of whale meat consumption in Japan, with some academics tracking the practice as far back as the Jōmon period (7–3000 BCE). During the Edo Period (1600–1867), whaling techniques were substantially improved, increasing the annual yield of whale meat. There was also a softening of the Buddhist prohibition on eating animal meats, although whale meat had traditionally been defined as a fish product. The real boom in whale meat consumption came at the end of the Second World War, when protein was hard to come by in the daily diet for average Japanese. Through the 1960s, whale meat constituted as much as 30 per cent of daily protein intake and it was used extensively in government-funded school lunch programmes into the 1970s. International Whaling Commission bans on whaling saw Japan forced to abandon commercial whaling. The level of whale meat on sale in Japan today appears to exceed the legal supply from the approved annual scientific (research) catch. It is difficult, however, to track illegal supply of frozen whale meat into Japan. In an attempt to meet domestic demand for this still popular food, Japan has concluded contracts with Russia to buy up to 200 beluga whales, and whaling permits have been issued in the face of extensive international protest against this rejuvenation of the international whale meat trade.

SANDRA BUCKLEY

whiskey

For the Japanese, the alcoholic beverages of choice are overwhelmingly **sake**, beer, *shōchū* (a native 'vodka' of about 50 per cent proof) and whiskey. Of these drinks, whiskey has the highest prestige. Japanese distillers, such as Suntory and Nikka, produce a variety of passable blended whiskeys that are reasonably priced and well received. Imported whiskeys, however, are considered most desirable, because of their exotic foreignness and identity as 'the real thing', and because of the exclusivity produced by exorbitantly high import tariffs. Bottles of whiskey are common gifts for men and some men make a hobby of collecting different brands of whiskey.

Whiskey is almost never drunk neat. It is ordinarily consumed in the form of whiskey and water (*mizuwari*) on the rocks. While ordering a single glass of whiskey and water is certainly possible at a bar or restaurant, many establishments have a system of 'whiskey keep'. At a 'keep' bar you buy your own bottle of whiskey from the house and get your name put on it. Your bottle is kept on a shelf and brought out when you request it. Having already paid for the whiskey, on any visit you pay only a nominal fee for the set up: glasses, ice and a jug of water. Some men keep bottles at several bars and take pleasure from – or reinforce business networks by – allowing others to call for their bottles.

Whiskey lends itself well to the Japanese practices of service accompanying drinking. Certain categories of bars, such as lounges known as *sunakku* ('snack'), have female employees who sit with the customers. The manifest job of such hostesses is to make sure that the customers enjoy themselves by instigating pleasant conversation, being a good listener and providing such indulgent services as lighting cigarettes, dishing out snack foods and pouring drinks. The latent purpose of the hostess is to stimulate business. Hostesses encourage drinking by regularly topping up drinks with a splash of water, a dollop of whiskey and another piece of ice. The constant topping up of the drinks normally creates a pressure on customers to drink (see 'drinking etiquette', described in **beer**), a pressure that may be underscored by the smiling hostess raising her own glass in an unspoken toast.

See also: alcoholism; beer; sake; *yobai*

STEPHEN R. SMITH

WOMAN IN THE DUNES *see Suna no onna*

women in film

'Women' are a prominent focus of Japanese cinema. Far from simply reflecting stereotypes of female subservience, directors such as **Mizoguchi Kenji** and **Naruse Mikio** allocated female characters subjectivity, and agency in the narrative development. However, even portrayals of 'active women' could be comfortably incorporated into male fantasy in the Japanese context, and the subject and the female spectator are still embedded with a certain displacement.

The **Allied Occupation**'s film policy strongly encouraged portrayals of Japanese women as liberated individuals. The heroine of **Kurosawa Akira**'s *Waga seishun ni kuinashi* (No Regrets for Our Youth) offers a clear example. She powerfully pursues her romantic love and her cause, and thus glorifies the ideals of post-war democracy. On the other hand, a genre called *haha-mono* (literally translated as 'mother thing'; maternal melodrama made mainly in the Daiei studio from 1948 to 1958) presents another facet of the early post-war period. Addressing the working-class female audience, it eulogises the self-sacrificing mother's sorrow in the ongoing process of Japanese modernisation. ***Nihon no higeki*** (The Japanese Tragedy) is a more cynical rendering of the same subject.

Towards the end of the 1950s, the representation of women underwent an important shift: the female body grew visible as both the object and the subject of desire. The rise of youth films enhanced public attention to the body and sexuality; the abolishing of legal prostitution in 1956 helped to undermine the wife (or mother)/whore dichotomy in cultural representations. **Imamura Shōhei**'s heroines, and the women embodied by **Wakao Ayako** in **Masumura Yasuzō**'s films actively seek to fulfil their sexual desires. In the 1960s, female sexuality provided politically and/or aesthetically militant male directors, such as **Ōshima Nagisa**, Yoshida Yoshishige and Wakamatsu Koji, with a fertile subject of inquiry. They attempted to break through to the depth of humanity (or inhumanity) via an encounter with the woman as the unknowable, opaque Other, vacillating between misogyny and fascination.

Commodification of the female body, accelerated by the decline of the studio system in Japan, culminated in Nikkatsu becoming a **pornography** studio in 1971. Soft porn made in Nikkatsu, though often staging sexual violence against women, sometimes ironically centred on female subjectivity and pleasure. The 1980s can be described as the decade of *shōjo*, or teenage girls. The destabilised sense of identity in late capitalist society found its manifestation in *shōjo* caught between adults and children, which appeared on the screen embodied by idol singers and young actresses, as in ***Taifu kurabū*** (The Typhoon Club). Unfortunately, many of the most innovative Japanese directors of the 1990s seem relatively uninterested in the representation of women, so the topic remains rather incompletely explored in more recent film.

See also: censorship and film; women in the film industry

Further reading

Hirano Kyoko (1991) *Mr Smith Goes to Tokyo*, Washington: Smithsonian Institution Press.

Turim, Maureen (1998) *The Films of Oshima Nagisa*, Berkeley and Los Angeles: University of California Press.

Ueno Koshi (1989) *Nikutai no jidai*, Tokyo: Tokyo Shokan.

KINOSHITA CHIKA

women in the film industry

Outside of acting, the Japanese film world is notoriously closed to women. The few women who establish professional careers in film usually have complicated – even antagonistic – relationships to feminism, even while embodying its ideals of independence and self-expression. Nowhere are the problems of breaking into the industry more clear than in directing. The standard reference book for directors lists only twenty-three women among its 1,000 entries. The female feature film directors generally established themselves as stars, most notably Tanaka Kinuyo, Kurisaki Midori and Hidari Sachiko. However, most women direct within the documentary and avant-garde, where independence allows a measure of freedom. Two pioneers whose careers straddle 1945 were Sakane Tazuko (Japan's first female director) and Atsugi Taka (one of the most important screenwriters and theorists of documentary, and a key leader in the women's movement). Other important directors include documentarists Haneda Sumiko and Tokieda Toshie, and video artist Idemitsu Mako.

Other fields of film-making where women have made their presence felt include screenwriting (Sakane, Wada Nattō) and foreign-film subtitling (Kamishima Kimi, Toda Natsuko), professions that carry considerable prestige in Japanese cinema.

In the 1980s and 1990s, women have made decisive contributions to the national cinema through programming and distribution, where they play a critical role in opening exhibition routes to women artists struggling outside of the mainstream industry. It was through these channels that Japan's youngest woman director, Sentō (Kawase) Naomi, rose from Super-8 experimental films to completion of a prize-winning feature film at Cannes in 1997.

ABÉ MARK NORNES

Women's Christian Temperance Union

The Japan Women's Christian Temperance Union (WCTU) (Nihon Kirisuto Kyō Kyōfūkai, or Kyōfūkai), established in 1886, is one of the oldest women's organisations in Japan. It promoted temperance, monogamy and reform of male sexual behaviour. It also campaigned against the licensed prostitution system, and attempted to assist women to leave this industry. In its centenary year, 1986, the WCTU set up a shelter for immigrant workers and victims of domestic violence (see **HELP Women's Shelter**).

Further reading

Ōshima, S. and Francis, C. (1990) *Japan through the Eyes of Women Migrant Workers*, Tokyo: HELP Asian Women's Shelter.

VERA MACKIE

women's history

Many of the pioneering works of women's history in the early twentieth century came from a socialist perspective, focusing on factory workers or farming women. After some involvement with anarchist women's organisations, **Takamure Itsue** retreated to her house in the woods and embarked on a lifelong mission to retrieve the history of women in Japan. For Takamure, the study of women's history demonstrated that women had not always been subordinated, and that it was therefore possible to imagine future societies that would not be based on patriarchal domination. A pioneering post-war work was Inoue Kiyoshi's 1948 Marxist-influenced history of women in Japan. Women's history was revived with the **Women's Liberation** movement of the 1970s, and was once again linked to imagining alternative visions of society. The recent revival of women's history has parallels with movements for 'people's history' and 'history from below'. Some historians link their histories with specific women's issues. Feminist historians have also entered into debates with conservative revisionists who have denied atrocities committed

during the Second World War and have denied the state's responsibility for the wartime military brothels.

See also: comfort women; feminism; feminist publishing; women's studies

VERA MACKIE

women's language

The Japanese language is heavily marked for gender. While some patterns of gender-differentiated speech duplicate the patterns of relations of hierarchy (where female speech adopts the inferior or respectful position), there are areas of gender differentiation that exceed the performance of honorific indicators.

Women's language is marked as softer, vaguer and generally more decorative and indirect. What can be said succinctly between two male interlocutors can require layers of gendered honorific inflection at the level of syntax and lexicon when spoken between a woman and her male superior/senior. Where a male speaker might simply say '*sensei ga kuru*' (the teacher is coming), either a male or female student could inflect the verb for respect and say '*sensei ga oide ni naru*', but only a female speaker would say '*sensei ga oide asobasu*' – where the verb is inflected for respect and the female gender of the speaker. Female speakers are far more likely to use honorific prefixes and suffixes. There is also a clearly gender-marked repertoire of final sentence particles and subject and object markers. Females use markedly less *kango* (words of Chinese origin) in both their written and spoken Japanese, and this reflects the historical association of *kango* with the language of authority and learning, and its use in official and scholarly documents, domains traditionally closed to women.

While there has been a gradual increase in the acceptability of younger women and girls utilising less honorifics and taking up what might traditionally have been considered more masculine patterns of speech, there has not been a similar shift in relation to men using forms marked as feminine. In other words, while enhanced awareness of the gender politics of language has created a trend towards females accessing what have been exclusively masculine patterns (the simplest example being the popular and playful use of the masculine first-person pronoun '*boku*' by teenage girls), there has been no equivalent reverse trend. This is generally seen as a reflection of the negative marking of women's speech. Men's speech continues to be the language of the public sphere of politics, business, education, publishing and the professions.

In literature and the arts, however, there are exceptions. The poetic form of *waka* was traditionally written in the feminine style in contrast to the masculine Chinese style of classical literature. *Kango* was avoided and the poems were rendered in the Japanese simple *hiragana* script and written in the fluid brush strokes of the femininely marked grass writing. This suit of feminine characteristics of the *waka* was used by male and female poets alike, creating what some have described as a literary cross-gendering. In the theatre, male *kabuki* and *nō* actors performing female roles have to master not only the feminine and historical dialogue meticulously captured by the great playwrights, but must also reproduce the highly stylised tonality, gestures and facial expressions that render the symbolic form of the feminine in these classic theatres.

Some feminist linguists and writers have argued that the artful use of women's speech can undermine the surface relations of power in language. There are others who explore in their writings and research the sense of disempowerment and outsider status experienced by women seeking to move beyond their traditional roles in Japanese society and having to constantly negotiate the gender gap in language. In film, poetry and fiction there are yet other women who work to explore the subtleties and beauty of women's language. The debate over the value and/or limitations of women's language continues across such diverse groups as educators, linguists, feminists, market researchers, media personalities, journalists and copy editors who each, in their very different contexts, struggle with the everyday implications of the gendered form of language.

Further reading

Ide Sachiko (1977) 'Women's language/men's language', in S. Buckley (ed.) *Broken Silence*,

Berkeley: University of California Press, pp. 32–65.

SANDRA BUCKLEY

Women's Liberation

The second wave of feminism in Japan started as 'Women's Lib' (*uuman ribu*) in the early 1970s. It was a movement that pursued social transformation through raising the individual consciousness of women. Although Japanese women had acquired constitutional equality after the war, the sexual division of labour and male dominance persisted in various aspects of social institutions. In accordance with rapid industrialisation and high economic growth, many women, including the university educated, entered the labour market, but were relegated to low-paid positions and had to manage the double burden of work and family. Those in the already established existing women's groups tended to have a socialist emphasis and privileged the class struggle rather than women's liberation. Women's liberationists advocated independence from existing organisations and sought to raise individual women's consciousness as a step towards liberation. The Lib Shinjuku Centre was opened in Tokyo in 1972 as the focal point for women's groups. Women's liberationists made sexual liberation a central philosophy of their movement. They argued that sex was a fundamental means of human subordination. A crucial goal was the recovery of women's sexual power from the control of the dominant patriarchal social system. They successfully fought against a proposed revision of the Eugenic Protection Law between 1972 and 1974. After this successful campaign, the movement shifted its focus from consciousness-raising strategies to direct-action campaigns centred on specific issues.

See also: feminism; reproductive control; Tanaka Mitsu; women's studies

Further reading

Tanaka, K. (1995) 'The new feminist movement in Japan, 1970–1990', in Kuniko Fujimura-Fanselow and Atsuko Kameda (eds) *Japanese Women: New Feminist Perspectives on the Past, Present and Future*, New York: The Feminist Press.

TANAKA KAZUKO

women's literature

The category of women's literature came into use in the early 1900s with the first publication of dedicated collections and histories of women's writing. Modern Japanese women writers had the unusual situation of a strong tradition of women's literature. The Heian period had seen a richness of women's writing across a range of genres including diaries, fictional tales and poetry. This was at least in part attributable to the influence of literary court salons sponsored by the well-placed and influential wives and concubines of the inner imperial family circle. The medieval period and ascendancy of a warrior culture saw the rapid marginalisation of both the old aristocracy and the literary production of the women of the court. It is not until the modern period that there is a resurgence of women's writing. Over the centuries, the most famous of the Heian works, Murasaki Shikibu's *Tale of Genji* being the most obvious example, had been encrusted with layer upon layer of commentary by male literary scholars. Moreover, the women writers' lives had been mythologised within a Buddhist morality that distorted and obscured any possible hint of a believable historical identity. They were assigned to the shallow stereotype of tragic 'fallen' beauties paying the price for the erotic excesses of their lives, and writing as lonely old women. Working within the category of *joryūbungaku*, the first feminist literary critics of the post-war period went back to the works of the Heian court and began to mount a challenge to much of the traditional scholarship and commentary.

The writings of modern women authors have also been collected under the category of *joryūbungaku*. The covers of these collections are often coloured pink, purple or similar shades traditionally associated with the feminine, the sensual and the erotic in Japan. From the appearance of the first *joryūbungaku* collections of individual writers and 'women's genres' there has been controversy over this categorisation. Some women writers and critics support a separate status for women's writing as a distinctive creative space that values and promotes women's literary creativity. Others reject the category as a marginalisation of women's writing that marks its difference, and by implication its inferiority or secondary status. *Joryūbungaku* allowed certain women's writing to be 'rescued' from the status of 'popular literature' (*taishū bungaku*) but still kept their texts segregated from the elite (and dominantly male) space of 'pure literature' (*junbungaku*).

Another dimension of *joryūbungaku* has been the establishment of specialised women's literature journals and prizes. Women are not excluded from other literary publications or awards, and have in fact more than held their own over the 1990s, but there is still a lingering sense of having to prove one can succeed outside the category of *joryūbungaku* and in order to be received as a 'serious' writer. To some extent, an author or poet can choose to work with a publisher to mainstream her work or self-select promotion as a *joryūbungaku* writer, but editors remain very powerful in these decision-making processes. Feminist publishing projects have proliferated since the 1970s, but have tended to specialise in non-fiction, although there have been some notable exceptions such as *La Mer* – a poetry journal that became an important vehicle for new women's poetry. More recently, the term '*joshi bungaku*'(another designation that still translates as women's literature) has been championed by some writers as a means of sustaining a separate category of women's writing but stepping outside the negative marking of *joryūbungaku* as 'just' light, romantic, emotional literature. Ironically, this stereotype cannot begin to capture the diversity and richness of writing that is reduced to this holistic category. The debate over the advantages and disadvantages of a separate category of women's writing are far from resolved, but for the moment the publishing and bookselling trades seem to have no intention of dismantling the ever-growing, and apparently lucrative, *joryūbungaku* section in bookshops and libraries.

Further reading

Buckley, S. (1955) 'Japanese women writing/

writing Japanese women', special issue, *Japan Women's Journal* (winter).

Schalow, P and Walker, J. (1996) *The Woman's Hand: Gender and Theory in Japanese Women's Writing*, Stanford: Stanford University Press.

SANDRA BUCKLEY

women's studies

Those who worked for the improvement of women's situation in the early twentieth century were also led into research in what was then called *fujin mondai* (the woman question). Many of these came from a socialist perspective, and were concerned with the situation of factory workers or farming women. After some involvement with anarchist women's organisations, **Takamure Itsue** retreated to her house in the woods and embarked on a lifelong mission to retrieve the history of women in Japan. Takamure's project would span the war years into the post-war period and play a key role in creating the intellectual space of women's studies in Japan. A pioneering early post-war work was Inoue Kiyoshi's Marxist-influenced history of women in Japan, which appeared in 1948. The current wave of women's studies in Japan can be traced to the **Women's Liberation** movements that grew out of the New Left activism of the 1970s, and the broader reformist feminist movements (see **feminism**). By the end of the 1970s, several women's studies associations had been established within Japan.

Although there are now a number of both women's studies associations, and academic women's studies journals, most teachers of women's studies are on the fringes of the academy, reflecting the already marginal place of women in most tertiary institutions. Women academics are more likely to be in part-time, casual or untenured positions, and women's studies courses are generally isolated subjects, with few co-ordinated interdisciplinary programmes and few universities that provide a major sequence in women's studies. As in many other countries, women's studies courses survive through the dedication of groups of feminist researchers who find solidarity in networks that cross several institutions, and bring together academics, activists, journalists, women in the law and other professions, and freelance writers

and researchers. The women's universities, such as Ochanomizu University, Japan Women's University and Tokyo Women's University, have provided a rather more hospitable environment for academic women's studies.

In addition to women's studies based in the academy, there is also a range of community-based, or grassroots women's studies activity, which often takes the form of the production of newsletters, journals, or monographs produced on a collaborative basis. **Women's history**, in particular, has developed such grassroots, community-based ways of writing history, while other community-based research is tied to specific issues such as sexual harassment, domestic violence, the situation of part-time workers, the situation of immigrant workers or support for claims for compensation by women forced into military prostitution in the Second World War. The local women's centres, which were established in many local government areas during the International Women's Decade, also host adult education classes on women's studies and women's history, and provide a focus for local study groups. Other types of publications try to bridge the perceived gap between academic research and feminist activism. While the publications of the Nihon Joseigaku Kenkyū Kai (Japan Women's Studies Association) remain on the academic side of the divide, the journal *Jūgo Shi Nōto* (Notes for a History of the Homefront) has been of interest to both feminist historians and activists. The group that produced this journal called themselves Women Questioning the Present. They came full circle with the final edition of the journal in 1996, bringing twenty years of feminist research to a close with an examination of the period of student left activism and women's liberation that had given birth to the group.

The **Asian Women's Association** also contributed to the development of feminist history with an activist emphasis through its journal *Asian Women's Liberation*. Like the journal *Feminist*, the producers of *Asian Women's Liberation* tried to integrate feminist groups in Japan into international channels of communication by producing regular English-language editions. With slightly different emphases, feminist thinkers now refer to women's studies (*joseigaku*), theories of women (*joseiron*) or research on women (*josei kenkyū*). The term gender (*jendaa*) was originally associated in Japan with a rather idiosyncratic use of the term by Ivan Illich. More recently, gender has come to be used in Japan to refer to the structured relationships between men and women in a given society, and the cultural constructions of masculinity and femininity. This has led to new coinages such as gender research (*jendaa kenkyū*). Recently, there has been an interest in the relationship between feminism and state institutions (*feminizumu to gyōsei*). Men's Studies (*danseigaku*) has also gained currency, as have gay, lesbian and queer studies. These are in addition to continued mainstream research and publishing on women's studies and gender studies.

See also: feminism; feminist publishing; Takamure Itsue; women's history

Further reading

Fujieda Mioko and Kumiko Fujimura-Fanselow, 'Women's Studies: An Overview', in Kuniko Fujimura-Fanselow and Atsuko Kameda (eds) *Japanese Women: New Feminist Perspectives on the Past, Present and Future*, New York: The Feminist Press, pp. 172–3.

VERA MACKIE

wrapping

The presentation of a gift or purchase has always carried great significance in Japan, where wrapping has long been an art form. Although supermarkets, and discount and convenience shops, have attempted to reduce wrapping costs, department stores and local merchants continue to place great importance on presentation and quality of wrapping. The consumer expectation of artful presentation and packaging has thwarted occasional campaigns by environmentalists to reduce waste levels through minimal, recyclable packaging.

Wrapping skills are built into store training programmes, and marketing campaigns will always include detailed product presentation strategies. Speedy service comes second to careful presentation and the foreign shopper is often frustrated by the long wait for a purchase to be handed over decked out in brand name or store logo paper, with matching ribbon or tape. In gift-giving season, companies and individuals seek out the latest trend in gifts wrapped and delivered from prestigious stores and the recognisable wrapping only adds value to the gift. Tailored-to-purpose wax paper, moulded containers, wooden and cardboard packing boxes protect and decorate everything from expensive meats, to kimono or pottery. A rare element of Japanese merchandising is the frequent lack of correspondence between purchase value and presentation. A single $2 rice cake purchased for morning tea will be wrapped in the same layers of bamboo leaf, wax paper and *washi*, and placed in the same logo carry bag as a $200 purchase.

SANDRA BUCKLEY

Wright, Frank Lloyd

Architect

b. 1867, Wisconsin, USA; d. 1959, Arizona, USA

Frank Lloyd Wright first visited Japan in 1905 but he always insisted that his work had not been derived from Japanese architecture and that any notable influence was limited to his admiration of traditional woodblock prints. He acknowledged a link between his own organic approach and Japanese aesthetics but preferred to see this link as a confirmation of a position he reached through his own development and not as something borrowed from Japan. Wright would continue to resist attempts among colleagues and critics to draw any closer association between his work and Japan. He reacted strongly to any suggestion of adaptation or derivation from Japanese building techniques or spatial aesthetics.

One of the so-called 'prairie school' of architects, Wright was an influential figure in the development of a US architecture. His work is often described as emerging at the juncture of early modernism and the arts and crafts movement, committedly exploring the potential of both US culture and its natural environment. His buildings and interiors are renowned for their integration of nature and structure. Some of his most striking works seem to unfold from the rock and tree around them in an expression of the principles of his organic architecture. The fixation on the extent to which he was or was not influenced by Japan often slips into little more than academic sleuthing. Wright's most explicit link to Japan is the Imperial Hotel in Tokyo, which was rebuilt according to his design. He was officially commissioned in 1916 but construction continued into the early 1920s. While insisting in various essays on this project that he was not imitating a Japanese style he also admonished Japanese modern architects for abandoning the potential and precedents of their tradition for imported models from Europe and the USA.

Further reading

Nute, K. (1993) *Frank Lloyd Wright and Japan: The Role of Traditional Japanese Art and Architecture in the Work of Frank Lloyd Wright*, New York: Van Nostrand Reinhold.

SANDRA BUCKLEY

Y

Yamada Eimi

b. 1959, Tokyo

Writer

Bestselling author Yamada Eimi is most famous in Japan for two things: her erotically explicit narrative portrayals of female sexuality and her favourite choice of African American men as her female protagonists' lovers. A popular writer read with hesitation by many critics, her *Beddo taimu aizu* (Bedtime Eyes, 1985), the story of Kim and her violent, heavy drinking and drug-taking African American lover, won the Bungei Prize and her *Sōru myūjikku, rabaazu on rii* (Soul Music: Lovers Only, 1987) the **Naoki Prize**. As her Japanised English titles indicate, Yamada takes her place among a younger generation of writers, who deviate from their predecessors by their unconcern with issues such as national identity and Japaneseness, or responsibility for the Second World War. Markedly non-intellectual, Yamada's narratives navigate physicality and emotionalism, qualities praised – when the author is a woman – by Japanese critics, and arguably by the reading public. After all, Yamada can boast terrific sales at a time when literature generally sells dismally.

Yamada's narratives describe, in raw erotic detail, the sensual and sexual experiences of her mostly female, cool, hip protagonists, paying scant attention to locales and socio-cultural or temporal context. The vagueness of time and place, which makes the fictions seem transnational (since they could take place anywhere), is often abetted by characters' nationally non-specific names like Kim (suggesting either Korea or the USA). Yamada shares this shift toward trans-Japanese narrative with, for example, the even more popular **Murakami Haruki**. At other times, Yamada identifies characters as American, South-East Asian, biracial or multinational, and chooses exotic locales for her tales of erotic passion. Here she follows the lead of the slightly senior **Murakami Ryū**.

Yamada's style is marked by minimalist plots, the extensive incorporation of English words, including African American urban slang, which is written in *katakana* (the phonetic syllabary used primarily for words of non-Chinese, non-Japanese origin). Yamada's portrayals of female sexuality and interracial relations involving minorities are what render her works controversial. She has been accused of stereotypical portrayals of African Americans and women, and of replicating colonialist models of power and desire. However, her attempt to detail honestly and passionately her female protagonists sexuality is also a bold, and in some ways, feminist gesture.

Further reading

Cornyetz, N. (1996) 'Power and gender in the narratives of Yamada Eimi', in P.G. Schalow and J.A. Walker (eds) *The Woman's Hand: Gender and Theory in Japanese Women's Writing*, Stanford: Stanford University Press, pp. 425–57.

NINA CORNYETZ

Yamakawa Kikue

b. 1890; d. 1980, Tokyo

Socialist writer

Yamakawa (née Aoyama) Kikue was the author and translator of numerous books on socialism and the so-called 'woman question'. Yamakawa contributed to the debate on the protection of motherhood, and argued for women's divisions in labour unions. With her husband, Yamakawa Hitoshi, she was affiliated with the Rōnō faction of the socialist movement in pre-war Japan. In the post-war period, Yamakawa was the first director of the Women's and Minors' Bureau of the Department of Labour.

Further reading

Shapcott, J. (1987) 'The red chrysanthemum: Yamakawa Kikue and the socialist women's movement in pre-war Japan', *Papers on Far Eastern History* 35: 1–30.

VERA MACKIE

Yamamoto Yōji

b. 1943, Tokyo

Fashion designer

Yamamoto Yōji was a contemporary of **Rei Kawakubo**. He graduated from the Bunkafukuso Institute of Keio University. He established Y's Incorporated, a now internationally recognised brand name in fashion design. He launched his first major collection at the same time as Kawakubo in Paris and they both quickly became part of the whirlwind taking 1980's fashion by storm. Of all the Japanese designers, he is the one who has most pursued traditional Western garment-making. Yet, at the same time, he has, one could say, drawn on Asian traditions and sensibilities to make sense of this tradition in new ways. His suits, shirts and dress designs are always playful and provocative reinventions of familiar forms and the Y's brand is renowned for the extraordinary quality of work-manship and textiles, something Yamamoto prides himself on. He has taken an active role in many diverse aspects of design including, among other things, costume design for theatre, opera and film. He has won many awards both within Japan and in other countries, including being honoured by the French government for his contribution to fine arts and culture.

AKIKO FUKAI

Yamashita Tatsurō

b. 1953

Singer

Yamashita Tatsurō has been a distinctive voice on the Japanese music scene since the mid-1970s. He is best known for his mastery of vocal harmony, chorus arrangement and pop-song craftsmanship.

Yamashita formed the band Sugar Babe in 1972, and began songwriting in 1973. The pop sound of Sugar Babe did not sell well in the mid-1970s due to the dominance of blues and R 'n' B in the non-idol singer music scene of the time. Sugar Babe supported themselves by touring as a vocal backing group for Ōtaki Eichi and performing session work for the many commercial jingles penned by Ōtaki. Sugar Babe's first album, *Songs*, was produced by Ōtaki and released in 1975. Yamashita released his first solo album, *Circus Town*, in October of the next year. While throughout the 1970s Yamashita remained a critic's and musician's favourite without much popular success, with the help of a Maxell commercial tie-in, his 1980, *Ride on Time*, sold 5,000,000 copies. His succeeding albums have all been bestsellers, particularly among college students. Yamashita is widely regarded as a popular music artist who has became a commercial success on his own terms. His 'Christmas Eve' has acquired perennial classic status.

MARK ANDERSON

Yano Akiko

b. 1955, Tokyo

Musician

A childhood piano prodigy, Yano Akiko had classical training and a familiarity with jazz, pop and R 'n' B by the time she reached high school. Upon entering high school she was a working musician in the Tokyo club scene. While performing with veteran jazzmen she began singing as well. She played on many albums as a session musician in Japan and also appeared in concert with Tin Pan Alley. While in Los Angeles to record her own material, Yano played on one track of an album by the US band Little Feat. She subsequently recorded her first solo album, *Japanese Girl*, which went on sale in 1976. Her unique, child-like voice and idiosyncratic rhythmic sensibility gained critical acclaim. After a series of important solo albums, in 1979 and 1980 she took part in the Yellow Magic Orchestra world tour. In 1980, she released a double solo album co-produced by herself and her husband **Sakamoto Ryūichi**, *Gohan dekita yo* (Dinner's Ready!). Yano Akiko is considered one of the major musical talents of the Japanese popular music world. Now living near New York, her solo work has returned to unaccompanied piano and compositions co-written with such artists as Pat Matheny.

MARK ANDERSON

Yasukuni Shrine

Yasukuni Shrine, in the heart of Tokyo, is far more than a religious institution: 'Yasukuni' has become an abbreviation for the problems associated with Japan's war legacy. Established in 1879, Yasukuni became the centre of a hierarchical organisation of shrines constituting **State Shintō**, which encompassed all imperial subjects. While other religions, notably Buddhism, were suppressed, State Shintō was dedicated to the crucial purpose of honouring death on the battlefield. Victory in the Sino-Japanese War (1894–5) and Russo-Japanese War (1904–5) entailed massive losses and an incipient pacifism. Apotheosis (deification) at Yasukuni of all

who died in battle, even the lowliest, expressed the ostensible egalitarianism of the emperor state.

The Allied Occupation dismantled State Shintō, deeming it ultranationalistic and militaristic. The new Constitution (1949) guaranteed freedom of religion and separation of church and state. From the early 1950s to the present day, conservative forces have sought to restore state sponsorship of Yasukuni, promoting official worship by Cabinet members or even suggesting that the Class-A war criminals there enshrined be 'removed' in order to neutralise reference to Japanese imperialism. Legal battles continue to be waged, with rare success, to challenge government sponsorship.

Further reading

Hardacre, Helen (1989) *Shinto and the State, 1868–1988*, Princeton: Princeton University Press.

NORMA FIELD

Yellow Magic Orchestra

The April 1978 session to record Hosono Haruomi's *Haraiso* was the departure point of Yellow Magic Orchestra (YMO). In this session, Hosono (bass and keyboards), the Sadistics' Takahashi Yukihiro (drums) and **Sakamoto Ryūichi** (keyboards) all came together. In November 1978, they released a self-titled album, *Yellow Magic Orchestra*. In 1979, they signed with A&M Records in the USA and in September of that year they released *Solid State Survivor* in both the USA and Japan. At this point they added two more members to the band, **Yano Akiko** (keyboard) and Watanabe Katsumi (guitar), and went on a world tour. The album broke into the Japanese charts during the tour, reaching number one and selling over 1,400,000 copies. It was one of the earliest postwar pop albums to sell over 1,000,000 copies.

The band released a live album, *Public Pressure*, in February 1980 and yet another album in June. Both reached number one on the Japanese charts. In the wake of YMO, the Japanese pop scene generally began to incorporate aspects of techno-pop style. They released a fourth album on BGM

Records in November 1981, *Technodelic*, which was successful as a combination of both pop and anti-pop. After this, the members concentrated on their solo careers. In May 1983, they released *Uwakina bokura* and in November of the same year another album, entitled *Service*. At this point, they announced they were suspending the band's activities.

The band's signature sound combined disco rhythms with the sound effects of the newly emerging computer games. Plugging self-consciously Orientalist melodies into their techno-pop apparatus, they joined the ranks of international superstardom. Synthesiser bands were not new, but YMO was one of the first to use them as an instrument in making pop music, or techno-pop, rather than to produce a specialised kind of synthesiser music. YMO was preceded by Kraftwerk and Brian Eno and was roughly contemporary with Gary Numan and Devo. It is said that Spandau Ballet and Duran Duran were among the bands influenced by YMO. YMO's music and image foregrounded issues of subject formation, culture and technology with both subtle irony and wall-to-wall overkill, the various proportions between them depending on the song or performance in question.

Further reading

Shinohara Akira (1996) *J-Rock 1968–1996: Best 123*, Tokyo: Kōdansha Bunko, pp. 162–3.

Yoshimura Eiichi and Satoh Kimitoshi (1998) *Compact YMO*, Tokyo: Tokuma Shoten.

MARK ANDERSON

yen

The yen (*en*, meaning round) was established as the unit of monetary account in Japan in 1871 by the Meiji government to replace the complex system of currency existing throughout the Edo Period. At that time, one hundredth of a yen was called a *sen*, and one-tenth of a *sen* was called a *rin*. After the Second World War, the government initiated currency reform and all old yen notes were taken out of circulation and replaced gradually with new yen notes. The exchange rate was fixed by the Allied Occupation authorities in 1949 at ¥360 to the US dollar. However, in 1973, the US dollar was devalued against gold, and the yen along with other major currencies moved to a floating exchange rate system. A key policy issue in recent years has been the various problems related to the 'internationalisation of the yen' and its role as a preferred currency in international trade and financial transactions. One of the factors contributing to the Asian currency crisis (1997–8) is said to have been the excessive dependence of Asian currencies on the US dollar. Consequently, an increase in the use of the yen in Asia could contribute to stabilising the exports and macro-economic performance of these countries. In the long run this could also help stabilise the Japanese economy.

DAVID EDGINGTON

Yi Hwe-Sung

b. 1935, Kabata Shinoka

Writer

Yi Hwe-Sung, also widely known by his Japanese name Ri Kai-Sei, was the first Korean resident in Japan to be awarded the Akutagawa Prize, which he received in 1972 for the work *Kunuta o utsu onna* (The Woman at the Washing Block). He was born in the then-Japanese territory of Kabata Shinoka, the third son of one parent from North Korea and one parent from the south. His mother died when he was nine years old, and after the war he moved with his father and other siblings to Hokkaidō where his father remarried. After completing senior high school in Sapporo, he entered Waseda University and graduated from the Russian literature department. His memories of the war years appear in his fiction.

Yi Hwe-Sung is concerned with externalised issues of cultural identity, particularly the tension between the public face of self and one's own inner sense of self. He believes that existence is difficult to resolve without an awareness of, if not a belief in ideology. Many of Hwe-Sung's works deal with the passage from youth to adulthood.

He is most well known for works that are rites of passage for young *zainichi* Koreans as they pass from youth into adulthood and consequently have to come to terms with their identity both as individuals and as part of the *zainichi* Korean community. They must confront a number of social issues if they are to find their own place in the world. He sets up dichotomies as a reflection of the *zainichi* Korean experience. He uses these dichotomies both thematically and structurally. In his works, self-awareness only becomes possible through an awareness of such dichotomies as truth/lies, childhood/adulthood, internal/external, beauty/ugliness, *nikoyon* or itinerant day labourer/gigolo.

His work includes *Warera no seishun no tojo nite* (Towards the Peak of Our Youth/On the Road to the End of Our Youth), first published in 1969. In this work he sets up a tension between externalised cultural identity and internalised self-identity. The enormous burden of nationhood and politics lies heavily on everything, even an individual's choice of name. The issue of naming can be seen as a metaphor for the *zainichi* Korean experience. First, one must choose a name, and then a language. Which language is one's mother tongue, the language one's mother or grandmother uses or the language one speaks? Will they define themselves as from North or South Korea and how will this affect how people treat them? Yi Hwe-Sung's work tells of the underside of Japanese society, of the *kitanai*, *kiken* and *kitsui* (dirty, dangerous and demanding) jobs that are left to the illegal foreign workers or the lowest of the lowest itinerant Japanese day labourers. One of his major themes is escapism. One way of dealing with the hard reality of the *zainichi* Korean experience is to escape through alcohol, insanity, anything that means the actor cannot be held responsible. Family is also an important motif in his work, as he uses family loyalties to reflect political positioning.

See also: Koreans in Japan; Korean-Japanese literature

CAROL HAYES

Yi Yang-Ji

b. 1945, Yamanashi; 1992, Tokyo

Writer

In January 1989, Yang-ji was awarded the 100th **Akutagawa Prize**, a prestigious prize for new authors, for her most well-known work *Yuhi*. She became, after **Yi Hwe-Sung**, only the second Korean-Japanese writer to be so recognised (see **Korean-Japanese literature**). Yang-ji's contribution to Korean literature in Japan lies in her ability to speak for her generation and stems from her narrative positioning of self, suspended between Korea and Japan, from which she explores the commonalities of the internal life of second-generation Koreans in Japan.

In her early teenage years, Yang-ji sought to reject all that was Korean within her in the hope of fitting into Japanese society, but in her early adulthood she tried the opposite, going to Korea to study its language and traditional music hoping to 'de-Japanify' herself. On a trip back to Japan in 1992 she was suddenly taken ill and died, tragically young.

Yang-ji felt caught between the reality of her life and the Utopian myth of her imagined homeland. She began to write in an attempt to gain some understanding of the duality between the Japan and the Korea within her, and her creativity fed on the emotional disparity between her own developing selfhood and the ethnic identity of Korean-Japanese as a group. Although her tragedy was that she rarely seemed able to find a balance between the two, Yang-ji's strength was in being able to weld the two sides warring within her into the synthesis of her own voice, what she referred to as her new mother tongue and to proudly present a new-found selfhood that was neither purely Korean nor purely Japanese.

Yang-ji published her first novel, *Nabi T'aryong* (Grieving Butterflies) in 1982. It is the story of Aiko, a young Korean-Japanese woman living in Japan. After a self-destructive early adulthood where her failures come to mirror those of her parents, Aiko discovers Korean music. It gives her the strength to break away from her life in Japan and take up the study of Korean music and dance, through which she finds the strength to make peace with her past and thus become a part of the historical continuum of her people.

Yuhi is set wholly in Korea and tells of another young Japan-born Korean woman, Yi Yuhi. Yuhi also travels to Korea in pursuit of the spirit of her motherland. Her primary goal is to master her mother tongue and the resultant identity struggle is fought between the Korean and the Japanese languages. The story is narrated by a young Korean woman, which, while highlighting Yuhi's marginalisation, allows Yang-ji to construct a narrative position that speaks for Korean natives, for Koreans resident in Japan and for Korean-Japanese in Korea, serving to underline the precarious nature of displaced identity. This strategy also allows Yang-ji to dispute the 'fixing' that categories such as ethnicity and geography exert on the formation of identity.

See also: Korean-Japanese literature; Yi Hwe-Sung; Yū Miri

Select bibliography

Yi, Y. (1993) *Yi Yang-Ji Zenshū* (Collected Works of Yi Yang-Ji), Tokyo: Kōdansha.
—— (1991) *Yu-hee* (extract), trans.C. Prenner, in H. Mitsios (ed.) *New Japanese Voices: The Best Contemporary Fiction from Japan*, New York: The Atlantic Monthly Press.

Further reading

Hayes, C. (2000) 'Cultural identity in the works of Yi Yang-Ji', in S. Ryang (ed.) *Koreans in Japan: Critical Voices from the Margin*, London: Routledge, pp. 119–39.

CAROL HAYES

yobai

Yobai (nightcrawling) is the practice of moving between restaurants, bars and clubs after work hours with colleagues, representatives of competitors or contractors or just with friends. It is part of a well-established culture of after-hours' socialisation

in the Japanese work environment. The heavy levels of alcohol consumption associated with *yobai* have often been criticised by health authorities as a form of corporate-sanctioned alcohol abuse. Feminists also target *yobai* for preventing men from playing a more active role in family life and for encouraging men to engage in extramarital flirtations and affairs with the bar hostesses and sex workers who are central figures in the night space of *yobai*. Although there is a growing tolerance of single female co-workers joining *yobai* activities, the stronger trend has been towards working women developing their own independent *yobai* circuits.

SANDRA BUCKLEY

yōga

Yōga (Western-style painting) is a story of 'East meets West', informed by a set of specific local Japanese conditions enmeshed in the global tide of modernisation. In practice, *yōga* is a form of painting created by using Western media, typically oil, on canvas. Broadly speaking, the term refers to works created in Western media in Japan after the late Edo Period as well as the entire tradition of Western painting. In the strictest sense, *yōga* means oil painting executed in Japan after the Meiji Period. Painting created using Western materials and/or techniques from pre-Meiji Japan is called *yōfūga* (literally, 'Western-mode painting').

Western painting techniques were first introduced to Japan along with Christianity in the late sixteenth century and practised until the early seventeenth century, when the country entered its isolationist period. A second wave of interest came with the expanding enthusiasm over Dutch studies, particularly science, in the late eighteenth century. Scientific perspective and modelling, both powerful tools for rendering the subject realistically, captivated the imagination of pre-Meiji *yōfūga* practitioners as well as traditional painters; the fascination with realism (*shajitsu*) continued to the late nineteenth century, among early *yōga* artists such as Takahashi Yuichi, and well into the twentieth century. The Meiji government even deemed the study of *yōga* a utilitarian necessity in attaining the national goal of Westernisation.

However, *yōga* was put on the defensive when the fervent nationalist movement rose during the 1880s, and it was at this time that both the term *yōga*, and the term **Nihonga** (Japanese-style painting) were coined.

While *yōga* and *Nihonga* have constituted two polarised camps of the art establishment, they are not so dissimilar in certain aspects. As with *Nihonga*, the evolution of *yōga* was closely entwined with that of art institutions. Furthermore, although the history of *yōga* may be equated with decades of adapting a gamut of European styles, from Impressionism to abstraction, *yōga* artists ultimately aspired to create 'Japanese expressions' in oil. The Japanised Fauvism by Umehara Ryūzaburō and the incorporation of Zen-derived *nanga* by Yorozu Tetsugorō and Kishida Ryūsei are but a few significant achievements. Perhaps due to its abiding interest in realism, *yōga* contributed, more visibly than *Nihonga*, to Japan's war efforts in the Second World War – the historical episode in the history of *yōga* that remains an unresolved issue to this day.

For a few decades after 1945, there were several new developments in *yōga*, ranging from Social Realism to surrealism to abstraction. However, *yōga* increasingly came to connote a range of increasingly 'academic practices', in light of the rise of alternative vanguard factions that are commonly referred to as 'contemporary painting' (*gendai kaiga*) (see **art, contemporary**).

Further reading

Higashi Ajia (1999) *Kaiga no kindai: Yuga no tanjō to sono tenkai / Oil Painting in the East Asia: Its Awakening and Development*, Shizuoka: Shizuoka Prefectural Museum of Art.

Takashina Shuuji, Rimer, J. Thomas and Bolas, Gerald D. (1987) *Paris in Japan: The Japanese Encounter with European Painting*, Tokyo: The Japan Foundation and St Louis: Washington University.

REIKO TOMII

Yokohama

Yokohama is Japan's second largest city, and the capital of Kanagawa Prefecture. Once a small fishing village, the destination of Commodore Perry, who arrived in his 'Black Ships' in 1853 to demand that Japan become more open to the rest of the world, Yokohama is now the centre of the Keihin Industrial Zone. It is a sea of industrial developments, office towers and massive residential apartment blocks that house both those who work in Yokohama and surrounding areas and those who commute daily to the **Tokyo** metropolitan area. On the southern edge of Tokyo Bay, Yokohama is Japan's largest port and one of the largest container facilities in the world. Its major industries include steel refineries, automobile factories, chemical plants, oil refineries, electronics manufacturers and food processors.

Partially because of its history as a port city, Yokohama has a reputation for exhibiting 'foreign' influences. It is a centre of newspaper production, which adds to the apparent worldly or international focus. It has some of the oldest universities, known for their collaboration with other parts of the world. It has one of the largest 'Chinatowns' in Japan, Chūkagai, and its large shopping arcades and many trendy boutiques are associated with the height of international fashion.

AUDREY KOBAYASHI

yokozuna

Yokozuna is the ranking of grand champion in **sumo wrestling**. All other rankings are temporary but this one. The promotion to *yokozuna* is determined by a committee within the Japan Sumo Association and the criteria include number of wins, technique and what might be called sumo etiquette or dignity (*hinkaku*). When a *yokozuna* begins to lose form he is expected to retire. Many move on to become sumo masters and train a stable (*heya*) of wrestlers. There was a long and often heated public controversy over the issue of non-Japanese being granted the rank of *yokozuna* but the 1990s finally saw the first promotions of foreign wrestlers.

See also: *basho*; sumo wrestling

SANDRA BUCKLEY

Yomiuri shinbun

The *Yomiuri*, founded in 1874, got its start as a gossip sheet that reported on everyday happenings in Tokyo. It was published on an alternate-day schedule. From its inception, the *Yomiuri* enjoyed wide popularity, and became a fully fledged daily in 1875.

In the Meiji Period (1868–1912), writers Tsubouchi Shōyō, Kōda Rohan and Ozaki Kōyō were among the regular contributors. The art and literature sections flourished, but news reportage remained weak. From the early 1900s, the creation of a news-gathering network became the *Yomiuri*'s top priority.

Shōriki Matsutarō bought control of the *Yomiuri* in 1924 after he resigned from the Tokyo Metropolitan Police Department. Reforms ensued and the *Yomiuri* became the first to include a woman's page and a radio page as regular features, sponsor a professional Japanese chess tournament and set up media events like baseball games and art exhibitions. At the time of the Manchurian Incident (1931), the *Yomiuri*'s news network was on a par with that of the **Asahi shinbun** and **Mainichi shinbun**.

After the Second World War, the *Yomiuri* promoted editorial policies similar to those of the *Asahi* and *Mainichi*, but its stance changed in the mid-1980s. Both the *Asahi* and *Mainichi* sharply criticised the *Yomiuri* for its support of the Nakasone Cabinet and the Reagan administration.

The *Yomiuri*'s circulation is the highest among Japan's national papers.

BARBARA HAMILL SATO

Yomota Inuhiko

b. 1953 Nishinomiya

Film critic

Since 1990, Yomota Inuhiko has been a lecturer on the history of cinema at the Meiji Gakuin University, Art Department. His main area of focus is on Japanese cinema, as indicated by his research on classical works (Ozu, Mizoguchi). He has written on the tendency of post-modern art in Japan and Asia, and has published some papers on **manga** and essays within the sphere of Japanese literature. In particular, starting from a year spent in Italy at DAMS (Performing Arts, University of Bologna), Yomota has contributed, with publications and participation in congresses and international festivals, promoting the diffusion of famous European cinema and theatre directors, including Fellini, Pasolini and Kantor.

MARIA ROBERTA NOVIELLI

Yoshida Takuro

b 5 April 1946, Kagoshima Prefecture

Musician

Yoshida Takuro led the move from folk to rock in the early 1970s, now known as New Music, and co-founded the first record label by and for artists. Although born in Kagoshima Prefecture, his family moved to Hiroshima when he was five. He began playing in bands during his high-school years. He was briefly a member of the student protest group, Zenkyōtō, while attending classes at Sophia University. His first album, *Seishun no Uta* (Song of Youth), was released in November 1968. In August 1971, at the All-Japan Folk Jamboree, in part due to PA problems, he performed the song 'Ningen nante' for over two hours to a feverish reception – a moment still remembered both as a highlight of his own career and the emerging music scene of the time.

During this famous performance he drew fans away from a larger stage featuring the then-leading folk singer, **Okabayashi Nobuyasu**. For many observers, this event signalled a change of the guard in the Japanese folk world. Where Okabayashi was overtly political but musically limited, Yoshida turned his attention to the drama of private life in a way that combined the lyrical intelligence of folk with the power and musicality of rock music. Yoshida's next album, *Ningen nante*, was released in November 1971 and sold over 100,000 copies. In 1972, Yoshida signed to a major label record company, the multinational CBS-Sony, and promptly released two hits, 'Kekkon sho yo' (Let's Get Married) and 'Tabi no yado' (Shelter on the

Road). The album that included those hits, *Genki desu* (I'm Fine), remained at number one on the album charts for thirteen straight weeks.

Those who supported anti-establishment folk music criticised Yoshida as a traitor. At various events he was heckled with calls of 'Go home!' On occasion he actually went home. Yoshida, however, sought to maintain his distance from the entertainment industry by refusing to make television appearances. Yoshida is credited with organising the first national rock 'n' roll concert tour in Japan featuring his own band, and not run by a talent manager or production company but by the artist himself. Yoshida was both a chart-topping idol of sorts and an artist in significant control of his own musical destiny. In 1974, one of his compositions won song of the year. (It was recorded by **Mori Shinichi**, so it represented an unprecedented meeting of the New Music and *enka* worlds.) In 1975, he made waves in the record industry by co-founding For Life Records as a record company run by and for artists. Yoshida has released over thirty albums, not including anthologies and collections. He has had an important influence on the themes and lyrical style of Japanese rock – he played a very large role in changing the direction of the Japanese popular music scene of the early 1970s.

MARK ANDERSON

Yoshimoto Banana

b. 1964, Tokyo

Writer

Yoshimoto was born in 1964 in Tokyo and named Yoshimoto Maiko, later choosing for herself the name Banana. She graduated from Nihon University in 1986. Her rise to literary fame is usually dated from the publication of *Kicchen* (Kitchen) in 1987 but she had already received the Izumi Kyoka Prize from her university for her work *Mūn raito shadou* (Moonlight Shadow) in 1986. *Kicchen* received the *Kaien* magazine New Writer Prize and was reported to be selling 10,000 hard-cover copies per day during the peak of what became known as 'Banana fever'. Her works have been taken up

extensively in translation with *Kicchen* appearing in English in 1992 to a warm reception that was at least in part attributable to an extensive and highly successful media campaign from Grove Press. Other works in translation include *N.P.* (1990, translation 1994), *Tokage* (*Lizard*, 1993, translation 1995) and *Amrita* (1994, translation 1997), but these represent only a small part of her prolific production in Japanese. Yoshimoto has become known as the literary voice of Japan's Generation X and the term perhaps most often, if loosely, used to describe her works is post-modern – not only in terms of the content but also the place her writing occupies in the consumer landscape of contemporary Japanese cultural production.

Yoshimoto quickly became known for a consistency of style, theme and characters. For her enthusiastic fans this became her literary trademark, while for her critics it was the mark of her limitations. Most are in agreement that she is at her strongest as a short-story writer and essayist. A longer work such as *Amrita* has been widely criticised for failing to sustain the techniques of her shorter format across an extended narrative. Her written style is consistently described as minimal, straightforward, concise, unadorned. She also relies heavily on dialogue in much of her fiction and is praised for her willingness to capture the vagueness and incompleteness of conversation without insisting on an artificially correct or complete formation of either the grammar or ideas of her characters. Conversations can seem disconnected and misdirected, as they often are in daily life. Ambiguity and indeterminacy often characterise actions and decisions in her storylines.

At the centre of her narratives is a young woman, and this character is almost always caught up in a struggle to locate herself in a set of relationships that undercut traditional and normative networks of support. If there is an anti-hero to Yoshimito's works it is the family, or at least the parent–child relationship. It is horizontal relationships that she explores tenaciously: siblings, friends, peers, lovers, ex-lovers. Yoshimoto's narratives never shy away from the extreme and the provocative: incestuous desires, the supernatural and occult, trans-sexuality, suicide. However, the extraordinary is always blended with the mundane, erupting into the everyday often without remark or response, accepted and negotiated along with the ordinary. Spirits, Bodhisattvas and mythical figures are interwoven into the lives of her characters as they move towards and away from one another. The allusiveness and risks of intimacy in contemporary life are constant themes as many of her key characters struggle with loss and longing. The family is represented as a broken myth rather than as a locus of nostalgia, as is so commonplace elsewhere in contemporary fiction and across Japanese consumer culture. Yoshimoto's writings focus on a longing for new formations and sites of belonging. Criticised by many in the *bundan* as a consumer phenomenon and not a literary figure, Yoshimoto, for her part, continues to enjoy a wide domestic and international following.

SANDRA BUCKLEY

youth hostels

Youth hostels form an important part of student life in Japan and are also a popular form of accommodation for young families when travelling. Not all hostels are open to adults and families, but there is a sufficiently dense network of hostels across the country with different regulations and clientele that most people can find an appropriate hostel within reach of their destination. This network includes a mix of Japan Youth Hostels Inc. facilities, and prefectural, municipal and privately operated hostels. In total there are some 480 hostels across the country with heavy concentrations in resort areas and larger urban centres. There are restrictions that apply when staying at hostels such as sex-segregated sleeping areas, night curfews and no alcohol. This still doesn't deter the many thousands of low-budget travellers who always set out on a trip with their youth hostel membership in hand. Hikers and mountain climbers make good use of the more remote hostels in areas where there is not enough tourism traffic to support an inn or hotel. There is an entire culture of youth hostel travel that may not appeal to everyone including group housework, night-time sing-alongs and games. For many, though, the hostels offer a chance to meet new

travelling companions while travelling safely and inexpensively.

SANDRA BUCKLEY

Yū Miri

b. 1968, Yokohama

Writer

In 1997, Yū Miri, was awarded the 116th **Akutagawa Prize**, a prestigious award for new writers, for her work *Kazoku Shinema* (Family Cinema). She was only the third Korean-Japanese writer to be awarded this prize (see **Korean-Japanese literature**). This award brought the issue of Koreans writing in Japanese to the forefront of critical debate and incited violent threats from Japanese right wingers who claimed that Japanese are portrayed as fools in her work. Her adolescence is a record of repeated anguish and her personal experiences mirror the ethnic discrimination other people of Korean descent suffer in Japan. She commented at the award ceremony that she has always felt a sense of estrangement and that her writing was an attempt to overcome this feeling.

When Yu was a middle-school student, she was ostracised by her classmates because she was Korean and attempted suicide several times; these suicide attempts resulted in her being expelled from high school without graduating. After leaving school, she tried acting with the theatre group, Tokyo Kid Brothers, but switched to writing plays when she found she could not speak on stage. In 1988, she helped to launch the theatre company Seishun Gogatsu To (The May Youth Group).

Yū Miri argues for a hybrid identity that includes the Japan in which she resides with the origins and language of the culture of her homeland. Yū Miri takes a firmly political stance, arguing for the right, as a second-generation Korean Japanese, to use contemporary Japanese language, as she works to carve out a new niche for herself within Japanese society and its literature. Without denying her own difference she refuses to be marginalised into that limited space somewhere between Korea, the notional homeland, and Japan.

She argues for more hybridity in the Japanese language, and that it be allowed to take on echoes from the cultural and ethnic diversity of those who choose to use it as their creative medium.

She firmly positions herself in and of Japanese society, while maintaining her right to the cultural diversity she inherits from her ethnicity. She cannot speak or write Korean.

Yu has worked in a variety of genres, beginning with plays and now increasingly working with novels, short stories and essays. She has been accused by the media of modelling her characters too closely on real people, and in 1994 with the publication of her first novel, *The Fish Who Swims in Stone*, she was taken to court by just such a claimant. Although the court ruled against the plaintiff, it was a disturbing experience and forced her to reconsider her relationship to writing.

Her major works include: novels such as, *Kazoku Shinema* (1997) and *Full House* (1996); essay collections such as *Kazoku no hyōhon* (Family Disunity, 1995), *Yū Miri no jisatsu* (Yū Miri's 'Suicide', 1995) and *Mado no aru shoten kara* (From the Bookshop with a Window, 1996); and plays, such as *Sakana no matsuri* (Fish Festival, 1996), *Himawari no hitsugi* (The Sunflowers' Coffin, 1993) and *Green Bench* (1993).

See also: Korean-Japanese literature; Yi Hwe-Sung; Yi Yang-Ji

Select bibliograpy

Yū Miri (1996) *Mado no aru shoten kara* (From a Bookshop with a Window), Tokyo: Kadokawa Shoten.

Further reading

Yoneyama, L. (2000) 'Writing against the bourgeois and national bodies: Family and residency in Yu Miri's texts', in S. Ryang (ed.) *Koreans in Japan: Critical Voices from the Margin*, London: Routledge, pp. 103–18.

CAROL HAYES

yukata

This is a lightweight summer kimono made from cotton. Although most Japanese now only rarely wear formal kimono, one of the pleasures of summer for many people is the opportunity to dress in this informal and comfortable style while vacationing in a resort town, enjoying a summer festival or fair, or even just donning a *yukata* for an evening stroll or after a bath while relaxing on a hot summer evening. *Yukata* are available in traditional patterns, but a number of Japanese and foreign designer brands have also launched *yukata* lines in bold and often very contemporary patterns and colours. Even United Colours of Benetton has developed a *yukata* line to compete in this specialised but highly popular segment of the Japanese fashion market. A *yukata* is worn with **geta** and tied with a lighter style of **obi**.

SANDRA BUCKLEY

Z

zaibatsu dissolution

Reforms were undertaken by the Occupation authorities and the Japanese government to break up family-owned financial and industrial conglomerates (*zaibatsu*) and their monopolistic control of the pre-war and wartime economy. Within the context of post-war democratisation and demilitarisation, *zaibatsu* were viewed as a culprit for Japan's militarisation and aggression, and concentration of capital was deemed anti-democratic. When General Douglas **MacArthur**'s intent to dissolve the *zaibatsu* became public, he was pre-empted by an industry-based plan to sell *zaibatsu* securities to the public and to prohibit *zaibatsu* executives from influential offices; a compromise aimed at securing the future of the *zaibatsu*. MacArthur accepted the plan in November 1945. In January 1947, MacArthur ordered a purge of *zaibatsu* executives and 1,535 were removed or resigned. Some anti-trust legislations were more extreme than comparable measures in the USA. For example, an April 1947 statute prohibited holding companies, monopolistic contracts and cartels.

By late 1947, anti-trust momentum had run its course. The US business community opposed splitting up monopolies under the Deconcentration Law of December 1947, such that only eleven of the 325 designated firms were broken up. Moreover, anti-trust reforms increasingly flew in the face of the 'reverse course'. Thus, eventually compromised, *zaibatsu* dissolution none the less forced alterations in corporate structures and encouraged greater competition.

See also: Allied Occupation

Further reading

Bisson, T.A. (1954) *Zaibatsu Dissolution in Japan*, Berkeley: University of California Press.

Dower, John W. (1999) *Embracing Defeat*, New York: Norton.

Edwards, Corwin (1966) *Trade Regulation Overseas*, Dobbs Ferry: Oceana.

Hadley, Eleanor (1970) *Antitrust in Japan*, Princeton: Princeton Uuniversity Press.

HIRAKU SHIMODA

zaikai

Zaikai, literally translated, means 'financial world' but in contemporary Japan is typically used to refer to the circle of individuals who are active in several specific Japanese business associations. These associations are: Keidanren (the Federation of Economic Organisations), the Keizai Dōyūkai (Japan Association of Corporate Executives), Nikkeiren (Japan Federation of Employers' Associations), Nisshō (Japan Chamber of Commerce and Industry) and, not infrequently, Kankeiren (Kansai Managers' Federation). All of these associations regularly release statements outlining positions on the key economic and political issues of the day, and these opinions are in turn thought to be extremely influential in the Japanese government policy making. Of the associations listed, Keidanren is by far the most prominent. It is, in effect, an 'association of associations', whose primary constituent members are trade associations representing the leading industries in the Japanese economy. Opinions issued by Keidanren are usually the product of painstaking deliberations carried out through its extensive committee structure. The end product is often characterised as constituting the 'general will' (*sōi*) of the big-business community, while the president of Keidanren is frequently referred to as the 'prime minister of *zaikai*' (*zaikai sōri*).

Nikkeiren focuses on industrial relations issues. Nisshō, the peak association for local chambers of commerce, is considered to be the somewhat curious voice of small business as filtered through the interests held by the big national firms headquartered in Tokyo. The latter dominate the Tokyo Chamber of Commerce and provide the staff and space for the Nisshō secretariat. The Keizai Dōyūkai, on the other hand, is an individual membership organisation with a reputation for liberal opinions, while Kankeiren is the voice of business in Japan's second largest industrial district, **Kansai**.

Implicit in the term *zaikai* is the idea that those who are actively involved in these associations are part of a close-knit circle of corporate executives who are the real decision makers in Japan. This perspective is the product of a number of factors, including a legacy of close personal relations between state officials and a small number of co-operative capitalists in the pre-Second World War era. Similar relationships were maintained by individuals who were active in *zaikai* associations during the three decades following the Second World War. From the 1980s onwards, *zaikai* has become a considerably less conspicuous presence and opinions voiced by the various *zaikai* associations have come to carry much less weight than they had earlier. The big-business community that *zaikai* ostensibly represents has itself become considerably more diversified, pluralistic and internationally oriented than was true in the past, with the consequence that *zaikai* is less likely to be understood to be the monolithic voice of Japanese capitalism that it was once assumed to be.

Further reading

Tanaka Yōsuke (1983). 'The world of zaikai', in *Politics and Economics in Contemporary Japan*, Tokyo: Kōdansha International, pp. 64–78.

Websites

Kankeiren: www.kankeiren.or.jp/index.html
Keidanren: www.keidanren.or.jp/index.html
Keizai Dōyūkai: www.doyukai.or.jp/Eindex.html
Nikkeiren: www.nikkeiren.or.jp
Nisshō: www.jcci.or.jp/home-e.html

LONNY E. CARLILE

Zen

Zen is a meditation-based form of Buddhism. It originated in China as a blend of Buddhism and Taoism but only developed into the form that is today widely recognised as Zen after its arrival in Japan, where it began to flourish over the Kamakura period. There are two major sects of Zen in Japan, Rinzai and Sōtō. It is Rinzai that is most familiar today outside Japan and combines the practice of *kōan* (the use of questions to focus meditation) and *zazen* (meditation in the sitting position). Sōtō rejects the use of *kōan*, using only *zazen*. During the twelfth and thirteenth centuries, there was a flow of Japanese Buddhist monks to China to study Zen with the Chinese masters. Although there was also some movement of Chinese Zen masters into Japan, the flourishing of Zen was primarily led by the new generations of Japanese masters. The Rinzai school crystallised its rapidly growing presence with the development of the Five Great Temples (Gozan) system. This originated with three monasteries in Kyōto and two in Kamakura, and finally five in each location. The Sōtō school distinguished itself from Rinzai by its founder's (Dōgen) rejection of the intrigue of politics and subsequent retreat from Kyōto to the Echizen region where he established the head temple of the sect, Eiheiji.

The Muromachi period saw a growing alliance between Zen and the shōgunate, culminating in the 1338 '*ankokuji* (temples to defend the nation) decree', which ordered the establishment of sixty-six Zen temples across the country. It was also during the Muromachi period that Zen came to exert an enduring influence on the culture of the ruling elite. Together with Neo-Confucianism, it promoted a return to Chinese classics while also fostering a Zen aesthetic that would become an essential element of a diversity of Japanese arts including tea ceremony, flower arrangement, gardening, ink painting, martial arts, poetry and *nō* theatre. The Edo Period saw the arrival of a third Zen sect from China, the Obaku school, which combined Zen meditation with the *nembutsu Amida* incantation techniques. There were two strong trends in the development of Zen over the Edo Period: first, the consolidation of the link between the martial arts of the samurai class and Zen aesthetic and meditation; and, second, the popularisation of Zen through a proliferation of local temples and the Edo shift of family registers to Buddhist temples. Zen suffered along with all other Buddhist sects under the government shift to State Shintō after the Meiji Restoration, and the Zen temples only began to fully recover their religious and financial position after 1945.

There are approximately 10 million Zen devotees in Japan today, but the number of practising monks living in Zen monasteries has declined. Many Zen temples and monasteries have opened their doors to foreign students of Zen wishing to work with Japanese Zen masters. Zen is the Japanese religion that has achieved considerable influence overseas with local and international meditation centres and schools offering different varieties of Zen instruction. There has been considerable influence from Zen on a number of alternative and New Age religions and lifestyle movements in the West. Hybrid practices of Zen and yoga are often at the heart of these meditation movements. Detoxification, and rehabilitation centres and health-related spas and clinics also often model core elements of their techniques on notional interpretations of a Zen aesthetic and methodology of meditation. These Western variations often oversimplify the very difficult and challenging meditational techniques of Zen, reducing them to a mere practice of 'centring' of the self through a discipline of isolation.

Both the *kōan* and *zazen* techniques are highly demanding and neither offers any assured passage to enlightenment and Buddahood. The Rinzai and Sōtō schools acknowledge that *satori* (enlightenment) is not limited to meditational practices and that it is the focus and discipline of *zazen* or *kōan* that guide a devotee towards a refinement of their inner mind or experience that may be conducive of *satori*. *Satori*, by nature, cannot be defined but only experienced by the individual. Zen meditation is meant to achieve an intensity of inner focus or concentration that excludes all else and therefore can only be defined negatively, in terms of what it is not. Perhaps the most famous *kōan* is 'What is the sound of one hand clapping?', which is attributted to the Rinzai master Hakuin (1686–1769). The *kōan* of Zen masters are collected and passed down within the various schools of Rinzai Zen. The aim of these questions is not to find an answer but to abandon rational processes of thought for a condition of focused 'unknowing'. It is widely acknowledged that the intensity of the experiences of Zen devotion can be traumatic and destabilising for the individual, and the role of the Zen master is to be taken very seriously in the processes of meditation. It is this area of cautious and timely guidance that can be lost in Western adaptations of Zen in healing and treatment centres, where the sectarian role of counsellor or analyst is simply substituted for the spiritual role of the Zen master, and a schedule of treatment (or predetermined departure date) replaces the open-endedness of Zen techniques.

The term Zen is widely and loosely applied today to an aesthetic of simplicity. Japanese architecture, interior and fashion design, contemporary landscaping, flower arrangement and cuisine are all often praised in and out of Japan for their Zen qualities. A rejection of visual excess does not, however, always equate with a Zen rejection of all excess. A recent restaurant review in Los Angeles described the Zen quality of a morsel of sushi wrapped in a simple thin sheet of gold leaf. Zen has become synonymous with a contemporary minimalist aesthetic now popular among a global elite. Flower shops, bookshops, design shops, cafés, restaurants and architect studios across the world have taken up the name of Zen in order to trade on some of the current cultural cache of this visual aesthetic.

SANDRA BUCKLEY

Zengakuren

Zengakuren (an abbreviation of Zen nihon gakusei jichikai sōrengō) began in September 1949 as an alliance of student autonomous councils. The councils and the Zengakuren organisation were part of the **Allied Occupation**'s democratising campaign, and broadly representative of so-called 'Potsdam Democracy'. The early post-war Zengakuren campaigned for improvements in student living conditions and democratisation of the university and society.

Until 1958, student autonomous councils were affiliated with the Japan Communist Party (JCP) and its student organisation, the Minsei (Democratic Youth). This changed during the Anpo protests (see **Anpo struggle**), when New Left students won the majority in many campus autonomous councils and in the national Zengakuren. Zengakuren students were at the forefront of the Anpo protests, and Zengakuren became synonymous with radical politics. In response, JCP-affiliated students split from the organisation. After the 1960 struggles, the JCP and its allies retook control and moved the Zengakuren away from direct confrontation with the state and towards campus issues. New Left activists left the JCP-affiliated Zengakuren, and formed their own Zengakuren. However, the New Left-affiliated Zengakuren split into several factions over the course of the 1960s, and by the time of the **Zenkyōtō** movement, all Zengakuren factions had lost much of their influence.

GUY YASKO

Zenkyōtō

Zenkyōtō is an abbreviation for *Zen(gaku) Kyōtō kaigi* or *iinkai*, which were names for the campus-wide student strike committees that formed during the student revolts of 1968–70. Zenkyōtō-style movements took root in student struggles for free speech at Keio University in 1965 and protests against tuition fee hikes at Waseda University in 1966–7. However, the most famous Zenkyōtō organisations grew out of student struggles at Tokyo University and Nihon University. The Tokyo University Zenkyōtō protested against the university's authoritarian bureaucracy and elitism. At Nihon University, the corruption of president, founder and owner incited student rage. Zenkyōtō-style organisations appeared at more than one hundred Japanese universities in 1968–9. Despite a failed attempt at forming a National Zenkyōtō, the Zenkyōtō form of organisation emphasised the local, the individual and minority politics. Zenkyōtō-style organisations and strikes later spread even to elements of the Japanese military and to high schools, where students protested against overly restrictive school rules.

Zenkyōtō-style organisation remained popular into the early 1970s. With no theoretical restrictions or formal requirements for membership, Zenkyōtō organisations were open to all who were willing to join in the struggle, including students who were members of New Left sects with more formal and rigid organisation.

GUY YASKO

zoku

Zoku functions as a suffix and is often translated as 'tribe' rather than the less sensational 'group'. It is used to describe groupings that can be characterised as non-conformist. Deviation from the mainstream can take many forms: behaviour, clothing, lifestyle, musical taste or politics. Most groupings designated as *zoku* in post-war Japan are sufficiently recognisable socio-cultural formations to warrant categorisation as sub-cultures. The term is most often applied to youth sub-cultures, such as the infamous *bōsōzoku* or bike and car gangs. The structured, hierarchical and ritualised nature of many *zoku* often appears to non-Japanese observers to be contradictory to a notion of sub-cultures as deviant groupings. *Zoku* identity is intimately linked today to consumerism, and the uniform fashion, hairstyles, favourite foods, cafés, travel destinations, etc. are fundamental to the defining elements of a group's sense of difference. The rapid commodification of markers of *zoku* identity is understood by members less as appropriation than as an indicator of group recognition and status. Over the 1990s, the term has been popularised in the media and by advertising agencies, and has increasingly come in to use to designate short lived, seasonal consumer trends.

Further reading

Sato Ikuya (1991) *Kamikaze Biker: Parody and Anomy in Affluent Japan*, Chicago: University of Chicago Press.

SANDRA BUCKLEY

Zunō keisatsu

Zunō keisatsu was practically the only politically oriented band of the early 1970s. Their startling name, Zunō keisatsu (Brain Police), comes from the title of a Frank Zappa song, 'Who Are the Brain Police?' from the album *Mothermania*. They are considered the first Japanese punk band and even today are still something of a legend. Their radical revolutionary spirit, critical posture and electrifying performances were all remarkable for the time.

Zunō keisatsu made their performing début on 1 April 1970 at the Head Lock Concert in Kanda. In May of the same year they appeared at the Western Carnival outdoor festival. The lead singer and guitar player, Panta, masturbated on stage. From this point on, their activities became the stuff of legend. They next played for the political assembly of the Communist League (Kyōsanshugisha dōmei) and for an outdoor festival in support of resistance to construction of Narita Airport. It was at this last concert that they débuted the songs that have become most representative of Zunō Keisatsu: 'Sekai kakumei sensō sengen' (Manifesto of World Revolutionary War), 'Akagun heishi no uta' (Song for a Soldier of the Red Army) and Jū wo tore! ('Take a Gun!'). The 1972 live album that included these songs, *1st Album*, was withdrawn from public sale because the lyrical content was found to be in violation of recording-industry regulations. In June of the same year, their officially recognised debut album, *Zunō Keisatsu/Second Album*, was released. The lyrics of this album were also found to violate regulations and less than one month later it was collected and withdrawn from public sale. (It was re-released in 1981.)

In October 1972, *Zuno Keisatsō 3* was released. They released six albums altogether before they disbanded in December 1975, but the anti-social spirit of their early period had become diluted. That was the spirit that became legendary, which lives on, and which was taken up again by the punk movement. They briefly reunited in 1990 for one year.

MARK ANDERSON

Index

Note: Japanese names have not been inverted unless Westernised.
Page numbers in **bold** refer to main subject entries.